Yearbook of American & Canadian Churches 2012

Previous Issues & Editors

1916, 1917
Federal Council Year Book, H. K. Carroll

1918, 1919
Yearbook of the Churches, C. F. Armitage

1920
Yearbook of the Churches, S. R. Warburton

1922, 1923, 1925
Yearbook of the Churches, E. O. Watson

1927
The Handbook of the Churches, B. S. Winchester

1931
The New Handbook of the Churches, Charles Steizle

1933, 1935, 1937, 1939
Yearbook of American Churches, H. C. Weber

1941, 1943, 1945
Yearbook of American Churches, B. Y. Landis

1947
Yearbook of American Churches, B. Y. Landis and G. F. Ketcham

1949, 1951
Yearbook of American Churches, G. F. Ketcham

1952–1965
Yearbook of American Churches, B. Y. Landis

1966
Yearbook of American Churches, C. H. Jacquet

1967, 1968
Yearbook of American Churches, L. B. Whitman

1969–1972
Yearbook of American Churches, C. H. Jacquet

1973–1990
Yearbook of American & Canadian Churches, C. H. Jacquet

1991
Yearbook of American & Canadian Churches, C. H. Jacquet and Alice M. Jones

1992
Yearbook of American & Canadian Churches, Kenneth B. Bedell and Alice M. Jones

1993–1997
Yearbook of American & Canadian Churches, Kenneth B. Bedell

1998–2011
Yearbook of American & Canadian Churches, Eileen W. Lindner

Eightieth Issue

Annual

YEARBOOK OF AMERICAN & CANADIAN CHURCHES 2012

Edited by Eileen W. Lindner

Prepared and edited for the
National Council of the Churches of Christ
in the U.S.A.
475 Riverside Drive, New York, NY 10115-0050

Published and distributed
by Abingdon Press
Nashville

Preparation of this *Yearbook* is an annual project of the National Council of the Churches of
Christ in the United States of America.

This is the seventy-ninth edition of a yearbook
that was first published in 1916. Previous edi-
tions have been entitled: *Federal Council
Yearbook* (1916–1917), *Yearbook of the
Churches* (1918–1925), *The Hand-book of the*
Churches (1927), *The New Handbook of the
Churches* (1928), *Yearbook of American
Churches* (1933–1972), and *Yearbook of
American & Canadian Churches* (1973–2011).

Eileen W. Lindner	*Editor*
Marcel A. Welty	*Associate Editor*
Elizabeth During	*Assistant Editor*

CONTENTS

Editor's Preface 7

I
PERSPECTIVES ON AMERICA'S RELIGIOUS LANDSCAPE

Trends & Developments, 2010 9
    Table 1. Longitudinal Inclusive Membership 1890–2010 10
    Table 2. U.S. Membership Church Ranking: Largest 25 Churches . . .12
    Table 3. Patterns of U.S. Membership Change of Selected
            Large Churches 2007–2010 14
    Table 4. U.S. Financial Summaries 2003–2010 14
Can the Church Log In with the "Connected Generation"? 16

II
DIRECTORIES

1. United States Cooperative Organizations, National 21
2. Canadian Cooperative Organizations, National 48
3. Religious Bodies in the United States 56
    Religious Bodies in the United States Arranged by Family 181
4. Religious Bodies in Canada 185
    Religious Bodies in the Canada Arranged by Family 215
5. Sources of Religion-Related Research 217
    I. Directory of Selected Research Organizations 217
    II. Directory of Selected Faith Communities in America 226
6. United States Regional and Local Ecumenical Bodies 238
    Index of Select Programs for U.S. Regional and
            Local Ecumenical Bodies 273
7. Canadian Regional and Local Ecumenical Bodies 292
8. Theological Seminaries and Bible Colleges in the United States 295
9. Theological Seminaries and Bible Colleges in Canada 317
10. Religious Periodicals in the United States 323
11. Religious Periodicals in Canada 346
12. Church Archives and Historical Records Collections 352

III
STATISTICAL SECTION

Guide to Statistical Tables 361
1. Membership Statistics in Canada 362
2. Membership Statistics in the United States 367
3. Membership Statistics for the National Council of Churches USA 378
4. Selected Statistics of Church Finances—Canadian Churches 380
5. Selected Statistics of Church Finances—United States Churches 382
Trends in Seminary Enrollment 388

IV
A CALENDAR FOR CHURCH USE

A Calendar for Church Use, 2012–2014 391

V
INDEXES

Organizations 395
Individuals 407

Editor's Preface

This eightieth edition of the *Yearbook of American & Canadian Churches* marks another anniversary that affirms the remarkable service this resource has played in preserving a fascinating record of our ever-changing religious institutions. We are especially conscious of the intense labors of previous editors and contributors who shaped this annual compilation of data in earlier years, and we are grateful to maintain their legacy. This 2012 edition is accessible in both hardcopy and electronically over the Internet using the unique pass code printed on the inside back cover of this volume. Updated information is reflected in the electronic edition twice during the year. In addition, a compact disc exists of data dating from 1916 through 2000, and brings these longitudinal data into ready availability.

Recognizing the Contributions of Many

The field of church statistics is complex and, of necessity, filled with inconsistencies. In recent years, electronic reporting has enabled greater amounts of time at each data collection level to raise questions and to recalculate and refine reports. We at the *Yearbook* are pleased to take our place in this important task of annually capturing a snapshot of American religious life. Reflection upon such findings tells us much about ourselves as well as the institutional religious life in a country which has been referred to as a "nation with the soul of a church."

Our colleagues in the compilation of each edition of the Yearbook are the thousands, perhaps tens of thousands, of individuals who keep church records. We rely and build upon the efforts of church pastors, deacons, secretaries and vestrymen and women who carefully review and report church membership statistics and financial giving. We acknowledge the contributions of those at congregational, regional and especially denominational levels who respond with good cheer and expeditiously in furnishing us with the detailed data we require in the format that we request. We hope that being a part of the record and analysis offered by the Yearbook contributes to their sense of satisfaction for a job well done.

For various chapters of the *Yearbook* we are indebted to specific individuals for their assistance in gathering, analyzing and corroborating the information we publish. We thank Eliza Smith Brown for her help in compiling the seminary enrollment data and providing insightful analysis. Our colleague Tracy DeLuca, Librarian of the Interchurch Center in New York is a regular and reliable consultant to us. We are grateful to Dale Dickerson who competently and expertly guides us through the maze and considerable complexity of the various religious calendars. Mark J. Duffy of the Episcopal Church Archives helps us accurately reflect the changes in religious archives and historical records collections. Cathy Lavendar of the United States Census Bureau assures that the Statistical Abstract remains current with *Yearbook* data.

Annual production of the *Yearbook* requires a variety of skills and commitments within our own editorial offices. Associate Editor, Marcel A. Welty gives leadership and prodigious effort to the logistics of researching, requesting, compiling, confirming, correcting, formatting and preparing data for analysis. Elizabeth During is the indefatigable Assistant Editor. Her careful attention to detail and efficient research and organization skills make the *Yearbook* possible. Almost as closely associated with us as those we see each day are our colleagues and friends of long standing, John and Sylvia Ronsvalle, of the *empty tomb, inc.* Nationally recognized for their steadfast attention to the patterns of church giving, the Ronsvalles are unfailingly gracious in providing expert assistance and in enabling our own analysis. As we went to press, their excellent analysis of church giving, *The State of Church Giving through 2009* (Twenty-first edition, October 2011), includes among other insightful analyses an exploration of the role of the U.S.A. Christian churches in addressing child mortality in 16 countries, and is highly recommended to those interested in understanding church benevolence.

On behalf of those readers, we extend our gratitude for the wisdom, skill, patience and generosity of those we acknowledge here. No small group of individuals could hope to have the knowledge needed to compile a text as far ranging as the *Yearbook*. Our efforts strengthened by the contributions of all those named above have led to the 80th edition of the *Yearbook of American & Canadian Churches*; we wish to express our deepest thanks to each of them.

The 2012 Edition Features

- Reports on 228 national church bodies, listing leadership and headquarters information in brief which itself is reflective of a remarkably robust immigrant history and the cultural and constitutional freedom of religion so characteristic of the United States.

- Signals that churches reporting in *Yearbook* statistics reflect an overall decline in churches' membership by 146,893 members from the previous reporting, representing a decline in total affiliation of -0.1%.

- Reports financial data for 63 US religious bodies showing a startling $1.23 billion decline in total giving from previous reporting, reflecting a decline of -3.5%.

- Reports longitudinal membership figures which suggest a relatively steady trend pattern for membership decline and growth between groups. Among the implications of these trends are confirming signs of continued displacement of mainline protestant denominations in the top twenty-five largest church bodies.

- Continues to offer an inclusive directory of 235 US local and regional ecumenical bodies with program and contact information.

- Provides listings of theological seminaries and bible schools, religious periodicals and guides to religious research including church archive listings.

- Access to accurate and timely information is available through the Yearbook's Internet edition, in its tenth year. Access is provided through a unique passcode printed inside the back cover of the *Yearbook*.

The 2012 Edition Updates

- Ranks the 25 largest churches by membership. Only three of the top ten are "mainline" protestant churches. Reports the fastest growing churches in this group as: the Assemblies of God. The Church of Jesus Christ of Latter-day Saints continued a steady growth pattern, as well the Seventh Day Adventists.

- We offer reports after extended hiatus by the Pentecostal Assemblies of the World, Inc., and the National Baptist Convention USA, Inc.

- Analyzes the financial data from 63 churches representing almost 45 million members and over $34 billion dollars.

The 2012 Edition Trends

- Reviews recent research on the Millennial Generation, their patterns of religious participation, and the implications for religious institutions' membership and mission (pp. 16–20).

- Notes a continued acceleration of church membership decline in mainline church traditions (p. 12).

- Notes a weakening in reported giving, with a relatively lower rate of decline in benevolence giving (p. 15).

- Reports on an overall decline in same-seminaries enrollment (p. 384).

- Despite an overall decline in seminary enrollment, the Association of Theological Seminaries figures reflect minority enrollment remains relatively strong. Hispanic and African American enrollment continues to rise, while Asian enrollment decreased in this report.

Eileen W. Lindner
Editor
New York, 2011

I

PERSPECTIVES ON AMERICA'S RELIGIOUS LANDSCAPE

Trends & Developments, 2011

Methodological Considerations

The *Yearbook of American & Canadian Churches* reports annually on data gathered from national religious bodies that reflect the religious affiliations and financial giving patterns of hundreds of millions of Americans. However, these data generally represent information gathered two calendar years prior to the year of publication. For instance, data reported in this 2012 edition of the *Yearbook* reflects information for 2010 that was collected by national church structures in 2011 and reported to the Yearbook at the end of 2011 for publication in this 2012 *Yearbook*. This "lag time" often leads our readers to ask if such data is out of date by the time it is printed. In response we would give a qualified "no." Massive national agencies such as the churches reporting through the *Yearbook* move in their institutional lives at nearly imperceptible rates of speed. Moreover, given the vast size and complexity of such diverse organizations, partial data reported more frequently might well have the unintended effect of conveying a sense of "trend" to momentary or regionally isolated patterns of reporting, affiliation and/or financial giving. Now in the 80th edition, the *Yearbook* believes that an annual review of data continues to provide an appropriate interval for tracking the changes in institutional patterns.

No single standard for data collection exists across the variety of ecclesiastical structures reported in the *Yearbook*. Moreover, the definitions of membership and related terms differ widely from one church structure to another. This lack of universal definition and collection methodology has frequently led to questions about the validity and reliability of self-reported data. Recognizing the limitations of the data reported herein, we continue to have confidence in the overall value of trends and other findings based on these figures and this methodology. While church data collection and analytical practices differ across various institutional and organizational margins, they tend to be remarkably consistent *within* specific organizations over time. (Where we are made aware of changes in a particular church's reporting methods, we will note them for the reader.) This consistency within organizations brings a greater degree of confidence to the relative data of a given church over time. For the same reason the *relative* size of one church to another as reported here, we believe, provides an accurate picture even while lacking a degree of absolute precision of membership statistics, particularly over time. Thus, we believe that the Southern Baptist Convention is roughly twice the size of the United Methodist Church, for example, and that changes relative to each other over several years are probably an accurate reflection of actual membership trends. Moreover, these data are the most exacting figures presently available, and thus serve as the national standard.

The first eight decades of record keeping represented by the Y*earbook of American & Canadian Churches* is contained on a comprehensive Historic Archive on CD-ROM (which contains membership and financial data from 1916–1999). This CD provides a longitudinal backdrop for the analysis that follows. Only through such a longitudinal study of growth and decline in membership are we able to capture and analyze the emerging patterns. Our annual trends analysis should be regarded as a snapshot taken at a discrete moment in history. The meaning of the figures within that snapshot will best be given definition by the larger and longer context of which they are a part.

The reader is invited to utilize both the current edition and the *Yearbook of American & Canadian Churches'* historic CD to test and amplify the analysis that follows. To obtain the Historic Archive on CD-ROM call (888) 870-3325.

Table 1
Longitudinal Inclusive Membership 1890–2010

Year	Membership	Source	Year	Membership	Source
1890	41,699,342	CRB	1970	131,045,053	YBAC
1906	35,068,058	CRB	1971	131,389,642	YBAC
1916	41,926,852	CRB	1972	131,424,564	YBAC
1926	54,576,346	CRB	1973	131,245,139	YBAC
1931	59,268,764	CH	1974	131,871,743	YBAC
1932	60,157,392	CH	1975	131,012,953	YBACC
1933	60,812,624	CH	1976	131,897,539	YBACC
1934	62,007,376	CH	1977	131,812,470	YBACC
1935	62,678,177	CH	1978	133,388,776	YBACC
1936	55,807,366	CRB	1979	133,469,690	YBACC
1936	63,221,996	CH	1980	134,816,943	YBACC
1937	63,848,094	CH	1981	138,452,614	YBACC
1938	64,156,895	YBAC	1982	139,603,059	YBACC
1940	64,501,594	YBAC	1983	140,816,385	YBACC
1942	68,501,186	YBAC	1984	142,172,138	YBACC
1944	72,492,699	YBAC	1985	142,926,363	YBACC
1945	71,700,142	CH	1986	142,799,662	YBACC
1946	73,673,182	CH	1987	143,830,806	YBACC
1947	77,386,188	CH	1988	145,383,739	YBACC
1948	19,435,605	CH	1989	147,607,394	YBACC
1949	81,862,328	CH	1990	156,331,704	YBACC
1950	86,830,490	YBAC	1991	156,629,918	YBACC
1951	88,673,005	YBAC	1992	156,557,746	YBACC
1952	92,277,129	YBAC	1993	153,127,045	YBACC
1953	94,842,845	YBAC	1994	158,218,427	YBACC
1954	97,482,611	YBAC	1995	157,984,194	YBACC
1955	100,162,529	YBAC	1996	159,471,758	YBACC
1956	103,224,954	YBAC	1997	157,503,033	YBACC
1957	104,189,678	YBAC	1998	150,105,525	YBACC
1958	109,557,741	YBAC	1999	151,161,906	YBACC
1959	112,226,905	YBAC	2000	152,134,407	YBACC
1960	114,449,217	YBAC	2001	158,952,292	YBACC
1961	116,109,929	YBAC	2002	161,202,780	YBACC
1962	117,946,002	YBAC	2003	163,128,935	YBACC
1963	120,965,238	YBAC	2004	163,438,911	YBACC
1964	123,307,449	YBAC	2005	163,677,894	YBACC
1965	124,682,422	YBAC	2006	163,698,507	YBACC
1966	125,778,656	YBAC	2007	162,555,074	YBACC
1967	126,445,110	YBAC	2008	163,325,722	YBACC
1968	128,469,636	YBAC	2009	160,012,464	YBACC
1969	12,505,084	YBAC	2010	159,848,057	YBACC

Source Key:
CRB- Census of Religious Bodies, Bureau of the Census, Washington
CH- *The Christian Herald*, New York
YBAC- *Yearbook of American Churches*, New York
YBACC- *Yearbook of American and Canadian Churches*, New York

Table 1 Longitudinal Inclusive Membership

This Table represents a longitudinal view of aggregated membership totals for all churches reporting to the *Yearbook*. These data do not reflect the entirety of national church membership since some churches either do not gather such data, or do not report them to the *Yearbook*. These figures moreover do not include membership of independent congregations including megachurches. Substantial numbers of church members, therefore, are not accounted for in nationally-gathered membership data. With almost 160 million adherents, the churches collectively continue to maintain a substantial organizational and institutional presence within the United States. Despite this institutional constancy this year's figure reflects a small decline in reported membership of 164,407 or -0.1%, but suggests a confirmation of a trend in the aggregate to fewer members.

Table 2 U.S Membership Church Ranking

This table allows comparison in size as determined by membership of the largest twenty-five churches in the nation. Dwarfing any single other church is the Catholic Church, reporting over 68.2 million adherents. The Southern Baptist Convention, with 16 million members is the largest Protestant denomination and is more than twice the size of the third ranked United Methodist Church. The Church of Jesus Christ of Latter-day Saints is ranked 4th with 6 million members. With the exception of the Greek Orthodox Archdiocese which is ranked 17th, and the Jehovah's Witnesses which is ranked 20th, the remainder of the top 25 are Protestant Churches.

The patterns of affiliation reflected in this table offer a numerical view and summary of American church history. Protestantism has, since the founding of the republic and until the present moment, enjoyed cultural hegemony accompanied throughout by a consistent substantial Catholic presence.

Four of the twenty-five largest churches are Pentecostal in belief and practice. Strong figures from the Assemblies of God, and a big jump in the Pentecostal Assemblies of the World (*which reflects four years of growth from last report in 2006*), balanced against relatively modest losses from the Church of God (Cleveland, Tennessee), might suggest a continuing increase in total numbers of adherents to Pentecostal groups. It is difficult to conclude, however, that a broad trend in Pentecostal groups is under way from this table since the largest Pentecostal church in this ranking has not reported since 1991. The four largest Pentecostal churches are: The Church of God in Christ, Assemblies of God, the Pentecostal Assemblies of the World, Inc., and the Church of God (Cleveland, Tennessee)

The last column in Table 2 presents increases (decreases) as a percentage change from the 79th Edition's reported membership figures. As the figures indicate, the direction of membership (growth or decline) remains very stable. That is, most churches which have been increasing in membership in recent years have continued to grow and likewise, those churches which have been declining in membership in recent years have continued to decline in membership.

Among the churches reporting increases in membership the largest single-year increase reported was 3.99% by the Assemblies of God, which has reported relatively more modest growth rates in recent years. The Church of Jesus Christ of Latter-day Saints continued a steady growth pattern, posting a solid 1.62% gain. Seventh Day Adventists also reported continued growth at 1.61%.The largest increase in this table of the 25 biggest groups was 20% reported by the Pentecostal Assemblies of the World, Inc., which increased its membership by 20% reflecting 4 years growth since last report in 2006. The National Baptist Convention USA, Inc. also reported a large, albeit multi-year increase of 3.95%, having last reported figures for 2004.

Among the churches reporting a decline in membership, two large churches, the Catholic Church (-0.44%), and the Church of God (Cleveland, Tennessee) (-0.21%), reflect a single year reversal from increases to decline. Of the other groups reporting declines, the four biggest declines were reported by mainline protestant denominations. The Evangelical Lutheran Church in America (-5.90%) shows an acceleration of the rate of decline. The second fastest decline was reported by the Presbyterian Church (U.S.A.) at -3.42%. The third and fourth fastest decliners were The Episcopal Church and the United Church of Christ, reporting -2.71% and -2.02% respectively. Rounding out the list of decliners are the Lutheran Church—Missouri Synod (-1.45%), The United Methodist Church (-1.22%), the American Baptist Churches in the U.S.A. (-0.19%), and the Southern Baptist Convention (-0.15%).

In terms of ranking, the 14 biggest groups maintained their places in the order, while the Pentecostal Assemblies of the World jumped from 17th place to 15th place. The Church of God (Cleveland, Tennessee) rose to 21st largest, and the Christian Churches and Churches of Christ,

Table 2

US MEMBERSHIP CHURCH RANKING: Largest 25 Churches

Denomination Nane	Inclusive Membership	Current Ranking [2010 Ed.]	Percentage Increase/ Decrease 2011–2012 Editions
The Catholic Church	68,202,492	1[1]	-0.44%
Southern Baptist Convention	16,136,044	2[2]	-0.15%
The United Methodist Church	7,679,850	3[3]	-1.22%
The Church of Jesus Christ of Latter-day Saints	6,157,238	4[4]	1.62%
The Church of God in Christ	5,499,875	5[5]	*0.00%*
National Baptist Convention, U.S.A., Inc.	5,197,512	6[6]	3.95%
Evangelical Lutheran Church in America	4,274,855	7[7]	-5.90%
National Baptist Convention of America, Inc.	3,500,000	8[8]	*0.00%*
Assemblies of God	3,030,944	9[9]	3.99%
Presbyterian Church (U.S.A.)	2,675,873	10[10]	-3.42%
African Methodist Episcopal Church	2,500,000	11[11]	*0.00%*
National Missionary Baptist Convention of America	2,500,000	11[11]	*0.00%*
The Lutheran Church— Missouri Synod (LCMS)	2,278,586	13[13]	-1.45%
The Episcopal Church	1,951,907	14[14]	-2.71%
Pentecostal Assemblies of the World, Inc.	1,800,000	15[17]	20.00%
Churches of Christ	1,639,495	16[15]	*0.00%*
Greek Orthodox Archdiocese of America	1,500,000	17[16]	*0.00%*
The African Methodist Episcopal Zion Church	1,400,000	18[18]	*0.00%*
American Baptist Churches in the U.S.A.	1,308,054	19[19]	-0.19%
Jehovah's Witnesses	1,184,249	20[20]	1.85%
Church of God (Cleveland, Tennessee)	1,074,047	21[22]	-0.21%
Christian Churches and Churches of Christ	1,071,616	22[23]	*0.00%*
Seventh-day Adventist Church	1,060,386	23[24]	1.61%
United Church of Christ	1,058,423	24[21]	-2.02%
Progressive National Baptist Convention, Inc.	1,010,000	25[25]	*0.00%*
TOTALS	**145,691,446**		**-0.10%**

Note: Percentage changes in *italic* signify that membership was not updated from previous reported figures.

as well the Seventh Day Adventist Church each rose one place in the ranking, to 22nd and 23rd respectively. The most significant drop in ranking was a move from 21st to 24th by the United Church of Christ.

Further discussion of these patterns is found in relation to Table 3 reported below. It should be noted that in the context of overall declining membership in the broadest aggregate in Table 1, all five mainline protestant denominations in this Table 2 are reporting declining membership.

In the last quarter century there has been much analysis and debate concerning the decline of "mainline" Protestantism. Despite the pattern of membership decline which predominates among these churches and in the aggregate, this ranking illustrates a continuing significant presence of mainline Protestantism in the American religious landscape. Of the top ten largest churches three are mainline protestant (The United Methodist Church, Evangelical Lutheran Church in America, and Presbyterian Church U.S.A.). In the top twenty-five churches, six are mainline protestant. In addition to the three noted above the mainline churches in the top twenty five largest churches include: American Baptist Churches in the U.S.A., The Episcopal Church, and the United Church of Christ.

The top fifteen churches, those with membership exceeding 1.5 million members, are reflective of the constancy of the Historic Black Churches. Five of the fifteen largest churches (The Church of God in Christ, National Baptist Convention USA Inc., National Baptist Convention of America Inc., African Methodist Episcopal Church, National Missionary Baptist Convention of America, and the African Methodist Episcopal Zion Church) are predominately African American churches. This of course is reflective of the historic and continuing strength of the church within the African American community.

12

Last Year's (2011 Edition) Ranking

Denomination Name	Inclusive Membership	Percentage Increase/Decrease, 2010–2011 Editions
The Catholic Church	68,503,456	0.57%
Southern Baptist Convention	16,160,088	-0.42%
The United Methodist Church	7,774,931	-1.01%
The Church of Jesus Christ of Latter-day Saints	6,058,907	1.42%
The Church of God in Christ	5,499,875	*0.00%*
National Baptist Convention, U.S.A., Inc.	5,000,000	*0.00%*
Evangelical Lutheran Church in America	4,542,868	-1.96%
National Baptist Convention of America, Inc.	3,500,000	*0.00%*
Assemblies of God	2,914,669	0.52%
Presbyterian Church (U.S.A.)	2,770,730	-2.61%
African Methodist Episcopal Church	2,500,000	*0.00%*
National Missionary Baptist Convention of America	2,500,000	*0.00%*
The Lutheran Church— Missouri Synod (LCMS)	2,312,111	-1.08%
The Episcopal Church	2,006,343	-2.48%
Churches of Christ	1,639,495	*0.00%*
Greek Orthodox Archdiocese of America	1,500,000	*0.00%*
Pentecostal Assemblies of the World, Inc.	1,500,000	*0.00%*
The African Methodist Episcopal Zion Church	1,400,000	*0.00%*
American Baptist Churches in the U.S.A.	1,310,505	-1.55%
Jehovah's Witnesses	1,162,686	4.37%
United Church of Christ	1,080,199	-2.83%
Church of God (Cleveland, Tennessee)	1,076,254	0.38%
Christian Churches and Churches of Christ	1,071,616	*0.00%*
Seventh-day Adventist Church	1,043,606	4.31%
Progressive National Baptist Convention, Inc.	1,010,000	-59.60%
TOTALS	**145,838,339**	**-1.05%**

Note: Percentage changes in *italic* signify that membership was not updated from previous reported figures.

Table 3 Patterns of Membership Gains and Losses

Table 3 offers longitudinal data on rate of growth or loss of church membership of a selected group of large churches for four years, 2007-2010.

The large churches reporting growth measured as a percentage of membership are: the Church of Jesus Christ of Latter-day Saints (1.62%), and the Assemblies of God (3.99%). Each of these churches report a steady trend of membership growth. Among the seven churches reporting a decline in membership, only one has reported any year-over-year growth since 2007, while four report faster rates of decline over the previous year (The United Methodist Church, Presbyterian Church (U.S.A.), Evangelical Lutheran Church, and Lutheran Church-Missouri Synod) and two churches (The United Methodist Church, and the Evangelical Lutheran Church in America) report an accelerated rate of decline in every successive year reflected in this reporting period. Some will wish to argue that the overall pattern of declining membership and sustained decline is evidence of an increasing secularization of American postmodern society. The finding reported for Table 1 (above) concerning an overall decline of -0.2% of membership offers further support for such a conclusion. Yet, caution in drawing such a conclusion is warranted. American society as whole has not experienced the kind and rate of secularization so clearly demonstrated during the last quarter century in Western Europe. Indeed, American church membership trends have defied gravity particularly when the Pentecostal experience is included. Alternative explanations for slowed membership growth are offered in this edition's focus chapter on the religious participation patterns of the Millennial Generation. These shifts in the ways young adults identify spiritually and relate to institutional religion must be carefully considered during the next few years if we are to make sense of the patterns which are now emerging.

Table 3

PATTERNS OF US MEMBERSHIP CHANGE OF SELECTED LARGE CHURCHES 2007–2010

Religious Body	2007 Membership Change	% Change	2008 Membership Change	% Change	2009 Membership Change	% Change	2010 Membership Change	% Change
The Catholic Church	-398,000	-0.59	997,985	1.49%	388,455	0.57%	-300,964	-0.44%
Southern Baptist Convention	-39,326	-0.24	-38,482	-0.24%	-68,350	-0.42%	-24,044	-0.15%
The United Methodist Church	-63,723	-0.80	-77,746	-0.98%	-79,056	-1.01%	-95,081	-1.22%
Evangelical Lutheran Church in America	-64,247	-1.35	-76,069	-1.62%	-91,019	-1.96%	-268,013	-5.90%
The Church of Jesus Christ of Latter-day Saints	94,092	1.63	100,633	1.71%	84,866	1.42%	98,331	1.62%
Presbyterian Church (U.S.A.)	-84,328	-2.79	-96,460	-3.28%	-74,222	-2.61%	-94,857	-3.42%
The Lutheran Church- Missouri Synod	-34,913	-1.44	-45,735	-1.92%	-25,238	-1.08%	-33,525	-1.45%
Assemblies of God	27,091	0.96	36,437	1.27%	14,967	0.52%	116,275	3.99%
American Baptist Churches in the U.S.A.	-12,927	-0.94	-62,804	-2.00%	-20,622	-1.55%	-2,451	-0.19%

Table 4

US FINANCIAL SUMMARIES 2003–2010

Year	Number Reporting	Full or Confirmed Members	Inclusive Members	Total Contributions	Per Capita Full or Confirmed Members	Per Capita Inclusive Members
2003	63	44,211,342	48,266,164	$32,269,713,588	$725.78	$667.34
2004	63	43,823,753	47,850,712	$33,214,186,254	$757.90	$694.12
2005	65	43,565,587	47,922,181	$34,170,801,942	$784.35	$713.05
2006	65	42,224,304	46,101,429	$34,219,114,885	$810.41	$742.26
2007	66	41,881,459	45,735,653	$35,949,676,148	$858.37	$786.03
2008	64	41,176,007	44,959,642	$35,922,818,150	$872.42	$786.03
2009	64	41,782,073	45,476,981	$35,472,748,189	$848.99	$780.02
2010	63	41,318,804	44,891,281	$34,248,155,335	$828.88	$762.91

Year	Total Congregational Contributions	Per Capita Full or Confirmed Members	Per Capita Inclusive Members	Total Benevolences	Per Capita Full or Confirmed Members	Per Capita Inclusive Members	Benevolence as a Percentage of Total Contributions
2003	$27,723,558,838	$627.07	$574.39	$4,748,202,343	$107.40	$98.38	15%
2004	$28,294,047,495	$645.63	$591.30	$4,921,921,435	$112.31	$102.86	15%
2005	$29,002,718,319	$665.73	$605.20	$5,168,083,623	$118.63	$107.84	15%
2006	$28,773,748,252	$681.45	$624.14	$5,389,573,754	$127.64	$116.91	16%
2007	$30,479,091,937	$727.75	$666.42	$5,470,584,375	$130.62	$119.61	15%
2008	$30,408,578,031	$738.50	$676.34	$5,514,242,844	$133.92	$122.65	15%
2009	$30,039,262,110	$718.95	$660.54	$5,406,158,561	$129.39	$118.88	15%
2010	$28,981,550,973	$701.41	$645.59	$5,266,604,587	$127.46	$117.32	15%

Several factors will need to be weighed afresh including the very centrality of the concept of church membership itself. For the age cohorts known as Gen X'ers and Millennials (people now in their 30s and 20s respectively) formal membership may lie outside of their hopes and expectations for their church relationships. For both of these age cohorts membership and commitment to institutions is no longer perceived as a mark of maturity or assumption of generational responsibility. Membership is sometimes perceived as an unnecessary and even undesirable exercise in over-institutionalization. Hence, for some young adults, church attendance, participation in fellowship or mission activities and even financial support of a local congregation does not translate into a desire to formally "join" and be listed among those in membership. Several other factors are at play, including diminished denominational structures and authority, which in turn, produce less complete membership reports, and emerging patterns of affiliation with independent congregations whose membership is not aggregated and reported, must be further explored in assessing overall decline in church membership.

Table 4 Financial Trends

Second only to the interest in membership trends is the interest of media and the church world alike in the financial trends reported in the *Yearbook*. While not all churches report their financial information to the *Yearbook*, 63 churches have provided full data for this 2012 edition providing an important glimpse into United States church giving. Over $34 billion dollars are accounted for in the reports of these churches and this is, of course, but a portion of the whole of church giving.

The financial reporting for this 2012 *Yearbook* is based on the financial income reports of 63 churches reporting essential figures. The records of those reporting churches are detailed in Table 4. The almost 45 million inclusive members contributed a total of almost $29 billion, marking a decrease in the total amount of income to the churches by $1.2 billion. This enormous loss of revenue dwarfs the $431 million decrease in giving reported last year and provides clear evidence of the impact of the deepening economic crises in the reporting period. All categories of Financial information declined: Total Giving, Giving to Congregations, and Giving for Benevolence.

Given that these figures reflect only a sample of churches, and that the number of churches reporting this year is reduced from 65 to 63, it is particularly useful to view this decrease in its *per capita* terms. The $763 contributed per person is a decrease of about $17 per person from the previous year. This 2.2 % decrease in *per capita* giving took place in the context of ongoing high unemployment and a protracted economic downturn. Yet it must be remembered that many individuals are contributing to parishes with a declining number of members. In such settings an increase in giving would be required to offset the financial loss associated with membership decline.

Benevolence giving for 2010 in our sample of United States churches is consistent with the last report and over several years, at 15%, but remains at the low end in the range of benevolent giving over the longer period of the last decade. A decline of -2.20% in the total funds contributed to congregations *per capita* was accompanied by a relatively lower decrease in *per capita* giving toward benevolences (-1.39%.) Overall, less total funding is available to support church-sponsored day care, soup kitchens, emergency help to persons with medical problems, or transportation to the elderly, even as the material need increases. In the midst of economic distress such decreases in benevolent giving are visited upon those least able to accommodate them. However, this year's reporting suggests that support for charitable purposes is not as adversely affected as the other parts of congregation's budgets: denominational support, buildings, salaries, etc.

An interesting comparison can be made with benevolence reported by Canadian churches. While admittedly reporting on a far smaller sample and reflecting a lower level of total giving, in the present reporting period characterized by economic hardship, the Canadian churches also report decreases in Total and Congregational giving, but significantly less decline in Benevolence giving. This relative support in charitable giving is reflected in the increase by 1 percent to 18% in Benevolences as a Percentage of Total Giving. US churches have likewise experienced declines in all types of church giving, but the share of giving for charitable purposes is remaining proportionally the same. Over the longer term, the percentage of benevolence giving for Canadian churches has remained in recent years in the 18%–20% range.

No one has given greater attention to church giving patterns than John and Sylvia Ronsvalle. For a fulsome discussion of the giving patterns of churches, see their The State of Church Giving series of publications, by writing: empty tomb, inc. P.O. Box 2404, Champaign, IL 61825, or through www.emptytomb.org.

Can the Church Log In with the "Connected Generation"?

The Church and Young Adults

Eileen W. Lindner, PhD

In each edition the Yearbook of American and Canadian Churches reviews current quantitative research which addresses some aspect of institutional church life within the contemporary American religious landscape. For this edition we have reviewed the rather extensive current research regarding the religious beliefs, practices and patterns of church affiliation of the Millennial Generation who are now in their mid twenties to early thirties. We have also examined the preliminary responses of the churches to these expressions of religious identity. Finally we conclude this theme chapter by pointing to promising areas for future research related to young adults and their relationship to the church.

Defining and locating Millennials within America Culture

To be sure, generational studies have their limitations and their own methodological challenges: Inclusive dates for specific generations are difficult to fix; intragenerational differences are easily overlooked; sampling issues and strategies emerge, and experiences common to the age cohort are often shared by other generational groups. Nonetheless, such studies have been productive of fresh insight and are broadly regarded as versatile tools of social science. Special caution must be exercised in generational studies to avoid formation of such tightly constructed generational archetypes that individual philosophic and psychological characteristics are lost within sweeping generational profiles.

Despite the limitations and cautions associated with generational studies, in the early years of the twenty-first century such approaches have gained new appeal and interest. Particular attention has been focused upon the age cohort variously known as the Millenials, the Echo (of the Baby Boomer) generation, the Net generation, the Dot.Com generation or the Y Generation. No common definition of the Millennials currently prevails with some researchers including those born as early as the mid 1970s to the mid 1990s and others using inclusive dates as late as 1980 to 2000. The Pew Research Center in its seminal study, *Millennials: A Portrait of Generation Next,* published in February of 2010 studied those born between 1981 and 1991 and defines the generation as those born after 1980. Now age 18-28, this age cohort is presently coming into young adulthood a decade into the twenty-first century. The largest cohort since the Baby Boomers, Millennials now comprise 25% of the US population and will exceed 30% by 2030. Racially and ethnically more diverse than previous generations, the social implications of their values, choices and aspirations will shape the culture and the church through the remainder of the century.

Scott Keeter and Paul Taylor, editors of the Pew study, offer a sweeping and comprehensive view of what makes this generation distinct, finding them "confident, connected and open to change." Despite being a post-9/11 cohort and launching careers in the midst of a deep economic recession, they remain optimistic about their economic prospects even in the face of the highest generational unemployment rates in thirty years. Their priorities accord with traditional American ambitions as they seek to be good parents in successful marriages, assisting those in need and owning a home and respecting their elders.

Their confidence may be tested by their economic circumstance. A 2009 MetLife *Study of the American Dream* found that, financially, Millennials have no expectation of an enduring governmental safety net and anticipate episodic unemployment and career changes throughout their lifetimes. With a higher percentage of college graduates, Millennials carry more indebtedness at graduation with $19,000 the average burden. Such a context fosters a high degree of skepticism with regard to the nation's primary institutions.

Despite this skepticism the political and social values trend toward the liberal among Millennials, and they voted in large numbers for the victor in the 2008 presidential election

16

and favor progressive policies on issues like abortion, homosexual marriage and expanding the role of government. A 2011 Brookings Institution study of 1000 Millennial leaders explored how this generation envisions leadership. Asked which historic figure best exemplifies the leadership needed in the twenty-first century, over one third named a civilian leader associated with wartime government. Franklin Roosevelt, Abraham Lincoln and John Kennedy were most frequently identified. Only 10% chose leaders of social change such as Martin Luther King, Jr., Nelson Mandela and Gandhi. When asked about current leaders as models for twenty-first century leadership, 49% named President Obama (62.8% of the sample were Democrats; 28% Republican).

Having been raised in the midst of a techno revolution, the Millennials are comfortable with digital technology and social media. As the first generation of "digital natives" they blog, email, text, download, upload and consume electronic messages at a rate and volume far in excess of any other cohort. They seek authenticity of relationships both online and offline with three quarters of them maintaining at least one social network profile. As a generation they are self aware of the distinctiveness of their ever-present connectedness and seek far-flung relationships with persons, electronic "friends," quite unlike themselves.

Belonging and Believing

The Pew study found that this age cohort is considerably less likely to maintain religious affiliation than older Americans. The diminution of religion in the lives of Millennials is measured not only by a decline in identification with a specific faith group but also by less frequent engagement in other religious practices such as prayer, meditation, worship attendance and Bible study. One quarter of this generation has no religious affiliation which is significantly higher than other generational groups at a similar point in their life cycle. Baby Boomers, for example, registered only 13% unaffiliated rate in the mid-1970s. It should be noted that it is very hard to measure religious non-participation and non-belief patterns since religious identity lingers long after participation has ceased. Moreover, some social stigma attaches to the acknowledgement of lack of religious identity in some quarters.

Suggestions that the Millennial generation are signaling the secularization of American culture are premature and ignore the rather nuanced religious identity of this age cohort. Belonging to a religious organization is a behavior. Belief is a conviction. As regards belief, Millennials have much in common with other Americans. Data from the General Social Surveys (GSS) show that 53% of Millennials profess a "certain" belief in God. Pew found that 64% of Millennials had "no doubt" about the existence of God compared to 73% of the population as a whole. Inasmuch as convictions of God's existence have tended to increase with age in other generations the religious belief of Millennials may not prove to be as distinct from other generations as it now appears. Pew found that adults under 30 are just as likely as older adults to believe in life after death (75% vs. 74%), heaven (74% each), hell (62% vs. 59%) and miracles (78% vs. 79%).

Millennials may frame their religious convictions in an idiom unique to their age cohort. A Lifeway study found that 72% of Millennials reported being "spiritual but not religious." Moreover, given their ethnic diversity, Millennials are exposed to a wide variety of religious expressions in an increasingly religiously plural environment. Only 7% of the age cohort reported that all or most of their friends were of their same religious identity as themselves.

Three quarters of the generation do maintain a religious identity with 68% identifying themselves as members of a Christian church (compared to 81% of adults over 30) and 43% describing themselves as Protestants, compared with 53% of those over 30, according to Pew. Among these affiliated Millennials, measures of religious *intensity* is as strong as for older Americans. Affiliated Millennials are actually more inclined than their elders to believe their own religion is the single true path to eternal life (29% vs. 23% for older adults) Yet, affiliated Millennials are more open to various interpretations of religious doctrine and less likely to perceive the Bible as *literal* truth. More Millennials who were once affiliated with mainline denominations now report being unaffiliated than those who were affiliated with more conservative evangelical traditions. As a result those in the age cohort who remain affiliated are more likely to have greater religious intensity and somewhat more conservative evangelical beliefs.

Religious Composition of Age Groups

	Total Pop. %	Total 18-29%	Total 30+%	30-39%	40-49%	50-59%	60-69%	70+%
Christian	**78**	**68**	**81**	**76**	**80**	**80**	**84**	**88**
Protestant	51	43	53	47	52	54	57	62
Evangelical Churches	*26*	*22*	*27*	*26*	*28*	*27*	*29*	*30*
Mainline Churches	*18*	*12*	*19*	*16*	*17*	*20*	*21*	*26*
Historically Black Churches	*7*	*8*	*7*	*6*	*7*	*7*	*7*	*6*
Catholic	24	22	24	25	25	23	24	23
Mormon	2	2	2	2	2	1	2	1
Jehovah's Witness	1	1	1	1	1	1	1	1
Orthodox	1	1	1	1	1	1	<0.5	1
Other Christian	<0.5	<0.5	<0.5	<0.5	<0.5	<0.5	1	<0.5
Other Religions	**5**	**6**	**4**	**5**	**4**	**5**	**5**	**4**
Jewish	2	2	2	1	1	2	2	2
Muslim	1	1	<0.5	1	<0.5	<0.5	<0.5	<0.5
Buddhist	1	1	1	1	1	1	1	<0.5
Hindu	<0.5	<0.5	<0.5	1	<0.5	<0.5	<0.5	<0.5
Other World Religions	<0.5	<0.5	<0.5	<0.5	<0.5	<0.5	<0.5	<0.5
Other Faiths	1	2	1	1	1	1	1	1
Unaffiliated	**16**	**25**	**14**	**19**	**15**	**14**	**10**	**8**
Religious Unaffiliated	6	9	5	7	6	5	3	3
Secular Unaffiliated	6	9	6	7	6	6	4	3
Atheist	2	3	1	2	1	1	1	1
Agnostic	2	4	2	2	2	2	2	1
DK/REF	**1**	**1**	**1**	**1**	**1**	**1**	**1**	**1**
	100	100	100	100	100	100	100	100
Total sample	**35,556**	**4,242**	**30,453**	**5,085**	**6,738**	**7,379**	**5,517**	**5,734**

Source: 2007 U.S. Religious Landscape Survey, Pew Forum on Religion & Public Life

Three quarters of all Millennials agree there are absolute standards of right and wrong—a finding that is consistent with the attitudes of older adults. Yet, on issues such as abortion, acceptability of homosexual marriage, evolution, pornography, and the role of government agencies, Millennials are more likely than older adults to take a tolerant view. These very attitudes may explain some of the tensions evident in the relationship of Millennials to religious denominations. Harvard's Robert Putnam, co-author with David Campbell of *American Grace: How Religion Divides and Unites Us*, contends that Millennials associate religion with intolerance and a kind of institutional rigor mortis. Alienated by religious institutional policies which address social issues from a perceived narrow perspective tends to increase Millennials indifference to religious institutions. Says Putnam, "Continuing to sound the trumpet for conservative social policy on issues such as homosexuality may or may not be the right thing to do from a theological point of view, but it is likely to mean saving fewer souls. " (Los Angeles Times)

Religious Affiliation Among Young Adults (18–29), by Decade				
	1970s %	1980s %	1990s %	2000s %
Unaffiliated (no religion)	12	12	16	23
Affiliated	88	88	84	77
Survey Size	2,722	3,434	2,525	2,711

Source: General Social Surveys

There remains much to learn about the religious identity of this large, diverse, inclusive and complex age cohort. The entrepreneurial aptitude they have applied to other areas of life is becoming evident in their religious expressions as well. Just as Millennials customize their smart phones and iPads with apps they find most useful to them, they may customize religious belief and practice in ways that enable them to best fashion a world view that sustains them. The decisions they make will once again reshape the American religious landscape.

The Quandary for Faith Organizations

Inasmuch as the church only survives from age to age on the strength of the nurture of new Christians, the defection of a single generation holds cataclysmic potential. With three quarters of the Millennials continuing to report that they are affiliated with a specific faith group such grim scenarios are not in the offing. Yet, the persistent membership loss among American Protestant churches over the last four decades places certain urgency on the church's task of recalibrating its ministry and mission to meet the needs, and quicken the commitment of Millennials to religious institutions. It will not be easy.

Many American churches, particularly mainline denominations, have long enjoyed cultural hegemony and often in the context of monocultural settings. With time honored traditions of communicating orally and in person or through periodic newsletters congregations will need to alter their very means of communication to even engage young adults in conversation. Although congregations increasingly have websites and social network profiles these are often poorly maintained. The cyber presence of denominational programs designed to meet the needs of a connected generation are also improving but still fall short of the state of the art proficiency Millennials themselves possess and expect of others.

Harder still will be the issues of adapting time-honored patterns of meeting in a fixed location at a regular time (usually Sunday morning) to participate in a highly predictable ritual of worship, to more flexible and varied online and offline options for spiritual enrichment. Many of these concerns have been under consideration at both denominational and congregational levels for at least two decades as the Gen Xers came of age. There are some indications that the megachurch, praise band, alternatively timed and located services of "celebration" that led to the rechurching of so many Gen Xers have little appeal for the Millennials. The Emergent Church movement may hold greater promise of addressing the spiritual longings of this generation. This movement, fully electronic from its inception has, at least, established a lingua franca the Millennials understand.

Pastoral care too holds promise of reaching Millennials in unexpected ways. Arriving at career launch just as the economy melted down their prospects of employment and the mortgage

19

industry, in freefall, evaporated their hopes of home ownership; Millennials are the first generation to have to lower their expectations of transcending their parents' level of occupational and economic attainment. Many live with parents, work one or more part time jobs, carry educational loans, lack health care insurance and are—in a characteristically entrepreneurial way—casting about for a life path of meaning and purpose. Indeed life online offers them a flexibility, access and freedom of action that the real time world is presently too burdened to afford them. A vigorous ongoing conversation is now taking place within theological seminaries, denominational offices and congregational settings concerning the nature, direction and goals of Young Adult ministry. While several mainline denominations have begun to devote substantial staff and resources to formulating a response to the Millennial generation, the conversation at hand is much broader. Eastern Orthodox prelates, rabbinical sources and African American church agencies are fully engaged in the dialogue. Catholic and Pentecostal contributions make clear that the quest for an adequate approach crosses all boundaries of doctrinal orientation and institutional organizational life. Models now proliferate ranging from social networking to Bible study in bars.

Rick Osmer of Princeton Theological Seminary typifies the thoughtful discussion. He says, "An important part of the dissatisfaction of today's young people with the mainline churches stems from the absence of a spiritually challenging and world-shaping vision that meets their hunger for the chance to participate in what Stanley Hauerwas has termed 'a worthy adventure'." Many options appeal to Millennnials interests in contributing to the common good through volunteer mission projects and especially projects which address environmental and/or social justice concerns. Yet the church is not the only potential source for such worthy adventures. The Peace Corps, Teach America, Bread for the World, Habitat for Humanity and hundreds of other causes clamor for the gifts and graces Millennials bring with them. At the close of 2011, the Occupyers protests, in over 100 American cities and more than 400 cities worldwide symbolizes other venues for Millennials to invest in their world and their future. The Occupyers (and many other protests today) were given rise through the technological and communications advances which have emerged in the last decades. These events have notably contributed to the global consciousness of the Millennials. Thus, the approach to civic life demonstrated by the Occupyers may offer hints of the ways in which this generation will organize, reshape and maintain its world.

Implications for Research

The potential for future research concerning religion and the Millennials is virtually limitless. Some immediate foci might well include;

- Gaining far more precise clarity about the meaning of the preference for the "spiritual" over the "religious." What meaning does this hold for Millennials and how does this group act on this conviction?
- Much more work needs to be done in teasing out the various strata within this large generation. Specifically, present research has often overrepresented affluent, white and urban Millennials. We need to move beyond the most easily captured data to gain a deeper understanding of the full range of those who comprise this generation.
- Longitudinal data on the religious participation and non-participation patterns of Millennials would allow some assessment of the social consequences of these patterns and their implications for civic engagement. Church members, historically, have voted, volunteered and donated to charity at rates higher than the population as a whole. How will the affiliation patterns of Millennials influence or fail to influence these behaviors?

How the Millennials define and pursue their various worthy adventures or abandon them for other pursuits will shape and reshape American culture and with it the American religious landscape for the remainder of twenty-first century.

II
DIRECTORIES
1. United States Cooperative Organizations, National

The organizations listed in this section are cooperative religious organizations that are national in scope. Regional cooperative organizations in the United States are listed in Directory 6, "United States Regional and Local Ecumenical Bodies."

The Alban Institute, Inc.

The Alban Institute is an independent, not-for-profit cradle of learning, grounded in faith and devoted to helping American congregations become greater communities of faithfulness, health, creativity, hospitality and leadership. Alban is the largest congregational resource and advocacy membership organization in the United States, reaching hundreds of thousands of congregants across all faith traditions with our signature of congregation building known as The Alban Way. From Alban's groundbreaking consulting practice, to original research, publications and seminars on leadership, conflict, planning and transitions, The Alban Institute knows what it takes to build vital, enduring communities of faith. Alban draws on a vast reservoir of congregational know-how and wisdom born on the firing line. Clergy and lay leaders seek guidance from the most respected problem solvers, strategists and teachers in the business.

Headquarters
2121 Cooperative Way, Suite 100, Herndon, VA 20171 Tel. (800)486-1318
Media Contact, Director of Research, Dr. Ian Evison

Officers
Pres., The Rev. James P. Wind, Ph.D.

The Alliance for Christian Media

The Alliance for Christian Media is an ecumenical organization dedicated to producing media resources from a mainline Protestant point of view. The flagship production is the weekly radio show, *Day 1*, formerly *The Protestant Hour*. The *Day 1* Website (day1.org) provides sermon transcripts and audio and video resources. *Day 1* features preachers from the Cooperative Baptist Fellowship, Episcopal Church, Evangelical Lutheran Church in America, Presbyterian Church (U.S.A.), United Church of Christ, and the United Methodist Church.

Headquarters
644 West Peachtree St, Suite 300, Atlanta, GA 30308-1925 Tel. (404)815-0640 Fax (404)815-0495
Media Contact, Peter Wallace

Officers
Bd. Chpsn., Michael L. Starr
Vice-Chpsn., Frank Troutman, Jr.
Pres., The Rev. Canon Louis C. Schueddig
V.P., The Rev. Peter M. Wallace
Treas., George Hauptfuhrer
Sec., Leslie G. Callahan

American Bible Society

After nearly 200 years of ongoing ministry, American Bible Society continues to invite people to experience the life-changing message of the Bible. Offering an increasing range of innovative ministries to address core life questions and struggles, the Bible Society works alongside ministry partners, Christian churches and national Bible Societies to share God's Word both in the United States and around the globe.

American Bible Society played a leading role in the founding of the United Bible Societies, a federation of 147 national Bible Societies around the world that enables global cooperation in Scripture translation, publication and distribution in more than 200 countries and territories. The Bible Society contributes generously to the support provided by the United Bible Societies to those national Bible Societies that request support to meet the total Scripture needs of people in their countries.

The work of American Bible Society is supported through gifts from individuals, local churches, denominations and foundations.

Headquarters
1865 Broadway, New York, NY 10023 Tel. (212)408-1200
Media Contact, Mindy Faustin, Tel. (212)408-8755 Fax (212)408-1456, mfaustin@american bible.org

Officers

Chpsn., Pieter J. Dearolf

Pres., Dr. R. Lamar Vest

Executive Vice Presidents, Simon Barnes, Robert L. Briggs, Stephen King, Julia Oliver

DEPARTMENT HEADS

Director of Domestic Ministries, Emilio Reyes

Director of International Ministries, Marco Herrera

Chief Legal Counsel, Peter Rathbun

Dean, Nida Institute for Biblical Scholarship, Dr. Phil Towner

Director of Internal Audit, Donald Cavanaugh

Director for Publishing Services, Bibles.com, Thomas Durakis

Chief Communications Officer, Geof Morin

Director of Global Scripture Impact, Mark Forshaw

Director of Building Management Services, Gary Schutz

Chief Technology Officer, Nicholas Garbidakis

Director of Bibles.com, Brian Sherry

Director of Investments, Nicholas Pagano

Director of Human Resources, Janet Grell

Director of Ministry Networks, Chris Thyberg

Director of Artist Advocacy, Karina Lucero

Director of Ministry Advancement, John Walter

Director of Field Team Development, Al Brill

Director of Mass Market Development, Joseph Pierce

American Council of Christian Churches

The American Council of Christian Churches is a Fundamentalist multidenominational organization whose purposes are to provide information, encouragement, and assistance to Bible-believing churches, fellowships, and individuals; to preserve our Christian heritage through exposure of, opposition to, and separation from doctrinal impurity and compromise in current religious trends and movements; to protect churches from religious and political restrictions, subtle or obvious, that would hinder their ministries for Christ; and to promote obedience to the inerrant Word of God.

Founded in 1941, The American Council of Christian Churches (ACCC) is a multi-denominational agency for fellowship and cooperation among Bible-believing churches in various denominations- fellowships, Bible Presby-terian Church, Evangelical Methodist Church, Fellowship of Fundamental Bible Churches (formerly Bible Protestant), Free Presbyterian Church of North America, Fundamental Methodist Church, Independent Baptist Fellowship of North America, Independent Churches Affiliated, along with hundreds of independent churches. The total membership nears 2 million. Each denomination retains its identity and full autonomy, but cannot be associated with the World Council of Churches, National Council of Churches or National Association of Evangelicals.

Headquarters

P.O. Box 5455, Bethlehem, PA 18015 Tel. (610)865-3009 Fax (610)865-3033

Media Contact, Exec. Dir., Dr. Ralph Colas

Officers

Pres., Dr. John McKnight

Vice-Pres., Rev. Randy Ardis

Exec. Sec., Dr. Ralph Colas

Sec., Rev. Jerry L. Johnson

Treas., Mr. Shane Burge

Commissions, Chaplaincy; Education; Laymen; Literature; Missions; Radio & Audio Visual; Relief; Youth

American Friends Service Committee

Founded 1917, Regional offices, 9. Founded by and related to the Religious Society of Friends (Quakers) but supported and staffed by individuals sharing basic values regardless of religious affiliation. Attempts to relieve human suffering and find new approaches to world peace and social justice through nonviolence. Work in 22 countries includes development and refugee relief, peace education, and community organizing. Sponsors off-the-record seminars around the world to build better international understanding. Conducts programs with U.S. communities on the problems of minority groups such as housing, employment, and denial of legal rights. Maintains Washington, D.C. office to present AFSC experience and perspectives to policymakers. The Quaker United Nations offices in New York City and Geneva, Switzerland arrange seminars, testimony before UN committees and behind-the-scence discussions with UN delegates. Seeks to build informed public resistance to militarism. A co-recipient of the Noble Peace Prize. Programs are multiracial, non-denominational, and international.

Headquarters

1501 Cherry St., Philadelphia, PA 19102 Tel. (215)241-7000 Fax (215)241-7275, Wesite:www.afsc.org

Director of Media Relations, Alexis Moore

Officers

Presiding Clerk., Paul Lacey

Treas., James Fletcher

General Secretary, Mary Ellen McNish

The American Theological Library Association

Established in 1946, the American Theological Library Association (ATLA) is a professional association of 1,000 individual, institutional and affiliate members providing programs, products

22

and services in support of theological and religious studies libraries and librarians. ATLA's ecumenical membership represents many religious traditions and denominations.

Headquarters

300 S. Wacker Dr., Suite 2100, Chicago, IL, 60606 Tel. (312)454-5100 Fax (312)454-5505 Media Contact, Sara Corkery, Communications Specialist

Officers

Pres., David R. Stewart, Luther Seminary Library
Vice Pres., Roberta Schaafsma, Perkins School of Theology, Southern Methodist University
Sec., Eileen K. Crawford, Vanderbilt University
Exec. Dir., Dennis A. Norlin, ATLA, 250

American Tract Society

The American Tract Society is a nonprofit, interdenominational organization, instituted in 1825 through the merger of most of the then-existing tract societies. As one of the earliest religious publishing bodies in the United States, ATS has pioneered in the publishing of Christian books, booklets and leaflets. The volume of distribution has risen to over 35 million pieces of literature annually. For free samples or a free catalog contact 1-800-54-TRACT.

Headquarters

P.O. Box 462008, Garland, TX 75046 Tel. (972)276-9408 Fax (972)272-9642
Media Contact, V.P. Evangelism/Outreach, David Leflore

The American Waldensian Society

The American Waldensian Society (AWS) promotes ministry linkages, broadly ecumenical, between U.S.A. churches and Waldensian (Reformed)-Methodist consti- tuencies in Italy and Waldensian constituencies in Argentina-Uruguay. Founded in 1906, AWS aims to enlarge mission discovery and partnership among overseas Waldensian-Methodist forces and denominational forces in the U.S.A.

AWS is governed by a national ecumenical board, although it consults and collaborates closely with the three overseas Waldensian and Waldensian-Methodist boards.

The Waldensian experience is the earliest continuing Protestant experience.

Headquarters

American Waldensian Society, 208 Rodoret Street, South, P.O. Box 398, Valdese, NC 28690 Toll-free Tel. (866)825-3373 Tel. (828)874-3500 Fax (828)874-3560 Voice (828)879-4100 Email: info@waldensian.org, www.waldensian.org
Media Contact, Rev. Francis Rivers Tel. (336) 716-4022 Fax (336)716-5075 Email: frivers@wfubmc.edu

Officers

Exec. Dir., The Rev. Francis Rivers PC(USA)
Pres., The Rev. Dr. Gabriella Lettini '09 WC
Vice Pres., Ms. June Rostan '09
Treas., Emile M. Jackumin, Jr. '09 PC(USA)
Sec., Rev. Peter Sulyok, '10 PC(USA)

Appalachian Ministries Educational Resource Center (AMERC)

The mission of AMERC is to promote contextual, cross-cultural education for theological students, faculties, ministers, and other Christian leaders. Working through an ecumenical consortium of theological schools and denominational judicatories, AMERC supports experiential learning about the theological, spiritual, social, economic and environmental aspects of Appalachian culture, especially for rural and small town settings for ministry.

Since 1985 AMERC, has provided quality educational programs and learning experiences for seminaries and other religious leaders interested in ministry in Appalachia and other rural areas. The centerpiece of these programs has been and continues to be in-depth, contextually based dialogue with local people engaged in creative ministries, exploring with them social, economic, political, ecological, cultural, and religious issues. Intense theological reflection is used to understand these issues through the eyes of faith, equipping students and other leaders for ministry in the Appalachian context.

In the new millennium AMERC's form of ministry has changed. AMERC is now supporting its consortium of members by providing program grants, technical and library support, and leadership consultation. The consortium seminaries and other groups, in turn, design and offer an even wider variety of experiential programs in rural and small town ministry in the context of Appalachia. Both seminary, for credit, and continuing education courses are offered. In 2000 AMERC launched its Grants Program for members of the consortium. Since that time AMERC has funded twenty-four winter and summer Travel Seminars, a spring course with an immersion component, a Seminary Faculty Immersion experience and a summer intern program. A consultation and six continuing education events with grants of up to $15,000.

Headquarters

400 Richmond Road, North, Suite E, Berea, KY 40403 Tel. (859)986-8789 Fax (859)986-2576, Email: loliver@amerc.org, Website: www.amerc.org
Media Contact, Rev. Dr. Lon D. Oliver, Executive Director
Executive Assistant, Marsha Baker

Officers

Chair, Rev. Dr. Barbara Blodgett, Yale Divinity School

Vice Chair, Rev. Dr. Jackie Johns, Church of God Theological Seminary

Secretary, Ms. Tena Willemsma, Commission on Religion in Appalachia

Treasurer, Mr. Jim Strand, Berea College

The Associated Church Press

The Associated Church Press was organized in 1916. Its membership includes periodicals and Web sites of major Protestant, Catholic, and Orthodox, and ecumenical groups in the U.S. and Canada, and abroad; individual members who supply publishing services on a freelance or student basis; and affiliate members who supply the Christian press with news, information, and vendor services. It is a professional Christian journalistic association seeking to promote excellence among editors and writers, recognize achievements, and represent the interests of the religious press. It sponsors seminars, conventions, awards programs, and workshops for editors, staff people, and business managers. It is active in postal rates and regulations on behalf of the religious press.

Headquarters

Media Contact, Exec. Dir., Mary Lynn Hendrickson, 1410 Vernon St. Stoughton , WI 53589-2248 Tel.(608)877-0011 Fax (608)877-0062, Website:www.theacp.org

Officers

Exec. Dir., Mary Lynn Hendrickson,1410 Vernon St. Stoughton, WI 53589-2248, Tel.608-877-0011, Fax 608-877-0062, acpoffice@earthlink.net

Pres., Jerry Van Marter, Presbyterian News Service, 100 Witherspoon St., Louisville, KY 40202-1396, Tel. (502)569-5493, Fax (502) 569-8073, Email: jvanmart@ctr.pcusa.org

Vice Pres., Terry DeYoung, The Church Herald, 4500-60th St. SE, Grand Rapids, MI 49512-9642, Tel. (616)698-7071, Fax (616)698-6606, Email: tdeyoung@rca.org

Past Pres., Victoria A. Rebeck, The Minnesota Connect, 122 W. Franklin, Ste. 400, Minneapolis, MN 55404-2472, Tel. (612)870-0058 ext. 232, Fax (612)870-1260, Email: victoria.rebeck@mnumc.org

Treas., Silvia Chavez, The Lutheran, 8765 W. Higgins Rd., Chicago, IL 60631-4189, Tel. (773)380-2543 Fax (773)380-2751, Email: schavez@elca.org

The Associated Gospel Churches

Organized in 1939, The Associated Gospel Churches (AGC) endorses chaplains primarily for strong evangelical Independent Baptist and Bible Churches to the U.S. Armed Forces. The AGC has been recognized by the U.S. Department of Defense for 65 years as an Endorsing Agency, and it supports a strong national defense. The AGC also endorses VA chaplains, police, correctional system and civil air patrol chaplains.

The AGC provides support for its constituent churches, seminaries, Bible colleges and missionaries.

The AGC believes in the sovereignty of the local church, the historic doctrines of the Christian faith and the infallibility of the Bible.

The AGC is a member of the National Conference on Ministry to the Armed Forces (NCMAF) and the Endorsers Conference for Veterans Affairs Chaplaincy (ECVAC).

Headquarters

Media Contact, Pres., Billy Baugham, D.D., National Hdqt., P.O. Box 733, Taylors, SC 29687 Tel. (864)268-9617 Fax (864)268-0166

Officers

Commission on Chaplains, Pres. and Chmn., Billy Baugham, D.D.

Vice-Pres., Rev. Chuck Flesher

Sec.-Treas., Eva Baugham

Executive Committee, Chaplain (Captain) James Poe, USN Member

Association of Catholic Diocesan Archivists

The Association of Catholic Diocesan Archivists, which began in 1979, has been committed to the active promotion of professionalism in the management of diocesan archives. The Association meets annually. In the even years it has its own summer conference; in the odd years it meets in conjunction with the Society of American Archivists. Publications include Standards for Diocesan Archives, Access Policy for Diocesan Archives and the quarterly Bulletin.

Headquarters

Joseph Cardinal Bernardin Archives & Records Center, 711 West Monroe, Chicago, IL 60661 Tel. (312)831-0711 Fax (312)831-0610

Media Contact, Brian P. Fahey

Officers

Episcopal Mod., Most Rev. Thomas J. Paprocki, Bishop, Diocese of Springfield in Illinois

Pres., Emilie Leumas, Rev. Mr. William Bissenden, Diocese of Bridgeport

Vice-Pres., Peggy Lavelle, Archdiocese of Chicago

Treas., Brian P. Fahey, Diocese of Charleston, P.O. Box 818, Charleston, SC 29402

Sec., Michele Levandoski, Diocese of Springfield in Illinois

Newsletter Editor, Ryan Rutkowski, Diocese of Whaling - Charleston

ADRIS-Association for the Development of Religious Information Services

The Association for the Development of Religious Information Services was established in 1971 to facilitate coordination and cooperation among information services that pertain to religion. Its goal is a worldwide network that is interdisciplinary, interfaith and interdenominational to serve both administrative and research applications. ADRIS publishes a blog and provides internet, open data, open source and open standards consulting services.

Headquarters

ADRIS Blog Office, P.O. Box 210735, Nashville, TN 37221-0735 Tel. (615)557-3975, Email: editor@adris.org
Media Contact, Editor., Ed Dodds, P.O. Box 210735, Nashville, TN 37221-0735 Tel. (615) 657-9359
AIM: ed1dodds
GoogleTalk: ed.dodds@gmail.com
ICQ: 49457096
Identica: http://identi.ca/eddodds
MSN: dodds@conmergence.com
SIP: ed_dodds_sip
SKYPE: ed_dodds_skype
Twitter: http://twitter.com/ed_dodds
VIBE: ed.dodds@vibe.novell.com
WAVE: ed.dodds@googlewave.com
Website: www.adris.org
Yahoo: ed_dodds@yahoo.com

Officers

Ed Dodds, P.O. Box 210735, Nashville, TN 37221-0735 Tel. (615)657-9359

Association of Gospel Rescue Missions

The Association of Gospel Rescue Missions (AGRM), formerly the International Union of Gospel Missions, is an association of 300 rescue missions and other ministries that serve more than 7 million homeless and needy people in the inner cities of the U.S., Canada and overseas each year. Since 1913, AGRM member ministries have offered emergency food and shelter, evangelical outreach, Christian counsel, youth and family services, prison and jail outreach, rehabilitation and specialized programs for the mentally ill, the elderly, the urban poor and street youth. The AGRM operates RESCUE College, an Internet-based distance education program to prepare and train rescue mission workers. The AGRM sponsors Alcoholics Victorious, a network of Christian support groups. AGRM is affiliated with the City Mission World Association, representing over 500 City Mission around the world.

Headquarters

7222 Commerce Center Drive, Suite 120, Colorado Springs, CO 80919 Tel. (719)266-8300 Fax (719)266-8600

Media Contact, Exec. Dir., Rev. John Ashmen or Phil Rydman

Officers

Exec. Dir., Rev. John Ashmen
Pres., Mr. Rick Alvis, Box 817, Indianapolis, IN 46206 Tel. (317)635-3575 Fax (317)687-3629
Sec., Mr. David Traedwell, 1350 R St NW, Washington DC 20009-4323, Tel. (202)745-7118 Fax (202)232-7072
Vice Pres., Mr. Perry Jones, IIIl, 259 s Pearl St., Albany, NY 12202, Tel. (518)462-0459 Fax (518)462-0489

Association of Statisticians of American Religious Bodies

This Association was organized in 1934 and grew out of personal consultations held by representatives from The Yearbook of American Churches, The National (now Official) Catholic Directory, the Jewish Statistical Bureau, The Methodist (now The United Methodist), the Lutheran and the Presbyterian churches.

ASARB has a variety of purposes: to bring together those officially and professionally responsible for gathering, compiling, and publishing denominational statistics; to provide a forum for the exchange of ideas and sharing of problems in statistical methods and procedure; and to seek such standardization as may be possible in religious statistical data. ASARB also conducts the decennial Religious Congregations Membership Study, a county listing of religious groups and their adherents.

Headquarters

Dale Jones, Church of the Nazarene, 17001 Prairie Star Parkway, Lenexa, KS 66220 Tel. (913)577-0651, Email: djones@nazarene.org
Media Contact, Sec.-Treas., Dale Jones

Officers

Pres., Richie Stanley, North American Mission Board, 4200 North Point PKWY., Alpharetta, GA 30022, Tel. (770)410-6381 Email: rstanley @namb.net
Immediate Past Pres., Destiny Hisey, United Church of Christ, 700 Prospect Ave., Cleveland, OH 44115, Tel. (216)736-2149 Fax (216)736-2276 Email: hiseyd@ucc.org
1st Vice Pres., Carl Royster, 21st Century Christian, 2309 12th Ave. S., Nashville, TN 37204, Tel. (615)383-3842 Fax (615)292-5983 Email: carlr@21stcc.com
2nd Vice Pres., Robert Stockman, Baha'I Faith USA, 224 Swanson Cir., South Bend, IN 46615, Tel. (847)337-7750 Email: rstockman@ usbnc.org

MEMBERS-AT-LARGE
Deborah Myers, Evangelical Lutheran Church in America, 8765 W. Higgins Rd., Chicago, IL 60631, Tel. (773)380-2915 Fax (773)380-2406 Email: Deborah.Myers@elca.org

Cynthia Woolever Molinari, U.S. Congregational Life Survey, 9 Indian Pipe Dr., Wynantskill, NY 12198 Tel. (518)336-6988 Email: Cynthia @cynthiawoolever.com

The Association of Theological Schools in the United States and Canada

The Association of Theological Schools in the United States and Canada (ATS) is a membership organization of more than 260 graduate schools that conduct post-baccalaureate professional and academic degree programs to educate persons for the practice of ministry and for teaching and research in the theological disciplines. The ATS Commission on Accrediting accredits schools and approves the degree programs they offer.

Headquarters
10 Summit Park Drive, Pittsburgh, PA 15275-1110 Tel. (412)788-6505 Fax (412)788-6510 Media Contact, Dir. of Communications and External Relations, Eliza Brown, Tel. (412) 788-6505 x244, Email: brown@ats.edu

Officers
President: Richard Mouw, President, Fuller Theological Seminary, Pasadena, CA
Vice President: Dorcas Gordon, Principal, Knox College, Toronto, ON
Secretary: Patricia Schoelles, President, St. Bernard's School of Theology and Ministry, Rochester, NY
Treasurer: Mary McNamara, Chief Executive Officer, United Theological Seminary of the Twin Cities, New Brighton, MN

Blanton-Peale Institute

Blanton-Peale Institute and Counseling Center is dedicated to helping people overcome emotional obstacles by joining mental health expertise with faith and values. The Blanton-Peale Graduate Institute provides advanced training in psychoanalysis and pastoral care for ministers, rabbis, sisters, priests, lay leaders, and other counselors. The Blanton-Peale Counseling Centers provide counseling for individuals, couples, families and groups. Blanton-Peale promotes interdisciplinary communication among theology, medicine and the behavioral sciences. Blanton-Peale was founded in 1937 by Dr. Norman Vincent Peale and psychiatrist Smiley Blanton, M.D.

Headquarters
3 W. 29th St., 5th Floor, New York, NY 10001 Tel. (212)725-7850 Fax (212)689-3212

Officers
Chpsn., Arthur Caliandro
Vice-Chpsn., Elizabeth Peale Allen
President and CEO: Rev. Dr. Paul W. Bradley

Bread For The World

Bread for the World is a collective Christian voice urging our nation's decision makers to end hunger at home and abroad. By changing policies, programs and conditions that allow hunger and poverty to persist, we provide help and opportunity far beyond the communities in which we live.

God's grace in Jesus Christ moves us to help our neighbors, whether they live in the next house, the next state or the next continent. Food is a basic need, and it is unjust that so many people do not have enough to eat.

Bread for the World members write personal letters and emails to Congress. We also meet with our representatives in Congress. Working through our churches, campuses, and other organizations, we engage more people in advocacy. Each year, Bread for the World invites churches across the country to take up a nationwide Offering of Letters to Congress on an issue that is important to hungry people.

Bread for the World has two affiliate organizations. Bread for the World Institute does analysis and education on hunger issues. The Alliance to End Hunger engages diverse institutions—Jewish and Muslim groups, charities, universities, corporations, and others—in building the political commitment needed to overcome hunger.

Bread for the World works in a bipartisan way. It enjoys the support of many different church bodies. Bread for the World collaborates with other organizations to build the political commitment needed to overcome hunger and poverty.

Headquarters
50 F St., NW, Ste. 500, Washington, DC 20001 Tel. (202)639-9400 Fax (202)639-9401 Media Contact, Adlai Amor

Officers
Pres., Rev. David Beckmann
Bd. Chpsn., Dave Miner
Bd. Vice-Chpsn.,

Campus Crusade for Christ International

Campus Crusade for Christ International is an interdenominational, evangelistic and discipleship ministry dedicated to helping fulfill the Great Commission through the multiplication strategy of "win-build-send." Founded in 1951 on the campus of UCLA, the organization now includes 60 plus ministries and special projects reaching out to almost every segment of society. There are more than 27,000 staff members and 226,000 trained volunteers in 190 countries.

Headquarters
100 Lake Hart Dr., Orlando, FL 32832 Tel. (407)826-2000 Fax (407)826-2120 Media Contact, James Woelbern

Chmn. & Pres., Steve Douglass
Chief Operating Officer, J. Roger Bruehl
Chief Financial Officer, Roger L.Craft

Center on Conscience & War

CCW, formed in 1940, is a nonprofit organization supported by individual contributions and related to more than thirty religious organizations. Its purpose is to defend and extend the rights of conscientious objectors to war. CCW provides information on how to register for the draft while documenting one's convictions as a conscientious objector, how to cope with penalties if one does not cooperate, and how to qualify as a conscientious objector while in the Armed Forces. It also provides information for counselors and the public about conscientious objection, military service and the operation of the draft. CCW provides information to and support for conscientious objectors in other countries, as well as individuals seeking US citizenship.

As a national resource center CCW assists research in its area of expertise including the peace witness of religious bodies. CCW staff provides referrals to local counselors and attorneys and professional support for them. Through publications and other outreach activities, CCW strives to provide support for people to decide for themselves what they believe about participation in war and to act on the basis of the dictates of their own informed consciences.

Headquarters

1830 Connecticut Ave. NW, Washington, DC 20009-5732 Tel. (202)483-2220 Fax (202)483-1246
Media Contact, Exec. Dir., Maria Santelli

Officers

Exec. Dir., Maria Santelli
Chpsn., Dallas Wisehaupt
Sec., Joan Broadfield
Treas., Jordan Blevins

Center for Parish Development

The Center for Parish Development is an ecumenical, non-profit research and development agency whose mission is to help church bodies learn to become faithful expressions of God's mission in today's post-modern, post-Christendom world. Founded in 1968, the Center brings a strong theological orientation, a missional ecclesial paradigm with a focus on faithful Christian communities as the locus of mission, research-based theory and practice of major change, a systems approach, and years of experience working with national, regional, and local church bodies.

Headquarters

General Mailing address: 738 East Dundee Rd., #210 Palatine, IL 60074 Tel. (773)752-1596, Email: cpde@missionalchurch.org, Website: www.missionalchurch.org
Media Contact, Managing Director Dale Ziemer

Officers

Chpsn.: Richard Putz, 1 Hawthorne Pl., Schererville, IN 46375
V. Chair: Calvert Audrain, 5743 S. Dorchester Ave., Chicago, IL 60615
Sec.: Raymond Schulte, 738 East Dundee Road, #210, Palatine, IL 60074
Managing Directors, Raymond Schulte and Dale Ziemer

Chaplaincy of Full Gospel Churches

The Chaplaincy of Full Gospel Churches (CFGC) is a unique coalition of 1500 nondenominational churches and networks of churches united for the purpose of being represented in military and civilian chaplaincies. Since its inception in 1984, CFGC has grown rapidly. Today CFGC represents over 7.5 million American Christians. Additionally, we are connected with another 144 fellowship groups consisting of another 7.5 million members, which gives CFGC the potential of representing a total 15 million.

Churches, fellowships and networks of churches which affirm the CFGC statement of faith that "Jesus is Savior, Lord and Baptizer in the Holy Spirit today, with signs, wonders and gifts following" may join the endorsing agency. CFGC represents its member-networks of churches (consisting of over 90,000 churches nation wide) before the Pentagon's Armed Forces Chaplains Board, the National Conference of Ministry to the Armed Forces, Endorsers Conference for Veterans Affairs Chaplaincy, Federal Bureau of Prisons, Association of Professional Chaplains, and other groups requiring professional chaplaincy endorsement (State/County/City Correctional, Healthcare, Law Enforcement, Workplace). The organization also ecclesiastically credentials professional counselors.

Headquarters

150 E. Highway 67 Ste. 250, Duncanville, TX 75137-4482 Tel. (214)331-4373 Fax (214)333-4401
Media Contact, Rev. Dr. Klon Kitchen Jr., PhD, DD

Officers

President, Rev. Dr. Klon Kitchen Jr., PhD, DD

Christian Endeavor International

Christian Endeavor International is a Christ-centered, youth-oriented ministry which assists local churches in reaching young people with the gospel of Jesus Christ, discipling them in the Christian faith, and equipping them for Christian ministry and service in their local church, community and world. It trains youth leaders for effective ministry and provides opportunities for Christian inspiration, spiritual growth, fellowship, and service. Christian Endevor International reaches across denominational, cultural, racial and geographical boundaries. All materials are on the internet at www.teamce.com

Headquarters
424 E. Main St., P.O. Box 377, Edmore, MI 48829 Tel. (989)427-3737 Fax (989)427-5530, Email: contact@teamce.com
Media Contact, Luke Sawyer

Officers
Chief Executive Officer, Timothy Eldred

Christian Management Association

Christian Management Association (CMA) provides leadership training, management resources and strategic networking relationships for leaders and managers of Christian organizations and growing churches. It's membership represents leaders and managers from more than 1,500 Christian organizations and larger churches in the U.S. CMA publishes Christian Management Report magazine, CMA Management Monthly e-newsletter, Total Compensation Survey Report for Christian Ministries, www.CMAonline.org website, CMA Management Tape Library and many other resources. CMA provides management training, resourcing and networking opportunities through its annual conference for Christian organizations and churches, CEO Dialogues one-day roundtables, chapters in selected cities, online Job Market, and many other programs. It also features annually the Best Christian Places to Work finalists and the CMA Management Award. Membership is open to Christian organizations, ministries and churches. Businesses that provide products or services for Christian organizations and churches may apply for a business membership. For complete membership information, go to www.CMAonline.org and click on "Membership."

Headquarters
P.O. Box 4090, San Clemente, CA 92674, Tel: (800)727-4262 Fax: (949)487-0927
John Pearson, CEO, Email: John@CMAonline.org
DeWayne Herbrandson, Director of Management Resources, Email: DeWayne@CMAonline.org
Dick Bahruth, Senior Consultant, Marketing, Email: Dick@CMAonline, org
Marsha Lyons, Director of Conferences & Meetings, Email: Marsha@CMAonline.org
Suzy West, Director of Administration/COO, Email: Suzy@CMAonline.org

Officers
Chairman, Mark G. Holbrook, Pres./CEO, ECCU
Vice-Chairman, C.E. Crouse, Managing Partner, Capin Crouse, LLP
Treas., Robert T. Lipps, Lockton Insurance Brokers of San Francisco
Sec., Mark A. Bankord, Managing Principal/ Chairman, Cap Trust Asset Management

A Christian Ministry in the National Parks

This ministry is recognized by over 40 Christian denominations and extends the ministry of Christ to the millions of people who live, work and vacation in our National Parks. Ministry Staff Members conduct services of worship in the parks on Sundays. The staff are employed by park concessionaires and have full-time jobs in which their actions, attitudes, and commitment to Christ serve as witness. Room and board are provided at a minimal cost; minimum commitment of 90 days needed.

Officers
Dir., The Rev. Richard P. Camp, Jr.
Deputy Director, Gordon Compton

Church Growth Center - Home of Church Doctor Ministries

The Church Growth Center is an interfaith, nonprofit, professional organization which exists to bring transformational change of the Christian church toward the effective implementation of the Lord's Great Commission, to make disciples of all people. This effort is done through consultations, resources, and educational events.

Founded in 1978 by leader Kent R. Hunter, the Church Growth Center offers over 17 different consultation services, including church consultations by experienced consultants, cutting edge resources through The Church Doctor™ Resource Center, and by providing educational events at churches and organizations in the way of providing speakers and resources at seminars, workshops, and conferences. The bi-monthly e-newsletter is the Church Doctor Report.

Headquarters
P.O.Box 145, 1230 U. S. Highway Six, Corunna, IN 46730 Tel. (800)626-8515 Fax (260)281-2167, Website: www.churchdoctor.org
Media Contact, Office Administrator, Jason Atkinson

Officers
President, Dr. Kent R. Hunter, D.Min, Ph.D.
Vice Pres., Greg Ulmer
Treas., Rob Olsen

Church Women United in the U.S.A.

Church Women United in the U.S.A. is a racially, culturally, theologically inclusive Christian women's movement, celbrating unity in diversity and working for a world of peace and justice. Founded in 1941, Church Women United is a movement representing Protestant, Roman Catholic, Orthodox and other Christian women; biblically based, shared Christian faith; organized into more than 1200 state and local units working for peace and justice in the United States and Puerto Rico; supported by constituents in state and local units and denominational women's organizations; impassioned by the Holy Spirit to act on behalf of women and children throughout the world; and recognized as a non-governmental organization by the United Nations.

Headquarters

NATIONAL OFFICE
475 Riverside Dr., Ste. 1626, New York, NY 10115 Tel. (800)CWU-5551 OR (212)870-2347 Fax (212)870-2338; Office manager: Julie Drews, juliedrews@churchwomen.org

LEGISLATIVE OFFICE
CWU Washington Office, 100 Maryland Ave. NE, Rm. 100, Washington, DC 20002 Tel. (202)544-8747, Fax (202)544-9133
Legislative Dir., Wash. Office, Patricia Burkhardt, Email: pburkhardt@churchwomen.org

Officers

Pres., Gail Mengel, Independence, MO
Vice-Pres., Vera Zander, Tucson, AZ
Secretary, Carol Kolsti, Austin, TX
Treasurer, Ann Kohler, Baldwinsville, NY
Regional Coordinators, Central, Susan Becker, Madison, WI; East Central, Margaret Tweet, Rock Island, IL; Mid-Atlantic, Blanche Simmons, Landover, MD; Northeast, Vivian Love-Jones, Newburg, NY; Northwest, Betty Luginbill, Boise, ID; South Central, Martha Moody Boone, Keithville, LA; Southeast, Pat Zangmeister, Tamarac, FL; Southwest, Jenny Ladefaged, Alisa Viego, CA

Churches Uniting in Christ

Churches Uniting in Christ (CUIC) was inaugurated on January 20, 2002, in Memphis Tennessee as a new relationship among nine communions which agreed to start living more fully into their unity in Christ. CUIC is the successor to the Consultation on Church Union (COCU) which was, in 1962 organized to explore the formation of a uniting church. At the 1999 COCU Plenary the nine member communions affirmed eight "Marks" of Churches Uniting in Christ and agreed to move into the new relationship of covenanted communion to be called Churches Uniting in Christ. Following confirmation actions by each of the communions, all nine communions officially constituted Churches Uniting in Christ. The nine member communions are: The African Methodist Episcopal Church, the African Methodist Episcopal Zion Church, the Christian Church (Disciples of Christ), the Christian Methodist Episcopal Church, The Episcopal Church, the International Council of Community Churches, the Presbyterian Church (USA), the United Church of Christ, and the United Methodist Church. Also participating at present are two Partners in Mission and Dialogue, the Evangelical Lutheran Church in America and the Moravian Church (Northern Province). The Catholic Church participates as an observer. Other communions are exploring various possibilities for relating to CUIC.

CUIC is a bold venture, expressed through the participating communions' covenant to seek to live a new relationship that bears witness to a church that is truly catholic, truly evangelical, and truly reformed. Among the goals for bearing witness to that unity are two very challenging endeavors: to heed the "emphatic call to `erase racism' by challenging the system of white privilege that has so distorted life in this society and in the churches themselves;" and to "provide a foundation for the mutual recognition and reconciliation of ordained ministry by the members of Churches Uniting in Christ by the year 2007. Notably, the commitment to address racism is named as a hallmark of the new relationship and, following the Inaugural ceremony,on Dr. Martin Luther King, Jr. Day, January 21, 2002, the Heads of Communion signed an Appeal to the Churches to work together for the eradication of racism.

The Ecumenical Officers of each of the communions will carry major responsibility for the engagement of their congregations and members in the CUIC relationship. Neighboring congregations are encouraged to celebrate the Eucharist together; invite the participation of each in services of baptism, ordinations and installation as well as other special events in the congregations' lives; and to discover ways in which they might witness together in combating social injustices, especially racism. In addition to the representational Coordinating Council, three task forces will work to enhance the collaborative endeavors of CUIC: Ministry, Racism, and Local and Regional Ecumenism.

Headquarters

475 E. Lockwood Ave, St. Louis MO 63119 Tel. (314)252-3160 Fax (314)252-3162 Email: jamesNTse@gmail.com or cuic@eden.org
Media Contact: Elder James Tse

Officers

President of the Coordinating Council The Reverend Dr. Suzanne Webb, Christian Church (Disciples of Christ)
Vice Pres., The Rt. Reverend Ronald Cunningham, Christian Methodist Episcopal Church
Sec., Mr. Abraham Wright, International Council of Community Churches
Trea., Elder James N. Tse (Presbyterian Church/USA)

COORDINATING COUNCIL REPRESENTA-TIVES FROM MEMBER COMMUNIONS
African Methodist Episcopal Church,
African Methodist Episcopal Zion Church, The Rev. Dr. Harrison Bonner

Christian Church (DISCIPLES OF CHRIST), The Rev. Dr. Suzanne Webb
Christian Methodist Episcopal Church, Bishop Ronald Cunningham
The Episcopal Church (USA), The Rev. C. Dana Krutz
International Council of Community Churches, Mr. Abraham Wright
Presbyterian Church (USA), Elder James N. Tse
United Church of Christ, The Rev. Lydia Veliko
The United Methodist Church, Bishop Albert F. Mutti

The Columbia Partnership, Inc.

Organized in 2005, The Columbia Partnership [TCP] is a non-profit Christian ministry that seeks to transform the capacity of the North American Church to pursue and sustain vital Christ-centered ministry. It works with lay and clergy leaders, congregations, denominations, and parachurch organizations to empower them to experience greater vitality and vibrancy in the fulfillment of their ministry vision. The 12 members of the TCP Ministry Community have worked with several thousand clients in approximately 50 denominations throughout North America.

The work and ministry of TCP is divided into teams around five emphases: Coaching Leaders, Funding Ministry, Sharing Knowledge, Transforming Congregations, and Transforming Denominations. A core value of TCP is that rather than doing something programmatic to religious organizations, it is much better to come alongside and join them in their journey using processes that increase their capacity to serve, and thus their vitality and vibrancy. Included in the Sharing Knowledge emphasis of TCP is a partnership with Chalice Press in St. Louis, MO which publishes books in the TCP Leadership Series, and digital manuscripts known as Chalice Pages. Also, TCP is in partnership with Northern Seminary in the Chicago, IL area to provide distance learning experiences for people in ministry, including two Doctor of Ministry degrees—one in Transforming Congregations and one in Transforming Denominations.

Headquarters
332 Valley Springs Road, Columbia, SC 29223-6934. Tel. 803.622.0923
Media Contact, Strategic Coordinator, Dr. George Bullard, Tel. 803.622.0923. E-mail: GBullard@TheColumbiaPartnership.org.

Officers
Pres. Dr. Ken Kessler, 2815 Aspinwald Drive, Henrico, VA 23233
Vice Pres., Dr. George Bullard, 332 Valley Springs Road, Columbia, SC 29223-6934
Sec., Dr. Richard Hamm, 8162 Winterset Circle, Indianapolis, IN 46214
Treas., Rev. Norman Jameson, 3116 Stone Gap Court, Raleigh, NC 2761

Evangelical Council for Financial Accountability

Founded in 1979, the Evangelical Council for Financial Accountability (ECFA) has the purpose of helping Christ-centered, evangelical, churches and other nonprofit organizations earn the public's trust through their ethical practices and financial accountability. ECFA assists its over 1,600 member organizations in making appropriate public disclosure of their financial practices and accomplishments, thus materially enhancing their credibility and support potential among present and prospective donors.

Headquarters
440 W. Jubal Early Drive Ste. 130, Winchester, VA 22601-6319 Tel. (540)535-0103 Fax (540)535-0533
Media Contact, Pres., Dan Busby

Officers
Pres., Dan Busby

Evangelical Press Association

The Evangelical Press Association is a professional association serving the evangelical periodical publishing industry. EPA provides a variety of services, including training and recognition of outstanding work.

Headquarters
P.O. Box 28129, Crystal, MN 55428 Tel. (763)535-4793 Fax (763)535-4794
Media Contact, Exec. Dir., Doug Trouten

Officers
President, Dean Ridings, Navigators, 3820 N. 30th St., Colorado Springs, CO 80904
President-elect, Theresa Keener, Christian Examiner, P.O. Box 2606, El Cajon, CA 92021
Treas., Dwight Widaman, Kansas City Metro Voice, P.O. Box 1114, Lee's Summit, MO 64063
Sec., D'Arcy Maher, ACSI, P.O. BOX 65130, Colorado Springs, CO 80962-5130
Advisor, Mark Winz, Worldwide Challenge, 100 Lake Hart Drive, #1600, Orlando, FL 32832-0100
Advisor, Ted Olsen, Christianity Today, 465 Gundersen Drive, Carol Stream, IL 60188
Exec. Dir., Doug Trouten

Faith & Values Media
(See also National Interfaith Cable Coalition, Inc.)

Faith & Values Media is a nation's largest coalition of Jewish and Christian faith groups dedicated to media production, distribution and promotion. It is a service of the National Interfaith Cable Coalition, Inc., established in 1987.

Faith & Values Media member association includes more than 40 faith groups and religious organizations representing 200,000 congregations and 120 million congregants. Its mission is to use television and other media to promote the vitality of religious experience in everyday life.

Award-winning programming from Faith & Values Media is available on Hallmark Channel and on www.faithstreams.com

Headquarters
74 Trinity Place, Suite 1550, New York, NY 10006 Tel. (212)406-4121 Fax (212)406-4105
Media Contact, Christine Luzano

Officers
Chair, Dr. Daniel Paul Matthews
Vice Chair, Elder Ralph Hardy Jr., Esq.
Secretary, Rabbi Daniel Freelander
Treasurer, Betty Elam

STAFF
President and CEO, Edward J. Murray
Exec. Vice President, Beverly Judge

Federation of Christian Ministries

The Federation of Christian Ministries (FCM)is a national ecumenical and inter-faith community founded in 1968. FCM stresses inclusiveness, opening its membership to women, men, and groups of varying faith backgrounds and interests who share its vision of an ecumenical, nondenominational ministerial community. FCM commissions its ministers for work in many capacities: pastoring house churches, local faith communities, and congregations/parishes; officiating at weddings, funerals, and baptisms; serving as endorsed chaplains in nursing homes, correctional facilities, and hospitals; leading retreats, giving spiritual direction, and counseling; offering healing ministries; organizing initiatives dedicated to peace and justice. FCM is a meeting place for faith communities and service organizations following Christ's directive to serve. FCM is a member of the International Council of Community Churches and a faith group member of the Association for Clinical Pastoral Education. Its educational branch, Global Ministries University, offers online degrees (delete completion) on the undergraduate, graduate, and doctoral levels for those seeking deeper levels of insight in the field of ministry.

Headquarters
1709 W. 69th Street #3, Cleveland, OH 44102-2957, (800)538-8923, centraloffice@FCMmail.org.
Website: federationofchristianministries.org
Contact: Thomas and Michaelita Quinn, Co-presidents, (203)792-4848, president@FCMmail.org

Officers
Chairperson:Antoinette Marold, (440)232-6212, chairperson@FCMmail.org.
President(s): Thomas and Michaelita Quinn, (203)792-4848, president@FCMmail.org.
Treasurer: Thomas Cusack, (732)329-3586, treasurer@FCMmail.org.

Secretary: Joyce McFadden, (781)925-3400, secretary@FCMmail.org.
Interim Chair, Commissioning Committee: William Manseau, (978)851-5547, certification chair@FCMmail.org.
Chair, Specialized Ministries Committee: Christy Howard-Steele, (708)747-6927, specmin@FCMmail.org.
Vice Chair, Specialized Ministries Committee: Carl Yusavitz, (215)248-2140, specmin@FCMmail.org.
Director at Large: William Manseau, (978)851-5547, directoratlarge@FCMmail.org.

REGIONAL VICE PRESIDENTS:
Pacific Region: Nick and Mary De Los Reyes, (562)547-0910, pacificvp@FCMmail.org.
Mountains & Plains: Michael Keefe, (219)221-9046, mts_plainsvp@FCMmail.org.
Great Lakes: Thomas Stricker, (937)855-4874, greatlakesvp@FCMmail.org and
and Amy Simpson Bennethum, (513)295-5506, greatlakesvp@FCMmail.org.
Southern: Virginia and Robert Graf, (304)728-2829, southernvp@FCMmail.org.
Northeast: Paul and Patricia Stubenbort, (215)752-7493, northeastvp@FCMmail.org.

Friends World Committee for Consultation (Section of the Americas)

The Friends World Committee for Consultation (FWCC) was formed in 1937. There has been an American Section as well as a European Section from the early days and an African Section was organized in 1971. In 1974 the name, Section of the Americas, was adopted by that part of the FWCC with constituency in North, Central, and South America and in the Caribbean area. In 1985 the Asia-West Pacific Section was organized. The purposes of FWCC are summarized as follows, To facilitate loving understanding of diversities among Friends while discovering together, with God's help, a common spiritual ground; and to facilitate full expression of Friends' testimonies in the world.

Headquarters
Section of the Americas Headquarters
1506 Race St., Philadelphia, PA 19102 Tel. (215)241-7250 Fax (215)241-7285 Email: americas@fwcc.quaker.org www.quaker.org/fwcc/americas/americas.html
Media Contact, Exec. Sec., Margaret Fraser
Latin American Office, Guerrero 223 Pte., Zona Centro, Cd. Mante, TAM 89800 Mexico

Officers
None-Just Exec. Secty, 5 Full-Time Employees

The Fund for Theological Education, Inc.

Begun in 1954 with the goal of supporting excellence in the profession of ministry. The

31

Fund for Theological Education has enjoyed a long and rich history, providing gifted women and men with more than 6000 pastoral fellowships and generating innovative new programs for support of young leaders preparing for ministry and theological teaching. Supported by individuals and grants foundations, FTE is an advocate for diversity and excellence in the congregations and seminaries of North America.

Headquarters
825 Houston Mill Rd., Suite 100, Atlanta, GA 30329 Tel. (404)727-1450 Fax (404)727-1490 Website: www.fteleaders.org

Officers
Interim President, Peg Birk

Glenmary Research Center
The Research Center is a department of the Glenmary Home Missioners, a Catholic society of priests and brothers. The Center was established in 1966 to serve the rural research needs of the Catholic Church in the United States. The Glenmary Research Center published the 2000 Religious Congregations and Membership Study as well as previous studies in 1971, 1980 and 1990. The research center was also responsible for collecting the Catholic data included in the past studies and is collecting the Catholic data for the 2010 study, which will be published in 2012. The Religious Congregations and Membership Study contains the most complete data available on U.S. religious affiliation.

Headquarters
P. O. Box 465418, Cincinnati, OH 45246-5618; Tel. (513)881-7497 Fax (513)874-1690, Email: grc@glenmary.org
Media Contact: Jean Bach

Officers
President: Fr. Chet Artysiewicz, P.O. Box 465418, Cincinnati, OH 45246-5618
1st Vice-President: Fr. Neil Pezzulo, P.O. Box 465418, Cincinnati, OH 45246-5618
2nd Vice-President: Br. Jack Henn, P.O. Box 465418, Cincinnati, OH 45246-5618
Treas.: Ms. Sandy Wissel, P.O. Box 465418, Cincinnati, OH 45246-5618
Staff: Coordinator, Lucy Putnam, P.O. Box 465418, Cincinnati, OH 45246-5618

Graymoor Ecumenical & Interreligious Institute (GEII)
Graymoor Ecumenical & Interreligious Institute has its roots in the Graymoor Ecumenical Institute which was founded in 1967 by the Franciscan Friars of the Atonement, to respond to the Friars' historical concern for Christian Unity in light of the theological and ecumenical developments arising from the Second Vatican Council.

In 1991, in response to developments in both the Institute and the wider ecumenical scene, the Graymoor Ecumenical Institute was expanded into an information and service organization with a mission of Christian Unity and interreligious dialogue. Today, the Graymoor Ecumenical & Interreligious Institute employs several means to accomplish this goal. Among these is the annual Week of Prayer for Christian Unity, "a world-wide observance initiated in 1908 by the Rev. Paul Wattson, co-founder of the Society of the Atonement," the theme and text of which are now chosen and prepared by the Pontifical Council for Promoting Christian Unity and representatives of the World Council of Churches. The Institute publishes the monthly journal Ecumenical Trends-to keep clergy and laity abreast of developments in the ecumenical and interreligious movements; provides membership in, and collaboration with, national and local ecumenical and interreligious organizations and agencies; and cooperates with individuals engaged in ecumenical and interreligious work. A new website, www.geii.org has been launched and will continue to be developed as a resource for ecumenical and interreligious research.

Over the years, the Graymoor Ecumenical & Interreligious Institute has sponsored and cosponsored meetings, colloquia, and workshops in areas of ecumenical and interreligious dialogue.

Headquarters
475 Riverside Dr., Rm. 1960, New York, NY 10115-1999 Tel. (212)870-2330 Fax (212)870-2001

Staff
Director, Rev. James Loughran, SA, Tel. (212)870-2330, Email: jlgeii@aol.com
Assoc. Director, Rev. Dr. Timothy MacDonald, SA, Tel. (212)870-2331, Email: tmdgeii@aol.com
Assoc. Dir., Week of Prayer for Christian Unity, Rev. Thomas Orians, SA, Tel. (212)870-2330, Email: togeii@aol.com
Editor, Ecumenical Trends, Rev. James Loughran SA., Graymoor, Route 9, P.O. Box 300 Garrison, NY 10524-0300 Tel. (845)424-3671 ext. 3323, Email: jlgeii@aol.com
Business Manager, Week of Prayer for Christian Unity Office, Mrs. Veronica Sullivan, Graymoor, Rt. 9, P.O. Box 300, Garrison, NY 10524-0300 Tel. (800)338.2620 ext. 2109 or (845)424-2109 Fax (845)424-2163, Email: rsullivan@atonementfriars.org

Interfaith Impact for Justice and Peace
Interfaith Impact for Justice and Peace is the religious community's united voice in Washington. It helps Protestant, Jewish, Muslim and Catholic national organizations have clout on

Capitol Hill and brings grassroots groups and individual and congregational members to Washington and shows them how to turn their values into votes for justice and peace.

Interfaith Impact for Justice and Peace has established the following Advocacy Networks to advance the cause of justice and peace, Justice for Women; Health Care; Hunger and Poverty; International Justice and Peace; Civil and Human Rights. The Interfaith Impact Foundation provides an annual Legislative Briefing for their members.

Members receive the periodic Action alerts on initiatives, voting records, etc., and a free subscription to the Advocacy Networks of their choice.

Headquarters
100 Maryland Ave. N.E., Ste. 200, Washington, DC 20002 Tel. (202)543-2800 Fax (202)547-8107
Media Contact, Jane Hull Harvey

Officers
Chpsn. of Bd., Jane Hull Harvey, United Methodist Church

MEMBERS
African Methodist Episcopal Church
African Methodist Episcopal Zion Church
Alliance of Baptists
American Baptist Churches, USA, Washington Office; World Relief Office
American Ethical Union
American Muslim Council
Center of Concern
Christian Methodist Episcopal (CME) Church
Christian Church (Disciples of Christ)
Church of the Brethren
Church Women United
Commission on Religion in Appalachia
Episcopal Church
Episcopal Urban Caucus
Evangelical Lutheran Church in America
Federation of Southern Cooperatives-LAF
Federation for Rural Empowerment
Graymoor Ecumenical and Interreligious Institute
Jesuit Social Ministries
Maryknoll Fathers and Brothers
Moravian Church in America
National Council of Churches of Christ, Church World Service; Washington Office
National Council of Jewish Women

NETWORK
Peoria Citizens Committee
Presbyterian Church (USA)
Progressive National Baptist Convention
Presbyterian Hunger Fund
Reformed Church in America
Rural Advancement Fund
Society of African Missions
Southwest Organizing Project
Southwest Voter Registration-Education Project
Toledo Metropolitan Ministries
Union of American Hebrew Congregations

Unitarian Universalist Association
Unitarian Universalist Service Committee
United Church of Christ, Bd. for Homeland Ministries; Bd. for World Ministries; Hunger Action Ofc.; Ofc. of Church in Society
United Methodist Church, Gen. Bd. of Church & Society; Gen. Bd. of Global Ministries Natl. Div.; Gen. Bd. of Global Ministries Women's Div.; Gen. Bd. of Global Ministries World Div.
Virginia Council of Churches
Western Organization of Resource Councils

Interfaith Worker Justice
Interfaith Worker Justice (IWJ) is a network of people of faith that calls upon their religious values in order to educate, organize, and mobilize the religious community in the United States on issues and campaigns that will improve wages, benefits, and conditions for workers, and give voice to workers, especially workers in low-wage jobs.

The organization supports and organizes local interfaith worker justice groups around the country, publishes Faith Works four times a year providing congregations resources and updates on religion-labor work.

Headquarters
1020 West Bryn Mawr, 4th floor, Chicago, IL 60660-4627 Tel. (773)728-8400 Fax (773)728-8409
Media Contact, Cynthia Brooke, cbrooke@iwj.org

Officers
President: Bishop Gabino Zavala, Archdiocese of Los Angeles
Vice-President: Dr. Edith Rasell, Economic Justice Minister, United Church of Christ
Finance Chair: Rev. Bennie Whiten Jr., United Church of Christ
Fundraising Chair: Rev. Jim Sessions, United Methodist Church
Public Policy Chair: Ms. Ros Pelles, Department of Civil, Human and Women's Rights, AFL-CIO
Communications Chair: Rabbi Jill Jacobs, Jewish Funds for Justice
Board Development Chair: Rev. Darren Cushman-Wood, Speedway United Methodist Church
Dr. Charles Amjad-Ali, Luther Seminary
Mr. Hussam Ayloush, Council on American-Islamic Relations – Southern California
Mr. Jules Bernstein, Bernstein & Lipsett, P.C.
Ms. Jennifer Butler, Faith In Public Life
Mr. Phil Cubeta,The American College
Imam Taha Hassane, Islamic Center of San Diego
Mr. John Hill, General Board of Church and Society, United Methodist Church
Ms. Arlene Holt Baker, AFL-CIO
Mr. John Howard, Ignatian Spirituality Project
Rev. Daryl Ingram, African Methodist Episcopal Church

Rev. Chris Johnson, Episcopal Church Center

Rev. Jarvis Johnson, New Prospect Family Praise and Worship Center

Sheikh Abdool Khan, Islamic Society of North America

Dr. Ken Brooker Langston, Christian Church (Disciples of Christ)

Ms. Susan Leslie, Unitarian Universalist Association

Rev. Dr. Leonard Lovett, Ecumenical Officer of Urban Affairs, Church of God in Christ

Dr. Joseph A. McCartin, Georgetown University

Rev. Aaron McEmrys, Unitarian Universalist Association

Rev. Dr. Lillian Daniel, First Congregational Church of Glen Ellyn

Sr. Jean Miller, Sisters of Charity

Mr. Todd O'Malley, O'Malley & Langan Law Offices

Sr. Mary Priniski, OP, Catholic Committee of the South

Rev. Frank Raines III, Gethsemane Missionary Baptist Church

Mr. Ibrahim Ramey, Muslim American Society's Freedom Foundation

Ms. Kathy Saile, United States Conference of Catholic Bishops

Rev. Dr. Martha Scott, United Methodist Church

Ms. Elena Segura, Office for Immigrant Affairs and Immigrant Education, Archdiocese of Chicago

Rev. Paul Sherry, United Church of Christ

Mr. Charles Whitaker, Northwestern University

Special Advisors

Bishop Jesse DeWitt**, Retired, United Methodist Church

Rev. Jim Lawson, Holman Untied Methodist Church

Rev. Joseph Echols Lowery, Southern Christian Leadership Conference

Rabbi Robert Marx**, Congregation Hakafa

Rev. Addie Wyatt, Vernon Park Church of God

Executive Director, Kim Bobo

* Former Board Officer

** Former Board President

Interreligious Foundation for Community Organization (IFCO)

IFCO is a national ecumenical agency created in 1966 by several Protestant, Roman Catholic and Jewish organizations, to be an interreligious, interracial agency for support of community organization and education in pursuit of social justice. Through IFCO, national and regional religious bodies collaborate in development of social justice strategies and provide financial support and technical assistance to local, national and international social-justice projects.

IFCO serves as a bridge between the churches and communities and acts as a resource for ministers and congregations wishing to better understand and do more to advance the struggles of the poor and oppressed. IFCO conducts workshops for community organizers and uses its national and international network of organizers, clergy and other professionals to act in the interest of justice.

Churches, foundations and individual donors use IFCO services as a fiscal agent to make donations to community organizing projects.

IFCO's global outreach includes humanitarian aid shipments through its Pastors for Peace program to Cuba, Haiti, Nicaragua, Honduras, and Chiapas, Mexico.

Headquarters

418 W. 145th St., New York, NY 10031 Tel. (212)926-5757 Fax (212)926-5842

Media Contact, Dir. of Communications, Lucia Bruno

Officers

Pres., Rev. Thomas Smith

Vice President & Treasurer, vacant

InterVarsity Christian Fellowship of the U.S.A.

InterVarsity Christian Fellowship is a nonprofit, interdenominational student movement that ministers to college and university students and faculty in the United States. InterVarsity began in the United States when students at the University of Michigan invited C. Stacey Woods, then General Secretary of the Canadian movement, to help establish an InterVarsity chapter on their campus. InterVarsity Christian Fellowship-USA was incorporated two years later, in 1941.

InterVarsity's uniqueness as a campus ministry lies in the fact that it is student-initiated and student-led. InterVarsity strives to build collegiate fellowships that engage their campus with the gospel of Jesus Christ and develop disciples who live out biblical values. InterVarsity students and faculty are encouraged in evangelism, spiritual discipleship, serving the church, multiethnicity, righteousness, vocational stewardship and world evangelization. The Urbana triennial missions convention has long been a launching point for missionary service. For more detials on urbana please visit www.urbana.org.

Headquarters

6400 Schroeder Rd., P.O. Box 7895, Madison, WI 53707 Tel. (608)274-9001 Fax (608)274-7882 www.intervarsity.org; info@intervarsity.org

Media Contact, Gordon Govier

Officers

Pres. & CEO, Alec Hill

Vice-Pres., C. Barney Ford; Robert A. Fryling; Karon Morton, Jim Lundgren, Paula Fuller, Paul Tokunaga, Tom Lin

Bd. Chpsn., Dennis O'Neal

Bd. Vice-Chpsn., E. Kenneth Nielson

The Kairos Institute, Inc.

The Kairos Institute provides quality support, consultation and in-depth educational opportunities to the professional, medical, mental health and religious communities and promotes assistance, consultation, education and care to families of exceptional children. It's clergy consultation service provides care to many denominations and clergy. "Career Path" offers candidate assessment for ordination and consultation for clergy in transition.

Headquarters
107 Green Ave., Madison, NJ 07940 Tel. (973)966-9099 Fax (973)377-8509

Officers
Executive Director, Kathryn (Penny) Vennard Clark, MSW, LCSW
Clergy Services: The Rev. Dr. Dan Bottorff & The Rev. Dr. Richard Crocker

Lift Disability Network

Created in 1988, the Christian Council on Persons with Disabilities (CCPD) is a coalition of churches, non-profit organizations and individuals advocating an evangelical perspective concerning people with disabilities and their place in God's world. The coalition provides a national voice for Christians involved in disability ministry, framing the Christian community's response to issues relating to disability.

CCPD provides information and responses on issues specifically relating to the church such as accessibility, disability theology and outreach; as well as disability-related issues of concern to the general public such as genetic research, end-of-life care and cloning.

Advocacy, professional development, networking and education are all part of the coalition's activities. Annual conferences (both national & regional), chapter groups and mentoring programs are part of the coalition's strategy in strengthening the network of disability ministry.

Headquarters
P.O. Box 770607, Winter Garden, FL 34777 Tel. (407)228-8343, Email: info@liftdisability.net, Website:www.liftdisability.net

Officers
Exec. Dir., Jim Hukill
Pres., Gary Wagner, Of Camp Verde, AZ
Treas., Stan Higgins, of Rohnert Park, CA

The Liturgical Conference

The Liturgical Conference advocates for the renewal of liturgy, supports the formation of liturgical people, seeks the unity of the Body of Christ, for the life of the world.

As an ongoing movement with the ecumenical church, founded in 1940, we seek to provide an ecumenical forum for articulating standards of liturgical excellence and for supporting persons who have a common interest and concern for the liturgical life and the liturgical arts of the church.

Headquarters
P.O.Box 31, Evanston, IL 60204

Officers
Pres., E. Byron Anderson
Vice-Pres., Todd Johnson
Sec., Fritz West
Treas., Lester Ruth

Lombard Mennonite Peace Center

The Lombard Mennonite Peace Center (LMPC) is a nonprofit organization with the mission "to proclaim Christ's good news, the gospel of peace and justice—and to be active in the sacred ministry of reconciliation." With an emphasis on equipping clergy and churches to function in healthy ways, LMPC offers training in conflict transformation and in a family systems approach to church leaders' management of themselves and their congregations.

One- and two-day educational workshops and a five-day "Mediation Skills Training Institute for Church Leaders" are offered throughout the U.S. Ongoing clergy clinics provide church leaders with regular opportunities to reflect on their own functioning. LMPC also provides educational events, consultation and mediation services for congregations and judicatories of all denominations, as well as consultation for individual clergy.

Founded in 1983 as a ministry of a local congregation, LMPC became an independent, 501(c)3 corporation in 1997.

Headquarters
101 W. 22nd St., Suite 206, Lombard, IL 60148 Tel. (630)627-0507 Fax (630)627-0519, Email: admin@LMPeaceCenter.org, Website: www. LMPeaceCenter.org

Officers
Executive Director, Richard G. Blackburn

The Lord's Day Alliance of the United States

The Lord's Day Alliance of the United States, founded in 1888 in Washington, D.C., is the only national organization whose sole purpose is the preservation and cultivation of Sunday, the Lord's Day, as a day of rest and worship. The Alliance also seeks to safeguard a Day of Common Rest for all people regardless of their faith. Its Board of Managers is composed of representatives from 25 denominations. It serves as an information bureau, publishes a magazine, Sunday, and furnishes speakers and a variety of materials such as pamphlets, videos, posters, radio spot announcements, cassettes, news releases, articles for magazines and television programs.

Headquarters

Mailing Address: P.O. Box 941745, Atlanta, GA 31141-0745, Phone: (404)693-5530, Website: www.ldausa.org

Media Contact: Tim Norton, tnorton@ldausa.org

Co-Executive Directors: Rev. Timothy A. Norton, tnorton@ldausa.org and Rev. Dr. Rodney L. Petersen, petersen@boston theological.org

Officers

President, Mr. David C. McNair
Immediate Past President, Mr. Brian W. Hanse
Vice President, Rev. Dr. J. N. Hollingsworth, III
Secretary, Rev. John Hinkle
Treasurer, Father Edward O'Flaherty SJ
Presidents Emeriti, Rev. Dr. Roger A. Kvam and Rev. Dr. W. David Sapp

Lutheran World Relief

Lutheran World Relief (LWR) is an overseas development and relief agency based in Baltimore which responds quickly to natural and man-made disasters and supports more than 160 long-range development projects in countries throughout Africa, Asia, the Middle East and Latin America. As its mission, Lutheran World Relief works with partners to help people grow food, improve health, strengthen communities, end conflict, build livelihoods, and recover from disasters.

Headquarters

700 Light Street, Baltimore, MD 21230-3850 Tel. (410)230-2800 Fax (410)230-2882

Officers

Pres., John A. Nunes

Mennonite Central Committee

Mennonite Cental Committee (MCC), a worldwide ministry of Anabaptist churches, shares God's love and compassion for all in the name of Christ by responding to basic human needs and working for peace and justice. MCC envisions communities in right relationship with God, one another and creation. Founded in 1920, MCC administers and participates in programs of agricultural and economic development, education, health, self-help, relief, peace and disaster service. MCC has about 1000 workers serving in 55 countries in Africa, Asia, Europe, Middle East and South, Central and North America.

MCC has service programs in North America that focus both on urban and rural poverty areas. There are also North American programs focusing on such diverse matters as community conciliation, employment creation and criminal justice issues. These programs are administered by two national bodies-MCC U.S. and MCC Canada.

Contributions from North American Mennonite and Brethren in Christ churches provide the largest part of MCC's support. Other sources of financial support include the contributed earnings of volunteers, grants from private and government agencies and contributions from Mennonite churches abroad. The total income in FYE2004, including material aid contributions, amounted to $69.4 million (US dollars).

MCC tries to strengthen local communities by working in cooperation with local churches or other community groups. Many personnel are placed with other agencies, including missions. Programs are planned with sensitivity to locally felt needs.

Headquarters

21 S. 12th St., P.O. Box 500, Akron, PA 17501-0500 Tel. (717)859-1151 Fax (717)859-2171 and 134 Plaza Dr., Winnipeg, MB R3T 5K9 Tel. (204)261-6381 Fax (204)269-9875

Media Coordinator at either address

Officers

Exec. Directors., Binational, Arli Klassen, Canada, Donald Peters; U.S., J. Ron Byler

National Association of Ecumenical and Interreligious Staff

NAEIS is an association of professional staff in ecumenical and interreligious work. Founded as the Association of Council Secretaries in 1940, the Association was widened to include program staff in 1971, and renamed the National Association of Ecumenical Staff. It has included staff of any faith engaged in interreligious work since 1994. NAEIS provides means for personal and professional growth, and for mutual support, through national and regional gatherings, a newsletter and exchange among its membership. NAEIS was established to provide creative relationships, mutual support and personal and professional growth of its members.

Headquarters

NAEIS, P.O. Box 95949, Seattle, WA 98145. Email: info@naeis.org

Officers

Pres.: The Rev. C. Dana Krutz, Louisiana Interchurch Conference, 527 North Blvd # 4 Baton Rouge, LA 70802-5720 Tel.(225)344-0134 Email: dankrutz@aol.com

Vice Pres.: The Rev. Scott Anderson, Wisconsin Council of Churches, 750 Windsor St #301, Sun Prairie, WI 53590-2149 Tel. (608)837-3108 Fax:(608)837-3038 Email: sanderson@ wichurches.org

Immediate Past Pres.: The Rev. Samuel Muyskens, Interfaith Ministers–Wichita, 820 North Market Street, Wichita, KS 67214-1157 Tel. (512)451-2062 Email: smuyskens@ ifmnet.org

Sec.: The Rev. Dr. Clark Lobenstine, Exec. Dir., Interfaith Conference of Metropolitan Washington, 1426 Ninth St. NW, 2nd Floor, Washington, DC 20001-3330 Tel. (202)234-6300 Email: clarkifc@aol.com

Treas.: Alice Woldt, Transitional Exec. Dir., Washington Association of Churches, P.O. Box 95949, Seattle, WA 98145 Email: woldt@thewac.org

The National Association of Evangelicals

The National Association of Evangelicals (NAE) is a voluntary fellowship of evangelical denominations, churches, organizations and individuals demonstrating unity in the body of Christ by standing for biblical truth, speaking with a representative voice, and serving the evangelical community through united action, cooperative ministry and strategic planning.

The association is composed of approximately 45,000 congregations nationwide from over 40 member denominations and fellowships. These ministries represent a broad range of theological traditions, but all subscribe to the distinctly evangelical NAE Statement of Faith. The association is a nationally recognized entity by the public sector with a reputation for integrity and effective service.

The cooperative ministries of the National Association of Evangelicals demonstrate the association's intentional desire to promote cooperation without compromise.

Headquarters

NAE-Washington, 701 G. St., SW, Washington, DC 20024 Tel. (202)789-1011 Fax (202)842-0392

Media Contact, Sarah Kropp, (202)789-1011

STAFF

President, Rev. Leith Anderson

National Bible Association

The National Bible Association is an autonomous, nonpolitical interfaith organization of lay people who advocate regular Bible reading and sponsors National Bible Week (Thanksgiving week) each November. Program activities include public service advertising, distribution of nonsectarian literature and thousands of local Bible Week observances by secular and religious organizations. The Association also urges constitutionally acceptable use of the Bible in public school classrooms, i.e. the study of the Bible in literature. All support comes from individuals, corporations and foundations.

Founded in 1940 by a group of business and professional people, the Association has the IRS nonprofit status of a 501(c)(3) educational association.

Headquarters

405 Lexington Avenue, 26th Floor, New York, NY 10174 Tel. (212)907-6427 Fax (212)898-1147

Media Contact, Pres., Richard Glickstein, Email: rglickstein@nationalbible.org

Officers

Cpsn., Sean Fieler
Pres., Richard Glickstein
Sec., J. Marshall Gage

The National Conference for Community and Justice

The National Conference for Community and Justice, founded in 1927 as the National Conference of Christians and Jews, is a human relations organization dedicated to fighting bias, bigotry and racism in America. The NCCJ promotes understanding and respect among all races, religions and cultures through advocacy, conflict resolution and education.

Programmatic strategies include interfaith and interracial dialogue, youth leadership workshops, workplace training, human relations research, and the building of community coalitions. NCCJ has 65 regional offices staffed by approximately 350 people. Nearly 200 members comprise the National Board of Advisors and members from that group form the 27-member National Board of Directors. Each regional office has its own Regional Board of Directors with a total of about 2,800. The National Board of Advisors meets once annually, the National Board of Directors at least three times annually.

Headquarters

NCCJ - The National Conference for Community and Justice of Connecticut and Western Massachusetts, Inc.

1095 Day Hill Road, Suite 100, Windsor, CT 06095, Tel: (860)683-1039, Fax: (860)683-1409

Email: agumbs@nccj.org, Web: www.nccj.org

Media Contact, Associate Director, Amanda Gumbs

Officers

Exec. Dir.: Dr. Andrea C. Kandel

National Conference on Ministry to the Armed Forces

The Conference is an incorporated civilian agency. Representation in the Conference with all privileges of the same is open to all endorsing or certifying agencies or groups authorized to provide chaplains for any branch of the Armed Forces.

The purpose of this organization is to provide a means of dialogue to discuss concerns and objectives and, when agreed upon, to take action with the appropriate authority to support the spiritual ministry to and the moral welfare of Armed Forces personnel.

Headquarters

4141 N. Henderson Rd., Ste. 13, Arlington, VA 22203 Tel. (703)276-7905 Fax (703)276-7906 Media Contact, Jack Williamson

STAFF

Coord., Jack Williamson
Admn. Asst., Maureen Francis

OFFICERS
Chpsn., David Peterson
Chpsn.-elect, Robert Jemerson
Sec., Lemuel Boyles
Treas., John Murdoch

National Council of the Churches of Christ in the U.S.A.

The National Council of the Churches of Christ in the U.S.A. is the preeminent expression in the United States of the movement toward Christian unity. The NCC's 37 member communions, including Protestant, Orthodox and Anglican church bodies, work together on a wide range of activities that further Christian unity, that witness to the faith, that promote peace and justice and that serve people throughout the world. Forty million U.S. Christians belong to churches that hold Council membership. The Council was formed in 1950 in Cleveland, Ohio, by the action of representatives of the member churches and by the merger of 12 previously existing ecumenical agencies, each of which had a different program focus. The roots of some of these agencies go back to the 19th century.

Headquarters

475 Riverside Dr., New York, NY 10115 Tel. (212)870-2141
Media Contact, Media Relations Specialist, Mr. Philip E. Jenks Tel. (212)870-2228 Fax (212) 870-2030, pjenks@ncccusa.org

Officers

GENERAL OFFICERS
NOTE: Dr. Kinnamon resigned effective December 31, 2011. All other officers began service on January 1, 2012.
Pres., Kathryn Mary Lohre
Gen. Sec., The Rev. Dr. Michael Kinnamon
Pres. Elect, The Rev. A. Roy Medley
Immediate Past Pres., The Rev. Canon Peg Chemberlin
Sec., The Rev. Dr. Karen Georgia Thompson
Vice Pres., Bishop John F. White
Vice Pres. at Large, The Rev. José Luis Casal
Vice Pres. at Large, The Rev. Dr. Rev. Earl D. Trent Jr.
Vice Pres. at Large, The Rev. Dr. Sharon Watkins

THE GENERAL SECRETARIAT
Deputy Gen. Sec. and General Counsel, Ms. Clare J.Chapman
Media Relations Specialist, Mr. Philip E. Jenks, Tel. (212)870-2228

ADMINISTRATION AND FINANCE
Senior Director, Ms. Karen Wang, Tel. (212)870-3351

RESOURCE DEVELOPMENT
Dir. of Development, Mr. Kurt Meyer, Tel. (212)870-2574, or (641)326-2255
Dir. of Donor Relations, The Rev. Deborah C. DeWinter, Tel. (212)870-2513
Dir. of Foundation Relations, Ms. Cassandra Carmichael, Tel. (202)481-6928
Dir. of Planned Giving, Mr. Kurt R. Kaboth, Esq., Tel. 212-870-2255

ADINISTRATION, FINANCE & LEGAL
Mr. Kurt R. Kaboth, Esq., Director of Administration & Associate General Counsel, Tel. (212)870-2255

YEARBOOK OF AMERICAN & CANADIAN CHURCHES
Editor, The Rev. Dr. Eileen W. Lindner, Tel. (212)567-0111
Assoc. Ed., Rev. Marcel A. Welty, Tel. (201)870-1492
Asst. Ed., Dr. Elizabeth During, Tel. (212)870-2031 Fax (212)870-2817

WASHINGTON OFFICE
110 Maryland Ave. NE Washington, D.C. 20002 Tel. (202)544-2350 Fax (202)543-1297
Dir. of Washington Office, Ms. Cassandra Carmichael, Tel. (202)481-6298
Office Manager, Mr. Kevin Williams, Tel. (202)544-2350

COMMUNICATION COMMISSION AND JUSTICE AND ADVOCACY COMMISSION
Media Relations Specialist, Mr. Philip E. Jenks, Tel. (212)870-2228
Coord. of Television Programming, Ms. Shirley W. Struchen, Tel. (212)870-2227
Eco-Justice Programs, Dir., Ms. Cassandra Carmichael, Tel. (202)481-6298
Poverty Initiative, the Rev. Michael Livingston, Dir., Tel. (202)-544-2375
Advocacy Officer and Ecumenical Peace Coordinator, Mr. Jordan Blevins, Tel. (202)-481-6943
Eco-Justice Programs, Asst. Dir., Climate Change and Energy Campaign Manager, Ms. Tyler Edgar, Tel. (202)544-2375
Eco-Justice Programs, Prog. Mgr., Environmental Health, Ms. Chloe Schwabe, Tel. (202)481-6932
Program for Women's Ministries, Dir., The Rev. Ann Tiemeyer, Tel. (202)870-3407

EDUCATION AND LEADERSHIP MINISTRIES COMMISSION
Associate General Secretary, Education and Leadership Ministries, (unfilled)

FAITH AND ORDER COMMISSION AND INTERFAITH RELATIONS COMMISSION
Associate General Secretary, Interfaith Relations and Faith & Order, Dr. Antonios Kireopoulos, Tel. (212)870-3422

RELATED ORGANIZATIONS

Agricultural Missions – Mr. Winston G. Carroo, Exec. Dir., Tel.(212)870-2553 Fax (212)870-2959

Church Women United, Ms. Djamillah Samad, National Exec., Tel. 800-298-5551; Dr. Robin Fillmore, CWU-NCC Advocacy Coordinator, Tel. (202)481-6929

Interfaith Center for Corporate Responsibility, Laura Berry, Exec. Dir., Tel.(212)870-2295

Let Justice Roll Poverty Initiative, Mr. Steve Copley, Chair of the Board, Tel. (501)626-9220

National Farm Workers Ministry, Ms. Virginia Nesmith, Exec. Dir., 438 N. Skinker, St. Louis, MD 63130, Tel. (314)726-6470

New Fire, Young Adult Ecumenists, c/o Mr. Jordan Blevins, Tel. (202)481-6943

U.S. Conference for the World Council of Churches, c/o Ms. Clare J. Chapman, Tel. 212-870-3366

World Day of Prayer-USA, Ms. Vivian Harrison, Tel. 212-870-2466

World Student Christian Federation, Mr. Luciano Kovacs, North American Regional Secretary, Tel. (212)870-2470

National Institute of Business and Industrial Chaplains

NIBIC is the professional organization for workplace chaplains, that includes members from a wide variety of faith groups and work settings, including corporations, manufacturing plants, air and sea ports, labor unions and pastoral counseling centers. NIBIC has six membership categories, including Certified, Clinical, Professional, Affiliates and Organizational.

NIBIC works to establish professional standards for education and practice; promotes and conducts training programs; provides mentoring, networking and chaplaincy information; encourages research and public information dissemination; communicates with business leaders and conducts professional meetings. NIBIC publishes a quarterly newsletter and co-sponsors The Journal of Pastoral Care and Counseling. A public membership meeting and training conference is held annually. NIBIC provides certification for qualified clinical members.

Headquarters

1900 St. James Place, Suite 880, Houston, TX 77056 Tel. (713)266-2456 Fax (713)266-0845
Media Contact, Rev. Diana C. Dale, D. Min., 1900 St. James Place, Suite 880 Houston, TX 77056 Tel. (713)266-2456 Fax (713)266-0845

Officers

Executive Dir., Rev. Diana C. Dale, D.Min., Ph.D.
Vice Pres., Rev. Dr. Juliette Jones, Ph.D.
President, Rev. Robert L. Lewis, Jr., STM

Treas., Rev. Gregory Edwards, M.Div.
Board Member, Timothy Bancroft, D.Min.

National Interfaith Cable Coalition, Inc. (NICC)

The National Interfaith Cable Coalition, Inc. (NICC) was formed as a not-for-profit 501(c)3 corporation, in December 1987, and is currently comprised of more than 40 faith groups and organizations from the Jewish and Christian traditions.

In September 1988, NICC launched a religious cable network called VISN (Vision Interfaith Satellite Network), later known as the Odyssey Network. Now known as the Hallmark Channel, it is owned and operated by Crown Media Holdings, Inc., in which NICC is a strategic investor. NICC provides regular and prime-time special programming on the network.

In 2000, NICC adopted Faith & Values Media as its service mark and expanded its mission to include a significant Web presence, www.FaithStreams.com, which features streaming video and video-on-demand service.

Headquarters

475 Riverside Drive, Ste. 530, New York, NY 10015 Tel. (212)870-1030
Media Contact, Desiree Frieson

Officers

Chair, Dr. Daniel Paul Matthews
Vice Chair, Elder Ralph Hardy Jr., Esq.
Secretary, Rabbi Daniel Freelander
Treasurer, Betty Elam

STAFF
President and CEO, Edward J. Murray
Exec. Vice President, Beverly Judge

National Interfaith Coalition on Aging

National Interfaith Coalition on Aging (NICA), a constituent unit of the National Council on Aging, is composed of Protestant, Roman Catholic, Jewish and Orthodox national and regional organizations and individuals concerned about the needs of older people and the religious community's response to problems facing the aging population in the United States. NICA was organized in 1972 to address spiritual concerns of older adults through religious sector action.

Mission Statement — The National Interfaith Coalition on Aging (NICA), affiliated with the National Council on the Aging (NCOA), is a diverse network of religious and other related organizations and individual members which promotes the spiritual well being of older adults and the preparation of persons of all ages for the spiritual tasks of aging. NICA serves as a catalyst for new and effective research, networking opportunities, resource development, service provision, and dissemination of information.

Headquarters

c/o NCOA, 1910 L Street, NW, 4th Floor, Washington, DC 20036 Tel. (202)479-6655 Fax (202)479-0735

Media Contact, Rita Chow, Ed.D.

Officers

Chpsn., Rev. Ronald Field
Chpsn.-Elect, Beth Schwartz
Past Chpsn., Jane Stenson
Sec., Donald R. Koepke
Dir., Dr. Rita K. Chow

National Religious Broadcasters

National Religious Broadcasters is an association of Christian communicators, 1,500 organizations which produce religious programs for radio and television and other forms of electronic mass media or operate stations carrying predominately religious programs. NRB member organizations are responsible for more than 75 percent of all religious radio and television in the United States, reaching an average weekly audience of millions by radio, television, and other broadcast media.

Dedicated to the communication of the Gospel, NRB was founded in 1944 to safeguard free and complete access to the broadcast media. By encouraging the development of Christian programs and stations, NRB helps make it possible for millions to hear the good news of Jesus Christ through the electronic media.

Headquarters

9510 Technology Drive, Manassas, VA 20110. Tel. (703)330-7000 Fax (703)330-7100

Media Contact, Pres., Dr. Frank Wright

Officers

Chmn., Ron. L. Harris
1st Vice Chmn., Janet Parshall
2nd Vice Chair: John Fuller
Sec.: Richard Bott
Treas.: Roger Kemp

National Woman's Christian Temperance Union

The National WCTU is a not-for-profit, nonpartisan, interdenominational organization dedicated to the education of our nation's citizens, especially children and teens, on the harmful effects of alcoholic beverages, other drugs and tobacco on the human body and the society in which we live. The WCTU believes in a strong family unit and, through legislation, education and prayer, works to strengthen the home and family.

WCTU, which began in 1874 with the motto, "For God and Home and Every Land," is organized in 58 countries.

Headquarters

1730 Chicago Ave., Evanston, IL 60201 Tel. (708)864-1396

Media Contact, Sarah F. Ward, Tel. (765)345-7600

Officers

Pres., Sarah F. Ward, 33 N. Franklin, Knightstown, IN 46148, Email: sarah@ wctu.org
Vice Pres., Rita Wert, 2250 Creek Hill Rd., Lancaster, PA 17601
Promotion Dir., Nancy Zabel, 1730 Chicago Ave., Evanston, IL 60201-4585
Treas., Faye Pohl, P.O. Box 739, Meade, KS 67864
Rec. Sec., Dorothy Russell, 18900 Nestueca Dr., Cloverdale, OR 97112

MEMBER ORGANIZATIONS

Loyal Temperance Legion (LTL), for boys and girls ages 6-12
Youth Temperance Council (YTC), for teens through college age

North American Baptist Fellowship

Organized in 1964, the North American Baptist Fellowship (NABF) is a voluntary organization of Baptist conventions and conferences, and other Baptist-related groups in Canada and the United States. It functions as one of the six regional bodies of the Baptist World Alliance. Its objectives are, (a) to promote fellowship and cooperation among Baptists in North America and (b) to further the aims and objectives of the Baptist World Alliance so far as these affect the life of the Baptist churches in North America. Its membership, however, is not identical with the North American membership of the Baptist World Alliance as various Baptist groups may affiliate with NABF who are not seeking membership in the Baptist World Alliance.

Church membership of the NABF bodies is more than 15 million.

The NABF assembles representatives of the member bodies twice each year for fellowship, dialogue, and strategic action. It develops networks around special interest areas that encourage the various member bodies to engage in synergistic efforts in areas of ministry such as disaster response, church planting movements, developing creative futures for denominations, the ministry of men, women, and youth, strengthening the identity of Baptists in North America, and in the traditional areas of support for evangelism, missions, and theological education. It also engages in partnership efforts with the other five regions of the Baptist World Alliance.

Headquarters

332 Valley Springs Road, Columbia, SC 29223-6934. Tel. 803.622.0923.

E-mail: NABF@TheColumbiaPartnership.org. Web Site: www.NABF.info.

Media Contact, Gen. Sec., Dr. George Bullard, Tel. 803.622.0923.

E-mail: GBullard@TheColumbiaPartnership.org.

Officers

Pres. Dr. David Emmanuel Goatley. 300 I Street, NE. Suite 104, Washington, DC 20002

Vice Pres., Dr. Stephen Thurston, 740 E. 77th St., Chicago, IL 60619

Vice Pres., Dr. Don Sewell, 3500 Gaston Ave., Dallas, TX 75227

Rec. Sec., Ms. Patty Lane, 222 N. Washington St., Dallas, Tx 75246-1798

Treas., Rev. Ralph Duke, 2472 Centreville Rd., Herndon, VA 22181

Oikocredit- Ecumenical Development Cooperative Society

Based in the Netherlands, EDCS is often called "the churches' bank for the poor." EDCS borrows funds from churches, religious communities and concerned individuals and re-lends the funds to enterprises operated by low-income communities. Launched in 1975 through an initiative of the World Council of Churches, EDCS is organized as a cooperative of religious institutions and is governed by annual membership meetings and an elected board of religious leaders and development and financial professionals.

An international network of 15 EDCS Regional Managers is responsible for lending funds to cooperative enterprises and microcredit institutions. At the present time over $530 million is at work in microloans. This includes coffee shops, fishing enterprises, handicraft production, truck farming, and many other commercial ventures owned and operated by poor people.

Oikocredit is represented in the United States by Oikocredit, a 501(c)3 non-profit corporation. American individuals and congregations can invest in Oikocredit by purchasing one, three, and five year notes paying 0-2% interest that are issued by Oikocredit USA.

U.S. HEADQUARTERS

P.O. Box 11000, Washington, D.C. 20008, Tel.(202)728-4140, Fax (202)728-4143 Email: office.usa@oikocredit.org, website:www.oiko credit.org

Media Contact, Regional Manager for North America, Rev. Terry Provance

Officers

OFFICERS, EDCS-USA

Exec. Dir., Rev. Terry Provance

Chair, Cathy Rowan

Treas., David Mesenbring

Parish Resource Center, Inc.

Parish Resource Center, Inc. promotes, establishes, nurtures and accredits local Affiliate Parish Resource Centers whose mission is to equip, coach, and train church leaders. Affiliate centers support and strengthen subscribing congregations of all faiths by providing professional consultants, resource materials and workshops. The Parish Resource Center was founded in 1976 and is located in Lancaster PA. In addition to the Lancaster PA Center, there are three additional free-standing affiliates located in Long Island, NY; Denver, CO.; and New York City. These centers serve congregations from 49 faith traditions.

Headquarters

633 Community Way, Lancaster, PA 17603 Tel. (717)299-9932 Fax (717)299-7229

Media Contact, Pres., Dr. H. David Loughery

Officers

Chairperson, Carolyn Pyfer

Vice-Chair, Dr. Robert Webber

Sec./Treas., David P. Harrison

Pres., Dr. H. David Loughery

Founder: Dr. D. Douglas Whiting

Pentecostal-Charismatic Churches of North America

The Pentecostal-Charismatic Churches of North America (PCCNA) was organized October 19, 1994, in Memphis TN. This organizational meeting came the day after the Pentecostal Fellowship of North America (PFNA) voted itself out of existence in order to make way for the new fellowship.

The PFNA had been formed in October 1948 in Des Moines, IA. It was composed of white-led Pentecostal denominations. The move to develop a multiracial fellowship began when the PFNA Board of Administration initiated a series of discussions with African-American Pentecostal leaders. The first meeting was held July 10-11, 1992, in Dallas, TX. A second meeting convened in Phoenix, AZ, January 4-5, 1993. On January 10-11, 1994, 20 representatives from each of the two groups met in Memphis to make final plans for a Dialogue which was held in Memphis, October 1994.

This racial reconciliation meeting has been called "The Memphis Miracle." During this meeting the PFNA was disbanded, and the PCCNA was organized. The new organization quickly adopted the "Racial Reconciliation Manifesto."

In an effort to further increase the spirit of reconciliation, the PCCNA meeting of 2000 was held during the North American Renewal Service committee (NARSC) Conference in St. Louis, Missouri. Furthermore, the PCCNA acted as host for the 19th Pentecostal World Conference held in Los Angeles, California, May 2001. PCCNA welcomes denominations, associations of churches, parachurch ministries, and local churches into membership. Its strategic vision includes "demonstrating unity in the power of the Spirit."

Headquarters

2020 Bell Ave., Des Moines, Iowa, Email: info@pccna.org

Media Contact, Dr. Jeff Farmer

PCCNA EXECUTIVE BOARD

Chairperson, Dr. Jeff Farmer, Open Bible Churches, 2020 Bell Ave., Des Moines, IA 50315 Tel. (515)288-6761 Fax (515)288-2510 Email: info@pccna.org

Co-Chairperson, Bishop Jerry Macklin, Church of God in Christ, 1027 W. Tennyson Rd, Hayward, CA 94544 Tel. (510)783-9377 Fax (510)783-8673 Email: PastorJWM@aol.com

Secretary, Dr. Cylde Hughes, Int'l Pentecostal Church of Christ, P.O. Box 439, London, OH 43140-0439 Tel. (740)852-4722 Email: hqipcc@aol.com

Treasurer, Bishop Randy Howard, Church of God of Prophecy, P.O. Box 2910, Cleveland, TN 39320-2910 Tel. (423)559-5102 Email: wmcogop@aol.com

EXECUTIVE COMMITTEE MEMBERS-AT-LARGE

Dr. Ron Carpenter, International Pentecostal Holiness Church, P.O. Box 12690, Oklahoma City, OK 73157-2609

Rev. Raymond Culpepper, Church of God, P.O. Box 2430, Cleveland, TN 37320

Rev. Glenn Burris, The Foursquare Church, 1910 W. Sunset Blvd., Los Angeles, CA 90026

Rev. David Wells, Pentecostal Assemblies of Canada, 2450 Milltower Court, Mississauga, ON L5N 5Z6

Bishop Elijah Williams, The United Holy Church of America, 901 Briarwood St., Reidsville, NC 27320

Dr. George Wood, Assemblies of God, 1445 N. Boonville, Springfield, MO 65802

Project Equality, Inc.

Project Equality is a national, non-profit, interfaith program for affirmative action and equal employment opportunity. Through a Buyer's Guide that is provided to sponsoring organizations and individuals, Project Equality serves as a registry for suppliers of goods and services who commit to equal employment practices. This allows members and friends to economically support those who practice equality and justice with their employees. Project Equality also provides consultation and training for workplace diversity, does EEO audits, and is a resource for Human Resource practices. Project Equality is a leader in creating inclusive and just communities.

Headquarters
7132 Main St., Kansas City, MO 64114-1406 Tel. (816)361-9222 Fax (816)361-8997

Officers
Board Chair, Salvador Mendoza
Interim Executive Director, Cathleen D. Cackler-Veazey, Ph.D.

Religion In American Life, Inc.

Religion In American Life (RIAL) is a unique cooperative program of some 50 major national religious groups (Catholic, Eastern Orthodox, Jewish, Protestant, Muslim, etc.). It provides services for denominationally-supported, congregation-based outreach and growth projects such as the current Invite a Friend program. These projects are promoted through national advertising campaigns reaching the American public by the use of all media. The ad campaigns are produced by a volunteer agency with production-distribution and administration costs funded by denominations and business groups, as well as by individuals.

Since 1949, RIAL ad campaign projects have been among the much coveted major campaigns of The Advertising Council. This results in as much as $35 million worth of time and space in a single year, contributed by media as a public service. Through RIAL, religious groups demonstrate respect for other traditions and the value of religious freedom. The RIAL program also includes seminars and symposia, research and leadership awards and produces a weekly syndicated radio broadcast, "SpiriTalk".

Headquarters
250 E 87th St., Suite 12F, New York, NY 10128-3116 Tel. (203)355-1220 Fax (203)355-1221
Media Contact, Exec. Admin., Martha Mesiti, Tel. (203)355-1220

EXECUTIVE COMMITTEE
Natl. Chpsn., Thomas S. Johnson, Chairman & CEO, Greenpoint Bank, NY
Chpsn. of Bd., Rev. Dr. Gordon Sommers
Vice-Chpsns., Bishop Khajag Barsamian, Primate (Armenian Church of America); Most Rev. William Cardinal Keeler, (Archbishop of Baltimore); Rabbi Ronald B. Sobel, (Cong. Emanu-El of the City of N.Y.)
Sec., Timothy A. Hultquist (Morgan Stanley Dean Witter)
Treas., Robertson H. Bennett (Smith Barney)
STAFF
Pres. & CEO, Robert B. Lennick, Rabbi, D.Min.
Exec. Admin., Martha Mesiti

The Religion Communicators Council, Inc.

RCC is an interfaith, interdisciplinary association of professional communicators who work for religious groups and causes. It was founded in 1929 and is the oldest non-profit professional public relations/communications organization in the world. RCC's more than 600 members include those who work in communications and related fields for church-related institutions, denominational agencies, non- and interdenominational organizations and communications firms who primarily serve religious organizations.

Members represent a wide range of faiths, including Presbyterian, Baptist, United Methodist, Lutheran, Episcopalian, Mennonite, Roman Catholic, Seventh-day Adventist, Jewish, Salvation

Army, Brethren, Bahá'í, Disciples, Muslim, Latter-day Saints and others.

On the national level, RCC sponsors an annual three-day convention, and has published seven editions of a Religious Public Relations Handbook for churches and church organizations, and a videostrip, The Church at Jackrabbit Junction. Members receive a quarterly newsletter (Counselor). There are 8 regional chapters.

RCC administers the annual Wilbur Awards competition to recognize high quality coverage of religious values and issues in the public media. Wilbur winners include producers, reporters, editors and broadcasters nationwide. To recognize communications excellence within church communities, RCC also sponsors the annual DeRose-Hinkhouse Awards for its own members.

In 1970, 1980, 1990, 2000, and 2010. RCC initiated a global Religious Communications Congress bringing together thousands of persons from western, eastern and third-world nations who are involved in communicating religious faith.

Headquarters
475 Riverside Dr., Rm. 1355, New York, NY 10115 Tel. (212)870-2985 Fax (212)870-2171
Exec. Dir., Shirley Whipple Struchen, Tel. (212) 870-2402, Email: SSTRUCHEN@RCN.com, Website: www.religioncommunicators.org

2011 - 2012 Officers
President., Deb K. Christian, Director, Custom Relations, UMR Communications, 1221 Profit Drive, Dallas, TX 75247, B: (800)947-0207 (x147), F: (214)631-6610, C:(214)662-6013, Email: dchristian@umr.org
Vice- Pres., Laura Flippen Tenzel, Communications Coordinator, GBHEM, United Methodist Endorsing Agency, P.O. Box 340007, Nashville, TN 37203-0007, 1001 197h Ave., So., B: (615)340-7364, F: (615)340-7358, C: (615)496-3875, Email: lflippen@gbhem.org
Treas., Brian E. Gray, APR, Editor, Momentum, National Catholic Educational Association, 1005 N. Glebe Rd., Ste. 525, Arlington, VA 22201, B: (571)257-0010, F: (703)243-0025, H: (703)750-3716, Emails: momentum@ncea.org or graybrain@aol.com
Sec., Terry Barone, Communications Group Leader, Calif. Southern Baptist Convention, 678 E. Shaw Ave. Fresno, CA 93710, B: (559)229-9533 (x218), F: (559)229-2824, C: (559)284-6236, Email: tbarone@csbc.com
Past Presiden, Douglas F. Cannon, PhD., APR+M, Assistant Professor, Department of Communication, Virginia Tech Shanks Hall (0311), Blacksburg, VA 24061 Tel. (540)231-2331 Fax (540)231-9817, Email: dcannon@cannonapr.com or dfcannon@vt.edu

Religion News Service
Religion News Service (RNS) has provided news and information to the media for MORE THAN 75 years. Owned by THE NONPROFIT RELIGION NEWS LLC, it is staffed by veteran jounalists who cover stories on all of the world religions as well as trends in ethics, morality and spirituality.

RNS provides a daily news service, a weekly news service, a web service and photo service. The daily service is also available via the AP Data Features wire, or e-mail. The weekly report is available by wire or e-mail. RNS's Photos Service features stock images and news photography. RNS also offers Religion Press Release Services, which distributes press releases and advisories to religion editors. RNS is syndicated in the United States by Universal Press Syndicate and in Canada by the Canadian Press.

Headquarters
529 14th Street NW, Suite 425 Washington, DC 20045 Tel. (202)463-8777, Email: info@religionnews.com, Website: www.religionnews.com

Officers
Editor-in-Chief, Kevin Eckstrom

Religion Newswriters Association and Foundation
Founded in 1949, the RNA is a professional association of journalist who write and edit about religion in the general circulating news media. It sponsors annual contests, conferences, online tools and Religion links. It also offers the Lilly Scholarships in Religion to journalists in the US and Canada to take religion courses of their choice. Annual meetings are held in the fall.

Our Mission: To promote excellence in religion reporting in the news media.

Our Vision: RNA will achieve its mission by providing education and other resources for its members by raising awareness of the importance of religion coverage in the secular media.

Headquarters
School of Journalism, 131 Neff Annex, University of Missouri, Columbia, MO 65211 Tel. (573)882-9257, Fax: (573)884-0977, Email: Mason@RNA.com, Websites: www.ReligionLink.com, www.religiionwriters.com, www.RNA.org
Media Contact, Exec. Dir., Debra Mason

Religions for Peace-USA, Inc.
Religions for Peace-USA, formerly the United States Conference of Religions for Peace, began in the 1970's as a program area and chapter of the World Conference of Religions for Peace (now known simply as Religions for Peace), the world's largest representative interreligious organization. Today, the organization is separately incorporated and registered as an independent 501(c)(3) and focuses its mandate on U.S.-based issues, while retaining a strong link to

the international work of the Religions for Peace. As the largest and most broadly based representative multi-religious forum in the United States, RFP-USA engages the religious leaders and experts in interreligious affairs and peace and justice of more than 50 religious traditions. By building on the spiritual, human, and institutional resources of these communities, RFP-USA establishes cooperative efforts among them to address shared challenges. Primary areas of concern for the organization include building interreligious relationships, creating mutual understanding amidst the country's increasing diversity, and examining the role of the U.S. as a citizen of the global community, with particular regard to peace, human rights, and development.

Headquarters
RFP-USA, 777 United Nations Plaza, 9th Floor, New York, NY 10017 Tel. (212)338-9140 Fax (212)983-0098

Officers
Interim Executive Director, Dr. Lucinda Mosher, Email: lmosher@rfpusa.org
Moderator, Dr. Tarnujit Singh Butalia

Religious Conference Management Association, Inc.

The Religious Conference Management Association, Inc. (RCMA) is a faith-based, nonprofit, professional organization of men and women who have responsibility for planning and-or managing meetings, seminars, conferences, conventions, assemblies or other gatherings for religious organizations.

Founded in 1972, RCMA is dedicated to promoting the highest professional performance by its members and associate members through the mutual exchange of ideas, techniques and methods. Today RCMA has 2,500 members who plan 14,000 conventions and meetings that annually attract over 10 million attendees.

The association conducts an annual world conference and exposition that provides a forum for its membership to gain increased knowledge in the arts and sciences of religious meeting planning and management.

RCMA publishes a bi-monthly magazine, Religious Conference Manager; a conference daily, RCMA Highlights; plus a semi-monthly e-newsletter.

Headquarters
7702 Woodland Drive, Suite 120, Indianapolis, IN 46278 Tel. (317)632-1888 Fax (317)632-7909, Website: www.RCMAWEB.ORG
Media Contact, Exec. Dir., Dr. DeWayne S. Woodring, CMP

Officers
Pres., Dr. Melvin L. Worthington, CMP, National Association of Free Will Baptists, 4878 Ayden Golf Club Road, Ayden, NC 28513-7423

Vice-Pres., The Rev. Harry Schmidt, Christian Life College, 400 E. Gregory, Mt. Prospect, IL 60056
Sec.-Treas., Mr. Lerry W. Fogle, Church of the Brethren, 1013 Mercer Place, Frederick, MD 21701
Exec. Dir., Dr. DeWayne S. Woodring, CMP, CEM

The Seminary Consortium for Urban Pastoral Education (SCUPE)

Founded in 1976, SCUPE is an inter-denominational agency committed to the development of individuals, congregations and organizations for leadership in urban ministry. For individuals, we offer five accredited graduate-level academic programs, the semester-and-or summer-term Graduate Theological Urban Studies program for seminary students; a M.A. in Social Justice and Community Development degree developed in partnership with the Institute of Pastoral Studies at Loyola University; Nurturing the Call, a year-long sequence of graduate courses in theology and ministry for urban pastors who have not previously attended seminary; the Center for African American Theological Studies, an Africentric 3-year M.Div program; and the Advanced Latino Theological Education program, a regional partnership of Instituto Biblico Ebnezer and Western Theolgical Seminary.

SCUPE also consults to other ministries and urban institutions, providing specially-designed training programs around issues including diversity, strategic planning, leadership development , and human resource mobilization. We operate an urban ministry resource center and occasionally publish resource materials as a service to the urban church. Every two years, SCUPE also organizes the Congress on Urban Ministry as a training and networking event for those in urban ministry.

Headquarters
200 N. Michigan Ave., Suite 502, Chicago, IL 60601 Tel. (312)726-1200 Fax (312)726-0425
Media Contact, President, Rev. Dr. Shanta Premawardhana; Director of Development, Nancy Renick

Officers
Chair, Ms. Cheryl Hammock
Vice Chair, Ms. Lydia Murray
Treasurer, Mr. Case Hoogendoorn
Secretary, Ben Dueholm
Lead Program Staff:
President, Rev. Dr. Shanta Premawardhana
Director, Graduate Theological Urban Studies (GTUS), Rev. Carol Ann McGibbon
Director, Masters of Arts in Social Justice and Community Development (MASJCD), Susan Rans
Director, Center for African American Theological Studies (CAATS), Dr. Sean McMillan

Director, Nurturing the Call (NtC), Cynthia Milsap

Director, Advanced Latino Theological Education (ALTE), Dr. Ramon Nieves

Registrar, Dody Finch

Transnational Association of Christian Colleges and Schools

Transnational Association of Christian Colleges and Schools (TRACS). TRACS was established in 1979 to promote the welfare, interests, and development of postsecondary institutions, whose mission is characterized by a distinctly Christian purpose, as defined in our Foundational Standards. TRACS is a voluntary, non-profit, self-governing organization that provides accreditation to Christian postsecondary institutions offering certificates, diplomas, and/or degrees. TRACS is recognized by the United States Department of Education, the Council for Higher Education Accreditation, and the International Network for Quality Assurance Agencies in Higher Education as a national accrediting body for Christian institutions, colleges, universities, and seminaries. The geographic territory of TRACS currently consists of the United States and its territories.

Headquarters
P.O. Box 328, Forest, Virginia 24551 Tel. (434)525-9539 Fax (434)525-9538, Email: info@tracs.org, Website:www.tracs.org

Media Contact: Exec. Dir., Dr. Russell G. Fitzgerald

Officers
Accreditation Commission Chairman, Dr. Charles T. Shoemaker

Exec. Dir., Dr. Russell G. Fitzgerald

Assoc. Exec. Dir., Dr. Paul Boatner

United Religions Initiative

The purpose of URI (www.uri.org) is to promote enduring, daily interfaith cooperation, to end religiously motivated violence and to create cultures of peace, justice and healing for the Earth and all living beings.

URI envisions a world at peace, sustained by engaged and interconnected communities committed to respect for diversity, nonviolent resolution of conflict and social, political, economic and environmental justice.

URI is a global grassroots interfaith network that cultivates peace and justice by engaging people to bridge religious and cultural differences and work together for the good of their communities and society.

We implement our mission through local and global initiatives that build the capacity of our member groups and organizations to engage in community action such as conflict resolution and reconciliation, environmental sustainability, education, women's and youth programs, and advocacy for human rights.

Headquarters
P.O. Box 29242, San Francisco, CA 94129-0242 Tel. (415)561-2300 Fax (415)562-2313

Media Contact, Kristin Swenson

STAFF
Ms. Yoland Trevino, Chairperson

Dr. Shlomo Alon, Vice-Chairperson

Ms. Perri Kathryn (P.K.) McCary, Secretary

Rabbi Doug Kahn, Treasurer

The Right Rev. William E. Swing, President and Founder

The Rev. Canon Charles P. Gibbs, Executive Director

Ms. Debra Ballinger Bernstein, Associate Executive Director

United States Conference for the World Council of Churches

The United States Conference of the World Council of Churches was formed in 1938 when the WCC itself was still in the "Process of Formation." Henry Smith Leiper, an American with many national and international connections, was given the title of "Associate General Secretary" of the WCC and asked to carry out WCC work in the U.S. After the World Council of Churches was officially born in 1948 in Amsterdam, Netherlands, Leiper raised millions of dollars for WCC programs.

Today the U.S. Conference of the WCC is composed of representatives of U.S. member churches of the worldwide body. The U.S. Office of the WCC works to develop relationships among the churches, advance the work of WCC and interpret the council in the United States.

Headquarters
475 Riverside Dr., Rm. 1370, New York, NY 10115 Tel. (212)870-3260 Fax (212)870-2528

Officers
Moderator: The Rev. Dr. Bernice Powell Jackson

Vice-Moderator: Rev. Tyrone Pitts

Vice-Moderator and Secretary/Treasurer: Ms. Anne Glynn Mackoul

Vellore Christian Medical College Foundation, Inc.

The Vellore Christian Medical College Foundation supports the wide range of programs at Christian Medical College (CMC), Vellore, Tamil Nadu, India, by securing contributions for its major capital equipment and construction goals; grants for educational, research and health care programs; and funds to support scholarships for medical, nursing and allied health students at Vellore and faculty study outside of India. The Board also facilitates opportunities for North Americans to volunteer at CMC and fosters working relationships between CMC and institutions in the U.S. Print, DVD and electronic materials about CMC's 110+ years as a leading medical college and hospital are available as part of the Board's public education program.

Headquarters
475 Riverside Dr., Rm.725, New York, NY 10115 Tel. (212)870-2640 Fax (212)870-2173
Media Contact, President, Dr. Louis L. Knowles
E-mail, foundation@vellorecmc.org

Officers
Pres., Dr. Louis L. Knowles
Chair, Mr. Anish Mathai, New York, NY
Vice-Chair, Dr. S. Balasubramaniam, Los Angeles, CA
Sec., Madelen Finkel, Weill/Cornell Medical School, New York, NY
Treas., Mr. Prasad Palla, New York, NY

World Day of Prayer International Committee

World Day of Prayer is an ecumenical movement initiated and carried out by Christian women in 170 countries who conduct a common day of prayer on the first Friday of March to which all people are welcome. There is an annual theme for the worship service that has been prepared by women in a different country each year. For March 4, 2011 the WDP Committee of Chile has prepared a worship service on the theme, "How Many Loaves Have You?". The offering at the WDP is gathered by each WDP National/Regional Committee and given to support projects for women and children and to help people who are in need.

Headquarters
World Day of Prayer International, 475 Riverside Dr., Suite 800, New York, NY 10115 Tel. (212)870-3049, Fax (212)864-8648, Email: info@wdp-usa.org, Website: wdp-usa.org
Media Contact, Exec. Dir., Eileen King
World Day of Prayer USA, 475 Riverside Dr., Suite 800, New York, NY 10115 Tel. (212)870-3049, Toll-free 866 WDP USA, (866)937-8720, Fax (212)864-8648, Email: info@wdp-usa.org, Website: wdp-usa.org

Officers
Chairperson, S. Annette Poitier
Treasurer, Marcia L. Florkey
Africa, Véronique Lusieboko Lutatabio, Assah E. Mgonja
Asia, Zenaida Maturan, Sheree, Suk-Ling Wong
Caribbean and North America, Alison Carter, Marilyn Fortin
Europe, Jean Hackett, Corinna Harbig
Latin America, Elisabeth Delmonte,Ormara Nolla
Middle East, Laila Carmi, Lucy Ishak Guirguis
Pacific, Vaieli Fuiono Piita, Pauline Smit

World Methodist Council-North American Section

The World Methodist Council, one of the 30 or so "Christian World Communions," shares a general tradition which is common to all Christians.

The world organization of Methodists and related United Churches is comprised of 76 churches with roots in the Methodist tradition. These churches found in 132 countries have a membership of more than 40 million.

The Council's North American Section, comprised of ten Methodist and United Church denominations, provides a regional focus for the Council in Canada, the United States and Mexico. The North American Section meets at the time of the quinquennial World Conference and Council, and separately as Section between world meetings.

North American Churches related to the World Methodist Council have a membership of approximately 16 million and a church community of more than 30 million.

Headquarters
P.O. Box 518, Lake Junaluska, NC 28745 Tel. (828)456-9432 Fax (828)456-9433
Media Contact, Gen. Sec., George H. Freeman

Officers
General Sec., Dr. George H. Freeman

World Vision

World Vision is a Christian relief and development organization dedicated to helping children and their communities worldwide reach their full potential by tackling the causes of poverty. Motivated by our faith in Jesus, we serve the poor as a demonstration of God's unconditional love for all people. World Vision works with communities in nearly 100 countries to develop long-term solutions that alleviate poverty, provides emergency assistance to children and families affected by natural disasters and civil conflict, and advocates for justice on behalf of the poor. World Vision U.S.—one of 52 national offices in the World Vision Partnership—serves in key United States metropolitan areas, providing intervention for challenged youth, tools that equip strong community leaders, and storehouses that provide essentials for living.

World Vision's Church Relations department facilitates chuch partnerships, connecting U.S. congregations with critical ministry among people in need locally and internationally. Church opportunities include partnerships with international projects, volunteer options through U.S. programs, and educational programs, including youth-oriented 30 Hour Famine and One Life Revolution, and child sponsorship.

Headquarters
P.O. Box 9716, Federal Way, WA 98063-9716 Tel. (253)815-1000
Church Relations Vice President, Steve Haas, Tel. (253)815-2698
Media Contact, Dean Owen, Tel. (253)815-2158

Officers
President, Richard Stearns
Senior Vice Presidents, Joan Mussa, Lawrence

Probus, Julie Regnier, Atul Tandon, George Ward, Michael Veitenhans

YMCA of the USA

The YMCA is one of the largest private voluntary organizations in the world, serving about 30 million people in more than 100 countries. In the United States, more than 2,000 local branches, units, camps and centers annually serve more than 14 million people of all ages, races and abilities. About half of those served are female. No one is turned away because of an inability to pay.

The Y teaches youngsters to swim, organizes youth basketball games and offers adult aerobics. But the Y represents more than fitness— it works to strengthen families and help people develop values and behavior that are consistent with Christian principles.

The Y offers hundreds of programs including day camp for children, child care, exercise for people with disabilities, teen clubs, environmental programs, substance abuse prevention, family nights, job training and many more programs from infant mortality prevention to overnight camping for seniors.

The kind of programs offered at a YMCA will vary; each is controlled by volunteer board members who make their own program, policy, and financial decisions based on the special needs of their community. In its own way, every Y works to build strong kids, strong families, and strong communities.

The YMCA was founded in London, England, in 1844 by George Williams and friends who lived and worked together as clerks. Their goal was to save other live-in clerks from the wicked life of the London streets. The first members were evangelical Protestants who prayed and studied the Bible as an alternative to vice. The Y has always been nonsectarian and today accepts those of all faiths at all levels of the organization.

Headquarters

101 N. Wacker Dr., Chicago, IL 60606 Tel. (312)977-0031 Fax (312)977-9063
Media Contact, Media Relations Manager, Arnie Collins

Officers

Board Chairman., Daniel E. Casey
Exec. Dir., Niel Nicoll
(Int.) Public Relations Assoc., Arnold Collins

YWCA of the U.S.A.

The YWCA of the U.S.A. is comprised of 313 affiliates in communities and on college campuses across the United States. It serves one million members and program participants. It seeks to empower women and girls to enable them, coming together across lines of age, race, religious belief, economic and occupational

status to make a significant contribution to the elimination of racism and the achievement of peace, justice, freedom and dignity for all people.

Headquarters

1015 18th St. Suite 1100, Washington, DC 20036. Tel. (202)467-0801 Fax: (202)467-0802
Media Contact, Khristina Lew Email: info@ywca.org

Officers

National Pres., Leticia Paez
Sec., Carol O. Markus
Chief Exec. Officer, Margaret Tyndall

Youth for Christ-USA

Founded in 1944, our mission is: YFC reaches young people everywhere, working together with the local church and other like-minded partners to raise up lifelong followers of Jesus who lead by their godliness in lifestyle, devotion to the Word of God and prayer, passion for sharing the love of Christ and commitment to social involvement.

Youth for Christ is active in 180 areas across the U.S., representing over 2,000 different locations where young people are being reached. There are over 70,000 teens involved each week in U.S. programs. Over 1,500 staff, 15,800 volunteers, and 6,300 student leaders are involved in the U.S. YFC/USA is part of an international movement involving over 100 countries, with each country having their own indigenous leadership. Worldwide, over 125,000 young people began a personal relationship with Jesus Christ last year as part of various YFC ministries.

Youth for Christ's core ministries are:
- Campus Life (high school) and Campus life (M) Middle School
- City Life reaching inner-city teens
- Teen Parents - ministry to expectant teens and their children
- Juvenile Justice Ministries - ministry to teens in correctional facilities, group homes,
- Emergency shelters, etc.
- Friend2Friend - Christian teens reaching their peers

Headquarters

U.S. Headquarters, P.O. Box 4478, Englewood, CO 80155 Tel. (303)843-9000 Fax (303)843-9002
Canadian Organization, c/o Tecsys, 87 Prince Street, 5th Floor, Montreal, QC H3C 2M7 Tel. (514)866-0001 x 4118 Fax (514)866-3033
Media Contact, VP of Communication, Mark Jevert

Officers

United States, President, Daniel S. Wolgemuth
Canada, National Dir., David Brereton
Youth for Christ Intl. Pres., David Wraight

2. Canadian Cooperative Organizations, National

In most cases, the organizations listed here work on a national level and cooperate across denominational lines. Regional cooperative organizations in Canada are listed in Directory 7, "Canadian Regional and Local Ecumenical Bodies."

Alcohol and Drug Concerns Inc.

Alcohol and Drug Concerns is a registered, non-profit, charitable organization that has a long association with the Christian Church. The organization's mission is to empower youth to make positive lifestyle choices relating to alcohol, tobacco, and other drugs.

The organization was granted a national charter in 1987, moving from an Ontario charter dating back to 1934. Among its services are, Choices F.I.T. (Fostering Independent Thinking)- a substance abuse prevention resource for grade 4 to 8 teachers; an Institute on Addiction Studies; Making the Leap- a substance abuse prevention resource for grade 7 to 8 teachers created by high school students; Drug and Alcohol Game Show for grades 6 to 9- a classroom activity; education and awareness courses for clients of the Ontario Ministry of Corrections.

Headquarters

4500 Sheppard Ave. E, Ste. 112, Toronto, ON M1S 3R6, Tel. (416)293-3400 Fax (416)293-1142

Media Contact, Robert Walsh, CEO

Officers

Pres., Jean Desgagne, Toronto
Treas., Peter Varley, Toronto
Vice-Pres., Nanci Harris, Toronto
Vice-Pres., Valerie Petroff, Oak Ridges
Vice-Pres., Heidi Stanley, Orillia
Past Pres., Larry Gillians, Napanee
CEO, Robert Walsh

Canadian Bible Society

The Canadian Bible Society is a non-denominational and inter-confessional organization that exists to translate, publish, distribute and encourage the use of the Scriptures, without doctrinal note or comment. Bible Society work was begun in Canada in 1804 by the British and Foreign Bible Society. In 1906, the various auxiliaries of the British and Foreign Bible Society joined together to form the Canadian Bible Society. Today, the Canadian Bible Society has 16 district offices across Canada, a Scripture Translation Office in Kitchener, a French Services Office in Montreal, and a National Support Office in Toronto. Additionally, the Bermuda Bible Society is constituted as an Associate District of the Canadian Bible Society. The Society holds quarterly Board meetings involving one elected representative from each of the districts and from the francophone sector. About 90% of the Society's revenue comes through the generosity of Canadian supporters in the form of donations, bequests and annuity income. Through the Canadian Bible Society's membership in the United States Societies' fellowship, over 67.5 million Bibles, Testaments and Portions were distributed globally in 2004. The complete Bible has been published in over 420 languages, with at least one book of the Bible available in 2377 languages.

Headquarters

C.B.S. National Support Office, 10 Carnforth Rd., Toronto, ON M4A 2S4, Tel. (416)757-4171 Fax (416)757-3376

Officers

National Director, Ted Seres, 10 Carnforth Rd., Toronto, ON M4A 2S4, Tel. (416)757-4171, Fax (416)757-1292, tseres@biblesociety.ca
Director of Finance, Mr. Nesa Gulasekharam, 10 Carnforth Rd., Toronto, ON M4A 2S4, Tel. (416)757-4171 Fax: (416)757-3376 ngulasekharam@biblesociety.ca
Director of Scripture Translation, Mr. Hart Wiens, Frederick Mall, 385 Frederick Street, Kitchener, ON N2H 2P2, Tel. (519)741-8285 Fax (519)741-8357, hwiens@biblesociety.ca
Director of Scripture Resources, Joel Coppieters, 10 Carnforth Rd., Toronto, ON M4A 2S4, Tel. (416)757-4171 Fax (416)757-3376, lcoppieters@biblesociety.ca
Human Resources Director/Volunteer Program, Ms. Meggy Kwok, 10 Carnforth Rd., Toronto, ON M4A 2S4, Tel. (416)757-4171 Fax (416)757-3376, mkwok@biblesociety.ca
Director of Strategic Services, Giorgio Gori, 10 Carnforth Rd., Toronto, ON M4A 2SA, Tel (416)757-4171 Fax (416)757-3376
Senior Consultant Development Major Gift, Jonh McLaverty, 10 Carnforth Rd., Toronto, ON M4A 2SA, Tel (416)757-4171 Fax (416)757-3376

Canadian Centre for Ecumenism

The Centre has facilitated understanding and cooperation among believers of various Christian traditions and world religions since 1963. An active interdenominational Board of Directors meets annually.

ECUMENISM, a quarterly publication, develops central themes such as Rites of Passage, Sacred Space, Interfaith Marriages, Care of the

Earth, etc. through contributions from writers of various churches and religions in addition to its regular ecumenical news summaries, book reviews and resources.

A specialized library is open to the public for consultation in the areas of religion, dialogue, evangelism, ethics, spirituality, etc.

Conferences and sessions are offered on themes such as Ecumenism and Pastoral Work, Pluralism, World Religions, Prayer and Unity.

Headquarters

1819 René-Lévesque West, Suite 003, Montreal, QC H3H 2P5, Tel. (514)937-9176 ext 21 Fax (514)937-4986
Email: info@ikoumene.ca
Website: www.oikoumene.ca

Officers

Media contact: Neala Vandermeulen
Executive Director: Deacon Anthony Mansour
Associate Director: Adèle Bordeur

The Canadian Council of Churches

The Canadian Council of Churches was organized in 1944. Its basic purpose is to provide the churches with an agency for conference and consultation and for such common planning and common action as they desire to undertake. It encourages ecumenical understanding and action throughout Canada through local councils of churches. It also relates to the World Council of Churches and other agencies serving the worldwide ecumenical movement.

The Council has a Governing Board which meets semiannually and an Executive Committee. Program is administered through two commissions—Faith and Witness, Justice and Peace.

Headquarters

47 Queen's Park Crescent East, Toronto, ON M5S 2C3, Tel. (416)972-9494 Fax (416)927-0405 or (800)822-7645
Media Contact, Lindsay Cox
Email: Cox@councilofchurches.ca
Website: www.councilofchurches.ca

Officers

Gen. Sec.: Rev. Dr. Karen Hamilton, 47 Queen's Park Crescent East, Toronto ON M5S 2C3, Tel. (416)972-9494, Email: Hamilton@ councilofchurches.ca
President: Rev. Bruce Adema, 47 Queen's Park Crescent East, Toronto ON M5S 2C3, Tel. (416)972-9494, Email: bruceadema@ crcna.org
Vice Presidents: Major Gillian Brown, 47 Queen's Park Crescent East, Toronto ON M5S 2C3, Tel. (416)972-9494, Email: gillian_brown@can.salvationarmy.org; Bishop Gilles Cazabon, O.M.I., 47 Queen's Park Crescent East, Toronto ON M5S 2C3, Tel. (416)972-9494 Fax: (416)922-9328, Email: gzcazomi@ yahoo.ca; Fr. John Jillions, 47 Queen's Park

Crescent East, Toronto, ON M5S 2C3, Tel. 416-972-9494, Email: jjillions@ustpaul.ca

MEMBER CHURCHES

The General Synod of The Anglican Church of Canada
Archdiocese of Canada of the Orthodox Church in America
Armenian Holy Apostolic Church, Canadian Diocese
British Methodist Episcopal Church of Canada (Associate Member)
Canadian Baptists of Ontario and Quebec
Canadian Baptists of Western Canada
Canadian Conference of Catholic Bishops
Canadian Yearly Meeting of the Religious Society of Friends (Quakers)
Christian Church (Disciples of Christ) in Canada
Christian Reformed Church in North America-Canada
The Coptic Orthodox Church of Canada
Ethiopian Orthodox Tewahedo Church of Canada
Evangelical Lutheran Church in Canada
Greek Orthodox Metropolis of Toronto (Canada)
Mennonite Church Canada
Polish National Catholic Church of Canada
The Presbyterian Church in Canada
Regional Synod of Canada - Reformed Church in America
The Salvation Army
Ukrainian Catholic Church
Ukrainian Orthodox Church of Canada
The United Church of Canada
Affiliate Members:
The Knowles-Woodsworth Centre for Theology and Public Policy
The Yonge Street Mission

Canadian Evangelical Theological Association

In May 1990, about 60 scholars, pastors and other interested persons met together in Toronto to form a new theological society. Arising out of the Canadian chapter of the Evangelical Theological Society, the new association established itself as a distinctly Canadian group with a new name. It sponsored its first conference as CETA in Kingston, Ontario, in May 1991.

CETA provides a forum for scholarly contributions to the renewal of theology and church in Canada. CETA seeks to promote theological work which is loyal to Christ and his Gospel, faithful to the primacy and authority of Scripture and responsive to the guiding force of the historic creeds and Protestant confessions of the Christian Church. In its newsletters and conferences, CETA seeks presentations that will speak to a general theologically-educated audience, rather than to specialists.

CETA has special interest in evangelical points of view upon and contributions to the wider conversations regarding religious studies and church life. Members therefore include pastors, students and other interested persons as well as professional academicians. CETA currently includes about 100 members, many of whom attend its annual conference in the early summer. It publishes the Canadian Evangelical Review and supports an active facebook.com page ("search" for Canadian Evangelical Theological Association) and webpage (www.ceta-cer.org).

Headquarters

Dr. Jeffrey A. McPherson, Division of Religion and Humanities, Roberts Wesleyan College, 2301 Westside Drive, Rochester, NY 14624
Email: McPherson_Jeffery@roberts.edu
Media Contact, Dr. Jeffrey McPherson

Officers

President: Dr. Jeffrey A. McPherson, Division of Religion and Humanities, Roberts Wesleyan College, 2301 Westside Drive, Rochester, NY 14624; Email: McPherson_Jeffery@roberts.edu
Media Contact, Dr. Jeffrey A. McPherson
President: Dr. J. Richard Middleton (ceta.president@gmail.com)
Secretary-Treasurer: Dr. Jeffery A.McPherson (McPherson_Jeffery@roberts.edu) Editor, Canadian Theological Review: Dr. Kent Clarke (kentc@twu.ca) Executive Members-at-large: David Ney (neydp@yahoo.ca) and Frank Emanuel (church@freedom vineyard.com)

Canadian Tract Society

The Canadian Tract Society was organized in 1970 as an independent distributor of Gospel leaflets to provide Canadian churches and individual Christians with quality materials proclaiming the Gospel through the printed page. It is affiliated with the American Tract Society, which encouraged its formation and assisted in its founding, and for whom it serves as an exclusive Canadian distributor. The CTS is a nonprofit international service ministry.

Headquarters

P.O. Box 2156, LCD 1, Brampton, ON L6T 3S4, Tel. (905)457-4559 Fax (905)457-0529
Media Contact, Mgr., Donna Croft

Officers

Director-Sec., Robert J. Burns
Director, John Neufeld
Director, Patricia Burns

Canadian Society of Biblical Studies-Société Canadienne des Études Bibliques

The object of the Society shall be to stimulate the critical investigation of the classical biblical literatures, together with other related literature, by the exchange of scholarly research both in published form and in public forum.

Headquarters

Media Contact, Exec. Sec., Michele Murray, Dept. of Religion, Bishop's University, Lennoxville, PQ J1M 1Z7, Email mmurray@ ubishops.ca, Website www.ccsr.ca/csbs

Officers

Pres., Mary Rose D'Angelo, Dept. of Theology, University of Notre Dame, Notre Dame, IN 46556, Tel. (219)631-7040 Fax: (219)631-6842
Vice-Pres., J. Glen Taylor, Wycliffe College, 5 Hoskin Ave., Toronto, ON M57 1H7, Tel. (416)946-3541 Fax: (416)946-3541, Email: glen.Taylor@utoronto.ca
Exec. Sec., Michele Murray, Dept. of Religion, Bishop's University, Lennoxville, QC J1M 1Z7, Tel. (819)822-9600 Fax: (819)822-9661, Email: mmurray@ubishops.ca
Treas., Robert A. Derrenbacker, Jr., Regent College, 5800 University Blvd, Vancouver, BC, V6T 2E4, Tel. (604)221-3349 Fax: (604)224-3097, Email: rderrenbacker@regent-college.edu
Prog. Coord., Christine Mitchell, St. Andrews College, 1121 College Dr., Saskatoon, SK S7N 0W3, Email: ckm365@duke.usask.ca
Comm. Officer, Richard Ascough, Queens' Theological College, Kingston, ON K7L 3N6, Tel. (613)533-6000 Fax: (613)533-6879, Email: rsa@post.queensu.ca
Student Liason Officer, Derek Suderman, Emmanuel College, 11739 McCowan Rd., Stouffville, ON L4A 7X5, Email: derek. suderman@utoronto.ca

The Church Army in Canada

The Church Army in Canada has been involved in evangelism and Christian social service since 1929. Church Army is a Society of Evangelists dedicated to helping bring people from all walks of life into a living relationship with Jesus Christ and His people. We are pressing on toward 80 years in Canada with these endeavours, and many more worldwide.

Headquarters

105 Mountain View Dr., Saint John, NB E2J 5B5, Tel. (888)316-8169 Fax (506)657-8217
Email: hello@churcharmy.com
Media Contact, National Director., Capt. R. Bruce Smith

Officers

National Dir., Capt. R. Bruce Smith
Bd. Chmn., Mr. Peter Bloom

The Churches' Council on Theological Education in Canada, An Ecumenical Foundation

It is the purpose of the Churches' Council on Theological Education in Canada: An Ecumenical Foundation (CCTE) to promote dialogue and discernment with respect to the content and practice of theological education in Canada, with a view to initiating collaborative and cooperative ventures which enrich that landscape. It pursues this purpose as Christian tradtion, with diverse faith communities, and with others.

In pursuit of this purpose, CCTE sponsors an annual conference for people involved in theological education in Canada and also co-sponsors the annual Canadian Theological Students' Conference. It also occasionally supports consultations and research related to the themes of these conferences.

Headquarters
47 Queen's Park Cres., E., Toronto, ON M5S 2C3, Tel. (416)928-3223 Fax (416)928-3563
Media Contact, Exec. Dir., Dr. Robert Faris
Web: www.ccte.ca Email: director@ccte.ca

Officers
Bd. of Dir., Chpsn., Dr. Glenn Wooden, Acadia Divinity College, 31 Horton Avenue, Wolfeville, NS B4P 2R6
Bd. of Dir., Vice-Chpsn., Rev. Steve Willey, United Church of Canada, 3250 Bloor Street, West, Toronto, ON M8X 2Y4
Treas., Mr. Brian Cox
Exec. Dir., Robert Faris

MEMBER ORGANIZATIONS
The Anglican Church of Canada
Canadian Baptist Ministries
The Evangelical Lutheran Church in Canada
The Presbyterian Church in Canada
The Canadian Conference of Catholic Bishops
The United Church of Canada

Evangelical Fellowship of Canada
The Fellowship was formed in 1964. There are 31 denominations, 124 organizations, 1,200 local churches and 11,000 individual members.

Its purposes are, "Fellowship in the gospel" (Phil. Ch.1 vs.5), "the defence and confirmation of the gospel" (Phil. Ch.1 vs.7) and "the furtherance of the gospel" (Phil. Ch.1 vs.12). The Fellowship believes the Holy Scriptures, as originally given, are infallible and that salvation through the Lord Jesus Christ is by faith apart from works.In national and regional conventions the Fellowship urges Christians to live exemplary lives and to openly challenge the evils and injustices of society. It encourages cooperation with various agencies in Canada and overseas that are sensitive to social and spiritual needs.The Evangelical Fellowship of Canada (EFC) is the national association of evangelical Christians in Canada. It gathers Evangelicals together for impact, influence and identity in ministry and public witness. Since 1964 the EFC has provided a national forum for Evangelicals and a constructive voice for biblical principles in life and society. The EFC affiliates include denominations, ministry organizations, educational institutions and individual

congregations, who uphold a common statement of faith. The EFC also has more than 15,000 supporting individuals.

Headquarters
Office, 600 Alden Rd. Ste. 300, Markham, ON L3R 0E7, Tel. (905)479-5885 Fax (905)479-4742; Mailing Address, M.I.P. Box 3745, Markham, ON L3R 0Y4
Media Contact, Pres., Dr. Gary Walsh, 600 Alden Rd., Ste. 300, Markham, ON L3R 0E7, Tel. (905)479-5885 Fax (905)479-4742

Officers
Pres., Bruce J. Clemenger
Chair, Dr. Paul Magnus
Vice-Chair, Dr. Rick Penner
Treas., Lt. Col. David Luginbuhl
Past Pres., Dr. Brian Stiller

EXECUTIVE COMMITTEE
Rev. Scott Campbell; Rev. Carson Pue; Ms. Ruth Andrews; Rev. Stewart Hunter; Ms. Jacqueline Dugas; Dr. Rick Penner; Lt. Col. David Luginbuhl; Dr. Ralph Richardson; Rev. Abe Funk; Rev. Gillis Killam; Dr. Paul Magnus; Rev. Winston Thurton
Task Force on Evangelism (Vision Canada), Interim Chair, Gary Walsh
Social Action Commission, Chpsn., Dr. James Read
Education Commission, Chpsn., Dr. Glenn Smith
Women in Ministry Task Force, Chpsn., Rev. Eileen Stewart-Rhude
Aboriginal Task Force, Co-Chairs, Ray Aldred; Wendy Peterson
Religious Liberties Commission, Chpsn., Dr. Paul Marshall
Task Force on Global Mission, Chpsn., Dr. Geoff Tunnicliffe

Inter-Varsity Christian Fellowship of Canada
Inter-Varsity Christian Fellowship is a non-profit, interdenominational student movement centering on the witness to Jesus Christ in campus communities, universities, colleges and high schools and through a Canada-wide Pioneer Camping program.

IVCF was officially formed in 1928-29 by the late Dr. Howard Guinness, whose arrival from Britain challenged students to follow the example of the British Inter-Varsity Fellowship by organizing themselves into prayer and Bible study fellowship groups. Inter-Varsity has always been a student-initiated movement emphasizing and developing leadership in the campus to call Christians to outreach, challenging other students to a personal faith in Jesus Christ and studying the Bible as God's revealed truth within a fellowship of believers. A strong stress has been placed on missionary activity, and the triennial conference held at Urbana, IL. (jointly sponsored by U.S. and Canadian IVCF) has been a means of challenging many young people to service in Christian vocations. Inter-Varsity works closely with and is a strong believer in the work of local and national churches.

Headquarters
1 International Blvd., Toronto, M9W 6H3, Tel. (416)443-1170 Fax (416)443-1499
Media Contact, Pres., Geri Rodman

Officers
President and CEO, Geri Rodman, 1 International Blvd., Toronto, M9W 6H3, Tel. (416)443-1170 ext. 117, Fax (416)443-1499, Email: grodman@ivcf.ca

Interchurch Communications
Interchurch Communications is made up of the communication units of the Anglican Church of Canada, the Evangelical Lutheran Church in Canada, the Presbyterian Church in Canada, the Canadian Conference of Catholic Bishops (English Sector), and the United Church of Canada. ICC members collaborate on occasional video or print coproductions and on addressing public policy issues affecting religious communications.

Headquarters
3250 Bloor St. W., Etobicoke, ON M8X 2Y4

MEMBERS
Mr. William Kokesch, Canadian Conference of Catholic Bishops, 90 Parent Ave., Ottawa, ON K1N 7B1, Tel. (613)241-9461 Fax (613)241-8117, Email: kokesch@cccb.ca
Religious Television Associates, 3250 Bloor St. W., Etobicoke, ON M8X 2Y4, Tel. (416)231-7680 Fax (416)232-6004

John Howard Society of Ontario
The John Howard Society of Ontario is a registered non-profit charitable organization providing services to individuals, families and groups at all stages in the youth and criminal justice system. The Society also provides community education on critical issues in the justice system and advocacy for reform of the justice system. The mandate of the Society is the prevention of crime through service, community education, advocacy and reform.

Founded in 1929, the Society has grown from a one-office service in Toronto to 19 local branches providing direct services in the major cities of Ontario and a provincial office providing justice policy analysis, advocacy for reform and support to branches.

Headquarters
603-111 Peter Street, Toronto, ON M5V 2H1, Tel (416)408-4282 ext 233, Fax (416)804-2991, Website: www.johnhoward.on.ca
Media Contact, Exec. Dir., Paula Osmok

Officers
See website: www.johnhoward.on.ca

LOCAL SOCIETIES
Collins Bay; Hamilton; Kingston; Lindsay; London; Niagara; Oshawa; Ottawa; Peel; Peterborough; Sarnia; Sault Ste. Marie; Sudbury; Thunder Bay; Toronto; Waterloo; Windsor

Lutheran Council in Canada
The Lutheran Council in Canada was organized in 1967 and is a cooperative agency of the Evangelical Lutheran Church in Canada and Lutheran Church-Canada.

The Council's activities include communications, coordinative service and national liaison in social ministry, chaplaincy and scout activity.

Headquarters
302-393 Portage Ave., Winnipeg, MB R3B 3H6, Tel. (204)984-9150 Fax (204)984-9185
Media Contact, Pres., Rev. Ralph Mayan, 3074 Portage Ave., Winnipeg, MB R3K 0Y2, Tel. (204)895-3433 Fax (204)897-4319

Officers
Pres., Bishop Susan Johnson
Treas., vacant
Sec., Rev. Leon C. Gilbertson
Vice Pres., Rev. Ralph Mayan

Mennonite Central Committee Canada (MCCC)
Mennonite Central Committee Canada was organized in 1964 to continue the work which several regional Canadian inter-Mennonite agencies had been doing in relief, service, immigration and peace. All but a few of the smaller Mennonite groups in Canada belong to MCC Canada.

MCCC is part of the Mennonite Central Committee (MCC) International which has its headquarters in Akron, Pa. from where most of the overseas development and relief projects are administered. In 2000-2001 MCCC's income was $25 million, about 47 percent of the total MCC income. There were 408 Canadians out of a total of 867 MCC workers serving in North America and abroad during the same time period.

The MCC office in Winnipeg administers projects located in Canada. Domestic programs of Voluntary Service, Native Concerns, Peace and Social Concerns, Food Program, Employment Concerns, Ottawa Office, Victim-Offender Ministries, Mental Health and Immigration are all part of MCC's Canadian ministry. Whenever it undertakes a project, MCCC attempts to relate to the church or churches in the area.

Headquarters
134 Plaza Dr., Winnipeg, MB R3T 5K9, Tel. (204)261-6381 Fax (204)269-9875
Communications, Rick Fast, 134 Plaza Dr.,

Winnipeg, MT R3T 5K9, Tel. (204)261-6381 Fax (204)269-9875

Officers
Exec. Dir., Donald Peters

Project Ploughshares

Project Ploughshares is an ecumenical peace centre of the Canadian Council of Churches, established in 1976 to implement the churches' imperative to seek and pursue peace. Project Ploughshares works with churches, governments, and non-governmental organizations, in Canada and internationally, to identify, develop, and advance approaches that build peace and prevent war, and promote the peaceful resolution of political conflict. Project Ploughshares is sponsored by eight national Canadian churches and is affiliated with the Institute of Peace and Conflict Studies, Conrad Grebel University College, University of Waterloo. Publications include The Ploughshares Monitor (quarterly), The Armed Conflicts Report (annually), Briefings and Working Papers (occasional).

Headquarters
Project Ploughshares, 57 Erb Street West, Waterloo, ON, Canada N2L 6C2, Tel. (519) 888-6541 Fax (519)888-0188, Email: plough @ploughshares.ca, Website: www.plough shares.ca

Media Contact: Director, John Siebert, (519)888-6541 x702, Email: jsiebert@ploughshares.ca

Officers
Executive Director, John Siebert
Associate Director, Nancy Regehr
Chair, Moira Hutchinson
Treasurer, Philip Creighton
Secretary, Rev. Dr. Martin Rumscheidt

SPONSORING ORGANIZATIONS
Anglican Church of Canada
Canadian Catholic Organization for Development & Peace
Canadian Unitarian Council
Canadian Voice of Women for Peace
Canadian Yearly Meeting, Religious Society of Friends
Evangelical Lutheran Church in Canada
Mennonite Central Committee Canada
Presbyterian Church in Canada
United Church of Canada

Religious Television Associates

Religious Television Associates was formed in the early 1960s for the production units of the Anglican, Baptist, Presbyterian, Roman Catholic Churches and the United Church of Canada. In the intervening years, the Baptists have withdrawn and the Lutherans have come in. RTA provides an ecumenical umbrella for joint productions in broadcasting and development education. The directors are the heads of the Communications Departments participating in Interchurch Communications.

Headquarters
c/o The United Church of Canada, 3250 Bloor St. W., Etobicoke, ON M8X 2Y4, Tel. (416)231-7680 ext. 4076 Fax (416)231-3103

Media Contact, Shane Chadden

Officers
The Anglican Church of Canada
Canadian Conference of Catholic Bishops
The Canadian Council of Churches
The Evangelical Lutheran Church in Canada
The Presbyterian Church in Canada
The United Church of Canada

Scripture Union

Scripture Union is an international interdenominational missionary movement working in 130 countries.

Scripture Union aims to work with the churches to make God's Good News known to children, young people and families and to encourage people of all ages to meet God daily through the Bible and prayer.

In Canada, a range of daily Bible guides are offered to individuals, churches, and bookstores from age four through adult. Sunday School curriculum and various evangelism and discipling materials are also offered for sale.

Children's ministry is offered to churches through summer sports camps and training for sports outreach programs.

Headquarters
1885 Clements Rd., Unit 226, Pickering, ON L1W 3V4, Tel. (905)427-4947 Fax (905)427-0334

Media Contact, President, John Irwin, Email: jirwinc617@rogers.com

Officers
Chair of the Board, Harold Murray, 216 McKinnon Pl. NE, Calgary, AB T2E 7B9, Tel. 403-276-4716, Email: hjmurray@home.com

President, Robert Szo, 1885 Clements Rd., Unit 226, Pickering, ON L1W 3V4, Email: robert@scriptureunion.ca

Student Christian Movement of Canada

The Student Christian Movement of Canada was formed in 1921 from the student arm of the YMCA. It has its roots in the Social Gospel movements of the late 19th and early 20th centuries. Throughout its intellectual history, the SCM in Canada has sought to relate the Christian faith to the living realities of the social and political context of each student generation.

The present priorities are built around the need to form more and stronger critical Christian communities on Canadian campuses within which individuals may develop their social and political analyses, experience spiritual growth and fellowship and bring Christian ecumenical witness to the university.

The Student Christian Movement of Canada is affiliated with the World Student Christian Federation.

Headquarters

310 Danforth Ave., Toronto, ON M4K 1N6, Tel. (416)463-4312 Fax (416)466-6854

Officers

Co-General Secretaries, Ryan Tristin Chapman and Jan Braun, Email: info@scmcanada.org

Women's Inter-Church Council of Canada

Women's Inter-Church Council of Canada is a national Christian women's council that encourages women to grow in ecumenism, to strengthen ecumenical community, to share their spirituality and prayer, to engage in dialogue about women's concerns and to stand in solidarity with one another. The Council calls women to respond to national and international issues affecting women and to take action together for justice. WICC sponsors the World Day of Prayer and Fellowship of the Least Coin in Canada. Human rights projects for women are supported and a quarterly magazine "Making Waves" distributed.

Headquarters

47 Queen's Park Cres. E, Toronto, ON M5S 2C3, Tel. (416)929-5184 Fax (416)929-4064
Media Contact, Communications Coordinator, Gillian Barfoot

Officers

Pres., Claire Heron
Exec. Dir., Pat Allinson

CHURCH MEMBER BODIES
African Methodist Episcopal, Anglican Church of Canada, Canadian Baptist Ministries, Christian Church (Disciples of Christ), Evangelical Lutheran Church in Canada, Mennonite Central Committee, Presbyterian Church in Canada, Religious Society of Friends, Roman Catholic Church, The Salvation Army in Canada, United Church of Canada

World Vision Canada

World Vision Canada is a Christian humanitarian relief and development organization. Although its main international commitment is to translate child sponsorship into holistic, sustainable community development, World Vision also allocates resources to help Canada's poor and complement the mission of the church.

World Vision's Reception Centre assists government-sponsored refugees entering Canada. The NeighbourLink program mobilizes church volunteers to respond locally to people's needs. A quarterly publication, Context, provides data on the Canadian family to help churches effectively reach their communities. The development education program provides resources on development issues. During the annual 30-Hour Famine, people fast for 30 hours while discussing poverty and raising funds to support aid programs.

Headquarters

1 World Dr., Mississauga, ON L5T 2Y4, Tel. (905)821-3030 Fax (905)821-1356
Media Contact, Philip Maher, Tel. (905)567-2726

Officers

Pres., Dave Toycen
Vice-Pres., Intl. & Govt. Relations, Linda Tripp; Natl. Programs, Don Posterski; Fin. & Admin., Charlie Fluit; Donor Development Group, Brian Tizzard

Young Men's Christian Association in Canada

The YMCA began as a Christian association to help young men find healthy recreation and meditation, as well as opportunities for education, in the industrial slums of 19th century England. It came to Canada in 1851 with the same mission in mind for young men working in camps and on the railways.

Today, the YMCA maintains its original mission, helping individuals to grow and develop in spirit, mind and body, but attends to those needs for men and women of all ages and religious beliefs. The YMCA registers 1.5 million participants in 250 communities that are served by 64 autonomous associations across Canada.

The program of each association differs according to the needs of the community, but most offer one or more programs in each of the following categories, health and fitness, child care, employment councelling and training, recreation, camping, community support and outreach, international development and short-term accommodation.

The YMCA encourages people of all ages, races, abilities, income and beliefs to come together in an environment which promotes balance in life, breaking down barriers and helping to create healthier communities.

Headquarters

42 Charles St. E., 6th Floor., Toronto, ON M4Y 1T4, Tel. (416)967-9622 Fax (416)967-9618
Media Contact, Sol Kasimer

Officers

Chpsn., Ray Mantha
CEO, Sol Kasimer

Young Women's Christian Association of-du Canada

The YWCA of-du Canada is a national voluntary organization serving 44 YWCAs and YM-YWCAs across Canada. Dedicated to the development and improved status of women and their families, the YWCA is committed to service delivery and to being a source of public education on women's issues and an advocate of social change. Services provided by YWCAs and YM-YWCAs include adult education programs, residences and shelters, child care, fitness activities, wellness programs and international development education. As a member of the World YWCA, the YWCA of-du Canada is part of the largest women's organization in the world.

Headquarters
80 Gerrard St. E., Toronto, ON M5B 1G6, Tel. (416)593-9886 Fax (416)971-8084
Media Contact, Int. CEO, Margaret MacKenzie

Officers
Pres., Ann Mowatt

Youth for Christ-Canada

Youth For Christ is an interdenominational organization founded in 1944 by Torrey Johnson. Under the leadership of YFC's 11 national board of directors, Youth For Christ-Canada cooperates with churches and serves as a mission agency reaching out to young people and their families through a variety of ministries.

YFC seeks to have maximum influence in a world of youth through high-interest activities and personal involvement. Individual attention is given to each teenager through small group involvement and counselling. These activities and relationships become vehicles for communicating the message of the Gospel.

Headquarters
325 Talbot Avenue, Winnipeg, MB R2L 0P9, Tel. (204)989-0056 Fax (204)661-4838

Officers
Exec. Dir., John Courtney

3. Religious Bodies in the United States

The United States, with its staunch constitutional stance on religious freedom and successive waves of immigrants over the last three centuries, has proved to be a fertile soil for the development of varied Christian traditions. In the directory that follows, some 227 distinct church traditions are represented. Many of these groups represent the processes of dividing and re-uniting that are a hallmark of American religious life. Many churches listed here represent those with a long tradition in Europe, Africa, or Asia predating their American tenure. Others are American-born churches. The researcher may be helped by consulting the churches grouped by tradition at the end of this directory in the section entitled, "Religious Bodies in the United States Arranged by Families." In this section, all the Baptists bodies are listed together, all the Lutheran bodies, Methodists, etc.

The following directory information is supplied by the national headquarters of each church. Each listing contains a brief description of the church, followed by the national headquarters contact information, which includes a mailing address, telephone and fax numbers, email and website addresses (when available), and the name of the media contact. After the headquarters, there are data regarding the church officers or leaders, including names, titles, and contact information (when contact information differs from the headquarters). There is a staggering array of churches, each with its own form of organization; not all of them refer to their leaders as "officers." In some places, the reader will find the term "Bishops," "Board Members," or "Executives" in place of "Officers."

Finally, when applicable, each entry contains a list of the names of church publications. The churches are printed in alphabetical order by the official name of the organization. There are a few instances in which certain churches are more commonly known by another name. In such cases, the reader is referred incidentally within the text to the appropriate official name. Churches that are member communions of the National Council of the Churches of Christ in the U.S.A. are marked with an asterisk (*).

Other useful information about the churches listed here can be found in other chapters or directories within the book: Statistical information for these churches can be found in the tables toward the end of this book in Section III. Further, more extensive information about the publications listed in this directory can be found in Directory 10, "Religious Periodicals in the United States."

The organizations listed here represent the denominations to which the vast majority of church members in the United States belong. It does not include all religious bodies functioning in the United States. *Melton's Encyclopedia of American Religions, 8th Edition* (Gale Cengage Learning, 1-800-877-GAL) contains names and addresses of additional religious bodies. The Encyclopedia of Religion in America (CQ Press, 2300 N St., NW, Suite 800, Washington, DC 20037) provides a multidisciplinary reference with an historical emphasis.

Advent Christian Church

The Advent Christian Church is a conservative, evangelical denomination which grew out of the Millerite movement of the 1830s and 1840s. The members stress the authority of Scripture, justification by faith in Jesus Christ alone, the importance of evangelism, disciple-making, and world missions and the soon visible return of Jesus Christ.

Organized in 1860, the Advent Christian Church maintains headquarters in Charlotte, N.C., with regional offices in Rochester, N. H., Princeton, N.C., Ellisville, MO., Sumas, WA, and Lenoir, N.C. Missions are maintained in India, Nigeria, Ghana, Japan, Liberia, Croatia, New Zealand, Malaysia, the Philippines, Mexico, South Africa, Namibia, Honduras, China, Kenya, Malawi, Mozambique, Congo, Romania, and Memphis, Tenn.

The Advent Christian Church maintains doctrinal distinctives in three areasconditional immortality, the sleep of the dead until the return of Christ and belief that the kingdom of God will be established on earth made new by Jesus Christ.

Headquarters

P.O. Box 690848, Charlotte, NC 28227, Tel. (704)545-6161 x202 Fax (704)573-0712 Media Contact, Exec. Director, Ronald P. Thomas, Jr.
Email: execdirect@adventchristian.org
Website: www.ecgc.us

Periodicals

Advent Christian News, Maranatha, Advent Christian Witness, Prayer & Praise, Weekly E-newsletter: www.ACGC.us

African Methodist Episcopal Church*

This church began in 1787 in Philadelphia when persons in St. George's Methodist Episcopal Church withdrew as a protest against color segregation. In 1816 the denomination was started, led by Rev. Richard Allen who had been ordained deacon by Bishop Francis Asbury and was subsequently ordained elder and elected and consecrated bishop.

Headquarters

3801 Market St., Suite 300, Philadelphia, PA 29204, Tel. (215)662-0506

56

Email: cio@ame-church.com
Website: www.AME-Church.com

Officers

Senior Bishop, Bishop John Richard Bryant, Presiding Bishop, Fourth Episcopal District, African Methodist Episcopal Church, 5627 South Michigan Ave., 3rd Floor, Chicago, IL 60637, Tel. (773)955-9825 Fax (773)955-9840.
Chief Ecumenical & Urban Affairs Officer, Bishop John F. White, African Methodist Episcopal Church, 4601 Sheridan St., Suite 318, Hollywood, FL 33021, Tel. (954)438-6378; Fax (954)438-9243.
Pres., Gen. Bd., Bishop Larry Kirkland, 4519 Admiralty Way, Suite 205, Marina Del Ray, CA 90292, Tel. (310)557-8530 Fax (310)577-8540.
Pres. Council of Bishops, Bishop David Rwhynica Daniels, Jr., 34 Camp-Johnson Rd., Monrovia, Liberia, West Africa, Tel. 011377467565679

GENERAL OFFICERS
Dr. Clement W. Fugh; Dr. Richard Allen Lewis; Dr. Daryl B. Ingram; Dr. Johnny Barbour; Jr., Dr. George F. Flowers; Dr. Dennis C. Dickerson; Dr. Jerome V. Harris; Dr. James Wade; Dr. Calvin H. Sydnor, III
Bishop John F. White, Ecumenical Officer/ Chaplains; Bishop Richard Franklin Norris (First Episcopal Dist.); Bishop Adam Jefferson Richardson, Jr. (Second Episcopal Dist.); Bishop Cornal Garnett Henning Sr. (Third Episcopal Dist.); Bishop John R. Bryant (Fourth Episcopal Dist.); Bishop T. Larry Kirkland (Fifth Episcopal Dist.); Bishop William Phillips DeVeaux (Sixth Episcopal Dist.); Bishop Preston Warren Williams, II (Seventh Episcopal Dist.); Bishop Carolyn Tyler Guidry (Eighth Episcopal Dist.); Bishop James L. Davis (Ninth Episcopal Dist.); Bishop Gregory Gerald McKinley Ingram (Tenth Episcopal Dist.); Bishop McKinley Young (Eleventh Episcopal Dist.); Bishop Samuel L. Green Sr. (Twelfth Episcopal Dist.); Bishop Vashti Murphy McKenzie (Thirteenth Episcopal Dist.); Bishop David Rwhynica Daniels, Jr. (Fourteenth Episcopal Dist.); Bishop Wilfred Jacobus Messiah (Fifteenth Episcopal Dist.); Bishop Sarah F. Davis (Sixteenth Episcopal Dist.); Bishop Paul Jones Mulenga Kawimbe (Seventeenth Episcopal Dist.); Bishop E. Earl McCloud Jr. (Eighteenth Episcopal Dist.); Bishop Jeffrey N. Leath (Nineteenth Episcopal Dist.); Bishop Julius McAllister Sr. (Twentieth Episcopal District)

Periodicals

The A.M.E. Review, The Christian Recorder, Journal of Christian Education, Women's Missionary Magazine, Secret Chamber, Voice of Mission

The African Methodist Episcopal Zion Church*

The A.M.E. Zion Church is an independent body, having withdrawn from the John Street Methodist Church of New York City in 1796. The first bishop was James Varick.

Headquarters

Dept. of Records & Research, 3225 West Sugar Creek Rd., Charlotte, NC 28269 Tel. (704)599-4630 Fax (704)688-2549, Email: j1gsa@aol.com
Media Contact, Gen. Sec.-Aud., Dr. W. Robert Johnson, III
Email: GENSEC17@yahoo.com
Website: www.amez.org

Officers

Sr. Bishop, Bishop George W.C. Walker, Sr.

BOARD OF BISHOPS OFFICERS
*Pres., Kenneth Monroe, 4633 Old Lowery Rd., Shannon, NC 28386; Tel. (910)843-8274; Fax (910)843-8702, Office Phone (910)987-1991, Episcopal Address: 1408 Jack White Dr., Rock Hill, SC 29732 Tel. (803)328-1068, Email: zion95@embarqmail.com
Sec., Louis Hunter, Sr., P.O. Box 2987, Suwanee, GA 30024, OR, 1314 Churchhill Downs Dr., Waxhaw, NC 28173, Office Tel. (678)482-5937 Fax (678)714-1686, Email: Bishoplhunter @aol.com
Treas., George W.C. Walker, Sr., 1314 Churchill Downs Dr., Waxhaw, NC 28173; Tel. (704)243-3880, Fax (704)243-3882; Mailing Address: P.O. Box 26770, Charlotte, NC 28221-6770, Office: 3225 W. Sugar Creek Rd., Charlotte, NC 28269 Tel. (704)599-4630, Fax (704)688-2540, Email: gwalker046@aol.com
Note: Presidency rotates every six (6) Months according to seniority.

ACTIVE MEMBERS
George Edward Battle Jr., 18403 Dembridge Lane, Davidson, NC 28036 Tel. (704)895-2236, Office: Two Wachovia Center, 301 South Tryon St., Suite 1755, Charlotte, NC 28202 Tel. (704)332-7600 Fax (704)343-3745 Email: gebjneed@bellsouth.net
Warren Matthew Brown, 12904 Canoe Ct., Ft. Washington, MD 20744 Tel. (301)203-1677, Office: 9500 Arena Dr., Suite 102, Largo, MD 20774; Tel. (301)322-3866 Fax (301)322-3862, Email: amezmidatlantic2@aol.com
Samuel Chuka Ekemam, Sr., Office-Mail: A.M.E. Zion Church Area Headquarters, 1 Zion Hill Plaza, (Ugwu Orji), Okigwe Rd., P.O. Box 8000, Owerri, Imo State, Nigeria. Home Phone from US: (1pm-5pm EST) 011-234-808-680-3447; Direct Line: 011-234-803-213-3767; Office from US: 011-234-803-301-8280, Email: bishopamezng@yahoo.com
Mildred B. Hines, 2011 Stearns Dr., Los Angeles, CA 90034 Tel. (323)559-0098, Email: mildred. hines@att.net

Roy A. Holmes, 22071 Sunset Dr., Richton Park, IL 60471 Tel. (708)679-1552 Fax (708)679-1562, Email: bishopraholmes92@sbcglobal.net

Louis Hunter, Sr., P.O. Box 2987, Suwanee, Georgia 30024 Office Tel. (678)482-5937 Fax (678)714-1686, Email: bishoplhunter@aol.com

James E. McCoy, 808 South Lawrence St., Montgomery, AL 36104-5055 Tel. (334)269-6365 Fax (334)269-6369, Email: aflamez@bellsouth.net

Kenneth Monroe, 4633 Old Lowery Rd., Shannon, NC 28386 Tel. (910)843-8274 Fax (910)843-8702; Office Phone (910)987-1991, Episcopal Address: 1408 Jack White Dr., Rock Hill, SC 29732 Tel. (803)328-1068, Email: Zion95@embarqmail.com

Dennis V. Proctor, 8369 Governor Grayson Way, Ellicott City, MD 21043 Tel. (410)418-4364 Fax (410)418-5834, Email: Bishopproctor@aol.com

Darryl B. Starnes, Sr., 3220 Brownes Creek Rd., Charlotte, NC 28269 Tel. (704)599-8718 Fax (704)599-5407, Email: BishopDBStarnes @aol.com

Richard Keith Thompson, Office: 3050 Berks Way, Raleigh, NC 27614 Tel. (919)554-8994; Fax (919)556-6049. Email: enced@ncrrbiz.com

George W.C. Walker, Sr., 1314 Churchill Downs Dr., Waxhaw, NC 28173; Tel. (704)243-3880, Fax (704)243-3882; Mailing Address: P.O. Box 26770, Charlotte, NC 28221-6770, Office: 3225 W. Sugar Creek Rd., Charlotte, NC 28269 Tel. (704)599-4630 Fax (704)688-2540, Email: gwalker046@aol.com

RETIRED MEMBERS

Cecil Bishop, P.O. Box 78535, Charlotte, NC 28271 Tel. (704)996-7669 Fax (704)770-0348

Clarence Carr, 965 Charlton Trace, Marietta, GA 30064 Tel. (770)420-9332

Nathaniel Jarrett, Jr., 18031 South Pheasant Lake Dr., Tinley Park, IL 60477 Tel. (708)802-9873 Fax (708)429-3911

Joseph Johnson, 320 Walnut Point Dr., Matthews, NC 28105 Tel. (704)849-0521; Email: djjj85@windstream.net

Marshall H. Strickland, 2000 Cedar Circle Dr., Baltimore, MD 21228 Tel. (410)744-7330 Fax (410)788-5510

EPISCOPAL ASSIGNMENTS

Piedmont Episcopal District: Blue Ridge, West Central North Carolina, Western North Carolina, Jamaica (all divisions) Conferences: Bishop George W. C. Walker, Sr.

Eastern West Africa Episcopal District: Central Nigeria, Lagos -West Nigeria, Nigeria, Northern Nigeria, Rivers, Mainland, Cross River, South Eastern, and Southern Conferences: Bishop Samuel Chuka Ekemam, Sr.

North Eastern Episcopal District: New England, New York, Western New York, and Bahamas Islands Conferences: Bishop George Edward Battle, Jr.

Eastern North Carolina Episcopal District: Albemarle, Cape Fear, Central North Carolina, North Carolina, Virgin Islands, and South Africa (Zimbabwe) Conferences: Bishop Richard Keith Thompson

Mid-Atlantic II Episcopal District: East Tennessee-Virginia, India, London-Midlands, Philadelphia-Baltimore, Virginia, East Angola, West Angola Conferences: Bishop Warren M. Brown

Mid-West Episcopal District: Indiana, Kentucky, Michigan, Missouri, Tennessee, and Central Africa: Bishop Roy A. Holmes

Mid-Atlantic I Episcopal District: Allegheny, New Jersey, Ohio, Guyana/Suriname, Trinidad-Tobago, and Barbados Conferences: Bishop Louis Hunter, Sr.

Alabama/Florida Episcopal District: Alabama, Cahaba, Central Alabama, North Alabama, South Alabama, West Montgomery Alabama, Florida, and South Florida Conferences: Bishop James E. McCoy

South Atlantic Episcopal District: Georgia, Palmetto, Pee Dee, and South Carolina Conferences: Bishop Kenneth Monroe

Southwestern Delta: Arkansas, Louisiana, Oklahoma, South Mississippi, West Tennessee-Mississippi and Texas Conferences: Bishop Darryl B. Starnes, Sr.

Western Episcopal District: Alaska, Arizona, California, Oregon-Washington, Southwest Rocky Mountains, and Colorado Conferences: Bishop Dennis V. Proctor

Western West Africa: Cote D'Ivoire, East Ghana, Liberia, Mid-Ghana, North Ghana, Togo, and West Ghana Conferences: Bishop Mildred B. Hines

GENERAL OFFICERS AND DEPARTMENTS

Address and telephone number for all Departments (except where indicated) is 3225 West Sugar Creek Rd., Charlotte, NC 28269 Tel. (704)599-4630 and Mailing Address for all Departments (except where indicated) is P.O. Box 26770, Charlotte, NC 28221

Department of Records and Research: W. Robert Johnson, III, Gen. Sec.-Aud., Fax (704)688-2549, Email: gensec17@yahoo.com or amezgsa17@aol.com

Department of Finance: Mrs. Shirley Welch, Chief Financial Officer, Fax (704)688-2553, Email: shwelch@amezhqtr.org

Star of Zion: Mike Lisby, Editor, Fax (704)688-2556, Email: sozbusiness@yahoo.com

A.M.E. Zion Quarterly Review and Secretary A.M.E. Zion Historical Society: James D. Armstrong, Sec.-Editor, P.O. Box 33247, Charlotte, NC 28233, Fax (704)688-2544, Email: jaarmstrong@amezhqtr.org

Heritage Hall, Livingstone College, 701 W. Monroe St., Salisbury, NC 28144 Tel. (704)216-6094

Department of Overseas Missions and Missionary Seer: Kermit DeGraffenreidt, Sec.-Editor, 475 Riverside Dr., Room 1935, New

York, NY 10115 Tel. (212)870-2952 Fax (212)870-2808

Department of Brotherhood Pensions and Ministerial Relief:

Christian Education Department: Raymon Hunt, Sec., Fax (704)688-2550, Email: rehunt@amezhqtr.org, Website: www.cedamezion.org.

Department of Church School Literature: Mary A. Love, Editor, Fax (704)688-2548, Email: malove@amezhqtr.org

Department of Church Extension and Home Missions: Terrence J. Jones, Sec.-Treas., Fax (704)688-2552, Email: tejones@amezhqtr.org

Bureau of Evangelism: Otis T. McMillan, Dir., P.O. Box 217258, Charlotte, NC 28221, Fax (704) 688-2547, Email: otmcmillan@embarqmail.com

Public Affairs and Convention Manager: George E. McKain, II, Dir., P.O. Box 1417, Summerville, SC 29484 Tel. (843)276-3411 Fax (843)821-1735, Email: zionpagem2@aol.com; Hqtrs. Tel. (704)599-4630

Department of Health and Social Concerns: Bernard Sullivan, Dir., Email: bernard sullivan2@yahoo.com

A.M.E. Zion Publishing House: David Baker, General Manager, Fax (704)688-2541, Email: dabaker@amezhqtr.org

JUDICIAL COUNCIL

Pres., Rev. Dr. E. Alex Brower, Esq. 235B State St., Hudson, NY 12534

Vice Pres., Rev. Dr. Richard Chapple, 1449 W. Adams Blvd., Los Angeles, CA 90007

Clerk, Ms. Monica S. Reed, 1641 Rosedale Ave., Knoxville, TN 37915-1929

Juraldine Battle-Hodge, Esq., 1017 North Burbank Dr., Montgomery, AL 26117. Email: battle@bellsouth.net

Rev. Dr. Charlotte Brown-Williams, Esq., 1131 Lynbrook Dr., Charlotte, NC 28221

Rachel R. Dawson, Esq. 4106 South Ellis, Chicago, IL

Elmira J. Jackson, Esq., 194 Wood Hollow Lane, New Rochelle, NY 10804

Rev. Dr. William McKenith, 247 Glove Ave., Union, NJ 07083

Rev. Dr. John L. Walker, Sr., Esq., 6510 Adak St., Seat Pleasant, MD 20743

Pres. Emeritus of Counsel, Hon. Adle M. Riley

CONNECTIONAL LAY COUNCIL

General President, Yvonne A. Tracey, 502 Ferndale Dr., Salisbury, NC 28144; (704)637-8687; Fax: (704)636-4562; Email: ytracey @bellsouth.net

First Vice Pres., Yvonne Baskerville, 1812 Allison St. NW, Washington, DC 20011; (202)726-5547; Email: eyb1022@yahoo.com

Second Vice-Pres., Effie B. Woodard, P.O. Box 662, Broadway, NC 27505; (919)258-6868; Tel: (919) 356-6608; Email: ebw108@windstream.net

Secretary, Delores Lancaster, 674 Azalea Dr., Rockville, MD 20850; (301)340-2590; Email: dlancaster674@aol.com

Treasurer, Trubbie R. Leeper, 2310 Yorktown Ave., Gastonia, NC 28054; (704)866-0742; Email: jessipoppy@yahoo.com

Financial Sec., Ira Rudolph Golden, 188 Hillside Ave., White Plains, NY 10603; Home: (914)285-9796; Cell; (914)960-7755; Email; IRBAGO@aol.com

Chaplain, Charles Montgomery, 11436 Studebaker Rd., Norwalk, CA 90650; (562)864-6180, Email: cpmonty@aol.com

Editor, "The Laity Speaks/The Connection", Rhandi M. Stith, Carrington Arms, 33 Lincoln Ave., Apt. 10L, New Rochelle, NY 10801. (914)235-3596; Fax (914)637-2518; Email: Rhandim@aol.com

GENERAL OFFICERS OF THE WOMEN'S HOME AND OVERSEAS MISSIONARY SOCIETY

General President, Dr. Sandra L. Gasdon

First Vice-President, Dr. Gloria G. Williams, 804 Prospect Ave., Raeford, NC 28376 Tel. (910)875-2205 Fax (910)875-8214. Email: gwilli5103@alol.com

Second Vice-President, Mrs. Joyce A. Reid, 5309 Dayan Dr., Charlotte, NC 28216 Tel. (704)596-3842 Fax (704)921-8323, Email: ejr5309@aol.com

Exec. Secretary, Mrs. Rosetta J. Dunham, P.O. Box 26846, Charlotte, NC 28221-6846 Tel. (704)599-4630 Fax (704)688-2554; Email: rodunham@amezhqtr.org

Recording Secretary, Ms. Dorothy McFarlane, 88 Fawcett Close, Wye St., Battersea London, England SW 112LU. Tel. +44207-228-8114/+447946292755. Email: dorothymc2 @yahoo-co-uk-

General Treasurer, Mrs. Jacqueline R. Pinkard

General Coordinator of YAMS, Mrs. Dawn L. Walker, 823 South Indiana Ave., Griffith, Indiana 46319 Tel. (219)922-1361, Email: dlwsweetspirit@aol.com

Secretary, Youth Missionary Society, Mrs. Vicki L. Lewis

Superintendent of Buds of Promise, Ms. Barbara Epps, 3204 Reid Ave., Charlotte, NC 28208. Tel. (704)372-7580. Fax (704)-372-7580. Email: bepps1@carolina.rr.com

Secretary, Bureau of Supply, Mrs. Sara S. Cherrington

Chairman, Life Members Council, Mrs. Loveleen "Dee" Perkins, 5303 Brewer Rd., Beltsville, MD 20705. Tel. (301)937-0244. Fax (301)937-4041. Email: dperkins02@yahoo.com

Editor, Women's Section, Missionary Seer, Mrs. Christina Penrose, 506 Fairdale St., Friendswood, TX 77546. Tel. (281)996-1304. Fax (832)201-8137. Fax (718)604-2094

Periodicals

Star of Zion, Quarterly Review, Church School Herald, Missionary Seer, Vision Focus, Evangel

Albanian Orthodox Archdiocese in America

The Albanian Orthodox Church in America traces its origins to the groups of Albanian immigrants which first arrived in the United States in 1886, seeking religious, cultural and economic freedoms denied them in the homeland. In 1908 in Boston, the Rev. Fan Stylian Noli (later Archbishop) served the first liturgy in the Albanian language in 500 years, to which Orthodox Albanians rallied, forming their own diocese in 1919. Parishes began to spring up throughout New England and the Mid-Atlantic and Great Lakes states. In 1922, clergy from the United States traveled to Albania to proclaim the self-governance of the Orthodox Church in the homeland at the Congress of Berat.

In 1971 the Albanian Archdiocese sought and gained union with the Orthodox Church in America, expressing the desire to expand the Orthodox witness to America at large, giving it an indigenous character. The Albanian Archdiocese remains vigilant for its brothers and sisters in the homeland and serves as an important resource for human rights issues and Albanian affairs, in addition to its programs for youth, theological education, vocational interest programs and retreats for young adults and women.

Headquarters
523 E. Broadway, S. Boston, MA 02127
Media Contact, Sec., Dorothy Adams, Tel. (617)268-1275 Fax (617)268-3184
Website: www.oca.org

Officers
Metropolitan Herman, Tel. (617)268-1275
Chancellor, V. Rev. Arthur E. Liolin, 60 Antwerp St., East Milton, MA 02186, Tel. (617)698-3366
Lay Chpsn., William Poist, 40 Forge Village Rd., Westford, MA 01885, Tel. (978)392-0759
Treas., Cynthia Vasil Brown, 471 Capt. Eames Circle, Ashland, MA 01721 (508)881-0072

Albanian Orthodox Diocese of America

This Diocese was organized in 1950 as a canonical body administering to the Albanian faithful. It is under the ecclesiastical jurisdiction of the Ecumenical Patriarchate of Constantinople (Istanbul).

Headquarters
P.O. Box 300158, Jamaica Plain, MA 02130, Tel. (775)348-6369 Fax (617)522-3878
Media Contact, His Grace Bishop Ilia Katra

Officers
His Grace Bishop Ilia Katra, P.O. Box 300158, Jamaica Plain, MA 02130, Tel. (775)348-6369 Fax (617)522-3878

The Allegheny Wesleyan Methodist Connection (Original Allegheny Conference)

This body was formed in 1968 by members of the Allegheny Conference (located in eastern Ohio and western Pennsylvania) of the Wesleyan Methodist Church, which merged in 1966 with the Pilgrim Holiness Church to form The Wesleyan Church. The Allegheny Wesleyan Methodist Connection is composed of persons "having the form and seeking the power of godliness, united in order to pray together, to receive the word of exhortation, and to watch over one another in love, that they may help each other to work out their salvation." There is a strong commitment to congregational government and to holiness of heart and life. There is a strong thrust in church extension within the United States and in missions worldwide.

Headquarters
P.O. Box 357, Salem, OH 44460, Tel. (330)337-9376 Fax (330)337-9700
Media Contact, Pres., Rev. William Cope
Email: awmc@juno.com

Officers
Pres., Rev. William Cope, P.O. Box 357, Salem, OH 44460
Vice Pres., Rev. David Blowers, 1856 Marion-Williamsport Rd., E, Marion, OH 43302
Sec., Rev. Jonathan Troyer, 2700 17th St., NW, Canton, OH 44708-2954
Treas., James Kunselman, 1022 Newgarden Ave., Salem, OH 44460

Periodicals
The Allegheny Wesleyan Methodist

Alliance of Baptists*

The Alliance of Baptists is an association of individuals and churches dedicated to the preservation of historic Baptist principles, freedoms, and traditions, and to the expression of our ministry and mission through cooperative relationships with other Baptist bodies and the larger Christian community.

From its inception in early 1987, the Alliance has stood for those values that have distinguished the Baptist movement from its beginnings nearly four centuries ago — the freedom and accountability of every individual in matters of faith; the freedom of each congregation under the authority of Jesus Christ to determine its own ministry and mission; and religious freedom for all in relationship to the state.

Headquarters
1328 16th St. N.W., Washington, DC 20036, Tel. (202)745-7609 Fax (202)745-0023
Media Contact, Exec. Dir., Rev. Dr. Stan Hastey
Email: shastey@allianceofbaptists.org
Website: www.allianceofbaptists.org

Officers

Exec. Dir., Rev. Dr. Stan Hastey
Assoc. Dir., Jeanette Holt
Pres., Rev. Jim Hopkins, Oakland, CA
Vice Pres., Kristy Arneson Pullen, Ashburn, VA
Sec., Amy Jacks Dean, Charlotte, NC

Periodicals

Connections

The American Association of Lutheran Churches

This church body was constituted on November 7, 1987. The AALC was formed by laity and pastors of the former American Lutheran Church in America who held to a high view of Scripture (inerrancy and infallibility). This church body also emphasizes the primacy of evangelism and world missions and the authority and autonomy of the local congregation.

Congregations of the AALC are distributed throughout the continental United States from Long Island, N.Y., to Los Angeles. The primary decision-making body is the General Convention, to which each congregation has proportionate representation.

Headquarters

The AALC National Office, 6600 N. Clinton St., Augustine Hall, #13, Fort Wayne, Indiana 46825, Tel. (260)452-3213 Fax (260)452-3215 Mailing Address: The AALC, 921 East Dupont Rd., #920, Fort Wayne, IN 46825-1551

Media Contact, Admn. Asst. to the AALC, Rev. Fred Balke, Email: fbalke@taalc.org

Email: theaalc@taalc.org; gstenzel@taalc.org
Website: www.taalc.org

Officers

Rev. Franklin E. Hays, Presiding Pastor, The American Association of Lutheran Churches, Tel. (260)452-3213, Email: presidingpastor@taalc.org

Rev. Richard Eddy, Assistant Presiding Pastor
Rev. Mark Homp, Secretary
Mr. Jim Daman, Treasurer
Rev. Richard Shields, ALTS President; Director of Pastoral Formation and Congregational Development; Administrative Ass't. to the Presiding Pastor, Tel. (260)452-3213, Email: rpshields@taalc.org

Rev. Fred Balke, Director of Communications, The AALC; Evangel Editor & Admn. Asst. to the AALC, Email: fbalke@taalc.org

American Lutheran Theological Seminary (ALTS), Pres., Rev. Richard Shields, 6600 N. Clinton St., Fort Wayne, IN 46825, Tel. (260)452-3213, Email: rpshields@taalc.org

Rev. Fred Balke, Registrar

Periodicals

The Evangel

The American Baptist Association

The American Baptist Association (ABA) is an international fellowship of independent Baptist churches voluntarily cooperating in missionary, evangelistic, benevolent and Christian education activities throughout the world. Its beginnings can be traced to the landmark movement of the 1850s. Led by James R. Graves and J.M. Pendleton, a significant number of Baptist churches in the South, claiming a New Testament heritage, rejected as extrascriptural the policies of the newly formed Southern Baptist Convention (SBC). Because they strongly advocated church equality, many of these churches continued doing mission and benevolent work apart from the SBC, electing to work through local associations. Meeting in Texarkana, TX, in 1924, messengers from the various churches effectively merged two of these major associations, the Baptist Missionary Association of Texas and the General Association, forming the American Baptist Association.

Since 1924, mission efforts have been supported in Australia, Africa, Asia, Canada, Central America, Europe, India, Israel, Japan, Korea, Mexico, New Zealand, South America and the South Pacific. An even more successful domestic mission effort has changed the ABA from a predominantly rural southern organization to one with churches in 48 states.

Through its publishing arm in Texarkana, the ABA publishes literature and books numbering into the thousands. Major seminaries include the Missionary Baptist Seminary, founded by Dr. Ben M. Bogard in Little Rock, AR; Texas Baptist Seminary, Henderson, TX; Oxford Baptist Institute, Oxford, MS; and Florida Baptist Schools in Lakeland, FL.

While no person may speak for the churches of the ABA, all accept the Bible as the inerrant Word of God. They believe Christ was the virgin-born Son of God, that God is a triune God, that the only church is the local congregation of scripturally baptized believers and that the work of the church is to spread the gospel.

Headquarters

4605 N State Line Ave. Texarkana, TX 75503, Tel. (903)792-2783

Media Contact, Steve Reeves, Public Relations Director

Email: bssc@abaptist.org
Website: www.abaptist.org

Officers

President, James Calhoun, 2105 Shadow Ridge Ct., Arkadelphia, AR 71923

Vice President, Darrel Owens, 388 CR 3201 W, Mt. Enterprise, TX 75681; James A.
Crain, 1520 Fincher Creek, Minden, LA 71055
Recording Clerks, Terry Parrish, 19 Eastwood, Bryant AR 72022

Publications, Editor in Chief, Larry Clements; Bus. Mgr., Wayne Sewell, 4605 N. State Line Ave., Texarkana, TX 75503

Meeting Arrangements Director, Edgar N. Sutton, P.O. Box 240, Alexander, AR 72002

Sec.-Treas. of Missions, Randy Cloud, P.O. Box 1050 Texarkana, TX 75504

American Baptist Churches in the U.S.A.*

Originally known as the Northern Baptist Convention, this body of Baptist churches changed the name to American Baptist Convention in 1950 with a commitment to hold the name in trust for all Christians of like faith and mind who desire to bear witness to the historical Baptist convictions in a framework of cooperative Protestantism. In 1972 American Baptist Churches in the U.S.A. was adopted as the new name. Although national missionary organizational developments began in 1814 with the establishment of the American Baptist Foreign Mission Society and continued with the organization of the American Baptist Publication Society in 1824 and the American Baptist Home Mission Society in 1832, the general denominational body was not formed until 1907. American Baptist work at the local level dates back to the organization by Roger Williams of the First Baptist Church in Providence, R. I. in 1638.

Headquarters

American Baptist Churches Mission Center

P.O. Box 851, Valley Forge, PA 19482-0851, Tel. (610)768-2000 Fax (610)768-2320

Media Contact, Assoc. Gen'l. Secretary for Mission Resource Development, the Rev. Dr. Leo S. Thorne, Tel. (610)768-2318 Fax (610)768-2320, Email: leo.thorne@abcusa. org

Email: richard.schramm@abc-usa.org

Website: www.abc-usa.org

Officers

Pres.,Ruth Clark, Email: pastorwifejbc @sbcglobal.net

Vice Pres., Don Ng, Email: DonN@abc-usa.org

Budget Review Officer, James Ratliff, Email: jamesratliff@abc-usa.org

Gen. Sec., A. Roy Medley;, Tel. (610)768-2273, Email: roy.medley@abc-usa.org

Assoc. Gen. Sec.-Treas., Alan Musoke, Tel. (610) 768-2280; Email: alan.musoke@abcusa. org

REGIONAL ORGANIZATIONS

Central Region, ABC of, John S. Williams, 5833 SW 29th St. Ste. A, Topeka, KS 66614-5500

Chicago, ABC of Metro, Larry L. Greenfield, P.O. Box 15127, Chicago, IL 60615

Cleveland Baptist Assoc., Leonard Thompson, 6060 Rockside Woods Blvd., Ste. 317, Cleveland, OH 44131

Connecticut, ABC of, Judy G. Allbee, 90 A North Main St., West Hartford, CT 06107-1924

Dakotas, ABC of, Riley H. Walker, 1101 W. 22nd St., Sioux Falls, SD 57105-1699

District of Columbia Bapt. Conv., Ricky O. Creech,1628 16th St., NW, Washington, DC 20009-3099

Evergreen Baptist Association, Marcia Patton, 409 Third Ave., South Ste. A, Kent, WA 98032

Great Rivers Region, ABC of, J. Dwight Stinnett, P.O. Box 3786, Springfield, IL 62708-3786

Indiana & Kentucky, ABC of, Don Scott, Interim, 1350 N. Delaware St., Indianapolis, IN 46202-2493

Indianapolis, ABC of Greater, Joan Friesen, Interim, P.O. Box 421487., Indianapolis, IN 46242-1487

Los Angeles, ABC of, Samuel S. Chetti, P.O. Box 1868, Glendale, CA 91209

Maine, ABC of, Alfred Fletcher, P.O. Box 6149, China Village, ME 04926-6149

Massachusetts, ABC of, Anthony Pappas, 167 Prescott St., Groton, MA 01450

Metropolitan New York, ABC of, James O. Stallings, 475 Riverside Dr., Rm. 432, New York, NY 10115-0432

Michigan, ABC of, Michael A. Williams, 4578 S. Hagadorn Rd., East Lansing, MI 48823-5396

Mid-American Baptist Churches, Marshall Peters, 2400 86th St. Ste. !5, Des Moines, IA 50322-4380

Nebraska, ABC of, Robin Stoops, 6404 Maple St., Omaha, NE 68104-4079

New Jersey, ABC of, Lee Spitzer, 3752 Nottingham Way, Ste. 101, Trenton, NJ 08690-3802

New York State, ABC of, Wayne Paulsen, Interim, 5865 E. Seneca Turnpike, Jamesville, NY 13078

Northwest, ABC of, Charles Revis, 601 S. Ross Point Rd., Post Falls, ID 83854-7726

Ohio, ABC of, Lawrence Swain, 136 N. Galway Dr., Granville, OH 43023-9579

Oregon, ABC of, Stephen Bils, 0245 SW Bancroft St., Ste. G, Portland, OR 97239

Pennsylvania & Delaware, ABC of, Frank Frischkorn, 106 Revere Lane, Coatesville, PA 19320

Philadelphia Baptist Assoc., James E. McJunkin, Jr., 8711 Ridge Ave., Philadelphia, PA 19128-2023

Puerto Rico, Iglesias Bautistads de, Roberto Dieppa-Baez, PMB 477, P.O. Box 6022, Carolina, PR 00984-6022

Rhode Island, ABC of, David M. Brown, Interim, P.O. Box 330, Exeter, RI 02822

Rochester-Genesee Region, ABC of, Alan Newton, 1100 S. Goodman, # 320 Rochester, NY 14620

Rocky Mountains, ABC of, Steven Van Ostran, 9085 E. Mineral Circle, Ste. 170, Centennial, CO 80112

South, ABC of the, Walter L. Parrish, II, 5124 Greenwich Ave., Baltimore, MD 21229-2393

Vermont-New Hampshire, ABC of, Dale Edwards, Interim, One Oak Ridge Rd., Bldg. B 3, Suite 4A, West Lebanon, NH 03784

West, Growing Healthy Churches, ABC of the, Paul D. Borden, 2420 Camino Ramon, Ste. 140, San Ramon, CA 94583-4207

West Virginia Baptist Convention, David L. Carrico, P.O. Box 1019, Parkersburg, WV 26102-1019

Wisconsin, ABC of, Arlo R. Reichter, 15330 Watertown Plank Rd., Elm Grove, WI 53122-2391

BOARDS

American Baptist Assembly, Green Lake, WI 54941; Pres., Ben Mott

American Baptist Historical Society, 3001 Mercer University Dr. Atlanta, GA 30341-4155

Admn. Archivist, Deborah B. VanBroekhoven; Pres., Trinette V. McCray

American Baptist Men, Pres., David Edwards

American Baptist Women's Ministries, Exec. Dir., Virginia Holmstrom; Pres., Barbara Anderson

Bd. of Intl. Ministries, Exec. Dir., Reid Trulson; Pres., Hopeton Scott

American Baptist Home Mission Societies, Exec. Dir., Aidsand F. Wright-Riggins; Pres., Clifford Johnson

Ministers & Missionaries Benefit Bd., Exec. Dir., Sumner M. Grant; Pres., George Tooze, 475 Riverside Dr., New York, NY 10115

Minister Council, Dir., Joseph Kutter; Pres., Jeffrey Savage

Periodicals

Tomorrow Magazine, The Secret Place, American Baptist Quarterly, The Christian Citizen, On Location, Mission in America

The American Carpatho-Russian Orthodox Greek Catholic Church

The American Carpatho-Russian Orthodox Greek Catholic Church is a self-governing diocese that is in communion with the Ecumenical Patriarchate of Constantinople. The late Patriarch Benjamin I, in an official Patriarchal Document dated Sept. 19, 1938, canonized the Diocese in the name of the Orthodox Church of Christ.

Headquarters

312 Garfield St., Johnstown, PA 15906, Tel. (814)539-4207 Fax (814)536-4699

Media Contact, Chancellor, V. Rev. Proto-presbyter Frank P. Miloro, Tel. (814)539-8086 Fax (814)536-4699

Email: archdiocese@goarch.org

Website: www.goarch.org

Officers

Bishop, Archbishop Demetrios (Locum Tenens), 312 Garfield St., Johnstown, PA 15906, Tel. (814)539-9143, Fax (814)536-4699

Chancellor, V. Rev. Protopresbyter Frank P. Miloro, 249 Butler Ave., Johnstown, PA

15906, Tel. (814)539-9143, Fax (814)536-4699, Email: acrod@helicon.net

Treas., V. Rev. Protopresbyter Ronald A. Hazuda, 1115 East Ave., Erie, PA 16503, Tel. (814)453-4902

Periodicals

The Church Messenger

American Evangelical Christian Churches

Founded in 1944, the A.E.C.C is composed of individual ministers and churches who are united in accepting "Seven Articles of Faith." These seven articles are-the Bible as the written word of God; the Virgin birth; the deity of Jesus Christ; Salvation through the atonement; guidance of our life through prayer; the return of the Saviour; the establishment of the Millennial Kingdom.

The American Evangelical Christian Churches offers the following credentials-Certified Christian Worker, Commission to Preach, Licensed Minister and Ordained Minister to those who accept the Seven Articles of Faith, who put unity in Christ first and are approved by A.E.C.C.

A.E.C.C seeks to promote the gospel through its ministers, churches and missionary activities. Churches operate independently with all decisions concerning local government left to the individual churches. The organization also has ministers in Canada, England, Bolivia, Philippines Thailand, Brazil and South America.

Headquarters

P.O. Box 47312, Indianapolis, IN 46227, Tel. (317)788-9280 Fax (317)788-1410

Media Contact, Dr. Charles Wasielewski, Sr., 51 Wells Rd, Barton, NY 13734-1818

Email: aeccoffice@earthlink.net

Website: www.aeccministries.com

Officers

INTERNATIONAL OFFICERS

Mod., Dr. Charles Wasielewski, Box 51, Wells Rd., Barton, NY 13734, Tel. (607)565-4074

Sec., Dr. Gene McClain, 520 Blooming Pike, Morgantown, IN 46160, Tel. (812)597-5021

Treas., Dr. Michael Ward, Sr., 4802 Chervil Ct., Indianapolis, IN 46237, Tel. (317)888-2095

Bd. Member, Dr. Allen Kent, 550 E. Shoeline Dr., Long Beach, CA 90802, Tel. (562)590-7294

Missions Coordinator, Dr. Douglas Schlemmer, P.O. Box 409, Twin Peaks, CA 92391, Tel. (909)338-6495

REGIONAL MODERATORS

Northwest Region, Rev. Alvin House, P.O. Box 393, Darby MT 59829 Tel. (406)821-3141

Central-West Region, Rev. Charles Clark, Box 314, Rockport, IL 62370 Tel. (217)437-2507

63

Far West Region, Pastor Richard Cuthbert, 1195 Via Serville, Cathedral City, CA 92234, Tel. (706)321-6682

Lowell Ford, 397 Shamrock Lane, Newark, OH, 43055, Tel. (614)309-3419

Northeast Region, Rev. John Merrill, P.O. Box 183, East Smithfield, PA 18817 Tel. (717)596-4598

East Region, James R. Brown, 17404 W. Washington, Hagerstown, MD 21740, Tel. (301)797812f1

Southeast Region, Rev. James Fullwood, 207 5th Ave., N.E., Lutz, FL 33549

STATE MODERATORS

Rev. James Brown, Maryland

Rev. John W. Coats, Delaware

Brenda Osborne, New York

Dr. Berton G. Heleine, Illinois

Rev. R. Eugene Hill, New Jersey

Rev. Kenneth Pope, Washington

Rev. Art Mirek, Michigan

Rev. Charles Jennings, Pennsylvania

Rev. Jerry Myers, Indiana

FOREIGN OUTREACH MINISTRIES

American Evangelical Christian Churches-Canada, Regional Moderator, Dr. Stephen K. Massey, 730 Ontario street, Suite 709, Toronto, Ontario M4X 1N3, Canada (416)323-9076

Philippine Evangelical Christian Churches, Director, Rev. Alan A. Olubalang, P.O. Box 540, Cotabato City, Philippines 9600

American Evangelical Christian Churches-Philippines, Regional Moderator, Rev. Oseas Andres, P.O. Box 2695, Central Post Office, 1166 Q.C. Metro Manila, Philippines

Periodicals

AECC Communique

American Rescue Workers

Major Thomas E. Moore was National Commander of Booth's Salvation Army when a dispute flared between Booth and Moore. Moore resigned from Booth's Army and due to the fact that Booth's Army was not incorporated at the time, Moore was able to incorporate under said name. The name was changed in 1890 to American Salvation Army. In 1913 the current name American Rescue Workers was adopted. It is a national religious social service agency which operates on a quasimilitary basis. Membership includes officers (clergy), soldiers-adherents (laity), members of various activity groups and volunteers who serve as advisors, associates and committed participants in ARW service functions.

The motivation of the organization is the love of God. Its message is based on the Bible. This is expressed by its spiritual Ministry, the purposes of which are to preach the gospel of Jesus Christ and to meet human needs in his name without discrimination. It is a branch of the Christian Church . . . A Church with a Mission.

Headquarters

Operational Headquarters, 25 Ross St., Williamsport, PA 17701, Tel. (570)323-8693 Fax (570)323-8694

National Field Office, 11116 Gehr Rd., Waynesboro, PA 17268-9101, Tel. (717)762-2965

Media Contact, Natl. Communication Sec./Natl Special Services Dir., Col. Robert N. Coles, Rev., Natl. Field Ofc., Fax (717)762-8109

Email: amerscwk@pcspower.net

Website: www.arwus.com

Officers

Commander-In-Chief & Pres. of Corp., General Claude S. Astin, Jr. Rev

Natl. Bd. Pres., Col. Sam Astin (Claude S. Astin, III)

Ordination Committee, Chpsn., Gen. Paul E. Martin, (Emeritus) Rev.

Natl. Chief Sec., Col. Dawn R. Astin, NQ-643 Elmira St., Williamsport, PA 17701

Periodicals

The Rescue Herald

Amish—please see Old Order Amish Church

Anglo-Lutheran Catholic Church

The Anglo-Lutheran Catholic Church (ALCC) was founded in November, 1997 as the Evangelical Community Church-Lutheran (ECCL) by former members of the Lutheran Church-Missouri Synod. It began as a single independent congregation, St. Michael's Lutheran Church, Kansas City Missouri. The first pastor of St. Michael's Lutheran Church was the Rev. Irl A. Gladfelter.

The Constitution and Canon Law of the ALCC require all clergy to be ordained (or re-ordained) into the historic apostolic succession upon their entry into the ALCC. Those already ordained in the historic apostolic succession in lineages considered technically valid by the Catholic Church are not re-ordained.

The ALCC officially changed its name to "Anglo-Lutheran Catholic Church" in October, 2007. The term, "Anglo" in the name reflects the fact that from its founding, this Church has been considerably influenced by the Anglo-Catholic ("high church") faction within Anglicanism.

Consistent with its ecumenical goal of eventual incorporation into the Catholic Church in whichever form is felt to be the most appropriate by the Vatican, through the years, the Anglo-Lutheran Catholic Church (ALCC) modified its theology, polity, worship, and spirituality to the point where it now rejects all aspects of Lutheran and Anglican faith, polity, worship, and spirituality which are not in full agreement with the faith, polity, worship, and spirituality of the Catholic Church and the teachings of the Catholic Magesterium.

The ecclesiastical government of the Anglo-Lutheran Catholic is hierarchal and episcopal (governed by bishops.) The structure of this Church at the international, national, diocesan, and parish levels, and the role of the laity is the same as that of the Catholic Church. The code of doctrine and discipline are contained in the ALCC's Constitution, Canon Law Code, Church Regulations, and in areas not covered by those documents, by the Code of Canon Law of the Catholic Church (Vatican Library Edition, 1989.) In July of 2008 it began requiring all clergy to sign the Mandatum, which is a vow in the form of a legal contract to not teach, preach, write, or publish nothing contrary to the Catholic Magisterium. Compliance with the Mandatum is enforced.

At this time, the ALCC has five (5) archdioceses, three (3) dioceses, and two (2) ethnic non-geographic archdioceses in the United States. It has a vicar general in Kenya, a priest in Germany, a significant presence in Sudan and South Sudan, and also has a presence in Canada, Northwest Uganda, and Northeast Congo. The ALCC has Archbishops with jurisdiction as Minor Metropolitans for Europe, Sub-Saharan Africa, North America, and Southeast Asia (though it has no Asian presence at this time.)

The ALCC is in Full Communion with the following "Continuing Anglican" Churches: Anglican Church of the Americas, Traditional Church of England, Anglican Church-Traditional Rite, Traditional Episcopal Church in Scotland, Traditional Church in Wales, Traditional English Church, and the Traditional Anglo-Catholic Communion. It is also in full communion with the Evangelical Marian Catholic Church.

The ALCC filed a formal petition to enter the Roman Catholic Church as a unified body in May of 2009, and in October of 2010 was directed by the Congregation for the Doctrine of the Faith to enter the Catholic Church through the U.S. Anglican Ordinariate. The ALCC has officially accepted that instruction in writing. All ALCC clergy and parishes have applied to enter the U.S. Ordinariate.

INTERNATIONAL HEADQUARTERS

Office of the Metropolitan Archbishop, Office of the Director of Temporal Administration, St. Michael's House, 1200 N. E. 81st Terrace, Kansas City, Missouri 64118-1361, Chancery Phone: (816)468-9691, Email: ALCC lutherans@kc.rr.com
Email: ALCClutherans@kc.rr.com
Website: www.anglolutherancatholic.org/

Officers

Metropolitan Archbishop, The Most Rev. Irl A. Gladfelter, C.S.P., M.Div., S.T.M., D.D., St. Michael's House, 1200 N. E. 81st Terrace, Kansas City, Missouri 64118-1361, Kansas City, Missouri 64118-1361, Tel. (816)468-9691, Email: ALCClutherans@kc.rr.com

Vicar General of the Anglo-Lutheran Catholic Church, Office of the Metropolitan Archbishop, The Most Rev. Robert W. Edmondson, C.S.P., M.Div., S.T.M., D.Min., Th.D., H.L.D., D.D., P. O. Box 6172, Pittsburgh, PA 15212, Tel. (412)741-9009, Email: DeoEtEcclesia@yahoo.com

Office of the Dean of the Holy Synod, The Most Rev. Tan Binh Phan Nguyen, O.S.A., S.T.L., M.A., S.T.M., D.D., 2389 Alden Woods Dr., Jonesboro, GA 30236, Tel. (770)210-9346, Email: lavanglutheran@yahoo.com

Treasurer: Mr. Dick Clemens, B.S., B.S. (Accounting), A.B.A., C.I.A., E.A., 200 NW Englewood, Gladstone, Missouri 64118, Tel. (816)454-4057, Website: www.bds accounting. com, Email: dclemens@ bdsaccounting.com

Office of the Director of Temporal Administration, Office of the Metropolitan Archbishop, L. J. Merrill, Mus.B., M.A.Mgt., D.D., St. Michael's House, 1200 N.E. 81st Terrace, Kansas City, Missouri 64118-1361, Tel. 816-468-9691, EMail: ALCClutherans@ kc.rr.com

Office for the Doctrine of the Faith, The Most Rev. Edward Steele, O.S.A., B.A., M.A.P.S., D.D., 2506 Astro Place, Seffner, FL 33584, Tel. (813) 217-3311; Email: edward.steele@saintled.edu

Office for the Promotion of Christian Unity, Office of the Metropolitan Archbishop, The Most Rev. Robert W. Edmondson, C.S.P., M.Div., S.T.M., D.Min., Th.D., H.L.D., D.D., Box 6172, Pittsburgh, PA 15212, Tel. (412)741-9009, Email: DeoEtEcclesia@yahoo.com

Director of Evangelism and Church Growth, Office of the Metropolitan Archbishop, The Rev. Msgr. Thomas Stover O.S.A., M.Div., D. Min., D.D., 1115 East 19th St., Minneapolis, MN 55404, Tel. (612)554-5368, Website: www.holytrinityalcc.org, Email: toms@holy trinityalcc.org

Office for Specialized Ministries, The Most Rev. Raymond W. Copp, O.S.A., M.Div., Ph.D., D.D., 564 Spring Oaks Dr., West Chester, PA 19382, Tel. (610)639-1082, Email: rwcopp@ gp4u.us

Director for Hospital and Hospice Chaplaincies, Office for Specialized Ministries: The Most Rev. Raymond W. Copp, O.S.A., M.Div., Ph.D., D.D, 564 Spring Oaks Dr., West Chester, PA 19382, Tel. (610)639-1082 Email: rwcopp@gp4u.us

Director for Police, Fire and Correctional Institution Chaplaincies, Office for Specialized Ministries: The Most Rev. Raymond W. Copp, O.S.A., M.Div., Ph.D., D.D, 564 Spring Oaks Dr., West Chester, PA 19382, Tel. (610)639-1082, Email: rwcopp@gp4u.us

Office for Pastoral Assistance to Health Care Workers, Office for Specialized Ministries: The Most Rev. Chaplen Luyimba Kweri, O.S.A., B.A.Th., M.Div., D.D., 4606 N. W.

Kenwood, Kansas City, MO 64116, Tel. (816)786-2742, Email: bishopweri@rocket mail.com

The Anglo-Lutheran Catholic Church is a member of the Augustana Catholic Communion.

The Antiochian Orthodox Christian Archdiocese of North America

The spiritual needs of Antiochian faithful in North America were first served through the Syro-Arabian Mission of the Russian Orthodox Church in 1895. In 1895, the Syrian Orthodox Benevolent Society was organized by Antiochian immigrants in New York City. Raphael Hawaweeny, a young Damascene clergyman serving as professor of Arabic language at the Orthodox theological academy in Kazan, Russia, came to New York to organize the first Arabic-language parish in North America in 1895, after being canonically received under the omophorion of the head of the Russian Church in North America. Saint Nicholas Cathedral, now located at 355 State St. in Brooklyn, is considered the "mother parish" of the Archdiocese.

On March 12, 1904, Hawaweeny became the first Orthodox bishop to be consecrated in North America. He traveled throughout the continent and established new parishes. The unity of Orthodoxy in the New World, including the Syrian Greek Orthodox community, was ruptured after the death of Bishop Raphael in 1915 and by the Bolshevik revolution in Russia and the First World War. Unity returned in 1975 when Metropolitan Philip Saliba, of the Antiochian Archdiocese of New York, and Metropolitan Michael Shaheen of the Antiochian Archdiocese of Toledo, Ohio, signed the Articles of Reunification, ratified by the Holy Synod of the Patriarchate. Saliba was recognized as the Metropolitan Primate and Shaheen as Auxiliary Archbishop. A second auxiliary to the Metropolitan, Bishop Antoun Khoury, was consecrated at Brooklyn's Saint Nicholas Cathedral, in 1983. A third auxiliary, Bishop Basil Essey was consecrated at Wichita's St. George Cathedral in 1992. Two additional bishops were added in 1994, Bishop Joseph Zehlaoui and Bishop Demetri Khoury.

The Archdiocesan Board of Trustees (consisting of 60 elected and appointed clergy and lay members) and the Metropolitan's Advisory Council (consisting of clergy and lay representatives from each parish and mission) meet regularly to assist the Primate in the administration of the Archdiocese. Currently, there are 256 parishes and missions in the Archdiocese.

Headquarters

358 Mountain Rd., Englewood, NJ 07631, Tel. (201)871-1355 Fax (201)871-7954

Media Contact, Very Rev. Fr Thomas Zain, 52 78th St., Brooklyn, NY 11209, Tel. (718)748-7940 Fax (718)855-3608

Email: FrJoseph@antiochian.org

Website: www.antiochian.org

Officers

Primate, Archbishop Philip Saliba, 358 Mountain Rd., Englewood, NJ 07631 -

Metropolitan of New York and all North America, Tel. (210)871-1355

Bishop Antoun Khouri, 358 Mountain Rd., Englewood, NJ 07631-Bishop of Miami and the Southeast, Tel. (201)871-1355

Bishop Joseph Zehlaoui, 454 S. Lorraine Blvd., Los Angeles, CA 90020 -Bishop of Los Angeles and the West, Tel. (323)934-3131

Bishop Basil Essey, 1559 N. Woodlawn, Wichita, KS 67208 -Bishop of Wichita and Mid-America, Tel. (316)687-3169

Bishop Thomas Joseph, 4407 Kanawa, Charleston WV 25304 -Bishop of Oakland, PA, Charleston, WV and the Mid Atlantic, Tel. (304)926-0009

Bishop Alexander Mufarrij, 10820 Rue La Verdue, Montreal, QC H3L2L9 -Bishop of Ottawa, Eastern Canada and Upstate New York, Tel. (514)388-4344

Periodicals

The Word, Again Magazine

Apostolic Catholic Assyrian Church of the East, North American Dioceses

The Holy Apostolic Catholic Assyrian Church of the East is the ancient Christian church that developed within the Persian Empire from the day of Pentecost. The Apostolic traditions testify that the Church of the East was established by Sts. Peter, Thomas, Thaddaeus and Bartholomew from among the Twelve and by the labors of Mar Mari and Aggai of the Seventy. The Church grew and developed carrying the Christian gospel into the whole of Asia and islands of the Pacific. Prior to the Great Persecution at the hands of Tamer'leng the Mongol, it is said to have been the largest Christian church in the world.

The doctrinal identity of the church is that of the Apostles. The church stresses two natures and two Qnume in the One person, Perfect God-Perfect man. The church gives witness to the original Nicene Creed, the Ecumenical Councils of Nicea and Constantinople and the church fathers of that era. Since God is revealed as Trinity, the appellation "Mother of God" is rejected for the "Ever Virgin Blessed Mary Mother of Christ," we declare that she is Mother of Emmanuel, God with us!

The church has maintained a line of Catholicos Patriarchs from the time of the Holy Apostles until this present time. Today the present occupant of the Apostolic Throne is His Holiness

66

Mar Dinkha IV, 120th successor to the See of Selucia Ctestiphon.

Headquarters

Catholicos Patriarch, His Holiness Mar Dinkha, IV, Metropolitanate Residence, The Assyrian Church of the East, Baghdad, Iraq
Media Contact, Father Sleiman Shequel, 7201 N. Ashland, Chicago, IL 60626, Tel. (773)465-4777 Fax (773)465-0776
Email: ABSoro@aol.com
Website: www.cired.org/ace

BISHOPS -NORTH AMERICA

Diocese Eastern USA, His Grace Bishop Mar Aprim Khamis, 8908 Birch Ave., Morton Grove, IL 60053, Tel. (847)966-0617 Fax (847)966-0012; Chancellor to the Bishop, Rev. Chancellor C. H. Klutz, 7201 N. Ashland, Chicago, IL 60626, Tel. (773)465-4777 Fax (773)465-0776
Diocese Western USA, St. Joseph Cathedral, 680 Minnesota Ave., San Jose, CA 95125, Tel. (408)286-7377 Fax (408)286-1236
Diocese of Canada, His Grace Bishop Mar Emmanuel Joseph, St. Mary Cathedral, 57 Apted Ave., Weston, ON M9L 2P2, Tel. (416)744-9311
Comm. on Inter-Church & Religious Ed., His Grace Bishop Mar Bawai, Diocese of Seattle in WA, 165 NW 65th, Seattle, WA 98117, Tel. (206)789-1843

Apostolic Catholic Church*

The Apostolic Catholic Church, rooted in the New Testament, affirms the empowerment and the dignity of the poor, the needy and the oppressed by adopting a preferential option for those who are disenfranchised and marginalized in this society. Apostolic Catholicism is radically committed to the unconditional acceptance of all who are in need.

The special mission of the Apostolic Catholic Church is to be Christ's arms and legs, reaching out to those who suffer and are ignored by the world. We choose to serve others, ever mindful of the example of Christ, who "did not cling to his equality with God, but emptied himself to assume the condition of a slave." (Philippians 2: 6-7) Member: The Council of North American Old Catholic Bishops, the Florida Council of Churches, and International Council of Community Churches.

Headquarters

Apostolic Catholic Church
7813 N. Nebraska Ave., Tampa, FL 33604
Media Contact: Bishop Charles Leigh 813-238-6060, Email: Bishop-Chuck@apostolic catholicchurch.com
Email: Bishop-Chuck@apostoliccatholic church. com
Website: www.apostoliccatholicchurch.com

Other Organizations

Family Counseling Center, Kids in Bible, St James Catholic Worker House, Kids in Balance, New Springs School, Pisgah View Community Services, National Ex-Offender Reentry Initiative.

Periodicals

The Shofar

Apostolic Catholic Orthodox Church

The Apostolic Catholic Orthodox Church (ACOC) is a communion of persons gathered for worship and public ministry outreach within the Christian Apostolic tradition. The ACOC is creedal, renewal-oriented, and is a part of the autocephalous (self-ruling) Old Catholic Movement, which has its origins in the ancient Catholic Church of the Netherlands. The immediate history of the Old Catholic churches comes out of the reform movement that took place after the First Vatican Council (1869-70). The ACOC maintains a friendly relationship with the Old Catholic Church in the Netherlands.

The bishops of the newly forming churches received episcopal consecration in valid Apostolic lines from the church of the Netherlands, based in Utrecht, which had been a fully autonomous Catholic church. These churches became known as "Old Catholic" in reference to their insistence upon return to the basic tenets of Apostolic Christianity, and as defined by the seven Ecumenical Councils of the undivided Eastern and Western Christian churches.

The Old Catholic independent church movement came to the United States as early as the 1880's. Bishop DeLandes Berghes, an Austrian nobleman, ordained and consecrated a bishop with valid Old Catholic Apostolic lines, was sent to North America in 1914. Two of the bishops he consecrated in 1916, Carmel Henry Carfora and William Francis Brothers, are from whom the ACOC derives its lines of Apostolic Succession. The Apostolic Catholic Orthodox Church's governance is collegial and synodal, with clergy and lay persons sharing in its spiritual leadership and pastoral outreach, in the Spirit of Christ. Clerical celibacy (which is a matter of discipline) is optional among Old Catholics. In the ACOC, Holy Orders are open to both women and men, single or married. Graduate, Seminary and Clinical Pastoral education are required for candidates for ordination. Decisions pertaining to family planning are left to the conscience of married couples, through prayer and counseling.

Matters of faith in the Apostolic Catholic Orthodox Church are the same as in other liturgical churches as formulated in the apostles and Nicene Creeds. The Offices of bishop, priest, and deacon exist for the service of spiritual leadership in facilitating expressions of life with

God -in the celebration of the sacraments, counseling and pastoral care, teaching, and public advocacy of Gospel values. The sacraments are never denied to any person on grounds of gender, race, or marital status. The Holy Eucharist is the center of worship for the ACOC and all who are baptized are welcomed at the Lord's Table.

The Apostolic Catholic Orthodox Church emphasizes the importance of the life of the church as community, that all may be one in Christ (John 17), through mutual helpfulness, ministering to one another and all creation in love, through the diversity of personal giftedness and sensitivity to the particular needs of those being served. The church values and promotes spiritually based, courageous, and compassionate ministry to both personal and global needs. Ongoing spiritual growth is to be nourished through sacred study and contemplative prayer. The ACOC values ecumenical dialogue as an expression of the life of the church.

Headquarters

1900 St. James Place, Suite 880, Houston, TX 77056-4129, Tel. (713)266-2456 or (713)977-2855 Fax (713)266-0845 Email: info@apostoliccatholic.org www.apostolic catholic.org
Email: info@apostoliccatholic.org
Website: www.apostoliccatholic.org

Officers

Presiding Bishop, Most Rev. Diana C. Dale, 1900 St. James Place, Suite 880, Houston, TX 77056-4125, Tel. (713)266-2456 Email: dcdale@apostoliccatholic.org
Tresurer, Elizabeth F. Burleigh, J.D., 1900 St. James Place, Suite 880, Houston, TX 77056-41291, Tel. (713)334-0499
Ecumenical Officer, Rev. Robert L. Lewis Jr., P.O. Box 10483, Rockville, MD 20849, Tel. (240)401-0178
Register Agent, Biz Filings (for CA incorporation), 8040 Excelsior Dr., Ste. 200, Madison, WI 53717

BOARD REGIONAL REPRESENTATIVES
West: The Rev. Art Jacobson, 307 S. Dickinson, Rock Rapids, IA 51246, Tel. (605)261-8230
Gulf: The Rev. Jonathan Scalone, D. Min., 15220, Royal Windsor Lane #704, Ft. Myers, FL 33919, Tel. (239)368-2040
East: The Rev. Danielline Martinez, 130 Malcolm X Blvd., #412, New York, NY 10026, Tel. (347)526-0808
Military Contact: The Rev. Steven L. Dundas, LCDR, CHC, U.S. Navy, 9 Naval Hospital Camp LeJeune, NC 28547, Tel. (910)450-4070

OTHER ORGANIZATIONS:
Institute of Worklife Ministry, 1900 St. James Place, Suite 880, Houston, TX 77056-4129, Tel. (713)266-2456 Fax(713)266-0855 Email: www.apostoliccatholic.org

Periodicals

ACOC Quarterly Bulletin; Worklife Quarterly Newsletter

Apostolic Christian Church (Nazarene)

This body was formed in America by an immigration from various European nations, from a movement begun by Rev. S. H. Froehlich, a Swiss pastor, whose followers are still found in Switzerland and Central Europe.

Headquarters

Apostolic Christian Church Foundation, 1135 Sholey Rd., Richmond, VA 23231, Tel. (804)222-1943 Fax (804)236-0642
Media Contact, Exec. Dir., James Hodges
Email: accf@sprynet.com

Officers

Exec. Dir., James Hodges

Apostolic Christian Churches of America

The Apostolic Christian Churches of America was founded in the early 1830s in Switzerland by Samuel Froehlich, a young divinity student who had experienced a religious conversion based on the pattern found in the New Testament. The church, known then as Evangelical Baptist, spread to surrounding countries. A Froehlich associate, Elder Benedict Weyeneth, established the church's first American congregation in 1847 in upstate New York. In America, where the highest concentration today is in the Midwest farm belt, the church became known as Apostolic Christian. Church doctrine is based on a literal interpretation of the Bible, the infallible Word of God. The church believes that a true faith in Christ's redemptive work at Calvary is manifested by a sincere repentance and conversion. Members strive for sanctification and separation from worldliness as a consequence of salvation, not as a means to obtain it. Security in Christ is believed to be conditional based on faithfulness. Uniform observance of scriptural standards of holiness are stressed. Holy Communion is confined to members of the church. Male members are willing to serve in the military, but do not bear arms. The holy kiss is practiced and women wear head coverings during prayer and worship. Doctrinal authority rests with a council of elders, each of whom serves as a local elder (bishop). Both elders and ministers are chosen from local congregations, do not attend seminary and serve without compensation. Sermons are delivered extemporaneously as led by the Holy Spirit, using the Bible as a text.

Headquarters

3420 N. Sheridan Rd., Peoria, IL 61604
Media Contact, Secretary., William R. Schlatter, 14834 Campbell Rd., Defiance, OH 43512,

Tel. (419)393-2621 Fax (419)393-2144 Email: wrschlatter@juno.com
Email: Questions@ApostolicChristian.org; wr schlatter@juno
Website: www.apostolicchristian.org

Officers

Sec., Elder William R. Schlatter, 14834 Campbell Rd., Defiance, OH 43512, Tel. (419)393-2621, Fax (419)393-2144
Apostolic Christian World Relief -Humanitarian Aid to the World -www.acworldrelief.org

Periodicals

The Silver Lining

Apostolic Episcopal Church

The Apostolic Episcopal Church on Sept. 23-24, 2000 in New York City signed Concordats of Intercommunion with the following Christian Churches-The Anglican Independent Communion, The Ethiopian Orthodox Coptic Archdiocese of North and South America, The Uniate Western Orthodox Catholic Church, and the Byelorussian Orthodox National Church in Exile under the administration of His Beatitude Yury I. In effect, the Apostolic Episcopal Church thus became a Uniate Western Rite of the Orthodox Church of the East, using the 1928 Book of Common Prayer. In 1905, under the guidance of Archbishop Tikhon Bellavin (later Patriarch of Moscow), the Holy Synod in St. Petersburg approved the use of the Anglican Liturgy for Western Rite Orthodox Christians. Today this usage is called the Rite of St. Tikhon and is in use among many Orthodox Western Rite Jurisdictions.

This Pilgrimage to Orthodoxy among Anglicans began in 1712 with the Non-Jurors Anglican Hierarchy and faithful. These Non-Jurors were Anglican Clergy who in 1689 refused allegiance to King William III and Queen Mary, the usurpers who had overthrown King James II. In 1712 Metropolitan-Bishop Arsenios of the Alexandrine Patriarchate visited England and received many of these "British Katholicks" into the Orthodox Church.

Headquarters

World Mission HQS: 80-46 234 St. Jamaica, NY 11427-2116, Attn.: The Rt. Rev. Francis C. Spataro DD, Tel. (917)373-4036
Ohio Vicariate: The V. Rev. Michael B. Reed, St. Peter the Aleut Mission, 3423 Hunter Dr., N. Olmstead, OH 44070, Tel. (440)779-0272
Pennsylvania Vicariate: Rev. Dr. Sam Guido DD, OCR, Sam Guido Evangelical Ministries, 4253 Carolyn Dr., Slatington, PA 18080, Tel. (610)760-8342
N.Y, Brooklyn Vicariate: Rt. Rev. Louis Milazzo, OCR, St. Lucy's, 802 Kent Ave., Clinton Hill, NY 11205. (718)246-4848
Shenouda Seminary Dir.: Rev. Dr. Paget Mack, OCR, OSBM, P.O. Box 673, New York, NY 10035: OSBM_NY@yahoo.com

Belarus Home Mission, AWP, 19 Aqueduct St, Ossining, NY 10562, Tel. (914)762-7093
Media Contact, Rt. Rev. F. C. Spataro, 80-46 234 St., Queens, NY 11427
Email: Vil11427@att.blackberry.net Website: www.bertilpersson.com

Officers

President, The Rt. Rev. Francis C. Spataro, DD, OCR Tel. (718)740 4134 (24 hour number) Email: vil11427@att.blackberry.net
Archbishop of the Central & Western Province, USA, Dr. Wayne Ellis, PhD, OCR Email: wayneellis@me.com
OCR Primate: The Rt. Rev. Peter P. Brennan, OCR, DD, Email: ddamdg@aol.com
Vicar for Ohio: The V. Rev. Michael B. Reed, OCR: mbr1946@aol.com
Emeritus Primate for the AEC, The M. Rev. Bertil Persson, ThD, OCR, Archbishop of Scandinavia & Baltic Republics, Illerstigen 22, S-170 71, Solna, Sweden: berper@bredband.net
Pennsylvania Vicariate: Rev. Dr. Sam Guido, DD LOC Email: samsamtheman@aol.com
Shenouda Seminary Dir.: Rev. Dr. Paget Mack, OSBM: (347)342-8484
Vicar for Belarus: M. Rev. Emigidiusz J. Ryzy, OCR, DD Email: amworldpat@Verizon.net
Representative in U.K.: Prof. Dr. John Kersey: innerchurch@gmail.com
The Order of Corporate Reunion; The Vilatte Guild/Society of St. Cassian;

Periodicals

www.bertilpersson.com

Apostolic Faith Mission Church of God

The Apostolic Faith Mission Church of God was founded and organized July 10, 1906, by Bishop F. W. Williams in Mobile, Alabama. Bishop Williams was saved and filled with the Holy Ghost at a revival in Los Angeles under Elder W. J. Seymour of The Divine Apostolic Faith Movement. After being called into the ministry, Bishop Williams went out to preach the gospel in Mississippi, then moved on to Mobile.

On Oct. 9, 1915, the Apostolic Faith Mission Church of God was incorporated in Mobile under Bishop Williams, who was also the general overseer of this church.

Headquarters

Ward's Temple, 806 Muscogee Rd., Cantonment, FL 32533
Media Contact, Natl. Sunday School Supt., Bishop Thomas Brooks, 3298 Toney Dr., Decatur, GA 30032, Tel. (404)284-7596

Officers

BOARD OF BISHOPS
Presiding Bishop, Donice Brown, 2265 Welcome Cir., Cantonement, FL 32535, Tel. (904)968-5225

Bishop John Crum, 4236 Jackson St., Birmingham, AL, 35217; Bishop Samuel Darden, 25 Taunton Ave., Hyde Park, MA 02136; Bishop James Truss, P.O. Box 495, Lincoln, AL, 35096; Bishop T.C. Tolbert, Jr., 768 Grayton Rd., Ohatchee, AL 36271; Bishop Thomas Brooks, 3298 Toney Dr., Decatur, GA. 30032, Tel. (404)284-7596, Fax: (404)284-7173; Bishop Johnny Cunningham, P.O. Box 472 Century, Fla. 32535, Tel. (850)256-2443; Bishop Wayne Smiley, 228 Seville Circle, Mary Ester, FL 32569

NATIONAL DEPARTMENTS
Missionary Dept., Pres., Rosa Tolbert, 226 Elston Ave., Anniston, AL 36201
Youth Dept., Pres., Erma McClain, 600 Spencer Ave., Pensacola, FL 32514
Sunday School Dept., Supt., Thomas Brooks, 3298 Toney Dr., Decatur, GA 30032
Mother Dept., Pres., Mother Brenda Brooks, 3298 Toney Dr., Decatur, GA 30032

INTERNATIONAL DEPARTMENTS
Monrovia, Liberia, Bishop Beter T. Nelson, Box 3646, Bush Rhode Islane, Monrovia, Liberia

Periodicals
The Three-Fold Vision

Apostolic Faith Mission of Portland, Oregon

The Apostolic Faith Mission of Portland, Oregon, was founded in 1907. It had its beginning in the Latter Rain outpouring on Azusa Street in Los Angeles in 1906. Some of the main doctrines are justification by faith which is a spiritual new birth, as Jesus told Nicodemus and as Martin Luther proclaimed in the Great Reformation; sanctification, a second definite work of grace; the Wesleyan teaching of holiness; the baptism of the Holy Ghost as experienced on the Day of Pentecost and again poured out at the beginning of the Latter Rain revival in Los Angeles.

Mrs. Florence L. Crawford, who had received the baptism of the Holy Ghost in Los Angeles, brought this Latter Rain message to Portland on Christmas Day 1906. It has spread to the world by means of literature which is still published and mailed everywhere without a subscription price. Collections are never taken in the meetings and the public is not asked for money.

Camp meetings have been held annually in Portland, Oregon since 1907, with delegations coming from around the world. Missionaries from the Portland headquarters have established churches in Korea, Japan, the Philippines, Romania and many countries in Africa.

Headquarters
6615 SE 52nd Ave., Portland, OR 97206, Tel. (503)777-1741 Fax (503)777-1743
Media Contact, Superintendent, Darrel D. Lee
Website: www.apostolicfaith.org

Officers
President, Rev. Darrel D. Lee

Periodicals
Higher Way

Apostolic Lutheran Church of America

Organized in 1872 as the Solomon Korteniemi Lutheran Society, this Finnish body was incorporated in 1929 as the Finnish Apostolic Lutheran Church in America and changed its name to Apostolic Lutheran Church of America in 1962. This body stresses preaching the Word of God. There is an absence of liturgy and formalism in worship. A seminary education is not required of pastors. Being called by God to preach the Word is the chief requirement for clergy and laity. The church stresses personal absolution and forgiveness of sins, as practiced by Martin Luther, and the importance of bringing converts into God's kingdom.

Headquarters
P.O. Box 2948, Battle Ground, WA 98604-2948
Media Contact, Secretary, Gary Bertham
Website: www.apostolic-lutheran.org

Officers
Chairman, Wilfred Sikkila, 57 Ashby Road #2, New Ipswich, N.H. 03071
Treas., Ben Johnson, 98920 Keller Rd., Astoria, OR 97103
Secretary, Gary Bertham, 124 Binney Hill Rd., New Ipswich, N.H. 03071

Periodicals
Christian Monthly

Apostolic Orthodox Catholic Church of North America

The Christian Church was established by the Lord Jesus Christ and His Holy Apostles in Jerusalem in 33 A.D. From Jerusalem, the Church spread to other centers of the known world, including Constantinople (founded in 37 A.D.) and Kiev (45 AD.), founded by St. Andrew the First-Called Holy Apostle. In 864, missionary of the Church of Constantinople further extended the Orthodox Christian Faith in present-day Russia. In 988, Rus' Prince Vladimir converted and declared Orthodoxy the State religion, while hundreds of thousands of people were baptized in the Dnieper River at Kiev. The resulting Russian Orthodox Church became the greatest safe-guard and body of Orthodox Christians in the world.

The history of Holy Synod for the American Diaspora began in 1794 when Russian Orthodox Church missionaries established the first Orthodox mission on North American soil at present-day Kodiak, Alaska. Their missionary efforts continued down the Pacific coast in 1824, then across the whole continent. Being the canonical founder of Orthodox Christianity in North America, the Russian Orthodox Church maintained and presided over all Orthodox missions, churches, and Christians throughout North America without question or challenge for over 100 years. However, the 1917 Bolshevik Revolution which resulted in severe persecution and imprisonment of the Russian Orthodox Mother Church also resulted in the unrestrained rise of old-country nationalism and great ethnic turbulence between Orthodox Catholic Christians and their churches in North America. They seperated and divided, often violently, along ethnic and nationalist lines with each creating their own old-world ethnic administrations. The once long-held unity and single Orthodox Church canonical administration in North America was destroyed.

The Holy Synod for the American Diaspora is canonically independent and indigenous to North America and comprised of bishops, clergy and faithful possessing unbroken Apostolic Succession since the time of Jesus Christ's appointment of His Twelve Holy Apostles to the present day through American Orthodoxy's Luminary and Defender, Russian Orthodox Prelate-Archbishop Aftimios Ofiesh of Blessed Memory. The Holy Synod for the American Diaspora maintains unquestionable, canonical Apostolic Succession passed on to its bishops through its Russian Orthodox Mother Church by Archbishop Aftimios Ofiesh, his succeeding Bishops Sophronios Beshara and Christopher Contogeorge, their legal successors and through consecrating support of such memorable Orthodox leaders as Russian Patriarchal Exarch of North America Metropolitan Benjamin Fedchenkov and Albanian Orthodox Church Metropolitan Theophan Noli. In 1945, the Apostolic Succession and Canonicity of these bishops "and their successors" were declared in binding agreement to be unquestionable, valid, authentic and independent by the Orthodox Church Ecumenical Patriarchate of Constantinople, and recognition was furthermore attested to in 1951. English-speaking and non-ethnic restrictive, the Holy Synod for the American Diaspora's further validity is evidenced by its life, mind, discourse and teaching all being governed and directed in accordance with the Sacred Canons of the Most Ancient Holy Orthodox Catholic Church. The Holy Synod for the American Diaspora embraces the ideals and theology of Orthodoxy and freedom which Archbishop Aftimios Ofiesh stood for, taught and passed on by selfless devotion and love for Christ and His Church, and by his personal example.

Headquarters
Holy Synod for the American Diaspora, P.O. Box 346, Seward, NE 68434, Tel. (503)375-6175

Media Contact, Most Rev. Aftimios (L. Sinclair), Presiding Archbishop, 4696 Horseshoe Court SE, Salem, OR 97301; Tel. (575)375-6175
Email: baftimii@aol.com

Officers
Archbishop, Most Rev. Mar Melchizedek
The Secretary of the Synod, Most. Rev. Bishop Aftimios
Synod of Bishops, Most Rev. Bishop Spyridon, Most Rev. Bishop Valerian, Most Rev. Bishop Maximus

SEMINARY
St Elias School of Orthodox Theology, P.O. Box 346, Seward, NE 68434, Tel. (402)-643-9365

Armenian Apostolic Church of America
Widespread movement of the Armenian people over the centuries caused the development of two seats of religious jurisdiction of the Armenian Apostolic Church in the World-the See of Etchmiadzin, in Armenia, and the See of Cilicia, in Lebanon. In America, the Armenian Church functioned under the jurisdiction of the Etchmiadzin See from 1887 to 1933, when a division occurred within the American diocese over the condition of the church in Soviet Armenia. One group chose to remain independent until 1957, when the Holy See of Cilicia agreed to accept them under its jurisdiction.

Despite the existence of two dioceses in North America, the Armenian Church has always functioned as one church in dogma and liturgy.

Headquarters
Eastern Prelacy, 138 E. 39th St., New York, NY 10016, Tel. (212)689-7810 Fax (212)689-7168 Email: email@armenianprelacy.org
Western Prelacy, 6252 Honolulu Ave., La Crecsenta, CA 91214, Tel. (818)248-7737; Fax (818)248-7745 Email: prelacy@aol.com
Media Contact, Vazken Ghougassian
Email: prelacy@gis.net
Website: www.armprelacy.org

Officers
Eastern Prelacy, Prelate, Archbishop Oshagan Choloyan
Eastern Prelacy, Chpsn., Stephen Hagopian
Western Prelacy, Prelate, Archbishop Moushegh Mardirossian
Western Prelacy, Chpsn., Mrs. Rima Boghosian

DEPARTMENTS
Eastern Prelacy Offices, Executive Director, Vazken Ghougassian
AREC, Armenian Religious Educ. Council, Exec. Coord., Deacon Shant Kazanjian
ANEC, Armenian Natl. Educ. Council, Exec. Coord., Valtan Matiosian

Periodicals
Outreach

Armenian Apostolic Church, Dioceses of America*

The Armenian Apostolic Church was established at the foot of the biblical Mount Ararat in the ancient land of Armenia, where two of Christ's Holy Apostles, Saints Thaddeus and Bartholomew, preached Christianity in the 1st century. In A.D. 301, the kingdom of Armenia became history's first Christian nation, when king Tiridates III was baptized by Saint Gregory the Illuminator. Gregory became the patron saint of Armenia, the first in a line of 132 Catholicoi of all Armenians, and founder, in A.D. 303, of the historic Mother See of Holy Etchmiadzin, which still serves as the central, pre-eminent shrine of the worldwide Armenian Church. The present day Catholicos of All Armenians is His Holiness Karekin II.

In 1891, in fulfillment of a petition to Holy Etchmiadzin, Armenian immigrants to America built and witnessed the consecration of the New World's first Armenian Church, in Worcester, Massachusetts. In 1898, the 125th Catholicos of All Armenians, Mgrdich Khrimian, established a diocesan jurisdiction for the burgeoning communities in North and South America.

Today, the Diocese of the Armenian Church of America (Eastern) administers parishes in the eastern half of the U.S., with separate dioceses governing parishes in California (the Western Diocese, established 1927), Canada (the Canadian Diocese, established 1984), and South America (various jurisdictions and dates). Other centers of major significance for the Armenian Apostolic Church are the Catholicate of Cilicia (located in Lebanon), the Armenian Patriarchate of Jerusalem, and the Armenian Patriarchate of Constantinople.

Headquarters

Eastern Diocese, 630 Second Ave., New York, NY 10016-4885, Tel. (212)686-0710, Fax (212)779-3558, Website: www.armenianchurch-ed.net

Western Diocese, 3325 North Glenoaks Blvd., Burbank, CA 91504, Tel. (818)558-7474, Fax (818)558-6333, Website: www.armenianchurchwd.com

Canadian Diocese, 615 Stuart Ave., Outremont, QC H2V 3H2, Tel. (514)276-9479, Fax (514)276-9960, Website: www.armenianchurch.ca

Eastern Diocese Media Contact: Christopher Zakian, Director of Communications, Tel. (212) 686-0710, E-mail: chrisz@armeniandiocese.org
Email: mgizlechyan@armenianchurchwd.com
Website: www.armenianchurch.org

Officers

Eastern Diocese:
Archbishop Khajag Barsamian, Primate
Oscar Tatosian, Diocesan Council Chair
Western Diocese:
Archbishop Hovnan Derderian, Primate
Armen Hampar, Diocesan Council Chair

Canadian Diocese:
Bishop Bagrat Galstanian, Primate

Periodicals

The Armenian Church Magazine (Eastern Diocese), The Mother Church Magazine (Western Diocese)

Assemblies of God

From a few hundred delegates at its founding convention in 1914 at Hot Springs, Ark., the Assemblies of God has become one of the largest church groups in the modern Pentecostal movement with over 61 million adherents worldwide. Throughout its existence it has emphasized the power of the Holy Spirit to change lives and the participation of all members in the work of the church.

The revival that led to the formation of the Assemblies of God and numerous other church groups early in the 20th century began during times of intense prayer and Bible study. Believers in the United States and around the world received spiritual experiences like those described in the Book of Acts. Accompanied by baptism in the Holy Spirit and its initial physical evidence of "speaking in tongues," or a language unknown to the person, their experiences were associated with the coming of the Holy Spirit at Pentecost (Acts 2), so participants were called Pentecostals.

The church also believes that the Bible is God's inspired infallible Word to man, that salvation is available only through Jesus Christ, that divine healing is made possible through Christ's suffering and that Christ will return again for those who love Him. In recent years, this Pentecostal revival has spilled over into almost every denomination in a wave of revival sometimes called the charismatic renewal.

Assemblies of God leaders credit their church's rapid and continuing growth to its acceptance of the New Testament as a model for the present-day church. Aggressive evangelism and missionary zeal at home and abroad characterize the denomination. Assemblies of God believers observe two ordinances-water baptism by immersion and the Lord's Supper, or Holy Communion. The church is Trinitarian, holding that God exists in three persons-Father, Son and Holy Spirit.

Headquarters

Media Contact: Juleen Turnage, Dir. of Public Relations, Assemblies of God, 1445 N. Boonville Ave., Springfield, MO 65802-1894, Tel. (417)862-2781 Fax (417)862-5554 Email: info@ag.org
Email: Statistics@ag.org
Website: www.ag.org/top

Officers

Gen. Supt., George O. Wood
Asst. Supt., L. Alton Garrison

Gen. Sec., James T. Bradford
Gen. Treas., Doug Clay
World Missions, Exec. Dir., L. John Bueno
AG U.S. Missions, Exec. Dir., Zollie L. Smith, Jr.
Great Lakes: Larry H. Griswold, P.O. Box 620, Carlinville IL, Tel. (217)854-4600 Fax (614)396-0701
Gulf: Douglas Fulenwider, P.O. Box 7388, Alexandria, LA 71306, Tel. (318)445-6238, Fax (318)473-9344
North Central: Clarence W. St John, 1315 Portland Ave. S., Minneapolis, MN 55404, Tel. (612)332-2409, Fax (612)332-2510
Northeast: H. Robert Rhoden, 3525 Corrotoman Rd., Glen Allen, VA 23060, Tel. (804)755-6181
Northwest: Warren Bullock, 3535 Auburn Way S, Auburn, WA 98092, Tel. (253)833-8252, Fax (253)351-2943
South Central: J. Don George, 4401 N. Highway 161, Irving, TX 75038, Tel. (972)261-1919 Fax (972)261-1895
Southeast: Dan Betzer, 6901 Harbor Ln., Ft. Myers, FL 33919, Tel. (239)936-6277, Fax (239)936-9365
Southwest, Richard Dresselhaus, 6126 Bernadette Ln., San Diego, CA 92120 Tel. (619)286-9361
Language Area –West Spanish, Jesse Miranda Jr., 55 Fair Dr., Costa Mesa, CA 92626, Tel. (714)556-3610, Fax (714)966-5471
Language Area Other, Nam Soo Kim, 13030 31st Ave Flushing NY 11354, Tel. (718)321-7800, Fax (718)321-9394
Ethnic Fellowship, John E. Maracle, P O Box 83387, Phoenix, AZ 85071, Tel. (602)216-6001, Fax (602)216-6004
Language Area – East Spanish, Saturnino Gonzalez, 830 California Woods Cir, Orlando FL 32824, Tel. (407)850-9861, Fax (407)852-9887
Ordained Female – A. Elizabeth Grant, P.O. Box 990, Springfield MO 65801, Tel. (417)833-5562, Fax (417)833-5568
Ordained Pastor under 40 – R Bryan Jarrett, P.O. Box 99, Wylie, TX 75098, Tel. (417)495-1116, Fax (972)495-4913
Division of the Treasury, Gen. Treas., Doug Clay
Division of Church Ministries and Discipleship, Executive Director, L. Alton Garrison
Division of World Missions, Exec Dir., L. John Bueno
Division of U.S. Missions, Exec. Dir., Zollie L. Smith, Jr.
Division of Publication, Gospel Publishing House, Natl. Dir., J. T. Wray
Division of Communications, Natl. Dir., Juleen Turnage

Periodicals

Enrichment -A Journal for Pentecostal Ministry, Rangers NOW, Today's Pentecostal Evangel, Heritage, On Course

Assemblies of God International Fellowship (Independent/Not affiliated)

April 9, 1906 is the date commonly accepted by Pentecostals as the 20th-century outpouring of God's spirit in America, which began in a humble gospel mission at 312 Azusa Street in Los Angeles. This spirit movement spread across the United States and gave birth to the Independent Assemblies of God (Scandinavian). Early pioneers instrumental in guiding and shaping the fellowship of ministers and churches into a nucleus of independent churches included Pastor B. M. Johnson, founder of Lakeview Gospel Church in 1911; Rev. A. A. Holmgren, a Baptist minister who received his baptism of the Holy Spirit in the early Chicago outpourings, was publisher of Sanningens Vittne, a voice of the Scandinavian Independent Assemblies of God and also served as secretary of the fellowship for many years; Gunnar Wingren, missionary pioneer in Brazil; and Arthur F. Johnson, who served for many years as chairman of the Scandinavian Assemblies.

In 1935, the Scandinavian group dissolved its incorporation and united with the Independent Assemblies of God of the U.S. and Canada which by majority vote of members formed a new corporation in 1986, Assemblies of God International Fellowship (Independent/Not Affiliated).

Headquarters

P. O. Box, San Diego, CA 92192, Tel. (858)677-9701 Fax (858)677-0038
Media Contact, Exec. Dir. & Ed., Rev. T. A. Lanes
Email: admin@agifellowship.org; info@agifellowship.org
Website: www.agifellowship.org

Officers

Exec. Dir., Rev. T. A. Lanes
Sec., Rev. George E. Ekeroth
Treas., M. J. Ekeroth
Canada, Sec., Harry Nunn, Sr., 15 White Crest Ct., St. Catherines, ON 62N 6Y1

Periodicals

Fellowship

Associate Reformed Presbyterian Church (General Synod)

The Associate Reformed Presbyterian Church (ARP) developed from two groups that formed in Scotland in the 17th and 18th Centuries — the Covenanters and Seceders. These two movements developed into the Reformed Presbyterian Church of Scotland and the Associate Church of Scotland respectively, and their members migrated to America because of religious and political upheaval in Britain. The two merged in 1782 and eventually became known as the Associate Reformed Presbyterian Church. The church continues its commitment to the fundamental truths on which it was founded: the Lordship of Jesus Christ and the free offer of the Gospel of grace.

We are a Presbyterian and Reformed Chuch rooted in the historic Reformed tradition as expressed in the Westminster Confession of Faith and Catechisms. Each local congregation elects ruling elders to the session, and deacons to the diaconate. In this representative form of government, the session oversees the total ministry of the congregation and is concerned primarily with the spiritual life of the church. The diaconate is concerned primarily with material needs.

The governing body above the local session is the presbytery, which oversees a group of congregations in a specific geographical area. The hightest governing body is the General Synod, composed of all ARP ministers and at least one elder from each congregation. The Synod meets annually to worship together and conduct business.

Headquarters

Associate Reformed Presbyterian Center, 1 Cleveland St., Greenville, SC 29601-3696, Tel. (864)232-8297
Email: modquery@arpsynod.org
Website: www.arpsynod.org

Officers

Moderator: The Rev. Andrew Putnam, 6161 Mount Gallant Rd., York, SC 29745, 803-366-5577, andrewputnan@mac.com
Moderator-Elect: Dr. Steven Suits, 116 Indian Ridge Ct., Irmo, SC 29063
Principal Clerk: The Rev. C. Ronald Beard, D.D., 3132 Grace Hill Rd., Columbia, SC 29204, 803-782-3896, rbcard1@sc.rr.com
Treasurer: Guy H. Smith, III, 1 Cleveland St., Greenville, SC 29601-3696, Tel. (864)232-8297

INSTITUTIONS

Agencies at ARP Center in Greenville, SC:
Central Services: Paul Bell, Executive Director, pbell@arpsynod.org
Christian Education Ministries: Rev. Brent Turner, D. Min., Exec. Director, bturner@arpsynod.org
Outreach North America: Rev. Alan Avera, D. Min., Executive Director, onadir@arpsynod.org
The Associate Reformed Presbyterian: Mrs. Delores McDonald, Editor, arpeditor@arpsynod.org
Word Witness, Board of Foreign Missions: Rev. Frank van Dalen, Executive Director, fvandalen@worldwitness.org

OTHER INSTITUTIONS

Bonclarken Conference Center, Pres., Joseph "Chip" Sherer, 500 Pine Drive., Flat Rock, NC 28731, Tel. (828)692-2223, csherer@bonclarken.com
Erskine College and Theological Seminary: Dr. David Norman, Ph.D., President, P.O. Box 72, Due West, SC 29639, 864-379-8833, norman@erskine.edu
ARP Women's Ministries: Mrs. Elaine Reed, President, 114 Dudley Lane, Goose Creek, SC 29445, 843-572-6427, jelainereed@comcast.net

Periodicals

The Associate Reformed Presbyterian, The Adult Quarterly

The Association of Free Lutheran Congregations

The Association of Free Lutheran Congregations, rooted in the northern European revival movements, was organized in 1962 by a Lutheran Free Church remnant which rejected merger with The American Lutheran Church. The original 42 congregations were joined by other like-minded conservative Lutherans, and there has been more than a sixfold increase in the number of congregations. Members subscribe to the Apostles', Nicene and Athanasian creeds; Luther's Small Catechism; and the Unaltered Augsburg Confession. The Fundamental Principles and Rules for Work (1897) declare that the local congregation is the right form of the kingdom of God on earth, subject to no authority but the Word and the Spirit of God.

Distinctive emphases are, (1) the infallibility and inerrancy of Holy Scriptures as the Word of God; (2) congregational polity; (3) the spiritual unity of all believers, resulting in fellowship and cooperation transcending denominational lines; (4) evangelical outreach, calling all to enter a personal relationship with Jesus Christ; (5) a wholesome Lutheran pietism that proclaims the Lordship of Jesus Christ in all areas of life and results in believers becoming the salt and light in their communities; (6) a conservative stance on current social issues.

A two-year Bible school and a theological seminary are in suburban Minneapolis. The AFLC is in fellowship with sister churches in Canada, Brazil, Mexico, and India.

Headquarters

3110 E. Medicine Lake Blvd., Minneapolis, MN 55441, Tel. (763)545-5631 Fax (763)545-0079
Media Contact, Pres., Rev. Elden K. Nelson
Email: webmaster@aflc.org
Website: www.aflc.org

Officers

Pres., Rev. Elden K. Nelson, 3110 E. Medicine Lake Blvd., Minneapolis, MN 55441, Tel. (763)545-5631, Fax (763)545-0079, Email: president@aflc.org
Vice Pres., Rev. Michael Brandt, 3110 E. Medicine Lake Blvd., Minneapolis, MN 55441, Tel(763)545-5631, Email: vpres@aflc.org

Sec., Rev. Brian Davidson, 3110 E. Medicine Lake Blvd., Minneapolis, MN 55441, Tel(763)545-5631 Fax(763)545-0079 Email: briand@aflc.org

Periodicals

The Lutheran Ambassador

Association of Independent Evangelical Lutheran Churches

The AIELC was established, as a response to the affiliation need of independent missions and churches originally of the Latino community in the USA and worldwide, which are commited to the learning and teaching of Lutheran Doctrine and Theology. We are a Lutheran denomination that provide support and guidance to independent missions and churches to be better prepared for the work in the Kingdom of God at the light of Lutheran understanding of Confessing Christ. As part of our affiliation process we don't ask independent missions and churches to surrender their buildings or administrative independency; nor do we require them to provide financial support to the main denomination itself.

Our current worlwide membership is estimated as approximately 35,000 members with Churches in Scotland, Channel Islands, India, South Africa, Argentina, Ecuador, Colombia, Puerto Rico, Haiti, Chile, Venezuela and the USA. We have active Concordat with religious bodies in the USA and abroad, among them the Evangelical Community Church-Lutheran, the Athanasian Catholic Church of the Augsburg Confession, and the Lutheran Orthodox Church. We hold active membership at the Queens Federation of Churches in New York.

Headquarters

14020 27th Avenue; Astoria, NY 11102, Tel. (718)278-3894

Email: mainoffice@aielc.org Website: www. associationofindependentevangelicallutheran churches.org

Officers

The Rev. Dr. Pedro Bravo-Guzmán, Presiding Bishop, 14-22 27th Ave, Astoria, NY 11102, Tel. (718)278-3894, Email: pbravoguzman @aielc.org

The Rev. Dr. Francis C. Spataro, Bishop Emeritus, 14-22 27th Ave, Astoria, NY 11102, Tel. (718)278-3894, Email: vil11427@my cingular.blackberry.net

The Rev. Dr. Peter P. Brennan, Bishop Visitor, 14-22 27th Ave, Astoria, NY 11102, Tel. (718)278-3894, Email: Ddamdg@aol.com

The Rev. Dr. Bishop Louis Marcel Pierre, Bishop for the Caribbean, 14-22 27th Ave, Astoria, NY 11102, Tel. (718)278-3894, Email: louispierre_73@hotmail.com

The Rev. Dr. Bishop Louis Mphahlele, Bishop for Africa, 14-22 27th Ave, Astoria, NY 11102, Tel. (718)278-3894, Email: lutheran united@webmail.co.za

The Rev. Dr. Bishop Adolfo Acuña, Bishop for South America, 14-22 27th Ave, Astoria, NY 11102, Tel. (718)278-3894, Email: icli_ comunicaciones@yahoo.com.ar

The Rev. Jesus Sierralta, Bishop for Venezuela, 14-22 27th Ave, Astoria, NY 11102, Tel. (718)278-3894, Email: icalve@yahoo.com.ve

The Rev. Paul Lorentzen, Assistant to the Presiding Bishop, 14-22 27th Ave, Astoria, NY 11102, Tel. (718)278-3894, Email: pal10314@aol.com

Miss Christine Dobush, Public Relations and Acting Secretary Director, 14-22 27th Ave, Astoria, NY 11102, Tel. (718)-278-3894, Email: cdobush@inch.com

Mr. Ivan Egas Alprecht, Treasurer, 14-22 27th Ave, Astoria, NY 11102, Tel. (718)278-3894, Email: aielcsecretariat@aielc.org

The Rev. Dr. Juan Verdugo Martinez, Lutheran Biblical Institute in Chile, Dean, 14-22 27th Ave, Astoria, NY 11102, Tel. (718)278-3894, Email: pentateuco754@hotmail.com

Global Aid Foundation

Association of Vineyard Churches — please see Vineyard USA

Baptist Bible Fellowship International

Organized on May 24, 1950, in Fort Worth, TX, the Baptist Bible Fellowship was founded by about 100 pastors and lay people who had grown disenchanted with the policies and leadership of the World Fundamental Baptist Missionary Fellowship, an outgrowth of the Baptist Bible Union formed in Kansas City in 1923 by fundamentalist leaders from the Southern Baptist, Northern Baptist and Canadian Baptist Conventions. The BBF elected W. E. Dowell as its first president and established offices and a threeyear (now four-year with a graduate school) Baptist Bible College.

The BBF statement of faith was essentially that of the Baptist Bible Union, adopted in 1923, a variation of the New Hampshire Confession of Faith. It presents an infallible Bible, belief in the substitutionary death of Christ, his physical resurrection and his premillennial return to earth. It advocates local church autonomy and strong pastoral leadership and maintains that the fundamental basis of fellowship is a missionary outreach. The BBF vigorously stresses evangelism and the international missions office reports 901 adult missionaries working on 110 fields throughout the world. There are BBF-related churches in every state of the United States, with special strength in the upper South, the Great Lakes region, southern states west of the Mississippi, Kansas and California. There are seven related colleges and one graduate school or seminary.

A Committee of Forty-Five, elected by pastors and churches within the states, sits as a representative body, meeting in three subcommittees, each chaired by one of the principal officers-an administration committee chaired by the president, a missions committee chaired by a vice-president and an education committee chaired by a vicepresident.

World Mission Service Center

Baptist Bible Fellowship Missions Bldg., 720 E. Kearney St., Springfield, MO 65803, Tel. (417)862-5001 Fax (417)865-0794; Mailing Address, P.O. Box 191, Springfield, MO 65801 Media Contact, Mission Dir., Dr. Jon Konnerup, P.O. Box 191, Springfield, MO 65801

Email: csbc@cherrystreet.org
Website: www.bbfi.org

Officers

Pres., Rev. Linzy Slayden, 14100 E 86th St N, Owasso, OK 74055, Tel. (918)272-2003

First Vice Pres., Rev. Mike Frazier, 515 Whipple Ave NW, Canton, OH 44708, Tel. (330)477-6267

Second Vice Pres., Rev. Keith Gillming, 3025 N Lindbergh Blvd, Saint Louis, MO 63074, Tel. (314)291-6919

Third Vice Pres., Rev. Dan Lamb, 8080 SR 124, Hillsboro, OH 45133-9303, Tel. (937)393-2911

Sec., Rev. Jim Goodman, 117 CR 3452, Clarksville, AR 72830, Tel. (479)754-3910

Treas., Rev. Howard Braymer, P.O. Box 2537, Harrison, AR 72602, Tel. (870)741-8755

Periodicals

The Baptist Bible Tribune

The Baptist General Conference — please see Converge Worldwide (BGC)

Baptist Missionary Association of America

A group of regular Baptist churches organized in associational capacity in May, 1950, in Little Rock, Ark., as the North American Baptist Association. The name changed in 1969 to Baptist Missionary Association of America. There are several state and numerous local associations of cooperating churches. In theology, these churches are evangelical, missionary, fundamental and for the most part premillennial.

Headquarters

9219 Sibley Hole Rd., Little Rock, AR, Tel. (501)455-4977 Fax (501)455-3636

Mailing Address, P.O. Box 30910, Little Rock, AR 72260-0910

Media Contact, Disciple Guide Information Services, Texarkana, AR 71854, Tel. (870)772-4550 Fax (870)772-5451

Email: bmaam@bmaam.com
Website: www.bmaam.com

Officers

Presiding Officers

President: Paul Bullock, 6710 Countryside Dr., Texarkana, AR 71854-2410, (870)330-9528 or (903)832-2063 Email: pastor.rrbc@yahoo.com

First Vice President: Ed Stephenson, 93 Elliott Rd., Greenbrier, AR 72058-9265, (501)679-5848, Email: ed@springhillbaptistchurch.info

Second Vice President: Jason Aultman, 660 Whispering Wind Cir., Conway, AR 72032-3482, (501)329-5153 or (501)327-0637, Email: jasonaultman@conwaycorp.net

Recording Secretaries: James Ray Raines, 5609 N. Locust St., North Little Rock, AR 72116-6229, (501)945-2640 or (501)758-4093, Email: jam@aristotle.net; Greg Medenwald, 310 Quail Hollow Pl., Hattiesburg, MS 39402-8974, (601)264-8087 or (601)264-8987, Email: magnoliabcms@aol.com; Jerome Cooper, 4613 Loop 245, Texarkana, Arkansas 71854-1263, Tel. (870)772-4550 or (903)278-9249, Email: jerome@discipleguide.org

BMA Theological Seminary, Department of Christian Education: Dr. Charley Holmes, President, 1530 East Pine Street; Mailing address: P.O. Box 670, Jacksonville, TX 75766-0670, Tel. (903)586-2501 Fax (903)586-0378

LIFEWORD MEDIA MINISTRIES
Department of Radio/Television, Executive Director: Steve Crawley, 611 Locust Ave.; Mailing Address: P.O. Box 6, Conway, AR 72033-0006, Tel. (501)329-6891 Fax (501)329-7951, Email: steve@lifeword.org, Website: www.lifeword.org

DISCIPLEGUIDE CHURCH RESOURCES
Department of Church Resources, Executive Director: Kevin W. Clayton, D.Min., 4613 Loop 245, Texarkana, AR 71854-1263, Tel. (870)772-4550 Fax (870)772-5451, Email: kevin@discipleguide.org, Website: www. DiscipleGuide.org Publishing Ministry, Jerome Cooper, publishing ministry director, jerome@discipleguide.org, 4613 Loop 245, Texarkana, AR 71854-1263, Website: www. DiscipleGuide.org, Tel. (870)772-4550; Orders (800)333-1442 Fax (870)772-5451

Conference Ministry, Donny Parrish, conference ministry director, Email: donny@disciple guide.org, P.O. Box 10356, Conway, AR 72034-0005, Website: www.DiscipleGuide.org, Tel. (501)513-3726 Fax (501)513-2159

Camp Ministry, Daniel Springs Baptist Encampment, James Speer, camp ministry director, Email: jspeer9064@discipleguide.org, P.O. Box 310, Gary, TX 75643-0310, Website: www.DiscipleGuide.org, Tel. (903)685-2433 or (800)332-2309 Fax (903)685-2422

Bobby Hudgens, research and development officer, bhudgens@discipleguide.org, 4613

Loop 245, Texarkana, AR 71854-1263, Tel. (870)772-4550 Fax (870)772-5451

BMAA DEPARTMENT OF MISSIONS
Executive Director: John D. Smith, D. Min. in Missiology, 9219 Sibley Hole Rd., Little Rock, AR; Mailing Address: P.O. Box 30910, Little Rock, AR 72260-0910, Tel. (501)455-4977 Fax (501)455-3636, Email: jdsmith@bmaam.com Website: www.bmaam.net
Director of Operations-North America: Larry Barker, 9219 Sibley Hole Rd., Little Rock, AR 72209; Mailing address: P.O. Box 30910, Little Rock, AR 72260), Tel. (501)455-4977 Fax (501)455-3636, Email: larry@bmaam.com
Director of Operations-Missions Support Ministries: Dr. Ralph Izard, 9219 Sibley Hole Rd., Little Rock, AR 72209; Mailing address: P.O. Box 30910, Little Rock, AR 72260, Tel. (501)455-4977 Fax (501)455-3636 Email: bmmi@bmaam.com
Director of Operations-Europe/Asia/Africa/Australia: Jerry D. Kidd, 9219 Sibley Hole Rd., Little Rock, AR 72209; Mailing address: P.O. Box 30910, Little Rock, AR 72260, Tel. (501)455-4977 Fax (501)455-3636, Email: jkidd@bmaam.com
Director of Operations-Latin America: Felix Knott, 9219 Sibley Hole Rd., Little Rock, AR 72209; Mailing address: P.O. Box 30910, Little Rock, AR 72260, Tel. (501)455-4977 Fax (501)455-3636, Email: knott@bmaam.com
Director of Operations-Armed Forces & Institutional Chaplaincy: David Norvell, CH LTC Retired, 687 S. Avila Heights, Alexander, AR 72002-8727, Tel. (501)213-6657, Email: arkatexs@gmail.com
Director of Student Ministries: Donny Parrish, P.O. Box 126, Forney, TX 75126-0126, Tel. (972) 564-9553, Email: donny@fellowshipforney.org

NATIONAL BROTHERHOOD
President: Collin Jones, 1016 N. Franklin St., Blytheville, AR 72315-1818

NATIONAL WOMEN'S MISSIONARY AUXILIARY
President: Valarie Fish, P.O. Box 66, Emerson, AR 71740, Tel. (870)547-2998, Email: dvfish@swat.coop

LIFEWORD MEDIA MINISTRIES
Department of Radio/Television, Executive Director: Steve Crawley, 611 Locust Ave.; Mailing Address: P.O. Box 6, Conway, AR 72033-0006, Tel. (501)329-6891 Fax (501)329-7951, Email: steve@lifeword.org, Website: www.lifeword.org

DISCIPLEGUIDE CHURCH RESOURCES
Department of Church Resources, Executive Director: Kevin W. Clayton, D.Min., 4613 Loop 245, Texarkana, AR 71854-1263, Tel. (870)772-4550 Fax (870)772-5451, Email: kevin@discipleguide.org, Website: www.DiscipleGuide.org

Publishing Ministry, Jerome Cooper, publishing ministry director, 4613 Loop 245, Texarkana, AR 71854-1263, Tel. (870)772-4550; Orders (800)333-1442 Fax (870)772-5451, Email: jerome@discipleguide.org, Website: www.DiscipleGuide.org,
Conference Ministry, Donny Parrish, conference ministry director, P.O. Box 10356, Conway, AR 72034-0005, Tel. (501)513-3726 Fax (501)513-2159, Email: donny@discipleguide.org, Website: www.DiscipleGuide.org
Camp Ministry -Daniel Springs Baptist Encampment: James Speer, camp ministry director, P.O. Box 310, Gary, TX 75643-0310, Tel. (903)685-2433, (800)332-2309 Fax (903)685-2422, Email: jspeer9064@discipleguide.org, Website: www.DiscipleGuide.org
Research and Development Officer: Bobby Hudgens, 4613 Loop 245, Texarkana, AR 71854-1263, Tel. (870)772-4550 Fax (870)772-5451, Email: bhudgens@discipleguide.org

BMAA DEPARTMENT OF MISSIONS
Executive Director: John David Smith, D. Min. in Missiology, 9219 Sibley Hole Rd., Little Rock, AR, Mailing Address: P.O. Box 30910, Little Rock, AR 72260-0016, Tel. (501)455-4977 Fax (501)455-3636, Email: jdsmith@bmaam.com or bmaam@bmaam.com, Website: www.bmaam.net
Director of Operations -North America: Larry Barker, 9219 Sibley Hole Rd., Little Rock, AR 72209; Mailing address: P.O. Box 30910, Little Rock, AR 72260), Tel. (501)455-4977 Fax (501)455-3636, Email: larry@bmaam.com
Director of Operations-Missions Support Ministries: Dr. Ralph Izard, 9219 Sibley Hole Rd., Little Rock, AR 72209; Mailing address: P.O. Box 30910, Little Rock, AR 72260, Tel. (501)455-4977 Fax (501)455-3636, Email: bmmi@bmaam.com
Director of Operations-Europe/Asia/Africa/Australia: Jerry D. Kidd, 9219 Sibley Hole Rd., Little Rock, AR 72209; Mailing address: P.O. Box 30910, Little Rock, AR 72260, Tel. (501)455-4977 Fax (501)455-3636, Email: jkidd@bmaam.com
Director of Operations-Latin America: Felix Knott, 9219 Sibley Hole Rd., Little Rock, AR 72209; Mailing address: P.O. Box 30910, Little Rock, AR 72260, Tel. (501)455-4977 Fax (501)455-3636, Email: knott@bmaam.com
Director of Operations-Armed Forces & Institutional Chaplaincy: David Norvell, CH LTC, Retired, 687 S. Avila Heights, Alexander, AR 72002-8727, Tel. (501)213-6657, Email: arkatexs@gmail.com
Director of Student Ministries: Donny Parrish, P.O. Box 126, Forney, TX 75126-0126, Tel. (972) 564-9553, Email: donny@fellowshipforney.org

Beachy Amish Mennonite Churches

The Beachy Amish Mennonite Church was established in 1927 in Somerset County, Pa. following a division in the Amish Mennonite Church in that area. As congregations in other locations joined the movement, they were identified by the same name. There are currently 97 churches in the United States, 9 in Canada and 34 in other countries. Membership in the United States is 7,059, according to the 1996 Mennonite Yearbook. Beachy Churches believe in one God eternally existent in three persons (Father, Son and Holy Spirit); that Jesus Christ is the one and only way to salvation; that the Bible is God's infallible Word to us, by which all will be judged; that heaven is the eternal abode of the redeemed in Christ; and that the wicked and unbelieving will endure hell eternally. Evangelical mission boards sponsor missions in Central and South America, Ireland, and in Kenya, Africa.

The Mission Interests Committee, founded in 1953 for evangelism and other Christian services, sponsors homes for handicapped youth and elderly people, mission outreaches among the North American Indians in Canada and a mission outreach in Europe.

Headquarters

Media Contact, Paul L. Miller, 7809 S. Herren Rd. Partridge, KS 67566, Tel. (620)567-2286
Email: ivanbeachy@emypeople.net

Officers

Amish Mennonite Aid, Sec.-Treas., Ivan Beachy, 8916 Mission Home Rd., Free Union, VA 22940, Tel. (434)985-4954
Mission Interests Committee, Sec.-Treas., Marvin Weirich, 13200, CR 20, Middlebury, IN 46540, Tel. (574)825-2877
Choice Books of Northern Virginia, Supervisor, Simon Schrock, 4614 Holly Ave., FairFax, VA 22030, Tel. (703)830-2800
Calvary Bible School, Sec., Treas., Timothy J. Stoltzfus, 5815 Sulfur Mt. Rd., Harrison, AR 72601, Tel. (870)741-1614
Penn Valley Christian Retreat, Bd. Chmn., Wayne Schrock, RR 2, Box 165, McVeytown, PA 17015, Tel. (717)529-2935

Periodicals

The Calvary Messenger

Berean Fellowship of Churches

Founded 1932 in North Platte, Nebraska, this body emphasizes conservative Protestant doctrines.

Headquarters

5 Camelot Way, Box 1264, Kearney, NE 68845
Tel. (308)234-5373 Fax (308)234-5373
Media Contact, Pres., Pastor Doug Shada
Email: BereanChurches@aol.com
Website: www.bereanfellowship.org

Officers

Pres., Doug Shada
Vice Pres., Richard Crocker, 419 Lafayette Blvd., Cheyenne, WY 82009, Tel. (307)635-5914
Sec., Frank Van Campen, 513 Education Dr., Malcolm, NE 68402
Treas., Virgil Wiebe, 125 Split Rock Cir., Hollister, MO 65672

The Bible Church of Christ, Inc.

The Bible Church of Christ was founded on March 1, 1961 by Bishop Roy Bryant, Sr. Since that time, the Church has grown to include congregations in the United States, Africa and India. The church is Trinitarian and accepts the Bible as the divinely inspired Word of God. Its doctrine includes miracles of healing, deliverance and the baptism of the Holy Ghost.

Headquarters

1358 Morris Ave., Bronx, NY 10456, Tel. (718)588-2284 Fax (718)992-5597
Media Contact, Pres., Bishop Roy Bryant, Sr.
Email: bccbookstore@earthlink.net
Website: www.thebiblechurchofchrist.org

Officers

Pres., Bishop Roy Bryant, Sr.
Vice Pres., Bishop Darue Bryant
Sec., Mother Sissieretta Bryant
Treas., Elder Artie Burney

EXECUTIVE TRUSTEE BOARD
Chpsn., Bishop Christopher Powell, 1069 Morris Ave., Bronx, NY 10456, Tel. (718)992-4653

OTHER ORGANIZATIONS
Christian Bookstore, Mgr., Deacon Kenneth Anderson, Tel. (718)293-1928
Foreign Missions, Pres., Sr. Autholene Smith, Tel. (914)664-4602
Home Missions: Pres., Evangelist Mary Jackson, Tel. (718)992-4653
Minister of Education: Minister Abraham Jones, Tel. (718)588-2284
Ministers of Music, Ray Crenshaw, Tyrone Sumter, Ann Dunston
Prison Ministry Team, Evangelist Marvin Smith
Public Relations, Minister Abraham Jones
Sunday Schools, Gen. Supt., Elder A. M. Jones
Alan Bryant Memorial Institute, Principal, Moses Tolborh, Chocolate City, Monrobia, Liberia
Theological Institute, Pres., Dr. Roy Bryant, Sr.; Dean, Elder A. M. Jones
Vessels Unto Honor Deliverance Ministries, Pres., Elder Antoinette Cannaday
Youth, Pres., Deacon Tommy Robinson
Bishops: Bishop Roy Bryant, Sr., Bishop Eddie Citronnelli, Bishop Christopher Powell
Presiding Elders: Delaware: Elder Edward Cannon, R R Box 70-B5, Daimond Acre, Dagsboro, DE 19939, Tel. (302)732-3351; Mount Vernon: Elder Artie Burney, 100 W. 2nd St., Mount Vernon, NY 10550, Tel. (914)664-4602; Bronx, Elder Anita Robinson,

1358 Morris Ave., Bronx, NY 10456, Tel. (718)588-2284; Annex, Elder Reginald Gullette, 1069 Morris Ave., Bronx, NY 10456, Tel. (718)992-4653; Schenectady, New York: Elder Monica Hope, 1132 Congress St., Schenectady, New York 12303, Tel. (518)382-5625; North Carolina: Elder Darue Bryant, 512 W. Vernon Ave., Kingston, N.C. 28502, Tel. (252)527-7739; India, Dr. B. Veeraswamy, 46-7-34, Danavaya Peta, Rajahmunry, India, 533103

Periodicals
The Gospel Light, The Challenge, The Voice

Bible Fellowship Church
The Bible Fellowship Church grew out of divisions in the Mennonite community in Pennsylvania in the 1850s. Traditional church leadership resisted the freedom of expression and prayer meetings initiated by several preachers and church leaders. These evangelical Mennonites formed the Evangelical Mennonite Society. Over the next two decades various like minded groups in Canada, Ohio and Pennsylvania joined the Society.

In 1959 the Conference became the Bible Fellowship Church and new articles of faith were ratified. They now hold a unique combination of Reformed doctrines with insistence on "Believer Baptism" and Premillennialism.

Headquarters
Bible Fellowship Church, 3000. Fellowship Dr., Whitehall, PA 18052
Media Contact, David T. Allen, 1640 Ashley Ct., Kutztown, PA 19530; Tel. (610)285-2964
Email: DTA10@aol.com
Website: www.bfc.org

Officers
Chairman., Randall A. Grossman, 1400 Oak Lane, Reading, PA 19604
Vice Chairman, Robert A. Sloan, Jr., 105 Charles Blvd., Sinking Spring, PA 19608
Executive Director, David T. Allen, 1640 Ashley Ct., Kutztown, PA 19530
Sec., Ronald L. Kohl, 53 Kenwood Circle, Quakertown, PA 18951

BOARDS AND COMMITTEES
Executive Board, Bible Fellowship Church
Christian Education Committee
Church Extension Ministries
Board of Pensions
Pinebrook Bible Conference
Board of Missions
Committee On Credentials
Board of Publication and Printing
Victory Valley Camp
Church Health Committee
Pinebrook Educational Foundation
Board of Youth & Adults
Ministerial Candidates Committee
Strategic Planning Committee
Ministerial Relations Committee

Conference Judicatory
Committee on Credentials
Committee on Nominations

Periodicals
Fellowship News, OneVoice

Bible Holiness Church
This church came into being about 1890 as the result of definite preaching on the doctrine of holiness in some Methodist churches in southeastern Kansas. It became known as The Southeast Kansas Fire Baptized Holiness Association. The name was changed in 1945 to The Fire Baptized Holiness Church and in 1995 to Bible Holiness Church. It is entirely Wesleyan in doctrine, episcopal in church organization and intensive in evangelistic zeal.

Headquarters
304 Camp Dr., Independence, KS 67301, Tel. (620)331-3049
Media Contact, Gen. Supt., Leroy Newport

Officers
Gen. Supt., Leroy Newport
Gen. Sec., Michael Schaper, 944 Linns Mill Rd., Troy, MO 63379
Gen. Treas., Philip Davolt, 10624 Bluestem, Wichita, KS 67207

Periodicals
The Flaming Sword, John Three Sixteen

Bible Way Church of Our Lord Jesus Christ World Wide, Inc.
This body was organized in 1957 in the Pentecostal tradition for the purpose of accelerating evangelistic and foreign missionary commitment and to effect a greater degree of collective leadership than leaders found in the body in which they had previously participated.

The doctrine is the same as that of the Church of Our Lord Jesus Christ of the Apostolic Faith, Inc., of which some of the churches and clergy were formerly members. This organization has churches and missions in Africa, England, Guyana, Trinidad and Jamaica, and churches in 25 states in America. The Bible Way Church is involved in humanitarian as well as evangelical outreach with concerns for urban housing, education and economic development.

Headquarters
4949 Two-Notch Rd., Columbia, SC 29204, Tel. (718)774-0401
Media Contact, Chief Apostle, Presiding Bishop Huie Rogers
Email: mr.ed5strings@worldnet.att.net
Website: www.biblewaychurch.org

Officers
Presiding Bishop, Bishop Huie Rogers, 4949 Two Notch Rd., Columbia, SC 29204, Tel. (800)432-5612 Fax (803)691-0583

Brethren in Christ Church

The Brethren in Christ Church was founded in Lancaster County, Pa. in about the year 1778 and was an outgrowth of the religious awakening which occurred in that area during the latter part of the 18th century. This group became known as "River Brethren" because of their original location near the Susquehanna River. The name "Brethren in Christ" was officially adopted in 1863. In theology they have accents of the Pietist, Anabaptist, Wesleyan and Evangelical movements.

Headquarters

General Church Office, P.O. Box A, Grantham, PA 17027, Tel. (717)697-2634 Fax (717)697-7714
Media Contact, Dr. Warren L. Hoffman, Mod., Tel. (717)697-2634 Fax (717)697-7714
Email: dmcniven@bic-church.org
Website: www.bic-church.org

Officers

Dr. Warren L. Hoffman, Mod. & Gen. Church Office Contact info.
Don McNiven, Gen. Sec. & Gen. Church Office Contact info.
Elizabeth Brown, Treas. & Gen. Church Office Contact info.

OTHER ORGANIZATIONS
General Conference Board, Chpsn., Dr. Mark Garis, 504 Swartley Rd., Hatfield, PA 19440
Bd. for World Missions, Dr. Grace Holland, Chair, 21A Junction Rd., Dillsburg, PA. 17019-9469; Exec. Dir., Rev. John Brubaker, P.O. Box 390, Grantham, PA 17027-0390
Bd. for Stewardship Services, Terry Hoke; Chair; Box A, Grantham, PA 17027; Pension Fund Trustees, Eric Mann, Chair
Brethren in Christ Foundation, Elvin H. Peifer, CEO, P.O. Box 290, Grantham, PA, 17027-0290

Brethren Church (Ashland, Ohio)

The Brethren Church (Ashland, Ohio) was organized by progressive-minded German Baptist Brethren in 1883. They reaffirmed the teaching of the original founder of the Brethren movement, Alexander Mack, and returned to limited congregational government.

Headquarters

524 College Ave., Ashland, OH 44805, Tel. (419)289-1708 Fax (419)281-0450
Media Contact, Rev. Ken Hunn Official Position: Executive Director Tel; (419)289-1708 Fax (419) 281-0450 Email: Ken@brethrenchurch.org
Email: brethren@brethrenchurch.org
Website: www.brethrenchurch.org

Officers

Executive Dir., Rev. Ken Hunn
Dir. of Administrative Services, Mr. Stanley Gentle

Periodicals

The Brethren Evangelist

Bruderhof Communities Inc. — please see Churches Communities International

Calvary Chapel

Calvary Chapel is a non-denominational Christian church which began in 1965 in Costa Mesa, California. Calvary Chapel's pastor, Chuck Smith became a leading figure in what has become known as the "Jesus Movement."

It has been estimated that in a two-year period in the mid '70s, Calvary Chapel of Costa Mesa had performed well over eight thousand baptisms. During that same period, we were instrumental in 20,000 conversions to the Christian faith. Our decadal growth rate had been calculated by church growth experts to be near the ten thousand percent level. Calvary Chapel also ministers over the airwaves, and this must account for many of those who travel long distances to fellowship here. A Nielsen survey indicated that our Sunday morning Calvary Chapel service is the most listened-to program in the area during the entire week. As of 1987, Calvary's outreach has included numerous radio programs, television broadcasts, and the production and distribution of tapes and records. The missions outreach is considerable. Calvary Chapel not only supports Wycliffe Bible Translators, Campus Crusade, Missionary Aviation Fellowship, and other groups, but we donate to Third World needs. We then built a radio station in San Salvador and gave it to the local pastors there. We also gave money to Open Doors to purchase the ship that, in tandem with a barge, delivered one million Bibles to mainland China. Our financial commitment to missions exceeds the local expense budget by over 50%.

Today, Calvary Chapel of Costa Mesa, the church which only had twenty-five members has established more than five hundred affiliate Calvary Chapels across the world and is among the world's largest churches with more than thirty-five thousand calling it their home church. It is one of the ten largest Protestant churches in the United States.

Headquarters

Calvary Chapel of Costa Mesa (Main Office), 3800 S. Fairview St., Santa Ana, CA 92704-7014, Tel. (714)979-4422
Email: costamesa@calvarychapel.com
Website: www.calvarychapel.com

The Catholic Church

The largest single body of Christians in the United States, The Catholic Church is under the spiritual leadership of His Holiness the Pope. Its establishment in America dates back to the priests who accompanied Columbus on his second voyage to the New World. A settlement, later discontinued, was made in 1565 at St. Augustine, Florida. The continuous history of this Church in the Colonies began at St. Mary's in Maryland, in 1634.

INTERNATIONAL ORGANIZATION

His Holiness the Pope, Bishop of Rome, Vicar of Jesus Christ, Supreme Pontiff of the Catholic Church: Pope Benedict XVI, Joseph Ratzinger (born April 16, 1927; installed April 24, 2005)

Apostolic Nuncio to the United States: Archbishop Pietro Sambi, 3339 Massachusetts Ave., N.W., Washington, DC 20008, Tel. (202)333-7121 Fax (202)337-4036

U.S. ORGANIZATION

United States Conference of Catholic Bishops, 3211 Fourth St NE, Washington, DC 20017-1194, Tel. (202)541-3000
Email: commdept@usccb.org
Website: www.usccb.org

The United States Conference of Catholic Bishops (USCCB) is an assembly of the hierarchy of the United States and the U.S. Virgin Islands who jointly exercise certain pastoral functions on behalf of the Christian faithful of the United States. The purpose of the Conference is to promote the greater good which the Church offers humankind, especially through forms and programs of the apostolate fittingly adapted to the circumstances of time and place. This purpose is drawn from the universal law of the Church and applies to the episcopal conferences which are established all over the world for the same purpose.

The bishops themselves constitute the membership of the Conference and are served by a staff of approximately 350 lay people, clerics and religious located at the Conference headquarters in Washington, DC. A film, television and video reviewer works in New York City and a branch office of Migration and Refugee Services is located in Miami. The bishops themselves form approximately 21 committees, each with its own particular responsibility.

The Conference is organized as a corporation in the District of Columbia. Its purposes under civil law are, "To unify, coordiante, encourage, promote and carry on Catholic activities in the United States; to organize and conduct religious, charitable and social welfare work at home and abroad; to aid in education; to care for immigrants; and generally to enter into and promote by education, publication and direction the objects of its being."

Officers

UNITED STATES CONFERENCE OF CATHOLIC BISHOPS (USCCB)

GENERAL SECRETARIAT
General Secretary, Msgr. Ronny Jenkins, 3211 4th St. NE, Washington DC 20017-1194, Tel. (202)541-3000, Email: CommDept@usccb.org

Assoc. Gen. Sec., Linda Hunt, Assoc. Gen. Sec., Nancy Wisdo, Assoc. Gen. Sec. Rev. Brian Bransfield, 3211 4th St. NE, Washington DC 20017-1194, Tel. (202)541-3000, Email: CommDept@usccb.org

OFFICERS
President, Archbishop Timothy Dolan of New York
Vice President, Archbishop Joseph Kurtz of Louisville, Kentucky
Treasurer, Bishop Michael Bransfield of Wheeling-Charleston, West Virginia
Secretary, Bishop George V. Murry, SJ, of Youngstown

COMMITTEES AND CHAIRS:
Committee on Canonical Affairs and Church Governance – Bishop Thomas John Paprocki
Committee on Catholic Education – Bishop Thomas J. Curry
Committee on Clergy, Consecrated Life, and Vocations – Archbishop Robert J. Carlson
Committee on Communications – Bishop Gabino Zavala
Committee on Cultural Diversity in the Church – Bishop Jaime Soto
Committee on Divine Worship – Archbishop Gregory M. Aymond
Committee on Doctrine –Cardinal Donald W. Wuerl
Committee on Domestic Justice and Human Development – Bishop Stephen E. Blaire
Committee on Ecumenical and Interreligious Affairs – Archbishop Wilton D. Gregory
Committee on Evangelization and Catechesis – Bishop Richard J. Malone
Committee on International Justice and Peace – Bishop Howard J. Hubbard
Committee on Laity, Marriage, Family Life, and Youth -Bishop Kevin C. Rhoades
Committee on Migration – Archbishop José H. Gomez
Committee on National Collections – Bishop Kevin J. Farrell
Committee on Pro-Life Activities – Cardinal Daniel N. DiNardo
Committee on the Protection of Children and Young People – Bishop Blase J. Cupich
Administrative Committee – Archbishop Timothy M. Dolan
Committee on Budget and Finance – Bishop Michael J. Bransfield
Committee on Priorities and Plans – Bishop George V. Murry, S.J.
Executive Committee – Archbishop Timothy M. Dolan

For information on related organizations and individual dioceses, consult the Official Catholic Directory (published annually by P.J. Kenedy and Sons) and the USCCB website (www.usccb.org).

Periodicals
Catholic News Service, Origins, Bishops Committee on the Liturgy Newsletter

Christ Catholic Church

The church is a catholic communion established in 1968 to minister to the growing number of people who seek an experiential relationship with God and who desire to make a total commitment of their lives to God. The church is catholic in faith and tradition. Participating cathedrals, churches and missions are located in several states.

Headquarters

405 Kentling Rd., Highlandville, MO 65669, Tel. (417)443-3951

Media Contact, Archbishop, Most Rev. Karl Pruter

Email: bishopkarl@juno.com

Website: www.christcatholicchurch.com

Officers

Archbishop, Most Rev. Karl Pruter, P.O. Box 63, Highlandville, MO 65669

Periodicals

St. Willibrord Journal

Christ Community Church (Evangelical-Protestant)

This church was founded by the Rev. John Alexander Dowie on Feb. 22, 1896 at Chicago, Ill. In 1901 the church founded the city of Zion, IL and moved their headquarters there. Theologically, the church is rooted in evangelical orthodoxy. The Scriptures are accepted as the rule of faith and practice. Other doctrines call for belief in the necessity of repentance for sin and personal trust in Christ for salvation. The Christ Community Church is a denominational member of The National Association of Evangelicals. It has work in six other nations in addition to the United States. Branch ministries are found in Tonalea, Arizona.

Headquarters

2500 Dowie Memorial Dr., Zion, IL 60099, Tel. (847)746-1411 Fax (847)746-1452

Email: frontoffice@ccczion.org

Website: www.ccczion.org

Officers

Senior Pastor, Ken Langley

Christadelphians

The Christadelphians are a body of people who believe the Bible to be the divinely inspired word of God, written by "Holy men who spoke as they were moved by the Holy Spirit" (2 Pet. 1:21). They believe that the Old Testament presents God's plan to establish His Kingdom on earth in accord with the promises He made to Abraham and David; and that the New Testament declares how that plan works out in Jesus Christ, who died a sacrificial death to redeem sinners. They believe in the personal return of Jesus Christ as King, to establish "all that God spoke by the mouth of his holy prophets from of old" (Acts 3:21). They believe that at Christ's return many of the dead will be raised by the power of God to be judged. Those whom God deems worthy will be welcomed into eternal life in the Kingdom on earth. Christadelphians believe in the mortality of man; in spiritual rebirth requiring belief and immersion in the name of Jesus; and in a godly walk in this life. They have no ordained clergy, and are organized in a loose worldwide confederation of autonomous congregations (ecclesias) in approximately 100 countries. They are conscientiously opposed to participation in war. They endeavor to be enthusiastic in work, loyal in marriage, generous in giving, dedicated in preaching, and cheerful in living.

The denomination was organized in 1844 by Dr. John Thomas, who came to the United States from England, and who devoted his life to a search for the truth of God from the Bible. Dr. Thomas claimed no special revelation or position. Although his Bible scholarship is highly respected, he is not revered as a prophet in any way. The name Christadelphian ("Brethren in Christ") was adopted in 1864. Initially limited mostly to English-speaking countries, the denomination now exists worldwide.

Primary activities in North America include Sunday worship and Sunday Schools, midweek Bible classes, Bible Schools, and inter-ecclesial gatherings. In addition, the Williamsburg Christadelphian Foundation (WCF) sponsors and assists charitable and preaching activities in many parts of the world, both by itself and in conjunction with the outreach work of the Christadelphian Bible Missions.

(In North America, there are two Christadelphian groups, Central and Unamended.)

Headquarters

Media Contact, Trustee, Norman D. Zilmer, Christadelphian Action Society, 904 Woodview Ct., Mahomet, IL 61853-3623, Tel. (217)590-4108 or (217)586-7592

Email: nzilmer@aol.com

Website: www.christadelphia.org

Officers

Co-Ministers:

Norman Fadelle, 904 Woodview Ct., Mahomet, IL 61853-3623

Norman D. Zilmer, 904 Woodview Ct, Mahomet, IL 61853-3623, Email: nzilmer@aol.com; nfadelle@gmail.com

Williamsburg Christadelphian Foundation (WCF) www.wcfoundation.org

Periodicals

Christadelphian Tidings (www.Tidings.org)

Christian Brethren (also known as Plymouth Brethren)

Christian Brethren churches are bound together by common beliefs and practices but not by central organization. They are committed to the inerrancy of Scripture, to Trinitarian doctrine, and to the evangelical message of salvation by faith apart from works or sacrament. Their most recognizable feature is the weekly observance of the Lord's Supper as the focus of a full length service of worship, not prearranged and not clergy-led.

Originating in England and Ireland in the late 1820s, the Brethren were influenced by the counsel of Anthony Norris Groves, an English dentist, and the teaching of John Nelson Darby, an Irish clergyman. They recovered aspects of church practice and simplicity that had been obscured in the course of the centuries, such as an unwillingness to establish denominational governing structures and a reluctance to accept sectarian names. The nickname Plymouth Brethren arose spontaneously when a large Plymouth congregation was evangelizing throughout the English countryside. In recent years the term Christian Brethren has replaced Plymouth Brethren for the open branch of the movement in Canada and the British Commonwealth and to some extent in the United States. Neither name has legal status, except where required by national governments. There are no central offices and no corporate property in the USA or Canada.

In the late 1840s the movement divided. The so-called open assemblies, led initially by George Mueller of orphanage fame, stressed evangelism and foreign missions. It has grown to be the larger of the two branches. The autonomy of local congregations permits variations in practice and generally avoids wide-ranging division. The other branch focused more on doctrinal and ecclesiastical issues. From it came notable Bible teachers like Darby, William Kelly, C.H. Mackintosh (CHM), and F. W. Grant. Their books have had a wide influence, espe cially among premillennialists. These assemblies stress the interdependency of congregations. Local church decisions on doctrine and discipline are generally held to be binding on all assemblies. At times, when actions were debatable, division spread throughout the group. By 1900, there were seven or eight main groups. Since 1925, some divisions have been healed, reducing that number to three or four.

CORRESPONDENT

John H. Rush, 2872 Illinois Ave., Dubuque, IA 52001 Tel. (563)557-8535
Email: jrush@emmaus.edu

RELATED ORGANIZATIONS

Believers' Bookshelf, P.O. Box 261 Sunbury, PA 17801
Believers' Stewardship Services, 2250 Chaney Rd., Dubuque, IA 50201, Tel. (563)582-4818
ECS Ministries, 2250 Chaney Rd., Dubuque, IA 50201, Tel. (563)585-2070

Emmaus Bible College, 2570 Asbury Rd., Dubuque, IA 52001-3044, Tel. (563)588-8000
Christian Missions in Many Lands, P.O. Box 13, Spring Lake, NJ 07762-0013, Tel. (732)449-8880
Interest Ministries, 2060 Stonington Ave., Suite 101, Hoffman Estates, IL 60195, Tel. (847)519-1495
Stewards Foundation, 14285 Midway Rd., Ste. 330, Addison, TX 75001-3622, Tel. (972)726-6550
Stewards Ministries, 18-3 E. Dundee Rd., Ste. 100, Barrington, IL 60010, Tel. (847)842-0227

Christian Church (Disciples of Christ) in the United States and Canada*

Born on the American frontier in the early 1800s as a movement seeking the unity of all Christians, this body drew its major inspiration from Thomas and Alexander Campbell in western Pennsylvania and Barton W. Stone in Kentucky. Developing separately, the "Disciples, led by Alexander Campbell, and the "Christians," led by Stone, came together in 1832 in Lexington, KY

The Christian Church (Disciples of Christ) is marked by openness, diversity, a reasoned faith, and a commitment to the priesthood of all believers. The Disciples claim no official doctrine or dogma, and have rejected the use of creeds as "tests of fellowship." Membership is granted after a simple confession of belief in Jesus Christ and baptism by immersion—although most congregations accept transfers baptized by other forms in other denominations. The Lord's Supper—generally called Communion—is open to all Christians, and is practiced weekly, although no church law insists upon it. Thoroughly ecumenical, the Disciples helped organize the National and World Councils of Churches. The church is a member of the Churches Uniting in Christ. The Disciples and the United Church of Christ have declared themselves to be in "full communion" through the General Assembly and General Synod of the two churches. Official theological conversations have been going on since 1967 directly with the Roman Catholic Church.

Disciples have vigorously supported world and national programs of education, agricultural assistance, medical care, urban reconciliation, and aid to victims of war and calamity. Operating ecumenically, Disciples' personnel or funds work in more than 100 countries outside North America.

Three expressions of the church (congregational, regional and general) operate within strong but voluntary covenantal ties to one another. Entities in each expression manage their own finances, own their own property, call their own staff, and conduct their own programs. A General Assembly meets every two years and has voting representation from each congregation.

Headquarters

Disciples Center, 130 E. Washington St., P.O. Box 1986, Indianapolis, IN 46206-1986, Tel. (317)635-3100 Fax (317)635-3700

Media Contact, Communication Ministries, Executive Director, Wanda Bryant Wills Email: cmiller@cm.disciples.org; hbowers@disciples.org

Officers

Gen. Minister & Pres., Rev. Dr. Sharon E. Watkins, Tel. (317)635-3100 Fax (317)713-2417, Email: swatkins@disciples.org

Mod., Larry Brown, 2806 Country Club Dr., Chickasha, OK 73018.

1st Vice Mod., Juan Rodriguez, 6936 Grand Ave., Hammond, IN 46323.

2nd Vice Mod., Marilyn F. Williams, 7908 McGuire Dr., Raleigh, NC 27616.

GENERAL OFFICERS

Gen. Minister & Pres., Rev. Dr. Sharon E. Watkins, Tel. (317)635-3100 Fax (317)713-2417, Email: swatkins@disciples.org

Assoc. Gen. Minister & Vice Pres., Todd A Adams, Tel. (317)635-3100 FAX (317)713-2417, Email: tadams@disciples.orgAssoc. Gen Min. & Admin. Sec. Of the National

Convocation, Timothy M. James, Email: tjames@disciples.org

GENERAL MINISTRIES

Board of Church Extension, dba Church Extension, Pres., Trans. Pres. Lori L. Adams, 130 E. Washington St., P.O. Box 7030, Indianapolis, IN 46207-7030, Tel. (317)635-6500 Fax (317)635-6534, Email: bce@churchextension.org

Christian Board of Publication (Chalice Press), Pres., Cyrus N. White, 1221 Locust St., Suite 1200, St. Louis, MO 63166-0179, Tel. (314)231-8500 or (800)366-3383 Fax (314) 231-8524, Email: customerservice@chalice press.com

Christian Church Foundation, Inc., Pres., Gary W. Kidwell, Tel. (317)635-3100 or (800)366-8016 Fax (317)635-1991, Email: jcullumb@ccf.disciples.org

Council on Christian Unity, Inc., Pres., Robert K. Welsh, Tel. (317)713-2586 Fax (317)713-2588, Email: rwelsh@ccu.disciples.org

Disciples Benevolent Services, Pres., Mark D. Anderson, 149 Weldon Parkway, Suite 115, Maryland Heights, MO 63043-3103, Tel. (314)993-9000 Fax (314)993-9018, Email: nba@nbacares.org

Disciples of Christ Historical Society, Pres., Glen T. Carson, 1101 19th Ave. S., Nashville, TN 37212-2196, Tel. (615)327-1444 Fax (615) 327-1445, Email: mail@discipleshistory.org

Division of Homeland Ministries, dba Disciples Home Missions, Pres., Ron Degges, Tel. (317)635-3100 or (888)346-2631, Fax (317)635-4426, Email: homelandministries@dhm.disciples.org

Division of Overseas Ministries, Pres., David A. Vargas, Tel. (317)635-3100, Fax (317)635-4323, Email: dom@disciples.org

Higher Education and Leadership Ministries (HELM), Pres., Dennis L. Landon, 11477 Olde Cabin Rd., Ste. 310, St. Louis, MO 63141-7130, Tel. (314)991-3000 Fax (314)991-2957, Email: helm@helmdisciples.org.

Pension Fund, Pres., James P. Hamlett, 130 E. Washington St., Indianapolis, IN 46204-3645, Tel. (317)634-4504 Fax (317)634-4071, Email: pfcc1@pension.disciples.org

REGIONAL UNITS OF THE CHURCH

Alabama-Northwest Florida, Regional Minister, John P. Mobley, 861 Highway 52, Helena, AL 35080-7743, Tel. (205)425-5245 Fax (205)425-5246, Email: alnwfl@aol.com

Arizona, Regional Minister, Dennis L. Williams, 4423 N. 24th St., Ste 700, Phoenix, AZ 85016-5544, Tel. (602)468-3815 Fax (602)468-3816, Email: region@arizonadisciples.com

California, Northern-Nevada, Regional Min. and Pres., Ben Bohren, 9260 Alcosta Blvd., C-18, San Ramon, CA 94583-4143, Tel. (925)556-9900 Fax (925)556-9904, Email: info@ccncn.org

Canada, P.O. Box 25087, London, ON N6C 6A8, Tel. (519)472-9083 Fax (519)637-6407 Email: ccic1@sympatico.ca

Capital Area, Regional Minister, Lari R. Grubbs, 8814 Kensington Pkwy, Suite 208, Chevy Chase, MD 20815-6743, Tel. (301)942-8266 Fax (301)942-8366, Email: lgrubbs@cccadisciples.org

Central Rocky Mountain Region, Trans. Regional Minister, Jose Morales, Jr., 2950 Tennyson #300, Denver, CO 80212-3029, Tel. (303)561-1790 Fax (303)561-1795, Email: crmr_admin@crmrdoc.org

Florida, Trans Regional Minister, Rebecca Hale, 924 N. Magnolia Ave., Ste. 200, Orlando, FL 32803-3845, Tel. (407)843-4652, Fax (407)843-0272, Email: RegionalOffice@floridadisciples.org

Georgia, Regional Minister, Ray Miles, 2370 Vineville Ave., Macon, GA 31204-3163, Tel. (478)743-8649 or (800)755-0485 Fax (478) 741-1508, Email: ccinga@bellsouth.net

Great River Region, Executive Regional Minister, Barbara E. Jones, 9302 Geyer Springs Rd, P.O. Box 192058, Little Rock, AR 72219-2058, Tel. (501)562-6053 & (888)241-5531, Fax (501)562-7089, Email: office@grrcc.org

Idaho, South, Regional Administrator, Brenda S. Lynch, 619 12th Ave S, P.O. Box 1092, Nampa, ID 83653, Tel. (208)468-8976, Fax (208)468-8973, Illinois and Wisconsin,

Regional Minister and Pres., Teresa Dulyea-Parker, 1011 N. Main St., Bloomington, IL 61701-1753, Tel. (309)828-6293 Fax (309) 829-4612, Email: teresa@cciwdisciples.org

Indiana, Regional Minister, Richard L. Spleth, 1100 W. 42nd St., Indianapolis, IN 46208-3375, Tel. (317)926-6051 Fax (317)931-2034, Email: cci@ccindiana.org

Kansas, Regional Minister/Pres., Paxton Jones, 2914 S.W. MacVicar Ave., Topeka, KS 66611-1787, Tel. (785)266-2914 Fax (785)266-0174, Email: cck@kansasdisciples.org

Kansas City, Greater, Regional Min./Pres., Paul J. Diehl, Jr., 7600 W. 75th St, Suite 6, Overland Park, KS 66204-2853, Tel. (913)432-1414, Fax (913)432-3598, Email: office@kc disciples.org

Kentucky, General Minister, J. Gregory Alexander, 1125 Red Mile Rd., Lexington, KY 40504-2660, Tel. (859)233-1391 Fax (859) 233-2079, Email: cck@ccinky.net

Michigan, Regional Minister, Interim Co-Regional Ministers, Eugene James & Margaret Mills, 2820 Covington Ct., Lansing, MI 48912-4830, Tel. (517)372-3220 Fax (517)372-2705, Email: ccmr@michigan disciples.org

Mid-America Region, Regional Minister, Danny Stewart, 3328 Bennett Ln., P.O. Box 104298, Jefferson City, MO 65110-4298, Tel. (573)636-8149 Fax (573)636-2889, Email: ccma@socket.net

Montana, Regional Minister, Ruth A. Fletcher, 1019 Central Ave., Great Falls, MT 59401-3784, Tel. (406)452-7404 Fax (406)452-7404, Email: ccmt@bresnan.net

Nebraska, Regional Ministers, Kenneth W. Moore, 1268 S. 20th St., Lincoln, NE 68502-1612, Tel. (402)476-0359 or (800)580-8851 Fax (402)476-0350, Email: ccnebraska@alltel

North Carolina, Regional Minister, John M. Richardson, 509 N.E. Lee St., P.O. Box 1568, Wilson, NC 27894-1568, Tel. (252)291-4047 Fax (252)291-3338, Email: ccnc@nc disciples.org

Northeastern Region, Regional Minister, Mary Anne Glover, 765 Lafayette Ave., Brooklyn, NY 11411-1414 Tel. (718)443-9120 Fax (718) 949-5460, Email: nedisciples@verizon.net

Northwest Region, Regional Minister and Pres., Sandra Messick, P. O. Box 23819, Federal Way, WA 98093, Tel. (253)893-7202 Fax (425) 251-4967, Email: nwrcc@disciplesnw.org

Ohio, Regional Pastor and Pres., William H. Edwards, 355 E. Campus View Blvd, Suite 110, Columbus, OH 43235-5616, Tel. (614)433-0343 Fax (614)433-7285, Email: ccio@ccinoh.org

Oklahoma, Regional Pastor, Thomas R. Jewell, 301 N.W. 36th St., Oklahoma City, OK 73118-8661, Tel. (405)528-3577 Fax (405)528-3584, Email: tjewell@okdisciples.org

Oregon, Co-Regional Ministers, Douglas Wirt & Cathy Myers-Wirt, 0245 S.W. Bancroft St.,

Ste. F, Portland, OR 97239-4267, Tel. (503)226-7648 Fax (503)226-0598, Email: odmail@oregondisciples.org

Pacific Southwest Region, Co-Regional Minister-Pres., Don & Susan Gonzales Dewey, 2401 N. Lake Ave., Altadena, CA 91001-2418, Tel. (626)296-0385, Fax (626)296-1280, Email: pswr@discipleswr

Pennsylvania, Interim Regional Minister, William Allen, 134 Mathews St, P O Box 90, Greensburg, PA 15601-0090, Tel. (724)925-1350 Fax (724)925-1358, Email: cjohns@ padisciples.org

South Carolina, Regional Minister, Sotello V. Long, 1293 Orange Grove Rd., Charleston, SC 29407-3947, Tel. (843)852-4537 Fax (843) 744-5787, Email: rcccsc@aol.com

Southwest Region, Regional Minister Dani Loving Cartwright, P.O. Box 1689, Fort Worth, TX 76101-1689, Tel. (817)926-4687 Fax (817)926-5121, Email: ccsw@ccsw.org

Tennessee, Regional Minister and Pres., Glen J. Stewart, 7980 Coley Davis Rd, Nashville, TN 37221-2397, Tel. (615)646-3705 Fax (615) 646-3707, Email: ccdctn@bellsouth.net

Upper Midwest Region, Regional Minister and Pres., Bill Spangler-Dunning, 5064 Lincoln St, Newton, IA 50208-8327, Tel. (515)255-3168 Fax (641)791-3009, Email: bsd@upper midwestcc.org

Virginia, Regional Minister, George Lee Parker, 1290 Enterprise Dr., Lynchburg, VA 24502-5744, Tel. (434)846-3400 Fax (434)528-4919, Email: regoffice.ccinva@verizon.net

West Virginia, Regional Minister, Thaddaeus B. Allen, 1402 Washington Ave. Parkersburg, WV 26101-3427, Tel. (304)428-1681 Fax (304) 428-1684, Email: tallen@wvdisciples.org

Periodicals
Call To Unity

Christian Churches and Churches of Christ

The fellowship, whose churches were always strictly congregational in polity, has its origin in the American movement to "restore the New Testament church in doctrine, ordinances and life" initiated by Thomas and Alexander Campbell, Walter Scott and Barton W. Stone in the early 19th century.

Headquarters
Media Contact, No. American Christian Convention Dir., Rod Huron, 4210 Bridgetown Rd., Box 11326, Cincinnati, OH 45211, Tel. (513)598-6222 Fax (513)598-6471

Email: Jowston@cwv.edu

Website: www.cctoday.com, and, www.naccthe connectingplace.org

CONVENTIONS
North American Christian Convention, Dir., Rod Huron, 4210 Bridgetown Rd., Box 11326,

Cincinnati, OH 45211, Tel. (513)598-6222; NACC Mailing Address, Box 39456, Cincinnati, OH 45239

National Missionary Convention, Coord., Walter Birney, Box 11, Copeland, KS 67837, Tel. (316)668-5250

Eastern Christian Convention, Kenneth Meade, 5300 Norbeck Rd., Rockville, MD 20853, Tel. (301)460-3550

Periodicals
Christian Standard, Restoration Herald, Horizons, The Lookout

The Christian Congregation, Inc.

The Christian Congregation is a denominational evangelistic association that originated in 1787 and was active on the frontier in areas adjacent to the Ohio River. The church was an unincorporated organization until 1887. At that time a group of ministers who desired closer cooperation formally constituted the church. The charter was revised in 1898 and again in 1970.

Governmental polity basically is congregational. Local units are semi-autonomous. Doctrinal positions, strongly biblical, are essentially universalist in the sense that ethical principles, which motivate us to creative activism, transcend national boundaries and racial barriers. A central tenet, John 13 vs.34-35, translates to such respect for sanctity of life that abortions on demand, capital punishment and all warfare are vigorously opposed. All wars are considered unjust and obsolete as a means of resolving disputes.

Early leaders were John Chapman, John L. Puckett and Isaac V. Smith. Bishop O. J. Read was chief administrative and ecclesiastic officer for 40 years until 1961. Rev. Dr. Ora Wilbert Eads has been general Superintendent since 1961. Ministerial affiliation for independent clergymen is provided.

Headquarters
804 W. Hemlock St., LaFollette, TN 37766

Media Contact, Gen. Supt., Rev. Ora W. Eads, D.D., Tel. (615)562-8511

Email: Revalnas@aol.com

Website: netministries.org/see/churches.exe/ch10619

Officers
Gen. Supt., Rev. Ora W. Eads, D.D., 812 W. Hemlock St. LaFollette, TN 37766

Christian Methodist Episcopal Church*

The Christian Methodist Episcopal Church (CME) is a historically African-American denomination that was established in Jackson, Tennessee in 1870 when a group of former slaves, representing eight annual conferences of the Methodist Episcopal Church South organized the Colored Methodist Episcopal Church in America. In 1954 at its General Conference in Memphis, Tennessee it was overwhelmingly voted to change the term "Colored" to "Christian". On January 3, 1956 the official name became Christian Methodist Episcopal Church. Its boundaries reach from the continental United States, Alaska, Haiti, Jamaica, and the West African countries of Nigeria, Ghana, and Liberia. One of its most significant witnessing arenas has been the education of African Americans. Today the CME Church supports Paine College, August, GA; Lane College, Jackson, TN; Miles College, Birmingham, AL; Texas College, Tyler, TX; and the Phillips School of Theology in Atlanta, GA.

Headquarters
First Memphis Plaza, 4466 Elvis Presley Blvd., Memphis, TN 38116

Media Contact, Exec. Sec., Attorney Juanita Bryant, 3675 Runnymede Blvd., Cleveland Hts., OH 44121, Tel. (216)382-3559 Fax (216)382-3516, Email: juanbr4law@aol.com

Email: juanbr4law@aol.com

Website: www.c-m-e.org

Officers
Exec. Sec., Attorney Juanita Bryant, 3675 Runnymede Blvd., Cleveland Hts., OH 44121, Tel. (216)382-3559 Fax (216)382-3516, Email: juanbr4law@aol.com

OTHER ORGANIZATIONS

Christian Education, Gen. Sec., Dr. Carmichael Crutchfield, 4466 Elvis Presley Blvd., Ste. 214, Box 193, Memphis, TN 38116-7100, Tel. (901)345-0580 Fax (901)345-4118

Lay Ministry, Gen. Sec., Dr. Victor Taylor, 9560 Drake Ave., Evenston, IL 60203, Tel. (800)782-4335 x. 6029, Fax (312)345-6056, Email:taylor617@comcast.net

Evangelism & Missions, Gen. Sec., Dr. Willie C. Champion, 102 Pearly Top Dr., Glen Heights, TX 75154, Tel. (214)372-9505, Email: champ_dr@sbcglobal.net

Finance, Sec., Dr. Joseph C. Neal, Jr., P.O. Box 75085, Los Angeles, CA 90075, Tel. (323)233-5050

Editor, The Christian Index, Dr. Kenneth E. Jones, P.O. Box 431, Fairfield, AL 35064, Tel. (205929-1640 Fax (205)791-1910, Email: Goodoc@aol.com

Publication Services, Gen. Sec., Rev. William George, 4466 Elvis Presley Blvd., Memphis, TN 38116, Tel. (901)345-0580 Fax (901)767-8514, Email: WEG38@aol.com

Personnel Services, Gen. Sec., Rev. Tyrone T. Davis, P.O. Box 74, Memphis, TN 38101-0074, Tel. (901)261-3228, Email: tyrone.t.davis@concast.net

Women's Missionary Council, Pres., Dr. Elnora P. Hamb, 11321 S. Aberdeen St., Chicago, IL 60643, Tel. (773)264-2273, Email: hamb@sbcglobal.net

Ministry to Men, Gen. Sec., Mr. Leo Pinkett, 2850 Shoreland De. S.W., Atlanta, GA 30331, Email: lpinkettace@yahoo.com

BISHOPS

First District, Bishop William H. Graves, Sr., 4466 Elvis Presley Blvd., Ste. 222, Memphis, TN 38116, Tel. (901)345-0580

Second District, Bishop E. Lynn Brown, 7030 Reading Rd., Suite 244, Cincinnati, OH 45237, Tel. (513)772-8622, Email: bishopelynnbrown 84@yahoo.com

Third District, Bishop Paul A. G. Stewart, Sr., 5925 W. Florissant Ave., St. Louis, MO 63136, Tel. (314)381-3111, Email: BishopPStewart@ aol.com

Fourth District, Bishop Thomas L. Brown Sr., P.O. Box 2793, Jackson, MS 39207, Tel. (601)398-3926, Email: thomasl30087@bellsooth.net

Fifth District, Bishop Lawerence L. Reddick III, 310 18th St., N, Ste. 400D, Birmingham, AL 35203, Tel. (205)655-0346 Fax (205)251-4371, Email: reddick3@bellsouth.net

Sixth District, Bishop Othal H. Lakey, 1776 Peachtree Rd. NW, Suite 210, South Tower, Atlanta, GA 30309, Tel. (404)745-9689, Fax (404)745-0691

Seventh District, Bishop Thomas L. Hoyt, Jr., 6524 16th St. N.W., Washington, DC, Tel. (318)820-9512 & (318)780-8467, Email: thoytjr@aol.com

Eighth District, Bishop Ronald M. Cunningham., 1616 E. Illinois, Dallas, TX 75216, Tel. (214)372-9073, Email: bishoprc7302@aol.com

Ninth District, Bishop Henry M. Williamson, 3844 W. Slauson Ave., Ste. 1, Los Angeles, CA 90043, Tel. (213)294-3830, Email: hwillia531 @aol.com

Tenth District, Bishop Kenneth Wayne Carter, 2202 Emerald Oaks Ct., Arlington, TX 76017, Tel. (817)468-1397, Email: KWCarter@ hotmail.com

Retired, Bishop Nathaniel L. Linsey, Canterbury Subdivision, 190 Squire Lane, Fayettsville, GA 30214, Tel. (770)460-6897, Email: linseyn@bellsouth.net; Bishop

Dotcy I. Isom, 4326 Richwood Place, Memphis, TN 36125, Tel. (901)753-8123; Bishop Marshall Gilmore, 683 Beacontree Ct., Concord, NC 28027, Tel. (704)786-3226

Periodicals

The Christian Index, The Missionary Messenger

The Christian and Missionary Alliance

The Christian and Missionary Alliance was formed in 1897 by the merger of two organizations begun in 1887 by Dr. Albert B. Simpson, The Christian Alliance and the Evangelical Missionary Alliance. The Christian and Missionary Alliance is an evangelical church that stresses the sufficiency of Jesus as Savior, Sanctifier, Healer, and Coming King and has earned a worldwide reputation for its missionary accomplishments. The Canadian districts became autonomous in 1981 and formed The Christian and Missionary Alliance in Canada.

NATIONAL OFFICE

P.O. Box 35000, Colorado Springs, CO 80935-3500, Tel. (719)599-5999 Fax (719)593-8234

Media Contact, Rick Hemphill, Director of Communications

Email: info@cmalliance.org

Website: www.cmalliance.org

Officers

Pres., Rev. Gary M. Benedict D.D.

Corp. Vice Pres., Rev. Jonathan G. Schaeffer, D. Min.

Corp. Sec., Rev. David L. Goodin

Vice Pres., for Development Dennis K. Whalen

Vice Pres. for International Ministries, Rev. Robert L. Fetherlin, D. Min.

Interim Vice Pres., for Church Ministries, Rev. Daniel R. Wetzel, MPS

Vice Pres. for Operations/Treasurer, Mr. Kenneth E. Baldes, MBA

BOARD OF DIRECTORS

Chpsn., Dr. Jonathan G. Schaeffer

Vice Chpsn., Rev. Jeffrey P. Brown

DISTRICTS

Cambodian, Rev. Sonly Goy, 1616 S. Palmetto Ave., Ontario, CA 91762-5972, Tel. (909)988-9434

Central, Rev. Jeffrey A Miller, 1231 High St., Wadsworth, OH 44281-9421, Tel. (330)336-2911

Central Pacific, Rev. R. Douglas Swinburne, JR., 715 Lincoln Ave., Woodland, CA 95695-4018 Tel. (530)662-2500

E. Pennsylvania, Rev. J. Wayne Spriggs, 1200 Spring Garden Dr., Middletown, PA 17057-3266, Tel. (717)985-9240

Great Lakes, Rev. Jeffrey P. Brown, 2250 Huron Parkway, Ann Arbor, MI 48104-5151 Tel. (734)677-8555

Hmong, Mr. Steven X. Her, DMin., 12287 Pennsylvania St., Thornton, CO 80241-3113, Tel. (303)252-1793

Korean, Rev. Han Young Baek, 550 Durie Ave., #201, Closter, NJ 07624-2012, Tel. (201)750-6750

Metropolitan, Rev. Bruce K. Terpstra, DMin., P.O. Box 7060, Newark, NJ 07107-0600, Tel. (973)412-7025

MidAmerica, Rev. Rodger L. Peck, 1301 S. 119th St., Omaha, NE 68144-1605, Tel. (402)330-1888

Mid-Atlantic, Rev. Randall B. Corbin, DMin., 292 Montevue Lane, Frederick, MD 21702-2812, Tel. (301)620-9934

Midwest, Rev. Jonathan W. Rich, 260 Glen Ellyn Rd., Bloomingdale, IL 60108-1826, Tel. (630)893-1355

New England, Rev. Thomas R. Flanders, P.O. Box 288, South Easton, MA 02375-0288 Tel. (508)238-3820

Northeastern, Rev. Daniel D. Miller, 6275 Pillmore Dr., Rome, NY 13440-7334 Tel. (315)336-4720

Northwestern, Rev. Donald A. Wiggins, DMin., 8860 College View Dr., St. Bonifacius, MN 55375-4504 Tel. (952)446-9318

Ohio Valley, Rev. P. David Klinsing, 7537 Burton Dr., Liberty Township, OH 45044-9032, Tel. (513)755-5950

Pacific NW, Rev. Matthew C. Boda, P.O. Box 3020, Wilsonville, OR 97070-3020 Tel. (503)685-9160

Puerto Rico, Rev. Luis A. Felipa, P.O. Box 1625 P.O. Box 1625, Sabana Hoyos, PR 00688-1625, Tel. (787)861-0101

Rocky Mountain, Rev. Timothy P. Owen, DMin., 2545 St. Johns Ave., Billings, MT 59102-4652, Tel. (406)656-4233

South Atlantic, Rev. Michael D. Noel, DMin., 10801 Johnston Rd., Ste. 125, Charlotte, NC 28226-4490, Tel. (704)543-0470

South Pacific, Rev. William W. Malick, 27377 Via Industria, Temecula, CA 92590-3699, Tel. (951)719-1191

Southeastern, Rev. Charles R. Hughes Jr, P.O. Box 720430, Orlando, FL 32872-0430 Tel. (407)823-9662

Southern, Rev. Fred G. King, 5998 Deerfoot Parkway, Trussville, AL 35173-2604 Tel. (205)661-9585

Southwestern, Rev. Mark R Searing, DMin, 5148 Treepoint Dr., Arlington, TX, 76017-1938 Tel. (817)561-0879

Spanish Central, Rev. Angel M. Garcia, P.O. Box 5477, McAllen, TX 78502-5477, Tel. (956)565-1600

Spanish Eastern, Rev. Jorge Cuevas, P.O. Box 865, Union City, NJ 07087-0865, Tel. (201)866-7202

Vietnamese, Dr. Tai Anh Nguyen, ThD., P.O. Box 2468, Fullerton, CA 92837-0468 Tel. (714)491-8007

W. Great Lakes, Rev. Gary E. Russell, W6107 Aerotech Dr., Appleton, WI 54914-7504, Tel. (920)734-1123

W. Pennsylvania, Rev. Jeffrey A. Norris, DMin., 341 Chestnut St., Punxsutawney, PA 15767-0600, Tel. (814)938-6920

NATIONAL ETHNIC ASSOCIATIONS

Association of African Churches, Dr. Amos B. Miamen, President, 3080 195th Ct., Lynwood, IL, 60411-6325 (708)252-5541

Association of African-American Churches, Rev. Terrence L. Nichols, President, 120 Lancaster Way, Vallejo, CA 94591-6836, Tel. (707)310-3926

Association of Filipino Churches, Rev. Lorenzo Collado, President,1618 Arkansas Ln, Arlington, TX 76013-6110 Tel. (817)704-4220

Association of Montagnard Churches, Rev. Glik Rahlan, President, 1100 Justice Ave.,

Charlotte, NC 28706-1824, Tel. (704)377-0425

Chinese Churches Association, Rev. Michael Y. K. Wu, Exec. Dir., 10515 Key West St., Temple City, CA 91780-3463, Tel. (626)319-9143

Haitian Association, Rev. Jean R. Jean, President, 6582 Springmeadow Dr., Greenacres, FL 33413-3400, Tel. (561)213-1637

Lao Association, Rev. Prasert Duangmala, President, 4838 Wild Grape Dr., Stockton, CA 95212-2711, (209)406-0943

Native American Association, Rev. Zane M. Williams, Acting President, 1600 Oak Hills Rd. SW, Bemidji, MN 56601-8826, (480)580-3945

Portuguese-Speaking Association of Churches, Rev. Santi E. Basiletti, 1100 Allenbrook Ln, Roswell, GA 30075-2996 (770)643-0180

Spanish Western Association, Rev. Samuel Calderon, President, 11157 S. Broadway, Apt. 4, Los Angeles, CA 90061-1963, Tel. (818)205-3647

ETHNIC/CULTURAL MINISTRIES

Alliance Jewish Ministries, Rev. Rosilio Roman, P.O. Box 35000, Colorado Springs, CO 80935-3500, Tel. (719)265-2053

Islamic-Hindu, Rev. Rosilio Roman, P.O. Box 35000, Colorado Springs, CO 80935-3500, Tel. (719)265-2053

Periodicals

Alliance Life

Christian Reformed Church in North America

The Christian Reformed Church represents the historic faith of Protestantism. Founded in the United States in 1857 and active in Canada since 1905, it asserts its belief in the Bible as the inspired Word of God, and is creedally united in the Belgic Confession (1561), the Heidelberg Catechism (1563), and the Canons of Dort (1618-19).

Headquarters

2850 Kalamazoo Ave., SE, Grand Rapids, MI 49560, Tel. (616)224-0832 Fax (616)224-5895

Media Contact, Exec. Dir., Rev. Joel R. Boot

Email: executive-director@crcna.org

Website: www.crcna.org

Officers

Executive Director, Maynard Wiersma

Representative: Western Canada, Ron Knol (Edmonton, AB)

Representative: Western Canada, Dave Broughton (Duncan, BC)

Representative: Ontario, Wayne DeBoer

Executive Assistant, Jill Jones

Finance and Systems Administrator, Mary Benn

Administrative Assistant, Laurinda Beimers

OTHER ORGANIZATIONS

Back to God Ministries International, Dir. Dr. Robert C. Heerspink

Christian Reformed Home Missions, Dir., Rev. Moses Chung
Christian Reformed World Missions, US, Dir., Dr. Gary Bekker
Christian Ref. World Missions, Canada, Dir., Vacant
Christian Reformed World Relief, US, Dir., Andrew Ryskamp
Christian Reformed World Relief, Canada, Dir., Ms. Ida Kaastra Mutoigo
Faith Alive Christian Resources, Dir., Mark Rice
Ministers' Pension Fund, Admn., Marjorie Csomor

Periodicals
The Banner

Christian Union

Organized in 1864 in Columbus, Ohio, the Christian Union stresses the oneness of the Church with Christ as its only head. The Bible is the only rule of faith and practice and good fruits the only condition of fellowship. Each local church governs itself.

Headquarters
455 Mill St., Greenfield, OH 45123, Tel. (937)981-2760
Media Contact: Rev. Jim Eschenbrenner, 308 North Waugh Rd., Hendrick, IA 52563, Tel. (641)653-4785, Email: jimesch@gmail.com or Rev. Marion Hunerdosse, Pres., 10619 N. Marsh Ave., Kansas City, MO 64157-7756, Tel. (816)781-5044, Email: mlh922@sbc global.net
Email: mlh922@sbcglobal.net
Website: www.christianunion.com

Officers
Pres., Rev. Marion Hunerdosse, 10619 N. Marsh Ave., Kansas City, MO 64157-7756, Tel. (816)781-5044, Email: mlh922@sbcglobal.net
Sec., Joseph Cunningham, 1005 N. 5th St., Greenfield, OH 45123, Tel. (937)981-3476, Email: joecuw@gmail.com
Asst. Sec., Jim Eschenbrenner, 308 North Waugh Road., Hedrick, IA 52563, Tel. (641)653-4785, Email: jimesch@gmail.com
Treas., Rev. Neal Skiles, 80 Licking View Dr., Heath, OH 43056-1530, Tel.740-522-4845 Fax (740)522-6076, Email: skiles@roadrunner.com

Periodicals
The Christian Union Witness; Christian Union Witness Express (bulletin)

Church of the Brethren*

Eight German Pietists/Anabaptists, including their leader, Alexander Mack, founded the Brethren movement in 1708 in Schwarzenau, Germany. Begun in reaction to spiritual stagnation in state churches, the Brethren formed their own movement, modeled on the first-century church. They practice believer baptism, anointing, and the love feast. They have no other creed than the New Testament, hold to principles of nonviolence, no force in religion, Christian service, and simplicity. They migrated to the colonies beginning in 1710 and settled at Germantown, Pennsylvania, moving westward and southward to plant congregations across the United States and Puerto Rico. Emphasis on religion in daily life led to the formation of Brethren Volunteer Service in 1948, which continues today. There are now sister denominations and missions in Nigeria, Haiti, India, Brazil, the Dominican Republic, and mission workers in several other places around the world.

Headquarters
Church of the Brethren General Offices, 1451 Dundee Ave., Elgin, IL 60120, Tel. (847)742-5100, Toll-free (800)323-8039, Fax (847)742-6103, Email: cobweb@brethren.org
Brethren Service Center: 500 Main St., P.O. Box 188, New Windsor, MD 21776, Tel. (410)635-8710, Fax (410)635-8789, Email: bsc@brethren.org
Media Contact: Cheryl Brumbaugh-Cayford, Director of News Services, 1451 Dundee Ave., Elgin, IL 60120, Tel. (847)742-5100, Toll-free (800)323-8039, Fax (847)742-1407, Email: cbrumbaugh-cayford@brethren.org
Email: cobweb@brethren.org; jclements@brethren.org
Website: www.brethren.org

Officers
Moderator: Timothy P. Harvey, 416 Church Ave., SW, Roanoke, VA 24016; Email: pastortim@central.roacoxmail.com
Moderator-elect: Robert W. Krouse, P.O. Box 437, Bethel, PA 19507; Email: bobkrouse@gmail.com
Secretary: Fred W. Swartz, 102 W. Rainbow Dr., Bridgewater, VA 22812; Email: acsecretary@brethren.org
Annual Conference Director: Chris Douglas, 1451 Dundee Ave., Elgin, IL 60120; Tel. (847)742-5100; Email: cdouglas@brethren.org

EXECUTIVE LEADERSHIP FORUM:
General Secretary: Stanley J. Noffsinger, 1451 Dundee Ave., Elgin, IL 60120; Tel. 847-742-5100; Email: snoffsinger@brethren.org
Executive Director, Centralized Resources & Chief Financial Officer/Treasurer: Judy E. Keyser, 1451 Dundee Ave., Elgin, IL 60120; Tel. 847-742-5100; Email: jkeyser@brethren.org
Executive Director & Publisher, Brethren Press: Wendy McFadden, 1451 Dundee Ave., Elgin, IL 60120; Tel. 847-742-5100; Email: wmcfadden@brethren.org
Executive Director, Congregational Life Ministries: Jonathan A. Shively, 1451 Dundee Ave., Elgin, IL 60120; Tel. 847-742-5100; Email: jshively@brethren.org

Executive Director, Global Mission Partnerships: Jay A. Wittmeyer, 1451 Dundee Ave., Elgin, IL 60120; Tel. 847-742-5100; Email: mission@brethren.org

Executive Director, Brethren Service Center: Roy E. Winter, P.O. Box 188, New Windsor, MD 21776; Tel. 410-635-8748; Email: rwinter@brethren.org

Executive Director, Ministry: Mary Jo Flory-Steury, 1451 Dundee Ave., Elgin, IL 60120; Tel. 847-742-5100; Email: mjflorysteury@brethren.org

Executive Director, Systems & Services & Assistant Treasurer: LeAnn Wine, 1451 Dundee Ave., Elgin, IL 60120; Tel. 847-742-5100; Email: lwine@brethren.org

Manager, Office Operations: Nancy B. Miner, 1451 Dundee Ave., Elgin, IL 60120; Tel. 847-742-5100; Email: nminer@brethren.org

Director, Human Resources: Karin Krog, 1451 Dundee Ave., Elgin, IL 60120; Tel. 847-742-5100; Email: kkrog@brethren.org

Periodicals

Messenger

Church of Christ

Joseph Smith and five others organized the Church of Christ on April 6, 1830 at Fayette, New York. In 1864 this body was directed by revelation through Granville Hedrick to return in 1867 to Independence, Missouri to the "consecrated land" dedicated by Joseph Smith. They did so and purchased the temple lot dedicated in 1831.

Headquarters

Temple Lot, 200 S. River St., P.O. Box 472, Independence, MO 64051, Tel. (816)833-3995

Media Contact, Gen. Church Rep., William A. Sheldon, P.O. Box 472, Independence, MO 64051, Tel. (816)833-3995

Website: church-of-christ.com

Officers

Council of Apostles, Secy., Apostle Smith N. Brickhouse, P.O. Box 472, Independence, MO 64051

Gen. Bus. Mgr., Bishop Alvin Harris, P.O. Box 472, Independence, MO 64051

Periodicals

Zion's Advocate

The Church of Christ (Holiness) U.S.A.

The Church of Christ (Holiness) U.S.A. has a Divine commission to propagate the gospel throughout the world, to seek the conversion of sinners, to reclaim backsliders, to encourage the sanctification of believers, to support divine healing, and to advance the truth for the return of our Lord and Savior Jesus Christ. This must be done through proper organization.

The fundamental principles of Christ's Church have remained the same. The laws founded upon these principles are to remain unchanged. The Church of Christ (Holiness) U.S.A. is representative in form of government; therefore, the final authority in defining the organizational responsibilities rests with the national convention. The bishops of the church are delegated special powers to act in behalf of or speak for the church. The pastors are ordained ministers, who under the call of God and His people, have divine oversight of local churches. However, the representative form of government gives ministry and laity equal authority in all deliberate bodies. With the leadership of the Holy Spirit, Respect, Loyalty and Love will greatly increase.

Headquarters

329 East Monument St., P.O. Box 3622, Jackson, MS 39207, Tel. (601)353-0222 Fax (601)353-4002

Media Contact, Maurice D. Bingham, Ed. D., Senior Bishop Emeritus

Email: Everything@cochusa.com

Website: www.cochusa.com

BOARD OF BISHOPS

Senior Bishop Emeritus, Maurice D. Bingham, Ed. D., P.O. Box 6182, Jackson, MS 39308, Tel. (601)353-0222, Email: Pminis3659@aol.com

Eastern Diocese, Bishop Lindsay E. Jones, 4053 Portland Ridge Dr., Florissant, MO 63034, Tel. (314)355-1775, Email: Ljones5@aol.com

North Central Diocese, Bishop Bennett Wolfe, 14315 River Oak Ct., Florissant, MO 63034, Tel. (314)741-4590, Email: Ned6@Hotmail.com

Senior Bishop, Northern Diocese, Bishop Emery Lindsay, 62 West 111th Place, Chicago, IL 60628, Tel. (773)821-0088, Email: Bpelind@aol.com

Pacific Northwest Diocese, Bishop Robert Winn, 1376 Oakwood Ave, Vallejo, CA 94591, Tel. (707)554-2493, Email: Awinner323@aol.com

South Central Diocese, Bishop Joseph Campbell, Jr., P.O. Box 3663, Jackson, MS 39207, Tel. (601)373-6223, Email: Bisjcsd@Bellsouth.net

Southeastern Diocese, Bishop Victor P. Smith, 3783 Treebark Trail, Decatur, GA 30034, Tel. (404)288-4885, Email: Victor@hotmail.com

Southwestern Diocese, President Bishop Vernon Kennebrew, 13900 Edgemond Dr., Little Rock, AR 72212, Tel. (501)954-7676

Western Diocese, Bishop Robert Winn, 1376 Oakwood Ave, Vallejo, CA 94591, Tel. (707)554-2493, Email: Awinner323@aol.com

Board Member, Bishop James K. Mitchell, 1580 Waite St., Gary, IN 46404, Tel. (219)944-0051, Email: Jasmitch9@aol.com

Periodicals

Truth

Church of Christ, Scientist

The Church of Christ, Scientist, was founded in 1879 by Mary Baker Eddy "to commemorate the word and works of our Master [Christ Jesus], which should reinstate primitive Christianity and its lost element of healing" (Church Manual, p. 17). Central to the Church's mission is making available worldwide Mrs. Eddy's definitive work on health and Bible-based Christian healing, Science and Health With Key to the Scriptures, as well as its publications, Internet sites, and broadcast programs, all of which respond to humanity's search for spiritual answers to today's pressing needs.

The Church also maintains an international speakers' bureau to introduce the public to Christian Science and Mrs. Eddy. Christian Science practitioners, living in hundreds of communities worldwide are available full-time to pray with anyone seeking comfort and healing. And Christian Science teachers hold yearly classes for those interested in a more specific understanding of how to practice the Christian Science system of healing. The worldwide activities and business of the Church are transacted by a five-member Board of Directors in Boston. About 2000 congregations, each democratically organized and governed, are located in approximately 80 countries. The church has no clergy.

Worship services are conducted by lay persons elected to serve as Readers. Each church maintains a Reading Room— a bookstore open to the community for spiritual inquiry and research; and a Sunday School where young people discuss the contemporary relevance of ideas from the Bible and Science and Health.

Headquarters
The First Church of Christ, Scientist, 210 Massachusetts Ave., Boston, MA 02115
Media Contact, Mgr., Committees on Publication, Phil Davis, Tel. (617)450-3300 Fax (617)450-3992
Website: www.spirituality.com and www.church ofchristscientist.org

Officers
Bd. of Directors: J. Thomas Black; Michael Pabst; Margaret Rogers; Mary Metzner Trammell; Nathan Talbot
President, Allison Phinney
Treas., Edward Odegaard
Clk., Nathan Talbot
First Reader, Curtis Wahlberg
Second Reader, Elizabeth Schaefer
Christian Science College Organizations, Website tmcyouth.com/cso

Periodicals
The Christian Science Monitor (www. csmonitor.com), The Christian Science Journal, Christian Science Sentinel, The Herald of Christian Science (13 languages), Christian Science Quarterly Bible Lessons (16 languages and English Braille)

Church Communities International
Church Communities International is a movement of Christian Church Communities

originating in Germany in 1920. Driven to England by Nazi persecution in 1937, Church Community members migrated to Paraguay in 1942 with the help of the Mennonite Church. In 1954 the first Church Community in the United States was founded in Rifton New York, where it continues to flourish. Today, a dozen Church Communities are located in New York and Pennsylvania as well as others in Australia, England, Germany and Thailand. Within each Church Community, residents practice their faith in the manner and spirit of the first-century Christians and the Reformation of the early 1500's, sharing everything in common and caring for each other and their neighbors. Members are baptized as adults on confession of the Apostolic Creed, making a voluntary lifetime commitment to living out the teachings of Jesus.

Headquarters
2032 Route 213, Rifton, NY 12471, Tel. (845)658-8351
Media Contact: Johann Huleatt, Tel. (845)658-7766
Email: johannh@rifton.com

Officers
Pedo Cavanna-Secretary Treasurer, 10 Hellbrook Lane, Ulster Park, NY 12487

The Church of God
The Church of God was established in about 28 A.D. by Jesus Christ on Mt. Kurn Hattin (Mark 3:13-15). It was endued with power on the Day of Pentecost, but was in operation prior to this point in time.

The true Church plunged into the Dark Ages on June 14th, 325 A.D. with the signing of the "Nicene Creed" and remained in darkness for 1578 years. From 325 A.D. to 1903, God was not asleep! He began revealing the truth to men once again: Martin Luther—justification by faith; John Wesley —sanctification; Dr. Albert Simpson—divine healing; (though some received the Holy Ghost prior to 1903, it is generally regarded the Pentecostal Movement began with a Holy Ghost revival in California in 1906 — Dr. Seymour).

On June 13,1903 The Church arose from darkness (as prophesied by Isaiah 60:1-5) in North Carolina. In 1923 a disruption caused a split in the Church, resulting in two groups both calling themselves the Church of God. In 1933 God gave the banner (Psalms 60:3, 4), the Church flag, to His Church; to those who feared Him too much to be led astray from the truth. (August 31, 2001 the Holy Ghost gave a new design for the banner of truth.)

On May 2nd, 1952 "of Prophecy" was added to the name Church of God. In 1990, the Church of God of Prophecy departed from theocratic government. Through the Holy Ghost, God called for a Solemn Assembly to be held July 23-25, 1993. On July 24th, the Holy Ghost gave direction to separate ourselves from the apostasy of the past three years, and to continue truly as The Church of God, clearly designating Robert J. Pruitt as the General Overseer. The Church of God thus returned to the true theocracy. This constituted not a new organization, but the reorganization of The Church of God as the true theocracy of God, the exclusive Body of Christ:

1. Which was set in order by Christ and functioned in theocratic order until A.D. 325;

2. Which arose from the Dark Ages on June 13, 1903;

3. Which continued true to God in "faith and practice, government and discipline" following the 1923 disruption;

4. Which is doing likewise since the similar disruption in 1993. Details of the future are, of course, unknown; but the prophecies of God are clear concerning His Church. The hour is late, but the brightness of the "Arise, Shine" lies just ahead. Without a doubt, perfection will be attained, for it has already been declared of the Church that Christ will "present it unto himself a glorious church, not having spot, or wrinkle, or any such thing; but that it should be holy and without blemish." (Ephesians 5:27; see also Revelations 19:6-9).

Headquarters

P.O. Box 450, Charleston, TN 37310, U.S.A., Tel. (423)339-8264

Officers

General Overseer, Stephen Smith, 197 Tillie Rd., Cleveland, TN
Field Secretary, Ray D. Dupre
Field Secretary, Robert F. Strong
Field Secretary, Donaldo Acosta
General Treasurer/ Assistant Editor of The Evening Light, Kevin D. Werkheiser
World Mission Coordinator/ Bible Training Institute Director, Herman D. Ard
Mission Representative (Africa, Asia & Europe), Robert J. Hawkins, Jr.
Assembly Band Movement Coordinator, Donald W. Branscum
Evangelism Coordinator, Lanny W. Carter
Church of Prophecy Marker Association Coordinator, Melvin Byers, Jr.
Sunday School Coordinator, Maudie E. Wood
Victory Leaders Band Coordinator, Sharon Griffin
Women's Missionary Band Coordinator, Betty Bishop

STATES

Alabama, James C. Anders
Alaska, Michael A. Grant
Arizona/Colorado/New Mexico/Texas (W), James R. Horne
Arkansas/Kansas/Missouri/Oklahoma/Texas (E), Dewayne Smith
Idaho (S)/California/Nevada/Utah, Serafin Pimentel
Idaho (N)/Montana (W)/Oregon/Washington, Ray D. Adams

Florida/Georgia, Melvin F. Kramer
Indiana/Illinois (S)/Kentucky/Ohio, Paul S. Jernigan
Louisiana/Mississippi, A. T. Dewberry
North Carolina, Melvin Byers, Jr.
South Carolina, Carl J. Neal
Pennsylvania/Delaware/Maryland/Massachusetts, James T. Smith
Virginia/ West Virginia, Clive Jared
N. Dakota/S. Dakota/Minnesota/Montana (E)/ Nebraska/Wyoming, Delbert G. Bock
Tennessee, Ray D. Dupre
Wisconsin/Illinois (N)/Iowa/Michigan, E. Roger Ammons

COUNTRIES

Argentina/Brazil/Paraguay/Uruguay, David Coronel
Bahamas/Cayman/Turks & Caicos Islands, George C. Forbes
Belize/Honduras/El Salvador/Spain, Donaldo Acosta
Bolivia/Ecuador, Benito Ramos Quispe
Canada East, E. Roger Ammons
Canada West, Ray Adams
Cameroon/Democratic Republic of Congo/ Republic of Congo, Patrice T. Kalamba
Chile, Javier Diaz
England, Robert J. Hawkins Jr.
Guatemala, Manuel S. Castro
Haiti, Louis E. Gaddis
India (South), Isaac Thomas Adimavunkal
India (North), Ch. Paul Sudhaker
Indonesia, Kalmen E. Nainggolan
Kenya/Ethiopia/Tanzania/Zimbabwe, Renison Mbogo Ngurukiri
Mexico, José G. Bañuelos
Nepal, Herman D. Ard
Nicaragua/Costa Rica/Panama, Caleb Hernández Ramírez
Nigeria, Matthew Ogunmola
Peru, Leonardo Luna
Philippines, Danilo M. Orcino
Puerto Rico/Dominican Republic/St. Vincent/ Netherlands Antilles, Juan Pimentel
Uganda/Burundi/Rwanda, Makohá F. Agati
Zambia, Alfred Nsofwa

Periodicals

The Evening Light

Church of God (Anderson, Indiana)

The Church of God (Anderson, Indiana) began in 1881 when Daniel S. Warner and several associates felt constrained to forsake all denominational hierarchies as formal creeds, trusting solely in the Holy Spirit as their overseer and the Bible as their statement of belief.

These people saw themselves at the forefront of a movement to restore unity and holiness to the church, not to establish another denomination, but to promote primary allegiance to Jesus Christ so as to transcend denominational loyalties. Deeply influenced by Wesleyan theology and Pietism, the Church of God has emphasized conversion, holiness and attention to the Bible. Worship services tend to be informal, accentuating expository preaching and robust singing. There is no formal membership. Persons are assumed to be members on the basis of witness to a conversion experience and evidence that supports such witness. The absence of formal membership is also consistent with the church's understanding of how Christian unity is to be achieved-that is, by preferring the label Christian before all others. The Church of God is congregational in its government. Each local congregation may call any recognized Church of God minister to be its pastor and may retain him or her as long as is mutually pleasing. Ministers are ordained and disciplined by state or provincial assemblies made up predominantly of ministers. National program agencies serve the church through coordinated ministries and resource materials. There are Church of God congregations in 89 foreign countries, most of which are resourced by one or more missionaries. There are slightly more Church of God adherents overseas than in North America.

Headquarters
General Director (President): Dr. Ronald V. Duncan, P.O. Box 2420, Anderson, IN 46018-2420, Tel. (765)642-0256 Fax (765)648-2191
Media Contact: David Farlow, Chief of Strategic Communications, Email: dfarlow@chog.org
Email: rduncan@chog.org
Website: www.chog.org

Officers
General Director (President): Dr. Ronald V. Duncan, D.Min. rduncan@chog.org
Vice President, Kenneth Hatch khatch@chog.org
Treasurer, Allan J. Smith asmith@chog.org
Secretary, Joni A. Burnett jburnett@chog.org; Mailing Address: P.O. Box 2420, Anderson, IN 46018-2420; Physical Address: 1201 E 5th St, Anderson, IN 46012, Tel. (765)642-0256
Media Contact: David Farlow, Chief of Strategic Communications, Email: dfarlow@chog.org

OTHER ORGANIZATIONS:
Board of Pensions, President: Jeffery A. Jenness, Box 2299, Anderson IN 46018
Warner Press, Inc., President: Eric King, Box 2499, Anderson IN 46018
Anderson University, President: James L. Edwards, 1100 E 5th St., Anderson IN 46012
Mid-America Christian University, President: John Fozard, 3500 SW 119th St., Oklahoma City OK 73170
Warner Pacific College, Interim President: Andrea Cook, 2219 SE 68th Ave, Portland OR 97215
Warner University, President: Gregory V. Hall, 13895 Hwy 27, Lake Wales, FL 33859

Christian Women Connection (CWC), Executive Director: Arnetta Bailey, P.O. Box 2328, Anderson, IN 46018
Children of Promise, President: Paul Maxfield, P.O. Box 2316, Anderson IN 46018

Periodicals
Pathways to God, People to People, YMI Update, CHOG News, Multiplication Moments, and Communion Together

The Church of God in Christ
The Church of God in Christ was founded in 1897 in Lexington, Mississippi by Bishop Charles Harrison Mason, a former Baptist minister, and organized as a Pentecostal Church during the early stages of the holiness movement and, more specifically, as an outgrowth of the Azusa Street Revival of Los Angeles, California, in 1906-9.

Initial growth of the church was attributable to the organization of four departments between 1910-1916, the Women's Department, the Sunday School, Young People's Willing Workers and Home and Foreign Missions.

The Church is Trinitarian and teaches the infallibility of Holy Scripture, the need for regeneration and baptism of the Holy Ghost evidenced by speaking in tongues. It emphasizes holiness as God's standard for Christian conduct and recognizes as ordinances Holy Communion, Water Baptism and Feet Washing. Its governmental structure is basically episcopal and consists of three branches. The General Board represents the Executive Branch, the General Assembly is the Legislative Branch, and the Judiciary Board represents the Judicial Branch

Headquarters
Mason Temple Church of God in Christ, 930 Mason St., Memphis, TN 38126, Tel. (901)947-9300
Elder J.H. Lyles, Jr., General Secretary, Mailing Address, P.O. Box 320, Memphis, TN 38101
Email: EJOHNCOGIC@aol.com
Website: www.cogic.com

Officers
THE PRESIDIUM:
Presiding Bishop, Bishop C.E. Blake, 3045 Crenshaw Blvd., Los Angeles, CA 90016, Tel. (323)733-8300
1st Assistant, Bishop N. Haynes, 1267 Whispering Oaks Dr., Desoto, TX 75115, Tel. (214)375-4105
2nd Assistant, Bishop P.A. Brooks, 30945 Wendbrook Ln., Beverly Hills, MI 48025, Tel. (313)835-5329
Secretary, Bishop W.W. Hamilton, 14570 Mountain Quail Rd., Salinas, CA 93908, Tel. (831)395-2774
Asst. Secretary, Bishop R.L.H. Winbush, 235 Diamond Dr., Lafayette, LA 70501, Tel. (318)232-6958

Member, Bishop C.D. Owens, 406 Roswell St., Marietta, GA 30060, Tel. (770)590-8510

Member, Bishop L.R. Anderson, 1023 E. Brook Hollow Dr., Phoenix, AZ 85022, Tel. (602)993-4906

Member, Bishop G.D. McKinney, 5825 Imperial Ave., San Diego, CA 92114, Tel. (619)262-2671

Member, Bishop S.L. Green, Jr., 41 St. Johns Dr., Hampton, VA 23666, Tel. (757)380-6118

Member, Bishop N.W. Wells, 717 Bridgeview Bay, Muskegon, MI 49441, Tel. (231)722-3219

Member, Bishop J.W. Macklin, 1027 W. Tennyson Rd., Haywood, CA 94544, Tel. (510)783-9377

GENERAL OFFICERS:

General Secretary, Elder A.Z. Hall, Jr., P.O. Box 320, Memphis, TN 38101, Tel. (901)947-9356

General Treasurer, Bishop S.L. Lowe, 938 Mason St., Memphis, TN 38126, Tel. (901)947-9319

Financial Secretary, Bishop F.O. White, 312 Grand Ave., Freeport, NY 11520, Tel. (516)623-7513

ELECTED OFFICERS, DEPARTMENTAL HEADS AND AUXILLIARY LEADERS

Chairman – General Assembly: Bishop J.O. Patterson, Jr., 229 Danny Thomas, Memphis, TN 38126

Chairman – Judiciary Board: Bishop T.L. Westbrook, 1623 S. 11th St., Tacoma, WA 98405

Chairman – Board of Bishops: Bishop J. Sheard, 19511 Afton Rd., Detroit, MI 48203

Chairman – Board of Trustees: Bishop C.M. Ford, 4525 S. Wabash, Chicago, IL 60653, Tel. (773)538-4526

Chief of Staff: Bishop J.L. Maynard, 930 Mason St., Memphis, TN 38126, Tel. (901)947-9338

Chief Accountant: Minister A. Perpener, P.O. Box 320, Memphis, TN 38126, Tel. (901)947-9361

National Properties: Elder D.L.S. Wells, 938 Mason St., Memphis, TN 38126, Tel. (901)947-9332

Chairman – Pastors/Elders: Elder D. Hutchins

Adjutant General: Bishop Matthew Williams, 1516 Dumont Dr., Valrico, FL 33594

President – Women's Dept.: Mother W.M. Rivers, P.O. Box 1052, Memphis, TN 38101

President – Missions Dept.: Bishop C.L. Moody, P.O. Box 320, Memphis, TN 38101, Tel. (901)947-9316

President – Evangelism: Bishop R. White, 4121 Thurman Dr., Conley, GA 30288, Tel. (404)361-7020

President – Youth Dept.: Elder Michael Hill, 23746 Riverside Dr., Lathrup, MI 48076

President – Sunday School: Elder Alton Gatlin, 229 Diamond Dr., Lafayette, LA 70501

President – Music Dept.: Professor I. Stevenson

President – Men's Conference: Bishop D. Hines, 8605 W. Goodhope Rd., Milwaukee, WI 53224

President – Sunshine Band: Dr. R.L. Howard

President – Purity: Missionary T. Cotton

Executive Director – Fine Arts: Mrs. S.J. Powell

CEO – Publishing House: Dr. D.A. Hall, Sr., 930 Mason St., Memphis, TN 38126

Chairman – Board of Pub.: Bishop R.L.H. Winbush, 235 Diamond Dr., Lafayette, LA 70501

Manager – COGIC Bookstore: Mrs. G. Miller, 285 S. Main, Memphis, TN 38101, Tel. (901)947-9304

EDUCATIONAL INSTITUTIONS:

Charles Harrison Mason Theological Seminary, 671 Beckwith St. SW, Atlanta, GA 30314 Attn: Dean O.L. Haney

C.H. Mason System of Bible Colleges, 930 Mason St., Memphis, TN 38126 Attn: Dr. M.L. Johnson

All Saints Bible College, 930 Mason St., Memphis, TN 38126 Attn: Dr. P. Little

Saints Academy, C.H. Mason Highway, Lexington, MS Attn: Elder L. Weems

Periodicals

The Whole Truth Magazine, The Voice of Missions, The McBrayer Report

Church of God in Christ, International

The Church of God in Christ, International was organized in 1969 in Kansas City, Mo., by 14 bishops of the Church of God in Christ of Memphis, Tenn. The doctrine is the same, but the separation came because of disagreement over polity and governmental authority. The Church is Wesleyan in theology (two works of grace) but stresses the experience of full baptism of the Holy Ghost with the initial evidence of speaking with other tongues as the Spirit gives utterance.

Headquarters

170 Adelphi St., Brooklyn, NY 11205, Tel. (718)625-9175

Media Contact, Natl. Sec., Rev. Sis. Sharon R. Dunn

Email: laity@cogic.org

Website: www.cogic.org/main

Officers

Presiding Bishop, Most Rev. Carl Williams, Jr.

Vice Presiding Bishop, Rt. Rev. J. C. White

Exec. Admn., Horace K. Williams, Word of God Center, Newark, NJ

Women's Dept., Natl. Supervisor, Evangelist Elvonia Williams

Youth Dept., Pres., Dr. Joyce Taylor, 137-17 135th Ave., S., Ozone Park, NY 11420

Music Dept., Pres., Isaiah Heyward

Bd. of Bishops, Chpsn., Bishop J. C. White, 360 Colorado Ave., Bridgeport, CT 06605

Church of God in Christ, Mennonite

The Church of God in Christ, Mennonite was organized by the evangelist-reformer John Holdeman in Ohio. The church unites with the faith of the Waldensians, Anabaptists and other such groups throughout history. Emphasis is placed on obedience to the teachings of the Bible, including the doctrine of the new birth and spiritual life, noninvolvement in government or the military, head-coverings for the women, beards for the men and separation from the world shown by simplicity in clothing, homes, possessions and lifestyle. The church has a worldwide membership of about 22,870, largely concentrated in the United States and Canada.

Headquarters

P.O. Box 313, 420 N. Wedel Ave., Moundridge, KS 67107, Tel. (620)345-2532 Fax (620)345-2582

Media Contact, Dale Koehn, P.O. Box 230, Moundridge, KS 67107, Tel. (620)345-2532 Fax (620)345-2582, Email: dalekoehn.gp@cogicm.org

Email: dalekoehn.gp@cogicm.org

Periodicals

Messenger of Truth

Church of God (Cleveland, Tennessee)

It is one of America's oldest Pentecostal churches founded in 1886 as an outgrowth of the holiness revival under the name Christian Union. In 1907 the church adopted the organizational name Church of God. It has its foundation upon the principles of Christ as revealed in the Bible. The Church of God is Christian, Protestant, foundational in its doctrine, evangelical in practice and distinctively Pentecostal. It maintains a centralized form of government and a commitment to world evangelization. The first church of Canada was established in 1919 in Scotland Farm, Manitoba. Paul H. Walker became the first overseer of Canada in 1931.

International Offices

2490 Keith St., NW, Cleveland, TN 37320, Tel. (423)472-3361 Fax (423)478-7066

Media Contact, Dir. of Communications, T. Scot Carter, P.O. Box 2430, Cleveland, TN 37320-2430; Tel. (423)478-7112 Fax (423)478-7066

Email: jrobinson@churchofgod.org

Website: www.churchofgod.org

Officers

General Overseer, Dr. Raymond F. Culpepper, P.O. Box 2430, Cleveland, TN 37320-2430, Tel. (423)478-7137, Fax (423)478-7275, gocog@churchofgod.org

First Assistant General Overseer, Dr. Timothy M. Hill, P.O. Box 2430, Cleveland, TN 37320-2430, Tel. (423)478-7136, Fax (423)478-7379, cog1a@churchofgod.org

Second Assistant General Overseer, Dr. Mark L. Williams, P.O. Box 2430, Cleveland, TN 37320-2430, Tel. (423)478-7126, Fax (423)478-7263, cog2a@churchofgod.org

Third Assistant General Overseer, Dr. David M. Griffis, P.O. Box 2430, Cleveland, TN 37320-2430, Tel. (423)478-7133, Fax (423)478-7247, cog3a@churchof god.org

Secretary General, Dr. Wallace J. Sibley, P.O. Box 2430, Cleveland, TN 37320-2430, Tel. (423)478-7127, Fax (423)478-7052, cogsec general@churchofgod.org

Canada-Eastern, Rev. Daniel J. Vassell, P.O. Box 2036, Brampton, ON L6T 3TO, Tel. (905)270-8083, Fax (905)270-6720

Canada-Western, Rev. Vaughn D. Mathews, Box 54055, 2640 52 St. NE, Calgary, AB T1Y 6S6, Tel. (403)293-8817 Fax (403)293-3466

Canada-Quebec-Maritimes, Rev. Jacques Houle, 19 Orly, Granby, QC J2H 1Y4, Tel. (450)378-4442 Fax (450)378-8646

Canada-National, Dr. Mark L. Williams, P.O. Box 2430, Cleveland, TN 37320-2430, Tel. (423)478-7126 Fax (423)478-7276

GENERAL MINISTRIES

Administrative Liaison to General Overseer, H. Lynn Stone

Legal Services-Attorney, Dennis W. Watkins

Communications-Director, T. Scot Carter

Church of God Foundation, Inc.-President/CEO, Donald S. Aultman

International Prayer Commission-Coordinator, P. Douglas Small

Division of World Evangelization

Executive Divisional Director-Timothy M. Hill

Black Ministries-Coordinator, Kenneth L. Hill

Hispanic Ministries-Director, Carlos S. Moran

Ministry to the Military-Director, Robert A. Moore

Multi-Cultural-Director, G. Dennis McGuire

Personal Evangelism-Coordinator, Leonard C. Albert

USA Missions-Director, Jimmy D. Smith

World Missions-Director, J. Douglas LeRoy

Division of Education

Executive Divisional Director-Mark L. Williams

European Theological Bible Seminary-Dir., Paul Schmidgall

International Bible College-Pres., Randy H. Krieger

Lee University-Pres., Charles Paul Conn

Patten University-Pres., Gary Moncher

Patten University/Internet Degree Program-Dir., Delton L. Alford

Pentecostal Theological Seminary, Pres., Steven J. Land

Ministerial Development/School of Ministry-Coord., Donald G. Bennett

USA Hispanic Education Ministries-Coord., Enrique de Jesus

Division of Discipleship

Executive Divisional Director-David M. Griffis

Youth Discipleship-Dir., Thomas A. Madden

Men's Discipleship-Coord., David H. Gosnell
Women's Discipleship-Coord., Lorna V. Gosnell
Publications-Dir., Terry R. Hart
Division of Care and Support Services
Care Ministries
Executive Divisional Director-Wallace J. Sibley
Executive Administrator-Donnie W. Smith
Chaplains Commission-Dir., Donnie W. Smith
Ministerial Care-Dir., Bill Leonard
Ministry to Israel-Dir., J. Michael Utterback
SpiritCare Ministries-Dir., Donnie W. Smith
Operation Compassion-Dir., David B. Lorency
Support Services
Executive Divisional Director-Wallace J. Sibley
Church of God Benefits Board, Inc.-Pres. &
CEO, Arthur D. Rhodes
Department of Business and Records-Dir., Julian
B. Robinson

Periodicals

Church of God Evangel, Church of God Editorial Evangelica, Save Our World, Ministry Now Profiles

Church of God by Faith, Inc.

Founded 1914, in Jacksonville Heights, Florida., by Elder John Bright, this church believes the word of God as interpreted by Jesus Christ to be the only hope of salvation and Jesus Christ the only mediator for people.

Headquarters

2409 Old Middleburg N., Jacksonville, FL 32210, Tel. (904)779-5469 Fax (904)779-5399
Media Contact, Ofc. Mgr., Sarah E. Lundy
Email: natl-hq@cogbf.org; info@cogbf.org
Website: www.cogbf.org

Officers

Presiding Bishop, James E. McKnight, P.O. Box 121, Gainesville, FL 32601
Treas., Elder John Robinson, 300 Essex Dr., Ft. Pierce, FL 34946
Exec. Sec., David C. Rourk, 207 Chestnut Hill Dr., Rochester, NY. 14617
Ruling Elder, James E. McKnight, Jr., P.O. Box 101, Starke, FL 32091

The Church of God of the Firstborn

The Church of God of the Firstborn was founded by Pentecostal evangelist Adolph Gustav Etterman in 1936. Headquarters are located in Newton, KS, where annual summer conferences are held. In 2002, the denomination consisted of 26 congregations, located primarily in the south central United States and in Mexico. In recent years, the number of Caucasian churches has declined and Hispanic membership has surged. James Etterman, the son of the founder, became president of the denomination in 1986.

Headquarters

P.O. Box 1041, 720 S. Kansas Ave., Newton, KS 671114-1041
Media Contact, Pres., Rev. James Etterman

Officers

Pres., Rev. James Etterman

Periodicals

The True Messenger

Church of God General Conference (McDonough, GA)

This church is the outgrowth of several independent local groups of similar faith. Some were in existence as early as 1800, and others date their beginnings to the arrival of British immigrants around 1847. Many local churches carried the name Church of God of the Abrahamic Faith. State and district conferences of these groups were formed as an expression of mutual cooperation. A national organization was instituted at Philadelphia in 1888. Because of strong convictions on the questions of congregational rights and authority, however, it ceased to function until 1921, when the present General Conference was formed at Waterloo, Iowa.

The Bible is accepted as the supreme standard of faith. Adventist in viewpoint, the second (premillenial) coming of Christ is strongly emphasized. The church teaches that the kingdom of God will be literal, beginning in Jerusalem at the time of the return of Christ and extending to all nations. Emphasis is placed on the oneness of God and the Sonship of Christ, that Jesus did not pre-exist prior to his birth in Bethlehem and that the Holy Spirit is the power and influence of God. Membership is dependent on faith, repentance and baptism by immersion.

The work of the General Conference is carried on under the direction of the board of directors. With a congregational church government, the General Conference exists primarily as a means of mutual cooperation and for the development of yearly projects and enterprises.

The headquarters and Bible College were moved from Oregon, IL to Morrow, GA in 1991 and then to McDonough, GA in 2009.

Headquarters

P.O. Box 2950, 2020 Avalon Parkway, Suite 400, McDonough, GA 30253, Tel. (678)833-1839 Fax (678)833-1853
Media Contact, Joe Martin
Email: info@abc-coggc.org
Website: www.abc-coggc.org

Officers

Chief Administrative Officer, Dr. Joe Martin, P.O. Box 2950, McDonough, GA 30253, Tel. (678)833-1839, Email: jmartin@abc-coggc.org
Chpsn., Pastor Joe Myers, 70 Knolls Ridge, Hampton, GA 30228, Tel. (770)280-5128, Email: pastorjoecbc@bellsouth.net

Vice Chpsn., Dr. Daniel Siderius, 19619 Galway Bay Circle, #404, Germantown, MD 20874, Tel. (314)956-7866, Email: dwsideri@yahoo.com

Sec., Carrie Briggs, 9222 Andean Ct., Jonesboro, GA 30236, Tel. (678)557-5597, Email carriebriggscpa@gmail.com

Treas., Richard McClain, 469 Empire SE, Kentwood, MI 49508, Tel. (616)698-2638, Email: rickmcc20@comcast.net

OTHER ORGANIZATIONS

Bus. Admn., Operations Manager, Mr. Gary Burnham, Box 2950, McDonough, GA 30253, Tel. (678)833-1839 Fax (678)833-1853, Email: gburnham@abc-coggc.org

Atlanta Bible College, President, Dr. Joe Martin, Box 2950, McDonough, GA 30253, Tel. (678)833-1839 Fax (678)833-1853, Email: jmartin@abc-coggc.org

Periodicals

The Restitution Herald and Progress Journal, A Journal From the Radical Reformation, Church of God

Church of God General Conference (Oregon, IL and Morrow, GA) —

please see Church of God General Conference (McDonough, GA)

Church of God, Mountain Assembly, Inc.

The church was formed in 1895 and organized in 1906 by J. H. Parks, S. N. Bryant, Tom D. Moses and William O. Douglas.

Headquarters

256 N. Florence Ave., P.O. Box 157, Jellico, TN 37762, Tel. (423)784-8260 Fax (423)784-3258 Media Contact, Gen. Sec.-Treas., Rev. James Kilgore

Email: cgmahdq@jellico.com
Website: www.cgmahdq.org

Officers

Gen. Overseer, Rev. Donnie Hill
Asst. Gen. Overseer, World Missions Dir., Rev. Lonnie Lyke
Gen. Sec.-Treas., Rev. James Kilgore
Youth Ministries & Camp Dir., Rev. James Coffey

Periodicals

The Gospel Herald

Church of God of Prophecy

The Church of God of Prophecy is one of the churches that grew out of the work of A. J. Tomlinson in the first half of the twentieth century. Historically it shares a common heritage with the Church of God (Cleveland Tennessee) and is in the mainstream of the classical Pentecostal-Holiness tradition.

At the death of A.J. Tomlinson in 1943, M.A. Tomlinson was named General Overseer and served until his retirement in 1990. He emphasized unity and fellowship unlimited by racial, social, or political differences. The next General Overseer, Billy D. Murray, Sr., who served from 1990 until his retirement in 2000, emphasized a commitment to the promotion of Christian unity and world evangelization. In July 2000, Fred S. Fisher, Sr. was duly selected to serve as the fourth General Overseer of the Church of God of Prophecy until his retirement in September 2006. In August 2006, Bishop Randall E. Howard, then Global Outreach Ministries Director, was selected as the fifth General Overseer of the Church.

From its beginnings, the Church has based its beliefs on "the whole Bible, rightly divided," and has accepted the Bible as God's Holy Word, inspired, inerrant and infallible. The church is firm in its commitment to orthodox Christian belief. The Church affirms that there is one God, eternally existing in three persons, Father, Son and Holy Spirit. It believes in the deity of Christ, His virgin birth, His sinless life, the physical miracles He performed, His atoning death on the cross, His bodily resurrection, His ascension to the right hand of the Father and his Second coming. The church professes that salvation results from grace alone through faith in Christ, that regeneration by the Holy Spirit is essential for the salvation of sinful men, and that sanctification by the blood of Christ makes possible personal holiness. It affirms the present ministry of the Holy Spirit by Whose indwelling believers are able to live godly lives and have power for service. The church believes in, and promotes, the ultimate unity of believers as prayed for by Christ in John 17. The church stresses the sanctity of human life and is committed to the sanctity of the marriage bond and the importance of strong, loving Christian families. Other official teachings include Holy Spirit baptism with tongues as initial evidence; manifestation of the spiritual gifts; divine healing; premillenial second-coming of Christ; total abstinence from the use of tobacco, alcohol and narcotics; water baptism by immersion; the Lord's supper and washing of the saints' feet; and a concern for moderation and holiness in all dimensions of lifestyle.

The Church is racially integrated on all levels, including top leadership. Women play a prominent role in church affairs, serving in pastoral roles and other leadership positions. The church presbytery has recently adopted plurality of leadership in the selection of a General Oversight Group. This group consists of eight bishops located around the world who, along with the General Overseer, are responsible for inspirational leadership and vision casting for the church body.

The Church has local congregations in all 50 states and more than 120 nations worldwide. Organizationally there is a strong emphasis on international missions, evangelism, youth and children's ministries, women's and men's ministries, stewardship, communications, publishing, leadership development and discipleship.

INTERNATIONAL OFFICES
P.O. Box 2910, Cleveland, TN 37320-2910
Email: betty@cogop.org
Website: www.cogop.org

Officers
Gen. Overseer: Bishop Randall E. Howard
General Presbyters: Sherman Allen, Sam Clements, David Browder, Clayton Endecott, Felix Santiago, Brice Thompson
International Offices Ministries Directors: Finance, Communications, and Publishing: Benjamin Feliz; Global Outreach Ministries: David Bryan

Periodicals
White Wing Messenger (English), White Wing Messenger (Spanish)

The Church of God (Seventh Day), Denver, Colorado — please see General Conference of the Church of God (Seventh Day), Denver, Colorado

The Church of Illumination
The Church of Illumination was organized in 1908 for the express purpose of establishing congregations at large, offering a spiritual, esoteric, philosophic interpretation of the vital biblical teachings, thereby satisfying the inner spiritual needs of those seeking spiritual truth, yet permitting them to remain in, or return to, their former church membership.

Headquarters
Beverly Hall, 5966 Clymer Rd., Quakertown, PA 18951, Tel. (800)779-3796
Media Contact, Dir. General, Gerald E. Poesnecker, P.O. Box 220, Quakertown, PA 18951, Tel. (215)536-7048 Fax (215)536-7058
Email: bevhall@comcat.net
Website: www.soul.org

Officers
Dir.-General, Gerald E. Poesnecker, P.O. Box 220, Quakertown, PA 18951

The Church of Jesus Christ (Bickertonites)
This church was organized in 1862 at Green Oak, PA, by William Bickerton, who obeyed the Restored Gospel under Sidney Rigdon's following in 1845.

Headquarters
Sixth St., Monongahela, PA 15063, Tel. (412)258-3066

Exec. Sec., Carl Frammolino

Officers
Pres., Paul Palmieri, 319 Pine Dr., Aliquippa, PA 15001 Tel.
First Counselor, Thomas M. Liberto, 6154 Stream View Dr., San Diego, CA 92115-6915
Second Counselor, Peter A. Scolaro, Ridge Way Dr., Rochester, MI 48307-1771
Exec. Sec., Carl J. Frammolino

ORGANIZATIONS
Missionary Benevolent Association, Ladies Uplift Circle

Periodicals
The Gospel News

The Church of Jesus Christ of Latter-day Saints
This church was organized April 6, 1830, at Fayette, N.Y., by Joseph Smith. Members believe Joseph Smith was divinely directed to restore the gospel to the earth, and that through him the keys to the Aaronic and Melchizedek priesthoods and temple work also were restored. Members believe that both the Bible and the Book of Mormon (a record of the Lord's dealings with His people on the American continent 600 B.C. -421 A.D.) are scripture. Membership is 14.1 million.

In addition to the First Presidency, the governing bodies of the church include the Quorum of the Twelve Apostles, the Presidency of the Seventy, the Quorums of the Seventy and the Presiding Bishopric.

Headquarters
47 East South Temple St., Salt Lake City, UT 84150, Tel. (801)240-1000 Fax (801)240-1167
Media Contact, Dir., Media Relations, Michael Purdy, Tel. (801)240-2363 Fax (801)240-1167
Email: PorterDS@ldschurch.org
Website: www.lds.org

Officers
Pres., Thomas S. Monson
1st Counselor, Henry B. Eyring
2nd Counselor, Dieter F. Uchtdorf
Quorum of the Twelve Apostles, Pres., Boyd K. Packer; L. Tom Perry; Russell M.
Nelson; Dallin H. Oaks; M. Russell Ballard; Richard G. Scott; Robert D. Hales;
Jeffrey R. Holland; David A. Bednar; Quentin L. Cook; D. Todd Christofferson; Neil L. Andersen

AUXILIARY ORGANIZATIONS
Sunday Schools, Gen. Pres., Russell T. Osguthorpe
Relief Society, Gen. Pres., Julie Beck
Young Women, Gen. Pres., Elaine Dalton
Young Men, Gen. Pres., David L. Beck
Primary, Gen. Pres., Rosemary M. Wixom

Periodicals
The Ensign, Liahona, New Era, Friend Magazine

Church of the Living God (Motto, Christian Workers for Fellowship)

The Church of the Living God was founded by William Christian in April 1889 at Caine Creek, Arkansas. It was the first black church in America without Anglo-Saxon roots and not founded by white missionaries.

Chief Christian, as he is now referred, was born a slave in Mississippi on Nov. 10, 1856 and grew up uneducated. In 1875, he united with the Missionary Baptist Church and began to preach. In 1888, he left the Baptist Church and began what was known as Christian Friendship Work. Believing himself to have been inspired by the Spirit of God through divine revelation and close study of the Scriptures, he was led to the truth that the Bible refers to the church as The Church of the Living God (I Timothy. Ch.3 vs.15). In 1889, he established the Church of the Living God organization.

The organization is nondenominational, non-sectarian and Trinitarian and believers in the infallibility of the Scriptures. It emphasizes believer's baptism by immersion, the use of water and unleavened bread element in the Lord's Supper and the washing of feet that is required only when one unites with the church.

The local organizations are know as "Temple" rather than as "Churches" and are subject to the authority of the general assembly. The presiding officer is styled as "chief bishop." The ministry includes bishops, overseers, evangelists, pastors, missionaries and local preachers. The Executive Board is in charge of the operation of the entire organization, in the absence of the Annual Assembly. Synod, Annual, General Assembly meets quadrennial.

The Church of the Living God, now headquartered in Cincinnati, Ohio, has been in existence for more than 114 years. It is represented by approximately 10,000 members throughout 25 states within the U.S. The presiding officer, Chief Bishop W. E. Crumes, has led the organization for more than 30 years.

Headquarters
430 Forest Ave., Cincinnati, OH 45229, Tel. (513)569-5660 Fax (513)569-5661;
MediaContact: Chief Bishop, Robert Tyler

EXECUTIVE BOARD
Chief Bishop, Robert Tyler, 430 Forest Ave., Cincinnati, OH 45229
Vice Chief Bishop, Robert D. Tyler, 3802 Bedford, Omaha, NE 68110
Exec. Sec., Bishop C. A. Lewis, 1360 N. Boston, Tulsa, OK 73111
Gen. Sec., Elder Raymond Powell, Sr., 2159 E. 95th St., Chicago, IL 60617
Gen. Treas., Elder Harry Hendricks, 11935 Cimarron Ave., Hawthorne, CA 90250
Bishop E. L. Bowie, 2037 N.E. 18th St., Oklahoma City, OK 73111
Bishop Leroy Smith, Jr., 1418 Faraday, Peoria, IL 61605

Bishop Jeff Ruffin, 302 E. Monte Way, Phoenix, AZ 85040
Bishop S. E. Shannon, 1034 S. King Hwy., St. Louis, MO 63110
Bishop, Elbert Jones, 4522 Melwood, Memphis, TN 38109
Bishop, Harold Edwards, P.O. Box 411489, Dallas, TX 75249

NATIONAL DEPARTMENTS
Convention Planning Committee
Young People's Progressive Union
Christian Education Dept.
Sunday School Dept.
Natl. Evangelist Bd.
Natl. Nurses Guild
Natl. Women's Work Dept.
Natl. Music Dept.
Natl. Usher Board
Natl. Sec. Office

Periodicals
The Gospel Truth

Church of the Lutheran Brethren of America

The Church of the Lutheran Brethren of America was organized in December 1900. Five independent Lutheran congregations met together in Milwaukee, Wisconsin, and adopted a constitution patterned very closely on that of the Lutheran Free Church of Norway.

The spiritual awakening in the Midwest during the 1890s crystallized into convictions that led to the formation of a new church body. Chief among the concerns were church membership practices, observance of Holy Communion, confirmation practices and local church government.

The Church of the Lutheran Brethren practices a simple order of worship with the sermon as the primary part of the worship service. It believes that personal profession of faith is the primary criterion for membership in the congregation. The Communion service is reserved for those who profess faith in Christ as savior. Each congregation is autonomous and the synod serves the congregations in advisory and cooperative capacities.

The synod supports an Internationa Mission program in Cameroon, Chad, Japan and Taiwan. Approximately 40 percent of the synodical budget is earmarked for international mission. A growing North American Regional Mission home mission ministry is planting new congregations in the United States and Canada. Affiliate organizations operate several retirement, nursing homes, conference and retreat centers.

Headquarters
1020 Alcott Ave., W., Box 655, Fergus Falls, MN 56538, Tel. (218)739-3336 Fax (218)739-5514
Media Contact, Pres., Rev. Joel Egge
Email: clb@clba.org; sdolsen@clba.org
Website: www.clba.org

Officers

Pres., Rev. Joel Egge

Vice Pres., Rev. Matthew Rogness

Sec., Rev. Paul Larson, 1020 Alcott Ave. W, Fergus Falls, MN 56537

Dir. of Finance and Personnel, Bradley Martinson

Lutheran Brethren Seminary President, Dr. David Veum

Dir. of International Mission, Exec. Dir., Rev. Matthew Rogness

Dir. of Communications and Prayer, Tim Mathiesen

Periodicals

Faith & Fellowship

Church of the Lutheran Confession

The Church of the Lutheran Confession held its constituting convention in Watertown, S.D., in August of 1960. The Church of the Lutheran Confession was begun by people and congregations who withdrew from church bodies that made up what was then known as the Synodical Conference over the issue of unionism. Following such passages as I Corinthians 1 vs.10 and Romans 16 vs.17-18, the Church of the Lutheran Confession holds the conviction that mutual agreement with the doctrines of Scripture is essential and necessary before exercise of church fellowship is appropriate.

Members of the Church of the Lutheran Confession uncompromisingly believe the Holy Scriptures to be divinely inspired and therefore inerrant. They subscribe to the historic Lutheran Confessions as found in the Book of Concord of 1580 because they are a correct exposition of Scripture.

The Church of the Lutheran Confession exists to proclaim, preserve and spread the saving truth of the gospel of Jesus Christ, so that the redeemed of God may learn to know Jesus Christ as their Lord and Savior and follow him through this life to the life to come.

Headquarters

501 Grover Rd., Eau Claire, WI 54701, Tel. (715)836-6622

Media Contact, Pres., Daniel Fleischer. Tel. (361)241-5147

Email: JohnHLau@juno.com

Website: www.clclutheran.org

Officers

Pres., Rev. John Schierenbeck, 3015 Ave. K NW, Winter Haven, FL 33881

Mod., Rev. Paul Nolting, 208 Gall Path, Mankato, MN 56001

Vice Pres., Rev. Mark Bernthal, 3232 West Point Rd., Middleton, WI 53562, Tel. (608)233-2244

Sec., Rev. Wayne Eichstadt, 417 Woodhaven Lane, Mankato MN 56001

Treas., Dr. James Sydow, 500 Grover Rd., Eau Claire, WI 54701

Archivist, Prof. David Lau, 507 Ingram Dr., Eau Claire, WI 54701

Statistician, Dr. James Sydow, 500 Grover Rd., Eau Claire, WI 54701

Periodicals

The Lutheran Spokesman, Journal of Theology

Church of the Nazarene

The Church of the Nazarene resulted from the merger of three independent holiness groups. The Association of Pentecostal Churches in America, located principally in New York and New England, joined at Chicago in 1907 with a largely West Coast body called the Church of the Nazarene and formed the Pentecostal Church of the Nazarene. A southern group, the Holiness Church of Christ, united with the Pentecostal Church of the Nazarene at Pilot Point, Texas, in 1908. In 1919 the word "Pentecostal" was dropped from the name. Principal leaders in the organization were Phineas Bresee, William Howard Hoople, H. F. Reynolds and C. B. Jernigan. Dr. H. F. Reynolds organized the first Canadian congregation in 1902 at Oxford, Nova Scotia. The Church of the Nazarene emphasizes entire sanctification or Christian Holiness. It stresses the importance of a devout and holy life and a positive witness through Christ-like character shaped by the Holy Spirit. Nazarenes express their faith through evangelism, compassionate ministries, and education. The church is connectional. Its polity combines episcopal, presbyterian, and congregational elements. Churches call pastors. Districts conduct annual assemblies and elect leaders. The quadrennial General Assembly, a delegated body, is international in scope and establishes doctrine and order, elects the general superintendents (currently six), and elects members to various church boards and agencies. Internationally the church has 13 liberal arts colleges and universities, five graduate seminaries, 34 Bible colleges, three schools of nursing, an education college, and a junior college. The church maintains 702 missionaries and has work in 156 world areas. World services include medical, educational and religious ministries. Books, periodicals and other Christian literature are published at the Nazarene Publishing House. The church is a member of the Christian Holiness Partnership, National Association of Evangelicals, the World Methodist Council, and the European Methodist Council.

Headquarters

Media Contact, Gen. Sec, Dr. David P. Wilson, Global Ministry Center, 17001 Prairie Star Parkway, Lenexa, KS, 66220 Tel. (913)577-0600, Fax (913)577-0848, Email: dwilson

Email: ssm@nazarene.org

Website: www.nazarene.org

Officers

Gen. Supts., D. Porter; Dr. Jesse C. Middendorf; Dr. J.K. Warrick; Dr. Eugénio R. Duarte; Dr. David W. Graves; Dr. Stan A. Toler; 17001 Prairie Star Parkway, Lenexa, KS 66220, Tel. (913)577-0500

Gen. Sec., Dr. David P. Wilson, Tel. (913)577-0500 Fax (816)822-9071 Email: dwilson@nazarene.org

Gen. Treas./Financial Officer (FO), Dr. Marilyn McCool (913)577-0500 FAX: (913)577-0843 Email: mmccool@nazarene.org

Sunday School and Discipleship Ministries International Director, Dr. Woodie Stevens, 17001 Prairie Star Parkway, Lenexa, KS 66220, Tel. (913)577-0500 FAX: (913)577-0891, Email: stevens@nazarene.org

Education Commissioner, Dr. Dan Copp, 17001 Prairie Star Parkway, Lenexa, KS 66220, Tel. (913)577-0500 Fax (913)577-0858, Email: dcopp@nazarene.org

Nazarene Youth International Director., Rev. Gary Hartke, 17001 Prairie Star Parkway, Lenexa, KS 66220, Tel. (913)577-0500 Fax (913)577-0858, Email: ghartke@nazarene.org

Global Mission Director., Dr. Louie Bustle, 17001 Prairie Star Parkway, Lenexa, KS 66220, Tel. (913)577-0500 Fax (913)577-0886, Email: lbustle@nazarene.org

Periodicals

Holiness Today, Grace & Peace Magazine, Engage Magazine

Church of Our Lord Jesus Christ of the Apostolic Faith, Inc.

This church body was founded by Bishop R.C. Lawson in Columbus, Ohio, and moved to New York City in 1919. It is founded upon the teachings of the apostles and prophets, Jesus Christ being its chief cornerstone.

Headquarters

2081 Adam Clayton Powell Jr. Blvd., New York, NY 10027, Tel. (212)866-1700

Media Contact, Exec. Sec., Bishop Thomas. E. Woolfolk, P.O. Box 119, Oxford, NC 27565, Tel. (919)693-9449 Fax (919)693-6115 Email: tewmsw@embarqmail.com Website: www.apostolic-faith.org

Officers

Board of Apostles: Bishop William L. Bonner; Chief Apostle; Bishop Matthew A Norwood., Presiding Apostle; Bishop Robert L Sanders Sr., Vice Pres; Bishop James I. Clark, Jr.; Bishop Gentle L. Groover; Bishop Fred Rubin; Bishop James A. Maye; Bishop Henry A. Moultrie, II; Bishop Wesley M. Taylor; Bishop Samuel R. Peters, Sr.; Bishop Walter L. Jackson; Bishop Bradford Berry; Bishop Herbert Edwards

Bd. of Bishops, Chmn., Bishop James Darby

Bd. of Presbyters, Chairman, Elder Willie Shy

Exec. Sec., Bishop Thomas E. Woolfolk
Natl. Rec. Sec., Bishop Raymond J. Keith, Jr.
Natl. Fin. Sec., Bishop Clarence Groover
Natl. Corr. Sec., Bishop Darryl Forhand
Natl Treas., Deacon Winston Knox

Periodicals

Contender For The Faith, Minute Book, and The Beacon

Church of the United Brethren in Christ, USA

The Church of the United Brethren in Christ had its beginning with Philip William Otterbein and Martin Boehm, who were leaders in the revival movement in Pennsylvania and Maryland from the late 1760s into the early 1800s.

On Sept. 25, 1800, they and others associated with them formed a society under the name of United Brethren in Christ. Subsequent conferences adopted a Confession of Faith in 1815 and a constitution in 1841. The Church of the United Brethren in Christ adheres to the original constitution as amended over the years.

Headquarters

302 Lake St., Huntington, IN 46750, Tel. (260)356-2312 Fax (260)356-4730 x 210

Media Contact, Communications Dir., Steve Dennie

Email: steve@ub.org
Website: www.ub.org

Officers

Bishop, Rev. Phil Whipple
Finance Director, Marci Hammel
Director of Higher Education, Dr. G. Blair Dowden
Global Ministries Director, Rev. Jeff Bleijerveld
Communications Director, Mr. Steve Dennie

Churches of Christ

Churches of Christ are autonomous congregations whose members follow the Bible alone in matters of faith and practice. There are no central offices or officers. Publications and institutions related to the churches are either under local congregational control or are independent of any congregation. Churches of Christ shared a common fellowship in the 19th century with the Christian Churches/Churches of Christ and the Christian Church (Disciples of Christ). This fellowship ended in the decades following the American Civil War due to erosion of confidence in Scripture among many of those who formed denominational ties. This shift in belief embraced theistic evolution, doubted the complete truth of Scripture, and permitted practices foreign to the New Testament into the work and worship of the church. Chief among the changes in practice were using instrumental music in worship, permitting women to officiate in worship services, and conducting the work of the church through centralized agencies. Churches of Christ, following this division, remained strongly united in their belief in the inerrancy and sufficiency of Scripture. From this standpoint, they affirm faith in one God who subsists in three persons: Father, Son, and Holy Spirit; they teach that salvation is through the sacrificial death of Christ and is available to all who come to God through repentance and faith, initially expressed through confession of faith and baptism by immersion. Churches of Christ follow the New Testament pattern to direct every facet of the teaching and work of the church.

Headquarters

Media Contact, Mr. Neil Anderson, Publisher, Gospel Advocate, 1006 Elm Hill Pike, Nashville, TN 37102, Tel. (800)251-8446 Fax (615)254-7411

Periodicals

Action, Christian Woman, Christian Bible Teacher, The Christian Chronicle, Firm Foundation, Gospel Advocate, Guardian of Truth, Restoration Quarterly, Think, 21st Century Christian, Rocky Mountain Christian, The Spiritual Sword, Word and Work.

Churches of Christ in Christian Union

Organized in 1909 at Washington Court House, Ohio, as the Churches of Christ in Christian Union, this body believes in the new birth and the baptism of the Holy Spirit for believers. It is Wesleyan, with an evangelistic and missionary emphasis. The Reformed Methodist Church merged with the Churches of Christ in Christian Union in 1952.

Headquarters

1553 Lancaster Pike, Circleville, OH 43113, Tel. (740)474-8856 Fax (740)477-7766

Media Contact, General Secreaty, Rev. Ralph Hux

Officers

Gen. Supt., Dr. Tom Hermiz

Asst. Gen. Supt., Rev. Mike Holbrook

General Secreaty, Rev. Ralph Hux

Gen. Treas., Rev. Bruce Crabtree

Gen. Bd. of Trustees, Chpsn., Dr. Tom Hermiz; Vice-Chpsn., Rev. Mike Holbrook

District Superintendents, West Central District, Rev. Joe Duvall; South Central District, Rev. Mike Holbrook; Northeast District, Rev. Brad Dixon; West Indies District, Joseph Atherly

Periodicals

The Evangelical Advocate

Churches of God, General Conference

The Churches of God, General Conference (CGGC) had its beginnings in Harrisburg, Pa., in 1825.

John Winebrenner, recognized founder of the Church of God movement, was an ordained minister of the German Reformed Church. His experience-centered form of Christianity, particularly the "new measures" he used to promote it, his close connection with the local Methodists, his "experience and conference meetings" in the church and his "social prayer meetings" in parishioners' homes resulted in differences of opinion and the establishment of new congregations. Extensive revivals, camp meetings and mission endeavors led to the organization of additional congregations across central Pennsylvania and westward through Ohio, Indiana, Illinois and Iowa.

In 1830 the first system of cooperation between local churches was initiated as an "eldership" in eastern Pennsylvania. The organization of other elderships followed. General Eldership was organized in 1845, and in 1974 the official name of the denomination was changed from General Eldership of the Churches of God in North America to its present name.

The Churches of God, General Conference, is composed of 5 Regions in the United States and 1 conference in Haiti. The polity of the church is presbyterial in form. The church has mission ministries in the southwest among native Americans and is extensively involved in church planting and whole life ministries in Bangladesh, Brazil, Haiti, India, Kenga, Sweden, Thailand, and Venezuela.

The General Conference convenes in business session triennially. An Administrative Council composed of 16 regional representatives is responsible for the administration and ministries of the church between sessions of the General Conference.

Headquarters

Legal Headquarters, United Church Center, Rm. 213, 900 S. Arlington Ave., Harrisburg, PA 17109, Tel. (717)652-0255

Administrative Offices, General Conf. Exec. Dir., Pastor Edward L. Rosenberry, P.O. Box 926, 700 E. Melrose Ave., P.O. Box 926, Findlay, OH 45840, Tel. (419)424-1961 Fax (419)424-3343, Email: director@cggc.org

Media Contact, Editor, Mrs. Rachel L. Foreman, P.O. Box 926, Findlay, OH 45839, Tel. (419)424-1961 Fax (419)424-3343, Email: communications@cggc.org

Email: director@cggc.org

Website: www.cggc.org

Officers

Pres., Pastor Douglas E. Nolt, Email: pastornolt@gmail.com

Sec., Pastor E. David Green, 700 E. Melrose Ave., P.O. Box 1132, Findlay, OH 45839, Tel. (419)423-7694 Fax (419)423-9092, Email: GLCdirector@cggc.org

102

Treas., Robert E. Stephenson, 700 E. Melrose Ave., P.O. Box 926, Findlay, OH 45839, Tel. (419)424-1961 Fax (419)424-3433, Email: treasurer@cggc.org

DEPARTMENTS
Cross-Cultural Ministries, Pastor Don Dennison
Pensions, Mr. James P. Thomas
Denominational Communications, Mrs. Rachel L. Foreman
Youth & Family Ministries, Pastor J. Lance Finley
Publications, Kris Cupp
CGWM -Churches of God Women's Ministries

Periodicals
The Church Advocate, The Gem, The Missionary Signal

Community of Christ*
Community of Christ's mission is to proclaim Jesus Christ and promote communities of joy, hope, love, and peace. Founded on April 6, 1830, this Christian denomination is present in nearly 50 nations with approximately 250,000 members worldwide. The church's Temple, located in the international headquarters complex, is dedicated to peace, reconciliation, and healing of the Spirit. Priesthood includes both men and women.

Headquarters
International Headquarters, 1001 W. Walnut, Independence, MO 64050-3562, Tel. (816) 833-1000 Fax (816)521-3096
Media Contact; Kendra Friend, Email: kfriend@cofchrist.org; or Jennifer Killpack, Email: jkillpack@cofchrist.org
Email: blindgren@CofChrist.org
Website: www.CofChrist.org

Officers
Mailing address for all officers is 1001 W. Walnut, Independence, MO 64050, Tel. (816)833-1000
First Presidency:
President, Stephen M. Veazey, Email: sveazey@cofchrist.org
Counselor, David D. Schaal, Email: dschaal@cofchrist.org
Counselor, Becky Savage, Email: bsavage@cofchrist.org
Council of Twelve Apostles
President, James E. Slauter, Email: jslauter@cofchrist.org
Presiding Bishopric:
Presiding Bishop, Stephen M. Jones, Email: sjones@cofchrist.org
Counselor, R. Paul Davis, Email: pdavis@cofchrist.org
Counselor, David J. Brown, Email: dbrown@cofchrist.org
Presiding Evangelist:
David R. Brock, Email: dbrock@cofchrist.org
World Church Secretary:
Andrew Shields, Email: ashields@cofchrist.org
Public Relations, Fax (816)521-3043

Kendra Friend, Email: kfriend@cofchrist.org
Jennifer Killpack, Email: jkillpack@cofchrist.org

Periodicals
Herald

Congregational Holiness Church
This body was organized in 1921 and embraces the doctrine of Holiness and Pentecost. It carries on mission work in Mexico, Honduras, Costa Rica, Cuba, Brazil, Guatemala, India, Nicaragua, El Salvador, Venezula, Panama, Chile, Argentina, Belize, Zimbabwe, Haiti, and Peru.

Headquarters
3888 Fayetteville Hwy., Griffin, GA 30223, Tel. (404)228-4833 Fax (404)228-1177
Media Contact, Gen. Supt., Bishop Ronald Wilson
Email: chchurch@bellsouth.net
Website: www.chchurch.com

EXECUTIVE BOARD
Gen. Supt., Bishop Ronald Smith
1st Asst. Gen. Supt., Rev. William L. Lewis
2nd Asst. Gen. Supt., Rev. Wayne Hicks
Gen. Sec., Rev. Leslee Bailey
Gen. Treas., Rev. Stephen Phillips
World Missions Supt., Rev. Billy Anderson

Periodicals
The Gospel Messenger

Conservative Baptist Association of America (CBAmerica)
The Conservative Baptist Association of America (now known as CBAmerica) was organized May 17, 1947 at Atlantic City, N.J. The Old and New Testaments are regarded as the divinely inspired Word of God and are therefore infallible and of supreme authority. Each local church is independent, autonomous and free from ecclesiastical or political authority.

CBAmerica provides wide-ranging support to its affiliate churches and individuals through nine regional associations. CBA offers personnel to assist churches in areas such as growth and health conflict resolution and financial analysis. The association supports its clergy with retirement planning, referrals for new places of ministry and spiritual counseling. The Conservative Baptist Women's Ministries assists women in the church to be effective in their personal growth and leadership.

Each June or July there is a National Conference giving members an opportunity for fellowship, inspiration and motivation.

Headquarters
1501 W. Mineral Ave., Suite B, Littleton, CO 80120-5612, Tel. (888)627-1995 or (720)283-3030 Fax (720)283-3333
Media Contact, Executive Director, Dr. Dennis L. Gorton

Email: cba@cbamerica.org
Website: www.cbamerica.org

OTHER ORGANIZATIONS
CBInternational, Exec. Dir., Dr. Hans Finzel, 1501 W. Mineral Ave., Littleton, CO 80120-5612
Mission to the Americas, Exec. Dir., Rev. Rick Miller, Box 828, Wheaton, IL 60189
Conservative Baptist Higher Ed. Council, Dr. Bert Downs, Western Seminary, 5511 S. E. Hawthorne Blvd., Portland, OR 97215

Periodicals
Front Line Turnings

Conservative Congregational Christian Conference

In the 1930s, evangelicals within the Congregational Christian Churches felt a definite need for fellowship and service. By 1945, this loose association crystallized into the Conservative Congregational Christian Fellowship, committed to maintaining a faithful, biblical witness.

In 1948 in Chicago, the Conservative Congregational Christian Conference was established to provide a continuing fellowship for evangelical churches and ministers on the national level. In recent years, many churches have joined the Conference from backgrounds other than Congregational. These churches include Community or Bible Churches and churches from the Evangelical and Reformed background that are truly congregational in polity and thoroughly evangelical in conviction. The CCCC welcomes all evangelical churches that are, in fact, congregational. The CCCC believes in the necessity of a regenerate membership, the authority of the Holy Scriptures, the Lordship of Jesus Christ, the autonomy of the local church and the universal fellowship of all Christians.

The Conservative Congregational Christian Conference is a member of the World Evangelical Congregational Fellowship (formed in 1986 in London, England) and the National Association of Evangelicals.

Headquarters
8941 Highway 5, Lake Elmo, MN 55042, Tel. (651)739-1474 Fax (651)739-0750
Media Contact, Conf. Min., Mrs. Diane Johnson
Email: ccc4@juno.com
Website: www.ccccusa.com

Officers
Pres., Rev. Paul McPheeters, 133 Floral Ave, Malden MA 02148
Vice Pres., Rev. Todd Venman, 2525 Swede Hill Rd, Russell PA 16354
Conf. Min., Rev. Dr. Ronald Hamilton, 8941 Highway 5, Lake Elmo MN 55042
Controller, Rev. Tay E. Kersey, 8450 Eastwood Rd., Moundsview, MN 55112
Treas., Mrs. Karen Sloat, 45505 Meadow Lake Dr, Indio, CA 92201

Sec., Rev. Gerard Kilyk, 3507 Bainbridge Blvd., Chesapeake, VA 23324
Editor, Rev. Ken McGarvey, 121 Chatuga Dr, Loudon, TN 37774
Historian, Rev. Alwyn York, 709 N. Cheyenne Ave., Hardin, MT 59034

Periodicals
Foresee

Conservative Lutheran Association

The Conservative Lutheran Association (CLA) was originally named Lutheran's Alert National (LAN) when it was founded in 1965 by 10 conservative Lutheran pastors and layman meeting in Cedar Rapids, Iowa. Its purpose was to help preserve from erosion the basic doctrines of Christian theology, including the inerrancy of Holy Scripture. The group grew to a worldwide constituency, similarly concerned with maintaining the doctrinal integrity of the Bible and the Lutheran Confessions.

Headquarters
Trinity Lutheran Church, 4101 E. Nohl Ranch Rd., Anaheim, CA 92807, Tel. (714)637-8370
Media Contact, Pres., Rev. P. J. Moore
Email: PastorPJ@ix.netcom.com
Website: www.tlcanaheim.com/CLA

Officers
Pres., Rev. P. J. Moore, 4101 E. Nohl Ranch Rd., Anaheim, CA 92807, Tel. (714)637-8370
Vice Pres., Rev. Dr. R. H. Redal, 409 Tacoma Ave. N., Tacoma, WA 98403, Tel. (206)383-5528
Faith Seminary, Dean, Rev. Dr. Michael J. Adams, 3504 N. Pearl St., P.O. Box 7186, Tacoma, WA 98407, Tel. (888)777-7675 Fax (206)759-1790

Converge Worldwide (BGC)

The Baptist General Conference, is now called Converge Worldwide, rooted in the pietistic movement of Sweden during the 19th century, traces its history to Aug. 13, 1852. On that day a small group of believers at Rock Island, Illinois, under the leadership of Gustaf Palmquist, organized the first Swedish Baptist Church in America. Swedish Baptist churches flourished in the upper Midwest and Northeast, and by 1879, when the first annual meeting was held in Village Creek, Iowa, 65 churches had been organized, stretching from Maine to the Dakotas and south to Kansas and Missouri.

By 1871, John Alexis Edgren, an immigrant sea captain and pastor in Chicago, had begun the first publication and a theological seminary. The Conference grew to 324 churches and nearly 26,000 members by 1902. There were 40,000 members in 1945 and in 2010 they have over 1100 churches.

104

Many churches began as Sunday schools. The seminary evolved into Bethel, a fouryear liberal arts university with 2,300 students, and theological seminaries in Arden Hills, Minnesota. and San Diego, California. Missions and the planting of churches have been main objectives both in America and overseas. Today churches have been established in the United States, Canada and Mexico, as well as twenty-four countries overseas. In 1985 the churches of Canada founded an autonomous denomination, The Baptist General Conference of Canada.

Converge Worldwide is a member of the Baptist World Alliance, the Baptist Joint Committee on Public Affairs and the National Association of Evangelicals. It is characterized by the balancing of a conservative doctrine with an irenic and cooperative spirit. Its basic objective is to seek the fulfillment of the Great Commission and the Great Commandment.

Headquarters
11002 Lake Hart Dr., Mail Code 200, Orlando, FL 32832, Tel. (407)563-6095
Email: gmarsh@baptistgeneral.org
Website: www.bgcworld.org

Officers
Pres. & Chief Exec. Officer, Dr. Gerald Sheveland, 11002 Lake Hart Dr., Mail Code 200, Orlando, FL 32832, Tel. (847)228-0200 Fax (847)228-5376; Email: Jerry. Sheveland@convergeww.org
Senior, Vice Pres., Dr. Doug Fagerstrom, (address/ph/fax same as above), Email: Doug.Fagerstrom@convergeww.org
Director of Finance, Stephen R. Schultz, 2002 S. Arlington Hts. Rd., Arlington Heights, IL 60005, Email: Steve.Schultz@convergeww.org
Exec. Director of National Ministries, Dr. John Jenkins, 11002 Lake Hart Dr., Mail Code 200, Orlando, FL 32832, Email: John.Jenkins@convergeww.org
Exec. Director of International Ministries: Mr. Steve Deggett, 11002 Lake Hart Dr., Mail Code 200, Orlando, FL 32832, Email: SteveD@convergeww.org

OTHER ORGANIZATIONS
Bd. of Trustees, Bethel University, Pres., Dr. Jay Barnes, III, 3900 Bethel Dr., St. Paul, MN 55112

Periodicals
Converge Point

Cooperative Baptist Fellowship
The Cooperative Baptist Fellowship is a fellowship of Baptist Christians and churches who share a passion for the Great Commission of Jesus Christ and a commitment to Baptist principles of faith and practice. Our mission is to serve Christians and churches as they discover and fulfill their God-given mission.

Made up of individuals and approximately 1,800 affiliated churches seeking to be the presence of Christ, the Fellowship serves a larger renewal movement among Baptists. Partnering with 15 theological schools, 18 autonomous state and regional organizations and more than 150 ministry organizations worldwide, CBF has an annual budget of $14.5 million and is based in Atlanta.

According to the CBF Constitution and Bylaws, affiliation is measured by contribution. Any church or individual who sends a contribution of any amount is considered a member of the Fellowship with voting rights at the annual General Assembly.

Headquarters
2930 Flowers Road South Suite 133 Atlanta, GA 30341 Tel. 800.352.8741
Media Contact: Lance Wallace, Director of Communications, Tel. (770)220-1641, Cell (404)644-2838
Email: contact@thefellowship.info
Website: www.thefellowship.info

2011-2012 CBF Coordinating Council
Colleen Burroughs, Moderator -Birmingham AL
Christy McMillin-Goodwin, Past Moderator - Rock Hill SC
Keith Herron, Moderator Elect -Kansas City, MO
Renee Bennett, Recorder -Macon GA

Periodicals
fellowship!, Form, Spark and Ignite

Coptic Orthodox Church*
This body is part of the ancient Coptic orthodox Church of Alexandria, Egypt which is currently headed by His Holiness Pope Shenouda III, 116th Successor to St. Mark the Apostle. Egyptian immigrants have organized many parishes in the United States. Copts exist outside Egypt in Africa, Europe, Asia, Australia, Canada and the United States. The total world Coptic community is estimated at 27 million. The church is in full communion with the other members of The Oriental Orthodox Church Family, The Syrian Orthodox Church, Armenian Orthodox Church, Ethiopian Orthodox Church, the Indian Orthodox Church and the Eritrean Orthodox Church.

Headquarters
427 West Side Ave., Jersey City, NJ 07304
Email: Webmaster@coptic.org
Website: www.coptic.org

Officers
Bishop of Los Angeles, Bishop Serapion, 3803 3803 W. Mission Blvd., Pomona, CA 91766, Tel. (909)865-8378 Fax (909)865-8348; Email: bishopserapion@lacopts.org

Periodicals
Agape Magazine, El Keraza

Cumberland Presbyterian Church

The Cumberland Presbyterian Church was organized in Dickson County, Tennessee, on Feb. 4, 1810. It was an outgrowth of the Great Revival of 1800 on the Kentucky and Tennessee frontier. The founders were Finis Ewing, Samuel King and Samuel McAdow, ministers in the Presbyterian Church who rejected the doctrine of election and reprobation as taught in the Westminster Confession of Faith.

By 1813, the Cumberland Presbytery had grown to encompass three presbyteries, which constituted a synod. This synod met at the Beech Church in Sumner County, Tenn., and formulated a "Brief Statement" which set forth the points in which Cumberland Presbyterians dissented from the Westminster Confession. These points are:

1. That there are no eternal reprobates;
2. That Christ died not for some, but for all people;
3. That all those dying in infancy are saved through Christ and the sanctification of the Spirit;
4. That the Spirit of God operates on the world, or as coextensively as Christ has made atonement, in such a manner as to leave everyone inexcusable.

From its birth in 1810, the Cumberland Presbyterian Church grew to a membership of 200,000 at the turn of the century. In 1906 the church voted to merge with the then-Presbyterian Church. Those who dissented from the merger became the nucleus of the continuing Cumberland Presbyterian Church.

Headquarters

8207 Traditional Place, Cordova, TN, 38016, Tel. (901)276-4572 Fax (901)272-3913
Media Contact, Stated Clk., Rev. Michael G. Sharpe, Fax (901)272-3913
Email: assembly@cumberland.org
Website: www.cumberland.org

Officers

Mod., Mr. Boyce Wallace, Cra 101 No. 15-93, Cali, Colombia, Email: hbwcali@yahoo.com
Stated Clk., The Rev. Michael G. Sharpe, Tel. (901)276-4572 x 225 Fax (901)272-3913, Email: mgs@cumberland.org

INSTITUTIONS
Cumberland Presbyterian Children's Home, Exec. Dir., Rev. Kevin Henson, Drawer G, Denton, TX 76202, Tel. (940)382-5112 Fax (940)387-0821; Email: cpch@cpch.org
Cumberland Presbyterian Center, Tel. (901)276-4572 Fax (901)272-3913 or (901) 276-4758
Memphis Theological Seminary, 168 E. Parkway S., Memphis, TN 38104, Tel. (901)458-8232 Fax (901)452-4051, Website: www.memphis seminary.edu, Pres., Dr. Jay Earheart-Brown

Bethel University, Pres., Dr. Robert Prosser, 325 Cherry St., McKenzie, TN 38201, Tel. (901)352-4004 Fax (901)352-4069; Email: prosserb@bethel-college.edu
Historical Foundation, Archivist, Susan K. Gore, 8207 Traditional Place, Cordova, TN, 38016, Tel. (901)276-8602 Fax (901)272-3913, Email: skg@cumberland.org

BOARDS
Ministry Council, Exec. Dir. Ms. Edith Gholson, 8207 Traditional Place, Cordova, TN, 38016, Email: emg@cumberland.org., Tel. (901)276-4572 Fax (901)276-4578
Communications Team: Team Leader: Mr. Mark Davis, 8207 Traditional Place, Cordova, TN, 38016, Email: MDavis@cumberland.org, Tel. (901)276-4572 Fax (901)276-4758
Discipleship Team: Team Leader: Rev. Frank Ward, 8207 Traditional Place, Cordova, TN, 38016, Email: Fdw@cumberland.org, Tel. (901)276-4572 Fax (901)276-4758
Missions Ministry Team: Team Leader: Rev. George R. Estes, 8207 Traditional Place, Cordova, TN, 38016, Email: gre@ cumberland.org, Tel. (901)276-4572 Fax (901) 276-4758
Pastoral Development Team: Team Leader: Rev. Milton Ortiz, 8207 Traditional Place, Cordova, TN, 38016, Email: Fdw@cumberland.org, Tel. (901)276-4572 Fax (901)276-4758

Periodicals

The Cumberland Presbyterian, The Missionary Messenger

Cumberland Presbyterian Church in America

This church, originally known as the Colored Cumberland Presbyterian Church, was formed in May 1874. In May 1869, at the General Assembly meeting in Murfreesboro, Tennessee, Moses Weir of the Black delegation sucessfully appealed for help in organizing a separate African church so that-Blacks could learn self-reliance and independence; they could have more financial assistance; they could minister more effectively among Blacks; and they could worship close to the altar, not in the balconies. He requested that the Cumberland Presbyterian Church organize Blacks into presbyteries and synods, develop schools to train black clergy, grant loans to assist Blacks to secure hymnbooks, Bibles and church buildings and establish a separate General Assembly. In 1874 the first General Assembly of the Colored Cumberland Presbyterian Church met in Nashville. The moderator was Rev. P. Price and the stated clerk was Elder John Humphrey.

The denomination's General Assembly, the national governing body, is organized around its three program boards and agencies-Finance, Publication and Christian Education, and

Missions and Evangelism. Other agencies of the General Assembly are under these three program boards.

The church has four synods (Alabama, Kentucky, Tennessee and Texas), 15 presbyteries and 153 congregations. The CPC extends as far north as Cleveland, Ohio, and Chicago, as far west as Marshalltown, Iowa, and Dallas, TX., and as far south as Selma, Ala.

Headquarters

Media Contact, Stated Clk., Rev. Dr. Robert. Stanley Wood, 226 Church St., Huntsville, AL 35801, Tel. (205)536-7481 Fax (205)536-7482
Email: mleslie598@aol.com
Website: www.cumberland.org/cpca

Officers

Mod., Rev. Endia Scruggs, 1627 Carroll Rd., Harvest, AL 35749
Stated Clk., Rev. Dr. Rorbert. Stanley Wood, 226 Church St., Huntsville, AL 35801, Tel. (205)536-7481

SYNODS

Alabama, Stated Clk., Arthur Hinton, 511 10th Ave. N.W., Aliceville, AL 35442
Kentucky, Stated Clk., Mary Martha Daniels, 8548 Rhodes Ave., Chicago, IL 60619
Tennessee, Stated Clk., Elder Clarence Norman, 145 Jones St., Huntington, TN 38334
Texas, Stated Clk., Arthur King, 2435 Kristen, Dallas, TX 75216

Disciples of Christ — please see Christian Church (Disciples of Christ) in the United States and Canada

Elim Fellowship

The Elim Fellowship, a Pentecostal Body established in 1947, is an outgrowth of the Elim Missionary Assemblies formed in 1933. It is an association of churches, ministers and missionaries seeking to serve the whole Body of Christ. It is of Pentecostal conviction and charismatic orientation, providing ministerial credentials and counsel and encouraging fellowship among local churches. Elim Fellowship sponsors leadership seminars at home and abroad and serves as a transdenominational agency sending long-term, short-term and tent-making missionaries to work with national movements.

Headquarters

1703 Dalton Rd., Lima, NY 14485, Tel. (585)582-2790 Fax (585)624-1229
Media Contact, Gen. Sec., Rev. Chris Ball
Email: executive@elimfellowship.org
Website: www.ElimFellowship.org

Officers

Pres., Rev. Dr. Ronald V. Burgio
Gen. Treas., Stephanie Zeller

Periodicals

Elim Herald

The Episcopal Church*

The Episcopal Church entered the colonies with the earliest settlers at Jamestown, Va., in 1607 as the Church of England. After the American Revolution, it became autonomous in 1789 as The Protestant Episcopal Church in the United States of America. (The Episcopal Church became the official alternate name in 1967.) Samuel Seabury of Connecticut was elected the first bishop and consecrated in Aberdeen by bishops of the Scottish Episcopal Church in 1784.

In organizing as an independent body, the Episcopal Church created a bicameral legislature, the General Convention, modeled after the new U.S. Congress. It comprises a House of Bishops and a House of Deputies and meets every three years. A 38-member Executive Council, which meets three times a year, is the interim governing body. An elected presiding bishop serves as Primate and Chief Pastor.

After severe setbacks in the years immediately following the Revolution because of its association with the British Crown and the fact that a number of its clergy and members were Loyalists, the church soon established its own identity and sense of mission. It sent missionaries into the newly settled territories of the United States, establishing dioceses from coast to coast, and also undertook substantial missionary work in Africa, Latin America and the Far East. Today, the overseas dioceses are developing into independent provinces of the Anglican Communion, the worldwide fellowship of 38 churches in communion with the Church of England and the Archbishop of Canterbury. The beliefs and practices of The Episcopal Church, like those of other Anglican churches, are both Catholic and Reformed, with bishops in the apostolic succession and the historic creeds of Christendom regarded as essential elements of faith and order, along with the primary authority of Holy Scripture and the two chief sacraments of Baptism and Eucharist.

EPISCOPAL CHURCH CENTER

815 Second Ave., New York, NY 10017, Tel. (212)716-6240 or (800)334-7626 Fax (212)867-0395 or (212)490-3298
Media Contact, Dir. of News Service., Robert Williams, Tel. (212)922-5385
Email: cepting@episcopalchurch.org
Website: www.ecusa.anglican.org

Officers

Presiding Bishop & Primate, The Most Rev. Katharine Jefferts Schori
Chief Operating Officer, The Rt. Rev. Stacy Sauls
Treas., Kurt Barnes, Tel. (212)922-5296 E-mail: kbarnes@episcopalchurch.org
Canon to the Presiding Bishop & Primate, The Rev. Canon Charles K. Robertson, Tel. (212)716-6278 Email: crobertson@episcopal church.org

House of Deputies, Pres., Bonnie Anderson

Exec. Officer and Sec. of the General Convention, Sec. of the House of Deputies, Sec. of the Domestic and Foreign Missionary Society, and Sec. of the Executive Council, The Rev. Gregory Straub

OFFICE OF THE PRESIDING BISHOP

Presiding Bishop, The Most Rev. Katharine Jefferts Schori, Tel. (212)716-6276

Chief Operating Officer, The Rt. Rev. Stacy Sauls, Tel. (212)922-5313 E-mail: ssauls@ episcopalchurch.org

Canon to the Presiding Bishop, The Rev. Canon Charles Robertson, Tel. (212)716-6278 E-mail: crobertson@episcopalchurch.org

Dir., Office for Transition Ministry, The Rev. Victoria Duncan, Tel. (212)922-5251

Exec. Dir., Office of Pastoral Dev., The Rt. Rev. Clayton Matthews, Tel. (212)716-6163

Exec. Sec., General Board of Examining Chaplains, Mr. Duncan C. Ely, Tel. (828)859-1205

Federal Ministries, Bishop Suffragan, The Rt. Rev. James B Magness, Tel. (646)434-0299

Convocation of American Churches in Europe, Bishop-in-Charge, Rt. Rev. Pierre Whalon, Tel. 011-33-1-472-01792

Deputy, Ecumenical and Interfaith Relations, VACANT, Tel. (212)716-6220

ADMINISTRATION AND FINANCE

Treasurer of the Domestic and Foreign Missionary Society and Chief Financial Officer, Kurt Barnes, Tel. (212)922-5296

Controller, Alpha Conteh, Tel. (212)922-5366

Archivist, Mark Duffy, Tel. (512)472-6816

Director, Human Resources Management, John Colon, Tel. (212)716-6331

MISSION

Deputy Chief Operating Officer and Director of Mission, Mr. Samuel A. McDonald, Tel. (212)716-6162

Associate Director of Mission, Ms. Antoinette (Toni) Daniels, Tel. (212)716-6332

Associate Director of Mission, The Rev. Margaret Rose, Tel. (212)922-5354

President, Episcopal Relief and Development, Robert Radtke, Tel. (212)716-6020

Includes Diocesan & Congregational Ministries; Diversity, Social & Environmental Ministries; Episcopal Migration Ministries; Formation & Vocation Ministries; Global Partnerships; and Government Advocacy for Peace & Justice

BISHOPS:

The Rt. Rev. Gladstone Adams III, Bishop of Central New York, 310 Montgomery St, Suite 200, Syracuse, NY 13202-2093

The Rt. Rev. J. Neil Alexander, Bishop of Atlanta, 2744 Peachtree Road NW, Atlanta, GA 30305

The Rt. Rev. Lloyd Allen, Bishop of Honduras, IMC-SAP; Dept. 215, Miami, FL 33152-3900

The Rt. Rev. David Alvarez, Bishop of Puerto Rico, P.O. Box 902, St Just, PR 00978-0902

The Rt. Rev. Marc Handley Andrus, Bishop of California, 1055 Taylor St., San Francisco, CA 94108

The Rt. Rev. David E. Bailey, Bishop of Navajoland Area Mission, P.O. Box 720, Farmington, NM 87499

The Rt. Rev. John Bauerschmidt, Bishop of Tennessee, 50 Vantage Way, Suite 107, Nashville, TN 37228

The Rt. Rev. Nathan Baxter, Bishop of Central Pennsylvania, P.O. Box 11937, Harrisburg, PA 17108

The Rt. Rev. Mark Beckwith, Bishop of Newark, 31 Mulberry St., Newark, NJ 07102

The Rt. Rev. Barry Beisner, Bishop of Northern California, 350 University Ave., Suite 280, Sacramento, CA 95825

The Rt. Rev. Larry Benfield, Bishop of Arkansas, P.O. Box 164668, Little Rock, AR 72216

The Rt. Rev. Charles E. Bennison, Jr., Bishop of Pennsylvania, 240 South 4th St., Philadelphia, PA 19106

The Rt. Rev. Scott Benhase, Bishop of Georgia, 611 East Bay St., Savannah, GA 31401

The Rt. Rev. Thomas Breidenthal, Bishop of Southern Ohio, 412 Sycamore St., Cincinnati, OH 45202

The Rt. Rev. C. Franklin Brookhart, Bishop of Montana, 515 North Park Ave., Helena, MT 59601

The Rt. Rev. J. Jon Bruno, Bishop of Los Angeles, P.O. Box 512164, Los Angeles, CA 90026

The Rt. Rev. John Buchanan, Provisional Bishop of Quincy, c/o St. Paul's Episcopal Cathedral, 3601 North North, Peoria, IL 61604

The Rt. Rev. John Chane, Bishop of Washington, Episcopal Ch. House, Mt. St. Alban, Washington, DC 20016-5094

The Rt. Rev. George Councell, Bishop of New Jersey, 808 West State St., Trenton, NJ 08618-5326

The Rt. Rev. Michael Curry, Bishop of North Carolina, 200 West Morgan St., Suite 300, Raleigh, NC 27601-1338

The Rt. Rev. Clifton Daniel, Bishop of East Carolina, P.O. Box 1336, Kinston, NC 28503

The Rt. Rev. Ian Douglas, Bishop of Connecticut, 1335 Asylum Ave., Hartford, CT 06105-2295

The Rt. Rev. C. Andrew Doyle, Bishop of Texas, 1225 Texas Ave., Houston, TX 77002

The Rt. Rev. Philip Duncan, Bishop of Central Gulf Coast, 102 N. Baylen St., Pensacola, FL 32591-3330

The Rt. Rev. Francisco Duque, Bishop of Colombia, Cra. 6 No. 49-85, Bogota, Colombia

The Rt. Rev. Jean Zache Duracin, Eglise Episcopal d'Haiti, 86 Rue Rigaud, Petion Ville, Haiti

The Rt. Rev. Dan Edwards, Bishop of Nevada, 9480 South Eastern Ave., Suite 236, Las Vegas, NV 89123

The Rt. Rev. Thomas Ely, Bishop of Vermont, 5 Rock Point Rd., Burlington, VT 05408

The Rt. Rev. Martin S. Field, Bishop of West Missouri, P.O. Box 413227, Kansas City, MO 64141-3227

The Rt. Rev. Robert Fitzpatrick, Bishop of Hawaii, 229 Queen Emma Square, Honolulu, HI 96813-2304

The Rt. Rev. Leopold Frade, Bishop of Southeast Florida, 525 NE 15th St., Miami, FL 33132

The Rt. Rev. R. William Franklin, Bishop of Western New York, 1064 Brighton Rd., Tonawanda, NY 14150

The Rt. Rev. Robert Gepert, Bishop of Western Michigan, 535 S. Burdick St., Kalamazoo, MI 49007

The Rt. Rev. Wendell Gibbs, Bishop of Michigan, 4800 Woodward Ave., Detroit, MI 48201-1399

The Rt. Rev. Duncan Gray, Bishop of Mississippi, P.O. Box 23107, Jackson, MS 39225-3107

The Rt. Rev. Mary Gray-Reeves, Bishop of El Camino Real, 1092 Noche Buena St., Seaside, CA 93955

The Rt. Rev. Orlando Guerrero, Bishop of Venezuela, 49-143 Colinas de Bello Monte, Caracas, VENEZUELA

The Rt. Rev. E. Ambrose Gumbs, Bishop of the Virgin Islands, P.O. Box 7488, Charlotte Amalie, St. Thomas, USVI 00801

The Rt. Rev. Michael J. Hanley, Bishop of Oregon, 11800 SW Military Lane, Portland, OR 97219-8436

The Rt. Rev. Scott B. Hayashi, Bishop of Utah, 75 South 200 East, P.O. Box 3090, Salt Lake City, UT 84110-3090

The Rt. Rev. Julio Holguin, Bishop of the Dominican Republic, DMG 13602, 100, Airport Rd., Venice, FL 34285

The Rt. Rev. Herman Hollerith, Bishop of Southern Virginia, 600 Talbot Hall Rd., Norfolk, VA 23505

The Rt. Rev. Mark Hollingsworth, Jr., Bishop of Ohio, 2230 Euclid Ave., Cleveland, OH 44115-2499

The Rt. Rev. S. Johnson Howard, Bishop of Florida, 325 Market St., Jacksonville, FL 32202

The Rt. Rev. John Howe, Bishop of Central Florida, 1017 East Robinson St., Orlando, FL 32801

The Rt. Rev. Russell Jacobus, Bishop of Fond du Lac, 1051 N. Lynndale Drive Suite 1B, Appleton, WI 54914-3094

The Rt. Rev. Don Johnson, Bishop of West Tennessee, 692 Poplar Avenue Memphis, TN 38105

The Rt. Rev. Shannon Johnston, Bishop of Virginia, 110 W. Franklin St., Richmond, VA 23220

The Rt. Rev. William Klusmeyer, Bishop of West Virginia, P.O. Box 5400, Charleston, WV 25361-0400

The Rt. Rev. Edward Konieczny, Bishop of Oklahoma, 924 North Robinson, Oklahoma City, OK 73102

The Rt. Rev. David J.H. Lai, Bishop of Taiwan, 7, Lane 105. Hangchow South Road Sec. 1, Taipei 10060, TAIWAN

The Rt. Rev. Stephen Lane, Bishop of Maine, 143 State St., Portland, ME 04101

The Rt. Rev. Mark A. Lattime, Bishop of Alaska, 1205 Denali Way, Fairbanks, AK 99701

The Rt. Rev. Mark Lawrence, Bishop of South Carolina, 126 Coming St., Charleston, SC 29413

The Rt. Rev. Jeffrey Lee, Bishop of Chicago, 65 East Huron St., Chicago, IL 60611

The Rt. Rev. Edwin M. Leidel, Jr., Provisional Bishop of Eau Claire, 510 South Farwell St., Eau Claire, WI 54701

The Rt. Rev. Gary Lillibridge, Bishop of West Texas, P.O. Box 6885, San Antonio, TX 78209

The Rt. Rev. Edward Little, Bishop of Northern Indiana, 117 North Lafayette Blvd., South Bend, IN 46601

The Rt. Rev. William Love, Bishop of Albany, 68 South Swan St., Albany, NY 12210

The Rt. Rev. D. Bruce MacPherson, Bishop of Western Louisiana, Box 2031, Alexandria, LA 71309

The Rt. Rev. Paul Marshall, Bishop of Bethlehem, 333 Wyandotte St., Bethlehem, PA 18015

The Rt. Rev. Daniel H. Martins, Bishop of Springfield, 821 South 2nd St., Springfield, IL 62704-2694

The Rt. Rev. James Mathes, Bishop of San Diego, 2728 Sixth Ave., San Diego, CA 92103

The Rt. Rev. J. Scott Mayer, Bishop of Northwest Texas, 1802 Broadway, Lubbock, TX 79401

The Rt. Rev. Steven Miller, Bishop of Milwaukee, 804 East Juneau Ave., Milwaukee, WI 53202

The Rt. Rev. Michael P. Milliken, Bishop of Western Kansas, 2 Hyde Park Dr., Hutchinson, KS 67502

The Rt. Rev. Alfredo Morante, Bishop of Litoral Ecuador, Apartado Aereo 0901-5250, Guayaquil, ECUADOR

The Rt. Rev. C. Wallis Ohl, Jr., Provisional Bishop of Fort Worth, 3550 Southwest Loop 820, Fort Worth, TX 76133

The Rt. Rev. Robert O'Neill, Bishop of Colorado, 1300 Washington St., Denver, CO 80203

The Rt. Rev. S. Todd Ousley, Bishop of Eastern Michigan, 924 North Niagara St., Saginaw, MI 48602

The Rt. Rev. Henry Parsley, Jr., Bishop of Alabama, 521 North 20th St., Birmingham, AL 35203

The Rt. Rev. F. Neff Powell, Bishop of Southwestern Virginia, P.O. Box 2279, Roanoke, VA 24009-2279

The Rt. Rev. Kenneth Price, Provisional Bishop of Pittsburgh, 4099 William Penn Highway, Suite 502, Monroeville, PA 15146

The Rt. Rev. Brian Prior, Bishop of Minnesota, 1730 Clifton Place, Suite 201, Minneapolis, MN 55403

The Rt. Rev. Lawrence Provenzano, Bishop of Long Island, 36 Cathedral Avenue P.O. Box 510, Garden City, NY 11530

The Rt. Rev. Rayford J. Ray, Bishop of Northern Michigan, 131 East Ridge St., Marquette, MI 49855

The Rt. Rev. Gregory Rickel, Bishop of Olympia, 1551 10th Avenue E, Seattle, WA 98102

The Rt. Rev. Bavi E. Rivera, Provisional Bishop of Eastern Oregon, 601 Union St., Box 1548, The Dalles, OR 97058

The Rt. Rev. V. Gene Robinson, Bishop of New Hampshire, 63 Green St., Concord, NH 03301 The Rt. Rev. Sean Rowe, Bishop of Northwestern Pennsylvania, 145 West 6th St., Erie,

PA 16501 The Rt. Rev. Luis Ruiz, Bishop of Central Ecuador, Calle Hernando Sarmiento N39-54 y

Portete, Sector El Batan, Quito, ECUADOR The Rt. Rev. Stacy Sauls, Bishop of Lexington, P.O. Box 610, Lexington, KY 40588-0610

The Rt. Rev. Alan Scarfe, Bishop of Iowa, 225 37th St., Des Moines, IA 50312-4399

The Rt. Rev. Gordon Scruton, Bishop of Western Massachusetts, 37 Chestnut St., Springfield, MA 01103

The Rt. Rev. James Shand, Bishop of Easton, 314 North St., Easton, MD 21601

The Rt. Rev. M. Thomas Shaw, Bishop of Massachusetts, 138 Tremont St., Boston, MA 02111

The Rt. Rev. Prince Singh, Bishop of Rochester, 935 East Ave., Rochester, NY 14607

The Rt. Rev. Mark Sisk, Bishop of New York, 1047 Amsterdam Ave., New York, NY 10025

The Rt. Rev. Dabney Smith, Bishop of Southwest Florida, 7313 Merchant Ct., Sarasota, FL 34240

The Rt. Rev. George Smith, Bishop of Missouri, 1210 Locust St., St. Louis, MO 63103

The Rt. Rev. Kirk Smith, Bishop of Arizona, 114 West Roosevelt St., Phoenix, AZ 85003-1406

The Rt. Rev. Michael Smith, Bishop of North Dakota, 3600 South 25th St., Fargo, ND 58104-6861

The Rt. Rev. John S. Smylie, Bishop of Wyoming, 123 South Durbin, Casper, WY 82601

The Rt. Rev. James Stanton, Bishop of Dallas, 1630 North Garrett Ave., Dallas, TX 75206

The Rt. Rev. Eugene Sutton, Bishop of Maryland, 4 East University Parkway, Baltimore, MD 21218

The Rt. Rev. Chester L. Talton, Provisional Bishop of San Joaquin, 1528 Oakdale Rd., Modesto, CA 95355

The Rt. Rev. John Tarrant, Bishop of South Dakota, 500 South Main Ave., Sioux Falls, SD 57104-6814

The Rt. Rev. G. Porter Taylor, Bishop of Western North Carolina, 900-B Centre Park Dr., Asheville, NC 28805

The Rt. Rev. Brian Thom, Bishop of Idaho, 1858 West Judith Lane, Boise, ID 83705

The Rt. Rev. Morris K. Thompson, Jr., Bishop of Louisiana, 1623 7th St., New Orleans, LA 70115

The Rt. Rev. Michael L. Vono, Bishop of the Rio Grande, 4304 Carlisle Blvd., Albuquerque, NM 87107

The Rt. Rev. James Waggoner, Jr., Bishop of Spokane, 245 East 13th Ave., Spokane, WA 99202-1114

The Rt. Rev. W. Andrew Waldo, Bishop of Upper South Carolina, 1115 Marion St., Columbia, SC 29201

The Rt. Rev. Catherine Waynick, Bishop of Indianapolis, 1100 West 42nd St., Indianapolis, IN 46208

The Rt. Rev. Terry Allen White, Bishop of Kentucky, 425 S. Second St., Louisville, KY 40202

The Rt. Rev. Geralyn Wolf, Bishop of Rhode Island, 275 North Main St., Providence, RI 02903

The Rt. Rev. Dean Wolfe, Bishop of Kansas, Bethany Place, Topeka, KS 66612-1688

The Rt. Rev. Wayne Wright, Bishop of Delaware, 2020 N. Tatnall St., Wilmington, DE 19802

The Rt. Rev. George D. Young III, Bishop of East Tennessee, 814 Episcopal School Way, Knoxville, TN 37932

Periodicals

Episcopal Life

The Episcopal Orthodox Church — please see The Orthodox Anglican Church

The Estonian Evangelical Lutheran Church — see the listing in Chapter 4, "Religious Bodies in Canada."

The Evangelical Church

The Evangelical Church was born June 4, 1968 in Portland, Oregon, when 46 congregations and about 80 ministers, under the leadership of V. A. Ballantyne and George Millen, met in an organizing session. Within two weeks a group of about 20 churches and 30 ministers from the Evangelical United Brethren and Methodist churches in Montana and North Dakota became a part of the new church. Richard Kienitz and Robert Strutz were the superintendents.

Under the leadership of Superintendent Robert Trosen, the former Holiness Methodist Church became a part of the Evangelical Church in 1969, bringing its membership and a flourishing mission field in Bolivia. The Wesleyan Covenant Church joined in 1977, with its missionary work in Mexico, in Brownsville, Texas and among the Navajos in New Mexico.

The Evangelical Church in Canada, where T. J. Jesske was superintendent, became an autonomous organization on June 5, 1970. In

1982, after years of discussions with the Evangelical Church of North America, a founding General Convention was held at Billings, Montana, where the two churches united. In 1993 the Canadian conference merged with the Canadian portion of the Missionary Church to form the Evangelical Missionary Church. The new group maintains close ties with their American counterparts. Currently there are nearly 150 U.S. congregations of the Evangelical Church. The headquarters is located in Minneapolis, Minnisota.

The following guide the life, program and devotion of this church-faithful, biblical and sensible preaching and teaching of those truths proclaimed by scholars of the Wesleyan-Arminian viewpoint; an itinerant system which reckons with the rights of individuals and the desires of the congregation; local ownership of all church properties and assets.

The church is officially affiliated with the Christian Holiness Partnership, the National Association of Evangelicals, Wycliffe Bible Translators, World Gospel Mission and OMS International. The denomination has nearly 150 missionaries.

Headquarters
Denominational Office, 9421 West River Rd., Minneapolis, MN 55444, Tel. (763)421-2589 Fax (763)424-9230
Media Contact, Gen. Supt., Brian Eckhardt
Email: ecdenom@usfamily.net
Website: www.TheEvangelicalChurch.org

Officers
Gen. Supt., Brian Eckhardt, 9421 West River Rd., Minneapolis, MN 55444
Denominational Secretary, Dr. Bruce Moyer, P.O. Box 29, University Park, IA 52595, Tel. (641)673-8391
Exectuive Director, Evangelical Church Mission, Rev. Duane Erickson, 9421 West River Rd., Minneapolis, MN 55444

Periodicals
HeartBeat, The Evangelical Challenge

The Evangelical Church Alliance
What is known today as the Evangelical Church Alliance began in 1887 under the name World's Faith Missionary Association. Years later, on March 28, 1928, a nonprofit organization was incorporated in the state of Missouri under the same name. In October, 1931, the name Fundamental Ministerial Association was chosen to reflect the organization's basis of unity.

On July 21, 1958, during the annual convention at Trinity Seminary and Bible College in Chicago, Illinois, a more comprehensive constitution was created and the name was changed to The Evangelical Church Alliance.

The ECA licenses and ordains ministers who are qualified providing them with credentials from a recognized ecclesiastical body; provides training courses through the Bible Extension Institute for those who have not had the opportunity to attend Seminary or Bible School; provides Associate Membership for churches and Christian organizations giving opportunity for fellowship and networking with other evangelical ministers and organizations who share the same goals and mission, while remaining autonomous; provides endorsement for military, prison, hospital & other institutional chaplains; provides Regional Conferences and an Annual International Conference where members can find fellowship, encouragement and training; cooperates with churches in finding new pastors when they have openings. ECA is an international, nonsectarian, Evangelical organization.

Headquarters
205 W. Broadway St., P.O. Box 9, Bradley, IL 60915, Tel. (815)937-0720 Fax (815)937-0001
Media Contact, Pres./CEO, Dr. Samuel Goebel
Email: info@ecainternational.org
Website: www.ecainternational.org

Officers
Pres./CEO, Dr. Samuel Goebel
Chairman, Dr. George L. Miller
First Vice Chairman, Dr. Rene Moreno
Vice Pres. Dr. Henry A. Roso

Periodicals
The Evangel

The Evangelical Congregational Church
This denomination had its beginning in the movement known as the Evangelical Association, organized by Jacob Albright in 1796. A division which occurred in 1891 in the Evangelical Association resulted in the organization of the United Evangelical Church in 1894. An attempt to heal this division was made in 1922, but a portion of the United Evangelical Church was not satisfied with the plan of merger and remained apart, taking the above name in 1928. This denomination is Wesleyan-Arminian in doctrine, evangelistic in spirit and Methodist in church government, with congregational ownership of local church property.

Congregations are located from New Jersey to Illinois. A denominational center, one retirement village and a seminary are located in Myerstown, Pennsylvania. Three summer youth camps and three camp meetings continue evangelistic outreach. A worldwide missions movement includes conferences in North East India, Liberia, Mexico, Costa Rica, and Japan. The denomination is a member of National Association of Evangelicals.

Headquarters

Evangelical Congregational Church Center, 100 W. Park Ave., Myerstown, PA 17067, Tel. (800)866-7581 Fax (717)866-7383
Media Contact, Chairman, National Conference, Frederick Moury, Jr., Tel. (717)866-7581
Email: eccenter@eccenter.com
Website: www.eccenter.com/church

Officers

Bishop, Rev. Bruce D. Hill
1st Vice Chpsn., Rev. Gary Brown
Sec., Rev. Kirk Marks
Conference Attorney, David Roland, Esquire
Treas., Deborah Patterson, Millersville, PA
New Dawn Christian Community Services, Pres., Steven J. Reiter, Fax (717)866-6448
Evangelical Theological Seminary, Pres., Michael W Sigman, Fax (717)866-4667

OTHER ORGANIZATIONS

Global Ministries Commission, Director., Rev. Randall L Sizemore
Controller, Kevin Henry, Myerstown, PA
ECC Benefits Coop, Pres., Rev. Franklin Schock

Periodicals

Window on the World (Global Ministries Commission)

The Evangelical Covenant Church

The Evangelical Covenant Church has its roots in historic Christianity as it emerged during the Protestant Reformation, in the biblical instruction of the Lutheran State Church of Sweden and in the great spiritual awakenings of the 19th century. The Covenant Church adheres to the affirmations of the Protestant Reformation regarding the Holy Scriptures, believing that the Old and the New Testament are the Word of God and the only perfect rule for faith, doctrine and conduct. It has traditionally valued the historic confessions of the Christian church, particularly the Apostles' Ethe Nicene Creed, while at the same time emphasizing the sovereignty of the Word over all creedal interpretations. It has especially cherished the pietistic restatement of the doctrine of justification by faith as basic to its dual task of evangelism and Christian nurture. It recognizes the New Testament emphasis upon personal faith in Jesus Christ as Savior and Lord, the reality of a fellowship of believers which acknowledges but transcends theological differences, and the belief in baptism and the Lord's Supper as divinely ordained sacraments of the church.

While the denomination has traditionally practiced the baptism of infants, in conformity with its principle of freedom it has also recognized the practice of believer baptism. The principle of personal freedom, so highly esteemed by the Covenant, is to be distinguished from the individualism that disregards the centrality of the Word of God and the mutual responsibilities and disciplines of the spiritual community.

Headquarters

5101 N. Francisco Ave., Chicago, IL 60625, Tel. (773)784-3000 Fax (773)784-4366
Media Contact, Donald L. Meyer, Email: don.meyer@covchurch.org
Email: Elliott.johnson@covchurch.org
Website: www.covchurch.org

Officers

Pres., Dr. Gary Walter
Exec. Vice Pres., Rev. Donn Engebretson
Vice Pres. Finance, Dr. Dean A. Lundgren

ADMINISTRATIVE BOARDS

Executive Board, Rev. D. Darrell Griffes, Chair
Bd. of Women Ministries, Exec. Minister, Rev. Ruth Y. Hill
Bd. Of Nominations, Advisory Member, (vacant)
Bd. of the Ordered Ministry, Exec. Minister, Rev. Dr. David Kersten
Bd. of Pensions & Benefits, Dir. of Pensions, Dean A. Lundgren
Bd. of Benevolence, Pres. of Covenant Ministries of Benevolence, David A. Dwight, 5145 N. California Ave., Chicago, IL 60625
North Park University, Pres., Dr. David l. Parkyn, 3225 W. Foster Ave., Chicago, IL 60625; North Park Theological Seminary, Pres. And Dean, Dr. John E. Phelan Jr.

SERVICE ORGANIZATIONS

National Covenant Properties, Pres., David W. Johnson, 5101 N. Francisco, Chicago, IL 60625, Tel. (773)784-3000
Covenant Trust Company, Pres., Charles A. Walles, 5215 Old Orchard Rd., Ste 725, Skokie, IL 60077 Tel.: (847)583-3200, (800)483-2177

REGIONAL CONFERENCES OF THE E.C.C.

Central Conference, Supt., Rev. Jerome O. Nelson, 3319 W. Foster Ave., Chicago, IL 60625, Tel. (773)267-3060
East Coast Conference, Supt., Rev. Howard K. Burgoyne, 52 Missionary Rd., Cromwell, CT 06416, Tel. (860)635-2691
Great Lakes Conference, Supt., Rev. Richard Lucco, 42219 Ann Arbor Road. E., Plymouth, MI 48170, Tel. (734)451-4670
Midwest Conference, Supt., Rev. Kenneth P. Carlson, 13304 W. Center Rd. #223, Omaha, NE 68144, Tel. (402)334-3060
North Pacific Conference, Supt., Rev. Mark A. Novak, 9311 SE 36th t., Ste 120, Mercer Island, WA 98040, Tel. (206)275-3903
Northwest Conference, Supt., Rev. James A. Fretheim, 3106 47th Avenue S., Minneapolis, MN 55406, Tel. (612)721-4893
Pacific Southwest Conference, Supt., Rev. Evelyn M. R. Johnson, 1333 Willow Pass Rd., Ste 212, Concord, CA 94502, Tel. (925)677-2140
Southeast Conference, Supt., Rev. Kurt A. Miericke, 1759 W. Broadway St., #7, Oviedo, FL 32765, Tel. (407)977-8009

Canada Conference, Supt., Rev. Jeffrey Anderson, P.O. Box 34025 RPO, Fort Richmond, Winnipeg, MB R3T, Tel. (204)269-3437
Midsouth Conference, Supt., Rev. Garth T Bolinder, 6119 E. 91st St., Ste. 2000, Tulsa, OK 74137, Tel. (918)481-9097
E.C.C. of Alaska, Field Dir., Rev. Rodney J. Sawyer, P.O. Box 770749, Eagle River, AK 99577, Tel. (907)694-6348
The Paul Carlson Partnership (affiliated)
Pres., Rev. Cartis D. Peterson
Exec. Dir., Rev. James V. Sundholm, 5101 N. Francisco Ave., Chicago, IL, 60625 Tel. (773)907-3302

Periodicals
Covenant Companion, Covenant Quarterly, Covenant Home Altar

The Evangelical Free Church of America

In October 1884, 27 representatives from Swedish churches met in Boone, Iowa, to establish the Swedish

Evangelical Free Church. In the fall of that same year, two Norwegian-Danish groups began worship and fellowship (in Boston and in Tacoma) and by 1912 had established the Norwegian-Danish Evangelical Free Church Association. These two denominations, representing 275 congregations, came together at a merger conference in 1950. The Evangelical Free Church of America is an association of local, autonomous churches across the United States and Canada, blended together by common principles, policies and practices. A 12-point statement addresses the major doctrines but also provides for differences of understanding on minor issues of faith and practice. Overseas outreach includes 500 missionaries serving in 31 countries.

Headquarters
901 East 78th St., Minneapolis, MN 55420-1300, Tel. (952)854-1300 Fax (952)853-8488
Media Contact, Exec. Dir. of International Mission, Timothy Addington
Email: president@efca.org
Website: www.efca.org

Officers
Pres., Dr. William J. Hamel, Minneapolis, MN
Senior Vice President, ReachGlobal: Timothy Addington, Minneapolis, MN
Senior Vice President, Finance and Operations: Jay O. Turner, Minneapolis, MN
Executive Director, ReachNational: Rev. Fritz Dale, Minneapolis, MN
Chairman: Rev. Robert Harrell, Austin, TX
Sececretary: Rev. David Rodquist, Minneapolis, MN
Moderator: Rev. Quintin Stieff, Des Moines, IA
Vice Moderator: Steven Hawn, St. Paul, MN

Periodicals
EFCA Today

Evangelical Friends International – North American Region

The organization adjusted its name from Evangelical Friends International in 2008 to better reflect that this ministry is assuredly a church movement. The North American Region ministers alongside other regions around the world under the banner of the Evangelical Friends Church International. The Strategic vision -as formulated by the North American Director, Dr. John P. Williams Jr. -reads "In joyful obedience to Jesus' Great Commission - and in the spirit of His Great Commandment -our movement purposes to serve the church and the world in love, multiplying disciples and churches in the power of the Holy Spirit so that our children's grandchildren and generations of the un-reached will be compelled to join.

Headquarters
5350 Broadmoor Cir. NW, Canton, OH 44709, Tel. (330)493-1660 Fax (330)493-0852
Media Contact, Gen. Supt., Dr. John P. Williams, Jr.
Email: efcer@aol.com
Website: www.evangelical-friends.org

YEARLY MEETINGS
Evangelical Friends Church, Eastern Region, Ron Johnson, 5350 Broadmoor Cir., N.W., Canton, OH 44709, Tel. (330)493-1660 Fax (330)493-0852
Rocky Mountain YM, John Brawner, 3350 Reed St., Wheatridge, CO 80033, Tel. (303)238-5200 Fax (303)238-5200
Mid-America YM, Duane Hansen, 2018 Maple, Wichita, KS 67213, Tel. (316)267-0391 Fax (316)267-0681
Northwest YM, Mark Ankeny, 200 N. Meridian St., Newberg, OR 97132, Tel. (503)538-9419 Fax (503)538-9410
Alaska YM, Sam Williams, P.O. Box 687, Kotzebue, AK 99752, Tel. (907)442-3906
Evangelical Friends Church Southwest, YM, Linda Coop, P.O. Box 1607, Whittier, CA 90609-1607, Tel. (562)947-2883 Fax (562)947-9385

Periodicals
The Friends Voice

Evangelical Lutheran Church in America*

The Evangelical Lutheran Church in America (ELCA) was organized April 30-May 3, 1987, in Columbus, Ohio, bringing together the 2.25 million-member American Lutheran Church, 2.85 million-member Lutheran Church in America, and the 100,000-member Association of Evangelical Lutheran Churches.

The ELCA is, through its predecessors, the oldest of the major U.S. Lutheran churches. In the mid-17th century, a Dutch Lutheran congregation was formed in New Amsterdam (now New York). Other early congregations were begun by German and Scandinavian immigrants to Delaware, Pennsylvania, New York and the Carolinas. The first Lutheran association of congregations, the Pennsylvania Ministerium, was organized in 1748 under Henry Melchior Muhlenberg. Numerous Lutheran organizations were formed as immigration continued and the United States grew.

In 1960, The American Lutheran Church (ALC) was created through a merger of an earlier American Lutheran Church, formed in 1930, the Evangelical Lutheran Church, begun in 1917, and the United Evangelical Lutheran Church started in 1896. In 1963 the Lutheran Free Church, formed in 1897, merged with the ALC.

In 1962, the Lutheran Church in America (LCA) was formed by a merger of the United Lutheran Church in America, formed in 1918, with the Augustana Evangelical Lutheran Church, begun in 1860, the American Evangelical Lutheran Church, founded in 1872, and the Finnish Evangelical Lutheran Church or Suomi Synod, founded in 1891. The Association of Evangelical Lutheran Churches arose in 1976 from a doctrinal split within the Lutheran Church-Missouri Synod.

The ELCA, through its predecessor church bodies, was a founding member of the Lutheran World Federation, the World Council of Churches, and the National Council of the Churches of Christ in the USA.

The church is divided into 65 geographical areas called synods. These 65 synods are grouped into nine regions for mission, joint programs and service.

Headquarters

8765 W. Higgins Rd., Chicago, IL 60631, Tel. (773)380-2700 Fax (773)380-1465
Email: info@elca.org
Website: www.elca.org

Officers

Presiding Bishop, Rev. Mark S. Hanson
Sec., Mr. David D. Swartling
Treas., vacant
Vice Pres., Mr. Carlos E. Pena
Exec. for Admn., Rev. Wyvetta Bullock
Office of the Presiding Bishop, Exec. Asst to the Presiding Bishop for Federal Chaplaincies, Rev. Darrell D. Morton; Exec. Asst. to the Presiding Bishop, Ms. Myrna J. Sheie

PROGRAM UNITS
Mission Advancement, Exec. Dir., Christina Jackson-Skeleton
Global Mission, Exec. Dir., Rev. Rafael Malpica Padilla
Congregational and Synodical Mission, Exec. Dir., Rev. Stephen P. Bouman
ELCA Publishing House, Exec. Dir., Ms. Beth A. Lewis

Women of the ELCA, Exec. Dir., Ms. Linda Post Bushkofsky; President., Ms. Jennifer Michael

OTHER CHURCHWIDE UNITS
Church Periodical, Editor, Mr. Daniel J. Lehmann
ELCA Bd. of Pensions

SYNODICAL BISHOPS
REGION 1
Alaska, Rev. Michael F. Keys, 1847 W. Northern Lights Blvd., #2, Anchorage, AK 99517-3343, Tel. (907)272-8899 Fax(907)274-3141
Northwest Washington, Rev. Wm Chris Boerger, 5519 Phinney Ave. N, Seattle, WA 98103-5899, Tel. (206)783-9292 Fax(206)783-9833
Southwestern Washington, Rev. Robert D. Hofstad, 420 121st St., S., Tacoma, WA 98444-5218, Tel. (253)535-8300 Fax (253)535-8315
Eastern Washington-Idaho, Rev. Martin D. Wells, 314 South Spruce St., Ste. A, Spokane, WA 19201-5823, Tel. (509)838-9871 Fax (509)838-0941
Oregon, Rev. David H. Brauer-Rieke, 2800 N. Vancouver Ave., Ste. 101, Portland, OR 97227-1630, Tel. (503)413-4191 Fax (503)413-2407
Montana, Rev. Jessica Crist-Graybill, 2415 13th Ave. S., Great Falls, MT 59405-5199, Tel. (406)453-1461 Fax (406)761-4632
Regional Coord., Rev. Shelley Wickstrom, Region 1, 4525 19th Ave, NE, Seattle, WA 98105-3301, Tel. (206)624-0093 Fax (206) 626-0987
REGION 2
Sierra Pacific, Rev. Mark W. Holmerod, P.O. Box 276648, Sacramento, CA 95827-6648, Tel. (916)756-1665, Fax(888)789-6434
Southwest California, Rev. Dean W. Nelson, 1300 E. Colorado St., Glendale, CA 91205-1406, Tel. (818)507-9591 Fax (818)507-9627
Pacifica, Rev. Murray D. Finck, 180-C1 Parkcourt Pl Bldg C, Santa Ana, CA 92701, Tel. (714)692-2791 Fax (714)692-9317
Grand Canyon, Rev. Stephen S. Talmage, Interchurch Center, 7227 N 16th St. Ste. 260, Phoenix, AZ 85020-5286, Tel. (602)957-3223 Fax (602)956-8104
Rocky Mountain, Rev. Allan C. Bjornberg, 455 Sherman St., Ste. 160, Denver, CO 80203, Tel. (303)777-6700 Fax (303)733-0750
Region 2, Ms. Margaret Schmitt Ajer, Region 2, 1801 Parkcourt Pl Bldg C, Santa Ana, CA 92701
REGION 3
Western North Dakota, Rev. Mark E. Narum, P.O. Box 370, Bismarck, ND 58502-0370, Tel. (701)223-5312 Fax (701)223-1435
Eastern North Dakota, Rev. William E. Rindy, 1703 32nd Ave., S., Fargo, ND 58103-5936, Tel. (701)232-3381 Fax (701)232-3180
South Dakota, Rev. David B. Zellmer, 2001 S Summit Ave, Sioux Falls, SD 57197-0001, Tel. (605)247-4011 Fax (605)274-4028

Northwestern Minnesota, Rev. Lawrence R. Wohlrabe, Concordia College, 901 8th St. S., Moorhead, MN 56562-0001, Tel. (218)299-3019 Fax (218)299-3363

Northeastern Minnesota, Rev. Thomas M. Aitken, 1105 E. Superior St., Upper Suite, Duluth, MN 55802-2204, Tel. (218)724-4424 Fax (218)724-4393

Southwestern Minnesota, Rev. Jon V. Anderson, P.O. Box 499, Redwood Falls, MN 56283-0499, Tel. (507)637-3904 Fax (507)637-2809

Minneapolis Area, Rev. Glenn W. Nycklemoe, 122 W. Franklin Ave., Ste. 600, Minneapolis, MN 55404-2474, Tel. (612)870-3610 Fax (612)870-0170

Saint Paul Area, Rev. Peter Rogness, 105 W. University Ave. W, St. Paul, MN 55103-2094, Tel. (651)224-4313 Fax (651)224-5646

Southeastern Minnesota, Rev. Harold L. Usgaard, Assisi Heights, 1001 14th St. NW, Ste. 300, Rochester, MN 55901-2551, Tel. (507)280-9457 Fax (507)280-8824

Regional Coord., Rev. Paul Baglyos, Region 3, Luther Seminary, 2481 Como Ave., St. Paul, MN 55108-1445, Tel. (651)649-0454 x 232, Fax (651)649-0468

REGION 4

Nebraska, Rev. David L. deFreese, 4980 S. 118th St., Ste. D, Omaha, NE 68137-2200, Tel. (402)896-5311 Fax (402)896-5354

Central States, Rev. Gerald L. Mansholt, 21 N 12th St. Ste. 210, 4th Fl., Kansas City, MO 66102-5161, Tel. (913)948-9701, Fax (913) 948-9707

Arkansas-Oklahoma, Rev. Michael K. Girlinghouse, 693 S. 66th E. Ave., Ste. 310, Tulsa, OK 74133-1760, Tel. (918)492-4288 Fax (918)491-6275

Northern Texas-Northern Louisiana, Rev. Kevin S. Kanouse, P.O. Box 560587, Dallas, TX 75356-0587, Tel. (214)637-6865 Fax (214) 637-4805

Southwestern Texas, Rev. Ray Tiemann, 1090 Oestreich Dr., Seguin, TX 78155, Tel. (830)379-9900 Fax (830)379-9990

Texas-Louisiana Gulf Coast, Rev. Michael W. Rinehart, 12941 I-45, North Freeway #210, Houston, TX 77060-1243, Tel. (281)873-5665 Fax (281)875-4716

Regional Coord., Rev. Herb Palmer, 10913 River Plantation Dr., Austin, TX, 78747-1492, Tel. (512)280-1093 Fax (512)272-9699

REGION 5

Metropolitan Chicago, Rev. Wayne N. Miller, 1420 West Dickens Ave., Chicago, IL 60614-3004, Tel. (773)248-0021 Fax (773)248-8455

Northern Illinois, Rev. Gary M. Wollersheim, 103 W. State St., Rockford, IL 61101-1105, Tel. (815)964-9934 Fax (815)964-2295

Central-Southern Illinois, Rev. S. John Roth, 524 S. Fifth St., Springfield, IL 62701-1822, Tel. (217)753-7915 Fax (217)753-7976

Southeastern Iowa, Rev. Michael L. Burk, Tel. (319)338-1273 Fax (319)351-8677

Western Iowa, Rev. Michael A. Last, P.O. Box 577, Storm Lake, IA 50588-0577, Tel. (712)732-4968 Fax (712)732-6540

Northeastern Iowa, Rev. Steven L. Ullestad, P.O. Box 804, Waverly, IA 50677-0804, Tel. (319)352-1414 Fax (319)352-1416

Northern Great Lakes, Rev. Thomas A. Skrenes, 1029 N. Third St. Ste. A, Marquette, MI 49855-3588, Tel. (906)228-2300 Fax (906)228-2527

Northwest Synod of Wisconsin, Rev. Duane C. Pederson, P.O. Box 107, Chetek, WI 54728-0107, Tel. (715)859-6810 Fax (715)859-6812

East-Central Synod of Wisconsin, Rev. James A. Justman, 16 Tri-Park Way, Appleton, WI 54914-1658, Tel. (920)734-5381 Fax (920)734-5074

Greater Milwaukee, Rev. Jeffrey S. Barrow, 1212 S. Layton Blvd., Milwaukee, WI 53215-1653, Tel. (414)671-1212 Fax (414)671-1756

South-Central Synod of Wisconsin, Rev. Bruce H. Burnside, 2909 Landmark Pl., Ste. 202, Madison, WI 53713-4200, Tel. (608)270-0201 Fax (608)270-0202

La Crosse Area, Rev. James A. Arends, 2301 South Ave., La Crosse, WI 54601-6229, Tel. (608)788-5000 Fax (608)788-4916

Regional Coord., Rev. Carl R. Evenson, Region 5, 130 Main St. Ste. 105, Menasha, WI 54952-3181, Tel. (920)720-9880 Fax (920)720-9881

REGION 6

Southeast Michigan, Rev. Donald P. Kreiss, 8115 E. Jefferson Ave., Detroit, MI 48214-3970, Tel. (313)821-1055 Fax (313)821-1425

Northwest Lower Michigan, Rev. John D. Schleicher, 2900 N. Waverly Rd., Ste. 2900 N, Lansing, MI 48906-3594, Tel. (517)321-5066 Fax (517)321-2632

Indiana-Kentucky, Rev. William O. Gafkjen, 911 E. 86th St., Ste. 200, Indianapolis, IN 46240-1800, Tel. (317)253-3522 Fax (317)254-5666

Northwestern Ohio, Rev. Marcus C. Lohrmann, 621 Bright Rd., Findlay, OH 45840-6940, Tel. (419)423-3664 Fax (419)423-8801

Northeastern Ohio, Rev. Elizabeth A. Eaton, 1890 Bailey Rd., Cuyahoga Falls, OH 44221-5259, Tel. (330)929-9022 Fax (330)929-9018

Southern Ohio, Rev. Callon W. Holloway, Jr., 300 S. 2nd St., Columbus, OH 43215-5196, Tel. (614)464-3532 Fax (614)464-3422

Regional Coord., Marilyn McCann Smith, Region 6, 911 86th St. Ste. 200, Indianapolis, IN 46240-1800, Tel. (317)253-3522 Fax (317)254-5666

REGION 7

New Jersey, Rev. E. Roy Riley, Jr., 1930 State Highway. 33, Hamilton Square, Trenton, NJ 08690-1714, Tel. (609)586-6800 Fax (609) 586-3357

New England, Rev. Margaret G. Payne, 20 Upland St., Worcester, MA 01607-2600, Tel. (508)791-1530 Fax (508)797-9295

Metropolitan New York, Rev. Robert A. Rimbo, Interchurch Center, 475 Riverside Dr.,

Ste.1620, New York, NY 10115-0037, Tel. (212)665-0732 Fax (212)877-6818

Upstate New York, Rev. Marie C. Jerge, 110 Hinsdale Rd., Camillus, NY 13031-1629, Tel. (315)446-2502 Fax (315)446-4642

Northeastern Pennsylvania, Rev. Samuel R. Zeiser, 2354 Grove Rd., Allentown, PA 18109-1723, Tel. (610)266-5101 Fax (610)266-5107

Southeastern Pennsylvania, Rev. Claire S. Burkat, Wiedemann Bldg., 7241 Germantown Ave., Philadelphia, PA 19119-1723, Tel. (267)232-3737 Fax (610)696-2782

Slovak Zion, Rev. Wilma S. Kucharek, P.O. Box 1003,Torrington, CT.06790-1003, Tel. (860) 482-6100 Fax (860)482-7463

Regional Coord., Rev. Peggy M. Wuertele, 7301 Germantown Ave., Philadelphia, PA 19119-1794, Tel. (215)248-6319 Fax (215)248-7377

REGION 8

Northwestern Pennsylvania, Rev. Ralph E. Jones, P.O. Box 43, Pleasantville, PA 16341-0043, Tel. (814)589-7660 Fax (814)589-7566

Southwestern Pennsylvania, Rev. Kurt F. Kusserow, 9625 Perry Hwy., Ste. 1, Pittsburgh, PA 15237-5590, Tel. (412)367-8222 Fax (412) 369-8840

Allegheny, Rev. Gregory R. Pile, 701 Quail Ave., Altoona, PA 16602-3010, Tel. (814)942-1042 Fax (814)941-9259

Lower Susquehanna, Rev. B. Penrose Hoover, 900 S. Arlington Ave., Ste. 200, Harrisburg, PA 17109-5031, Tel. (717)652-1852 Fax (717) 652-2504

Upper Susquehanna, Rev. Robert L. Driesen, P.O. Box 36, Lewisburg, PA 17837-0036, Tel. (570) 524-9778 Fax (570)524-9757

Delaware-Maryland, Rev. Wolfgang D. Herz-Lane, 700 Light St., Baltimore, MD 21230-3850, Tel. (410)230-2869 Fax (410)230-2871

Metropolitan Washington, D.C., Rev. Richard H. Graham, 1025 Connecticut Ave. NW., Ste. 904, Washington, DC 20036-5433, Tel. (202) 822-1901 Fax (202)822-1902

West Virginia-Western Maryland, Rev. Ralph W. Dunkin, The Atrium, 503 Morgantown Ave., Ste. 200, Fairmont, WV 26554-4389, Tel. (304)363-4030 Fax (304)363-4042

Regional Coord., Rev. Nancy Gable, Lutheran Theological Sem. at Gettysburg, 61 Seminary Ridge, Gettysburg, PA 17325-1795, Tel. (717) 338-3033 Fax (717)334-0323

REGION 9

Virginia, Rev. James F. Mauney, Roanoke College, P.O. Drawer 70, Salem, VA 24153-0070, Tel. (540)389-1000 Fax (540)389-5962

North Carolina, Rev. Leonard H. Bolick, 1988 Lutheran Synod Dr., Salisbury, NC 28144-5734, Tel. (704)633-4861 Fax (704)638-0508

South Carolina, Rev. Herman R. Yoos III, 1003 Richland St., P.O. Box 43, Columbia, SC 29202-0043, Tel. (803)765-0590 Fax (803) 252-5558

Southeastern, Rev. H. Julian Gordy, 100 Edgewood Ave., NE, Ste. 1600, Atlanta, GA 30303-3066, Tel. (404)589-1977 Fax (404) 521-1980

Florida-Bahamas, Rev. Edward R. Benoway, 3838 W. Cypress St., Tampa, FL 33607-4803, Tel. (813)876-7660 Fax (813)870-0826

Caribbean, Rev. Felipe Lozada Montañez, PMB Num 359 Ste. 1, 425 CARR 693, Dorado, PR 00646-4802, Tel. (787)278-8300 Fax (787) 796-3365

Regional Coord., Rev. Harvey L. Huntley Jr., Region 9, Lutheran Theological Southern Seminary, 4201 N. Main St., Columbia, SC 29203-5863, Tel. (803)461-3263 Fax (803) 461-3380

Periodicals
The Lutheran, Gather Seeds for the Parish

Evangelical Lutheran Synod

The Evangelical Lutheran Synod had its beginning among the Norwegian settlers who brought with them their Lutheran heritage. The synod was organized in 1853. It was reorganized in 1918 by those who desired to adhere to the synod's principles not only in word but also in deed.

The synod owns and operates Bethany Lutheran College and Bethany Lutheran Theological Seminary. It has congregations in 20 states and maintains foreign missions in Peru, Chile, India, Korea, the Czech Republic, Latvia, and Ukraine. It operates a seminary in Lima, Peru and in Ternopil, Ukraine.

Headquarters
6 Browns Ct., Mankato, MN 56001, Tel. (507)344-7356 Fax (507)344-7426

Media Contact, Pres., John A. Moldstad

Email: jamjr@blc.edu

Website: www.EvLuthSyn.org

Officers
Pres., Rev. John A. Moldstad, 6 Browns Ct., Mankato, MN 56001

Sec., Rev. Craig Ferkenstad, 37777 State Hwy 22, St. Peter, MN 56082

Vice Pres., Rev. Glenn Obengerger, 12309 Pacific Ave., Tacoma, WA 98444

Lutheran Synod Book Co., Bethany Lutheran College, 700 Luther Dr., Mankato, MN 56001

Bethany Lutheran Theological Seminary, 6 Browns Ct., Mankato, MN 56001

Periodicals
Lutheran Sentinel, Lutheran Synod Quarterly, Young Branches, Oak Leaves, Mission News

Evangelical Methodist Church

The Evangelical Methodist Church was organized in 1946 at Memphis, Tenn., largely as a movement of people who opposed modern liberalism and wished for a return to the historic Wesleyan position. In 1960, it merged with the Evangel Church (formerly Evangelistic Tabernacles) and with the People's Methodist Church in 1962.

Headquarters

P.O. Box 17070, Indianapolis, IN 46217, Tel. (317)780-8017 Fax (317)780-8078
Media Contact, Gen. Conf. Sec.-Treas., Rev. James A. Coulston
Email: headquarters@emchurch.org
Website: www.emchurch.org

Officers

Gen. Supt., Dr. Edward W. Williamson
Gen. Conf. Sec.-Treas., Rev. James A. Coulston

Periodicals

The Connection

Evangelical Presbyterian Church

The Evangelical Presbyterian Church (EPC), established in March 1981, is a conservative denomination of 8 geographic presbyteries. From its inception with 12 churches, the EPC has grown to 250 churches with a membership of over 90,000. Planted firmly within the historic Reformed tradition, evangelical in spirit, the EPC places high priority on church planting and development along with world missions. Over Eighty missionaries serve the church's mission.

Based on the truth of Scripture and adhering to the Westminster Confession of Faith plus its Book of Order, the denomination is committed to the "Essentials of the faith." The historic motto "In essentials, unity; in nonessentials, liberty; in all things charity" catches the irenic spirit of the EPC, along with the Ephesians theme, "truth in love." The Evangelical Presbyterian Church is a member of the World Reformed Fellowship, World Alliance of Reformed Churches, National Association of Evangelicals, World Evangelical Fellowship and the Evangelical Council for Financial Accountability.

Headquarters

Office of the General Assembly, 17197 N. Laurel Park Dr., Suite 567, Livonia, MI 48152, Tel. (734)742-2020 Fax (734)742-2033
Media Contact, Stated Clerk, Dr. Jeffrey Jeremiah
Email: EPCHURCH@epc.org
Website: www.epc.org

Officers

Administration Committee, Chmn., Bill Vogles, 1314 Stonecreek Dr., Lawrence, KS 66049
Board of Benefits, Chmn., Rev. Ron Horgan, c/o EPC, 17197 N. Laurel Park Dr. Suite 567, Livonia, MI 48152
Comm. on Christian Educ. & Publ., Chmn., Rev. Tommy Overton, First Presbyterain Church of Rome, 101 E. Third Avenue 77459
College Ministries Committee, Chmn., Rev. Pedro Govantes, Grace Presbyterain, 133 Shrewsbury Ct., Pennington, NJ 08534
Committee on Fraternal Relations, Chmn., Dr. Don Fortson, 400 Leighton Ct., Matthews, NC 28105-6586

Committee on National Outreach, Chmn., Dr. Shawn Robinson, Clayton Community Church, 6055 Main St., Clayton, CA 94517
Committee on World Outreach, Chmn., Mr. Jim Thomason, 3470 Wrights Valley Rd., Bluefield VA 24605
Committee on Ministerial Vocation, Chmn., Mr. Bill Meeks, 712 E. Monroe, St. Louis MO 63122
Committee on Women's Ministries, Chmn., Libby Cooper, 2030 Ralston Ct., Florence, SC 29505
Committee on Theology, Chmn., Rev. Paul Husband, Tunica Presbyterain Church, Tunica, MS 38676-1095
Committee on Student Ministries, Chmn., Rev. Brandor Bates, Lakeside Presbyterain Church, 2070 Sillway Rd., Brandon MS 39047

PRESBYTERIES
Central South, Stated Clk., Rev. Ken Van Kampen, Atoka Presbyterain Church, 1041 Atoka Idaville Rd., Atoka, TN 38004
East, Stated Clk., Rev. Ron Meyer, Fourth Presbyterian Church, 5500 River Rd., Bethesda, MD 20816
Florida, Stated Clk., Rev. Robert Garment, Hope EPC, 4680 Thomasville Rd., Tallahassee, FL 32309
Mid-America, Stated Clk., Mr. Dexter Kuhlman, 1926 Prospector Ridge, Ballwin, MO 63011
Mid-Atlantic, Stated Clk., Dr. Howard Shockley, P.O. Box 10, Moore, SC 29369
Midwest, Stated Clk., Mr. John C. Manon, P.O. Box 6047, Auburn, IN 46706-6047
Southeast, Stated Clk., Mr. Walter "Jerry" Clothier, 1605 Verdi Lane, Knoxville, TN 37922
West, Stated Clk., Rev. Marc Huebl, 1250 S. Buckely Rd., Suite # 146, Aurora, CO 80017

Fellowship of Evangelical Bible Churches

This Fellowship grew out of the immigration of Mennonites from Russia/Ukraine into the praire states and provinces between 1874-1880. Established with an emphasis on true repentance, conversion, and a life committed to Jesus as Savior and Lord, the Fellowship was founded in 1889 under the leadership of Isaac Peters and Aaron Wall. The founding churches were located in Mountain Lake, Minnesota, and in Henderson and Jansen, Nebraska. The Fellowship has since grown to 43 churches with approximately 5000 members in Canada, Paraguay and the United States.

World evangelization has been an integral part of the Fellowship since its beginning. Today, for every 50 members in the home churches, one missionary is serving. The Fellowship does not direct its own mission efforts, but participates with existing evangelical "faith" mission agencies. Personnel from Fellowship churches serve under in 22 countries under almost 40 agencies.

Doctrinally, the Fellowship has its roots in historic Anabaptism but was strongly influenced by the Bible School Movement. Believer's baptism is by immersion. The Fellowship is holding fast to the inerrancy of Scripture; the deity of Christ; and the need for spiritual regeneration by faith in the death, burial and resurrection of Jesus Christ as payment for sin. Members look forward to the imminent return of Jesus Christ and retain a sense of urgency to share the gospel with those who have never heard of God's redeeming love.

Headquarters
11605 W. Dodge Rd., Ste. 3, Omaha, NE 68154, Tel. (402)965-3860 Fax (402)965-3871 Admn., Paul Boeker, 3339 N 109th Plz., Omaha, NE 68164, Tel. (402)965-3860 Fax (402)965-3871, Email: info@febcministries.org
Email: info@febcministries.org
Website: www.febcministries.org

Officers
President, Mr. Blaine Donaldson, 11605 W. Dodge Rd., Ste. 3, Omaha, NE, 68154, Tel. (402)965-3860, Email: president@febcministries.org
Vice President, Mr. Don Krehbiel, 801 S 52nd St, Apt. 813, Omaha, NE 68106-1804, Email: don.febc@cox.net
Admn., Paul Boeker, 11605 W. Dodge Rd., Ste. 3., Omaha, NE 68154, Tel. (402)965-3860 Fax (402)965-3871,Email: info@febcministries.org
Ministries Coordinator, Harvey Schultz, 3011 3rd Ave. East, P.O. Box 8, Waldheim, SK S0K 4R0, Tel. (306)945-2220, Fax (306)945-2008, Email: ministries@febcministries.org

Periodicals
Fellowship Focus

Fellowship of Evangelical Churches
The Evangelical Mennonite Church is an American denomination in the European free church tradition, tracing its heritage to the Reformation period of the 16th century. The Swiss Brethren of that time believed that salvation could come only by repentance for sins and faith in Jesus Christ; that baptism was only for believers; and that the church should be separate from controls of the state. Their enemies called them Anabaptists, since they insisted on rebaptizing believers who had been baptized as infants. As the Anabaptist movement spread to other countries, Menno Simons became its principal leader. In time his followers were called Mennonites.

In 1693 a Mennonite minister, Jacob Amman, insisted that the church should adopt a more conservative position on dress and style of living and should more rigidly enforce the "ban" -the church's method of disciplining disobedient members. Amman's insistence finally resulted in a division within the South German

Mennonite groups; his followers became known as the Amish.

Migrations to America, involving both Mennonites and Amish, took place in the 1700s and 1800s, for both religious and economic reasons. The Evangelical Mennonite Church was formed in 1866 out of a spiritual awakening among the Amish in Indiana. It was first known as the Egly Amish, after its founder Bishop Henry Egly. Bishop Egly emphasized regeneration, separation and nonconformity to the world. His willingness to rebaptize anyone who had been baptized without repentance created a split in his church, prompting him to gather a new congregation in 1866. The conference, which has met annually since 1895, united a number of other congregations of like mind. This group became The Defenseless Mennonite Church in 1898 and has been known as the Evangelical Mennonite Church since 1948. At the 2003 convention the delegates voted to change the name to Fellowship of Evangelical Churches.

Resource Center
1420 Kerrway Ct., Fort Wayne, IN 46805, Tel. (260)423-3649 Fax (260)420-1905
Media Contact, Admn. Asst., Lynette Augsburger
Email: FECministries@aol.com
Website: www.fecministries.org

Officers
Pres., Rev. Rocky Rocholl, 3324 Rockwood Dr., Fort Wayne, IN 46815
Chpsn., Rev. Matt Boyers, 22130 Co Rd. A, Archbold, OH 43502
Vice-Chpsn., Rev. Mike Heiniger, 1602 N. 1125 E. Rd., Monticello, IL 61856
Sec., Rev. Doug Witzig, 754 Taylor St., Morton, IL 61550

Periodicals
FEConnections

Fellowship of Fundamental Bible Churches
The churches in this body represent the 1939 separation from the Methodist Protestant Church, when some 50 delegates and pastors (approximately one-third of the Eastern Conference) withdrew to protest the union of the Methodist Protestant Church with the Methodist Episcopal Church and the Methodist Episcopal Church South, and what they considered the liberal tendencies of those churches. These churches subsequently changed their name to the Bible Protestant Church. In 1985, this group again changed its name to the Fellowship of Fundamental Bible Churches to more accurately define their position.

As fundamentalists, this group strongly adheres to the historic fundamentals of the faith, including the doctrine of separation. This group accepts a literal view of the Bible and, consequently, accepts premillennial theology and a pre-tribulational rapture. The churches are currently located in New Jersey, New York, Pennsylvania, Virginia, Michigan, and California. It is a fellowship of independent Bible and Baptist churches. Baptism, by immersion, and the Lord's Supper, as a memorial, are recognized as ordinances. There are currently 22 churches representing 1200 members. This constituent body is a member of the American Council of Christian Churches.

The Fellowship of Fundamental Bible Churches owns and operates Tri-State Bible Camp and Conference Center in Montague, New Jersey, oversees a mission board called Fundamental Bible Missions, and conducts a Bible Institute called Fundamental Bible Institute.

Headquarters
P.O. Box 206, Penns Grove, NJ 08069
Media Contact, Sec., Rev. Edmund G. Cotton, 80 Hudson St., Port Jervis, NY 12771, Tel. (845)856-7695
Email: ecotton@citlink.net
Website: www.churches-ffbc.org

Officers
Pres., Rev. Daniel Boyle, 16 Little Brooklyn Rd., Warwick, NY 10990, Tel. (845)258-2111, Email: boyce@cleaninter.net
Vice-Pres., Rev. Mr. Frank D'Agostino, 104 Memorial Lane, Mount Laurel, NJ 08054, Tel. (856)802-9542, Email: Frankthecarguy@verizon.net
Sec., Rev. Edmund G. Cotton, 80 Hudson St., Port Jervis, NY 12771, Tel. (845)856-6795, Email: ecotton@citlink.net
Treas., Rev. Stepehn Racite, 6 Tamara Lane, Cornwall, NY 12518, Tel. (845)534-3335, Email: sracite@verizon.net

Fellowship of Grace Brethren Churches
A division occurred in the Church of the Brethren in 1882 on the question of the legislative authority of the annual meeting. It resulted in the establishment of the Brethren Church under a legal charter requiring congregational government. This body divided in 1939 with the Grace Brethren establishing headquarters at Winona Lake, Ind., and the Brethren Church at Ashland, Ohio.

Headquarters
Media Contact, Fellowship Coord., Rev. Thomas Avey, P.O. Box 386, Winona Lake, IN 46590, Tel. (219)269-1269 Fax (219)269-4066
Email: fgbc@fgbc.org
Website: www.fgbc.org

Officers
Mod., Dr. Galen Wiley, 22713 Ellsworth Ave., Minerva, OH 44657

1st Mod.-Elect, Dr. James Custer, 2515 Carriage Rd., Powell, OH 43065
2nd Mod.-Elect, Dr. Ron Manahan, 2316 E. Kemo Ave., Warsaw, IN 46580
Fellowship Coord., Rev. Thomas Avey, P.O. Box 386, Winona Lake, IN 46590, Tel. (219)269-1269 Fax (219)269-4066
Sec., Fellowship Coord., Rev. Thomas Avey, P.O. Box 386, Winona Lake, IN 46590
Treas., Thomas Staller, 2311 S. Cost-a-Plenty Dr., Warsaw, IN 46580

OTHER BOARDS
Grace Brethren International Missions, Exec. Dir., Rev. Tom Julien, P.O. Box 588, Winona Lake, IN 46590
Grace Brethren Home Missions, Exec. Dir., Larry Chamberlain, P.O. Box 587, Winona Lake, IN 46590
Grace College & Seminary, Pres., Ronald E. Manahan, 200 Seminary Dr., Winona Lake, IN 46590, Tel. (210)372-5100
Brethren Missionary Herald Co., Pub. & Gen. Mgr., James Bustram, P.O. Box 544, Winona Lake, IN 46590
CE National, Exec. Dir., Rev. Ed Lewis, P.O. Box 365, Winona Lake, IN 46590
Grace Brethren Navajo Ministries, Dir., Steve Galegor, Counselor, NM 87018
Grace Village Retirement Community, Admn., Jeff Carroll, P.O. Box 337, Winona Lake, IN 46590
Natl. Fellowship of Grace Brethren Ministries, Pres., Dr. Steve Taylor, 132 Summerall Ct., Aiken, SC 29801
Women's Missionary Council, Pres., Janet Minnix, 3314 Kenwick Tr., S.W., Roanoke, VA, 24015
Grace Brethren Men International, Pres., Morgan Burgess, 163 N. Franklin St., Delaware, OH 43015

Free Christian Zion Church of Christ
This church was organized in 1905 at Redemption, Ark., by a company of African-American ministers associated with various denominations. Its polity is in general accord with that of Methodist bodies.

Headquarters
1316 S. Hutchinson St., Nashville, AR 71852
Media Contact, Gen. Sec., Shirlie Cheatham

Officers
Chief Pastor, Willie Benson, Jr.

Free Methodist Church—USA
The Free Methodist Church was organized in 1860 near Rochester, New York. Arising out of controversy within the Methodist Episcopal Church over the Wesleyan interpretation of the doctrine of entire sanctification as well as issues such as slavery, free pews, secret societies, and freedom in

worship, concerned ministers and laypersons in eastern New York State encouraged Benjamin Titus Roberts to lead them in forming a new church.

The church is Wesleyan in doctrine and evangelical in spirit. Episcopal in basic orientation, the church is organized into sixteen general or provisional general conferences on four continents, each led by a national bishop or bishops.

The Free Methodist Church sponsors both educational and benevolent institutions in North America and around the world. With a ministry support center in Indianapolis, Indiana, world membership stands at approximately 982,000, with a total contituency of 1,200,000. The Free Methodist World Conference, composed of bishops and delegates from the several general conferences, meets each quadrennium for fellowship, worship, and global ministries support.

Headquarters
World Ministries Center, 770 N. High School Rd., Indianapolis, IN 46214, Tel. (800) 342-5531 or (317)244-3660 Fax (317)244-1247
Mailing Address, P.O. Box 535002, Indianapolis, IN 46253, Tel. (800)342-5531
Media Contact, Yearbook Ed., P.O. Box 535002, Indianapolis, IN 46253
Email: info@fmcna.org
Website: www.freemethodistchurch.org

Officers
Bishop David W. Kendall; Bishop David T. Roller; Bishop Matthew A. Thomas
General Conference Secretary, Mrs. Barb Sands
Exec, Dir. of Administraion and Finance, Mr. Dale Hill
Exec. Dir. of Free Methodist Communications, Mr. Jason Archer
Free Methodist World Missions, Rev. Bishop David Roller
Men's Ministries International, Exec. Dir., Rev. Jeffrey Johnson
Women's Ministries International, President, LaWanda Bullock

Periodicals
Light and Life Magazine; Free Methodist World Mission People

Friends General Conference

Friends General Conference (FGC) is an association of fifteen yearly meetings open to all Friends meetings which wish to be actively associated with FGC's programs and services. Friends General Conference includes Baltimore, Canadian, Illinois, Intermountain, Lake Erie, New England, New York, Northern, Ohio Valley, Philadelphia, South Central and Southeastern Yearly Meetings; Alaska Friends Conference, Southern Appalachian Yearly Meeting and Association, and Piedmont Friends Fellowship; plus ten independently affiliated monthly meetings. Friends General Conference is primarily a service organization with the stated purpose of nurturing the spiritual life within its constituency of predominantly unprogrammed Friends. FGC offers services to all Friends, but has no authority over constituent meetings. A Central Committee, to which constituent Yearly Meetings name appointees (in proportion to membership), and its Executive Committee, are responsible for the direction of FGC's programs and services which include a bookstore, conferences, and traveling ministries program. The 2009 Central Committee approved the following Minute of Purpose, Friends General Conference, with Divine guidance, nurtures the spiritual vitality of the Religious Society of Friends (Quakers) by providing programs and services for Friends, meetings, and seekers.

Major Goals

1. Nurture meetings and worship groups.

2. Provide resources and opportunities for meetings, Friends, and seekers to experience the Light, the living presence of God.

3. Help meetings guide Friends to discern the leadings of the Inward Teacher and to grow into ministry.

4. Transform our awareness so that our corporate and individual attitudes and actions fully value and encompass the blessed diversity of our human family.

5. Work to grow and sustain a vital, diverse, and loving community of Friends based on a shared search for unity in the Spirit.

6. Articulate, communicate, and exemplify Friends' practices, core experiences, and the call to live and witness to our faith.

7. Promote dialogue with others, sharing with them our corporate experience of Divine Truth and listening to and learning from their experience of the same.

Headquarters
1216 Arch St., 2B, Philadelphia, PA 19107, Tel. (215)561-1700 Fax (215)561-0759 Email: Friends@fgcquaker.org
Media Contact, Gen. Sec., Barry Crossno
Email: friends@fgcquaker.org
Website: www.fgcquaker.org

Officers
Gen. Sec., Barry Crossno, 1216 Arch St., 2B Philadelphia, PA 19107
Presiding Clerk, Sue Regen, 10 Hillside Rd, Penfield, NY 14526-2502
Treas., Stoph Hallward, 4446 Dallas St, Acworth, GA 30101-5310

YEARLY MEETINGS
Alaska Friends Conference, Clerk, Douglas Mertz, 11380 N Douglas Hwy, Juneau, AK 99801-7615, Email: dkmertz@ak.net
*Baltimore, Clerk, Elizabeth Meyer; 17100 Quaker Ln., Sandy Spring, MD 20860, Tel. (301)774-7663 Email: admin@bym-rsf.org
*Canadian, Clerk, Anne Mitchelle; Staff, Kerry McAdam, 91A Fourth Ave., Ottawa, ON K1S

2L1, Tel. (613)235-8553, Email: cym-office@quaker.ca

Illinois, Clerk, Janice Domanik; Staff, Sharon Haworth, 608 W. Illinois St. Urbana, Il. 61801, Tel. (217)384-9591 Email: shaworth@sbcglobal.net

Intermountain, Clerk, Claire Leonard, P.O. Box 5662, Santa Fe, NM 87502-5662 Email: imymclerk@hotmail.com

Lake Erie, Clerk, Peggy Daub, 1246 Masonic Dr Alma, MI 48801-1167, Email: peggydaub@hotmail.com

*New England, Clerk, Jackie Stillwell; Staff, Jeffery Hipp, 901 Pleasant St., Worcester, MA 01602-1908, Tel. (508)754-6760, Email: adminsec@neym.org

*New York, Clerk, Heather Cook; Staff, Helen Garay Toppins, 15 Rutherford Pl., New York, NY 10003, Tel. (212)673-5750, Email: office@nyym.org

Northern, Clerk, Robin Greenler, 1602 Wicklowway Madison, WI 53711, Tel. (608)442-1642, Email: clerk@northernyearlymeeting.org

Ohio Valley, Clerk, Paul Kriese; Staff, Deborah Jordan, Community Friends, Cincinnati, OH 45229-1950, Email: djordan@fuse.net

Philadelphia, Clerk, Thomas Swain, 1515 Cherry St., Philadelphia, PA 19102, Tel. (215)241-7210, Email: tswain@ccil.org

Piedmont Friends Fellowship, Clerk, Wendy Michener, 223 Hillside Ave, Fayetteville, NC 28301-4829, Email: wkm4peace@aol.com

South Central, Clerk, Claudia Wilson, 3802 Gardendale Dr, Houston, TX 77092-7921, Email: kenandnan@sbcglobal.net

*Southeastern, Clerk, Phoebe Andersen; Staff, Lyn Cope P.O. Box 510975, Melbourne Beach, FL 32951, Tel. (321)724-1162, Email: admin@seym.org

Southern Appalachian, Clerk, Tim Lamm; P.O. Box 5848 Savannah, GA 31404 Email: clerk@sayma.org

*also affiliated with Friends United Meeting

Periodicals
FGConnections; Religious Education Newsletter

Friends United Meeting*

Friends United Meeting was organized in 1902 (the name was changed in 1963 from the Five Years Meeting of Friends) as an association of North American yearly meetings to facilitate a united Quaker witness in missions, peace work, Christian education and outreach.

Today Friends United Meeting is comprised of 30 full-member and 3 association member yearly meetings representing about half the Friends in the world. FUM's current work includes programs of mission and service, leadership development and outreach. FUM publishes Christian education curriculum, books of Quaker history and religious thought and a magazine, Quaker Life.

Headquarters
101 Quaker Hill Dr., Richmond, IN 47374-1980, Tel. (765)962-7573 Fax (765)966-1293, Website: www.fum.org
Media Contact, Interim General Secretary, Sylvia Graves
Email: info@fum.org
Website: www.fum.org

Officers
Presiding Clk., Kelly Kellum
Treas., John Norris
Gen. Sec., Sylvia Graves

DEPARTMENTS
Global Ministries, Sylvia Graves
Quaker Life, Ed., Katie Terrell
Friends United Press, Ed., Katie Terrell

YEARLY MEETINGS
Baltimore Yearly Meeting, 17100 Quaker Ln., Sandy Spring, MD 20860-1296, Tel. (301)774-7663, (800)962-4766 Fax (301)774-7087 www.bym-rsf.org, Howard Fullerton, clerk; Riley Robinson, Gen. Sec.

Bware Yearly Meeting, P.O. Box 179, Suna-Migori 40400, Kenya East Africa; Samuel Kaguli Omondi, Gen. Sect., Epainitus Adego Ominde, Gen Supt., Daniel Ole Siakati, Presiding Clerk

Canadian Yearly Meeting, 91-A Fourth Ave., Ottawa ON K1S 2L1, Canada;, Tel. & Fax (888)296-3222 Fax (613)235-1753; Ann Mitchell, clerk; Email: cym@web.net

Central Yearly Meeting, P.O. Box 1510, Kakamega 50100, Kenya, E. Africa, Seth Shikunzi Okang'a, Gen Sect., Evans Nyenzo, Gen. Supt., Joseph Mmbwavi, Presiding Clerk

Chavakali Yearly Meeting, P.O. Box 102, Chavakali 50317, Kenya, East Africa; Elijah Mwavalie Vieliza, Gen. Sect., Hezekiah Ngadi Buliva, Gen. Supt., Gerishom Mwavali, Presiding Clerk

Cuba Yearly Meeting, Calle 20 #118 Esquina Paz, Reparto Vista, Alegre 80300, Hoguin, Cuba; Ramon Gonzalez-Longoria, Presiding Clerk

Chwele Yearly Meeting, P.O. Box 428 Chwele 50202, Kenya, East Africa, Stephen Sikulu Kisiangani, Gen. Sect., Alex Waliaula, Gen. Supt., Joseph Mamai Makokha, Presiding Clerk

East Africa Yearly Meeting of Friends, (Kaimosi) P.O. Box 35, Tiriki 50309, Kenya, East Africa; Ephraim Konzolo Muhadi, Gen. Sec., Erastus Kesohole, Gen Supt., Lucas Mudoga, Presiding Clerk

East Africa Yearly Meeting of Friends (North), P.O. Box 544, Kitale, Kenya, East Africa; James Mugalavai, Gen. Sec., Billy Wekesa, Gen. Supt., John Walukhu, Presiding Clerk

Elgon East Yearly Meeting, P.O. Box 2322, Kitale 30200, Kenya, East Africa; Philip Wasike Musungu, Gen. Sec., Isaac Wangila, Gen. Supt, Humphrey Mutende, Presiding Clerk.

Elgon Religious Society of Friends, (West) P.O. Box 4, Lugulu Via Webuye, Kenya, East Africa, Peter Kiliswa Keya, Gen. Sec., John W. Ngoya, Gen. Supt., Amos A. Dodo, Presiding Clerk

Great Plains Yearly Meeting, 2611 Bader Dr, Central City, NE 68826, (316)262-0471; Email: greatplainsyearlymeeting.org, Laura Dugan, Clerk

Indiana Yearly Meeting, 4715 N. Wheeling Ave., Muncie, IN 47304-1222; Tel. (765)284-6900 Fax (765)284-8925, Email: iyminfo@iym.org; Greg Hinshaw, Clerk; Doug Shoemaker, Gen. Supt.

Iowa Yearly Meeting, Box 657, Oskaloosa, IA 52577-0657; Tel. (641)673-6830 Fax (641)673-9718; Email: iaym@mahaska.org; John Rainocs, Clerk, Ron Bryan, Gen. Superintendent

Jamaica Yearly Meeting, 4 Worthington Ave., Kingston 5, Jamaica West Indies; Tel. (876)926-7371, Horace Hall, Presiding Clerk

Kakamega Yearly Meeting, P.O. Box 465, Kakamega 50100, Kenya, East Africa; Harun Wesley Sasita, Gen. Sec., Patrick L Muganda, Gen. Supt., Jared Waudo Wangila, Presiding Clerk

Lugari Yearly Meeting, P.O. Box 483, Turbo 30106, Kenya, East Africa; Enock Were, Gen. Sec., Jotham Nyongesa Situma, Gen. Supt., Alex Kimiya, Presiding Clerk Malava Yearly Meeting, P.O. Box 26, Malava 50103, Kenya, East Africa; Simon Belengu, Gen. Sec., Stephen Koikoi, Gen. Supt., Andrew Mulupi Khayisie, Presiding Clerk

Nairobi Yearly Meeting, P.O. Box 8321, Nairobi 00300, Kenya, East Africa; Churchill Malimo, Gen. Sec., Henry Apencha, Gen. Supt., Midikira Churchil Kibisu, Presiding Clerk

New England Yearly Meeting, 901 Pleasant St., Worcester, MA 01602-1908, Tel. (508)754-6760, Email: neym@neym.org; Linda Jenkins, Clerk; Jonathan Vogel-Borne, Field Secretary

New York Yearly Meeting, 15 Rutherford Pl., New York, NY 10003, Tel. (212)673-5750, Email: office@nyym.org; Heather Cook, Clerk; Christopher Sammond, General Secretary

North Carolina Yearly Meeting,4811 Hilltop Rd, Greensboro, NC 27407; Tel. (336)292-6957 Fax (336)292-1905, Email: ncfriends@ncym-fum.org; Judy Ritter, Clerk; John Porter, Gen. Superintendent

Southeastern Yearly Meeting, P.O. Box 510795, Melbourne Beach, FL 32951-0795, Tel. (321)724-1162; Susan Taylor, Clerk; Lyn Cope-Robinson, Adm. Sec., Sec: admin@seym.org

Tuloi Yearly Meeting, P.O. Box 128, Kapsabet 50305, KENYA, East Africa; Moses S. Khayumbi, Gen. Sec., John Musanga Kidziiri, Gen. Supt., Simon Vuhasio, Presiding Clerk

Uganda Yearly Meeting, P.O. Box 2384, Mbale, UGANDA, East Africa; Nambafu Julius, Gen. Sec., Wopicho Apollo, Clerk, Francis Wamalia, Gen. Supt.

VIHIGA Yearly Meeting of Friends, P.O. Box 160, Vihiga 50310, KENYA, East Africa, Lam Kisanya Osodo, Gen. Sec., Zebedee Musudia, Gen. Supt., Hezekiah Atsiaya, Presiding Clerk

Vokoli Yearly Meetings, P.O. Box 266, Wodanga 50311, KENYA, East Africa; Ephraim Mudoga Ludeki, Gen. Sec., Timothy Kisago, Gen Supt., Gerishom Lumasia, Presiding Clerk

Western Association of the Religious Society of Friends, 13205 E Philadelphia St, Whittier, CA 90601 Tel. (562)698-9805, Email: warsf@inreach.com

Western Yearly Meeting, P.O. Box 70, Plainfield, IN 46168; Tel. (800)909-3452 & (317)839-2789 Fax (317)839-2616, Email: westernym@sbcglobal.net; Steve and Marlene Pediso, Co-Superintendents, Jim Crew, Clerk

Wilmington Yearly Meeting, Pyle Center Box 1194, Wilmington, OH 45177; Tel. (937)382-2491 Fax (937)382-7077, Email: patwym@aol.com; Lois Hackney, Clerk; Marvin Hall, Ex. Sec.

Periodicals

Quaker Life

Full Gospel Assemblies International

The Full Gospel Assemblies International was founded in 1962 under the leadership of Dr. Charles Elwood Strauser. The roots of Full Gospel Assemblies may be traced to 1947 the beginning of the Full Gospel Church of Coatesville, Pennsylvania. As an Assemblies of God Pentecostal church, the Full Gospel Church of Coatesville was active in evangelization and educational ministries to the community. In service to the ministers and students of the Full Gospel Church ministries, the Full Gospel Trinity Ministerial Fellowship was formed in 1962, later changing its name to Full Gospel Assemblies International.

Retaining its original doctrine and faith, Full Gospel Assemblies is Trinitarian, believing that the Bible is God's infallible Word to mankind, baptism in the Holy Spirit according to Acts 2, divine healing is made possible by the sufferings of our Lord Jesus Christ, and in the imminent return of Christ for those who love him. The body of Full Gospel Assemblies is an evangelical missionary fellowship sponsoring ministry at home and abroad, composed of self governing ministries and churches. Congregations, affiliate ministries and clerical body are located throughout the United States and over 15 countries of the world.

Headquarters

International Headquarters: 3018 E Lincoln Hwy, Parkesburg, PA

Mailing Address, P.O. Box 1230, Coatesville, PA 19320, Tel. (610)857-2357, Fax (610)857-3109

Media Contact, Simeon Strauser

Officers

Chairman, Simeon J. Strauser

Exec. Dir. of Ministry, Edward Popovich

Exec. Sec., Carol Strauser

Exec. Trustee, J. Victor Fisk

National Ministers Council

Chpsn., Simeon Strauser, Sadsburyville, PA

J. Victor Fisk, Apollo, PA

Bette Elgin, Zenia, CA

Reginald Licht, Prairie du Sac, WI

Raymond Favicha, Spring Hill, FL

Edward Popovich, Burgesttstown, PA

Periodicals

Full Gospel Ministries Outreach Report, Denominational Code

Full Gospel Fellowship of Churches and Ministers International

In the early 1960s a conviction grew in the hearts of many ministers that there should be closer fellowship between the people of God who believed in the apostolic ministry. At the same time, many independent churches were experiencing serious difficulties in receiving authority from the IRS to give governmentally accepted tax-exempt receipts for donations.

In September 1962 a group of ministers met in Dallas, Texas, to form a Fellowship to give expression to the essential unity of the Body of Christ under the leadership of the Holy Spirit— a unity that goes beyond individuals, churches or organizations. This was not a movement to build another denomination, but rather an effort to join ministers, churches and ministry organizations of like mind across denominational lines. To provide opportunities for fellowship and to support the objectives and goals of local and national ministries-regional conventions and an annual international convention are held.

Headquarters

1000 N. Belt Line Rd., Irving, TX 75061, Tel. (214)492-1254

Media Contact & Convention Planner, Sec., Dr. Harry Schmidt, 400 E. Gregory, Mt. Prospect, IL 60056

Email: TheFellowship@fgfcmi.org

Website: www.fgfcmi.org

Officers

Pres., Rev. Gene Evans, P.O. Box 813, Douglasville, GA 30133

1st Vice Pres, Dr. Harry Schmidt, 400 E. Gregory, Mt. Prospect, IL 60056

Sec., Rev. Phillip Vance, 1035 S. Grand, Pullamn, WA 99163-2161

Treas., Rev. Steve Biffle, 3833 Westerville Rd., Columbus, OH 43224

Business Admin., Bryan Crowson, 1000 N. Belt Line Rd., Irving, TX 75061

Assist. Bus. Admin., S.K. Biffle, 1000 N. Belt Line Rd., Irving, TX 75061

Office Manager, Mrs. Anita Sullivan, 1000 N. Belt Line Rd., Irving, TX 75061

Vice-Pres. at Large, Rev. Don Westbrook, 3518 Rose of Sharon Rd., Durham, NC 27712

Chmn. of Evangelism, Rev. Billy Gibson, 4249 Winding Brook Dr., Plano, TX 75093

Chmn of Mission, Rev. David Robinson, 1121 Shuler St., Elgin. IL 60123

Chmn of Youth, Rev. Steven K. Biffle, 3833 Westerville Rd., Columbus, OH 43224

Past Pres., Rev. Don Arnold, 1001 Lake Carolyn Parkway # 403, Irving TX 75039

REGIONAL VICE PRESIDENTS

Southeast, Rev. Steve Holder, 103 Hawkins Dr., Pikeville, NC 27863

South Central, Rev. Billy Gibson, 4249 Winding Brook Dr., Plano, TX 75093

Southwest, Dr. George Stover, 4870 Janell Dr., Las Vegas, NV 89149

Northeast, Rev. Derwin Lowe, 6099 Ocean Gateway, Trappe, MD 21673

North Central, Rev. David Robinson, 1121 Shuler St., Elgin, IL 60123

Northwest, Rev. Jon R. Engstrom, 19605 12th Ave. W, Lynnwood, WA 98036

Periodicals

Fellowship Tidings

Fundamental Methodist Church, Inc.

This group traces its origin through the Methodist Protestant Church. It withdrew from The Methodist Church and organized on August 27, 1942.

Headquarters

1034 N. Broadway, Springfield, MO 65802

Media Contact, Betty Nicholson, 2497 North Farm Road 17, Nashville, TN 65604, Tel. (417)751-2268

Officers

Treas., and Sec., Betty Nicholson, 2497 North Farm Road 17, Nashville, TN 65604, Tel. (417)751-2268

General Association of General Baptists

Similar in doctrine to those General Baptists organized in England in the 17th century, the first General Baptist churches were organized on the Midwest frontier following the Second Great Awakening. The first church was established by the Rev. Benoni Stinson in 1823 at Evansville, Ind.

Stinson's major theological emphasis was general atonement -Christ tasted death for every man. The group also allows for the possibility of apostasy. It practices open Communion and believer's baptism by immersion.

Called 'liberal' Baptists because of their emphasis on the freedom of man, General Baptists organized a General Association in 1870 and invited other 'liberal' Baptists (e.g., 'Free Will' and Separate Baptists) to participate. The

123

policy-setting body is composed of delegates from local General Baptist churches and associations. Each local church is autonomous but belongs to an association. The group currently consists of more than 60 associations in 16 states, as well as associations in the Philippines, Guam, Saipan, Jamaica, Honduras, and India. Ministers and deacons are ordained by a presbytery.

The denomination operates Oakland City University in Oakland City, Indiana, and Nursing Homes in Illinois and Missouri. General Baptists belong to the Baptist World Alliance, the North American Baptist Fellowship and the National Association of Evangelicals.

Headquarters

100 Stinson Dr., Poplar Bluff, MO 63901, Tel. (573)785-7746 Fax (573)785-0564
Media Contact, Interim Exec. Dir., Dr. James W. Murray
Email: james.murray@generalbaptist.com
Website: www.generalbaptist.com

Officers

Mod., Dr. Terrell Somerville
Clk., Rev. Dennis Powell
Exec. Dir., Dr. James W. Murray
International Missions, Dir., Rev. Sean Warren,100 Stinson Dr., Poplar Bluff, MO 63901, Tel. (573)785-7746, sean.warren@generalbaptist.com
National Missions, Dir., Rev. Donald Key, 100 Stinson Dr., Poplar Bluff, MO 63901, Tel. (573)785-7746, don.key@generalbaptist.com
Womens Ministries, Dir., Patti Thornton, 100 Stinson Dr., Poplar Bluff, MO 63901, Tel. (573) 785-7746, patti.thornton@generalbaptist.com
Oakland City University, Dr. Ray Barber, President, 138 North Lucretia St., Oakland City, IN 47660, Tel. (812)749-4781
Congregational Ministries, Dir., Dr. Franklin Dumond, 100 Stinson Dr., Poplar Bluff, MO 63901, Tel. (573)785-7746, franklin.dumond @generalbaptist.com
Pastoral Ministries, Dir., Dr. John Sloan, 100 Stinson Dr., Poplar Bluff, MO 63901, Tel. (573)785-7746, john.sloan@generalbaptist.com
Admin., Financial Services, Financial Officer, Linda McDonough, 100 Stinson Dr., Poplar Bluff, MO 63901, Tel. (573)785-7746 linda.mcdonough@generalbaptist.com
Stinson Press, Inc., Pres., Rev. Dale Bates, 400 Stinson Dr., Poplar Bluff, MO 63901, bates@stinsonpress.com
Nursing Home Board, CEO Scott Cole, Rt. #3, Box 650, Campbell, MO 63933, gbnh1@sbcglobal.net
Compassionate Care Adoption Agency, Dir., Rev. Darrell Hillouse, 26 Jones Rd., Sebree, KY 42455
General Baptist Investment Fund Dir., Rev. Stephen Naff, 100 Stinson Dr., Poplar Bluff, MO 63901, Tel. (573)785-7746, steve.naff@generalbaptist.com

Periodicals

Capsule, Voice, Woman to Woman, Messenger

General Association of Regular Baptist Churches

This association was founded in May, 1932, in Chicago by a group of churches which had withdrawn from the Northern Baptist Convention (now the American Baptist Churches in the U.S.A.) because of doctrinal differences. Its Confession of Faith, which it requires all churches to subscribe to, is essentially the old, historic New Hampshire Confession of Faith with a premillennial ending applied to the last article. The churches of the General Association of Regular Baptist Churches voluntarily join together to accomplish four goals. (1) Champion Biblical truth—committed to communicating the whole counsel of God in its timeless relevance. (2) Impact the world for Christ — obeying the Lord's Great Commission to take the life-changing gospel to the entire world. (3) Perpetuate Its Baptist heritage—faithfully promoting its Scriptural legacy and identity. (4) Advancing GARBC churches—strengthening existing churches and planting new churches for the purposes of evangelism and edification.

Headquarters

1300 N. Meacham Rd., Schaumburg, IL 60173, Tel. (847)843-1600 Fax (847)843-3757
Media Contact, Natl. Rep., Dr. John Greening
Email: garbc@garbc.org
Website: www.garbc.org

Officers

Chpsn., Rev. Richard Van Heukelum, Waterloo IA
Vice Chpsn., Rev. Bradley Quick, Elyria OH
Treas., Michael Nolan, Schaumburg IL
Sec., Dr. John Hartag, III, Cambridge IA
Natl. Rep., Dr. John Greening, Schaumburg IL

Periodicals

Baptist Bulletin, Synergy Newsletter, E-Info Newsletter

General Church of the New Jerusalem

The General Church of the New Jerusalem, also called the New Church, was founded in 1897. It is based on the teachings of the 18th Century scientist Emanuel Swedenborg, and stresses the oneness of God, who is the Lord Jesus Christ, a life of faith and love in service to others, in true married love, and in life after death.

Headquarters

1100 Cathedral Rd, P.O. Box 743, Bryn Athyn, PA 19009, Tel. (267)502-2682
Media Contact, Ed., Church Journal, Rev. Erik E. Sandström, Box 743, Bryn Athyn, PA 19009, Tel. (267)502-4998 Fax (267)502-2616

Email: svsimpso@newchurch.edu
Website: www.newchurch.org

Officers
Presiding Bishop, Rt. Rev. Thomas L. Kline
Sec., Alaine F. York
Treas., David Frazier

Periodicals
New Church Life

General Conference of The Church of God (Seventh Day), Denver, Colorado

General Conference of the Church of God (Seventh Day) began in southwestern Michigan in 1858, when a group of Sabbath-keepers led by Gilbert Cranmer refused to give endorsement to the visions and writings of Ellen G. White, a principal in the formation of the Seventh-Day Adventist Church. Another branch of Sabbath-keepers, which developed near Cedar Rapids, Iowa, in 1860, joined the Michigan church in 1863 to publish a paper called The Hope of Israel, the predecessor to the Bible Advocate, the church's present publication. As membership grew and spread into Missouri and Nebraska, it organized the General Conference of the Church of God in 1884. The words "Seventh Day" were added to its name in 1923. The headquarters of the church was in Stanberry, Missouri, from 1888 until 1950, when it moved to Denver.

The Church teaches salvation is a gift of God's grace, and is available solely by faith in Jesus Christ, the Savior; that saving faith is more than mental assent, it involves active trust and repentance from sin. Out of gratitude, Christians will give evidence of saving faith by a lifestyle that conforms to God's commandments, including the seventh-day Sabbath, which members observe as a tangible expression of their faith and rest in God as their Creator and Redeemer. The church believes in the imminent, personal, and visible return of Christ; that the dead are in an unconscious state awaiting to be resurrected, the wicked to be destroyed, and the righteous to be rewarded to eternal life in the presence of God on a restored earth. The church observes two ordinances, baptism by immersion and an annual Communion service accompanied by foot washing.

Headquarters
330 W. 152nd Ave., P.O. Box 33677, Denver, CO 80233, Tel. (303)452-7973 Fax (303)452-0657
Media Contact, Pres., Whaid Rose
Email: whaidrose@cog7.org
Website: www.cog7.org

Ministries
Missions Ministries, Dir., William Hicks,
Publications/Bible Advocate Press, Dir., Keith Michalak

Lifespring School of Ministry, Interium Dir., Richard Jensen, PhD.
Young Adult Ministry, Dir., Christy Lang
Youth Ministry, Dirs., Kurt & Kristi Lang
Women's Ministry, Dir., Grace Sanchez

Periodicals
The Bible Advocate (English & Spanish),
Churchright (English & Spanish)

General Conference of Mennonite Brethren Churches

A small group, requesting that closer attention be given to prayer, Bible study and a consistent lifestyle, withdrew from the larger Mennonite Church in the Ukraine in 1860. Anabaptist in origin, the group was influenced by Lutheran pietists and Baptist teachings and adopted a quasi-congregational form of church government. In 1874 and years following, small groups of these German-speaking Mennonites left Russia, settled in Kansas and then spread to the Midwest west of the Mississippi and into Canada. Some years later the movement spread to California and the West Coast. In 1960, the Krimmer Mennonite Brethren Conference merged with this body.

Today the General Conference of Mennonite Brethren Churches conducts services in many European languages as well as in Vietnamese, Mandarin and Hindi. It works with other denominations in missionary and development projects in 25 countries outside North America.

Headquarters
4812 E. Butler Ave., Fresno, CA 93727, Tel. (209)452-1713 Fax (209)452-1752
Media Contact, Exec. Sec., Marvin Hein

Officers
Mod., Ed Boschman, 12630 N. 103rd Ave., Suite 215, Sun City, AZ 85351
Asst. Mod., Herb Kopp, 200 McIvor Ave., Winnipeg, NB R20 028
Sec., Valerie Rempel
Exec. Sec., Marvin Hein

Periodicals
Christian Leader

Grace Gospel Fellowship

The Grace Gospel Fellowship was organized in 1944 by a group of pastors who held to a dispensational interpretation of Scripture. Most had ministries in the Midwest. Two prominent leaders were J. C. O'Hair of Chicago and Charles Baker of Milwaukee. Subsequent to 1945, a Bible Institute was founded (now Grace Bible College of Grand Rapids, Mich.), and a previously organized foreign mission (now Grace Ministries International of Grand Rapids) was affiliated with the group. Churches have now been established in most sections of the country.

The body has remained a fellowship, each church being autonomous in polity. All support for its college, mission and headquarters is on a contributory basis. The binding force of the Fellowship has been the members' doctrinal position. They believe in the Deity and Saviorship of Jesus Christ and subscribe to the inerrant authority of Scripture. Their method of biblical interpretation is dispensational, with emphasis on the distinctive revelation to and the ministry of the apostle Paul.

Headquarters

Media Contact, Pres., Frosty Hansen, 2125 Martindale SW, P.O. Box 9432, Grand Rapids, MI 49509, Tel. (616)245-0100 Fax (616)241-2542

Email: ggfinc@aol.com

Website: www.ggfusa.org

Officers

Pres., Traynor ("Frosty") Hansen, Jr.

OTHER ORGANIZATIONS

Grace Bible College, Pres., Rev. Ken Kemper, 1011 Aldon St. SW, Grand Rapids, MI 49509

Grace Ministries Intl., Exec. Dir., Dr. Samuel Vinton, 2125 Martindale Ave. SW, Grand Rapids, MI 49509

Prison Mission Association, Gen. Dir., Donald Sommer, P.O. Box 1587, Port Orchard, WA 98366-0140

Grace Publications Inc., Exec. Dir., Wayne Schoonover, 2125 Martindale Ave. SW, Grand Rapids, MI 49509

Bible Doctrines to Live By, Exec. Dir., Lee Homoki, P.O. Box 2351, Grand Rapids, MI 49501

Periodicals

Truth

Greek Orthodox Archdiocese of America*

The Orthodox Church today, numbering over 250 million worldwide, is a communion of self-governing Churches, each administratively independent of the other, but united by a common faith and spirituality. Their underlying unity is based on identity of doctrines, sacramental life and worship, which distinguishes Orthodox Christianity. All recognize the spiritual preeminence of the Ecumenical Patriarch of Constantinople who is acknowledged as primus inter pares, first among equals. All share full communion with one another. The living tradition of the Church and the principles of concord and harmony are expressed through the common mind of the universal episcopate as the need arises. In all other matters, the internal life of each independent Church is administered by the bishops of that particular Church. Following the ancient principle of the one people of God in each place and the universal priesthood of all believers, the laity share equally in the responsibility for the preservation and propagation of the Christian faith and Church.

THE GREEK ORTHODOX ARCHDIOCESE OF AMERICA:

Before the establishment of an Archdiocese in the Western Hemisphere there were numerous communities of Greek Orthodox Christians. The first Greek Orthodox community in the Americas was founded in New Orleans, LA by a small colony of Greek merchants. History also records that on June 26, 1768 the first Greek colonists landed at St. Augustine, FL, the oldest city in America. The first permanent community was founded in New York City in 1892, today's Archdiocesan Cathedral of the Holy Trinity and the See of the Archbishop of America. The Greek Orthodox Archdiocese of North and South America was incorporated in 1921 and officially recognized by the State of New York in 1922.

The Greek Orthodox Archdiocese of America is composed of the Direct Archdiocesan District —New York and eight Metropolises: Chicago, Pittsburgh, Boston, Denver, Atlanta, Detroit, San Francisco and New Jersey. It is governed by the Archbishop and the Synod of Bishops. The Synod of Bishops is headed by the Archbishop and comprised of the Metropolitans who are in charge of a metropolis. It has all the authority and responsibility which the Church canons provide for a provincial synod.

Headquarters

8-10 E. 79th St., New York, NY 10021, Tel. (212)570-3500 Fax (212)570-3569

Media Contact, Nikki Stephanopoulos, Director, News and Information/Public Affairs, Tel. (212)570-3530 Fax (212)774-0215 Email: nikki@goarch.org

Email: archdiocese@goarch.org; stavros@goarch.org

Website: www.goarch.org

Officers

HOLY EPARCHIAL SYNOD OF BISHOPS

His Eminence Archbishop Demetrios, Primate of the Greek Orthodox Archdiocese of America, Exarch of the Atlantic and Pacific Oceans, Chairman of the Holy Synod of Bishops, Greek Orthodox Church in America, 8-10 East 79th St., New York, NY 10021, Tel. (212)570-3500, Fax (212)570-3592

METROPOLIS'

His Eminence Metropolitan Iakovos of Chicago, Metropolis of Chicago, 40 East Burton Place, Chicago, IL 60610, Tel. (312)337-4130 Fax (312)337-9391

His Eminence Metropolitan Maximos of Pittsburgh, Metropolis of Pittsburgh, 5201 Ellsworth Ave., Pittsburgh, PA 15232, Tel. (412)621-5529 Fax (412)621-1522

His Eminence Metropolitan Methodios of Boston, Metropolis of Boston, 162 Goddard Ave., Brookline, MA 02146, Tel. (617)277-4742, Fax (617)739-9229

His Eminence Metropolitan Isaiah of Denver, Metropolis of Denver, 4610 East Alameda Ave., Suite D1, Denver, CO 80222, Tel. (303)333-7794 Fax (303)333-7796

His Eminence Metropolitan Alexios of Atlanta, Metropolis of Atlanta, 2480 Clairmont Road NE, Atlanta, GA 30329, Tel. (404)634-9345 Fax (404)634-2471

His Eminence Metroplitan Nicholas of Detroit, Metropolis of Detroit, 19405 Renfrew Rd., Detroit, MI 48221, Tel. (313)664-5433 Fax (313)864-5543

His Eminence Metropolitan Gerasimos of San Francisco, Metropolis of San Francisco, 372 Santa Clara Ave., San Francisco, CA 94127, Tel. (415)753-3075 Fax (415)753-1165

His Eminence Metropolitan Evangelos of New Jersey, Metropolis of New Jersey 629 Springfield Rd., Kenilworth, NJ 07033, Tel. (908)686-0003 Fax (908)686-0046

Auxiliary Bishops: His Grace Bishop Dimitrios of Xanthos, His Grace Bishop Savas of Troas, His Grace Bishop Andonios of Phasiane, His Grace Bishop Demetrios of Mokissos.

CLERGY-LAITY CONGRESS

The Clergy-Laity Congress, the highest legislative body of the Archdiocese, is convened biennially and presided over by the Archbishop. It is concerned with all matters, other than doctrinal or canonical, affecting the life, growth and unity of the Church, the institutions, finances, administration, educational and philanthropic concerns and its increasing growing role in the life of the nations of the Western Hemisphere. The delegates are the pastors and elected lay representatives. There are 560 parishes, 840 priests and approximately 1.5 million faithful in the Greek Orthodox Archdiocese of America

THE ARCHDIOCESAN COUNCIL

The Archdiocesan Council is the deliberative body of the Greek Orthodox Archdiocese which meets in the interim period between Clergy-Laity Congresses, held every two years.

Executive Committee, His Eminence Archbishop Demetrios Chairman

The Holy Synod of Bishops

Vice Chairman, Michael Jaharis; Nicholas Bouras, Treasurer; Catherine Bouffides-Walsh, Secretary; George Behrakis, Elini Huszagh, Peter Kikis, George Mathews, Anthony Stefanis, George Vourvoulias; Emanuel G. Demos, General Counsel to the Archdiocese.

INSTITUTIONS

Archdiocesan Cathedral of the Holy Trinity
The Rev. Frank Marangos, Dean, 319-337 East 74th St., New York, NY 10021, Tel. (212)288-3215 Fax (212)288-5876 Website: www.the cathedral.goarch.org

Hellenic College/Holy Cross School of Theology, The Rev. Nicholas Triantafilou, President, 50 Goddard Ave., Brookline, MA 02445, Tel. (617)731-3500 Fax (617)850-1460, Email: admission@hchc.edu

Saint Basil Academy, The Rev. Constantine L. Sitaras, Director, 79 Saint Basil Road Garrison, NY 10524, Tel. (845)424-3500 Fax (845)424-4172, Email: stbasil@bestweb.net, Website: www.stbasil.goarch.org

St. Michael's Home, His Grace Bishop Andonios of Phasiane, Director, 3 Lehman Terrace, Yonkers, NY 10705, Tel. (914)476-3374 Fax (914)476-1744, Email: Stmichaelshome@ msn.com, Website: stmichael.goarch.org

ARCHDIOCESE OF NEW YORK

Office of the Archbishop, Alice Keurian; Director; Office of the Chancellor,His Grace Bishop Savas of Troas, Chancellor; Office of Administration, Jerry Dimitriou, Executive Director.

ARCHDIOCESAN DEPARTMENTS

Registry, Finance, Stewardship & LOGOS, Religious Education, Greek Education, Communications, Internet Ministries, Information Technologies, Youth and Young Adults, Camping Ministry, Ionian Village Ecumenical, Interfaith/Interchurch Marriages, Archives, Benefits Related Organizations, auxiliaries Ladies Philoptochos Society, Presbyters Council, Sisterhood of Presvyteres, Retired Clergy of America, National Forum of Greek Orthodox Musicians, Hellenic Cultural Center, Archons of the Ecumenical Patriarchate, Archbishop Iakovos Leadership 100 Endowment Fund, St. Photios National Shrine, International Orthodox Christian Charities (IOCC), Orthodox Christian Mission Center, Trinity Children & Family Services.

OTHER JURISDICTIONS OF THE ECU-MENICAL PATRIARCHATE IN THE USA

Albanian Orthodox Diocese in America; Belarusian Council of Orthodox Churches in North America; American Carpatho-Russian Orthodox Greek Catholic Diocese of the USA; Ukrainian Orthodox Church of the USA

Periodicals
THE ORTHODOX OBSERVER

The Holy Eastern Orthodox Catholic and Apostolic Church in North America, Inc.

We were Canonically established as The Holy Eastern Orthodox Catholic and Apostolic Church in North America on Feb. 2, 1927 by the Russian Syod of Bishops in North America. We were incorporated in Boston, MA in 1928 with this same name "The Holy Eastern Orthodox Catholic and Apostolic Church in North America".

Our names as listed in the 1927 Church Constitution are as follows; Our Corporate name

127

"The Holy Eastern Orthodox Catholic and Apostolic Church in North America". Our short name from our 1927 Constitution is "American Orthodox Catholic Church". In 2003 the North American Holy Synod declared this Church to be the "American Orthodox Patriarchate and elected Abp. Nikon to be the first Patriarch of the Church. If you list American Orthodox Patriarchate please say "see The Holy Eastern Orthodox Catholic and Apostolic Church in North America". This is our original name and our 1928 Corporate name and we still use this name first.

Also "The Society of Clerks Secular of Saint Basil" was established by Abp. Ofiesh and Bp. Ignatius within this Church ad continues in this Church. There are a few in the independent movement who use our names improperly.

We are recognized by the Roman and Byzantine Catholics and the Episcopal Church USA who accepted one of our former priests without re-ordination. We have a letter, dated 1996, that we can provide communion to Roman Catholics within our own liturgy. On Feb. 2, 2011 we celebrated our 84th Anniversary. The North American Holy Synod consists of 4 bishops in the U.S.

In Dec. 2009 we asked a few bishops to leave for refusing to obey the Sacred and Divine Canons as well as the canons of the Church. It may be noted that we view certain SCOBA Orthodox as being Schismatics for the 1929 schism caused by the Archbishop of their church, their continued violations of the Canons and allowing priests to attack the good name and memory of bishops who died years ago.

Headquarters
Monastery: St. Pachomius Monastery, P.O. Box 121, Sudan, TX 79371, Tel. (806)227-2214
Primate, Metropolitan Victor
Email: theocacna@yahoo.com; theocacna@webtv.net
Website: www.theocacna.org; www.theocacna.us

Officers
Archbishop Peter Mar Kepa -Archdiocese of the East
Metropolitan Victor -Archdiocese of the West
Bishop Christopher -Diocese of Houston, TX.
Bishop Cassian -Diocese of Columbus, OH.
Bishop Arthur -Diocese of Michigan

SYNOD ADVISORS
Archbishop James
Bishop Donald
Society: The Society of Clerks Secular of St. Basil, est. 1931

Holy Ukrainian Autocephalic Orthodox Church in Exile

This church was organized in a parish in New York in 1951 by Ukrainian laymen and clergy who settled in the Western Hemisphere after World War II. In 1954 two bishops, immigrants from Europe, met with clergy and laymen and formally organized the religious body.

Headquarters
103 Evergreen St., W. Babylon, NY 11704

Officers
Admn., Rt. Rev. Serhij K. Pastukhiv

House of God, Which is the Church of the Living God, the Pillar and Ground of the Truth, Inc.

This body, founded by Mary L. Tate in 1919, is episcopally organized.

Headquarters
1301 N. 58th St., Philadelphia, PA 19131
Media Contact, Sec., Rose Canon, 515 S. 57th St., Philadelphia, PA 19143, Tel. (215)474-8913

Officers
Bishop, Raymond W. White, 6107 Cobbs Creek Pkwy., Philadelphia, PA 19143, Tel. (215)748-6338

Hungarian Reformed Church in America*

A Hungarian Reformed Church was organized in New York in 1904 in connection with the Reformed Church of Hungary. In 1922, the Church in Hungary transferred most of its congregations in the United States to the Reformed Church in the U.S. Some, however, preferred to continue as an autonomous, self-supporting American deno-mination, and these formed the Free Magyar Reformed Church in America. This group changed its name in 1958 to Hungarian Reformed Church in America. This church is a member of the World Alliance of Reformed Churches, Presbyterian and Congregational, the World Council of Churches and the National Council of Churches of Christ.

Headquarters
Bishop's Office, 13 Grove St., Poughkeepsie, NY 12601, Tel. (914)454-5735
Email: bozsiujj@yahoo.com

Officers
Bishop, Rt. Rev. Alexander Forro
Chief Lay-Curator, Prof. Stephen Szabo, 464 Forest Ave., Paramus, NJ 07652
Gen. Sec. (Clergy), Rt. Rev. Stefan M. Torok, 331 Kirkland Pl., Perth Amboy, NJ 08861, Tel. (908)442-7799
Gen Sec. (Lay), Zoltan Ambrus, 3358 Maple Dr., Melvindale, MI 48122
Eastern Classes, Dean (Senior of the Deans, Chair in Bishop's absence), Very Rev. Imre Bertalan, 10401 Grosvenor Pl., #1521, Rockville, MD 20852, Tel. (301)493-5036 Fax (301)571-5111; Lay-Curator, Balint Balogh, 519 N. Muhlenberg St., Allentown, PA 18104

128

New York Classes, Supervisor, Rt. Rev. Alexander Forro; Lay-Curator, Laszlo B. Vanyi, 229 E 82nd St., New York, NY 10028 Western Classes, Dean, V. Rev. Andor Demeter, 3921 W. Christy Dr., Phoenix, AZ 85029; Lay-Curator, Zolton Kun, 2604 Saybrook Dr., Pittsburgh, PA 15235

Periodicals
Magyar Egyhaz

Hutterian Brethren

Small groups of Hutterites derive their names from Jacob Hutter, a 16th-century Anabaptist who taught true discipleship after accepting Jesus as Saviour, advocated communal ownership of property and was burned as a heretic in Austria in 1536. Many believers are of German descent and still use their native tongue at home and in church. Much of the denominational literature is produced in German and English. "Colonies" share property, practice non-resistance, dress plainly, do not participate in politics and operate their own schools. There are 428 colonies with 42,000 members in North America. Each congregation conducts its own youth work through Sunday school. Until age 15, children attend German and English school which is operated by each colony. All youth ages 15 to 20 attend Sunday school. They are baptized as adults upon confession of faith, around age 20.

Headquarters
Media Contact, Philip J. Gross, 3610 N. Wood Rd., Reardon, WA 99029, Tel. (509)299-5400 Fax (509)299-3099
Email: philsjg@juno.com

Officers
Smiedleut Chmn., No. 1, Jacob Waldner—Blumengard Colony, Box 13 Plum Coulee, MB R0G 1R0, Tel. (204)829-3527
Smiedleut Chmn., No. 2, Jacob Wipf, Spring Creek Colony, 36562 102 St., Forbes, ND 58439, Tel. (701)358-8621
Dariusleut, Chmn., No. 1, Martin Walter, Springpoint Colony, Box 249, Pincher Creek, AB T0K 1W0 Phone (403)553-4368
Lehrerleut, Chmn., Rev. John Wipf, Rosetown Colony, Box 1509, Rosetown, SK S0L 2V0, Tel. (306)882-3344

IFCA International, Inc.

This group of churches was organized in 1930 at Cicero, Illinois, by representatives of the American Council of Undenominational Churches and representatives of various independent churches. The founding churches and members had separated themselves from various denominational affiliations. Founders included J. Oliver Buswell of Wheaton College, Billy McCarrell of Cicero Bible Church and Moody Bible Institute, and M. R. DeHaan of Grand Rapids, MI and Radio Bible Class. Members have included J. Vernon McGee, Charles Ryrie, John Walvoord, and John MacArthur.

The IFCA provides a way for independent churches and ministers to unite in close fellowship and cooperation, in defense of the fundamental teachings of Scripture and in the proclamation of the gospel of God's grace.

Today it consists of 1000 associated churches and 1200 individual members (pastors, professors, missionaries, chaplains, and other Christian workers.)

Headquarters
3520 Fairlanes, Grandville, MI 49418, Tel. (616)531-1840 Fax (616)531-1814
Mailing Address, P.O. Box 810, Grandville, MI 49468-0810
Media Contact, Exec. Dir., Dr. Les Lofquist
Email: office@ifca.org
Website: www.ifca.org

Officers
Exec. Dir., Dr. Les Lofquist
Pres. of Board, Rev. Earl Brubaker

Periodicals
The Voice

International Church of the Foursquare Gospel

Founded by Aimee Semple McPherson in 1927, the International Church of the Foursquare Gospel proclaims the message of Jesus Christ the Savior, Healer, Baptizer with the Holy Spirit and Soon-coming King. Headquartered in Los Angeles, this evangelistic missionary body of believers consists of nearly 1,900 churches in the United States and Canada. The International Church of the Foursquare Gospel is incorporated in the state of California and governed by a Board of Directors who direct its corporate affairs. A Foursquare Cabinet, consisting of the Corporate Officers, Board of Directors and District Supervisors of the various districts of the Foursquare Church in the United States and other elected or appointed members, serves in an advisory capacity to the President and the Board of Directors. Each local Foursquare Church is a subordinate unit of the International Church of the Foursquare Gospel. The pastor of the church is appointed by the Board of Directors and is responsible for the spiritual and physical welfare of the church. To assist and advise the pastor, a church council is elected by the local church members. Foursquare churches seek to build strong believers through Christian education, Christian day schools, youth camping and ministry, Foursquare Women International who support and encourage Foursquare missionaries abroad, local radio and television ministries, the Foursquare World *ADVANCE* Magazine and over

550 Bible colleges worldwide. Worldwide missions remains the focus of the Foursquare Gospel Church with 38,217 churches and meeting places, 49,287 national pastors, leaders and 4,113,981 members with a combined constituency nearing 5 million in over 140 countries of the world. The Church is affiliated with the Pentecostal/Charismatic Churches of North America, the National Association of Evangelicals and the Pentecostal World Conference.

Headquarters

1910 W. Sunset Blvd., Ste. 200, P.O. Box 26902, Los Angeles, CA 90026-0176, Tel. (213)989-4234 Fax (213)989-4590
Media Contact, Editor, Dr. Ron Williams
Email: comm@foursquare.org
Website: www.foursquare.org

Officers

President: Dr. Jack W. Hayford
Vice President/General Supervisor: Rev. Glenn C. Burris Jr.
Vice President/Director of Global Operations and Missions: Rev. Michael Larkin
Vice President/Church Operations: Rev. James C. Scott Jr.
Vice President/Director of Urban and Multicultural Ministries: Rev. Arthur J. Gray II
Vice President/Corporate Secretary-Treasurer: Dr. Sterling Brackett
Chief Financial Officer: Rev. Jeffrey L. Bird
Vice President/Chief Information Technologies Officer: Rev. Dan Ussery
All of the above can be reached through the corporate address: International Church of the Foursquare Gospel, P.O. Box 26902, Los Angeles, CA 90026, Tel. (888)635-4234 Fax: 213-989-4590, Email: comm@foursquare.org, Website: www.foursquare.org

Periodicals

Foursquare World ADVANCE

International Council of Community Churches*

This body is a fellowship of locally autonomous, ecumenically minded, congregationally governed, non-creedal Churches. The Council came into being in 1950 as the union of two former councils of community churches, one formed of black churches known as the Biennial Council of Community Churches in the United States and Elsewhere and the other of white churches known as the National Council of Community Churches.

Headquarters

21116 Washington Pky., Frankfort, IL 60423-3112, Tel. (815)464-5690 Fax (815)464-5692
Media Contact, Exec. Dir., Rev. Michael E. Livingston
Email: icccml@sbcglobal.net

Officers

Pres., Mrs. Saundra Nelson
Vice Pres., Rev. Paul Drake
Sec., Rev. Dick Griffith
Treas., Nick Brame
Commission on Laity and Church Relations, Emma Smith
Commission on Ecumenical and Inter-faith Relations, Rev. Herman Harmelink, III
Commission on Clergy Relations, Rev. Glenn Clay
Commission on Faith, Justice & Mission, Rev. Dr. Richard Griffith
Women's Christian Fellowship, Pres., Rev. Cay Randall-May
Samaritans (Men's Fellowship), Pres., Abraham Wright
Youth Fellowship, Pres., Danielle Bailey

Periodicals

The Christian Community, The Inclusive Pulpit, Key Lay Notes, Clergy communique

International Fellowship of Bible Churches, Inc

Founded August, 1988 from three groups of ministers and churches of conservative Wesleyan holiness tradition. Sponsor mission works in six countries on four continents. Locally autonomous congregations cooperate for missions, education, youth camps, religious gatherings, etc. Congregational goverment at Assembly level. International Assembly held biannually on even numbered years. Officers include General Superintendent and a 20-member Board comprised of 10 clergy and 10 non-clergy, elected by the International Assembly. The International Fellowship of Bible Churches, Incorporated is an association of autonomous congregations and parachurch ministries joined together by common persuasions, purposes and principles. International refers to our commitment to maintaining a consciousness of the global and universal nature of the Church of Jesus Christ, as well as our firm commitment to active service as part of that universal and international church. The Fellowship currently operates an international ministry in several locations across the globe. Fellowship refers to our commitment to the autonomy of the local congregation while maintaining the belief that we really do need each other. Bible refers to our commitment to the authority of Scripture as the final guide for all matters of faith and practice, both public and private. Churches refers to our belief that ministry occurs most efficiently and effectively at the local church level, not at the denominational or organizational level.

Headquarters

3511 N. Geraldine Ave., Oklahoma City, OK 73112, Tel. & Fax (405)948-9388
Media Contact, Gen. Superintendent, William Harrison Sillings

Email: williamsillins@ibfc.org
Website: www.ifbc.org

Officers

Gen. Superintendent, William Harrison Sillings, 3511 N. Geraldine Ave., Oklahoma City, OK 73112, Tel. & Fax (405)948-9388, Email: williamsillings@ibfc.org

Secretary, Rev. Howard Russell, 16163 Galehouse Rd., Doylesville, OH 44230, Tel. (330)798-5248 Fax (330)658-1431, Email: hrussell@cbnews.org

Treasurer, Rev. Ronald Ruyle, 7512 S. Villa, Oklahoma City, OK 73159, Tel. (405)681-7475

Director of Missions, Rev. Robert Gilbert, 8103 Dudley Rd., Chattanooga, TN 3741, Tel. (423)296-8612 Fax (423)499-0357, Email: rgilbert@precept.org

Director of Chaplains, Rev. Gary Hedges, P.O. Box 5555, Ft. Oglethorpe, GA 30742, Tel. (706)861-7733 Fax (706)861-7777, Email: gary@chswebsite.com

International Fellowship of Christian Assemblies

Originally known as the Italian Christian Church, its first General Council was held in 1927 at Niagara Falls, N.Y. This body was incorporated in 1948 at Pittsburgh, Pa., and is described as Pentecostal but does not engage in the "the excesses tolerated or practiced among some churches using the same name."

The movement recognizes two ordinances-baptism and the Lord's Supper. Its moral code is conservative and its teaching is orthodox. Members are exhorted to pursue a life of personal holiness, setting an example to others. A conservative position is held in regard to marriage and divorce. The governmental form is, by and large, congregational. District and National officiaries, however, are referred to as Presbyteries led by Overseers.

The group functions in cooperative fellowship with the Italian Pentecostal Church of Canada and the Evangelical Christian Churches-Assemblies of God in Italy. It is an affiliate member of the Pentecostal Fellowship of North America and of the National Association of Evangelicals.

Headquarters

1294 Rutledge Rd., Transfer, PA 16154-2299, Tel. (724)962-3501 Fax (724)962-1766

Exec. Sec., Christine Marini; Asst., Candace Tarr

Email: ifcahq@verizon.net

Website: www.ifcaministry.com

Officers

Executive Bd., Gen. Overseer, Rev. Michael Player, 1294 Rutledge Rd., Transfer, PA. 16154

Exec. Vice Pres., Rev. Warren Day, 16679, Sandy Creek Valley Rd., Watertown, NY 13601

Asst. Gen. Overseers, Rev. Carmine Zottoli, 270 Sheer Hill Rd., Mahopac, NY 10541

Rev. Timothy Tyler, 20840 Bon Heur, St. Clair Shores, MI 48081

Rev. John King, 59 Bellwood Circle, Bellingham, MA 02019

Rev. Warren Day, 16678 Sandy Creek Valley Rd., Watertown, NY 13601

Rev. Richard George, 3395 Waterside Dr., Akron, OH 44319

Rev. Douglas Bedgood, 442 Trinidad Lane, Largo, FL 33770

DEPARTMENTS

Benevolence, Rev. Michael Player, 1294 Rutledge Rd., Transfer, PA 16154

Home Missions, Rev. Dale Russo, 1294 Rutledge Rd., Transfer, PA 16154

Faith, Order & Credentials, Rev. Warren Day, 16678 Sandy Creek Valley Rd., Watertown, NY 13601

Missions, Rev. Dale Russo, 1294 Rutledge Rd., Transfer, PA 16154

Publications Relations, vacant, Lay Ministries, vacant

Education, Rev. Lucian Gandolfo, P.O. Box 230606, Brooklyn, NY 11223

Periodicals

Vista

The International Pentecostal Church of Christ

At a General Conference held at London, Ohio, Aug. 10, 1976, the International Pentecostal Assemblies and the Pentecostal Church of Christ consolidated into one body, taking the name International Pentecostal Church of Christ.

The International Pentecostal Assemblies was the successor of the Association of Pentecostal Assemblies and the International Pentecostal Missionary Union. The Pentecostal Church of Christ was founded by John Stroup of Flatwoods, Ketucky, on May 10, 1917 and was incorporated at Portsmouth, Ohio, in 1927. The International Pentecostal Church of Christ is an active member of the Pentecostal/Charismatic Churches of North America, as well as a member of the National Association of Evangelicals.

The priorities of the International Pentecostal Church of Christ are to be an agency of God for evangelizing the world, to be a corporate body in which people may worship God and to be a channel of God's purpose to build a body of saints being perfected in the image of His Son. The Annual Conference is held each year during the third full week of July in London, Ohio.

Headquarters

2245 St. Rt. 42 SW, P.O. Box 439, London, OH 43140, Tel. (740)852-4722 Fax (740)852-0348

Media Contact, Gen. Overseer, Clyde M. Hughes

Email: hqipcc@aol.com
Website: members.aol.com/hqipcc

Officers

EXECUTIVE COMMITTEE
Gen. Overseer, Clyde M. Hughes, P.O. Box 439, London, OH 43140, Tel. (740)852-4722 Fax (740)852-0348 Email: c.hughes@ipcc.cc
Asst. Gen. Overseer, B.G. Turner, 87 Old Taylor Lane, Harpers Ferry, WV 25425, Tel. (304)535-2221 Fax (304)535-1357 Email: bolipcc@citlink.net
Gen. Sec., Anthony S. Ralph, P.O. Box 141, Manns Habor, NC 27953-1041, Tel. (252)473-2720 Email: cheslight@yahoo.com
Gen. Treas., Ervin Hargrave, P.O. Box 439, London, OH 43140, Tel. (740)852-4722 Fax (740)852-0348 Email: compipcc@aol.com
Dir. of Global Missions, Aaron Turner, P.O. Box 177, South Charleston, OH 45638, Tel. (937)462-8654 Email: scccipcc@aol.com
Dir. of Church Ministries, Randall Davis, 333 Country Lake Dr., McDough, GA 30252-2695, Tel. (770)954-1287, Email: DavisOne Heart@aol.com

DISTRICT OVERSEERS
Central District, Ervin Hargrave, P.O. Box 439, London, OH 43140, Tel. (740)852-4722 Fax (740)852-0348 Email: compipcc@aol.com
Mid-Eastern District, H. Gene Boyce, 705 W. Grubb St., Hertford, NC 27944, Tel. (252)426-5403
Mountain District, Terry Lykins, P.O. Box 131, Staffordsville, KY 41256, Tel. (606)297-3282 Email: tlykins@auddenlink.net
New River District, Calvin Weikel, RR. 2, Box 300, Ronceverte, WV 24970, Tel. (304)647-4301
North Central District, Jack Bowen, 6334 W. Mt. Morris Rd., Mt. Morris, MI 48458-9431 Email: jackbowendo@comcast.net
North Eastern District, Wayne Taylor, 806 8th St., Shenandoah, VA 22849, Tel. (540)652-8090 Email: revwayne@embarqmail.com
South Eastern District, Frank Angié, 2507 Old Peachtree Rd., Duluth, GA 30097, Tel. (678)429-2313 Email: franklyn_ahotmail.com
Tri-State District, Clyde M. Hughes, P.O. Box 439, London, OH 43140, Tel. (740)852-4722 Fax (740)852-0348 Email: c.hughes@ipcc.cc

OTHER ORGANIZATIONS
Women's Ministries Department, Gen. Pres., Janice Boyce, 121 W. Hunters Tr., Elizabeth City, NC 27909, Tel. and Fax (252)338-3003 Email: jwboyce@inteliport.com
National Youth and Christian Education Dept., Dir., Brenton Hubbard, Tel. (740)852-0448 Fax (740)852-0348 Email: kingscommission@ipcc.cc
King's Commission, Dir., Brenton Hubbard, Tel. (740)852-0448 Fax (740)852-0348 Email: kingscommission@ipcc.cc

Periodicals
The Bridegroom's Messenger, The Pentecostal Leader

International Pentecostal Holiness Church

This body grew out of the National Holiness Association movement of the nineteenth century, with roots in Methodism. Beginning in the South and Midwest, the church represents the merger of the Fire-Baptized Holiness Church founded by B. H. Irwin in Iowa in 1895; the Pentecostal Holiness Church founded by A. B. Crumpler in Goldsboro, North Carolina, in 1898; and the Tabernacle Pentecostal Church founded by N. J. Holmes in 1898.

All three bodies joined the ranks of the pentecostal movement as a result of the Azusa Street revival in Los Angeles in 1906 and a 1907 pentecostal revival in Dunn, N.C., conducted by G. B. Cashwell, who had visited Azusa Street. In 1911, the Fire-Baptized and Pentecostal Holiness bodies merged in Falcon, N.C., to form the present church; the Tabernacle Pentecostal Church was added in 1915 in Canon, Georgia.

The church stresses the new birth, the Wesleyan experience of sanctification, the pentecostal baptism in the Holy Spirit, evidenced by speaking in tongues, divine healing and the premillennial second coming of Christ.

Headquarters
P.O. Box 12609, Oklahoma City, OK 73157-2609, Tel. (405)787-7110 Fax (405)789-3957
Media Contact, Joe Iaguinta.
Email: RCarpenter@iphc.org
Website: www.iphc.org

Officers
Gen. Supt., Bishop Ronald W. Carpenter, Sr
Vice Chpsn. Executive Director of Evangelism USA, Dr. Ronald W. Carpenter, Sr.
Exec. Dir. Of World Missions Ministries, Dr. A.D. Beacham Jr.
Executive Director of Church Education Ministries, Rev. Talmadge Gardner
OTHER ORGANIZATIONS
The Publishing House (LifeSprings Resources), CEO, Greg Hearn, Franklin Springs, GA 30639
Women's Ministries, Exec. Dir., Mrs. Jewelle Stewart
Men's Ministries, Exec. Dir., Rev. Bill Terry, P.O. Box 12609, Oklahoma City, OK 73157

Periodicals
IPHC Experience

Jehovah's Witnesses

Modern-day Jehovah's Witnesses began in the early 1870s when Charles Taze Russell was the leader of a Bible study group in Allegheny City, Pennsylvania. In July 1879, the first issue of Zion's Watch Tower and Herald of Christ's Presence (now called The Watchtower which is published in 188 languages with a circulation of 42,162,000 appeared. In 1884 Zion's Watch Tower Tract Society was incorporated, later changed to Watch Tower Bible and Tract Society. Congregations spread into other states and countries, and followers witnessed from house to house.

By 1913, printed sermons were in four languages in 3,000 newspapers in the United States, Canada and Europe. Hundreds of millions of books, booklets and tracts were distributed. Publication of the magazine now known as Awake! Began in 1919. Today, it is published in more than 80 languages and has a circulation of upwards of 38,451,000. In 1931 the name Jehovah's Witnesses, based on Isaiah 43 vs.10-12, was adopted. During the 1930s and 1940s, and as recently as 2002, Jehovah's Witnesses fought many court cases in the interest of preserving freedom of speech, press, assembly and worship. They have won a total of 50 cases before the United States Supreme Court. A missionary training school was established in 1943, and it has been a major factor in the international expansion of the Witnesses. There are now 7.5 million Witnesses in 236 lands.

Jehovah's Witnesses believe in one almighty God, Jehovah, who is the Creator of all things. They believe in Jesus Christ as God's Son, the first of His creations. While Jesus is now an immortal spirit in heaven, ruling as King of God's Kingdom, he is still subject to his heavenly Father, Jehovah God. Christ's human life was sacrificed as a ransom to open up for obedient mankind the opportunity of eternal life. With Christ in heaven, 144,000 individuals chosen from among mankind will rule in righteousness over an unnumbered great crowd who will survive the destruction of wickedness and receive salvation into an earth cleansed of evil. (Rev. Ch.7 vs.9, 10; Ch.14 vs.1-5). These, along with the resurrected dead, will transform the earth into a global earthly paradise and will have the prospect of living forever on it.

Headquarters
25 Columbia Heights, Brooklyn, NY 11201-2483, Tel. (718)560-5000 x25263
Media Contact, Office of Public Information, J. R. Brown
Editorial Contact, Writing Department, James N. Pellechia
Website: www.watchtower.org

Officers
Pres. Watch Tower Bible and Tract Society of Pennsylvania, Don Adams

Periodicals
Awake!, The Watchtower

The Korean Presbyterian Church Abroad*
This body came into official existence in the United States in 1976 and is currently an ethnic church, using the Korean and English language.

Headquarters
General Assembly of the Korean Presbyterian Church in America
17200 Clark Ave., Bellflower, CA 90706
Tel. (443)502-2950 Fax (714)816-1120
Email: jacobjang@yahoo.com
Website: www.kpca.org

Officers
General Secretary, Rev. Jacob Se Jang, 5848 Pimlico Rd., Baltimore, MD 21209, Tel. (410)236-8939
Moderator, Rev. Dr. Young Chin Huh, 12601 Leda Lane, Garden Grove, CA 92840, Tel. (714)537-2687

The Latvian Evangelical Lutheran Church in America
This body was organized into a denomination on Aug. 22, 1975 after having existed as the Federation of Latvian Evangelical Lutheran Churches in America since 1955. This church is a regional constituent part of the Lutheran Church of Latvia Abroad, a member of the Lutheran World Federation and the World Council of Churches.

The Latvian Evangelical Lutheran Church in America works to foster religious life, traditions and customs in its congregations in harmony with the Holy Scriptures, the Apostles', Nicean and Athanasian Creeds, the unaltered Augsburg Confession, Martin Luther's Small and Large Catechisms and other documents of the Book of Concord. The LELCA is ordered by its Synod (General Assembly), executive board, auditing committee and district conferences.

Headquarters
1853 N. 75th St., Milwaukee, WI 53213, Tel. (414)258-8070
Media Contact, Juris Pulins, 9531 Knoll Top Rd., Union, IL 60180, Tel. (815)923-5919,
Email: pulins@earthlink.net
Email: pulins@earthlink.net

Officers
Pres., Dean Lauma Zusevics, Tel. (414)421-3934
Email: pastorlauma@gmail.com
Vice Pres., Rev. Anita Varsberga-Paza, Email: macavp@yahoo.com
Sec., Tija Abuls, 2910 Pomona Ct., Brookfield, WI 53005, Email: tabuls@att.net
Treas., Vilmars Beinikis, 17 John Dr., Old Bethpage, NY 11804, Tel. (516)293-8432

Periodicals
Cela Biedrs, Lelba Zinas

The Liberal Catholic Church— Province of the United States of America

The Liberal Catholic Church was founded Feb. 13, 1916 as a reorganization of the Old Catholic Church in Great Britain with the Rt. Rev. James I. Wedgwood as the first Presiding Bishop. The first ordination of a priest in the United States was Fr. Charles Hampton, later a Bishop. The first Regionary Bishop for the American Province was the Rt. Rev. Irving S. Cooper (1919-1935).

Headquarters

Pres., The Rt. Rev. William S.H. Downey, 1206 Ayers Ave., Ojai, CA 93023, Tel. (805)646-2573 Fax (805)646-2575

Media Contact, Regionary Bishop, The Rt. Rev. William S.H. Downey

Email: W.Downey@sbcglobal.net

Website: www.thelcc.org

Officers

Pres. & Regionary Bishop, The Rt. Rev. William S.H. Downey

Vice Pres., Rev. L. Marshall Heminway, P.O. Box 19957 Hampden Sta., Baltimore, MD 21211-0957

Sec. (Provincial), Rev. Lloyd Worley, 1232 24th Avenue Ct., Greeley, CO 80631, Tel. (303)356-3002

Provost, Rev. Lloyd Worley

Treas., Rev. Milton Shaw

BISHOPS

Regionary Bishop for the American Province, The Rt. Rev. William S.H. Downey

Aux. Bishops of the American Province, Rt. Rev. Dr. Robert S. McGinnis, Jr., 3612 N. Labarre Rd., Metaire, LA 70002; Rt. Rev. Joseph L. Tisch, P.O. Box 1117, Melbourne, FL 32901; Rt. Rev. Dr. Hein VanBeusekom, 12 Krotona Hill, Ojai, CA 93023; Rt. Rev. Ruben Cabigting, P.O. Box 270, Wheaton, IL 60189; The Rt. Rev. Lawrence Smith 9740 S. Avers Ave., Evergreen Park, IL.

Periodicals

Ubique

The Lutheran Church— Missouri Synod (LCMS)

The Lutheran Church --Missouri Synod (LCMS), which was founded in 1847, has nearly 6,200 congregations in the United States and has active work or mission relationships in nearly 100 countries. It has 2.3 million members and is the second-largest Lutheran denomination in North America.

The LCMS is a mission-oriented, Bible-based, confessional Christian denomination. It accepts the teachings of Martin Luther that inspired the Protestant Reformation of the Christian church in the 16th century. The Synod's beliefs can be summed up in three phrases: Grace alone, Scripture alone, Faith alone.

The church has nearly 9,000 rostered pastors and some 11,600 additional rostered (called) church workers. Women are active in church work, although they do not occupy clergy positions. Serving in positions such as teachers, deaconesses, and social workers, women account for more than half of all commissioned rostered workers.

The members' responsibility for congregational leadership is a distinctive characteristic of the LCMS. Power is vested in voters' assemblies, generally comprised of adults of voting age. Synod decision making is given to the delegates at triennial national and district conventions, where the franchise is equally divided between lay and pastoral representatives.

LCMS educational institutions serve all ages from pre-school to college. LCMS congregations operate one of the largest Protestant early childhood, elementary and secondary school system in the nation and more than 28,000 students are enrolled in the LCMS' 10 colleges and universities and two seminaries.

The LCMS is known for mass-media outreach through "The Lutheran Hour," broadcast around the world by Lutheran Hour Ministries; syndicated and streaming programming on KFUO radio; "This Is The Life" dramas on television; and the products of Concordia Publishing House, the third-largest Protestant, church-owned publisher, whose Arch Books children's series alone has sold more than 60 million copies. The LCMS works with some 270 Recognized Service Organizations (RSOs) which foster the church's mission and ministry. These organizations include social service agencies, educational institutions, retreat centers, summer camps and mission societies. The LCMS also is a founding partner of Lutheran Services of America, a social service organization that serves one in every 50 Americans.

Headquarters

The Lutheran Church -Missouri Synod, International Center, 1333 S. Kirkwood Rd., St. Louis, MO 63122-7295, Tel. (888)THE-LCMS (843-5267), Fax (314)996-1016

Media Contact, Director, Integrated Communications, Ms. Vicki Biggs, Tel. (314)996-1236

Managing Editor, Reporter, Mr. Joe Isenhower, Tel. (314)996-1231 Fax (314)996-1126

Managing Editor, The Lutheran Witness, Ms. Adriane Dorr, Tel. (314)996-1229 Fax (314)996-1126

Managing Editor, Witness, Mercy, Life Together, Deaconess Pamela Nielsen, Tel. (314)996-1215 Fax (314)996-1126

Email: infocenter@lcms.org

Website: www.lcms.org

Officers

Pres., Rev. Dr. Matthew C. Harrison, St. Louis, MO, Tel. (314)965-9000

1st Vice Pres., Rev. Herbert C. Mueller, St. Louis, MO, Tel. (314)965-9000

2nd Vice Pres., Dr. John C. Wohlrabe, Jr., Geneso, IL, Tel. (314)965-9000

3rd Vice Pres., Dr. Paul. L. Maier, Kalamazoo, MI, Tel. (314)965-9000

4th Vice Pres., Rev. Daniel Preus, St. Louis, MO, Tel. (314)965-9000

5th Vice Pres., Dr. Scott R. Murray, Houston, TX, Tel. (314)965-9000

Sec., Dr. Raymond L. Hartwig, St. Louis, MO, Tel. (314)965-9000

Treas., Mr. Jerald Wulf, St. Louis, MO, Tel. (314)965-9000

Chief Admn. Officer, Mr. Ronald Schultz, St. Louis, MO, Tel. (314)965-9000

Legal Counselor, Mrs. Sherri Strand, Thompson Coburn, LLP, 1 US Bank Plaza, St. Louis, MO 63101, Tel. (314)552-6000

BOARD OF DIRECTORS

Dr. Victor T. Belton, Decatur, GA; Mr. Walter Brantz, Cody, WY; Mr. Kermit Brashear, Omaha, NE; Mr. James Carter Jr., Arlington Heights, IL; Dr. Gloria Edwards, Portola Valley, CA; Mr. Ed Everts, Daytona Beach Shores, FL; Mr. Keith Frndak, Cabot, PA; Rev. Dr. Matthew C. Harrison, St. Louis, MO; Dr. Raymond L. Hartwig, St. Louis, MO; Dr. Robert Kuhn, Oviedo, FL; Rev. Michael Kumm, Milstadt, IL; Chaplain Donald Muchow, Buda, TX; Rev. Herbert C. Mueller Jr., St. Louis, MO; Mr. Curtis Pohl, St. Michael, MN; Mr. Warren Puck, Manning, IA; Dr. Kurt Senske, Austin, TX

BOARDS AND COMMISSIONS

National Mission, Board Chairman, Rev. Steven C. Briel

International Mission, Board Chairman, Rev. Bernhard M. Seter

Concordia University System, Board Chairman, Vacant

Theology & Church Relations, Exec. Dir., Dr. Joel D. Lehenbauer

Constitutional Matters, Commission Chairman, Dr. Wilbert J. Sohns

RELATED ORGANIZATIONS

Concordia Plan Services, Pres., Mr. Jim Sanft, St. Louis, MO, Tel. (314)965-9000

LCMS Foundation, Interim Pres., Mr. Wayne Price, St. Louis, MO, Tel. (314)965-9000

Lutheran Church Extension Fund, Pres., Mr. Richard C. Robertson, St. Louis, MO, Tel. (314)965-9000

Concordia Publishing House, Pres., Mr. Bruce Kintz, 3558 S. Jefferson Ave., St. Louis, MO 63118-3968, Tel. (314)268-1000

Concordia Historical Institute, Dir., Mr. Larry Lumpe, 804 Seminary Place, St. Louis, MO 63105, Tel. (314)505-7900

Lutheran Hour Ministries, Exec. Dir., Mr. Bruce Wurdeman, 660 Mason Ridge Ctr. Dr., St. Louis, MO, 63141-8557, Tel. (314)317-4100

Lutheran Women's Missionary League, Pres., Ms. Kay Krekau, 3558 S. Jefferson Ave., St. Louis, MO 63118, Tel. (314)268-1530

KFUO Radio, Interim General Manager, Rev. Michael Kumm, 85 Founders Lane, St. Louis, MO 63105, Tel. (314)725-3030

Periodicals

The Lutheran Witness (www.lcms.org/witness), Reporter (www.lcms.org/reporter)

Lutheran Evangelical Protestant Church (GCEPC)

General Conference

Concordia Theologica Institute International, P.O. Box 5184, West Columbia SC 29171 USA, Telephone: (803)739-6960, Fax (803)739-0847

Email: generalconference@lutheranepc.com

Website: www.lutheranepc.com

Officers

Presiding Bishop/President: Rev. Nancy K. Drew, General Conference

Executive Bishop/Vice President: Rev. Jessica L. Johnston, General Conference

Regional Bishops:

Council and Board of Advisors

Rev. Dr. David A. Church, California

Rev. Dennis Overlien, Wisconsin

Rev. Dr. Michael Norton, South Carolina

Rev. Dr. Ralf Muller, New Zealand

Rev. Dr. Harvey A.Menden,Georgia

Rev. Dr. Bob E. Tutrone, Pennsylvania

Rev. Dr. William Dorn, Wisconsin

Rev. Linda Dabney, Arkansas

Ecumenical Affairs:

Rev. Pat Pierce, Wisconsin

Caribbean and All Regions-Ambassador: Rev. Earline Parsons

Trinidad-Tabago, West Indies

New Zealand and All Regions-Ambassador: Rev. Ralf Muller

Wisconsin, USA and All Regions-Ambassador: Rev. Patrick Pierce

LEPC Chaplaincy:Bishop of Chaplaincy: Rev. Dr. Robert E. Tutrone

Director of Missions: Rev. Dr. David Church, Representative to Gospel for Asia.

LEPC Kenya National Bishop: Rev. Dr. Fred M. Macharia, Concordia Theologica Kenya, Nairobi, Kenya

LEPC Nigeria, National Bishop: Rev. Israel Ilpeka, CTI Affiliate Freedom School, Lagos, Nigeria

LEPC Espana, National Bishop: Rev. Dr. Francesco Reale, Pego (Alicante) Spain

Technology and Web Media: Rev. Tom Dickerson, Arizona

Apostolic Lutheran Church of America — listed under "A."

Conservative Lutheran Association — listed under "C."

Evangelical Lutheran Church in America — listed under "E."

Evangelical Lutheran Synod — listed under "E."

The American Association of Lutheran Churches — listed under "A."

Malankara Orthodox Syrian Church, Diocese of America*

Malankara (Indian) Orthodox Church is an ancient Church of India and it traces its origin to as far back as A. D. 52 when St. Thomas one of the Disciples of Jesus Christ came to India and established Christanity in the South Western parts of the sub-continent. The St. Thomas Christians or the Syrian Christians exist at present in different churches and denominations. But a major section of the parent body of St. Thomas Christians which has maintained its independent nature constitute the Orthodox Church under the Catholicos of the East and Malankara Metropolitan, whose seat is at Devalokam, Kottayam, Kerala, India. The Church has dioceses and churches in most parts of India as well as in the United States, Canada, United Kingdom, Western Europe, Persian Gulf nations, South Africa, Malaysia, Singapore, Australia and New Zealand. The official title of the head of the Church is the "Catholicos of the East, Catholicos of the Apostolic throne of St. Thomas and the Malankara Metropolitan". The present Catholicos of the East and Malankara Metropolitan is H.H. Mar Baselios Mar Thoma Didymos I.

The Church, though modern in its vision and outlook, keeps the traditional Orthodox faith and liturgy. It accepts the first three Ecumenical Synods. The liturgy now in use is the translation of the liturgy adopted from the Antiochian Church in the 17th century. However, the liturgical rites are uniquely Indian. Today the Church uses liturgy in Malayalam, Syriac, Hindi, and English.

The Indian Orthodox community inherited many aspects of Indian civilization and they are as any other member of any other community in India, in their customs, manners, and life style. The Church has a Theological Seminary at Kottayam, Kerala, which was established in AD 1815. Another seminary is situated in Nagpur, Maharashtra. The latter was established fairly recently in the later part of the 20th century.

Headquarters

Indian Orthodox Church Center, 80-34 Commonwealth Blvd., Bellerose, NY 11426, Tel. (718)470-9844 Fax (718)470-9219
Media Contact, His Grace Mathews Mar Barnabas, Diocesan Metropolitan
Email: Malankara@malankara.org
Website: www.malankara.org/american

Officers

Diocesan Metropolitan: His Grace Mathews Mar Barnabas
Assistant Metropolitan: His Grace Zachariah Mar Nicholovos
Diocesan Sec., The Rev. Fr. John Thomas
Secretary to the Metropolitan: The Rev. Dn. Ciby Mathew
Public Relations Director: The Very Rev. Dr. P. S. Samuel Cor Episcopos

Periodicals

Diocesan Voice, Family and Youth Conference Souvenir

Mar Thoma Syrian Church of India*

According to tradition, the Mar Thoma Church was established as a result of the apostolic mission of St. Thomas, the apostle in 52 AD. Church history attests to the continuity of the community of faithful, throughout the long centuries in India. The liturgy and faith practices of the Church were based on the relationship between the Church in Kerala, India, which St. Thomas founded, with the East-Syrian and Persian Churches. This started in the 3rd century and continued up to the 16th century. In the 17th century, the Malabar Church of St. Thomas (as the Church in Kerala was known) renewed her relationship with the Orthodox Patriarchate of Antioch as part of the resistance to forced Latinization by the Portuguese. This process also led to the development of the Kerala Episcopacy, whereby the first Indian Bishop Mar Thoma I was consecrated in Kerala.

The Mar Thoma Church retains her Eastern Orthodoxy. She follows an Orthodox worship form and liturgy, believes in the catholicity of grace, is missionary and evangelistic in approach. She derives Episcopal succession from the Syrian Orthodox Church of Antioch and follows Eastern Reformed Theology. She is independent, autonomous, and indigenous, constitutionally combining democratic values and Episcopal authority. She has been in full communion with the Anglican Church since 1954.

The Mar Thoma Church has been dynamically involved in the socio-cultural settings of North America and Europe for the past 30 years. Fundamentally an immigrant Church, she has contextualized her ministry in her new life situation without compromising the rich ethos and tradition received from her motherland of Kerala, India. Currently, under the rubric of the

Diocese, there are 67 parishes and 13 congregations. In order to cater to the ministerial needs of the Diocese, there are 70 clergy as well as functioning organizations for children, youth, women, and evangelistic work. The Diocese is presided over by the Diocesan Bishop, The Rt. Rev. Dr. Geevarghese Mar Theodosius Episcopa. The history of the Mar Thoma Church in the North American and European continent represents the dreams and aspirations of the faithful members of the Church.

Commencing as a small prayer group in Queens, New York, in 1972, the first approved parish was recognized in New York in 1976. The churches in North America and United Kingdom have become constituents of the newly formed "Diocese of North America and United Kingdom." The Headquarters has subsequently moved to its current location at 2320 South Merrick Ave., Merrick, N.Y.

Headquarters
Sinai Mar Thoma Center, 2320 S. Merrick Ave., Merrick, New York 11566, Tel. (516)377-3311 Fax (516)377-3322
Email: webmaster@marthomachurch.org
Website: www.marthomanae.org

Officers
Diocesan Bishop, Rt. Rev. Dr. Geevarghese Mar Theodosius 2320 Merrick Ave, Merrick, NY 11566, Tel.: 516-377-3311 Cell: 516-655-1852 Fax: 516-377-3322 Email: mtcmartheo@ yahoo.com.ph, or marthomadiocese@gmail.com
Diocesan Bishop's Sec., Rev.K.E Geevarghese 2320 Merrick Ave, Merrick NY 11566, Tel. :516-377-3311 Cell:516-754-6110 Fax :516-377-3322 Email: revkeg@gmail.com or marthomadiocese@gmail.com
Diocesan Treasurer, Mr. Chacko Mathew 18 Park Drive East, Syosset NY 11791, Tel. :516-364-1854 Cell:917-578-4679 Fax :516-377-3322 Email: sunnysusan2@gmail.com.ph, or marthomadiocese@gmail.com

Periodicals
Mar Thoma Messenger

Mennonite Church USA
Mennonite Church USA, with 109,000 members, is one of several denominations that traces their beginnings to the Protestant Reformation in the early 1500s. Mennonites hold common core beliefs with other Christian denominations, but they live out God's call in some ways that make them distinct. Mennonites believe in giving ultimate loyalty to God rather than to the nations in which they live. They believe that Jesus revealed a way for people to live peacefully and nonviolently, and they seek to be peacemakers in everyday life.

Mennonite church USA is committed to sharing its faith and passion for Jesus with others and is open to anyone who confesses Jesus Christ as Lord and Savior and wants to live as Jesus taught.

The vision statement of Mennonite Church USA reads, "God calls us to be followers of Jesus Christ and, by the power of the Holy Spirit, to grow as communities of grace, joy, and peace, so that God's healing and hope flow through us to the world." Mennonite Church USA — its congregations, area conferences, Executive Board, ministry offices and churchwide agencies — focus on four priorities as it seeks to nurture missional congregations that join in God's activity in the world:

1. In our holistic witness we practice and proclaim the Gospel of Jesus Christ through a seamless web of evangelism, justice and peacebuilding.

2. We create a culture of call by calling, training anf nurturing new leaders.

3. We honor the dignity and value of all people, regardless of their race or ethnicity and denounce racist behavior.

4. We build global connections by fostering and developing partnerships with the broader body of Christ around the world.

Mennonite Church USA lists as its strengths a high level of integrity recognized in both society and the religious community; high church attendance (90% of members attend church regularly); expanded global awareness through exposure to other world cultures; strong commitment to nonviolence and use of conflict resolution skills; above average giving to the work of the church; a natural communitarian impulse demonstrated by an emphasis on congregational relationships and mutual accountabilities; strong support of volunteer efforts, relief and service activities; and a holistic theology that holds word and deed together.

Headquarters
Newton office: 722 Main St., Newton KS 67114, Tel. (316)283-5100, Fax (316)283-0454, Email: info@mennoniteusa.org, Website: www.mennoniteusa.org, toll free number for all churchwide agencies (866)866-2872
Elkhart office: P.O. Box 1245, 1601 W. Beardsley Ave., Elkhart IN 46515-1245, Tel. (574)523-3041, Fax (574)293-1892, Email: info@mennoniteusa.org, Website: www. mennoniteusa.org, toll free number for all churchwide agencies (866)866-2872
Email: info@MennoniteUSA.org
Website: www.MennoniteChurchUSA.org

Officers
Moderator, Edward Diller, 30 Thomas Point Dr., Ft. Thomas KY 41075, Tel. (859)781-2796, Email: edd@mennoniteusa.org
Moderator-elect, Dick Thomas, 2176 Lincoln Hwy. East, Lancaster PA 17602, Tel. (717)299-0436, ext. 306, Email: richardt@mennonite usa.org

Acting Executive Director, J. Ron Byler, P.O. Box 1245, 1601 W. Beardsley Ave., Elkhart IN 46515-1245, Tel. (574)523-3040, Fax (574)293-1892, Email: ronb@mennoniteusa.org

Mennonite Education Agency, Executive Director, Carlos Romero, 63867 County Rd. 35, Suite 1, Goshen IN 46528-9621, Tel. (574)642-3164, Fax (574)642-4863, Email: info@mennoniteeducation.org

Mennonite Mission Network, Executive Director, Stanley Green, P.O. Box 370, 1601 W. Beardsley Ave., Elkhart IN 46515-0370, Tel. (574)294-7523, Fax (574)294-8669, Email: info@mennonitemission.net

Mennonite Mission Network, President, Larry Miller, P. O. Box 486, Goshen IN 46527, Tel. (574)533-9511, Fax (574)533-5264, Email: mma@mma-online.org

Mennonite Publishing Network, Executive Director, Ron Rempel, 616 W. Walnut Ave., Scottdale PA 15683-1999, Tel. (800)245-7894, Fax (724)887-3111, Email: info@mpn.net

Periodicals
The Mennonite, Leader, Rejoice!, Mennonite Historical Bulletin, Mennonite Quarterly Review, Purpose

The United Methodist Church is listed under "U"

The Missionary Church
The Missionary Church was formed in 1969 through a merger of the United Missionary Church (organized in 1883) and the Missionary Church Association (founded in 1898). It is evangelical and conservative with a strong emphasis on missionary work and church multiplication.

There are three levels of church government with local, district and general conferences. There are 13 church districts and 7 mission districts in the United States. The general conference meets every two years. The denomination operates one college [Bethel College, Mishawaka, IN] in the United States.

Headquarters
3811 Vanguard Dr., P.O. Box 9127, Ft. Wayne, IN 46899-9127, Tel. (260)747-2027 Fax (260)747-5331
Media Contact, Pres., Rev. William Hossler
Email: ronphipps@mcusa.org
Website: www.mcusa.org

Officers
Pres., Rev. William Hossler
Sec., Rev. Dave Engbrecht
Treas., Darrel Schlabach
Director of U.S. Ministries, Rev. Robert Ransom
Director of World PartnersUSA, Rev. David Mann
Healthy Church Initiatives Coordinator, Dr. Dan Riemenschneider

Servant Leadership Coordinator, Rev. Greg Getz
Support Ministries Coordinator, Rev. Ron Phipps
Pastoral Leadership Institute Director, Rev. Greg Getz
Director of Development/Communications, Dr. Tom Murphy
Dir. of Ad. Services, Eric Smith
Director of Financial Services, Neil Rinehart
Coordinator of Church Multiplication, Rev. Jeff Getz
Coordinator of Ethnic Ministries, Rev. Jose Manuel Mendez
Missionary Men Liaison, Rev. Ron Phipps
Missionary Women Intl., Pres., Sharon Moore
Missionary Church Investment Foundation, Mr. Eric Smith

Periodicals
Missionary Church Today

Moravian Church in America (Northern Province, Southern Province)*
In 1735 German Moravian missionaries of the pre-Reformation faith of Jan Hus came to Georgia, in 1740 to Pennsylvania, and in 1753 to North Carolina. They established the American Moravian Church, which is broadly evangelical, ecumenical, liturgical, "conferential" in form of government and has an episcopacy as a spiritual office. The Northern and Southern Provinces of the church operate on a semi-autonomous basis.

Headquarters
Denominational offices or headquarters are called the Provincial Elders' Conference. See addresses for Northern Province

NORTHERN PROVINCE HEADQUARTERS
1021 Center St., P.O. Box 1245, Bethlehem, PA 18016-1245, Tel. (610)867-7566 Fax (610)866-9223
Media Contact, Mr. Mike Riess

PROVINCIAL ELDERS' CONFERENCE, NORTHERN PROVINCE
Pres., Rev. Dr. Elizabeth Miller, Email: betsy@mcnp.org
Other Members: Stephen Gohdes, James Hicks, David Bennett, Jill Westbrook, Wilton Grannum, Judy Kaaua, Thomas Zimmer
Comptroller, Christina Giesler, 1021 Center St., P.O. Box 1245, Bethlehem, PA 18016-1245

NORTHERN PROVINCE
1021 Center St., P.O. Box 1245, Bethlehem, PA 18016-1245, Tel. (610)867-7566 Fax (610)866-9223
Northern Province Pres., Rev. Dr. Elizabeth Miller, P.O. Box 1245, Bethlehem, PA 18016-1245, Email: betsy@mcnp.org
Eastern District Pres., Rev. David Bennett P.O. Box 1245, Bethlehem, PA 18016-1245
Western District Pres., Rev. James T. Hicks, P.O. 12677, Green Bay, WI 54307

Canadian District Pres., Rev. Stephen Gohdes, 600 Arcadia Dr. SE, Calgary, AB T2J 0B8, Email: sgohdes@shaw.ca

SOUTHERN PROVINCE HEADQUARTERS
459 S. Church St., Winston-Salem, NC 27101
Winston-Salem, NC 27108, Tel. (336)725-5811 Fax (336)723-1029 Website, www.moravian.org (for Moravian Church, Northern and Southern Provinces)

PROVINCIAL ELDERS' CONFERENCE, SOUTHERN PROVINCE
Pres., Rev. David Guthrie

ALASKA PROVINCE
P.O. Box 545, 361 3rd Ave., Bethel, AK 99559

PROVINCIAL ELDERS' CONFERENCE, ALASKA PROVINCE
Pres., vacant

Periodicals
The Moravian

Mormons — please see The Church of Jesus Christ of Latter-day Saints; see also Community of Christ

National Association of Congregational Christian Churches

This association was organized in 1955 in Detroit, Michigan, by delegates from Congregational Christian Churches committed to continuing the Congregational way of faith and order in church life. Participation by member churches is voluntary.

Headquarters
P.O. Box 288, Oak Creek, WI 53154, Tel. (414)764-1620 Fax (414)764-0319
Media Contact, Assoc. Exec. Sec., Rev. Dr. Donald P. Olsen, 8473 So. Howell Ave., Oak Creek, WI 53154, Tel. (414)764-1620 Fax (414)764-0319
Email: trichard@naccc.org; naccc@naccc.org
Website: www.naccc.org

Officers
Exec. Sec., Rev. Dr. Thomas M. Richard, 8473 South Howell Ave., Oak Creek, WI 53154
Assoc. Exec. Secs., Rev. Phil Jackson and Rev. Dr. Donald P. Olsen

Periodicals
The Congregationalist

National Association of Free Will Baptists

This evangelical group of Armenian Baptists was organized by Paul Palmer in 1727 at Chowan, North Carolina. Another movement (teaching the same doctrines of free grace, free salvation and free will) was organized June 30, 1780, in New Durham, N.H., but there was no connection with the southern organization except for a fraternal relationship.

The northern line expanded more rapidly and extended into the West and Southwest. This body merged with the Northern Baptist Convention Oct. 5, 1911, but a remnant of churches reorganized into the Cooperative General Association of Free Will Baptists Dec. 28, 1916, at Pattonsburg, Mo.

Churches in the southern line were organized into various conferences from the beginning and finally united in one General Conference in 1921. Representatives of the Cooperative General Association and the General Conference joined Nov. 5, 1935 to form the National Association of Free Will Baptists.

Headquarters
5233 Mt. View Rd., Antioch, TN 37013-2306, Tel. (615)731-6812 Fax (615)731-0771
Mailing Address, P.O. Box 5002, Antioch, TN 37011-5002
Media Contact, Exec. Sec., Keith Burden CMP
Email: webmaster@nafwb.org
Website: www.nafwb.org

Officers
Exec. Sec., Keith Burden CMP
Mod., Tim York, 623 Knollwood Dr., LaVergne, TN 37086

DENOMINATIONAL AGENCIES
Free Will Baptist Foundation, Dir., David Brown
Free Will Baptist Bible College, Pres., Mathew Pinson
International Missions Dept., Dir., Rev. James Forlines
Home Missions Dept., Dir., Rev. Larry Powell
Bd. of Retirement, Dir., Rev. D. Ray Lewis
Historical Commission, Chpsn., Dr. Darrell Holley, 3606 West End Ave., Nashville, TN 37205
Comm. for Theological Integrity, Chpsn., Rev. Leroy Forlines, 3606 West End Ave., Nashville, TN 37205
Music Commission, Chpsn., Chris Truett, 1936 Banks School Rd., Kinston, NC 28504
Media Comm., Chpsn., Keith Fletcher, P.O. Box 17306, Nashville, TN 37217
Randall House Publications, Dir., Rev. Ron Hunter
Women Nationally Active for Christ, Exec. Sec., Danita High
Master's Men Dept., Dir., Kenneth Akers

Periodicals
ONE Magazine, Co-Laborer

National Baptist Convention of America, Inc.*

The National Baptist Convention of America, Inc., was organized in 1880. Its mission is articulated through its history, constitution, articles of incorporation and by-laws. The Convention (corporate churches) has a mission statement with fourteen (14) objectives including fostering unity throughout its membership and the world Christian community by proclaiming the gospel of Jesus Christ; validating and propagating the Baptist doctrine of faith and practice, and its distinctive principles throughout the world; and harnessing and encouraging the scholarly and Christian creative skills of its membership for Christian writing and publications.

Headquarters

777 S. R.L. Thornton Fwy., Ste. 205, Dallas, TX 75203, Tel. (214)946-8913 Fax (214)946-9619 Email: LaJuanda.jones@tx.twcbc.com Website: www.nbcamerica.net

Officers

Pres., Rev. Stephen J. Thurston, President, 1327 Pierre Ave., Shreveport, LA 71103, Tel. (773)224-5570 Fax (773)224-8200 Gen. Rec. Sec., Rev. Tolbert
Historian, Dr. Clarence C. Pennywell, 2016 Russell Rd., Shreveport, LA 71107
Corres. Sec., 6614 South Western Ave., Los Angeles, CA 90047
Administrative Assistant, Ms. LaJuanda Jones, Tel. (800)543-4019 x 10 / (214)942-3311 Fax (318)222-7512; Email: LaJuanda.jones@tx.twcbc.com

Periodicals

The Lantern

National Baptist Convention, U.S.A., Inc.*

The National Baptist Convention, one of the oldest African American organization in the nation, traces it history back to 1895. It was formed as a cosolidation of the Baptist Foreign Mission Convention (1880), Consolidated American Baptist Convention (1896), and the National Baptist Educational Convention (1882). Rev. W. H. Alpine of Alabama was the first president of the Baptist Foreign Mission Board which later became the Baptist Foreign Mission Convention, USA.

The constitution of the convention 1895 states: Whereas, It is the sense of the Colored Baptists of the United States of America, convened in the city of Atlanta, Georgia, September 28, 1895 in the several organizations as "The Baptist Foreign Mission Convention of the United States of America," hithero engaged in Mission work on the West Coast of Africa: and the `National Baptist Convention' which has been engaged in mission work in the United States of America; and the `National Baptist Educational Convention,' which has sought to look after the educational interest that the interest of the way of the Kingdom of God requires that the several bodies above named should, and do now, unite in one body. Therefore, we do now agree to and adopt the following constitution: This body shall become known and styled, The National Baptist Convention of the United States of America.

The object of this convention shall be "to do mission work in the United States of America, in Africa, and elsewhere and to foster the cause of education. "Dr. L.M. Luke was elected the first Corresponding Secretary of the Foreign Board. In October, 1896 Rev. L.G. Jordan, pastor of the Union Baptist Church of Philadelphia was selected successor of Luke" (The Epoch of Negro Baptists and The Foreign Mission Board, NBC, USA, Inc. Dr. Edward A. Freeman, The Central Seminary Press 1953.) In September 1915 at the annual meeting of the convention the constitution was revised with the following changes:

The particular business and object of this Convention shall be to promote a growth and propagamation of religion, morality, and intelligence among the races of mankind, by engaging in missionary work in the United States of America, and elsewhere, by fostering the cause of education and publishing and circulating literature, and in providing the necessary ways and means for carrying on such work.

Headquarters

1700 Baptist World Center Dr., Nashville, TN 37207, Tel. (615)228-6292, Fax (615)262-3917

Officers

Pres., Dr. Julius Scruggs, First Missionary Baptist Church, 3509 Blue Spring Rd., Huntsville, AL 35810, Tel. (256)428-1255 Fax (256)428-5975, Email: jscruggs@national baptist.com
Gen. Sec., Dr. Calvin McKinney, Calvary Baptist Church, 217-245 Passaic St., Garfield, NJ 07026, Tel. (973)773-2444 Fax (973)773-2424, Email: mckinneycalvary@aol.com

Periodicals

Mission Herald

National Missionary Baptist Convention of America*

The National Missionary Baptist Convention of America was organized in 1988 as a separate entity from the National Baptist Convention of America, Inc., after a dispute over control of the convention's publishing efforts. The new organization intended to remain committed to the National Baptist Sunday Church School and Baptist Training Union Congress and the National Baptist Publishing Board.

The purpose of the National Missionary Baptist Convention of America is to serve as an agency of Christian education, church extension and missionary efforts. It seeks to maintain and safeguard full religious liberty and engage in social and economic development.

Headquarters

4269 S. Figueroa St., Los Angeles, CA 90037, Tel. (323)846-1950 Fax (323)846-1964

Media Contact, Dr. Melvin Von Wade, Sr.

Email: president@top2000.org

Website: www.nmbca.com

Officers

Pres., Dr. C.C. Robertson, President, Dallas, Texas

Vice President-at-Large, Dr. Nehemiah Davis, Fort Worth, Texas

Vice Pres., Ecumenical Affairs, Dr. L.C. Firle Collins, MS

Vice Pres., Auxiliaries, Dr. Bernard Black, Phoenix, AZ

Vice Pres., Boards, Dr. A. Charles Bowie, Cleveland, OH

Vice Pres., Financial Affairs, Dr. Ray W. Williams, Oakland, CA

Pres., National Baptist Publishing Bd., Dr. T. B. Boyd, III, 6717 Centennial Blvd., Nashville, TN 37209

Gen. Sec., Dr. A. Wayne Johnson, 106 NE Ivy St., Portland, OR 97212, Tel. (503)281-4925 Fax (503)281-6520, Email: gensec@jiacom.net

Corres. Sec., Dr. Walter Houston, Houston, TX

Treas., Dr. William R. Lott, Chicago, IL

Rec. Sec., Dr. T.L. Brown, Dallas, TX

National Organization of the New Apostolic Church of North America

The New Apostolic Church of North America claims common origin with the Catholic Apostolic movement in England, which began with the calling of an apostle in 1832. The New Apostolic Church distinguished itself from the parent body in 1863 by recognizing a succession of Apostles.

Headquarters

3753 N. Troy St., Chicago, IL 60618

Media Contact: Winfred Jacob, Tel. (814)833-6063 Fax (814)833-6308

Email: info@nak.org

Website: www.nak.org

Officers

Pres., Rev. Leonard R. Kolb, 1703 Peninsula Dr., Erie, PA 16505-4242

Vice Pres., Rev. John W. Fendt, Jr., 2 Willets Ln., Plandome, NY 11030-1023

Treas. & Secretary: Mr. K. Stefan Heinzelmann, 3753 N. Troy St. Chicago, IL 60618

Periodicals

Our Family; Vision

National Primitive Baptist Convention, Inc.

Throughout the years of slavery and the Civil War, the Negro population of the South worshiped with the white population in their various churches. At the time of emancipation, their white brethren helped them establish their own churches, granting them letters of fellowship, ordaining their deacons and ministers and helping them in other ways.

The doctrine and polity of this body are quite similar to that of white Primitive Baptists, yet there are local associations and a national convention, organized in 1907. Each church is independent and receives and controls its own membership. This body was formerly known as Colored Primitive Baptists.

Headquarters

6433 Hidden Forest Dr., Charlotte, NC 28213, Tel. (704)596-1508

Media Contact, Elder T. W. Samuels

Email: TurbanLeague@yahoo.com

Officers

Natl. Convention, Pres., President – Elder Ernest Ferrell, Tallahassee, FL

Natl. Convention, Vice Pres., Elder Bernard Yates, Pensacola, FL

Natl. Convention, Secretary, Elder W. J. Williams, Tampa, Florida

Natl. Church School Training Union, Pres., Dr. Jonathan Yates, Mobile, AL

Natl. Ushers Congress, Pres., Dea. Carl Batts, 21213 Garden View Dr., Maple Heights, OH 44137

Publishing Bd., Chpsn., Elder John R. Cox, Birmingham, AL

Women's Congress, Pres., Mother Ann Cartes, Dallas, TX

Natl. Laymen's Council, Pres., Dea. Densimore Robinson, Huntsville, AL

Natl. Youth Congress, Pres., Minister Jacques Mood, Concord, NC

National Spiritualist Association of Churches

This organization is made up of believers that Spiritualism is a science, philosophy and religion based upon the demonstrated facts of communication between this world and the next.

Headquarters

NSAC General Offices, Rev. Sharon L. Snowman, Secretary, P.O. Box 217, Lily Dale, NY 14752-0217

Media Contact, Rev. Lelia Cutler, 7310 Midfield St. #1, Norfolk, VA 23505-4126

Email: nsac@nsac.org; secretary@nsac.org

Website: www.nsac.org

Officers

Pres., Rev. Lelia Cutler, 7310 Midfield St. #1, Norfolk, VA 23505-4126

Vice Pres., Rev. Catherine Snell 23 Pleasant St. Windham, NH 03087

Sec., Rev. Sharon L. Snowman, P.O. Box 217, Lily Dale, NY 14752, Tel. (716)595-2000 Fax (716)595-2020

141

Treas., Peter Berg, 20916 Bellerive Dr., Pflugerville, TX 78660

OTHER ORGANIZATIONS
Department of Education, Rev. Barbara Starr, Director, 4245 Woodmont Rd., Great Cacapon, WV 25422

Department of Lyceums, Rev. Arsenia Williams, Director, 10913 S. Parnell, Chicago, IL 60628

Department of Missionaries, Rev. E. Ann Otzelberger, Director, 4332 Woodlynne Lane, Orlando, FL 32812-7562

Department of Phenomenal Evidence, Revs. Brian and Lynn Kent, Directors 28-3rd Street 4308, Warren, RI 02885

Department of Public Relations, Mary Montgomery Clifford, Director, 2426 North Kimball St., Chicago, IL 60647

Department of Publications, Joe Owen, Director, 5 Third St. Suite 724, San Francisco, CA 94103

NSAC Healing Center, Rev. Kathleen Rottino, President, 74 Scenic Dr., Lebanon, CT 06249

NSAC Minsterial Association, Rev. Barbara Star, NST, Pres., 4245 Woodmont Rd., Great Cacapon, WV 25422

National Spiritualist Teachers Club, Rev. E. Ann Otzelberger, NST, Pres., 4332 Woodlynne Lane, Orlando, FL 32812

Spiritualist Healers League, Rev. E. Annotzelberger, NST President Licentiate Ministers & Certified Mediums Society, Rev. Janet Tisdale, NST, Pres., 1616 N. Alta Mesa Drive #51, Mesa, AZ 85205

The Stow Memorial Foundation, Sec., Rev. Sharon L. Snowman, P.O. Box 217, Lily Dale, NY 14752, Tel. (716)595-2000 Fax (716)595-2020

Spiritualist Benevolent Society, Inc., P.O. Box 217, Lily Dale, NY 14752

Periodicals
The National Spiritualist, Spotlight

Netherlands Reformed Congregations

The Netherlands Reformed Congregations trace their denominational origin to several U.S. congreagtions in the latter half of the nineteenth century. In the early 1900s several more congregations were organized. After the Second World War, immigration from the Netherlands gave rise to still more congregations, especially in Canada. Currently a little over half the membership resides in Canada. Their sister denomination in the Netherlands is the Gereformeerde Gemeenten, which were organized in 1907.

Doctrinal standards are the Confession of Faith (1561), the Heidelberg Catechism (1563), and the Canons of Dordt (1618-1619). This indicates the denomination is rooted in the Reformation of 1517. The congregations are divided into three Classes, which meet at least one a year. Every two years a Synod is held.

Headquarters
Media Contact, Rev. A.H. Verhoef, 1142 Lakeshore Rd. W, RR#3, St. Catharines, ON L2R 6P9 CANADA, Tel. (905)935-4934

OTHER ORGANIZATIONS
Netherlands Reformed Book and Publishing, 7638 Park Ridge Dr., Jenison, MI 49428

Periodicals
The Banner of Truth, Paul (mission magazine), Insight Into, Learning and Living

The New Church — please see General Church of the New Jerusalem

North American Baptist Conference

Churches belonging to this conference emanated from Germany Baptist immigrants of more than a century ago. Although scattered across Canada and the U.S., they are bound together by a common heritage, a strong spiritual unity, a Bible-centered faith and a deep interest in missions. Their two main priorities are Leadership Development and Church Multiplication. Note, The details of general organization, officers, and periodicals of this body will be found in the North American Baptist Conference directory in the "Religious Bodies in the United States" section of this Yearbook.

Headquarters
1 S. 210 Summit Ave., Oakbrook Terrace, IL 60181, Tel. (630)495-2000 Fax (630)495-3301
Media Contact, Marlene Minor, Senior Leader/Stewardship and Communications
Email: serve@nabconf.org
Website: www.nabconference.org

Officers
Exec. Dir., Rev. Ron Berg, 1 So 210 Summit Ave., Oakbrook Terrace, IL 60181, Tel. (630)495-2000 Fax (630)475-3301, Email: RBerg@nabconf.org

OTHER ORGANIZATIONS
Church Extension Investors Fund, Dir., Les D. Collins

Periodicals
NABtoday

North American Old Roman Catholic Church (Archdiocese of New York)

This body is identical with the Roman Catholic Church in faith but differs from it in discipline and worship. The Mass is offered with the appropriate rite either in Latin or in the vernacular. All other sacraments are taken from the Roman Pontifical. This jurisdiction allows for married clergy.

PRIMATIAL HEADQUARTERS
60 ST. Felix St., Brooklyn, NY 11217-1206, Tel. (718)855-0600

Media Contact, Primate, Most Rev. Albert J. Berube
Email: info@orccna.org
Website: www.orccna.org

Officers
Primate, The Most Rev. Albert J. Berube
Diocese of New York, Ordinary, Most Rev. Albert J. Berube
Diocese of Montreal & French Canada, Ordinary, Most Rev. Gerard Marcoux

Old Calender Orthodox Church of Greece (Holy Synod in Resistance), American Exarchate

The American Exarchate of the Old Calendar Orthodox Church of Greece (Holy Synod in Resistance) adheres to the tenets of the Eastern Orthodox Church, which considers itself the legitimate heir of the historical Apostolic Church.

When the Orthodox Church of Greece adopted the New, or Gregorian, Calendar in 1924, many felt that this breach with tradition compromised the Church's festal calendar, based on the Old, or Julian, Calendar, and its unity with world Orthodoxy. In 1935, three State Church Bishops returned to the Old Calendar and established a Synod in Resistance, the True Orthodox Church of Greece. When the last of these Bishops died, the Russian Orthodox Church Abroad consecrated a new Hierarchy for the Greek Old Calendarists and, in 1969, declared them a Sister Church.

In the face of persecution by the State Church, some Old Calendarists denied the validity of the Mother Church of Greece and formed two synods, now under the direction of Archbishop Kallinikos of Athens and Archbishop Nicholas of Athens. A moderate faction under Metropolitan Cyprian of Oropos and Fili does not maintain communion with the Mother Church of Greece, but recognizes its validity and seeks a restoration of unity by a return to the Julian Calendar and traditional ecclesiastical polity by the State Church. About 1.5 million Orthodox Greeks belong to the Old Calendar Church.

The first Old Calendarist communities in the United States were formed in the 1930s. The Exarchate under Metropolitan Cyprian was established in 1986. Placing emphasis on clergy education, youth programs, and recognition of the Old Calendarist minority in American Orthodoxy, the Exarchate has encouraged the establishment of monastic communities and missions. Cordial contacts with the New Calendarist and other Orthodox communities are encouraged. A center for theological training and Patristic studies has been established at the Exarchate headquarters in Etna, California. In July 1994, the Old Calendar Orthodox Church of Greece (Holy Synod in Resistance), the Old Calendar Orthodox Church of Romania, the Old Calendar Orthodox Church of Bulgaria, and the Russian Orthodox Church Abroad entered into liturgical union, forming a coalition of traditionalist Orthodox bodies several million strong.

Headquarters
St. Gregory Palamas Monastery, P.O. Box 398, Etna, CA 96027-0398, Tel. (530)467-3228 Fax (530)467-5828
Media Contact, Exarch in America, His Eminence, Archbishop Chrysostomos

Officers
Acting Synodal Exarch in America, His Grace Bishop Auxentios
Chancellor of the Exarchate, The Very Rev. Raphael Abraham, 3635 Cottage Grove Ave. S.E., Cedar Rapids, IA 52403-1612

Periodicals
Orthodox Tradition

The Old Catholic Orthodox Church

The Old Catholic Orthodox Church (formerly, the Apostolic Orthodox Old Catholic Church) was founded in Illinois in the year 1985, originally as a Spanish speaking community of faith. It has now grown to include English speaking and other international provinces. We subscribe to the Apostles', Nicene and Athanasian Creeds as matters of faith. Along with upholding all sacraments of the One, Holy, Catholic and Apostolic Church.

Headquarters
The Most Reverend Jorge Rodriguez-Villa, Apostolic Primate (Presiding Bishop) P.O. Box 80193, Rancho Santa Margarita, CA 92688, Tel. (323)806-4045
Website: www.oldcatholicorthodoxchurch.org

Officers
The Most Reverend Jorge Rodriguez-Villa, Apostolic Primate (Presiding Bishop)
The Most Rev. William Anthony Harrison, Apostolic Vicar General

Old German Baptist Brethren Church

This group separated from the Church of the Brethren (formerly German Baptist Brethren) in 1881 in order to preserve and maintain historic Brethren Doctrine.

Headquarters
Vindicator Ofc. Ed., Steven L. Bayer, 6952 N. Montgomery County Line Rd., Englewood, OH 45322-9748, Tel. (937)884-7531

Periodicals
The Vindicator

Old Order Amish Church

The congregations of this Old Order Amish group have no annual conference. They worship in private homes. They adhere to the older forms of worship and attire. This body has bishops, ministers and deacons.

Correspondence
Der Neue Amerikanische Calendar, c-o Raber's Book Store, 2467 C R 600, Baltic, OH 43804, LeRoy Beachy, Beachy Amish Mennonite Church, 4324 SR 39, Millerburg, OH 44654, Tel./Fax (330)893-2883

Old Order (Wisler) Mennonite Church
This body arose from a separation of Mennonites dated 1872, under Jacob Wisler, in opposition to what were thought to be inno- vations. The group is in the Eastern United States and Canada. Each state, or district, has its own organization and holds semi-annual conferences.

Headquarters
Media Contact, Amos B. Hoover, 376 N. Muddy Creek Rd., Denver, PA 17517, Tel. (717)484- 4849 Fax (717)484-104

Periodicals
Home Messenger, Exchange Messenger

Open Bible Churches
Open Bible Churches (formerly, Open Bible Standard Churches) originated from two revival movements, Bible Standard Conference, founded in Eugene, Oregon, under the leadership of Fred L. Hornshuh in 1919, and Open Bible Evangelistic Association, founded in Des Moines, Iowa, under the leadership of John R. Richey in 1932. Similar in doctrine and government, the two groups amalgamated on July 26, 1935 as "Open Bible Standard Churches, Inc." with headquarters in Des Moines, Iowa. The original group of 210 ministers has enlarged to incorporate over 2,500 ministers and 1,509 churches in 40 countries. The first missionary left for India in 1926. The church now ministers in Asia, Africa, South America, Europe, Canada, Mexico, Central America, and the Caribbean Islands.

Historical roots of the parent groups reach back to the outpouring of the Holy Spirit in 1906 at Azusa Street Mission in Los Angeles and to the full gospel movement in the Midwest. Both groups were organized under the impetus of pentecostal revival. Simple faith, freedom from fanaticism, emphasis on evangelism and missions and free fellowship with other groups were characteristics of the growing organizations.

The highest governing body of Open Bible Churches meets biennially and is composed of all ministers and one voting delegate per 100 members from each church. A National Board of Directors, elected by the national and regional conferences, conducts the business of the organization. Official Bible College is New Hope Christian College in Oregon.

Open Bible Churches is a charter member of the National Association of Evangelicals and of the Pentecostal/Charismatic Churches of North America. It is a member of the Pentecostal World Conference.

NATIONAL OFFICE
2020 Bell Ave., Des Moines, IA 50315, Tel. (515)288-6761 Fax (515)288-2510
Media Contact, Exec. Dir., Communications & Resources, Jeff Farmer, Tel. (515)288-6761 Fax (515)288-2510
Email: info@openbible.org
Website: www.openbible.org

Officers
Pres., Jeffrey E. Farmer, 2020 Bell Ave., Des Moines, Iowa 50315, Tel. (515)288-6761 Fax (515)288-2510, Email: jeff@openbible.org
Esq., Sec.-Treas., Teresa A. Beyer, 2020 Bell Ave., Des Moines, Iowa 50315, Tel. (515)288-6761 Fax (515)288-2510, Email: tbeyer@openbible.org
Dir., of Intl. Min., Vince S. McCarty, 2020 Bell Ave., Des Moines, Iowa 50315, Tel. (515)288-6761 Fax (515)288-2510, Email: missions@openbible.org

Periodicals
Message of the Open Bible

The (Original) Church of God, Inc.
This body was organized in 1886 as the first church in the United States to take the name "The Church of God." In 1917 a difference of opinion led this particular group to include the word (Original) in its name. It is a holiness body and believes in the whole Bible, rightly divided, using the New Testament as its rule and government.

Headquarters
P.O. Box 592, Wytheville, VA 24382
Media Contact, Gen. Overseer, Rev. William Dale

Officers
Gen. Overseer, Rev. William Dale
Asst. Gen. Overseer, Rev. Alton Evans

The Orthodox Anglican Church
The Orthodox Anglican church was incorporated in 1964 to provide a religious body faithful to historic Anglican doctrine and practice as dogmatically set forth in the Book of Common Prayer (1928 US and 1662 English editions), the Ordinal of the Church of England, AD 1662 , and the Articles of Religion set forth in AD 1562. The Church thus affirms the inspiration of the Holy Scriptures and confesses the three ancient creeds of the Universal Church (the Apostles', Nicene, and Athanasian Creeds). Clergy are trained at St. Andrew's Theological College and Seminary, which the Church established in 1971. The Church is a member of the Orthodox Anglican

Communion, founded in 1967. The Orthodox Anglican Communion is a fellowship of churches around the world that adhere to historic Anglican faith and order. With more than a million lay members, the Communion is the largest such fellowship of Churches not affiliated with the See of Canterbury. The Presiding Bishop of the Orthodox Anglican Church serves as the Primate of the international Communion.

Headquarters

14 West Main St., P. O. Box 1980, Thomasville, NC 27361-1980, Tel. (336)472-2343, Fax (336)472-2351, Website: www.orthodox anglican.net
Email: abpmclaughlin@orthodoxanglican.net
Website: www.orthodoxanglican.net

Officers

Presiding Bishop, The Most Rev. Scott McLaughlin, 14 West Main St., P. O. Box 1980, Thomasville, NC 27361-1980, Tel. (336)472-2343, Fax (336)474-235, Email: abpmclaughlin@orthodoxanglican.net
St. Andrew's Theological College and Seminary
The Orthodox Anglican Society of St. Francis
The Cathedral Priory of St. Stephen

Periodicals

The Orthodox Anglican Herald

The Orthodox Church in America*

The Orthodox Church of America entered Alaska in 1794 before its purchase by the United States in 1867. Its canonical status of independence (autocephaly) was granted by its Mother Church, the Russian Orthodox Church, on April 10, 1970, and it is now known as The Orthodox Church in America.

Headquarters

P.O. Box 675, Syosset, NY 11791-0675, Tel. (516)922-0550 ext. 129, Fax (516)922-0954
Media Contact, Secretary, Archpriest Eric G. Tosi, P.O. Box 675, Syosset, NY 11791, Tel. (516)922-0550 ext. 129, Fax (516)922-0954, Email: egtosi@oca.org
Email: ajarmus@oca.org
Website: www.oca.org

Officers

HOLY SYNOD OF BISHOPS
RULING BISHOPS
Primate, Archbishop of Washington, Metropolitan of All America & Canada, His Beatitude Metropolitan Jonah, P.O. Box 675, Syosset, NY 11791; Tel. (516)922-0550
Archbishop of Detroit and the Romanian Episcopate, His Eminence Archbishop Nathaniel, P.O. Box 309, Grass Lake, MI 49240-0309; Tel. (517)522-4800
Bishop of Boston, New England and the Albanian Archdiocese, His Grace Bishop Nikon, P.O. Box 149, Southbridge, MA 01550; Tel. (508)764-3222

Bishop of Philadelphia and Eastern Pennsylvania, His Grace Bishop Tikhon, P.O. Box C, South Canaan, PA 18459; Tel. (570)937-9331
Bishop of San Francisco and the West, His Grace Bishop Benjamin, 1520 Green St., San Fransisco, CA 94123; Tel. (415)567-9378
Bishop of Mexico City and Exarchate of Mexico, His Grace Bishop Alejo, Rio Consulado e Irapuato, Col. Penon de los banos, 15520 Mexico D.F.
Bishop of Pittsburgh and Western Pennsylvania, His Grace Bishop Melchisedek, P.O. Box 1769, Cranberry Township, PA 16006; Tel. (724)776-5555
Bishop of New York and the Diocese of New York and New jersey, His Grace Bishop Michael, 33 Hewitt Ave, Bronxville, NY 10708; Tel. (914)779-6580
Archbishop of Chicago and the Midwest, His Grace Bishop Matthias, 927 N. LaSalle, Chicago, IL 60610; Tel. (312)202-0424
Bishop of Ottawa and the Archdiocese of Canada, Administrator His Grace Bishop Irenee of Quebec City, P.O. Box 179, Spencerville, ON K0E 1X0, Tel. (613)925-5226
Bishop of Anchorage and the Diocese of Alaska, Open, Locum tenens His Grace Bishop Benjamin, P.O. Box 210569, Anchorage, AK 99521; Tel. (907)270-0025
Bishop of Dallas and the South, Open, Locum tenens His Grace Bishop Nikon, 4112 Throckmorton St., Dallas, TX 75219; Tel. (214)522-4149
Bishop of Toledo and the Bulgarian Archdiocese, Bishop-Elect Archinadrite Alexander, 286 E. Woodsdale Ave, Akron, OH 44301; Tel. (330)724-7009

AUXILIARY BISHOPS
Bishop of Dearborn Heights, His Grace Bishop Irineu, 23300 Davison Ave. West, Detriot, MI 48223; Tel. (517)522-4800
Bishop of Quebec City, His Grace Bishop Irenee, 9600 rue St-Denis Apt A101, Montreal, Quebec, Canada H2M 1P2; Tel. (514)382-1804
Bishop of Bethesda, His Grace Bishop Mark, 414 SE 14th St., Apt. 8, Ft. Lauderdale, FL 33316; Tel. (214)522-4149

RETIRED BISHOPS
Retired Metropolitan, His Beatitude Metropolitan Theodosius, 156 Rifgon Dr., Canonsburg, PA 15317
Retired Metropolitan, His Beatitude Metropolitan Herman, P.O. Box 130, South Canaan, PA 18459
Retired Archbishop, His Eminence Archbishop Lazar, 37323 Hawkins Pickle Rd., Dewdney, BC, Canada V0M 1H0
Retired Bishop, His Grace Bishop Seraphim, 320 S. Broadway Unit P7, Tarrytown, NY 10591
Retired Bishop, His Grace Bishop Mark, 9511 Sun Pointe Dr., Boynton Beach, FL 33437

145

Retired Bishop, His Grace Bishop Tikhon, 649 Robinson St., Los Angeles, CA 90026

Retired Bishop, His Grace Bishop Nikolai, 5170 Evaline St., Las Vegas, NV 89120

Retired Bishop, His Grace Bishop Varlaam, 37323 Hawkins Pickle Rd., Dewdney, BC, Canada V0M 1H0

OFFICERS OF THE CHURCH

Archprist, John A. Jillions, Chancellor, P.O. Box 675, Syosset, NY 11791; Tel. (516)922-0550 ext. 130; Email: jjillions@OCA.org

Archpriest Eric G. Tosi, Secretary, P.O. Box 675, Syosset, NY 11791; Tel. (516)922-0550 ext 129; Email: egtosi@oca.org

Melanie Ringa, Treasurer, P.O. Box 675, Syosset, NY 11791; Tel. (516)922-0550 ext. 128; Email: mringa@oca.org

Archpriest Leonid Kishkovsky, Willow Shore Ave., Sia Cliff, NY 11579, Tel. (516)528-7637; Email: leonid@OCA.org

Alumni Association of St. Herman Seminary, 414 Mission Rd., Kodiak, AK 99615

Alumni Association of St. Tikhon Seminary, South Canaan, PA 18459

Alumni Association of St. Vladimir Seminary, 575 Scarsdale Rd., Crestwood, NY 10707

American Romanian Orthodox Youth, P.O. Box 309, Grass Lake, MI 49240

Association of Romanian Orthodox Ladies' Auxiliaries of America, P.O. Box 309, Grass Lake, MI 49240

Association of Romanian Canadian Orthodox Ladies' Auxiliaries, Box 4023, Regina, SK, Canada S4P 3R9

Fellowship of Orthodox Christians in America, 10 Downs Dr., Wilkes-Barre, PA 18705

Fellowship of Orthodox Stewards, P.O. Box 675, Syosset, NY 11791

Orthodox Brotherhood of USA, P.O. Box 309, Grass Lake, MI 49240

Orthodox Brotherhood of Canada, Box 4023, Regina, SK, Canada S4P 3R9

Project Mexico, P.O. Box 120028, Chula Vista, CA 91912

Russian Brotherhood Organization of the USA, 1733 Spring Garden St., Phildelphia, PA, 19130

Russian Orthodox Catholic Mutual Aid Society of the USA, 10 Downs Dr., Wilkes-Barre, PA 18705

Periodicals
The Orthodox Church

The Orthodox Presbyterian Church

On June 11, 1936, certain ministers, elders and lay members of the Presbyterian Church in the U.S.A. withdrew from that body to form a new denomination. Under the leadership of the late Rev. J. Gresham Machen, noted conservative New Testament scholar, the new church determined to continue to uphold the Westminster Confession of Faith as traditionally understood by Presbyterians and to engage in proclamation of the gospel at home and abroad.

The church has grown modestly over the years although having suffered early defections, most notably one in 1937 that resulted in the formation of the Bible Presbyterian Church under the leadership of Dr. Carl McIntire. It now has congregations throughout the states of the continental United States and in the Canadian provinces of Alberta and Ontario.

The denomination is a member of the North American Presbyterian and Reformed Council and the International Conference of Reformed Churches.

Headquarters
607 N. Easton Rd., Bldg. E, Willow Grove, PA 19090-2539, Tel. (215)830-0900 Fax (215) 830-0350

Media Contact, Stated Clerk., Rev. George R. Cottenden

Email: cottenden.1@opc.org; gcottenden@verizon.net

Website: www.opc.org

Officers
Moderator of General Assembly, The Rev. Danny E. Olinger, 607 N. Easton Rd., Bldg. E, Willow Grove, PA 19090-2539, Tel. (215)830-0900.

Email: olinger.1@opc.org

Stated Clk., Rev. George R. Cottenden (see contact information above)

Periodicals
New Horizons in the Orthodox Presbyterian Church

Patriarchal Parishes of the Russian Orthodox Church in the U.S.A.*

This group of parishes is under the direct jurisdiction of the Patriarch of Moscow and All Russia, His Holiness Aleksy II, in the person of a Vicar Bishop, His Grace Mercurius, Bishop of Zaraisk.

Headquarters
St. Nicholas Cathedral, 15 E. 97th St., New York, NY 10029, Tel. (212)996-6638 Fax (212)427-5003

Media Contact, Sec. to the Bishop, Igumen Joseph, Tel. (212)996-6638

Email: bmercurius@ruscon.com

Website: www.russianchurchusa.org

Officers
Secretary to the Bishop, Igumen Joseph

Secretary of the Representation, Very Rev. Alexander Abramov

Pentecostal Assemblies of the World, Inc.

This organization is an interracial Pentecostal nature subscribing to the Apostles doctrine with later-day roots dating back to Azusa Street revival in the early 1900s. We believe in repentence from sin; baptism in water by emerging in the name of Jesus Christ; and the infilling of the Holy Spirit with the evidence of speaking in unknown tongues.

Headquarters
3939 N. Meadows Dr., Indianapolis, IN 46205, Tel. (317)547-9541 Fax (317)543-0513
Interim Office Manager, Ms. Roxanne McDaniel
Email: dana.felton@greatergrace.org
Website: www.pawinc.org

Officers
Presiding Bishop, Charles H. Ellis III
1st Assistant Presiding Bishop, Richard E. Young
2nd Assistant Presiding Bishop, Theodore L. Brooks
Secretary A. Glenn Brady
Assist. Sec., Donald L. Golder
Gen. Treas.,Carl A. Turner
Asst. Treas., Stewart Reese

Pentecostal Church of God

Growing out of the pentecostal revival at the turn of the 20th century, the Pentecostal Church of God was organized in Chicago on Dec. 30, 1919, as the Pentecostal Assemblies of the U.S.A. The name was changed to Pentecostal Church of God in 1922; in 1934 it was changed again to The Pentecostal Church of God of America, Inc.; and finally the name became the Pentecostal Church of God (Incorporated.) in 1979. The International Headquarters was moved from Chicago, Illinois to Ottumwa, Iowa, in 1927, then to Kansas City, Missouri, in 1933 and finally to Joplin, Missouri, in 1951. The denomination is evangelical and pentecostal in doctrine and practice. Active membership in the National Association of Evangelicals and the Pentecostal/Charismatic Churches North America is maintained.

The church is Trinitarian in doctrine and teaches the absolute inerrancy of the Scripture from Genesis to Revelation. Among its cardinal beliefs are the doctrines of salvation, which includes regeneration; divine healing, as provided for in the atonement; the baptism in the Holy Ghost, with the initial physical evidence of speaking in tongues; and the premillennial second coming of Christ.

Headquarters
4901 Pennsylvania, P.O. Box 850, Joplin, MO 64802, Tel. (417)624-7050 Fax (417)624-7102
Media Contact, Gen. Sec., Wayman C. Ming Jr.
Email: generalsecretary@pcg.org
Website: www.pcg.org

Officers
Gen. Bishop., Dr. Charles G. Scott
Gen. Sec., Wayman C. Ming Jr.

OTHER GENERAL EXECUTIVES
Dir. of World Missions, Rev. Loyd L. Naten
Dir. of Indian Missions, Dr. C. Don Burke
Dir. of Youth Ministries, Rev. Joe Skiles, Jr.
Dir. of National Missions, Rev. David "Andy" Hunte

ASSISTANT GENERAL SUPERINTENDENTS/BISHOPS
Northwestern Division, Rev. Donald Manning
Southwestern Division, Rev. Jan Lake
North Central Division, Rev. Joseph Skiles, Sr.
South Central Division, Rev. John Norvell
Northeastern Division, Rev. Thomas E. Branham
Southeastern Division, Rev. C.W. Goforth

OTHER DEPARTMENTAL OFFICERS
Bus. Mgr., Gabriel Espinoza
Director of Women's Ministry, Mrs. Janice Scott

Periodicals
The Pentecostal Messenger

The Pentecostal Churches of Christ

In a time when the Church of Jesus Christ is challenged to send the "Evening Light Message" to the uttermost part of the Earth, a group of men and women came together on May 29, 1992 at the Pentecostal Church of Christ in Cleveland, Ohio to form what is now called The Pentecostal Churches of Christ.

Organized and established by Bishop J. Delano Ellis, II, the Pentecostal Churches of Christ is about the business of preparing people to see the Lord of Glory. The traditional barriers of yesteryear must not keep saints of like faith apart ever again and this fellowship of Pentecostal, Apostolic Independent Churches have discovered the truth of Our Lord's Prayer in the seventeenth chapter of Saint John, "that they may all be One." The Pentecostal Churches of Christ is a fellowship of holiness assemblies which has membership in the universal Body of Christ. As such, we preserve the message of Christ's redeeming love through His atonement and declare holiness of life to be His requirement for all men who would enter into the Kingdom of God. We preach repentance from sin, baptism in the Name of Jesus Christ, a personal indwelling of the Holy Spirit, a daily walk with the Lord and life after death. Coupled with the cardinal truths of the Church are the age old customs of ceremony and celebration.

Headquarters
10515 Chester Ave., Cleveland, OH 44106, Tel. (216)721-5935 Fax: (216)721-6938
Contact Person, Secretary General, Bishop Benjamin T. Douglass

APOSTOLIC OFFICES
10605 Chester Avenue – Suite 510, Cleveland, OH 44106, Tel. (216)721-5554, Fax (216)721-5517

147

Contact Person, Secretary General, Bishop Benjamin T. Douglass

Email: godsquad77@spcglobal.net; terwood2@aol.com

Website: www.pcccleveland.com

Officers

Presiding Prelate, Bishop J. Delano Ellis, II, Cleveland, OH

Secretary General, Bishop Benjamin T. Douglass

General Treasurer, Elder Jessie R. Woodson, Memphis, TN

Periodicals

The Pentecostal Flame

Pentecostal Fire-Baptized Holiness Church

Organized in 1918, this group consolidated with the Pentecostal Free Will Baptists in 1919. It maintains rigid discipline over members.

Headquarters

P.O. Box 261, La Grange, GA 30241-0261, Tel. (706)884-7742

Media Contact, Gen. Mod., Wallace B. Pittman, Jr.

Officers

Gen. Treas., Alan Sparkman, 1961 Norjon circle, Clio, SC 29525, Tel. (843)586-9095

Gen. Sec., Joel Powell, 16841 Springs Mill Rd. Lauringbury, NC 28352, Tel. (901)462-3379

Gen. Mod., Wallace B. Pittman, Jr.

Gen. Supt. Mission Bd., Jerry Powell, Rt. 1, Box 384, Chadourn, NC 28431

The Pentecostal Free Will Baptist Church, Inc.

The Cape Fear Conference of Free Will Baptists, organized in 1855, merged in 1959 with The Wilmington Conference and The New River Conference of Free Will Baptists and was renamed the Pentecostal Free Will Baptist Church, Inc. The doctrines include regeneration, sanctification, the Pentecostal baptism of the Holy Ghost, the Second Coming of Christ and divine healing.

Headquarters

P.O. Box 1568, Dunn, NC 28335, Tel. (910)892-4161 Fax (910)892-6876

Media Contact, Gen. Supt., Preston Heath

Email: pheath@intrstar.net

Website: www.pfwb.org

Officers

Gen. Supt., Rev. Preston Heath

Asst. Gen. Supt., Jim Wall

Gen. Sec., Mr. Stephen Garriss

Gen. Treas., Mr. Dewayne Weeks

Christian Ed. Dir., Rev. Randy Barker

World Witness Dir., Rev. Hobbs

Gen. Services Dir., Ms. Cathy Muzingo

Ministerial Council Dir., Rev. Ed Taturn

Ladies' Auxiliary Dir., Dollie Davis

Heritage Bible College, Pres., Dr. Dwarka Ramphal

Crusader Youth Camp, Dir., Rev. Randy Barker

OTHER ORGANIZATIONS

Heritage Bible College

Crusader Youth Camp

Blessings Bookstore, 1006 W. Cumberland St., Dunn, NC 28334, Tel. (910)892-2401

Periodicals

The Messenger

Philadelphia Yearly Meeting of the Religious Society of Friends*

PYM traces its roots to the yearly meeting of 1681 in Burlington, New Jersey. For more than three centuries, PYM has served Monthly Meetings and Quarterly Meetings throughout eastern Pennsylvania, southern New Jersey, eastern Maryland and Delaware.

Headquarters

Philadelphia Yearly Meeting, 1515 Cherry St., Philadelphia, PA 19102-1479, Tel. (215)241-7210 Fax (215)241-7045 Website: www.pym.org

Website: www.pym.org

Officers

Presiding Clerk, Thomas Swain, 1515 Cherry St., Philadelphia, PA 19102-1479

General Secretary, Arthur M. Larrabee

Periodicals

PYM News

Pillar of Fire

The Pillar of Fire was founded by Alma Bridwell White in Denver on Dec. 29, 1901 as the Pentecostal Union. In 1917, the name was changed to Pillar of Fire. Alma White was born in Kentucky in 1862 and taught school in Montana where she met her husband, Kent White, a Methodist minister, who was a University student in Denver. Because of Alma White's evangelistic endeavors, she was frowned upon by her superiors, which eventually necessitated her withdrawing from Methodist Church supervision. She was ordained as Bishop and her work spread to many states, to England, and since her death to Liberia, West Africa, Malawi, East Africa, Yugoslavia, Spain, India and the Philippines.

The Pillar of Fire organization has a college and two seminaries stressing Biblical studies. It operates eight separate schools for young people. The church continues to keep in mind the founder's goals and purposes.

Headquarters

P.O. Box 9159, Zarephath, NJ 08890, Tel. (732)356-0102

Western Headquarters, 1302 Sherman St., Denver, CO 80203, Tel. (303)427-5462

Media Contact, 1st Vice Pres., Robert B. Dallenbach, 3455 W. 83 Ave., Westminster, CO 80031, Tel. (303)427-5462 Fax (303)429-0910
Email: info@zarephath.edu
Website: www.gospelcom.net/pof

Officers

Pres. & Gen. Supt., Dr. Robert B. Dallenbach
1st Vice Pres. & Asst. Supt., Rev. Joseph Gross
2nd Vice Pres./Sec.-Treas., Lois R. Stewart
Trustees, Kenneth Cope; S. Rea Crawford; Lois Stewart; Dr. Donald J. Wolfram; Robert B. Dallenbach; Rob W. Cruver; Joseph Gross

Plymouth Brethren—please see Christian Brethren

Polish National Catholic Church of America*

After a number of attempts to resolve differences regarding the role of the laity in parish administration in the Roman Catholic Church in Scranton, Pennsylvania, this Church was organized in 1897. With the consecration to the episcopacy of the Most Rev. Francis Hodur, this Church became a member of the Old Catholic Union of Utrecht in 1907.

Headquarters

Office of the Prime Bishop, 1006 Pittston Ave., Scranton, PA 18505, Tel. (570)346-9131
Media Contact, Prime Bishop, Most Rev. Robert M. Nemkovich, 1006 Pittston Ave., Scranton, PA 18505, Tel. (570)346-9131, Fax (570)346-2188
Email: PNCCCenter@adelphia.net
Website: www.PNCC.org

Officers

Prime Bishop, The Most Rev. Anthony A. Mikovsky, 1006 Pittston Ave., Scranton, PA 18505, Tel. (570)346-9131, Fax (570)346-2188, Email: mikovskyac@hotmail.com; Home Address: 115 Lake Scranton Rd., Scranton, PA 18505, Tel. (570)344-0916
Eastern Diocese, Bishop, Rt. Rev. Thomas J. Gnat, 166 Pearl St., Manchester, NH 03104
Buffalo-Pittsburgh Diocese, Bishop, Rt. Rev. Thaddeus S. Peplowski, 5776 Broadway, Lancaster, NY 14086
Western Diocese, Rt. Rev. Anthony D. Kopka, 920 N. Northwest Hwy., Park Ridge, IL 60068
Canadian Diocese, Bishop, Rt. Rev. Sylvester Bigaj, 880 Barton Steet East, Hamilton, ON L8L3B7, Canada
Ecumenical Officer, Rev. Robert M. Nemkovich, Jr. Home Address: 37 Winthrop St., Fall River, MA 02721, Tel. (508)672-4854, Fax (508)672-2350, Email: RobNem21@aol.com
Savonarola Theological Seminary, 1031 Cedar Ave., Scranton, PA 18505; Rector: Most Rev. Robert M. Nemkovich; Vice Rector: Rev. Dr. Czeslaw Kuliczkowski

Periodicals
God's Field, Polka

Presbyterian Church in America

The Presbyterian Church in America is an Evangelical, Reformed covenant community of churches in the United States and Canada committed to a common doctrinal standard (The Westminster Standards), mutual accountability (representative church government), and cooperative ministry. The PCA traces its historical roots to the First General Assembly of the Church of Scotland of 1560, the establishment of the Presbytery of Philadelphia, 1789, and the General Assembly of the Southern Presbyterian Church, Augusta in 1861. Organized in 1973 by conservative churches formerly associated with the Presbyterian Church in the United States, the Church was first known as the National Presbyterian Church but changed its name in 1974 to the Presbyterian Church in America. The PCA seeks to be "Faithful to the Scriptures, True to the Reformed Faith, and Obedient to the Great Commission." In 1982 the Reformed Presbyterian Church, Evangelical Synod joined the PCA bringing with it a rich tradition that had antecedents in colonial America.

The PCA holds to the ancient creeds of the Church such as the Apostles' Creed and the Nicene Creed and has a firm commitment to its doctrinal standards, The Westminster Confession of Faith, Larger and Shorter Catechisms, that have been significant in Presbyterianism since 1645, These doctrinal standards reflect the distinctives of the Reformed tradition, Calvinism, and Covenant Theology. Ministers, ruling elders, and deacons are required to subscribe to the Westminster Standards in good faith. Individuals are received by a Session as communing members of the Church upon their profession of faith in Jesus Christ as Lord and Saviour, their promise to live a Christian lifestyle, and their commitment to worship and service in the Church.

The PCA is a connectional Church, led by ruling elders (lay leaders) and teaching elders (ministers). The Session governs a local congregation; the Diaconate carries out mercy ministries. The Presbytery is responsible for regional matters and the General Assembly is responsible for national matters in the USA and Canada. Cooperative ministry is carried out through over seventy Presbyteries and ten General Assembly Ministries.

The educational institutions of the Church are Covenant College of Lookout Mountain,GA and Covenant Theological Seminary of St. Louis, MO. The PCA and the Orthodox Presbyterian Church participate in a joint publication venture, Great Commission Publications, for the publication of Christian Education materials. In its ecumenical relations the PCA is a member of the North American Presbyterian and Reformed Council, the National Association of Evangelicals, and the World Reformed Fellowship.

The General Assembly approved a statement of purpose, "It is the purpose of the PCA to bring glory to God as a worshipping and serving community until the nations in which we live are filled with churches that make Jesus Christ and His word their chief joy, and the nations of the world, hearing the Word, are discipled in obedience to the Great Commission."

The Church has grown beyond its origin in the southeastern states to have congregations in forty-nine states in the USA and in several provinces of Canada. Growth is due to the PCA's ministry in evangelism, discipleship, church planting, church renewal, and campus ministry. Indicative of her concern for cross-cultural ministry, the PCA has the largest international missionary force in Presbyterian Church history.

Headquarters
1700 N. Brown Rd., Lawrenceville, GA 30043-8122, Tel. (678)825-1000
Email: ac@pcanet.org
Website: www.pcanet.org

Officers
Moderator: RE Dan Carrell, c/o Carrell Blanton Law Firm, 7275 Glen Forest Drive #310, Richmond, VA 23226, Tel. (804)285-7900, Email:lexrex3dac@aol.com.
Stated Clerk/Coordinator of Administration – Dr. L. Roy Taylor, 1700 N. Brown Rd., Suite 105, Lawrenceville, GA 30043-8143, Tel. (678)825-1000, Email: ac@pcanet.org
Christian Education & Publications Coordinator – Dr. Charles Dunahoo, 1700 N. Brown Rd., Suite 102, Lawrenceville, GA 30043-8143, Tel. (678)825-1100, Email: cep@pacnet.org
Mission to the World Coordinator – Dr. Paul D. Kooistra, 1600 N. Brown Rd., Lawrenceville, GA 30043-8141, Tel. (678)-823-0004, Email: mtw@mtw.org
Mission to North America Coordinator – Dr. James C. Bland, 1700 N. Brown Rd., Suite 101, Lawrenceville, GA 30043-8143, Tel. (678)825-1200, Email: mna@pcanet.org
Reformed University Ministries Coordinator – Dr. Rod Mays, 1700 N. Brown Rd., Suite 104, Lawrenceville, GA 30043-8143, Tel. (678)825-1070, Email: rum@pcanet.org
PCA Foundation President – Mr. Randel Stair, 1700 N. Brown Rd., Suite 103, Lawrenceville, GA 30043-8143, Tel. (678)825-1040, Email: pcaf@pcanet.org
PCA Retirement and Benefits Inc., Pres., Mr. Gary D. Campbell, 1700 North Brown Rd., Suite 106, Lawrenceville, GA 30043-8143, Tel. (678)825-1260, Email: gcampbell@pcanet.org

Ridge Haven Conference Director – RE Wallace Anderson, Executive Director, 214 Ridge Haven Rd., Brevard, NC 28712, Tel. (828)862-3916, Fax:828-884-6988, Email:wallace@ridgehaven.org
Covenant College President-Dr. Niel Nielson, 14049 Scenic Highway, Lookout Mountain, GA 30750-4164, Tel. (706)820-1117, Fax:706-820-2165, Email:webmaster@ covenant.edu
Covenant Theological Seminary President – Dr. Bryan Chapell, 12330 Conway Rd., St. Louis, MO 63141-8609, Tel. (314)434-4044, Fax (314)434-4819, Email: president@covenant seminary.edu

Periodicals
ByFaith, Equip, Covenant, Mission Report, The View

Presbyterian Church (U.S.A.)*
The Presbyterian Church (U.S.A.) was organized June 10, 1983, when the Presbyterian Church in the United States and the United Presbyterian Church in the United States of America united in Atlanta. The union healed a major division which began with the Civil War when Presbyterians in the South withdrew from the Presbyterian Church in the United States of America to form the Presbyterian Church in the Confederate States.

The United Presbyterian Church in the United States of America had been created by the 1958 union of the Presbyterian Church in the United States of America and the United Presbyterian Church of North America. Of those two uniting bodies, the Presbyterian Church in the U.S.A. dated from the first Presbytery organized in Philadelphia, about 1706. The United Presbyterian Church of North America was formed in 1858, when the Associate Reformed Presbyterian Church and the Associate Presbyterian Church united.

Strongly ecumenical in outlook, the Presbyterian Church (U.S.A.) is the result of at least 10 different denominational mergers over the last 250 years. A restructure, adopted by the General Assembly meeting in June 1993, has been implemented. The Presbyterian Church (U.S.A.) dedicated its new national offices in Louisville, Kentucky in 1988.

Headquarters
100 Witherspoon St., Louisville, KY 40202, Tel. (888)728-7228 Fax (502)569-5018
Media Contact, Assoc. Dir. for Communications, Barry Creech, Tel. (502)569-5515 Fax (502)569-8073
Email: presytel@pcusa.org
Website: www.pcusa.org

Officers
Mod., Eld Cynthia Bolbach, 100 Witherspoon St, Louisville KY 40202, Tel. (888)728-7228

Vice Mod., Rev. Landon Whitsitt, 100 Witherspoon St, Louisville KY 40202, Tel. (888)728-7228

Stated Clk., Rev. Gradye Parsons, 100 Witherspoon St, Louisville KY 40202, Tel. (888)728-7228

THE OFFICE OF THE GENERAL ASSEMBLY
100 Witherspoon St, Louisville KY 40202-1396, Tel. (888)728-7228 x. 5424 Fax (502)569-8005
Stated Clk., Rev. Gradye Parsons
Strategic Operations, Dir., Rev. Thomas Hay
Middle Governing Body Relations, Coord., Rev. Jill Hudson
Dept. of the Stated Clerk, Dir., Loyda Aja
Dept. of Constitutional Services, Dir., Vacant
Ecumenical & Agency Relations, Dir., Rev. Robina Winbush
Dept. of Communication, Development & Technology, Dir., Rev. Kerry Clements
Dept. of Hist., Philadelphia, 425 Lombard St., Philadelphia, PA 19147, Tel. (215)627-1852 Fax (215)627-0509; Dir., Frederick J. Heuser, Jr.

GENERAL ASSEMBLY MISSION COUNCIL
Exec. Dir., Linda Valentine
Deputy Exec. Dir. for Mission, Rev. Roger Dermody
Deputy Exec. Dir. for Communication & Funds Development, Eld Karen Schmidt
Deputy Exec. Dir. for Shared Services & Chief Financial Officer, Eld Joey Bailey
Theology, Worship & Education, Dir.,Vacant
Evangelism & Church Growth, Dir., Rev. Eric Hoey
Peace & Justice, Dir, Eld Sara Lisherness
Relief & Development, Int Dir., Eld Sara Lisherness
World Mission, Dir., Rev. Hunter Farrell
Racial Ethnic & Women's Ministries/ Presbyterian Women, Dir., Rev. Rhashell Hunter

BOARD OF PENSIONS
200 Market St., Philadelphia, PA 19103-3298, Tel. (800)773-7752 Fax (215)587-6215
Pres., & CEO, Robert W. Maggs, Jr.

PRESBYTERIAN CHURCH (U.S.A.) FOUNDATION
200 E. Twelfth St., Jeffersonville, IN 47130, Tel. (812)288-8841 Fax (502)569-5980
Pres. & CEO, Rev. Thomas Taylor

PRESBYTERIAN CHURCH (U.S.A.) INVESTMENT & LOAN PROGRAM, INC.
Tel. (800)903-7457 Fax (502)569-8868
Pres. & CEO, James L. Hudson

PRESBYTERIAN PUBLISHING CORPORATION
Pres. & CEO, Marc Lewis

SYNOD EXECUTIVES
Alaska-Northwest, Rev. Joyce Emery Martin, Int., 217 6th Ave. N., Seattle, WA 98109, Tel. (206)448-6403

Boriquen in Puerto Rico, Rev. Edwin Quiles Rodriquez Int., Ave. Hostos Edificio 740, Cond. Medical Center Plaza, Ste. 216, Mayaguez, PR 00680, Tel. (787)832-8375

Covenant, Eld. Rev Raafat Zaki, 1911 Indian Wood Cir #B, Tel. (419)754-4050

Lakes & Prairies, Rev. Philip Brown, 2115 Cliff Dr #210, Eagan, MN 55122-3327, Tel. (651)357-1140

Lincoln Trails, Rev. Carol McDonald and Rev. David Crittenden, 1100 W. 42nd St., Indianapolis, IN 46208-3381, Tel. (317)923-3681

Living Waters, Rev. Terry Newland, 5016 Spedale Ct #339, Spring Hill TN 37174 Tel. (615)261-4008

Mid-America, Rev. Nancy Kahaian, 7301 Mission Rd #107, Prairie Village KS 66208 Tel. (913)384-3020

Mid-Atlantic, Rev. David McKee, 3218 Chamberlayne Ave, Richmond, VA 23227, Tel. (804)342-0016

Northeast, Eld Mary Lynne Flowers, 5811 Heritage Landing Dr., East Syracuse, NY 13057-9360, Tel. (315)446-5990

Pacific, Rev. Robert Brinks, 200 Kentucky St #B, Petaluma CA 94952-2879 Tel. (707)765-1772

Rocky Mountains, Rev Daivd Ezekiel, Int, 7061 S University Blvd #206., Centennial, CO 80211, Tel. (303)477-9070

South Atlantic, Rev. Reginald Parsons, 118 E. Monroe St., Ste. 3, Jacksonville, FL 32202, Tel. (904)356-6070

Southern California & Hawaii, Eld Doska Ross, 1501 Wilshire Blvd., Los Angeles, CA 90017-2293, Tel. (213)483-3840

Southwest, Eld Conrand Rocha, 401 E. 4th St. #A, Tucson, AZ 85705, Tel. (520)791-9600

The Sun, Rev. Judy R. Fletcher, 6100 Colwell Blvd #200, Irving, TX 75039, Tel. (214)390-1894

The Trinity, Rev. Bruce G. Stevens, 3040 Market St., Camp Hill, PA 17011-4599, Tel. (717)737-0421

Periodicals
Journal of Presbyterian History, Presbyterian News Service, Church & Society Magazine, Horizons, Presbyterians Today, Interpretation, Presbyterian Outlook

Primitive Advent Christian Church

This body split from the Advent Christian Church. All its churches are in West Virginia. The Primitive Advent Christian Church believes that the Bible is the only rule of faith and practice and that Christian character is the only test of fellowship and communion. The church agrees with Christian fidelity and meekness; exercises mutual watch and care; counsels, admonishes, or reproves as duty may require and receives the same from each other as becomes the household of faith. Primitive Advent Christians do not believe in taking up arms.

The church believes that three ordinances are set forth by the Bible to be observed by the Christian church, (1) baptism by immersion; (2) the Lord's Supper, by partaking of unleavened bread and wine; (3) feet washing, to be observed by the saints' washing of one another's feet.

Headquarters

Media Contact, Sec.-Treas., Roger Wines, 1971 Grapevine Rd., Sissonville, WV 25320, Tel. (304)988-2668

Officers

Pres., Herbert Newhouse, 7632 Hughart Dr., Sissonville, WV 25320, Tel. (304)984-9277

Vice Pres., Roger Hammons, 273 Frame Rd., Elkview, WV 25071, Tel. (304)965-6247

Sec. & Treas., Roger Wines, 1971 Grapevine Rd., Sissonville, WV 25320, Tel. (304)988-2668

Primitive Baptists

This group of Baptists has churches in the United States, the Philippines, India and Africa. While they oppose centralization and modern mission boards, they believe in the circulation of the gospel. They preach salvation by grace alone.

Headquarters

P.O. Box 38, Thornton, AR 71766, Tel. (501)352-3694

Media Contact, Elder W. Hartsel Cayce

Officers

Elder W. Hartsel Cayce

Elder Lasserre Bradley, Jr., Box 17037, Cincinnati, OH 45217, Tel. (513)821-7289

Elder S. T. Tolley, P.O. Box 68, Atwood, TN 38220, Tel. (901)662-7417

Periodicals

Baptist Witness

Primitive Methodist Church in the U.S.A.

Hugh Bourne and William Clowes, local preachers in the Wesleyan Church in England, organized a daylong meeting at Mow Cop in Staffordshire on May 31, 1807, after Lorenzo Dow, an evangelist from America, told them of American camp meetings. Thousands attended and many were converted but the Methodist church, founded by the open-air preacher John Wesley, refused to accept the converts and reprimanded the preachers.

After waiting for two years for a favorable action by the Wesleyan Society, Bourne and Clowes established The Society of the Primitive Methodists. This was not a schism, Bourne said, for "we did not take one from them ... it now appeared to be the will of God that we ... should form classes and take upon us the care of churches in the fear of God." Primitive

Methodist missionaries were sent to New York in 1829. An American conference was established in 1840.

Missionary efforts reach into Guatemala, Spain and other countries. The denomination joins in federation with the Evangelical Congregational Church, the United Brethren in Christ Church and the Southern Methodist Church and is a member of the National Association of Evangelicals.

The church believes the Bible is the only true rule of faith and practice, the inspired Word of God. It believes in one Triune God, the Deity of Jesus Christ, the Deity and personality of the Holy Spirit, the innocence of Adam and Eve, the Fall of the human race, the necessity of repentance, justification by faith of all who believe, regeneration witnessed by the Holy Spirit, sanctification by the Holy Spirit, the second coming of the Lord Jesus Christ, the resurrection of the dead and conscious future existence of all people and future judgments with eternal rewards and punishments.

Headquarters

Media Contact, Pres., Rev. Frank Hrabak, 1122 Frosty Hollow Rd., Langhorne, PA 19047-5719, Tel. (215)757-3049

Email: pmconf@juno.com

Website: www.primitivemethodistchurch.org

Officers

Pres., Rev. Frank Hrabak, 1122 Frosty Hollow Rd., Langhorne, PA 19047-5719, Tel. (215)757-3049

Vice Pres., Rev. Allen Rupert, 207 Whitmore Ave., Mayfield, PA 18433-1738, Tel. (570)876-2234

Recording Secretary, Rev. David Sargent, 5021 Willow Ave., Bowling Green, FL 33834-2880, Tel. (863)375-9913

General. Secretary., Rev. David Allen, Jr., 1199 Lawrence St., Lowell, MA 01852-5526, Tel. (978)453-2052 Email: pahson@verizon.net

Treas., Mr. Raymond C. Baldwin, 18409 Mill Run Ct., Leesburg, VA 20176-4583, Email: Rbaldwin32@aol.com

Progressive National Baptist Convention, Inc.*

This body held its organizational meeting in Cincinnati in November, 1961. Subsequent regional sessions were followed by the first annual session in Philadelphia in 1962.

Headquarters

601-50th St., N.E., Washington, DC 20019, Tel. (202)396-0558 Fax (202)398-4998

Media Contact, Gen. Sec., Dr. Walter L. Parrish III

Email: infor@pnbc.org

Website: www.pnbc.org

Officers

Periodicals

Baptist Progress, The Worker

Protestant Reformed Churches in America

The Protestant Reformed Churches (PRC) have their roots in the sixteenth century Reformation of Martin Luther and John Calvin, as it developed in the Dutch Reformed churches. The denomination originated as a result of a controversy in the Christian Reformed Church in 1924 involving the adoption of the "Three Points of Common Grace." Three ministers in the Christian Reformed Church, the Reverends Herman Hoeksema, George Ophoff, and Henry Danhof, and their consistories (Eastern Ave., Hope, and Kalamazoo, respectively) rejected the doctrine. Eventually these men were deposed, and their consistories were either deposed or set outside the Christian Reformed Church. The denomination was formed in 1926 with three congregations. Today the denomination is comprised of some twenty-eight churches (more than 7,000 members) in the USA and Canada. The presbyterian form of church government as determined by the Church Order of Dordt is followed by the PRC. The doctrinal standards of the PRC are the Reformed confessions -the Heidelberg Catechism, Belgic Confession of Faith, and Canons of Dordrecht. The doctrine of the covenant is a cornerstone of their teaching. They maintain an unconditional, particular covenant of grace that God establishes with His elect.

Headquarters

4949 Ivanrest Ave. SW, Grandville, MI 49418
Tel. (616)531-1490
Media Contact, Stated Clerk, Don Doezema, 4949 Ivanrest Ave., Grandville, MI 49418, Tel. (616)531-1490
Email: doezema@prca.org
Website: www.prca.org

Officers

Stat. Clk., Don Doezema, 4949 Ivanrest Ave., Grandville, MI 49418, Tel. (616)531-1490, Fax (616)531-3033, Email: doezema@ prca.org

Periodicals

The Standard Bearer

Quakers—please see Friends

Reformed Catholic Church

The Reformed Catholic Church was founded in 1988, and incorporated in 1989, as an alternative to the structures and strictures of the Roman Catholic Church, yet without denying basic catholic beliefs of faith and love, spirituality and community, prayer and sacramentality. The Reformed Catholic Church is a federation of independent churches offering a progressive alternative in the Catholic tradition. It is a newly formed rite, as in the tradition of the Orthodox churches of the Catholic tradition and the Old Catholic Church of Utrecht. It remains a Catholic Church, and its priests are considered Catholic priests.

Headquarters

P.O. Box 5554, Toledo, OH 43613-0554
Email: holycrossrcc@aol.com
Website: www.reformedcatholicchurch.org

Officers

Metropolitan Archbishop, Wm. Quinlan, DD RFC P.O. Box 5554, Toledo, OH 43613-0554
Presiding Archbishop M Heckman, DD RSJ, P.O. Box 5554, Toledo, OH 43613-0554
Archbishop John Bell DD OSBr 3156 Mapleleaf Ave. Cincinnati OH 45213
Archbishop Francis Fontenot 119 St. Fabian Dr.Carencro, LA 70520
Bishop Bill Heller, DD, P.O. Box 5554, Toledo, OH 43613-0554
Bishop Obispo José Israel, DD, PMB #114 P.O. Box 4960 Caguas, PUERTO RICO 00726-4960 Bishop Shane Price, DD RSJ, 825 N. 26th St. Bismark, ND 58501
Bishop Chris Carpenter, DD, P.O. Box 40217 Long Beach, CA 90814
Bishop Peter Posthumus, DD OPJB, 255 Plymouth SE East Grand Rapids, MI 49506

Reformed Church in America*

The Reformed Church in America was established in 1628 by the earliest settlers of New York. It is the oldest Protestant denomination with a continuous ministry in North America. Until 1867 it was known as the Reformed Protestant Dutch Church. The first ordained minister, Domine Jonas Michaelius, arrived in New Amsterdam from The Netherlands in 1628. Throughout the colonial period, the Reformed Church lived under the authority of the Classis of Amsterdam. Its churches were clustered in New York and New Jersey. Under the leadership of Rev. John Livingston, it became a denomination independent of the authority of the Classis of Amsterdam in 1776. Its geographical base was broadened in the 19th century by the immigration of Reformed Dutch and German settlers in the midwestern United States. The Reformed Church now spans the United States and Canada.

The Reformed Church in America accepts as its standards of faith the Heidelberg Catechism, Belgic Confession and Canons of Dort and the Belhar Confession. It has a rich heritage of world mission activity. It claims to be loyal to reformed tradition which emphasizes obedience to God in all aspects of life.

Although the Reformed Church in America has worked in close cooperation with other churches, it has never entered into merger with any other denomination. It is a member of the World Alliance of Reformed Churches, the World Council of Churches and the National Council of the Churches of Christ in the United States of America. In 1998 it also entered into a relationship of full communion with the Evangelical Lutheran Church in America, Presbyterian Church (U.S.A.), and the United Church of Christ by way of Formula of Agreement. In 2007 it also entered into full communion with the Christian Reformed Church in North America.

Headquarters

475 Riverside Dr., New York, NY 10115, Tel. (212)870-3243 Fax (212)870-2499

Media Contact, Communication Officer, Paul Boice, 4500 60th St. SE, Grand Rapids, MI 49512, Tel. (616)698-7071 Fax (616)698-6606
Email: dmorris@rca.org
Website: www.rca.org

Officers

President, the Rev. Lisa Vaner Wal, 475 Riverside Dr., 18th Floor, New York, NY 10115

General Synod Council; Moderator, the Rev. Donald Poest, 475 Riverside Dr., 18th Floor, New York, NY 10115

General Secretary, the Rev. Thomas De Vries, 475 Riverside Dr., 18th Floor, New York, NY 10115; 4500 60th St. S.E., Grand Rapids, MI 49512

Operations and Support, Director & Assistant Secretary, The Rev. Kenneth Bradsell

Global Mission, Director, The Rev. Jhonny Alicea-Baez

Leadership/Revitalization, Director, The Rev. Kenneth Eriks

Church Multiplication/Discipleship, Director, The Rev. Kenneth Eriks

Finance Services, Treasurer, Ms. Barbara Boers
World Council of Churches
World Communion of Reformed Churches
National Council of Churches of Christ in the U.S.A.
Christian Churches Together
Global Christian Forum
Roman Catholic/Reformed Dialogue

Periodicals

Perspectives, RCA Today

Reformed Church in the United States

Lacking pastors, early German Reformed immigrants to the American colonies were led in worship by "readers." One reader, schoolmaster John Philip Boehm, organized the first congregations near Philadelphia in 1725. A Swiss pastor, Michael Schlatter, was sent by the Dutch Reformed Church in 1746. Strong ties with the Netherlands existed until the formation of the Synod of the German Reformed Church in 1793.

The Eureka Classis, organized in North and South Dakota in 1910 and strongly influenced by the writings of H. Kohlbruegge, P. Geyser and J. Stark, refused to become part of the 1934 merger of the Reformed Church with the Evangelical Synod of North America, holding that it sacrificed the Reformed heritage. (The merged Evangelical and Reformed Church became part of the United Church of Christ in 1957.) Under the leadership of pastors W. Grossmann and W. J. Krieger, the Eureka Classis in 1942 incorporated as the continuing Reformed Church in the United States.

The growing Eureka Classis dissolved in 1986 to form a Synod with four regional classes. An heir to the Reformation theology of Zwingli and Calvin, the Heidelberg Catechism, the Belgic Confession and the Canons of Dort are used as the confessional standards of the church. The Bible is strictly held to be the inerrant, infallible Word of God.

The RCUS supports Dordt College, Mid-America Reformed Seminary, New Geneva Theological Seminary, West Minster Theological Seminary in California, and Hope Haven. The RCUS is the official sponsor to the Reformed Confessing Church of Zaire.

Headquarters

Media Contact, Rev. Frank Walker Th.M., 6121 Pine Vista Way, Elk Grove City, CA 95758-4205, Tel. (661)827-9885
Email: TriWheeler@aol.com
Website: www.rcus.org

Officers

Pres., Rev. Vernon Pollema, 235 James St., Shafter, CA 93263, Tel. (661)746-6907

Vice Pres., Rev. Robert Grossmann, Th.M., 1905 200th St., Garner, IA 50438, Tel. (515)923-3060

Stated Clk., Rev. Frank Walker Th.M., 5601 Spring Blossom St., Bakersfield, CA 93313-6025, Tel. (661)827-9885

Treas., Clayton Greiman, 2115 Hwy. 69, Garner, IA 50438, Tel. (515)923-2950

Reformed Episcopal Church

The Reformed Episcopal Church was founded December 2, 1873 in New York City by Bishop George David Cummins, an assistant bishop in the Protestant Episcopal Church from 1866 until his departure to found the new jurisdiction. Cummins and other evangelical Episcopalians were concerned about the exclusiveness propagated by what they perceived to be an excessive ritualism sweeping the church. Throughout the late 1860's evangelicals and ritualists clashed over ceremonies, vestments, open or closed communion, the Articles of Religion, interpretation of the meaning of the sacraments, and the understanding of Apostolic Succession.

In October, 1873, other bishops of the Protestant Episcopal Church publically attacked Cummins in major newspapers for his participation in an ecumenical communion service sponsored by the Evangelical Alliance. Cummins resigned from the Episcopal Church and drafted a call to organize a new Episcopal Church for the "purpose of restoring the old paths of their fathers". On December 2, 1873, a Declaration of Principle which expressed the evangelical understanding of the Articles of Religion was adopted. Dr. Charles Edward Cheney of Chicago was elected bishop to serve with Bishop Cummins. The Second General Council, meeting in May, 1874 in New York City, approved a Constitution and Canons and adopted the 1785 Proposed Book of Common Prayer for use in the New Church. Other notable early bishops (1876) included Rufus Nicholson, Edward Cridge, of Victoria, B.C., and Samuel Fallows through whom the episcopate of the church was perpetuated.

In recent years the Reformed Episcopal Church has revised the Book of Common Prayer to conform to the 1662 and 1928 Prayer Books. The Church continues to embrace the Thirty-Nine Articles of Religion, and has affirmed the Chicago-Lambeth Quadrilateral of 1886-1888.

From 1993 until 2003 the Reformed Episcopal Church was in dialogue with the Episcopal Church U.S.A. at which time it was discontinued. The Reformed Episcopal Church subsequently became a member of the Common Cause Partnership, an association of traditional Anglicans, becoming a founding subjurisdiction of the Anglican Church in North America officially formed from that body in Ft. Worth, Texas in June, 2009.

The Reformed Episcopal Church presently consists of six geographic dioceses and one domestic missionary diocese in the United States and Canada. Active missionary work continues in several countries including Germany and Cuba. Previous missionary jurisdictions in India and Liberia have been granted autonomy.

Seminaries operated by the church are located in Philadelphia, PA, Houston, TX, and Summerville, SC. The Reformed Episcopal Church is a member of the National Association of Evangelicals and the Anglican Church in North America.

Headquarters

826 2nd Ave, Blue Bell, PA 19422-1257, Tel. (215)483-1196 Fax (215)483-5235

Media Contact, Rt. Rev. Leonard Riches

Media Contact, Rt. Rev. Royal U. Grote, Jr., Church Growth Office, 211 Byrne Ave., Houston, TX 77009, Tel. (713)862-4929

Email: wycliffe@jps.net

Website: recus.org

Officers

PRESIDENT AND PRESIDING BISHOP
The Right Reverend Leonard W. Riches, M. Div., D.D., 85 Smithtown Rd., Pipersville, PA 18947, Tel. (610)294-8001 Fax (610)294-8009

VICE PRESIDENT & MEDIA OFFICER
The Right Reverend Royal U. Grote, Jr., 4142 Dayflower, Katy, Texas 77449, Tel. (281)463-9454 or (800)732-3433 Fax (281)463-2304, Email: Royalrec1@aol.com

SECRETARY
Mrs. Tonya M. Forsberg, 826 Second Avenue Blue Bell, PA 19422, Tel. (610)292-9581 Fax (610)292-9853

ASSISTANT SECRETARY
Mrs. Bonnie C. Abboud, 826 Second Avenue Blue Bell, PA 19422, Tel. (610)292-9581 Fax (610)292-9853

TREASURER
The Venerable Dr. Jon W. Abboud, 826 Second Avenue Blue Bell, PA 19422, Tel. (610)292-9581 Fax (610)292-9853

ECUMENICAL OFFICER
The Rt. Reverend Ray R. Sutton

BOARD OF FOREIGN MISSIONS
The Rt. Reverend Royal U. Grote

COMMISSION ON THEOLOGICAL EDUCATION
The Venerable Dr. Jon W. Abboud

COMMITTEE ON DOCTRINE & WORSHIP
The Rt. Reverend Royal U. Grote

COMMITTEE ON CONSTITUTION & CANONS
The Venerable Dr. James T. Payne, P.O. Box 973 Missouri City, TX 77459, Tel. (713)434-1117

BISHOPS
The Most Rev. Leonard W. Riches, 85 Smithtown Rd., Pipersville, PA 18947-1604, Email: nicaea@aol.com, Presiding Bishop of the Reformed Episcopal Church

The Rt. Rev. Royal U. Grote, Jr., 2818 Shadow Canyon Lane, Katy, TX 77494, Email: Royal REC1@aol.com, DMA: Bishop Ordinary

The Rt. Rev. Richard Boyce, 2340 N. 155th St., Seattle, WA 98133, Email: bpboyce1@ msn.com, DOW: Bishop Ordinary

The Rt. Rev. Charles W. Dorrington, 70-7570 Tetayut, Saanichton, BC, Canada V8M 2H4, Email: recwcan@island.net, DWC-A: Bishop Ordinary

The Rev. George B. Fincke, 1902 Centre Square, Moorhead, MN 56560, Email: KOGvicar@yahoo.com, DMA: Bishop, Asst; King of Glory RE Mission

The Rt. Rev. William White, 1260 Peru Road, St. Stephen, S.C. 29479, Email: wwjwhite@ yahoo.com, DSE: Bishop Suffragan

The Rt. Rev. Alphonza Gadsden, Sr., P.O. Box 657, St. Stephen, SC 29479-0657, Email: bishopgadsden@att.net, DSE: Bishop Ordinary, Liberty RE Church

The Rt. Rev. David L. Hicks, 117 Redford Rd., Oreland, PA 19075, Email: bishophicks@ comcast.net, DNE-MA: Bishop Ordinary

The Rt. Rev. Gerhard Meyer, Richberg Str. #11, 34639 Schwarzenborn, Germany, Email: bischof.Meyer@rekd.de, REK: Bishop, Asst.; GERMANY

The Rt. Rev. Daniel R. Morse, 4011 Farmingham Woods Dr., Hermitage, TN 37076, Email: dmorse3738@aol.com, MDCS: Missionary Bishop

The Rt. Rev. Winfield Mott, P.O. Box 2325, Deming, NM 88031, Email: staugustine@ zianet.com, DOW: Bishop, St. Augustine Church

The Rt. Rev. Ray R. Sutton, 4327 Hollow Oak Dr., Dallas, TX 75287, Email: psalm whosoever@aol.com, DMA: Bishop Suffragan; Church of the Holy Communion

DIOCESE OF MID-AMERICA (DMA)
The Rt. Rev. Royal U. Grote, Jr., Ordinary, 4142 Dayflower, Katy, Texas 77449, Tel. (281)463-9454 or (800)732-3433, Email: royalrec1@ aol.com

Rt. Rev. Ray R. Sutton, Suffragan

Rt. Rev. George B. Fincke, Assistant Bishop

DIOCESE OF THE NORTHEAST & MID-ATLANTIC (DNE-MA)
The Most Rev. Leonard W. Riches, Presidig, 826 Second Ave, Blue Bell, PA 19422-125 Tel.

(610)292-9581 Fax (610)292-9853, Email: nicaea@aol.com

Rt. Rev. David Hicks, Coadjutor

Rt. Rev. Daniel G. Cox, (semi-Retired)

DIOCESE OF THE WEST (DOW)
The Rt. Rev. Richard Boyce, Ordinary, 2340 N. 155th St., Seattle, WA Tel. (206)525-1618, Email: bpboyce1@msn.com

Rt. Rev. Winfield Mott

DIOCESE OF THE SOUTHEAST (DSE)
The Rt. Rev. Al Gadsden, Ordinary, 705 S. Main St., Summerville, SC 2948 Tel. (843)873-3451, Email: bishopgadsden@att.net

MISSIONARY DIOCESE OF THE CENTRAL STATES (MDCS)
The Rt. Rev Daniel R. Morse, Missionary Bishop, 4011 Famingham Woods Dr., Hermitage, TN 370 Email: dmorse3738@ aol.com

DIOCESE OF CENTRAL & EASTERN CANADA (DC-EC)
The Rt. Rev. David Hicks, Tel. (705)645-4565, Email: trinityfed@hotmail.com

DIOCESE OF WESTERN CANADA & ALASKA (DWC-A)
The Rt. Rev. Charles W. Dorrington, Ordinary, 70-7570 Tetayut Rd., Saanichton, BC V8M 2H4, Tel. (250)727-3722 Email: recwcan@ islandnet.com

OTHER ORGANIZATIONS
Bd. of Foreign Missions, Pres., Dr. Barbara J. West, 316 Hunters Rd., Swedesboro, NJ 08085, Tel. (609)467-1641

Bd. of Natl. Church Extension, Pres., Rt. Rev. Royal U. Grote, Jr., 211 Byrne Ave., Houston, TX 77009, Tel. (713)862-4929

Publication Society, Pres., Rt. Rev. Royal U. Grote; 211 Byrne Ave., Houston, TX 77009, Tel. (713)862-4929, 7372 Henry Ave., Philadelphia, PA 19128 25-956-0655

The Reapers, Pres., Susan Higham, 472 Leedom St., Jenkintown, PA 19046

Committee on Women's Work, Pres., Joan Workowski, 1162 Beverly Rd., Rydal, PA 19046

Committee on Constitutions and Canons, Rev. Canon James T. Payne, P.O. Box 973, Missouri City TX 77495

BISHOPS
Leonard W. Riches, Sr., 85 Smithtown Rd., Pipersville, PA 18947, Tel. (215)483-1196 Fax (215)294-8009

Royal U. Grote, Jr., 211 Byrne Ave., Houston, TX 77009

James C. West, Sr., 408 Red Fox Run, Summerville, SC 29485

Robert H. Booth, 1611 Park Ave., #212, Quakertown, PA 18951

Gregory K. Hotchkiss, 318 E. Main St., Somerville, NJ 08876

George B. Fincke, 155 Woodstock Circle, Vacaville, CA 95687-3381

Daniel R. Morse, 11259 Wexford Dr., Eads, TN 38025

Michael Fedechko, Box 2532, New Liskeard, ON P0J 1P0

Charles W. Dorrington, 626 Blanshard St., Victoria, BC V8W 3G6

Ray R. Sutton, 17405 Muirfield Dr., Dallas TX 75287, Tel. (972)248-6505

Periodicals
Reformed Episcopalians

Reformed Mennonite Church

This is a small group of believers in Pennsylvania, Ohio, Michigan, Illinois, and Ontario, Canada who believe in non-resistance of evil, and non-conformity to the world and who practice separation from unfaithful worship. They believe that Christian unity is the effect of brotherly love and are of one mind and spirit. Their church was established in 1812 by John Herr who agreed with the teachings of Menno Simon as well as those of Jesus Christ.

Headquarters
Lancaster County only, Reformed Mennonite Church, 602 Strasburg Pike, Lancaster, PA 17602

Media Contact, Bishop, Glenn M. Gross, Tel. (717)697-4623

Email: beehlerg@quadro.net

Website: www.reformedmennonitechurch.org

Officers
Bishop Glenn M. Gross, 906 W. Grantham Rd., Mechanicsburg, PA 17055

Reformed Methodist Union Episcopal Church

The Reformed Methodist Union Episcopal church was formed after a group of ministers withdrew from the African Methodist Episcopal Church following a dispute over the election of ministerial delegates to the General Conference.

These ministers organized the Reformed Methodist Union church during a four-day meeting beginning on January 22, 1885 at Hills Chapel (now known as Mt. Hermon RMUE church), in Charleston, South Carolina. The Rev. William E. Johnson was elected president of the new church. Following the death of Rev. Johnson in 1896, it was decided that the church would conform to regular American Methodism (the Episcopacy). The first Bishop, Edward Russell Middleton, was elected, and "Episcopal" was added to the name of the church. Bishop Middleton was consecrated on Dec. 5, 1896, by Bishop P. F. Stephens of the Reformed Episcopal Church.

Headquarters
1136 Brody Ave., Charleston, SC 29407

Media Contact, Gen. Secretary, Brother Willie B. Oliver, P.O. Box 1995, Orangeburg, SC 29116, Tel. (803)536-3293

Officers
Bishop, Rt. Rev. Leroy Gethers, Tel. (803)766-3534

Asst. Bishop, Rt. Rev. Jerry M. DeVoe, Jr.

Gen. Sec., Brother Willie B. Oliver

Treas., Rev. Daniel Green

Sec. of Education, Rev. William Polite

Sec. of Books Concerns, Sister Ann Blanding

Sec. of Pension Fund, Rev. Joseph Powell

Sec. of Church Extension, Brother William Parker

Sec. of Sunday School Union, Sister Wine

Sec. of Mission, Rev. Warren Hatcher

Reformed Presbyterian Church of North America

Also known as the Church of the Covenanters, this church's origin dates back to the Reformation days of Scotland when the Covenanters signed their Covenants in resistance to the king and the Roman Church in the enforcement of state church practices. The Church in America has signed two Covenants in particular, those of 1871 and 1954. The Westminster Confession of Faith and the Larger and Shorter Catechism are among the subordinant standards of the denomination.

Headquarters
Media Contact, Stated Clk., James K. McFarland, 7408 Penn Ave., Pittsburgh, PA 15208, Tel. (412)731-1177 Fax (412)731-8861

Email: RPTrustees@aol.com

Website: www.reformedpresbyterian.org

Officers
Mod., Mr. Steven C. McMahan, P. O. Box 805, Clay Center, KS 67432, Tel. (785)632-2177 ext. 232

Clk., J. Bruce Martin, 310 Main St., Ridgefield Park, NJ 07660, Tel. (201)440-5993

Asst. Clk., Raymond E. Morton, 411 N. Vine St., Sparta, IL 62286, Tel. (618)443-3419

Stated Clk., James K. McFarland, 7408 Penn Ave., Pittsburgh, PA 15208, Tel. (412)731-1177

Geneva College, 3200 College Ave, Beaver Falls, PA 15010, Tel. (724)846-5100 Pres., Kenneth A. Smith, Ph.D.

Reformed Presbyterian Theological Seminary, 7418 Penn Ave., Pittsburgh, 15208, Tel. (412)731-8690, Pres., The Rev. Jerry F. O' Neill, D.D.

Reformed Presbyterian Home, 2344 Perrysville Ave., Pittsburgh, PA 15214, Tel. (412)321-4139 Director, Margaret Hemphill

Crown and Covenant Publications, 7408 Penn Ave., Pittsburgh, PA 15208, Tel. (412)241-0436 Drew and Lynne Gordon Managing Editors.

Periodicals
The Witness, The Reformed Presbyterian Witness

Reformed Zion Union Apostolic Church

This group was organized in 1869 at Boydton, VA., by Elder James R. Howell of New York, a minister of the A.M.E. Zion Church, with doctrines of the Methodist Episcopal Church.

Headquarters

Rt. 1, Box 64D, Dundas, VA 23938, Tel. (804)676-8509

Media Contact, Bishop G. W. Studivant

Officers

Exec. Brd., Chair, Rev. Hilman Wright, Tel. (804)447-3988

Sec., Joseph Russell, Tel. (804)634-4520

Religious Society of Friends (Conservative)

These Friends mark their present identity from separations occurring by regions at different times from 1845 to 1904. They hold to a minimum of organizational structure. Their meetings for worship, which are unprogrammed and based on silent, expectant waiting upon the Lord, demonstrate the belief that all individuals may commune directly with God and may share equally in vocal ministry.

They continue to stress the importance of the Living Christ and the experience of the Holy Spirit working with power in the lives of individuals who obey it.

YEARLY MEETINGS

North Carolina YM, Sidney Lee Kitchens, P.O. Box 4591, Greensboro, NC 27404, Tel. (252)587-2571

Iowa YM, Deborah Frisch, Clerk, 3400 King Dian Blvd, Des Moines, Iowa 50311

Ohio YM, Seth Hinshaw, Clerk, 61830 Sandy Ridge Rd., Barnesville, OH 43713

Religious Society of Friends (Unaffiliated Meetings)

Though all groups of Friends acknowledge the same historical roots, 19th-century divisions in theology and experience led to some of the current organizational groupings. Many newer yearly meetings, have chosen not to identify with past divisions by affiliating in traditional ways with the larger organizations within the Society.

Headquarters

Central Yearly Meeting [Friends Evangel] (I), Supt., Michael Williams, P.O. Box 122, Westfield, IN 46074, Tel. (765)857-2347 Fax (765)857-2347, Website: www.centralyearly meetingoffriends.org

Intermountain Yearly Meeting (I), Clerk and Contact: Claire Leonard, Email: imymclerk @hotmail.com, Website: www. imym.org

North Pacific Yearly Meeting (I), Clerk, Helen Dart, Contact Person: Turtle Robb, P.O. Box 5023, Bellingham, WA 98227, Tel. (360)312-8234, Email: secretary@npym.org

Pacific Yearly Meeting (I), Clerk & Contact, Marilee Eusebio, Website: www.pacific yearlymeeting.org Email: margaretf@fwcc americas.org

Officers

Central Yearly Meeting, 150 Members

Intermountain Yearly Meeting, 1,083 Members

North Pacific Yearly Meeting, 850 Members

Pacific Yearly Meeting, 1,453 Members

Periodicals

Western Friend, Friends Evangel

The Roman Catholic Church — please see The Catholic Church under "C"

The Romanian Orthodox Church in America

The Romanian Orthodox Church in America is an autonomous Archdiocese chartered under the name of "Romanian Orthodox Archdiocese in America." The diocese was founded in 1929 and approved by the Holy Synod of the Romanian Orthodox Church in Romania in 1934. The Holy Synod of the Romanian Orthodox Church granted ecclesiastical autonomy in American Diocese on July 12, 1950. The Diocese continues to hold dogmatic and canonical ties with the Holy Synod and the Romanian Orthodox Patriarchate of Romania.

In 1951, approximately 40 parishes with their clergy from the United States and Canada separated from this church. In 1960, they joined the Russian Orthodox Greek Catholic Metropolia, now called the Orthodox Church in America, which reordained for these parishes a bishop with the title "Bishop of Detroit and Michigan."

On June 11, 1973 the Holy Synod of the Romanian Orthodox church elevated the Bishop of Romanian Orthodox Missionary Episcopate in America to the rank of Archbishop.

Headquarters

5410 N. Newland Ave. Chicago IL 60656, Tel. (773)774-1677 Fax (773)774-1805

Media Contact, Archdiocesan Secretary, V. Rev. Fr. Daniel Adrian Ene, 56 Andrews St., Victor, NY 14564-1262 Tel/Fax: 585-924-8737, Email: frdaniel@romanianholytrinity.org

Email: ArchNicolae@aol.com; romarch67@ aol.com

Website: www.romarch.org

Officers

Archbishop: His Eminence Dr. Nicolae Condrea, 5410 N. Newland Ave. Chicago IL 60656, Tel. (773)774-1677 Fax (773)774-1805; Email: romarch67@aol.com

Vicar: V. Rev. Fr. Nicholas Apostola, 44 Midland St., Worcester, MA 01602-4217, Tel.

(508)845-0088 Fax (508)845-8850, Email: frnick@stnicholaschurch.org
Inter-Church Relations, Dir., V. Rev. Fr. Nicholas Apostola, 44 Midland St., Worcester, MA 01602-4217, Tel. (508)845-0088; Fax (508)845-8850, Email: frnick@stnicholas church.org

Periodicals
Credinta-The Faith

The Romanian Orthodox Episcopate of America
This body of Eastern Orthodox Christians of Romanian descent is part of the Autocephalous Orthodox Church in America.

Headquarters
2535 Grey Tower Rd., Jackson, MI 49201, Tel. (517)522-4800, Website: www.roea.org
Mailing Address, P.O. Box 309, Grass Lake, MI 49240-0309
Media Contact, Ed. -Sec., Rev. Archdeacon David Oancea, P.O. Box 185, Grass Lake, MI 49240-0185, Tel. (517)522-3656
Email: chancery@roea.org
Website: www.roea.org

Officers
Ruling Hierarch, Most Rev. Archbishop Nathaniel Popp
P.O. Box 309, Grass Lake, MI 49240-0309

Periodicals
Solia-The Herald, Good News-Buna Vestire (in Canada only)

The Russian Orthodox Church Outside of Russia
This group was organized in 1920 to unite in one body of dioceses the missions and parishes of the Russian Orthodox Church outside of Russia. The governing body, set up in Constantinople, was sponsored by the Ecumenical Patriarchate. In November 1950, it came to the United States. The Russian Orthodox Church Outside of Russia emphasizes being true to the old traditions of the Russian Church. In May 2007, it re-established communion with the Moscow Patriarchate.

Headquarters
75 E. 93rd St., New York, NY 10128, Tel. (212)534-1601 Fax (212)426-1086
Media Contact, Dep. Sec., Nicholas A. Ohotin, Tel. (212)534-1610 x 37
Email: nohotin@synod.com

SYNOD OF BISHOPS
Pres., His Eminence Metropolitan Hilarion
Vice Pres., His Eminence Archbishop Kyrill, Tel. (212)534-1601

Periodicals
Living Orthodoxy, Orthodox Family, Orthodox Russia, Pravoslavnaya Rus, Pravoslavnaya Zhisn, Orthodox America

The Salvation Army
The Salvation Army, founded in 1865 by William Booth (1829-1912) in London, England, and introduced into America in 1880, is an international religious and charitable movement organized and operated on a paramilitary pattern and is a branch of the Christian church. To carry out its purposes, The Salvation Army has established a widely diversified program of religious and social welfare services which are designed to meet the needs of children, youth and adults in all age groups.

Headquarters
615 Slaters Ln., Alexandria, VA 22313, Tel. (703)684-5500 Fax (703)684-5538
Media Contact: National Community Rel. & Dev. Secretary, Major George Hood, Tel. (703)684-5526 Fax (703)684-5538 Email: george_hood@usn.salvationarmy.org
Email: george_hood@usn.salvationarmy.org
Website: www.salvationarmyusa.org

Officers
Natl. Commander, Commissioner William A. Roberts
Natl. Chief Sec., Colonel William Harfoot
Natl. Community Relations and Develepment Secretary, Dir., Major George Hood

TERRITORIAL ORGANIZATIONS
Central Territory, 10 W. Algonquin Rd., Des Plaines, IL 60016, Tel. (847)294-2000 Fax (847)294-2299; Territorial Commander, Commissioner Paul Seiler
Eastern Territory, 440 W. Nyack Rd., P.O. Box C-635, West Nyack, NY 10994, Tel. (914)620-7200 Fax (914)620-7766; Territorial Commander, Commissioner Steve Hedgren
Southern Territory, 1424 Northeast Expressway, Atlanta, GA 30329, Tel. (404)728-1300 Fax (404)728-1331; Territorial Commander, Commissioner David Jeffrey
Western Territory, 180 E. Ocean Blvd., Long Beach, CA, Tel. (562)436-7000 Fax (562)491-8792; Territorial Commander, Commissioner James Knaggs

Periodicals
The War Cry

The Schwenkfelder Church
The Schwenkfelders are the spiritual descendants of the Silesian nobleman Caspar Schwenkfeld von Ossig (1489-1561), a scholar, reformer, preacher and prolific writer who endeavored to aid in the cause of the Protestant Reformation. A contemporary of Martin Luther, John Calvin, Ulrich Zwingli and Phillip Melanchthon, Schwenkfeld sought no following, formulated no creed and did not attempt to organize a church based on his beliefs. He labored for liberty of religious belief, for a fellowship of all believers and for one united Christian church.

159

He and his cobelievers supported a movement known as the Reformation by the Middle Way. Persecuted by state churches, ultimately 217 Schwenkfelders exiled from Silesia emigrated to Pennsylvania in six migrations, 1731 -1734. The largest migration, about 180 landed at Philadelphia Sept. 22, 1734. In 1782, the Society of Schwenkfelders, the forerunner of the present Schwenkfelder Church, was formed. The church was incorporated in 1909.

The Schwenkfelder Church is a voluntary association of six Schwenkfelder Churches at Palm, Worcester, Lansdale, Norristown and two in Philadelphia, Pennsylvania. They practice adult baptism, dedication and baptism of children, and observe the Lord's Supper regularly with open Communion. In theology, they are Christo-centric; in polity, congregational; in missions, world-minded; in ecclesiastical organization, ecumenical.

The ministry is recruited from graduates of accredited theological seminaries. The churches take leadership in ecumenical concerns through ministerial associations, community service and action groups, councils of Christian education and other agencies.

Headquarters
105 Seminary St., Pennsburg, PA 18073, Tel. (215)679-3103
Media Contact, David W. Luz
Email: info@schwenkfelder.com

Officers
Mod., H. Drake Williams, Jr., Paoli, PA
Vice Mod., Darlene Jones, Green Lane, PA
Sec., Leah Tyson, Norristown, PA
Treas., Pat McGinnis, Central Schwenkfelder Church, Worcester, PA 19490

Periodicals
The Schwenkfeldian

Separate Baptists in Christ
The Separate Baptists in Christ are a group of Baptists found in Indiana, Ohio, Kentucky, Tennessee, Virginia, West Virginia, Florida and North Carolina dating back to an association formed in 1758 in North Carolina and Virginia.

Today this group consists of approximately 100 churches. They believe in the infallibility of the Bible, the divine ordinances of the Lord's Supper, feetwashing, baptism and that those who endureth to the end shall be saved. The Separate Baptists are Arminian in doctrine, rejecting both the doctrines of predestination and eternal security of the believer.

At the 1991 General Association, an additional article of doctrine was adopted. "We believe that at Christ's return in the clouds of heaven all Christians will meet the Lord in the air, and time shall be no more," thus leaving no time for a literal one thousand year reign. Seven

associations comprise the General Association of Separate Baptists.

Headquarters
Media Contact, Clk., Greg Erdman, 10102 N. Hickory Ln., Columbus, IN 47203, Tel. (812)526-2540
Email: mail@separatebaptist.org
Website: www.separatebaptist.org

Officers
Mod., Rev. Jim Goff, 1020 Gagel Ave., Louisville, KY 40216
Asst. Mod., Rev. Jimmy Polston, 785 Kitchen Rd., Mooresville, IN 46158, Tel. (317)831-6745
Clk., Greg Erdman, 10102 N. Hickory Ln., Columbus, IN 47203, Tel. (812)526-2540
Asst. Clk., Rev. Mattew Cowan, 174 Oak Hill School Rd., Lot 30, Smiths Grove, KY 42171, Tel. (270)678-5599

Serbian Orthodox Church in the U.S.A. and Canada*
The Serbian Orthodox Church is an organic part of the Christian Orthodox Church. As a local church it received its autocephaly from Constantinople in 1219 A.D. In 1921, a Serbian Orthodox Diocese in the United States of America and Canada was organized. In 1963, it was reorganized into three dioceses, and in 1983 a fourth diocese was created for the Canadian part of the church. The Serbian Orthodox Church in the USA and Canada received its administrative autonomy in 1928. However, it remains canonically an integral part of the Serbian Orthodox Patriarchate with its see in Belgrade. The Serbian Orthodox Church is in absolute doctrinal unity with all other local Orthodox Churches.

Headquarters
St. Sava Monastery, P.O. Box 519, Libertyville, IL 60048, Tel. (847)367-0698
Email: oea@oea.serbian-church.net
Website: www.serborth.org/midwestdiocese.html

BISHOPS
Metropolitan of Midwestern America, Most Rev. Metropolitan Christopher
Bishop of Canada, Georgije, 5A Stockbridge Ave., Toronto, ON M8Z 4M6, Tel. (416)231-4009
Bishop of Eastern America, Rt. Rev. Bishop Mitrophan, 138 Carriage Hill Dr., Mars, PA 16046, Tel. (724)772-8866
Diocese of Western America, Bishop Maxim, 2541 Crestline Terr., Alhambra, CA 91803, Tel. (818)264-6825

OTHER ORGANIZATIONS
Brotherhood of Serbian Orth. Clergy in U.S.A. & Canada, Pres., V. Rev. Dennis Pavichevich
Federation of Circles of Serbian Sisters
Serbian Singing Federation

Seventh-day Adventist Church

The Seventh-day Adventist Church grew out of a worldwide religious revival in the mid-19th century. People of many religious persuasions believed Bible prophecies indicated that the second coming or advent of Christ was imminent.

When Christ did not come in the 1840s, a group of these disappointed Adventists in the United States continued their Bible studies and concluded they had misinterpreted prophetic events and that the second coming of Christ was still in the future. This same group of Adventists later accepted the teaching of the seventh-day Sabbath and became known as Seventh-day Adventists. The denomination organized formally in 1863. The church was largely confined to North America until 1874, when its first missionary was sent to Europe. Today, over 70,000 congregations meet in 206 countries and areas of the world. Membership exceeds 17 million.

In addition to a mission program, the church has the largest worldwide Protestant parochial school system with approximately 7,802 schools with more than 1,680,000 students on elementary through college and university levels.

The Adventist Development and Relief Agency (ADRA) helps victims of war and natural disasters, and many local congregations have community service facilities to help those in need close to home.

The church also has a worldwide publishing ministry with 63 printing facilities producing magazines and other publications in over 370 languages and dialects. In the United States and Canada, the church sponsors a variety of radio and television programs, including *Christian Lifestyle* Magazine, *It Is Written, Breath of Life, Ayer, Hoy y Mañana, Voice of Prophecy*, and *La Voz de la Esperanza.*

The North American Division of Seventh-day Adventist includes 58 Conferences which are grouped together into nine organized Union Conferences. The various Conferences work under the general direction of these Union Conferences.

Headquarters

12501 Old Columbia Pike, Silver Spring, MD 20904-6600, Tel. (301)680-6000
Media Contact, Dir., Communication, Williams S. Costa, Jr.
Email: JonesK@gc.adventist.org
Website: www.adventist.org

WORLD-WIDE OFFICERS

Pres.,Ted N. C. Wilson
Sec., G. T. Ng
Treas., Robert E. Lemon

WORLD-WIDE DEPARTMENTS

Adventist Chaplaincy Ministries, Dir., Gary R Councell
Children's Ministries, Dir., Linda Mei Lin Koh
Education, Dir., Lisa M. Beardsley
Communication, Dir., Williams S. Costa, Jr.
Family Ministries, Dir., Willie Oliver
Health Ministries, Dir., Allan R. Handysides
Ministerial Assoc., Dir., Jerry N. Page
Public Affairs and Religious Liberty, Dir., John Graz
Publishing Ministries, Dir., Howard F Faigao
Sabbath School and Personal Ministries, Jonathan Kuntaraf
Stewardship Ministries, Dir., Erika F. Puni
Planned Giving and Trust Services, Gary W. Dodge
Women's Ministries, Heather-Dawn Small
Youth Ministries, Gilbert R. Cangy

NORTH AMERICAN OFFICERS

Pres., Daniel R. Jackson
Vice Pres., Larry D. Blackmer; Paul S. Brantley; Debra C. Brill; Alvin M. Kibble; R. Ernest Castillo
Sec., G. Alexander Bryant
Treas., G. Thomas Evans
Assoc. Treas., C. Michael Park; Delbert L. Johnson; Michael R. Jamieson, Patricia L. Horst

NORTH AMERICAN ORGANIZATIONS

Atlantic Union Conf., P.O. Box 1189, South Lancaster, MA 01561-1189; Pres., Donald G. King
Canada, Seventh-day Adventist Church in Canada (see Ch. 4)
Columbia Union Conf., 5427 Twin Knolls Rd., Columbia, MD 21045; Pres., Dave Weigley
Lake Union Conf., P.O. Box 287, Berrien Springs, MI 49103; Pres., Don Livesay
Mid-America Union Conf., P.O. Box 6128, Lincoln, NE 68506; Pres., Thomas L. Lemon
North Pacific Union Conf., Pres., 5709 N 20th St., Ridgefield, WA 98642-7742; Pres., Max C Torkelsen II
Pacific Union Conf., P.O. Box 5005, Westlake Village, CA 91359; Pres., Ricardo B. Graham
Southern Union Conf., P.O. Box 849, Decatur, GA 30031; Pres., Gordon L. Retzer
Southwestern Union Conf., P.O. Box 4000, Burleson, TX 76097; Pres., Larry R. Moore

Periodicals

ADRA Works, The Adventist Chaplain, Adventist Review, ASI Magazine, CQ, Children's Friend, Christian Record, College and University Dialogue, Collegiate Quarterly, Cornerstone Youth Resource Magazine, Cornerstone Connections, Elder's Digest, Encounter, For God and Country, Geoscience Newsletter, Evangelist, Message, Ministry, Mission Post, Origins, Our Little Friend, Primary Treasure, Publishing Mirror, Shabbat Shalom, Shepherdess International Journal, Signs of the Times, Transmis-

sions, *Vibrant Life, Voice of Prophecy News, Winner, Women of Spirit, Young and Alive, Youth Ministry ACCENT*

Seventh Day Baptist General Conference, USA and Canada

Seventh Day Baptists emerged during the English Reformation, organizing their first churches in the mid-1600s. The first Seventh Day Baptists of record in America were Stephen and Ann Mumford, who emigrated from England in 1664. Beginning in 1665 several members of the First Baptist Church at Newport, R.I. began observing the seventh day Sabbath, or Saturday. In 1671, five members, together with the Mumfords, formed the first Seventh Day Baptist Church in America at Newport.

Beginning about 1700, other Seventh Day Baptist churches were established in New Jersey and Pennsylvania. From these three centers, the denomination grew and expanded westward. They founded the Seventh Day Baptist General Conference in 1802. The organization of the denomination reflects an interest in home and foreign missions, publications and education. Women have been encouraged to participate. From the earliest years religious freedom has been championed for all and the separation of church and state, advocated.

Seventh Day Baptists are members of the Baptist World Alliance and Baptist Joint Committee. The Seventh Day Baptist World Federation has 17 member conferences on six continents.

Headquarters

Seventh Day Baptist Center, 3120 Kennedy Rd., P.O. Box 1678, Janesville, WI 53547-1678, Tel. (608)752-5055 Fax (608)752-7711 Media Contact, Ex. Dir., Robert Appel
Financial Dir., Morgan D. Shepard
Email: sdbgen@inwave.com; robappel@seventh daybaptist.org
Website: www.seventhdaybaptist.org

OTHER ORGANIZATIONS

Seventh Day Baptist Missionary Society, Exec. Dir., Clint Brown, 19 Hillside Ave., Ashaway, RI 02804
Seventh Day Bapt. Bd. of Christian Ed., Exec. Dir., Rev. Andrew Camenga, Box 115, Alfred Station, NY 14803
Women's Soc. of the Gen. Conference, Pres., Mrs. Althea Rood, P.O. Box 122, Dodge Center, MN 55927
American Sabbath Tract & Comm. Council, Dir. of Communications, Rev. Kevin J. Butler, 3120 Kennedy Rd., P.O. Box 1678, Janesville, WI 53547
Seventh Day Baptist Historical Society, Historian, Nicholas Kersten, 3120 Kennedy Rd., P.O. Box 1678, Janesville, WI 53547

Seventh Day Baptist Center on Ministry, Dir. of Pastoral Services, Rev. Gordon Lawton, 3120 Kennedy Rd., P.O. Box 1678, Janesville, WI 53547

Periodicals

Sabbath Recorder

Southern Baptist Convention

The Southern Baptist Convention was organized on May 10, 1845, in Augusta, Georgia. Cooperating Baptist churches are located in all 50 states, the District of Columbia, Puerto Rico, American Samoa and the Virgin Islands. The members of the churches work together through 1,175 district associations and 42 state conventions or fellowships. The Southern Baptist Convention has an Executive Committee and 12 national entities -four boards, six seminaries, one commission, and one auxiliary organization.

The purpose of the Southern Baptist Convention is "to provide a general organization for Baptists in the United States and its territories for the promotion of Christian missions at home and abroad and any other objects such as Christian education, benevolent enterprises, and social services which it may deem proper and advisable for the furtherance of the Kingdom of God" (Constitution, Article II). The Convention exists in order to help the churches lead people to God through Jesus Christ.

From the beginning, there has been a mission desire to share the Gospel with the peoples of the world. The Cooperative Program is the basic channel of mission support. In addition, the Lottie Moon Christmas Offering for Foreign Missions and the Annie Armstrong Easter Offering for Home Missions support Southern Baptists' world mission programs.

In 2010, there were 5,031 foreign missionaries serving in foreign countries and 5,096 home missionaries serving in North America.

Headquarters

901 Commerce St., Nashville, TN 37203, Tel. (615)244-2355
Media Contact, Vice Pres. for Convention Communications, and Relations, Roger S. Oldham, Tel. (615)244-2355 Fax (615)782-8684
Email: soldham@sbc.net
Website: www.sbc.net

Officers

Pres., Bryant Wright, 955 Johnson Ferry Rd., Marietta, GA 30068
Recording Sec., John Yeats, 1250 MacArthur Dr., Alexandria, LA 71303
Executive Committee, Pres., Frank S. Page; Exec. Vice Pres., Convention Policy, Augie Boto; Vice Pres., Convention Communications and Relations, Roger S. Oldham; Vice Pres., Convention Finance, Bill Townes

GENERAL BOARDS AND COMMISSION
International Mission Board, Acting Interim Pres., Thomas D. Elliff, 3806 Monument Ave, Richmond, VA 23230, Tel. (804)353-6655
North American Mission Board, Pres., Kevin Ezell, 4200 No. Point Pkwy., Alpharetta, GA 30022-4176, Tel. (770)410-6519
Guidestone Financial Resources, Pres., O. S. Hawkins, 2401 Cedar Springs Rd, Dallas, TX 75201, Tel. (214)720-4700
LifeWay Christian Resources, Pres., Thom Rainer, One Lifeway Plaza, Nashville, TN 37234, Tel. (615)251-2605
Ethics and Religious Liberty Commission, Pres., Richard D. Land, 901 Commerce St., Suite 550, Nashville, TN 37203, Tel. (615)782-8404

STATE CONVENTIONS
Alabama, Rick Lance, 2001 E. South Blvd., Montgomery, AL 36116, Tel. (334)288-2460
Alaska, Mike Procter, 1750 O'Malley Rd., Anchorage, AK 99507, Tel. (907)344-7044
Arizona, State Executive Director, 2240 N. Hayden Rd., Ste. 100, Scottsdale, AZ 85257, Tel. (480)945-0880
Arkansas, Emil Turner, 10 Remington Dr., Little Rock, AR 72204, Tel. (501)376-4791
California, Fermin A. Whittaker, 678 E. Shaw Ave., Fresno, CA 93710, Tel. (559)229-9533 x 230
Colorado, Mark Edlund, 7393 So. Alton Way, Centennial, CO 80112, Tel. (303)771-2480
Dakota Baptist Convention, Garvon Golden, Interim, 503 N. Weber Ave., Sioux Falls, SD 57103, Tel. (605)271-9224
District of Columbia, Ricky O. Creech, 1628 Sixteenth St. NW, Washington, DC 20009, Tel. (202)265-1526
Florida, John Sullivan, 1230 Hendricks Ave., Jacksonville, FL 32207, Tel. (904)396-2351 x 8101
Georgia, J. Robert White, 6405 Sugarloaf Pkwy., Duluth, GA 30097, Tel. (770)455-0404
Hawaii, Veryl F. Henderson, 2042 Vancouver Dr., Honolulu, HI 96822, Tel. (808)946-9581 x 229
Illinois, Nate Adams, 3085 Stevenson Dr, Springfield, IL 62794, Tel. (217)786-2600
Indiana, Cecil Seagle, Interim, 900 N. High School Rd., Indianapolis, IN 46214, Tel. (317)241-9317
Iowa, Jimmy Barrentine, 2400 86th St., Suite #27, Des Moines, IA 50322, Tel. (515)278-4369
Kansas-Nebraska, Bob Mills, 5410 W. Seventh St., Topeka, KS 66606, Tel. (785)228-6800
Kentucky, Paul Chitwood, 13420 Eastpoint Centre Dr., Louisville, KY 40223, Tel. (502)245-4101
Louisiana, David E. Hankins, 1250 MacArthur Dr., Alexandria, LA 71303, Tel. (318)448-3402
Maryland-Delaware, David H. Lee, 10255 Old Columbia Rd., Columbia, MD 21046, Tel. (410)290-5290

Michigan, Bobby Gilstrap, 8420 Runyan Lake Rd., Fenton, MI 48430, Tel. (810)714-1907
Minnesota-Wisconsin, Leo Endel, 519 16th St. SE, Rochester, MN 55904, Tel. (507)282-3636
Mississippi, James R. Futral, 515 Mississippi St., Jackson, MS 39201, Tel. (601)968-3800
Missouri, Jay Huges, Interim, 400 E. High St., Jefferson City, MO 65101, Tel. (573)636-0400
Montana, Fred Hewett, 1130 Cerise Rd., Billings, MT 59101, Tel. (406)252-7537
Nevada, Terry Arnold, Interim, 406 California Ave., Reno, NV 89509, Tel. (775)786-0406
New England, James Wideman, 87 Lincoln St., Northborough, MA 01532, Tel. (508)393-6013 x 224
New Mexico, Joseph L. Bunce, P.O. Box 94485, Albuquerque, NM 87199, Tel. (505)924-2300 x 11
New York, Terry M. Robertson, 6538 Baptist Way, East Syracuse, NY 13057, Tel. (315)433-1001
North Carolina, Milton A. Hollifield Jr., 205 Convention Dr., Cary, NC 27511, Tel. (919)467-5100 x 102
Northwest, Bill Crews, 3200 NE 109th Ave., Vancouver, WA 98682, Tel. (360)882-2100
Ohio, Jack P. Kwok, 9000 Antares Ave, Columbus, OH 43240, Tel. (614)258-8491
Oklahoma, Anthony L. Jordan, 3800 N. May Ave., Oklahoma City, OK 73112, Tel. (405)942-3800
Pennsylvania-South Jersey, David C. Waltz, 4620 Fritchey St., Harrisburg, PA 17109, Tel. (717)652-5856
Puerto Rico/Virgin Islands, Carlos Rodriguez, URB Crown HLS, 138 W. Churchhill PMB 811, San Juan, PR 00926-6013, Tel. (787)731-5010
South Carolina, James W. Austin, 190 Stoneridge Dr., Columbia, SC 29210, Tel. (803)765-0030
Tennessee, Randy Davis, 5001 Maryland Way, Brentwood, TN 37027, Tel. (615)373-2255
Texas, (BGCT) Baptist General Convention of Texas, Steve Vernon, Interim, 333 N. Washington, Dallas, TX 75246, Tel. (214)828-5100
Texas, (SBTC) Southern Baptists of Texas, James W. Richards, 4500 State Hwy. 360, Grapevine, TX 76051, Tel. (817)552-2500
Utah-Idaho, Rob Lee, 12401 South 450 East #G-1, Draper, UT 84020, Tel. (801)572-5350
Virginia, (BGAV) Baptist General Association of Virginia, John V. Upton Jr., 2828 Emerywood Pkwy, Richmond, VA 23226, Tel. (804)915-5000
Virginia, (SBCV) Southern Baptist Conservatives of Virginia, Doyle Chauncey, Interim, 4101 Cox Rd., Suite 100, Glen Allen, VA 23060, Tel. (804)270-1848
West Virginia, Terry L. Harper, One Mission Way, Scott Depot, WV 25560, Tel. (304)757-0944
Wyoming, Lynn Nikkel, 3925 Casper Mountain Rd., Casper, WY 82601, Tel. (307)472-4087

Periodicals
The Commission, SBC Life, On Mission

Southern Methodist Church

Organized in 1939, this body is composed of congregations desirous of continuing in true Biblical Methodism and preserving the fundamental doctrines and beliefs of the Methodist Episcopal Church, South. These congregations declined to be a party to the merger of the Methodist Episcopal Church, The Methodist Episcopal Church, South and the Methodist Protestant Church into The Methodist Church.

Headquarters

425 Broughton St., Orangeburg, SC 29115, Tel. (803)536-1378 Fax (803)535-3881
Media Contact, Pres., Rev. John T. Hucks, Jr.
Email: smpresid@bellsouth.net; smchq@juno.com

Officers

Pres., Rev. John T. Hucks, Jr.
Dir. Of Admin. & Finance, Rev. Cecil Clark, 425 Broughton St., Orangeburg, SC 29115
Director of Foreign Missions, Rev. Marvin Clark, 425 Broughton St., Orangeburg, SC 29115
Southern Methodist College Pres., Rev. Gary Briden, P.O. Box 1027, Orangeburg, SC 29116-1027

Periodicals
The Southern Methodist

Sovereign Grace Believers

The Sovereign Grace Believers are a contemporary movement which began its stirrings in the mid-1950s when some pastors in traditional Baptist churches returned to a Calvinist-theological perspective.

The first "Sovereign Grace" conference was held in Ashland, Kentucky, in 1954 and since then, conferences of this sort have been sponsored by various local churches on the West Coast, Southern and Northern states and Canada. This movement is a spontaneous phenomenon concerning reformation at the local church level. Consequently, there is no interest in establishing a Sovereign Grace Baptist "Convention" or "Denomination." Each local church is to administer the keys to the kingdom.

Most Sovereign Grace Believers formally or informally relate to the "First London" (1646), "Second London" (1689) or "Philadelphia" (1742) Confessions.

There is a wide variety of local church government in this movement. Many Calvinist Baptists have a plurality of elders in each assembly. Other Sovereign Grace Believers, however, prefer to function with one pastor and several deacons.

Membership procedures vary from church to church but all require a credible profession of faith in Christ, and proper baptism as a basis for membership. Calvinistic Baptists financially support gospel efforts (missionaries, pastors of small churches at home and abroad, literature publication and distribution, radio programs, etc.) in various parts of the world.

Headquarters

Media Contact, Corres., Jon Zens, P.O. Box 548, St. Croix Falls, WI 54024, Tel. (651)465-6516 Fax (651)465-5101
Email: jon@searchingtogether.org
Website: www.searchingtogether.org

Periodicals
Searching Together, Sound of Grace

The Swedenborgian Church*

Founded in North America in 1792 as the Church of the New Jerusalem, the Swedenborgian Church was organized as a national body in 1817 and incorporated in Illinois in 1861. Its biblically-based theology is derived from the spiritual, or mystical, experiences and exhaustive biblical studies of the Swedish scientist and philosopher Emanuel Swedenborg (1688-1772).

The church centers its worship and teachings on the historical life and the risen and glorified present reality of the Lord Jesus Christ. It looks with an ecumenical vision toward the establishment of the kingdom of God in the form of a universal Church, active in the lives of all people of good will who desire and strive for freedom, peace and justice for all. It is a member of the NCCC and active in many local councils of churches.

With churches and groups throughout the United States and Canada, the denomination's central administrative offices and its seminary, "Swedenborg House of Studies" are located in Newton, Massachusetts and Berkeley, California. Affiliated churches are found in Africa, Asia, Australia, Canada, Europe, the United Kingdom, Japan, South Korea and South America. Many philosophers and writers have acknowledged their appreciation of Swedenborg's teachings.

Headquarters

11 Highland Ave., Newtonville, MA 02460, Tel. (617)969-4240 Fax (617)964-3258
Media Contact, Operations. Mgr., Renee Hellenbrecht
Email: manager@swedenborg.org
Website: www.swedenborg.org

Officers

Pres., Rev. Kenneth O. Turley, P. O. Box 594, Bridgton, ME 04009-0594, Tel. (603)986-3609, Email: revken@swedenborg.org
Vice Pres., Betsy Coffman, 3156 Adell Dr., Urbana, OH 43078-9732-5054, Tel. (937)653-5054; Email: bcoffman@woh.rr.com
Rec. Sec., Rev. Susannah Currie, 54 Wannisett Ave., Riverside, RI 02915-2939, Tel. (401) 369-7732, Email: secretary@swedenborg.org

Treas., Polly Baxter, 305 Prospect Hill, 24-C, Frederiksted, VI 00840-3652, Tel. (340)227-6069, Email: treasure@swedenborg.org
Operation Mgr., Renee Hellenbrecht, 11 Highland Ave., Newtonville, MA 02460, Tel. (617)969-4240, Email: manager@swedenborg.org

Periodicals
The Messenger, Our Daily Bread

Syriac-Greek Antiochian Orthodox Catholic Church

The Syriac-Greek Antiochian Orthodox Catholic Church was established in May of 1892 as the American Orthodox Catholic Archdiocese of America, and was canonized by His Holiness Ignatius Peter III, Patriarch of Antioch. It was this same Patriarch that issued the Bull for the consecration of its first Archbishop Metropolitan, Timotheos Vilathi, as Patriarch Ignatius later named him. The Syriac-Greek Antiochian Orthodox Catholic Church is an Eastern Rite jurisdiction but its Liturgy of St Gregory is one of the Byzantinized forms. It has elements from both the Byzantine and Occidental traditions. In August of 2008 the Synod of Bishops voted unanimously to return to the original mandate of the Archdiocese – to be an American Orthodox Archdiocese using a Western Liturgy. Since 1892, the Liturgy went through some changes from time-to-time, i.e., Western Rite to Byzantine Rite, to the current Syriac-Greek Antiochene Rite. The current Liturgy used is in English or the vernacular except for a few hymns and chants in Greek. The Liturgy is a successful blend of East and West. However, the faith taught by the Church is one with the One, Holy, Catholic and Apostolic Church of Orthodox Faith. The Synod of Bishops is referred to as the "Syriac-Greek Antiochian Synod of Bishops." First parishes of this jurisdiction were established in Wisconsin among Belgians, Italians, Slavs, and other ethnic groups. After Archbishop Timotheos' consecration, parishes were later formed in Ohio, Indiana, Illinois, and New York, and some missionary work begun in Canada. Today parishes exist throughout the United States and several foreign countries.

After much disagreement with the Syriac Patriarchate concerning administration, especially in the appointing of bishops, and the Christology issue, i.e., Christ's two Natures that surfaced at the Council of Chalcedon, Archbishop Timotheos separated from the Patriarchate. A Consistory was convened on January 1, 1910 concerning the future of the Archdiocese of America. The Bishops agreed upon and decided that, "Our reality as a branch, a part of the true Catholic and Orthodox Church of God, is not dependent upon the recognition of any ecclesiastical authority outside the Councils of our own American Ecclesiastical Consistory and National Synod of Bishops and Clergy." Archbishop Timotheos believed strongly in the truths of the Council of Chalcedon and all the Ecumenical Councils, and the right of the American Church to name its own bishops, and from then on the Church was known as Autocephalous and severed from the Patriarchate of Antioch. However, after this time several schisms occurred that gave way to some heretical and newly established "churches" that caused the Church to eventually be renamed "Syriac-Greek Antiochian Orthodox Catholic." In 1960, the Greek Apostolic Succession of Antioch was added to the Church when Bishop Joseph John Skureth was elevated to Archbishop. This was done at St Nicholas Russian Orthodox Greek Catholic Cathedral in New York New York. It was presided over by Archbishop Konstantin (Nikolaevich Wendland) and assisted by Bishop Dositheus (Ivanchenko). His Holiness Patriarch Aleksij of the Russian Orthodox Church, consecrated Archbishop Konstantin in 1958. Although this was done through the Russian Orthodox Church, the Apostolic Succession of Archbishop Konstantin is traced back to His Holiness Gregorios (Haddad) IV, Greek Patriarch of Antioch through Patriarch Aleksij.

In 1980, after the retirement for health reasons of Archbishop John, Archbishop Joseph of Blessed Memory became the newly enthroned Metropolitan Primate of the Church. He possessed Apostolic Succession from both the Syrian and Greek Antiochian Orthodox Churches later giving the Synod the name Syriac-Greek Antiochian Orthodox Catholic Church. In 1987, before the death of Metropolitan Joseph, a meeting was held at St. Paul's Monastery in LaPorte, Indiana and Very Right Reverend Archimandrite Stephen (Thomas) was canonically and duly elected the new Metropolitan Primate. He was consecrated Bishop on October 18th, 1987, by Metropolitan Joseph assisted by Archbishop George of Chicago (IL) and Bishop Norman of Central Indiana at St. Mary's Chapel, LaPorte, Indiana. In the following year Bishop Stephen was enthroned as V Metropolitan Primate. Metropolitan Archbishop Stephen has caused the Church to grow throughout the world. In 1994-96, he endured many sufferings in Colorado as the result of some clergy who went astray and who took part in a conspiracy to ruin the name of the Archbishop and the Church for their own gain. These clergy were since deposed from their faculties and offices. An Old Catholic group in Canada quickly made some of the deposed men, which were not yet ordained deacons or priests, instant priests. Some of these, within days, were made bishops, and most left this Old Catholic group to create their own groups. Since that time, the Church has experienced peace, growth, and new viability except in 2010 some other deposed clergy once again tried to damage the good image of the Church using an attentive reporter to join in their smear tactics.

There are two monastic orders, The Community of Saint Basil, which is open to men, and the Sisters of St Basil which is open to women, and both are currently headquartered in Canfield Ohio. The Metropolis and Chancery Center is located in Canfield Ohio at St Sophia Moanstery Inn. The Church has 1 monastery and 4 convents: St Sophia Moanstery, Canfield Ohio; St Mary Mother of God Convent, Democratic Republic of the Congo in Africa; Holy Archangels Convent, Democratic Republic of the Congo in Africa; St Anne Convent, Lagos Nigeria; and St Barbara Convent, London England. At the Synod of Bishops meeting in 2008, it was decided to amend the name of the Church from Syro-Russian Orthodox Catholic Church to Syriac-Greek Antiochian Orthodox Catholic Church. This was done to better describe the Church and the sources of its Apostolic Succession, i.e., the Syriac and Greek Patriarchates of Antioch. The original source comes from the Syriac Orthodox Patriarchate of Antioch. The Synod of Bishops currently consists of His Beatitude Metropolitan Stephen, His Eminence Archbishop Timothy, His Grace Bishop John (India), His Grace Bishop Joshua (North Carolina), Bishop-elect Samson (Tanzania), and Right Reverend Chorbishop Haralambos (Alaska). His Grace Bishop Andreas, who has been separated from the Metropolis for over five years has petitioned to be accepted back into the canonicity of the Church. Missions and parishes exist in Canada, Cuba, Democratic Republic of the (African) Congo, Cameroon, India, Kenya Africa, Nigeria Africa, Pakistan, Tanzania Africa, Uganda Africa, Zimbabwe, and the United States.

Headquarters

Metropolis and Chancery, 7815 Akron Canfield Rd., Canfield OH 44406; 330.533.4048; 216.543.6377
Primate: Metropolitan Stephen
Coadjutor: Archbishop Timothy of Cleveland
Email: rbsocc@juno.com
Website: www.rbsocc.org

Officers

His Beatitude Metropolitan Archbishop Stephen, Primate, 7815 Akron Canfield Rd., Canfield OH 44406 Email: rbsocc@juno.com .
His Eminence Archbishop Timothy, Archdiocese of the Americas & Dependencies; 7815 Akron Canfield Rd., Canfield OH 44406 Tel. (216)543.6377
V.R. Father Patrick Lemming, Archdiocesan Chaplain, St James the Apostle House & Chapel, 304 Grace Ave., Sevierville TN 37862, Tel. (865)429-3641.

His Grace Bishop Joshua, Eastern Vicariate, Salem-Winston North Carolina
Changes made in the following:
Father Stephen Lawrence DDS JCD, Metropolis Judicial Vicar -Carlsbad CA
Father Demetrios E Wruck DC, Senior Advisor to Metropolitan -Maui Hawaii
Father Padraig Kneafsey, Archdiocesan Advisor - County Mayo Ireland

SYNODAL COUNCIL ADVISORS:
VR Father Paul Jensen, Honorary -Texas
Dr Peter Smyth, Honorary -Ontario Canada
Father Stephen Lawrence -California
Dr Andrew Gill -Texas
Dr Audrey Daniel -South Carolina
Dr Hamptom Bumgarner -New Jersy
Dr Janet Maus -Maryland
Dr Sandra Dobiash -Colorado
Christ the Pantocrator Sovereign Order of Chivalry; Father Demetrios E Wruck DC, Protector of Chivalric Orders of the Metropolia.
Commission on Religious Counseling and Healing; Father Stephen Lawrence, DDS DCh, President, Dr. Peter Smyth (Canadian Liaison).
Community of St Basil and Sisters of the Community of St Basil; and Sisters of St Basil, Mother Helena (Abbess, St Mary Mother of God Convent, Democratic Republic of the Congo, Africa).

Periodicals

Orthodox Christian Herald; Sophia Newsletter

Syrian (Syriac) Orthodox Church of Antioch*

The Syrian Orthodox Church of Antioch traces its origin to the Patriarchate established in Antioch by St. Peter the Apostle. It is under the supreme ecclesiastical jurisdiction of His Holiness the Syrian Orthodox Patriarch of Antioch and All the East, now residing in Damascus, Syria. The Syrian Orthodox Church—composed of several archdioceses, numerous parishes, schools and seminaries—professes the faith of the first three Ecumenical Councils of Nicaea, Constantinople and Ephesus, and numbers faithful in the Middle East, India, the Americas, Europe, Australia and New Zealand. The first Syrian Orthodox faithful came to North America during the late 1800s, and by 1907 the first Syrian Orthodox priest was ordained to tend to the community's spiritual needs. In 1949, His Eminence Archbishop Mor Athanasius Y. Samuel came to America and was appointed Patriarchal Vicar in 1952. The Archdiocese was officially established in 1957. In 1995, the Archdiocese of North America was divided into three separate Patriarchal Vicariates (Eastern United States, Western United States and Canada), each under a hierarch of the Church.

There are 32 official archdiocesan parishes in the United States, located in Arizona, California, District of Columbia, Florida, Georgia, Indiana, Illinois, Massachusetts, Michigan, Nevada, New

Jersey, New York, Oregon, Rhode Island, Texas and Virginia. In Canada, there are six official parishes -three in the Province of Ontario and two in the Province of Quebec and one in the Province of Alberta.

Headquarters

Archdiocese for the Eastern U.S., 260 Elm Ave., Teaneck, NJ 07666, Tel. (201)801-0660 Fax (201)801-0603, Email: inquiries@syrian orthodoxchurch.org
Archdiocese of the Western U.S., 417 E. Fairmount Rd., Burbank, CA 91501, Tel. (818)845-5089 Fax (818)953-7203, Email: MorClemis@hotmail.com
Media Contact, Ecumenical Officer, Very Rev. Chorepiscopus John Meno, 771 Cedarwood Ct., Stanley, NC 28164, Tel. (704)951-8225, Email: vrjmeno@aol.com
Email: inquiries@syrianorthodoxchurch.org
Website: www.syrianorthodoxchurch.org

Officers

Archdiocese for Eastern U.S., Archbishop, Mor Cyril Aphrem Karim
Archdiocese of the Western U.S., Archbishop, Mor Clemis Eugene Kaplan

Triumph the Church and Kingdom of God in Christ Inc. (International)

This church was given through the wisdom and knowledge of God to the Late Apostle Elias Dempsey Smith on Oct. 20, 1897, in Issaquena County, Mississippi, while he was pastor of a Methodist church.

The Triumph Church, as this body is more commonly known, was founded in 1902. Its doors opened in 1904 and it was confirmed in Birmingham, Alabama, with 225 members in 1915. It was incorporated in Washington, D.C. in 1918 and currently operates in 31 states and overseas. The General Church is divided into 13 districts, including the Africa District.

Triumphant doctrine and philosophy are based on the principles of life, truth and knowledge; the understanding that God is in man and expressed through man; the belief in manifested wisdom and the hope for constant new revelations. Its concepts and methods of teaching the second coming of Christ are based on these and all other attributes of goodness.

Triumphians emphasize that God is the God of the living, not the God of the dead.

Headquarters

213 Farrington Ave. S.E., Atlanta, GA 30315
Media Contact, Bishop Zephaniah Swindle, 7114 Idlewild, Pittsburg, PA 15208, Tel. (412)731-2286

Officers

Chief Bishop, Bishop Zephaniah Swindle, Rt. 1, Box 1927, Shelbyville, TX 75973, Tel. (936)598-3082

Gen. Bd of Trustees, Chmn., Rev. Oprah Francis
Gen. Rec. Sec., Bishop R.D. Clarke
Gen. Treas., Bishop W.R. Matt Malcolm

True Orthodox Church of Greece (Synod of Metropolitan Cyprian), American Exarchate —please see Old Calendar Orthodox Church of Greece (Holy Synod in Resistance), American Exarcharte

Ukrainian Orthodox Church of the U.S.A.*

The Ukrainian Orthodox Church of the USA has its origin in the ancient lands of Rus-Ukraine (present day Ukraine). It was to the inhabitants of these lands that the Apostle Andrew first preached the Gospel. Christianization began early in the history of Rus-Ukraine by missionaries from the Orthodox Christian See of Constantinople. In 988 AD, the Saintly Prince Volodymyr, crowned a process of Christian Evangelization begun in the 4th century, by personally accepting Orthodox Christianity and inspiring his subjects to do the same. The baptism of Volodymyr, his household and the inhabitants of Kyiv, altered the face of Kyivan Rus-Ukraine and Slavic history for all time. Kyiv became the spiritual heart of Orthodox Christians in Rus-Ukraine. It was from this See that missionaries were sent into every corner of St. Volodymyr's realm. Through their efforts the Gospel was preached and new communities were established. The Mother Church of Kyiv and its See of Saint Sophia, modeled after Constantinople's See of the same name, gave birth to many Orthodox Christian centers and communities in the west, east and north of the Dnipro river, among them the Orthodox Christian See of Moscow, Russia (Rosia).

The Ukrainian Orthodox Church of USA ministers to the needs of the faithful whose ancestral roots are in Ukraine. The Church found haven in America in the early 1920's. Its first bishop, Metropolitan Ioan (John) Teodorovych, arrived from Ukraine in 1924 and shepherded the Church as Metropolitan until his death in 1971. His successor, Archbishop Mstyslav, arrived in the USA in 1950, and shepherded the Church as Metropolitan from 1971 until his death in 1993. It was Metropolitan Mstyslav who, as a consequence of Ukraine's independence, was named Patriarch of Kyiv and All Ukraine, in 1990. Previous to 1996 there were two Ukrainian Orthodox jurisdictions in the USA. Formal unification of the Ukrainian Orthodox Church of the USA, shepherded by His Beatitude Metropolitan Constantine, and the Ukrainian Orthodox Church of America, shepherded by His Grace Bishop Vsevolod, was concluded in November 1996.

Headquarters

Saint Andrew the Firstcalled Apostle Ukrainian Orthodox Church Center, P.O. Box 495, South Bound Brook, NJ 08880, Tel. (732)356-0090 Fax (732)356-5556
Media Contact, His Eminence Antony, Archbishop of New York, Consistory President
Email: consistory@verizon.net
Website: www.uocofusa.org

Officers

Metropolitan, His Beatitude Constantine, 1803 Sidney St., Pittsburgh, PA 15203

CENTRAL EPARCHY
Eparchial Bishop, Metropolitan Constantine
Eparchial See, St. Volodymyr Cathedral, 5913 State Rd., Parma, OH 44134, Tel. (440)885-1509
Eparchial Territory: Florida, Georgia, Ohio, Western Pennsylvania

EASTERN EPARCHY
Eparchial Bishop, Archbishop Antony.
Eparchial Seat, St. Volodymyr Cathedral, 160 West 82nd St. New York, NY 10024, Tel. (212)873-8550
Eparchial Territory: Connecticut, Deleware, Massachusetts, Maryland, New Jersey, New York, Pennsylvania and Rhode Island

WESTERN EPARCHY
Eparchial Bishop, Archbishop Vsevolod
Eparchial Seat, St. Volodymyr Cathedral, 2230-50 West Cortez St. Chicago, IL 60622, Tel. (312)278 2827
Eparchial Territory: Arizona, California, Colorado, Illinois, Indiana, Michigan, Minnesota, North Dakota, Nebraska, Oregon, Washington, Wisconsin, Ontario Province

COUNCIL OF BISHOPS OF THE UKRAINIAN ORTHODOX CHURCH OF THE USA
Metropolitan Constantine -Chair
Achbishop Antony -Secretary
Achbishop Vsevolod -Member

METROPOLITAN COUNCIL MEMBERS
Archimandrite Andriy -Vice-chairman
Protopresbyter William Diakiw
Protopresbyter Frank Estocin, JCB
Protopriest John Nakonachny
Protopriest Michael Kochis
Protopriest Eugene Meschisen
Protopriest Bazyl Zawierucha
Dr. Gayle Woloschak -English Language Secretary
Mr. Emil Skocypec
Dr. Paul Micevych
Dr. George Krywolap-Ukrainian Language Secretary
Dr. Anatol Lysyj
Mrs. Helen Greenleaf

Mr. Michael Kapeluck
Daria Pishko, Ukrainian Orthodox League President
Mrs. Nadia Mirchuk, United Ukrainian Orthodox Sisterhoods President
Mr. Michael Heretz, Saint Andrew Society, President

CONSISTORY
Consistory President, His Eminence Antony, Archbishop of New York, P.O. Box 495, South Bound Brook, NJ 08880, Tel. (732)356-0090 Fax (732)356-5556, Email: uocofusa@aol.com
Vice Pres., Protopresbyter Willam Diakiw
Sec., Protopriest Frank Estocin
Treas., Mr. Emil Skocypec
Member, Protopriest John Nakonachny
Member, Protopriest Bazyl Zawierucha
Member, Dr. George Krywolap
Deaneries: New England – Protopriest Roman Tarnavsky, Dean; New York/New York, Protopresbyter Taras Chubenko, Dean; Mid-Atlantic, Protopresbyter Frank Estocin, Dean; Pittsburgh, Protopresbyter George Hnatko, Dean; Penn-Ohio, V. Rev. Dennis Kristof, Dean; Upstate New York, V. Rev. Mykola Krywonos, Dean; Florida, Protopresbyter Michael Petlak, Dean; Chicago, V. Rev. Bohdan Kalyniuk, Dean; Minneapolis, V. Rev. Evhen Kumka, Dean; West Coast, Rev. Vasile Sauciur, Dean
Ecclesiastical Court: Rev. Stephen Masliuk, President, Rev. Vasile Sauciur, Rev. Myroslav Schirta, Mr. Michael Slavich, Mr. Wesley Dunn
Audit Commission: Ms. Hanja Cherniak, Chairman, V. Rev. Yurij Siwko, V. Rev. Timothy Tomson, Mr. Edward Zetick, Mrs. Mary Lee Leszczuk
Office of Youth and Young Adult Ministry: Natalie Kapeluck-Nixon, Director
Office of Missions and Christian Ministry: Rev. Deacon Dr. Ihor Mahlay, Director
Office of Family and Adult Ministry: Rev. Harry Linsinbigler, Director
Office of Religious Education: Rev. Harry Linsinbigler, Temporary Director
Office of Development: Dr. Stephen Sivulich, Director
Office of Financial Affairs: Eng. Emil Skocypec, Director
Office of External Affairs and Interchurch Relations: Protopresbyter Frank Estocin, Director
Office of Publications: Protopresbyter William Diakiw, Director
Office of Archival and Historical Information: Dr. George Krywolap
Office of Public Relations: Hieromonk Daniel, Director
All Saints Camp: Stephen Sheptak, Director
Historical and Educational Museum Complex: Natalia Honcharenko, Director
St. Sophia Seminary: V. Rev. Bazyl Zawierucha, Rector

St. Sophia Seminary – Ukrainian Orthodox Church Library: Larissa Bulya, Librarian

Jr. Ukrainian Orthodox League: Mark Meschisen, President

St. Andrew Cemetery: Anastasia Hrybowych, Director

St. Andrew Bookstore: Shirley Skocypec, Director

Periodicals
Ukrainian Orthodox Word; Vira

Unitarian Universalist Association of Congregations

History: The Unitarian Universalist Association (UUA), created in 1961 through a consolidation of the Universalist Church of America with the American Unitarian Association, combines two liberal religious traditions. The religion traces its roots back to Europe where in 1569, the Transylvanian king, John Sigismund (1540-1571), issued an edict of religious freedom. The religious philosophy led to the organization of the Universalists in this country in 1793, and the Unitarians (organized here in 1825). Beliefs: Founders of Universalism believed in universal salvation of all humans by God, while founders of Unitrarianism believed in the unity of God (as opposed to the Trinity). Unitarian Universalism is a liberal, creedless religion with Judeo-Christian roots. It draws also from Eastern, humanist, and other religious traditions, and encourages its members to seek religious truth out of their own reflection and experience. The denomination teaches tolerance and respect for other religious viewpoints and affirms the worth and dignity of every person.

Organization and Government: The Unitarian Universalist Association consists of 1,048 congregations in the United States and Canada, with over 221,000 members, and is served by more than 1,700 ministers. The Association is the fastest-growing liberal religion in North America, at an average annual rate of between 1 and 2 percent. Each member congregation within the UUA is governed independently. In North America, the Association is made up of 19 Districts (served by a District Executive who is a member of the UUA staff), with each congregation having district affiliation. The Association is governed by an elected Board of Trustees, chaired by an elected Moderator. An elected President, three vice presidents, and directors of five departments form the Executive Staff that administers the daily activities of the Association.

The General Assembly, held each June in a different UUA District, serves as the Association's annual business meeting. The UUA includes Departments of Ministry and Professional Leadership; Lifespan Faith Development; Congregational Services; Identity Based Ministries; District Services; Advocacy and Witness; Financial Development; and Communications. "UU World", published quarterly, is the denominational journal. Beacon Press, an internationally honored trade publishing house, is wholly owned by the Unitarian Universalist Association.

Headquarters
25 Beacon St., Boston, MA 02108, Tel. (617)742-2100 Fax (617)367-3237
Media Contact, Daisy Kincaid, Public Relations Director, Tel. (617)948-4386
Email: info@uua.org
Website: www.uua.org

Officers
President, The Rev. Peter Morales
Moderator, Gini Courter
Executive Vice President, Kathleen C. Montgomery

Periodicals
UU World, InterConnections

The United Catholic Church, Inc.

In 1996, a group of autocephalous Catholic Bishops, meeting in Synod, asked Archbishop Robert Bowman to draw up guidelines to support inclusivity. The United Catholic Church was convened under these guidelines and was incorporated in the State of Florida in August 1996. The church is apostolic, conciliar, and synodal. In fulfillment of its understood mission as a renewal church while holding to a faith base that is framed by scripture, the historic creeds, and Early Church tradition, the United Church supports conventional parishes and ministries, as well as non-traditional and experimental mission outreach designs that are directed toward supporting the spiritual needs of underserved populations and promoting ecumenism.

Headquarters
Media Contact: Bishop Rose Tressel, 51 Hilltop Rd., Bethany, CT 06524, Tel. (203)393-3260, Email: unitedcatholic@snet.net
Email: catholic@rmbowman.com
Website: www.united-catholic-church.org

Officers
Bishop Rose Tressel, Presiding Bishop, 51 Hilltop Rd., Bethany CT 06524, Tel. 203-393-3260, Email: unitedcatholic@snet.net

Bishop Hollis Dodge, Jurisdiction Bishop, 802 Donaghue St., Staunton, VA 24401, Tel. 540-448-4623, Email: hollisdodge@msn.com

Bishop Bernardo Morales, Jurisdiction Bishop, 6315 Bass Highway, P.O. Box 702192, St. Cloud, FL 34771, Tel. 407-498-0333, Email: bmorales3@cfl.rr.com

Bishop Peter Orlando, Jurisdiction Bishop, 716 W. Moore Ave., Gilbert AZ, 85233, Tel. 480-558-3039, Email: pandborlando@q.com

Bishop Terry Boyer, Jurisdiction Bishop, 5960 SE 15th Loop, Gresham, OR 97080, Tel. 971-322-8032, Email: Revboyertm@grosb.org

Periodicals
The United Catholic Quarterly

United Christian Church

The United Christian Church originated about 1864. There were some ministers and laymen in the United Brethren in Christ Church who disagreed with the position and practice of the church on infant baptism, voluntary bearing of arms and belonging to oath-bound secret combinations. This group developed into United Christian Church, organized at a conference held in Campbelltown, Pennsylvania, on May 9, 1877. The principal founders of the denomination were George Hoffman, John Stamn and Thomas Lesher. Before they were organized, they were called Hoffmanites.

The United Christian Church has district conferences, a yearly general conference, a general board of trustees, a mission board, a board of directors of the United Christian Church Home, a camp meeting board, a young peoples' board and local organized congregations.

It believes in the Holy Trinity and the inspired Holy Scriptures with the doctrines they teach. The church practices the ordinances of Baptism, Holy Communion and Foot Washing.

It welcomes all into its fold who are born again, believe in Jesus Christ as Savior and Lord and have received the Holy Spirit.

Headquarters
Media Contact, Presiding Elder, John W. Graybill, 35 Oakwood Dr. Palmyra, PA. 17078, Tel. (717)838-4798, Email: graybilly@aol.com

Officers
Presiding Elder, Elder John W. Graybill

Conf. Sec., Mr. Lee Wenger, 1625 Thompson Ave., Annville, PA 17003

Conf. Moderator, Elder Gerald Brinser, 2360 Horseshoe Pike, Annville, PA 17003

OTHER ORGANIZATIONS

Mission Board, Pres., Elder John Graybill, 35 Oakwood Dr., Palmyra, PA 17078 Email: raybilly@aol.com; Sec., Elder David Heagy, 4129 Oak St., Lebanon, PA 17042;

Treas., Mr. Robert Morgan, 1413 Harding Ave., Hershey, PA 17033

United Church of Christ*

The United Church of Christ was constituted on June 25, 1957 by representatives of the Congregational Christian Churches and of the Evangelical and Reformed Church, in Cleveland, Ohio.

The Preamble to the Constitution states, "The United Church of Christ acknowledges as its sole head, Jesus Christ . . . It acknowledges as kindred in Christ all who share in this confession. It looks to the Word of God in the Scriptures, and to the presence and power of the Holy Spirit . . . It claims

. . . the faith of the historic Church expressed in the ancient creeds and reclaimed in the basic insights of the Protestant Reformers. It affirms the responsibility of the Church in each generation to make this faith its own in . . . worship, in honesty of thought and expression, and in purity of heart before God. . . . it recognizes two sacraments, Baptism and the Lord's Supper."

The creation of the United Church of Christ brought together four unique traditions:

(1) Groundwork for the Congregational Way was laid by Calvinist Puritans and Separatists during the late 16th-early 17th centuries, then achieved prominence among English Protestants during the civil war of the 1640s. Opposition to state control prompted followers to emigrate to the United States, where they helped colonize New England in the 17th century. Congregationalists have been self-consciously a denomination from the mid-19th century.

(2) The Christian Churches, an 18th-century American restorationist movement emphasized Christ as the only head of the church, the New Testament as their only rule of faith, and "Christian" as their sole name. This loosely organized denomination found in the Congregational Churches a like disposition. In 1931, the two bodies formally united as the Congregational Christian Churches.

(3) The German Reformed Church comprised an irenic aspect of the Protestant Reformation, as a second generation of Reformers drew on the insights of Zwingli, Luther and Calvin to formulate the Heidelberg Catechism of 1563. People of the German Reformed Church began immigrating to the New World early in the 18th century, the heaviest concentration in Pennsylvania. Formal organization of the American denomination was completed in 1793. The church spread across the country. In the Mercersburg Movement, a strong emphasis on evangelical catholicity and Christian unity was developed.

(4) In 19th-century Germany, Enlightenment criticism and Pietist inwardness decreased long-standing conflicts between religious groups. In Prussia, a royal proclamation merged Lutheran and Reformed people into one United Evangelical Church (1817). Members of this new church way migrated to America. The Evangelicals settled in large numbers in Missouri and Illinois, emphasizing pietistic devotion and unionism; in 1840 they formed the German Evangelical Church Society in the West. After union with other Evangelical church associations, in 1877 it took the name of the German Evangelical Synod of North America.

On June 25, 1934, this Synod and the Reformed Church in the U.S. (formerly the German Reformed Church) united to form the Evangelical and Reformed Church. They blended the

Reformed tradition's passion for the unity of the church and the Evangelical tradition's commitment to the liberty of conscience inherent in the gospel.

Headquarters

700 Prospect Ave., Cleveland, OH 44115, Tel. (216)736-2100 Fax (216)736-2103 Tollfree 866-822-8224 (866-UCC-UCC4) Media Contact, Rev. J. Bennett Guess, 700 Prospect Ave., Cleveland, OH 44115, Tel. (216)736-2177 Fax (216)736-2223 Email: kellys@ucc.org; hiseyd@ucc.org Website: www.ucc.org

Officers

Gen. Minister and Pres., Rev. Geoffrey A. Black
Assoc. Gen. Minister, Ms. Edith A. Guffey
Exec. Minister, Wider Church Ministries, Rev. Cally Rogers-Witte
Exec. Minister, Justice and Witness Ministries, Rev. M. Linda Jaramillo
Exec. Minister, Local Church Ministries, Rev. Stephen L. Sterner

ORGANIZATIONS

Office of General Ministries, National Office, 700 Prospect Ave., Cleveland, Ohio 44115, Tel. (216)736-2100 Fax (216)736-2103, General Minister and President, Rev. Geoffrey A. Black; Associate General Minister, Ms. Edith A. Guffey
Justice and Witness Ministries, National Offices (as above), Tel. (216)736-3700 Fax (216)736-3703, Franklinton Center at Bricks, P.O. Box 220, Whitakers, NC 27891, Tel. (252)437-1723 Fax (252)437-1278, Washington Office, 100 Maryland Avenue North East, Suite 330, Washington, DC. 20002 Tel. (202)543-1517 Fax (202)543-5994, Centro Romero, 173 W. Hall Ave., San Ysidro, CA 92173, Tel. (619)428-8700 Fax (619)428-8705, Executive Minister, Rev. M. Linda Jaramillo
Local Church Ministries, National Offices, Tel. (216)736-3800 Fax (216)736-3803.
Executive Minister, Rev. Stephen L. Sterner
Wider Church Ministries, National Offices (as above), Tel. (216)736-3200 Fax (216)736-3203, Global Ministries of the Christian Church and United Church of Christ, P.O. Box 1986, Indianapolis, IN 46206, Tel. (317)635-3100 Fax (317)635-4323, Executive Minister, Rev. Cally Rogers-Witte;
Pension Boards, Main Office, 475 Riverside Dr., New York, NY 10115., Tel. (212)729-2700 Fax (212)729-2701; National Office, 700 Prospect Ave., Cleveland, OH 44115, Tel. (216)736-2274 Fax (216)736-2274, President/Chief Executive Officer, Mr. Michael A. Downs
United Church Funds., 475 Riverside Dr., Room 1020, New York, NY 10115., Tel. (212)729-2600 Fax (212)729-2601, President, Mr. Donald G. Hart

Council for Health and Human Services Ministries, National Office (as above)., Tel. (216)736-2250 Fax (216)736-2251, President and Chief Executive Officer, Rev. Bryan W. Sickbert

CONFERENCES

WESTERN REGION

California, Nevada Northern, Rev. Phillip Hart, 21425 Birch St., Hayward, CA 94541-2131
California, Nevada Southern, Rev. Felix Villanueva, 2401 N. Lake Ave., Altadena, CA 91001
Central Pacific, Rev. Dr. Walter John Boris, 0245 SW Bancroft St. Ste. E, Portland, OR 97239
Hawaii, Rev. Charles Buck, 1848 Nu'uanu Ave., Honolulu, HI 96817
Montana-Northern Wyoming, Rev. Randall Hyvonen, 2016 Alderson Ave., Billings, MT 59102
Pacific Northwest, Rev. Michael Denton, 325 N. 125th St., Seattle, WA 98133
Rocky Mountain, Rev. Dr. Tom Rehling, 1140 W. 5th Ave., Denver, CO 80204
Southwest, Rev. Dr. John Dorhauer, 4423 N. 24th St., # 600, Phoenix, AZ 85016

WEST CENTRAL REGION

Iowa, Rev. Rich Pleva, 5609 Douglas Ave., Des Moines, IA 50310
Kansas-Oklahoma, Rev. Krista Betz, (Interim), 1245 Fabrique, Wichita, KS 67218
Minnesota, Rev. Dr. Karen Smith Sellers, 122 W. Franklin Ave., Rm. 323, Minneapolis, MN 55404
Missouri, Mid-South, Rev. Jeffrey Whitman, 483 E. Lockwood Ave., #15, St. Louis, MO 63119
Nebraska, Rev. Roddy Dunkerson, 3151 South St., Ste. B, Lincoln, NE 68502
Northern Plains, Rev. Dr. Wade Schemmel, 1200 E. Highland Acres Rd., Bismarck, ND 58501
South Dakota, Rev. Dr. David Felton (Interim), 3500 S. Phillips Ave., #100, Sioux Falls, SD 57105-6864

GREAT LAKES REGION

Illinois, Rev.Jorge Morales, 1840 Westchester Blvd., Westchester, IL 60154
Illinois South, Rev. Sheldon Culver, 1312 Broadway, Highland, IL 62249
Indiana-Kentucky, Rev. John Gantt (Interim), 1100 W. 42nd St. #350, Indianapolis, IN 46208
Michigan, Judith Youngman (Interim), P.O. Box 1006, 5945 Park Lake Rd., East Lansing, MI 48826
Ohio, Rev. Robert Molsberry, 6161 Busch Blvd., #100, Columbus, OH 43229
Wisconsin, Rev. David Moyer, 4459 Gray Rd., P.O. Box 435, De Forest, WI 53532-0435

SOUTHERN REGION

Florida, Rev. Kent Siladi, 924 N. Magnolia Ave. #250, Orlando, FL 32803
South Central, Rev. Doug Anders, 9022 Long Point Rd., Houston, TX 77055

Southeast, Rev. Timothy C. Downs, 1330 W. Peachtree St., Ste. 350, Atlanta, GA 30309

Southern, Rev. Vertie Powers (Interim), 252 -B West Fifth St., Burlington, NC 27215

MIDDLE ATLANTIC REGION

Central Atlantic, Rev. Dr. John R. Deckenback, 916 S. Rolling Rd., Baltimore, MD 21228

New York, Rev. Dr. Rita Root (Interim), 5575 Thompson Rd., DeWitt, NY 13214

Penn Central, Rev. Dr. Marja Coons-Torn, 900 S. Arlington Ave. 227A, Harrisburg, PA 17109

Penn Northeast, Rev. Alan C. Miller, 431 Delaware Ave., Palmerton, PA 18071

Pennsylvania Southeast, Rev. Geneva M. Butz (Acting), 505 S. Second Ave., P.O. Box 26400, Collegeville, PA 19426-0400

Penn West, Rev. Alan McLarty, 320 Maple Ave., Greensburg, PA 15601

NEW ENGLAND REGION

Connecticut, Rev. Charles L. Wildman (Interim), 125 Sherman St., Hartford, CT 06105

Maine, Rev. David R. Gaewski, 28 Yarmouth Crossing Dr., Yarmouth, ME 04096

Massachusetts, Rev. Dr. Jim Antal, 1 Badger Rd., Framingham, MA 01702

New Hampshire, Rev. Gary Schulte, 140 Sheep Davis Rd, Pembroke, NH 03275

Rhode Island, Rev. Charles Barnes, 8 Summer St., Pawtucket, RI 02860

Vermont, Rev. Lynn Bujnak, 36 N. Main St., Randolph, VT 05060

Nongeographic

Calvin Synod, Rt. Rev. Béla Poznán, 7319 Tapper Ave., Hammond, IN 46324

Periodicals

United Church News, Common Lot

United Holy Church of America, Inc.

The United Holy Church of America, Inc. is an outgrowth of the great revival that began with the outpouring of the Holy Ghost on the Day of Pentecost. The church is built upon the foundation of the Apostles and Prophets, Jesus Christ being the cornerstone. During a revival of repentence, regeneration and holiness of heart and life that swept through the South and West, the United Holy Church was born. The founding fathers had no desire to establish a denomination but were pushed out of organized churches because of this experience of holiness and testimony of the Spirit-filled life. On the first Sunday in May 1886, in Method, North Carolina, what is today known as the United Holy Church of America, Inc. was born. The church was incorporated on Sept. 25, 1918.

Baptism by immersion, the Lord's Supper and feet washing are observed. The premillennial teaching of the Second Coming of Christ, Divine healing, justification by faith, sanctification as a second work of grace and Spirit baptism are accepted.

Headquarters

5104 Dunstan Rd., Greensboro, NC 27405, Tel. (336)621-0669

Media Contact, Gen. Statistician, Ms. Jacquelyn B. McCain, 1210 N. Euclid Ave., Apt. A, St. Louis, MO 63113-2012, Tel. (314)367-8351 Fax (314)367-1835

Email: books@mohistory.org

Officers

GENERAL ADMINISTRATION

Gen. Pres., The Rt. Rev. Odell McCollum, 707 Woodmark Run, Gahanna, OH 43230, Tel. (614)475-4713, Fax (614)475-4713

Gen. Vice Pres., Bishop Elijah Williams, 901 Briarwood St., Reidsville, NC 27320, Tel. (919)349-7275

Gen. 2nd Vice-Pres., The Rt. Rev. Kenneth O. Robinson, Sr., 33 Springbrook Rd., Nanuet, NY 10954-4423, Tel. (914)425-8311, Fax (914) 352-2686

Gen. Rec. Sec., Rev. Mrs. Elsie Harris, 2304 Eighth St., Portsmouth, VA 23704 Tel. (757)399-0926

Asst. Rec. Sec., Mrs. Cassandra Jones, 3869 JoAnn Dr., Cleveland, OH 44122, Tel. (216)921-0097

Gen. Fin. Sec., Vera Perkins-Hughes, P.O. Box 6194, Cleveland, OH, Tel. (216)851-7448

Asst. Fin. Sec., Bertha Williams, 4749 Shaw Dr., Wilmington, NC 28405, Tel. (919)395-4462

Gen. Corres. Sec., Ms. Gwendolyn Lane, 3069 Hudson St., Columbus, OH 43219

Gen. Treas., Louis Bagley, 8779 Wales Dr., Cincinnati, OH 45249, Tel. (513)247-0588

GENERAL OFFICERS

Gen Pres. Missionary Dept., Rev. Ardelia M. Corbett, 519 Madera Dr., Youngstown, OH 44504, Tel. (216)744-3284

Gen. Evangelism & Extension Dept., Pres., Elder Clifford R. Pitts, 3563 North 14th St., Milwaukee, WI 53206, Tel. (414)244-1319

Gen. Bible Church School Dept., Superintendent, Robert L. Rollins, 1628 Avondale Ave., Toledo, OH 43607, Tel. (419)246-4046

Gen. Y.P.H.A., Pres., Elder James W. Brooks, Rt. 3 Box 105, Pittsboro, NC 27312, Tel. (919)542-5357

Gen. Ushers Department, Pres., Ms. Sherly M. Hughes, 1491 East 191st St., #H-604, Euclid, OH 44117, Te. (216)383-0038

Gen. Educ. Dept., Elder Roosevelt Alston, 168 Willow Creek Run, Henderson, NC 27636, Tel. (919)438-5854

Gen. Music Dept., Chair, Rosie Johnson, 2009 Forest Dale Dr., Silver Spring, MD 20932

Gen. Historian, Dr. Chester Gregory, Sr., 1302 Lincoln Woods Dr., Baltimore, MD 21228, Tel. (410)788-5144

Gen. Counsel, Mr. Joe L. Webster, Esquire, Attorney-At-Law, P.O. Box 2301, Chapel Hill, NC 27515-2301, Tel. (919)542-5150

UHCA Academy, Dir., Ms. Stephanie Davis, The United Holy Church of America, Inc., 5104

Dunstan Rd., Greensboro, NC 27405, Tel. (336)621-0069

Gen. Statistician, Ms. Jacquelyn B. McCain, 1210 N. Euclid Ave., Apt. A, St. Louis, MO 63113-2012, Tel. (314)367-8351 Fax (314) 367-1835

PRESIDENTS OF CONVOCATIONAL DISTRICTS

Barbados District; The Rt. Rev. Jestina Gentles, 5 West Ridge St., Britton's Hill, St. Michael, BH2 Barbados, West Indies, Tel. (246)427-7185

Bermuda Dist., The Rt. Rev. Calvin Armstrong, P.O. Box 234, Paget, Bermuda, Tel. (441)296-0828 or (441)292-8383

Central Western Dist., Bishop Bose Bradford, 6279 Natural Bridge, Pine Lawn, MO 63121, Tel. (314)355-1598

Ghana, West Africa Dist., The Rt. Rev. Robert Blount, 231 Arlington Av., Jersey City, NJ 07035, Tel. (201)433-5672

New England Dist., The Rt. Rev. Lowell Edney, 85 Woodhaven St., Mattapan, MA 02126, Tel. (617)296-5366

Northern Dist., The Rt. Rev. Kenneth O. Robinson, Sr., 33 Springbrook Rd., Nanuet, NY 10954, Tel. (914)425-8311

Northwestern Dist., The Rt. Rev. M. Daniel Borden, 8655 North Melody Lane, Macedonia, OH 44056, Tel. (330)468-0270

Pacific Coast Dist., The Rt. Rev. Irvin Evans, 235 Harvard Rd., Linden, NJ 07036, Tel. (908)925-6138

Southeastern Dist., The Rt. Rev. James C. Bellamy, 1825 Rockland Dr., SE, Atlanta, GA 30316, Tel. (404)241-1821

Southern Dist.-Goldsboro, The Rt. Rev. Ralph E. Love, Sr., 200 Barrington Rd., Greenville, NC 27834, Tel. (252)353-0495

Southern Dist.-Henderson, The Rt. Rev. Jesse Jones, 608 Cecil St., Durham, NC 27707, Tel. (919)682-8249

St. Lucia Dist., The Rt. Rev. Carlisle Collymore, P.O. Box 51, Castries, St. Lucia, West Indies, Tel. (758)452-5835

Virginia Dist., The Rt. Rev. Albert Augson, 1406 Melton Ave., Richmond, VA 23223, Tel. (804)222-0463

West Virginia Dist., The Rt. Rev. Alvester McConnell, Route 3, Box 263, Bluefield, WV 24701, Tel. (304)248-8046

Western North Carolina Dist., The Rt. Rev. Elijah Williams, 901 Briarwood St., Reidsville, NC 27320-7020, Tel. (336)349-7275

United House of Prayer

Today, the United House of Prayer is headed by Bishop C. M. Bailey, CEO & Sole Trustee, and consists of 138 Congregations, variously located in 28 States across the Nation. It was founded and organized as a hierarchical church in the 1900s by the late Bishop C. M. Grace, who built the first House of Prayer in 1919 in West

Wareham, MA, with his own hands.The purpose of the organization is to establish, maintain and perpetuate the doctrine of Christianity and the Apostolic Faith throughout the world among all people; to erect and maintain houses of prayer and worship where all people may gather for prayer and to worship the almighty God in spirit and in truth, irrespective of denomination or creed, and to maintain the Apostolic faith of the Lord and Savior, Jesus Christ.

Headquarters

628 M St. NW, Washington, DC 20001, Tel. (202)289-9890 Fax (202)289-3690
Media Contact, Apostle S. Green
Email: apostlegreen@hotmail.com

Officers

CEO & Sole Trustee, Bishop C. M. Bailey, 1665 N. Portal Dr. NW, Washington, DC 20012, Tel. (202)882-3956 Fax (202)829-4717

NATIONAL PROGRAM STAFF

General Assembly Secretary, Apostle A. D. Cunningham,The General Assembly,

Presiding Officer, Bishop C. M. Bailey, 1665 N. Portal Dr. NW, Washington, DC 20012, Tel. (202)882-3956 Fax (202)829-4717

General Council Ecclesiastical Court, Clerk, Apostle R. Price, 1665 N. Portal Dr. NW, Washington, DC 20012, Tel. (202)882-3956 Fax (202)829-4717

Nationwide Building Program, General Builder, Bishop C. M. Bailey, 1665 N. Portal Dr. NW, Washington, DC 20012, Tel. (202)882-3956 Fax (202)829-4717

Special Projects, Dir., Apostle S. Green

Annual Truth & Facts Publication, Exec. Editor, Bishop C. M. Bailey, 1665 N. Portal Dr. NW, Washington, DC 20012, Tel. (202)882-3956 Fax (202)829-4717

Periodicals

Bailey Magazine, ARE YOU AWARE?

The United Methodist Church*

The United Methodist Church was formed April 23, 1968, in Dallas by the union of The Methodist Church and The Evangelical United Brethren Church. The two churches shared a common historical and spiritual heritage. The Methodist Church resulted in 1939 from the unification of three branches of Methodism -the Methodist Episcopal Church, the Methodist Episcopal Church, South, and the Methodist Protestant Church. The Methodist movement began in 18th-century England under the preaching of John Wesley, but the Christmas Conference of 1784 in Baltimore is regarded as the date on which the organized Methodist Church was founded as an ecclesiastical organization. It was there that Francis Asbury was elected the first bishop in this country.

The Evangelical United Brethren Church was formed in 1946 with the merger of the Evangelical

Church and the Church of the United Brethren in Christ, both of which had their beginnings in Pennsylvania in the evangelistic movement of the 18th and early 19th centuries. Philip William Otterbein and Jacob Albright were early leaders of this movement among the German-speaking settlers of the Middle Colonies.

Headquarters

Media Contact, Director of Public Relations, Diane Degnan, Tel. (615)742-5406, Email: ddegnan@umcomm.org

General Information, Director, InfoServ, Vicki Wallace, (800)251-8140, Fax (615)742-5423, Email: infoserv@umcom.org

Website: www.umc.org

Officers

General Conference, Sec., Rev. L. 'Gere' Fitzgerald Reist II, 216 State St, Harrisburg, PA 17101-1109, Tel. (570)724-3113, Email: freist@cpcumc.org

Council of Bishops: Pres., Bishop Larry M. Goodpaster, P.O. Box 18750, Charlotte, NC 28218-0750, Tel. (704)-535-2260, Fax 704-535-9160, Email: bishop@wnccumc.org

Sec., Robert E. Hayes, Jr. 1501 NW 24th St, 73106, P.O. Box 60467, Oklahoma City, OK 73146-0467, Tel. (405)530-2025 Fax (405) 530-2040, Email: jharris@okumc.org

JURISDICTIONAL BISHOPS:

NORTH CENTRAL JURISDICTION

Chicago Episcopal Area, Bishop Hee-Soo Jung, 77 W. Washington St., Ste. 1820, Chicago, IL 60602-3181, Tel. (312)346-9766 x 102 Fax (312)214-9031, Email: hsjung@umcnic.org

Dakotas Episcopal Area, Bishop Deborah L. Kiesey, 1331 W. University Ave., P.O. Box 460, Mitchell, SD 57301-0460, Tel. (605)996-6552, Fax (605)996-1766, Email: bishop@dakotasumc.org

Illinois Episcopal Area, Bishop Gregory V. Palmer, (5900 S 2nd St., 62711), P.O. Box 19215, Springfield, IL 62794-9215, Tel. (217)529-3820, Fax (217)529-4190, Email: ILareaoffice@igrc.org

Indiana Episcopal Area, Bishop Michael J. Coyner, 301 Pennsylvania Pkwy, Ste 300, Indianapolis, IN 46280-1396, Tel. (317)564-3239, Fax (317)735-4225, Email: bishop coyner@inumc.org

Iowa Episcopal Area, Bishop Julius C. Trimble, 2301 Rittenhouse St, Des Moines, IA 50321-3101, Tel. (515)974-8902, Fax (515)974-8952, Email: bishopjc.trimble@iaumc.org

Michigan Episcopal Area, Bishop Jonathan D. Keaton 2164 University Park Dr., Ste. 250, Okemos, MI 48864, Tel. (517)347-4030, Fax (517)347-4003, Email: bishopsoffice@miareaumc.org

Minnesota Episcopal Area, Bishop Sally Dyck, 122 W. Franklin Ave., Ste. 200, Minneapolis, MN 55404-2472, Tel. (612)870-4007, Fax (612)870-3587, Email: sally.dyck@minnesota umc.org

Ohio East Episcopal Area, Bishop John L. Hopkins (8800 Cleveland Ave. NW 44720-4598), P.O. Box 2800, North Canton, OH 44720-0800, Tel. (330)499-3972 x 112, Fax (330)497-4911, Email: bishop@eocumc.com

Ohio West Episcopal Area, Bishop Bruce R. Ough, 32 Wesley Blvd., Worthington, OH 43085-3585, Tel. (614)844-6200 x 215 Fax (614)781-2625, Email: Bishop@wocumc.org

Wisconsin Episcopal Area, Bishop Linda Lee, 750 Windsor St., Ste. 303, Sun Prairie, WI 53590-2149, Tel. (608)837-8526, Fax (608) 837-0281, Email: bishoplee@wisconsinumc.org

NORTHEASTERN JURISDICTION

Boston Episcopal Area, Bishop Peter D. Weaver (276 Essex St. 5th Fl., 01840-1516), P.O. Box 249, Lawrence, MA 01842-0449, Tel. (978)682-7555 x 250 Fax (978)682-9555, Email: bishopsoffice@neumc.org

Harrisburg Episcopal Area, Bishop Jane Allen Middleton, 303 Mulberry Dr., Ste. 100, Mechanicsburg, PA 17050-3141, Tel. (717)766-7871 x 3100 Fax (717)766-3210, Email: bishop@susumc.org

New Jersey Episcopal Area, Bishop Sudarshana Devadhar, 1001 Wickapecko Dr., Ocean, NJ 07712-4733, Tel. (732)359-1010 Fax (732) 359-1019, Email: Bishop@gnjumc.org

New York Episcopal Area, Bishop Jeremiah J. Park, 20 Soundview Ave., White Plains, NY 10606-3302, Tel. (914)615-2221 Fax (914) 615-2246, Email: Bishop@nyac.com

Upper New York Episcopal Area, Bishop Marcus Matthews, 324 University Ave, 3rd Fl, Syracuse, NY 13210-1811, Tel. (315)422-5027 Fax (315)422-5304, Email: bishopmatthews@unyumc.org

Philadelphia Episcopal Area, Bishop Peggy Johnson (980 Madison Ave, Norristown, 19403), P.O. Box 820, Valley Forge, PA 19482-0820, Tel. (610)666-9090 x 233, Fax (610)666-9181, Email: peggy.johnson@epaumc.org

Pittsburgh Episcopal Area, Bishop Thomas J. Bickerton (1204 Freedom Rd., 16066-4999), P.O. Box 5002, Cranberry Township, PA 16066-1902, Tel. (724)776-1499/1599, Fax (724) 776-1683, Email: umbishop@wpaumc.org

Washington Episcopal Area (DC), Bishop John R. Schol, 11711 E Market Pl, Fulton, MD 20759-2594, Tel. (410)309-3400 x 300, Fax (410) 309-9759, Email: bishopsoffice@bwcumc.org

West Virginia Episcopal Area, Bishop Ernest S. Lyght, United Methodist Center, 900 Washington St. E., Ste. 300, Charleston, WV 25301-1710, Tel. (304)344-8330, Fax (304)344-8330, Email: WVareaumc@aol.com

SOUTH CENTRAL JURISDICTION:

Arkansas Episcopal Area, Bishop Charles N. Crutchfield, 800 Daisy Gatson Bates Dr, Little Rock, AR 72202-3770, Tel. (501)324-8007,

174

Fax (501)324-8021, Email: bishopcnc@arumc.org

Dallas Episcopal Area, Bishop Earl W. Bledsoe, P.O. Box 866188, Plano, TX 75086-6188, Tel. (972)526-5015, Fax (972)526-5014, Email: bishop@ntcumc.org

Fort Worth Episcopal Area, Bishop Michael J. Lowry, 464 Bailey Ave., Fort Worth, TX 76107-2153, Tel. (817)877-5222, Fax (817) 332-4609, Email: bishop@ctcumc.org

Houston Episcopal Area, Bishop Janice Riggle Huie, 5215 Main St., Houston, TX 77002-9792, Tel. (713)528-6881, Fax (713)529-7736, Email: bishop.huie@txcumc.org

Kansas Episcopal Area, Bishop Scott J. Jones, 9440 E. Boston St, Ste 160, Wichita, KS 67207-3603, Tel. (316)686-0600, Fax (316) 684-0044, Email: kansasbishop@kswestumc.org

Louisiana Episcopal Area, Bishop William W. Hutchinson, 527 North Blvd., Baton Rouge, LA 70802-5700, Tel. (225)346-1646 x 212, Fax (225)387-3662, Email: enixmore@bellsouth.net

Missouri Episcopal Area, Bishop Robert C. Schnase, 3601 Amron Ct, Columbia, MO 65202-1918, Tel. (573)441-1770, Fax (573) 441-0765, Email: rschnase@moumethodist.org

Nebraska Episcopal Area, Bishop Ann Brookshire Sherer, 3333 Landmark Circle, Lincoln, NE 68504-4760, Tel. (402)466-4955, Fax (402)466-7931, Email: bishopsherer@umcneb.org

Northwest Texas-New Mexico Episcopal Area, Bishop D. Max Whitfield, 11816 Lomas Blvd NE, Albuquerque, NM 87112-5614, Tel. (505)255-8786, Fax (505)255-8738, Email: whitmax@nmconfum.com

Oklahoma Episcopal Area, Bishop Robert E. Hayes, Jr. (1501 NW 24th St, 73106), P.O. Box 60467, Oklahoma City, OK 73146-0467, Tel. (405)530-2025, Fax (405)530-2040, Email: jharris@okumc.org

San Antonio Episcopal Area, Bishop James E. Dorff 16400 Huebner Rd, 78248-1694, San Antonio, TX 78248-1694, Tel. (210)408-4502, Fax (210)408-4501, Email: bishop@umcswtx.org

SOUTHEASTERN JURISDICTION:

Alabama-West Florida Episcopal Area, Bishop Paul L. Leeland, 100 Interstate Park Dr., Ste 120 A, Montgomery, AL 36109-5488, Tel. (334)277-1787, Fax (334)277-0109, Email: bishop@awfumc.org

Birmingham Episcopal Area, Bishop William H. Willimon, 898 Arkadelphia Rd., Birmingham, AL 35204-5011, Tel. (205)226-7991, Fax (205) 226-7998, Email: wwillimon@northalabamaumc.org

Charlotte Episcopal Area, Bishop Larry M. Goodpaster (3400 Shamrock Dr., 28215), P.O. Box 18750, Charlotte, NC 28218-0750, Tel. (704)535-2260 x 138, Fax (704)535-9160, Email: bishop@wnccumc.org

Columbia Episcopal Area, Bishop Mary Virginia Taylor, 4908 Colonial Dr., Ste. 121, Columbia, SC 29203-6080, Tel. (803)786-9486, Fax (803)754-9327, Email: bishop@umcsc.org

Florida Episcopal Area, Bishop Timothy W. Whitaker 450 Martin L King Jr Ave, Lakeland, FL 38815-1522, Tel. (863)688-4427, Fax (863)687-0568, Email: bishop@flumc.org

Holston Episcopal Area, Bishop James E. Swanson, Sr. (217 S Rankin Rd., 37701-2633) P.O. Box 850, Alcoa, TN 37701-0850, Tel. (865)690-4080 Fax (865)690-7112, Email: bishop@holston.org

Louisville Episcopal Area, Bishop Lindsey Davis, 7400 Floydsburg Rd., Crestwood, KY 40014-8202, Tel. (502)425-4240 Fax (502) 425-9232, Email: bishop@kyumc.org

Mississippi Episcopal Area, Bishop Hope Morgan Ward (321 Mississippi St., 39201), P.O. Box 931, Jackson, MS 39205-0931, Tel. (601)948-4561 Fax (601)948-5981, Email: bishop@mississippi-umc.org

Nashville Episcopal Area, Bishop Richard J. Wills, Jr., 520 Commerce St., Ste. 201, Nashville, TN 37203-3714, Tel. (615)742-8834 Fax (615)742-3726, Email: bishop@nasharea.org

North Georgia Episcopal Area, Bishop B. Michael Watson 4511 Jones Bridge Cir. NW, Norcross, GA 30092-1406 Tel. (678)533-1360 Fax (678)533-1361, Email: bishop@ngumc.org

Raleigh Episcopal Area, Bishop Alfred W. Gwinn, Jr. (700 Waterfield Ridge Place), P.O. Box 1970, Garner, NC 27529-1970, Tel. (919)779-6115 X 242, Fax (919)773-2416, Email: bishopgwinn@nccumc.org

Richmond Episcopal Area, Bishop Charlene Payne Kammerer (10330 Staples Mill Rd.), P.O. Box 5606, Glen Allen, VA 23058-5606, Tel. (804)521-1102, Fax (804)521-1171, Email: bishopk@vaumc.org

South Georgia Episcopal Area, Bishop James R. King, Jr., 3370 Vineville Ave., Ste. 101, Macon, GA 31204-2331, Tel. (478)475-9286, Fax (478)475-9248, Email: jking@sgaumc.org

WESTERN JURISDICTION:

Denver Episcopal Area, Bishop Elaine J.W. Stanovsky 6110 Greenwood Plaza Blvd, Greenwood Village, CO 80111-4803, Tel. (303)733-0083, Fax (303)733-5047, Email: bishop@rmcumc.com

Los Angeles Episcopal Area, Bishop Mary Ann Swenson (110 S. Euclid Ave., 91101-2421), P.O. Box 6006, Pasadena, CA 91102-6006, Tel. (626)568-7312, Fax (626)568-7377, Email: bishop@cal-pac.org

Phoenix Episcopal Area, Bishop Minerva G. Carcaño, 1550 E. Meadowbrook Ave., Phoenix, AZ 85014-4040, Tel. (602)266-6956 x 209, Fax (602)279-1355, Email: Bishopmc@desertsw.org

Portland Episcopal Area, Bishop Robert T. Hoshibata, 1505 SW 18th Ave., Portland, OR 97201-2599, Tel. (503)226-1530, Fax (503) 228-3189, Email: bishop@umoi.org

San Francisco Episcopal Area, Bishop Warner H. Brown, Jr., (1276 Halyard Dr., 95691), P.O. Box 980250, West Sacramento, CA 95798-0250, Tel. (916)374-1510, Fax (916)372-9062, Email: bishop@calnevumc.org

Seattle Episcopal Area, Bishop Grant Hagiya, (816 S 216th St #2, 98198-6331), P.O. Box 13650, Des Moines, WA 98198-1009, Tel. (206)870-6810, Fax (206)870-6811, Email: bishop@pnwumc.org

Periodicals

Mature Years, El Intérprete; New World Outlook; Newscope; Interpreter; Methodist History; Pockets; Response; Social Questions Bulletin; United Methodist Reporter; Quarterly Review; Alive Now; Circuit Rider; El Aposento Alto; Weavings-A Journal of the Christian Spiritual Life; The Upper Room, Faith in Action -online publication

United Pentecostal Churches of Christ —
please see The Pentecostal Churches of Christ

United Pentecostal Church International

The United Pentecostal Church International came into being through the merger of two oneness Pentecostal organizations -the Pentecostal Church, Inc., and the Pentecostal Assemblies of Jesus Christ. The first of these was known as the Pentecostal Ministerial Alliance from its inception in 1925 until 1932. The second was formed in 1931 by a merger of the Apostolic Church of Jesus Christ with the Pentecostal Assemblies of the World.

The church contends that the Bible teaches that there is one God who manifested himself as the Father in creation, in the Son in redemption, and as the Holy Spirit in regeneration; that Jesus is the name of this absolute deity and that water baptism should be administered in his name, not in the titles Father, Son and Holy Ghost (Acts Ch.2 vs.38, Ch.8 vs.16, and Ch.19 vs.6).

The Fundamental Doctrine of the United Pentecostal Church International, as stated in its Articles of Faith, is "the Bible standard of full salvation, which is repentance, baptism in water by immersion in the name of the Lord Jesus Christ for the remission of sins, and the baptism of the Holy Ghost with the initial sign of speaking with other tongues as the Spirit gives utterance."

Further doctrinal teachings concern a life of holiness and separation, the operation of the gifts of the Spirit within the church, the second coming of the Lord, and the church's obligation to take the gospel to the whole world.

Headquarters

8855 Dunn Rd., Hazelwood, MO 63042, Tel. (314)837-7300 Fax (314)837-4503

Media Contact, Gen. Sec.-Treas., Rev.Jerry Jones Email: rfuller@upci.org

Officers

Gen. Supt., Rev. Kenneth F. Haney
Asst. Gen. Supts., Rev. Paul. Mooney and Rev. Randy Keyes
Gen. Sec.-Treas., Rev. Jerry Jones
Dir. of Foreign Missions, Rev. Bruce Howell
Gen. Dir. of Home Missions, Rev. Carlton Coon
Editor-in-Chief, Rev. Robert H. Fuller
Gen. Sunday School Dir., Rev. Gary Erickson
Youth Pres., Rev. Todd Gaddy

OTHER ORGANIZATIONS

Pentecostal Publishing House, Mgr., Rev. Robert H. Fuller
Ladies Ministries, Pres., Gwyn Oakes
Stewardship Dept., Dir., Rev., Stephen Drury
Division of Education, Supt., Rev. Don Batchelor
Word Aflame Publications, Editor, Rev. Richard Davis
Media Missions Asst. Dir., Rev. Morman R. Paslay II
Media Missions Announcer, Rev. J. Hugh Rose
Public Relations, Contact Church Administration
Historical Society & Archives
Urshan Graduate School of Theology

Periodicals

The Pentecostal Herald, World Harvest Today, The North American Challenge, Conqueror, Reflections, Forward, Apostolic Man

United Zion Church

A branch of the Brethren in Christ which settled in Lancaster County, Pennsylvania, the United Zion Church was organized under the leadership of Matthias Brinser in 1855.

Headquarters

United Zion Retirement Community, 722 Furnace Hills Pk., Lititz, PA 17543
Media Contact, Bishop Charles Brown, 4041 Shanamantown Rd., Annville, PA 17003, Tel. (717)867-1133
Website: www.unitedzionchurch.org

Officers

Gen. Conf. Mod., Bishop Charles Brown, 4041 Shanamantown Rd., Annville, PA 17003, Tel. (717)867-1133
Asst. Mod., Rev. Paul H. Martin
Gen. Conf. Sec., Rev. Clyde Martin
Gen. Conf. Treas., Kenneth Kleinfelter, 919 Sycamore Lane, Lebanon, PA 17042

Unity of the Brethren

Czech and Moravian immigrants in Texas (beginning about 1855) established congregations which grew into an Evangelical Union in 1903, and with the accession of other Brethren in

176

Texas, into the Evangelical Unity of the Czech-Moravian Brethren in North America. In 1959, it shortened the name to the original name used in 1457, the Unity of the Brethren (Unitas Fratrum, or Jednota Bratrska).

Headquarters
4009 Hunter Creek, College Station, TX 77845
Media Contact, Sec. of Exec. Committee, Ginger McKay, 148 N. Burnett, Baytown, TX 77520
Email: lkoslovsky@teleshare.net
Website: www.unityofthebrethren.org

Officers
President: Claren Kotrla, 1501 Echo Bluff Cove, Austin Texas 78754, Tel. (512)491-7802, Email: kotrla@flash.net
1st Vice President: Rev. Linda Chandler, 13108 N. Ridge Circle, Leander, TX 78641, Tel. (512)267-4826, Email: L77c@aol.com
2nd Vice President: Pastor Joe Emerson, P.O. Box 4615, Temple, TX 76505, Tel. (254)791-0420, Email: pastorjde@juno.com
3rd Vice President: Rev. James Hejl, 309 Cherrywood Circle, Taylor, TX 76574, Tel. (512)365-6890, Email: jhejl@austin.rr.com
Secretary: Kathy Harrison, P.O. Box 593, Little River-Academy, Texas 76554, Tel. (254)721-1815, Email: kathy@pearson-lawfirm.com
Financial Secretary: Dewyan Weise, 6006 FM Hwy 765, San Angelo, TX 76905, Email: DWeise@academicplanet.com
Treasurer: James Marek, 1304 T.H. Johnson Dr., Taylor, Texas 76574, Tel. (512)352-6165, Email: james@cnbt.com

OTHER ORGANIZATIONS
Bd. of Christian Educ., Dr., Donald Ketcham, 900 N. Harrison, West, TX 76691
Brethren Youth Fellowship, Pres., Jamie Brooke Bryan, 1231 Four Corners, West, TX 76691
Friends of the Hus Encampment, Jim Baletka, 727 San Benito, College Station, TX 77845
Christian Sisters Union, Pres., Janet Pomykal, P.O. Box 560, Brenham, TX 77834
Sunday School Union, Pres., Dorothy Kocian, 107 S. Barbara Dr., Waco, TX 76705
Youth Director, Kimberly Stewart, 1500 Lawnmont Dr., Apt. 208, Round Rock, TX 78664

Periodicals
Brethren Journal

Universal Catholic Church
Founded as a reorganization of the Dutch Old Catholic Church in 1915-16. In 1941 a controversy broke out in the Church regarding whether or not certain teachings of Theosophy (reincarnation, etc.) were to become official teachings of the Church. The Liberal Catholic Church International split in 2007 into two bodies

Headquarters
741 Cerro Gordo Ave., San Diego, CA 92102, USA., Tel. & Fax (619)239-0637

Officers
The Most Rev. Deab Bekken, 741 Cerro Gordo Ave., San Diego, CA 92102, USA., Tel. & Fax (619)239-0637, Email: bekken@sbcglobal.net
The Most Rev. Robert Winters, VP and Teasurer, 741 Cerro Gordo Ave., San Diego, CA 92102, USA., Tel. & Fax (619)239-0637
St. Alban Press, 741 Cerro Gordo Ave., San Diego, CA 92102, USA., Tel. & Fax (858)689-8610, Email: info@stalbanpress.com

Universal Fellowship of Metropolitan Community Churches
The Universal Fellowship of Metropolitan Community Churches was founded Oct. 6, 1968 by the Rev. Troy D. Perry in Los Angeles, with a particular but not exclusive outreach to the gay community. Since that time, the Fellowship has grown to include congregations throughout the world.

The simple declaration of faith of what MCC believes, as stated in our By-Laws and accepted by our General Conference is that "Christianity is the revelation of God in Jesus Christ and is the religion set forth in the scriptures. Jesus Christ is foretold in the Old Testament, presented in the New Testament, and proclaimed by the Christian Church in every age and in every land."

Founded in the interest of offering a church home to all who confess and believe, Metropolitan Community Churches moves in the mainstream of Christianity. Our faith is based on the principles outlined in the historic creeds: Apostles and Nicene. The government of this Fellowship is vested in its tri-annual General Conference, comprised of clergy and lay church delegates, who exert the right of control in all of its affairs, subject to the provisions of its Articles of Incorporation and By-Laws. Ongoing leadership is provided by the Board of Elders and Board of Administration.

Headquarters
Mailing address: P.O. Box 1374, Abilene, TX 79604
Location: 500 Chestnut St., Suite 1513, Abilene, TX 79602
Tel. (310)360-8640 Fax (325)675-8977, Email: info:mccchurch.net
Media Contact, Email: communications@mcccurch.net
Email: StanKimer@MCCchurch.net
Website: www.mcchurch.org

Officers
Moderator: Rev. Elder Nancy Wilson, 3293 Fruitville Road #105, Sarasota, FL 34237, Tel. (941)755-5771 Fax (941)847-0867, Email: RevNancyWilson@MCCchurch.net
Council of Elders: Rev. Elder Ken Martin, Email: RevKenMartin@MCCchurch.net; Rev. Elder Diane Fisher (MCC Ecumenical Officer),

Email: RevDianeFisher@MCCchurch.net;
Rev. Elder Darlene Garner, Email:
RevDarleneGarner@MCCchurch.net; Rev.
Elder Lillie Brock, Email: RevLillieBrock@
MCCchurch.net
Director of Operations: Barbara Crabtree, P.O.
Box 1374, Abilene, TX 79604, Tel. (310)861-
4658 Fax (310)388-1252, Email: Barbara
Crabtree@MCCchurch.net
Chair, Global Justice Team: Rev. Pat Bumgardner,
Email: Rvpatmccny@aol.com
Chair, Ecumenical and Inter-Religious Team: Stan
Kimer, Email: StanKimer@MCCchurch.net
Chair, MCC Theologies Team: Rev. Kharma
Amos, Email: KharmaAmos@aol.com
Office of Formation and Leadership
Development: Rev. Dr. Mona West, Email:
RevMonaWest@MCCchurch.net

Periodicals
MCC Impact

Vineyard USA
Vineyard USA is a community of
approximately 600 churches committed to
building the church and living under the reign of
God. It officially started in Southern California in
1982 under the leadership of John Wimber. The
Board of Directors is the governing Board for
Vineyard USA. The form of government is Free
Church and thus the local Vineyards are free to
govern as they desire as long as they do not
violate the faith or practices of the Vineyard
community. Vineyard USA consists of 8 regions
under the direction of a Regional Overseer in
each. Each region also has Area Pastoral Care
Leaders who give oversight to a small group of
pastors in a geographic area. The National
Director is the CEO of Vineyard USA and works
with the National Board to see that Vineyard
USA achieves its purpose.

Headquarters
5115 Grove West Blvd., Stafford, TX 77477, Tel.
(281)313-8463 Fax (281)313-8464
Email: info@vineyardusa.org; lucierosser@
vineyardusa.org
Website: vineyardusa.org

Officers
National Dir., Berten A. Waggoner, Email:
lucierosser@vineyardusa.org
Secretary, Doug Anderson, Email:
doug@vineyardusa.org
Treasurer, Brian Anderson
Vineyard Music USA, Vineyard Resources USA,
Mercy Response

Periodicals
Cutting Edge

Volunteers of America
Volunteers of America is a Christian Church
that answers God's call to transform the world
through a ministry of service that feeds, clothes,

shelters and demonstrates to all people that they
are beloved children of God. As part of that
ministry, Volunteers of America provides local
human service programs and opportunities for
individual and community involvement through
local affiliate offices and the National Services
Housing and Health Care Division. Volunteers of
America has become the largest non profit
provider of housing (affordable/senior/homeless
shelters) in the US.

Founded in 1896 by Christian social reformers
Ballington and Maud Booth, Volunteers of
America provides over 100 different types of
programs and services in more than 400
communities nationwide. Programs include
services for abused and neglected children, youth
at risk, the elderly, people with disabilities,
homeless individuals and families, and many
others. It also provides a national Prison After-
Care program that engages local congregations of
all denominations as mentors to newly released
prisoners. It employs 16,000 individuals whose
work is assisted by over 90,000 committed
volunteers.

Headquarters
1660 Duke St., Alexandria, VA 22314-3427, Tel.
(800)899-0089
Email: voa@voa.org
Website: www.voa.org

Officers
Chpsn., Nancy Gofus
Pres., Mike King, 1660 Duke St., Alexandria,
VA. 22314, Tel. (703)341-5000, Email:
mking@voa.org
Vice President, Ministry, Harry V. Quiett, 1660
Duke St., Alexandria, VA. 22314, Tel.
(703)341-5084 Fax (703)341-7000, Email:
hquiett@voa.org
*39 local affiliate offices and one National
Services Division. Information accessible
through the national website: www.voa.org*

Periodicals
Spirit Magazine, Gazette

The Wesleyan Church
The Wesleyan Church was formed on June 26,
1968, through the union of the Wesleyan
Methodist Church of America (1843) and the
Pilgrim Holiness Church (1897). The headquarters
was established at Marion, Ind., and relocated to
Indianapolis in 1987,and relocated again in
Fishers, Indiana in 2004.

The Wesleyan movement centers around the
beliefs, based on Scripture, that the atonement in
Christ provides for the regeneration of sinners and
the entire sanctification of believers. John Wesley
led a revival of these beliefs in the 18th century.
When a group of New England Methodist
ministers led by Orange Scott began to crusade for
the abolition of slavery, the bishops and others

178

sought to silence them. This led to a series of withdrawals from the Methodist Episcopal Church. In 1843, the Wesleyan Methodist Connection of America was organized and led by Scott, Jotham Horton, LaRoy Sunderland, Luther Lee and Lucius C. Matlack.

During the holiness revival in the last half of the 19th century, holiness replaced social reform as the major tenet of the Connection. In 1947 the name was changed from Connection to Church and a central supervisory authority was set up. The Pilgrim Holiness Church was one of many independent holiness churches which came into existence as a result of the holiness revival. Led by Martin Wells Knapp and Seth C. Rees, the International Holiness Union and Prayer League was inaugurated in 1897 in Cincinnati. Its purpose was to promote worldwide holiness evangelism and the Union had a strong missionary emphasis from the beginning. It developed into a church by 1913.

The Wesleyan Church is now spread across most of the United States and Canada and in over 90 other countries. The International Conference of The Wesleyan Church, originally named Wesleyan World Fellowship, was organized in 1972 to unite Wesleyan mission bodies developing into mature churches. The Wesleyan Church is a member of the National Association of Evangelicals and the World Methodist Council.

Headquarters
P.O. Box 50434, Indianapolis, IN 46250, Tel. (317)774-7900
Media Contact, Gen. Sec., Dr. Ronald D. Kelly, Tel. (317)774-7907 Fax (317)744-3924 Email: kellyr@wesleyan.org
Mailing Address: P.O. Box 50434, Indianapolis, IN 46250
Email: generalsecretary@wesleyan.org
Website: www.wesleyan.org

Officers
GENERAL SUPERINTENDENTS
Dr. Jo Anne Lyon, Tel. (317)774-3932 Fax (317)774-3931, Email: lyonja@wesleyan.org
Dr. Thomas E. Armiger, Tel. (317)774-3934 Fax (317)774-3931, Email: armigert@wesleyan.org
Dr. Jerry G. Pence, Tel. (317)774-3933 Fax (317)774-3931, Email: pencej@wesleyan.org
General Officers
Gen. Sec., Dr. Ronald D. Kelly, Tel. (317)774-7907 Fax (317)744-3924, Email: kellyr@wesleyan.org
Gen. Treas., Kevin J. Batman, Tel. (317)774-3941 Fax (317)744-3948, Email: batmank@wesleyan.org
Gen. Publisher, Mr. Donald D. Cady, Tel. (317)774-3853 Fax (317)774-3865, Email: cadyd@wesleyan.org
Gen. Director of Communications, Dr. Ronald D. Kelly, Tel. (317)774-7907 Fax (317)774-3924, Email: kellyr@wesleyan.org

Gen. Dir. of Spiritual Formation, Dr. James A. Dunn, Tel. (317)744-3888 Fax (317)774-3880, Email: dunnj@wesleyan.org
Gen. Dir. of Education & the Ministry, Dr. Kerry D. Kind, Tel. (317)774-3911 Fax (317)774-3915, Email: kindk@wesleyan.org
Gen. Dir. of World Missions, Dr. H. C. Wilson, Tel. (317)774-7980 Fax (317)774-7958, Email: wilsonhc@wesleyan.org

AUXILIARIES/SUBSIDIARY AGENCIES
Wesleyan Investment Foundation, Gen. Dir., Dr. Craig A. Dunn, Tel. (317)774-7300 Fax (317)774-7321 Email: wif@wesleyan.org
Wesleyan Pension Fund, Gen. Dir., Dr. Craig A. Dunn, Tel. (317)774-7300 Fax (317)774-7321, Email: dunnc@wesleyan.org
Wesleyan Women, Mrs. Martha Blackburn, Tel. (317)774-7970 Fax (317)774-7975, Email: blackbma@wesleyan.org
Wesleyan Kids for Mission, Mrs. Peggy Ann Camp, Tel. (704)892-3744 Fax (317)570-5254, Email: camppeg@aol.com
Address Service, Tel. (317)744-7900
Archives & Historical Library, Tel. (317)774-7996
Computer Information Services, Tel. (317)774-7931
Wesleyan Publishing House, Tel. (317)774-3853

Periodicals
Wesleyan Life, GP World View

Wesleyan Holiness Association of Churches
This body was founded Aug. 4, 1959 near Muncie, Indiana by a group of ministers and laymen who were drawn together for the purpose of spreading and conserving sweet, radical, scriptural holiness. These men came from various church bodies. This group is Wesleyan in doctrine and standards.

Headquarters
1141 North US Hwy 27, Fountain City, IN 47341-9757, Tel. (765)584-3199
Media Contact, Gen. Sec.-Treas., Rev. Nathan D. Schockley, 6014 N. US Hwy 31, Columbus, IN 47201

Officers
Gen. Supt., Rev. John Brewer
Asst. Gen. Supt., Rev. Robert W. Wilson, 2346 Neitz Valley Rd., Selinsgrove, PA 17870, Tel. (570)539-9821
Gen. Sec.-Treas., Rev. Nathan D. Shockley, 6014 North U.S. Hwy. 31, Columbus, IN 47201, Tel. (812)376-3019
Gen. Youth Pres., Rev. Nathan Shockley, 6014 North U.S. Hwy. 31, Columbus, IN 47201, Tel. (812)376-3019

Periodicals
Eleventh Hour Messenger

Wisconsin Evangelical Lutheran Synod

Organized in 1850 at Milwaukee, Wisconsin, by three pastors sent to America by a German mission society, the Wisconsin Evangelical Lutheran Synod still reflects its origins, although it now has congregations in 50 states and three Canadian provinces. It supports missions in 26 countries.

The Wisconsin Synod federated with the Michigan and Minnesota Synods in 1892 in order to more effectively carry on education and mission enterprises. A merger of these three Synods followed in 1917 to give the Wisconsin Evangelical Lutheran Synod its present form.

Although at its organization in 1850 WELS turned away from conservative Lutheran theology, today it is ranked as one of the most conservative Lutheran bodies in the United States. WELS confesses that the Bible is the verbally inspired, infallible Word of God and subscribes without reservation to the confessional writings of the Lutheran Church. Its interchurch relations are determined by a firm commitment to the principle that unity of doctrine and practice are the prerequisites of pulpit and altar fellowship and ecclesiastical cooperation. It is a founding member of the Confessional Evangelical Lutheran Conference, a federation of 21 like-minded bodies worldwide.

Headquarters

2929 N. Mayfair Rd., Milwaukee, WI 53222, Tel. (414)256-3888 Fax (414)256-3899

MCG Director, Rev. J.D. Liggett
Email: webbin@wels.net
Website: www.wels.net

Officers

Pres., Rev. Mark G. Schroeder, 2929 N Mayfair Rd., Milwaukee, WI 53222, Tel. (414)256-3888, Fax (414)256-3899, Email: mark.schroeder@wels.net

1st Vice Pres., Rev. James R. Huebner, 7318 W. Bluemound Rd., Milwaukee, WI 53213, Tel. (414)271-3006, Email: welsvpl@wels.net

2nd Vice Pres., Rev. Joel R. Voss, 6700 Crossbrook Dr., Centerville, OH 45459-6963, Tel. (937)434-9876, Email: revjrvoss@aol.com

Sec., Rev. Robert Pasbrig, 876 Fairview Dr., Hartford, WI 53027, Tel. (414)259-8122, Email: sec@wels.net

OTHER ORGANIZATIONS

Bd. for Ministerial Education, Admn., Rev. Paul T. Prange

Congregation and Ministry Support Group, Coordinator, Rev. Bryan Gerlach

Bd. for Home Missions, Admn., Rev. Keith A. Free

Bd. for World Missions, Admn., Rev. Daniel Koelpin

Missions Operations, Director, Mr. Mel Schuler

Periodicals

Forward in Christ, Wisconsin Lutheran Quarterly, The Lutheran Educator, Lutheran Leader, Mission Connections

Religious Bodies in the United States Arranged by Families

The following list of religious bodies appearing in the Directory Section of the *Yearbook* shows the "families," or related clusters into which American religious bodies can be grouped. For example, there are many communions that can be grouped under the heading "Baptist" for historical and theological reasons. It should not be assumed, however, that all denominations under one family heading are necessarily consistent in belief or practice. The family clusters tend to represent historical factors more often than theological or practical ones. These family categories provide one of the major pitfalls when compiling church statistics because there is often a tendency to combine the statistics by "families" for analytical and comparative purposes. Such combined totals are deeply flawed, even though they are often used as variables for sociological analysis. The arrangement by families offered here is intended only as a general guide for conceptual organization when viewing the broad sweep of American religious culture.

Religious bodies that cannot be categorized under family headings appear alphabetically and are not indented in the following list.

Adventist Bodies
Advent Christian Church
Church of God General Conference
(McDonough, GA)
Primitive Advent Christian Church
Seventh-day Adventist Church

American Evangelical Christian Churches

American Rescue Workers

Anglican Bodies
The Episcopal Church
The Orthodox Anglican Church
Reformed Episcopal Church

Anglo-Lutheran Catholic Church

Apostolic Catholic Church

Apostolic Christian Church (Nazarene)

Apostolic Christian Churches of America

Apostolic Episcopal Church

Baptist Bodies
Alliance of Baptists
The American Baptist Association
American Baptist Churches in the U.S.A.
Baptist Bible Fellowship International
Baptist Missionary Association of America
Conservative Baptist Association of America
(CBAmerica)
Converge Worldwide (BGC)
Cooperative Baptist Fellowship
General Association of General Baptists
General Association of Regular Baptist
Churches
National Association of Free Will Baptists
National Baptist Convention of America, Inc.
National Baptist Convention, U.S.A., Inc.
National Missionary Baptist Convention of
America
National Primitive Baptist Convention, Inc.
North American Baptist Conference

Primitive Baptists
Progressive National Baptist Convention, Inc.
Separate Baptists in Christ
Seventh Day Baptist General Conference,
USA and Canada
Southern Baptist Convention
Sovereign Grace Believers

Berean Fellowship of Churches

Brethren (German Baptist
Brethren Church (Ashland, Ohio)
Church of the Brethren
Fellowship of Grace Brethren Churches
Old German Baptist Brethren Church

Brethren, River
Brethren in Christ Church
United Zion Church

The Catholic Church

Christ Community Church (Evangelical-Protestant)

Christadelphians

Christian Brethren (also known as Plymouth Brethren)

The Christian Congregation, Inc.

The Christian and Missionary Alliance

Christian Union

The Church of Christ (Holiness) U.S.A.

Church of Christ, Scientist

Church Communities International

The Church of Illumination

Church of the Living God (Motto: Christian Workers for Fellowship)

Church of the Nazarene

181

Churches of Christ - Christian Churches
Christian Church (Disciples of Christ)
Christian Churches and Churches of Christ
Churches of Christ

Churches of Christ in Christian Union

Churches of God
Church of God (Anderson, Indiana)
Churches of God, General Conference
General Conferences of the Churches of God (Seventh Day), Denver, Colorado

Churches of the New Jerusalem
General Church of the New Jerusalem
The Swedenborgian Church

Conservative Congregational Christian Conference

Eastern Orthodox Churches
Albanian Orthodox Archdiocese in America
Albanian Orthodox Diocese of America
The American Carpatho-Russian Orthodox Greek Catholic Church
The Antiochian Orthodox Christian Archdiocese of North America
Apostolic Catholic Assyrian Church of the East, North American Dioceses
Apostolic Episcopal Church
Apostolic Orthodox Catholic Church of North America
Greek Orthodox Archdiocese of America
The Holy Eastern Orthodox Catholic and Apostolic Church in North America, Inc.
Holy Ukrainian Autocephalic Orthodox Church in Exile
Old Calendar Orthodox Church of Greece (Holy Synod in Resistance), American Exarchate
The Orthodox Church in America
Patriarchal Parishes of the Russian Orthodox Church in the U.S.A.
The Romanian Orthodox Church in America
The Romanian Orthodox Episcopate of America
The Russian Orthodox Church Outside of Russia
Serbian Orthodox Church in the U.S.A. and Canada
Syriac-Greek Antiochian Orthodox Catholic Church
Ukrainian Orthodox Church of the U.S.A.

The Evangelical Church

The Evangelical Church Alliance

The Evangelical Congregational Church

The Evangelical Covenant Church

The Evangelical Free Church of America

Fellowship of Fundamental Bible Churches

Free Christian Zion Church of Christ

Friends
Evangelical Friends International – North American Region
Friends General Conference
Friends United Meeting
Religious Society of Friends (Conservative)
Religious Society of Friends (Unaffiliated Meetings)

Grace Gospel Fellowship

IFCA International, Inc.

International Council of Community Churches

International Fellowship of Bible Churches, Inc

Jehovah's Witnesses

Latter Day Saints (Mormons)
Church of Christ
The Church of Jesus Christ (Bickertonites)
The Church of Jesus Christ of Latter-day Saints
Community of Christ

The Liberal Catholic Church— Province of the United States of America

Lutheran Bodies
The American Association of Lutheran Churches
Apostolic Lutheran Church of America
The Association of Free Lutheran Congregations
Association of Independent Evangelical Lutheran Churches
Church of the Lutheran Brethren of America
Church of the Lutheran Confession
Conservative Lutheran Association
The Estonian Evangelical Lutheran Church
Evangelical Lutheran Church in America
Evangelical Lutheran Synod
The Latvian Evangelical Lutheran Church in America
The Lutheran Church— Missouri Synod (LCMS)
Lutheran Evangelical Protestant Church (GCEPC)
Wisconsin Evangelical Lutheran Synod

Mennonite Bodies
Beachy Amish Mennonite Churches
Bible Fellowship Church
Church of God in Christ, Mennonite
Fellowship of Evangelical Bible Churches
Fellowship of Evangelical Churches
General Conference of Mennonite Brethren Churches

Hutterian Brethren
Mennonite Church USA
Old Order Amish Church
Old Order (Wisler) Mennonite Church
Reformed Mennonite Church

Methodist Bodies

African Methodist Episcopal Church
The African Methodist Episcopal Zion Church
The Allegheny Wesleyan Methodist
Connection (Original Allegheny Conference)
Bible Holiness Church
Christian Methodist Episcopal Church
Evangelical Methodist Church
Free Methodist Church of North America
Fundamental Methodist Church, Inc.
Primitive Methodist Church in the U.S.A.
Reformed Methodist Union Episcopal Church
Reformed Zion Union Apostolic Church
Southern Methodist Church
The United Methodist Church
The Wesleyan Church

The Missionary Church

Moravian Bodies

Moravian Church in America (Northern
Province, Southern Province)
Unity of the Brethren

**National Association of Congregational
Christian Churches**

**National Organization of the New
Apostolic Church of North America**

**National Spiritualist Association of
Churches**

**North American Old Roman Catholic
Church (Archdiocese of New York)**

Old Catholic Churches

Apostolic Catholic Orthodox Church
Christ Catholic Church
The Old Catholic Orthodox Church
The United Catholic Church, Inc.
Universal Catholic Church

Oriental Orthodox Churches

Armenian Apostolic Church of America
Armenian Apostolic Church, Dioceses of
America
Coptic Orthodox Church
Malankara Orthodox Syrian Church, Diocese
of America
Syrian (Syriac) Orthodox Church of Antioch

Pentecostal Bodies

Apostolic Faith Mission Church of God
Apostolic Faith Mission of Portland, Oregon
Assemblies of God
Assemblies of God International Fellowship
(Independent/Not affiliated)

The Bible Church of Christ, Inc.
Bible Way Church of Our Lord Jesus Christ
World Wide, Inc.
Calvary Chapel
The Church of God
The Church of God in Christ
Church of God in Christ, International
Church of God (Cleveland, Tennessee)
Church of God by Faith, Inc.
The Church of God of the Firstborn
Church of God, Mountain Assembly, Inc.
Church of God of Prophecy
Church of Our Lord Jesus Christ of the
Apostolic Faith, Inc.
Congregational Holiness Church
Elim Fellowship
Full Gospel Assemblies International
Full Gospel Fellowship of Churches and
Ministers International
House of God, Which is the Church of the
Living God, the Pillar and Ground of the
Truth, Inc.
International Church of the Foursquare
Gospel
International Fellowship of Christian
Assemblies
The International Pentecostal Church of
Christ
International Pentecostal Holiness Church
Open Bible Churches
The (Original) Church of God, Inc.
Pentecostal Assemblies of the World, Inc.
Pentecostal Church of God
The Pentecostal Churches of Christ
Pentecostal Fire-Baptized Holiness Church
The Pentecostal Free Will Baptist Church, Inc.
United Holy Church of America, Inc.
United House of Prayer
United Pentecostal Church International
Vineyard USA

Pillar of Fire

**Polish National Catholic Church of
America**

Reformed Bodies

Associate Reformed Presbyterian Church
(General Synod)
Christian Reformed Church in North America
Cumberland Presbyterian Church
Cumberland Presbyterian Church in America
Evangelical Presbyterian Church
Hungarian Reformed Church in America
The Korean Presbyterian Church Abroad
Netherlands Reformed Congregations
The Orthodox Presbyterian Church
Presbyterian Church in America
Presbyterian Church (U.S.A.)
Protestant Reformed Churches in America
Reformed Church in America
Reformed Church in the United States

183

Reformed Presbyterian Church of North America
United Church of Christ

Reformed Catholic Church

The Salvation Army

The Schwenkfelder Church

Thomist Churches
Mar Thoma Syrian Church of India

Triumph the Church and Kingdom of God in Christ Inc. (International)

Unitarian Universalist Association of Congregations

United Brethren Bodies
Church of the United Brethren in Christ, USA
United Christian Church

Universal Fellowship of Metropolitan Community Churches

Volunteers of America

Wesleyan Holiness Association of Churches

184

4. Religious Bodies in Canada

A large number of Canadian religious bodies were organized by immigrants from Europe and elsewhere, and a smaller number sprang up originally on Canadian soil. In the case of Canada, moreover, many denominations that transcend the U.S.-Canada border have headquarters in the United States.

A final section in this directory lists churches according to denominational families. This can be a helpful tool in finding a particular church if you don't know the official name. Complete statistics for Canadian churches are found in the statistical section in Chapter 3: Table 1 contains memberhsip figures, and Table 4 contains giving figures. Addresses for periodicals are found in Directory 4 entitled, "Religious Periodicals in Canada."

The Anglican Church of Canada

Anglicanism came to Canada with the early explorers such as Martin Frobisher and Henry Hudson. Continuous services began in New-foundland about 1700 and in Nova Scotia in 1710. The first Bishop, Charles Inglis, was appointed to Nova Scotia in 1787 The Anglican Church of Canada includes a large number of the original inhabitants of Canada (Indians, Inuit and Metis) and has been a strong advocate of their rights.

The Anglican Church of Canada has enjoyed self-government for over a century since 1893 and is an autonomous member of the worldwide Anglican Communion. The Church also has a strong international role in development and disaster relief through the Primate's World Relief and Development Fund (PWRDF). The General Synod, which normally meets triennially (next meeting 2010), consists of the Archbishops, Bishops and elected clerical and lay representatives of the 30 dioceses. Each of the Ecclesiastical Provinces—Canada, Ontario, Rupert's Land and British Columbia—is organized under a Metropolitan and has its own Provincial Synod and Executive Council. Each diocese has its own Diocesan Synod.

Headquarters
Church House, 80 Hayden St., Toronto, ON M4Y 3G2, Tel. (416)924-9192 (Switchboard) (416)924-9199 (Voice mail) Fax (416)968-7983, Website: www.anglican.ca
Media Contact: Mr. Vianney (Sam) Carriere
General Email: info@national.anglican.ca

Officers
GENERAL SYNOD OFFICERS
Primate of the Anglican Church of Canada, The Most Rev. Fred J. Hiltz
Prolocutor, Canon Robert Falby
Gen. Sec., vacant
Treas., Gen. Synod, Ms. Michèle George

DEPARTMENTS AND DIVISIONS
Faith, Worship & Ministry, Interim Dir., The Rev. Dr. Eileen Scully
Financial Management and Dev., Dir., Ms. Michèle George
Inform. Resources Dir., Mr. Vianney (Sam) Carriere
Pensions, Dir., Ms. Judith Robinson

Philanthropy, Interim Dir., Mr. Vianney (Sam) Carriere
Primate's World Relief and Dev. Fund, Exec. Dir., Ms. Adele Finney

METROPOLITANS (ARCHBISHOPS)
British Columbia, The Most Rev. John E. Privett, Metropolitan, 1876 Richter St., Kelowna BC V1Y 2M9, Tel. (250)762-3306 Fax: (250)762-4150, Email: diocese_of_kootenay@telus.net
Canada, The Most Rev. Claude E.W. Miller, Metropolitan, 115 Church St., Fredericton NB E3B 4C8, Tel. (506)459-1801 Fax: (506)460-0520, Email: diocese@anglican.nb.ca
Ontario, The Most Rev. Colin R. Johnson, 135 Adelaide St. East, Toronto, ON M5C 1L8, Tel. (416)363-6021 Fax: (416)363-7678 Email: diocese@toronto.anglican.ca
Rupert's Land, The Most Rev. David Ashdown, 915 Ottawa St., Box 567, Keewatin, ON P0X 1C0, Tel. (807)547-3353 Fax (807)547-3356, Email: keewatinbishop@shaw.ca

DIOCESAN BISHOPS
Algoma, The Rt. Rev. Stephen Andrews, Box 1168, Sault Ste. Marie, ON P6A 5N7, Tel. (705)256-5061 Fax (705)946-1860, Email: secretary@dioceseofalgoma.com
Arctic, The Rt. Rev. Andrew P. Atagotaaluk, 4910 51st St., Box 190, Yellowknife, NT X1A 2N2, Tel. (867)873-5432 Fax (867)873-8478, Email: diocese@arcticnet.org
Athabasca, The Rt. Rev. Fraser W. Lawton, Box 6868, Peace River, AB T8S 1S6, Tel. (780) 624-2767 Fax (780)624-2365, Email: bpath@ telusplanet.net
Brandon, The Rt. Rev. James D. Njegovan, Box 21009 WEPO, Brandon, MB R7B 3W8, Tel. (204)727-7550 Fax (204)727-4135, Email: bishopbdn@mts.net
British Columbia, The Rt. Rev. James A.J. Cowan, 900 Vancouver St., Victoria, BC V8V 3V7, Tel. (250)386-7781 Fax (250)386-4013, Email: synod@bc.anglican.ca
Caledonia, The Rt. Rev. William J. Anderson, #201 – 4716 Lazelle Ave., Terrace, BC V8G 1T2, Tel. (250)635-6016 Fax (250)635-6026, Email: caledonia@telus.net
Calgary, Bishop, The Rt. Rev. Derek B.E. Hoskin, #180, 1209 59th Ave., SE, Calgary, AB T2H 2P6, Tel. (403)243-3673 Fax (403) 243-2182, Diocesan Email: diocese@calgary.anglican.ca

Central Interior, Anglican Parishes (APCI) The Rt. Rev. Barbara Andrews, 360 Nicole St., Kamloops, BC V2C 2P5, Tel. (778)471-5573 Fax (778)471-5586 Email: apci@shaw.ca

Central Newfoundland, The Rt. Rev. F. David Torraville, 34 Fraser Rd., Gander, NF A1V 2E8, Tel. 709-256-2372 Fax 709-256-2396, Email: bishopcentral@nfld.net

Eastern Newfoundland and Labrador, The Rt. Rev. Cyrus C.J. Pitman , 19 King's Bridge Rd., St. John's, NF A1C 3K4, Tel. (709)576-6697 Fax (709)576-7122, Email: cpitman@anglican enl.nf.net

Edmonton, The Rt. Rev. Jane Alexander, 10035 - 103 St., Edmonton, AB T5J 0X5, Tel. (780) 439-7344 Fax (780)439-6549, Email: bishop@edmonton.anglican.ca

Fredericton, The Most Rev. Claude E.W. Miller, 115 Church St., Fredericton, NB E3B 4C8, Tel. (506)459-1801 Fax (506)459-8475, Email: diocese@anglican.nb.ca

Huron, The Rt. Rev. Robert F. Bennett, 190 Queens Ave., London, ON N6A 6H7, Tel. (519)434-6893 Fax (519)673-4151, Email: bishops@huron.anglican.ca

Keewatin, The Most Rev. David N. Ashdown, 915 Ottawa St., P.O. Box 567, Keewatin, ON P0X 1C0, Tel. (807)547-3353 Fax (807)547-3356 Email: dioceseofkeewatin@shaw.ca

Kootenay, The Most Rev. John E. Privett, 1876 Richter St., Kelowna, BC V1Y 2M9, Tel. (250)762-3306 Fax (250)762-4150, Email: diocese_of_kootenay@telus.net

Montreal, The Rt. Rev. Barry B. Clarke, 1444 Union Ave., Montreal, QC H3A 2B8, Tel. (514)843-6577 Fax (514)843-3221, Email: bishops.office@montreal.anglican.ca

Moosonee, The Rt. Rev. Thomas A. Corston, Box 841, Schumacher, ON P0N 1G0, Tel. (705)360-1129 Fax (705)360-1120, Email: executiveassistant@moosoneeanglican.ca

New Westminster, The Rt. Rev. Michael C. Ingham, 580-401 W. Georgia St., Vancouver, BC V6B 5A1, Tel. (604)684-6306 Fax (604) 684-7017, Email: bishop@vancouver.anglican.ca

Niagara, The Rt. Rev. Michael A. Bird, 252 James St. N., Hamilton, ON L8R 2L3, Tel. (905)527-1278 Fax (905)527-1281, Email: bishop@niagara.anglican.ca

Nova Scotia and Prince Edward Is., The Rt. Rev. Susan E. Moxley, 6017 Quinpool Rd., Halifax, NS B3K 5J6, Tel. (902)420-0717 Fax (902) 425-0717, Email: office@nspeidiocese.ca

Ontario, The Rt. Rev. Michael D. Oulton, 90 Johnson St., Kingston, ON K7L 1X7, Tel. (613)544-4774 Fax (613)547-3745, Email: synod@ontario.anglican.ca

Ottawa, The Rt. Rev. John H. Chapman, 71 Bronson Ave., Ottawa, ON K1R 6G6, Tel. (613)232-7124 Fax (613)232-7088, Email: bishopsoffice@ottawa.anglican.ca

Qu'Appelle, The Rt. Rev. Gregory K. Kerr-Wilson, 1501 College Ave., Regina, SK S4P

1B8, Tel. (306)522-1608 Fax (306)352-6808, Email: bpgregory@sasktel.net

Quebec, The Rt. Rev. Dennis Drainville, 31 rue des Jardins, Quebec, QC G1R 4L6, Tel. (418) 692-3858 Fax (418)692-3876, Email: bishop@quebec.anglican.ca

Rupert's Land, The Rt. Rev. Donald D. Phillips, 935 Nesbitt Bay, Winnipeg, MB R3T 1W6, Tel. (204)922-4200 Fax (204)922-4219, Email: general@rupertsland.ca

Saskatchewan, The Rt. Rev. Michael W. Hawkins, 1308 5th Ave. East, Prince Albert, SK S6V 2H7, Tel. (306)763-2455 Fax (306) 764-5172, Email: synod@sasktel.net

Saskatoon, The Rt. Rev. David M. Irving, Box 1965, Saskatoon, SK S7K 3S5, Tel. (306)244-5651 Fax (306)933-4606, Email: anglican synod@sasktel.net

Toronto, The Most Rev. Colin R. Johnson, 135 Adelaide St. East, Toronto, ON M5C 1L8, Tel. (416)363-6021 Fax (416)363-3683, Email: cjohnson@toronto.anglican.ca

Western Newfoundland, The Rt. Rev. Percy D. Coffin, 25 Main St., Corner Brook, NF A2H 1C2, Tel. (709)639-8712 Fax (709)639-1636, Email: dsown@nf.aibn.com

Yukon, The Rt. Rev. Larry Robertson, Box 31136, Whitehorse, YT Y1A 5P7, Tel. (867) 667-7746 Fax (867)667-6125, Email: synod office@klondiker.com

Periodicals
Anglican Journal (National Newspaper); Ministry Matters

The Antiochian Orthodox Christian Archdiocese of North America

The approximately 130,000 members of the Antiochian Orthodox community in Canada are under the jurisdiction of the Antiochian Orthodox Christian Archdiocese of North America with headquarters in Englewood, N.J. There are churches in Edmonton, Halifax, London, Ottawa, Toronto, Windsor, Montreal, Saskatoon, Charlottestown, PEI, Calgary, and Mississauga.

Headquarters
Metropolitan Philip Saliba, 358 Mountain Rd., Englewood, NJ 07631, Tel. (201)871-1355 Fax (201)871-7954

Website: www.antiochian.org

Media Contact, Rev. Fr. Thomas Zain, 355 State Street, Brooklyn, NY 11217, Tel. (718)855-6225 Fax (718)855-3608 Email: abouna@aol.com

Officers
Bishop Alexander, 10820 Rue Laverdure, Montreal, PQ H3L2L9, Tel. (514)388-4344 Fax (514)388-4051

Periodicals
The Word; Again; Handmaiden

Apostolic Christian Church (Nazarene)

This church was formed in Canada as a result of immigration from various European countries. The body began as a movement originated by the Rev. S. H. Froehlich, a Swiss pastor, whose followers are still found in Switzerland and Central Europe.

Headquarters

Apostolic Christian Church Foundation, 1135 Sholey Rd., Richmond, VA 23231, Tel. (804) 222-1943

Media Contact, James Hodges

Officers

Exec. Dir., James Hodges

The Apostolic Church in Canada

The Apostolic Church in Canada is affiliated with the worldwide organization of the Apostolic Church with headquarters in Great Britain (www.apostolicworld.net). A product of the Welsh Revival (1904 to 1908), its Canadian beginnings originated in Nova Scotia in 1927. Today its main centers are in Nova Scotia, Ontario and Quebec. This church is evangelical, fundamental and Pentecostal, with special emphasis on the ministry gifts listed in Ephesians 4:11-12.

Headquarters

27 Castlefield Ave., Toronto, ON M4R 1G3
Media Contact, Pres., Rev. D. Karl Thomas, 220 Adelaide St. London, ON N6B-3H4, Tel. (519) 438-7036 Fax (705)742-2948
Email: nlcrevival@goldon.net
Website: www.apostolic.ca

Officers

Pres., Rev. D. Karl Thomas, 220 Adelaide St., London, ON N6B 344, Tel. (519)438-7036 Fax (519)438-5800, Email: nlcrevival@goldon.net
Natl. Sec., Rev. Phillip Woolridge, 27 Castlefield Ave., Toronto, ON M4R 1G3, Tel. (519)438-7036 Fax (519)438-5800

Periodicals

Canadian News Up-Date

Apostolic Church of Pentecost of Canada Inc.

The Apostolic Church of Pentecost, Incorporated, was founded in 1921 at Winnipeg, Manitoba, by Pastor Frank Small and is a network of ministers and churches providing fellowship, encouragement and accountability in the proclamation of the Gospel of Jesus Christ by the power of the Holy Spirit.

Headquarters

#119-2340 Pegasus Way NE, Calgary, AB T2E 8M5
Email: acop@acop.ca

Website: www.acop.ca
Media Contact, President, Rev. Wes Mills, Tel. (403)273-5777 Fax (403)273-8102

Officers

President., Rev. Wes Mills
Administrator, Mrs. Darla Matchett

Periodicals

This Week in ACOP (a weekly email newsletter)

Armenian Evangelical Church of Toronto

Founded in 1960 by immigrant Armenian evangelical families from the Middle East, this body is conservative doctrinally, with an evangelical, biblical emphasis. The polity of churches within the group differ with congregationalism being dominant, but there are presbyterian Armenian Evangelical churches as well. Most of the local churches have joined main-line denominations. All of the remaining Armenian Evangelical (congregational or presbyterian) local churches in the United States and Canada have joined with the Armenian Evangelical Union of North America.

Headquarters

Armenian Evangelical Church of Toronto, 2600 14th Avenue, Markham, ON L3R 3X1, Tel. (905)305-8144 Fax (905)305-8125
Media Contact, Chief Editor, Rev. Samuel Albarian

Officers

Min., Rev. Samuel Albarian
A.E.U.N.A. OFFICERS
Min. to the Union, Rev. Joseph D. Matossian, 411 E. Acacia St., Suite 200, Glendale, CA 91205-2821
Mod., Rev. Mgedich Melkonian, 430 South First Street, Fresno, CA 93702-1056, Tel. (559)237-6638. Fax (559)237-9526

Periodicals

Armenian Evangelical Church, Our Church News Letter

Armenian Holy Apostolic Church - Canadian Diocese

The Canadian branch of the ancient Church of Armenia founded in A.D. 301 by St. Gregory the Illuminator was established in Canada at St. Catharines, Ontario, in 1930. The diocesan organization is under the jurisdiction of the Holy See of Etchmiadzin, Armenia. The Diocese has churches in St. Catharines, Hamilton, Toronto, Ottawa, Van-couver, Mississauga, Montreal, Laval, Windsor, Halifax, Winnipeg, Edmonton and Calgary.

Headquarters

Diocesan Offices, Primate, Canadian Diocese, Archbishop Hovnan Derderian, 615 Stuart

Ave., Outremont, QC H2V 3H2, Tel. (514) 276-9479 Fax (514)276-9960
Email adiocese@aol.com
Website: www.canarmdiocese.org
Media Contact, Exec. Dir. Deacon Hagop Arslanian; Silva Mangassarian, Secretary

Officers
Sec., Silva Mangassarian
Webmaster, Albert Yeglikian

Periodicals

Associated Gospel Churches

The Associated Gospel Churches (AGC) traces its historical roots to the 1890s. To counteract the growth of liberal theology evident in many established denominations at this time, individuals and whole congregations seeking to uphold the final authority of the Scriptures in all matters of faith and conduct withdrew from those denominations and established churches with an evangelical ministry. These churches defended the belief that "all Scripture is given by inspiration of God" and also declared that the Holy Spirit gave the identical word of sacred writings of holy men of old, chosen by Him to be the channel of His revelation to man.

At first this growing group of independent churches was known as the Christian Workers' Churches of Canada, and by 1922 there was desire for forming an association for fellowship, counsel and cooperation. Several churches in southern Ontario banded together under the leadership of Dr. P. W. Philpott of Hamilton and Rev. H. E. Irwin, K. C. of Toronto.

When a new Dominion Charter was obtained on March 18, 1925, the name was changed to Associated Gospel Churches. Since that time the AGC has steadily grown, spreading across Canada by invitation to other independent churches of like faith and by actively beginning new churches.

Headquarters
1500 Kerns Rd., Burlington, ON L7P 3A7, Tel. (905)634-8184 Fax (905)634-6283
Email: admin@agcofcanada.com
Website: www.agcofcanada.com
Administrative Assistant, Donna Leung, 1500 Kerns Rd., Burlington, ON L7P 3A7, Tel. (905)634-8184 Fax (905)634-6283, Email: donna@agcofcanada.com

Officers
Pres., Dr. Bill Fietje, 1500 Kerns Rd., Burlington, ON L7P 3A7, Tel. (905)634-8184 Fax (905) 634-6283
Mod., Rev. Randy Jost , 1500 Kerns Rd, Burlington, L7P3A7, el. (905)634-8184 Fax (905)634-6283

Periodicals
Insidedge

Association of Regular Baptist Churches (Canada)

The Association of Regular Baptist Churches was organized in 1957 by a group of churches for the purpose of mutual cooperation in missionary activities. The Association believes the Bible to be God's word, stands for historic Baptist principles, and opposes modern ecumenism.

Headquarters
17 Laverock St., Tottenham, ON L0G 1W0, Tel. 905-936-3786

Officers
Chmn., Rev. S. Kring, 67 Sovereen St., Delhi, ON N4B 1L7

Baptist Convention of Ontario and Quebec

The Baptist Convention of Ontario and Quebec is a family of 365 churches in Ontario and Quebec, united for mutual support and encouragement and united in missions in Canada and the world.

The Convention was formally organized in 1888. Its one educational institution—McMaster Divinity College was founded in 1887. The Convention works through the all-Canada missionary agency, Canadian Baptist Ministries. The churches also support the Sharing Way, the relief and development arm of Canadian Baptist Ministries.

Headquarters
195 The West Mall, Ste. 414, Etobicoke, ON M9C 5K1, Tel. (416)620-2940 Fax (416)622-2308
Media Contact, Exec. Min., Dr. Ken Bellous, Website: www.Baptist.ca

Officers
Past Pres., Rev. John Torrance
President, Mr. Evan Whitehead
1st Vice-Pres., Mrs. Marie Toompuu
2nd Vice Pres., Mr. Don Hallman
Treas.-Bus. Admn., Nancy Bell
Exec. Min., Dr. Ken Bellous

Periodicals
The Canadian Baptist

Baptist General Conference of Canada

The Baptist General Conference was founded in Canada by missionaries from the United States. Originally a Swedish body, BGC Canada now includes people of many nationalities and is conservative and evangelical in doctrine and practice.

Headquarters
#205 15824 131 Avenue Edmonton, AB T5V 1J4, Tel. (780)438-9127 Fax (780)435-2478
Media Contact, Exec. Dir., Jamey S. McDonald

Officers

Exec. Dir., Jamey S. McDonald , #205 15824 131 Avenue Edmonton, AB T5V 1J4, Tel. (780) 438-9127 Fax (780)435-2478

Exec. Dir., Gordon H. Sorensen, BGC Stewardship Foundation, #205 15824 131 Avenue Edmonton, AB T5V 1J4, Tel. (780) 438-9127 Fax (780)435-2478

DISTRICTS

Baptist Gen. Conf.- Central Canada, Exec. Min., Lorne Meisner, 877 Wilkes Avenue, Winnipeg, MB R3P 1B8, Tel. (204)772-6742 Fax (204) 269-5505

Baptist General Conference in Alberta, Exec. Min., Cal Netterfield, 11525 23 Ave., Edmonton, AB T6J 4T3, Tel. (780)438-9126 Fax (780)438-5258

British Columbia Baptist Conference, Exec. Min., Walter W. Wieser, 7600 Glover Rd., Langley, BC V2Y 1Y1, Tel. (604)888-2246 Fax (604)888-0046

Baptist General Conf. in Saskatchewan, Exec. Min., Abe Funk

The Bible Holiness Movement

The Bible Holiness Movement, organized in 1949 as an outgrowth of the city mission work of the late Pastor William James Elijah Wakefield, an early-day Salvation Army officer, has been headed since its inception by his son, Evangelist Wesley H. Wakefield, its Bishop-General.

It derives its emphasis on the original Methodist faith of salvation and scriptural holiness from the late Bishop R. C. Horner. It adheres to the common evangelical faith in the Bible, the Deity and the atonement of Christ. It stresses a personal experience of salvation for the repentant sinner, of being wholly sanctified for the believer and of the fullness of the Holy Spirit for effective witness.

Membership involves a life of Christian love and evangelistic and social activism. Members are required to totally abstain from liquor and tobacco. They may not attend popular amusements or join secret societies. Divorce and remarriage are forbidden. Similar to Wesley's Methodism, members are, under some circumstances, allowed to retain membership in other evangelical church fellowships. Interchurch affiliations are maintained with a number of Wesleyan-Arminian Holiness denominations.

Year-round evangelistic outreach is maintained through open-air meetings, visitation, literature and other media. Noninstitutional welfare work, including addiction counseling, is conducted among minorities. There is direct overseas famine relief, civil rights action, environment protection and antinuclearism. The movement sponsors a permanent committee on religious freedom and an active promotion of Christian racial equality.

The movement has a world outreach with branches in the United States, India, Nigeria, Philippines, Ghana, Liberia, Cameroon, Kenya, Zambia, South Korea, Mulawi, and Tanzania. It also ministers to 29 countries in 42 languages through literature, radio and audiocassettes.

Headquarters

Box 223, Postal Stn. A, Vancouver, BC V6C 2M3, Tel. (250)492-3376

Media Contact, Bishop-General, Evangelist Wesley H. Wakefield, P.O. Box 223, Postal Station A, Vancouver, BC V6C 2M3, Tel. (250)492-3376

Website: www.bible-holiness-movement.com

Directors

Bishop-General, Evangelist Wesley H. Wakefield, (Intl. Leader)

Evangelist M. J. Wakefield, Penticton, BC

Pastor Vincente and Mirasal Hernando, Phillipines

Pastor and Mrs. Daniel Stinnett, 1425 Mountain View W., Phoenix, AZ

Pastor Monday S. Attai, Abak, Akwalbom, Nigeria, West Africa

Pastor Choe Chong Dae, Iksun City, S. Korea

Pastor T. Chandra, Sekhor-Rao, India

Pastor Victor Freeman Holmquist, Vancouver, B.C., Canada

Bro. Aaron Louis Birch, Vancouver, B.C., Canada

Evangelist and Mrs. Stephen Richards, Uyo, Akwa Iborn State, Nigeria, West Africa

Periodicals

Hallelujah!

Brethren in Christ Church, Canadian Conference

The Brethern in Christ, formerly known as Tunkers in Canada, arose out of a religious awakening in Lancaster County, Pennsylvania late in the 18th century. Representatives of the new denomination reached Ontario in 1788 and established the church in the southern part of the present province. Presently the conference has congregations in Ontario, Alberta, Quebec and Saskatchewan. In theology they have accents of the Pietist, Anabaptist, Wesleyan and Evangelical movements.

Headquarters

Brethren in Christ Church, Gen. Ofc., P.O. Box A, Grantham, PA 17027-0901, Tel. (717)697-2634 Fax (717)697-7714

Canadian Headquarters, Bishop's Ofc., 416 North Service Rd. E., Suite 1, Oakville, ON L6H 5R2,, Tel. (905)339-2335

Media Contact, Mod., Dr. Warren L. Hoffman, Brethren in Christ Church Gen. Ofc.

Officers

Mod., Bishop Brian Bell, 416 North Service Road, Suite 1, Oakville, ON L6H 5R2, Tel. (905)339-2335 Fax (905)337-2120

Sec., Betty Albrecht, RR 2, Petersburg, ON N0B 2H0

Sec., Carole Phillips, 416 North Service Rd. E., Suite 1, Oakville, ON L6H 5R2

Periodicals

Evangelical Visitor; "Yes", Shalom

British Methodist Episcopal Church of Canada

The British Methodist Episcopal Church was organized in 1856 in Chatham, Ontario and incorporated in 1913. It has congregations across the Province of Ontario.

Headquarters

430 Grey Street, London, ON N6B 1H3

Media Contact, Gen. Sec., Rev. Jacqueline Collins, 47 Connolly St., Toronto, ON M6N 4Y5, Tel. (416)653-6339

Officers

Gen. Supt., Rt. Rev. Dr. Douglas Birse, R.R. #5, Thamesville, ON N0P 2K0, Tel. (519)692-3628

Asst. Gen. Supt., Maurice M. Hicks, 3 Boxdene Ave., Scarborough, ON M1V 3C9, Tel. (416) 534-3831/ (416)534-8257

Gen. Sec., Rev. Jacqueline Collins, 47 Connolly St., Toronto, ON M6N 4Y5, Tel. (416)653-6339

Gen. Treas., Ms. Hazel Small, 7 Wood Fernway, North York, ON M2J 4P6, Tel. (416)491-0313

Periodicals

B.M.E. Church Newsletter

Canadian and American Reformed Churches

The Canadian and American Reformed Churches accept the Bible as the infallible Word of God, as summarized in The Belgic Confession of Faith (1561), The Heidelberg Catechism (1563) and The Canons of Dort (1618-1619). The federation was founded in Canada in 1950 and in the United States in 1955.

Headquarters

Contact church for the federation of churches, 607 Dynes Rd., Burlington, ON L7N 2V4

Canadian Reformed Churches, Ebenezer Canadian Reformed Church, 607 Dynes Rd., Burlington, ON L7N 2V4

Canadian Reformed Churches, Ebenezer Canadian Reformed Church, 607 Dynes Rd., Burlington, ON L7N 2V4

Theological College, Dr. G. H. Visscher, 110 W. 27th St., Hamilton, ON L9C 5A1, Tel. (905)575-3688 Fax (905)575-0799

Media Contact, Rev. Dr. G. Nederveen, 3089 Woodward Ave., Burlington, ON L7N 2M3, Tel. (905)681-7055 Fax (905)681-7055

Related Organizations

Anak-Anak Terang (Timor childrens aid), Anchor Canadian Reformed Association for the Handicapped, Association for Reformed Political Action, Campfire Summer Bible Camp, Canadian Reformed Broadcasting Association,Canadian Reformed Home Registry, Canadian Reformed Teachers Association,Canadian Reformed World Relief Fund, Faithworks, Christian Young Adults Retreat, Coram Deo International Aid - Adoration Christian Centre, Covenant Canadian Reformed Teachers College, Guido De Bres Christian High School, Emmanuel Christian High School, Harvest Endowment Foundation, Canadian Reformed Society for a Home for the Aged, Canadian Reformed Senior Citizens' Home Society, Inter-League Publication Board, International Conference of Reformed Churches, League of Canadian Reformed Men's Societies in Ontario, League of Canadian Reformed School Societies, League of Canadian Reformed Women's Societies in Ontario, Middle East Reformed Fellowship-Canada, Reformed Evangelism Taskforce, Reformed Library Association, Reformed Perspective Foundation, Spindleworks, Youth Conference Committee

Periodicals

Reformed Perspective, A Magazine for the Christian Family; Evangel, The Good News of Jesus Christ; Clarion, The Canadian Reformed Magazine; Diakonia-A Magazine of Office-Bearers; Book of Praise; Koinonia, A periodical of the Ministers of the CanRC; Horizon, A quaterly magazine published by the League of CanRC Women Societies; A Gift from Heaven, A Reformed Bible course; Mission News; Roadside Assistance, a magazine for young people; Sermon Series,published sermons for officebearers; Yearbook of Canadian & American Reformed Churches and the Free Reformed Churches of Australia.

Canadian Baptist Ministries

The Canadian Baptist Ministries has four federated member bodies, (1) Baptist Convention of Ontario and Quebec, (2) Baptist Union of Western Canada, (3) the United Baptist Convention of the Atlantic Provinces, (4) Union d'Églises Baptistes Françaises au Canada (French Baptist Union). Its main purpose is to act as a coordinating agency for the four groups for mission in all five continents.

Headquarters

7185 Millcreek Dr., Mississauga, ON L5N 5R4, Tel. (905)821-3533 Fax (905)826-3441

Website: www.cbmin.org

Media Contact, Communications, David Rogelstad

Email: daver@cbmin.org

Officers

Pres., Doug Coomas

Gen. Sec., Rev. Gart Nelson

Email: NelsonG@cbmin.org

190

Canadian Baptists of Western Canada

Headquarters
#1100 550 11TH. Ave, SW, Calgary, Alberta T2R 1K9, Tel.(800)820-2479/(403)228-9559
Media Contact, Exec. Min., Rev. Jeremy Bell, Tel. (403)228-9559 ext. 310

Officers
President: Rev. David Simpson (until April 2009), 8025 Sherwood Dr., Regina, SK S4Y 1G1
Executive Minister; Rev. Jeremy Bell, 5920 Iona Drive, Vancouver BC, V6T 1J6
Alberta Regional Minister: Rev. Dennis Stone, 212, 9333 – 50th St., Edmonton, Alberta T6B 2L5
BCY Regional Minister: Rev. Rob Ogilvie, 201, 20349 88th Ave, Langley, British Columbia V1M 2K5
Heartland Regional Minister: Rev. Devin Seghers, 3–4621 Rae St., Regina, Saskatchewan S4S 6K6
Carey Theological College: President, Dr. Brian Stelck, 5920 Iona Drive, Vancouver BC, V6T 1J6

Canadian Conference of Mennonite Brethren Churches

The conference was incorporated November 22, 1945.

Headquarters
1310 Taylor Ave., Winnipeg, MB R3M 3Z6, Tel. (204)669-6575 Fax (204)654-1865 Toll Free: 888-669-6575 www.mbconf.ca
Media Contact, Exec. Dir., Dave Wiebe

Periodicals
Mennonite Brethren Herald; Le Lien; Chinese Herald; Mennonite Historian

Canadian District of the Moravian Church in America, Northern Province

The work in Canada is under the general oversight and rules of the Moravian Church, Northern Province, general offices for which are located in Bethlehem, Pennsylvania. For complete information, see "Religious Bodies in the United States" section of the Yearbook.

Headquarters
1021 Center St., P.O. Box 1245, Bethlehem, PA 18016-1245
Media Contact, Mr. Mike Riess

Officers
Pres., Rev. Stephen Gohdes, 600 Acadia Dr. SE Calgary, AB T2J OB8, Email: sgohdes@shaw.ca

Periodicals
The Moravian

Canadian Convention of Southern Baptists

The Canadian National Baptist Convention was formed at the Annual Meeting, May 7-9, 1985, in Kelowna, British Columbia. It was formerly known as the Canadian Baptist Conference, founded in Kamloops, British Columbia, in 1959 by pastors of existing churches.

Headquarters
100 Convention Way, Cochrane, AB T4C 2G2, Tel. (403)932-5688 Fax (403)932-4937
Email: office@cnbc.ca

Officers
National Ministry Leader, Gerald Taillon, 17 Riverview Close, Cochrane, AB T4C 1K7
Pres., Richard Lamothe, 31 Koho Drive, Ashton, ON K0A 1B0

Periodicals
The Baptist Horizon

Canadian Yearly Meeting of the Religious Society of Friends

Canadian Yearly Meeting of the Religious Society of Friends was founded in Canada as an offshoot of the Quaker movement in Great Britain and colonial America. Genesee Yearly Meeting, founded 1834, Canada Yearly Meeting (Orthodox), founded in 1867, and Canada Yearly Meeting, founded in 1881, united in 1955 to form the Canadian Yearly Meeting. Canadian Yearly Meeting is affiliated with Friends United Meeting and Friends General Conference. It is also a member of Friends World Committee for Consultation.

Headquarters
91A Fourth Ave., Ottawa, ON K1S 2L1, Tel. (613)235 - 8553 OR, Tel. (888)296 - 3222 Fax (613)235-1753, Email: cym-office@quaker.ca

Officers
Clerk, Anne Mitchell
Archivist, Jane Zavitz Bond
Archives, Arthur G. Dorland, Pickering College, 389 Bayview St., Newmarket, ON L3Y 4X2, Tel. (416)895-1700

Periodicals
The Canadian Friend; Quaker Concern

Christ Catholic Church International

Christ Catholic Church International now has churches and-or missions in 14 countries spread over four continents. They are located in the United States, Canada, Poland, Bahamas, Ukraine, Trinidad-Tobago, Colombia, Australia, Slovakia, Belarus, Kenya and the Phillipines. Some countries have active churches and missions; some just missions and-or prayer groups.

CCCI is an Orthodox-Catholic Communion tracing Apostolic Succession through the Old Catholic and Orthodox Catholic Churches.

The church ministers to a growing number of people seeking an experiential relationship with their Lord and Savior Jesus Christ in a Sacramental and Scripture based church.

Headquarters

4695 St. Lawrence Ave., Niagara Falls, ON L2G 1Y4
Email: dioceseofniagara@cogeco.net
Website: www3.sympatico.ca/dwmullan
Media Contact, The Rt. Rev. John W. Brown, 1504-75 Queen St., Hamilton, ON L8R 3J3, Tel. (905)527-9089 Fax (905)522-6240, bishopjohn@primus.ca

Officers

PRESIDING ARCHBISHOP
The Most Rev. Donald Wm. Mullan, 6190 Barker St., Niagara Falls, ON L2G 1Y4, Tel. 905-354-2329 Fax 905-357-9934, dmullan1@cogeco.net

ARCHBISHOPS
The Most Rev. Jose Ruben Garcia Matiz, Calle 52 Sur #24A-35-Bq. #1, Ap. 301, Santa Fe de Bogota, D.C., Colombia, South America, Tel. 57-71447 87, jorugama@col1.telecom.com.co

BISHOPS
The Rt. Rev. John Wm. Brown, 1504-75 Queen St., N. Hamilton, ON L8R 3J3, Tel. 905-522-6240, bishopjohn@primus.ca
The Rt. Rev. Luis Fernando Hoyos Maldonado, A. A. 24378 Santa Fe de Bogota, D.C., Colombia, South America, Tel. 57-276-68-16, jourgama@col1.telecom.com.co
The Rt. Rev. Jose Moises Moncada Quevedo, A.A. 24378 Santa Fe de Bogota, D.C., Colombia, South America, Tel. 57-276-68-16, jourgama@col1.telecom.com.co
The Rt. Rev. Jerome Robben, Vicar General, P.O. Box 566, Chesterfield, MO 63006-0566, Tel. 314-205-8422, abbajn17@aol.com
The Rt. Rev. Andrzej J. Sarwa, ul. Krucza 16 27-600 Sandomierz, Poland, Tel./Fax 084 (015)833-21-41, andrzej-san@poczta.wp.pl
The Rt. Rev. Robert Smith, 824 Royal Oak Dr., Orlando, FL 32809, Tel 407-240-7833, yshwa@webtv.net
The Rt. Rev. Ted Lorah Jr., 430 Wawassan Drive, P.O. Box 208, Honey Brook, PA 19344, Tel 610 273-7209, tlorah@temple.edu
The Rt. Rev. John Gilbert-Cougar, Box 7305, D. L. Atkinson Station, Pasadena, TX 77508-7305

Periodicals

St. Luke Magazine

Christian Brethren (also known as Plymouth Brethren)

The Christian Brethren are a loose grouping of autonomous local churches, often called "assemblies." They are firmly committed to the inerrancy of Scripture and to the evangelical doctrine of salvation by faith alone apart from works or sacrament. Characteristics are a weekly Breaking of Bread and freedom of ministry without a requirement of ordination. For their history, see Directory 3, "Religious Bodies in the United States" in this Yearbook.

CORRESPONDENT

John Rush, 2872 Illinois Avenue., Debuque, IL 52001, USA, Tel.(563)557-8535

RELATED ORGANIZATIONS
Christian Brethren Churches in Quebec, P.O. Box 1054, Sherbrooke, QC J1H 5L3, Tel. (819) 820-1693 Fax (819)821-9287
Kawartha Lakes Bible College, Box 1101, Peterborough, ON K9J 7H4, Tel. (705)742-2437
Mount Carmel Bible School, 4725 106th Ave., Edmonton, AB T6A 1E7, Tel. (780)465-3015
MSC Canada, 509-3950 14th Ave., Markham, ON L3R 0A9, Tel. (905)947-0468 Fax (905) 947-0352
Vision Ministries Canada, 145 Lincoln Road, Waterloo, ON N2J 2N8, Tel. (519)725-1212 Fax (519)725-9421

Periodicals

News of Quebec

Christian Church (Disciples of Christ) in Canada

Disciples have been in Canada since 1810, and were organized nationally in 1922. This church served the Canadian context as a region of the whole Christian Church (Disciples of Christ) in the United States and Canada.

Headquarters

Christian Church in Canada, P.O. Box 23030, 417 Wellington St., St. Thomas, ON N5R 6A3, Tel. 519-633-9083 Fax 519-637-6407, Email ccic@netrover.com
Media Contact, Reg. Min., F. Thomas Rutherford

Officers

Mod., Peter Fountain, P.O. Box 344, Milton, NS B0T 1P0, Tel. 902-354-5988, pjfountain@auracom.com
Reg. Min., F. Thomas Rutherford, P.O. Box 23030, 417 Wellington St., St. Thomas, ON N5R 6A3, Tel. 519-633-9083 Fax 519-637-6407, ccic@netrover.com

Christian Churches / Churches of Christ

First congregation organized: Cross Roads Christian Church, Cross Roads, Prince Edward Island, Canada, 1810, by "Scotch Baptists" influenced by James and Robert Haldane of Edinburgh. Since the 1820s when the writings of Thomas and Alexander Campbell were widely circulated and reprinted in periodicals, these congregations have identified with the 19th-c. "Restoration Movement" (also known as, "Stone-Campbell Movement") which came to be known as "Disciples of Christ." In late 19th-c. Ontario, some congregations separated over the use of musical instruments into a group known as the a capella Churches of Christ. From the 1880s to the 1930s, Disciples of Christ migrating from Ontario and emigrating from the United States organized congregations in Manitoba, Saskatchewan, Alberta, and British Columbia. From about 1948, when the Disciples of Christ in Canada first moved toward and, then, declared a formal denominational structure in 1968, 65-70 congregations across Canada did not identify with this structure preferring to remain free, congregationally governed fellowships. While especially in western Canada these congregations cooperate and fellowship with congregations identified with the Disciples of Christ in Canada, a capella Churches of Christ, and people and congregations of several other traditions, they generally tend to identify with the interpretation of the Restoration or Stone-Campbell Movement as exemplified by U.S. Christian Churches and Churches of Christ in affinity with the North American Christian Convention, an annual, non-delegated, preaching and teaching convention. (See "The Movement in Canada", *Encyclopedia of the Stone-Campbell Movement*. Grand Rapids, Mich.: Eerdmans, 2004, pp. 151-163).

Headquarters
Media Contact: Russell E. Kuykendall, 13 Roseglen Private, Ottawa, ON K1H 1B5 Tel (416)895-1098, Email: russkuyk@primus.ca

Other Organizations
All of the following are free-standing, para-church institutions. Mortgage financing for congregations and para-church institutions: Church of Christ Development Company, Edmonton, Alberta. Church-planting associations: Partners in Atlantic Canada Evangelism, Impact Ontario, and Alberta Church Planting Association. Degree-granting colleges: Maritime Christian College, Charlottetown, PEI, and Alberta Bible College, Calgary, AB. Cross-cultural missions: Church of Christ Mission Jamaica; Church of Christ Mission India; Global Missionary Ministries (Central Europe); Frontier Labourers for Christ Canada (Thailand, Laos, and Myanmar); Graceland Ministries (Poland); Terri Scruggs, Partners with Nationals, Wycliffe Bible Translators; Benevolent Social Services of India; and others. Christian camps: Canoe Cove (PEI), Ontario Christian Assembly, Camp Christian (Pine Lake, AB), Pine Ridge Christian (Grande Prairie, AB), and Double VM (Lumby, BC). Annual fellowship meetings: Maritime Christian Fellowship, Ontario Christian Missionary Conference, Western Canada Christian Convention (with Disciples of Christ and a capella Churches of Christ), and the North American Christian Convention.

Christian and Missionary Alliance in Canada
A Canadian movement, dedicated to the teaching of Jesus Christ the Saviour, Sanctifier, Healer and Coming King, commenced in Toronto in 1887 under the leadership of the Rev. John Salmon. Two years later, the movement united with The Christian Alliance of New York, founded by Rev. A. B. Simpson, becoming the Dominion Auxiliary of the Christian Alliance, Toronto, under the presidency of the Hon. William H. Howland. Its four founding branches were Toronto, Hamilton, Montreal, and Quebec. The movement focused on the deeper life and missions. In 1980, the Christian and Missionary Alliance in Canada became autonomous. Its General Assembly is held every two years.

National Office
30 Carrier Dr, Suite 100, Toronto, ON M9W 5T7, Tel. 416-674-7878 Fax 416-674-0808
Email: info@cmacan.org
Media Contact, Director of Communications, Barrie Doyle

Officers
Pres., Dr. Franklin Pyles, pylesf@cmacan.org
Vice-Pres.-Global Ministries, Rev. Jim Foster, fosterj@cmacan.org
Vice-Pres.-Fin., Paul D. Lorimer, lorimerp@cmacan.org
Vice-Pres.- Strategic Interface, Rev. David Freeman, freemand@cmacan.org

Periodicals
Alliance.ca

Christian Reformed Church in North America
Canadian congregations of the Christian Reformed Church in North America have been formed since 1905. For detailed information about this denomination, please refer to the listing for the Christian Reformed Church in North America in Directory 3, "Religious Bodies in the United States."

Headquarters
United States Office, 2850 Kalamazoo Ave., S.E., Grand Rapids, MI 49560, Tel. (616)224-0832 Fax (616)224-5895
Canadian Office, 3475 Mainway, P.O. Box 5070 STN LCR 1, Burlington, ON L7R 3Y8, Tel. (905)336-2920 Fax (905)336-8344
Website: www.crcna.org
Media Contact, Exec. Dir., Rev. Gerard Dykstra, U.S. Office; Director of Communication, Mr. Henry Hess, Canadian Office

Executive Director: Rev. Gerard Dykstra
Director of Finance & Administration: Mr. John Bolt, U.S. Office
Director of Denominational Ministries: Mrs. Sandy Johnson

Periodicals
The Banner

Church of God (Anderson, Ind.)

This body is one of the largest of the groups which have taken the name "Church of God." Its headquarters are at Anderson, Indiana. It originated about 1880 and emphasizes Christian unity.

Headquarters
Western Canada Assembly, Chpsn., Egbert Lubek, 4717- 56th St., Camrose, AB T4V 2C4, Tel. (780)672-0772 Fax (780)672-6888
Eastern Canada Assembly, Chpsn., Jim Wiebe, 38 James St., Dundas, ON L9H 2J6
Email: admincoo@telsu.net
Website: www.chog.ca
Media Contact for Western Canada, Executive Dir. of Ministry Services, Ken Wiedrick, 4717 56th St., Camrose, AB T4V 2C4, Tel. (780) 672-0772 Fax (780)672-6888

Periodicals
The Gospel Contact; The Messenger

Church of God in Christ (Mennonite)

The Church of God in Christ, Mennonite was organized by the evangelist-reformer John Holdeman in Ohio. The church unites with the faith of the Waldenses, Anabaptists and other such groups throughout history. Emphasis is placed on obedience to the teachings of the Bible, including the doctrine of the new birth and spiritual life, noninvolvement in government or the military, a head-covering for women, beards for men and separation from the world shown by simplicity in clothing, homes, possessions and lifestyle. The church has a worldwide membership of about 22,870, largely concentrated in the United States and Canada.

Headquarters
P.O. Box 313, 420 N. Wedel Ave., Moundridge, KS 67107, Tel. (620)345-2532 Fax (620)345-2582
Media Contact, Dale Koehn, P.O. Box 230, Moundridge, KS 67107, Tel. (620)345-2532 Fax (620)345-2582

Periodicals
Messenger of Truth

Church of God (Cleveland, Tenn.)

It is one of America's oldest Pentecostal churches founded in 1886 as an outgrowth of the holiness revival under the name Christian Union.

In 1907 the church adopted the organizational name Church of God. It has its foundation upon the principles of Christ as revealed in the Bible. The Church of God is Christian, Protestant, foundational in its doctrine, evangelical in practice and distinctively Pentecostal. It maintains a centralized form of government and a commitment to world evangelization.

The first church in Canada was established in 1919 in Scotland Farm, Manitoba. Paul H. Walker became the first overseer of Canada in 1931.

Headquarters
Intl. offices, 2490 Keith St., NW, Cleveland, TN 37320, Tel. (423)472-3361 Fax (423)478-7066
Media Contact, Dir. of Communications, T. Scot Carter, P.O. Box 2430, Cleveland, TN 37320-2430, Tel. (423)478-7112 Fax (423)478-7066

Officers

EXECUTIVES
General Overseer, Dr. Raymond F. Culpepper, P.O. Box 2430, Cleveland, TN 37320-2430, Tel. 423-478-7137 Fax 423-478-7275, gocog @churchofgod.org.
First Assistant General Overseer, Dr. Timothy M. Hill, P.O. Box 2430, Cleveland, TN 37320-2430, Tel. 423-478-7136 Fax 423-478-7379, cog1a@churchofgod.org
Second Assistant General Overseer, Dr. Mark L. Williams, P.O. Box 2430, Cleveland, TN 37320-2430, Tel. 423-478-7126 Fax 423-478-7263, cog2a@churchofgod.org
Third Assistant General Overseer, Dr. David M. Griffis, P.O. Box 2430, Cleveland, TN 37320-2430, Tel. 423-478-7133 Fax 423-478-7247, cog3a@churchofgod.org
Secretary General, Dr. Wallace J. Sibley, P.O. Box 2430, Cleveland, TN 37320-2430, Tel. 423-478-7127 Fax 423-478-7052, cogsec general@churchofgod.org
Canada-Eastern, Reverend Daniel J. Vassell, P.O. Box 2036, Brampton, ON L6T 3TO, Tel. (905)270-8083 Fax (905)270-6720
Canada-Western, Reverend Vaughn D. Mathews, Box 54055, 2640 52 St. NE, Calgary, AB T1Y 6S6, Tel. (403)293-8817 Fax (403)293-3466
Canada-Quebec-Maritimes, Reverend Jacques Houle, 19 Orly, Granby, QC J2H 1Y4, Tel. (450)378-4442 Fax (450)378-8646
Canada-National, Dr. Mark L. Williams, P.O. Box 2430, Cleveland, TN 37320-2430, Tel. (423)478-7126 Fax (423)478-7276

GENERAL MINISTRIES
Administrative Liaison to General Overseer, H. Lynn Stone
Legal Services-Attorney, Dennis W. Watkins
Communications-Dir., T. Scot Carter
Church of God Foundation, Inc.-Pres./CEO Donald S. Aultman
International Prayer Commission-Coord., P. Douglas Small

194

DIVISION OF WORLD EVANGELIZATION
Executive Divisional Director-Timothy M. Hill
Black Ministries-Coordinator, Kenneth L. Hill
Hispanic Ministries-Director, Carlos S. Moran
Ministry to the Military-Director, Robert A. Moore
Multi-Cultural-Director, G. Dennis McGuire
Personal Evangelism-Coordinator, Leonard C. Albert
USA Missions-Director, Jimmy D. Smith
World Missions-Director, J. Douglas LeRoy

DIVISION OF EDUCATION
Executive Divisional Director-Mark L. Williams
European Theological Bible Seminary-Dir., Paul Schmidgall
International Bible College-Pres., Randy H. Krieger
Lee University-Pres., Charles Paul Conn
Patten University-Pres., Gary Moncher
Patten University/Internet Degree Program-Dir., Delton L. Alford
Pentecostal Theological Seminary, Pres., Steven J. Land
Ministerial Development/School of Ministry-Coord., Donald G. Bennett
USA Hispanic Education Ministries-Dir., Enrique de Jesus

DIVISION OF DISCIPLESHIP
Executive Divisional Director-David M. Griffis
Youth Discipleship-Dir., Thomas A. Madden
Men's Discipleship-Coord., David H. Gosnell
Women's Discipleship-Coord., Lorna V. Gosnell
Publications-Dir., Terry R. Hart

DIVISION OF CARE AND SUPPORT SERVICES
Care Ministries:
Executive Divisional Director-Wallace J. Sibley
Executive Administrator-Donnie W. Smith
Chaplains Commission-Dir., Donnie W. Smith
Ministerial Care-Dir., Bill Leonard
Ministry to Israel-Dir., J. Michael Utterback
SpiritCare Ministries-Dir., Donnie W. Smith
Operation Compassion-Dir., David B. Lorency
Support Services:
Executive Divisional Director-Wallace J. Sibley
Church of God Benefits Board, Inc.-Pres. & CEO, Arthur D. Rhodes
Department of Business and Records-Dir., Julian B. Robinson

Periodicals
Church of God Evangel, Editorial Evangelica, Save Our World, Ministry Now Profiles

The Church of God of Prophecy Canada East

The Church of God of Prophecy is one of the churches that grew out of the work of A. J. Tomlinson in the first half of the twentieth century. Historically it shares a common heritage with the Church of God (Cleveland Tennessee) and is in the mainstream of the classical Pentecostal-holiness tradition.

At the death of A.J. Tomlinson in 1943, M.A. Tomlinson was named General Overseer and served until his retirement in 1990. He emphasized unity and fellowship unlimited by racial, social, or political differences. The next General Overseer, Billy D. Murray, Sr., who served from 1990 until his retirement in 2000, emphasized a commitment to the promotion of Christian unity and world evangelization. In July 2000, Fred S. Fisher, Sr. Was duly selected to serve as the fourth General Overseer of the Church of God of Prophecy.

From its beginnings, the Church has based its beliefs on "the whole Bible, rightly divided," and has accepted the Bible as God's Holy Word, inspired, inerrant and infallible. The church is firm in its commitment to orthodox Christian belief. The Church affirms that there is one God, eternally existing in three persons, Father, Son and Holy Spirit. It believes in the deity of Christ, His virgin birth, His sinless life, the physical miracles He performed, His atoning death on the cross, His bodily resurrection, His ascension to the right hand of the Father and his Second coming. The church professes that salvation results from grace alone through faith in Christ, that regeneration by the Holy Spirit is essential for the salvation of sinful men, and that sanctification by the blood of Christ makes possible personal holiness. It affirms the present ministry of the Holy Spirit by Whose indwelling believers are able to live godly lives and have power for service. The church believes in, and promotes, the ultimate unity of believers as prayed for by Christ in John 17. The church stresses the sanctity of human life and is committed to the sanctity of the marriage bond and the importance of strong, loving Christian families. Other official teachings include Holy Spirit baptism with tongues as initial evidence; manifestation of the spiritual gifts; divine healing; premillenial second-coming of Christ; total abstinence from the use of tobacco, alcohol and narcotics; water baptism by immersion; the Lord's supper and washing of the saints' feet; and a concern for moderation and holiness in all dimensions of lifestyle.

The Church is racially integrated on all levels, including top leadership. Women play a prominent role in church affairs, serving in pastoral roles and other leadership positions. The church presbytery has recently adopted plurality of leadership in the selection of a General Oversight Group. This group consists of eight bishops located around the world who, along with the General Overseer, are responsible for inspirational leadership and vision casting for the church body.

The Church has local congregations in all 50 states and more than 100 nations worldwide. Organizationally there is a strong emphasis on

195

international missions, evangelism, youth and children's ministries, women's and men's ministries, stewardship, communications, publishing, leadership development and discipleship.

Church of God of Prophecy International Offices

P.O. Box 2910, Cleveland, TN 37320-2910
Media Contact, National Overseer, Levi Clarke, 5145 Tomken Rd, Mississauga, ON L4 W1P1, Tel. (905)625-1278 Fax (905)-625-1316
Website: www.cogop.ca

Officers

Gen. Overseer, Bishop Randy E. Howard, Sr.; General Presbyters, Sherman Allen, Sam Clements, Daniel Corbett, Clayton Endecott, Miguel Mojica, José Reyes, Sr., Felix Santiago, Brice Thompson
International Offices Ministries Dirs., Finance, Communications, and Publishing, Perry Gillum; Global Outreach and Administrative Asst. to the General Presbyters, Randy Howard; Leadership Development and Discipleship Ministries, Larry Duncan.

Periodicals

White Wing Messenger (ENG), Victory (Youth Magazine/ Sunday School Curriculum); The Happy Harvester, White Wing Messenger (Spanish).

The Church of Jesus Christ of Latter-Day Saints in Canada

The Church has had a presence in Canada since the early 1830's. Joseph Smith and Brigham Young both came to Eastern Canada as missionaries. There are now 157,000 members in Canada in more than 400 congregations.

Leading the Church in Canada are the presidents of over 40 stakes (equivalent to a diocese). World headquarters is in Salt Lake City, UT (See U.S. Religious Bodies chapter of the Directories section of this Yearbook).

Headquarters

50 East North Temple St., Salt Lake City, UT 84150
Media Contact, Public Affairs Dir., Ellen Warner, 1185 Eglinton Ave., Box 116, North York, ON M3C 3C6, Tel. (905)793-3675 Fax (416)438-2723

Church of the Lutheran Brethren

The Church of the Lutheran Brethren of America was organized in December 1900. Five independent Lutheran congregations met together in Milwaukee, Wisconsin, and adopted a constitution patterned very closely to that of the Lutheran Free Church of Norway.

The spiritual awakening in the Midwest during the 1890s crystallized into convictions that led to the formation of a new church body. Chief among the concerns were church membership practices,

observance of Holy Communion, confirmation practices and local church government.

The Church of the Lutheran Brethren practices a simple order of worship with the sermon as the primary part of the worship service. It believes that personal profession of faith is the primary criterion for membership in the congregation. The Communion service is reserved for those who profess faith in Christ as savior. Each congregation is autonomous and the synod serves the congregations in advisory and cooperative capacities.

The synod supports an Internation Mission program in Cameroon, Chad, Japan and Taiwan. Approximately 40 percent of the synodical budget is earmarked for International mission. A growing North American Regional mission ministry is planting new congregations in the United States and Canada. Affiliate organizations operate several retirement-nursing homes, conference and retreat centers.

Headquarters

1020 Alcott Ave., W., P.O. Box 655, Fergus Falls, MN 56538, Tel. (218)739-3336 Fax (218)739-5514
Email: clb@clba.org
Website: www.clba.org
Media Contact, Rev. Joel Egge

Officers

Regional Pastor: Art Hundeby, 206 Bayview Cres., Saskatoon, Sk S7V 1B6 Canada
Regional Chairman: Jon Overland, 114 Waldron Ave., Okotoks, AB T0L 1T1
Vice-Chairman: Harold Rust, 3810 65th Street, Camrose, AB T4V 3S1
Sec./Dir. of Comm: Dean Rostad, 4620 61st Street, Camrose, AB T4V 2H7
Treas., Edwin Rundbraaten, Box 739, Birch Hills, SK S0J 0G0

Periodicals

Faith and Fellowship

Church of the Nazarene in Canada

The Church of the Nazarene in Canada was organized in Nova Scotia in November, 1902 by Rev. H.F. Reynolds. The 160 churches today are organized in five districts, with the Canada National Office located in Brampton, Ontario. The Church of the Nazarene is Methodist in theology, representative in church government and warmly evangelistic. It is a a part of the Church of the Nazarene International.

Headquarters

20 Regan Rd., Unit 9, Brampton, ON L7A 1C3, Tel. (905)846-4220 Fax (905)846-1775
Email: national@nazarene.ca
Website: www.nazarene.ca
Media Contact, Gen. Sec., /Operations Officer, Dr. David Wilson, 17001 Prairie Star Parkway, Lenexa, KS 66220, Tel. (913)577-0600 Fax (913)577-0548

Natl. Dir., Dr. Clair MacMillan, 20 Regan Rd. Unit 9, Brampton, ON L7A 1C3, Tel. (905) 846-4220 Fax (905)846-1775, Email: cmacmillan@nazarene.ca

Exec. Asst., Allan McAlpin, 20 Regan Rd. Unit 9, Brampton, ON L7A 1C3, Tel. (905)846-4220 Fax (905)846-1775, Email: national@nazarene.ca

Churches of Christ in Canada

Churches of Christ are autonomous congregations, whose members appeal to the Bible alone to determine matters of faith and practice. There are no central offices or officers. Publications and institutions related to the churches are either under local congregational control or independent of any one congregation.

Churches of Christ shared a common fellowship in the 19th century with the Christian Churches-Churches of Christ and the Christian Church (Disciples of Christ). Fellowship was broken after the introduction of instrumental music in worship and centralization of church-wide activities through a missionary society. Churches of Christ began in Canada soon after 1800, largely in the middle-eastern provinces. The few pioneer congregations were greatly strengthened in the mid-1800s, growing in size and number.

Members of Churches of Christ believe in the inspiration of the Scriptures, the divinity of Jesus Christ, and immersion into Christ for the remission of sins. The New Testament pattern is followed in worship and church organization.

Headquarters

Media Contact, Man. Ed., Gospel Herald, Max Craddock, 5 Lankin Blvd., ON M4J 4W7, Tel. (416)461-7406 Fax (416)424-1850, Email: maxc@strathmorecofc.ca

Periodicals

Gospel Herald

Community of Christ

Founded April 6, 1830, by Joseph Smith, Jr., the church was reorganized under the leadership of the founder's son, Joseph Smith III, in 1860. The Church is established in nearly 50 countries including the United States and Canada, with nearly a quarter of a million members. A world conference is held every three years in Independence, Missouri. The current president is Stephen M. Veazey.

Headquarters

International Headquarters, 1001 W. Walnut, Independence, MO 64050, Tel. (816)833-1000 Fax (816)521-3043

Ontario Regional Ofc., 390 Speedvale Ave. E., Guelph, ON N1E 1N5

Media Contact, Media Relations, Kendra Friend

Officers

Canada East Mission Centre

Ken Barrows, Mission Centre President, 390 Speedvale Ave E., Guelph, ON N1E 1N5 CANADA, (519)822-4150, Email: kbarrows@CofChrist.org

Michael Hewitt, Mission Centre Financial Officer, 390 Speedvale Ave. E., Guelph, ON N1E 1N5 CANADA, (519)822-4150, Email: mhewitt@CofChrist.org

Canada West Mission Centre

Darrell Belrose, Mission Centre President, 6415 Ranchview Drive NW, Calgary AB T3G 1B5 CANADA, Tel. (877)411-2632, Email: dbelrose@CofChrist.org

Jim Poirier, Mission Centre Financial Officer, Email: jpoirier@CofChrist.org

Periodicals

Herald

Congregational Christian Churches in Canada

This body originated in the early 18th century when devout Christians within several denominations in the northern and eastern United States, dissatisfied with sectarian controversy, broke away from their own denominations and took the simple title "Christians." First organized in 1821 at Keswick, Ontario, the Congregational Christian Churches in Canada was incorporated on Dec. 4, 1989, as a national organization. In doctrine the body is evangelical, being governed by the Bible as the final authority in faith and practice. It believes that Christian character must be expressed in daily living; it aims at the unity of all true believers in Christ that others may believe in Him and be saved. In church polity, the body is democratic and autonomous. It is also a member of The World Evangelical Congregational Fellowship.

Headquarters

241 Dunsdon St. Ste. 405, Brantford, ON N3R 7C3, Tel. (519)751-0606 Fax (519)751-0852

Media Contact, Rev. David Schrader, 241 Dunsdon St. Ste. 405, Brantford, ON N3R 7C3, Tel. (519)751-0606 Fax (519)751-0852

Officers

Pres., Rev. Jim Potter

Exec. Dir., Rev. David Schrader

Sec., Rev. Ron Holden

Convention of Atlantic Baptist Churches

The Convention of Atlantic Baptist Churches is the largest Baptist Convention in Canada. Through the Canadian Baptist Ministries, it is a member of the Baptist World Alliance.

In 1763 two Baptist churches were organized in Atlantic Canada, one in Sackville, New Brunswick and the other in Wolfville, Nova

Scotia. Although both these churches experienced crises and lost continuity, they recovered and stand today as the beginning of organized Baptist work in Canada.

Nine Baptist churches met in Lower Granville, Nova Scotia in 1800 and formed the first Baptist Association in Canada. By 1846 the Maritime Baptist Convention was organized, consisting of 169 churches. Three streams of Baptist life merged in 1905 to form the United Baptist Convention. This is how the term "United Baptist" was derived. Today there are 511 churches within 21 associations across the Convention.

The Convention has two educational institutions, Crandall University in Moncton, New Brunswick, a Christian Liberal Arts University, and Acadia Divinity College in Wolfville, Nova Scotia, a Graduate School of Theology. The Convention engages in world mission through Canadian Baptist Ministries, the all-Canada mission agency. In addition to an active program of home mission, evangelism, training, social action and stewardship, the Convention operates senior citizen complexes and a Christian bookstore.

Headquarters
1655 Manawagonish Rd., Saint John, NB E2M 3Y2, Tel. (506)635-1922 Fax (506)635-0366 Email: cabc@baptist-atlantic.ca
Media Contact, Communications Manager, Andrew Myers, Email: andrew.myers@baptist-atlantic.ca
Website: www.baptist.atlantic.ca

Officers
Executive Minister, Dr. Peter Reid, 1655 Manawagonish Road, Saint John NB E2M 3Y2, Tel. (506)635-1922 Fax: (506)635-0366, Email: peter.reid@baptist-atlantic.ca
Dir. of Operations, Mr. Daryl MacKenzie, 1655 Manawagonish Rd., Saint John, NB E2M 3Y2, Tel. (506)635-1922 Fax (506)635-0366, Email: daryl.mackenzie@baptist-atlantic.ca
Dir. of Atlantic Baptist Mission, Dr. Malcolm Beckett, 1655 Manawagonish Rd., Saint John, NB E2M 3Y2, Tel. (506)635-1922 Fax (506) 635-0366 Email: malcolm.beckett@baptist-atlantic.ca
Dir. of Youth and Family, Rev. Dale O. Stairs, 1655 Manawagonish Road, Saint John NB E2M 3Y2, Tel. (506)635-1922 Fax: (506)635-0366, Email: dale.stairs@baptist-atlantic.ca
Dir. of Development, Rev. Greg Jones, 1655 Manawagonish Rd., Saint John, NB E2M 3Y2, Tel. (506)635-1922 Fax (506)635-0366, Email: greg.jones@baptist-atlantic.ca
Dir. of Public Witness and Social Concern, Dr. Lois P. Mitchell, 1655 Manawagonish Rd., Saint John, NB E2M 3Y2, Tel. (506)635-1922; Fax (506)635-0366, Email: lois.mitchell@baptist-atlantic.ca
Communications Manager: Mr. Andrew Myers, 1655 Manawagonish Road, Saint John NB E2M

3Y2, Tel. (506)635-1922 Fax: (506)635-0366, Email: andrew.myers@baptist-atlantic.ca

The Coptic Orthodox Church in Canada

The Coptic Orthodox Church in North America was begun in Canada in 1964 and was registered in the province of Ontario in 1965. The Coptic Orthodox Church has spread rapidly since then. The total number of local churches in both Canada and the USA has exceeded one hundred and ninety. Two dioceses, two monasteries with monks and novices, and two theological seminaries were established in the USA.

The Coptic Orthodox Church is the church of Alexandria founded in Egypt by St. Mark the Apostle in the first century A.D. She is a hierarchical church and the administrative governing body of each local church is an elected Board of Deacons approved by the Bishop. The current patriarch of the church is H. H. Pope Shenouda III, Pope of Alexandria and Patriach of the see of St. Mark. The Coptic Orthodox Church is a member of the Canadian Council of Churches.

Headquarters
St. Mark's Coptic Orthodox Church, 41 Glendinning Ave., Toronto, ON M1W 3E2 4449, Tel. (416)494-4449 Fax (416)494-2631, Email: mail@coptorthodox.ca, Website: www.stmark.toronto.on.coptorthodox.ca
Media Contact, Fr. Ammonius Guirguis, Tel. (416) 494-4449 Fax (416)494-4196, frammonius@coptorthodox.ca

Elim Fellowship Canada

The Elim Fellowship Canada, a Pentecostal body, was established in 1984 as a sister organization of Elim Fellowship in the United States.

This is an association of churches, ministers and missionaries seeking to serve the whole body of Christ. It is Pentecostal and has a charismatic orientation.

Headquarters
379 Golf Road, RR#6, Brantford, ON N3T 5L8, Tel. (519)753-7266, Email: admin@elim.ca
Website: www.elim.ca
Ofc. Mgr., Larry Jones

Officers
Pres., Rev. Ralph Byma
Vice-Pres., Rev. Bob Warriner
Sec./Treas., Larry Jones

COUNCIL OF ELDERS
Ralph Byma, Brantford, Ontario
Ron Burgio, Lima, New York
Claude Favreau, Drummondville, Quebec
Daniel St. Laurent, Montreal, Quebec
Bob Warriner, Millgrove, Ontario

BOARD OF DIRECTORS
Yves Alarie, Montreal, Quebec

John Brooks, Whitby, Ontario
Al Craig, Hamilton, Ontario
Hendrina Dockalek, Brampton, Ontario
Claude Favreau, Drummondville, Quebec
Silas Lazar, Montreal, Quebec
Daniel St. Laurent, Montreal, Quebec
Bob Warriner, Millgrove, Ontario

The Estonian Evangelical Lutheran Church Abroad

The Estonian Evangelical Lutheran Church (EELC) was founded in 1917 in Estonia and reorganized in Sweden in 1944. The teachings of the EELC are based on the Old and New Testaments, explained through the Apostolic, Nicean and Athanasian confessions, the unaltered Confession of Augsburg and other teachings found in the Book of Concord.

Headquarters
383 Jarvis St., Toronto, ON M5B 2C7, Tel. (416) 925-5465 Fax (416)925-5688
Media Contact, Archbishop, Rev. Udo Petersoo
Email: udo.petersoo@eelk.ee
Website: www.eelk.ee/e.e.l.k./

Officers
Archbishop, The Rev. Udo Petersoo
Gen. Sec., Mr. Ivar Nippak
Sec./Clerk, Mrs. Eerika Lage

Periodicals
Eesti Kirik

Evangelical Christian Church in Canada

The Evangelical Christian Church in Canada (Christian Disciples) as a religion in Canada can be traced to the formal organization of the Christian Church in 1804, in Bourbon County, Kentucky, under the leadership of Barton Warren Stone (1772-1844). The Stone Movement later merged with the efforts of Thomas Campbell (1774-1854) and his son Alexander Campbell (1788-1844) to become the Restoration Movement that gave birth to the Churches of Christ (Non-Instrumental), the Christian Churches and Churches of Christ, and the Christian Church (Disciples of Christ). The Evangelical Christian Church (Christian Disciples) as a new group within the Restoration tradition was recognized in 2001.

Headquarters
General Superintendent, Rev. David P. Lavigne, 410-125 Lincoln Rd., Waterloo, ON N2J 2N9, Tel. (519)880-9110 Toll free (888)981-8881
Email: cecc@rogers.com
Website: www.cecconline.net

Officers
Bishop., Rev. Dr. David P. Lavigne, 410-125 Lincoln Rd., Waterloo, ON N2J 2N9, Tel. (519)880-9110 or (888)981-8881, Email: cecc@rogers.com

Gen. Sec., Rev. Gordon Horsely, 213 Homestead Drive, Shelburne, On LON1SO, Tel. (519)925-3651

The Evangelical Covenant Church of Canada

A Canadian denomination organized in Canada at Winnipeg in 1904 which is affiliated with the Evangelical Covenant Church of America and with the International Federation of Free Evangelical Churches, which includes 31 federations in 26 countries.

This body believes in the one triune God as confessed in the Apostles' Creed, that salvation is received through faith in Christ as Saviour, that the Bible is the authoritative guide in all matters of faith and practice. Christian Baptism and the Lord's Supper are accepted as divinely ordained sacraments of the church. As descendants of the 19th century northern European pietistic awakening, the group believes in the need of a personal experience of commitment to Christ, the development of a virtuous life and the urgency of spreading the gospel to the "ends of the world."

Four Core Values: To be a Missional Church; To be a Biblical Church; To be a Devotional Church; and to be a Connnectional Church.

Four Ministry Priorities: Leadership Development; Church Planting & Mission; Church Renewal/ Transition; and Christian Services.

Headquarters
P.O. Box 34025, RPO Fort Richmond, Winnipeg, MB R3T 5T5, Tel.(204)269-3437 Fax (204)269-3584
Media Contact, Supt., Jeff Anderson

Officers
Pres./Supt., Rev. Jeff Anderson, PO 34025, RPO Fort Richmond, Winnipeg, MB R3T 5T5

Evangelical Free Church of Canada

The Evangelical Free Church of Canada traces its beginning back to 1917 when the church in Enchant, Alberta opened its doors. Today the denomination has 140 churches from the West Coast to Quebec. Approximately 80 missionaries are sponsored by the EFCC in 17 countries. The Evangelical Free Church is the founding denomination of Trinity Western University in Langley, British Columbia. Church membership is 8,441, average attendance is 18,455

Headquarters
Mailing Address: P.O. Box 850 LCD1, Langley, BC V3A 8S6, Tel. (604)888-8668 Fax (604)888-3108
Location, 7600 Glover Rd., Langley, BC
Email: efcc@twu.ca
Website: www.efcc.ca
Media Contact, Executive Assistant Maureen Wilson, P.O. Box 850 LCD1, Langley, BC V3A 8S6, Tel. (604)888-8668 Fax (604)888-3108

Officers
President, Dr. Ron Unruh, P.O.Box 850 LCD 1, Langley, BC, Canada V3A 8S6, Tel (604)888-8668 Fax (604)888-3108 efcc@twu.ca

Periodicals
The Pulse

Evangelical Lutheran Church in Canada

The Evangelical Lutheran Church in Canada was organized in 1985 through a merger of The Evangelical Lutheran Church of Canada (ELCC) and the Lutheran Church in America—Canada Section.

The merger is a result of an invitation issued in 1972 by the ELCC to the Lutheran Church in America—Canada Section and the Lutheran Church—Canada. Three-way merger discussions took place until 1978 when it was decided that only a two-way merger was possible. The ELCC was the Canada District of the ALC until autonomy in 1967.

The Lutheran Church in Canada traces its history back more than 200 years. Congregations were organized by German Lutherans in Halifax and Lunenburg County in Nova Scotia in 1749. German Lutherans, including many United Empire Loyalists, also settled in large numbers along the St. Lawrence and in Upper Canada. In the late 19th century, immigrants arrived from Scandinavia, Germany and central European countries, many via the United States. The Lutheran synods in the United States have provided the pastoral support and help for the Canadian church.

Headquarters
302-393 Portage Avenue, Winnipeg, MB R3B 3H6, Tel. (204)984-9150 Fax (204)984-9185
Media Contact, Bishop, Rev. Raymond L. Schultz

Officers
Evangelical Lutheran Women Inc., ELCIC Group Services Inc.

Periodicals
Canada Lutheran; Esprit

Evangelical Mennonite Conference

The Evangelical Mennonite Conference is a modern church of historic Christian convictions, tracing its indebtedness to the Radical Reformation, which, in turn, is rooted in the Protestant Reformation of the 16th century. The Centre of faith, and of Scripture, is found in Jesus Christ as Saviour and Lord.

The church's name was chosen in 1959. Its original name, Kleine Gemeinde, which means "small church", reflected its origins as a renewal movement among Mennonites in southern Russia. Klaas Reimer, a minister, was concerned about a decline of spiritual life and discipline in the church, and inappropriate involvement in the Napoleanic War. About 1812, Reimer and others began separate worship services, and two years later were organized as a small group.

Facing increasing government pressure, particularly about military service, the group migrated to North America in 1874 to 1875. Fifty families settled in Manitoba and 36 in Nebraska. Ties between the groups weakened and eventually the U.S. group gave up its KG identity. The KG survived several schisms and migrations, dating from its years in Russia through the 1940s.

As an evangelical church, The Evangelical Mennonite Conference holds that Scripture has final authority in faith and practice, a belief in Christ's finished work, and that assurance of salvation is possible. As Mennonite, the denomination has a commitment to discipleship, baptism upon confession of faith, community, social concern, non-violence and the Great Commission. As a conference, it seeks to encourage local churches, to work together on evangelism and matters of social concern, and relates increasingly well to other denominations.

In the year 2006 its membership surpassed 7270, with many more people as treasured adherents and a wider circle of ministry influence. Membership is for people baptized on confession of faith (usually in adolescence or older). Children are considered safe in Christ until they reach an age where they are accountable for their own spiritual decision and opt out; they are considered part of the church, while full inclusion occurs upon personal choice.

The Conference has 60 churches from British Columbia to Ontario (37 in Manitoba) and roughly 149 mission workers in 25 countries. The cultural make-up of the Conference is increasingly diverse, though its Dutch-German background remains dominant nationally. Twelve churches have pastors or leaders who are of non-Dutch-German background.

Some churches have a multiple leadership pattern (ministers and deacons can be selected from within the congregation); others have new patterns. Most churches support their leading minister full time. Its church governance moved from a bishop system to greater local congregational autonomy. It currently functions as a conference of churches with national boards, a conference council, and a moderator.

Women can serve on most national boards, as conference council delegates, as missionaries, and within a wide range of local church activities; while they can be selected locally, they cannot currently serve as nationally recognized or commissioned ministers.

It is a supporting member of Mennonite Central Committee and the Evangelical Fellowship of Canada. About 80 percent of its national budget goes toward mission work in Canada and other countries.

440 Main St., Steinbach, MB R5G 1Z5, Tel. (204)326-6401 Fax (204)326-1613
Email: emconf@mts.net
Media Contact, Conf. Pastor, David Thiessen

Officers
Conf. Mod., Ron Penner
General Sec., Tim Dyck
Conference Pastor, Bd. of Leadership and Outreach, David Thiessen
Bd. of Missions, Exec. Sec., Tim Dyck
Bd. of Missions, Foreign Sec., Ken Zacharias
Bd. of Church Ministries, Exec. Sec.-Editor, Terry M. Smith
Bd. of Trustees, Exec. Sec. Tim Dyck
Canadian Church Planting Coordinator, Exec. Sec. - Ward Parkinson
Conference Youth Minister, Gerald Reimer

Periodicals
The Messenger

Evangelical Mennonite Mission Conference

This group was founded in 1936 as the Rudnerweider Mennonite Church in Southern Manitoba and organized as the Evangelical Mennonite Mission Conference in 1959. It was incorporated in 1962. The Annual Conference meeting is held in July.

Headquarters
Box 52059, Niakwa P.O., Winnipeg, MB R2M 5P9, Tel. (204)253-7929 Fax (204)256-7384
Email: info@emmc.ca
Media Contact, Lil Goertzen
Email: lil@emmc.ca

Officers
Mod., Jake Thiessen, Box 215, Altona MB R0G 0B0 204-324-6209, Email: jmcath@mts.net
Vice-Mod., Frank Friesen, Box 1392, Altona MB R0G 0B0 204-324-8389, Email: frankf@mts.net
Sec., Gin Thiessen, 818-77 University Cres, Winnipeg MB R3T 3N8, 204-475-3107, Email: vjthies@mts.net
Conference Pastor, Allen Kehler, Box 52059, Niakwa PO, Winnipeg MB R2M 5P9, 204-253-7929, Email: al@emmc.ca
Business Admin., Bob Milks, Box 52059, Niakwa PO, Winnipeg MB R2M 5P9, 204-253-7929, Email: al@emmc.ca
The Gospel Message, Box 1760, Warman SK S0K 4S0, Tel. (306)242-5001 Fax (306)242-6115;
Radio Pastor, Rev. Ed Martens

Periodicals
EMMC Recorder

The Evangelical Missionary Church of Canada

This denomination was formed in 1993 with the merger of The Evangelical Church of Canada and The Missionary Church of Canada. The Evangelical Missionary Church of Canada maintains fraternal relations with the worldwide body of the Missionary Church, Inc. and with the Evangelical Church of North America. The Evangelical Church of Canada was among those North American Evangelical United Brethren Conferences which did not join the EUB in merging with the Methodist Church in 1968. The Missionary Church of Canada is Anabaptist in heritage. Its practices and theology were shaped by the Holiness Revivals of the late 1800s. The Evangelical Missionary Church consists of 135 churches in two conferences in Canada.

Headquarters
214 Highland Road E, Kitchener, ON N2M 2W3, Tel. (519)894-9800 Fax (519)894-0941,
Email: info@emcc.ca
Media Contact, Communications

Officers
Pres., Rev. Phil Delsaut, 214 Highland Road E, Kitchener, ON N2M 2W3,2H2, Tel. (519)894-9800, Email: pdelsaut@emcc.ca

The Fellowship of Evangelical Baptist Churches in Canada

The Fellowship is a family of 500 Evangelical Baptist Churches across Canada, holding worship services in 13 different languages.

Headquarters
P.O. Box 457, Guelph ON, Canada, N1H 6K9, Tel. (519)821-4830 Fax (519)821-9829

Periodicals
B.C. Fellowship Baptist; The Evangelical Baptist Magazine; Intercom

Foursquare Gospel Church of Canada

The Western Canada District was formed in 1964 with the Rev. Roy Hicks as supervisor. Prior to 1964 it had been a part of the Northwest District of the International Church of the Foursquare Gospel with headquarters in Los Angeles, California.

A Provincial Society, the Church of the Foursquare Gospel of Western Canada, was formed in 1976; a Federal corporation, the Foursquare Gospel Church of Canada, was incorporated in 1981 and a national church formed. The provincial society was closed in 1994.

Headquarters
B-307 2099 Lougheed Highway, Port CoQuituam, BC V3B 1A8, Tel. (604)941-8414
Email: info@foursquare.ca
Media Contact, Pres., Barry J. Buzza, B-307 2099 Lougheed Highway, Port CoQuituam, BC V3B 1A8

Pres., Barry J. Buzza, B-307 2099 Lougheed Highway, Port CoQuituam, BC V3B 1A8

Free Methodist Church in Canada

The Free Methodist Church was founded in New York in 1860 and expanded into Canada in 1880. It is Methodist in doctrine, evangelical in ministry and emphasizes the teaching of holiness of life through faith in Jesus Christ.

The Free Methodist Church in Canada was incorporated in 1927 after the establishment of a Canadian Executive Board. In 1959 the Holiness Movement Church merged with the Free Methodist Church. Full autonomy for the Canadian church was realized in 1990 with the formation of a Canadian General Conference. Mississauga, Ontario, continues to be the location of the Canadian Headquarters.

The Free Methodist Church ministers in 80 countries through its World Ministries Center in Indianapolis, Indiana.

Headquarters

4315 Village Centre Ct., Mississauga, ON L4Z 1S2, Tel. (905)848-2600 Fax (905)848-2603
Email: ministrycentre@fmcic.ca
Website: www.fmcic.ca
Media Contact, Lisa Howden

Officers

Bishop, Rev. Keith Elford
Dir. of Admn. Ser., Mark Molczanski
Dir. of Global and Intercultural Ministries, Rev. Dan Sheffield
Dir., Personnel, Rev. Kim Henderson
Dir., Growth Ministries, Rev. Jared Siebert

Periodicals

Mosaic

Free Will Baptists

As revival fires burned throughout New England in the mid- and late 1700s, Benjamin Randall proclaimed his doctrine of Free Will to large crowds of seekers. In due time, a number of Randall's converts moved to Nova Scotia. One such believer was Asa McGray, who was to become instrumental in the establishment of several Free Baptist churches. Local congregations were organized in New Brunswick. After several years of numerical and geographic gains, disagreements surfaced over the question of music, Sunday school, church offerings, salaried clergy and other issues. Adherents of the more progressive element decided to form their own fellowship. Led by George Orser, they became known as Free Christian Baptists.

The new group faithfully adhered to the truths and doctrines which embodied the theological basis of Free Will Baptists. Largely through Archibald Hatfield, contact was made with Free Will Baptists in the United States in the 1960s.

The association was officially welcomed into the Free Will Baptist family in July 1981, by the National Association.

Headquarters

5233 Mt. View Rd., Antioch, TN 37013-2306, Tel. (615)731-6812 Fax (615)731-0771
Media Contact, Mod., Rev. Oral McAssee, 1039 Route 560, Jacksontown, New Brunswick E7M 3L3, Tel. (506)325-9381

Officers

Mod., Rev. Oral McAssee

General Church of the New Jerusalem

The Church of the New Jerusalem, also called The New Church, is a Christian Church founded on the Bible and the Writings of Emanuel Swedenborg (1688-1772). These Writings were first brought to Ontario in 1835 by Christian Enslin.

Headquarters

c/o Olivet Church, 279 Burnhamthorpe Rd., Etobicoke, ON M9B 1Z6, Tel. (416)239-3054 Fax (416)239-4935
Email: mgladish@shaw.ca
Website: www.newchurch.org
Media Contact, Exec. Vice-Pres., Rev. Michael D. Gladish

Officers

Pres., Rt. Rev. T. Kline, Bryn Athyn, PA 19009
Exec. Vice-Pres., Rev. Michael D. Gladish
Sec., Carolyn Bellinger, 110 Chapel Hill Dr., Kitchener, ON N2G 3W5

General Conference of the Canadian Assemblies of God

This body had its beginnings in Hamilton, Ontario, in 1912 when a few people of an Italian Presbyterian Church banded themselves together for prayer and received a Pentecostal experience of the baptism in the Holy Spirit. Since 1912, there has been a close association with the teachings and practices of the Pentecostal Assemblies of Canada.

The work spread to Toronto, then to Montreal, where it also flourished. In 1959, the church was incorporated in the province of Quebec. The early leaders of this body were the Rev. Luigi Ippolito and the Rev. Ferdinand Zaffuto. The churches carry on their ministry in both the English and Italian languages.

Headquarters

6724 Fabre St., Montreal, QC H2G 2Z6, Tel. (514)279-1100 Fax (514)279-1131
Media Contact, Gen. Sec., Rev. Raymond Narula, 190 Lynden Rd., Brantford ON N3R 8A3, Tel. (519)759-7990 Fax (519)759-8163

Officers

Gen. Supt., Rev., Rev. David DiStaulo, P. O. Box Marquette # 37315, Montreal QC H2E 3B5, Tel. (514)279-1100 Fax (514)279-1131

Gen. Sec., Rev. Raymond Narula, 190 Lynden Rd., Brantford ON N3R 8A3, Tel. (519)759-7990 Fax (519)759-8163

Gen. Treas., Rev. David Quackenbush, 686 Ossington, Toronto ON M6G 3T7, Tel. (416)532-3951 Fax (416)532-0267

Overseer, Rev. Mario Catalano, 6550 Maurice-Duplessis, Montreal-North QC H1G 6K9; Tel (514)323-3087 Fax (514)323-3074

Overseer, Rev. David Hortelliti, P.O. Box Marquette # 37315, Montreal QC H2E 3B5, Tel. (514)279-1100 Fax (514)279-1131

Greek Orthodox Metropolis of Toronto (Canada)

Greek Orthodox Christians in Canada are under the jurisdiction of the Ecumenical Patriarchate of Constantinople (Istanbul).

Headquarters

86 Overlea Blvd., Toronto, ON M4H 1C6, Tel. (416)429-5757 Fax (416)429-4588

Email: metropolis@gocanada.org

Officers

Metropolitan Archbishop of the Greek Orthodox Metropolis of Toronto (Canada), His Eminence Metropolitan Archbishop Sotirios

Periodicals

Orthodox Way

Independent Assemblies of God International (Canada)

This fellowship of churches has been operating in Canada for over 60 years. Each church within the fellowship is completely independent.

Headquarters

Media Contact, Gen. Sec., Rev. Paul McPhail, Box 653 Chatham, ON, N7M 5K8, Phone (519)352-1743 Fax (519)351-6070, Email: pmcphail@ciaccess.com

Officers

Gen. Sec., Rev. Paul McPhail, Box 653 Chatham, ON, N7M 5K8, Phone (519)352-1743 Fax (519)3516070

Treas., Rev. David Ellyatt, 1795 Parkhurst Ave., London, ON N5V 2C4

Email: david.ellyatt@odyssey.on.ca

Periodicals

The Mantle

Independent Holiness Church

The former Holiness Movement of Canada merged with the Free Methodist Church in 1958. Some churches remained independent of this merger and they formed the Independent Holiness Church in 1960, in Kingston, Ontario. The doctrines are Methodist and Wesleyan. The General Conference is every three years, next meeting in 2004.

Headquarters

Media Contact, Rev. R. E. Votary, 1564 John Quinn Rd., R.R.1, Greely, ON K4P 1J9, Tel. (613)821-2237

Website: www.holiness.ca

Officers

Gen. Supt., Rev. R. E. Votary, 1564 John Quinn Rd., Greeley, ON K4P 1J9

Additional Officers:

E. Brown, 104-610 Pesehudoff Cresc., Saskatoon, SK S7N 4H5

T. Gibbons, P O Box 775, Brighton, ON K0K 1H0

A. Clark, 899, 15 St. West, Prince Albert, SK S6V 3S1

N. Fradley, 83 5820 Hastings St., Burnaby, BC V5B 1R6

A. Gordon, P O Box 15, Elgin, ON K0G 1E0

Periodicals

Gospel Tidings

Jehovah's Witnesses

For a description of Jehovah's Witnesses see Directory 3, "Religious Bodies in the United States" in this Yearbook.

Headquarters

25 Columbia Heights, Brooklyn, NY 11201-2483, Tel. (718)560-5600 Fax (718)560-8850

Canadian Branch Office, Box 4100, Halton Hills, ON L7G 4Y4, Tel. (888)301-4259

Media Contact, Office of Public Information, J. Richard Brown

Media Contact, Office of Public Information in Canada, Mark Ruge

Editorial Contact, Writing Department, James N. Pellechia

Lutheran Church-Canada

Lutheran Church-Canada was established in 1959 at Edmonton, Alberta, as a federation of Canadian districts of the Lutheran Church - Missouri Synod; it was constituted in 1988 at Winnipeg, Manitoba, as an autonomous church.

The church confesses the Bible as both inspired and infallible, the only source and norm of doctrine and life and subscribes without reservation to the Lutheran Confessions as contained in the Book of Concord of 1580.

Headquarters

3074 Portage Ave., Winnipeg, MB R3K 0Y2, Tel. (204)895-3433 Fax (204)832-3018, Email: info@lutheranchurch.ca

Media Contact, Dir. of Comm., Ian Adnams, communications@lutheranchurch.ca

Officers

Pres.: Rev. Robert Bugbee, 3074 Portage Ave, Winnipeg, MB, R3K 0Y2, Tel. 204-895-3433 ext 2212 Fax 204-832-3018 president@ lutheranchurch.ca,

Pres. Emeritus: Rev. Dr. Ralph Mayan, 6565 Willoughby Way, Langley, BC V2Y 1K3, Tel. 778-278-2094, missions@lutheranchurch.ca

Pres. Emeritus: Rev. Dr. Edwin Lehman, 686 Lee Ridge Road, Edmonton, AB, T6K 0P2, Tel. 780-462-9608 Fax 780-468-2172 edwin lehman@shaw.ca

Honorary Pres.:

Vice-Pres.: Rev. Daryl Solie, 935 McCarthy Blvd N, Regina, SK, S4X 3L2, Tel. 306-543-9898, poplc@sasktel.net

Vice Pres.: Rev. Robert C. Krestick, 78 John St., W. Waterloo, ON N2L 1B8, Tel. 519-745-5027 Fax 519-745-7165, krestick@redeemer-church.ca

Vice Pres.: Rev. Thomas Kruesel, 201 Birch St, Campbell River, BC, V9W 2S4, Tel. 250-287-7771, bethany.lutheran.1@gmail.com

Treas.: Mr. Dwayne Cleave, 3074 Portage Avenue, Winnipeg, MB R3K 0Y2, treasure r@lutheranchurch.ca, Tel. (204)-895-3433 Fax (204)897-4319

DISTRICT OFFICES

Alberta-British Columbia, Pres., Rev. D. Schiemann, 7100 Ada Blvd., Edmonton, AB T5B 4E4, Tel. (780)474-0063 Fax (780)477-9829, info@lccabc.ca

Central, Pres., Rev. T. Prachar, 1927 Grant Dr., Regina, SK S4S 4V6, Tel. (306)586-4434 Fax (306)586-0656, tprachar@accesscomm.ca

East, Pres., Rev. Paul Zabel, 275 Lawrence Ave., Kitchener, ON N2M 1Y3, Tel. (519)578-6500 Fax (519)578-3369, pzabel@lcceastdistrict.ca

Periodicals

The Canadian Lutheran

Mennonite Church Canada

Mennonite Church Canada is a successor denomination of the Conference of Mennonites in Canada, and the bi-national denominations (USA and Canada) of the General Conference Mennonite Church and the Mennonite Church. These groups merged in the late 1990's to become Mennonite Church Canada.

The first Mennonites came to Canada in 1786, moving from Pennsylvania in Conestoga wagons. Over the next 150 years, more arrived by ship from Europe, in at least four successive waves.

Its members hold to traditional Christian beliefs, believer's baptism and congregational polity. They emphasize practical Christianity, opposition to war, service to others and personal ethics.

Some people who have joined the Canadian Mennonite body in recent years have arrived from Asia, from Africa, or from Latin and South America. Native brothers and sisters, whose people were here long before the first conastoga wagons arrived, have added their voices to the mix.

Meanwhile, French-speaking and English-speaking Canadians from the wider community have enriched the Mennonite people. Together we are Christian believers moving into the future under the umbrella of the Mennonite Church Canada. Today we worship in 14 different languages across Canada.

Mennonite Church Canada is affiliated with Mennonite Church USA whose offices are at Newton, Kansas and Elkhart, Indiana. (See, Mennonite Church USA description in the section "Religious Bodies in the United States")

Headquarters

600 Shaftesbury Blvd., Winnipeg, MB R3P 0M4, Tel. (204)888-6781 Fax (204)831-5675

Media Contact, Dan Dyck

Email: ddyck@mennonitechurch.ca

Website: www.mennonitechurch.ca

Officers

Chpsn., Andrew Reesor McDowell

Gen. Sec., Willard Metzger

Periodicals

Canadian Mennonite; Intotemak

North American Baptist Conference

Churches belonging to this conference emanated from German Baptist immigrants of more than a century ago. Although scattered across Canada and the U.S., they are bound together by a common heritage, a strong spiritual unity, a Bible-centered faith and a deep interest in missions. Their two main priorities are Leadership Development and Church Multiplication.

Note, The details of general organization, officers, and periodicals of this body will be found under the listing for the North American Baptist Conference in Directory 3, "Religious Bodies in the United States" of this Yearbook.

Headquarters

1 S. 210 Summit Ave., Oakbrook Terrace, IL 60181, Tel. (630)495-2000 Fax (630)495-3301

Media Contact, Ron Norman

Officers

Exec. Dir., Dr. Rob McCleland

Periodicals

N.A.B. Today

The Old Catholic Church of Canada

The church was founded in 1948 in Hamilton, Ontario. The first bishop was the Rt. Rev. George Davis. The Old Catholic Church of Canada accepts all the doctrines of the Eastern Orthodox Churches and, therefore, not Papal Infallibility or the Immaculate Conception. The ritual is Western (Latin Rite) and is in the vernacular language. Celibacy is optional.

Headquarters

715 East 51st Ave., Vancouver, BC V5X 1E2, Tel. (905)855-3643, Tel. (905)855-3643

Media Contact, Bishop, The Right Rev. Pat Davies, Presiding Bishop

Officers

Presiding Bishop, The Rt. Rev. Patricia Davis, 715 East 51st Ave., Vancouver, BC V5X 1E2, Tel. (905)855-3643, Email: bishoppat@oldcatholic.ca

Old Order Amish Church

This is the most conservative branch of the Mennonite Church and direct descendants of Swiss Brethren (Anabaptists) who emerged from the Reformation in Switzerland in 1525. The Amish, followers of Bishop Jacob Ammann, became a distinct group in 1693. They began migrating to North America about 1737; all of them still reside in the United States or Canada. They first migrated to Ontario in 1823 directly from Bavaria, Germany and later from Pennsylvania and Alsace-Lorraine. Since 1953 more Amish have migrated to Ontario from Ohio, Indiana and Iowa.

As of 2009 there are 35 congregations in Ontario, each being autonomous. No membership figures are kept by this group, and there is no central headquarters. Each congre-gation is served by a bishop, two ministers and a deacon, all of whom are chosen from among the male members by lot for life.

Correspondent

Pathway Publishers, David Luthy, Rt. 4, Aylmer, ON N5H 2R3

Periodicals

Blackboard Bulletin; Herold der Wahreit; The Budget; The Diary; Die Botschaft; Family Life; Young Companion, Plain Interests.

Open Bible Faith Fellowship of Canada

This is an Evangelical, Full Gospel Fellowship of Churches and Ministries emphasizing evangelism, missions and the local church for success in the present harvest of souls. OBFF was chartered January 7, 1982.

Headquarters

4490 7th Concession, Windsor, Ontario, N9A 6J3, Tel. (519)972-5385 Fax (519)972-0075, Email: obff@wcf.ca

Officers

President, David Youngren
Vice President, Lindsey Burt
Sec./Treasurer, George Woodward
Director, Jim Buslon
Director, Lindsey Burt
Director, Mike Welch
Director, Christer Ihreborg

Orthodox Church in America (Archdiocese of Canada)

The Archdiocese of Canada of the Orthodox Church in America was established in 1916. First organized by St. Tikhon, martyr Patriarch of Moscow, previously Archbishop of North America, it is part of the Russian Metropolia and its successor, the autocephalous Orthodox Church in America.

The Archdiocesan Council meets twice yearly, the General Assembly of the Archdiocese takes place every three years. The Archdiocese is also known as "Orthodox Church in Canada."

Headquarters

P.O. Box 179, Spencerville, ON K0E 1X0, Tel. (613)925-5226, Email: zoe@ripnet.com

Officers

Bishop of Ottawa & Canada, The Rt. Rev. Seraphim; Chancellor, V. Rev. Dennis Pihach, 15992-107A Ave, Edmonton, AB T5P 0Z2
Treas., Nikita Lopoukhine, P.O. Box 179, Spencervillt, ON K0E 1X0
Sec., Archpriest Cyprian Hutcheon, P.O. Box 179, Spencerville, ON K0E 1X0

ARCHDIOCESAN COUNCIL
Clergy Members, Rev. Lawrence Farley; Rev. R.S. Kennaugh; Rev. Larry Reinheimer; Igumen Irenee Rochon; Rev. John Jillions, Rev. Ovest Olekshy
Lay Members, David Grier, John Hadjinicolaou, Mother Sophia (Zion), David Rystephanuk, Rod Tkachuk, Sandra Ellis, Alexei Vassiouchkine
Ex Officio, Chancellor; Treas.; Sec.

Periodicals

Canadian Orthodox Messenger

Patriarchal Parishes of the Russian Orthodox Church in Canada

This is the diocese of Canada of the former Exarchate of North and South America of the Russian Orthodox Church. It was originally founded in 1897 by the Russian Orthodox Archdiocese in North America.

Headquarters

St. Barbara's Russian Orthodox Cathedral, 10105 96th St., Edmonton, AB T5H 2G3
Media Contact, Roman Lopushinsky, 11620 134 Ave., Edmonton, AB T5E 1K9, Tel./Fax (780) 455-6314

Officers

Admn., Bishop of Kashira, Most Rev. Iov, 10812-108 St., Edmonton, AB T5H 3A6, Tel. (780)420-9945

The Pentecostal Assemblies of Canada

The PAOC received its federal charter in 1919. It is currently the largest Pentecostal organization in Canada with more than 1,100 local churches across the nation which are served by eight regional offices. Missions is a high priority in the organization which supports 265 missionaries located in 55 countries. The PAOC also serves 35 language groups in Canada as well as 80 French and 85 First Nations churches. The International Office is located in Mississauga, Ontario.

In the tradition of Classical Pentecostalism, the PAOC emphasizes a Baptism in the Holy Spirit subsequent to conversion with the initial evidence of speaking in tongues. Theologically it is aligned with the Reformed branch of Pentecostalism which views sanctification as a process of daily spiritual growth where the believer becomes more conformed to the image of Christ.

Historically, the PAOC has enjoyed fraternal relationships with the Pentecostal Assemblies of Newfoundland and Labrador and the Assemblies of God, Springfield, Missouri. It is a member of the Pentecostal/Charismatic Church of North America, the Pentecostal World Fellowship, and the World Assemblies of God Fellowship. Nationally, it holds membership in the Evangelical Fellowship of Canada. Its Emergency Relief and Development Organization (ERDO) responds to social needs around the world.

Headquarters
2450 Milltower Court, Mississauga, ON L5N 5Z6, Tel. (905)542-7400 Fax (905)542-7313

Officers
EXECUTIVE OFFICERS
Gen. Supt., Rev. David R. Wells, 2450 Milltower Crt, Mississauga, ON L5N 5Z6, Tel.: (905) 542-7400, Email: info@paoc.org
Asst. Supt., for Fellowship Services, Rev. David E. Hazzard,2450 Milltower Crt, Mississauga, ON L5N 5Z6, Tel.: (905)542-7400, Email: info@paoc.org
Asst. Supt. for International Missions, Rev. D. Murray Cornelius, 2450 Milltower Crt, Mississauga, ON L5N 5Z6, Tel.: (905)542-7400, Email: info@paoc.org

DISTRICT SUPERINTENDENTS
British Columbia & Yukon Districts, Rev. Ken Russell, 20411 Douglas Crescent, Langley, BC V3A 4B6, Tel. (604)533-2232 Fax (604)533-5405, Email: office@bc.paoc.org
Alberta & Northwest District, Rev. Kenneth A. Solbrekken, 10585-111 St., Edmonton, AB T5H 3E8, Tel. (780)426-0081 Fax (780)420-1318, Email: info@abnwt.paoc.org
Saskatchewan District, Rev. John Drisner, 3488 Fairlight Dr., Saskatoon, SK S7M 3Z4, Tel. (306)683-4646 Fax (306)683-3699, Email: paocsk@sasktel.net
Manitoba & North West Ontario District, Rev. James S. Poirier, 187 Henlow Bay, Winnipeg, MB R3Y 1G4, Tel. (204)940-1000 Fax (204)940-1009, Email: info@paoc.net
Western Ontario District, Rev. Lorrie H. Gibbons, 3214 S. Service Road., Burlington, ON L7N 3J2, Tel. (905)637-5566 Fax (905) 637-7558, Email: reception@wodistrict.org
Eastern Ontario District, Rev. Craig Burton, Box 337, Cobourg, ON K9A 4K8, Tel. (905)373-

7374 Fax (905)373-1911, Email: info@eod.paoc.org
Quebec District, Rev. Michael Bisaillon, 839 rue La Salle Longueil, QC J4K 3G6, Tel (4005) 442-2732 Fax (405)442-3818, Email: info@dq.paoc.org
Maritime District, Rev. Kevin H. Johnson, Box 1184, Truro, NS B2N 5H1, Tel. (902)895-4212 Fax (902)897-0705, Email: maritimepaoc@ns.aliantzinc.ca

BRANCH CONFERENCES
Finnish Conference, Rev. Paavo A. Korpela, 2570 Bayview Ave, Toronto, ON M2L1B3 Tel (416)222-2291 Fax (416)222-3356
The Slavic Branch of the PAOC, Rev. Adolfo Muravski, 445 Stevenson Rd., Oshawa, ON L1J 5N8 Tel (905)576-6130 Fax (905)576-3584

Periodicals
testimony (Official magazine of The Pentecostal Assemblies of Canada); Enrich; Contact

The Pentecostal Assemblies of Newfoundland
This body began in 1911 and held its first meetings at Bethesda Mission at St. John's. It was incorporated in 1925 as The Bethesda Pentecostal Assemblies of Newfoundland and changed its name in 1930 to The Pentecostal Assemblies of Newfoundland.

Headquarters
57 Thorburn Rd., Box 8895, Stn. "A", St. John's, NF A1B 3T2, Tel. (709)753-6314 Fax (709) 753-4945
Email: paon@paon.nf.ca
Media Contact, Gen. Sup't., H. Paul Foster, 57 Thorburn Rd., Box 8895, Stn. "A", St. John's, NF A1B 3T2

Officers
GENERAL EXECUTIVE OFFICERS
Gen. Sup't.: H. Paul Foster, 57 Thorburn Rd., Box 8895, Stn. "A", St. John's, NF A1B 3T2
Gen. Sec.-Treas.: Clarence Buckle, 57 Thorburn Rd., Box 8895, Stn. "A", St. John's, NF A1B 3T2
Ex. Dir. of Home Missions: Andrew R. Anstey, 57 Thorburn Rd., Box 8895, Stn. "A", St. John's, NF A1B 3T2
Ex. Dir. of Ch. Ministries: Robert H. Dewling, 57 Thorburn Rd., Box 8895, Stn. "A", St. John's, NF A1B 3T2

PROVINCIAL DIRECTORS
Sunday School & Children's Ministries: Kelly L. Brenton, 42 Franks Road, Conception Bay South, NL A1X 6W8
Women's Ministries: Catherine J. Snow, 14 Jeddores Lane, Deer Lake, NL A8A 1P4
Men's Ministries: Wilfred S. Buckle, 52 Premier Dr., Corner Brook, NL A2H 1S4
Youth Ministries: B. Dean Brenton, Box 21100, St. John's, NF A1B 3L5

Mature Adult Ministries: Barry D. Pelley, Box 1715, Lewisporte, NL A0G 3A0
Family Ministries: Sharmaine R. Reid, Box 2, Hant's Harbour, NL A0B 1Y0

AUXILIARY SERVICES

Chaplain of Institutions: Robert G. Parsons, 29 Caster's Drive, Mount Pearl, NL A1N 4X3
Pentecostal Senior Citizens Home Administrator: Beverley Bellefleur, Box 130, Clarke's Beach, NF A0A 1W0
Evergreen Manor, Summerford, NF A0G 4E0
Chaplain: Memorial University of Newfoundland, Gregory R. Dewling, Memorial University of Newfoundland, Box 102, St. John's, NF A1C 5S7
Emmanuel Convention Centre Administrator: Sterling E. Warr, P.O. Box 1409, Lewisporte, NL A0G 3A0
Managing Editor, Good Tidings: Burton K. Janes, 57 Thornburn Rd., Box 8895, Stn. "A", St. John's, NF A1B 3T2

Periodicals

Good Tidings

Presbyterian Church in America (Canadian Section)

Canadian congregations of the Reformed Presbyterian Church, Evangelical Synod, became a part of the Presbyterian Church in America when the RPCES joined PCA in June 1982. Some of the churches were in predecessor bodies of the RPCES, which was the product of a 1965 merger of the Reformed Presbyterian Church in North America, General Synod and the Evangelical Presbyterian Church. Others came into existence later as a part of the home missions work of RPCES. Congregations are located in seven provinces, and the PCA is continuing church extension work in Canada. The denomination is committed to world evangelization and to a continuation of historic Presbyterianism. Its officers are required to subscribe to the Reformed faith as set forth in the Westminster Confession of Faith and Catechisms.

Headquarters

Media Contact, Dr. Dominic Aquila, Editor Byfaithonline Newletter, New Geneva Seminary, 3622 East Galley Rd, Colorado Springs, CO, 80909, Tel. (719)573-5395 Fax (719)573-5398, Email daquila6@aol.com

Periodicals

Equip for Ministry; Multiply; Network; byFaith

Presbyterian Church in Canada

This is the nonconcurring portion of the Presbyterian Church in Canada that did not become a part of The United Church of Canada in 1925.

Headquarters

50 Wynford Dr., Toronto, ON M3C 1J7, Tel. (416)441-1111 Fax (416)441-2825

Website: www.presbyterian.ca
Media Contact, Principal Clk., Rev. Stephen Kendall or Associate Secretary for Resource Production & Communication, Mr. Colin Carmichael

Officers

Principal Clk., Rev. Stephen Kendall, 50 Wynford Dr., Toronto, ON M3C 1J7, Tel. (416)441-1111 Fax (416)441-2825, Website: www.presbyterian.ca

Periodicals

Channels; The Presbyterian Message; Presbyterian Record; Glad Tidings; La Vie Chrétienne

Reformed Church in Canada

The Canadian region of the Reformed Church in America was organized under the General Synod of the Reformed Church in America. The RCA in Canada has 40 churches which includes three classes (lower assemblies). The Reformed churches in Canada are member congregations of the Reformed Church in America and the Regional Synod of Canada (one of eight RCA regional synods established by its General Synod) and three classes, Ontario, Canadian Prairies and British Columbia.

The first ordained minister, Domine Jonas Michaelius, arrive in New Amsterdam from The Netherlands in 1628. Throughout the colonial period, the Reformed Church lived under the authority of the Classis of Amsterdam. Its churches were clustered in New York and New Jersey. Under the leadership of Rev. John Livingston, it became a denomination independent of the authority of the Classis of Amsterdam in 1776. Its geographical base was broadened in the 19th century by the immigration of Reformed Dutch and German settlers in the midwestern United States. The Reformed Church now spans the United States and Canada. The Reformed Church in America accepts as its standards of faith the Heidelberg Catechism, Belgic Confession, the Canons of Dort, and the Belhar Confession. It has a rich heritage of world mission activity. It claims to be loyal to Reformed tradition which emphasizes obedience to God in all aspects of life.

Although the Reformed Church in America has worked in close cooperation with other churches, it has never entered into merger with any other denomination. It is a member of the World Alliance of Reformed Churches, the World Council of Churches and the National Council of the Churches of Christ in the United States of America. In 1998 it also entered into a relationship of full communion with the Evangelical Lutheran Church in America, Presbyterian Church (U.S.A.), and the United Church of Christ by way of the Formula of Agreement. It also entered into full communion with the Christian Reformed Church in North America in 2007.

Headquarters

475 Riverside Dr., 18th Floor, New York, NY 10115, Tel. (212)870-3243 Fax (212)870-2499 Media Contact, Communications Officer, Paul Boice, 4500 60th St., SE, Grand Rapids, MI 49512, Tel. (616)698-7071 Fax (616)698-6606 Website: www.rca.org

OFFICERS AND STAFF OF GENERAL SYNOD

Regional Synod of Canada, Synod Executive, Mr. John Kapteyn, 201 Paradise Rd N, Hamilton, ON L8S 3T3
President, The Rev. Lisa Vander Wal, 475 Riverside Dr., 18th Floor, New York, NY 10115
General Synod Council; Moderator, The Rev. Donald Poest, 475 Riverside Dr., 18th Floor, New York, NY 10115
General Secretary, The Rev. Thomas De Vries, 475 Riverside Dr., 18th Floor, New York, NY 10115; 4500 60th St. S.E., Grand Rapids, MI 49512
Operations and Support, Director & Assistant Secretary, The Rev. Kenneth Bradsell
Global Mission, Director, The Rev. Jhonny Alicea-Baez
Leadership/Revitalization, Director, The Rev. Kenneth Eriks
Church Multiplication/Discipleship, Director, The Rev. Kenneth Eriks
Finance Services, Treasurer, Ms. Barbara Boers
Related Organizations:
World Council of Churches
World Communion of Reformed Churches
National Council of Churches of Christ in the U.S.A.
Christian Churches Together
Global Christian Forum
Roman Catholic/Reformed Dialogue

Periodicals

RCA Today, Perspectives

The Reformed Episcopal Church of Canada

The Reformed Episcopal Church is a separate entity. It was established in Canada by an act of Parliament given royal assent on June 2, 1886. It maintains the founding principles of episcopacy (in historic succession from the apostles), Anglican liturgy and Reformed doctrine and evangelical zeal. In practice it continues to recognize the validity of certain nonepiscopal orders of evangelical ministry. The Church has reunited with the Reformed Episcopal Church and is now composed of two Dioceses in this body - the Diocese of Central and Eastern Canada and the Diocese of Western Canada and Alaska.

Headquarters

Box 2532, New Liskeard, ON P0J 1P0, Tel. (705) 647-4565 Fax (705)647-1340
Email: fed@nt.net
Website: www.rececan.org

Media Contact, Pres., The Rt. Rev. Michael Fedechko, M. Div., D.D.

Officers

Pres., The Rt. Rev. Michael Fedechko, 320 Armstrong St., Temiskaming Shores, ON P0J 1P0
Vice-Pres., Bob Harrold, St. Catharines, ON.
Sec., Allison Buffet, Hamilton, ON.

BISHOPS

Diocese of Central & Eastern Canada, The Rt. Rev. Michael Fedechko, 320 Armstrong St., Temiskaming Shores, ON P0J 1P0, Tel. (705)647-4565 Fax (705)647-1340
Diocese of Western Canada & Alaska, Rt. Rev. Charles W. Dorrington, 54 Blanchard St., Victoria, BC V8X 4R1, Tel. (604)744-5014 Fax (604)388-5891

Periodicals

The Messenger

Reinland Mennonite Church

This group was founded in 1958 when 10 ministers and approximately 600 members separated from the Sommerfelder Mennonite Church. In 1968, four ministers and about 200 members migrated to Bolivia. The church has work in five communities in Manitoba and one in Ontario

Headquarters

Bishop William H. Friesen, P.O. Box 96, Rosenfeld, MB R0G 1X0, Tel. (204)324-6339
Media Contact, Deacon, Henry Wiebe, Box 2587, Winkler, MB R6W 4C3, Tel. (204)325-8487

The Roman Catholic Church in Canada

The largest single body of Christians in Canada, the Roman Catholic Church is under the spiritual leadership of His Holiness the Pope. Catholicism in Canada dates back to 1534, when the first Mass was celebrated on the Gaspé Peninsula on July 7, by a priest accompanying Jacques Cartier. Catholicism had been implanted earlier by fishermen and sailors from Europe. Priests came to Acadia as early as 1604. Traces of a regular colony go back to 1608 when Champlain settled in Quebec City. The Récollets (1615), followed by the Jesuits (1625) and the Sulpicians (1657), began the missions among the native population. The first official Roman document relative to the Canadian missions dates from March 20, 1618. Bishop François de Montmorency-Laval, the first bishop, arrived in Quebec in 1659. The church developed in the East, but not until 1818 did systematic missionary work begin in western Canada.

In the latter 1700s, English-speaking Roman Catholics, mainly from Ireland and Scotland, began to arrive in Canada's Atlantic provinces.

208

After 1815 Irish Catholics settled in large numbers in what is now Ontario. The Irish potato famine of 1847 greatly increased that population in all parts of eastern Canada.

By the 1850s the Catholic Church in both English- and French-speaking Canada had begun to erect new dioceses and found many religious communities. These communities did educational, medical and charitable work among their own people as well as among Canada's native peoples. By the 1890s large numbers of non-English and non-French-speaking Catholics had settled in Canada, especially in the Western provinces. In the 20th century the pastoral horizons have continued to expand to meet the needs of what has now become a very multicultural church.

The Canadian Conference of Catholic Bishops is the national association of the Latin and Eastern Catholic Bishops of Canada. Its main offices are in Ottawa, Ontario.

CANADIAN ORGANIZATION

Conférence des évêques catholiques du Canada - Canadian Conference of Catholic Bishops, 2500 Don Reid Drive, Ottawa, ON k1H 2J2, Tel. (613)241-9461 Fax (613)241-9048, cecc@cccb.ca, website:www.cccb.ca
Media Contact, Mr. Gérald Baril, gbaril@ cecc.ca, Tel. (613)241-9461 cecc@cccb.ca

Officers
General Secretariat of the Canadian Conference of Catholic Bishops
General Secretary: Msgr. Mario Paquette, P.H.
Associate General Secretaries: vacant (French Sector); Mr. Bede Hubbard (English Sector)

EXECUTIVE COMMITTEE
Pres., Most Rev. V. James Weisgerber; Vice-Pres., Most Rev. Pierre Morissette; Co-Treas., Most Rev. Richard Smith and Most Rev. V. Paul-André Durocher

EPISCOPAL COMMISSIONS - NATIONAL LEVEL
Justice and Peace: Most Rev. Brendan O'Brien
Doctrine: Most Rev. Most Rev. Michael Miller, C.S.B.
Christian Unity, Religious Relations with the Jews, and Interfaith Dialogue: Most Rev. Martin Veillette

EPISCOPAL COMMISSIONS - SECTOR LEVEL
Christian Education: Most Rev. Richard Smith
Liturgie et sacrements: Most Rev. Louis Dicaire
Liturgy: Most Rev. Albert LeGatt

NATIONAL COMMITTEES
Canon Law: Most Rev. Peter Hundt
Relations with Catholic Movements and Associations: Most Rev. Pierre-André Fournier
Communications: Most Rev. Pierre Morissette
Government Relations: Most Rev. V. James

Weisgerber

OFFICES
Justice, Paix et Missions – Justice Peace and Missions, Mr. François Poitras, Dir.
Communications: Mr. Gérald Baril, Dir.
Droit canonique—inter-rites-Canon Law—Inter-rite: Msgr. Mario Paquette, P.H. Secr.
Éditions-Publications: Dr. Vicki Bennett, Dir.
Liturgie-Liturgy: M. Gaëtan Baillargeon, Dir. (French Sector); Rev. William Burke, Dir. (English Sector)
National Office of Religious Education: Ms. Joanne Chafe, Dir.
Relations ecclésiales et doctrine – Ecclesial Relations and Doctrine: Mr. Jonas Abromaitis
Tribunal d'appel du Canada - The Canadian Appeal Tribunal: Msgr. Alan McCormack, P.H., Vicaire judiciaire-Judicial Vicar

REGIONAL EPISCOPAL ASSEMBLIES
Atlantic Episcopal Assembly - Assemblée des évêques de l'Atlantique: Pres., Most Rev. François Thibodeau, C.J.M.; Vice Pres., Most Rev. Martin William Currie and Most Claude Champagne, O.M.I.; Secretary-Treasurer: Fr. Léo Grégoire, I.V. Dei, Tel. 506-735-5578 Fax 506-735-4271
Assemblée des évêques catholiques du Québec: Pres., Most Martin Veillette; Vice Prés., Most Jean Gagnon; Secrétaire général, M. Bertrand Ouellet, Tel. 514-274-4323 Fax 514-274-4383
Ontario Conference of Catholic Bishops - Conférence des évêques catholiques de l'Ontario: Pres., Most Rev. Thomas Collins, Vice Pres., Most Rev. Anthony Daniels; Secretary-Treasurer, Mr. Luciano Piovesan, Tel. (416)923-1423 Fax (416)923-1509
Assembly of Western Catholic Bishops - Assemblée des évêques catholiques de l'Ouest: Pres., Most Rev. Daniel Bohan; Vice Pres., Most Rev. Larence Huculak, O.S.B.M.; Sec.-Treasurer, Rt. Rev. Peter Novecosky, O.S.B., Tel. (306)682-1788 Fax (306)682-1766

MILITARY ORDINARIATE-ORDINARIAT MILITAIRE
Bishop, Most Rev. Donald J. Theriault, Military Ordinariate of Canada, Canadian Forces Support Unit (Ottawa), Uplands Site Building 469, Ottawa, ON K1A 0K2, Tel. (613)990-7824 Fax 613-991-1056
Canadian Religious Conference, Sec. Gen., Sr. Margaret Toner, SCIC.
4135, rue de Rouen, Montréal, Québec H1V 1G5, Tel. (514)259-0856 Fax (514)259-0857
Organisme catholique pour la vie et la famille/Catholic Organization for Life and Family, co-directors: Ms. Michèle Boulva, Tel. (613)241-9461 Fax (613)241-9048, mboulva @colf.ca

Periodicals
Foi et Culture (Bulletin natl. de liturgie)

Romanian Orthodox Church in America (Canadian Parishes)

The first Romanian Orthodox immigrants in Canada called for Orthodox priests from their native country of Romania. Between 1902 and 1914, they organized the first Romanian parish communities and built Orthodox churches in different cities and farming regions of western Canada (Alberta, Saskatchewan, Manitoba) as well as in the eastern part (Ontario and Quebec).

In 1929, the Romanian Orthodox parishes from Canada joined with those of the United States in a Congress held in Detroit, Michigan, and asked the Holy Synod of the Romanian Orthodox Church of Romania to establish a Romanian Orthodox Missionary Episcopate in America. The first Bishop, Policarp (Morushca), was elected and consecrated by the Holy Synod of the Romanian Orthodox Church and came to the United States in 1935. He established his headquarters in Detroit with jurisdiction over all the Romanian Orthodox parishes in the United States and Canada.

In 1950, the Romanian Orthodox Church in America (i.e. the Romanian Orthodox Missionary Episcopate in America) was granted administrative autonomy by the Holy Synod of the Romanian Orthodox Church of Romania, and only doctrinal and canonical ties remain with this latter body.

In 1974 the Holy Synod of the Romanian Orthodox Church of Romania recognized and approved the elevation of the Episcopate to the rank of the Romanian Orthodox Archdiocese in America and Canada and completed the administrative autonomy.

Headquarters
Romanian Orthodox Archdiocese in the Americas, 5410 N. Newland Ave., Chicago, IL 60656 USA

Officers
Archbishop, Most Rev. Nicolae Condrea,5410 N. Newland Ave., Chicago, IL 60656 USA, Tel. 773-774-1677 Fax 773-774-1805, Email: arch nicolae@aol.com

Auxiliary Bishop, Right Rev. ioan Casian Tunaru, 168 Chemin Louisa, Wentworth, QC J8H 0C7, Canada, Email: tcasian@yahoo.com

Vicar, V. Rev. Fr. Nicholas Apostola, 44 Midland St. Worchester, MA 01602-4217, Tel. (508) 845-0088 Fax (508)752-8180

Secretary, V. Rev. Fr. Daniel Ene, 56 Andrews Street, Victor, NY, 14565, Tel. (585)924-8737, Email: frdaniel@romanianholytrinity.org

Periodicals
Credinta - The Faith

The Romanian Orthodox Episcopate of America (Jackson, MI)

This body of Eastern Orthodox Christians of Romanian descent is part of the Autocephalous Orthodox Church in America. For complete description and listing of officers, please see chapter 3, "Religious Bodies in the United States."

Headquarters
2535 Grey Tower Rd., Jackson, MI 49201, Tel. (517)522-4800

Mailing Address: P.O. Box 309, Grass Lake, MI 49240-0309

Email: chancery@roea.org

Website: www.roea.org

Media Contact, Ed.-Sec., Rev. Archdeacon David Oancea, P.O. Box 185, Grass Lake, MI 49240-0185, Tel. (517)522-3656

Officers
Ruling Hierarch, Most. Rev. Archbishop Nathaniel Popp

Dean of All Canada, Very Rev. Daniel Nenson, 2855 Helmsing St., Regina, SK S4V 0W7, Tel. (306)761-2379

Periodicals
Solia - The Herald; Good News- Buna Vestire (in Canada only)

The Salvation Army in Canada

The Salvation Army, an evangelical branch of the Christian Church, is an international movement founded in 1865 in London, England. The ministry of Salvationists, consisting of clergy (officers) and laity, comes from a commitment to Jesus Christ and is revealed in practical service that is offered without discrimination.

The Salvation Army began its work in Canada in 1882 and has grown to become the largest non-governmental direct provider of social services in the country. The Salvation Army gives hope and support to vulnerable people today and everyday in 400 communities across Canada and 115 countries around the world. The Salvation Army offers practical assistance for children and families, often tending to the basic necessities of life, provides shelter for homeless people and rehabilitation for people who have lost control of their lives to an addiction.

Headquarters
2 Overlea Blvd., Toronto, ON M4H 1P4, Tel. (416)425-2111

Media Contact, Andrew Burditt, Tel. (416)422-6208 Fax (416)422-6217

Email: andrew_burditt@can.salvationarmy.org

Website: www.SalvationArmy.ca

Officers
Territorial Commander, Commissioner William W. Francis

Territorial President, Women's Organizations, Commissioner Marilyn Francis

Chief Secretary, Lt.-Colonel Donald J. Copple

Secretary for Personnel, Major Jean Moulton

Secretary for Business Administrtaion, Major Neil Watt

Financial Secretary, Paul Goodyear
Secretary for Program, Lt.-Colonel David
Hiscock
Secretary for Public Realtions and Development,
Graham Moore
Property Secretary, Major Pearce Samson
Social Services Secretary, Mary Ellen Eberlin

Periodicals
Salvationist; Faith & Friends

Serbian Orthodox Church in the U.S.A. and Canada, Diocese of Canada

The Serbian Orthodox Church is an organic part of the Eastern Orthodox Church. As a local church it received its autocephaly from Constantinople in A.D. 1219. The Patriarchal seat of the church today is in Belgrade, Yugoslavia. In 1921, a Serbian Orthodox Diocese in the United States of America and Canada was organized. In 1963, it was reorganized into three dioceses, and in 1983 a fourth diocese was created for the Canadian part of the church. The Serbian Orthodox Church is in absolute doctrinal unity with all other local Orthodox Churches.

Headquarters
7470 McNiven Rd., RR 3, Campbellville, ON
L0P 1B0, Tel. (905)878-0043 Fax (905)878-1909
Email: vladika@istocnik.com
Website: www. istocnik.com
Media Contact, Rt. Rev. Georgije

Officers
Serbian Orthodox Bishop of Canada, Rt. Rev.
Georgije
Dean of Western Deanery, V. Rev. Drago
Knezevic, 12936 - 112th St., Edmonton, AB
T5E 6J1, Tel. (780)454-6513
Dean of Eastern Deanery, V. Rev. Zivorad
Subotic, 351 Mellville Ave., Westmount, QC
H3Z 2Y7, Tel./Fax (514)931-6664

Periodicals
*Istocnik, Herald of the Serbian Orthodox Church
— Canadian Diocese*

Seventh-day Adventist Church in Canada

The Seventh-day Adventist Church in Canada is part of the worldwide Seventh-day Adventist Church with headquarters in Silver Spring, Maryland (See "Religious Bodies in the United States" section of this *Yearbook* for a fuller descri-ption.) The Seventh-day Adventist Church in Canada was organized in 1901 and reorganized in 1932.

Headquarters
1148 King Street East, Oshawa, ON L1H 1H8,
Tel. (905)433-0011 Fax (905)433-0982
Media Contact, Nilton D. Amorim

Officers
Pres., Mark Johnson
Sec., Dragan Stojanovic
Treas., John Ramsay

DEPARTMENTS
Undertreasurer, Joyce Jones
Education, Dennis Marshall
Family Ministries, Hebert Valiame
Trust Services
ADRA Canada

Periodicals
Canadian Adventist Messenger

Syriac Orthodox Church of Antioch

The Syriac Orthodox Church professes the faith of the first three ecumenical councils of Nicaea, Constantinople and Ephesus and numbers faithful in the Middle East, India, the Americas, Europe and Australia. It traces its origin to the Patriarchate established in Antioch by St. Peter the Apostle and is under the supreme ecclesiastical jurisdiction of His Holiness the Syrian Orthodox Patriarch of Antioch and All the East, now residing in Damascus, Syria.

The Archdiocese of the Syrian Orthodox Church in the U.S. and Canada was formally established in 1957. In 1995, the Archdiocese of North America was divided into three separate Patriarchal Vicariates, including one for Canada. The first Syrian Orthodox faithful came to Canada in the 1890s and formed the first Canadian parish in Sherbrooke, Quebec. Today five official parishes of the Archdiocese exist in Canada—two in Quebec and three in Ontario. There is also an official mission congregation in Calgary, Alberta and Ottawa, Ontario.

Headquarters
Archdioces of Canada, 4375 Henri-Bourassa
West, Montreal, Quebec H4L 1A5, Canada,
Tel. (514)334-6993 Fax (514)334-8233

Officers
Archbishop Mor Athanasius Elia Bahi

Ukrainian Orthodox Church of Canada

Toward the end of the 19th century many Ukrainian immigrants settled in Canada. In 1918, a group of these pioneers established the Ukrainian Orthodox Church of Canada (UOCC), today the largest Ukrainian Orthodox Church beyond the borders of Ukraine. In 1990, the UOCC entered into a eucharistic communion with the Ecumenical Patriarchate of Constantinople (Istanbul).

Headquarters
Ukrainian Orthodox Church of Canada, Office of the Consistory, 9 St. Johns Ave., Winnipeg, MB R2W 1G8, Tel. (204)586-3093 Fax

(204)582-5241, Email: consistory@uocc.ca, Website: www. uocc.ca

Media Contacts, Rev. Fr. Gene Maximiuk, 9st. John's Ave., Winnipeg, MB R2W 1G8, Tel. (204)586-3093 Fax (204)582-5241

Officers

Primate, Most Rev. Metropolitan Yurij (Kalistchuk), 9 St. Johns Ave., Winnipeg, MB R2W 1G8, Tel. (204)586-3093 Fax (204)582-5241

Chancellor, RT. Rev. Victor Lakusta

Periodicals

Visnyk-The Herald-Le Messager; Ridna Nyva

Union d'Eglises Baptistes Françaises au Canada

Baptist churches in French Canada first came into being through the labors of two missionaries from Switzerland, Rev. Louis Roussy and Mme. Henriette Feller, who arrived in Canada in 1835. The earliest church was organized in Grande Ligne (now St.-Blaise), Quebec in 1838.

By 1900 there were 7 churches in the province of Quebec and 13 French-language Baptist churches in the New England states. The leadership was totally French Canadian.

By 1960, the process of Americanization had caused the disappearance of the French Baptist churches in the New England states. During the 1960s, Quebec as a society, began rapidly changing in all its facets, education, politics, social values and structures. Mission, evangelism and church growth once again flourished. In 1969, in response to the new conditions, the Grande Ligne Mission passed control of its work to the newly formed Union of French Baptist Churches in Canada, which then included 8 churches. By 2005 the French Canadian Baptist movement had grown to include 34 congregations present in three provinces: Quebec, New Brunswick, and Ontario.

The Union d'Églises Baptistes Françaises au Canada is a member body of the Canadian Baptist Ministries and thus is affiliated with the Baptist World Alliance.

Headquarters

2285 Avenue Papineau, Montreal, QC H2K 4J5, Tel. (514)526-6643 Fax (514)526-9269

Media Contact, Gen. Sec., Rev. Roland Grimard

Officers

Sec. Gen., Rev. Roland Grimard

Periodicals

www.UnionBaptiste.com (Internet)

Union of Spiritual Communities of Christ (Orthodox Doukhobors in Canada)

The Doukhobors are Canadians of Russian origin living primarily in the western provinces of Canada, but their beginnings in Russia are unknown. The name "Doukhobors," or "Spirit Wrestlers," was given them in derision by the Russian Orthodox clergy in Russia as far back as 1785. The Doukhobors were persecuted by the church for rejecting Orthodoxy, and following the counsel of their leader, Peter V. Verigin, earned the wrath of the Tsarist government by destroying all of their weapons and adopting pacifism in 1895. In 1899 the Tsarist government allowed 8,000 Doukhobors to leave Russia in response to an international uproar over their persecution by the church and state. They made their way to Canada with the assistance of Count Leo Tolstoy, who saw in these people the living embodiment of his philosophy, the Religious Society of Friends, commonly known as Quakers and other people of good will. Originally settled in Saskatchewan, by 1911 the majority followed Verigin to Bristish Columbia because of government efforts to assismilate them.

The teaching of the Doukhobors is penetrated with the Gospel spirit of love. Worshiping God in the spirit, they affirm that the outward church and all that is performed in it and concerns it has no importance for them; the church is where two or three are gathered together, united in the name of Christ. They do not believe in icon worship or in intermediaries between themselves and God. Their spiritual teachings are founded on ancient tradition, which they call the "Book of Life," because it lives in their memory and hearts. In this book are psalms composed by their elders and leaders, partly formed out of the contents of the Bible partly out of their historical experience. These are committed to memory by each succeeding generation. Doukhobors observe complete pacifism and non-violence, are lacto-vegetarians, and attempt to maintain a communal lifestyle.

The majority of Canadian Doukhobors were reorganized in 1938 by Peter P. Verigin, son of P.V. Verigin, shortly before his death, into the Union of Spiritual Communities of Chris to distinguish themselves from a radical off shoot who call themselves Sons of Freedom, and whose embrace of nudity and depradations has been sensationalized by the media and has stigmatized all Doukhobors. Today the USCC is governed by Trustees elected from member communities and administered by an elected Executive Committee headed by Honourary Chairman, John J. Verigin, CM OBC. The USCC executes the will and protects the interests of its member communities and its members living beyond south central British Columbia where the USCC is headquartered. The USCC is the largest organization of Doukhobors and maintains relations with other Doukhobor groups across Canada, in the USA, the Russian Federation, the Ukraine, and Georgia. The USCC also cooperates with other non governmental organizations working non violently to promote peace and justice, and respect for human didgnity and ecological integrity.

Headquarters
USCC Central Office, Box 760, Grand Forks, BC V0H 1H0, Tel. (250)442-8252 Fax (250)442-3433
Media Contact, John J. Verigin, Sr.

Officers
Hon. Chmn. of the Exec. Comm., John J. Verigin, Sr.
Chpsn., Fred Bojey

Periodicals
ISKRA

United Brethren Church in Canada
Founded in 1767 in Lancaster County, Pennsylvania, missionaries came to Canada about 1850. The first class was held in Kitchener in 1855, and the first building was erected in Port Elgin in 1867.

The Church of the United Brethren in Christ had its beginning with Philip William Otterbein and Martin Boehm, who were leaders in the revivalistic movement in Pennsylvania and Maryland during the late 1760s.

Headquarters
302 Lake St., Huntington, IN 46750, Tel. (219) 356-2312 Fax (219)356-4730

GENERAL OFFICERS
Pres., Rev. Brian Magnus, 120 Fife Rd., Guelph, ON N1H 6Y2, Tel. (519)836-0180
Treas., Brian Winger, 2233 Hurontario St., Apt. 916, Mississauga, ON L5A 2E9, Tel. (905) 275-8140

The United Church of Canada
The United Church of Canada was formed on June 10, 1925, through the union of the Methodist Church, Canada, the Congregational Union of Canada, the Council of Local Union Churches and 70 percent of the Presbyterian Church in Canada. The union culminated years of negotiation between the churches, all of which had integral associations with the development and history of the nation.

In fulfillment of its mandate to be a uniting as well as a United Church, the denomination has been enriched by other unions during its history. The Wesleyan Methodist Church of Bermuda joined in 1930. On January 1, 1968, the Canada Conference of the Evangelical United Brethren became part of The United Church of Canada. At various times, congregations of other Christian communions have also become congregations of the United Church.

The United Church of Canada is a full member of the World Methodist Council, the World Alliance of Reformed Churches (Presbyterian and Congregational), and the Canadian and World Councils of Churches. The United Church is the largest Protestant denomination in Canada.

NATIONAL OFFICES
General Council Office, 3250 Bloor St. W., Ste. 300, Toronto, ON M8X 2Y4, Tel. (416)231-5931 Fax (416)231-3103, 1-(800)268-3781
Media Contact, Communications Officer, Mary-Frances Denis

GENERAL COUNCIL
Mod., Mardi Tindal
Gen. Sec., Nora M. Sanders

GENERAL COUNCIL OFFICERS
Conciliar Relations, Rev. Carol L. Hancock
Programs, Rev. Bruce Gregersen

ADMINISTRATIVE UNITS (EXECUTIVE MINISTERS OR OFFICERS)
Aboriginal Ministries Circle, Rev. Maggie McLeod
Communications, Dan Benson
Communities in Ministry, Rev. Michael Blair
Finance, William Kennedy
Ministry and Employment, Rev. Alan Hall
Partners in Mission
Omega Bula Philantropy, David Amour

CONFERENCE EXECUTIVE SECRETARIES
Alberta and Northwest, Rev. Lynn I. Maki, 9911-48 Ave., NW, Edmonton, AB T6E 5V6, Tel. (780)435-3995 Fax (780)438-3317, Email: coffice@anwconf.com
All Native Circle, Speaker, Cheryl Jourdain, 367 Selkirk Ave., Winnipeg, MB R2W 2M3, Tel. (204)582-5518 Fax (204)582-6649, Email: allnative@ancconline.ca
Bay of Quinte, Rev. William Steadman, P.O. Box 700, 67 Mill St., Frankford, ON K0K 2C0, Tel. (613)398-1051 Fax (613)398-8894, E-mail: officeadmin@bayofquinteconference.ca
British Columbia, Rev. Douglas Goodwin, 4383 Rumble St., Burnaby, BC V5J 2A2, Tel. (604)431-0434 Fax (604)431-0439, Email: reception@bc.united-church.ca
Hamilton, Rev. Fred Monteith, Box 100, Carlisle, ON L0R 1H0, Tel. (905)659-3343 Fax (905)659-7766, Email: office@hamconf.org
London, Rev. Heather McLean, 747 Hyde Park Rd., Ste 111, London, ON N6H 3S3, Tel. (519)672-1930 Fax (519)439-2800, Email: office@londonconference.ca
Manitoba and Northwestern Ontario, Rev. Bruce Faurschou, 1470 Willson Place, Winnipeg, MB R3T 3N9, Tel. (204)233-8911 Fax (204) 233-3289, Email: office@confmnwo.mb.ca
Manitou, Rev. William Kunder, 319 McKenzie Ave., North Bay, ON P1B 7E3, Tel. (705)474-3350 Fax (705)497-3597, Email: office@manitouconference.ca
Maritime, David Hewitt, 21 Wright St., Sackville, NB E4L 4P8, Tel. (506)536-1334 Fax (506)536-2900, Email: info@marconf.ca
Montreal and Ottawa, Rev. Rosemary Lambie, 225-50 Ave., Lachine, QC H8T 2T7, Tel.

(514)634-7015 Fax (514)634-2489, Email: moconferenceuccmt1@gmail.com

Newfoundland and Labrador, Rev. Faith March-MacCuish, 320 Elizabeth Ave., St. John's, NL A1B 1T9, Tel. (709)754-0386 Fax (709)754-8336, Email: unitedchurch@nfld.net

Saskatchewan, Rev. William Doyle, 418 A McDonald St., Regina, SK S4N 6E1, Tel. (306)721-3311 Fax (306)721-3171, Email: ucskco@skconf.ca

Toronto, Rev. David W. Allen, 65 Mayall Ave., Downsview, ON M3L 1E7, Tel. (416)241-2677 Fax (416)241-2689, Email: tco-office @united-church.ca

Periodicals

United Church Observer; Mandate; Aujourd'hui Credo

United Pentecostal Church in Canada

This body, which is affiliated with the United Pentecostal Church, International, with headquarters in Hazelwood, Missouri, accepts the Bible standard of full salvation, which is repentance, baptism by immersion in the name of the Lord Jesus Christ for the remission of sins and the baptism of the Holy Ghost, with the initial signs of speaking in tongues as the Spirit gives utterance. Other tenets of faith include the Oneness of God in Christ, holiness, divine healing and the second coming of Jesus Christ.

Headquarters

United Pentecostal Church Intl., 8855 Dunn Rd., Hazelwood, MO 63042, Tel. (314)837-7300 Fax (314)837-4503

Media Contact, Gen. Sec.-Treas., Rev. C. M. Becton

District Superintendents

Atlantic, Rev. Harry Lewis, P.O. Box 1046, Perth Andover, NB E0J 1V0

British Columbia, Rev. Paul V. Reynolds, 13447-112th Ave., Surrey, BC V3R 2E7

Canadian Plains, Rev. Johnny King, 615 Northmount Dr., NW, Calgary, AB T2K 3J6

Central Canadian, Rev. Clifford Heaslip, 4215 Roblin Blvd., Winnipeg, MB R3R 0E8

Newfoundland, Jack Cunningham

Nova Scotia, Superintendent, Rev. John D. Mean, P.O. Box 2183, D.E.P.S., Dartmouth, NS B2W 3Y2

Ontario, Rev. Carl H. Stephenson, 63 Castlegrove Blvd., Don Mills, ON M3A 1L3

Universal Fellowship of Metropolitan Community Churches

The Universal Fellowship of Metropolitan Community Churches is a Christian church which directs a special ministry within, and on behalf of, the gay and lesbian community. Involvement, however, is not exclusively limited to gays and lesbians; U.F.M.C.C. tries to stress its openness to all people and does not call itself a "gay church."

Founded in 1968 in Los Angeles by the Rev. Troy Perry, the U.F.M.C.C. has over 300 member congregations worldwide. Congregations are in Vancouver, Edmonton, Windsor, London, Toronto, Ottawa (2), Guelph, Fredericton, Winnipeg, Halifax, Barrie and Belleville.

Theologically, the Metropolitan Community Churches stand within the mainstream of Christian doctrine, being "ecumenical" or "interdenominational" in stance (albeit a "denomination" in their own right).

The Metropolitan Community Churches are characterized by their belief that the love of God is a gift, freely offered to all people, regardless of sexual orientation and that no incompatibility exists between human sexuality and the Christian faith.

The Metropolitan Community Churches in Canada were founded in Toronto in 1973 by the Rev. Robert Wolfe.

Headquarters

Media Contact: The Rev. Diane Fisher, 530 Salem Street, Willimington, DE 01887, Tel. (213)447-2953

The Wesleyan Church of Canada

This group is the Canadian portion of The Wesleyan Church which consists of the Atlantic and Central Canada districts. The Central Canada District of the former Wesleyan Methodist Church of America was organized at Winchester, Ontario, in 1889 and the Atlantic District was founded in 1888 as the Alliance of the Reformed Baptist Church, which merged with the Wesleyan Methodist Church in July, 1966.

The Wesleyan Methodist Church and the Pilgrim Holiness Church merged in June, 1968, to become The Wesleyan Church. The doctrine is evangelical and Wesleyan Arminian and stresses holiness beliefs. For more details, consult the U.S. listing under The Wesleyan Church.

Headquarters

The Wesleyan Church Intl. Center, P.O. Box 50434, Indianapolis, IN 46250-0434

Media Contact, Dist. Supt., Central Canada, Rev. Donald E. Hodgins, 3545 County Road 27, RR # 2, Lyn, ON K0E 1M0, Tel. (613)966-7527 Fax (613)968-6190

District Superintendents

Central Canada, Rev. Donald E. Hodgins, 3545 County Road 27, RR # 2, Lyn, ON K0E 1M0, Email: ccd@on.aibn.com

Atlantic, Rev. Dr. H. C. Wilson, 1600 Main St., Ste. 216, Moncton, NB E1E 1G5, Email: ncwilson@nbnet.nb.ca

Periodicals

Central Canada; The Clarion

Religious Bodies in Canada Arranged by Families

The following list of religious bodies appearing in the Directory Section of the *Yearbook* shows the "families," or related clusters into which Canadian religious bodies can be grouped. For example, there are many communions that can be grouped under the heading "Baptist" for historical and theological reasons. It should not be assumed, however, that all denominations under one family heading are necessarily consistent in belief or practice. The family clusters tend to represent historical factors more often than theological or practical ones. These family categories provide one of the major pitfalls when compiling church statistics because there is often a tendency to combine the statistics by "families" for analytical and comparative purposes. Such combined totals are deeply flawed, even though they are often used as variables for sociological analysis. The arrangement by families offered here is intended only as a general guide for conceptual organization when viewing the broad sweep of Canadian religious culture.

Religious bodies that cannot be categorized under family headings appear alphabetically and are not indented in the following list.

The Anglican Church of Canada
Apostolic Christian Church (Nazarene)
Armenian Evangelical Church
Associated Gospel Churches

Baptist Bodies

Association of Regular Baptist Churches (Canada)
Baptist Convention of Ontario and Quebec
Baptist General Conference of Canada
Baptist Union of Western Canada
Canadian Baptist Ministries
Canadian Convention of Southern Baptists
Convention of Atlantic Baptist Churches
The Fellowship of Evangelical Baptist Churches in Canada
Free Will Baptists
North American Baptist Conference
Union d'Eglises Baptistes Françaises au Canada

Brethren in Christ Church, Canadian Conference
Canadian District of the Moravian Church in America, Northern Province
Canadian Evangelical Christian Churches
Canadian Yearly Meeting of the Religious Society of Friends
Christ Catholic Church International
Christian Brethren (also known as Plymouth Brethren)
Christian and Missionary Alliance in Canada
Church of God (Anderson, Ind.)
Church of the Nazarene in Canada

Churches of Christ-Christian Churches

Christian Church (Disciples of Christ) in Canada
Christian Churches / Churches of Christ
Churches of Christ in Canada

Congregational Christian Churches in Canada

Eastern Orthodox Churches

The Antiochian Orthodox Christian Archdiocese of North America
Greek Orthodox Metropolis of Toronto (Canada)
Orthodox Church in America (Archdiocese of Canada)
Orthodox Church in America (Canada Section)
Patriarchal Parishes of the Russian Orthodox Church in Canada
Romanian Orthodox Church in America (Canada)
The Romanian Orthodox Episcopate of America (Jackson, MI)
Serbian Orthodox Church in the U.S.A. and Canada, Diocese of Canada
Ukrainian Orthodox Church of Canada

The Evangelical Covenant Church of Canada
Evangelical Free Church of Canada
The Evangelical Missionary Church of Canada
General Church of the New Jerusalem
Jehovah's Witnesses

Latter Day Saints (Mormons)

The Church of Jesus Christ of Latter Day Saints in Canada
Community of Christ

Lutheran Bodies

Church of the Lutheran Brethren
The Estonian Evangelical Lutheran Church Abroad
Evangelical Lutheran Church in Canada
Lutheran Church—Canada

Mennonite Bodies

Canadian Conference of Mennonite Brethren Churches
Church of God in Christ (Mennonite)
The Evangelical Mennonite Conference

Evangelical Mennonite Mission Conference
Mennonite Church Canada
Old Order Amish Church
Reinland Mennonite Church

Methodist Bodies

British Methodist Episcopal Church
of Canada
Free Methodist Church in Canada
Independent Holiness Church
The Wesleyan Church of Canada

The Christ Catholic Church International
The Old Catholic Church of Canada
Open Bible Faith Fellowship of Canada

Oriental Orthodox Churches

Armenian Holy Apostolic Church - Canadian
Diocese
The Coptic Orthodox Church in Canada
Syriac Orthodox Church of Antioch

Pentecostal Bodies

The Apostolic Church in Canada
Apostolic Church of Pentecost of Canada Inc.
The Bible Holiness Movement
Canadian Assemblies of God (formerly The
Italian Pentecostal Church of Canada)
Church of God (Cleveland, Tenn.)

The Church of God of Prophecy
in Canada East
Elim Fellowship Canada
Foursquare Gospel Church of Canada
General Conference of the Canadian
Assemblies of God
Independent Assemblies of God International
(Canada)
The Pentecostal Assemblies of Canada
Pentecostal Assemblies of Newfoundland
United Pentecostal Church in Canada

Reformed Bodies

Canadian and American Reformed Churches
Christian Reformed Church in North America
Presbyterian Church in America (Canadian
Section)
Presbyterian Church in Canada
Reformed Church in Canada

The Reformed Episcopal Church of Canada
The Roman Catholic Church in Canada
The Salvation Army in Canada
Seventh-day Adventist Church in Canada
Union of Spiritual Communities of Christ
(Orthodox Doukhobors in Canada)
United Brethren Church in Canada
The United Church of Canada
Universal Fellowship of Metropolitan
Community Churches

5. Sources of Religion-Related Research
I. Directory of Selected Research Organizations

The editorial office of the *Yearbook of American & Canadian Churches* receives innumerable requests for data about churches, religious organizations, attendance patterns, and comparative religion concerns. Sometimes we are able to furnish the requested data, but more often we refer the inquirer to other research colleagues in the field. We are always interested in and aided by such requests, and we find ourselves informed by each question.

In response to such inquiries, the "Sources in Religion-Related Research" directory was initiated in the 1999 edition of the *Yearbook*. In addition to asking each organization to provide a brief overall description, each was also asked to indicate any special research foci (i.e. denominational, congregational, interfaith, gender, etc.). Further, each organization is asked to identify the sociological, methodological, or theological approaches that serve to guide their research, and to describe any current or recent research projects. Lastly, we asked for a list of recurrent publications. Below the organizations' responses to these questions are reported as clearly and completely as is possible. Contact information appears just beneath the title of each organization. In most cases, the organization's website provides very detailed information about current research projects.

Numerous other research centers in the area of American religious life, each with specific areas of concern, conduct timely and significant research. We hope that readers will find utility in this directory and we invite them to identify additional sources by email: yearbook@ncccusa.org or by Fax: (212) 870-2817.

American Academy of Religion (AAR)

AAR Executive Office
825 Houston Mill Rd., Ste. 300
Atlanta, GA 30329
Tel. (404)727-7920
Fax (404)727-7959
Email: aar@aarweb.org
Website: www.aarweb.org
President: Dr. Diana Eck
Exec. Dir.: Dr. John Fitzmier

The AAR is the major learned society and professional association for scholars whose object of study is religion. Its mission—in a world where religion plays so central a role in social, political and economic events, as well as in the lives of communities and individuals—is to meet a critical need for ongoing reflection upon and understanding of religious traditions, issues, questions and values. As a learned society and professional association of teachers and research scholars, the American Academy of Religion has over 8500 members who teach in some 1,500 colleges, universities, seminaries, and schools in North America and abroad. The Academy is dedicated to furthering knowledge of religion and religious institutions in all their forms and manifestations. This is accomplished through Academy-wide and regional conferences and meetings, publications, programs, and membership services. Within a context of free inquiry and critical examination, the Academy welcomes all disciplined reflection on religion—both from within and outside of communities of belief and practice—and seeks to enhance its broad public understanding.

The AAR's annual meeting, over 8,000 scholars gather to share research and collaborate on scholarly projects. The annual meeting sessions are grouped into over 70 program units, each representing an ongoing community of scholars who are collectively engaged in pursuing knowledge about a specific religious tradition or a specific aspect of religion. In addition, the AAR's ten regional organizations sponsor smaller annual meetings that are similar in structure to the Academy-wide meeting. All of the world's major religious traditions, as well as indigenous and historical religions, are explored in the work of AAR members.

Current or Recent Research

Currently, for example, the AAR offers Teaching Workshops for both junior and senior scholars. It is organizing efforts to gather data on the field to facilitate departmental planning and funding. A full explanation of the many current research projects is available on the AAR website, which is listed above.

Periodicals

The *Journal of the American Academy of Religion* is the scholarly periodical of the AAR. In addition, the AAR publishes a quarterly newsletter, *Religious Studies News, AAR Edition.*

Association of Religion Data Archives (ARDA)

Department of Sociology
The Pennsylvania State University
211 Oswald Tower
University Park, PA 16802-6207
Tel. (814)865-6258
Fax (814)863-7216
Email: arda@pop.psu.edu
Website: www.TheARDA.com
Director: Dr. Roger Finke

The ARDA allows you to interactively explore the highest quality data on American and international religion using online features for generating national profiles, maps, church membership overviews, denominational heritage trees, tables, charts, and other summary reports. Nearly 500 data files are available for online preview and most can be downloaded for additional review. The ARDA (www.theARDA.com) is supported by the Lilly Endowment and the John Templeton Foundation and is housed in the Social Science Research Institute at the Pennsylvania State University. All services are provided free of charge.

Association of Theological Schools (ATS)

10 Summit Park Dr.
Pittsburgh, PA 15275-1103
Tel. (412)788-6505
Fax (412)788-6510
Email: ats@ats.edu
Website: www.ats.edu
Exec. Dir.: Daniel O. Aleshire
Dir. of Communications and External Relations: Eliza Smith Brown

The mission of The Association of Theological Schools in the United States and Canada (ATS) is to promote the improvement and enhancement of theological schools to the benefit of communities of faith and the broader public. The Association seeks to fulfill this mission by engaging in four core areas of work, (1) accreditation, (2) leadership education for administrative officers and faculty, (3) development of theological education, which involves the study of critical issues in theological education, and (4) communications and data.

The Association is a membership organization of approximately 260 graduate schools of theology, including Protestant, Roman Catholic, and Orthodox schools, both freestanding seminaries and university-related divinity schools. A full list of members is available on the above website.

Targeted areas of the Association's work currently include Institutional Viability and Financially Stressed Schools; Christian Hospitality and Pastoral Practices in a Multifaith Society; Race and Ethnicity in Theological Education; Women in Leadership in Theological Education; and Technology and Educational Practices.

Current or Recent Research

The Institutional Viability and Financially Stressed Schools project seeks to identify underlying issues that result in chronic financial stress and patterns of institutional effort that could provide for healthier financial futures for affected schools. The Christian Hospitality and Pastoral Practices in a Multifaith Society project seeks to identify those practices that theological schools should undertake in training ministers and priests to ensure religion's positive contribution to an increasingly diverse religious landscape. An ongoing project on Technology and Educational Practices is identifying best practices in the use of educational technology in theological education, conducting events that provide information about and skill development in the use of educational technology, and creating resources about education and technology for use by theological schools.

Periodicals

The Association publishes *Theological Education*, a bi-annual journal; *Colloquy*, a bi-annual magazine; and the *Bulletin*, which contains the formal institutional documents of the Association, including its membership list. Additional data is available at the ATS website, www.ats.edu.

Auburn Theological Seminary

3041 Broadway
New York, NY 10027
Tel. (212)662-4315

218

Fax (212)663-5214
Email: cste@auburnsem.org
Website: www.auburnsem.org
President: Rev. Dr. Katharine R. Henderson
Director, The Center for the Study of Theological Education (CSTE): Dr. Barbara G. Wheeler

Auburn Theological Seminary's mission is to strengthen religious leadership. It carries out its mission through programs of non-degree theological education for clergy and laity; through programs for Presbyterian students enrolled at its partner institution, Union Theological Seminary in New York City; and by conducting research on theological education at its Center for the Study of Theological Education. Auburn was founded in 1818 in Auburn, New York; it is currently located on Union Seminary's campus.

Auburn Seminary is related by covenant agreement with the Presbyterian Church (U.S.A.), but most of its programs are ecumenical, and many have a multi-faith focus. The Center for the Study of Theological Education includes Protestant and Roman Catholic seminaries and divinity schools as well as rabbinical schools in its research.

Research is conducted using a variety of methods, including survey and ethnographic research, structured interviews and case studies. Reports of findings are distributed widely to denominations, church agencies and theological schools.

Current or Recent Research

Leadership That Works (2010) identifies the characteristics of leadership that create stable, forward-looking theological institutions. The five-member research team, using site visits, interviews and surveys, studied seminary presidents and their senior administrative teams.. The team followed ten new presidents as they began their tenure in office, visiting them annually for three years. They also conducted case studies of six "well-functioning" schools and surveyed presidents, academic deans and chief financial officers.

Periodicals

Auburn Studies, an occasional bulletin in which the Center publishes its research results. Research reports are also available on Auburn's website (listed above).

The Barna Group, Ltd.

1957 Eastman Ave., Suite B
Ventura, CA 93003
Tel. (805)658-8885
Fax (805)658-7298
Email: barna@barna.org
Website: www.barna.org
President: George Barna
President: David Kinnaman

The Barna Group conducts primary research related to cultural change, people's lifestyles, values, attitudes, beliefs and religious practices. Its vision is to provide current accurate and reliable information, in bite-sized pieces and at reasonable costs, to its clients to facilitate strategic decisions. Barna also produces many research-based books, reports, and ministry tools to help churches understand the national context of ministry. The organization works with churches from all Christian denominations.

It conducts projects based upon existing needs in the Church at-large, or for its clients specifically. Methodologically, The Barna Group uses both qualitative approaches (focus groups, depth interviews) and quantitative approaches (cross-sectional surveys, longitudinal studies, panel research).

Data collection methods include telephone surveys, mail surveys, in-person interviews, on-line surveys, self-administered surveys, focus groups.

Current or Recent Research

The Barna Group conducts more than 50 studies each year, covering a broad range of topics. Some of the recent non-proprietary studies completed are focused on understanding the state of the Church; the habits of highly effective churches; worship efficacy; the unchurched; strategies and techniques for developing lay leaders; understanding effective discipleship processes; pastoral profiles; beliefs, behaviors and core attitudes of ministry donors; Biblical knowledge, and many others.

Periodicals

The Barna Group offers a free bi-weekly report—*The Barna Update*—on current information related to faith matters from its national non-proprietary research. This information is free to those who register for it at the website (listed above).

Center for Applied Research in the Apostolate (CARA)

Georgetown University
Washington, DC 20057
Tel. (202) 687-8080
Fax (202) 687-8083
Email: cara@georgetown.edu
Website: www. Cara.georgetown.edu
Executive Director: Thomas P. Gaunt, S. J., Ph.D.
Sr. Research Associate: Mary Gautier

CARA-the Center for Applied Research in the Apostolate is a not-for-profit research organization of the Roman Catholic Church. It operates on the premise that not only theological principles but also findings of the social sciences must be the basis for pastoral care.

CARA's mission since its founding in 1964 has been "To discover, promote, and apply modern techniques and scientific informational resources for practical use in a coordinated and effective approach to the Church's social and religious mission in the modern world, at home and overseas."

CARA performs a wide range of research studies and consulting services. Since its roots are Roman Catholic, many of its studies are done for dioceses, religious orders, parishes, and the United States Conference of Catholic Bishops. Interdenominational studies are also performed. Publishes The CARA Report, a research newsletter on Catholic Church related topics, four times a year and The Catholic Ministry Formation Directory, a guide and statistical compilation of enrollments for Catholic seminaries, diaconate formation programs, and lay ministry formation programs.

Periodicals

The Catholic Ministry Formation Directory

Center for the Study of Religion and American Culture

Indiana University
Purdue University at Indianapolis
425 University Blvd, Room 341
Indianapolis, IN 46202-5140
Tel. (317)274-8409
Fax (317)278-3354
Email: pgoff@iupui.edu
Website: www.iupui.edu/~raac
Director: Dr. Phillip Goff
Program Coordinator: Rebecca Vasko

The Center for the Study of Religion and American Culture is a research and public outreach institute devoted to the promotion of the understanding of the relation between religion and other features of American culture. Research methods are both inter-disciplinary and multi-disciplinary. Established in 1989, the Center is based in the School of Liberal Arts and Indiana University–Purdue University at Indianapolis. Center activities include national conferences and symposia, commissioned books, essays, bibliographies, and research projects, fellowships for younger scholars, data based communication about developments in the field of American religion, a newsletter devoted to the promotion of Center activities, and the semi-annual scholarly periodical, Religion and American Culture, A Journal of Interpretation.

Current or Recent Research

The Center is presently overseeing two initiatives. The "Young Scholars in American Religion Program" is a multi-year project to assist early-career scholars in developing their teaching skills and research agendas. The "Centers and Institutes Project," meanwhile, brings together those organizations dedicated to the academic study of religion in the U.S. in order to discuss common problems and solutions, as well as to identify areas for cooperative efforts. The work of these various centers and institutes will be highlighted in future issues of the Newsletter from the Center for the Study of Religion and American Culture and the Center's reception at the annual meeting of the American Academy of Religion.

We continue to explore other areas of potential research in the relation between religion and other aspects of American culture. As these projects materialize, they will be announced on this website and in the Newsletter.

Periodicals

Religion and American Culture, A Journal of Interpretation. Center books include the series, The Public Expressions of Religion in America.

Collegeville Institute for Ecumenical & Cultural Research

14027 Fruit Farm Road
PO Box 2000
Collegeville, MN 56321-2000
Tel. (320)363-3366
Fax (320)363-3313
Email: staff@CollegevilleInstitute.org
Website: CollegevilleInstitute.org
Exec. Dir.: Dr. Don B. Ottenhoff
Administrative Assistant: Elisa Schneider

The Collegeville Institute for Ecumenical and Cultural Research brings together well-trained, creative, articulate men and women for careful thought and dialogue in a place of inquiry and prayer. The Resident scholars Program welcomes researchers and their families for either individual semesters or for an entire academic year. Resident scholars work on their own projects but meet once a week for seminars, and have other occasions for conversation. Each scholar presents a public lecture or presentation.

Ecumenism happens at the Institute as people come to know one another in community. The Institute is an independent corporation, but shares in the Benedictine and academic life of Saint John's Abbey and University, and of nearby Saint Benedict's Monastery and the College of Saint Benedict. In the summer the Institute uses its facilities for summer writing workshops and seminars.

In the Resident Scholars Program, the subjects of research are determined by the interests of the applicants who are invited to come by the Admissions Committee. While most of the work tends to be in traditional theological areas, we encourage people in all fields to consider applying, both because ecumenism is of concern across the spectrum of disciplines, and because the term "cultural" in our title extends our reach beyond theology and religious studies. In particular cases, work done here may have a denominational, congregational, or interfaith focus, but the Institute does not prescribe or delimit, in any narrow way, what is appropriate.

Current or Recent Research

Individual research conducted by scholars.

Periodicals

Bearings

empty tomb, inc.

301 North Fourth Street
P.O. Box 2404
Champaign, IL 61825-2404
Tel. (217)356-9519
Fax (217)356-2344
Email: research@emptytomb.org
Website: www.emptytomb.org
CEO: John L. Ronsvalle
Exec.Vice-Pres.: Sylvia Ronsvalle

empty tomb, inc. is a Christian research and service organization. On a local level, it coordinates direct services to people in need in cooperation with area congregations. On a national level, it studies church member giving patterns of historically Christian churches, including Roman Catholic, mainline and evangelical Protestant, Anabaptist, Pentecostal, Orthodox, and fundamentalist communions. empty tomb publishes the annual State of Church Giving series. Also, empty tomb offers a mission funding incentive program, Mission Match, in an effort to help reverse the negative giving trends indicated by national data.

Current or Recent Research

Current research monitors and analyzes church member giving patterns, and is published in *The State of Church Giving* series produced by empty tomb, inc.

Periodicals

The State of Church Giving series is an annual publication. It considers denominational giving data, analysis of giving and membership trends, and other estimates of charitable giving. Each edition has featured a special focus chapter, which discusses giving issues relevant to church giving patterns. Past *State of Church Giving* special focus chapters are posted on the www.emptytomb.org website.

SOURCES

221

The Hartford Institute for Religion Research of Hartford Seminary

Hartford Seminary
77 Sherman Street
Hartford, CT 06105
Tel. (860)509-9543
Fax (860)509-9551
Email: hirr@hartsem.edu
Website: www.hirr.hartsem.edu
Director of Research: Dr. David A. Roozen
Administrative Assistant: Mary Jane Ross

The Hartford Institute for Religion Research of Hartford Seminary was established in 1981, formalizing a research program initiated by the Seminary in 1974. Until recently it was known as The Center for Social and Religious Research. The Institute's work is guided by a disciplined understanding of the interrelationship between (a) the inner life and resources of American religious institutions and (b) the possibilities and limits placed on those institutions by the social and cultural context into which God has called them.

Its twenty-one year record of rigorous, policy-relevant research, anticipation of emerging issues, commitment to the creative dissemination of learning, and strong connections to both theological education and the church has earned the Institute an international reputation as an important bridge between the scholarly community and the practice of ministry.

Current or Recent Research

Some of the titles of current projects at the Institute are, "Organizing Religious Work for the 21st Century, Exploring 'Denominationalism;'" "Cooperative Congregational Studies Project;" "Congregational Consulting Services;" "New England Religion Discussion Society (NERDS);" "Congregational Studies Team." Descriptions of these programs are available on the Institute's website, listed above.

Periodicals

Praxis is Hartford Seminary's magazine, which focuses on the activities and faculty of the seminary.

Institute for the Study of American Evangelicals (ISAE)

ISAE, Wheaton College
Wheaton, IL 60187
Tel. (630)752-5437
Fax (630)752-5294
Email: isae@wheaton.edu
Website: www.isae@wheaton.edu
Director: Dr. Edith Blumhofer
Associate Director: Larry Eskridge

Founded in 1982, the Institute for the Study of American Evangelicals is a center for research and functions as a program of Wheaton College. The purpose of the ISAE is to encourage and support research on evangelical Christianity in the United States and Canada. The institute seeks to help evangelicals develop a mature understanding of their own heritage and to inform others about evangelicals' historical significance and contemporary role. For the most part, the ISAE focuses on historical research, with input from scholars across a number of disciplines in the humanities and the social sciences.

Current or Recent Research

Currently the Institute is finishing up a project funded by the Lilly Endowment that examines changes in American Protestant missions in the century since the great Edinburgh Missions Conference of 1910. A conference on this topic at Duke Divinity School in 2011 will yield a specifically-dedicated issue of the International Bulletin of Missionary Research, and the Institute is seeking publication for another set of conference-derived essays with a university press. A 6-part ISAE-produced DVD video study curriculum entitled *People of Faith: Christianity in America* is now completed and will be available by January 2012.

Periodicals

The *Evangelical Studies Bulletin (ESB)* is designed to aid both the scholar and the layman in his or her education and research of evangelicalism. Issued quarterly, the bulletin contains articles, book reviews, notices, a calendar of events, and bibliographic information on the latest dissertations, articles and books related to the study of evangelicals and American religion.

Institute for the Study of American Religion

P.O. Box 90709
Santa Barbara, CA 93190-0709
Tel. (805)967-7721
Email: jgordon@linkline.com
Website: www.americanreligion.org
Director: Dr. J. Gordon Melton
Associate Director: Dr. James Beverley

The Institute for the Study of American Religion was founded in 1968 in Evanston, Illinois as a religious studies research facility with a particular focus upon the smaller religions of the United States. Those groups that it has concentrated upon have been known under a variety of labels including sect, cult, minority religion, alternative religion, non-conventional religion, spiritual movement and new religious movement.

In the 1970s the Institute extended its attention to Canada and in the1990s developed an even more global focus. In 1985, the institute moved to its present location in Santa Barbara, California. Over the years the institute built a large collection of both primary and secondary materials on the religious groups and movements it studied. In 1985 this collection of more than 40,000 volumes and thousands of periodicals and archival materials was deposited with the Davidson Library at the University of California in Santa Barbara. The reference material exists today as the American Religions Collection and is open to scholars and the interested public. The institute continues to support the collection with donations of additional materials.

Current or Recent Research

Today the institute has two main foci. It monitors all of the religious denominations, organizations, and movements functioning in North America and regularly publishes reports drawing from that activity in a series of reference books. The most important of these reference books is the *Encyclopedia of American Religions* (Detroit, Gale Group, 7th edition, 2002).

Among the most called for information is factual data on the many new and more controversial religious movements, which are popularly labeled as "cults." The institute's second focus developed out of its more recent refocusing on the international scene, provoked by the international life of most of the religious groups which it has studied in previous decades.

J.M. Dawson Institute of Church-State Studies at Baylor University

P.O. Box 97308
Waco, TX 76798-7308
Tel. (254)710-1510
Fax (254)710-1571
Email: derek_davis@baylor.edu
Website: www.baylor.edu/~Church_State
Director: Dr. Derek Davis
Administrative Assistant: Wanda Gilbert

Baylor University established the J.M. Dawson Institute of Church-State Studies in 1957, so named in honor of an outstanding alumnus, an ardent advocate of religious liberty, and a distinguished author of publications on church and state. The Institute is the oldest and most well-established facility of its kind located in a university setting. It is exclusively devoted to research in the broad field of church and state and the advancement of religious liberty around the world.

From its inception in 1957, the stated purpose of the Institute has been to stimulate academic interest and encourage research and publication in the broad area of church-state relations. In carrying out its statement of purpose, the Institute has sought to honor a threefold commitment, to be interfaith, interdisciplinary, and international.

Current or Recent Research

Some current research includes, Government persecution of minority religions in Europe; original intent of Founding Fathers regarding religion and public life; Christian Right views on political activism; conservative versus moderate Baptist views on church-state relations; role of civil religion in America; international treaties and religious liberty.

Periodicals

Journal of Church and State is the only scholarly journal expressly devoted to church-state relations.

The Louisville Institute

1044 Alta Vista Road
Louisville, KY 40205-1798
Tel. (502) 992-9341

Fax (502) 894-2286
Email: jlewis@louisville-institute.org
Website: www.louisville-institute.org
Exec. Dir.: Dr. James W. Lewis
Assoc. Dir.: Dr. Don Richter

The Louisville Institute is a Lilly Endowment-funded program for the study of American religion based at the Louisville Presbyterian Seminary. The distinctive mission of the Louisville Institute is to enrich the religious life of American Christians and to encourage the revitalization of their institutions by bringing together those who lead religious institutions with those who study them, so that the work of each might inform and strengthen the other. The Louisville Institute offers funding through five grant programs to serve three strategic constituencies: pastors, younger scholars, and researchers and scholars for the broader church. These programs also seek to advance our understanding of three important issues: Christian faith and life, pastoral leadership, and religious institutions. In addition, a new emphasis of the Louisville Institute is the identification and support of a new generation of ecclesially engaged scholars for theological schools and colleges.

Current or Recent Research

Please see the Louisville Institute website (listed above) for lists of recent grants made by the Louisville Institute.

Periodicals

Intersections

The Pluralism Project

Harvard University
1531 Cambridge St.
Cambridge, MA 02139
Tel. (617)496-2481
Fax (617)496-2428
Email: staff@pluralism.org
Website: www.pluralsm.org
Director: Dr. Diana L. Eck
Assistant Manager: Kathryn Lohre

The Pluralism Project was developed by Dr. Diana L. Eck at Harvard University to study and document the growing religious diversity of the United States, with a special view to its new immigrant religious communities. The religious landscape of the U.S. has radically changed in the past forty years; in light of these changes, how Americans of all faiths begin to engage with one another in shaping a positive pluralism is one of the most important questions American society faces in the years ahead. In addressing these phenomena, the Project has four goals: 1) To document and better understand the changing contours of American religious demography, focusing especially on those cities and towns where the new plurality has been most evident and discerning the ways in which this plurality is both visible and invisible in American public life. 2) To study the religious communities themselves ¬ their temples, mosques, gurudwaras and retreat centers, their informal networks and emerging institutions, their forms of adaptation and religious education in the American context, their encounter with the other religious traditions of our common society, and their encounter with civic institutions. 3) To explore the ramifications and implications of America's new plurality through case studies of particular cities and towns, looking at the response of Christian and Jewish communities to their new neighbors; the development of interfaith councils and networks; the new theological and pastoral questions that emerge from the pluralistic context; and the recasting of traditional church-state issues in a wider context. 4.) To discern, in light of this work, the emerging meanings of religious "pluralism," both for religious communities and for public institutions, and to consider the real challenges and opportunities of a public commitment to pluralism in the light of the new religious contours of America.

The Pluralism Project has the most comprehensive archive anywhere of the print materials of America's new immigrant religious communities, including newsletters, serial publications, anniversary programs, handbooks, prayer books, calendars, and educational materials donated directly by centers. The Project files also include numerous research papers, profiles of centers, and information on events, all available at www.pluralism.org.

The Pluralism Project On-Line Directory maintains an extensive directory of religious centers in the United States. At present, this directory exists in a searchable database, with listings of over six thousand centers across the U.S.

Current or Recent Research

The Pluralism Project produced a CD-ROM, *On Common Ground- World Religions in America*, to present some of the wide range of work that had emerged from three years of research. Numerous affiliate research reports from a wide network of university professors and students are available on their website. *Religious Diversity News* summarizes news stories on pressing issues in the United States including most minority faiths, with a companion *International News*; both of these resources are available online in searchable databases, with archives back to 1997. In 2005 the Pluralism Project released, *Acting on Faith: Women's New Religious Activism*, available on VHS and DVD. *World Religions in Boston: A Guide to Communities and Resources*, is an online resource that profiles many of the diverse religions centers in the Boston area. Current research includes The Interfaith Initiative, The City Hall Initiative, The Women's Initiative, and The International Initiative. One can subscribe to their monthly e-newsletter online.

II. Directory of Selected Faith Communities in the USA

Compiling a directory of faith communities is an arduous but rewarding task in religiously plural America. In part, because the very self-understanding and definition of community varies so greatly from tradition to tradition. In order to present a reasonably parallel and well-balanced listing of organizations for each faith, care must be taken not to impose categories or terms from one's own universe of understanding upon other contexts. The very terms, "church," "membership," "denomination," and "hierarchy", which are essential constructs of certain Christian universes of understanding, are rendered meaningless when applied to other faith groups.

Further, it is important to remember that many religious communities lack a centralized organization that speaks for the whole. Often, this lack of centralization reflects the existence of several distinct forms or branches of the religion. In some instances, different ethnic groups immigrating to the U.S., bring with them a distinctive form of their religion, which is particular to their culture of origin. In other cases, plural forms of a faith exist resulting from theological, political, or economic differences. Still other faith groups may be more tightly organized, but the religious center that provides guidance in matters of faith and, perhaps, even organizational discipline may not be in the United States. Hence, the organizations before us are not necessarily religious hierarchical organizations, but are often groups assembled for other purposes that are associated with a particular faith group, or subdivision of that faith group. Caution is advised in regarding these entries as one might regard a "church headquarters."

The compilation of any directory relies upon the existence of some common organizational structure within all the entities listed. Yet, when compiling a directory of faith groups, it cannot be assumed such organizational parallels exist. Oblique ways must be found to adequately represent individual faith groups. The many religious communities in the United States are associated with myriad organizations of all different types. Some of these are primarily places of worship; others are organizations seeking to represent either the religious community as a whole or some particular constituency within it. Others are community centers; some are educational groups; some are organizations particularly for women or youths; and some are political action groups. Still others are peace organizations or relief organizations.

That said, a directory of this sort cannot include an exhaustive list of organizations for each faith group nationwide. The omission of any particular organization or branch of any of the major faith groups listed does not reflect a deliberate attempt to homogenize the rich pluralities that exist within faith groups. Instead, the listings that follow are intended to provide the interested reader with a few initial contacts within each religious community, in alphabetical order within the tradition.

Despite the above cautions, this directory provides a rich resource for readers and researchers who wish to learn more about other faith groups. The agencies listed here consist of organizations of importance within the communities they represent, and serve as excellent introductory points of contact with those communities. In some cases, these religious communities are in a state of flux; the Internet is an excellent way to keep contact with changing religious organizations. There is a plethora of information available about nearly all religious traditions online, but sites vary widely in their accuracy and reliability. Nearly any Internet search engine will provide extensive links to information about specific religious traditions. For directory information about national Interfaith organizations in the United States, please see Directory 1, "U.S. Cooperative Organizations" For directory information on local interfaith organizations, please see Directory 6, "U.S. Regional and Local Ecumenical Bodies."

BAHÁ'Í FAITH

The Bahá'í Faith arose in 19th-century Persia, and refers to followers of Mirza Hussein Ali Nuri, whom they call Baha'ullah (Arabic for Glory of God). In 1863, Bahá'u'lláh proclaimed himself to be the Manifestation of God for the present age. His coming had been heralded in 1844 by Mirza Ali Muhammad, also known as the Báb (the Door) whom Bahá'ís consider a Manifestation of God as well. Shortly afterward there was a severe persecution. The Báb was executed in 1850; Bahá'u'lláh died in exile, under house arrest in Acre, Palestine, in 1892. Bahá'ís believe in Progressive Revelation. Thus, as the manifestation of God for the present age, Bahá'u'lláh is considered to be the most recent in a lineage of messengers which includes Abraham, Krishna, the Buddha, Zarathustra, Jesus, and Muhammad. The oneness of God, the oneness of religion, and the oneness of humanity (with stress on racial and gender equality) are key principles of the Bahá'í Faith. Bahá'u'lláh's son

Abd-al-Baha organized the religion's sacred texts, and established its system of representative governance through consensus, collaboration, and consultation. This includes the Universal House of Justice (the supreme administrative body, which meets in Haifa, Israel), National Spiritual Assemblies, and Local Spiritual Assemblies.

The Baha'i National Center of the U.S.A. and **The National Spiritual Assembly of the Bahà'ìs of the United States**
1233 Central Street
Evanston, IL 60201
Tel. (847)733-3559/3400 Fax (847)733-3578
Website: www.bahai.usa
The home of the National Spiritual Assembly of the Bahá'ís of the United States the center is an official source of information about the Bahá'í Faith, resources on many issues (such as peace, justice, economic development, racial unity, and education), and networking with Bahá'í spiritual assemblies throughout the world, of which there are more than 1700 in the U.S.A.

BUDDHISM

Buddhism is a Western term for the many and varied expressions of practices based on the teachings of Siddhartha Gautama, who lived in northern India c. 563-483 B.C.E.. Called the Buddha (the Enlightened One) by his followers, Siddhartha proposed a Middle Way between self-indulgence and extreme Hindu asceticism. Central to Buddhist teaching are the Four Noble Truths: that life inevitably involves suffering; that the origin of suffering is desire; that suffering can be eradicated by extinguishing desire; and that the way to accomplish this is to follow the Noble Eightfold Path of morality, concentration, and wisdom. Buddhists "take refuge" in the Triple Gem: the Buddha, the dhamma (his teachings), and the sangha (the community). Buddhism has two major branches. Theravada (Way of the Elders) which defines the sangha primarily as the community of ascetics. Mahayana (Great Vehicle) defines the sangha as all Buddhists, and includes the many schools Pure Land, Zen (Ch'an), and Tibetan Buddhism. Vajrayana (Diamond Vehicle) is a rigorous form of Mahayana associated frequently (but not exclusively) with Tibetan practice. Distinctive Western eclectic forms have emerged in recent decades. While there is much variation, Buddhist practice is characterized by meditation, chanting, and emphasis on compassion. Although most practice-groups and temples function autonomously and some are affiliated with a particular teacher or movement, there are continuing local or regional attempts to bridge philosophical differences.

American Buddhist Association
4524 N. Richmond Street
Chicago, IL 60625
Tel: (773)583-5794
Contact: Richard Brandon (Zenyo)
Email: brightdawn_1@juno.org
Website: www.awakenedone.org
Founded in 1955 for the study and propagation of Buddhism and to encourage the understanding and application of Buddhist principles in the general American public, this organization's roots are in Japanese Buddhism (Jodo Shinshu and Zen), but is now independent and nonsectarian. It publishes books, pamphlets, and audio-visual materials, sponsors seminars, and acts as a resource center.

American Buddhist Congress
3835 E. Thousand Oaks Blvd., Ste. 450
Westlake Village, CA 91362
Tel. (877)7BUDDHA, (877)728-3342
Email: BuddhistCongress@adelphia.net
Website: www.americanbuddhistcongress.org
Founded in 1987 to bring together individuals and organizations of various Buddhist traditions, denominations, and ethnic backgrounds, this organization is dedicated to developing an "American" Buddhism which, while paying respect and acknowledging its debt to Buddhist traditions of other cultures, seeks to synthesize American values and traditions with the basic Buddhism of the tripitaka (scripture) without the linguistic and cultural aspects which are not understood or confusing to most Americans.

Buddhist Churches of America
1710 Octavia St.
San Francisco, CA 94109
Tel. (415)776-5600
Fax (415)771-6293
Email: bcahq@pacbell.net

SOURCES

Website: buddhistchurchesofamerica.org

Founded in 1899, this is a national headquarters and resource center for temples in the Japanese Shin (Pure Land) tradition. It also serves as a regional center of the World Fellowship of Buddhists

Buddhist Council of the Midwest

1812 Washington Street
Evanston, IL 60202
Tel. (847)869-5806
Fax (847)869-5806
Email: infor@buddhistcouncilmidwest.org
Website: www.buddhistcouncilmidwest.org

Incorporated as a non-profit religious organization in 1987, the Buddhist Council of the Midwest includes 95 Buddhist groups in Chicago and the Midwest area. Its purpose is to foster the learning and practice of Buddhism; to represent the Midwest Buddhist community in matters affecting its membership; and to pool resources and coordinate efforts by its membership to create an atmosphere of fellowship and cooperation.

Buddhist Council of the Northwest

1530 184th Ave NE
Bellevue, WA 98008
Tel: (425)442-0986
Fax: (425)643-2490
Email: info@buddhistcouncilnw.org
Website: www.buddhistcouncilnw.org

Founded in 2002, the Buddhist Council of the Northwest is a non-profit organization formed to pool resources and coordinate efforts by its membership. It serves as a consultant to and advocate for Buddhist temples, study groups, and individuals on matters of cultural, legal, and government concern related to the preservation and promotion of the Buddha Dhamma (teaching) in the Pacific Northwest, with special focus on the Asian-American Buddhist temples and communities, and realizing and respecting the diversity of Buddhist traditions within the Pacific Northwest. It initiates and supports religious, cultural or social welfare project which will help to disseminate the spirit of the Buddha Dhamma, and works ecumenically with over religious groups.

The Buddhist Peace Fellowship

P.O. Box 3470
Berkeley, CA 94703
Tel. (510)655-6169
Fax (510)655-1369
Email: membership@bpf.org
Website: www.bpf.org

Founded in 1978, the Buddhist Peace Fellowship's purpose is to serve as a catalyst for socially engaged Buddhism, striving for peace where there is conflict, promoting communication and cooperation among Buddhist sanghas, and seeking to alleviate suffering wherever possible. BPF's programs, publications, and practice groups link Buddhist teachings of wisdom and compassion with progressive social change.

Insight Meditation Society

1230 Pleasant St.
Barre, MA 01005
Tel: (978)355-4378
Email: RC@dharma.org
Website: www.dharma.org

Dedicated to Vipassana (insight meditation), a practice associated with Theravada Buddhism, this is a loosely associated network of groups, including major centers in New York, Washington DC, Seattle, San Francisco, Los Angeles, and Boston, and smaller centers and practice groups in many other cities and towns.

New York Buddhist Council

c/o Staten Island Buddhist Vihara
115 John Street
Staten Island, NY 10302
Tel: (718)556-2051

Email: heenko@yahoo.com
Website: www.newyorkbuddhistcouncil.com
An umbrella organization bringing together the leaders of New York City's Buddhist organizations across traditions and ethnicities.

Soka Gakkai International-USA

National Headquarters
606 Wilshire Blvd.
Santa Monica, CA 90401
Tel: (310)260-8900
Fax: (310)260-8917
Website: www.sgi-usa.org
An American Buddhist association that promotes world peace and individual happiness based on the teachings of the Nichiren school of Mahayana Buddhism. Its members reflect a cross section of our diverse American society, representing a broad range of ethnic and social backgrounds.

Soto Zen Buddhist Association (SZBA)

8058 Mill Station Rd
Sebastopol, CA 95472
Tel.: (707)827-3757
Email: korin108@gmail.com
Website: www.szba.org
Director: Charlie Korin Pokorny
Soto Zen traces its lineage back to the Chinese founder, Zen master Tung-shan Liang-jie (807-869). The Soto Zen school was established in Japan by Zen master Eihei Dogen (1200-1253). A number of lineages descended from Dogen have been established in the U.S. with over 12 distinct lineages represented by the membership of the SZBA. Essential practices upheld by the Soto Zen tradition include "just sitting" (shikan-taza), "actualizing the fundamental point" (genjo koan), and "the style of mindful attention to each thing" (memmitsu-no-kafu). The Soto Zen Buddhist Association is organized to preserve and promote the Buddha-dharma through the teaching and practice of Soto Zen Buddhism in North America, and to facilitate trust, respect, communication, ethical conduct, and education among the many sanghas of Soto Zen lineages and in the wider community.

Texas Buddhist Council

6007 Spindle Dr.
Houston, TX 77086
Tel. (281)445-5773
A regional coordinating body and advocacy agency for Buddhists of all traditions, it seeks to unify Buddhist practitioners across Texas by increasing communication between temples, study groups, and individuals from various schools and by providing opportunities for mutually beneficial interaction. It also strives to bring Buddhist teachings into the Texas mainstream through education and opportunities for social service.

Unified Buddhist Church, Inc.

c/o Blue Cliff Monastery
3 Mindfulness Rd
Pine Bush, New York 12566
Phone: (845)733-4959
Email: office@bluecliffmonastery.org
Website: www.bluecliffmonastery.org
This organization of Thich Nhat Hanh and his Sangha (network of practitioners and practice-groups) in the United States of America is also known as the Community of Mindful Living.

Won Buddhism of America Headquarters

143-42 Cherry Avenue
Flushing, NY 11355
Tel: (718)762-4103
Email: info@wonbuddist.org
Won Buddhism is a Korean reform movement with many non-Korean adherents and an abiding commitment to promoting interreligious understanding. While this is the seat of the U.S. branch of the Won movement, English-speakers may find it easier to contact the Manhattan temple, 431 East 57th Street, New York, NY 10022, Tel: (212)750-2773

HINDUISM

Hinduism is a western term for Sanatana Dharma (Eternal Law), the various streams of practice, ancient texts, and theological traditions associated with the Indian subcontinent. Hindus worship Brahman (Ultimate Reality) which is both the formless Absolute and the divine-as-personal. Hindus fall into schools of devotion to particular forms of the ultimate-as-personal: Vaishnavites (devotees of Vishnu, known also through his avatars [manifestations] such as Rama and Krishna), Shaivites (devotees of Shiva), and devotees of the Parashakti, the Divine Feminine (embodied variously as Durga, Parvati, Kali, and more). Other deities may be regarded as subordinate to, or as personifications of various functions of, the ultimate-as-personal. In the U.S.A., an ecumenical Hindu theology which sees all deities as pointers to the one Brahman, and emphasizes the non-duality of all things is also prevalent. Hindus agree for the most part on notions of karma and reincarnation, but fall into various philosophical schools of thought regarding the nature of the divine-human relationship. Yoga can take the form of intellectual or physical discipline, selfless service, or devotional practices. Most Hindus acknowledge the authority of the Vedas, but some pay more attention to the Bhaghavad-Gita, the Yoga Sutras of Patanjali, or the writings of the founding guru of their movement. Most North American mandirs (temples) are autonomous, but some are affiliated with a national or international movement.

American Hindus Against Defamation

P.O. Box 611
Inselin, NJ 08830
Tel. (858)866-9661
Email: director_ahad@vhp-america.org
Website: www.hindunet.org/ahad
Director, Mr. Ajay Shah
An organization devoted to defending Hindus from stereotyping and discriminatory or defamatory acts or speech.

Bochasanwasi Shri Akshar Purushottam Swaminarayan Sanstha (B.A.P.S.)

BAPS Swaminarayan Sanstha
81 Suttons Lane
Piscattaway, NJ 08854-5723
Tel. (732)777-1414
Fax (732)777-1616
Website: www.swaminarayan.org
B.A.P.S. is a reform movement within the Vaishnava Visishtadvaita tradition. This North American headquarters serves about 50 temples in US & Canada.

Council of Hindu Temples of North America

Sri Siva Vishnu Temple
6905 Cipriano Road
Lanham, MD 20706
Tel. (301)552-3335
Email: info@councilofhindutemples.org
Website: www.councilofhindutemples.org
President: Dr. Siva Subramanian
The council is an independent association of autonomous temples and Hindu religious organizations which promotes the establishment of Hindu temples, encourages interfaith dialogue, and aids in instruction in Indian languages and culture.

The International Society for Krishna Consciousness (ISKCON)

26 Second Avenue
New York, NY 10003
Tel. (212)253-6182
Email: nycpandit@gmail.com
A modern expression of Vaishnavite belief and practice established by A. C. Bhaktivedanta Swami (called Prabhubapa by devotees), ISKCON is one of many Indian spiritual movements planted in North America during the 20th century. The Second Avenue temple, which dates from 1966, was the movement's first in the U.S.

Vedanta Society of New York

34 West 71st Street
New York, NY 10023

Tel. (212)877-9197
Fax: (212)877-9198
Email: mail@vedantany.org
Website: www.vedanta.org
Founded in 1894, Vedanta Society of New York is the first Vedanta Center in the West, and has been joined by many other such centers. The various centers of the Vedanta Society are affiliates of the worldwide network of the Ramakrishna Order, headquartered in Belur Math, India. Adherents follow the teachings and example of Sri Ramakrishna (1836-1886), his wife and spiritual companion Holy Mother Sri Sarada Devi (1853-1920), and Ramakrishna's chief disciple Swami Vivekananda.

ISLAM

Islam dates to 7th-century Arabia and the Prophet Muhammad's receipt of the Qur'an. The word islam means submission, and is related linguistically to salaam, the Arabic word for peace. A Muslim is one who practices Islam by following the Qur'an and the Prophet's sunna (example). Muslims consider the Qur'an (in its original Arabic) to be God's speech. They place great emphasis on tawhid (God's absolute oneness and its implications). They use the Arabic word Allah for God, stressing that it refers to God as worshiped by Jews and Christians as well. Muslims are to maintain Five Pillars of practice. The first of these is iman, the profession of faith called the shahadah, which states "There is no God but God, and Muhammad is his prophet." The second, salah is the ritual prayer, done five times a day, facing Mecca. Third, is zakah, the returning of a portion of one's wealth to the community annually. Fourth, is swam, the fasting from dawn to dusk during the holy month of Ramadan. Fifth, is Hajj, the pilgrimage to Mecca once in one's lifetime (health and means permitting). Early in its history, Islam split into two branches, Sunni and Shi'ah (and several subgroups of the latter) which differ on some matters of belief and practice, and notions of transmission of authority.

The Islamic Society of North America (ISNA)
P.O. Box 38
Plainfield, IN 46168
Tel. (317)839-8157
Fax (317)839-1840
Website: www.isna.net
President: Dr. Mohamed Magid
The Islamic Society of North America grew out of the Muslim Students Association and is one of the oldest national Muslim organizations in the United States. It has a varied program primarily serving the Muslim community, but also seeks to promote relations between Muslims and non-Muslims. It has a speakers' bureau, film loans, library assistance program, and several other services. It has also has a number of publications. Its annual convention during Labor Day weekend usually in Chicago attracts over 35,000 participants.

Council for American-Islamic Relations (CAIR)
453 New Jersey Ave. SE
Washington, DC 20003-4034
Tel. (202)488-8787
Fax (202)488-0833
Email: info@cair.com
Website: www.cair.com
CAIR's mission is to enhance understanding of Islam, encourage dialogue, protect civil liberties, empower American Muslims and build coalitions that promote justice and mutual understanding.

Islamic Circle of North America (ICNA)
166-26 89th Avenue
Jamaica, NY 11432
Tel. (718)658-1199
Fax (718)658-1255
Website: www.icna.org
A non-ethnic, non-sectarian grassroots organization with a varied program of education and support for Muslims. Its subsidiary, ICNA Relief, provides humanitarian aid wherever it is needed.

The Mosque Cares (Ministry of Imam W. Deen Mohammed)
P.O. Box 1061
Calumet City, IL 60409

Tel. (708)798-6750
Fax (708)798-6827
Email: WdMinistry@sbcglobal.net
Website: www.wdmministry.org
Also known as the American Society of Muslims, this is the headquarters of the community in association with the leadership of W. D. Mohammed.

Muslim American Society

1325 G Street NW
Washington, DC 20005
Tel. (202)552-7414
Email for General Information: info@masfreedom.org
Website: www.muslimamericansociety.org
Founded in 1992, this is a charitable, religious, social, cultural, and educational, not-for-profit organization. It is a pioneering Islamic organization, an Islamic revival, and reform movement that uplifts the individual, family, and society. This organization is not to be confused with the ministry of W. D. Mohammad, which once used this name.

Muslim Peace Fellowship

P.O. Box 271
Nyack, New York 10960 USA
Tel. (845)358-4601
Fax (845)358-4924
Email: mpf@mpfweb.org
Website: www.forusa.org
The Muslim Peace Fellowship (Ansar as-Salam) is a network of peace and justice-oriented Muslims of all backgrounds who are dedicated to making the beauty of Islam evident in the world.

Muslim Public Affairs Council (MPAC)

3010 Wilshire Blvd. Ste. 217
Los Angeles, CA 90010
Tel. (323)258-6722
Fax (323)258-5879
Email: contact@mpac.org
Website: www.mpac.org
Exec. Dir. Salam Al-Marayati
MPAC seeks to establish a vibrant Maerican Msulim community that will enrich American society through promoting the Islamic values of mercy, justice, peace, human dignity, freedom and equality for all.

JAINISM

Jainism is an ancient Indian religion based on the notion that, periodically, humanity is blessed with a series of twenty-four tirthankaras (crossing-makers)—great spiritual leaders who attain infinite knowledge; revive a way of life that is based on the principles of non-harming, non-attachment, and openmindedness, and directed by right knowledge, right faith, and right conduct; establish an order of renunciates; and assist in the liberation of countless other human beings from the cycle of reincarnation. Vardhamana (599–527 B.C.E.), a contemporary of the Buddha, was the twenty-fourth and last tirthankara for the current eon, and is known as Mahavira (Great Hero). His sermons provide the core of Jain scriptures, the Agam Sutras, but Jainism's two main branches differ over the exact contents. Jainism stresses asceticism. Digambara (sky-clad) monks renounce all clothing; Svetambara (whiteclad) monks and nuns wear simple, white robes. Both branches may use murtis (images) of tirthankaras in devotional practice, but Digambara murtis will be plainer. The doctrine of ahimsa (non-harming) leads to strict vegetarianism, avoidance of animal products of any kind, and avoidance of interpersonal conflicts. Mahatma Gandhi was influenced greatly by Jain teachings.

JAINA: Federation of Jain Associations in North America

Jaina HQ 43-11 Ithaca Street
Elmhurst, NY 11373
Tel. (718)606-2885

Email: jainahq@jaina.org
Website: www.jaina.org
An umbrella organization linking local U.S. and Canadian Jain associations. It seeks to promote Jain principles and better understanding of Jainism. It also engages in humanitarian work.

Siddhachalam International Mahavira Jain Mission
65 Mud Pond Road
Blairstown, NJ 07825
Tel. (908)362-9793, (908)362-5487
Fax (908)362-9649
Email: presidentimjm@gmail.com or president@siddhachdam.org
Website: www.siddhachalam.org
Founded by Acharya Shri Shushil Kumarji in 1983, this resident community for monks, nuns, laymen, and laywomen is described as the first Jain pilgrimage site outside India. It promotes ahimsa for world peace, vegetarianism, and nonviolence to animals; and is headquarters for the International Jain Mission, the World Fellowship of Religions, and the World Jain Congress.

JUDAISM
Judaism is one of the world's oldest religions, encompassing a rich and complex tradition that has evolved over centuries and has given rise to, or influenced, other major world traditions. Numerous expressions of Judaism have always coexisted with one another, as they do today. The central concern shared by all is to live in relation to God and to follow God's will. Jews understand themselves to be in covenant with God, who is the one transcendent God, Creator of the Universe. God revealed the Torah to the people of Israel as his way of life. History brought the Jewish people into contact with many cultures and civilizations, contacts that continuously transformed the nature of their worship, the understanding of God's law, and even their conceptualization of peoplehood. At the time of the second Diaspora, or great migration of Jews throughout the Middle East, North Africa, and Europe at the beginning of the common era, was the rise of the Rabbinical Tradition, with its emphasis on the study of scripture. Today's Judaism has grown out of these roots. In the 19th century, Reform Judaism arose in Europe and the United States as one Jewish response to modernity. Conservative Judaism and Reconstructionism are branches of Jewish practice that first developed in America. Orthodox Judaism also has a number of modern forms.

ALEPH Administrative Office
7000 Lincoln Drive #B2
Philadelphia, PA 19119-3046
Tel: (215)247-9700
Fax: (215)247-9703
Email: aleph-info@aleph.org
Website: www.aleph.org
Exec. Dir., Ms. Debra Kolodny
A core institution of the Jewish Renewal movement dedicated to the Jewish people's sacred purpose of partnership with the Divine in the inseparable tasks of healing the world and healing our hearts.

The American Jewish Committee
P.O. Box 705
New York, NY 10150
Tel. (212)751-4000
Fax (212)891-1454
Email: pr@ajc.org
Website: www.ajc.org
Exec. Dir., David A. Harris
Founded in 1906, The AJC protects the rights and freedoms of Jews world-wide; combats bigotry and anti-Semitism and promotes democracy and human rights for all. It is an independent community-relations organization, with strong interest in interreligious relations and public-policy advocacy. The AJC publishes the American Jewish Yearbook, and Commentary magazine.

The Anti-Defamation League of B'nai B'rith
605 Third Avenue
New York, NY 10158

Tel. (212)885-7707 or (212)490-2525
Fax (212)867-9406
Website: www.adl.org
National Dir., Abraham H. Foxman
Since 1913, the Anti-Defamation League has been involved in combating and documenting anti-Semitism. It also works to secure fair treatment for all citizens through law, education and community relations.

Jewish Council for Public Affairs
116 East 27th St.10th Floor
New York, NY 10016
Tel. (212)684-6950
Fax (212)686-1353
Email: contactus@thejcpa.org
Website: www.jewishpublicaffairs.org
This national coordinating body for the field of Jewish community relations comprises 13 national and 122 local Jewish communal agencies. Through the Council's work, and in its collaboration with other religious groups, its constituent agencies work on public policy issues, both international and domestic.

Jewish Reconstructionist Federation
Beit Devora, 101 Greenwood Avenue Suite 430
Jenkintown, PA 19046
Tel. (215)885-5601
Fax:(215)885-5603
Email: info@jrf.org
Website: www.jrf.org
Fosters the establishment and ongoing life of Reconstructionist congregations and fellowship groups. Publishes The Reconstructionist and other materials. Rabbis who relate to this branch of Judaism are often members of the Reconstructionist Rabbinical Association.

Religious Action Center of Reform Judaism
2027 Massachusetts Ave. NW at Kivie Kaplan Way
Washington, DC 20036
Tel. (202)387-2800
Fax (202)667-9070
Website: www.rac.org
Exec. Dir., Rabbi David Saperstein
The Religious Action Center pursues social justice and religious liberty by mobilizing the American Jewish community and serving as its advocate in the capitol of the United States.

The Union of Orthodox Jewish Congregations of America
11 Broadway
New York, NY 10004-1003
Tel. (212)563-4000
Fax (212)564-9058
Website: www.ou.org
Exec. Vice-Pres., Rabbi Steven Weil
The national central body of Orthodox synagogues since 1898, providing kashrut supervision, women's and youth organizations, and a variety of educational, religious and public policy programs and activities. Publishers of Jewish Action magazine and other materials. The Rabbinical Council of America is the related organization for Orthodox Rabbis.

Union of Reform Judaism
633 Third Ave.
New York, NY 10017
Tel. (212)650-4000
Email: urj@urj.org
Website: www.urj.org
Pres., Rabbi Eric H. Yoffie
The central congregational body of Reform Judaism, founded in 1873. It serves approx. 875 affiliated temples and its members through religious, educational, cultural and administrative

programs. Women's Men's and Youth organizations. Reform Judaism is one of its publications. The Central Conference of American Rabbis is the affiliated rabbinical body.

The United Synagogue of Conservative Judaism
820 Second Avenue
New York, NY 10017-7800
Tel. (212)533-7800
Fax (212)353-9439
Website: www.uscj.org
Exec. Vice-Pres., Rabbi Steven Wernick
The International organization of 800 congregations, founded in 1913. Provides religious, educational, youth, community and administrative programming. Publishes United Synagogue Review and other materials. The Rabbinical Assembly is the association of Conservative Rabbis.

NATIVE AMERICAN
TRADITIONAL SPIRITUALITY

Native American spirituality is difficult to define or categorize because it varies so greatly across the continent. Further, it is deeply entwined with elements of nature which are associated with different geographical regions. For example, while Plains Indians possess a spiritual relationship with the buffalo, Indigenous Peoples from the Northwest share a similar relationship with salmon. Hence, the character of Native American spirituality is dependent, to some extent, on the surrounding geography and its incumbent ecosystems. Despite this great variety, there are some similarities which allow us to consider the many Native American forms of spirituality together: Contrary to popular belief, Native American peoples are monotheistic; they do not worship the sun or buffalo or salmon, but rather understand that these elements of nature are gifts from the "Great Mystery," and are parts of it. Today, while still working toward religious freedom in the United States, Native Americans are also struggling to protect sacred sites, which they consider to be comparable to "churches." But since these sites are actually part of the land, not man-made structures, many are constantly under attack for the natural resources they contain. Such exploitation of these resources is an offense to the Native American sense of spirituality, which views resources like timber, oil, and gold, as gifts from the Great Mystery. The struggle to protect and respect these sacred sites is a universal and essential part of Native American spirituality.

National Congress of American Indians (NCAI)
1516 P Street NW
Washington, DC 20005
Tel. (202)466-7767
Fax (202)466-7797
Email: ncia@ncia.org
Website: www.ncai.org
Exec. Dir., Jacqueline Johnson-Pata
The National Congress of American Indians (NCAI), founded in 1944, is the oldest, largest and most representative national Indian organization serving the needs of a broad membership of American Indian and Alaska Native governments. NCAI stresses the need for unity and cooperation among tribal governments and people for the security and protection of treaty and sovereign rights. As the preeminent national Indian organization, NCAI is organized as a representative congress aiming for consensus on national priority issues. The NCAI website contains links for a directory of Indian nations in the continental U.S. and Alaska as well as a directory of tribal governments. There are also links to other Native American websites.

Native American Rights Fund (NARF)
1506 Broadway
Boulder, CO 80302-6296
Tel. (303)447-8760
Fax (303)433-7776
Website: www.narf.org
Exec. Dir., Jacqueline Johnson Pata
The Native American Rights Fund is the non-profit legal organization devoted to defending and promoting the legal rights of the Indian people. NARF attorneys, most of whom are Native Americans, defend tribes who otherwise cannot bear the financial burden of obtaining justice in the courts of the United States. The NARF mission statement outlines five areas of concentration: 1) Preservation of tribal existence; 2) Protection of tribal natural resources; 3) Promotion of human rights; 4) Accountability of government; 5) Development of Indian law.

SIKHISM

Sikhism was founded by Guru Nanak during the 15th and 16th centuries C.E. in the state of Punjab in northwestern India. Nanak was greatly influenced by the teachings of Kabir, a Muslim who became deeply inspired by Hindu philosophies. Kabir's poems called for a synthesis between Islam and Hinduism. In the footsteps of Kabir's wisdom, Nanak drew upon elements of Bhakti Hinduism and Sufi Islam: He stressed the existence of a universal, single God, who transcends religious distinctions. Union with God is accomplished through meditation and surrender to the divine will. Nanak also called for the belief in reincarnation, karma, and also the cyclical destruction and recreation of the universe. However, he rejected the caste system, the devotion to divine incarnations, priesthood, idol worship, all of which were elements of the Hindu tradition. Nanak was the first of ten gurus, or teachers. The fourth guru, built the Golden Temple in Amritsar, the Sikh religious center. The fifth guru compiled the Adi Granth, a sort of hymn-book of spiritual authority. All male sikhs are initiated into the religious brotherhood called the Khalsa. Members of this order vow never to cut their beard or hair, to wear special pants, to wear an iron bangle as an amulet against evil, to carry a steel dagger, and a comb.

Sikh American Heritage Organization (SAHO)

P.O. Box 63
Wayne, IL 60184-0063
Tel. (630)377-5893
Fax (630)377-5893
Email: SikhAmerican@aol.com
Promotes and fosters fellowship with the American mainstream and minority communities while maintaining Sikh values, heritage, and identity; participates in Asian American events, interfaith programs, community affairs, social services, and other civic activities.

Sikh American Legal Defense and Education Fund (SALDEF)

1012 14th Street, NW Suite 450
Washington, DC 20005
Tel. (202)393-2700
Fax (202)318-4433
Website: www.saldef.org
Formerly Sikh Mediawatch and Research Task Force (SMART), SALDEF is a national civil rights and educational organization which provides legal assistance, educational outreach, legislative advocacy, and media relations.

Sikh Coalition

40 Exchange Place, Suite 728
New York, N.Y. 10005
Tel. (212)655-3095, ext. 83
Email: info@sikhcoalition.org
Website: www.sikhcoalition.org
Exec. Dir., Sapreet Kaur
Founded in response to bias attacks following the September 11, 2001, Sikh Coalition defends civil rights and liberties, educates the broader community about Sikhs and diversity, promotes local community empowerment, and fosters civic engagement amongst Sikh Americans.

Sikh Foundation

580 College Avenue
Palo Alto, CA 94306
Tel. (650)494-7454
Fax (650)494-3316
Email: info@sikhfoundation.org
Website: www.sikhfoundation.org
Founded in 1967 to promote the heritage and future of Sikhism, the Sikh Foundation's sponsor's academic courses, conferences and chairs of Sikh studies at leading universities in the West; promotes Sikh art exhibitions and the establishing permanent Sikh art galleries at major museums worldwide; and works to provide the community with highest quality of educational products on Sikhism.

Sikh Research Institute

7800 IH 10 West Suite #105
San Antonio, TX 78230

Tel. (210)582-3371
Fax (469)324-2954
Email: info@sikhri.org
Website: www.sikhri.org
The goals of this organization are leadership enhancement, community revival, and facilitation of connections between various Sikh organizations. It is active in interfaith work, and education of Americans about Sikhism.

World Sikh Council – America Region
P.O. Box 3635,
Columbus, Ohio 43210
Tel. (614)210-0591
Fax (419)535-6794
Email: contact@worldsikhcouncil.org
Website: www.worldsikhcouncil.org
Secretary General, Anahat Kaur
A national unit of the World Sikh Council, WSC-AR is a representative and elected body of Sikh Gurudwaras and institutions in the US. Its members include 31 Gurudwaras (Sikh places of worship) and 6 other Sikh institutions across the nation. Its mission is to promote Sikh interests at the national and international level focusing on issues of advocacy, education, and well-being of humankind.

ZOROASTRIANISM
The western name for "The Good Religion" based on the teachings of the Prophet Zarathustra, who lived sometime between 1200 and 550 B.C.E., in what is now Iran. Zoroastrians from India are often called Parsis (Parsees). Zoroastrians worship Ahura Mazda (Wise Lord): the one God, the uncreated, immanent and transcendent source of all that is good, true, and beautiful, for whom the only appropriate symbol is fire. Zoroastrians fall into two streams: traditionalists, for whom all ancient Zoroastrian texts are scripture; and progressives, for whom only the Gathas (the oldest texts) have authority. The two streams differ sharply in beliefs and practices. There are also informal denominations according to which of several Zoroastrian calendars one prefers.

Federation of Zoroastrian Associations of North America (FEZANA)
8615 Meadowbrook Drive
Burr Ridge, IL 60527
Tel/Fax. (630)468-2705
Email: admin@fezana.org
Website: www.fezana.org
President, Dr. Bomi Patel
A coordinating organization for Zoroastrian Associations of North America.

6. United States Regional and Local Ecumenical Bodies

One of the many ways Christians and Christian churches relate to one another locally and regionally is through ecumenical bodies. The membership in these ecumenical organizations is diverse. Historically, councils of churches were formed primarily by Protestants, but many local and regional organizations now include Orthodox and Roman Catholics. Many are made up of congregations or judicatory units of churches. Some have a membership base of individuals. Others foster cooperation between ministerial groups, community ministries, coalitions, or church agencies. While "council of churches" is a term still commonly used to describe this form of cooperation, other terms such as "conference of churches," "ecumenical councils," "churches united," "metropolitan ministries," are coming into use. Ecumenical organizations that are national in scope are listed in Directory 1, "United States Cooperative Organizations."

An increasing number of ecumenical bodies have been exploring ways to strengthen the interreligious aspect of life in the context of religious pluralism in the U.S. today. Some organizations in this listing are fully interfaith agencies primarily through the inclusion of Jewish congregations in their membership. Other organizations nurture partnerships with a broader base of religious groups in their communities, especially in the areas of public policy and interreligious dialogue.

This list does not include all local and regional ecumenical and interfaith organizations in existence today. The terms regional and local are relative, making identification somewhat ambiguous. Regional councils may cover sections of large states or cross-state borders. Local councils may be made up of several counties, towns, or clusters of congregations. State councils or state-level ecumenical contacts exist in 45 of the 50 states. These state-level or multi-state organizations are marked with a "*". The organizations are listed alphabetically by state.

ALABAMA

Greater Birmingham Ministries
2304 12th Ave. N, Birmingham, AL 35234-3111, Tel. (205)326-6821 Fax (205)252-8458
Email: info@gbm.org
Website: www.gbm.org
Exec. Dir., Scott Douglas
Economic Justice, Co-Chpsn., Helen Holdefer, Betty Likis
Direct Services, Chpsn., Patty Warren
Faith in Community, Chpsn., Patricia Ross
Finance & Fund-Raising, Chpsn., Richard Ambrose
Pres., Tom Forsee
Treas., Helen Tibbs Wilson
Major Activities: Direct Service Ministries (Food, Utilities, Rent and Nutrition Education, Shelter); Alabama Arise (Statewide legislative network focusing on low income issues); Economic Justice Issues (Low Income Housing and Advocacy, Health Care, Community Development, Jobs Creation, Public Transportation); Faith in Community Ministries (Interchurch Forum, Interpreting and Organizing, Bible Study)

Interfaith Mission Service
701 Andrew Jackson Way NE, Huntsville, AL 35801-3504, Tel. (256)536-2401 Fax (256)536-2284
Email: ims@hiwaay.net
Exec. Dir., Susan J. Smith
Pres., Richard C. Titus
Major Activities: Foodline & Food Pantry; Local FEMA Committee; Ministry Development; Clergy Luncheon; Workshops; Response to Community Needs; Information and Referral; Interfaith Understanding; Christian Unity; Homeless Needs; School Readiness Screenings

ALASKA

Alaska Christian Conference
P.O. Box 112944, Anchorage, AK 99511, Tel. (907)240-6154 Fax (907)349-3426
Email: phyllisfs@juno.com
Website: www.ak-acc.org
Media Contact, Rev. Phyllis Sullivan
Pres., Chaplain James Stephens (Retired) (Disciple), 1231 Surray Circle #A, Anchorage, Alaska 99515; Cell (907)240-6154; Email: jim56@gci.net
Vice-Pres., vacant
Sec., Phyllis Sullivan (United Methodist), 1725 Tillicum, Wasilla, AK 99654; Cell (907)232-2634; Email: phyllisfs@juno.com
Treas., Phyllis Sullivan, (United Methodist), 1725 Tillicum, Wasilla, AK 99654; Cell (907)232-2634; Email: phyllisfs@juno.com
Special Asst. Web Master, Rev. David Blanchette, 1100 Pullman Drive, Wasilla, AK 99654; wwww. Ak-acc.org; Cell (907)232-2634; Email: revdavid@gci.net
Special Asst. RurAL CAP Rep., Rev. David Fison, 6800 O'Malley Road, Anchorage, Alaska 99516, Tel. (907)346-2975 (Home).
Major Activities: Legislative & Social Concerns; Resources and Continuing Education; New Ecumenical Ministries; Communication;

Alcoholism (Education & Prevention); Family Violence (Education & Prevention); Native Issues; Ecumenical-Theological Dialogue; HIV-AIDS Education and Ministry; Criminal Justice.

ARIZONA

Arizona Ecumenical Council*

7227 N. 16th St., Ste 260, Phoenix, AZ 85020, Tel. (602)468-3818 Fax (602)314-7950
Email: aec@aecunity.net
Website: www.aecunity.net
Media Contact, Exec. Dir., Rev. Jan Olav Flaaten, Tel. (602)468-3818, Fax (602)314-7950, Cell (602)670-1594
Exec. Dir., Rev. Jan Olav Flaaten (ELCA Lutheran)
Pres. Bishop Stephen Talmage (ELCA Lutheran)
Vice-Pres: Fr. Michael Diskin (Roman Catholic)
Sec., Sr. Gaye Moorhead (Roman Catholic)
Treas., Ed Davis (ELCA Lutheran)
Major Activities: Ecumenical Dialogue, e.g. Donohoe Forum, Healthcare Reform, Comprehensive Immigration Reform, Ecu-menical Prayer and Worship, Week of Prayer for Christian Unity, Earth Care, Disaster Response and Preparedness in the Faith Communities

ARKANSAS

Arkansas Interfaith Conference*

P.O. Box 151, Scott, AR 72142, Tel. (501)961-2626
Email: aicark@aol.com
Media Contact, Conf. Exec., Mimi Dortch
Conf. Exec., Mimi Dortch
Pres., Rev. Steve Copley. 6701 JFK Blvd., N. Little Rock, AR. 72116 (Methodist)
Sec., Imam John Hasan. P.O. Box 1607, Little Rock, AR 72203. (Muslim)
Treas., Jim Davis, Box 7239, Little Rock, AR 72217 (Catholic)
Major Activities: Institutional Ministry; Interfaith Executives' Advisory Council; Interfaith Relations; Church Women United; Our House-Shelter; Legislative Liaison; Ecumenical Choir Camp; Tornado Disaster Relief; Camp for Jonesboro School Children Massacre; Welfare Reform Work; Med Center Chaplaincy; Peace Service

CALIFORNIA

California Council of Churches-California Church Impact*

2715 K Street, Suite D, Sacramento, CA 95816, Tel. (916)488-7300 Fax (916)488-7310
Email: cccinfo@calchurches.org
Website: www.calchurches.org
Media Contact, Exec. Dir., The Rev. Rick Schlosser
Exec. Dir., The Rev. Rick Schlosser
Major Activities: Monitoring State Legislation; California IMPACT Network; Legislative Principles; Food Policy Advocacy; Family Welfare Issues; Health; Church-State Issues; Violence Prevention; Child Care Program-Capacity Coordinator to Increase Quality Child Care within California for the Working Poor; Building Bridges of Understanding: An Interfaith Response to Septerber 11.

The Council of Churches of Santa Clara County

1710 Moorpark Avenue, San Jose, CA 95128, Tel. (408)297-2660 Fax (408)297-2661
Email: councilofchurches@sbcglobal.net
Website: www.councilofchurches-scc.org
Media Contact, Co-executive Directors: Rev. Margo Tenold, Rev. Diana Gibson
Chair, Board of Directors, Rev. Jerry Fox
Major Activities: Social Education-Action; Ecumenical and Interfaith Witness; Affordable Housing; Environmental Ministry; Family-Children; Convalescent Hospital Ministries; Gay Ministry; Strengthening Congregations for Ministry

The Ecumenical Council of Pasadena Area Churches

P.O. Box 41125, 444 E. Washington Blvd., Pasadena, CA 91114-8125, Tel. (626)797-2402 Fax (626)797-7353
Email: info@ecpac.net
Exec. Dir., Rev. Pat O'Reilly
Major Activities: Christian Education; Community Worship; Community Concerns; Christian Unity; Ethnic Ministries; Hunger; Peace; Food, Clothing Assistance for the Poor; Emergency Shelter

Ecumenical Council of San Diego County

3530 Camino del Rio North, # 301, San Diego, CA 92108, Tel. (619)238-0649 Fax (619)238-1526
Email: info@ecsd.org
Website: www.ecsd.org
Exec. Dir. vacant
Pres. Red. Dr. Richard Freeman
Treas., Rev. Tim Tiffany
Major Activities: Interfaith Shelter Network-Rational Shelter and El Nido Transitional Living Program; Emerging Issues; Faith Order & Witness; Worship & Celebration; Ecumenical Tribute Dinner; Advent Prayer Breakfast; Seminars and Workshops; Continuing Education for clergy and laypersons; Inter-Religious Council.

Fresno Metro Ministry

1055 N. Van Ness, Ste. H, Fresno, CA 93728, Tel. (559)485-1416 Fax (559)485-9109
Email: metromin@fresnometmin.org
Website: www.fresnometmin.org
Media Contact, Exec. Dir., Richard P. Yanes
Exec. Dir., Richard P. Yanes
Pres., Tony Gonzalez
Major Activities: Hunger Relief & Nutrition Advocacy; Cultural Diversity and Anti-Racism;

239

Health Care Advocacy; Environmental Health and Quality; Access and Public Health; Public Education Concerns; Children's Needs; Air Quality; Ecumenical & Interfaith Celebrations & Cooperation; Youth Needs; Community Network Building; Human Services Facilitation; Anti-Poverty Efforts; Low-Income and Immigrant Leadership Development related to public policies

Inland Valley Hope Partners
1753 N. Park Ave., Pomona, CA 91768, Tel. (909)622-3806 Fax (909)622-0484
Email: info@inlandvalleyhopepartners.org
Website: www.inlandvalleyhopepartners.org
Media Contact, Dir. of Dev., Fran Robertson
Pres., Michael Light
Acting Exec. Dir., Wytske G. Visser
Sec., Herbert Rosenzweig
Treas., Rev. Michael Frank
Major Activities: Advocacy and Education for Social Justice; Ecumenical Celebrations; Hunger and Housing Advocacy; Emergency Food and Shelter Assistance; Farmer's Market

Interfaith Council of Contra Costa County
1543 Sunnyvale Ave., Walnut Creek, CA 94596, Tel. (925)933-6030 Fax (925)952-4554
Email: eye4cee@aol.com
Chaplains, The Rev. Charles Tinsley
Pres., Rev. Steve Harms, Rabi Raphael Asher
Treas., Myrdell Dybdal
Major Activities: Youth Chaplaincies, Community Education, Interfaith Cooperation, Social Justice, Winter Shelter

Interfaith Service Bureau
2212 K. St., Sacramento, CA 95816-4923, Tel. (916)448-2212 Fax (916)456-3816
Email: info@isbsacramento.org
Media Contact, Exec. Dir., Dexter McNamara
Executive Dir., Dexter McNamara
Pres., Richard Montgomery
Vice-Pres., Lloyd Hanson
Major Activities: Religious and Racial Cooperation and Understanding; Welfare Reform Concerns; Refugee Resettlement & Support; Religious Cable Television; Violence Prevention; Graffiti Abatement

Marin Interfaith Council
1510 5th Avenue, San Rafael, CA 94901-1807, Tel. (415)456-6957 Fax (415)456-6959
Email: programs@marinifc.org
Website: www.marinifc.org
Media Contact, Exec. Dir., Rev. Carol Hovis
Exec. Dir., Rev. Carol Hovis
Major Activities: Interfaith Dialogue; Education; Advocacy; Convening; Interfaith Worship Services & Commemorations

Northern California Interreligious Conference
534 22nd St., Oakland, CA 94612, Tel. (510)433-0822 Fax (510)433-0813

Email: NCIC@igc.org
Website: ncic.home.igc.org
Media Contact, Pres., Rev. Phil Lawson
Exec. Dir., Catherine Coleman
Pres., Rev. Phil Lawson
Vice-Pres., Esther Ho
Sec., Robert Forsberg
Major Activities: Peace with Justice Commission; Interreligious Relationships Commission; Public Policy Advocacy; Welfare Reform, Founding member of California Council of Churches and of California Interfaith Power and Light; Soul of Justice, a spiritual and leadership concepts interactive performance troupe of teens and young adults; death penalty moratorium; video produced for sale for congregations-organizations to study legal, theological and social implications of marriage and same gender marriage, widening our circle of religious groups participating; a cooperating circle of URL.

San Fernando Valley Interfaith Council
10824 Topanga Canyon Blvd., No. 7, Chatsworth, CA 91311, Tel. (818)718-6460 Fax (818)718-0734
Email: info@vic-LA.org
Website: www.vic-LA.org
Media Contact, Comm. Coord., Eileen Killoren, ext. 3002
Pres., Barry Smedberg; Ext. 3011
Chair, Board of Dir., Earl Fagin, Esq.
Major Activities: Seniors Multi-Purpose Centers; Nutrition & Services; Meals to Homebound; Meals on Wheels; Interfaith Reporter; Interfaith Relations; Social Adult Day Care; Hunger-Homelessness; Volunteer Care-Givers; Clergy Gatherings; Food Pantries and Outreach; Social Concerns; Aging; Hunger; Human Relations; Immigration Services; Self-Sufficiency Program for Section 8 Families

South Coast Interfaith Council
759 Linden Ave., Long Beach, CA 90813, Tel. (562)983-1665 Fax (562)983-8812
Email: SouthCoastInterfaith@gmail.com
Website: www.SCInterfaith.org
Media Contact, Exec. Dir., Milia Islam-Majeed

STAFF
Exec. Dir., Milia Islam-Majeed
President, Cantor Ilan Davidson
Farmers' Markets, Rev. Dale Whitney
Centro Shalom, Amelia Nieto
Good Samaritan Counseling Center, Dr. William Scar
Major Activities: Farmers' Markets; CROP Hunger Walks; Church Athletic Leagues; Community Action; Interreligious Dialogue; Justice Advocacy; Martin Luther King, Jr. Celebration; Violence Prevention; Long Beach Interfaith Clergy; Crop Hunger; Walks; Counseling services

Southern California Ecumenical Council

195 So. Hill Ave., Pasadena, CA 91106, Tel. (626) 578-6371 Fax (626)578-6358
Email: scec1@scec1.net
Website: www.scec1.net
Media Contact, Exec. Dir., Rev. Albert G. Cohen
Exec. Dir., The Rev. Albert G. Cohen
Pres., Mrs. Lucy Guernsey
Treas., The Rev. Larry Hixon
Sec., Fr. Arshag Khatchadourian
Vice Pres. The Rev. Dr. Gwynne Guibord
Second Vice Pres., Carol Kostura
Members at Large, The Rev. Dr. Dagmar Grefe, Pr. Kenny Bowen, Fr. Alexei Smith
Faith and Order Chair, The Rev Dr. Tamara Rodenberg
Past Pres., The Rev. Dr. Paul Lance
Major Activities: Consultation with the regional religious sector concerning the well being and spiritual vitality of this most diverse and challenging area

Westside Interfaith Council

P.O. Box 1402, Santa Monica, CA 90406, Tel. (310)394-1518 Fax (310)576-1895
Media Contact, Rev. Janet A. Bregar
Exec. Dir., Rev. Janet A. Bregar
Major Activities: Meals on Wheels; Community Religious Services; Convalescent Hospital Chaplaincy; Homeless Partnership; Hunger & Shelter Coalition

COLORADO

Colorado Council of Churches*

3690 Cherry Creek S. Dr., Denver, CO 80209, Tel. (303)825-4910 Fax (303)744-8605
Email: jryan@COchurches.org
Website: www.Cochurches.org
Media Contact, Council Exec., Rev. Dr. James R. Ryan
Pres., Rev. Gordon Kieft
Staff Assoc, Dori Wilson
Major Activities: Addressing issues of Christian Unity, Justice, and Environment, Interfaith Relations. Bullying, Health Care Reform, Suicide Prevention, Returning Military and Families

Interfaith Council of Boulder

3700 Baseline Rd., Boulder, CO 80303, Tel.
Media Contact, Pres., Stan Grotegut, 810 Kalma Ave., Boulder, CO 80304, Tel. (303)443-2291
Pres., Stan Grotegut
Major Activities: Interfaith Dialogue and Programs; Thanksgiving Worship Services; Food for the Hungry; Share-A-Gift; Monthly Newsletter

CONNECTICUT

Association of Religious Communities

325 Main St., Danbury, CT 06810, Tel. (203)792-9450 Fax (203)792-9452

Email: arc325@sbcglobal.net
Media Contact, Exec. Dir., Rev. Phyllis J. Leopold
Exec. Dir., Rev. Phyllis J. Leopold
Pres., The Rev. Angelo S. Arrando
Major Activities: Refugee Resettlement; Family Counseling; Family Violence Prevention; Affordable Housing, Inter-Faith Dialogue, Racial Justice

The Capitol Region Conference of Churches

60 Lorrain St., Hartford, CT 06105, Tel. (860)236-1295 Fax (860)236-8071
Email: crcc@conferenceofchurches.org
Website: www.conferenceofchurches.org
Media Contact, Exec. Dir., Rev. Shelley Copeland
Exec. Dir., The Rev. Shelley Copeland
Pastoral Care & Training, Dir., The Rev. Kathleen Davis
Aging Project, Dir., Barbara Malcolm
Community Organizer, Joseph Wasserman
Broadcast Ministry Consultant, Ivor T. Hugh
Pres., Mr. David O. White
Major Activities: Organizing for Peace and Justice; Aging; Legislative Action; Cooperative Broadcast Ministry; Ecumenical Cooperation; Interfaith Reconciliation; Chaplaincies; Low-Income Senior Empowerment; Anti-Racism Education

Center City Churches

40 Pratt Street, Ste. 210, Hartford, CT 06103-1601, Tel. (860)728-3201 Fax (860)549-8550
Email: raiello@handsonhartford.org
Website: www.centercitychurches.org
Media Contact, Exec. Dir., Barbara Shaw
Exec. Dir., Barbara Shaw
Pres., Jeannette L. Brown
Treas., Rusty Spears
Major Activities: Senior Services; Family Resource Center; Food Pantry; Assistance & Advocacy; After School Tutoring and Arts Enrichment; Summer Day Camp; Housing for persons with AIDS; Community Soup Kitchen

Christian Community Action

168 Davenport Ave., New Haven, CT 06519, Tel. (203)777-7848 Fax (203)777-7848
Email: cca@ccahelping.org
Website: www.ccahelping.org
Media Contact, Exec. Dir., The Rev. Bonita Grubbs
Exec. Dir., The Rev. Bonita Grubbs
Major Activities: Emergency Food Program; Used Furniture & Clothing; Security and Fuel; Emergency Housing for Families; Advocacy; Transitional Housing for Families

Christian Conference of Connecticut*

999 Asylum Avenue, Hartford, CT 06105, Tel. (860)560-0125 Fax (860)236-9977
Email: ctchurches@att.net
Media Contact, Interim Exec. Dir., Rev. Dr. Robert D. McNaughton, Email: rdm.ctchurches@att.net

Interim Exec. Dir., Rev. Dr. Robert D. McNaughton
Pres., Ms. Alberta Hoagland, pro tem
Vice Pres., TBD
Sec., The Rev. Dr. Sandra Olsen
Treas., Ms. Alberta Hoagland
Major Activities: Communications; Institutional Ministries; Connecticut Ecumenical Small Church Project; Ecumenical Forum; Faith & Order; Social Concerns; Public Policy; Peace and Justice Convocation; Restorative Justice & Death Penalty; Interreligious Dialogue ; Anti—Nuclear Activities; Problem Gambling; Jewish-Christian Dialogue, Muslim-Christian Dialogue

The Council of Churches of Greater Bridgeport, Bridgeport, CT
1100 Boston Avenue, Bldg. 5 A, Bridgeport, CT 06610, Tel. (203)334-1121 Fax (203)367-8113
Email: brianbodt@ccgb.org
Website: www.ccgb.org
Media Contact, President & CEO, Rev. Dr. Brian R. Bodt
President & CEO., Rev. Dr. Brian R. Bodt
Chairman, Carl F. Johnson, Jr.
Vice Chair, Donald E. Gibson, PhD
Sec., Valzie Peterkin
Treas., Phil Norgren
Major Activities: Youth in Crisis; Youth In Crisis Hotline, Responses & Safe Places; Host Home Shelter Care; Criminal Justice Services for Ex-offenders; Jail Ministry; Hunger Outreach and Networking; Ecumenical & Inter-Religious Relations, Prayer and Celebration; Covenantal Ministries; Homework Help; Summer Programs; Race Relations-Bridge Building

Council of Churches and Synagogues of Southwestern Connecticut
1 Canterbury Green, Box 7, Stamford, CT 06901, Tel. (203)348-2800 Fax (203)358-0627
Email: interfaith.council@sbcglobal.net
Website: www.interfaithcouncil.org
Media Contact, Comm. Ofc., Kate Heichler
Exec. Dir., Jack Penfield, Interim Director
Major Activities: Partnership Against Hunger; The Food Bank of Lower Fairfield County; Friendly Visitors and Friendly Shoppers; Senior Neighborhood Support Services; Christmas in April; Interfaith Programming; Prison Visitation; Friendship House; Help a Neighbor; Operation Fuel; Teaching Place

Greater Waterbury Interfaith Ministries, Inc.
16 Church St, Waterbury, CT 06702, Tel. (203) 756-7831 Fax (203)419-0024
Media Contact, Exec. Dir., Carroll E. Brown
Exec. Dir., Carroll E. Brown
Pres., The Rev. Dr. James G. Bradley
Major Activities: Emergency Food Program; Emergency Fuel Program; Soup Kitchen; Ecumenical Worship; Christmas Toy Sale; Annual Hunger Walk

Manchester Area Conference of Churches
P.O. Box 3804, Manchester, CT 06045-3804, Tel. (860)647-8003 Fax (860) 646-9631
Email: bstafford@macc-ct.org
Website: www.macc-ct.org
Media Contact, Exec. Dir., Beth Stafford
Exec. Dir., Beth Stafford
Pres., Rev. Carol Gregory
Vice Pres., Ed Sutton
Sec., Dough Mantz
Treas., Dave Russell
Major Activities: Provision of Basic Needs (Food, Fuel, Clothing, Furniture); Emergency Aid Assistance; Emergency Shelter; Soup Kitchen; Reentry Assistance to Sex-Offenders; Pastoral Care in Local Institutions; Interfaith Day Camp; Advocacy for the Poor; Ecumenical Education and Worship

New Britain Area Conference of Churches (NEWBRACC)
830 Corbin Ave., New Britain, CT 06052, Tel. (860)229-3751 Fax (860)223-3445
Media Contact, Acting Exec. Dir., Rev. Teresa A. Hughes
Acting Exec. Dir., The Rev. Teresa A. Hughes
Pastoral Care-Chaplaincy, The Rev. Ron Smith; The Rev. Will Baumgartner
Pres., The Rev. Charles Tillet
Treas., Dierdre Elloian
Major Activities: Worship; Social Concerns; Emergency Food Bank Support; Communications-Mass Media; Hospital; Elderly Programming; Homelessness and Hunger Programs; Telephone Ministry

DELAWARE

The Christian Council of Delaware and Maryland's Eastern Shore*
2020 N. Tatnall Street, Wilmington, DE 19802, Tel. (302)656-5441
Website: www.DeMdSynod.org
Media Contact, Pres., Bishop Wayne P. Wright, Diocese of Delaware, 2020 N. Tatnall Street, Wilmington, DE 19802
Pres., Bishop Wayne P. Wright, Diocese of Delaware, 2020 N. Tatnall Street, Wilmington, DE 19802
Major Activities: Exploring Common Theological, Ecclesiastical and Community Concerns; Racism; Prisons

DISTRICT OF COLUMBIA

The Council of Churches of Greater Washington
5 Thomas Circle N.W., Washington, DC 20005, Tel. (202)722-9240 Fax (202)722-9240
Media Contact, Exec. Dir., The Rev. Rodger Hall Reed, Sr.
Pres., The Rev. Lewis Anthony
Exec. Dir., The Rev. Rodger Hall Reed, Sr.

Program Officer, Daniel M. Thompson
Major Activities: Promotion of Christian Unity-Ecumenical Prayer & Worship; Coordination of Community Ministries; Summer Youth Employment; Summer Camping-Inner City Youth; Supports wide variety of social justice concerns

InterFaith Conference of Metropolitan Washington

100 Allison St., N.W., Washington, DC 20011, Tel. (202)234-6300 Fax (202)234-6303
Email: ifc@ifcmw.org
Website: www.ifcmw.org
Media Contact, Exec. Dir., Rev. Dr. Clark Lobenstine
Exec. Dir., Rev. Dr. Clark Lobenstine
Admn. Sec., Judy Bond
Pres., Mrs. Carole Miller
1st Vice-Pres., Siva Subramanian, M.D.
Chpsn., Rev. Dr. Robert Maddo
Sec., Mrs. Iris Lav
Treas., Sheikh Bassam Estwani
Major Activities: Helps end hunger, homelessness, and racism. Strengthens families and youth and deepens understanding by bringing together 10 world religions to build a just, compassionate community in metropolitan Washington D.C.

FLORIDA

Christian Service Center for Central Florida, Inc.

808 W. Central Blvd., Orlando, FL 32805-1809, Tel. (407)425-2523 Fax (407)425-9513
Website: www.christianservicecenter.org
Media Contact, Exec. Dir., Robert F. Stuart
Exec. Dir., Robert F. Stuart
Family Emergency Services, Dir.,Rev. Haggeo Gautier
Fresh Start, Dir., Rev. Haggeo Gautier
Pres., Dr. Bryan Fulwider
Treas., Peter Reinert
Sec., Terry Bitner
Major Activities: Provision of Basic Needs (food, clothing, shelter); Emergency Assistance; Noon-time Meals; Collection and Distribution of Used Clothing; Shelter & Training for Homeless; Children After-School and Summer Programs

Florida Council of Churches*

3838 West Cypress Street, Tampa, FL 33607, Tel. (813)435-5335 Fax (928)268-8765
Email: rmeyer@floridachurches.org
Website: www.floridachurches.org
Media Contact, Exec. Dir., Rev. Russell L. Meyer
Exec. Dir., Rev. Russell Meyer, ELCA
Pres. Bishop Charles Leigh, Apostolic Catholic Church
Sec., Rev. Wilma Israel, Moravian Unity Southern Province
Treas., Lynda Mack, CPA
Other: Bishop Timothy Whitaker, Dean, College of Judicatory Leaders

Major Activities: Christian Ecumenism, Farm-worker Advocacy, Immigration Advocacy, Eco-Justice Advocacy

GEORGIA

Georgia Christian Council*

P.O. Box 7193 (2370 Vineville Ave.), Macon, GA 31209-7193, Tel. (478)743-2085 Fax (478)743-2085
Email: GAChristiancouncil@alltel.net
Media Contact, Exec. Dir., Rev. Leland C. Collins
Exec. Dir., Rev. Leland C. Collins
Pres., Bishop B. Michael Watson, 3370 Vineville, Ave., Suite 101, Macon, GA 31204
Sec., Dr. Willis Moore, 5312 W. Mountain St., Suite 200, Stone Mountain, GA 30083-2073
Major Activities: Local Ecumenical Support and Resourcing; Legislation; Rural Development; Racial Justice; Networking for Migrant Coalition; Aging Coalition; GA To GA With Love; Medical Care; Prison Chaplaincy; Training for Church Development; Souper Bowl; Disaster Relief; Clustering; Development of Local Ecumenism; Prison Ministry; Hunger Advocacy; Family Advocacy; Developing Discipleship

The Regional Council of Churches of Atlanta

100 Edgewood Avenue, Suite 812, Atlanta, GA 30303, Tel. (404)523-5554 x 231 Fax (404)523-7330
Email: ecarter@rccatl.org
Website: www.rccatl.org
Media Contact, Program Director, Ethel Ware Carter
Executive and Officers:
Pres. The Rev. Gerald Durley (Baptist)
Vice-Pres: The Rev. George Wirth ,co President (PCUSA)
Major Activities: Monthly Pastors Breakfast Dialogue, Christian Ecumenism, Interfaith Relations, FaithWorks Mental Health Initiative, Collaboration and coalition building, Weekly Church Action eNewsletter to 14,000 faith and community leaders, Website with resources and community calendar

IDAHO

The Regional Council for Christian Ministry, Inc.

237 N. Water, Idaho Falls, ID 83403, Tel. (208)524-9935
Email: rccm@tumcif.org
Exec. Sec., Daniel Sene
Major Activities: Island Park Ministry; Community Food Bank; Community Observances; F.I.S.H.

ILLINOIS

Community Renewal Society

332 South Michigan Ave. Suite 500, Chicago, IL 60604, Tel. (312) 427-4830 Fax (312)427-6130

Email: bborst@communityrenewalsociety.org
Website: www.communityrenewalsociety.org
Media Contact, Exec. Dir., Dr. Calvin S. Morris, PhD

John Purdy, Jr.; Vice President: Rev. Bobbie Taylor; Treasurer: Yolanda Waggoner Foreman; Secretary: Dr. David Mussatt

Major Activities: Community Organizing, Advocacy, Training, Investigative Journalism with focus on race and poverty ("The Chicago Reporter") and Education ("Catalyst Chicago")

Contact Ministries of Springfield

1100 E. Adams, Springfield, IL 62703, Tel. (217) 753-3939 Fax (217)753-8643
Email: rtarrcm@springnetl.com
Website: www.contactministries.net
Media Contact, Interim Exec. Dir., Cindy Drum
Interim Exec. Dir., Cindy Drum
Major Activities: Information; Referral and Advocacy; Ecumenical Coordination; Low Income Housing Referral; Food Pantry Coordi-nation; Prescription & Travel Emergency; Low Income Budget Counseling; 24 hours on call; Emergency Shelter On-site Women with Children

Greater Chicago Broadcast Ministries

112 E. Chestnut St., Chicago, IL 60611-2014, Tel. (312)988-9001 Fax (312)988-9004
Email: gcbm@ameritech.net
Website: www.gcbm.org
Media Contact, Exec. Dir., Lydia Talbot
Pres., Bd. of Dir., Rev. Phil Blackwell
Exec. Dir., Lydia Talbot
Major Activities: Television, Interfaith-Ecumenical Development; Social-Justice Concerns

The Hyde Park & Kenwood Interfaith Council

5745 S. Blackstone Ave., Chicago, IL 60637, Tel. (773)752-1911 Fax (773)752-2676
Media Contact, Exec. Dir., Lesley M. Radius
Exec. Dir., Lesley M. Radius
Pres., The Rev. David Grainger
Sec., Barbara Krell
Major Activities: Interfaith Work; Hunger Projects; Community Development

Illinois Conference of Churches*

2160 South 6th Street, Suite D-2, Springfield, IL 62703, Tel. (217)522-7099
Website: www.ilconfchurches.org
Media Contact, Media Contact: Laurie Vital
Exec. Dir., Laurie Vital
Other: Co-Chair, Leadership Team, Bishop Gary Wollersheim (Evangelical Lutheran Church in America)
Other: Co-Chair, Leadership Team, Rev. Terry Clark (United Methodist Church)
Other: Administrative Coordinator, Pamela Tackett (Disciples of Christ)
Major Activities: Christian Ecumenism; Address issues impacting the economically distressed;

Address racial concerns; Bi-Annual Statewide Gathering-Seeing with New Eyes: the Changing Faces of Poverty and the new challenge of ministry

Interfaith Action of Evanston

P.O. Box 1414, Evanston, IL 60204, Tel. (847)475-1150 Fax (847)475-2526
Email: ia@interfaithactionofevanston.org
Website: www.interfaithactionofevanston.org
Media Contact, Director: Susan Murphy
Dir. Hospitality Cntr. for the Homeless, Sue Murphy
Pres.: Carolyn Gifford
Major Activities: Interfaith Communication and Education; Peace and Justice Ministries; Coordinated Social Action; Soup Kitchens; Multi-Purpose Hospitality Center for the Homeless; Worship and Renewal, Racial Reconciliation, Youthwork

Oak Park-River Forest Community of Congregations

P.O. Box 3365, Oak Park, IL 60303-3365, Tel. (708)386-8802 Fax (708)386-1399
Website: http://lgrossman.comcomcong.htm
Media Contact, The Rev. Marguerite Rourke
Pres., The Rev. Marguerite Rourke
Treas., The Rev. Dwight Bailey
Major Activities: Community Affairs; Ecumenical-Interfaith Affairs; Youth Education; FOOD PANTRY; Senior Citizens Worship Services; Interfaith Thanksgiving Services; Good Friday Services; Literacy Training; CROP-CWS Hunger Walkathon; Work with Homeless Through PADS (Public Action to Deliver Shelter; Diversity Education; Walk-in Ministry

Peoria Friendship House of Christian Service

800 N.E. Madison Ave., Peoria, IL 61603, Tel. (309)671-5200 Fax (309)671-5206
Email: bhartnett@peoriafriendshiphouse.org
Website: www.peoriafriendshiphouse.org
Media Contact, Exec. Dir., Barbara Hartnett
Pres. of Bd., David Dadds
Major Activities: Children's After-School; Teen Programs; Recreational Leagues; Senior Citizens Activities; Emergency Food-Clothing Distri-bution; Emergency Payments for Prescriptions, Rent, Utilities; Community Outreach; Economic Development; Neighborhood Empowerment; GED Classes; Family Literacy; Mother's Group; Welfare to Work Programs

INDIANA

The Associated Churches of Fort Wayne & Allen County, Inc.

602 E. Wayne St., Fort Wayne, IN 46802, Tel. (260)422-3528 Fax (260)-422-6721
Email: associatedchurches@comcast.net
Website: www.associatedchurches.org

Media Contact, Exec. Dir., Rev. Roger Reece
Exec. Dir., Rev. Roger Reece
Administrative Assistant, Elaine Williamson
Foodbank- Director, John Lassen; Isaac Nickleson; Gordon Matoon
Dir. Of Prog. Development & Mission Outreach, Theresa Tracey
Dir. Of Weekday Religious Education, Kathy Rolf
Pres., Rev. Richard Hartman, 3923 Nottingham Dr., Fort Wayne, IN 46815
Treas., Mary Jo Mikulski
Major Activities: Weekday Religious Ed.; Baby's Closet; Hunger Walk; Food Bank System; Peace & Justice Commission; Welfare Reform; Endowment Development; Child Care Advocacy; Advocates Inc.

Christian Ministries of Delaware County
401 E. Main St., Muncie, IN 47305, Tel. (317)288-0601 Fax (317)282-4522
Email: christianministries@netzero.net
Website: www.christianministries.ws
Media Contact, Exec. Dir., Becki Clock
Exec. Dir., Becki Clock
Pres., David Abrams
Treas., Joan McKee
Major Activities: Baby Care Program; Youth Ministry at Detention Center; Community Church Festivals; Food Pantry; Emergency Assistance; CROP Walk; Social Justice; Family Life Education; Homeless Shelter (sleeping room only); Clothing and household items available free; workshops for low income clients; homeless apartments available- short stays only at no cost; provide programs and workshops for pastors and churches in community; work with schools sponsoring programs.

Church Community Services
629 S. 3rd Street, Elkhart, IN 46516-3241, Tel. (574)295-3673 Fax (574)295-5593
Email: ccs6293rd@aol.com
Website: www.soupofsuccess.com
Exec. Director, Dean Preheim-Bartel
Major Activities: Financial Assistance for Emergencies; Food Pantry; Information and Referral; Clothing Referral; Rent Assistance; Utility Assistance; Medication Vouchers; Transportation Vouchers; Job and Life Skills Training Program for Women

The Church Federation of Greater Indianapolis, Inc.
1100 W. 42nd St., Ste. 345, Indianapolis, IN 46208, Tel. (317)926-5371 Fax (317)926-5371
Email: churches@churchfederationindy.org
Website: www.churchfederationindy.org
Media Contact, Pres., Rev. Alan Goertemiller
Exec. Dir., Rev. Dr. Angelique Walker-Smith
Pres., Rev. Alan Goertemiller
Treas., Hugh Moore
Major Activities: Founded in 1912 (John 17: 20-23); Benevolence Ministry-C.R.O.P. (Church

World Service; Sacred Conversations (Racial Reconciliation); Clergy ID Badge Program; Community Organizing; Faith and Fathers Juvenile Prison Ministry; Hispanic-Latino Forum; Faith and Education Initiative; Centennial Committee; Project Reconnect: Church and Neighborhood Partnership; Greater Indianapolis Prayer Network to Stop the Violence-Ecumenical Project for Reconciliation and Healing; IndyFaith.Com/net/org; TV Broadcasts; Interfaith Hunger Network; Caring Churches Network; Indianapolis Prayer Breakfast (Partnership).

Indiana Partners for Christian Unity and Mission
P.O. Box 88790, Indianapolis, IN 46208-0790, Tel. (800)746-2310 Fax (315)292-5990
Email: INDUnity@aol.com
Website: www.ipcum.org
Media Contact, Rev. Janet Wanner
Executive Dir., The Rev. Dennis Frische-Mouri
Pres., The Rev. Janet Wanner
Treas., Mrs. Marilyn Moffett
Major Activities: Initiating dialogue on issues of social concern by organizing conferences on the death penalty, racism, welfare reform and violence; facilitating communication through an electronic newsletter and web site; promoting the National Day of Prayer and the Week of Prayer for Christian Unity; and advancing Churches Uniting in Christ.

Interfaith Community Council, Inc.
702 E. Market St., New Albany, IN 47150, Tel. (812)948-9248 Fax (812)948-9249
Email: info@interfaithinc.org
Website: www.interfaithinc.org
Media Contact, Exec. Dir., Christine Harbeson
Exec. Dir., Christine Harbeson
Programs - Emergency Assistance
RSVP, Dir., Ceil Sperzel
Major Activities: Emergency Assistance; Retired Senior Volunteer Program; New Clothing and Toy Drives; Emergency Food Distribution; Homeless Prevention; Kids' Café; Youth Development Services

Kentuckiana Interfaith Community (see listing under Kentucky)

Lafayette Urban Ministry
420 N. 4th St., Lafayette, IN 47901-2213, Tel. (317)423-2691 Fax (317)423-2693
Media Contact, Exec. Dir., Joseph Micon
Exec. Dir., Joseph Micon
Advocate Coord., Rebecca Smith
Public Policy Coord., Harry Brown
Pres., John Wilson
Major Activities: Social Justice Ministries with and among the Poor

United Religious Community of St. Joseph County
501 North Main St., South Bend, IN 46601, Tel. (574)282-2397 Fax (574)282-8014

Email: urc@urcsjc.org
Website: www.urcsjc.org
Media Contact, Exec. Dir., William J. Wassner
Exec. Dir., William J. Wassner
Pres., Rabbi Michael Friesllow
Refugee Program Director, Carol McDonnell
Victim Impact Panel Director, Marchell Wesaw
Advocacy Centers Director, Marchell Wesaw
Major Activities: Religious Understanding; Interfaith-Ecumenical Education; Interfaith Newsletter "Torch"; CROP Walk; On-site Prayer Ministry; Peacemaker Awards; Hunger Education; Housing and Homelessness Issues; Clergy Education and Support; Refugee Resettlement; Victim Assistance; Advocacy for the Needy; Family Justice Center (Partner addressing chaplaincy), Housing Project for Grandparents raising Grandchildren

Weekday Christian Education
2001 Bayard Park Drive, Evansville, IN 47714, Tel. (812)425-3524 Fax (812)425-3524
Email: weekdayce@gmail.com
Website: www.weekdayevansville.org
Media Contact, Weekday Executive Director, Donna K. Carr
Weekday Exec. Dir., Donna K. Carr
Pres., Karen Moore
V. Pres., Nancy Sanderson
Sec., Sandy Danks
Treas., Nancy Keeney
Major Activities: Food Pantry System; Weekday Christian Education

Wellspring Interfaith Social Services, Inc. (previously West Central Neighborhood Ministry, Inc.)
1316 Broadway, Fort Wayne, IN 46802-3304, Tel. (219)422-6618 Fax (219)422-9319
Email: fzirille@wellspringinterfaith.org
Media Contact, Exec. Dir., Francis M. Zirille
Exec. Dir., Francis M. Zirille
Ofc. Mgr., J. R. Stopperich
Neighborhood Services Dir., Carol Salge
Senior Citizens Dir., Gayle Mann
Youth Director, Lois Ehinger
Major Activities: After-school Programs; Teen Drop-In Center; Summer Day Camp; Summer Overnight Camp; Information and Referral Services; Food Pantry; Nutrition Program for Senior Citizens; Senior Citizens Activities; Tutoring; Developmental Services for Families & Senior Citizens; Parent Club

IOWA

Churches United, Inc.
1035 3rd Ave., Suite 202, Cedar Rapids, IA 52403-2463, Tel. (319)366-7163 Fax (319)366-7163
Email: churchesunited@yahoo.com
Website: www.churchesunitedcr.org
Media Contact, Exec. Dir., Darci Morin
Exec. Dir., Darci Morin

Pres., Rev. David Loy
Treas., Ellen Bruckner
Major Activities: Communication-resource center for member churches; Community Information and Referral; Ecumenical City-wide Celebrations; Restorative Justice programs

Churches United of the Quad City Area
2535 Tech Drive, Suite 205, Bettendorf, IA 52722, Tel. (563)332-5002 Fax (563)332-5075
Email: rquay@cuqca.org
Website: www.rquay@cuqca.org
Media Contact, Exec. Dir., Rev. Ronald c. Quay
Exec. Dir., Rev. Ronald C. Quay (American Baptist Churches)
Pres., Rev. Brian Fischer (American Baptist Churches)
Sec., Rev. Lisa Dietrich (Evangelical Lutheran Church of America)
Treas., Rev. Travis Fisher (Evangelical Lutheran Church of America)
Other: Rev. Parker Lewis, (United Church of Christ)
Other: Vicki Felger (Evangelical Lutheran Church of America)
Major Activities: Food Pantries, Emergency Financail Assistance, Homeless Shelter for Women with or without children, Crop Walk Coordinator, Ecumenical Worship Services, Interfaith Relations, Jail Ministries, Justice Issues Advocacy

Des Moines Area Religious Council
3816 36th St., Ste. 202, Des Moines, IA 50310, Tel. (515)277-6969 Fax (515)274-8389
Email: info@dmreligious.org
Website: dmreligious.org
Media Contact, Exec. Dir., Sarai Schnucker-Rice
Exec. Dir., Sarai Schnucker-Rice
Pres., James Swanstrom
Pres. Elect, Faith Ferre
Treas., Leonara Waller
Major Activities: Education; Social Initiatives Advocacy; Mission; Emergency Food Pantry; Ministry to Widowed; Child Care Assistance, Compassion in Action, Cross-cultural

Ecumenical Ministries of Iowa (EMI)*
P.O. Box 41487, Des Moines, IA 50311, Tel. (515)274-2278 Fax (515)274-2278
Email: emofiowa@aol.com
Website: www.iowachurches.org
Media Contact, Comm. Coord., Mary Swalla Holmes
Exec. Dir., Rev. Sarai Schnucker Beck
Major Activities: Facilitating the denomi-nations'cooperative agenda of resourcing local expression of the church; Assess needs & develop responses through Justice and Unity Commissions

Iowa Religious Media Services
3116 104th Street, Urbandale, IA 50322-3818, Tel. (515)277-2920 Fax (515)277-0842

Email: questions@irms.org
Website: www.irms.org
Media Contact, Exec. Dir., Sharon E. Strohmaier
Exec. Dir., Sharon E. Strohmaier
Major Activities: Media Library for Churches supported by six denominations in Iowa and the upper Midwest (details on the website)

KANSAS

Cross-Lines Cooperative Council
736 Shawnee Ave., Kansas City, KS 66105, Tel. (913)281-3388 Fax (913)281-2344
Email: theresa@cross-lines.org
Website: www.cross-lines.org
Media Contact, Dir. of Public Relations & Marketing, Theresa Swartwood
Exec. Dir., Roberta Lindbeck
Dir.of Emergency Services, Carey Sterrett
Dir. of Volunteer Services & Commodities, Amber Glasgow
Major Activities: Emergency Assistance; Hunger Relief; Community Garden/Nutrition Project; Thrift Store; Highlight Programs such as Prom Attire Distribution, School Supplies; Christmas Store. A Thrift Store is also available for all shoppers.

Inter-Faith Ministries-Wichita
829 N. Market, Wichita, KS 67214-3519, Tel. (316)264-9303 Fax (316)264-2233
Email: smuyskens@ifmnet.org
Website: www.ifmnet.org
Media Contact, Exec. Dir., Sue Castile
Exec. Dir., Sue Castile
Adm. Asst., Kathy Freed
ASAP Haiti, Dir. Bonnie Chadick
Homeless and Housing Services, Dir., Sandy Swank
Special Projects, Dir., Ashley Davis
Development, Dir., Karen Dobbin
Campaign to End Childhood Hunger, Karole Bradford
Community Ministry/Restorative Justice/Family Group Conferencing/Racial Justice Coord., Jeannine Little
Faith in Action, Coord., Richard Hanley
GoZones! Dir., Johanna Wilson
Major Activities: Communications; Urban Education; Inter-religious Understanding; Community Needs and Issues; Theology and Worship; Hunger; Family Life; Multi-Cultural Concerns

Kansas Ecumenical Ministries*
1248 SW Buchanan Street, Topeka, KS 66604, Tel. (785)272-9531
Email: LK331@aol.com
Website: www.kansasecuminical.com
Media Contact, Director
Pres. Sean Weston
Vice-Pres: Ray Moore
Sec., Rev.Jane Siebert
Treas., Rev. Sam Muyskens
Major Activities: State Council of Churches; Legislative Activities, Program Facilitation and Coordination; Education; Kansas Christian Leaders Forum; Grassroots Ecumenical Young Adult Ministry, Faith and Order

Eastern Area Community Ministries
P.O. Box 43049, Louisville, KY 40253-0049, Tel. (502)244-6141 Fax (502)254-5141
Email: eacmexdir@bellsouth.net
Media Contact, Exec. Dir., Carrie Gerard
Exec. Dir., Carrie Gerard
Board Pres., Rev. Elwood Sturtevant
Board Sec., Mary Stephens
Board Treas., Homer Lacy, Jr.
Youth and Family Services,Rachael Elrod
Older Adult Services, Associate Program Dir., Joni Snyder
Neighborhood Visitor Program, Acting Prog. Dir., Jane Parker
Major Activities: Emergency Assistance; Clothes Closet; Meals on Wheels; Community Worship Services; Good Start for Kids; Juvenile Court Diversion; Community Development; Transient Fund; Ministerial Association; Juvenile Court Diversion

KENTUCKY

Fern Creek-Highview United Ministries
7502 Tangelo Dr., Louisvlle, KY 40228, Tel. (502)239-7407 Fax (502)239-7454
Email: FernCreek.Ministries@crnky.org
Media Contact, Exec. Dir., Kay Sanders, 7502 Tangelo Dr., Louisville, KY 40228, Tel. (502)239-7407
Exec. Dir., Kay Sanders
Pres., David Pooler
Major Activities: Ecumenically supported social service agency providing services to the community, including Emergency Financial Assistance, Food-Clothing, Health Aid Equipment Loans, Information-Referral, Advocacy, Checks; Holiday Programs, Life Skills Training; Mentoring; Case Management; Adult Day-Care Program

Hazard-Perry County Community Ministries, Inc.
P.O. Box 1506, Hazard, KY 41702-1506, Tel. (606)436-0051 Fax (606)436-0071
Media Contact, Gerry Feamster-Roll
Exec. Dir., Gerry Feamster-Roll
Chpsn., Sarah Hughes
V. Chpsn., Susan Duff
Sec., Virginia Campbell
Treas., Margaret Adams
Major Activities: Food Pantry-Crisis Aid Program; Day Care; Summer Day Camp; After-school Program; Christmas Tree; Family Support Center; Adult Day Care; Transitional Housing

Highlands Community Ministries
1140 Cherokee Rd., Louisville, KY 40204, Tel. (502)451-3695 Fax (502)451-3609

247

Email: hcmexecu@hotmail.com
Website: www.hcmlou.org
Media Contact, Exec. Dir., Stan Esterle
Exec. Dir., Stan Esterle
Major Activities: Welfare Assistance; Children Day Care; Adult DayHealth Care; Social Services for Elderly; Housing for Elderly and Handicapped; Ecumenical Programs; Interfaith Programs; Community Classes; Activities for Children; Neighborhood and Business organization

Kentuckiana Interfaith Community

PO BOX 7128, Louisville, KY 40257, Tel. (502)587-6265 Fax (502)451-9827
Email: churchoffice@salemucc.com
Website: www.neighborhoodlink.com/org/kic
Media Contact, Exec. Dir., Rev. Douglas Fowler
Pres., Ron Gaddie
Vice-Pres., Laura Metzger
Treas., Charles Hawkins
Major Activities: Christian-Jewish, Islamic, Bahai Ministries in KY, Southern IN; Consensus Advocacy; Interfaith Dialogue; Community Hunger Walk; Racial Justice Forums; Network for Neighborhood-based Ministries; Hunger & Racial Justice Commission; Faith Channel-Cable TV Station, Horizon News Paper; Police-Comm. Relations Task Force; Ecumenical Strategic Planning; Networking with Seminaries & Religious-Affiliated Institutions

Kentucky Council of Churches*

1500 Leestown Rd., Suite 316, Lexington, KY 40511, Tel. (859)269-7715 Fax (859)269-1240
Email: kcc@kycouncilofchurches.org
Website: www.kycouncilofchurches.org
Media Contact, Exec. Dir., Marian M. Taylor
Exec. Dir., The Rev. Marian McClure Taylor (Presbyterian)
Pres. The Rev. Mike Ward (Presbyterian)
Vice-Pres: Dr. John Lepper (Baptist)
Sec., Rev. Amy Real Coultas (Episcopalian)
Treas., Mr. Michael Watts (United Methodist)
Major Activities: Legislative Advocacy, Clergy peer groups, Disaster response coordination, Support to local ecumenical initiatives

Ministries United South Central Louisville (M.U.S.C.L., Inc.)

1207 Hart Avenue, Louisville, KY 42013, Tel. (502)363-9087 Fax (502)363-9087
Media Contact, Exec. Dir., Rev. Antonio (Tony) Aja, M.Div., Tel. (502)363-2383, Email Tony_Aja@pcusa.org
Ex. Dir., Rev. Antonio (Tony) Aja, M.Div.
Airport Relocation Ombudsman, Rev. Phillip Garrett, M.Div., Tel. (502)361-2706; E-mail, philombud@aol.com
Senior Adults Programs, Dir., Mrs. Jeannine Blakeman, BSSW
Emergency Assistance, Dir., Mr. Michael Hundley
Low-Income Coord., Ms. Wanda Irvio
Youth Services, Dir., The Rev. Bill Sanders, M.Div.
Volunteers Coord., Mrs. Carol Stemmle

Northern Kentucky Interfaith Commission, Inc.

901 York St., P.O. Box 72296, Newport, KY 41072-0296, Tel. (859)581-2237 Fax (859)261-6041
Website: www.nkyinterfaith.com
Media Contact, Exec. Dir., Rev. James A. Bishop
Pres., Mr. Paul Whalen
Sec., Ms.Cordelia Koplow
Treas., Mr. John Wilgus
Admin. Asst., Pat McDermott
Major Activities: Understanding Faiths; Meeting Spiritual and Human Needs; Enabling Churches to Greater Ministry

Paducah Cooperative Ministry

402 Legion Drive, Paducah, KY 42003, Tel. (270)442-6795 Fax (270)442-6812
Email: pcministry@hcis.net
Website: www.paducahcooperativeministry.org
Media Contact, Dir., Heidi Suhrheinrich
Dir., Heidi Suhrheinrich
Chairman., Don Barger
Vice-Chpsn., Rev. David Comperry
Major Activities: Programs for Hungry, Elderly, Poor, Homeless, Handicapped, Undereducated

St. Matthews Area Ministries

201 Biltmore Rd., Louisville, KY 40207, Tel. (502)893-0205 Fax (502)893-0206
Email: danglane@stman.com
Website: www.stmam.com
Media Contact, Exec. Dir., Dan G. Lane
Exec. Dir., Dan G. Lane
Child Care, Dir., Julie Abbott
Dir. Assoc., Danette Baker
Major Activities: Child Care; Emergency Assistance (Financial +); Family Services; Divorce Family Transition Sessions (F.I.T.); Early Essentials for Infants/Toddlers; Case Management; Counseling; Information & Referral; Meals on Wheels; Medical Equipment Loan; Early Essentials For Infants/Toddlers; School Supplies Program; Financial/Budgeting Classes; Families in Transition (Divorce Sessions For Families); Volunteer Organization Active in Disaster (St. MAM V.O.A.D.).

South East Associated Ministries (SEAM)

6500 Six Mile Ln., Ste. A, Louisville, KY 40218, Tel. (502)499-9350
Website: www.seam.com
Media Contact, Mary Beth Helton
Exec. Dir., Mary Beth Helton
Life Skills Center, Dir., Robert Davis
Youth Services, Dir., Bill Jewel
Pres., David Ehresman
Treas., Bill Trusty
Major Activities: Emergency Food, Clothing and Financial Assistance; Life Skills Center (Programs of Prevention and Case Management and Self-Sufficiency Through Education, Empowerment, Support Groups, etc.); Bloodmobile;

Ecumenical Education and Worship; Juvenile Court Diversion; TEEN Court; Teen Crime & the Community

South Louisville Community Ministries

Peterson Social Services Center,4803 Southside Dr., Louisville, KY 40214, Tel. (502)367-6445 Fax (502)361-4668
Email: slcm@slcm.org
Website: www.slcm.org
Media Contact, Exec. Dir., J. Michael Jupin
Bd. Chair., Rev. Michelle Elfers
Bd. Vice-Chair., Craig Oeswein
Bd. Treas., Greg Greenwood
Exec. Dir., Rev. J. Michael Jupin
Major Activities: Food, Clothing & Financial Assistance; Home Delivered Meals; Ecumenical Worship; Affordable Housing; Adult Day Care; Dare to Care Kids Café

LOUISIANA

Greater New Orleans Federation of Churches

4640 S. Carrollton Ave, Suite 2B, New Orleans, LA 70119-6077, Tel. (504)488-8788 Fax (504)488-8823
Exec. Dir., The Rev. J. Richard Randels
Major Activities: Information and Referral; Food Distribution(FEMA); Forward Together TV Program; Sponsors seminars for pastors (e.g. church growth, clergy taxes,etc.); Police Chaplaincy; Fire Chaplaincy

Interfaith Federation of Greater Baton Rouge

3112 Convention St., Baton Rouge, LA 70806, Tel. (225)267-5600 Fax (225)267-5100
Email: director@ifedgbr.com
Website: www.ifedgbr.com
Media Contact, Exec. Dir., Rev. Jeff Day
Exec. Dir., Rev. Jeff Day
Admn. Asst., Ashley Griffin
Pres., Rev. Amy Mercer
Pres.-Elect, Joyce Robinson
Treas., Melvin Davis
Major Activities: Combating Hunger; Interfaith Relations; Interfaith Concert; Race Relations; Interfaith Caregivers (Faith in Action)

Louisiana Interchurch Conference*

527 North Boulevard, Fourth Floor, Baton Rouge, LA 70802, Tel. (225)344-0134 Fax (225)344-0142
Email: lainterchurch@aol.com
Website: www.lainterchurch.org
Media Contact, Exec. Dir., Rev. C. Dana Krutz
Exec. Dir., Rev. C. Dana Krutz
Pres., Bishop Thomas Brown
Major Activities: Ecumenical Dialogue; Prison Reform; Liaison with State Agencies; Institutional Chaplains; Racism; Environmental; Public Policy Advocacy

MAINE

Maine Council of Churches*

156 High Street, Portland, ME 04101, Tel. (207) 772-1918 Fax (207)772-1918
Email: info@mainecouncilofchurches.org
Website: www.mainecouncilofchurches.org
Media Contact, Executive Director, Jill Saxby or Associate Director, Eric C. Smith
Exec. Dir., The Rev. Jill Job Saxby (Unitarian Universalist)
Pres. Silver Moore-Leamon (UCC)
Vice-Pres: Leslie Manning (Religious Society of Friends)
Sec., Eric C. Smith (UCC) (MCC staff)
Treas., Kenneth McAfee (UCC)
Major Activities: Religious Campaign Against Torture, including Maine prison project (solitary confinement); Economic Justice program—advocacy for programs supporting low-income, low food secure and homeless Mainers, Environmental Justice program—various projects and coalitions, Giving Winds project (Native American economic development), Local Foods Bean Suppers project, "Fishes and Loaves"—environmental education resource for congregational study, ecumenical relationships, interfaith relationships, Maine Immigration Reform Coalition (founding member), Coalition for Affordable Health Care (foiunding member), Maine Citizens for Clean Elections (member), Maine Partners for Cool Communities (founding member)

MARYLAND

Central Maryland Ecumenical Council*

Cathedral House, 5400 Loch Raven Blvd, Baltimore, MD 21218, Tel. (410)467-6194 Fax 410-464-6194
Email: cmecouncil@gmail.com
Website: www.cmecouncil.org
Media Contact, Exec. Dir., Reverend John R. Sharp
Pres., The Rev. Iris Farabee-Lewis
Major Activities: Interchurch Communications and Collaboration; Information Systems; Ecumenical and Interfaith Relations; Urban Mission and Advocacy; Staff for Judicatory Leadership Council; Commission on Dialogue; Commission on Church & Society; Commission on Admin. & Dev.; Ecumenical Awards & Choral Concerts; Ecumenical Worship Services,Thanksgiving Interfaith Awards Breakfast presenting the Agus-Shenan Interfaith Leadership Award. Interfaith Clergy Dialogue on Israel in Partnership with the Baltimore Jewish Council, Ecumenical All-Church June Picnic, Advocacy in Annapolis, Partner in "Heeding God's Call," program to enlist congregations in stopping "straw gun purchases."

The Christian Council of Delaware and Maryland's Eastern Shore (see listing under Delaware)

Community Ministries of Rockville
1010 Grandin Ave. Suite a-1, Rockville, MD 20850, Tel. (301)762-8682 Fax (301)762-2939
Email: asaenz@cmrocks.org
Website: www.cmrocks.org
Media Contact, Managing Dir., Agnes Saenz
Exec. Dir. & Comm. Min., Mansfield M. Kaseman
Managing Dir., Agnes Aaenz
Major Activities: Shelter Care; Emergency Assistance; Elderly Home Care; Affordable Housing; Political Advocacy; Community Education; Education to Recent Immigrants

Community Ministry of Montgomery County
114 West Montgomery Ave., Rockville, MD 20850, Tel. (301)762-8682 Fax (301)762-2939
Email: rwagner@iworksmc.org
Media Contact, Exec. Dir., Rebecca Wagner
Exec. Dir., Rebecca Wagner
Major Activities: Interfaith Clothing Center; Emergency Assistance Coalition; The Advocacy Function; Information and Referral Services; Friends in Action; The Thanksgiving Hunger Drive; Thanksgiving in February; Community Based Shelter

MASSACHUSETTS

Attleboro Area Council of Churches, Inc.
95 Pine Street Suite # 10, Attleboro, MA 02703, Tel. (508)222-2933 Fax (508)222-2008
Email: aaccoffice@verizon.net
Website: www.attleborocouncilofchurches.org
Media Contact, Executive Director, Kat Wright
Executive Director, Kat Wright
Exec. Adm., Kathleen Trowbridge
Pamela Tarallo, Food n Friends Coordinator (foodnfriends@attleborocouncilofchurches.org)
Susan Smith, Homes with Heart Case Manager (casemanager1@attleborocouncilof churches.org)
Steve Wright, Homes with Heart Assistant Case Manager (casemanager2@attleborocouncilof churches.org)
Patti Sparrow, Administrative Assistant (office@ attleborocouncilof churches.org)
Bill MacLagan, Assistant Chaplain
Pres., Rev. Ruth Shaver, Minister of Christian Ed. And Family Life, Second Congregational Ch.,
Treas., Mr. Richard Shaw, 70 Stanson Dr., N. Attleboro, MA 02760
Major Activities: Hospital Chaplaincy; personal Growth-Skill Workshops; Ecumenical Worship; Interfaith Worship; Media Resource Center; Referral Center; Communications-Publications; Community Social Action; Food'n Friends Kitchens; Nursing Home Volunteer Visitation Program; Clergy Fellowship-Learning Events

The Cape Cod Council of Churches, Inc.
P.O. Box 758, Hyannis, MA 02601, Tel. (508)775-5073 Fax (508)775-5073
Email: capecodcouncil@verizon.net
Website: www.capecouncilofchurches.org
Media Contact, Exec. Dir., Diane Casey-Lee
Pres., Rev. Bette Anne
Vice Pres., G/ Thomas Ryan
Treasurer, Al Grorud
Corp. Secretary, Shirley Lamson
Major Activities: Human Services; Social Witness; Spirituality; Ecumenism; Interfaith Relations

Cooperative Metropolitan Ministries
474 Centre St., Newton, MA 02458, Tel. (617)244-3650 Fax (617)630-9172
Email: info@coopmet.org
Website: www.coopmet.org
Media Contact, Exec. Dir., Alexander Levering Kern
Exec. Dir., Alexander Levering Kern
Bd. Pres., Rev. Anne Rousseau
Major Activities: Low Income; Suburban-Urban Bridges; Racial and Economic Justice, Leadership Training, Interfaith Dialogue, Poverty, Violence Prevention, Religious Intolerance

Council of Churches of Greater Springfield
39 Oakland St., Springfield, MA 01108, Tel. (413) 733-2149 Fax (413)733-9817
Email: info@councilofchurchesgs.org
Media Contact, Asst. to Dir., Andrea Skeene
Exec. Dir., Rev. Paula Alexander
Community Min., Dir. Don A. Washington
Pres., The Rev. Paula Alexander
Treas., John Pearson, Esq
Major Activities: Advocacy; Emergency Fuel Fund; Peace and Justice Division; Community Ministry; Hospital and Jail Chaplaincies; Pastoral Service; Crisis Counseling; Christian Social Relations; Relief Collections; Ecumenical and Interfaith Relations; Church-Community Projects and Community Dialogues; Publication, "Knowing My Neighbor- Religious Beliefs and Traditions at Times of Death"

Greater Lawrence Council of Churches
276 Essex Street, Lawrence, MA 01842, Tel. 978-686-4012 Fax 978-689-2006
Email: ctstaff276@comcast.net
Website: greater-lawrence-churches.org
Media Contact, Exec. Dir., David Edwards
Exec. Dir., David Edwards
Pres., Jane Barlow
Vice-Pres., Rev. Dr. Richard Haley
Admn. Asst., Barbara Payson
Major Activities: Ecumenical Worship; Radio Ministry; Hospital and Nursing Home Chaplaincy; Afterschool Children's Program; Vacation Bible School, Interfaith care givers of Greater Lawrence

Inter-Church Council of Greater New Bedford

412 County St., New Bedford, MA 02740-5096, Tel. (508)993-6242 Fax (508)991-3158
Email: pastor@iccgnb.org
Website: www.inter-churchcouncil.org
Media Contact, Min., Rev. David Lima
Exec. Min., Rev. David Lima
Pres., vacant
Treas., George Mock
Major Activities: Counseling; Spiritual Direction; Chaplaincy; Housing for Elderly and Disabled; Urban Affairs; Community Spiritual Leadership; Parish Nurse Ministry; Accounting and Spiritual Care for the Developmentally Challenged; Ecumenical and Interfaith Ministries; Advocacy for the Homeless; Support for Urban Schhol District; Opposition to Expanded Gambling

Massachusetts Commission on Christian Unity

82 Luce St, Lowell, MA 01852, Tel. (978)453-5423 Fax (978)453-5423
Email: kgordonwhite@msn.com
Media Contact, Exec. Dir., Rev. K. Gordon White
Exec. Sec., Rev. K. Gordon White
Pres., Rev. Fr. Edward O'Flaherty, Ecumenical Officer, Roman Catholic Archdiocese of Boston
Major Activities: Faith and Order Dialogue with Church Judicatories; Guidelines & Pastoral Directives for Inter-Church Marriages; Guidelines for Celebrating Baptism in an Ecumenical Context

Massachusetts Council of Churches*

14 Beacon St., Suite 416, Boston, MA 02108, Tel. (617)523-2771 Fax (617)523-1483
Email: council@masscouncilofchurches.org
Website: www.masscouncilofchurches.org
Media Contact, Dir., Rev. Jack Johnson
Exec. Dir., The Rev. Jack Johnson
Assoc. Dir., Ms. Laura Everett
Pres., Mr. Richard Harter
Vice-Pres., The Rev. Joel Matthew Anderle
Sec., The Rev. Karen Coleman
Treas., The Rev. Kenneth G. Y. Grant
Major Activities: Christian Unity; Education and Evangelism; Social Justice & Individual Rights; Ecumenical Worship; Services and Resources for Individuals and Churches

Worcester County Ecumenical Council

128 Providence Street, Worcester, MA 01604-5432, Tel. (508)757-8385 Fax (508)795-7704
Email: wcec@verizon.net
Media Contact, Exec. Dir., Rev. Allyson D. Platt
The Rev. Allyson D. Platt, Email: wcec.Allyson@verizon.net
Pres., Mrs. Fran Langille
Major Activities: Ecumenical worship and dialogue networking congregations together in partnerships of mission, education and spiritual renewal. Clusters of Churches; Ecumenical

Worship and Dialogue; Interfaith Activities; Resource Connection for Churches; Group Purchasing Consortium

MICHIGAN

Bay Area Ecumenical Forum

103 E. Midland St., Bay City, MI 48706, Tel. (989) 686-1360 Fax (989)686-0178
Email: wpccares@sbcglobal.net
Website: www.wpcbc.org
Media Contact, Jena Windiate
Major Activities: Ecumenical Worship; Community Issues; Christian Unity; Education; CROP Walk

Berrien County Association of Churches

200 E. Empire, P.O. Box 1081, Benton Harbor, MI 49023-1081, Tel. (616)926-0030 Fax (616)926-2159*51
Email: bcac_cweb@sbcglobal.net
Website: www.berrienchurches.org
Media Contact, Sec., Mary Ann Hinz
Pres., Yvonne Wood
Dir., Street Ministry, The Rev. Yvonne Hester
Major Activities: Street Ministry; CROP Walk; Community Issues; Fellowship; Christian Unity; Publish Annual County Church Directory and Monthly Newsletter; Resource Guide for Helping Needy; Distribution of Worship Opportunity— Brochure for Tourists, GED Programs, Food Pantry, Morning Prayer Groups - Women/Ministers.

Grand Rapids Area Center for Ecumenism (GRACE)

183 Lakeside Dr., N.E., Grand Rapids, MI 49503, Tel. (616)643-0117 Fax (616)774-2883
Email: grace@graceoffice.org
Website: www.graceoffice.org
Media Contact, Lisa H. Michelle
Leadership Team: Rev. David P. Baak; Lisa H. Mitchell; Rev. David G. May
Major Activities: AIDS Care Network; Volunteer Transportation; Hunger Walk ; Education; Christian Unity Worship (Ecumenical Lecture, Christian Unity Worship Events, Interfaith Dialogue Conference); (Affiliate, FISH for My People-transportation); Racial Justice Institute; West Michigan Call to Renewal (Response to Poverty Advocacy); Publications (Grace In~Site); Faith In Motion (Mass Transit and Land Use); Restorative Justice Coalition

Greater Flint Council of Churches

P.O. Box 126, Flint, MI 48501, Tel. (810)238-3691 Fax (810)238-4463
Email: greaterflintcouncilofchurches@yahoo.com
Media Contact, Coord., Ms. Barbara Shackelford
Barbara Spaulding Westcott, Publicity Chairperson
President, Overseer Barbara Shackelford
Major Activities: Christian Education; Christian Unity; Christian Missions; Nursing Home

251

Visitor; Church in Society; American Bible Society Materials; Interfaith Dialogue; Church Teacher Exchange Sunday; Directory of Area Faiths and Clergy; Thanksgiving & Easter Sunrise Services; CROP Walks

The Jackson County Interfaith Council
425 Oakwood, P.O. Box 156, Clarklake, MI 49234-0156, Tel. (517)529-9721
Media Contact, Exec. Dir., vacant
Exec. Dir., vacant
Major Activities: Chaplaincy at Institutions and Senior Citizens Residences; Martin L. King, Jr. Day Celebrations; Ecumenical Council Representation; Radio and TV Programs; Food Pantry; Interreligious Events; Clergy Directory

The Metropolitan Christian Council: Detroit-Windsor
4750 Woodward Ave., Suite 215, Detroit, MI 48201, Tel. (313)870-9550
Email: councilweb@sbcglobal.net
Website: users.aol.com/councilweb
Media Contact, Exec. Dir.,Rev. Pricilla Carey-Tucker
Exec. Dir., Rev. Pricilla Carey-Tucker
Meals for Shut-ins, Prog. Dir., John Simpson; Office. Asst., Ms. Gwen Hunter
Major Activities: Theological and Social Concerns; Ecumenical Worship; Educational Services; Electronic Media; Print Media; Meals for Shut-Ins; Summer Feeding Program

Muskegon County Cooperating Churches
1095 Third St., Suite 10, Muskegon, MI 49441-1976, Tel. (231)727-0841 Fax (231)727-0841
Email: delphine.mccc@frontier.com
Website: www.cooperatingchurches.com
Media Contact, Prog. Coord., Delphine Hogston
President: Amy Hart
Major Activities: Local Faith Community Information Source, Racial Reconciliation, Dialogue, & Healing; Multiracial Family Support; Ecumenical Worship; Faith News TV Ministry; CROP Walk Against Hunger; Jewish-Christian Dialogue; Environmental Issues, Social Justice Issues, Pastoral Support, Homeless Sheltering, Second Harvest Gleaners Food Trucks, Mentoring School Children

SUBSIDIARY ORGANIZATION
Interfaith Hospitality Network in Muskegon now called "Family Promise of the Lakeshore"
Media Contact: Delphine Hogston
Major Activities: Helping congregations shelter homeless families
Community Connects Choir
Media Contact: Darlene Collett
Major Activities: Winter Holiday Concert. Intentionally interracial, intergenerational, ecumenical singing blending gospel and traditional music. Supports other diverse music opportunities for the community. Shoah Remembrance Committee Muskegon (SRCM)

MINNESOTA

Arrowhead Interfaith Council*
102 W. 2nd St., Duluth, MN 55802, Tel. (218)722-7166
Email: dbb@digiterp.com
Website: www.arrowheadinterfaith.org
Media Contact, President - Rev. Erik Nordgren
President - Rev. Erik Nordgren
Vice-President - Rev. Sharon Osborn
Co-Secretary - Liana Salima Rael Swenson
Treasurer - Gary Wise
Major Activities: InterFaith Dialogue; Joint Religious Legislative Coalition; Corrections Chaplaincy; Human Justice and Community Concerns; Community Seminars; Children's Concerns

Community Emergency Assistance Program (CEAP)
6840 78th Ave N, Brooklyn Park, MN 55445, Tel. (763)566-9600 Fax (763)566-9604
Email: smklein@isd.net
Website: www.ceap.homestead.com
Media Contact, Exec. Dir., Stephen Klein
Exec. Dir., Stephen Klein
Major Activities: Provision of Basic Needs (Food, Clothing); Emergency Financial Assistance for Shelter; Home Delivered Meals; Chore Services and Homemaking Assistance; Family Loan Program; Volunteer Services

Greater Minneapolis Council of Churches
1001 E. Lake St., P.O. Box 7509, Minneapolis, MN 55407-0509, Tel. (612)276-8687 Fax (612)276-1534
Email: info@gmcc.org
Website: www.gmcc.org
Media Contact, Marketing and Communications Manager, Randy Miranda
President and CEO, Rev. Dr. Gary B. Reierson
    Email: reierson@gmcc.org
Chair, Susan Sands
Vice Chair, Simon Foster
Treasurer, John Ratelle
Secretary, Ron McKinley
Senior Vice President & Exec. Dir., Division Indian Work, Noya Woodrich
Advancement, Vice President, Tracy Elftmann
Finance & Administration, Vice President and CFO, Peter Lee
Program Development, Exec. Dir., Bruce Bjork
Program Manager, Bridget Ryan
Minnesota FoodShare, Dir., Sara Nelson-Pallmeyer
HandyWorks, Dir., Megan Nolan-Elliasen
Clinical Pastoral Education, Dir., Rev. Dr. Susan Allers Hatlie
Division of Indian Work, Youth Leadership Development Program, Dir., Louise Matson
Division of Indian Work Health Services, Dir., George Spears
Division of Indian Work Strengthening Family Circles, Dir., Suzanne Tibbetts Young

Division of Indian Work Healing Spirit, Dir., Kirk Crow Shoe

Urban Immersion Service Retreats, Dir., Gennae Falconer

Metro Paint-A-Thon, Dir., Deidre Pope

Discover Parenting, Coord., LaDonna White

Community Justice Project, Co-Dirs., Rev. Brian Herron, Rev. Hillary Freeman

Center for Families, Dir. of Programs, Edmund Ocansey

Project Preserve, Coord., Deborah Easter

Early Childhood Programming, Coord., LaDonna White

Major Activities: American Indian Work (Emergency Assistance, Youth Leadership, Self-sufficiency, American Indian parents, Healing Spirit Program - Foster Care, Youth tutoring and school success, Supportive Housing, Health Services, Winter Clothing Distribution, Food Shelf and Family Violence Program; Minnesota FoodShare; Metro Paint-A-Thon and HandyWorks – Senior Services; Clinical Pastoral Education (in social justice and community settings), Social Justice Advocacy; Urban Immersion Service Retreats; Welfare Reform; Economic Self-Sufficiency; Parent Support and Early Childhood Programming; Center for Families (Immigrant and Refugee Services); Community Health Promotion; Correctional Aftercare

The Joint Religious Legislative Coalition

122 W. Franklin Ave., Ste 315, Minneapolis, MN 55404, Tel. (612)870-3670 Fax (612)870-3671

Email: info@jrlc.org

Website: www.jrlc.org

Media Contact, Exec. Dir., Brian A. Rusche

Exec. Dir., Brian A. Rusche

Board Chair, Mr. Owais Bayunus

Major Activities: Lobbying at State Legislature; Researching Social Justice Issues and Preparing Position Statements; Organizing Grassroots Citizen's Lobby, Social Justice Advocacy.

Mall Area Religious Council (MARC)

Mall of America, 7200 York Avenue South, #416, Edina, MN 55435-4406, Tel. (952)831-0447

Email: jchell@manrol.com

Website: www.meaningstore.org

Media Contact, Rev. John Chell, Executive Director

Metropolitan Interfaith Council on Affordable Housing (MICAH)

122 W. Franklin Ave., #310, Minneapolis, MN 55404, Tel. (612)871-8980 Fax (612)871-2634

Email: info@micah.org

Website: www.micah.org

Media Contact, Interim Exec. Dir., Shelley Jacobson

Interim Ex. Dir., Shelley Jacobson

Congregational Organizer, Jodi Nelson, Renee Lundgren, John Slade, Cheryl Wilson

Sec., B. Aaron Parker

Pres., Jean Mac Farland

Treas., Barbara Brooks

Past Pres., Rev. Nancy L. Anderson

Major Activities: The Metropolitan Interfaith Council on Affordable Housing, MICAH, seeks to live out the prophetic vision that calls us "to do justice, to love mercy and to walk humbly with God." (Micah 6:8). We envision a metropolitan area where everyone without exception has a safe, decent and affordable home. MICAH will realize this vision through organizing congregations of faith and community partners to change the political climate and public policies so that all communities preserve and build affordable housing. MICAH's faith-based organizing creates power that produces results. During the past five years MICAH: Mobilized congregations to build community support for 1,348 affordable homes for families with very low incomes. Increased investment in affordable housing by leading successful campaigns for housing trust funds in Minneapolis, Anoka and Hennepin counties. Twenty-seven (27) comprehensive land use plans have been strangthened to reduce regulatory barriers to affordable housing.

Minnesota Council of Churches*

122 W. Franklin Ave., Rm. 100, Minneapolis, MN 55404, Tel. (612)870-3600 Fax (612)870-3622

Email: mcc@mnchurches.org

Website: www.mnchurches.org

Media Contact, Exec. Dir., Rev. Peg Chemberlin, Email: peg.chemberlin@mnchurches.org

Exec. Dir., Rev. Peg Chemberlin, Enail: peg.chemberlin@mnchurches.org

Unity & Relationships, Director, Gail Anderson, Email: gail.anderson@mnchurches.org

Refugee Services, Dir., Rachele King, Email: rachele.king@mnchurches.org

Communications, Emily Jarrett Hughes, Email: emily.jarretthughes@mnchurches.org

Finance & Facilities, Dir., Douglas Swanson, Email: doug.swanson@mnchurches.org

Joint Religious Legislative Coalition, Exec., Brian A. Rusche

Pres. Bishop Sally Dyck

Major Activities: Minnesota Church Center, Rural Life-Ag Crisis; Indian Ministry; Legislative Advocacy; Refugee Services; Service to Newly Legalized-Undocumented persons; Unity & Relationships, Sexual Exploitation within the Religious Community; Jewish-Christian Relations; Muslim-Christian Relations; Hindu-Christian Relations; Minnesota Foodshare; A Minnesota Without Poverty, Healthy Homes Healthy Congregations

Saint Paul Area Council of Churches

1671 Summit Ave, St. Paul, MN 55105, Tel. (651)646-8805 Fax (651)646-8866

Email: info@spacc.org

253

Website: www.spacc.org

Media Contact, Executive Director, Rev. Patricia J. Lull

Major Activities: Project Home Family Shelters (Direct Service), Project SPIRIT & Freedom School: out-of-school time programming for African American youth (Direct Service), Department of Indian Work: out-of-school time enrichment, parenting education, diabetes education, food shelf (Direct Service), Interfaith Youth Leadership Coalition (Interfaith Relations, Christian Ecumenism), CROP/ Hunger Walk (Christian Ecumenism), Minnesota Collaborative Anti-Racism Initiative (MCARI), Gateways to Service donation drives (Christian Ecumenism)

Tri-Council Coordinating Commission

122 W. Franklin, Rm. 100, Minneapolis, MN 55404, Tel. (612)871-0229 Fax (612)870-3622

Email: naja@gmcc.org

Website: www.gmcc.org/tcc.html

Media Contact, Co.-Dir., R. James Addington, Assoc. Rev. Carmen Valenzuela

Exec. Cmte.: The Rev. Peg Chemberlin, The Rev. Gary Reierson and The Rev. Thomas Duke

Major Activities: Anti-Racism training and organizational consultation; Institutional anti-racism team development and coaching; training and coaching of anti-racism trainers and organizers (in cooperation with cross roads ministry)

MISSISSIPPI

Mississippi Religious Leadership Conference*

P.O. Box 68123, Jackson, MS 39286-8123, Tel. (601)924-7430 Fax (601)924-7430

Email: chancery@jacksondiocese.org

Website: www.msrlc.org

Media Contact, Exec. Dir., Rev. Paul Griffin Jones, II, Th.D., PhD.

Exec. Dir.,The Rev. Paul Griffin Jones, II, Th.D., PhD.

Chair, Bishop Duncan Gray, III

Treas., The Rev. Jim White

Major Activities: Cooperation among Religious Leaders; Lay-Clergy Retreats; Social Concerns Seminars; Disaster Task Force; Advocacy for Disadvantaged

Council of Churches of the Ozarks

P.O. Box 3947, Springfield, MO 65808-3947, Tel. (417)862-3586 Fax (417)862-2129

Email: ccozarks@ccozarks.org; bgardner@cc ozarks.org

Website: www.ccozarks.org

Media Contact, Comm. Dir., vacant

Exec. Dir., Dr. David W. Hockensmith, Jr.

Chief Operating Officer, Julie Guillebeau

Major Activities: Ministerial Alliance; Child Care Food Program-FDA Food Program; Child Care Resource & Referral; Connections Handyman Service; Crosslines-Food and Clothing Pantry; Daybreak Adult Day Care Center; Long-Term Care Ombudsman Programs; Ozarks Food Harvest; Retired and Senior Volunteer Program; Sigma House-Treatment Center for Alcohol and Drug Abuse; Therapeutic Riding of the Ozarks

MISSOURI

Interfaith Community Services

200 Cherokee St., P.O. Box 4038, St. Joseph, MO 64504-0038, Tel. (816)238-4511 Fax (816)238-3274

Email: rsharp@inter.serv.org

Website: www.inter-serv.org

Media Contact, Exec. Dir., David G. Howery

Exec. Dir., David G. Howery

Dir. of Operations, Randy Sharp

Major Activities: Child Development; Neighborhood Family Services; Immigration Services; Retired Senior Volunteer Program; Nutrition Program; Mobile Meals; Southside Youth Program; Church and Community; Housing Development; Homemaker Services to Elderly; Emergency Food, Rent, Utilities; AIDS Assistance; Family Respite; Family and Individual Casework

Interfaith Partnership of Metropolitan St. Louis

4144 Lindell Blvd Ste 221, St. Louis, MO 63108, Tel. (314)531-4784 Fax (314)531-4785

Email: bdrodriguez@faithbeyondwalls.org

Website: http://www.interfaithpartnership.org

Media Contact, Director of Service Learning and Projects, Mandy Ellis

Cabinet Chair, Cynthis Holmes

President, Rev. Dr. Dieter Heinzl.

Executive Director, Beth Damsgaard-Rodriguez

Major Activities: Speaking out with a concerted faith voice on public issues, Celebrating our diversity encouraging respect for our faith traditions through interfaith dialogue, service projects, health initiatives and health care advocacy. Projects that promote bridge building across racial, religious, and cultural divides, and health promotion through congregational health initiatives.

MONTANA

Montana Association of Churches*

25 South Ewing, Ste. 408, Helena, MT 59714, Tel. (406)449-6010 Fax (406)449-6657

Email: mac@montana-chuches.net

Website: http://montana-churches.net

Media Contact, Administator: Pam Shelden

Exec. Dir., Administrator, Pam Shelden (Lutheran)

Pres., Rev. Dan Krebill (Presbyterian)

Vice-Pres: Pres. Elect, Rev. Peter Shober (United Church of Christ)

Sec., Laurie Croghan (Roman Catholic)

Treas., Judy Reel (Presbyterian)

Other: Judicatory Exec Rep., Rev Su DeBree (United Methodist)

Major Activities: Montana Abolition Coalition, Montana National Guard Yellow Ribbon Program, The Tributary Fund - Greening Our Faith, Montana State HHS Tobacco Prevention Program, Warm Springs Chapel Project Montana State Prison Chaplain Program, Montana Organizing Project (labor, community, faith collaboration on issues for middle & low income families), Christian Ecumenism Projects

NEBRASKA

Interchurch Ministries of Nebraska*

215 Centennial Mall S., Suite 300, Lincoln, NE 68508-1810, Tel. (402)476-3391 Fax (402)416-9310
Email: im50427@windstream.net
Website: www.interchurchministries.org
Media Contact, Exec., Ms. Marilyn P. Mecham
Pres., Ms. Susan Gilles
Treas., Rev. Dr. Kenneth W. Moore
Exec., Ms. Marilyn Mecham
Adm. Asst., Sharon K. Kalcik
Major Activities: Indian Ministry; Disaster Response; Rural Response Hotline; Health Ministry; Peace with Justice; Angel Connection; Domestic Violence Resources; Annual Ecumenical Legislative Briefing Day; Social Ministries; Ministry to Returning Military Persons and their Families; Suicide Prevention Program

Lincoln Interfaith Council

140 S. 27th St., Ste. B, Lincoln, NE 68510-1301, Tel. (402)474-3017 Fax (402)475-3262
Email: mail@lincolninterfaith.org
Website: www.lincolninterfaith.org
Media Contact, Doug Boyd
Interim Coordinator, Kim Beyer Nelson
Pres., Sue Howe
Vice-Pres., Gene Crump
Sec., Stephanie Dohner
Treas.,Terri Lee
Major Activities: MLK, Jr. Observance; Week of Prayer Christian Unity; Festival of Faith & Culture; Holocaust Memorial Observance; Citizens Against Racism & Discrimination; Community organization; Multi-Faith & Multi-Cultural Training; New Clergy Orientation; Directory of Clergy, Congregations & Religious Resources; Multi-Faith Planning Calendar Publication

NEW HAMPSHIRE

New Hampshire Council of Churches*

140 Sheep Davis Road, Ste. 1, Pembroke, NH 03275, Tel. (603)224-1352 Fax (603)224-9161
Email: churches@nhchurches.org
Website: www.nhchurches.org
Media Contact, Exec. Dir., David Lamarre-Vincent, P.O. Box 1087, Concord, NH 03302-1087, Tel. (603)224-1352 Fax (603)224-9161, Email david@nhchurches.org

Pres., The Rev. Susan Ackley, Concord, NH 03302
Treas., Mr. Thomas Madson
Major Activities: Statewide Ecumenical Work For Christian Unity, Interfaith Understanding, and Social Justice

NEW JERSEY

Bergen County Council of Churches

457 Division Ave., Carlstadt, NJ 07072, Tel. (201) 438-5526 Fax (201)438-3161
Email: bergencouncilofchurches@yahoo.com
Website: www.bergenccc.org
Media Contact, Pres., Rev. Dr. Stephen T. Giordano, Clinton Avenue Reformed Church, 457 Division Ave., Carlstadt, NJ 07072, Tel. (201)438-5526 Fax (201)438-3161
Pres., Donald M. Pitches
Major Activities: Ecumenical and Religious Institute; Brotherhood-Sisterhood Breakfast; Center for Food Action; Homeless Aid; Operation Santa Claus; Aging Services; Boy & Girl Scouts; Easter Dawn Services; Music; Youth; Ecumenical Representation; Support of Chaplains in Jails & Hospitals; Faith & Values Online project www.njfaithandvalues.org; Welfare into Workplace

Ecclesia

700 West State St., Trenton, NJ 08618, Tel. (609) 394-9229 Fax (609)394-8231
Email: team@teamtrenton.org
Media Contact, Sec., Mrs. Tina Swan
Pres., Rev. Joseph P. Ravenell
Campus Chaplains- Rev. Nancy Schulter; Rev. Robert Wittin, Rev. Richard Kocses
Major Activities: Racial Justice; Children & Youth Ministries; Advocacy; CROP Walk; Ecumenical Worship; Hospital Chaplaincy; Church Women United; Campus Chaplaincy; Congregational Empowerment; Prison Chaplaincy; Substance Abuse Ministry Training

Metropolitan Ecumenical Ministry

525 Orange St., Newark, NJ 07107, Tel. (973)485-8100 Fax (973)485-1165
Media Contact, Consultant, Rev. M. L. Emory
Exec. Dir., C. Stephen Jones
Major Activities: Community Advocacy (education, housing, environment); Church Mission Assistance; Community and Clergy Leadership Development; Economic Development; Affordable Housing

Metropolitan Ecumenical Ministry Community Development Corp.

525 Orange St., Newark, NJ 07107, Tel. Fax (201)481-7883
Email: memcdc@juno.com
Exec. Dir., Jacqueline Jones
Major Activities: Housing Development; Neighborhood Revitalization; Commercial-Small Business Development; Economic Development; Community Development; Credit

255

Union; Home Ownership Counseling; Credit Repair; Mortgage Approval; Technical Assitance To Congregations

New Jersey Council of Churches*
176 W. State St., Trenton, NJ 08608, Tel. (609) 396-9546 Fax (609)396-7646
Media Contact, Public Policy Dir., Joan Diefenbach, Esq.
Pres., Rev. Jack Johnson
Sec., Beverly McNally
Treas., Marge Christie
Major Activities: Racial Justice; Children's Issues; Theological Unity; Ethics Public Forums; Advocacy; Economic Justice

NEW MEXICO

Faith Community Assistance Center
P.O. Box 15517, Santa Fe, NM 87592, Tel. (505) 438-4782 Fax (505)473-5637
Media Contact, Barbara A. Robinson
Major Activities: Faith Community Assistance Center; providing emergency assistance to the poor; Interfaith Dialogues-Celebrations-Visitations; Peace Projects; Understanding Hispanic Heritage; Newsletter

New Mexico Conference of Churches*
336 N Camino del Pueblo, P O Box 606, Bernalillo, NM 87004-0606, Tel. (505)867-2956 Fax (505)867-6379
Email: nmcc@nmchurches.org
Website: www.nmchurches.org
Media Contact, Exec. Dir., Rev. Donna McNiel
Pres., Dr. Robert S. Turner
Treas., Robert Sandoval
Exec. Dir., Rev. Dr. Donna McNiel
Major Activities: Affordable Housing; Social Justice Coalitions; Spiritual Life & Ministries

NEW YORK

Brooklyn Council of Churches
125 Ft. Greene Place, Brooklyn, NY 11217, Tel. (718)625-5851 Fax (718)522-1231
Media Contact, Dir., Charles Henze
Program Dir., Charles Henze (Deacon)
Pres., The Rev. James H. Eggleston
Treas., The Rev. Charles H. Straut , Jr.
Major Activities: Education Workshops; Food Pantries; Hospital and Nursing Home Chaplaincy; Church Women United; Legislative Concerns; Directory of Churches; Ecumenical Dialogue

Broome County Council of Churches, Inc.
William H. Stanton Center, 3 Otseningo St., Binghamton, NY 13903, Tel. (607)724-9130 Fax (607)724-9148
Email: mfrick@broomecouncil.net
Website: www.broomecouncil.net
Media Contact, Rev. Dr. Murray Frick

Exec. Dir., Rev. Dr. Murray Frick
Exec. Asst., Brigitte Stella
Hospital Chaplains, Betty Pomeroy; Rev. David Rockwell
Jail Chaplain, Rev. Cris Mogenson
Aging Ministry Coord., Linda McColgin
CHOW Prog. Coord., Wendy Primavera
Pres., Dr. Thomas Kelly
Treas., Rey Hull
Caregiver Program Coord., Joanne Kays
Community and Donor Relations, Dir., Dr. Murray Frick
Major Activities: Hospital and Jail Chaplains; Youth and Aging Ministries; Broome Bounty (Food Rescue Program); Emergency Hunger & Advocacy Program; Faith & Family Values; Ecumenical Worship and Fellowship; Media; Community Affairs; Peace with Justice; Day by Day Marriage Prep Program; Interfaith Coalition; Interfaith Volunteer Caregiver Program

Capital Area Council of Churches, Inc.
646 State St., Albany, NY 12203-1217, Tel. (518) 462-5450 Fax (518)462-5450
Email: CapAreaCC@aol.com
Website: www.CapAreaCC.org
Media Contact, Admin. Director, Kitt Jackson
Exec. Dir., the Rev. Dr. George Brennan, D. Min.
Pres.: Board of Dir., Deb Riitano (RC)
Sec., Board Sec., Nancy Scholes (PCUSA)
Treas., Board Treas., William B. Hedberg (Episcopalian)
Major Activities: Campus Ministry, CROP Hunger Walk, Emergency Homeless Shelter, Christian Ecumenism, Martin Luther King, Jr. Memorial Service & Scholarship Program, Court & Jail Ministry, Ecumenical Witnesses at Baptism Program

Capital Region Ecumenical Organization (CREO)
102 Arrow Wood Place, Malta, NY 12020, Tel. (518)729-0278 Fax (518)382-7505
Email: mishamarvel@gmail.com
Website: www.albanypresbytery.org/about_creo.html
Media Contact, Coord., Misha Marvel
Pres. Ian Leet (Reformed Church in America)
Vice-Pres: Barbara DiTommaso (Roman Catholic)
Sec., Kitt Jackson (Reformed Church in America)
Treas., Kay Victorson (Evangelical Lutheran Church in America)
Other: The Rev. Cass Shaw (Presbyterian Church USA)
Other: The Rev. Marian Shearer (United Church of Christ)
Other: The Most Rev. Howard Hubbard (Roman Catholic)
Major Activities: Judicatory Executives Forum, Ecumenical Retreats and Pentecost Events, Ecumenical Connections and Relationship Building, One Table - quarterly resource publicizing advocacy issues and ecumenical

opportunities, Promote Ecumenical Mission Trips, Issue information sharing

Chautaugua County Rural Ministry
127 Central Ave., P.O. Box 362, Dunkirk, NY 14048, Tel. (716)366-1787 Fax (716)366-1787
Email: ccrm@netsync.net
Website: www.ccrm.netsync.net
Exec. Dir., Kathleen Peterson
Major Activities: Chautaugua County Food Bank; Collection-Distribution of Furniture, Clothing, and Appliances; Homeless Services; Advocacy for the Poor; Soup Kitchen; Emergency Food Pantry; Thrift Store

Concerned Ecumenical Ministry to the Upper West Side
286 Lafayette Ave., Buffalo, NY 14213, Tel. (716) 882-2442 Fax (716)882-2477
Email: information@cembuffalo.org
Website: www.cembuffalo.org
Media Contact, Exec. Dir., The Rev. Catherine Rieley-Goddard
Pres., Mr. Peter Hogan
Major Activities: Community Center Serving Youth, Families, Seniors and the Hungry

Cortland County Council of Churches, Inc.
7 Calvert St., Cortland, NY 13045, Tel. (607)753-1002 Fax (607)758-8780
Email: cortlandchurches@gmail.com
Media Contact, Office Mgr., Joy Niswender
Exec. Dir., The Rev. Donald M. Wilcox
Major Activities: College Campus Ministry; Hospital Chaplaincy; Nursing Home Ministry; Newspaper Column; Interfaith Relationships; Hunger Relief; CWS; Crop Walk; Leadership Education; Community Issues; Mental Health Chaplaincy; Grief Support; Jail Ministry

Council of Churches of Chemung County, Inc.
1009 Maple Ave., Elmira, NY 14904, Tel. (607) 733-4374 Fax (607)734-2294
Email: chemungcouncilchurches@yahoo.com
Media Contact, Exec. Dir., Joan Geldmacher, Tel. (607)734-7622
Exec. Dir., Joan Geldmacher
Pres., Rev. Horace Stoddard, 23 AutumnView, NY 14871
Major Activities: CWS Collection/Health Kits etc.; ANNUAL CROP WALK; Radio "Tower of Faith" Easter Dawn Service; Communications Network (produce and distribute Church Directories; Representation on community boards and agencies; Ecumenical Services; Interfaith Coalition; Taskforce on Children & Families; Compeer and Interfaith Hospitality Center (at the Prison).

Council of Churches of the City of New York
475 Riverside Dr., Rm. 727, New York, NY 10115, Tel. (212)870-1020 Fax (212)870-1025

Email: cccny@cccny.net
Website: www.cccny.net
Media Contact, Exec. Dir., Rev. Jimmy Seong G. Lim
Exec. Dir., Rev. Jimmy Seong G. Lim
Pres., The Rev. A. R. Bernard, Sr.
1st Vice-Pres., Mr. G. Morris Gurley, Esq.
2nd Vice-Pres., The Rev. Dr. Young Choon Chang
3rd Vice-Pres., Rev. Dr. Adolfo Carrion, Sr.
Sec., The Rev. N. J. "Skip" L'Heureux
Treas., The Rev. Jon Norton
Major Activities: Clergy Training, Radio & TV; Pastoral Care; Christ for the World Chapel, Kennedy International Airport; Coordination and Strategic Planning; Interfaith Coordinator, Religious Conferences; Interfaith Commission of Religious Leaders; Referral & Advocacy; Youth Development; Directory of Churches and Database Available

Dutchess County Interfaith Council, Inc.
9 Vassar St., Poughkeepsie, NY 12601, Tel. (845) 471-7333 Fax (845)471-5253
Email: dic@bestweb.net
Website: www.dutchessinterfaithcouncil.org
Media Contact, Exec. Dir., Edward Koziol
Exec. Dir., Edward Koziol
Pres., Rabbi Paul Golumb
Treas., Amy Harding King
Major Activities: CROP Hunger Walk; Interfaith Music Festival; Public Worship Events; Interfaith Story Circles; Oil Purchase Group; Tour Of Houses Of Worship; Weekly Radio Program; Racial Unity Work; Poverty Forums

The Faith In Action Network of Rochester, NY
2 Riverside St., Rochester, NY 14613-1222, Tel. (585)254-2570 Fax (585)254-6551
Email: grcc1@frontiernet.net
Website: www.grcc.org
Media Contact, Executive Director, Marie E. Gibson
Dr. Marvin K. Mich, President
Robert Crystal, VP for Organization
Rev. William Wilkinson, VP for Social Justice Ministry
Tim Calkins, Secretary
Kenneth Anderson, Treasurer
Elizabeth LeValley SSJ, Officer-at-Large
Rev. Gordon V. Webster, Officer-at-Large
Major Activities: Faith-based information-resources for the greater Rochester area; Social Justice Ministry; Anti-Racism and Peace initiatives; Ecumenical Worship; Interfaith Health Care Coalition; Commission on Christian Jewish Relations, Commission on Christian Muslim Relations, Christian Hindu Dialogue, Faith in Action Annual Celebration; Rochester Supplemental Burial Fund, Annual Community Walk: Stations of the Cross.

FOCUS Churches of Albany, Inc.
275 State Street, Albany, NY 12110, Tel. (518)443-0460 Fax (518)443-0461

257

Email: info@focuschurches.net
Website: www.focuschurches.net
Media Contact, Exec. Dir., Debra Jameson
Exec. Dir., Debra Jameson (Reformed)
Vice-Pres., Allan Tedrow (Presbyterian USA)
Sec., Nancy Horan (American Baptist)
Treas., Richard Moneymaker (United Methodist)
Pres., Irving Smith Jr., (Presbyterian USA)
Major Activities: Pantry - feeding program, interfaith direct service; Soup Kitchen - feeding program, interfaith direct service; Common Worship - Christian Ecumenism; Legislative Advocacy; Computers for Kids Intensive - direct service; School Supply Project - direct service; Educational Forums - Christian and interfaith relations.

Genesee County Churches United, Inc.
P.O. Box 547, Batavia, NY 14021, Tel. (716)343-6763
Media Contact, Pres.,Captain Leonard Boynton, Salvation Army, 529 East Main St., Batavia, NY 14020, Tel. (716)343-6284
Pres., James Woodruff
Exec. Sec., Cheryl Talone
Chaplain, The Rev. Peter Miller
Major Activities: Jail Ministry; Food Pantries; Serve Needy Families; Radio Ministry; Pulpit Exchange; Community Thanksgiving; Ecumenical Services at County Fair

Genesee-Orleans Ministry of Concern
Arnold Gregory Memorial Complex, Suite 271
243 South Main St., Albion, NY 14411, Tel. (585) 589-9210 Fax (585)589-9617
Email: director@ministryofconcern.org
Website: www.ministryofconcern.org
Media Contact, Exec. Dir., Lisa Ireland
Exec. Dir., Lisa Ireland
Pres., John W. Cebula, Esq.
Vice Pres., Rev. Joseph Fifagrowicz
Sec., Jane Balbick
Treas., Mary Grace Demarse
Major Activities: Advocacy Services for the Disadvantaged, Homeless, Ill, Incarcerated and Victims of Family Violence; Emergency Food, Shelter, Utilities, Medicines, Just Friends (a mentoring program for children), Parenting Program, Furniture Program.

InterFaith Works of Central New York
3049 E. Genesee St., Syracuse, NY 13224, Tel. (315)449-3552 Fax (315)449-3103
Email: mbowles@interfaithworkscny.org
Website: www.interfaithworkscny.org
Media Contact, Dir. of Advancement, Ms. Gloria Heffernan
Executive Dir., Ms. Beth A. Broadway
Pres., Ms. Millicent Davis
CFO, John Ashby
Director for Resource Development, Ms. Gloria Heffernan
Spiritual Care Program Director, The Rev. Roberta Yackel

Center for New Americans, Dir., Ms. Helen Malina
Senior Companion Prog., Dir., Mr. Larry Crinnin
InterFaith Housing Prog., Dir., Mr. Michael Collins
Community Wide Dialogue on Racism, Mr. Derrick Dorsey
Interfaith Education and Engagement, Dir., Ms. Beth Broadway
InterFaith Works News, Ed., Ms. Gloria Heffernan
Major Activities: Pastoral Ministries; Community Ministries; Interrreligious and Ecumenical Relations; Diversity Education; Worship; Community Advocacy and Planning

The Long Island Council of Churches
1644 Denton Green, Hempstead, NY 11550, Tel. (516)565-0290 Fax (516)565-0291
Email: licc@optonline.net
Website: www.liccny.org
Media Contact, Exec. Dir., Thomas W. Goodhue
Exec. Dir., Rev. Thomas W. Goodhue
Head Chaplain, Rev. Nancy Schaffer
Hempstead Office Manager, Yolanda Murray, Tel: (516) 565-0290
Riverhead Office Manager Carolyn Gumbs, Tel: (631)727-2210
Major Activities: Pastoral Care in Jails; Emergency Food; Family Support & Advocacy; Church World Service; Multifaith Education; Financial Education; Clergy-Laity Training; Newsletter; Church Directory

Network of Religious Communities
1272 Delaware Ave., Buffalo, NY 14209-2496, Tel. (716)882-4793 Fax (716)882-3797
Email: nrc@religiousnet.org
Website: www.ReligiousNet.org
Media Contact, Exec. Dir., CEO, Rev. Dr. G. Stanford Bratton
Exec. Dir. & CEO, The Rev. Dr. G. Stanford Bratton
Associate Executive., The Rev. Francis X. Mazur (Ecumenical Officer, Diocese of Buffalo-Roman Catholic)
President, Dr. Vijay Chakravarthy, Hindu Cultural Society,Western New York
Immediate Past Co-Presidents, Rev. Dr. Kenneth Neal, WNY Churches in Covenant and Rev. Mary Masters, Unity Church of Practical Christianity
Vice-Pres. For Outreach, Deacon James Anderson, National Baptist
Vice-Pres. For Administration, Rev. Msgr. Paul A. Litwin, Chancellor, Diocese of Buffalo
Vice-Pres. For Finance, Dr. Nasir Khan, Ahmadiyya Muslim Community
Vice-Pres. For Program, Dr. Douglas Bunker, Church of Jesus Christ of Latter Day Saints
Secretary, Mr. Raymond Herman, Westminster Presbyterian Church
Treasurer, Mr Dennis Smith, Spiritual Assembly of Baha'is of Amherst
Chpsn., Interreligious Concerns, Dr. Othman Shibly, Islamic Society of the Niagara Frontier

Chpsn., Membership, The Rev. Jeff Carter, Ephesis Ministries (Pentecostal)

Chpsn., Christian Concerns, The Rev. Dr Kenneth Neal, WNY Churches in Covenant (Disciples/UCC)

Chpsn., Communications, Ms. Susan Dayton, Church of Jesus Christ of Latter Day Saints

Chpsn., Riefler Enablement Fund, Rev. Dr. Robert L Graham, Ruling Elder, AME Zion Churches

Chpsn., Public Issues, Ms Judy Metzger, Episcopal Diocese of WNY

Chpsn., Nominating Committee, Ms Marlene Glickman, Temple Beth Am

President., Church Women United, Holy Angels Roman Catholic Church

STAFF (Other than Executive Directors)

Financial/office administrator, Ms. Bonnie Jehle

Church Women United Coordinator, Ms. Sally Giordano

Food For All, Coordinator, Ms. Kelly Kowalski

Nutrition Outreach, Marlyn Moore

Major Activities: Hunger Advocacy, Food Distribution, Food Stamp Promotion and coordination, Summer Food Program for Children, Spirituality and End of Life Program for University at Buffalo Medical Students, Spirituality and Health Initiative with Niagara University Department of Nursing, Diabetes Initiative, Radio-TV Production and Broadcast (3 TV and 2 weekly radio Programs), Indigenous Women's Initiatives, Church Women United, Festivals of Faiths, Community Development, Yom Hashoah Commemoration Service, Aids Memorial Service, CROP Walks, Interfaith Thanksgiving Service, Legal action against opening of Casino in Buffalo and Ecumenical and Interreligious Relations and Celebrations.

New York State Council of Churches, Inc.*

1580 Central Ave, Albany, NY 12205, Tel. (518)436-9319 Fax (518)427-6705

Email: nyscoc@aol.com

Website: www.nyscoc.org

Media Contact, Ms. Mary Lu Bowen

Pres., Bishop Marie C. Jerge

Vice Pres., The Rev. Dr. William Levering

Vice Pres., The Rev. Stuart Buisch

Corp. Sec., The Rev. Dr. Jon Norton

Treas., The Rev. Dr. John Hiemstra

Convener of Collegium, Heather Cook

STAFF:

Coordinator of Chaplaincy Services, Ms. Damaris McGuire

Public Policy and Communications Consultant, The Rev. Daniel Hahn

Admin. Asst., Karen Lapierre

Book Keeper, Charlene Schaffer

Major Activities: State Chaplaincy; Public Policy Advocacy in the following areas; Anti-Racism; Campaign Reform; Criminal Justice System Reform; Disability; Economic-Social Justice; Environmental; Health care; Homelessness-Shelter; Hunger-Food; Immigrant Issues; Public Education; Rural Issues; Substance Abuse; Violence; Women's Issues; Peace

The Niagara Council of Churches Inc.

St. Paul UMC, 723 Seventh St., Niagara Falls, NY 14301, Tel. (716)285-7505

Media Contact, Pres., Nessie S. Bloomquist, 7120 Laur Rd., Niagara Falls, NY 14304, Tel. (716)297-0698 Fax (716)298-1193

Exec. Dir., Ruby Babb

Pres., Nessie S. Bloomquist

Treas., Shirley Bathurst

Trustees Chpsn., The Rev. Vincent Mattoni, 834 19th St., Niagara Falls, NY 14304

Major Activities: Ecumenical Worship; Bible Study; Christian Ed. & Social Concerns; Church Women United; Evangelism & Mission; Institutional Min. Youth Activities; Hymn Festival; Week of Prayer for Christian Unity; CWS Projects; Audio-Visual Library; UNICEF; Food Pantries and Kitchens; Community Missions, Inc.; Political Refugees; Eco-Justice Task Force; Migrant-Rural Ministries; Interfaith Coalition on Energy

Queens Federation of Churches

86-17 105th St., Richmond Hill, NY 11418-1597, Tel. (718)847-6764 Fax (718)847-7392

Email: info@queenschurches.org

Website: www.queenschurches.org

Media Contact, The Rev. N. J. L'Heureux, Jr.

Exec. Dir., The Rev. N. J. L'Heureux, Jr.

Pres., Edward Middendorf

Treas., Annie Lee Phillips

Major Activities: Queens Interfaith Hunger Network—Emergency Food Service; Interfaith Campus Ministry; Scouting & Youth Ministry; Christian Education Workshops; Planning and Strategy; Church Women United; Community Consultations; Seminars for Church Leaders; Online Directory of Congregations; Christian Relations (Prot-RC); Chaplaincies; Public Policy Issues; N.Y.S. Interfaith Commission on Landmarking of Religious Property; "The Nexus of Queens" (online, weekly newspaper); Religious Liberty Issues

Rural Migrant Ministry

P.O. Box 4757, Poughkeepsie, NY 12602, Tel. (845)485-8627 Fax (845)485-1963

Email: hope@ruralmigrantministry.org

Website: ruralmigrantministry.org

Media Contact, Exec. Dir., Rev. Richard Witt

Exec. Dir., The Rev. Richard Witt

Pres., Melinda Trotti

Major Activities: Serving the Rural Poor and Migrants Through a Ministry of Advocacy & Empowerment; Youth Program; Latino Committee; Organization and Advocacy with and for Rural Poor and Migrant Farm Workers

Schenectady Inner City Ministry

930 Albany St., Schenectady, NY 12307-1514, Tel. (518)374-2683 Fax (518)382-1871
Email: INFORMATION@SICM.US
Website: www.sicm.us
Media Contact, Janet Mattis
Urban Agent, Rev. Phillip N. Grigsby
Business Manager, Barbara Bieniek
Emergency Food, Gail Van Vallenburgh
Pres., Peter Notch
Damien Center, Daniel Butterworth
Summer Food, Crystal Hamelink
Housing Task Force, Rev. Phil Grigsby
Spiritually Sound and Physically Fit, Rev. Phillip Grugsby
Safe Parks and Eligible Playgrounds, Rev. Dr. Van I. W. Stuart
Healthy Homes and Healthy People, Nancy Peterson
Major Activities: Food Security; Advocacy; Housing; Neighborhood and Economic Issues; Ecumenical Worship and Fellowship; Community Research; Education in Congregations on Faith Responses to Social Concerns; Legislative Advocacy; CROP Walk; HIV-AIDS Ministry; Summer Lunch for Youth; Study Circles Initiative on Embracing Diversity; Community Crisis Nework; Housing Services and Advocacy; Youth Initiative; After-School Program; Committee for Social Justice; Theological Center; Computer for Kids; Faith Based Nutrition and Wellness; Environmental Justice

Southeast Ecumenical Ministry

25 Westminster Rd., Rochester, NY 14607, Tel. (585)271-5350 Fax (585)271-8526
Email: sem@frontiernet.net
Media Contact, Laurie Jenkins
Dir., Laurie Jenkins
Pres., Ronald K. Fox
Major Activities: Transportation of Elderly & Disabled; Emergency Food Cupboard for Case Managers to access for their clients; Supplemental Nutrition Program for seniors; Community Health and Pharmacy Partnership (CHAPP).

Staten Island Council of Churches

2187 Victory Blvd., Staten Island, NY 10314, Tel. (718)761-6782
Email: sicoc@verizon.net
Media Contact, Pres., Rev. Virginia Kaada, 2187 Victory Blvd., Staten Island, NY 10314, Tel. (718)761-6782
Pres., The Rev. Virginia Kaada
Exec. Sec., Rebekah A. Ellis
Major Activities: Congregational Support & Outreach; Education & Pastoral Care; Ecumenical & Interfaith Witness; Social Witness

Troy Area United Ministries

392 Second St., Troy, NY 12180, Tel. (518)274-5920 Fax (518)271-1909

Email: info@TAUM.org
Website: www.taum.org
Media Contact, Exec. Dir., Rev. Donna Elia
Pres., Rev. Arthur Hagy Jr.
Chaplain, R.P.I. And Russel Sage, Rev. Beth Illingworth
Damien Center, Dir., Terri Conhue
Furniture Program, Dir., Michael Barrett
Major Activities: College Ministry; CROP Walk; Homeless and Housing Concerns; Community Worship Celebrations; Racial Relations; Furniture Program; Damien Center of Troy Hospitality for persons with HIV-AIDS; Computer Ministries; Youth Ministry

Wainwright House

260 Stuyvesant Ave., Rye, NY 10580, Tel. (914)967-6080 Fax (914)967-6114
Email: frandavies@wainwright.org
Website: www.wainwright.org
Media Contact, Exec. Dir., Fran Davies
Exec. Dir., Fran Davies
Pres., Robert Laughlin
Vice-Pres., Michael Standen
Major Activities: Educational Programs, Retreat and Conference Center; Intellectual, Psychological, Physical and Spiritual Growth; Healing and Health

NORTH CAROLINA

Asheville-Buncombe Community Christian Ministry (ABCCM)

30 Cumberland Ave., Asheville, NC 28801, Tel. (828)259-5300 Fax (828)259-5923
Email: srogers@abccm.org
Website: www.abccm.org
Media Contact, Exec. Dir., Rev. Scott Rogers, Fax (828)259-5323
Exec. Dir., The Rev. Scott Rogers
Pres., Stephen Williamson
Major Activities: Crisis Ministry; Jail-Prison Ministry; Shelter Ministry; Medical Ministry

Greensboro Urban Ministry

305 West Lee St., Greensboro, NC 27406, Tel. (910)271-5959 Fax (910)271-5920
Email: Guministry@aol.com
Website: www.greensboro.com/gum
Media Contact, Exec. Dir., Rev. Mike Aiken
Exec. Dir., The Rev. Mike Aiken
Major Activities: Emergency Financial Assistance; Emergency Housing; Hunger Relief; Inter-Faith and Inter-Racial Understanding; Justice Ministry; Chaplaincy with the Poor

North Carolina Council of Churches*

27 Horne St., Raleigh, NC 27607, Tel. (919)828-6501 Fax (919)828-9697
Email: nccofc@nccouncilofchurches.org
Website: www.nccouncilofchurches.org
Media Contact, Comm. Assoc., Aleta Payne
Exec. Dir., J. George Reed
Program Associate, Chris Liu-Beers

Program Associate for Peace, David LaMotte
Program Associate for Administration, Rose Gurkin
NC Interfaith Power & Light Director [vacant]
Communications Associate, Aleta Payne
Program Associate for Health, Willona Stallings
Program Associate for Christian Unity, Rollin Russell
Pres., The Rev. Jean Rodenbough
Treas., The Rev. Owen Peeler
Major Activities: Health Care Justice; Health Education and Promotion; Christian Unity; Legislative Program; Farmworker Ministry; Rural Crisis; Immigration; Racial and Ethnic Justice; Climate Change; Public Education; Economic Justice; Peace

NORTH DAKOTA

North Dakota Conference of Churches*
9195 70th Avenue, SE, Ashley, ND 58413-9600, Tel. (701)647-2063
Email: exe_sec.ndcc@yahoo.com
Website: ndconference.org
Media Contact, Exec. Sec., Renee Gopal
Pres., Bishop Paul Zipfel
Vice Pres. I, Dr. Wade Schemmel
Vice Pres. II, Grace Wisthoff
Treas., The Rev. Michael Hicken
Secretary, Bishop Duane Danielson
Major Activities: Rural Life Ministry; Faith and Order; North Dakota 101; Victims & Offenders Ministry; Rural Life Convocation; Restorative Justice

OHIO

Akron Area Association of Churches
800 East Market Street, Akron, OH 44305-2424, Tel. (330)535-3112 Fax (330)374-5041
Email: akronchurches@earthlink.net
Website: www.triple-ac.org
Media Contact, Exec. Dir., Chloe Ann Kriska
Bd. of Trustees, Pres., Rev. Dr. J. Wayman Butts
Vice-Pres., The Rev. Mark Frey
Sec., Dale Kline
Treas., Ms. Sherrie Petrochuk
Major Activities: Messiah Sing; Interfaith Council; Newsletters; Resource Center; Community Worship; Training of Local Church Leadership; Radio Programs; Clergy and Lay Fellowship Luncheons; Neighborhood Development; Community Outreach; Church Interracial Partnerships; Pastor Peer Group Program; Advocacy, Social Justice

Alliance of Churches
470 E. Broadway, Alliance, OH 44601, Tel. (330)821-6648 Fax (330)821-7288
Email: dcarter@fbcalliance.org
Media Contact, Betty Rush
Pres., Rev. Peggy Hawkins
Treas., Betty Rush
Major Activities: Christian Education; Community Relations & Service; Ecumenical Worship;

Community Ministry; Peacemaking; Medical Transportation for Anyone Needing It; Emergency Financial Assistance

Churchpeople for Change and Reconciliation
Box 488, Lima, OH 45802-0488, Tel. (419)224-2086 Fax (419)224-2086
Media Contact, Exec. Dir., The Rev. Darwin Ralston
Exec. Dir., The Rev. Darwin Ralston
Major Activities: Developing Agencies for Minorities, Poor, Alienated and Despairing; especially Our Daily Bread Soup Kitchen

Council of Christian Communions of Greater Cincinnati
7030 Reading Road
Suite 642, Cincinnati, OH 45237, Tel. (513)351-6789 Fax (513)458-2252
Email: joellengrady@zoomtown.com
Website: www.cccgc.org
Media Contact, Exec. Dir., Joellen W. Grady
Exec. Dir., Joellen W. Grady
Justice Chaplaincy, Assoc. Dir., Rev. Jack Marsh
Educ., Assoc., Lillie D. Bibb
Pres., Rev. Damon Lynch III
Major Activities: Christian Unity & Interfaith Cooperation; Justice Chaplaincies; Police-Clergy Team; Adult and Juvenile Jail Chaplains; Religious Education

Greater Dayton Christian Connections
915 Salem Avenue, Dayton, OH 45406, Tel. (937) 222-4322 Fax (937)227-9407
Email: gdcc@Christianconnections.org
Website: www.christianconnections.org
Media Contact, Exec. Dir., Rev. Darryl Fairchild
Exec. Dir., Rev. Darryl Fairchild
Major Activities: Ecumenical and Interfaith Dialogue; Peace Making; Environmental Justice; Racial Reconciliation; Pastoral Leadership Resources; Ministry Recruitment and Placement; Communication

Mahoning Valley Association of Churches
2214 Mahoning Avenue, Youngstown, OH 44509, Tel. (330)788-5914
Email: mvacchurch@gmail.com
Website: mvaconline.org
Media Contact, Exec. Dir., Elsie L. Dursi
Exec. Dir., Elsie L. Dursi
Pres., Rev. Bob Bonnot
Treasurer Sr Isabel Rudge
Sec., Monica Spelich
Major Activities: Communications; Christian Education; Ecumenism; Social Action; Advocacy; Initiating Inter Faith Youth Core chapter at Youngstown State University, the Leader is Mr. Cary Dabney.

Metropolitan Area Church Council
760 E. Broad St., Columbus, OH 43205, Tel. (614)461-7103 Fax (614)280-0352

261

Email: church_council@yahoo.com
Media Contact, Exec. Dir., Alvin Hadley
President: The Rev. Melvin Richardson
Vice-Pres.: The Rev. Ken Coy
Secretary: Ms. Margaret Stansbery
Treasurer: Mr. Brian Shaffer
Exec. Dir., Alvin Hadley
Major Activities: Newspaper; Published nine times annually; Annual Living Faiths Awards; Quarterly Racial unity Services; Clergy Hospital Indentification Badges; Community Computer Center; Social Concerns relating to human needs in our community; Older Adult ministries; Collaborations to facilitate unity among religious denominations.

Metropolitan Area Religious Coalition of Cincinnati

632 Vine Street, Suite 606, Cincinnati, OH 45202-2423, Tel. (513)721-4843 Fax (513)721-4891
Email: marcc@fuse.net
Website: www.marcconline.com
Media Contact, Dir., vacant
Pres., Mr. Adam Hall
Dir., Margaret A. Fox
Major Activities: Local social policy decisions chosen annually

Ohio Council of Churches*

6230 Busch Blvd., Ste 430, Columbus, OH 43229-1879, Tel. (614)885-9590 Fax (614)885-6097
Email: rtollefson@ohcouncilchs.org
Website: www.ohcouncilchs.org
Media Contact, Executive Director, Rebecca J. Tollefson
Exec. Dir., Rev. Rebecca J. Tollefson (PCUSA)
Pres. The Rev. William F. Schnell, Ohio Fellowship of Community Churches (ICCC)
Vice-Pres: The Rev. Dr. Bill Edwards, CC(DC)
Sec., The Rev. Deborah Oskins, Church of the Brethren, Southern Ohio District
Treas., Mr. Steve Salt, Christian Science Committee on Publication
Major Activities: Faith and Order Commission, Justice and Advocacy Commission, Ohio Ministries Convocation; Public Policy, Ohio Interfaith Power and Light

Pike County Outreach Council

107-9 West Second Street, Waverly, OH 45690, Tel. (740)941-4348
Email: pikecountyoutreachcouncil@yahoo.com
Website: www.pikecountyoutreach.com
Dir., Judy Dixon
Major Activities: Emergency Service Program; Self Help Groups; Homeless Shelter, Food Pantry

Toledo Area Ministries

444 Floyd St., Toledo, OH 43620, Tel. (419)242-7401 Fax (419)242-7404
Email: santhony@tamohio.org
Website: www.tamohio.org
Media Contact, Executive Director, Rev. Stephen D. Anthony

Major Activities: Ecumenical Relations; Interfaith Relations; Food Program; Housing Program; Social Action- Public Education; Urban Ministry; Youth Leadership; Elimination of Discrimination

Tuscarawas County Council for Church and Community

1458 5th St. NW, New Philadelphia, OH 44663, Tel. (330)343-6012 Fax (330)343-9845
Email: t4c66@neohio.twcbc.com
Website: www.tyeconline.net
Media Contact, Janet Downin
Exec. Dir., Janet Downin
Pres., Dr. Fran Halder
Treas., Ms. Terry Miller
Major Activities: Emergency Assistance, Abstinence Education,Youth Boosters

West Side Ecumenical Ministry

5209 Detroit Ave, Cleveland, OH 44102, Tel. (216)651-2037 Fax (216)651-4145
Email: jpeters@wsem.org
Website: www.wsem.org
Media Contact, Dir. of Marketing and Public Relations, Kami L. Marquardt
Pres., & CEO, Judith Peters
Chief Operation Officer, Adam Roth
Major Activities: WSEM is dedicated to serving urban low-income families by providing programs that encourage self-sufficiency. Three food pantries and outreach centers, a job-training program, early childhood, preschool, and school-age child care, crisis intervention, counseling, youth services, a theatre education program and a senior nutrition program are among the services available. WSEM serves more than 56,000 children, families, and individuals annually with a staffing of more than 300 employees and 3,200 volunteers.

OKLAHOMA

Oklahoma Conference of Churches*

301 Northwest 36th St., Oklahoma City, OK 73118, Tel. (405)525-2928 Fax (405)525-2636
Email: wtabbernee@okchurches.org
Website: www.okchurches.org
Media Contact, The Rev. Dr. William Tabbernee, Email: joanne.kurklin@okchurches.org
Exec. Dir., The Rev. Dr. William Tabbernee
Pres., The Rev. Dr. Rockford Johnson
Major Activities: Christian Unity Issues; Community Building Among Members; Rural Community Care; Children's Advocacy; Day at the Legislature; Impact; Criminal Justice; Hunger & Poverty; Legislative Advocacy; Aging; Women's Issues; Interfaith Coalition and Activities

Tulsa Metropolitan Ministry

221 S. Nogales, Tulsa, OK 74127, Tel. (918)582-3147 Fax (918)582-3159
Email: info@tumm.org
Website: www.TUMM.org

Media Contact, Exec. Dir., The Rev. Mark Gibbens-Rickman

Exec. Dir., The Rev. Mark Gibbens-Rickman

Pres., The Rev. Marlin Lavanhar

Treas., Virginia Katz

Major Activities: Religious Understanding; Legislative Issues; Christian Unity; Criminal and Justice Issues; Committee against Racism; Disability Awareness; Directory of Metropolitan Religious Community; Airport Interfaith Chapel; Native American Issues.

OREGON

Ecumenical Ministries of Oregon*

0245 S.W. Bancroft St., Ste. B, Portland, OR 97239, Tel. (503)221-1054 Fax (503)223-7007

Email: emo@emoregon.org

Website: www.emoregon.org

Media Contact, Dir. Of Development & Communications, Carla Starrett Bigg

Exec. Dir., David A. Leslie

Finance and Administrative Services, Dir., Kathie Titzler

Development & Communications, Carla Starrett Bigg

Community Ministries, Lowen Berman

Sponsors Organized to Assist Refugees, Vesna Vila

Russian Oregon Social Services, Yelena Hansen

Portland International Community School, Skip Adams

Public Policy Dir., Kevin Finney

Interfaith Network for Earth Concerns, Jenny Holmes

HIV Day Center, Lindsay Ross-Hunt

Shared Housing, Barbara Stone

Northeast Emergency Food Program, Howard Kenyon

President, The Rev. Aleida Jernigan

Major Activities: Ecumenical Ministries of Oregon is a statewide association of Christian denominations - including Protestant, Roman Catholic and Orthodox bodies - congregations, ecumenical organizations and interfaith partners working together to improve the lives of Oregonians through community ministry programs, ecumenical and interreligious dialogue, environmental ministry and public policy advocacy.

PENNSYLVANIA

Allegheny Valley Association of Churches

1913 Freeport Rd., Natrona Heights, PA 15065, Tel. (724)226-0606 Fax (724)226-3197

Email: avac@avaoc.org

Website: www.avaoc.org

Media Contact, Exec. Dir., Karen Snair

Exec. Dir., Karen Snair

Pres., The Rev. Dr. W. James Legge

1st Vice President: The Rev James Gascoine

2nd Vice President: Mrs. Darlene Benn

Secretary: The Rev. Stephen Smalley

Treasurer: Mrs. Libby Grimm

Major Activities: Ecumenical Services; Dial-a-Devotion; Walk for Hunger; Food Bank; Emergency Aid; Cross-on-the-Hill; AVAC Hospitality Network for Homeless Families; Senior Citizen Housing-Pine Ridge Heights Senior Complex, AVAC Chaplaincy Program; Summer Camp for Children, Case Management, Faith-in-Action

Anchor Point Counseling Ministry

802 McKnight Park Dr., Pittsburgh, PA 15237, Tel. (412)366-1300 Fax (412)366-1333

Email: nhym@nhymcc.org

Website: www.nhymcc.org

Media Contact, Exec. Dir., Rev. Ronald B. Barnes

Exec. Dir., Ronald B. Barnes

Major Activities: Elementary, Junior and Senior High School Individual and Family Counseling; Elementary Age Youth Early Intervention Counseling; Educational Programming for Churches and Schools; Youth Advocacy; Parent Education; Marital Counseling; Tutoring for Elementary, Junior and Senior High Students; Healthy Communities-Healthy Youth Training and workshops based on Search Institutes (out of Mineaplis, MN); 40 Assets

Christian Associates of Southwest Pennsylvania

204 37th St., Suite 201, Pittsburgh, PA 15201, Tel. (412)688-9070 Fax (412)688-9091

Email: info@casp.org

Website: www.casp.org

Media Contact, Dir. of Television Ministry, Monica Kao

Exec. Dir., Exec. Dir. Rev. Dr. Donald B. Green (Evangelcial Lutheran Church in America)

Pres. Chair of Council, Major Robert A. Reel (The Salvation Army)

Vice-Pres: Vice Chair of Council, Rev. Alan McLarty (Uunite Church of Christ)

Sec., Secretary of Council Rev. Wayne A. Yost (Presbyterian Church-USA)

Treas., President Baord of Delegates, Rev. Dr. Eric Brown (African Methodist Episcopal Church)

Major Activities: Jail Chaplaincy, Pre-release & post release jail inmate mentoring, Youth-incarceration, Theological Dialogue - Religious Education, Television Ministry, Christian Ecumenism, Interfaith Relations, Disaster Preparedness and Response

Christian Churches United of the Tri-County Area

413 South 19th St.

P.O. Box 60750, Harrisburg, PA 17106-0750, Tel. (717)230-9550 Fax (717)230-9554

Email: ccuhbg@aol.com

Website: www.ccuhbg.org

Media Contact, Exec. Dir., Jacqueline P. Rucker

Exec. Dir., Jacqueline P. Rucker

Pres., Rev. Dr. Thomas Johnston

Vice-Pres., Rev. Monica Dawkins-Smith

Sec., Alice Anne Schwab

HELP & LaCasa Ministries, John Scarpato, Program Director, P.O. Box 60750, Harrisburg, PA 17106-0750, Tel. (717)238-2851 Fax (717)238-1916

Major Activities: Volunteer Ministries to Prisons; HELP (Housing, Rent, Food, Medication, Transportation, Home Heating, Clothing); La Casa de Amistad (The House of Friendship) Social Services; Prison Chaplaincy; Susquehanna Harbor Safe Haven (Homeless Shelter)

Christians United in Beaver County

1098 Third St., Beaver, PA 15009, Tel. (724)774-1446 Fax (724)774-1446

Email: cubc@access995.com

Media Contact, Exec. Sec., Lois L. Smith

Exec. Sec., Lois L. Smith

Chaplains- The Rev. Dennis Ugoletti; The Rev. Anthony Massey; The Rev. Arthur Peters; John Pusateri, Rev. Bertha Lay

Pres., Mrs. Delores Tisdale, 1021-5th Street, New Brighton, PA. 15066

Treas., Mr. Richard Puryear, 2 McCabe Street, Sewickley, PA. 15143

Major Activities: Christian Education; Evangelism; Social Action; Church Women United; United Church Men; Ecumenism; Hospital, Detention Home and Jail Ministry, Behavioral Health Clinic.

East End Cooperative Ministry

250 N. Highland Ave., Pittsburgh, PA 15206, Tel. (412)361-5549 Fax (412)361-0151

Email: eecm@eecm.org

Website: www.eecm.org

Media Contact, Exec. Dir., Myrna Zelenitz

Exec. Dir., Myrna Zelenitz

Ass. Dir., Rev. Darnell Leonard

Major Activities: Food Pantry; Soup Kitchen; Men's Emergency Shelter; Drop-In Shelter for Homeless; Meals on Wheels; Information and Referral; Programs for Children and Youth; Bridge Housing Program for Men and PennFree Housing for Women in Recovery

Ecumenical Conference of Greater Altoona

P.O. Box 771, Altoona, PA 16693, Tel. (814)942-0512 Fax (814)942-0512

Email: ecumenaltoona@charter.net

Media Contact, Exec. Dir., Susanna M. Tomlinson

Pres., Eillen Becker

Major Activities: Religious Education; Workshops; Ecumenical Activities; Religious Christmas Parade; Campus Ministry; Community Concerns; Peace Forum; Religious Education for Mentally Challenged, and Inter-faith Committee

Hanover Area Council of Churches

136 Carlisle St., Hanover, PA 17331-2406, Tel. (717)633-6353 Fax (717)633-1992

Email: opsmanhacc@comcast.net

Website: www.hanoverareacouncilofchurches.org

Exec. Dir. & Operations Manager, Carol Hinkle

Major Activities: Meals on Wheels, Provide a Lunch Program, Fresh Air Program, Clothing Bank, Hospital Chaplaincy Services; Congregational & Interfaith Relations, Public Ecumenical Programs and Services, State Park Chaplaincy Services & Children's Program; Compeer; Faith at Work; CROP Walk; Stolte Scholarship Fund; Community Needs; Cold Weather Shelter; AA

Inter-Church Ministries of Erie County

250 W. 7th St., Erie, PA 16501, Tel. (814)454-2411 Fax (814)454-2412

Email: icm@icmeriecounty.com

Website: www.icmeriecounty.com

Pres., The Rev. Katie White

Treas., The Rev. J. David Mumford

Major Activities: Local Ecumenism; Social Ministry; Continuing Education; North West Pennsylvania Conference of Bishops and Judicatory Execs.; Theological Dialogue; Coats for Kids; Voucher Program for Emergency Assistance; Worship; Advocacy

Lancaster County Council of Churches

344 N. Marshall St., Lancaster, PA 17602, Tel. (717)291-2261 Fax (717)291-2261

Email: asone@lcchurches.org

Website: www.lccouncilofchurches.org

Media Contact, Exec. Dir., Rev. Scott Fischer

Pres.: Dean Zerbe

DROP: Service Ministry Interim Director: Doug Hopwood

Assistant Executive Director: Bethany Woodcock

Major Activities: Ministering to human needs; Addressing community and societal issues; Ecumenical Collaboration

Lebanon County Christian Ministries

250 South 7th St., Lebanon, PA 17042, Tel. (717) 272-4000 Fax (717)274-1361

Email: info@lccm.us

Website: www.lccm.us

Media Contact, Exec. Dir., Troy Williams

Exec. Dir., Troy Williams

Client Services Manager, Wenda Dinatale

Major Activities: Food Bank, Clothing Bank, and Other Emergency Services; Free Noon Meal; Prescription Aid; Utility Assistance (Heating Oil, Natural Gas, Water/Saver).

Lehigh County Conference of Churches

534 Chew St., Allentown, PA 18104, Tel. (610)433-6421 Fax (610)439-8039

Email: info@lehighchurches.org

Website: www.lehighchurches.org

Media Contact, Exec. Dir. The Rev. Dr. Christine L Nelson

Exec:. Dir.: The Rev. Dr. Christine L. Nelson (UCC)

Pres. Richard Focht (Lutheran)

Vice-Pres: Eunice Schermerhorn (Lutheran)

Sec., Ken Mohr (UCC)
Treas., Theresa Racek (Roman Catholic)
Major Activities: Homelessness Direct Services, Mentoring Direct Services, Soup Kitchen Hunger Direct Services
Mental Health Direct Services, Christian Ecumenism worship, lectures, educational events, Interfaith in Action activities, Justice and Advocacy Activities including legislative action and workshops

Lewisburg Council of Churches
5. S. Asper Place, Lewisburg, PA 17837, Tel. (570) 524-2834
Media Contact, Guy Temple, 139 Iron Cave Lane, Lewisburg, PA 17837, Tel. (570)-524-4877
Pres., Mrs. Gail Pepper, First Baptist Church, 51 S. 3rd St, Lewisburg, PA 17837, Tel. (570)524-7438
Treas., Mrs. Jan Temple, 139 Iron Cave Lane, Lewisburg, PA 17837, Tel. (570)524-4877
Major Activities: Supplementary and Emergency Food Pantries; Clothing Bank; CROP Walk; Week of Prayer for Christian Unity; Soup & Scripture Lenten Series; 3-hour Good Friday Service; Human Services Directory; Transient-Homeless Aid

Metropolitan Christian Council of Philadelphia
1501 Cherry St., Philadelphia, PA 19102-1429, Tel. (215)563-7854 Fax (215)563-6849
Email: geiger@mccp.org
Website: www.mccp.org
Media Contact, Assoc. Communications, Nancy L. Nolde
Exec. Dir., Rev. C. Edward Geiger
Assoc. Communications, Nancy L. Nolde
Office Mgr., Joan G. Shipman
Pres., Rev. Steven B. Laurence
First Vice-Pres., Rev. G. Daniel Jones
Treas., A. Louis Denton, Esq.
Major Activities: Congregational Clusters; Public Policy Advocacy; Communication; Theological Dialogue (Christian & Interfaith); Women's Issues

Northside Common Ministries
P.O. Box 99861, Pittsburgh, PA 15233, Tel. (412) 323-1163 Fax (412)323-1749
Email: jay.poliziani@ncmin.com
Media Contact, Exec. Dir., Jay Poliziani
Exec. Dir., Jay Poliziani
Major Activities: Pleasant Valley Shelter for Homeless Men; Advocacy around Hunger, Housing, Poverty, and Racial Issues; Community Food Pantry and Service Center; Supportive Housing

Northwest Interfaith Movement
6757 Greene St., Philadelphia, PA 19119, Tel. (215)843-5600 Fax (215)843-2755
Email: jjohnson@nim-phila.org
Website: www.nim-phila.org

Media Contact, Exec. Dir., Rabbi George M. Stern
Exec. Dir., Rabbi George M. Stern
Chpsn., Judy Weinstein
Long Term Care Program, Dir., Donald Carlin
Neighborhood Child Care Resource Prog., Dir., Leslie S. Eslinger
Major Activities: Resources amd Technical Assistance for Child Care Programs; Conflict Mediation and Support for Nursing and Boarding Home Residents

Pennsylvania Conference on Interchurch Cooperation
P.O. Box 2835, 223 North St., Harrisburg, PA 17105, Tel. (717)238-9613 Fax (717)238-1473
Email: info@pacatholic.org
Website: www.pacatholic.org/ecumenism
Media Contact, Amy Hill
Co-Staff, Dr. Robert J. O'Hara, Jr., Rev. Gary Harke
Co-Chpsns., Bishop Joseph Martino; Bishop Donald Main.
Major Activities: Theological Consultation; Social Concerns; Public Policy; Conferences and Seminars

The Pennsylvania Council of Churches*
900 S. Arlington Ave., Ste. 211A, Harrisburg, PA 17109-5024, Tel. (717)545-4761 Fax (717)545-4765
Email: pcc@pachurches.org
Website: www.pachurches.org
Media Contact, Exec. Dir.,The Rev. Gary L. Harke
Exec. Dir., The Rev. Gary L. Harke
Dir. of Public Advocacy, The Rev. Sandra L. Strauss
Dir. of Finance & Facilities, Janet A. Gulick
Pres., Bishop Robert L. Driesen
Vice-Pres., The Rev. David A. Steele
Sec., The Rev. Lavette Paige
Treas., Mr. David Hoffman, CPA
Major Activities: Inter-church dialogue; trade association activities; faith and order; seasonal farmworker ministry; trucker-traveler ministry; public policy advocacy and education; leisure ministry (summer park chaplaincy); conferences and continuing education events

Project of Easton, Inc.
330 Ferry St., Easton, PA 18042, Tel. (215)258-4361 Fax 610)258-7502
Email: jkomisor@projecteaston.org
Pres., Dr. John H. Updegrove
Vice-Pres. Public Relations, Rev. Charles E. Staples
Vice-Pres. Operations, Don Follett
Sec., Rosemary Reese
Treas., Steve Barsony
Exec. Dir., Maryellen Shuman
Major Activities: Food Bank; Adult Literacy Program; English as a Second Language; Children's Programs; Parents as Student Support; CROP Walk; Interfaith Council; Family Literacy; Emergency Assistance; Even Start Family Literacy

Reading Berks Conference of Churches

519 Elm St., P.O. Box 957, Reading, PA 19603, Tel. (610)375-6108 Fax (610)375-6205
Email: rdgbrkscc@comcast.net
Website: www.readingberksconferenceof churches.com
Media Contact, Exec. Dir., Rev. Calvin Kurtz
Admin Asst., Donna Boyajcan
Exec. Dir., Rev. Calvin Kurtz
Pres., John Roland
Treas., William Maslo
Major Activities: Institutional Ministry; Social Action; CROP Walk for Hunger; Emergency Assistance; Prison Chaplaincy; Hospital Chaplaincy; Interchurch-Intercultural Services; Children & Youth Ministry; Healthy Family & Marriage Initiatives; Lazarus Project

South Hills Interfaith Ministries

5301 Park Ave., Bethel Park, PA 15102, Tel. (412) 854-9120 Fax (412)854-9123
Website: www.shim-centers.org
Media Contact, Exec. Dir., Jerry Ellis
Prog. Dir., Director of Youth Programs, Sarah Henkel
Psychological Services, Don Zandier
Family Assistance Coordinator, Harry Dietz
Business Mgr., Amy Puglisi
Volunteer Coordinator, Barbara Houston
Major Activities: Basic Human Needs; Community Organization and Development; Inter-Faith Cooperation; Personal Growth; At-Risk Youth Development; Women in Transition; Elderly Support; After School Homework Club; Early Childhood Program (Pre-School); Interfaith Educational Programs & Observances

United Churches of Lycoming County

202 E. Third St., Williamsport, PA 17701, Tel. (570)322-1110 Fax (570)326-4572
Email: uclc@sunlink.net
Website: www.uclc.org
Media Contact, Exec. Dir., Rev. Gwen Nelson Bernstine
Exec. Dir., Rev. Gwen Nelson Bernstine
Ofc. Sec., Linda Winter
Pres., Rev. Maurice C. Frontz III, 324 South Howard Street, South Williamsport PA 17702
Treas., Mrs. Madeline Bird, 407 South Market Street, Muncy PA17756
Shepherd of the Streets, Rev. Dr. J. Morris Smith, 669 Center Street., Williamsport, PA 17701
Ecumenism, Dir., Rev. Maurice C. Frontz, 324 Howard Street, South Williamsport, PA 17702
Educ. Ministries, Dir., Mr. James Foran, 711 Edwin Street, Williamsport PA 17701
Institutional Ministry, Dir., Pastor Constance Waugh, 4570 Rt 87 Hwy, Williamsport PA 17701
Radio-TV, Dir., Rev. Dr. James Behrens, 1971 Lycoming Creek Rd., Williamsport, PA 17701
Prison Ministry, Dir., Mrs. Evadna Cline, 3336 West Fourth St., Williamsport, PA 17701
Christian Social Concerns, Dir., Pastor Kathy Behrens, 21 Casey Drive, Williamsport APA 17701

Prison Ministry, Dir., Rev. Danesta Whaley, Williamsport, PA 17701
Christian Social Concerns, Dir., Dr. Danial Doyle, 301 South Main Street, Muncy PA 17756
Major Activities: Ecumenism; Educational Ministries; Church Women United; Church World Service and CROP; Prison Ministry; Radio-TV; Nursing Homes; Fuel Bank; Food Pantry; Family Life; Shepherd of the Streets Urban Ministry; Peace Concerns; Housing Initiative; Interfaith Dialogue, Youth Ministry, Campus Ministry

Wilkinsburg Community Ministry

704 Wood Street, Pittsburgh, PA 15221, Tel. (412) 241-8072 Fax (412)241-8315
Email: caring@wcm15221.org
Website: wcm15221.org
Media Contact, Ann Greider
Acting Dir., Elizabeth Mulvaney, MSW, LSW
Pres. Of Bd., Glenna Wilson, MSW, LSW
Major Activities: Hunger Ministry;Summer Reading Camp; Teen-Moms Infant Care; Meals on Wheels; Church Camp Scholarships; Utility Assistance; Clothing-Furniture Assistance; Case Management for Elderly Homebound Persons and Families, Soup Kitchen

Wyoming Valley Council of Churches

70 Lockhart St., Wilkes-Barre, PA 18702, Tel. (570)825-8543
Media Contact, Exec. Dir., Beth Titus
Exec. Dir., Beth Titus
Ofc. Sec., Sandra Karrott
Pres., Very Rev. Joseph Martin
Treas., Rev. Dr. Robert Zanicky
Major Activities: Nursing Home Chaplaincy; Hospital Referral Service; CROP Hunger Walk; Pastoral Care Ministries; Clergy Retreats and Seminars; Meals on Wheels Fuel Service; Citizen's Voice articles

York County Council of Churches

30 East King St, 2nd Floor, P.O. Box 1865, York, PA 17405, Tel. (717)854-9504
Email: gwdunham@ycchurches.org
Website: www.ycchurches.org
Media Contact, Rev. Guy W. Dunham
Exec. Dir., Rev. Guy W. Dunham
Major Activities: Partners for Sacred Places; York Ecumenical Choral Society; Festival of Trees; York County Hunger Fund, OPEN - HIV/AIDS, Four Chaplains Prayer Breakfast; Faith Is Alive Radio Program; Bulk Paper Ordering for Churches; York Fair Ecumenical Celebration of Faith; York Metro CROP Walk for the Hungry; Parish Resource Center/York Affiliate; York/Adams American Red Cross-partnership; York County Circles - Lutheran Social Services - partnership; York City Safer York/Weed & Seed - partnership; Volunteer Organizations Active in Disaster (VOAD) - partnership; York Habitat for Humanity - partnership; Emergency Food & Shelter Program/United Way-

partnership; Communities of Shalom/United Methodist Church - partnerhship; Communities That Care/Truancy Prevention Initiative/York Bar Association - partnership

RHODE ISLAND

The Rhode Island State Council of Churches*
100 Niantic Avenue Suite 101, Providence, RI 02907, Tel. (401)461-5558 Fax (401)461-5233
Email: riscc@councilofchurchesri.org
Website: www.councilof churchesri.org
Media Contact, Exec. Minister, Dr. Donald C. Anderson
Exec. Min., Dr. Donald C. Anderson
Admn. Asst., Dolores Taylor
Pres., Rev. Matthew Kai
Treas., George Weavill
Major Activities: Urban Ministries; Institutional Chaplaincy; Advocacy-Justice & Service, Legislative Liaison; Faith & Order; Community Network; Campus Ministries; Prison Ministry

SOUTH CAROLINA

South Carolina Christian Action Council, Inc.*
P.O. Drawer 3248, 4209 N. Main St., Columbia, SC 29230, Tel. (803)786-7115 Fax (803) 786-7116
Email: sccouncil@sccouncil.net
Website: www.sccouncil.net
Media Contact, Exec. Minister, Brenda Lynn Kneece
Exec. Minister, The Rev. Brenda Kneece
Exec. Dir., The Rev. Brenda Lynn Kneece (Cooperative Baptist Fellowship)
Pres., Missie Walker (Roman Catholic)
Vice-Pres: The Rev. Dr. Carl Evans (United Methodist)
Sec., The Rev. Andy Sidden (United Church of Christ)
Treas., The Rev, Joseph Cobb (Christian Church (Disciples))
Other: Past President: The Rev. Dr. Joseph Darby (African Metodist Episcopal)
Secretary, The Rev. Terry Brooks, CBF
Treas., The Rev. Dr. Carl Evans, UMC
Pres. Elect: Mrs. Melissa (Missie) Walker
Past Pres., Mrs. Debbie Dantzler, Attorney, CBF
Major Activities: Christian Ecumenism, Legislative Advocacy, Racial Healing

United Ministries
606 Pendleton St., Greenville, SC 29601, Tel. (864)232-6463 Fax (864)370-3518
Email: info@united-ministries.org
Website: www.united-ministries.org
Media Contact, Exec. Dir., Keith Trout
Exec. Dir., Keith Trout
Pres., Nancy Orders Smith
Vice-Pres., Anne Ellefson
Sec., Becky Bouton
Treas., Lan Nix

Major Activities: Assistance with rent, utilities, prescriptions, food, heat; Place of Hope (A day shelter for people who are homeless); Assistance with getting and keeping jobs; A GED program for adults; Case Management as part of all activities, College assistance with books and scholarships.

SOUTH DAKOTA

Association of Christian Churches of South Dakota*
100 S. Spring Ave., Suite 106, Sioux Falls, SD 57104-3626, Tel. (605)334-1980
Email: office@accsd.org
Website: www.accsd.org
Media Contact, Gene E. Miller, 100 S. Spring Ave., Sioux Falls, SD 57104, Tel. (605)334-1980
Pres., Bd. of Directors, Ms. Ann Smith
Major Activities: Ecumenical Forums; Continuing Education for Clergy; Legislative Information; Resourcing Local Ecumenism; Native American Issues; Ecumenical Fields Ministries; Rural Economic Development; Children at Risk

TENNESSEE

Metropolitan Inter Faith Association (MIFA)
910 Vance Ave, Memphis, TN 38216, Tel. (901) 527-0208 Fax (901)527-3202
Email: jseacat@mifa.org
Website: www.mifa.org
Media Contact, Communications Dir., Jim Seacat
Exec. Dir., Sally Jones Heinz
Major Activities: Emergency Services (Rent, Utility, Food, Clothing Assistance); Home-Delivered Meals and Senior Support Services; Youth Services; Homeless Programs

Tennessee Association of Churches*
103 Oak St., Ashland City, TN 37015, Tel. (615)792-4631
Ecumenical Admn., vacant
Pres., Rev. Steve Mosley
Treas., Paul Milliken
Major Activities: Faith and Order; Christian Unity; Social Concern Ministries; Governmental Concerns; Governor's Prayer Breakfast

Volunteer Ministry Center
103 South Gay St., Knoxville, TN 37902, Tel. (423)524-3926 Fax (423)524-7065
Media Contact, Exec. Dir., Angelia Moon
Exec. Dir., Angelia Moon
Pres., David Leech
Vice-Pres., John Moxham
Treas., Doug Thompson
Major Activities: Homeless Program; Food Line; Crisis Referral Program; Subsidized Apartment Program; Counselling Program; Parenting Education for Single Parents

TEXAS

Austin Area Interreligious Ministries
701 Tillery St., Ste. 8, Austin, TX 78705, Tel.
(512)386-9145 Fax (512)385-1430
Email: aaim@aaimaustin.org
Website: www.aaimaustin.org
Media Contact, Chief Executive Officer, Tom
Spencer
Exec. Dir., Tom Spencer
Pres., Rev. Mel Waxler
Treas., Anita Maxwell
Major Activities: Youth at Risk Mentoring;
Housing Rehabilitation; Broadcast Ministry;
Interfaith Dialogues; Family Issues; Homeless
Issues; Hunger Issues; Racial Reconciliation,
ESL

Border Association for Refugees from Central America (BARCA), Inc.
P.O. Box 1725, Edinburg, TX 78540, Tel. (956)
631-7447 Fax (956)631-7447
Email: barcainc@aol.com
Media Contact, Exec. Dir., Ninfa Ochoa-Krueger
Exec. Dir, Ninfa Ochoa-Krueger
Outreach Services, Dir., Juanita Ledesma
Major Activities: Direct assistance and referral
service to Newly Arrived Indigent Immigrants
& Refugees; Medical and Other Emergency
Aid; Special Services to Children; Speakers on
Refugee and Immigrant Concerns for Church;
School and other social service agencies and
Groups; Orientation, Advocacy and Legal
Services for Immigrants and Refugees

Corpus Christi Metro Ministries
1919 Leopard St., P.O. Box 78469, Corpus Christi,
TX 78408, Tel. (361)887-0151 Fax (361)887-
7900
Email: rpizzi@ccmetroministries.org; info@cc
metro.org
Website: www.ccmetroministries.com
Media Contact, Exec. Dir., Rosa E. Pizzi
Exec. Dir., Rosa E. Pizzi, Email: rpizzi@
ccmetroministries.org; info@ccmetro.org
Volunteer Dir., Ann Cox
Fin. Coord., Sue McCown
Loaves & Fishes Dir., Ray Gomez
Emergency Services Mgr., Ann Cox
Employment Dir., Larry Curtis
Health and Human Services, Dir., Ann Cox
Major Activities: Clothing Distribution, Employ-
ment Assistance, Healthcare, Homelessness/
Shelter, and Hunger/Food Programs.

East Dallas Cooperative Parish
P.O. Box 720305, Dallas, TX 75372-0305, Tel.
(214)823-9149 Fax (214)823-2015
Email: edcp@swbell.net
Media Contact, Exec. Dir., Nancy Jellinek
Pres., Debbie Thorpe
Major Activities: Emergency Food, Clothing, Job
Bank; Medical Clinic; Legal Clinic, Tutorial
Education; Home Companion Service; Pre-
School Education; Hispanic Ministry; Activity
Center for Low Income Older Adults; Pastoral
Counseling; English Language Ministry, Pre-
GED program

Family Endeavors
535 Bandera Rd., San Antonio, TX 78228, Tel.
(210)431-6466 Fax (210)431-6470
Media Contact, Sue Kelly
Exec. Dir., Sue Kelly
Pres., Rev. Leslie Ellison
Major Activities: Homes for Discharged Mental
Patients; After School Care for Latch Key
Children; Christian Based Community Ministry

Greater Dallas Community of Churches
624 N. Good-Latimer #100, Dallas, TX 75204-
5818, Tel. (214)824-8680 Fax (214)824-8726
Email: gdcc@churchcommunity.org
Media Contact, Exec. Dir., Rev. Elzie Odom
Exec. Dir., Rev. Elzie Odom
AmeriCorps-Building Blocks Dir., Venita Allen-
Kent
Development Vice Pres., Charlotte Coyle
Pres., Richard Selby
Treas., John Rutzler
Major Activities: Interdenominational, Interfaith
and Interracial Understanding and Joint Work;
AmeriCorps-Building Blocks (Direct Service to
Develop Inner City Children, Youth &
Families); Summer Food & Reading; Hunger;
Peacemaking; Public Policy; Social Justice;
Faith & Life; Children's Health Outreach; Child
Advocacy; Dismantaling Racism

Interfaith Ministries for Greater Houston
3217 Montrose Blvd., Houston, TX 77006, Tel.
(713)522-3955 Fax (713)520-4663
Media Contact, Exec. Dir., Betty P. Taylor
Exec. Dir., Betty P. Taylor
Pres., Charles R. Erickson
Development, Dir., Sharon Ervine
Assoc. Exec. Dir., Larry Norton
Treas., Fort D. Flowers, Jr.
Sec., Darlene Alexander
Major Activities: Community Concerns, Hunger;
Older Adults; Families; Youth; Child Abuse;
Refugee Services; Congregational Relations
and Development; Social Service Programs,
Refugee Services; Hunger Coalition; Youth
Victim Witness; Family Connection; Meals on
Wheels; Senior Health; RSVP; Foster
Grandparents

North Dallas Shared Ministries
2530 Glenda Ln., #500, Dallas, TX 75229, Tel.
(214)620-8696 Fax (214)620-0433
Media Contact, Exec. Dir., J. Dwayne Martin
Exec. Dir., J. Dwayne Martin
Pres., vacant
Major Activities: Emergency Assistance; Job
Counseling; ESL

Northside Inter-Church Agency (NICA)
1600 Circle Park Blvd., Fort Worth, TX 76164,
Tel. (817)626-1102 Fax (817)626-9043
Email: info@nicaagency.org
Website: www.nicaagency.org
Media Contact, Exec. Dir., Connie Nahoolewa
Exec. Dir., Connie Nahoolewa
Major Activities: Food; Clothing; Counseling;
Information and Referral; Furniture and
Household Items; Nutrition Education; Employ-
ment Services; Thanksgiving Basket Program;
"Last Resort" Christmas Program; Community
Networking; Ecumenical Worship Services;
Volunteer Training; Newsletter; Senior Home
Repairs; School Clothing Program; Advocacy;
GED Preparation; Literacy; Computer Training;
English as a Second Language

San Antonio Community of Congregations
1101 W. Woodlawn, San Antonio, TX 78201, Tel.
(210)733-9159 Fax (210)733-5780
Email: sacommchurches@sbcglobal.net
Website: www.sacoc.info
Media Contact, Exec. Dir., Mrs. Jeanne Goodlin
Exec. Dir., Mrs. Jeanne Goodlin
Pres., Rev. Mike Cave
Major Activities: Infant Formula Program for "at
risk" infants; Social Issues; Disaster Recovery;
Marriage Education; Environmental Concerns;
Sponsor annual CROP Walk for Hunger; Peace
and Anti-Violence Initiatives

Southeast Area Churches (SEARCH)
P.O. Box 51256, Fort Worth, TX 76105, Tel. (817)
531-2211
Exec. Dir., Dorothy Anderson-Develrow
Major Activities: Emergency Assistance; Advo-
cacy; Information and Referral; Community
Worship; School Supplies; Direct Aid to Low
Income and Elderly

Tarrant Area Community of Churches
2601 Clover Lane, Fort Worth, TX 76107, Tel.
(817)737-5554 Fax (817)534-1995
Email: melindav@tarrantareacc.org
Website: www.tarrantareacc.org
Media Contact, Kelly Kirkendoll Shafer of Results
in Sight
Exec. Dir., Reverend Melinda Veatch
Pres. Reverend Jorene Swift
Sec., Cynthia Fisher Miller
Major Activities: Christian Ecumenism; Congre-
gational online & mentoring resource centers;
Homeless transitioning off the streets congre-
gational mentoring network; CROP Walk for
hunger; Week of Prayer for Christian Unity;
Educational forums & opportunities for dialogue;
Interfaith engagement in community projects

Texas Conference of Churches*
6800 Woodrow Avenue, Austin, TX 78757, Tel.
(512)451-0991 Fax (512)451-0991
Email: tcc@txconfchurches.org

Website: www.txconfchurches.org
Media Contact, Ms. Natalie Redle
Exec. Dir., Laura Vaught Lincoln
Pres., Rev. Mark McNeese
Major Activities: Building Relationships -
Building Unity; Faith & Order; Building and
Supporting Regional Ecumenical Networks at
the grass-roots level; Promoting Healthy
Congregational Organizations; Judicatory
Leaders Retreat; Regional Assemblies; Ecu-
menical Worship

United Board of Missions
1701 Bluebonnet Ave., P.O. Box 3856, Port
Arthur, TX 77643-3856, Tel. (409)982-9412
Fax (409)985-3668
Media Contact, Admin. Asst., Carolyn Schwarr
Exec. Dir., Clark Moore
Pres., Glenda McCoy
Major Activities: Emergency Assistance (Food
and Clothing, Rent and Utility, Medical, Dental,
Transportation); Share a Toy at Christmas;
Counseling; Back to School Clothing
Assistance; Information and Referral; Hearing
Aid Bank; Meals on Wheels; Super Pantry;
Energy Conservation Programs; Job Bank
Assistance to Local Residents Only

VERMONT

Vermont Ecumenical Council and Bible Society*
P.O. Box 728, Richmond, VT 05477, Tel. (802)
434-7307 Fax (802)434-7307
Email: info@vecbs.org
Website: www.vecbs.org
Media Contact, Administrator, Betsy Hardy
Pres., Mr. Chistopher McCandles
Treas., Mr. Roy V. Hill II
Treas., Mrs. Mary Margaret Hamlin
Major Activities: Christian Unity; Bible Distri-
bution; Social Justice; Committee on Faith and
Order; Committee on Peace, Justice and the
Integrity of Creation; Committee on Prayer and
Worship

Virginia Council of Churches, Inc.*
1214 W. Graham Rd., Richmond, VA 23220-1409,
Tel. (804)321-3300 Fax (804)329-5066
Email: barton@vacouncilofchurches.org
Website: www.vacouncilofchurches.org
Media Contact, Gen. Min., Rev. Jonathan Barton
President, The Rev. David McKea
Vice President, The Rev. Reginald Terry
Treasurer, The Rev. David Shumate
Secretary, Ms. Jean James
Gen. Min., The Rev. Jonathan Barton
Rural Family Development, Ex Dir. Mr. Ed
Rossmoore
Refugee Resettlement, Dir., Mr. Viktor Sokolyuk
Campus Ministry Forum, Coord., The Rev. Steve
Darr
Major Activities: Faith and Order; Network
Building & Coordination; Ecumenical Com-

269

munications; Justice and Legislative Concerns; Rural Concerns; Refugee Resettlement; Migrant Ministries and Migrant Head Start; Disaster Coordination and Response; Infant Mortality Prevention; Interfaith Dialogue; Native American Outreach

Associated Ministries of Tacoma-Pierce County

1224 South I St., Tacoma, WA 98405-5021, Tel. (253)383-3056 Fax (253)383-2672
Email: info@associatedministries.org
Website: www. associatedministries.org
Media Contact, Executive Director, Rev. Christopher Morton
Director of Communications, Kitty Gibbs
Pres., Carol Baarsma
Vice-Pres. Kathy Russell
Sec., Ernie Bianco
Treas., Connie Robey
Exec. Dir., Rev. Christopher Morton
Dir. of Mission & Development, Rev. Heidi Calhoun
Director of Communication, Kitty Gibbs
Dir. of Project Interdependence, Valorie Crout
Director of Pierce County Asset Building Coalition, Barbara Gorzinski
Director of Housing & Shelter Services, Yvonne Eden
Director of Paint Tacoma-Pierce Beautiful, Sallie Shawl
Major Activities: Associated Ministries Hunger Walk; Paint Tacoma-Pierce Beautiful; Project Interdependence; Homeless mail services; Protective payee services; Utility assistance: Family Emergency Fund;   Housing services and advocacy; Case management; Help accessing other public benefits and community resources; Housing and Shelter Services; Community Resource Connections; Pierce County Asset Building Coalition; Disaster Preparedness and Recovery

WASHINGTON

Church Council of Greater Seattle

2701 First Ave., Suite 240, Seattle, WA 98121, Tel. (206)525-1213 Fax (206)525-1218
Email: info@thechurchcouncil.org
Website: www.thechurchcouncil.org
Media Contact, Exec. Dir., Michael Ramos
Exec. Dir., Exec. Dir., Michael Ramos (Roman Catholic)
Pres. Pres., Verlene Jones (American Baptist)
Treas., Interim Treas., The Rev. M. Christopher Boyer (American Baptist)
Other: President-Elect., The Rev. M. Christopher Boyer (American Baptist)
Major Activities: Christian Ecumenism, Direct Service, Legislative Advocacy, HomeStep (Transitional Housing), The Sharehouse (Furniture Bank), Friend to Friend, Sound Youth VISTA, Social Justice Ministries, Rauschenbusch Center for Spirit and Action

Faith Action Network: A Partnership for the Common Good*

766 John St., Suite B, Seattle, WA 98109, Tel. (206)625-9790 Fax (206)625-9791
Email: fan@fanwa.org
Website: www.fanwa.org
Media Contact, Co-Exec. Dir., Alice Woldt, Email: awoldt@fanwa.org
Co-Exec. Dir., Rev. Paul Benz, Email: pbenz@fanwa.org
Co-Exec. Dir., Alice Woldt
Co-Exec. Dir., Rev. Paul Benz
Co-Chair: Rev. Carol Jensen (ELCA Lutheran)
Co-Chair: Rev. Rich Gamble (United Church of Christ)
Treas., Rev. Sharon Moe (United Methodist)
Major Activities: Legislative Advocacy, Veterans Support Training, Interfaith Relations, Mental Health Training, Ecumenical Relations, Issues Education

FaithTrust Institute

2400 N. 45th St, Suite 101, Seattle, WA 98103, Tel. (206)634-1903 Fax (206)634-0115
Email: info@faithtrustinstitute.org
Website: www.faithtrustinstitute.org
Media Contact, Ko-Eun Kim
Executive Director, Rev. Kathryn J. Jans, info@faithtrustinstitute.org
Founder & Senior Analyst, Rev. Dr. Marie M. Fortune, mfortune@faithtrustinstitute.org
Director of Training & Education, Rev. Thelma Burgonio-Watson, burgonio@faithtrustinstitute.org
Director of the Jewish Program, Rabbi Cindy Enger, cenger@faithtrustinstitute.org
Clearinghouse Coordinator, Dinah Hall, dhall@faithtrustinstitute.org
Finance Director, Marion J. Ward
Major Activities: Training - Domestic Violence; Healthy teen relationships; Child Abuse; Sexual Abuse by Clergy and Religious Leaders; Sexual Violence Consultation (Expertise to develop policies to address and prevent sexual abuse by clergy, guidance on integrating issues of sexual and domestic violence into religious education); Educational Materials (multicultural and multi-faith educational materials, extensive resource catalog includes videos, books and curricula)

The Interfaith Association of Northwest Washington

2301 Hoyt, P.O. Box 12824, Everett, WA 98206, Tel. (206)252-6672
Email: execdir@interfaithwa.org
Website: www.interfaithwa.org
Media Contact, Exec. Dir., Mary Ellen Wood
Exec. Dir., Mary Ellen Wood
Pres.,Ted Lombard
Major Activities: Housing and Shelter for homeless and low-come families; increase united action among faith groups including interfaith devotional gatherings and service to those in need.

Interfaith Council
1620 N. Monroe, Spokane, WA 99205, Tel. (509) 329-1410 Fax (509)329-1409
Email: info@interfaithnw.org
Website: www.interfaithnw.org
Media Contact, Dir., Kateri Caron
Director: Kateri Caron
Board President: Stephen Rorie
Vice President: Elliot Fabric
Sec., Rev. Dr. Richard Erhardt
Major Activities: Camp PEACE; Multi-Cultural Human Relations; High School Youth Camp; Eastern Washington Legislative Conference; CROP Walk; Interfaith Thanksgiving Worship; Easter Sunrise Service; Dir. Of Churches & Community Agencies; Circle of Caring (for Women in Domestic Violence); Guatemala Dialogues

Interfaith Works
P.O. Box 1221, Olympia, WA 98507, Tel. (360) 357-7224
Email: office@interfaith-works.org
Website: www.interfaith-works.org
Media Contact, Exec. Dir., Daniel Kadden
Exec. Dir., Daniel Kadden
Pres., Barnett Kalikow
Treas., Susan Kavanaugh
Major Activities: Interfaith Relations; Social and Health Concerns; Community Action; Social Justice

Northwest Harvest-E. M. M.
P.O. Box 12272, Seattle, WA 98102, Tel. (206) 625-0755 Fax (206)625-7518
Email: nharvest@blarg.net
Website: www. northwestharvest.org
Media Contact, Comm. Affairs Dir., Ellen Hansen
Exec. Dir., Ruth M. Velozo
Chpsn., Patricia Barcott
Major Activities: Northwest Harvest (Statewide Hunger Response); Cherry Street Food Bank (Community Hunger Response); Northwest Infants Corner (Special Nutritional Products for Infants and Babies)

WEST VIRGINIA

Greater Fairmont Council of Churches
P.O. Box 108, Fairmont, WV 26554, Tel. (304)367-0962
Media Contact, Pres., Rev. Jeremiah Jasper
President, Rev. Jeremiah Jasper
Major Activities: Community Ecumenical Services; Youth and Adult Sports Leagues; CROP Walk Sponsor; Weekly Radio Broadcasts

West Virginia Council of Churches*
2207 Washington St. E., Charleston, WV 25311, Tel. (304)344-3141 Fax (304)342-1506
Email: dsparks@wvcc.org
Website: www.wvcc.org
Media Contact, Exec. Dir. Rev. Dennis Sparks
Exec. Dir., Reverend Dennis D. Sparks (Disciples of Christ/ United Church of Christ)

Pres. Monsignor Frederick Annie (Roman Catholic)
Vice-Pres: Bishop Ernest Lyght (United Methodist)
Sec., Rev. Dr. William Wilson (United Methodist)
Treas., Rev. Thaddaeus Allen (Disciple of Christ)
Other: Personnel: Bishop Ralph Dunkin (Evangelical Lutheran Church in America)
Other: Nominating: Rev. Don Snyder (Disciples of Christ)
Other: Second Vice President: Delores Alt Probst (Church Women United, Church of Breathren)
Major Activities: Faith and Order (One in the Spirit for 130 Years); Interfaith Relations; Government Concerns (Peace and Justice-Public Policy); Healthy Kids and Families Coalition; Care Net: Caring Beyond the Yellow Ribbon (for military and families); Prison Ministry and Corrections Advocacy; Disaster Recovery and Preparedness

WISCONSIN

Christian Youth Council
1715-52nd St., Kenosha, WI 53140, Tel. (262) 654-6200 x120 Fax (414)652-4461
Media Contact, Exec. Dir., Steven L. Nelson
Exec. Dir., Steven L. Nelson
Sports Dir., Jerry Tappen
Outreach Dir., Linda Osborne
Accountant, Debbie Cutts
Class Director, Jill Cox
Pres. & Chmn. of Board, Lon Knoedler
Gang Prevention Dir., Sam Sauceda
Major Activities: Leisure Time Ministry; Institutional Ministries; Ecumenical Committee; Social Concerns; Outreach Sports (with a Christian Philosophy)

Interfaith Conference of Greater Milwaukee
1442 N. Farwell Ave., Ste. 200, Milwaukee, WI 53202, Tel. (414)276-9050 Fax (414)276-8442
Email: th@interfaithconference.org
Website: interfaithconference.org
Media Contact, Exec. Dir., Tom Heiman
Chpsn., Rev. Velma Smith
First Vice-Chair, Archbishop Rembert G. Weakland
Second Vice-Chair, Rev. Charles Graves
Sec., Paula Simon
Treas., The Rev. Mary Ann Neevel
Exec. Dir., Marcus White
Consultant in Communications, Rev. Robert P. Seater
Major Activities: Economic Issues; Racism; CROP Walk; Public Policy; Suburban and Urban Partnerships; TV Programming; Peace and International Issues Committee; Annual Membership Luncheon; Religion Diversity; Restorative Justice

Madison-area Urban Ministry
2300 S. Park St. # 5, Madison, WI 53713, Tel. (608)256-0906 Fax (608)256-4387

Email: mum@emum.org
Website: www.emum.org
Media Contact, Office Mgr., Linda Ketcham
Exec. Dir., Linda Ketcham
Major Activities: Community Projects; Dialogue-Forums; Prisoner Re-Entry

Wisconsin Council of Churches*

750 Windsor St. Ste. #301, Sun Prairie, WI 53530-2149, Tel. (608)837-3108 Fax (608)837-3038
Email: wcoc@wichurches.org
Website: www.wichurches.org
Media Contact, Executive Director, Scott Anderson
Exec. Dir., Executive Director, Scott Anderson (PC (USA))
Coordinator for Public Policy, Peter Bakken, PhD
Major Activities: Ecumenical Relationships

WYOMING

Wyoming Association of Churches*

P. O. Box 1473, Laramie, WY 82073, Tel. (307) 761-0755
Email: wychurches@wyoming.com
Website: www.wyomingassociationofchurches.org
Media Contact, Director - Chesie Lee
Dir., Chesie Lee
Chair, The Rev. Tim Trippel
Treasurer, Bill Mankin
Admin. Assistant, Rose Hackett
Major Activities: Alternatives to Violence; Beyond Tolerance; Malicious Harrasment; Domestic Violence; Empowering the Poor and Oppressed; Peace and Justice; Public Health Issues; Welfare Reform; Anti-Death Penalty, Community Networking Facilitation, Environmental Justice, Immigration, Anti-Gambling

Index of Select Programs for U.S. Regional and Local Ecumenical Bodies

For many years the *Yearbook of American & Canadian Churches* has published the previous chapter, The Directory of U.S. Regional and Local Ecumenical Bodies. Each entry of that directory contains a brief description of the diverse programs offered by each agency. However, researchers, pastors, service organizations and theological seminaries often inquire about specific programs and which agencies carry out such programs. In response we have created this chapter, which indexes the various regional and local ecumenical agencies by twenty-seven different program areas. These program areas are the twenty-seven that have been the most frequent subjects of inquiry in our office. We have collected this program information directly from these organizations by means of a simple response form. There is an enormous diversity of ministries and missions conducted by these diverse organizations. Most organizations pursue several kinds of programs at once. However, some of these may focus their efforts most especially on only one of their programs; their other programs may be less well developed than their specialty. Consequently, the extent to which any of these ministries is a priority for any particular organization cannot be inferred from this list. For detailed information about the nature and extent of any particular ministry, the reader is urged to contact the organization directly using the directory of "U.S. Regional and Local Ecumenical Bodies," which is found in the pages just prior to this index.

AIDS/HIV Programs

Center City Churches—Hartford, CT
The Council of Churches of Santa Clara County—San Jose, CA
East Dallas Cooperative Parish—Dallas, TX
Ecumenical Ministries of Oregon—Portland, OR
Grand Rapids Area Center for Ecumenism (GRACE)—Grand Rapids, MI
Greater Chicago Broadcast Ministries—Chicago, IL
Interfaith Community Services—St. Joseph, MO
Interfaith Federation of Greater Baton Rouge—Baton Rouge, LA
Lehigh County Conference of Churches—Allentown, PA
Metropolitan Ecumenical Ministry—Newark, NJ
Network of Religious Communities—Buffalo, NY
Schenectady Inner City Ministry—Schenectady, NY
Southeast Ecumenical Ministry—Rochester, NY
Troy Area United Ministries—Troy, NY
Virginia Council of Churches, Inc.—Richmond, VA
Wyoming Valley Council of Churches—Wilkes-Barre, PA
York County Council of Churches—York, PA

Anti-Gambling Programs

The Associated Churches of Fort Wayne & Allen County, Inc.—Fort Wayne, IN
Association of Christian Churches of South Dakota—Sioux Falls, SD
The Cape Cod Council of Churches, Inc.—Hyannis, MA
Christian Associates of Southwest Pennsylvania—Pittsburgh, PA
Ecumenical Ministries of Iowa (EMI)—Des Moines, IA
Ecumenical Ministries of Oregon—Portland, OR
Genesee County Churches United, Inc.—Batavia, NY
Greater Chicago Broadcast Ministries—Chicago, IL
Greater Lawrence Council of Churches—Lawrence, MA
The Joint Religious Legislative Coalition—Minneapolis, MN

Kentuckiana Interfaith Community—Louisville, KY
Kentucky Council of Churches—Lexington, KY
Mahoning Valley Association of Churches—Youngstown, OH
Massachusetts Council of Churches—Boston, MA
Mississippi Religious Leadership Conference—Jackson, MS
Montana Association of Churches—Helena, MT
Network of Religious Communities—Buffalo, NY
New Hampshire Council of Churches—Pembroke, NH
New Mexico Conference of Churches—Bernalillo, NM
North Carolina Council of Churches—Raleigh, NC
Ohio Council of Churches—Columbus, OH
The Pennsylvania Council of Churches—Harrisburg, PA
West Virginia Council of Churches—Charleston, WV
Worcester County Ecumenical Council—Worcester, MA
Wyoming Association of Churches—Laramie, WY

Anti-Racism Programs

Akron Area Association of Churches—Akron, OH
Alaska Christian Conference—Anchorage, AK
Associated Ministries of Tacoma-Pierce County—Tacoma, WA
Association of Christian Churches of South Dakota—Sioux Falls, SD
Association of Religious Communities—Danbury, CT
Austin Area Interreligious Ministries—Austin, TX
Broome County Council of Churches, Inc.—Binghamton, NY
The Capitol Region Conference of Churches—Hartford, CT
Central Maryland Ecumenical Council—Baltimore, MD
Christian Associates of Southwest Pennsylvania—Pittsburgh, PA
Christian Ministries of Delaware County—Muncie, IN

273

Church Council of Greater Seattle—Seattle, WA

The Church Federation of Greater Indianapolis, Inc.—Indianapolis, IN

Community Emergency Assistance Program (CEAP)—Brooklyn Park, MN

Community Renewal Society—Chicago, IL

Cooperative Metropolitan Ministries—Newton, MA

Council of Churches of the City of New York—New York, NY

The Council of Churches of Santa Clara County—San Jose, CA

Council of Churches and Synagogues of Southwestern Connecticut—Stamford, CT

Dutchess County Interfaith Council, Inc.—Poughkeepsie, NY

East Dallas Cooperative Parish—Dallas, TX

Ecclesia—Trenton, NJ

Ecumenical Conference of Greater Altoona—Altoona, PA

Ecumenical Ministries of Oregon—Portland, OR

Faith Action Network: A Partnership for the Common Good—Seattle, WA

Faith Community Assistance Center—Santa Fe, NM

The Faith In Action Network of Rochester, NY—Rochester, NY

FaithTrust Institute—Seattle, WA

Florida Council of Churches—Tampa, FL

Fresno Metro Ministry—Fresno, CA

Georgia Christian Council—Macon, GA

Grand Rapids Area Center for Ecumenism (GRACE)—Grand Rapids, MI

Greater Birmingham Ministries—Birmingham, AL

Greater Chicago Broadcast Ministries—Chicago, IL

Greater Dallas Community of Churches—Dallas, TX

Greater Dayton Christian Connections—Dayton, OH

Greensboro Urban Ministry—Greensboro, NC

Illinois Conference of Churches—Springfield, IL

Indiana Partners for Christian Unity and Mission—Indianapolis, IN

Inter-Church Council of Greater New Bedford—New Bedford, MA

Interfaith Conference of Greater Milwaukee—Milwaukee, WI

InterFaith Conference of Metropolitan Washington—Washington, DC

Interfaith Council—Spokane, WA

Interfaith Federation of Greater Baton Rouge—Baton Rouge, LA

Inter-Faith Ministries-Wichita—Wichita, KS

Interfaith Mission Service—Huntsville, AL

Interfaith Service Bureau—Sacramento, CA

Interfaith Works—Olympia, WA

InterFaith Works of Central New York—Syracuse, NY

The Joint Religious Legislative Coalition—Minneapolis, MN

Kentuckiana Interfaith Community—Louisville, KY

Kentucky Council of Churches—Lexington, KY

Lehigh County Conference of Churches—Allentown, PA

Lincoln Interfaith Council—Lincoln, NE

Madison-area Urban Ministry—Madison, WI

Mahoning Valley Association of Churches—Youngstown, OH

Massachusetts Council of Churches—Boston, MA

The Metropolitan Christian Council: Detroit-Windsor—Detroit, MI

Metropolitan Christian Council of Philadelphia—Philadelphia, PA

Metropolitan Ecumenical Ministry—Newark, NJ

Metropolitan Interfaith Council on Affordable Housing (MICAH)—Minneapolis, MN

Mississippi Religious Leadership Conference—Jackson, MS

Montana Association of Churches—Helena, MT

Muskegon County Cooperating Churches—Muskegon, MI

Network of Religious Communities—Buffalo, NY

New Britain Area Conference of Churches (NEW-BRACC)—New Britain, CT

New Hampshire Council of Churches—Pembroke, NH

New Mexico Conference of Churches—Bernalillo, NM

North Carolina Council of Churches—Raleigh, NC

Northern California Interreligious Conference—Oakland, CA

Northside Common Ministries—Pittsburgh, PA

Ohio Council of Churches—Columbus, OH

Oklahoma Conference of Churches—Oklahoma City, OK

St. Matthews Area Ministries—Louisville, KY

Saint Paul Area Council of Churches—St. Paul, MN

South Carolina Christian Action Council, Inc.—Columbia, SC

South Hills Interfaith Ministries—Bethel Park, PA

Tri-Council Coordinating Commission—Minneapolis, MN

Troy Area United Ministries—Troy, NY

Tulsa Metropolitan Ministry—Tulsa, OK

Virginia Council of Churches, Inc.—Richmond, VA

Wainwright House—Rye, NY

West Virginia Council of Churches—Charleston, WV

Wisconsin Council of Churches—Sun Prairie, WI

Christian Education Programs

Akron Area Association of Churches—Akron, OH

Arizona Ecumenical Council—Phoenix, AZ

Arkansas Interfaith Conference—Scott, AR

The Associated Churches of Fort Wayne & Allen County, Inc.—Fort Wayne, IN

Associated Ministries of Tacoma-Pierce County—Tacoma, WA

Attleboro Area Council of Churches, Inc.—Attleboro, MA

Berrien County Association of Churches—Benton Harbor, MI

Brooklyn Council of Churches—Brooklyn, NY

Christian Ministries of Delaware County—Muncie, IN

Christians United in Beaver County—Beaver, PA

Church Council of Greater Seattle—Seattle, WA

Council of Christian Communions of Greater Cincinnati—Cincinnati, OH

The Council of Churches of Santa Clara County—San Jose, CA

Council of Churches and Synagogues of Southwestern Connecticut—Stamford, CT

274

East Dallas Cooperative Parish—Dallas, TX
Ecclesia—Trenton, NJ
Ecumenical Conference of Greater Altoona—Altoona, PA
Ecumenical Council of San Diego County—San Diego, CA
FaithTrust Institute—Seattle, WA
FOCUS Churches of Albany, Inc.—Albany, NY
Georgia Christian Council—Macon, GA
Grand Rapids Area Center for Ecumenism (GRACE)—Grand Rapids, MI
Greater Chicago Broadcast Ministries—Chicago, IL
Greater Fairmont Council of Churches—Fairmont, WV
Greater Flint Council of Churches—Flint, MI
Greater Lawrence Council of Churches—Lawrence, MA
Greater Minneapolis Council of Churches—Minneapolis, MN
Greater New Orleans Federation of Churches—New Orleans, LA
Greensboro Urban Ministry—Greensboro, NC
Inter-Church Council of Greater New Bedford—New Bedford, MA
Inter-Church Ministries of Erie County—Erie, PA
Interchurch Ministries of Nebraska—Lincoln, NE
Iowa Religious Media Services—Urbandale, IA
Lehigh County Conference of Churches—Allentown, PA
Marin Interfaith Council—San Rafael, CA
The Metropolitan Christian Council: Detroit-Windsor—Detroit, MI
Metropolitan Christian Council of Philadelphia—Philadelphia, PA
Metropolitan Ecumenical Ministry—Newark, NJ
Montana Association of Churches—Helena, MT
New Britain Area Conference of Churches (NEW-BRACC)—New Britain, CT
New Mexico Conference of Churches—Bernalillo, NM
Northern Kentucky Interfaith Commission, Inc.—Newport, KY
Oklahoma Conference of Churches—Oklahoma City, OK
Peoria Friendship House of Christian Service—Peoria, IL
Reading Berks Conference of Churches—Reading, PA
South Carolina Christian Action Council, Inc.—Columbia, SC
Staten Island Council of Churches—Staten Island, NY
Tarrant Area Community of Churches—Fort Worth, TX
Texas Conference of Churches—Austin, TX
Troy Area United Ministries—Troy, NY
United Churches of Lycoming County—Williamsport, PA
Wainwright House—Rye, NY
Weekday Christian Education—Evansville, IN
Wyoming Valley Council of Churches—Wilkes-Barre, PA
York County Council of Churches—York, PA

Clothing Distribution Programs

Asheville-Buncombe Community Christian Ministry (ABCCM)—Asheville, NC
Attleboro Area Council of Churches, Inc.—Attleboro, MA
The Cape Cod Council of Churches, Inc.—Hyannis, MA
Chautauqua County Rural Ministry—Dunkirk, NY
Christian Community Action—New Haven, CT
Christian Ministries of Delaware County—Muncie, IN
Christian Service Center for Central Florida, Inc.—Orlando, FL
Community Emergency Assistance Program (CEAP)—Brooklyn Park, MN
Community Ministry of Montgomery County—Rockville, MD
Contact Ministries of Springfield—Springfield, IL
Cooperative Metropolitan Ministries—Newton, MA
Corpus Christi Metro Ministries—Corpus Christi, TX
Council of Churches of the Ozarks—Springfield, MO
Cross-Lines Cooperative Council—Kansas City, KS
East Dallas Cooperative Parish—Dallas, TX
Eastern Area Community Ministries—Louisville, KY
The Ecumenical Council of Pasadena Area Churches—Pasadena, CA
Ecumenical Ministries of Oregon—Portland, OR
Fern Creek-Highview United Ministries—Louisvlle, KY
Greater Birmingham Ministries—Birmingham, AL
Greater Fairmont Council of Churches—Fairmont, WV
Greater Lawrence Council of Churches—Lawrence, MA
Greater Minneapolis Council of Churches—Minneapolis, MN
Greensboro Urban Ministry—Greensboro, NC
Hanover Area Council of Churches—Hanover, PA
Highlands Community Ministries—Louisville, KY
Inter-Church Ministries of Erie County—Erie, PA
Interfaith Community Services—St. Joseph, MO
Lebanon County Christian Ministries—Lebanon, PA
Lehigh County Conference of Churches—Allentown, PA
Lewisburg Council of Churches—Lewisburg, PA
The Long Island Council of Churches—Hempstead, NY
Madison-area Urban Ministry—Madison, WI
Metropolitan Ecumenical Ministry—Newark, NJ
New Mexico Conference of Churches—Bernalillo, NM
Northside Inter-Church Agency (NICA)—Fort Worth, TX
Peoria Friendship House of Christian Service—Peoria, IL
Reading Berks Conference of Churches—Reading, PA
St. Matthews Area Ministries—Louisville, KY
Saint Paul Area Council of Churches—St. Paul, MN
South East Associated Ministries (SEAM)—Louisville, KY
South Hills Interfaith Ministries—Bethel Park, PA
West Side Ecumenical Ministry—Cleveland, OH
Wilkinsburg Community Ministry—Pittsburgh, PA

CROP Walks

Akron Area Association of Churches—Akron, OH
Alaska Christian Conference—Anchorage, AK
Alliance of Churches—Alliance, OH
Arizona Ecumenical Council—Phoenix, AZ
Asheville-Buncombe Community Christian Ministry (ABCCM)—Asheville, NC
Attleboro Area Council of Churches, Inc.—Attleboro, MA
Austin Area Interreligious Ministries—Austin, TX
Berrien County Association of Churches—Benton Harbor, MI
Broome County Council of Churches, Inc.—Binghamton, NY
Capital Area Council of Churches, Inc.—Albany, NY
Central Maryland Ecumenical Council—Baltimore, MD
Chautauqua County Rural Ministry—Dunkirk, NY
Christian Ministries of Delaware County—Muncie, IN
Christian Service Center for Central Florida, Inc.—Orlando, FL
Church Community Services—Elkhart, IN
Churches United, Inc.—Cedar Rapids, IA
Churches United of the Quad City Area—Bettendorf, IA
Community Emergency Assistance Program (CEAP)—Brooklyn Park, MN
The Council of Churches of Greater Bridgeport, Bridgeport, CT—Bridgeport, CT
Council of Churches of Greater Springfield—Springfield, MA
The Council of Churches of Santa Clara County—San Jose, CA
Dutchess County Interfaith Council, Inc.—Poughkeepsie, NY
East Dallas Cooperative Parish—Dallas, TX
East End Cooperative Ministry—Pittsburgh, PA
Ecclesia—Trenton, NJ
The Ecumenical Council of Pasadena Area Churches—Pasadena, CA
Ecumenical Ministries of Oregon—Portland, OR
The Faith In Action Network of Rochester, NY—Rochester, NY
FOCUS Churches of Albany, Inc.—Albany, NY
Greater Dayton Christian Connections—Dayton, OH
Greater Fairmont Council of Churches—Fairmont, WV
Greater Flint Council of Churches—Flint, MI
Greater Waterbury Interfaith Ministries, Inc.—Waterbury, CT
Greensboro Urban Ministry—Greensboro, NC
Hanover Area Council of Churches—Hanover, PA
Inter-Church Ministries of Erie County—Erie, PA
Interfaith Action of Evanston—Evanston, IL
The Interfaith Association of Northwest Washington—Everett, WA
Interfaith Conference of Greater Milwaukee—Milwaukee, WI
Interfaith Council—Spokane, WA
Interfaith Council of Contra Costa County—Walnut Creek, CA
Inter-Faith Ministries-Wichita—Wichita, KS
Interfaith Works—Olympia, WA
InterFaith Works of Central New York—Syracuse, NY
Lehigh County Conference of Churches—Allentown, PA
Lewisburg Council of Churches—Lewisburg, PA
The Long Island Council of Churches—Hempstead, NY
Mahoning Valley Association of Churches—Youngstown, OH
Marin Interfaith Council—San Rafael, CA
Metropolitan Ecumenical Ministry—Newark, NJ
Muskegon County Cooperating Churches—Muskegon, MI
Network of Religious Communities—Buffalo, NY
New Mexico Conference of Churches—Bernalillo, NM
Northside Inter-Church Agency (NICA)—Fort Worth, TX
Oak Park-River Forest Community of Congregations—Oak Park, IL
Peoria Friendship House of Christian Service—Peoria, IL
Pike County Outreach Council—Waverly, OH
Reading Berks Conference of Churches—Reading, PA
Saint Paul Area Council of Churches—St. Paul, MN
San Fernando Valley Interfaith Council—Chatsworth, CA
Schenectady Inner City Ministry—Schenectady, NY
South Coast Interfaith Council—Long Beach, CA
Staten Island Council of Churches—Staten Island, NY
Tarrant Area Community of Churches—Fort Worth, TX
Troy Area United Ministries—Troy, NY
United Churches of Lycoming County—Williamsport, PA
United Religious Community of St. Joseph County—South Bend, IN
Virginia Council of Churches, Inc.—Richmond, VA
Wilkinsburg Community Ministry—Pittsburgh, PA
Worcester County Ecumenical Council—Worcester, MA
Wyoming Valley Council of Churches—Wilkes-Barre, PA
York County Council of Churches—York, PA

Domestic Violence

Alaska Christian Conference—Anchorage, AK
Anchor Point Counseling Ministry—Pittsburgh, PA
Asheville-Buncombe Community Christian Ministry (ABCCM)—Asheville, NC
Associated Ministries of Tacoma-Pierce County—Tacoma, WA
Association of Religious Communities—Danbury, CT
Border Association for Refugees from Central America (BARCA), Inc.—Edinburg, TX
Central Maryland Ecumenical Council—Baltimore, MD
Chautauqua County Rural Ministry—Dunkirk, NY
Churches United of the Quad City Area—Bettendorf, IA
Colorado Council of Churches—Denver, CO

Contact Ministries of Springfield—Springfield, IL

The Council of Churches of Greater Bridgeport, Bridgeport, CT—Bridgeport, CT

The Council of Churches of Santa Clara County—San Jose, CA

Dutchess County Interfaith Council, Inc.—Poughkeepsie, NY

The Ecumenical Council of Pasadena Area Churches—Pasadena, CA

Ecumenical Council of San Diego County—San Diego, CA

Ecumenical Ministries of Oregon—Portland, OR

FaithTrust Institute—Seattle, WA

Genesee-Orleans Ministry of Concern—Albion, NY

Greater Chicago Broadcast Ministries—Chicago, IL

Greater Minneapolis Council of Churches—Minneapolis, MN

Indiana Partners for Christian Unity and Mission—Indianapolis, IN

Inter-Church Council of Greater New Bedford—New Bedford, MA

Interchurch Ministries of Nebraska—Lincoln, NE

Interfaith Council—Spokane, WA

Interfaith Service Bureau—Sacramento, CA

Metropolitan Ecumenical Ministry—Newark, NJ

Mississippi Religious Leadership Conference—Jackson, MS

Montana Association of Churches—Helena, MT

New Hampshire Council of Churches—Pembroke, NH

New Mexico Conference of Churches—Bernalillo, NM

North Carolina Council of Churches—Raleigh, NC

Oklahoma Conference of Churches—Oklahoma City, OK

Peoria Friendship House of Christian Service—Peoria, IL

Southeast Ecumenical Ministry—Rochester, NY

Tarrant Area Community of Churches—Fort Worth, TX

Troy Area United Ministries—Troy, NY

Tulsa Metropolitan Ministry—Tulsa, OK

United Religious Community of St. Joseph County—South Bend, IN

West Side Ecumenical Ministry—Cleveland, OH

York County Council of Churches—York, PA

Economic/Social Justice Programs

Alaska Christian Conference—Anchorage, AK

Arizona Ecumenical Council—Phoenix, AZ

Arkansas Interfaith Conference—Scott, AR

Asheville-Buncombe Community Christian Ministry (ABCCM)—Asheville, NC

The Associated Churches of Fort Wayne & Allen County, Inc.—Fort Wayne, IN

Associated Ministries of Tacoma-Pierce County—Tacoma, WA

Association of Christian Churches of South Dakota—Sioux Falls, SD

Austin Area Interreligious Ministries—Austin, TX

Berrien County Association of Churches—Benton Harbor, MI

Border Association for Refugees from Central America (BARCA), Inc.—Edinburg, TX

Brooklyn Council of Churches—Brooklyn, NY

Broome County Council of Churches, Inc.—Binghamton, NY

California Council of Churches-California Church Impact—Sacramento, CA

The Cape Cod Council of Churches, Inc.—Hyannis, MA

Capital Area Council of Churches, Inc.—Albany, NY

Capital Region Ecumenical Organization (CREO)—Malta, NY

The Capitol Region Conference of Churches—Hartford, CT

Central Maryland Ecumenical Council—Baltimore, MD

Chautauqua County Rural Ministry—Dunkirk, NY

Christian Community Action—New Haven, CT

Christian Ministries of Delaware County—Muncie, IN

Christian Service Center for Central Florida, Inc.—Orlando, FL

Church Council of Greater Seattle—Seattle, WA

The Church Federation of Greater Indianapolis, Inc.—Indianapolis, IN

Churches United, Inc.—Cedar Rapids, IA

Churches United of the Quad City Area—Bettendorf, IA

Colorado Council of Churches—Denver, CO

Community Emergency Assistance Program (CEAP)—Brooklyn Park, MN

Community Ministry of Montgomery County—Rockville, MD

Community Renewal Society—Chicago, IL

Contact Ministries of Springfield—Springfield, IL

Cooperative Metropolitan Ministries—Newton, MA

Council of Churches of the City of New York—New York, NY

Council of Churches of Greater Springfield—Springfield, MA

The Council of Churches of Santa Clara County—San Jose, CA

Eastern Area Community Ministries—Louisville, KY

Ecclesia—Trenton, NJ

Ecumenical Conference of Greater Altoona—Altoona, PA

The Ecumenical Council of Pasadena Area Churches—Pasadena, CA

Ecumenical Council of San Diego County—San Diego, CA

Ecumenical Ministries of Oregon—Portland, OR

Faith Action Network: A Partnership for the Common Good—Seattle, WA

Faith Community Assistance Center—Santa Fe, NM

The Faith In Action Network of Rochester, NY—Rochester, NY

Florida Council of Churches—Tampa, FL

FOCUS Churches of Albany, Inc.—Albany, NY

Fresno Metro Ministry—Fresno, CA

Grand Rapids Area Center for Ecumenism (GRACE)—Grand Rapids, MI

Greater Birmingham Ministries—Birmingham, AL

Greater Chicago Broadcast Ministries—Chicago, IL

Greater Dallas Community of Churches—Dallas, TX

Greater Dayton Christian Connections—Dayton, OH

Greater Minneapolis Council of Churches—Minneapolis, MN

Highlands Community Ministries—Louisville, KY
Illinois Conference of Churches—Springfield, IL
Inland Valley Hope Partners—Pomona, CA
Inter-Church Council of Greater New Bedford—New Bedford, MA
Interchurch Ministries of Nebraska—Lincoln, NE
Interfaith Action of Evanston—Evanston, IL
Interfaith Community Council, Inc.—New Albany, IN
Interfaith Conference of Greater Milwaukee—Milwaukee, WI
InterFaith Conference of Metropolitan Washington—Washington, DC
Interfaith Council—Spokane, WA
Interfaith Council of Contra Costa County—Walnut Creek, CA
Inter-Faith Ministries-Wichita—Wichita, KS
Interfaith Mission Service—Huntsville, AL
Interfaith Service Bureau—Sacramento, CA
Interfaith Works—Olympia, WA
InterFaith Works of Central New York—Syracuse, NY
The Joint Religious Legislative Coalition—Minneapolis, MN
Kentuckiana Interfaith Community—Louisville, KY
Kentucky Council of Churches—Lexington, KY
Lehigh County Conference of Churches—Allentown, PA
Lincoln Interfaith Council—Lincoln, NE
Madison-area Urban Ministry—Madison, WI
Mahoning Valley Association of Churches—Youngstown, OH
Maine Council of Churches—Portland, ME
Marin Interfaith Council—San Rafael, CA
Massachusetts Council of Churches—Boston, MA
Metropolitan Christian Council of Philadelphia—Philadelphia, PA
Metropolitan Ecumenical Ministry—Newark, NJ
Metropolitan Interfaith Council on Affordable Housing (MICAH)—Minneapolis, MN
Minnesota Council of Churches—Minneapolis, MN
Mississippi Religious Leadership Conference—Jackson, MS
Montana Association of Churches—Helena, MT
Muskegon County Cooperating Churches—Muskegon, MI
Network of Religious Communities—Buffalo, NY
New Britain Area Conference of Churches (NEW-BRACC)—New Britain, CT
New Hampshire Council of Churches—Pembroke, NH
New Mexico Conference of Churches—Bernalillo, NM
North Carolina Council of Churches—Raleigh, NC
North Dakota Conference of Churches—Ashley, ND
Northern California Interreligious Conference—Oakland, CA
Northside Inter-Church Agency (NICA)—Fort Worth, TX
Northwest Interfaith Movement—Philadelphia, PA
Oak Park-River Forest Community of Congregations—Oak Park, IL
Oak Park-River Forest Community of Congregations—Oak Park, IL

Ohio Council of Churches—Columbus, OH
Oklahoma Conference of Churches—Oklahoma City, OK
Pennsylvania Conference on Interchurch Cooperation—Harrisburg, PA
The Pennsylvania Council of Churches—Harrisburg, PA
Peoria Friendship House of Christian Service—Peoria, IL
Rural Migrant Ministry—Poughkeepsie, NY
St. Matthews Area Ministries—Louisville, KY
San Antonio Community of Congregations—San Antonio, TX
San Fernando Valley Interfaith Council—Chatsworth, CA
Schenectady Inner City Ministry—Schenectady, NY
South Carolina Christian Action Council, Inc.—Columbia, SC
South Coast Interfaith Council—Long Beach, CA
South East Associated Ministries (SEAM)—Louisville, KY
Southern California Ecumenical Council—Pasadena, CA
Tarrant Area Community of Churches—Fort Worth, TX
Troy Area United Ministries—Troy, NY
United Churches of Lycoming County—Williamsport, PA
United Religious Community of St. Joseph County—South Bend, IN
Virginia Council of Churches, Inc.—Richmond, VA
Wainwright House—Rye, NY
West Virginia Council of Churches—Charleston, WV
Wilkinsburg Community Ministry—Pittsburgh, PA
Wisconsin Council of Churches—Sun Prairie, WI
Wyoming Association of Churches—Laramie, WY
York County Council of Churches—York, PA

Employment Assistance Programs

Asheville-Buncombe Community Christian Ministry (ABCCM)—Asheville, NC
Associated Ministries of Tacoma-Pierce County—Tacoma, WA
Chautauqua County Rural Ministry—Dunkirk, NY
Community Emergency Assistance Program (CEAP)—Brooklyn Park, MN
Contact Ministries of Springfield—Springfield, IL
Corpus Christi Metro Ministries—Corpus Christi, TX
The Council of Churches of Greater Bridgeport, Bridgeport, CT—Bridgeport, CT
East Dallas Cooperative Parish—Dallas, TX
East End Cooperative Ministry—Pittsburgh, PA
Eastern Area Community Ministries—Louisville, KY
Fern Creek-Highview United Ministries—Louisvlle, KY
Genesee-Orleans Ministry of Concern—Albion, NY
Greater Chicago Broadcast Ministries—Chicago, IL
Greater Dallas Community of Churches—Dallas, TX
Greensboro Urban Ministry—Greensboro, NC
Illinois Conference of Churches—Springfield, IL
Interfaith Action of Evanston—Evanston, IL
Kentuckiana Interfaith Community—Louisville, KY
Lehigh County Conference of Churches—Allentown, PA

The Long Island Council of Churches—Hempstead, NY

Madison-area Urban Ministry—Madison, WI

Metropolitan Ecumenical Ministry—Newark, NJ

Minnesota Council of Churches—Minneapolis, MN

Northside Inter-Church Agency (NICA)—Fort Worth, TX

Peoria Friendship House of Christian Service—Peoria, IL

St. Matthews Area Ministries—Louisville, KY

South East Associated Ministries (SEAM)—Louisville, KY

Southeast Ecumenical Ministry—Rochester, NY

United Ministries—Greenville, SC

West Side Ecumenical Ministry—Cleveland, OH

Environmental Programs

Akron Area Association of Churches—Akron, OH

Arizona Ecumenical Council—Phoenix, AZ

California Council of Churches-California Church Impact—Sacramento, CA

The Cape Cod Council of Churches, Inc.—Hyannis, MA

Capital Region Ecumenical Organization (CREO)—Malta, NY

The Capitol Region Conference of Churches—Hartford, CT

Central Maryland Ecumenical Council—Baltimore, MD

Christian Associates of Southwest Pennsylvania—Pittsburgh, PA

Colorado Council of Churches—Denver, CO

The Council of Churches of Santa Clara County—San Jose, CA

Ecumenical Ministries of Iowa (EMI)—Des Moines, IA

Ecumenical Ministries of Oregon—Portland, OR

Faith Action Network: A Partnership for the Common Good—Seattle, WA

Florida Council of Churches—Tampa, FL

Fresno Metro Ministry—Fresno, CA

Georgia Christian Council—Macon, GA

Greater Chicago Broadcast Ministries—Chicago, IL

Greater Dayton Christian Connections—Dayton, OH

Inter-Church Council of Greater New Bedford—New Bedford, MA

Interfaith Conference of Greater Milwaukee—Milwaukee, WI

InterFaith Conference of Metropolitan Washington—Washington, DC

Interfaith Council of Contra Costa County—Walnut Creek, CA

Interfaith Mission Service—Huntsville, AL

Interfaith Works—Olympia, WA

Kentucky Council of Churches—Lexington, KY

The Long Island Council of Churches—Hempstead, NY

Maine Council of Churches—Portland, ME

Massachusetts Council of Churches—Boston, MA

Metropolitan Christian Council of Philadelphia—Philadelphia, PA

Metropolitan Ecumenical Ministry—Newark, NJ

Minnesota Council of Churches—Minneapolis, MN

Mississippi Religious Leadership Conference—Jackson, MS

Montana Association of Churches—Helena, MT

Muskegon County Cooperating Churches—Muskegon, MI

Network of Religious Communities—Buffalo, NY

New Hampshire Council of Churches—Pembroke, NH

New Mexico Conference of Churches—Bernalillo, NM

North Carolina Council of Churches—Raleigh, NC

Northern California Interreligious Conference—Oakland, CA

Ohio Council of Churches—Columbus, OH

The Pennsylvania Council of Churches—Harrisburg, PA

San Antonio Community of Congregations—San Antonio, TX

South Carolina Christian Action Council, Inc.—Columbia, SC

South Coast Interfaith Council—Long Beach, CA

Southern California Ecumenical Council—Pasadena, CA

United Churches of Lycoming County—Williamsport, PA

Vermont Ecumenical Council and Bible Society—Richmond, VT

West Virginia Council of Churches—Charleston, WV

Wyoming Association of Churches—Laramie, WY

Faith and Order Programs

Akron Area Association of Churches—Akron, OH

Alaska Christian Conference—Anchorage, AK

Arizona Ecumenical Council—Phoenix, AZ

The Associated Churches of Fort Wayne & Allen County, Inc.—Fort Wayne, IN

Associated Ministries of Tacoma-Pierce County—Tacoma, WA

Association of Christian Churches of South Dakota—Sioux Falls, SD

The Cape Cod Council of Churches, Inc.—Hyannis, MA

Capital Area Council of Churches, Inc.—Albany, NY

Capital Region Ecumenical Organization (CREO)—Malta, NY

Christian Associates of Southwest Pennsylvania—Pittsburgh, PA

The Church Federation of Greater Indianapolis, Inc.—Indianapolis, IN

Churches United, Inc.—Cedar Rapids, IA

Colorado Council of Churches—Denver, CO

Council of Churches of the City of New York—New York, NY

Council of Churches of Greater Springfield—Springfield, MA

The Council of Churches of Santa Clara County—San Jose, CA

Council of Churches and Synagogues of Southwestern Connecticut—Stamford, CT

East Dallas Cooperative Parish—Dallas, TX

Ecclesia—Trenton, NJ

Ecumenical Council of San Diego County—San Diego, CA

Ecumenical Ministries of Iowa (EMI)—Des Moines, IA

279

Florida Council of Churches—Tampa, FL
Georgia Christian Council—Macon, GA
Greater Chicago Broadcast Ministries—Chicago, IL
Greater Dallas Community of Churches—Dallas, TX
Greater Lawrence Council of Churches—Lawrence, MA
Greater New Orleans Federation of Churches—New Orleans, LA
Greater Waterbury Interfaith Ministries, Inc.—Waterbury, CT
Illinois Conference of Churches—Springfield, IL
Inter-Church Council of Greater New Bedford—New Bedford, MA
Interchurch Ministries of Nebraska—Lincoln, NE
Interfaith Action of Evanston—Evanston, IL
InterFaith Conference of Metropolitan Washington—Washington, DC
InterFaith Works of Central New York—Syracuse, NY
Kentuckiana Interfaith Community—Louisville, KY
Lehigh County Conference of Churches—Allentown, PA
Mahoning Valley Association of Churches—Youngstown, OH
The Metropolitan Christian Council: Detroit-Windsor—Detroit, MI
Metropolitan Christian Council of Philadelphia—Philadelphia, PA
Metropolitan Ecumenical Ministry—Newark, NJ
Minnesota Council of Churches—Minneapolis, MN
Montana Association of Churches—Helena, MT
New Britain Area Conference of Churches (NEW-BRACC)—New Britain, CT
New Hampshire Council of Churches—Pembroke, NH
New Mexico Conference of Churches—Bernalillo, NM
North Carolina Council of Churches—Raleigh, NC
North Dakota Conference of Churches—Ashley, ND
Northern California Interreligious Conference—Oakland, CA
Northern Kentucky Interfaith Commission, Inc.—Newport, KY
Ohio Council of Churches—Columbus, OH
Oklahoma Conference of Churches—Oklahoma City, OK
The Pennsylvania Council of Churches—Harrisburg, PA
San Antonio Community of Congregations—San Antonio, TX
Southern California Ecumenical Council—Pasadena, CA
Texas Conference of Churches—Austin, TX
Troy Area United Ministries—Troy, NY
Tulsa Metropolitan Ministry—Tulsa, OK
United Churches of Lycoming County—Williamsport, PA
United Religious Community of St. Joseph County—South Bend, IN
Vermont Ecumenical Council and Bible Society—Richmond, VT
Virginia Council of Churches, Inc.—Richmond, VA
Wainwright House—Rye, NY
West Virginia Council of Churches—Charleston, WV

Wisconsin Council of Churches—Sun Prairie, WI
Wyoming Valley Council of Churches—Wilkes-Barre, PA

Health Care Issues

Arizona Ecumenical Council—Phoenix, AZ
Asheville-Buncombe Community Christian Ministry (ABCCM)—Asheville, NC
California Council of Churches-California Church Impact—Sacramento, CA
Christian Associates of Southwest Pennsylvania—Pittsburgh, PA
Christian Churches United of the Tri-County Area—Harrisburg, PA
Churchpeople for Change and Reconciliation—Lima, OH
Colorado Council of Churches—Denver, CO
Community Ministries of Rockville—Rockville, MD
Corpus Christi Metro Ministries—Corpus Christi, TX
Council of Churches of the City of New York—New York, NY
The Council of Churches of Santa Clara County—San Jose, CA
East Dallas Cooperative Parish—Dallas, TX
Eastern Area Community Ministries—Louisville, KY
Ecumenical Ministries of Iowa (EMI)—Des Moines, IA
Faith Action Network: A Partnership for the Common Good—Seattle, WA
Fresno Metro Ministry—Fresno, CA
Greater Chicago Broadcast Ministries—Chicago, IL
Greensboro Urban Ministry—Greensboro, NC
Highlands Community Ministries—Louisville, KY
Inter-Church Council of Greater New Bedford—New Bedford, MA
Inter-Church Ministries of Erie County—Erie, PA
Interchurch Ministries of Nebraska—Lincoln, NE
Interfaith Conference of Greater Milwaukee—Milwaukee, WI
Interfaith Council of Contra Costa County—Walnut Creek, CA
Interfaith Federation of Greater Baton Rouge—Baton Rouge, LA
Kansas Ecumenical Ministries—Topeka, KS
Kentucky Council of Churches—Lexington, KY
The Long Island Council of Churches—Hempstead, NY
Madison-area Urban Ministry—Madison, WI
Maine Council of Churches—Portland, ME
The Metropolitan Christian Council: Detroit-Windsor—Detroit, MI
Metropolitan Ecumenical Ministry—Newark, NJ
Metropolitan Ecumenical Ministry Community Development Corp.—Newark, NJ
Mississippi Religious Leadership Conference—Jackson, MS
Network of Religious Communities—Buffalo, NY
New Hampshire Council of Churches—Pembroke, NH
New Mexico Conference of Churches—Bernalillo, NM
North Carolina Council of Churches—Raleigh, NC
Ohio Council of Churches—Columbus, OH
Oklahoma Conference of Churches—Oklahoma City, OK

The Pennsylvania Council of Churches—Harrisburg, PA

Peoria Friendship House of Christian Service—Peoria, IL

Pike County Outreach Council—Waverly, OH

Schenectady Inner City Ministry—Schenectady, NY

South Carolina Christian Action Council, Inc.—Columbia, SC

Southeast Ecumenical Ministry—Rochester, NY

Tuscarawas County Council for Church and Community—New Philadelphia, OH

United Churches of Lycoming County—Williamsport, PA

United Religious Community of St. Joseph County—South Bend, IN

West Virginia Council of Churches—Charleston, WV

Wyoming Association of Churches—Laramie, WY

Homelessness/Shelter Programs

Alaska Christian Conference—Anchorage, AK

Allegheny Valley Association of Churches—Natrona Heights, PA

Alliance of Churches—Alliance, OH

Arkansas Interfaith Conference—Scott, AR

Asheville-Buncombe Community Christian Ministry (ABCCM)—Asheville, NC

Associated Ministries of Tacoma-Pierce County—Tacoma, WA

Attleboro Area Council of Churches, Inc.—Attleboro, MA

Austin Area Interreligious Ministries—Austin, TX

Border Association for Refugees from Central America (BARCA), Inc.—Edinburg, TX

The Cape Cod Council of Churches, Inc.—Hyannis, MA

Capital Area Council of Churches, Inc.—Albany, NY

The Capitol Region Conference of Churches—Hartford, CT

Center City Churches—Hartford, CT

Chautauqua County Rural Ministry—Dunkirk, NY

Christian Associates of Southwest Pennsylvania—Pittsburgh, PA

Christian Churches United of the Tri-County Area—Harrisburg, PA

Christian Community Action—New Haven, CT

Christian Ministries of Delaware County—Muncie, IN

Christian Service Center for Central Florida, Inc.—Orlando, FL

Church Council of Greater Seattle—Seattle, WA

Churches United, Inc.—Cedar Rapids, IA

Churches United of the Quad City Area—Bettendorf, IA

Community Emergency Assistance Program (CEAP)—Brooklyn Park, MN

Community Ministries of Rockville—Rockville, MD

Community Ministry of Montgomery County—Rockville, MD

Contact Ministries of Springfield—Springfield, IL

Cooperative Metropolitan Ministries—Newton, MA

Corpus Christi Metro Ministries—Corpus Christi, TX

Council of Churches of the City of New York—New York, NY

The Council of Churches of Greater Bridgeport, Bridgeport, CT—Bridgeport, CT

Council of Churches of Greater Springfield—Springfield, MA

The Council of Churches of Santa Clara County—San Jose, CA

East End Cooperative Ministry—Pittsburgh, PA

The Ecumenical Council of Pasadena Area Churches—Pasadena, CA

Ecumenical Council of San Diego County—San Diego, CA

Ecumenical Ministries of Oregon—Portland, OR

Faith Action Network: A Partnership for the Common Good—Seattle, WA

Faith Community Assistance Center—Santa Fe, NM

Genesee-Orleans Ministry of Concern—Albion, NY

Grand Rapids Area Center for Ecumenism (GRACE)—Grand Rapids, MI

Greater Chicago Broadcast Ministries—Chicago, IL

Greater Dayton Christian Connections—Dayton, OH

Greater Minneapolis Council of Churches—Minneapolis, MN

Greensboro Urban Ministry—Greensboro, NC

Hanover Area Council of Churches—Hanover, PA

Highlands Community Ministries—Louisville, KY

Illinois Conference of Churches—Springfield, IL

Inland Valley Hope Partners—Pomona, CA

Inter-Church Ministries of Erie County—Erie, PA

Interfaith Action of Evanston—Evanston, IL

The Interfaith Association of Northwest Washington—Everett, WA

Interfaith Community Council, Inc.—New Albany, IN

Interfaith Community Services—St. Joseph, MO

Interfaith Conference of Greater Milwaukee—Milwaukee, WI

InterFaith Conference of Metropolitan Washington—Washington, DC

Interfaith Council of Contra Costa County—Walnut Creek, CA

Inter-Faith Ministries-Wichita—Wichita, KS

Interfaith Mission Service—Huntsville, AL

Interfaith Works—Olympia, WA

InterFaith Works of Central New York—Syracuse, NY

Lehigh County Conference of Churches—Allentown, PA

Lewisburg Council of Churches—Lewisburg, PA

The Long Island Council of Churches—Hempstead, NY

Madison-area Urban Ministry—Madison, WI

Maine Council of Churches—Portland, ME

Marin Interfaith Council—San Rafael, CA

Metropolitan Ecumenical Ministry—Newark, NJ

Metropolitan Inter Faith Association (MIFA)—Memphis, TN

Metropolitan Interfaith Council on Affordable Housing (MICAH)—Minneapolis, MN

Minnesota Council of Churches—Minneapolis, MN

Mississippi Religious Leadership Conference—Jackson, MS

Muskegon County Cooperating Churches—Muskegon, MI

New Britain Area Conference of Churches (NEWBRACC)—New Britain, CT

New Hampshire Council of Churches—Pembroke, NH

New Mexico Conference of Churches—Bernalillo, NM

North Carolina Council of Churches—Raleigh, NC

Northside Common Ministries—Pittsburgh, PA

Northside Inter-Church Agency (NICA)—Fort Worth, TX

Paducah Cooperative Ministry—Paducah, KY

Peoria Friendship House of Christian Service—Peoria, IL

Pike County Outreach Council—Waverly, OH

Reading Berks Conference of Churches—Reading, PA

St. Matthews Area Ministries—Louisville, KY

Saint Paul Area Council of Churches—St. Paul, MN

Schenectady Inner City Ministry—Schenectady, NY

Tarrant Area Community of Churches—Fort Worth, TX

Troy Area United Ministries—Troy, NY

Tuscarawas County Council for Church and Community—New Philadelphia, OH

United Ministries—Greenville, SC

United Religious Community of St. Joseph County—South Bend, IN

West Virginia Council of Churches—Charleston, WV

Wyoming Valley Council of Churches—Wilkes-Barre, PA

York County Council of Churches—York, PA

Hunger/Food Program

Alaska Christian Conference—Anchorage, AK

Allegheny Valley Association of Churches—Natrona Heights, PA

Alliance of Churches—Alliance, OH

Arizona Ecumenical Council—Phoenix, AZ

Arkansas Interfaith Conference—Scott, AR

Asheville-Buncombe Community Christian Ministry (ABCCM)—Asheville, NC

The Associated Churches of Fort Wayne & Allen County, Inc.—Fort Wayne, IN

Associated Ministries of Tacoma-Pierce County—Tacoma, WA

Attleboro Area Council of Churches, Inc.—Attleboro, MA

Austin Area Interreligious Ministries—Austin, TX

Berrien County Association of Churches—Benton Harbor, MI

Border Association for Refugees from Central America (BARCA), Inc.—Edinburg, TX

Brooklyn Council of Churches—Brooklyn, NY

Broome County Council of Churches, Inc.—Binghamton, NY

California Council of Churches-California Church Impact—Sacramento, CA

The Cape Cod Council of Churches, Inc.—Hyannis, MA

Capital Area Council of Churches, Inc.—Albany, NY

Capital Region Ecumenical Organization (CREO)—Malta, NY

Center City Churches—Hartford, CT

Chautauqua County Rural Ministry—Dunkirk, NY

Christian Churches United of the Tri-County Area—Harrisburg, PA

Christian Community Action—New Haven, CT

Christian Ministries of Delaware County—Muncie, IN

Christian Service Center for Central Florida, Inc.—Orlando, FL

Church Community Services—Elkhart, IN

The Church Federation of Greater Indianapolis, Inc.—Indianapolis, IN

Churches United of the Quad City Area—Bettendorf, IA

Community Emergency Assistance Program (CEAP)—Brooklyn Park, MN

Community Ministry of Montgomery County—Rockville, MD

Concerned Ecumenical Ministry to the Upper West Side—Buffalo, NY

Contact Ministries of Springfield—Springfield, IL

Corpus Christi Metro Ministries—Corpus Christi, TX

Council of Churches of the City of New York—New York, NY

The Council of Churches of Greater Bridgeport, Bridgeport, CT—Bridgeport, CT

Council of Churches of the Ozarks—Springfield, MO

The Council of Churches of Santa Clara County—San Jose, CA

Council of Churches and Synagogues of Southwestern Connecticut—Stamford, CT

Cross-Lines Cooperative Council—Kansas City, KS

Des Moines Area Religious Council—Des Moines, IA

Dutchess County Interfaith Council, Inc.—Poughkeepsie, NY

East Dallas Cooperative Parish—Dallas, TX

East End Cooperative Ministry—Pittsburgh, PA

Eastern Area Community Ministries—Louisville, KY

Ecclesia—Trenton, NJ

The Ecumenical Council of Pasadena Area Churches—Pasadena, CA

Ecumenical Council of San Diego County—San Diego, CA

Ecumenical Ministries of Oregon—Portland, OR

Faith Action Network: A Partnership for the Common Good—Seattle, WA

Faith Community Assistance Center—Santa Fe, NM

Fern Creek-Highview United Ministries—Louisvlle, KY

Florida Council of Churches—Tampa, FL

FOCUS Churches of Albany, Inc.—Albany, NY

Fresno Metro Ministry—Fresno, CA

Genesee County Churches United, Inc.—Batavia, NY

Genesee-Orleans Ministry of Concern—Albion, NY

Grand Rapids Area Center for Ecumenism (GRACE)—Grand Rapids, MI

Greater Birmingham Ministries—Birmingham, AL

Greater Chicago Broadcast Ministries—Chicago, IL

Greater Dallas Community of Churches—Dallas, TX

Greater Minneapolis Council of Churches—Minneapolis, MN

Greater New Orleans Federation of Churches—New Orleans, LA

Greater Waterbury Interfaith Ministries, Inc.—Waterbury, CT

Greensboro Urban Ministry—Greensboro, NC

Hanover Area Council of Churches—Hanover, PA

Highlands Community Ministries—Louisville, KY

Illinois Conference of Churches—Springfield, IL

Inland Valley Hope Partners—Pomona, CA

Inter-Church Ministries of Erie County—Erie, PA
Interchurch Ministries of Nebraska—Lincoln, NE
Interfaith Action of Evanston—Evanston, IL
Interfaith Community Council, Inc.—New Albany, IN
Interfaith Community Services—St. Joseph, MO
InterFaith Conference of Metropolitan Washington—Washington, DC
Interfaith Federation of Greater Baton Rouge—Baton Rouge, LA
Inter-Faith Ministries-Wichita—Wichita, KS
Interfaith Mission Service—Huntsville, AL
InterFaith Works of Central New York—Syracuse, NY
Kentuckiana Interfaith Community—Louisville, KY
Lebanon County Christian Ministries—Lebanon, PA
Lehigh County Conference of Churches—Allentown, PA
Lewisburg Council of Churches—Lewisburg, PA
The Long Island Council of Churches—Hempstead, NY
Madison-area Urban Ministry—Madison, WI
Maine Council of Churches—Portland, ME
The Metropolitan Christian Council: Detroit-Windsor—Detroit, MI
Metropolitan Ecumenical Ministry—Newark, NJ
Metropolitan Inter Faith Association (MIFA)—Memphis, TN
Minnesota Council of Churches—Minneapolis, MN
Mississippi Religious Leadership Conference—Jackson, MS
Muskegon County Cooperating Churches—Muskegon, MI
Network of Religious Communities—Buffalo, NY
New Britain Area Conference of Churches (NEW-BRACC)—New Britain, CT
New Hampshire Council of Churches—Pembroke, NH
New Mexico Conference of Churches—Bernalillo, NM
Northside Common Ministries—Pittsburgh, PA
Northside Inter-Church Agency (NICA)—Fort Worth, TX
Northwest Harvest-E. M. M.—Seattle, WA
Northwest Harvest-E. M. M.—Seattle, WA
Oak Park-River Forest Community of Congregations—Oak Park, IL
Ohio Council of Churches—Columbus, OH
Oklahoma Conference of Churches—Oklahoma City, OK
Paducah Cooperative Ministry—Paducah, KY
Peoria Friendship House of Christian Service—Peoria, IL
Pike County Outreach Council—Waverly, OH
Queens Federation of Churches—Richmond Hill, NY
Reading Berks Conference of Churches—Reading, PA
The Regional Council for Christian Ministry, Inc.—Idaho Falls, ID
St. Matthews Area Ministries—Louisville, KY
Saint Paul Area Council of Churches—St. Paul, MN
San Antonio Community of Congregations—San Antonio, TX
San Fernando Valley Interfaith Council—Chatsworth, CA

Schenectady Inner City Ministry—Schenectady, NY
South East Associated Ministries (SEAM)—Louisville, KY
South Hills Interfaith Ministries—Bethel Park, PA
South Louisville Community Ministries—Louisville, KY
Southeast Ecumenical Ministry—Rochester, NY
Staten Island Council of Churches—Staten Island, NY
Tuscarawas County Council for Church and Community—New Philadelphia, OH
United Churches of Lycoming County—Williamsport, PA
United Ministries—Greenville, SC
United Religious Community of St. Joseph County—South Bend, IN
Virginia Council of Churches, Inc.—Richmond, VA
Weekday Christian Education—Evansville, IN
Wellspring Interfaith Social Services, Inc. (previously West Central Neighborhood Ministry, Inc.)—Fort Wayne, IN
West Side Ecumenical Ministry—Cleveland, OH
Wilkinsburg Community Ministry—Pittsburgh, PA
Wyoming Valley Council of Churches—Wilkes-Barre, PA
York County Council of Churches—York, PA

Immigration Issues

Arizona Ecumenical Council—Phoenix, AZ
Arkansas Interfaith Conference—Scott, AR
Association of Religious Communities—Danbury, CT
Austin Area Interreligious Ministries—Austin, TX
Border Association for Refugees from Central America (BARCA), Inc.—Edinburg, TX
Central Maryland Ecumenical Council—Baltimore, MD
Chautauqua County Rural Ministry—Dunkirk, NY
Church Council of Greater Seattle—Seattle, WA
Colorado Council of Churches—Denver, CO
Community Emergency Assistance Program (CEAP)—Brooklyn Park, MN
Community Ministries of Rockville—Rockville, MD
Council of Churches of the City of New York—New York, NY
East Dallas Cooperative Parish—Dallas, TX
Eastern Area Community Ministries—Louisville, KY
The Ecumenical Council of Pasadena Area Churches—Pasadena, CA
Ecumenical Ministries of Oregon—Portland, OR
Faith Action Network: A Partnership for the Common Good—Seattle, WA
Florida Council of Churches—Tampa, FL
Greater Minneapolis Council of Churches—Minneapolis, MN
Illinois Conference of Churches—Springfield, IL
Interfaith Community Services—St. Joseph, MO
InterFaith Works of Central New York—Syracuse, NY
Kansas Ecumenical Ministries—Topeka, KS
Kentucky Council of Churches—Lexington, KY
Maine Council of Churches—Portland, ME
Minnesota Council of Churches—Minneapolis, MN
Mississippi Religious Leadership Conference—Jackson, MS

Network of Religious Communities—Buffalo, NY

New Hampshire Council of Churches—Pembroke, NH

New Mexico Conference of Churches—Bernalillo, NM

North Carolina Council of Churches—Raleigh, NC

Northside Inter-Church Agency (NICA)—Fort Worth, TX

Oklahoma Conference of Churches—Oklahoma City, OK

Peoria Friendship House of Christian Service—Peoria, IL

Reading Berks Conference of Churches—Reading, PA

San Fernando Valley Interfaith Council—Chatsworth, CA

South Carolina Christian Action Council, Inc.—Columbia, SC

South Coast Interfaith Council—Long Beach, CA

Tulsa Metropolitan Ministry—Tulsa, OK

United Religious Community of St. Joseph County—South Bend, IN

Virginia Council of Churches, Inc.—Richmond, VA

West Virginia Council of Churches—Charleston, WV

Interfaith Dialogue/Relationships

Akron Area Association of Churches—Akron, OH

Arizona Ecumenical Council—Phoenix, AZ

Arkansas Interfaith Conference—Scott, AR

The Associated Churches of Fort Wayne & Allen County, Inc.—Fort Wayne, IN

Associated Ministries of Tacoma-Pierce County—Tacoma, WA

Association of Christian Churches of South Dakota—Sioux Falls, SD

Association of Religious Communities—Danbury, CT

Attleboro Area Council of Churches, Inc.—Attleboro, MA

Austin Area Interreligious Ministries—Austin, TX

Border Association for Refugees from Central America (BARCA), Inc.—Edinburg, TX

Brooklyn Council of Churches—Brooklyn, NY

Broome County Council of Churches, Inc.—Binghamton, NY

California Council of Churches-California Church Impact—Sacramento, CA

The Cape Cod Council of Churches, Inc.—Hyannis, MA

Capital Area Council of Churches, Inc.—Albany, NY

Capital Region Ecumenical Organization (CREO)—Malta, NY

The Capitol Region Conference of Churches—Hartford, CT

Central Maryland Ecumenical Council—Baltimore, MD

Christian Associates of Southwest Pennsylvania—Pittsburgh, PA

Christian Ministries of Delaware County—Muncie, IN

Church Council of Greater Seattle—Seattle, WA

Churches United, Inc.—Cedar Rapids, IA

Churches United of the Quad City Area—Bettendorf, IA

Colorado Council of Churches—Denver, CO

Community Emergency Assistance Program (CEAP)—Brooklyn Park, MN

Community Ministries of Rockville—Rockville, MD

Community Ministry of Montgomery County—Rockville, MD

Community Renewal Society—Chicago, IL

Cooperative Metropolitan Ministries—Newton, MA

Council of Churches of Chemung County, Inc.—Elmira, NY

Council of Churches of the City of New York—New York, NY

The Council of Churches of Greater Bridgeport, Bridgeport, CT—Bridgeport, CT

Council of Churches of Greater Springfield—Springfield, MA

The Council of Churches of Santa Clara County—San Jose, CA

Council of Churches and Synagogues of Southwestern Connecticut—Stamford, CT

Des Moines Area Religious Council—Des Moines, IA

Dutchess County Interfaith Council, Inc.—Poughkeepsie, NY

East Dallas Cooperative Parish—Dallas, TX

Eastern Area Community Ministries—Louisville, KY

Ecclesia—Trenton, NJ

Ecumenical Conference of Greater Altoona—Altoona, PA

The Ecumenical Council of Pasadena Area Churches—Pasadena, CA

Ecumenical Council of San Diego County—San Diego, CA

Ecumenical Ministries of Iowa (EMI)—Des Moines, IA

Ecumenical Ministries of Oregon—Portland, OR

Faith Action Network: A Partnership for the Common Good—Seattle, WA

Faith Community Assistance Center—Santa Fe, NM

The Faith In Action Network of Rochester, NY—Rochester, NY

FaithTrust Institute—Seattle, WA

Florida Council of Churches—Tampa, FL

Fresno Metro Ministry—Fresno, CA

Georgia Christian Council—Macon, GA

Grand Rapids Area Center for Ecumenism (GRACE)—Grand Rapids, MI

Greater Birmingham Ministries—Birmingham, AL

Greater Chicago Broadcast Ministries—Chicago, IL

Greater Dallas Community of Churches—Dallas, TX

Greater Dayton Christian Connections—Dayton, OH

Greater Flint Council of Churches—Flint, MI

Greater Lawrence Council of Churches—Lawrence, MA

Greater New Orleans Federation of Churches—New Orleans, LA

Greater Waterbury Interfaith Ministries, Inc.—Waterbury, CT

Greensboro Urban Ministry—Greensboro, NC

Highlands Community Ministries—Louisville, KY

Illinois Conference of Churches—Springfield, IL

Inter-Church Council of Greater New Bedford—New Bedford, MA

Inter-Church Ministries of Erie County—Erie, PA

Interchurch Ministries of Nebraska—Lincoln, NE

Interfaith Action of Evanston—Evanston, IL

The Interfaith Association of Northwest Washington—Everett, WA

Interfaith Community Services—St. Joseph, MO

Interfaith Conference of Greater Milwaukee—Milwaukee, WI

InterFaith Conference of Metropolitan Washington—Washington, DC

Interfaith Council—Spokane, WA

Interfaith Council of Contra Costa County—Walnut Creek, CA

Interfaith Federation of Greater Baton Rouge—Baton Rouge, LA

Inter-Faith Ministries-Wichita—Wichita, KS

Interfaith Mission Service—Huntsville, AL

Interfaith Service Bureau—Sacramento, CA

Interfaith Works—Olympia, WA

InterFaith Works of Central New York—Syracuse, NY

The Joint Religious Legislative Coalition—Minneapolis, MN

Kentuckiana Interfaith Community—Louisville, KY

Lehigh County Conference of Churches—Allentown, PA

Lewisburg Council of Churches—Lewisburg, PA

Lincoln Interfaith Council—Lincoln, NE

The Long Island Council of Churches—Hempstead, NY

Madison-area Urban Ministry—Madison, WI

Mahoning Valley Association of Churches—Youngstown, OH

Maine Council of Churches—Portland, ME

Massachusetts Council of Churches—Boston, MA

The Metropolitan Christian Council: Detroit-Windsor—Detroit, MI

Metropolitan Christian Council of Philadelphia—Philadelphia, PA

Metropolitan Ecumenical Ministry—Newark, NJ

Metropolitan Interfaith Council on Affordable Housing (MICAH)—Minneapolis, MN

Minnesota Council of Churches—Minneapolis, MN

Mississippi Religious Leadership Conference—Jackson, MS

Muskegon County Cooperating Churches—Muskegon, MI

Network of Religious Communities—Buffalo, NY

New Britain Area Conference of Churches (NEW-BRACC)—New Britain, CT

New Hampshire Council of Churches—Pembroke, NH

New Mexico Conference of Churches—Bernalillo, NM

North Carolina Council of Churches—Raleigh, NC

North Dakota Conference of Churches—Ashley, ND

Northern California Interreligious Conference—Oakland, CA

Northern Kentucky Interfaith Commission, Inc.—Newport, KY

Northwest Interfaith Movement—Philadelphia, PA

Oak Park-River Forest Community of Congregations—Oak Park, IL

Oklahoma Conference of Churches—Oklahoma City, OK

Pennsylvania Conference on Interchurch Cooperation—Harrisburg, PA

Peoria Friendship House of Christian Service—Peoria, IL

Queens Federation of Churches—Richmond Hill, NY

Reading Berks Conference of Churches—Reading, PA

St. Matthews Area Ministries—Louisville, KY

Saint Paul Area Council of Churches—St. Paul, MN

San Fernando Valley Interfaith Council—Chatsworth, CA

South Carolina Christian Action Council, Inc.—Columbia, SC

South Coast Interfaith Council—Long Beach, CA

South Hills Interfaith Ministries—Bethel Park, PA

Staten Island Council of Churches—Staten Island, NY

Tarrant Area Community of Churches—Fort Worth, TX

Troy Area United Ministries—Troy, NY

Tulsa Metropolitan Ministry—Tulsa, OK

Tuscarawas County Council for Church and Community—New Philadelphia, OH

United Churches of Lycoming County—Williamsport, PA

United Religious Community of St. Joseph County—South Bend, IN

Wainwright House—Rye, NY

West Side Ecumenical Ministry—Cleveland, OH

West Virginia Council of Churches—Charleston, WV

Wisconsin Council of Churches—Sun Prairie, WI

Worcester County Ecumenical Council—Worcester, MA

Wyoming Valley Council of Churches—Wilkes-Barre, PA

Peace Advocacy

Arizona Ecumenical Council—Phoenix, AZ

Arkansas Interfaith Conference—Scott, AR

The Associated Churches of Fort Wayne & Allen County, Inc.—Fort Wayne, IN

Associated Ministries of Tacoma-Pierce County—Tacoma, WA

Association of Christian Churches of South Dakota—Sioux Falls, SD

Border Association for Refugees from Central America (BARCA), Inc.—Edinburg, TX

The Cape Cod Council of Churches, Inc.—Hyannis, MA

Central Maryland Ecumenical Council—Baltimore, MD

Church Council of Greater Seattle—Seattle, WA

The Church Federation of Greater Indianapolis, Inc.—Indianapolis, IN

Colorado Council of Churches—Denver, CO

Council of Churches of the City of New York—New York, NY

Council of Churches of Greater Springfield—Springfield, MA

The Council of Churches of Santa Clara County—San Jose, CA

Ecumenical Conference of Greater Altoona—Altoona, PA

Ecumenical Ministries of Iowa (EMI)—Des Moines, IA

Ecumenical Ministries of Oregon—Portland, OR

Faith Action Network: A Partnership for the Common Good—Seattle, WA

The Faith In Action Network of Rochester, NY—Rochester, NY

Florida Council of Churches—Tampa, FL

FOCUS Churches of Albany, Inc.—Albany, NY

Greater Chicago Broadcast Ministries—Chicago, IL

Greater Dallas Community of Churches—Dallas, TX

Illinois Conference of Churches—Springfield, IL

Interchurch Ministries of Nebraska—Lincoln, NE

Interfaith Council of Contra Costa County—Walnut Creek, CA

InterFaith Works of Central New York—Syracuse, NY

Kentuckiana Interfaith Community—Louisville, KY

Lehigh County Conference of Churches—Allentown, PA

Lincoln Interfaith Council—Lincoln, NE

Madison-area Urban Ministry—Madison, WI

Muskegon County Cooperating Churches—Muskegon, MI

Network of Religious Communities—Buffalo, NY

New Hampshire Council of Churches—Pembroke, NH

New Mexico Conference of Churches—Bernalillo, NM

North Carolina Council of Churches—Raleigh, NC

Oklahoma Conference of Churches—Oklahoma City, OK

The Pennsylvania Council of Churches—Harrisburg, PA

San Fernando Valley Interfaith Council—Chatsworth, CA

South Carolina Christian Action Council, Inc.—Columbia, SC

Southern California Ecumenical Council—Pasadena, CA

Staten Island Council of Churches—Staten Island, NY

Tarrant Area Community of Churches—Fort Worth, TX

Tulsa Metropolitan Ministry—Tulsa, OK

United Religious Community of St. Joseph County—South Bend, IN

Vermont Ecumenical Council and Bible Society—Richmond, VT

West Virginia Council of Churches—Charleston, WV

Worcester County Ecumenical Council—Worcester, MA

Prison Chaplaincy

Akron Area Association of Churches—Akron, OH

Asheville-Buncombe Community Christian Ministry (ABCCM)—Asheville, NC

Broome County Council of Churches, Inc.—Binghamton, NY

The Cape Cod Council of Churches, Inc.—Hyannis, MA

Capital Area Council of Churches, Inc.—Albany, NY

Christian Associates of Southwest Pennsylvania—Pittsburgh, PA

Christian Churches United of the Tri-County Area—Harrisburg, PA

Christians United in Beaver County—Beaver, PA

The Church Federation of Greater Indianapolis, Inc.—Indianapolis, IN

Churches United of the Quad City Area—Bettendorf, IA

Churchpeople for Change and Reconciliation—Lima, OH

Council of Christian Communions of Greater Cincinnati—Cincinnati, OH

Council of Churches of the City of New York—New York, NY

The Council of Churches of Greater Bridgeport, Bridgeport, CT—Bridgeport, CT

Council of Churches of Greater Springfield—Springfield, MA

The Council of Churches of Santa Clara County—San Jose, CA

Ecclesia—Trenton, NJ

Genesee County Churches United, Inc.—Batavia, NY

Greater Chicago Broadcast Ministries—Chicago, IL

Interfaith Council of Contra Costa County—Walnut Creek, CA

InterFaith Works of Central New York—Syracuse, NY

The Long Island Council of Churches—Hempstead, NY

Montana Association of Churches—Helena, MT

New Hampshire Council of Churches—Pembroke, NH

New Mexico Conference of Churches—Bernalillo, NM

Oklahoma Conference of Churches—Oklahoma City, OK

Reading Berks Conference of Churches—Reading, PA

United Churches of Lycoming County—Williamsport, PA

United Religious Community of St. Joseph County—South Bend, IN

West Virginia Council of Churches—Charleston, WV

Programs with/for Persons with Disabilities

Christian Ministries of Delaware County—Muncie, IN

Greater Chicago Broadcast Ministries—Chicago, IL

Inter-Church Council of Greater New Bedford—New Bedford, MA

Inter-Faith Ministries-Wichita—Wichita, KS

InterFaith Works of Central New York—Syracuse, NY

Massachusetts Council of Churches—Boston, MA

Metropolitan Ecumenical Ministry—Newark, NJ

New Hampshire Council of Churches—Pembroke, NH

Reading Berks Conference of Churches—Reading, PA

Schenectady Inner City Ministry—Schenectady, NY

Southeast Ecumenical Ministry—Rochester, NY

Public Education

Akron Area Association of Churches—Akron, OH

The Associated Churches of Fort Wayne & Allen County, Inc.—Fort Wayne, IN

Austin Area Interreligious Ministries—Austin, TX

Border Association for Refugees from Central America (BARCA), Inc.—Edinburg, TX

California Council of Churches-California Church Impact—Sacramento, CA

The Cape Cod Council of Churches, Inc.—Hyannis, MA

Center City Churches—Hartford, CT

Christian Ministries of Delaware County—Muncie, IN

Church Council of Greater Seattle—Seattle, WA

The Church Federation of Greater Indianapolis, Inc.—Indianapolis, IN

Colorado Council of Churches—Denver, CO

Community Emergency Assistance Program (CEAP)—Brooklyn Park, MN

Community Ministries of Rockville—Rockville, MD

Community Ministry of Montgomery County—Rockville, MD

Community Renewal Society—Chicago, IL

Concerned Ecumenical Ministry to the Upper West Side—Buffalo, NY

Contact Ministries of Springfield—Springfield, IL

Council of Churches of the City of New York—New York, NY

The Council of Churches of Greater Bridgeport, Bridgeport, CT—Bridgeport, CT

Council of Churches of Greater Springfield—Springfield, MA

Faith Action Network: A Partnership for the Common Good—Seattle, WA

The Faith In Action Network of Rochester, NY—Rochester, NY

FOCUS Churches of Albany, Inc.—Albany, NY

Greater Birmingham Ministries—Birmingham, AL

Greater Chicago Broadcast Ministries—Chicago, IL

Greater Fairmont Council of Churches—Fairmont, WV

Greater Waterbury Interfaith Ministries, Inc.—Waterbury, CT

Illinois Conference of Churches—Springfield, IL

Inter-Church Council of Greater New Bedford—New Bedford, MA

Interchurch Ministries of Nebraska—Lincoln, NE

Interfaith Conference of Greater Milwaukee—Milwaukee, WI

InterFaith Conference of Metropolitan Washington—Washington, DC

Interfaith Council—Spokane, WA

Interfaith Federation of Greater Baton Rouge—Baton Rouge, LA

InterFaith Works of Central New York—Syracuse, NY

The Joint Religious Legislative Coalition—Minneapolis, MN

Lehigh County Conference of Churches—Allentown, PA

The Long Island Council of Churches—Hempstead, NY

Madison-area Urban Ministry—Madison, WI

Maine Council of Churches—Portland, ME

Metropolitan Christian Council of Philadelphia—Philadelphia, PA

Metropolitan Ecumenical Ministry—Newark, NJ

Metropolitan Interfaith Council on Affordable Housing (MICAH)—Minneapolis, MN

Mississippi Religious Leadership Conference—Jackson, MS

New Hampshire Council of Churches—Pembroke, NH

New Mexico Conference of Churches—Bernalillo, NM

North Carolina Council of Churches—Raleigh, NC

Oak Park-River Forest Community of Congregations—Oak Park, IL

Oklahoma Conference of Churches—Oklahoma City, OK

The Pennsylvania Council of Churches—Harrisburg, PA

Peoria Friendship House of Christian Service—Peoria, IL

Queens Federation of Churches—Richmond Hill, NY

South Carolina Christian Action Council, Inc.—Columbia, SC

Tarrant Area Community of Churches—Fort Worth, TX

Tuscarawas County Council for Church and Community—New Philadelphia, OH

United Churches of Lycoming County—Williamsport, PA

United Religious Community of St. Joseph County—South Bend, IN

West Virginia Council of Churches—Charleston, WV

Wisconsin Council of Churches—Sun Prairie, WI

Refugee Assistance Programs

Associated Ministries of Tacoma-Pierce County—Tacoma, WA

Association of Religious Communities—Danbury, CT

Austin Area Interreligious Ministries—Austin, TX

Border Association for Refugees from Central America (BARCA), Inc.—Edinburg, TX

The Capitol Region Conference of Churches—Hartford, CT

Community Emergency Assistance Program (CEAP)—Brooklyn Park, MN

Ecumenical Ministries of Oregon—Portland, OR

Greater Chicago Broadcast Ministries—Chicago, IL

Interfaith Service Bureau—Sacramento, CA

InterFaith Works of Central New York—Syracuse, NY

Kentuckiana Interfaith Community—Louisville, KY

Metropolitan Ecumenical Ministry—Newark, NJ

Minnesota Council of Churches—Minneapolis, MN

Network of Religious Communities—Buffalo, NY

New Hampshire Council of Churches—Pembroke, NH

Oklahoma Conference of Churches—Oklahoma City, OK

United Religious Community of St. Joseph County—South Bend, IN

Virginia Council of Churches, Inc.—Richmond, VA

Rural Issues

Alaska Christian Conference—Anchorage, AK

Association of Christian Churches of South Dakota—Sioux Falls, SD

287

Berrien County Association of Churches—Benton Harbor, MI

Border Association for Refugees from Central America (BARCA), Inc.—Edinburg, TX

Chautauqua County Rural Ministry—Dunkirk, NY

Ecumenical Ministries of Iowa (EMI)—Des Moines, IA

Ecumenical Ministries of Oregon—Portland, OR

Faith Action Network: A Partnership for the Common Good—Seattle, WA

Georgia Christian Council—Macon, GA

Interchurch Ministries of Nebraska—Lincoln, NE

Interfaith Conference of Greater Milwaukee—Milwaukee, WI

Kentucky Council of Churches—Lexington, KY

Minnesota Council of Churches—Minneapolis, MN

Mississippi Religious Leadership Conference—Jackson, MS

Montana Association of Churches—Helena, MT

New Hampshire Council of Churches—Pembroke, NH

New Mexico Conference of Churches—Bernalillo, NM

North Carolina Council of Churches—Raleigh, NC

North Dakota Conference of Churches—Ashley, ND

Oklahoma Conference of Churches—Oklahoma City, OK

Pike County Outreach Council—Waverly, OH

Reading Berks Conference of Churches—Reading, PA

United Churches of Lycoming County—Williamsport, PA

United Religious Community of St. Joseph County—South Bend, IN

Virginia Council of Churches, Inc.—Richmond, VA

West Virginia Council of Churches—Charleston, WV

Senior Citizen Programs

Allegheny Valley Association of Churches—Natrona Heights, PA

Alliance of Churches—Alliance, OH

Attleboro Area Council of Churches, Inc.—Attleboro, MA

Capital Area Council of Churches, Inc.—Albany, NY

The Capitol Region Conference of Churches—Hartford, CT

Center City Churches—Hartford, CT

Christian Ministries of Delaware County—Muncie, IN

Church Council of Greater Seattle—Seattle, WA

Community Emergency Assistance Program (CEAP)—Brooklyn Park, MN

Community Ministries of Rockville—Rockville, MD

Concerned Ecumenical Ministry to the Upper West Side—Buffalo, NY

Council of Churches of Greater Springfield—Springfield, MA

Council of Churches of the Ozarks—Springfield, MO

Council of Churches and Synagogues of Southwestern Connecticut—Stamford, CT

Cross-Lines Cooperative Council—Kansas City, KS

East Dallas Cooperative Parish—Dallas, TX

East End Cooperative Ministry—Pittsburgh, PA

Eastern Area Community Ministries—Louisville, KY

Faith Action Network: A Partnership for the Common Good—Seattle, WA

Fern Creek-Highview United Ministries—Louisvlle, KY

Georgia Christian Council—Macon, GA

Greater Chicago Broadcast Ministries—Chicago, IL

Greater Lawrence Council of Churches—Lawrence, MA

Greater Minneapolis Council of Churches—Minneapolis, MN

Highlands Community Ministries—Louisville, KY

Illinois Conference of Churches—Springfield, IL

Inter-Church Council of Greater New Bedford—New Bedford, MA

Interfaith Community Council, Inc.—New Albany, IN

Interfaith Community Services—St. Joseph, MO

Interfaith Council of Contra Costa County—Walnut Creek, CA

Interfaith Federation of Greater Baton Rouge—Baton Rouge, LA

Inter-Faith Ministries-Wichita—Wichita, KS

InterFaith Works of Central New York—Syracuse, NY

Lebanon County Christian Ministries—Lebanon, PA

The Long Island Council of Churches—Hempstead, NY

Marin Interfaith Council—San Rafael, CA

The Metropolitan Christian Council: Detroit-Windsor—Detroit, MI

Metropolitan Ecumenical Ministry—Newark, NJ

Metropolitan Inter Faith Association (MIFA)—Memphis, TN

Mississippi Religious Leadership Conference—Jackson, MS

New Hampshire Council of Churches—Pembroke, NH

New Mexico Conference of Churches—Bernalillo, NM

Northside Inter-Church Agency (NICA)—Fort Worth, TX

Northwest Interfaith Movement—Philadelphia, PA

Oklahoma Conference of Churches—Oklahoma City, OK

Paducah Cooperative Ministry—Paducah, KY

Peoria Friendship House of Christian Service—Peoria, IL

St. Matthews Area Ministries—Louisville, KY

San Fernando Valley Interfaith Council—Chatsworth, CA

Schenectady Inner City Ministry—Schenectady, NY

South Hills Interfaith Ministries—Bethel Park, PA

South Louisville Community Ministries—Louisville, KY

Southeast Ecumenical Ministry—Rochester, NY

Troy Area United Ministries—Troy, NY

Tuscarawas County Council for Church and Community—New Philadelphia, OH

United Religious Community of St. Joseph County—South Bend, IN

Wainwright House—Rye, NY

Wellspring Interfaith Social Services, Inc. (previously West Central Neighborhood Ministry, Inc.)—Fort Wayne, IN

West Side Ecumenical Ministry—Cleveland, OH
Wilkinsburg Community Ministry—Pittsburgh, PA

Substance Abuse Programs

Anchor Point Counseling Ministry—Pittsburgh, PA
Central Maryland Ecumenical Council—Baltimore, MD
Community Ministries of Rockville—Rockville, MD
Corpus Christi Metro Ministries—Corpus Christi, TX
Council of Churches of the Ozarks—Springfield, MO
East End Cooperative Ministry—Pittsburgh, PA
Ecumenical Ministries of Iowa (EMI)—Des Moines, IA
Greater Chicago Broadcast Ministries—Chicago, IL
Greater Minneapolis Council of Churches—Minneapolis, MN
Greensboro Urban Ministry—Greensboro, NC
Hanover Area Council of Churches—Hanover, PA
Interchurch Ministries of Nebraska—Lincoln, NE
Interfaith Action of Evanston—Evanston, IL
Lehigh County Conference of Churches—Allentown, PA
Metropolitan Ecumenical Ministry—Newark, NJ
Metropolitan Ecumenical Ministry Community Development Corp.—Newark, NJ
Mississippi Religious Leadership Conference—Jackson, MS
New Hampshire Council of Churches—Pembroke, NH
Pike County Outreach Council—Waverly, OH
Southeast Ecumenical Ministry—Rochester, NY
United Religious Community of St. Joseph County—South Bend, IN
Vermont Ecumenical Council and Bible Society—Richmond, VT
West Side Ecumenical Ministry—Cleveland, OH
West Virginia Council of Churches—Charleston, WV

Theology and Worship Programs

Akron Area Association of Churches—Akron, OH
Allegheny Valley Association of Churches—Natrona Heights, PA
Arizona Ecumenical Council—Phoenix, AZ
Arkansas Interfaith Conference—Scott, AR
The Associated Churches of Fort Wayne & Allen County, Inc.—Fort Wayne, IN
Association of Christian Churches of South Dakota—Sioux Falls, SD
Attleboro Area Council of Churches, Inc.—Attleboro, MA
Brooklyn Council of Churches—Brooklyn, NY
Broome County Council of Churches, Inc.—Binghamton, NY
The Cape Cod Council of Churches, Inc.—Hyannis, MA
Capital Area Council of Churches, Inc.—Albany, NY
Capital Region Ecumenical Organization (CREO)—Malta, NY
Christian Associates of Southwest Pennsylvania—Pittsburgh, PA
Christian Churches United of the Tri-County Area—Harrisburg, PA
Christians United in Beaver County—Beaver, PA
The Church Federation of Greater Indianapolis, Inc.—Indianapolis, IN

Churches United of the Quad City Area—Bettendorf, IA
Colorado Council of Churches—Denver, CO
Council of Churches of the City of New York—New York, NY
The Council of Churches of Santa Clara County—San Jose, CA
Council of Churches and Synagogues of Southwestern Connecticut—Stamford, CT
Dutchess County Interfaith Council, Inc.—Poughkeepsie, NY
East Dallas Cooperative Parish—Dallas, TX
The Ecumenical Council of Pasadena Area Churches—Pasadena, CA
Ecumenical Council of San Diego County—San Diego, CA
Ecumenical Ministries of Iowa (EMI)—Des Moines, IA
Ecumenical Ministries of Oregon—Portland, OR
Faith Action Network: A Partnership for the Common Good—Seattle, WA
The Faith In Action Network of Rochester, NY—Rochester, NY
FaithTrust Institute—Seattle, WA
Florida Council of Churches—Tampa, FL
Georgia Christian Council—Macon, GA
Grand Rapids Area Center for Ecumenism (GRACE)—Grand Rapids, MI
Greater Chicago Broadcast Ministries—Chicago, IL
Greater Dallas Community of Churches—Dallas, TX
Greater Dayton Christian Connections—Dayton, OH
Greater Fairmont Council of Churches—Fairmont, WV
Greater Lawrence Council of Churches—Lawrence, MA
Greater New Orleans Federation of Churches—New Orleans, LA
Greensboro Urban Ministry—Greensboro, NC
Illinois Conference of Churches—Springfield, IL
Inter-Church Council of Greater New Bedford—New Bedford, MA
Inter-Church Ministries of Erie County—Erie, PA
Interchurch Ministries of Nebraska—Lincoln, NE
Interfaith Council—Spokane, WA
Interfaith Mission Service—Huntsville, AL
InterFaith Works of Central New York—Syracuse, NY
Iowa Religious Media Services—Urbandale, IA
Kentuckiana Interfaith Community—Louisville, KY
Lehigh County Conference of Churches—Allentown, PA
The Long Island Council of Churches—Hempstead, NY
Mahoning Valley Association of Churches—Youngstown, OH
The Metropolitan Christian Council: Detroit-Windsor—Detroit, MI
Metropolitan Christian Council of Philadelphia—Philadelphia, PA
Metropolitan Ecumenical Ministry—Newark, NJ
Muskegon County Cooperating Churches—Muskegon, MI
New Britain Area Conference of Churches (NEW-BRACC)—New Britain, CT

New Hampshire Council of Churches—Pembroke, NH

New Mexico Conference of Churches—Bernalillo, NM

North Carolina Council of Churches—Raleigh, NC

Northern Kentucky Interfaith Commission, Inc.—Newport, KY

Oak Park-River Forest Community of Congregations—Oak Park, IL

Oklahoma Conference of Churches—Oklahoma City, OK

The Pennsylvania Council of Churches—Harrisburg, PA

Reading Berks Conference of Churches—Reading, PA

The Regional Council for Christian Ministry, Inc.—Idaho Falls, ID

The Regional Council of Churches of Atlanta—Atlanta, GA

The Rhode Island State Council of Churches—Providence, RI

San Antonio Community of Congregations—San Antonio, TX

Schenectady Inner City Ministry—Schenectady, NY

South Carolina Christian Action Council, Inc.—Columbia, SC

South East Associated Ministries (SEAM)—Louisville, KY

Tarrant Area Community of Churches—Fort Worth, TX

Texas Conference of Churches—Austin, TX

Troy Area United Ministries—Troy, NY

United Churches of Lycoming County—Williamsport, PA

United Religious Community of St. Joseph County—South Bend, IN

Vermont Ecumenical Council and Bible Society—Richmond, VT

Wainwright House—Rye, NY

Worcester County Ecumenical Council—Worcester, MA

York County Council of Churches—York, PA

Women

Berrien County Association of Churches—Benton Harbor, MI

California Council of Churches-California Church Impact—Sacramento, CA

Chautaugua County Rural Ministry—Dunkirk, NY

Christian Ministries of Delaware County—Muncie, IN

Church Community Services—Elkhart, IN

Colorado Council of Churches—Denver, CO

Community Ministries of Rockville—Rockville, MD

Council of Churches of the City of New York—New York, NY

The Council of Churches of Santa Clara County—San Jose, CA

Cross-Lines Cooperative Council—Kansas City, KS

East Dallas Cooperative Parish—Dallas, TX

Ecumenical Council of San Diego County—San Diego, CA

Ecumenical Ministries of Oregon—Portland, OR

FaithTrust Institute—Seattle, WA

Genesee-Orleans Ministry of Concern—Albion, NY

Georgia Christian Council—Macon, GA

Greater Birmingham Ministries—Birmingham, AL

Greater Chicago Broadcast Ministries—Chicago, IL

Greater Dallas Community of Churches—Dallas, TX

Inter-Church Council of Greater New Bedford—New Bedford, MA

Interfaith Community Services—St. Joseph, MO

Interfaith Council—Spokane, WA

InterFaith Works of Central New York—Syracuse, NY

Madison-area Urban Ministry—Madison, WI

Metropolitan Christian Council of Philadelphia—Philadelphia, PA

Metropolitan Ecumenical Ministry—Newark, NJ

Mississippi Religious Leadership Conference—Jackson, MS

Network of Religious Communities—Buffalo, NY

New Hampshire Council of Churches—Pembroke, NH

New Mexico Conference of Churches—Bernalillo, NM

North Carolina Council of Churches—Raleigh, NC

Oklahoma Conference of Churches—Oklahoma City, OK

Peoria Friendship House of Christian Service—Peoria, IL

The Regional Council of Churches of Atlanta—Atlanta, GA

South Hills Interfaith Ministries—Bethel Park, PA

Wainwright House—Rye, NY

West Side Ecumenical Ministry—Cleveland, OH

Youth

Austin Area Interreligious Ministries—Austin, TX

Berrien County Association of Churches—Benton Harbor, MI

The Cape Cod Council of Churches, Inc.—Hyannis, MA

Center City Churches—Hartford, CT

Christian Ministries of Delaware County—Muncie, IN

Church Council of Greater Seattle—Seattle, WA

The Church Federation of Greater Indianapolis, Inc.—Indianapolis, IN

Churches United of the Quad City Area—Bettendorf, IA

Concerned Ecumenical Ministry to the Upper West Side—Buffalo, NY

Cooperative Metropolitan Ministries—Newton, MA

Council of Churches of the City of New York—New York, NY

The Council of Churches of Greater Bridgeport, Bridgeport, CT—Bridgeport, CT

The Council of Churches of Santa Clara County—San Jose, CA

Cross-Lines Cooperative Council—Kansas City, KS

Dutchess County Interfaith Council, Inc.—Poughkeepsie, NY

East Dallas Cooperative Parish—Dallas, TX

East End Cooperative Ministry—Pittsburgh, PA

Eastern Area Community Ministries—Louisville, KY

Ecclesia—Trenton, NJ

Genesee-Orleans Ministry of Concern—Albion, NY

Greater Chicago Broadcast Ministries—Chicago, IL

Greater Dallas Community of Churches—Dallas, TX

Greater Fairmont Council of Churches—Fairmont, WV

Greater Minneapolis Council of Churches—Minneapolis, MN

Highlands Community Ministries—Louisville, KY

Inter-Church Council of Greater New Bedford—New Bedford, MA

Interfaith Action of Evanston—Evanston, IL

Interfaith Community Council, Inc.—New Albany, IN

Interfaith Community Services—St. Joseph, MO

Interfaith Conference of Greater Milwaukee—Milwaukee, WI

Interfaith Conference of Metropolitan Washington—Washington, DC

Interfaith Council—Spokane, WA

Inter-Faith Ministries-Wichita—Wichita, KS

InterFaith Works of Central New York—Syracuse, NY

Lehigh County Conference of Churches—Allentown, PA

Marin Interfaith Council—San Rafael, CA

Metropolitan Ecumenical Ministry—Newark, NJ

Metropolitan Ecumenical Ministry Community Development Corp.—Newark, NJ

Metropolitan Inter Faith Association (MIFA)—Memphis, TN

New Hampshire Council of Churches—Pembroke, NH

New Mexico Conference of Churches—Bernalillo, NM

Northern California Interreligious Conference—Oakland, CA

Oklahoma Conference of Churches—Oklahoma City, OK

Peoria Friendship House of Christian Service—Peoria, IL

Queens Federation of Churches—Richmond Hill, NY

Reading Berks Conference of Churches—Reading, PA

Rural Migrant Ministry—Poughkeepsie, NY

St. Matthews Area Ministries—Louisville, KY

Saint Paul Area Council of Churches—St. Paul, MN

Schenectady Inner City Ministry—Schenectady, NY

South East Associated Ministries (SEAM)—Louisville, KY

South Hills Interfaith Ministries—Bethel Park, PA

South Louisville Community Ministries—Louisville, KY

Southeast Ecumenical Ministry—Rochester, NY

Staten Island Council of Churches—Staten Island, NY

Troy Area United Ministries—Troy, NY

Tuscarawas County Council for Church and Community—New Philadelphia, OH

United Churches of Lycoming County—Williamsport, PA

Wainwright House—Rye, NY

Wellspring Interfaith Social Services, Inc. (previously West Central Neighborhood Ministry, Inc.)—Fort Wayne, IN

West Side Ecumenical Ministry—Cleveland, OH

7. Canadian Regional and Local Ecumenical Bodies

Most of the organizations listed below are councils of churches in which churches participate officially, whether at the parish or judicatory level. They operate at the city, metropolitan area, or county level. Parish clusters within urban areas are not included.

Canadian local ecumenical bodies operate without paid staff, with the exception of a few which have part-time staff. In most cases, the name and address of the president or chairperson is listed. As these offices change from year to year, some of the information may be out of date by the time the *Yearbook of American and Canadian Churches* is published.

ALBERTA

Calgary Council of Churches
120 17th Ave., Calgary, AB T2S 2T2 Tel. (403)218-5521
Media Contact: Kristoph Franz Dobrowolski
Email: ecumenism@rcdiocese-calgary.ab.ca

Calgary Inter-Faith Community Action Association
2405 Macleod Trail SW, Calgary, AB T2G 2P3 Tel. (403)262-5171
Media Contact: J. McGrath
Email: jmcgrath@shawcable.com
Website: www.calgary-interfaith.ab.ca

BRITISH COLUMBIA

Multifaith Action Society of British Columbia
#5-305 West 41st Ave., Vancouver, BC V5Y 2S5 Tel. (604)321-1302
Media Contact: Marcus Hynes
Email: admin@multifaithaction.org
Website: www.multifaithaction.org

NEW BRUNSWICK

Atlantic Ecumenical Council of Churches
170 Daniel Ave., Saint John, NB E2K 4S7 Tel. (506)538-2491
Media Contact: Rev. Rufus Onyewuchi
Email: mknowles@ ns.sympatico.ca

First Miramichi Inter-Church Council
Doaktown, NB E0C 1G0
Media Contact: Ellen Robinson

Moncton Area Council of Churches
135 Mount Royal Blvd., Moncton, NB E1E 2V5 Tel. (506)382-7725
Media Contact: Rev. Donald Routledge

NEWFOUNDLAND

St. John's Area Council of Churches
21 Adams Avenue, St. John's, NL A1C 4Z1 Tel. (709)579-0536

Media Contact: The Very Rev. Dr. Marion Pardy, President
Mr. George H. Powell, Secretary
Email: councilofchurhces@nl.rogers.com

NOVA SCOTIA

Atlantic Ecumenical Council of Churches
Box 637, 90 Victoria St., Amherst, NS B4H 4B4 Tel. (902)864-1834
Media Contact: Rev. Dr. Chris Coffin
Email: jhtye@isn.net

Bridgewater Inter-Church Council
P.O. Box 11, B4V 2W6 Bridgewater, Lunenburg, NS B4V 2W6 Tel. (902)543-5441
Media Contact: Rosemary Veinotte
Email: rosemary_veinot@hotmail.com

Cornwallis District Inter-Church Council
Centreville, RR 2, Kings County, NS B0T 1J0
Media Contact: Mr. Tom Regan

Industrial Cape Breton Council of Churches
24 Huron Ave., Sydney Mines, NS B1S 1V2
Media Contact: Rev. Karen Ralph

Kentville Council of Churches
325-325 Main St., Kentville, NS B4N 1C5
Media Contact: Rev. Canon S.J.P. Davies

Lunenburg Queens Baptist Association of Convention Baptist Churches
66 Hillside Dr., Conquerall Bank, NS v0G 9 Tel. (902)543-3328
Media Contact: Mrs. Nilda Chute
Email: nrchute@eastlink.ca

Mahone Bay Interchurch Council
RR 1, Blockhouse, NS B0J 1E0
Media Contact: Patricia Joudrey

Pictou Council of Churches
P.O. Box 70, Pictou, NS B0K 1H0
Media Contact: Rev. D.J. Murphy

Queens County Association of Churches
Box 537, Liverpool, NS B0T 1K6
Media Contact: Mr. Donald Burns

ONTARIO

Burlington Inter-Church Council
425 Breckenwood, Burlington, ON L7L 2J6
Media Contact: Mr. Fred Townsend
Email: eandbwheeler@sympatico.ca

Christian Leadership Council of Downtown Toronto
40 Homewood Ave. #509, Toronto, ON M4Y 2K2
Media Contact: Ken Bhagan

Ecumenical Committee
76 Eastern Ave., Sault Ste. Marie, ON P6A 4R2
Media Contact: Rev. William B. Kidd

Glengarry-Prescott-Russell Christian Council
St. Eugene's, Prescott, ON K0B 1P0
Media Contact: Rev. G. Labrosse

The Greater Toronto Council of Christian Churches
1155 Yonge St., Toronto, ON M4T 1W2 Tel. (416)934-3400 ext. 344
Media Contact: Father Damian MacPherson
Email: dmacpherson@archtoronto.org

Ignace Council of Churches
Box 5, 205 Pine St., Ignace, ON P0T 1H0

Inter Church Council of Burlington
P.O. Box 62120, Burlington Mall R.P.O., Burlington, ON L7R 4K2 Tel. (905)333-0515
Media Contact: Rev. Moe Anderson
Email: webmaster@iccb.ca
Website: www.iccb.ca

Kitchener-Waterloo Council of Churches
53 Allen St. E., Waterloo, ON N2J 1J3
Media Contact: Rev. Clarence Hauser, CR

London Inter-City Faith Team
United Church, 711 Colbourne St., London, ON N6A 3Z4
Media Contact: David Carouthers

Massey Inter-Church Council
Box 238, Massey, ON P0P 1P0 Tel. (705)865-2202
Media Contact: Rev. Brian Sonnenburg

Ottowa Christian Council of the Capital Area
1247 Kilborn Ave., Ottawa, ON K1H 6K9

St. Catharines & District Clergy Fellowship
663 Vince St., St. Catharines, ON L2M 3V8
Media Contact: Rev. Victor Munro

Spadina-Bloor Interchurch Council
Bathurst St. United Church, 427 Bloor St. W., Toronto, ON M5S 1X7
Media Contact: Rev. Frances Combes

Stratford & District Council of Churches
202 Erie St., Stratford, ON N5A 2M8
Media Contact: Rev. Ted Heinze

Thorold Inter-Faith Council
1 Dunn St., St. Catharines, ON L2T 1P3

Thunder Bay Council of Churches
1800 Moodie St. E., Thunder Bay, ON P7E 4Z2
Media Contact: Rev. Richard Darling

PRINCE EDWARD ISLAND

Atlantic Ecumenical Council
Immaculate Conception Church, St. Louis, PEI C0B 1Z0 Tel. (902)963-2202 or (902)882-2610
Media Contact: Rev. Arthur J. Pendergast

Summerside Christian Council
P.O. Box 1551, Summerside, PEI C1N 4K4
Media Contact: Ms. A. Kathleen Miller

QUEBEC

Action des Chrétiens pour l'Abolition de la Torture
ACAT Canada, 2715, ch. Cote-Sainte-Catherine, Montréal, QC H3T 1B6 Tel. (514)890-6169 Fax (514)890-6484
Media Contact: Guy Gauthier
Email: info@acatcanada.org
Website: www.acatcanada.org

AGAPÉ Deux-Montagnes
1002 chemin d'Oka, Deux-Montagnes, QC J7R 1L7 Tel. (450)473-9877
Media Contact: Donald Tremblay

Canadian Centre for Ecumenism
1819, boul. René-Lévesque Ouest, Suite 003, Montreal, QC H3H 2P5 Tel. (514)937-9176 Fax (514)937-4986
Media Contact: Neala Vandermeulen, Assistant to the Exec. Dir.
Email: info@oikoumene.ca
Website: www.oikoumene.ca

Centre Emmaüs
Centre Emmaüs de Méditation et spiritualité hésychaste, 3774 chemin Queen-Mary, 3e étage, Montréal, QC H3V 1A6 Tel. (514)276-2144

Media Contact: Dir., Stephane Vaillancourt,
Email: info-emmaus@gmail.com
Website: www.centre-emmaus.org

Christian-Jewish Dialogue of Montreal

c/oTemple Emanu-El-Beth Sholom, 4100
Sherbrooke St. West, Westmount, QC H3Z
1A5 Tel. (514)937-3575 or (514)937-3708 Fax
(514)937-7058
Media Contact: Pres., Prof. Jean Duhaime,
Faculté de Théologie, Université de Montréal,
3333, ch. Queen-Mary,
6e étage (620-4), Montréal, QC H3V 1A2, Tel.
(514)343-7616, Email: jean.duhaime@
umontreal.ca
Email: rabbi@templemontreal.ca

Comité Québécois du Dialogue musulman-chrétien

1640 rueSt. Hubert, Montréal, QC H2L 3Z3 Tel.
(514)849-1167 Fax (514)284-2034
Media Contact: RP Gilles Barrette
Email: gilbar1945@yahoo.ca
Website: www.interreligion.com

Direction Chrétienne

1450 rue City Councillors, bureau 520, Montréal,
QC H3A 2E6 Tel. (514)878-3035 Fax (514)
878-8048
Media Contact: Rev. Dr. Glenn Smith
Email: info@direction.ca
Website: www.direction.ca

Hemmingford Ecumenical Committee

Box 300, Hemmingford, QC J0L 1H0
Media Contact: Catherine Priest

Interfaith Council of Montréal

1819 René-Lévesque West Suite 003, Montréal,
QC H3H 2P5 Tel. (514)937-9176 Fax (514)
937-4986
Media Contact: Mandit Singh, President
Email: info@oikoumene.ca
Website: www.oikoumene.ca

Montreal Association for the Blind Foundation

7000 Sherbrooke St. W., Montréal, QC H4B 1R3
Tel. (514)489-8201 Fax (514)489-3477
Media Contact: Nicole Halpert
Email: nhalpert@mabmackay.va
Website: www.mab.ca

Radio Ville-Marie

Radio religieuse, 4020, rue Saint-Ambroise,
Suite 199, Montréal, QC H4C 2C7 Tel.
(514)382-3913 or (877)668-6601 Fax (514)
858-0965

Media Contact: Friends
Email: cira@radiovm.com
Website: www.radiovm.com

Réseau Oecuménique Justice et Paix

C.P. 55029, 1580, rue Ontario Est, Montréal, QC
H2L 0C1 Tel. (514)937-2683 Fax (514)937-2683
Media Contact: Jean-Luc Djigo or Julie
Sabourault
Email: info@justicepaix.org
Website: www.justicepaix.org

Réseau Oecuménique du Québec (Quebec Ecumenical Network)

Centre canadien d'oecuménisme en assure le
secretariat, 1819 rue René-Lévesque W #003,
Montréal, QC H3H 1G6 Tel. (514)937-9176
Fax (514)937-4986
Media Contact: Friends
Email: info@oikoumene.ca
Website: www.oikoumene.ca

The St. Bruno Ecumenical Group

Holy Trinity Anglican Church, 140 Beaumont St.
East, St. Bruno, QC J3V 5L9 Tel. (450)653-4531

UNITAS

Centre oecuménique de meditation chrétienne et
de spiritualité, 1950 rue St. Antoine Ouest,
Montréal, QC H3J 1A5 Tel. (514)485-0009
Media Contact: Friends
Email: info@unitasmeditation.ca
Website: www.unitasmeditation.ca

SASKETCHEWAN

Humboldt Clergy Council

Box 1989, Humboldt, SK S0K 2A0
Media Contact: Fr. Leo Hinz, OSB

Melville Association of Churches

Box 878, Melville, SK S0A 2P0 Tel. (306)728-
5081
Media Contact: Catherine Gaw

Prairie Centre for Ecumenism

600 45th Street W., Saskatoon, SK S7L 5W9 Tel.
(306)653-1633 Fax (306)653-1821
Media Contact: vacant
Email: pce@ecumenism.net
Website: www.ecumenism.net

Regina Council of Churches

2660 Albert St, Regina, SK S4P 2V9 Tel.
(306)545-3375
Media Contact: Joan Galvin
Email: jegalvin@saskatel.net

9. Theological Seminaries and Bible Colleges in the United States

The following list includes theological seminaries, Bible colleges and departments in colleges and universities in which ministerial training is given. Many denominations have additional programs.

Inclusion in or exclusion from this list implies no judgment about the quality or accreditation of any institution. Those schools that are members of the Association of Theological Schools are marked with a †. Those schools that are accredited by the Transnational Association of Christian Colleges and Schools are marked with a ‡. Additional information about enrollment patterns in ATS member schools can be found in the "Trends in Seminary Enrollment" section of chapter III. Information about TRACS and ATS as institutions can be found in the United States Cooperative Organizations section of chapter II.

Each of the listings include when available: the institution name, denominational sponsor, location, the president or dean of the institution, telephone and fax numbers and email and website addresses.

Abilene Christian University Graduate School of Theology† (Churches of Christ), Jack R. Reese, Dean, College of Biblical Studies, ACU Box 29422, 1850 N. Judge Ely Boulevard, CBS Room 297, Abilene, TX 79699-9422 Tel. (325)674-3700 Fax (325)674-6180
Email: reesej@acu.edu
Website: www.acu.edu/GST

Alaska Bible College (Nondenominational), Nick Ringger, President, P.O. Box 289, Glennallen, AK 99588 Tel. (907)822-3201 Fax (907)822-5027
Email: info@akbible.edu
Website: www.akbible.edu

Alliance Theological Seminary† (The Christian and Missionary Alliance), Michael G. Scales, President, 350 N. Highland Ave., Nyack, NY 10960-1416 Tel. (845)353-2020 Fax (845)727-3002
Email: president@nyack.edu
Website: www. nyack.edu

American Baptist College (National Baptist Convention USA, Inc.), Dr. Forrest E. Harris, Sr., President, 1800 Baptist World Center Dr., Nashville, TN 37207 Tel. (615)256-1463 Fax (615)226-7855
Email: forrest.harris@gmail.com
Website: www.abcnash.edu

American Baptist Seminary of the West† (American Baptist Churches in the USA), Paul M. Martin, President, 2606 Dwight Way, Berkeley, CA 94704-3029 Tel. (510)841-1905 Fax (510)841-2446
Email: pmartin@absw.edu
Website: www.absw.edu

Amridge University (Churches of Christ), Dr. Michael C. Turner, President, 1200 Taylor Rd., Montgomery, AL 36117-3553 Tel. (334)387-3877 Fax (334)387-3878
Email: mcturner@amridgeuniversity.edu
Website: www.amridgeuniversity.edu

Anderson University School of Theology† (Church of God (Anderson, Ind.)), James L. Edwards, President, 1100 East Fifth Street, Anderson, IN 46012-3495 Tel. (765)641-4010 Fax (765)641-3851
Email: mtan@anderson.edu
Website: www.anderson.edu/academics/sot

Andover Newton Theological School† (American Baptist Churches in the USA; United Church of Christ), Nick Carter, President, 210 Herrick Rd., Newton Centre, MA 02459 Tel. (617)964-1100 Fax (617)558-9785
Email: admissions@ants.edu
Website: www.ants.edu

Apex School of Theology (Interdenominational), Dr. Joseph E. Perkins, President, 5104 Revere Road, Durham, NC 27713 Tel. (919)572-1625 Fax (919)572-1762
Email: info@apexsot.edu
Website: www.apexsot.edu

Appalachian Bible College (Nondenominational), Daniel L. Anderson, President, 161 College Drive, Mt. Hope, WV 25880 Tel. (304)877-6428 Fax (304)877-5082
Email: abc@abc.edu,
Website: www.abc.edu

Aquinas Institute of Theology† (Catholic Church), The Rev. Richard A. Peddicord, O.P., President, 23 S. Spring, St. Louis, MO 63108-3323 Tel. (314)256-8800 Fax (314)256-8888
Email: info@ai.edu
Website: www.ai.edu

Arlington Baptist College (Baptist), David Bryant, President, 3001 W. Division, Arlington, TX 76012-3425 Tel. (817)461-8741 Fax (817)274-1138
Email: info@abconline.org
Website: www.abconline.edu

Asbury Theological Seminary† (Inter/ Multidenominational), Timothy C. Tennent, President, 204 N. Lexington Ave., Wilmore, KY 40390-1199 Tel. (859)858-3581
Website: www.asburyseminary.edu

Ashland Theological Seminary† (Brethren Church (Ashland, Ohio)), John C. Shultz, President, 910 Center St., Ashland, OH 44805 Tel. (419)289-5161 Fax (419)289-5969
Email: jshultz@ashland.edu
Website: www.ashland.edu/seminary or seminary.ashland.edu

Assemblies of God Theological Seminary† (Assemblies of God), Byron D. Klaus, President, 1435 North Glenstone Avenue, Springfield, MO 65802-2131 Tel. (417)268-1000 Fax (417)268-1001
Email: agts@agseminary.edu
Website: www.agts.edu

Associated Mennonite Biblical Seminary† (Mennonite Church USA; Mennonite Church Canada), Sara Wenger Shenk, President, 3003 Benham Ave., Elkhart, IN 46517-1999 Tel. (574)295-3726 Fax (574)295-0092
Email: swshenk@ambs.edu
Website: www.ambs.edu

Athenaeum of Ohio† (The Catholic Church), Edward P. Smith, President and Rector, 6616 Beechmont Ave., Cincinnati, OH 45230-2091 Tel. (513)231-2223 Fax (513)231-3254
Email: esmith@athenaeum.edu
Website: www.athenaeum.edu

Atlanta Christian College (Christian Churches and Churches of Christ), Dean Collins, President, 2605 Ben Hill Rd., East Point, GA 30344 Tel. (404)761-8861 Fax (404)669-2024
Email: admissions@acc.edu
Website: www.acc.edu

Austin Presbyterian Theological Seminary† (Presbyterian Church (USA)), Theodore J. Wardlaw, President, 100 E. 27th St., Austin, TX 78705-5797 Tel. (512)472-6736 Fax (512)479-0738
Email: admissions@austinseminary.edu
Website: www.austinseminary.edu

Azusa Pacific Graduate School of Theology† (Interdenominational), David W. Wright, President, 901 E. Alosta, P.O. Box 7000, Azusa, CA 91702-7000 Tel. (845)969-3434 Fax (845)969-7180
Email: ezone@apu.edu
Website: www.apu.edu/theology

Bakke Graduate University‡ (Non-Denominational), Brad Smith, President, 1013 Eighth Ave, Suite 401, Seattle, WA 98104 Tel. (206)264-9100 Fax (206)264-8828

Email: bgu@bgu.edu
Website: www.bgu.edu

Bangor Theological Seminary† (United Church of Christ; Ecumenical; Interfaith), Kent J. Ulery, President, Two College Circle, P.O. Box 411, Bangor, ME 04402-0411 and 159 State Street, Portland ME 04101, Tel. (207)942-6781 Fax (207)942-4914
Email: mhuddy@bts.edu
Website: www.bts.edu

Baptist Bible College (Baptist Bible Fellowship International), Jim Edge, President, 628 E. Kearney, Springfield, MO 65803 Tel. (417) 268-6060 Fax (417)268-6694
Email: jedge@gobbc.edu
Website: www.baptist.edu

Baptist Bible College and Seminary (Baptist), Jim Jeffery, President, 538 Venard Rd., Clarks Summit, PA 18411 Tel. (570)586-2400 Fax (570)586-1753
Email: webmaster@bbc.edu
Website: www.bbc.edu

Baptist Missionary Association Theological Seminary† (Baptist Missionary Association of America), Charley Holmes, President, 1530 E. Pine St., Jacksonville, TX 75766 Tel. (903) 586-2501 Fax (903)586-0378
Email: bmatsem@bmats.edu
Website: www.bmats.edu

Baptist Theological Seminary at Richmond† (Cooperative Baptist Fellowship), Ronald W. Crawford, President, 3400 Brook Rd., Richmond, VA 23227 Tel. (804)355-8135 Fax (804)355-8182
Email: rcrawford@btsr.edu
Website: www.btsr.edu

Barclay College (Interdenominational), Maurice G. Chandler, President, 607 N Kingman, Haviland, KS 67059 Tel. (620)862-5252 Fax (620)862-5403
Email: herb.frazier@barclaycollege.edu
Website: www.barclaycollege.edu

Barry University Department of Theology and Philosophy† Mark E. Wedig, Chair of the Department of Theology and Philosophy, 11300 Northeast Second Avenue, Miami Shores, FL 33161-6695 Tel. (305)899-3469 Fax (305)899-3385
Email: theology@mail.barry.edu
Website: www.barry.edu/Theology Philosophy/default

Bay Ridge Christian College (Church of God (Anderson Ind.)), Dr. Verda Beach, President, P.O. Box 726, Kendleton, TX 77451 Tel. (979)532-3989 Fax (979)532-4352

Email: jwalker@bayridgedchristiancollege.org
Website: brcconline.org

Beeson Divinity School of Samford University† (Inter/Multidenominational), Timothy George, Dean, 800 Lakeshore Dr., Birmingham, AL 35229-2252 Tel. (205)726-2991 Fax (205)726-2260
Email: JTPrince@samford.edu
Website: www.beesondivinity.com

Berkeley Divinity School† (Episcopal Church), Joseph H. Britton, Dean, 409 Prospect Street, New Haven, CT 06511 Tel. (203)432-9285 Fax (203)432-9353
Email: joseph.britton@yale.edu
Website: www.yale.edu/berkeleydivinity

Bethany Lutheran Theological Seminary (Evangelical Lutheran Synod), G. R. Schmeling, President, 6 Browns Court, Mankato, MN 56001 Tel. (507)344-7354 Fax (507)344-7426
Email: gschmeli@blc.edu
Website: www.blts.edu

Bethany Theological Seminary† (Church of the Brethren), Ruthann K. Johansen, President, 615 National Rd. W., Richmond, IN 47374 Tel. (765)983-1800 Fax (765)983-1840
Email: president@bethanyseminary.edu
Website: www.bethanyseminary.edu

Bethel Seminary† (Coverge Worldwide (Baptist General Conference)), James Barnes III, President, 3949 Bethel Dr., St. Paul, MN 55112 Tel. (651)638-6180 Fax (651)638-6002
Email: s-wible@bethel.edu
Website: www.bethel.edu

Bethel Seminary of the East (Converge Worldwide (Baptist General Conference); Conservative Baptist Association of America Baptist General Conference), Douglas W. Fombelle, Dean and Executive Officer, 3600 Brightseat Rd., Landover, MD 20785-2414 Tel. (215)659-1000 Fax (215)659-1066
Email: d-fombelle@bethel.edu
Website: www.seminary.bethel.edu

Bethel Seminary San Diego† (Bapist General Conference), Jay Barnes, President, 6116 Arosa Street, San Diego, CA 92115-3902 Tel. (619)325-5200 Fax (619)325-5238
Email: bsem-admit@bethel.edu
Website: seminary.bethel.edu/sandiego

Beulah Heights Bible College‡ (The International Pentecostal Church of Christ), Dr. Benson M. Karanja, Ed. D., President, 892 Berne St. SE, Atlanta, GA 30316 Tel. (404)627-2681 Fax (404)627-0702
Email: Benson.Karanja@beulah.org
Website: www.beulah.org

Bexley Hall Seminary† (Episcopal Church), Robert Bottoms, President and Dean, 583 Sheridan Avenue, Columbus, OH 43209-2325 Tel. (614)231-3095 Fax (614)231-3236
Email: bexleyhall@bexley.edu
Website: www.bexley.edu

Bible Church of Christ Theological Institute (Nondenominational), Roy Bryant, Sr., Pres., 1358 Morris Ave., Bronx, NY 10456-1402 Tel. (718)588-2284 Fax (718)992-5597
Email: info@biblechurchofchrist.org
Website: www.thebiblechurchofchrist.org

Biblical Theological Seminary† (Inter/Multidenominational), David G. Dunbar, President, 200 N. Main St., Hatfield, PA 19440 Tel. (215)368-5000 Fax (215)368-2301
Email: president@biblical.edu
Website: www.biblical.edu

Blessed John XXIII National Seminary† (Catholic Church), Francis D. Kelly, Rector, 558 South Avenue, Weston, MA 02493-2699 Tel. (781)899-5500 Fax (781)899-9057
Email: seminary@blessedjohnxxiii.edu
Website: www.blessedjohnxxiii.edu

Boise Bible College (Christian Churches and Churches of Christ), Dr. Charles A. Crane, President, 8695 Marigold St., Boise, ID 83714 Tel. (208)376-7731 Fax (208)376-7743
Email: boisebible@boisebible.edu
Website: www.boisebible.edu

Boston Baptist College‡ (Baptist), Rev. David Melton, President, 950 Metropolitan Avenue, Boston, MA 02136 Tel. (617)364-3510 Fax (617)364-0723
Email: mail@boston.edu
Website: www.boston.edu

Boston College Institute of Religious Education and Pastoral Ministry and Department of Theology (Catholic Church), Thomas H. Groome, Director, 31 Lawrence Ave., Chestnut Hill, MA 02467-3931 Tel. (617)552-8440 Fax (617)552-0811
Email: lambmb@bc.edu
Website: www.bc.edu/sem

Boston College School of Theology and Ministry† (Catholic Church), Mark Massa, SJ, Dean, 140 Commonwealth Avenue, Chestnut Hill, MA 02467 Tel. (617)552-6509 Fax (617)492-5833
Email: terry.lima@bc.edu
Website: www.bc.edu/schools.html

Boston University School of Theology† (The United Methodist Church), Ray L. Hart, Dean, 745 Commonwealth Ave., Boston, MA 02215 Tel. (617)353-3050 Fax (617)353-3061
Website: www.bu.edu/STH

Brite Divinity School, Texas Christian University† (Christian Church (Disciples of Christ)), Newell Williams, President, TCU Box 298130, Ft. Worth, TX 76129-0002 Tel. (817)257-7575 Fax (817)257-7305
Email: k.winter@tcu.edu
Website: www.brite.tcu.edu

Byzantine Catholic Seminary of SS. Cyril and Methodius† (Byzantine Catholic Archeparchy of Pittsburgh), John G. Petro, Rector, 3605 Perrysville Ave., Pittsburgh, PA 15214 Tel. (412)321-8383 Fax (412)321-9936
Email: m.andrako@verizon.net
Website: www.byzcathsem.org

California Christian College‡ (Free Will Baptist), Wendell Walley, President, 4881 E. University Avenue, Fresno, CA 93703 Tel. (559)251-4215 Fax (559)251-4231
Email: cccregistrar@sbcglobal.net
Website: www.calchristiancollege.org

Calvary Bible College and Calvary Theological Seminary (Independent Fundamental Churches of America, International), James L. Clark, PhD, President, 15800 Calvary Rd., Kansas City, MO 64147-1341 Tel. (800)326-3960 Fax (816)331-4474
Email: president@calvary.edu
Website: www.calvary.edu

Calvin Theological Seminary† (Christian Reformed Church in North America), The Rev. Cornelius Plantinga, Jr., Ph.D., President, 3233 Burton St. S.E., Grand Rapids, MI 49546-4387 Tel. (616)957-6036 or (616)957-6044 Fax (616)957-8621
Email: sempres@calvinseminary.edu
Website: www.calvinseminary.edu

Campbell University Divinity School† (Baptist State Convention of North Carolina), Andrew H. Wakefield, Dean, 116 T. T. Lanier Street, PO Drawer 4050, Buies Creek, NC 27506 Tel. (910)893-1830 Fax (910)893-1835
Email: cogdill@campbell.edu
Website: www.campbell.edu/divinity

Candler School of Theology of Emory University† (The United Methodist Church), Jan Love, Dean, Emory University, 1531 Dickey Drive, Atlanta, GA 30322 Tel. (404)727-6324 Fax (404)727-3182
Email: candler@emory.edu
Website: www.emory.edu/candler

Capital Bible Seminary† (Nondenominational), Dr. George Harton, Interim President, Interim President, 6511 Princess Garden Parkway, Lanham, MD 20706 Tel. (301)552-1400 Fax (301)614-1024
Email: bfox@bible.edu
Website: www.bible.edu

Carolina Graduate School of Divinity† (Religious Society of Friends), Frank P. Scurry, President, P.O. Box 7841, High Point, NC 27417 Tel. (336)315-8660 Fax (336)882-3370
Email: fscurry@ceds.edu
Website: www.ceds.edu

Catholic Theological Union at Chicago† (Roman Catholic Church), Donald Senior, C.P., President, 5401 S. Cornell Ave., Chicago, IL 60615-5664 Tel. (773)371-5400 Fax (773)324-8490
Email: donald@ctu.edu
Website: www.ctu.edu

Catholic University of America School of Theology† (Catholic Church), Rev. Magr. Kevin W. Irwin, Dean, 620 Michigan Avenue NE, Washington, DC 20064 Tel. (202)319-5683 Fax (202)319-4967
Email: cua-deansrs@cua.edu
Website: www.trs.cua.edu

Central Baptist College (Baptist Missionary Association of Arkansas), Terry Kimbrow, President, 1501 College Ave., Conway, AR 72032 Tel. (501)329-6872 Fax (501)329-2941
Email: TKimbrow@cbc.edu
Website: www.cbc.edu

Central Baptist Theological Seminary† (Baptist), The Rev. Dr. Molly T. Marshall, President, 6601 Monticello Road, Shawnee, KS 66226-3513 Tel. (913)667-5700 Fax (913)371-8110
Email: central@cbts.edu
Website: www.cbts.edu

Central Baptist Theological Seminary in Indiana (National Baptist Convention USA, Inc.), Dr. Robert Lee, President-Dean, 1535 Dr. A. J. Brown Ave. N., Indianapolis, IN 46202 Tel. (317)636-6622
Email: henriettabrown@webtv.net

Central Bible College (Assemblies of God), In Transition, President, 3000 N. Grant Ave., Springfield, MO 65803 Tel. (417)833-2551 Fax (417)833-5141
Email: info@cbcag.edu
Website: www.cbcag.edu

Central Christian College of the Bible (Christian Churches and Churches of Christ), Ronald L. Oakes, D.Min, President, 911 E. Urbandale Dr., Moberly, MO 65270-1997 Tel. (660)263-3900 Fax (660)263-3936
Email: president@cccb.edu
Website: www.cccb.edu

Chapman Seminary of Oakland City University† (General Association of General Baptists), Ray G. Barber, President, 138

Lucretia Street, Oakland City, IN 47660 Tel. (812)749-4781 Fax (812)749-1233 Email: bbenson@oak.edu Website: www.oak.edu

Chicago Theological Seminary† (United Church of Christ), Susan Brooks Thistlethwaite, President, 5757 South University Ave., Chicago, IL 60637-1507 Tel. (773)752-5757 Fax (773)752-5925 Email: kjohnson@ctschicago.edu Website: www.ctschicago.edu

Christ the King Seminary† (Catholic Church), Rev. Peter J. Drilling, President and Rector, 711 Knox Rd., P.O. Box 607, East Aurora, NY 14052-0607 Tel. (716)652-8900 Fax (716)652-8903 Email: pdrilling@cks.edu Website: www.cks.edu

Christ the Savior Seminary (The American Carpatho-Russian Orthodox Greek Catholic Church), Nicholas Smisko, President, 225 Chandler Ave., Johnstown, PA 15906 Tel. (814)539-0116 Fax (814)536-4699 Email: csseminary@atlanticbb.net Website: www.acrod.org/seminary

Christian Life College‡ (Non-Denominational), Harry Schmidt, President, 400 E. Gregory Street, Mount Prospect, IL 60056 Tel. (847) 259-1840 Fax (847)259-3888 Email: admissions@christianlifecollege.edu Website: www.christianlifecollege.edu

Christian Theological Seminary† (Christian Church (Disciples of Christ)), Dr. Edward L. Wheeler, President, 1000 W. 42nd St., Indianapolis, IN 46208-3301 Tel. (317)924-1331 Fax (317)923-1961 Email: wheeler@cts.edu Website: www.cts.edu

Christian Witness Theological Seminary† (Nondenominational), Rev. Daniel Tan, President, 1975 Concourse Drive, San Jose, CA 95131 Tel. (408)433-2280 Fax (408)433-9855 Email: admin@cwts.edu Website: www.cwts.edu

Church Divinity School of the Pacific† (Episcopal Church), Donn F. Morgan, President, 2451 Ridge Rd., Berkeley, CA 94709-1217 Tel. (510)204-0700 Fax (510)644-0712 Email: jrobinson@cdsp.edu Website: www.cdsp.edu

Cincinnati Bible Seminary of Cincinnati Christian University† (Christian Churches and Churches of Christ), David M. Faust, President, 2700 Glenway Ave., Cincinnati, OH 45204-3200 Tel. (513)244-8100 or 800-949-4228 Fax (513)244-8140 Email: president@ccuniversity.edu Website: www.CCuniversity.edu

Circleville Bible College (Churches of Christ in Christian Union), Dr. Mark Smith, President, 1476 Lancaster Pike, Circleville, OH 43113 Tel. (740)474-8896 Fax (740)477-7755 Email: enroll@ohiochristian.edu Website: www.ohiochristian.edu

Claremont School of Theology† (The United Methodist Church), Jerry D. Campbell, President, 1325 N. College Ave., Claremont, CA 91711-3199 Tel. (909)447-2500 Fax (909)621-2552 Email: jcampbell@cst.edu Website: www.cst.edu

Clear Creek Baptist Bible College (Southern Baptist Convention), President Bill Whittaker, President, 300 Clear Creek Rd., Pineville, KY 40977 Tel. (606)337-3196 Fax (606)337-2372 Email: ccbbc@ccbbc.edu Website: www.ccbbc.edu

Clinton Junior College‡ (African Methodist Episcopal Zion Church), Dr. Elaine Johnson Copeland, President, 1029 Crawford Road, Rock Hill, SC 29730 Tel. (803)327-7402 ext. 223 Fax (803)327-3261 Email: ecopeland@clintonjuniorcollege.edu Website: www.clintonjuniorcollege.edu

Colegio Biblico Pentecostal de Puerto Rico (Church of God (Cleveland, Tenn.)), Francisco Ortiz, President, P.O. Box 901, Saint Just, PR 00978 Tel. (787)761-0640 Fax (787)748-9228 Email: presidente.utc@gmail.com Website: www.cbp.edu

Colgate Rochester Crozer Divinity School† (American Baptist Churches in the USA), Eugene C. Bay, President, 1100 S. Goodman St., Rochester, NY 14620 Tel. (585)271-1320 Fax (585)271-8013 Email: ebay@crcds.edu Website: www.crcds.edu

Colorado Christian University (Nondenominational), Bill William Armstrong, President, 180 S. Garrison St., Lakewood, CO 80226 Tel. (303)202-0100 Fax (303)274-7560 Email: warmstrong@ccu.edu Website: www.ccu.edu

Columbia International University Seminary & School of Missions† (Multidenominational), William H. Jones, President, P.O. Box 3122, Columbia, SC 29230-3122 Tel. (803)754-4100 Fax (803)786-4209

Email: publicrelations@ciu.edu
Website: www.ciu.edu

Columbia Theological Seminary† (Presbyterian Church (USA)), Dr. Stephen A. Hayner, President, 701 Columbia Dr., P.O. Box 520, Decatur, GA 30031 Tel. (404)378-8821 Fax (404)377-9696
Email: hayner@CTSnet.edu
Website: www.CTSnet.edu

Concordia Seminary† (The Lutheran Church-Missouri Synod), Dale A. Meyer, President, 801 Seminary Place, St. Louis, MO 63105 Tel. (314)505-7010 Fax (314)505-7002
Email: bartelta@csl.edu
Website: www.csl.edu

Concordia Theological Seminary† (The Lutheran Church-Missouri Synod), Dean O. Wenthe, President, 6600 N. Clinton St., Ft. Wayne, IN 46825-4996 Tel. (260)452-2100 Fax (260)452-2121
Email: dean.wenthe@ctsfw.edu
Website: www.ctsfw.edu

Corban University School of Ministry‡ (Baptist), Dr. Reno Hoff, President, 4301 North Stevens St., Tacoma, WA 98407 Tel. (253)759-6104 Fax (253)759-3299
Email: cusm@corban.edu
Website: www.corban.edu/ministry

Covenant Theological Seminary† (Prebyterian Church in America), Dr. Bryan Chapell, President, 12330 Conway Rd., St. Louis, MO 63141-8697 Tel. (314)434-4044 Fax (314)434-4819
Email: kathy.woodard@covenantseminary.edu
Website: www.covenantseminary.edu

Cranmer Seminary (The Episcopal Orthodox Church; The Anglican Rite Synod in the Americas; The Orthodox Anglican Communion), The Most Rev. Scott E. McLaughlin, D.D., Ph.D., President, 901 English Rd., High Point, NC 27262 Tel. (336)885-6032 Fax (336)885-6021
Email: seminaryinfo@orthodoxanglican.net
Website: orthodoxanglican.net;
divinityschool.org

Criswell Center for Biblical Studies (Southern Baptist Convention), Dr. Lamar Cooper, Interim President, 4010 Gaston Ave., Dallas, TX 75246 Tel. (214)821-5433 Fax (214)370-0497
Email: reception@criswell.edu
Website: www.criswell.edu

Crossroads College (Christian Churches and Churches of Christ - Non-denominational), Mike Kilgallin, President, 920 Mayowood Rd.

S.W., Rochester, MN 55902 Tel. (507)288-4563 Fax (507)288-9046
Email: academic@crossroadscollege.edu
Website: www.crossroadscollege.edu

Crown College (The Christian and Missionary Alliance), Rick Mann, President, 8700 College View Dr., St. Bonifacius, MN 55375-9001 Tel. (952)446-4100 Fax (952)446-4149
Email: crown@crown.edu
Website: www.crown.edu

Cummins Theological Seminary (Reformed Episcopal Church), The Rt. Rev. Al Gadsden, President, 1016 S. Elm Ave., Webster Groves, MO 63119 Tel. (314)566-8642 Fax (843)875-6200
Email: bishopgadsden@att.net
Website: www.recus.org

Dallas Christian College (Christian Churches and Churches of Christ), Dustin "Dusty" Rubeck, President, 2700 Christian Pkwy, Dallas, TX 75234 Tel. (972)241-3371 Fax (972)241-8021
Email: dcc@dallas.edu
Website: www.dallas.edu

Dallas Theological Seminary† (Inter/Multidenominational), Dr. Mark L. Bailey, President, 3909 Swiss Ave., Dallas, TX 75204 Tel. (214)824-3094 Fax (214)841-3625
Email: kgrassmick@dts.edu
Website: www.dts.edu

Davis College (Practical Bible College) (Independent Baptist), Dr. George Miller, President, 400 Riverside Drive, Johnson City, NY 13790 Tel. (607)729-1581 Fax (607)729-2962
Website: www.davisny.edu

Denver Seminary† (Nondenominational), Mark S. Young, PhD, President, 6399 S. Santa Fe Drive, Littleton, CO 80120 Tel. (303)761-2482 Fax (303)761-8060
Email: admissions@denverseminary.edu
Website: www.denverseminary.edu

The Disciples Divinity House of the University of Chicago (Christian Church (Disciples of Christ)), Dr. Kristine A. Culp, Dean, 1156 E. 57th St., Chicago, IL 60637-1536 Tel. (773)643-4411 Fax (773)643-4413
Email: ddhadmin@gmail.com
Website: ddh.uchicago.edu

Dominican House of Studies† (Catholic Church), Dwight Reginald Whitt, O.P., President, 487 Michigan Ave. N.E., Washington, DC 20017-1585 Tel. (202)529-5300 Fax (202)636-1700
Email: assistant@dhs.edu
Website: www.dhs.edu

Dominican School of Philosophy and Theology† (Catholic Church), Michael Sweeney, President, 2301 Vine Street, Berkeley, CA 94708 Tel. (510)883-2083 Fax (510)849-1372
Email: msweeney@dspt.edu
Website: www.dspt.edu

Dominican Study Center of the Caribbean† (Catholic Church), Rev. Dr. Yamil Samalot Rivera, O.P., Dean, Apartado Postal 1968, Bayamon, PR 00960-1968 Tel. (787)787-1826 Fax (787)798-2712
Email: info@cedoc.edu
Website: www.cedocpr.org

Drew University Theological School† (The United Methodist Church), Jeoffery Ku, Dean, 36 Madison Ave., Madison, NJ 07940-4010 Tel. (973)408-3258 Fax (973)408-3534
Email: miannuzzi@drew.edu
Website: www.drew.edu/theo

Duke University Divinity School† (The United Methodist Church), Richard B. Hays, Dean, P.O. Box 90968, Durham, NC 27708-0968 Tel. (919)660-3400 Fax (919)660-3473
Email: admissions@div.duke.edu
Website: www.divinity.duke.edu

Earlham School of Religion† (Interdenominational-Friends), Jay Wade Marshall, Dean, 228 College Ave., Richmond, IN 47374 Tel. (800)432-1377 Fax (765)983-1688
Email: esr@earlham.edu
Website: www.esr.earlham.edu

Eastern Mennonite Seminary of Eastern Mennonite University† (Mennonite Church USA), Michael A. King, Dean, 1200 Park Road, Harrisonburg, VA 22802 Tel. (540)432-4260 Fax (540)432-4598
Email: swartlej@emu.edu
Website: www.emu.edu/seminary

Ecumenical Theological Seminary† (Inter/Multidenominational), Marsha Foster Boyd, President, 2930 Woodward Ave., Detroit, MI 48201 Tel. (313)831-5200 Fax (313)831-1353
Email: lhannum@etseminary.edu
Website: www.etseminary.edu

Eden Theological Seminary† (United Church of Christ), David M. Greenhaw, President, 475 E. Lockwood Ave., St. Louis, MO 63119-3192 Tel. (314)961-3627 Fax (314)918-2626
Email: dgreenhaw@eden.edu
Website: www.eden.edu

Emmanuel Christian University† (Christian Churches and Churches of Christ), Michael L. Sweeney, President, One Walker Dr., Johnson City, TN 37601-9438 Tel. (423)926-1186 Fax (423)926-6198

Email: sweeneym@esr.edu
Website: www.esr.edu

Emmaus Bible College (Christian Brethren (also known as Plymouth Brethren)), Kenneth Alan Daughters, President, 2570 Asbury Rd., Dubuque, IA 52001 Tel. (563)588-8000 Fax (563)588-1216
Email: info@emmaus.edu
Website: www.emmaus.edu

Episcopal Divinity School† (Episcopal Church), The Rev. Dr Randall Chase, Acting President and Dean, 99 Brattle St., Cambridge, MA 02138-3494 Tel. (617)868-1511 Fax (617)864-5385
Email: rchase@eds.edu
Website: www.eds.edu

Seminary of the Southwest† (Episcopal Church), Douglas Travis, Dean and President, P.O. Box 2247, Austin, TX 78768-2247 Tel. (512)472-4133 Fax (512)472-3098
Email: seminary@ssw.edu
Website: www.ssw.edu

Erskine Theological Seminary† (Associate Reformed Presbyterian Church (General Synod)), Dr. David A. Norman, President, P.O. Box 668, Due West, SC 29639 Tel. (864)379-8833 Fax (864)379-6658
Email: norman@erskine.edu
Website: www.erskineseminary.org

Eugene Bible College (Open Bible Churches, Inc.), David Cole, President, 2155 Bailey Hill Rd., Eugene, OR 97405 Tel. (541)485-1780 Fax (541)343-5801
Email: davidcole@ebc.edu
Website: www.ebc.edu

Evangelical Theological Seminary† (The Evangelical Congregational Church), President, 121 S. College St., Myerstown, PA 17067 Tel. (717)866-5775 Fax (717)866-4667
Website: www.evangelical.edu

Evangelical Seminary of Puerto Rico† (Inter/Multidenominational), Sergio Ojeda-Carcamo, President, Ponce de Leon Avenue 776, San Juan, PR 00925 Tel. (787)763-6700 Fax (787)751-0847
Email: meperez@se-pr.org
Website: www.seminarioevangelicopr.org

Faith Baptist Bible College and Theological Seminary (Baptist), James D. Maxwell III, President, 1900 N.W. 4th St., Ankeny, IA 50023 Tel. (515)964-0601 Fax (515)964-1638
Email: schmidtg@faith.edu
Website: www.faith.edu

Faith Evangelical Lutheran Seminary‡ (Conservative Lutheran Association), R. H. Redal, President, 3504 N. Pearl St., Tacoma,

301

WA 98407 Tel. (253)752-2020 or (888)777-7675 Fax (206)759-1790
Email: fsinfo@faithseminary.edu
Website: wwwfaithseminary.edu

Florida Center for Theological Studies† (Inter/Multidenominational), Patrick H. O'Neill, President, 111 NE First St., Eighth Floor, Miami, FL 33132 Tel. (305)379-3777 Fax (305)379-1006
Email: budrew@fcts.edu
Website: www.fcfts.org

Florida Christian College (Christian Churches and Churches of Christ), A. Wayne Lowen, President, 1011 Bill Beck Blvd., Kissimmee, FL 34744 Tel. (407)847-8966 Fax (407)847-3925
Email: fcc@fcc.edu
Website: www.fcc.edu

Franciscan School of Theology† (Catholic Church), Mario DiCicco, President, 1712 Euclid Ave., Berkeley, CA 94709 Tel. (510) 848-5232 Fax (510)549-9466
Email: mdicicco@fst.edu
Website: www.fst.edu

Free Will Baptist Bible College (National Association of Free Will Baptists), J. Matthew Pinson, President, 3606 West End Ave., Nashville, TN 37205 Tel. (615)844-5000 Fax (615)269-6028
Email: president@fwbbc.edu
Website: www.fwbcc.edu

Fuller Theological Seminary† (Multidenominational), Richard J. Mouw, President, 135 N. Oakland Ave., Pasadena, CA 91182 Tel. (626)584-5200 Fax (626)795-8767
Email: mgiven@fuller.edu
Website: www.fuller.edu

Garrett-Evangelical Theological Seminary† (The United Methodist Church), Philip A. Amerson, President, 2121 Sheridan Rd., Evanston, IL 60201-3298 Tel. (847)866-3900 Fax (847)866-3957
Email: seminary@garrett.edu
Website: www.garrett.edu

The General Theological Seminary† (Episcopal Church), Ward B. Ewing, Dean and President, 175 Ninth Ave., New York, NY 10011-4977 Tel. (212)243-5150 Fax (212)647-0294
Email: ewing@gts.edu
Website: www.gts.edu

George Fox Evangelical Seminary† (Inter/Multidenominational), Charles Conniry Jr, Vice President & Dean, 12753 SW 68th Ave., Portland, OR 97223 Tel. (503)554-6150 Fax (503)554-6155

Email: cconniry@georgefox.edu
Website: www.seminary.georgefox.edu

George Mercer Jr. Memorial School of Theology (Episcopal Church), The Very Reverend David B. Lowry, PhD, Interim Dean, 65 Fourth St., Garden City, NY 11530 Tel. (516)248-4800 Fax (516)248-4883
Email: merceroffice@dioceseli.org
Website: www.mercerschool.org

George W. Truett Theological Seminary of Baylor University† (Baptist General Convention of Texas), David E. Garland, Dean, One Bear Place # 97126, Waco, TX 76798-7126 Tel. (254)710-3755 Fax (254)710-3753
Email: Angela_Bailey@baylor.edu
Website: www.baylor.edu/truett

God's Bible School and College (Nondenominational), Dr. Michael Avery, President, 1810 Young St., Cincinnati, OH 45202 Tel. (513)721-7944 Fax (513)721-3971
Email: president@gbs.edu
Website: www.gbs.edu

Golden Gate Baptist Theological Seminary† (Southern Baptist Convention), Jeff Iorg, President, 201 Seminary Dr., Mill Valley, CA 94941-3197 Tel. (415)380-1300 Fax (415)380-1302
Email: seminary@ggbts.edu
Website: www.ggbts.edu

Gonzaga University Department of Religious Studies (Catholic Church), Pat McCormick, Dept. Head, Spokane, WA 99258-0001 Tel. (509)328-6782 Fax (509)323-5718
Email: McCormick@Gonzaga.edu
Website: www.gonzaga.edu

Gordon-Conwell Theological Seminary† (Inter/Multidenominational), James Emery White, President, 130 Essex St., South Hamilton, MA 01982 Tel. (978)468-7111 Fax (978)468-6691
Email: info@gcts.edu
Website: www.gordonconwell.edu

Grace Bible College (Grace Gospel Fellowship), Kenneth B. Kemper, President, P.O. Box 910, Grand Rapids, MI 49509 Tel. (616)538-2330 Fax (616)538-0599
Email: info@gbcol.edu
Website: www.gbcol.edu

Grace Theological Seminary† (Fellowship of Grace Brethren Churches), Ronald E. Manahan, President, 200 Seminary Dr., Winona Lake, IN 46590-1294 Tel. (574)372-5100 Fax (574)372-5139
Email: rmanahan@grace.edu
Website: www.grace.edu

Grace University (Interdenominational), Dr. James Eckman, President, 1311 South 9th St., Omaha, NE 68108 Tel. (402)449-2809 Fax (402)341-9587
Email: jofast@graceu.edu
Website: www.graceuniversity.edu

Graduate Theological Foundation (Interdenominational/Interfaith), Kendra E. Clayton, Ed.D., Director of Academic Affairs, Dodge House, 415 Lincoln Way East, Mishawaka, IN 46544 Tel. (800)423-5983 or (574)255-3642 Fax (574)255-7520
Email: info@gtfeducation.org
Website: www.gtfeducation.org

Graduate Theological Union† (Interdenominational), James A. Donahue, President, 2400 Ridge Rd., Berkeley, CA 94709-1212 Tel. (510)649-2400 Fax (510)649-1417
Email: president@gtu.edu
Website: www.gtu.edu

Grand Rapids Theological Seminary of Cornerstone University† (Nondenominational), Dr. Joseph M. Stowell, President, 1001 East Beltline Ave., NE, Grand Rapids, MI 49525 Tel. (616)222-1428 Fax (616)222-1502
Email: joe.stowell@conerstone.edu
Website: www.grts.cornerstone.edu

Great Lakes Christian College (Christian Churches and Churches of Christ), Larry Carter, President, 6211 W. Willow Hwy., Lansing, MI 48917 Tel. (517)321-0242 Fax (517)321-5902
Email: lcarter@glcc.edu
Website: www.glcc.edu

Greenville College (Free Methodist Church of North America), Dr. Larry Linamen, President, 315 E. College Ave., P.O. Box 159, Greenville, IL 62246 Tel. (618)664-2800 Fax (618)664-1748
Website: www.greenville.edu

Harding School of Theology† (Churches of Christ), Evertt W. Huffard, Executive Director, 1000 Cherry Rd., Memphis, TN 38117-5499 Tel. (901)761-1352 Fax (901)761-1358
Email: dean@hst.edu
Website: www.hst.edu

Hartford Seminary† (Interdenominational), Heidi Hadsell, President, 77 Sherman St., Hartford, CT 06105-2260 Tel. (860)509-9500 Fax (860)509-9509
Email: info@hartsem.edu
Website: www.hartsem.edu

Harvard University Divinity School† (Multidenominational/Multireligious), Professor William A. Graham, Dean, 45 Francis Ave., Cambridge, MA 02138 Tel. (617)495-4513 Fax (617)496-8026
Email: suzanne_rom@harvard.edu
Website: www.hds.harvard.edu

Hebrew Union College-Jewish Institute of Religion (Jewish), Rabbi David Ellenson, President, 3077 University Ave., Los Angeles, CA 90007 Tel. (213)749-3424 Fax (213)747-6128
Email: presoff@huc.edu
Website: www.huc.edu

Hebrew Union College - Jewish Institute of Religion, NY (Reform Judaism), Rabbi David Ellenson, President, One West 4th St., New York, NY 10012 Tel. (212)824-2201 Fax (212)388-1720
Email: presoff@huc.edu
Website: www.huc.edu

Heritage Bible College‡ (Pentecostal Free Will Baptist), Dr. Elvin R. Butts, President, 1747 Bud Hawkins Road, P.O. Box 1628, Dunn, NC 28335 Tel. (910)892-3178 Fax (910)892-1809
Email: generalinfo@heritagebiblecollege.edu
Website: www.heritagebiblecollege.edu

Hillsdale Free Will Baptist College‡ (Free Will Baptist), Carl Cheshier, President, P.O. Box 7208, Moore, OK 73153-1208 Tel. (405)912-9000 Fax (405)912-9050
Email: hillsdale@hc.edu
Website: www.hc.edu

Hobe Sound Bible College (Nondenominational), P. Daniel Stetler, President, P.O. Box 1065, Hobe Sound, FL 33475 Tel. (407)546-5534 Fax (407)545-1421
Email: lavernegagnon@hsbc.edu
Website: www.hsbc.edu

Holy Cross Greek Orthodox School of Theology† (Greek Orthodox Archdiocese of America), Rev. Nicholas C. Triantafilou, President, 50 Goddard Ave., Brookline, MA 02445-7495 Tel. (617)731-3500 Fax (617)850-1460
Email: pres_office@hchc.edu
Website: www.hchc.edu

Holy Trinity Orthodox Seminary (The Russian Orthodox Church Outside of Russia), Archimandrite Luke (Murianka), President, P.O. Box 36, Jordanville, NY 13361 Tel. (315)858-0945 Fax (315)858-0945
Email: info@hts.edu
Website: www.hts.edu

Hood Theological Seminary† (African Methodist Episcopal Zion Church), Albert J. D. Aymer, President, 1810 Lutheran Synod Drive, Salisbury, NC 28144 Tel. (704)636-7611 Fax (704)636-7699

Email: pwells@hoodseminary.edu
Website: www.hoodseminary.edu

Hope International University (Christian Churches and Churches of Christ), Dr. John Derry, President, 2500 E. Nutwood Ave., Fullerton, CA 92831-3104 Tel. (714)879-3901 Fax (714)681-7451
Email: tmurray@hiu.edu
Website: www.hiu.edu

Houston Graduate School of Theology† (Friends/Nondenominational), Keith A. Jenkins, President, 2501 Central Parkway, Suite A-19, Houston, TX 77092 Tel. (713)942-9505 Fax (713)942-9506
Email: hgst@hgst.edu
Website: www.hgst.edu

Howard University School of Divinity† (Nondenominational), Alton B. Pollard III, Dean, 1400 Shepherd St. N.E., Washington, DC 20017 Tel. (202)806-0500 Fax (202)806-0711
Email: apollard@howard.edu
Website: www.divinity.howard.edu

Huntington University (Church of the United Brethren in Christ), Blair Dowden, President, 2303 College Ave., Huntington, IN 46750 Tel. (260)356-6000 Fax (260)359-4126
Email: webmaster@huntington.edu
Website: www.huntington.edu/gscm

Iliff School of Theology† (The United Methodist Church), David Trickett, President, 2201 S. University Blvd., Denver, CO 80210-4798 Tel. (303)744-1287 Fax (303)777-3387
Email: dgtrickett@iliff.edu
Website: www.iliff.edu

Immaculate Conception Seminary School of Theology, Seton Hall University† (Catholic Church), Rev. Msgr. Robert F. Coleman, J. C. D., Rector and Dean, 400 S. Orange Ave., South Orange, NJ 07079 Tel. (973)761-9575 Fax (973)761-9577
Email: theology@shu.edu
Website: www.shu.edu/academics/theology/

Indiana Wesleyan University (The Wesleyan Church), Dr. Henry L. Smith, President, 4201 S. Washington, Marion, IN 46953-4974 Tel. (765)674-6901 Fax (765)677-2465
Email: henry.smith@indwes.edu
Website: www.indwes.edu

Institute for Ministry Development (Assemblies of God), Robert Koscak, President, P.O. Box 2180, Rapid City, SD 57709 Tel. (605)342-6180 Fax (605)845-7744

Inter-American Adventist Theological Seminary† (Seventh-day Adventist), Jaime Castrejon, Ph.D., President, P.O. Box 830518, Miami, FL 33283 Tel. (305)403-4575 Fax (305)403-4646
Email: castrejon@interamerica.org
Website: www.interamerica.org

Interdenominational Theological Center† (Interdenominational), Ronald E. Peters, Ed.D., President, 700 Martin Luther King, Jr. Dr. S.W., Atlanta, GA 30314-4143 Tel. (404)527-7702 Fax (404)527-7770
Email: ydowery@itc.edu
Website: www.itc.edu

International Baptist College‡ (Baptist), Pastor David Brock, President, 2211 West Germann Rd, Chandler, AZ 85286 Tel. (480)245-7903 Fax (480)245-7908
Email: info@ibconline.edu
Website: www.ibconline.edu

International College & Graduate School (Nondenominational), Dr. Rick Stinton, President, 20 Dowsett Avenue, Honolulu, HI 96817 Tel. (808)595-4247 Fax (808)595-4779
Email: icgs@hawaii.rr.com
Website: www.icgshawaii.org

International Theological Seminary† (Nondenominational), Mel Loucks, President, 3215-3225 N. Tyler Ave., El Monte, CA 91731 Tel. (626)448-0023 Fax (626)350-6343
Email: dean@itsla.edu
Website: www.itsla.edu

James and Carolyn McAfee School of Theology of Mercer University† (Cooperative Baptist Fellowship), R. Alan Culpepper, Dean of the School of Theology, 3001 Mercer University Drive, Atlanta, GA 30341-4115 Tel. (678)547-6470 Fax (678)547-6478
Email: culpepper_ra@mercer.edu
Website: theology.mercer.edu

Jesuit School of Theology of Santa Clara University† (Catholic Church), Joseph P. Daoust, President, 1735 LeRoy Ave., Berkeley, CA 94709-1193 Tel. (510)549-5000 Fax (510)841-8536
Email: cdodson@jstb.edu
Website: www.jstb.edu

Jewish Theological Seminary of America (Jewish), Arnold Eisen, President, 3080 Broadway, New York, NY 10027-4649 Tel. (212)678-8000 Fax (212)678-8947
Email: areisen@jtsa.edu
Website: www.jtsa.edu

The John Leland Center for Theological Studies† (Baptist), Mark Olson, President, 405 N. Washington St., Suite 200, Falls Church, VA 22046 Tel. (703)812-4757 ext. 201 Fax (703)812-4764

Email: molson@leland.edu
Website: www.leland.edu

John Wesley College (Interdenominational), Brian C. Donley, President, 2314 N. Centennial St., High Point, NC 27265 Tel. (336)889-2262 Fax (336)889-2261 Email: admissions@johnwesley.edu Website: www.johnwesley.edu

Johnson University (Christian Churches and Churches of Christ), Gary E. Weedman, President, 7900 Johnson Dr., Knoxville, TN 37998 Tel. (865)573-4517 Fax (865)251-2336 Email: tnice@jbc.edu Website: www.johnsonu.edu

Kansas City College and Bible School (Church of God (Holiness)), Gayle Woods, President, 7401 Metcalf Ave., Overland Park, KS 66204 Tel. (913)722-0272 Fax (913)722-2135 Email: pastorchad@eldochurch.com Website: www.kccbs.edu

Kenrick-Glennon Seminary† (Catholic Church), Ted L. Wojcicki, President-Rector, 5200 Glennon Dr., St. Louis, MO 63119-4399 Tel. (314)792-6100 Fax (314)792-6500 Email: wojcicki@kenrick.edu Website: www.kenrick.edu

Kentucky Christian University (Christian Churches and Churches of Christ), Jeffrey K. Metclaf, Ed. D., President, 100 Academic Parkway, Grayson, KY 41143 Tel. (606)474-3000 Fax (606)474-3155 Email: krobinette@kcu.edu Website: www.kcu.edu

Kentucky Mountain Bible College (Inter-denominational), Philip Speas, President, Box 10, Vancleve, KY 41385 Tel. (606)666-5000 Fax (606)666-7744

King's University‡ (Non-Denominational), Paul G. Chappell, Ph.D., Chief Academic Officer, 14800 Sherman Way, Los Angeles, CA 91405 Tel. (818)779-8040 Fax (818)779-8241 Email: admissions@kingsseminary.edu Website: www.kingsseminary.edu www.kingscollege.edu

Knox Theological Seminary† (Presbyterian Church in America), R. Fowler White, Administrator and Dean of the Faculty, 5554 North Federal Highway, Fort Lauderdale, FL 33308 Tel. (954)771-0376 Fax (954)351-3343 Email: knox@crpc.org Website: www.knoxseminary.org

Kuyper College (Interdenominational), Nicholas V. Kroeze, President, 3333 East Beltline N.E., Grand Rapids, MI 49525-9749 Tel. (616)222-3000 Fax (616)988-3608

Email: jheyboer@kuyper.edu
Website: www.kuyper.edu

La Sierra University School of Religion† (Seventh-day Adventist Church), Randal R. Wisbey, President, 4500 Riverwalk Parkway, Riverside, CA 92515-8247 Tel. (951)785-2041 Fax (951)785-2199 Email: religion@lasierra.edu Website: www.lasierra.edu/religion

Lancaster Bible College (Nondenominational), Peter W. Teague, President, 901 Eden Road, Lancaster, PA 17601 Tel. (717)560-8278 Fax (717)560-8260 Email: president@lbc.edu Website: www.lbc.edu

Lancaster Theological Seminary† (United Church of Christ), Dr. Carol E. Lytch, President, 555 W. James St., Lancaster, PA 17603-2897 Tel. (717)393-0654 Fax (717)393-4254 Email: seminary@lancasterseminary.edu Website: www.lancasterseminary.edu

Lexington Theological Seminary† (Christian Church (Disciples of Christ)), R. Robert Cueni, President, 631 S. Limestone St., Lexington, KY 40508 Tel. (859)252-0361 Fax (859)281-6042 Email: rlowery@lextheo.edu Website: www.lextheo.edu

Liberty Theological Seminary and Graduate School (Independent Baptist), Dr. Ergun Caner, Dean, 1971 University Blvd., Lynchburg, VA 24502-2269 Tel. (434)592-4140 Fax (434)522-0415 Email: ecaner@liberty.edu Website: www.liberty.edu/Academics/Religion/Seminary

Liberty University (Baptist), Dr. John Borek, President, 1971 University Boulevard, Lynchburg, VA 24502 Tel. (434)582-2000 Fax (434)582-2304 Email: admissions@liberty.edu Website: www.liberty.edu

Life Pacific College (International Church of the Foursquare Gospel), Dan R. Stewart, President, 1100 Covina Blvd., San Dimas, CA 91773 Tel. (909)599-5433 Fax (909)599-6690 Email: info@lifepacific.edu Website: www.lifepacific.edu

Lincoln Christian University-The Seminary† (Christian Churches and Churches of Christ), Keith H. Ray, President, 100 Campus View Dr., Lincoln, IL 62656 Tel. (217)732-3168 ext.2274 Fax (217)732-5718 Email: semadmis@Lincolnchristian.edu Website: www.LincolnChristian.edu

Hazelip School of Theology of Lipscomb University† (Churches of Christ), L. Randolph Lowry, III, President, 1 University Park Drive, Nashville, TN 37204-3951 Tel. (615)966-6053 Fax (615)279-6052
Email: melissa.cox@lipscomb.edu
Website: http://hazelip.lipscomb.edu

Logos Evangelical Seminary† (Evangelical Formosan Church), Felix Liu, President, 9358 Telstar Ave., El Monte, CA 91731 Tel. (626) 571-5110 Fax (626)571-5119
Email: logos@les.edu
Website: www.logos-seminary.edu

Logsdon Seminary of Logsdon School of Theology† (Baptist General Convention of Texas), Donald D. Williford, Interim Dean, P.O. Box 16235, Abilene, TX 79698-6235 Tel. (325)670-1287 Fax (325)670-1406
Email: willifrd@hsutx.edu
Website: www.hsutx.edu/academics/logsdon

Louisville Presbyterian Theological Seminary† (Presbyterian Church (USA)), Michael Jinkins, President, 1044 Alta Vista Rd., Louisville, KY 40205 Tel. (502)895-3411 Fax (502)895-1096
Email: melton@lpts.edu
Website: www.lpts.edu

Loyola Marymount University Department of Theological Studies† (Catholic Church), Jeffrey S. Siker, Chair, One LMU Drive, Los Angeles, CA 90045-2659 Tel. (310)338-7670 Fax (310)338-1947
Email: jsiker@lmu.edu
Website: bellarmine.lmu.edu/theology

Loyola University Chicago Institute of Pastoral Studies (Catholic Church), Robert A. Ludwig, Director, 820 N. Michigan Ave., Chicago, IL 60611 Tel. (312)915-7400 Fax (312) 915-7410
Email: rludwig@luc.edu
Website: www.luc.edu/depts/ips

Luther Rice Bible College & Seminary‡ (Baptist), Dr. James Flanagan, President, 3038 Evans Mill Road, Lithonia, GA 30038 Tel. (770)484-1204 Fax (770)484-1155
Email: LRU@LRU.edu
Website: www.LRU.edu

Luther Seminary† (Evangelical Lutheran Church in America), Richard H. Bliese, President, 2481 Como Ave., St. Paul, MN 55108 Tel. (651)641-3456 Fax (651)641-3425
Email: admissions@luthersem.edu
Website: www.luthersem.edu

Lutheran Bible Institute in California (Intersynodical Lutheran), Samuel Giesy, Acting President, 5321 University Dr., Ste. G, Irvine, CA 92612-2942 Tel. (949)262-9222 or (800)261-5242 Fax (949)262-0283
Email: info@lbic.org
Website: www.lbic.org

Lutheran Brethren Seminary (Church of the Lutheran Brethren of America), David Veum, D. Min, President, 815 W. Vernon, Fergus Falls, MN 56537 Tel. (218)739-3375 Fax (218)739-1259
Email: lbs@lbs.edu
Website: www.lbs.edu

Lutheran School of Theology at Chicago† (Evangelical Lutheran Church in America), James Kenneth Echols, President, 1100 E. 55th St., Chicago, IL 60615-5199 Tel. (773)256-0700 Fax (773)256-0782
Email: jechols@lstc.edu
Website: www.lstc.edu

Lutheran Theological Seminary at Gettysburg† (Evangelical Lutheran Church in America), The Rev. Michael L. Cooper-White, President, 61 Seminary Ridge, Gettysburg, PA 17325-1795 Tel. (717)334-6286 Fax (717)334-3469
Email: ctroyer@ltsg.edu
Website: www.ltsg.edu

Lutheran Theological Seminary at Phila-delphia† (Evangelical Lutheran Church in America), Philip D.W. Krey, President, 7301 Germantown Ave., Philadelphia, PA 19119 Tel. (215)248-4616 Fax (215)248-4577
Email: mtairy@ltsp.edu
Website: www.ltsp.edu

Lutheran Theological Southern Seminary† (Evangelical Lutheran Church in America), Marcus J. Miller, President, 4201 North Main St., Columbia, SC 29203 Tel. (803)786-5150 Fax (803)786-6499
Email: Mmiller@ltss.edu
Website: www.ltss.edu

M. Christopher White School of Divinity of Gardner-Webb University† (Baptist State Convention of North Carolina Cooperative Baptist Fellowship), Robert W. Canoy, Dean, 110 N. Main Street, Noel Hall, Boiling Springs, NC 28017 Tel. (704)406-4400 Fax (704)406-3935
Email: rcanoy@gardner-webb.edu
Website: www.divinity.gardner-webb.edu

Manhattan Christian College (Christian Churches and Churches of Christ), Jolene Rupe, Secretary, Institutional Advancement, 1415 Anderson Ave., Manhattan, KS 66502 Tel. (785)539-3571 Fax (785)539-0832
Email: jrupe@mccks.edu
Website: www.mccks.edu

Maple Springs Baptist Bible College and Seminary‡ (Non-Denominational), Dr. Larry W. Jordan, President, 4130 Belt Road, Capital Heights, MD 20743 Tel. (301)736-3631 Fax (301)735-6507
Email: larry.jordan@msbbcs.edu
Website: www.msbbcs.edu

McCormick Theological Seminary† (Presbyterian Church (USA)), Cynthia M. Campbell, President, 5460 S. University Ave., Chicago, IL 60615-5108 Tel. (773)947-6300 Fax (773)288-2612
Email: ccampbell@mccormick.edu
Website: www.mccormick.edu

Meadville Lombard Theological School† (Unitarian Universalist), Lee Barker, President, 5701 S. Woodlawn Ave., Chicago, IL 60637 Tel. (773)256-3000 Fax (773)753-1323
Email: LBarker@meadville.edu
Website: www.meadville.edu

Memphis Theological Seminary† (Cumberland Presbyterian Church), Daniel J. Earheart-Brown, President, 168 E. Parkway S at Union, Memphis, TN 38104-4395 Tel. (901)458-8232 Fax (901)452-4051
Email: jebrown@memphisseminary.edu
Website: www.memphisseminary.edu

Mennonite Brethren Biblical Seminary† (General Conference of Mennonite Brethren Churches), Jim Holm, President, 4824 E. Butler Ave. (at Chestnut Ave.), Fresno, CA 93727-5097 Tel. (559)251-8628 Fax (559)251-7212
Email: fresno@mbseminary.edu
Website: www.mbseminary.edu

Messenger College‡ (Pentecostal Church of God), Patricia Pentecost, Dir. of Admissions, 300 E. 50th Street, Joplin, MO 64804 Tel. (417)624-7070 Fax (417)624-5070
Email: info@messengercollege.edu
Website: www.messengercollege.edu

Methodist Theological School in Ohio† (The United Methodist Church), Jay Rundell, President, 3081 Columbus Pike, Delaware, OH 43015-8004 Tel. (740)363-1146 Fax (740)362-3135
Email: admit@mtso.edu
Website: www.mtso.edu

Moody Theological Seminary and Graduate School† (Non-Denominational), Paul Nyquist, President, 41550 E. Ann Arbor Trail, Plymouth, MI 48170-4308 Tel. (734)207-9581 Fax (734)207-9582
Email: admissions@mts.edu
Website: www.mts.edu

Mid-America Christian University (The Church of God - Anderson, IN), Dr. John D. Fozard, President, 3500 S.W. 119th St., Oklahoma City, OK 73170 Tel. (405)691-3800 Fax (405)692-3165
Email: info@macu.edu
Website: www.macu.edu

Mid-America Reformed Seminary†‡ (Inter-/Multidenominational), Cornelius P. Venema, President, 229 Seminary Drive, Dyer, IN 46311 Tel. (219)864-2400 Fax (219)864-2410
Email: info@midamerica.edu
Website: www.midamerica.edu

Mid-Atlantic Christian University (Christian Churches and Churches of Christ), Kevin W. Larsen, Ph.D., V P Academic Affairs, 715 N. Poindexter St, Elizabeth City, NC 27909-4054 Tel. (252)334-2000 Fax (252)334-2071
Email: kevin.larsen@macuniversity.edu
Website: www.macuniversity.edu

Midwest University‡ (Interdenominational), Dr. James Song, President, 851 Parr Road, Wentzville, MO 63385 Tel. (636)327-4645 Fax (636)327-4715
Email: usa@midwest.edu
Website: www.midwest.edu

Midwestern Baptist Theological Seminary† (Southern Baptist Convention), Dr. R. Philip Roberts, President, 5001 N. Oak Trafficway, Kansas City, MO 64118 Tel. (816)414-3700 Fax (816)414-3799
Email: president@mbts.edu
Website: www.mbts.edu

Moody Bible Institute (Interdenominational), Michael J. Easley, President, 820 N. La Salle Blvd., Chicago, IL 60610 Tel. (312)329-4000 Fax (312)329-4109
Email: pr@moody.edu
Website: www.moody.edu

Moravian Theological Seminary† (Moravian Church in America (Unitas Fratrum)), Christopher M. Thomforde, President, 1200 Main St., Bethlehem, PA 18018 Tel. (610)861-1516 Fax (610)861-1569
Email: seminary@moravian.edu
Website: www.moravianseminary.edu

Moreau Seminary (Congregation of Holy Cross) (Catholic Church), Rev. Peter A. Jarret, C.S.C., Rector, Moreau Seminary University of Notre Dame, Notre Dame, IN 46556 Tel. (574)631-7735 Fax (574)631-9233
Email: morseml@nd.edu
Website: www.vocation.nd.edu

Morehouse School of Religion (Inter-denominational Baptist), William T. Perkins, President, 645 Beckwith St. S.W., Atlanta, GA 30314 Tel. (404)527-7777 Fax (404)681-1005
Website: www.itc.edu

Mount Angel Seminary† (Catholic Church), Very Rev. Fr. Richard Paperini, President Rector, St. Benedict, OR 97373 Tel. (503)845-3951 Fax (503)845-3126
Email: seminary@mountangelabbey.org
Website: www.mountangelabbey.org/seminary

Mt. St. Mary's Seminary† (Catholic Church), Steven P. Rohlfs, Rector, 16300 Old Emmitsburg Rd., Emmitsburg, MD 21727-7797 Tel. (301)447-5295 Fax (301)447-5636
Email: rhoades@msmary.edu
Website: www.msmary.edu

Mt. St. Mary's Seminary of the West (Catholic Church), Rev. Edward P. Smith, President, 6616 Beechmont Ave., Cincinnati, OH 45230 Tel. (513)231-2223 Fax (513)231-3254
Email: esmith@mtsm.org
Website: mtsm.org

Multnomah Biblical Seminary† (Multnomah Biblical Seminary), Dr. Daniel R. Lockwood, President, 8435 N.E. Glisan St., Portland, OR 97220 Tel. (503)255-0332 Fax (503)251-6701
Email: dlockwood@multnomah.edu
Website: www.multnomah.edu

The University of St. Mary of the Lake/Mundelein Seminary† (The Catholic Church), Dennis J. Lyle, Rector-President, 1000 E. Maple, Mundelein, IL 60060-1174 Tel. (847)566-6401 Fax (847)566-7330
Email: rector@usml.edu
Website: www.usml.edu

Nashotah House (Theological Seminary)† (Episcopal Church), Robert S. Munday, President and Dean, 2777 Mission Rd., Nashotah, WI 53058-9793 Tel. (262)646-6500 Fax (262)646-6504
Email: smills@nashotah.edu
Website: www.nashotah.edu

Nazarene Bible College (Church of the Nazarene), Hiram Sanders, President, 1111 Academy Park Loop, Colorado Springs, CO 80910-3704 Tel. (719)884-5000 Fax (719)884-5199
Email: info@nbc.edu
Website: www.nbc.edu

Nazarene Theological Seminary† (Church of the Nazarene), Ron Benefiel, President, 1700 E. Meyer Blvd., Kansas City, MO 64131-1246 Tel. (816)268-5400 Fax (816)268-5500
Email: lneely@nts.edu
Website: www.nts.edu

Nebraska Christian College (Christian Churches and Churches of Christ), Richard D. Milliken, President, 12550 S. 114th Street, Papillion, NE 68046 Tel. (402)935-9400 ext. 400 Fax (402)935-9500
Email: rcmilliken@nechristian.edu
Website: www.nechristian.edu

New Brunswick Theological Seminary† (Reformed Church in America), Gregg A. Mast, President, 17 Seminary Pl., New Brunswick, NJ 08901-1196 Tel. (732)247-5241 Fax (732)247-5412
Email: gmast@nbts.edu
Website: www.nbts.edu

New Orleans Baptist Theological Seminary† (Southern Baptist Convention), Charles S. Kelley, President, 3939 Gentilly Blvd., New Orleans, LA 70126 Tel. (504)282-4455 Fax (504)816-8023
Email: nobts@nobts.edu
Website: www.nobts.edu

New York Theological Seminary† (Inter/Multidenominational), Dale T. Irvin, President, 475 Riverside Drive, Ste. 500, New York, NY 10115 Tel. (212)870-1223 Fax (212)870-1236
Email: dirvin@nyts.edu
Website: www.nyts.edu

North Central Bible College (Assemblies of God), Gordon L. Anderson, President, 910 Elliot Ave. S., Minneapolis, MN 55404 Tel. (612)332-3491 Fax (612)343-4778
Email: INFO@NCBC.EDU
Website: www.NCBC.EDU

North Park Theological Seminary† (The Evangelical Covenant Church), Timothy Johnson, Acting President, 3225 W. Foster Ave., Chicago, IL 60625 Tel. (773)244-6214 Fax (773)244-6244
Email: gbrown@northpark.edu
Website: www.northpark.edu

Northeastern Seminary at Roberts Wesleyan College† (Nondenominational), John A. Martin, President, 2265 Westside Dr., Rochester, NY 14624-1977 Tel. (585)594-6800 Fax (585)594-6801
Email: seminary@roberts.edu
Website: www.nes.edu

Northern Baptist Theological Seminary† (American Baptist Churches in the USA), Dr. Alister Brown, President, 660 E. Butterfield Rd., Lombard, IL 60148-5698 Tel. (630)620-2100 Fax (630)620-2194
Email: info@seminary.edu
Website: www.seminary.edu

Northwest College (Assemblies of God), Don H. Argue, Ed.D., President, 5520 108th Ave. N.E., P.O. Box 579, Kirkland, WA 98083-0579 Tel. (425)822-8266 Fax (425)827-0148 Email: receptionist@NorthwestU.edu Website: www.nwcollege.edu

Notre Dame Seminary† (Catholic Church), Patrick J. Williams, M. Div., M.S., President and Rector, 2901 S. Carrollton Ave., New Orleans, LA 70118-4391 Tel. (504)866-7426 Fax (504)866-3119 Email: pjwilliams@nds.edu Website: www.nds.edu

Oak Hills Christian College (Interdenominational), Dr. Steven Hostetter, President, 1600 Oak Hills Rd. S.W., Bemidji, MN 56601 Tel. (218)751-8670 Fax (218)751-8825 Email: stevehostetter@oakhills.edu Website: www.oakhills.edu

Oblate School of Theology† (Catholic Church), Ronald Rolheiser, President, 285 Oblate Dr., San Antonio, TX 78216-6693 Tel. (210)341-1366 Fax (210)341-4519 Email: oblate@connecti.com Website: www.ost.edu

Oral Roberts University Graduate School of Theology and Ministry† (Inter/Multidenominational), Dr. Thomson K. Mathew, Dean, 7777 S. Lewis Ave., Tulsa, OK 74171 Tel. (918)495-7016 Fax (918)495-6259 Email: jcope@oru.edu Website: www.oru.edu

Ozark Christian College (Christian Churches and Churches of Christ), Matt Proctor, President, 1111 N. Main St., Joplin, MO 64801 Tel. (417)626-1234 Fax (417)624-0090 Email: pres@occ.edu Website: www.occ.edu

Pacific Islands Bible College‡ (Inter denominational), The Rev. David L. Owen, President, P.O. Box 22619, GMF, GU 96921 Tel. (671)734-1812 Fax (671)734-1813 Email: GuamCampus@pibc.edu Website: www.piu.edu

Pacific Lutheran Theological Seminary† (Evangelical Lutheran Church in America), Phyllis Anderson, President, 2770 Marin Ave., Berkeley, CA 94708-1530 Tel. (510)524-5264 Fax (510)524-2408 Email: president@plts.edu Website: www.plts.edu

Pacific School of Religion† (Inter/Multidenominational), Riess Potterveld, President, 1798 Scenic Ave., Berkeley, CA 94709 Tel. (510)849-8200 Fax (510)845-8948

Email: rpotterveld@psr.edu Website: www.psr.edu

Palmer Theological Seminary: The Seminary of Eastern University† (American Baptist Churches in the USA), Christopher A. Hall, Dean, 6 E. Lancaster Ave., Wynnewood, PA 19096 Tel. (610)896-5000 Fax (610)649-3834 Email: semdean@Eastern.edu Website: www.palmerseminary.edu

Payne Theological Seminary† (African Methodist Episcopal Church), Leah Gaskin Fitchue, Ed.D., President, P.O. Box 474 1230 Wilberforce-Clifton Rd., Wilberforce, OH 45384-0474 Tel. (937)376-2946 Fax (937)376-3330 Email: LFitchue@payne.edu Website: www.payne.edu

Pentecostal Theological Seminary† (Church of God (Cleveland, Tenn.)), Steven J. Land, President, P.O. Box 3330, Cleveland, TN 37320-3330 Tel. (423)478-1131 Fax (423)478-7711 Email: tgilbert@ptseminary.edu Website: www.ptseminary.edu

Pepperdine University (Churches of Christ), Dr. Tim Willis, Chair of Religion Division, Religion Division, Malibu, CA 90263-4352 Tel. (310)506-4352 Fax (310)317-6907 Email: timothy.willis@pepperdine.edu Website: pepperdine.edu/religion

Perkins School of Theology (Southern Methodist University)† (The United Methodist Church), William B. Lawrence, Dean, P.O. Box 750133, Dallas, TX 75275-0133 Tel. (214)768-2335 Fax (214)768-2117 Email: Rcox@smu.edu Website: www.smu.edu/perkins

Philadelphia Biblical University (Nondenominational), Todd J. Williams, President, 200 Manor Ave., Langhorne, PA 19047-2990 Tel. (215)752-5800 Fax (215)702-4341 Email: president@pbu.edu Website: www.pbu.edu

Phillips Theological Seminary† (Christian Church (Disciples of Christ)), Gary Peluso-Verdend, President, 901 North Mingo Road, Tulsa, OK 74116 Tel. (918)610-8303 Fax (918) 610-8404 Email: linda.ford@ptstulsa.edu Website: www.ptstulsa.edu

Phoenix Seminary† (Nondenominational), Dr. Darryl DelHousaye, President, 4222 E. Thomas Road, Ste 400, Phoenix, AZ 85018-Tel. (602)850-8000 Fax (602)850-8080 Email: ddel@ps.edu Website: www.phoenixseminary.edu

Piedmont Baptist College‡ (Baptist (Independent)), Charles W. Petitt, President, 716 Franklin St., Winston-Salem, NC 27101 Tel. (336)725-8344 Fax (336)725-5522
Email: admissions@pbc.edu
Website: www.pbc.edu

Pittsburgh Theological Seminary† (Presbyterian Church (USA)), William J. Carl III, President, 616 N. Highland Ave., Pittsburgh, PA 15206 Tel. (412)362-5610 Fax (412)363-3260
Email: wcarl@pts.edu
Website: www.pts.edu

Pontifical College Josephinum† (Catholic Church), Msgr. Paul J. Langsfeld, Rector and President, 7625 N. High St., Columbus, OH 43235 Tel. (614)885-5585 Fax (614)885-2307
Email: plangsfeld@pcj.edu
Website: www.pcj.edu

Pope John XXIII National Seminary (Catholic Church), Francis D. Kelly, President, 558 South Ave., Weston, MA 02193 Tel. (617)899-5500 Fax (617)899-9057
Email: seminary@blessedjohnxxiii.edu
Website: www.blessedjohnxxiii.edu

Princeton Theological Seminary† (Presbyterian Church (USA)), Iain R. Torrance, President, P.O. Box 821, Princeton, NJ 08542-0803 Tel. (609)921-8300 Fax (609)924-2973
Email: comm-pub@ptsem.edu
Website: www.ptsem.edu

Protestant Episcopal Theological Seminary in Virginia† (Episcopal Church), Martha J. Horne, Dean and President, 3737 Seminary Rd., Alexandria, VA 22304 Tel. (703)370-6600 Fax (703)370-6234
Email: mhorne@vts.edu
Website: www.vts.edu

Puget Sound Christian College (Christian Churches and Churches of Christ), Randy J. Bridges, Ph.D., President, P.O. Box 13108, Everett, WA 98206-3108 Tel. (425)257-3090 Fax (425)258-1488
Email: president@pscc.edu
Website: www.pscc.edu

Rabbi Isaac Elchanan Theological Seminary (Jewish), Dr. Norman Lamm, President, 2540 Amsterdam Ave., New York, NY 10033 Tel. (212)960-5344 Fax (212)960-0061
Email: amlevin@ymail.yu.edu
Website: www.yu.edu/riets

Reconstructionist Rabbinical College (Jewish), Dan Ehrenkrantz, President, 1299 Church Rd, Wyncote, PA 19095 Tel. (215)576-0800 Fax (215)576-6143

Email: admissions@rrc.edu
Website: www.rrc.edu

Reformed Episcopal Seminary† (Reformed Episcopal Church), Wayne A. Headman, President, 826 Second Ave., Blue Bell, PA 19422-1257 Tel. (610)292-9852 Fax (610)292-9853
Email: wayne.headman@reseminary.edu
Website: www.reseminary.edu

Reformed Presbyterian Theological Seminary† (Reformed Presbyterian Church of North America), Jerry F. O'Neill, President, 7418 Penn Ave., Pittsburgh, PA 15208-2594 Tel. (412)731-8690 Fax (412)731-4834
Email: info@rpts.edu
Website: www.rpts.edu

Reformed Theological Seminary† (Inter/Multidenominational), Dr. Robert C. Cannada, Jr., President, 5422 Clinton Blvd., Jackson, MS 39209-3099 Tel. (601)923-1600 Fax (601)923-1654
Email: rts.orlando@rts.edu
Website: www.rts.edu

Regent University School of Divinity† (Non-denominational/Evangelical), Michael Palmer, Dean, 1000 Regent University Dr, Virginia Beach, VA 23464-9870 Fax (757)226-4597
Email: mpalmer@regent.edu
Website: www.regent.edu/acad/schdiv

Sacred Heart Major Seminary† (Catholic Church), Very Rev. Msgr. Jeffrey M. Monforton, President, 2701 Chicago Blvd., Detroit, MI 48206 Tel. (313)883-8501 Fax (313)868-6440
Email: Information@shms.edu
Website: www.shmsonline.org

Sacred Heart School of Theology† (Catholic Church), Very Rev. Thomas Knoebel, Acting President-Rector, P.O. Box 429, Hales Corners, WI 53130-0429 Tel. (414)425-8300 Fax (414)529-6999
Email: rector@shst.edu
Website: www.shst.edu

St. Bernard's School of Theology and Ministry† (Catholic Church), Patricia A. Schoelles, President, 120 French Road, Rochester, NY 14618 Tel. (585)271-3657 Fax (585)271-2045
Email: pschoelles@sbi.edu
Website: www.stbernards.edu

St. Charles Borromeo Seminary† (Catholic Church), Rev. Msgr. Joseph G. Prior, M.Div., M.A., S.S.L., S.T.D., President and Rector, 100 East Wynnewood Rd., Wynnewood, PA 19096-3001 Tel. (610)667-3394 Fax (610)667-0452

Email: developmentscs@adphila.org
Website: www.scs.edu

St. Francis Seminary† (Catholic Church), Very Rev.Donald J. Hying, Rector, 3257 S. Lake Dr., St. Francis, WI 53235 Tel. (414)747-6404 Fax (414)747-6442
Email: dhying@sfs.edu
Website: www.sfs.edu

St. John Vianney Theological Seminary† (Catholic Church), Michael Glenn, Rector, 1300 S. Steele St., Denver, CO 80210-2599 Tel. (303)282-3427 Fax (303)282-3453
Website: www.sjvdenver.com

St. John's Seminary† (Catholic Church), John Farren, Rector and President, 127 Lake St., Brighton, MA 02135 Tel. (617)254-2610 Fax (617)787-2336
Email: Reverend_John_L_Sullivan@rcab.org
Website: www.sjs.edu

St. John's Seminary† (Catholic Church), Monsignor Craig Cox, Rector and President, 5012 Seminary Rd., Camarillo, CA 93012-2500 Tel. (805)482-2755 Fax (805)482-0637
Email: rector@stjohnsem.edu
Website: www.stjohnsem.edu

St. John's University, School of Theology - Seminary† (Catholic Church), William J. Cahoy, Dean, Box 7288, Collegeville, MN 56321-7288 Tel. (320)363-2622 Fax (320)363-3145
Email: bduffy@csbsju.edu
Website: www.csbsju.edu/sot

St. Joseph's Seminary† (Catholic Church), Peter G. Finn, President, 201 Seminary Ave., Yonkers, NY 10704 Tel. (914)968-6200 Fax (914)968-7912
Email: sjsirs@aol.com
Website: www.ny-archdiocese.org/pastoral/seminary.cfm

St. Louis Christian College (Christian Churches and Churches of Christ), Dr. Guthrie Veech, President, 1360 Grandview Dr., Florissant, MO 63033 Tel. (314)837-6777 Fax (314)837-8291
Email: agall@slcconline.edu
Website: www.slcconline.edu

St. Mary Seminary and Graduate School of Theology† (Catholic Church), Thomas W. Tifft, President, 28700 Euclid Ave., Wickliffe, OH 44092-2585 Tel. (440)943-7600 Fax (440)943-7577
Email: ttifft@dioceseofcleveland.org
Website: www.stmarysem.edu

St. Mary's Seminary (Catholic Church), Very Rev. Brendan Cahill, Rector, 9845 Memorial Dr., Houston, TX 77024-3498 Tel. (713)686-4345 Fax (713)681-7550
Email: cahillb@stthom.edu
Website: www.diocese-gal-hou.org/education_stmarysseminary

St. Mary's Seminary and University† (Catholic Church), Robert F. Leavitt, President and Rector, 5400 Roland Ave., Baltimore, MD 21210 Tel. (410)864-4000 Fax (410)864-4278
Email: rleavitt@stmarys.edu
Website: www.stmarys.edu

Saint Meinrad School of Theology† (Catholic Church), Fr. Denis Robinson, OSB, President, 200 Hill Drive, St. Meinrad, IN 47577 Tel. (812)357-6611 Fax (812)357-6964
Email: theology@saintmeinrad.edu
Website: www.saintmeinrad.edu

St. Patrick's Seminary and University† (Catholic Church), Gerald L. Brown, President and Rector, 320 Middlefield Rd., Menlo Park, CA 94025 Tel. (650)325-5621 Fax (650)322-0997
Email: jennifer@stpatricksseminary.org
Website: www.stpatricksseminary.org

Saint Paul School of Theology† (The United Methodist Church), Myron F. McCoy, President, 5123 E. Truman Rd., Kansas City, MO 64127-2499 Tel. (816)483-9600 Fax (816)483-9605
Email: spst@spst.edu
Website: www.spst.edu

St. Paul Seminary School of Divinity of the University of St. Thomas† (Catholic Church), The Rev.Msgr. Aloysius R. Callaghan, Rector and Vice-President, 2260 Summit Ave., St. Paul, MN 55105 Tel. (651)962-5050 Fax (651)962-5790
Email: spssod@stthomas.edu
Website: www.stthomas.edu/spssod

St. Petersburg Theological Seminary‡ (Inter/Multidenominational), Dr. John Guedes, President, 10830 Navajo Dr., St. Petersburg, FL 33708 Tel. (727)399-0276 Fax (727)399-1324
Email: sptseminary@tampabay.rr.com
Website: www.sptseminary.edu

St. Tikhon's Orthodox Theological Seminary† (The Orthodox Church in America), Metropolitan Herman (Swaiko), President and Very Rev. Michael G. Dahulich, Ph.D., Dean and Bishop Tikhon (Mollard), Rector, President, Box 130, St. Tikhon's Rd., South Canaan, PA 18459-0130 Tel. (570)937-4411 Fax (570)937-3100
Email: info@stots.edu
Website: www.stots.edu

St. Vincent de Paul Regional Seminary† (Catholic Church), Msgr. Keith R. Brennan, Rector and President, 10701 South Military Trail, Boynton Beach, FL 33436-4899 Tel. (561)732-4424 Fax (561)737-2205 Email: Kbrennan@svdp.edu Website: www.svdp.edu

St. Vincent Seminary† (Catholic Church), Very Rev. Kurt Belsole, O.S.B., Rector, 300 Fraser Purchase Rd., Latrobe, PA 15650-2690 Tel. (724)537-4592 Fax (724)532-5052 Email: kurt.belsole@email.stvincent.edu Website: benedictine.stvincent.edu/seminary

St. Vladimir's Orthodox Theological Seminary† (The Orthodox Church in America), John Behr, Dean, 575 Scarsdale Rd., Crestwood, NY 10707-1699 Tel. (914)961-8313 Fax (914)961-4507 Email: info@svots.edu Website: www.svots.edu

SS. Cyril and Methodius Seminary† (Catholic Church), Very Rev. Charles G Kosanke, Rector, 3535 Indian Trail, Orchard Lake, MI 48324-1623 Tel. (248)683-0310 Fax (248)738-6735 Email: info@sscms.edu Website: www.sscms.edu

Samuel DeWitt Proctor School of Theology of Virginia Union University† (American Baptist Churches in the USA, National Baptist Convention, Progressive National Baptist Convention), Dr. John W. Kinney, Dean, 1500 North Lombardy Street, Richmond, VA 23330 Tel. (804)257-5715 Fax (804)342-3911 Email: JWKinney@vuu.edu Website: www.vuu.edu

San Diego Christian College (Southern Baptist), Paul Ague, President, 2100 Greenfield Drive, El Cajon, CA 92019 Tel. (619)441-2200 Fax (619)440-0209 Email: chcadm@christianheritage.edu Website: www.christianheritage.edu

San Francisco Theological Seminary† (Presbyterian Church (USA)), Rev. Dr. Philip W. Butin, President, 105 Seminary Rd., San Anselmo, CA 94960 Tel. (415)451-2800 Fax (415)451-2811 Email: sftsinfo@sfts.edu Website: www.sfts.edu

Savonarola Theological Seminary (Polish National Catholic Church of America), Most Rev. Anthony A. Mikovsky, Prime Bishop, Rector, 1006 Pittston Avenue, Scranton, PA 18505-4109 Tel. (570)346-9131 Fax (570)346-2188 Email: PBMikovsky@hotmail.com Website: pncc.org

Seabury-Western Theological Seminary† (Episcopal Church), Dr. Robert G. Bottoms, Interim Dean and President, 2122 Sheridan Rd., Evanston, IL 60201-2976 Tel. (847)328-9300 Fax (847)328-9624 Email: seabury@seabury.edu Website: www.seabury.edu

The Seattle School of Theology and Psychology†‡ (Non-Denominational/Inter-Denominational), Keith R. Anderson, D.Min, President, 2501 Elliott Ave, Seattle, WA 98121 Tel. (206)876-6100 or (888)977-2002 Fax (206)876-6195 Email: info@mhgs.edu Website: www.mhgs.edu

Seattle University School of Theology and Ministry† (Catholic Church and 10 Mainline Protestant Denominations and Associations), Mark S Markuly, Dean, 901 12th Avenue, P.O. Box 222000, Seattle, WA 98122-1090 Tel. (206)296-5330 Fax (206)296-5329 Email: sueh@seattleu.edu Website: www.seattleu.edu/stm

Seminario Evangelico de Puerto Rico (Inter-denominational), Sergio Ojeda-Cárcamo, President, 776 Ponce de León Ave., San Juan, PR 00925 Tel. (787)763-6700 Fax (787)751-0847 Email: drsojeda@se-pr.edu Website: netministries.org/see/charmin/CM01399

Seminary of the Immaculate Conception† (Catholic Church), Msgr. Francis J. Schneider, J.C.D., Rector/President, 440 West Neck Rd., Huntington, NY 11743 Tel. (631)423-0483 Fax (631)423-2346 Email: eluckstone@icseminary.edu Website: www.icseminary.edu

Seventh-day Adventist Theological Seminary of Andrews University† (Seventh-day Adventist Church), Denis Fortin, Dean, Andrews University, 4145 E. Campus Circle Drive, Berrien Springs, MI 49104-1502 Tel. (269)471-3537 Fax (269)471-6202 Email: seminary@andrews.edu Website: www.andrews.edu/sem

Seventh Day Baptist School of Ministry (Seventh Day Baptist General Conference USA and Canada Ltd.), Gordon P. Lawton, Dean of School of Ministry, 3120 Kennedy Rd., P.O. Box 1678, Janesville, WI 53547 Tel. (608)752-5055 Fax (608)752-7711 Email: dean@sdbministry.org Website: www.sdbministry.org

Sewanee: The University of the South School of Theology† (Episcopal Church), The Dean, 335 Tennessee Ave., Sewanee, TN 37383-0001 Tel. (800)722-1974 Fax (931)598-1412 Email: theology@sewanee.edu Website: www.theology.sewanee.edu

Shasta Bible College and Graduate School‡ (Baptist), Dr. David Nicholas, President, 2951 Goodwater Avenue, Redding, CA 96002 Tel. (530)221-4275 Fax (530)221-6929 Email: sbcadm@shasta.edu Website: www.shasta.edu

Shaw University Divinity School† (General Baptist State Convention, N.C.; American Baptist Churches), James T. Roberson, Jr., Dean, P.O. Box 2090, Raleigh, NC 27602 Tel. (919)546-8569 Fax (919)546-8571 Email: JTRob@ShawU.edu Website: www.shawuniversity.edu

Simpson College (The Christian and Missionary Alliance), James M. Grant, President, 2211 College View Dr., Redding, CA 96003 Tel. (916)224-5600 Fax (916)224-5608 Email: rerickson@simpsonuniversity.edu Website: www.simpsonuniversity.edu

Sioux Falls Seminary† (North American Baptist Conference), G. Michael Hagan, President, 2100 S. Summit Avenue, Sioux Falls, SD 57105-2729 Tel. (605)336-6588 Fax (605)335-9090 Email: shandas@sfseminary.edu Website: www.sfseminary.edu

Southeastern Baptist College (Baptist Missionary Association of America), Dr. Medrick Savell, President, 4229 Highway 15N, Laurel, MS 39440 Tel. (601)426-6346 Fax (601)426-6347 Email: info@southeasternbaptist.edu Website: www.southeasternbaptist.edu

Southeastern Baptist Theological Seminary† (Southern Baptist Convention), Daniel L. Akin, President, P.O. Box 1889, Wake Forest, NC 27588-1889 Tel. (919)556-3101 Fax (919)556-8550 Email: president@sebts.edu Website: www.sebts.edu

Southeastern Bible College (Interdenominational), Dr. Don Hawkins, President, 2545 Valleyvale Rd., Birmingham, AL 35244 Tel. (205)408-7073 or (205)970-9200 Fax (205)970-9207 Email: President@sebc.edu Website: www.sebc.edu

Southeastern University (Assemblies of God), Mark Rutland, President, 1000 Longfellow Blvd., Lakeland, FL 33801 Tel. (863)667-5000 Fax (863)667-5200

Email: info@seuniversity.edu Website: www.seuniversity.edu

Southern Baptist Theological Seminary† (Southern Baptist Convention), R. Albert Mohler, Jr., President, 2825 Lexington Rd., Louisville, KY 40280- Tel. (502)897-4011 Fax (502)899-1770 Email: communications@sbts.edu Website: www.sbts.edu

Southern California Seminary (Southern Baptist Convention), Dr. Gary F. Coombs, President, 2075 East Madison Avenue, El Cajon, CA 92019 Tel. (619)201-8999 Fax (619)201-8975 Email: eherrelko@socalsem.edu Website: www.socalsem.edu

Southern Evangelical Seminary‡ (Interdenominational), Dr. Norman Geisler, President, 3000 Tilley Morris Road, Matthews, NC 28104 Tel. (704)847-5600 Fax (704)845-1747 Email: ses@ses.edu Website: www.ses.edu

Southern Methodist College (Southern Methodist Church), The Rev. Gary Briden, President, 541 Broughton Street, Orangeburg, SC 29115 Tel. (803)534-7826 Fax (803)534-7827 Email: gbriden@smcollege.edu Website: www.smcollege.edu

Southern Wesleyan University (The Wesleyan Church), President David J. Spittal, President, 907 Wesleyan Dr., P.O. Box 1020, Central, SC 29630-1020 Tel. (864)644-5000 Fax (864)644-5900 Email: dspittal@swu.edu Website: www.swu.edu

Southwestern Assemblies of God University (Assemblies of God), Kermit S. Bridges, President, 1200 Sycamore St., Waxahachie, TX 75165 Tel. (972)937-4010 Fax (972)923-0488 Email: president@sagu.edu Website: www.sagu.edu

Southwestern Baptist Theological Seminary† (Southern Baptist Convention), Paige Patterson, President, 2001 W. Seminary Dr., Fort Worth, TX 76115 Tel. (817)923-1921 Fax (817)923-0610 Email: PresidentsOffice@swbts.edu Website: www.swbts.edu

Southwestern College (Conservative Baptist Association of America), Brent D. Garrison, President, 2625 E. Cactus Rd., Phoenix, AZ 85032 Tel. (602)992-6101 Fax (602)404-2159 Email: swc@swcaz.edu Website: www.southwesterncollege.edu

Starr King School for the Ministry† (Unitarian Universalist Association), Rebecca Parker, President, 2441 LeConte Ave., Berkeley, CA 94709 Tel. (510)845-6232 Fax (510)845-6273 Email: rparker@sksm.edu Website: www.sksm.edu

Swedenborgian House of Studies at the Pacific School of Religion (The Swedenborgian Church), Dr. James F. Lawrence, Dean, 1798 Scenic Ave., Berkeley, CA 94709 Tel. (510)849-8228 Fax (510)849-8296 Email: jlawrence@shs.psr.edu Website: www.shs.psr.edu

Talbot School of Theology of Biola University† (Inter/Multidenominational), Dr. Barry H. Corey, President, 13800 Biola Ave., La Mirada, CA 90639-0001 Tel. (562)903-6000 Fax (562)903-4759 Email: talbot.receptionist@biola.edu Website: www.talbot.edu

Temple Baptist Seminary‡ (Interdenominational), Dr. Jim O'Neill, President, 1815 Union Ave., Chattanooga, TN 37404 Tel. (800)553-4050 Fax (423)493-4471 Email: tbsinfo@templebaptistseminary.edu Website: www.tntemple.edu

Tennessee Temple University‡ President, 1815 Union Avenue, Chattanooga, TN 37404 Tel. (800)553-4050 Fax (423)493-4114 Email: ttuinfo@tntemple.edu Website: www.tntemple.edu

Theological School of the Protestant Reformed Churches (Protestant Reformed Churches in America), Ronald L. Cammenga, President, 4949 Ivanrest Ave., Grandville, MI 49418 Tel. (616)531-1490 Fax (616)531-3033 Email: doezema@prca.org Website: www.prca.org/seminary

Toccoa Falls College (The Christian and Missionary Alliance), Dr. W. Wayne Gardner, President, P.O. Box 800777, Toccoa Falls, GA 30598 Tel. (706)886-6831 Fax (706)282-6005 Email: president@tfc.edu Website: www.tfc.edu

Trevecca Nazarene University (Church of the Nazarene), Dan Boone, President, 333 Murfreesboro Rd., Nashville, TN 37210-2877 Tel. (615)248-1200 Fax (615)248-7728 Email: atwining@trevecca.edu Website: www.trevecca.edu

Trinity Baptist College‡ (Baptist), Tom Messer, Pastor, 800 Hammond Boulevard, Jacksonville, FL 32221 Tel. (904)596-2400 Fax (904)596-2531 Email: trinity@tbc.edu Website: www.tbc.edu

Trinity Bible College (Assemblies of God), Dennis D. Niles, President, 50 S. 6th Ave., Ellendale, ND 58436 Tel. (701)349-3621 or (800)523-1603 Fax (701)349-5443 Email: president@trinitybiblecollege.edu Website: www.trinitybiblecollege.edu

Trinity College of Florida (Nondenominational), Mark T. O'Farrell, President, 2430 Welbilt Blvd., Trinity, FL 34655-4401 Tel. (727)376-6911 Fax (727)376-0781 Email: admissions@trinitycollege.edu Website: www.trinitycollege.edu

Trinity Episcopal School for Ministry† (Episcopal Church), The Very Rev. Dr. Paul F.M. Zahl, Dean and President, 311 Eleventh St., Ambridge, PA 15003 Tel. (724)266-3838 Fax (724)266-4617 Email: tesm@tesm.edu Website: www.tesm.edu

Trinity Evangelical Divinity School of Trinity International University† (Evangelical Free Church of America), Jeanette Hsieh, Interim President, 2065 Half Day Rd., Deerfield, IL 60015 Tel. (847)945-8800 Fax (847)317-8141 Email: gwaybrig@tiu.edu Website: www.tiu.edu/divinity

Trinity Lutheran College (Interdenominational-Lutheran), John W. Reed, President, 2802 Wetmore Avenue, Everett, WA 98201 Tel. (425)249-4800 Fax (425)249-4801 Email: info@tlc.edu Website: www.tlc.edu

Trinity Lutheran Seminary† (Evangelical Lutheran Church in America), Mark R. Ramseth, President, 2199 East Main Street, Columbus, OH 43209-2334 Tel. (614)235-4136 Fax (614)238-0263 Email: mramseth@TLSohio.edu Website: www.TLSohio.edu

Union Theological Seminary† (Inter/Multidenominational), Serene Jones, President, 3041 Broadway at 121st Street, New York, NY 10027-0003 Tel. (212)662-7100 Fax (212)280-1440 Email: sjones@uts.columbia.edu Website: www.utsnyc.edu

Union Presbyterian Seminary† (Presbyterian Church (USA)), Brian K. Blount, President, 3401 Brook Rd., Richmond, VA 23227 Tel. (800)229-2990 Fax (804)355-3919 Email: gbirch@union-psce.edu Website: www.union-psce.edu

United Theological Seminary† (The United Methodist Church), Dr. Wendy J. Deichmann Edwards, President, 4501 Denlinger Rd,

Dayton, OH 45426 Tel. (937)529-2201 Fax (866)433-8235
Email: utscom@united.edu
Website: www.united.edu

United Theological Seminary of the Twin Cities† (United Church of Christ), Mary E. McNamara, President, 3000 Fifth St. N.W., New Brighton, MN 55112 Tel. (651)633-4311 Fax (651)633-4315
Email: info@unitedseminary.edu
Website: www.unitedseminary.edu

University of Chicago Divinity School† (Inter-denominational), Richard A. Rosengarten, Dean, 1025 E. 58th St., Chicago, IL 60637 Tel. (773)702-8221 Fax (773)702-6048
Email: raroseng@midway.uchicago.edu
Website: www.uchicago.edu/divinity

University of Dubuque Theological Seminary† (Presbyterian Church (USA)), Jeffrey Bullock, President, 2000 University Ave., Dubuque, IA 52001-5099 Tel. (563)589-3122 Fax (563)589-3110
Email: udtsadms@dbq.edu
Website: www.UDTSeminary.net

University of Notre Dame Department of Theology† (Catholic Church), John C. Cavadini, Department Chair, 130 Malloy Hall, Notre Dame, IN 46556-5639 Tel. (574)631-6662 Fax (574)631-4291
Email: Cavadini.1@nd.edu
Website: theology.nd.edu

University of St. Mary of the Lake Mundelein Seminary† (Catholic Church), Dennis J. Lyle, Rector and President, 1000 E. Maple, Mundelein, IL 60060-1174 Tel. (847)566-6401 Fax (847)566-7330
Email: rector@usml.edu
Website: www.usml.edu

University of St. Thomas School of Theology at St. Mary's Seminary† (Catholic Church), Sandra Magie, Dean, 9845 Memorial Dr., Houston, TX 77024 Tel. (713)686-4345 Fax (713)683-8673
Email: sms@stthom.edu
Website: www.stthom.edu/stmary

Urshan Graduate School of Theology† (United Pentecostal Church International), David K. Bernard, President, 704 Howdershell Road, Florissant, MO 63031 Tel. (314)921-9290 Fax (314)921-9203
Email: info@ugst.org
Website: www.ugst.org

Valley Forge Christian College (Assemblies of God), Don Meyer, President, 1401 Charlestown Rd., Phoenixville, PA 19460 Tel. (610)935-0450 Fax (610)935-9353

Email: admissions@vfcc.edu
Website: www.vfcc.edu

Vanderbilt University Divinity School† (Inter/Multidenominational), James Hudnut-Beumler, Dean, 411 21st Av. So., Nashville, TN 37240 Tel. (615)322-2776 Fax (615)343-9957
Email: james.hudnut-beumler@vanderbilt.edu
Website: divinity.lib.vanderbilt.edu/vds/vds-home

Vennard College (Interdenominational), Dr. Bruce Moyer, President, Box 29, University Park, IA 52595 Tel. (641)673-8391 Fax (641)673-8365
Email: bruce.moyer@vennard.edu
Website: www.vennard.edu

Virginia Union University (School of Theology) (American Baptist Churches in the USA, National Baptist Convention, USA, Inc., Progressive National Baptist Convention, Inc., National Baptist Convention of America), Dr. John W. Kinney, Dean, 1500 N. Lombardy St., Richmond, VA 23220 Tel. (804)257-5715 Fax (804)342-3911
Email: JWKinney@vuu.edu
Website: www.vuu.edu/theology

Wake Forest University Divinity School† (Inter/Multidenominational), Gail R. O'Day, Dean, P.O. Box 7719 Reynolda Station, Winston-Salem, NC 27109-7719 Tel. (336)758-3957 Fax (336)758-4316
Email: odaygr@wfu.edu
Website: www.wfu.edu

Walla Walla College (School of Theology) (Seventh-day Adventist Church), Dr. Jon Dybdahl, President, 204 S. College Ave., College Place, WA 99324-1198 Tel. (509)527-2194 Fax (509)527-2253
Email: dybdjo@wwc.edu
Website: www.wwc.edu

Wartburg Theological Seminary† (Evangelical Lutheran Church in America), Duane H. Larson, President, 333 Wartburg Pl., P.O. Box 5004, Dubuque, IA 52004-5004 Tel. (563)589-0200 Fax (563)589-0333
Email: mailbox@wartburgseminary.edu
Website: www.wartburgseminary.edu

Washington Baptist College and Seminary† (Baptist), Jacob S. Shin, President, 4300 Evergreen Lane, Annandale, VA 22003 Tel. (703)333-5904 Fax (703)333-5906
Email: info@wbcs.edu
Website: www.wbcs.edu

Washington Theological Consortium (Non-denominational), The Rev. John W. Crossin, O.S.F.S., Executive Director, 487 Michigan

315

Ave. N.E., Washington, DC 20017 Tel. (202)832-2675 Fax (202)526-0818 Email: wtc@washtheocon.org Website: www.washtheocon.org

Washington Theological Union† (Catholic Church), Frederick J. Tillotson, O. CARM., President, 6896 Laurel St. N.W., Washington, DC 20012-2016 Tel. (202)726-8800 Fax (202) 726-1716 Email: ftillotson@wtu.edu Website: www.wtu.edu

Wesley Biblical Seminary† (Interdenominational), Ronald E. Smith, President, P.O. Box 9938, Jackson, MS 39286-0938 Tel. (601)366-8880 Fax (601)366-8832 Email: rsmith@wbs.edu Website: www.wbs.edu

Wesley Theological Seminary† (The United Methodist Church), David F. McAllister-Wilson, President, 4500 Massachusetts Ave. N.W., Washington, DC 20016-5690 Tel. (800)885-8600 or (800)882-4987 Fax (202) 885-8605 Email: caldridge@wesleysem.edu Website: www.Wesleysem.edu

Western Seminary† (Conservative Baptist Association of America), Randal R. Roberts, President, 5511 S.E. Hawthorne Blvd., Portland, OR 97215 Tel. (877)517-1800 or (503)517-1800 Fax (503)517-1801 Email: admiss@westernseminary.edu Website: www.westernseminary.edu

Western Theological Seminary† (Reformed Church in America), Timothy L. Brown, President, 101 E. 13th St., Holland, MI 49423 Tel. (616)392-8555 Fax (616)392-7717 Email: tim.brown@westernsem.edu Website: www.westernsem.edu

Westminster Theological Seminary† (various Reformed), Peter A. Lillback, President, Chestnut Hill, P.O. Box 27009, Philadelphia, PA 19118 Tel. (215)887-5511 Fax (215)887-5404 Email: admissions@wts.edu Website: www.wts.edu

Westminster Seminary California† (Nondenominational), W. Robert Godfrey, President, 1725 Bear Valley Pkwy, Escondido, CA

92027-4128 Tel. (760)480-8474 Fax (760)480-0252 Email: info@wscal.edu Website: www.wscal.edu

William Jessup University (Christian Churches and Churches of Christ), Dr. John Jackson, Phd, President, 333 Sunset Blvd., Rocklin, CA 95765 Tel. (916)577-2210 Fax 916-577-2213 Email: bjessup@jessup.edu Website: www.jessup.edu

William Tyndale College (Interdenominational), Robert E. Hagerty, President, 35700 W. Twelve Mile Rd., Farmington Hills, MI 48331 Tel. (248)553-7200 Fax (248)553-5963 Website: www.williamtyndale.edu

Williamson Christian College (Nondenominational), Dr. Ed Smith, President, 200 Seaboard Lane, Franklin, TN 37067 Tel. (615) 771-7821 Fax (615)771-7810 Email: info@williamsoncc.edu Website: www.williamsoncc.edu

Winebrenner Theological Seminary† (Churches of God, General Conference), David E. Draper, President, 950 N. Main Street, Findlay, OH 45840 Tel. (419)434 4200 Fax (419)434 4267 Email: wts@winebrenner.edu Website: www.winebrenner.edu

Wisconsin Lutheran Seminary (Wisconsin Evangelical Lutheran Synod), Paul O. Wendland, President, 11831 N. Seminary Dr., 65W, Mequon, WI 53092-1597 Tel. (262)242-8100 Fax (262)242-8110 Email: president@wls.wels.net Website: www.wls.wels.net

Word of Life Bible Institute‡ (Nondenominational), Dr. Joe Jordan, Chancellor, P.O. Box 129, 4200 Glendale Road, Pottersville, NY 12860 Tel. (518)494-4723 Fax (518)494-7474 Email: admissions@wol.org Website: www.wol.org

Yale University Divinity School† (Inter/Multidenominational), Harold W. Attridge, Dean, 409 Prospect Sreet, New Haven, CT 06511-2167 Tel. (203)432-5360 Fax (203)432-7475 Email: divinity.admissions@yale.edu Website: www.yale.edu/divinity

9. Theological Seminaries and Bible Colleges in Canada

The following list includes theological seminaries and departments in colleges and universities in which ministerial training is provided. Many denominations have additional programs. The list has been developed from direct correspondence with the institutions. Inclusion in or exclusion from this list implies no judgment about the quality or accreditation of any institution. Those schools that are members of the Association of Theological Schools are marked with an asterisk (*). Each of the listings include: the institution name, denominational sponsor when appropriate, location, the president or dean, telephone and fax numbers when known and email and website addresses when available.

Acadia Divinity College* (Convention of the Atlantic Baptist Church), Dr. Harry G. Gardner, Principal and Dean of the Faculty of Theology, 31 Horton Street, Wolfville, NS B4P 2R6, Tel. (866)875-8975 (902)585-2210 Fax (902)585-2233
Email: adcinfo@acadiau.ca
Website: adc.acadiau.ca

Alberta Bible College (Christian Churches and Churches of Christ in Canada), Rob Pittman, President, 635 Northmount Dr. NW, Calgary, AB T2K 3J6, Tel. (877)542-9492/(403)282-2994 Fax (403)282-3084
Email: president@abccampus.ca
Website: www.abccampus.ca

Ambrose Seminary of Ambrose University College* (Christian and Missionary Alliance in Canada), Dr. George Durance, President, 833-4th Avenue SW #630, Calgary, AB T2P 3T5, Tel. (403)410-2000 Fax (403)571-2556
Email: hwilson@ambrose.edu
Website: www.auc-nuc.ca

Ambrose University College (Church of the Nazarene Canada), Howard Wilson, President, 150 Ambrose Circle SW, Calgary, AB T3H 0L5, Tel. (403) 410-2000 Fax (403)571-2556
Email: ewick@ambrose.edu
Website: www.auc-nuc.ca

Arthur Turner Training School (The Anglican Church of Canada), Principal, Principal, Box 378, Pangnirtung, NU X0A 0R0, Tel. (867)873-5432 Fax (867)473-8375
Email: arctic@arcticnet.org

Associated Canadian Theological Schools of Trinity Western University* (Baptist General Conference of Canada, Evangelical Free Church of Canada, The Fellowship of Evangelical Baptist Churches in Canada, Christian and Missionary Alliance, Canadian Conference of Mennonite Brethren Churches), Dr. Phil Zylla, Principal, 7600 Glover Rd., Langley, BC V2Y 1Y1, Tel. (888)468-6898 (604)513-2044 Fax (604)513-2045
Email: acts@twu.ca
Website: www.acts.twu.ca

Atlantic School of Theology* (Ecumenical, (Anglican Church of Canada, Roman Catholic Church, and United Church of Canada)), The Rev. Canon Eric Beresford, President, 660 Francklyn St., Halifax, NS B3H 3B5, Tel. (902)423-6939 Fax (902)492-4048
Email: academicoffice@astheology.ns.ca
Website: www.astheology.ns.ca

Baptist Leadership Training School (Canadian Baptist Ministries), Hugh Fraser, President, 4330 16th St. S.W., Calgary, AB T2T 4H9
Email: blts@imag.net
Website: www.yet.ca

Bethany Bible College-Canada (The Wesleyan Church), Dr. Arthur W. Maxwell, President, 26 Western St., P.O. Box 5125, Sussex, NB E4E 5L2, Tel. (506)432-4400 Fax (506)432-4425
Email: president@bbc.ca
Website: www.bbc.ca

Bethany College (Canadian Conference of Mennonite Brethren Churches (Saskatchewan and Alberta Conferences)), Howie Wall, President, Box 160, Hepburn, Saskatchewan S0K 1Z0, Tel. (306)947-2175 Fax (306)947-4229
Email: info@bethany.sk.ca
Website: www.bethany.sk.ca

Briercrest Seminary* (Interdenominational), Dwayne Uglem, President, 510 College Dr., Caronport, SK S0H 0S0, Tel. (800)667-5199 Fax (306)756-5500
Email: admissions@briercrest.ca
Website: www.briercrest.ca

Canadian Lutheran Bible Institute (Lutheran), Pastor Harold Rust, President, 4837 52A St., Camrose, AB T4V 1W5, Tel. (780)672-4454 Fax (780)672-4455
Email: clbi@clbi.edu
Website: www.clbi.edu

Canadian Mennonite University (Mennonite Brethren Churches, Mennonite Church Canada), Gerald Gerbrandt, President, 500 Shaftesbury Blvd, Winnipeg, MB R3P 2N2, Tel. (204)487-3300 Fax (204)487-3858

Email: reception@cmu.ca
Website: www.cmu.ca

Canadian Southern Baptist Seminary* (Canadian Convention of Southern Baptists), Robert Blackaby, President, 200 Seminary View, Cochrane, AB T4C 2G1, Tel. (877)922-2727 or (403)932-6622 Fax (403)932-7049 Email: Rob.Blackaby@@csbs.ca Website: www.csbs.edu

Canadian Theological Seminary* (Christian and Missionary Alliance in Canada), Dr. Riley Coulter, Acting President, 150 Ambrose Circle, SW, Calgary, AB T3H 0L5, Tel. (403)410-2000 Fax (403)571-2556 Email: reception@ambrose.edu Website: www.ambrose.edu

Carey Theological College* (Canadian Baptists of Western Canada), Brian F. Stelck, President, 5920 Iona Drive, Vancouver, BC V6T 1J6, Tel. (604)224-4308 Fax (604)224-5014 Email: info@carey-edu.ca Website: www.carey-edu.ca

Centre for Christian Studies (The Anglican Church of Canada, The United Church of Canada), Megan McKenzie, Principal, 60 Maryland, Winnipeg, MB R3G 1K7, Tel. (204) 783-4490 Fax (204)786-3012 Email: info@ccsonline.ca Website: www.ccsonline.ca

Collège Dominicain de Philosophie et de Théologie (The Roman Catholic Church in Canada), Father Maxine Allard, President, 96 Avenue Empress, Ottawa, ON K1R 7G3, Tel. (613)233-5696 ext. 206 Fax (613)233-6064 Email: info@collegedominicain.ca Website: www.collegedominicain.ca

College of Emmanuel and St. Chad* (The Anglican Church of Canada), The Rev. Terry Wieve, Principal, 114 Seminary Crescent, Saskatoon, SK S7N 0X3, Tel. (306)975-3753 Fax (306)934-2683 Email: emmanuel.stchad@usask.ca Website: www.usask.ca/stu/emmanuel

Columbia Bible College (BC Conference of Mennonite Brethren Churches & Mennonite Church in BC), Dr. Ron Penner, President, 2940 Clearbrook Rd., Abbotsford, BC V2T 2Z8, Tel. (604)853-3358 Fax (604)853-3063 Email: info@columbiabc.edu Website: www.columbiabc.edu

Concordia Lutheran Seminary* (Lutheran Church-Canada), Dr. Manfred Zeuch, President, 7040 Ada Blvd., Edmonton, AB T5B 4E3, Tel. (780)474-1468 Fax (780)479-3067 Email: info@concordiasem.ab.ca Website: www.learngrowserve.ca

Concordia Lutheran Theological Seminary* (Lutheran Church-Canada), Thomas Winger, President, 470 Glenridge Ave., St. Catharines, ON L2T 4C3, Tel. (905)688-2362 Fax (905)688-9744 Email: concordia@brocku.ca Website: www.brocku.ca/concordiaseminary

Ecole de Theologie Evangelique de Montreal (Canadian Conference of Mennonite Brethren Churches), Kristen Corrigan, President, 4824, ch. de la Cote-des-Neiges, Suite 301, Montreal, QC H3V 1G4, Tel. (514)331-0878 Fax (514)331-0879 Email: info@etem.ca Website: www.etem.ca

Emmanuel Bible College (The Evangelical Missionary Church of Canada), Thomas E. Dow, President, 100 Fergus Ave., Kitchener, ON N2A 2H2, Tel. (519)894-8900 Fax (519) 894-5331 Email: admin@ebcollege.on.ca Website: www.ebcollege.on.ca

Emmanuel College of Victoria University* (The United Church of Canada), The Rev. Dr. Mark G. Toulouse, Principal, 75 Queens Park Crescent East, Toronto, ON M5S 1K7, Tel. (416)585-4539 Fax (416)585-4516 Email: ec.office@utoronto.ca Website: vicu.utoronto.ca

Eston College (Apostolic Church of Pentecost of Canada Inc.), Brian Fuller, President, Box 579, Eston, SK S0L 1A0, Tel. (306)962-3621 Fax (306)962-3810 Email: info@estoncollege.ca Website: www.estoncollege.ca

Faculté De Théologie Évangélique (Interdenominational), Amar Djaballah, President, 2285 Avenue Papineau, Montréal, QC H2K 4J5, Tel. (514)526-2003 Fax (514)526-6887 Email: reg@fteacadia.ca Website: www.fteacadia.ca

Faith Alive Bible College (Nondenominational), Dr. David Pierce, Dean, 637 University Dr., Saskatoon, SK S7N 0H8, Tel. (306)652-2230 Fax (306)665-1125 Email: info@fabc.ca Website: www.fabc.ca

Gardner College, A Centre for Christian Studies (Church of God (Anderson, Ind.)), Donnalyn Froese, President, 4707 56th St., Camrose, AB T4V 2C4, Tel. (780)672-0171 Fax (780)672-2465 Email: info@gardnercollege.org Website: www.gardnercollege.org

Grand Seminaire de Montréal (The Roman Catholic Church in Canada), Charles Langlois, P.S.S., Rector, 2065, Sherbrooke Ouest,

Montréal, QC H3H 1G6, Tel. (514)935-1169
Fax (514)935-5497
Email: charlan7@mac.com
Website: www.gsdm.qc.ca

Great Lakes Bible College (Churches of Christ in Canada), Mr. J. Arthur Ford, Board of Trustees Chairman, 470 Glenelm Crescent, Waterloo, ON N2L 5C8, Tel. (519)884-4310 Fax (519)884-4412
Email: learn@glbc.on.ca
Website: www.glbc.on.ca

Heritage Theological Seminary* (Fellowship of Evangelical Baptist Churches in Canada and the Ontario region.), Marvin R. Brubacher, President, 175 Holiday Inn Dr., Cambridge, ON N3C 3T2, Tel. (519)651-2869 or 800-465-1961 Fax (519)651-2870
Email: discover@heritageseminary.net
Website: www.DiscoverHeritage.ca

Horizon College and Seminary, Affiliated College of the University of Saskatchewan* (The Pentecostal Assemblies of Canada), Jeromey Martini, PhD., Academic Dean, 1303 Jackson Ave., Saskatoon, SK S7H 2M9, Tel. (306)374-6655/(879)374-6655 Toll Free Fax (306)373-6968
Email: admissions@horizon.edu
Website: www.horizon.edu

Huron University College Faculty of Theology* (The Anglican Church of Canada), Dr. Stephen McClatchie, Principal, 1349 Western Rd., London, ON N6G 1H3, Tel. (519)438-7224 Fax (519)438-9981
Email: huron@uwo.ca
Website: www.huronuc.on.ca

Institut Biblique Beree (The Pentecostal Assemblies of Canada), André L. Gagnon, President, 1711 Est Boul. Henri-Bourassa, Montréal, QC H2C 1J5, Tel. (514)385-4238 Fax (514)385-4238
Email: mlecompte@ibq-canada.org
Website: http://www.ibq-canada.org

Institut Périchorèse Atelier d'iconographie Michèle Lévesque, Director, 10 rue du Postillon, Saint-Jean-sur-Richelieu, QC J2W 1L5, Tel. (450)348-7879
Email: contact@perichorese-icones.org
Website: www.perichorese-icones.org

Institute Biblique Québec (The Pentecostal Assemblies of Canada), Rév. Patrick St-Onge, President, 839 La Salle, Longueuil, QC J4K 3G6, Tel. (450)651-4200 Fax (450)651-6300
Email: pstonge@ibq-canada.org
Website: http://www.ibq-canada.org/

Institute for Christian Studies (Nondenominational), Harry Fernhout, President, 229 College St., Suite 200, Toronto, ON M5T 1R4,

Tel. (416)979-2331 or 1 (888)326-5347 Fax (416)979-2332
Email: info@icscanada.edu
Website: www.icscanada.edu

International Bible College (Church of God (Cleveland, Tenn.)), Randy Krieger, President, 401 Trinity La., Moose Jaw, SK S6H 0E3, Tel. (306)692-4041 Fax (306)692-7968
Email: ibc.administrator@saktel.net
Website: www.ibiblecollege.com

Key-Way-Tin Bible Institute (Nondenominational), Eric Sinclair, Interim Administrator, Site 633 Comp 8 RR1, Lac La Biche, AB T0A 2C1, Tel. (780)623-4565 Fax (780)623-1788
Email: kbi@telus.net
Website: www.keywaytinbibleinstitute.org

Knox College* (The Presbyterian Church in Canada), J. Dorcas Gordon, Principal, 59 St. George St., Toronto, ON M5S 2E6, Tel. (416)978-4500 Fax (416)971-2133
Email: knox.college@utoronto.ca
Website: www.utoronto.ca/.knox

Living Faith Bible College (Fellowship of Christian Assembles (Canada)), Paul Reich, M.A, President, Box 100, Caroline, AB T0M 0M0, Tel. (403)722-2225 or (800)838-2975 Fax (403)722-2459
Email: office@lfbc.net
Website: www.lfbc.net

Lutheran Theological Seminary* (Evangelical Lutheran Church in Canada), Kevin A. Ogilvie, President, 114 Seminary Crescent, Saskatoon, SK S7N 0X3, Tel. (306)966-7850 Fax (306)966-7852
Email: lutheran.seminary@usask.ca
Website: www.usask.ca/stu/luther

Maritime Christian College (Christian Churches and Churches of Christ), Fred C. Osborne, President, 503 University Ave., Charlottetown, PE C1A 7Z4, Tel. (902)628-8887 Fax (902)892-3959
Email: registrar@maritimechristian college.pe.ca
Website: www.maritimechristiancollege.pe.ca

Master's College and Seminary (The Pentecostal Assemblies of Canada), Dr. William Morrow, President, 780 Argyle Street, Peterborough, ON K9H 5T2, Tel. (705)749-0725 Fax (705)749—0417
Email: info@mcs.edu
Website: www.mcs.edu

McGill University Faculty of Religious Studies* (Interdenominational), Ellen B. Aitken, Dean, 3520 University St., Montréal, QC H3A 2A7, Tel. (514)398-4121 Fax (514)398-6665
Email: web.relgstud@mcgill.ca
Website: www.mcgill.ca/religiousstudies

319

McMaster Divinity College* Stanley E. Porter, President/Dean, 1280 Main St. West, Hamilton, ON L8S 4K1, Tel. (905)525-9140 ext. 24401 Fax (905)577-4782
Email: divinity@mcmaster.ca
Website: www.macdiv.ca

Millar College of the Bible (Interdenominational), A. Brian Atmore, President, Box 25, Pambrun, SK S0N 1W0, Tel. (306)582-2033 Fax (306)582-2027
Email: info@millarcollege.ca
Website: www.millarcollege.ca

Montreal Diocesan Theological College* (The Anglican Church of Canada), Bishop of Montreal, President, 3475 University St., Montreal, QC H3A 2A8, Tel. (514)849-3004 Fax (514)849-4113
Email: diocoll@netrover.com
Website: www.dio-mdtc.ca

Montreal School of Theology* (Inter/Multidenominational), Dr. John Vissers, Administrative Officer, 3475 University St., Montréal, QC H3A 2A8, Tel. (514)849-8511 Fax (514)849-4113
Email: info@mst-etm.ca
Website: www.mst-etm.ca

Mount Carmel Bible School (Transdenominational), Wayne Tomalty, President, 4725 106 Ave., Edmonton, AB T6A 1E7, Tel. (780)465-3015 or (800) 561-6443 Fax (780)466-2485
Email: mail@mountcarmel.net
Website: www.mountcarmel.net

Newman Theological College* (The Catholic Church in Canada), Rev. Shayne Craig, p.s.s., President, 10012-84 Street NW, Edmonton, AB T6A 0B2, Tel. (780)392-2450 Fax (780)462-4013
Email: registrar@newman.edu
Website: www.newman.edu

Nipawin Bible College (Interdenominational), Mr. Wes Fehr, President, Box 1986, Nipawin, SK S0E 1E0, Tel. (306)862-5095 Fax (306) 862-3651
Email: info@nipawin.org
Website: www.nipawin.org

Northwest Baptist Theological College and Seminary (The Fellowship of Evangelical Baptist Churches of Canada), Dr. Larry Perkins, President, 7600 Glover Rd., Langley, BC V2Y 1Y1, Tel. (604)888-7592 Fax (604) 637-3212
Email: larry@nbseminary.com
Website: www.nbseminary.ca

Ontario Christian Seminary (Christian Churches and Churches of Christ in Canada), James R. Cormode, President, 260 High Park

Ave., Toronto, ON M6P 3J9, Tel. (416)769-7115 Fax (416)769-7047

Pacific Life Bible College (Foursquare), Rob Buzza, President, 15030 66 A Ave., Surrey, BC V3S 2A5, Tel. (604)597-9082 Fax (604) 597-9090
Email: plbc@pacificlife.edu
Website: www.pacificlife.edu

Parole de Vie Bethel/Word of Life Bethel (Nondenominational), Mark Strout, Director, 1175, ch. Thomas - Woodward, Sherbrooke, QC J1M 0B4, Tel. (819)823-8435 Fax (819) 823-2468
Email: quebec@pdvb.org
Website: www.pdvb.org

Peace River Bible Institute* (Interdenominational), Waldie Neufeld, President, Box 99, Sexsmith, AB T0H 3C0, Tel. (780)568-3962 Fax (780)568-4431
Email: prbi@prbi.edu
Website: www.prbi.edu

Prairie Graduate School (Interdenominational), Dr. Dennis Punter, Interim-President, 330 6th Ave., Three Hills, AB T0M 2N0, Tel. (403) 443-5511 Fax (403)443-5540
Email: prairie@prairie.edu
Website: www.pbi.ab.ca

The Presbyterian College, Montreal* (Presbyterian Church in Canada), John Vissers, Principal, 3495 University St., Montreal, QC H3A 2A8, Tel. (514)288-5256 Fax (514)288-8072
Email: info@presbyteriancollege.ca
Website: www.presbyteriancollege.ca

Providence College and Theological Seminary* (Inter/Multidenominational), August H. Konkel, President, 10 College Crescent, Otterburne, MB R0A 1G0, Tel. (204) 433-7488 Fax (204)433-7158
Email: info@prov.ca
Website: www.prov.ca

Queens College Faculty of Theology* (The Anglican Church of Canada), John Mellis, President, 210 Prince Philip Dr., Suite 3000, St. Johns, NL A1B 3R6, Tel. (709)753-0116 Fax (709)753-1214
Email: queens@mun.ca
Website: www.mun.ca/queens

Queen's School of Religion* (The United Church of Canada), Pamela Dickey Young, Principal, Room 212 Theological Hall, Kingston, ON K7L 3N6, Tel. (613)533-2110 Fax (613)533-6879
Email: youngpd@queensu.ca
Website: www.queensu.ca/religion

Reformed Episcopal Theological College (The Reformed Episcopal Church of Canada), Rt.

320

Rev. Michael Fedechko, President, PO Box 2532, Hwy 11 North, New Liskeard, ON P0J 1P0, Tel. (705)647-4565 Fax (705)647-4565 Email: fed@nt.net
Website: www.retcc.com

Reformed Episcopal Theological College (Reformed Episcopal Church of Canada), Rt. Rev. Michael Fedechko, President, PO Box 2532, New Liskeard, ON P0J 1P0, Tel. (705)630-2071 Fax (705)647-4481 Email: bishopfedechko@yahoo.com
Website: www.rececan.org

Regent College* (Interdenominational), Rod Wilson, PhD, President, 5800 University Blvd., Vancouver, BC V6T 2E4, Tel. (800)663-8664 or (604)224-3245 Fax (604) 224-3097 Email: presidentsoffice@regent-college.edu
Website: www.regent-college.edu

Regis College* (The Roman Catholic Church in Canada), John E. Costello, S.J, President, 100 Wellesley St. West, Toronto, ON M5S 2Z5, Tel. (416)922-5474 Fax (416)922-2898 Email: regis.registrar@utoronto.ca
Website: www.regiscollege.ca

Rocky Mountain College, Centre for Biblical Studies (The Evangelical Missionary Church of Canada), Kerry Belt, President, 4039 Brentwood Rd. NW, Calgary, AB T2L 1L1, Tel. (403)284-5100 ext.233 Fax (403)220-9567 Email: admissions@rockymountaincollege.ca
Website: www.rockymountaincollege.ca

St. Andrew's College* (The United Church of Canada), Rev. Lorne Calvert, Principal, 1121 College Drive, Saskatoon, SK S7N 0W3, Tel. (306)966-8970; (877)644-8970 Fax (306)966-8981
Email: lorne.calvert@usask.ca
Website: www.standrews.ca

St. Augustine's Seminary of Toronto* (The Roman Catholic Church in Canada), Rev. Msgr. A. Robert Nusca, President and Rector, 2661 Kingston Rd., Toronto, ON M1M 1M3, Tel. (416)261-7207 Fax (416)261-2529 Email: tehil@web.net
Website: www.staugustines.on.ca

St. John's College, Univ. of Manitoba, Faculty of Theology (The Anglican Church of Canada), Dr. Janet A. Hoskins, Warden & Vice Chancellor, 92 Dysart Rd., Winnipeg, MB R3T 2M5, Tel. (204)474-8531 Fax (204)474-7610 Email: stjohns_college@umanitoba.ca
Website: www.umanitoba.ca/colleges/st_johns

Saint Paul University, Faculty of Theology* (The Roman Catholic Church), Fr. Andrea Spatafora, MSF, Ph.D., Dean, 223 Main St., Ottawa, ON K1S 1C4, Tel. (613)236-1393 x. 2247 Fax (613)751-4016

Email: fquesnel@ustpaul.ca
Website: www.ustpaul.ca

St. Peter's Seminary* (The Roman Catholic Church in Canada), Steven A. Wlusek, Rector, 1040 Waterloo St. North, London, ON N6A 3Y1, Tel. (519)432-1824 Fax (519)432-0964 Email: jslawek@uwo.ca
Website: www.stpetersseminary.ca

St. Stephen's College* (The United Church of Canada), Dr. Earle Sharam, President, 8810 112th St., Edmonton, AB T6G 2J6, Tel. (800) 661-4956 Fax (780)433-8875 Email: st.stephens@ualberta.ca
Website: www.ststephenscollege.ca

Salvation Army College for Officer Training (The Salvation Army in Canada), Wayne N. Pritchett, Principal, 2130 Bayview Ave., North York, ON M4N 3K6, Tel. (416)481-6131 Fax (416)481-6810; (416)481-2895 (Library) Email: sandra_rice@can.salvationarmy.org

The Salvation Army William and Catherine Booth College (The Salvation Army in Canada), Dr. Jonathan S. Raymond, President, 447 Webb Pl., Winnipeg, MB R3B 2P2, Tel. (204)947-6701 Fax (204)942-3856 Email: wcbc@boothcollege.ca
Website: www.boothcollege.ca

Steinbach Bible College (Mennonite), Rob Reimer, President, 50 PTH 12 N, Steinbach, MB R5G 1T4, Tel. (204)326-6451 Fax (204) 326-6908 Email: info@sbcollege.ca
Website: www.sbcollege.ca

Summit Pacific College (The Pentecostal Assemblies of Canada), David Demchuk, President, Box 1700, Abbotsford, BC V2S 7E7, Tel. (604)853-7491 Fax (604)853-8951 Email: pr@summitpacific.ca
Website: www.summitpacific.ca

Taylor College of Mission and Evangelism (Non-Denominational), Reed Fleming, Director of Formation, 105 Mountain View Drive, Saint John, NB E2J 5B5, Tel. (506)642-2210 or 1-888-316-8169 Fax (506)657-8217 Email: info@taylorcollege.ca
Website: www.taylorcollege.ca

Theological College of the Canadian Reformed Churches (Canadian and American Reformed Churches), Dr. G. H. Visscher, President, 110 West 27th St., Hamilton, ON L9C 5A1, Tel. (905)575-3688 Fax (905)575-0799 Email: theocollege@seminary.canrc.org
Website: www.theologicalcollege.ca

Toronto Baptist Seminary and Bible College (Baptist), Dr. Glendon G. Thompson, President, 130 Gerrard St., E., Toronto, ON M5A 3T4, Tel. (416)925-3263 Fax (416)925-8305

Email: inquiry@tbs.edu
Website: www.tbs.edu

Toronto School of Theology* (Inter/Multidenominational), Alan Hayes, Director, 47 Queens Park Crescent E., Toronto, ON M5S 2C3, Tel. (416)978-4039 Fax (416) 978-7821
Email: alan.hayes@utoronto.ca
Website: www.tst.edu

Trinity College Faculty of Divinity* (The Anglican Church of Canada), David Neelands, Dean, 6 Hoskin Ave., Toronto, ON M5S 1H8, Tel. (416)978-2133 Fax (416)978-4949
Email: divinity@trinity.utoronto.ca
Website: www.trinity.utoronto.ca/divinity

Tyndale University College & Seminary* (Trans-denominational), Dr. Gary V. Nelson, President, 25 Ballyconnor Ct., Toronto, ON M2M 4B3, Tel. (416)226-6620 or (877)896-3253 Fax (416)226-6746
Email: info@tyndale.ca
Website: www.tyndale.ca

United Theological College/Le Séminaire Uni* (The United Church of Canada), Rev. Philip Joudrey, President, 3521 rue Université, Montréal, QC H3A 2A9, Tel. (514)849-2042 Fax (514)849-8634
Email: admin@utc.ca
Website: www.utc.ca

Université Laval, Faculté de Théologie et de Sciences Religieuses* (The Roman Catholic Church in Canada), Marc Pelchat, Doyen, Pavillon Felix-Antoine Savard, 2325 Rue Des Bibliotheques, Hocal 846, Quebec, QC G1V 0A6, Tel. (418)656-2131 Fax (418)656-3273
Email: marc.pelchat@ftsr.ulaval.ca
Website: www.ftsr.ulaval.ca

Université de Montréal, Faculté de théologie et de sciences des religion (The Roman Catholic Church in Canada), Jean-Claude Breton, Doyen, President, C. P. 6128 Succ. Centre Ville, Montréal, QC H3C 3J7, Tel. (514)343-7160 Fax (514)343-5738
Email: ftsr@umontreal.ca
Website: www.ftsr.umontreal.ca

Université de Sherbrooke, Faculté de theologié, d'éthique et de philosophie (The Roman Catholic Church in Canada), Jean-François Malherbe, President, 1111, rue Saint-Charles Ouest, Tourquest - Bureau 310, Longueuil, QC J4K 5G4, Tel. (450)670-7157 Fax (450)670-1959

Email: rectrice@usherbrooke.ca
Website: www.usherb.ca/longueuil

University of St. Michael's College Faculty of Theology* (Roman Catholic Church), Rev. Dr. Mario O. D'Souza, C.S.B., Dean, 81 St. Mary St., Toronto, ON M5S 1J4, Tel. (416)926-7140 Fax (416)926-7294
Email: usmctheology.registrar@utoronto.ca
Website: http://stmikes.utoronto.ca/theology/

The University of Winnipeg Faculty of Theology* (Multi-denominational and the United Church of Canada), James T. Christie, Dean, 515 Portage Ave., Winnipeg, MB R3B 2E9, Tel. (204)786-9390 Fax (204)772-2584
Email: theology@uwinnipeg.ca
Website: www.theology/uwinnipeg.ca

Vancouver School of Theology* (Inter/Multidenominational), Rev. Dr. Wendy Fletcher, Principal, 6000 Iona Dr., Vancouver, BC V6T 1L4, Tel. (866)822-9031 Fax (604)822-9212
Email: vstinfo@vst.edu
Website: www.vst.edu

Vanguard College (The Pentecostal Assemblies of Canada), Stephen Hertzog, President, 12140 103 St., Edmonton, AB T5G 2J9, Tel. (780)452-0808 Fax (780)452-5803
Email: info@vanguardcollege.com
Website: www.vanguardcollege.com

Waterloo Lutheran Seminary* (Evangelical Lutheran Church in Canada), David Pfrimmer, Principal Dean, 75 University Ave. W., Waterloo, ON N2L 3C5, Tel. (519)884-1970 Fax (519)725-2434
Email: seminary@wlu.ca
Website: www.seminary.wlu.ca

Western Christian College (Churches of Christ in Canada), Kevin Vance, President, 100-4400 4th Ave., Regina, SK S4T 0H8, Tel. (306)545-1515 Fax (306)352-2198
Email: bschwarz@westernchristian.ca
Website: www.westernchristian.ca

Wycliffe College* (The Anglican Church of Canada), Rev. Canon. Dr. George R. Sumner, Jr., Principal, 5 Hoskin Ave., Toronto, ON M5S 1H7, Tel. (416)946-3535 Fax (416)946-3545
Email: info@wycliffe.utoronto.ca
Website: www.wycliffecollege.ca

10. Religious Periodicals in the United States

This directory lists 405 publications, primarily of the organizations listed in Directory 3, "Religious Bodies in the United States." Some independent publications are also listed. The list does not include all publications prepared by religious bodies, and not all the publications listed here are necessarily the official publication of a particular church. Regional publications and newsletters are not ordinarily included. A more extensive list of religious periodicals published in the United States can be found in *Gale Directory of Publications and Broadcast Media*, (Gale Research, Inc., P.O. Box 33477, Detroit MI 48232-5477).

Each entry in this directory contains: the title of the periodical, frequency of publication, religious affiliation, editor's name, address, telephone and fax number and email and website addresses when available. The frequency of publication, which appears in parenthesis after the name of the publication is represented by a "D" for daily, "W" for weekly; "M" for monthly; "Q" for quarterly; "Y" for yearly, and "I" for Internet.

21st Century Christian, (M) Churches of Christ, M. Norvel Young and Prentice A. Meador, Jr., Box 40304, Nashville, TN 37204 Tel. (800)331-5991 Fax (615)385-5915 Email: eric@nafwb.org

Action, (6-Y) Churches of Christ, John D. Reese, P.O. Box 2169, Cedar Park, TX 78630-2169 Tel. (512)345-8191 Fax (512)401-8265 Email: wbsinfo@wbschool.org Website: www.wbschool.org

Adra Works, (Q) Seventh-day Adventist Church, Tina Hudgins, 12501 Old Columbia Pike, Silver Spring, MD 20904-6600 Tel. (301)680-6355 Email: tina.hudgins@adra.org Website: www.adra.org

Adra's World, (Q) Seventh-day Adventist Church, Tina Hudgins, 12501 Old Columbia Pike, Silver Spring, MD 20904-6600 Tel. (800)424-2372 Email: tina.hudgins@adra.org Website: www.adra.org

The Adult Quarterly, (Q) Associate Reformed Presbyterian Church (General Synod), The Rev. William B. Evans, PhD, P.O. Box 275, Due West, SC 29639 Tel. (864)379-8896 Email: wbevans@erskine.edu

Advent Christian News, (M) Advent Christian Church, Rev. Keith D. Wheaton, P.O. Box 23152, Charlotte, NC 28227 Tel. (704)545-6161 Fax (704)573-0712 Email: Acpub@Adventchristian.org

The Adventist Chaplain, (Q) Seventh-day Adventist Church, Deena Bartel-Wagner, Editor, Adventist Chaplaincy Ministries, General Conference of Seventh-day Adventists, 12501 Old Columbia Pike, Silver Spring, MD 20904-6600 Tel. (301)680-6780 Fax (301)680-6783

Email: acm@gc.adventist.org Website: www.adventistchaplains.org

Adventist Review, (3-M) Seventh-day Adventist Church, Bill Knott, 12501 Old Columbia Pike, Silver Spring, MD 20904-6600 Tel. (301)680-6560 Fax (301)680-6638 Email: letters@adventistreview.org Website: www.adventistreview.org

Adventist World, (M) Seventh-day Adventist Church, Bill Knott, 12501 Old Columbia Pike, Silver Spring, MD 20904-6600 Tel. (301)680-6560 Fax (301)680-6638 Email: letters@adventistworld.org Website: www.AdventistWorld.org

Agape Magazine, (bi-M) Coptic Orthodox Church, Bishop Serapion, 4909 Cleland Ave, Los Angeles, CA 90050 Tel. (909)865-8378 Fax (909)865-8348 Email: agape@lacopts.org Website: lacopts.org

Alive Now, (bi-M) The United Methodist Church, JoyAnn Miller (Interim), P.O. Box 340004, Nashville, TN 37203-0004 Tel. (615)340-7218 Email: alivenow@upperroom.org Website: www.alivenow.org

The Allegheny Wesleyan Methodist, (M) The Allegheny Wesleyan Methodist Connection (Original Allegheny Conference), William Cope, P.O. Box 357, Salem, OH 44460 Tel. (330)337-9376 Fax (330)337-9700 Email: awmc@juno.com

Alliance Life, (M) The Christian and Missionary Alliance, Mark Failing, P.O. Box 35000, Colorado Springs, CO 80935 Tel. (719)599-5999 Fax (719)599-8234 Email: alife@cmalliance.org Website: www.alliancelife.org

American Baptist Quarterly, (Q) American Baptist Churches in the USA American Baptist Historical Society, Dr. Robert E. Johnson, 3001 Mercer University Drive, Atlanta, GA 30341 Tel. (678)547-6680 Fax (678)547-6682 Website: www.abhsarchives.org

American Baptists In Mission, (Q) American Baptist Churches in the USA, Richard W. Schramm, P.O. Box 851, Valley Forge, PA 19482-0851 Tel. (610)768-2000 Fax (610)768-2320
Email: richard.schramm@abc-usa.org
Website: www.abc-usa.org

American Bible Society Record, (4-Y) Nondenominational, Liz Smith, 1865 Broadway, New York, NY 10023 Tel. (610)647-8080 Fax (484)654-3503
Email: absrecord@americanbible.org
Website: www.AmericanBible.org

Annual Catholic Directory, The, (Y) The Catholic Church, Michelle Laque Johnson, 222 N. 17th St., Philadelphia, PA 19103 Tel. (215)587-3660 Fax (215)587-3979

El Aposento Alto, (bi-M) The United Methodist Church, Carmen Gaud, P.O. Box 340004, Nashville, TN 37203-0004 Tel. (615)340-7253 Fax (615)340-7267
Email: ElAposentoAlto@upperroom.org
Website: www.upperroom.org

The Armenian Church, (2-Y) Diocese of the Armenian Church of America, Arpie McQueen, 630 Second Avenue, New York, NY 10016 Tel. (212)686-0710 Fax (212)779-3558
Email: tac@armeniandiocese.org
Website: www.armenianchurch.org

Around the Fellowship, (M) Universal Fellowship of Metropolitan Community Churches, Director of Communications: James N. Birkitt, Jr., P.O. Box 1374, Abilene, TX 79604 Tel. (310)360-8640 Fax (310)388-1252
Email: info@mccchurch.org
Website: www.mccchurch.org

Assemblies of God Heritage, (Y) Assemblies of God, Darrin Rodgers, 1445 Boonville Ave., Springfield, MO 65802 Tel. (417)862-1447 Ext. 4400 Fax (417)862-6203
Email: drodgers@ag.org
Website: www.iFPHC.org

The Associate Reformed Presbyterian, (M) Associate Reformed Presbyterian Church (General Synod), Delores McDonald, One Cleveland St., Greenville, SC 29601 Tel. (864)232-8297 ext. 236 Fax (864)271-3729
Email: arpeditor@arpsynod.org
Website: www.arpmagazine.org

Attack, A Magazine for Christian Men, (Q) National Association of Free Will Baptists, James E. Vallance, P.O. Box 5002, Antioch, TN 37011-5002 Tel. (615)731-4950 Fax (615)731-0771

Awake!, (M) Jehovah's Witnesses, Watch Tower Society, 25 Columbia Heights, Brooklyn, NY 11201-2483 Tel. (718)560-5000
Website: watchtower.org

The Banner, (M) Christian Reformed Church in North America, Robert DeMoor, 2850 Kalamazoo Ave., S.E., Grand Rapids, MI 49560 Tel. (616)224-0732 Fax (616)224-0834
Email: editorial@thebanner.org
Website: www.thebanner.org

The Banner of Truth, (M) Netherlands Reformed Congregations, J. den Hoed, P.O. Box 621, Carlisle, PA 17013 Tel. (717)249-5747 Fax (360)354-7565

The Baptist Bible Tribune, (M) Baptist Bible Fellowship International, Keith Bassham, P.O. Box 309, Springfield, MO 65801-0309 Tel. (417)831-3996 Fax (417)831-1470
Email: editors@tribune.org
Website: www.tribune.org

Baptist Bulletin, (6-Y) General Association of Regular Baptist Churches, Sr Editor: Norman A. Olson Mg. Editor: Kevin Mungons, 1300 N. Meacham Rd., Schaumburg, IL 60173-4806 Tel. (847)843-1600 Fax (847)843-3757
Email: baptistbulletin@garbc.org
Website: www.garbc.org

Baptist History and Heritage Society, (3-Y) Baptist, Doug Weaver, 151 Broadleaf Dr., Macon, GA 31210 Tel. (615)371-7937 Fax (615)371-7939
Email: bhhs@baptisthistory.org
Website: www.baptisthistory.org

Baptist Peacemaker, (Q) Baptist, Katie Cook, 4800 Wedgewood Dr., Charlotte, NC 28210 Tel. (704)521-6051 Fax (704)521-6053
Email: bpfna@bpfna.org
Website: www.bpfna.org

The Baptist Preacher, (bi-M) Baptist Bible Fellowship International, Mike Randall, P.O. Box 309 HSJ, Springfield, MO 65801 Tel. (417)831-3996 Fax (417)831-1470
Email: editors@tribune.org
Website: www.tribune.org

The Baptist Preacher's Journal, (Q) Baptist Bible Fellowship International, Keith Bassham, P.O. Box 309, Springfield, MO 65801 Tel. (417)831-3996 Fax (417)831-1470
Email: editor@tribune.org
Website: tribune.org

Baptist Progress, (Q) Progressive National Baptist Convention, Inc., Justus Y. Reeves, 601 50th St. NE, Washington, DC 20019 Tel. (202)396-0558 Fax (202)398-4998
Email: infor@pnbc.org
Website: www.PNBC.org

Baptist Witness, (M) Primitive Baptists, Lasserre Bradley, Jr., P.O. Box 17037, Cincinnati, OH 45217 Tel. (513)821-7289 Fax (513)821-7303
Email: bbh45217@aol.com
Website: www.BaptistBibleHour.org

The Bible Advocate, (6-Y) The Church of God (Seventh Day), Denver, CO, Calvin Burrell, P.O. Box 33677, Denver, CO 80233 Tel. (303)452-7973 Fax (303)452-0657
Email: bibleadvocate@cog7.org
Website: www.baonline.org

The Brethren Evangelist, (4-6-Y) The Brethren Church, 524 College Ave., Ashland, OH 44805 Tel. (419)289-1708 Fax (419)281-0450
Email: brethren@brethrenchurch.org
Website: www.brethrenchurch.org

Brethren Journal, (10-Y) Unity of the Brethren, Rev. Milton Maly, 6703 FM 2502, Brenham, TX 77833-9803 Tel. (409)830-8762
Website: www.unityofthebrethren.org

Brethren Life and Thought, (Q) Church of the Brethren, Karen Garrett, Bethany Seminary, 615 National Road West, Richmond, IN 47374-4019 Tel. (765)983-1811 Fax (765)983-1840
Email: blt@bethanyseminary.edu
Website: www.bethanyseminary.edu/blt

The Bridegroom's Messenger, (bi-M) The International Pentecostal Church of Christ, Janice Boyce, 121 W. Hunters Trail, Elizabeth City, NC 27909 Tel. (919)338-3003 Fax (919)338-3003

The Burning Bush, (Q) The Metropolitan Church Association, Inc. (Wesleyan), Rev. Gary Bowell, The Metropolitan Church Assoc., 126 Stadia Drive, Franklin, OH 45005-1502 Tel. (937)746-3287 Fax (937)550-0171
Email: metrochurch assn@zoomtown.com
Website: www.TheMCA.net

Call to Unity: Resourcing the Church for Ecumenical Ministry, (Annual) Christian Church (Disciples of Christ), Robert K. Welsh, P.O. Box 1986, Indianapolis, IN 46206-1986 Tel. (317)713-2586 Fax (317)713-2588
Email: rwelsh@ccu.disciples.org
Website: www.disciples.org/ccu

Calvary Messenger, (M) Beachy Amish Mennonite Churches, Paul L. Miller, 7809 South Herren Road, Partridge, KS 67566 Tel. (620)567-2286 Fax (620)567-2286
Email: paullmiller@btsskynet.com

Caring, (Q) Assemblies of God, Owen Wilkie, Gospel Publishing House, 1445 N. Boonville Ave., Springfield, MO 65802 Tel. (417)862-2781 Fax (417)862-0503
Email: benevolences@ag.org
Website: www.benevolences.ag.org

Cathedral Age, (Q) Interdenominational, Craig W. Stapert and Richard Weinberg, Washington National Cathedral, 3101 Wisconsin Ave., NW, Washington, DC 20016-5098 Tel. (202)537-5681 Fax (202)364-6600
Email: cathedral_age@cathedral.org
Website: www.cathedralage.org

Catholic Chronicle, (1st Friday, no Jy) The Catholic Church, Angela Kessler, 1933 Spielbusch Avenue, Toledo, OH 43604-5360 Tel. (419)244-6711 ext. 138 Fax (419)244-0468
Email: ccnews@toledodiocese.org
Website: www.catholicchronicle.org

Catholic Digest, (M) The Catholic Church, Dan Connors, P.O. Box 6015, New London, CT 06320 Tel. (800)321-0411 Fax (860)536-5600
Email: dconnors@catholicdigest.com
Website: www.CatholicDigest.org

Catholic Herald (Milwaukee), (W) The Catholic Church, Brian T. Olszewski, 3501 S. Lake Dr., St. Francis, WI 53235-0913 Tel. (414)769-3500 Fax (414)769-3468
Email: chnonline@archmil.org
Website: www.chnonline.org

Catholic Light, (17-Y) The Catholic Church, William R. Genello, 300 Wyoming Ave., Scranton, PA 18503 Tel. (570)207-2229 Fax (570)207-2271
Email: william-genello@dioceseofscranton.org
Website: www.dioceseofscranton.org

The Catholic Peace Voice, (bi-M) The Catholic Church, Dave Robinson, 532 W. 8th Street, Erie, PA 16502 Tel. (814)453-4955 Fax (814)452-4784
Email: info@paxchristiusa.org
Website: www.paxchristiusa.org

The Catholic Review, (W) The Catholic Church, Christopher Gunty - Associate Publisher, P.O. Box 777, Baltimore, MD 21203 Tel. (443)524-3150 Fax (443)524-3155
Email: mail@catholicreview.org
Website: www.catholicreview.org

Catholic Standard and Times, (W) The Catholic Church, Mathew Gambino, 222 N.

17th St., Philadelphia, PA 19103 Tel. (215) 587-3660 Fax (215)587-3979
Email: standard@adphila.org
Website: www.cst-phl.com

The Catholic Worker, (7-Y) The Catholic Church, Sarah Brook, Joanne Kennedy, Ted Walker, Managing Editors, 36 E. First St., New York, NY 10003 Tel. (212)777-9617

Cela Biedrs, (bi-M) The Latvian Evangelical Lutheran Church in America, Vieturs Bambans, 7630 S.W. 26th Ave., Portland, OR 97219 Tel. (503)781-6724
Email: celabiedrs@yahoo.com or celabiedrs@lelba.org
Website: www.lelba.org

Celebration: An Ecumenical Worship Resource, (M) Interdenominational, Patrick Marrin, 115 East Armor Blvd., Kansas City, MO 64111 Tel. (816)531-0538 Fax (816)968-2291
Email: patmarrin@aol.com
Website: www.ncrpub.com

The Challenge, (Q) The Bible Church of Christ, Inc., A.M. Jones, 1358 Morris Ave., Bronx, NY 10456 Tel. (718)588-2284 Fax (718)992-5597
Website: www.thebiblechurchofchrist.org

Charisma, (M) Nondenominational, J. Lee Grady, 600 Rinehart Rd., Lake Mary, FL 32746 Tel. (407)333-0600 Fax (407)333-7133
Email: grady@strang.com
Website: www.charismamag.com

The Children's Friend, (English Braille), (Q) Seventh-day Adventist Church, Richard Clark Jr., Christian Record Services for the Blind, P.O. Box 6097, Lincoln, NE 68506 Tel. (402)488-0981 Fax (402)488-7582
Email: editorial@christianrecord.org
Website: www.christianrecord.org

The Christadelphian Advocate, (M) Christadelphians, Jim Washeck, 12 Westwood Est. Drive, St. Peters, MO 63376 Tel. (636)397-4430 Fax (802)885.2319
Email: washecks@juno.com
Website: www.christadelphian-advocate.org

Christadelphian Tidings, (M) Christadelphians, Donald H. Styles, 42076 Hartford Dr., Canton, MI 48187 Tel. (313)844-2426 Fax (313)844-8304

The Christian Baptist, (Q) Primitive Baptists, Elder S. T. Tolley, P.O. Box 68, Atwood, TN 38220 Tel. (901)662-7417
Email: cbl@aeneas.net

Christian Bible Teacher, (Q) Churches of Christ, J.E. Snelson, P.O. Box 7385, Ft. Worth, TX 76111 Tel. (817)838-2644 Fax (817)838-2644

The Christian Century, (bi-W) Nondenominational, John Buchanan, 104 South Michigan Ave. Suite 700, Chicago, IL 60603 Tel. (312)263-7510 Fax (312)263-7540
Email: main@christiancentury.org
Website: www.christiancentury.org

The Christian Chronicle, (M) Churches of Christ, Lynn McMillon, P.O. Box 11000, Oklahoma City, OK 73136-1100 Tel. (405)425-5070 Fax (405)425-5076
Website: www.christianchronicle.org

The Christian Community, (8-Y) International Council of Community Churches, DeAnn Chatlosh, 21116 Washington Pkwy., Frankfort, IL 60423 Tel. (815)464-5690 Fax (815)464-5692
Email: ICCC60423@sbcglobal.net
Website: icccusa.com

The Christian Contender, (M) Mennonite Church, John David Martin, Box 3, Highway 172, Crockett, KY 41413 Tel. (606)522-4348 Fax (606)522-4896

The Christian Index, (M) Christian Methodist Episcopal Church, Dr. Kenneth E. Jones, P.O. Box 431, Fairfield, AL 35064 Tel. (205)504-6120
Email: goodoc@aol.com
Website: www.c-m-e.org; thechristianindexonline.blogspot.com

Christian Journal, (Q) Churches of Christ, J.E. Snelson, P.O. Box 7385, Ft. Worth, TX 76111 Tel. (817)838-2644

Christian Leader, (bi-M) U.S. Conference of Mennonite Brethren Churches, Connie Faber, P.O. Box 155, Hillsboro, KS 67063 Tel. (316)947-5543
Email: editor@usmb.org

Christian Monthly, (M.-Online) Apostolic Lutheran Church of America, Lois Matson, P.O. Box 2996, Battle Ground, WA 98604 Tel. (360)904-6951 Fax (503)686-4131
Email: cm@apostoliclutheran.org
Website: www.Apostolic-Lutheran.org

Christian Record, (English Braille), (Q) Seventh-day Adventist Church, Richard Clark Jr., Christian Record Services for the Blind, P.O. Box 6097, Lincoln, NE 68506 Tel. (402)488-0981 Fax (402)488-7582
Email: editorial@christianrecord.org
Website: www.christianrecord.org

The **Christian Recorder**, (bi-W) African Methodist Episcopal Church, Dr. Calvin H. Sydnor III, 500 Eighth Ave. South, Nashville, TN 37215-6167 Tel. (615)714-0986
Email: chsydnor@bellsouth.net
Website: www.the.christian.recorder.org

The **Christian Science Journal**, (M) Church of Christ, Scientist, Mary M. Trammell, Editor in Chief: William G. Dawley, Editor, 210 Massachusetts Avenue, Boston, MA 02115-3195 Tel. (617)450-2000 Fax (617)450-2930
Email: trammellm@csps.com OR dawleyw@csps.com
Website: www.csjournal.com

The **Christian Science Monitor**, (D & W) Church of Christ, Scientist, David T. Cook, One Norway St., Boston, MA 02115 Tel. (617)450-2000 Fax (617)450-7575
Website: www.csmonitor.com

Christian Science Quarterly Bible Lessons, (M & Q) First Church of Christ, Scientist, Christian Harder, Manager, 210 Massachusetts Ave., Boston, MA 02115 Tel. (617)450-2651 Fax (617)450-2203
Email: service@csps.com
Website: www.BibleLesson.com

Christian Science Sentinel, (W) Church of Christ, Scientist, Mary M. Trammell, Editor in Chief; William G. Dawley, Editor, 210 Massachusetts Avenue, Boston, MA 02115-3195 Tel. (617)450-2000 Fax (617)450-2930
Email: sentinel@csps.com; trammellm@csps.com (the Editor)
Website: www.cssentinel.com

Christian Standard, (W) Christian Churches and Churches of Christ, Mark A. Taylor, 8805 Governor's Hill Drive, Cincinnati, OH 45249 Tel. (513)931-4050 Fax (513)931-0950
Email: christianstandard@standardpub.com
Website: www.christianstandard.com

The **Christian Union Witness**, (M. (except Jy-Ag)) Christian Union, Joseph Cunningham, P.O. Box 361, Greenfield, OH 45123 Tel. (937)981-2760 Fax (937)981-2760
Email: ohiocu@bright.net
Website: christianunionbright.net

Christian Woman, (bi-M) Churches of Christ, Sandra Humphrey, Box 150, Nashville, TN 37202 Tel. (615)254-8781 Fax (615)254-7411

Christianity Today, (Online) Nondenominational, Christopher Lutes, 465 Gunderson Dr., Carol Stream, IL 60188 Tel. (630)260-6200 Fax (630)480-2004
Website: www.chritianitytoday.com

The **Church Advocate**, (Q) Churches of God, General Conference, Rachel L. Foreman, P.O. Box 926, 700 E. Melrose Ave., Findlay, OH 45839 Tel. (419)424-1961 Fax (419)424-3433
Email: communications@cggc.org
Website: www.cggc.org

Church of God Evangel, (M) Church of God (Cleveland, Tenn.), Lance Colkmire, P.O. Box 2250, Cleveland, TN 37320-2250 Tel. (423)478-7592 Fax (423)478-7616
Email: editor@pathwaypress.org
Website: www.pathwaypress.org

The **Church Herald**, (11-Y) Reformed Church in America, Christina Van Eyl, 4500 60th St. SE, Grand Rapids, MI 49512 Tel. (616)698-7071 Fax (616)698-6606
Email: herald@rca.org
Website: herald.rca.org

Church History: Studies in Christianity and Culture, (Q) Scholarly, John Corrigan, Amanda Porterfield, Florida State Univesity, Dept of Religion, M05 Dodd Hall, FSU, Tallahassee, FL 32306-1520 Tel. (850)644-1020 Fax (850)644-7225
Email: church-history@admin.fsu.edu
Website: www.churchhistory.org/churchhistory.html

The **Church Messenger**, (bi-W) The American Carpatho-Russian Orthodox Greek Catholic Church, V. Rev. Michael Rosco, 145 Broad St., Perth Amboy, NJ 08861 Tel. (732)826-4442
Email: mrosco2@excite.com
Website: www.acrod.org/news/messenger1.html

Church School Herald, (Q) African Methodist Episcopal Zion Church, Ms. Mary A. Love, P.O. Box 26769, Charlotte, NC 28221-6769 Tel. (704)599-4630 ext. 324 Fax (704)688-2548
Email: MaLove@amezhqtr.org

Church & Society Magazine, (bi-M) Presbyterian Church (U.S.A.), Rev. Dr. Bobbi Wells Hargleroad, 100 Witherspoon St., Louisville, KY 40202-1396 Tel. (502)569-5810 Fax (502)569-8116
Email: c-s@ctr.pcusa.org
Website: www.pcusa.org/churchsociety

ChurchRite, (6-Y) The Church of God (Seventh Day), Denver, CO, P.O. Box 33677, 330 W. 152nd Ave., Denver, CO 80233 Tel. (303)452-7973 Fax (303)452-0657
Email: churchrite@cog7.org

Churchwoman, (Q) Interdenominational, Julie Drews, 475 Riverside Dr., Suite 500, New York, NY 10115 Tel. (212)870-2347 Fax (212)870-2338

Email: cwu@churchwomen.org
Website: www.churchwomen.org

Circuit Rider, (bi-M) The United Methodist Church, Jessica Kelley, 201 Eighth Ave. S, Nashville, TN 37203 Tel. (615)749-6538 Fax (615)749-6061
Email: jkelley@umpublishing.org
Website: www.circuitrider.com

Clarion Herald, (W./45-Y) The Catholic Church, Peter P. Finney, Jr., P.O. Box 53247, 1000 Howard Ave. Suite 400, New Orleans, LA 70153 Tel. (504)596-3035 Fax (504)596-3020
Email: clarionherald@clarionherald.org
Website: www.clarionherald.org

Clergy Comminique, (2-Y) International Council of Community Churches, DeAnn Chatlosh, 21116 Washington Pky., Frankfort, IL 60423-3112 Tel. (815)464-5690 Fax (815)464-5692
Email: iccc60423@sbcglobal.net
Website: icccusa.com

The Clergy Journal, (9-Y) Nondenominational, Sharon L. Firle, Managing Editor & Clyde J. Steckel, Executive Editor, 6160 Carmen Avenue E, Inver Grove Heights, MN 55076-4422 Tel. (800)328-0200 Fax (651)457-4617
Email: editor@logostaff.com
Website: www.logosproductions.com

Club Connection, (Q) Assemblies of God, Debby Seler, 1445 Boonville Ave., Springfield, MO 65802-1894 Tel. (417)862-2781 Fax (417)862-0503
Email: clubconnection@ag.org
Website: www.missionettes.ag.org

College and University Dialogue, (3-Y) Seventh-day Adventist Church, John M. Fowler, 12501 Old Columbia Pike, Silver Spring, MD 20904-6600 Tel. Fax (301)622-9627
Website: dialogue.adventist.org

Collegiate Quarterly, (Q) Seventh-day Adventist Church, Lyndelle Brower Chiomenti, 12501 Old Columbia Pike, Silver Spring, MD 20904 Tel. (301)680-6160 Fax (301)680-6155

Columbia, (M) The Catholic Church, Tim S. Hickey, One Columbus Plaza, New Haven, CT 06510 Tel. (203)752-4398 Fax (203)752-4109
Email: info@kofc.org
Website: www.kofc.org

CommissionStories, (Q) International Mission Board, Southern Baptist Convention, Bill Bangham, Box 6767, Richmond, VA 23230-6767 Tel. (804)219-1373 Fax (804)219-1410

Email: commission@imb.org
Website: www.tconline.org

Common Lot, (Q) United Church of Christ, Martha J. Hunter, 700 Prospect Ave., Cleveland, OH 44115 Tel. (216)736-2150 Fax (216)736-2156

Commonweal, (bi-W) The Catholic Church, Paul Baumann, 475 Riverside Drive, Rm 405, New York, NY 10115 Tel. (212)662-4200 Fax (212)662-4183
Email: editors@commonwealmagazine.org
Website: www.commonwealmagazine.org

Communion Together, (bi-M) Church of God (Anderson, Indiana), David Farlow, P.O. Box 2420, 1201 E. 5th Street, Anderson, IN 46018-2420 Tel. (765)648-2182 Fax (765)648-2191
Email: dfarlow@chog.org
Website: Chog.org/Publications/Communion Together

The Congregationalist, (Q) National Association Congregational Christian Churches, Larry F. Sommers, P.O.Box 288, Oak Creek, WI 53154-0288 Tel. (800)262-1620 Fax (860)887-5715
Email: larry.sommers@charter.net
Website: www.congregationalist.org

Connections, (M Online) Alliance of Baptists, Mary Andreolli, 3939 Lavista Rd. Ste. E-122, Atlanta, GA 30084 Tel. (866) 7457609
Email: mary@allianceofbaptists.org
Website: www.allianceofbaptists.org

Context, (M) Nondenominational, Martin Marty, 205 W. Monroe St., Chicago, IL 60606-5013 Tel. (312)236-7782 Fax (312)236-8207
Email: editors@uscatholic.org
Website: www.contextonline.org

Covenant, (2-Y) Presbyterian Church in America, Jackie Fogas, Covenant Theological Seminary, 12330 Conway Road, St. Louis, MO 63141 Tel. (314)434-4044 Fax (314)434-4819
Email: covenantmagazine@covenant seminary.edu
Website: www.convenantseminary.edu

Converge Point, (4-Y) Converge Worldwide (Baptist General Conference), Bob Putman, 2002 S. Arlington Heights Rd., Arlington Heights, IL 60005 Tel. (847)228-0200 Fax (847)228-5376
Email: bob.putman@convergeww.org
Website: www.convergeworldwide.org

Cook Partners, (bi-M) Nondenominational online magazine on Christian publishing worldwide, David Cook, P.O. Box 36720, Colorado Springs, CO 80936-3672 Tel. (719)536-0100 x3519 Fax (719)536-3266

Email: Global@DavidCCook.org
Website: www.cookinterntional.org/
www.cook-partners.org

Cornerstone Connections, (Q) Seventh-day Adventist Church, Gary B. Swanson, 12501 Old Columbia Pike, Silver Spring, MD 20904 Tel. (301)680-6160 Fax (301)680-6155

The Covenant Companion, (M) Evangelical Covenant Church, Cathy Norman Peterson, Features Editor; Jane K. Swanson-Nystrom, Managing Editor, 8303 W. Higgins Rd.,, Chicago, IL 60631 Tel. (773)906-3328 Fax (773)907-3328
Email: communication@covchurch.org
Website: www.covchurch.org/cov/companion

Covenant Home Altar, (Q) Evangelical Covenant Church, Jane K. Swanson-Nystrom and Cathy Norman Peterson, 8303 W. Higgins Rd., Chicago, IL 60631 Tel. (773)784-3000 Fax (773)907-3328
Email: communication@covchurch.org
Website: www.covchurch.org

Covenant Quarterly, (Q) Evangelical Covenant Church, Paul E. Koptak, 3225 W. Foster Ave., Chicago, IL 60625-4895 Tel. (773)244-6242
Email: info@covenantbookstore.com

The Covenanter Witness, (11-Y) Reformed Presbyterian Church of North America, Drew Gordon and Lynne Gordon, 7408 Penn Ave., Pittsburgh, PA 15208 Tel. (412)241-0436 Fax (412)731-8861
Email: info@psalms4u.com
Website: www.psalms4u.com

Credinta—The Faith, (Q) The Romanian Orthodox Church in America, V. Rev. Archim. Dr. Vasile Vasilac, 45-03 48th Ave., Woodside, Queens, NY 11377 Tel. (313)893-8390

The Cumberland Presbyterian, (11-Y) Cumberland Presbyterian Church, Mark J. Davis, Cumberland Presbyterian Church, 8207 Traditional Place, Cordova, TN 38016-7414 Tel. (901)276-4572 x216 Fax (901)276-4578
Email: cp.editor@cumberland.org
Website: cpmag.org

Currents in Theology and Mission, (bi-M) Evangelical Lutheran Church in America, Kathleen D. Billman, Kurt K. Hendel, and Mark N. Swanson, Lutheran School of Theology at Chicago (w/Pacific Lutheran Theo. Seminary & Wartburg Theo. Seminary, 1100 E. 55th St., Chicago, IL 60615 Tel. (773)256-0751 Fax (773)256-0782
Email: currents@lstc.edu
Website: currentsjournal.org

Cutting Edge, (Q) Association of Vineyard Churches, Jeff Bailey, 2495 Howard St., Evanston, IL 60202 Tel. (847)328-4544 Fax (847)328-5153
Email: cuttingedge@vineyardusa.org
Website: www.vineyardusa.org/ publications/newsletters/cutting_edge

Decision, (11-Y) Nondenominational, Bob Paulson, 35 E 21st Street, 6th Floor, Charlotte, NC 28201-0001 Tel. (704)401-2426 Fax (704)401-3009
Email: decision@bgea.org
Website: www.billygraham.org/decisionmag

DisciplesWorld, (10-Y) Christian Church (Disciples of Christ) in the United States and Canada, Verity A. Jones, 6325 N. Guilford Ave Suite 213, Indianapolis, IN 46220 Tel. (317)375-8846 Fax (317)375-8849
Email: info@disciplesworld.com
Website: www.disciplesworld.com

EcuLink, (M online newsletter) Interdenominational, Melissa Dixon, 475 Riverside Drive, 8th Floor, New York, NY 10115-0050 Tel. (212)870-2227 Fax (212)870-2030
Email: mdixon@ncccusa.org
Website: www.eculink.org

Ecumenical Trends, (M) The Catholic Church, Rev. James Loughran, SA, Graymoor Ecumenical & Interreligious Institute, P.O. Box 300, Garrison, NY 10524-0300 Tel. (845)424-3671 ext. 3303 Fax (845)424-2163
Email: jlgeii@aol.com
Website: www.geii.org

EFCA Today, (bi-M) The Evangelical Free Church of America, Mr. Tim Addington, 901 East 78th St., Minneapolis, MN 55420 Tel. (877)293-5653 Fax (952)853-8488
Email: today@efca.org
Website: www.efca.org

El Centinela, (Q) Seventh-day Adventist Church, Miguel Valdivia/Milton Peverini, Christian Record Services for the Blind, P.O. Box 6097, Lincoln, NE 68506-0097 Tel. (402)488-0981 Fax (402)488-7582
Email: editorial@christianrecord.org
Website: www.christianrecord.org

Eleventh Hour Messenger, (bi-M) Wesleyan Holiness Association of Churches, John Brewer, 11411 N US Hwy 27, Fountain City, IN 47341-9757 Tel. (317)584-3199

Encounter (Audio), (Q) Seventh-day Adventist Church, Bert Williams, Christian Record Services for the Blind, P. O. Box 6097, Lincoln, NE 68506 Tel. 402-488-0981 Fax (402)488-7582

Email: editorial@christianrecord.org
Website: www.christianrecord.org

Enrichment: A Journal for Pentecostal Ministry, (Q) Assemblies of God, George P. Wood, Rick Knoth, Managing Editors, 1445 N. Boonville Ave., Springfield, MO 65802 Tel. (417)862-2781 Fax (417)862-0416
Email: rKnoth@ag.org
Website: www.enrichmentjournal.ag.org

The Ensign, (M) The Church of Jesus Christ of Latter-day Saints, Don L. Searle, Managing Editor, 50 E North Temple Street, Room 2420, Salt Lake City, UT 84150 Tel. (801)240-2950 Fax (801)240-2270
Email: ensign@ldschurch.org
Website: www.magazines.lds.org

Episcopal Life, (M) The Episcopal Church, Jerrold Hames, 815 Second Ave., New York, NY 10017-4503 Tel. (800)334-7626 Fax (212)949-8059
Email: jhames@episcopalchurch.org
Website: www.episcopal-life.org

Equip, (bi-M) Presbyterian Church in America, Dr. Charles Dunahoo, 1700 N. Brown Road Ste. 102, Lawrenceville, GA 30043 Tel. (678)825-1100 Fax (678)825.1101
Email: cep@pcanet.org
Website: pcanet.org

The Evangel, (Q) The Evangelical Church Alliance, Dr. Henry A. (Hank) Roso, 205 W. Broadway, P. O. Box 9, Bradley, IL 60915 Tel. (815)937-0720 Fax (815)937-0001
Email: hank@ecainternatinal.org
Website: www.ecainternational.org

The Evangel, (bi-M) American Association of Lutheran Churches, The, Rev. Richard Shields, 921 East Dupont Road, Suite 920, Ft. Wayne, IN 46825-1551 Tel. (260)465-3213 Fax (260)465-3215
Email: theaalc@aol.com; evangel@taalc.org
Website: www.taalc.com

The Evangelical Advocate, (bi-M) Churches of Christ in Christian Union, Ralph Hux, P.O. Box 10, Circleville, OH 43113 Tel. (740)474-8856 ext. 712 Fax (740)477-7766
Email: doc@cccuhq.org
Website: www.cccuhq.org

Evangelical Challenge, (Q) The Evangelical Church, Shirley Roehl, 9421 West River Road, Minneapolis, MN 55444 Tel. (763)424-2589 Fax (763)424-9230
Email: ecdenom@usfamily.net
Website: www.theevangelicalchurch.org

The Evangelist, (W) The Roman Catholic Church, Kate Blain, 40 N. Main Ave., Albany, NY 12203 Tel. (518)453-6688 Fax (518)453-8448
Email: k.blain@rcda.org
Website: www.evangelist.org

Explorations, (Q) Nondenominational, Irvin J. Borowsky, 321 Chestnut Street, 4th Floor, Philadelphia, PA 19106-2779 Tel. (215)925-2800 Fax (215)925-3800
Email: aii@interfaith-scholars.org

Extension, (M) The Catholic Church, Bradley Collins, Editor, 150 S. Wacker Drive, 20th Floor, Chicago, IL 60606 Tel. (312)236-7240 Fax (312)236-5276
Email: magazine@catholic-extension.org
Website: www.catholic-extension.org

Faith & Fellowship, (6-Y) Church of the Lutheran Brethren of America, Brent Julliot, P.O. Box 655, Fergus Falls, MN 56538 Tel. (218)736-7357 Fax (218)736-2200
Email: ffpress@clba.org
Website: www.faithandfellowship.org

Faith in Action, (I) The United Methodist Church, vacant, 100 Maryland Ave. NE, Washington, DC 20002 Tel. (202)488-5621 Fax (202)488-1617
Website: http://www.umc-gbcs.org/site/c.frLJK2PKLqF/b.2798475/k.7A8F/Faith_in_Action.htm

Faith-Life, (bi-M) Lutheran, Pastor Marcus Albrecht, 2107 N. Alexander St., Appleton, WI 54911 Tel. (920)733-1839 Fax (920)733-4834
Email: malbrecht@milwpc.com

FEConnections, (3-Y) Fellowship of Evangelical Churches, Rocky Rocholl, 1420 Kerrway Ct., Fort Wayne, IN 46805 Tel. (260)423-3649 Fax (260)420-1905
Email: FECMinistries@FECMinistries.org
Website: www.fecministries.org

Fellowship, (Q) Interfaith, Ethan Vesely-Flad, Box 271, Nyack, NY 10960-0271 Tel. (845)358-4601 Fax (845)358-4924
Email: fellowship@forusa.org
Website: www.forusa.org

Fellowship Focus, (bi-M) Fellowship of Evangelical Bible Churches, Sharon K. Berg, 3339 N 109th Plz, Omaha, NE 68164-2908 Tel. (402)965-3860 Fax (402)965-3871
Email: fellowshipfocus@febcministries.org
Website: www.febcministries.org

Fellowship Tidings, (Q) Full Gospel Fellowship of Churches and Ministers International, Anita Sullivan, 1000 N. Beltline Road, Irving, TX 75061 Tel. (214)492-1254 Fax (214)492-1736

Email: FGFCMI@aol.com
Website: www.thefellowshiptoday.com

FGConnections, (2-Y) Friends General Conference, Lucy Duncan, Deborah Fisch, 1216 Arch Street 2B, Philadelphia, PA 19107 Tel. (215)561-1700 Fax (215)561-0759 Email: connections@fgcquaker.org Website: www.fgcquaker.org/fgconnections

Firm Foundation, (M) Churches of Christ, H. A. Dobbs, P.O. Box 690192, Houston, TX 77269-0192 Tel. (713)469-3102 Email: had@worldnet.att.net

First Monday, (M) Seventh-day Adventist Church, Ken Flemmer, 12501 Old Columbia Pike, Silver Spring, MD 20904-6600 Tel. (800)424-2372 Fax (301)680-6370 Email: ken.flemmer@adra.org Website: www.adra.org

First Things: A Monthly Journal of Religion & Public Life, (10-Y) Interdenominational, Russell R. Reno, 35 East 21st Street, 6th Floor, New York, NY 10010 Tel. (212)627-1985 Fax (212)627-2184 Email: ft@firstthings.com Website: www.firstthings.com

The Flaming Sword, (M) Bible Holiness Church, Susan Davolt, 10th St. & College Ave., Independence, KS 67301 Tel. (316)331-2580 Fax (316)331-2580

For God and Country, (Q) Seventh-Day Adventist Church, Deena Bartel-Wagner - Editor; Gary R. Councell - Executive Editor, Adventist Chaplaincy Ministries, General Conference of Seventh-day Adventists, 12501 Old Columbia Pike, Silver Spring, MD 20904-6600 Tel. (301)860-6780 Fax (301)680-6783 Email: acm@gc.adventist.org Website: www.nad.adventistchaplains.org

Foresee, (bi-M) Conservative Congregational Christian Conference, Ken McGarvey, 8941 Highway 5, Lake Elmo, Lake Elmo, MN 55042 Tel. (651)739-1474 Fax (651)739-0750 Email: dmjohnson@ccccusa.com Website: www.ccccusa.com

Forum Letter, (M) Independent, Intra-Lutheran (companion publication to the quarterly, Lutheran Forum), Pastor Richard O. Johnson, Peace Lutheran Church, P. O. Box 1394, Grass Valley, CA 95945 Tel. (530)273-9631 Fax (530)274-2772 Email: roj@nccn.net Website: www.alpb.org

Forward, (Q) United Pentecostal Church International, Rev. J. L. Hall, 8855 Dunn Rd., Hazelwood, MO 63042 Tel. (314)837-7300

Fax (314)837-4503 Email: info@upci.org Website: www.upci.org

Forward in Christ, (M) Wisconsin Evangelical Lutheran Synod, Rev. John A. Braun, 2929 N. Mayfair Rd., Milwaukee, WI 53222 Tel. (414)256-3230 Fax (414)256-3230 Email: fic@wels.net Website: www.wels.net

Foursquare World Advance, (Q, w/ a bonus issue) International Church of the Foursquare Gospel, Dr. Ron Williams, P.O. Box 26902, 1910 W. Sunset Blvd., Ste 400, Los Angeles, CA 90026-0176 Tel. (213)989-4230 Fax (213) 989-4544 Email: comm@foursquare.org Website: www.advancemagazine.org

Free Will Baptist Gem, (M) National Association of Free Will Baptists, Gary Fry, P.O. Box 991/ 100 E. Commercial Street, Lebanon, MO 65530 Tel. (417)532-9131 Fax (417)588-7911 Email: gwfry@webound.com; gwfry@mofwb.org Website: www.mofwb.org

Friend Magazine, (M) The Church of Jesus Christ of Latter-day Saints, Vivian Paulsen, 50 E South Temple Street, 24th Fl, Salt Lake City, UT 84150 Tel. (801)240-2210 Fax (801)240-2270

Friends Bulletin, (10-Y) Religious Society of Friends, Anthony Manousos, 3223 Danaha St., Torrance, CA 90505 Tel. (310)-325-3581 Email: friendsbul@aol.com Website: www.quaker.org/western/

Friends Journal, (M) Religious Society of Friends, Susan Corson-Finnerty, Publisher & Exec. Editor, 1216 Arch St., 2A, Philadelphia, PA 19107-2835 Tel. (215)563-8629 Fax (215) 568-1377 Email: info@friendsjournal.org Website: www.friendsjournal.org

The Friends Voice, (3-Y) Evangelical Friends International—North America Region, Dr. Becky Towne, Sr. Editor, Dr. Kathy Roblyer, Assoc. Editor, 2748 E. Pikes Peak Ave, Colorado Springs, CO 80909 Email: thevoice@evangelicalfriends.org Website: www.evangelical-friends.org/ www.quaker.org/periodicals.html

Front Line, (3-Y) Conservative Baptist Association of America, Al Russell, P.O. Box 68, Clearbrook, MN 56634 Tel. (218)776-2513 Fax (509)356-7112 Email: chapruss@cbamerica.org Website: www.cbchaplains.net

Full Gospel Ministries Outreach Report, (Q) Full Gospel Assemblies International, Simeon Strauser, P.O. Box 1230, Coatsville, PA 19320 Tel. (610)857-2357 Fax (610)857-3109

The Gem, (W) Churches of God, General Conference, Rachel Foreman, P.O. Box 926, Findlay, OH 45839 Tel. (419)424-1961 Fax (419)424-3433
Email: communications@cggc.org
Website: www.cggc.org

God's Field, (bi-W, except Dec.) Polish National Catholic Church of America and Canada, Most Rev. Anthony Mikovsky, 1006 Pittston Ave., Scranton, PA 18505-4109 Tel. (570)346-9131 Fax (570)346-2188
Email: bpmikovsky@pncc.org
Website: www.pncc.org

Good News - Buna Vestire, (Q) The Romanian Orthodox Episcopate of America, The Romanian Orthodox Deanery of Canada, 11400 88St. SE, Regina, SK S4V 0W7 Tel. (403)203-7033 Fax (306)525-9650
Email: fatherlupu@shaw.ca
Website: www.romanianorthodoxdeanery.org

Gospel Advocate, (M) Churches of Christ, Neil W. Anderson, 1006 Elm Hill Pike, Nashville, TN 37202 Tel. (615)254-8781 Fax (615)254-7411
Email: info@gospeladvocate.com
Website: www.gospeladvocate.com

The Gospel Herald, (M) Church of God, Mountain Assembly, Inc., J. Jon Waldon IV, P.O. Box 157, Jellico, TN 37762 Tel. (423)784-8260 Fax (423)784-3258
Email: cgmahdq@jellico.com
Website: www.cgmahdq.org

The Gospel Light, (2-Y) The Bible Church of Christ, Inc., Carole Crenshaw, 1358 Morris Ave., Bronx, NY 10456 Tel. (718)588-2284 Fax (718)992-5597
Website: www.thebiblechurchofchrist.org

The Gospel Messenger, (Q) Congregational Holiness Church, Inc., Rev. Danny K. Jones, Congregational Holiness Church, 3888 Fayetteville Highway, Griffin, GA 30223 Tel. (770-228-4833 Fax (770-228-1177
Email: messenger@CHChurch.com
Website: www.CHChurch.com

The Gospel Truth, (bi-Y) Church of the Living God, C.W.F.F., Robert D. Tyler, 430 Forest Avenue, Cincinnati, OH 45229 Tel. (513)569-5660 Fax (513)569-5661
Email: national@ctlgcwff.org
Website: www.ctlgcwff.org

Grow Magazine, (Q) Church of the Nazarene, Bryon K. McLaughlin, 6401 The Paseo, Kansas City, MO 64131 Tel. (816)333-7000 ext. 2828 Fax (816)523-1872
Email: gpeditor@nazarene.orgg
Website: www.graceandpeacemagazine.org

Guide, (W) Seventh-day Adventist Church, Randy Fishell, 55 W. Oak Ridge Dr., Hagerstown, MD 21740 Tel. (301)393-4035 Fax (301)393-4055
Email: guide@rhpa.org
Website: www.guidemagazine.org

The Handmaiden, (Q) The Antiochian Orthodox Christian Archdiocese of North America, Virginia Nieuwsma, P.O. Box 748, Chesterton, IN 46304 Tel. (800)967-7377 Fax (831)336-8882
Email: czell@conciliarpress.com
Website: www.conciliarpress.com

The Happy Harvester, (M) Church of God of Prophecy, Diane Pace, P.O. Box 2910, Cleveland, TN 37320-2910 Tel. (423)559-5435 Fax (423)559-5444
Email: JoDiPace@wingnet.net

Herald, (M) Community of Christ, Editorial Board, 1001 W. Walnut, Independence, MO 64050 Tel. (816)833-1000 Fax (816)521-3043
Email: Herald@cofochrist.org
Website: www.heraldhouse.org or www.cofchrist.org

The Herald of Christian Science, (M, bi-M, Q, I) Church of Christ, Scientist/ Christian Science, Mary M. Trammell, Editor-in-Chief, The Christian Science Publishing Society, 210 Massachusetts Avenue, Boston, MA 02115-3195 Tel. (617) 450-2000 Fax (617) 450-2893
Email: lessal@csps.com or herald@csps.com
Website: www.csherald.com

Higher Way, (Q) Apostolic Faith Mission of Portland, Oregon, Darrel D. Lee, 6615 S.E. 52nd Ave., Portland, OR 97206 Tel. (503)777-1741 Fax (503)777-1743
Email: kbarrett@apostolicfaith.org
Website: www.apostolicfaith.org

Holiness Today, (bi-M) Church of the Nazarene, David J. Felter, 17001 Prairie Star Parkway, Lenexa, KS 66220 Tel. (913)577-0500 Fax (913)577-0857
Email: HolinessToday@nazarene.org
Website: www.HolinessToday.com

Homiletic and Pastoral Review, (M) The Roman Catholic Church, Kenneth Baker, 50 S Franklin Tpk, P. O. Box 297, Ramsey, NJ 07446 Tel. (201)236-9336

Horizons, (M) Christian Churches and Churches of Christ, Leah Ellison Bradley, Susan Jackson Dowd, 100 Witherspoon St, Louisville, KY 40202-1396 Tel. (505)569-5368 Fax (502)569-8085
Email: msa@missionservices.org
Website: www.missionservices.org

Horizons, (7-Y) Presbyterian Church (U.S.A.), Susan Jackson Dowd, Presbyterian Women, 100 Witherspoon St., Louisville, KY 40202 Tel. (502)569-5368 Fax (502)569-8085
Email: susan.jackson-dowd@pcusa.org
Website: wwwhorizons.pcusa.org

The Inclusive Pulpit, (Y) International Council of Community Churches, Larry and Carolyn Dipboye, 21116 Washington Pky., Frankfort, IL 60423-3112 Tel. (815)464-5690 Fax (815) 464-5692
Email: iccc60423@fbcglobal.net
Website: icccusa.com

Insight Into, (bi-M) Netherlands Reformed Congregations, Mr. Schipper, 4732 E. C Avenue, Kalamazoo, MI 49004 Tel. (269)349-9448

International Bulletin of Missionary Research, (Q) Nondenominational, Jonathan J. Bonk, Overseas Ministries Study Center, 490 Prospect St., New Haven, CT 06511-2196 Tel. (203)624-6672 Fax (203)865-2857
Email: ibmr@OMSC.org
Website: www.OMSC.org
www.DACB.org
www.internationalbulletin.org

Interpretation: A Journal of Bible and Theology, (Q) Presbyterian, Sam Balentine, 3401 Brook Rd., Richmond, VA 23227 Tel. (804)278-4296 Fax (804)278-4208
Email: email@interpretation.org
Website: www.interpretation.org

el Intérprete, (bi-M) The United Methodist Church, Amanda M. Bachus, Director/Editor, Spanish Resources, United Methodist Communications P.O. Box 320, Nashville, TN 37202-0320 Tel. (615)742-5113 Fax (615)742-5460
Email: abachus@umcom.org
Website: www.interpretermagazine.org;
www.noticias.umc.org

El Interprete (Spanish), (6-Y) United Methodist Church, Amanda Bachus, UM Communications, P.O. Box 320, Nashville, TN 37202-0320 Tel. (615)742.5113 Fax 615-742-5469
Email: abachus@umcom.org
Website: umc.org/elinterprete

Interpreter, (6-Y) United Methodist Church, Kathy Noble, United Methodist Communi-cations, P.O. Box 320, Nashville, TN 37202-0320 Tel. (615)742-5441 Fax (615)742-5469
Email: knoble@umcom.org
Website: www.interpretermagazine.org

IPHC Experience, (bi-M) International Pentecostal Holiness Church, Shirley Spencer, P.O. Box 12609, Oklahoma City, OK 73157 Tel. (405)787-7110 Fax (405)789-3957
Website: www.iphc.org/wms

John Three Sixteen, (Q) Bible Holiness Church, Ms. Diane Baber, Old Pathes Tract Society INC, 11298 Old Paths Lane, Shoals, IN 47581-7234 Tel. (812)247-2560 Fax (812) 247-2476
Email: optskem@juno.com

Journal of Adventist Education, (5-Y) Seventh-day Adventist Church, Beverly J. Robinson-Rumble, 12501 Old Columbia Pike, Silver Spring, MD 20904-6600 Tel. (301)680-5075 / (301)680-5069 Fax (301)622-9627
Email: rumbleb@gc.adventist.org;
goffc@gc.adventist.org
Website: http://jae.adventist.org

Journal of the American Academy of Religion, (Q) Nondenominational, Charles T. Mathewes, Department of Religous Studies, University of Virginia, P. O. Box 400126, Charlottesville, VA 22904-4126
Email: jaar@virginia.edu
Website: www.aarweb.org

Journal of Christian Education, (Q) African Methodist Episcopal Church, Kenneth H. Hill, 500 Eighth Ave., S., Nashville, TN 37203 Tel. (615)242-1420 Fax (615)726-1866
Email: cedoffice@ameced.com
Website: www.ameced.com

Journal of Ecumenical Studies, (Q) Interdenominational/Interfaith, Leonard Swidler, Temple Univ. (022-38), 1114 West Berks St., Philadelphia, PA 19122-6090 Tel. (215)204-7714 Fax (215)204-4569
Email: nkrody@temple.edu
Website: http://journal.jesdialogue.org/

The Journal of Pastoral Care & Counseling, (Q) Nondenominational, Orlo Strunk, Jr., 1068 Harbor Dr., SW, Calabash, NC 28467 Tel. (910)579-5084 Fax (910)579-5084
Email: jpcp@jpcp.org
Website: www.jpcp.org

Journal of Presbyterian History, (bi-Y) Presbyterian Church (U.S.A.), James H. Moorhead; Frederick J. Heuser, Jr., 425 Lombard St., Philadelphia, PA 19147 Tel. (215)627-1852 Fax (215)627-0509
Email: jph@history.pcusa.org
Website: www.history.pcusa.org

Journal From the Radical Reformation, (Periodic via e-mail) Church of God General Conference (Morrow, GA), Kent Ross, Sr. Editor, 2020 Avalon Parkway, Suite 400, McDonough, GA 30253 Tel. (678)833-1839 Fax (678)833-1853
Email: info@abc-coggc.org
Website: www.abc-coggc.org

Journal of Theology, (Q) Church of the Lutheran Confession, Prof. Steve Sippert, Immanuel Lutheran College, 501 Grover Rd., Eau Claire, WI 54701-7199 Tel. (715)832-9936 Fax (715)836-6634
Email: ilcgreekprof@yahoo.com
Website: www.clcpub/clc/clc.html

The Joyful Noiseletter, (10-Y) Interdenominational, Cal Samra, P.O. Box 895, Portage, MI 49081-0895 Tel. (269)324-0990
Email: joyfulnz@aol.com
Website: www.joyfulnoiseletter.com

Judaism, (Q) Jewish (Sponsored by the American Jewish Conference), Rabbi Shammai Engelmayer, 15 E. 84th St., New York, NY 10028 Tel. (212)879-4500 Fax (212)249-3672
Email: contact@ajcongress.org
Website: humwww.ucsc.edu/judaism/judaism.html

Key Lay Notes, (2-Y) International Council of Community Churches, DeAnn Chatlosh, 21116 Washington Pky., Frankfort, IL 60423-3112 Tel. (815)464-5690 Fax (815)464-5692
Email: iccc60423@sbcglobal.net
Website: icccusa.com

The Lantern, (bi-M) National Baptist Convention of America, Inc., Robert Jeffrey, 1320 Pierre Avenue, Shreveport, LA 71103 Tel. (318)221-3701 Fax (318)222-7512

Leadership: Real Ministry in a Complex World, (Q) Nondenominational, Marshall Shelley, 465 Gundersen Dr., Carol Stream, IL 60188 Tel. (630)260-6200 Fax (630)260-8428
Email: LJeditor@leadershipjournal.net
Website: www.Leadershipjournal.net

Learning and Living, (Q) Netherlands Reformed Congregations, David Engelsma, 1000 Ball, Northeast, Grandrapids, MI 49505 Tel. (616)458-4367 Fax (616)458-8532
Email: engelsma@plymouthchristian.us

Liberty, (bi-M) Seventh-day Adventist Church, Clifford R. Goldstein, 12501 Old Columbia Pike, Silver Spring, MD 20904 Tel. (301)680-6691 Fax (301)680-6695

Lifeglow, Large Print, (6-Y) Seventh-day Adventist Church, Bert Williams, Christian Record Services for the Blind, P.O. Box 6097, Lincoln, NE 68506 Tel. (402)488-0981 Fax (402)488-7582
Email: editorial@christianrecord.org
Website: www.christianrecord.org

Light and Life Magazine, (bi-M) Free Methodist Church, Douglas M. Newton, P.O. Box 535002, Indianapolis, IN 46253-5002 Tel. (317)244-3660
Email: llmeditor@fmcna.org
Website: www.freemethodistchurch.org

Liguorian, (10-Y) The Catholic Church, Publisher: Mathew Kessler, C.SS.R., 1 Liguori Dr., Liguori, MO 63057 Tel. (636)464-2500 Fax (636)464-8449
Email: liguorianeditor@liguori.org
Website: www.liguorian.org

Listen, (Sep.-May) Seventh-day Adventist Church, Céleste Walker, 55 W. Oak Ridge Dr., Hagerstown, MD 21740 Tel. (301)393-4082 Fax (301)393-4055
Email: listen@healthconnection.org
Website: www.listenmagazine.org

Living Orthodoxy, (bi-M) The Russian Orthodox Church Outside of Russia, Fr. Gregory Williams, 1180 Orthodox Way, Liberty, TN 37095 Tel. (615)536-5239 Fax (615)536-5945
Email: info@sjkp.org
Website: www.sjkp.org

The Long Island Catholic, (W) The Roman Catholic Church, Richard Hinshaw, P.O. Box 9000, 200 W Centennial Ave Suite 201, Roosevelt, NY 11575 Tel. (516)594-1000 Fax (516)594-1092
Website: www.licatholic.org

The Lookout, (W) Christian Churches and Churches of Christ, Shawn McMullen, 8805 Governor's Hill Drive, Suite 400, Cincinnati, OH 45249 Tel. (513)931-4050 ext. 6839 Fax (513)931-0950
Email: lookout@standardpub.com
Website: www.lookoutmag.com

Lumicon Digital Productions, (I) Independent, Protestant, Rev. Dr. Tom Boomershine, UMR Communications, P.O. Box 660275, Dallas, TX 75266-0275 Tel. (214)630-6495 Fax (214)630-0079
Email: tboom@umr.org
Website: www.lumicon.org

The Lutheran, (M) Evangelical Lutheran Church in America, Daniel J. Lehmann, 8765 W. Higgins Rd., Chicago, IL 60631-4183 Tel. (773)380-2540 Fax (773)380-2751
Email: lutheran@elca.org
Website: www.thelutheran.org

334

The Lutheran Ambassador, (16-Y) The Association of Free Lutheran Congregations, Craig Johnson, 575 34th Street, Astoria, OR 97103 Tel. (541)687-8643 Fax (541)683-8496 Email: cjohnson@efn.org

Lutheran Forum, (Q) Interdenominational Lutheran, Ronald B. Bagnall, 207 Hillcrest Ave., Trenton, NJ 08618 Tel. (856)696-0417

The Lutheran Layman, (bi-M) The Lutheran Church—Missouri Synod, Gerald Perschbacher, 660 Mason Ridge Center Dr, St. Louis, MO 63141-8557 Tel. (314)317-4100 Fax (314)317-4295
Website: www.lhm.org

Lutheran Partners, (bi-M) Evangelical Lutheran Church in America, William A. Decker, 8765 W. Higgins Rd., Chicago, IL 60631-4101 Tel. (773)380-2884 Fax (773)380-2829
Email: lutheran.partners@elca.org
Website: www.elca.org/lutheranpartners

Lutheran Sentinel, (M) Evangelical Lutheran Synod, Theodore Gullixson, 5530 Englewood Dr., Madison, WI 53705 Tel. (641)585-1683 Fax (641)585-1683
Email: Theodore Gullixson

Lutheran Spokesman, (M) Church of the Lutheran Confession, Rev. Paul Fleischer, 1741 E. 22nd St., Cheyenne, WY 82001 Tel. (307)638-8006
Email: paulgf@qwestoffice.net
Website: www.lutheranspokesman.org

Lutheran Synod Quarterly, (Q) Evangelical Lutheran Synod, G.R. Schmeling, Bethany Lutheran Theological Semi, 6 Browns Ct., Mankato, MN 56001 Tel. (507)344-7855 Fax (507)344-7426
Email: elsynod@blc.edu
Website: www.blts.edu

The Lutheran Witness, (M, Ju/Jy combined) The Lutheran Church—Missouri Synod, Adriane Dorr, 1333 S. Kirkwood Road, St. Louis, MO 63122-7295 Tel. (314)965-9000 Fax (314)966-1126
Email: lutheran.witness@lcms.org
Website: www.lcms.org/witness

Lutheran Woman Today, (10-Y) Evangelical Lutheran Church in America, Kate Sprutta Elliott, Women of the ELCA, 8765 W. Higgins Rd., Chicago, IL 60631-4101 Tel. (773)380-2730 Fax (773)380-2419
Email: lwt@elca.org
Website: www.lutheranwomantoday.org

Lyceum Spotlight, (10-Y) National Spiritualist Association of Churches, Rev. Cosie Allen,

P.O.Box 93252, Las Vegas, NV 89193 Tel. (616)241-2761 Fax (616)241-4703
Email: Spotlight@NSAC.Org
Website: www.nsac.org

Magyar Egyhaz—Magyar Church, (Q) Hungarian Reformed Church in America, Stephen Szabo, 464 Forest Ave., Paramus, NJ 07652 Tel. (201)262-2338 Fax (845)359-5771

Mar Thoma Messenger, (Q) Mar Thoma Syrian Church of India, Eapen Daniel, 2320 S. Merrick Ave, Merrick, NY 11566 Tel. (516)377-3311 Fax (516)377-3322
Email: marthoma@aol.com

Maranatha, (Q) Advent Christian Church, Justin Nash, P.O. Box 690848, Charlotte, NC 28227 Tel. (704)545-6161 Fax (704)573-0712
Email: jnash@acgc.us
Website: www.acgc.us

Marriage Partnership, (I) Nondenominational, Ginger Kolbaba, 465 Gundersen Dr., Carol Stream, IL 60188 Tel. (630)260-6200 Fax (630)260-0114
Email: mp@marriagepartnership.com
Website: www.marriagepartnership.com

Mature Years, (Q) The United Methodist Church, Marvin W. Cropsey, 201 Eighth Ave. S, Nashville, TN 37202 Tel. (615)749-6292 Fax (615)749-6512
Email: matureyears@umpublishing.org

The Mennonite, (24-Y) Mennonite Church USA, Everett J. Thomas, 1700 S. Main St., Goshen, IN 46526 Tel. (574)535-6051 Fax (574)535-6050
Email: editor@themennonite.org
Website: www.themennonite.org

Mennonite Historical Bulletin, (Q) Mennonite Church USA, Richard Preheim, 1700 South Main St., Goshen, IN 46526 Tel. (574)523-3080 Fax (574)535-7756
Email: archives@mennoniteusa.org
Website: www.MennoniteUSA.org/history

Mennonite Quarterly Review, (Q) Mennonite Church, John D. Roth, 1700 S. Main St., Goshen, IN 46526 Tel. (574)535-7433 Fax (574)535-7438
Email: MQR@goshen.edu
Website: www.goshen.edu/mqr

Message, (bi-M) Seventh-day Adventist Church, Dr. Washington Johnson II, D.Min., Review and Herald Publishing Association, 55 West Oak Ridge Dr., Hagerstown, MD 21740 Tel. (301)393-3000 Fax 301-393-4103
Email: wjohnson@rhpa.org
Website: messagemagazine.org

Message of the Open Bible, (bi-M) Open Bible Standard Churches, Inc., Andrea Johnson, 2020 Bell Ave., Des Moines, IA 50315-1096 Tel. (515)288-6761 Fax (515)288-2510
Email: message@openbible.org
Website: www.openbible.org

The Messenger, (M) The Swedenborgian Church, Herb Ziegler, Central Office, 11 Higland Ave, Newtonville, MA 02460 Tel. (617)969-4240
Email: messenger@swedenborg.org
Website: www.swedenborg.org

The Messenger, (M) Pentecostal Free Will Baptist Church, Inc., Herb Ziegler, Central Office, 11 Higland Ave, Newtonville, MA 02460 Tel. (617)969-4240 Fax (910)892-6876
Email: messenger@swedenborg.org

Messenger, (10-Y) Church of the Brethren, Randy Miller (Interim), 1451 Dundee Ave., Elgin, IL 60120 Tel. (847)742-5100 Fax (847)742-1407
Email: messenger@brethren.org
Website: www.brethren.org/messenger

Messenger of Truth, (bi-W) Church of God in Christ (Mennonite), Gladwin Koehn, P.O. Box 230, Moundridge, KS 67107 Tel. (620)345-2532 Fax (620)345-2582
Email: gospelpublishers@cogicm.org

Methodist History, (Q) The United Methodist Church, Robert J. Williams, P.O. Box 127, Madison, NJ 07940 Tel. (973)408-3189 Fax (973)408-3909
Email: rwilliams@gcah.org
Website: www.gcah.org

Ministry, (M) Seventh-day Adventist Church, Derek J. Morris, 12501 Old Columbia Pike, Silver Spring, MD 20904 Tel. (301)680-6510 Fax (301)680-6502
Email: ministrymagazine@gc.adventist.org
Website: www.MinistryMagazine.org

Mission, Adult, and Youth Children's Editions, (Q) Seventh-day Adventist Church, Charlotte Ishkanian, 12501 Old Columbia Pike, Silver Spring, MD 20904 Tel. (301)680-6167 Fax (301)680-6155
Email: information@adventistmission.org; missioneditor@gt.adventist.org
Website: www.adventistmissions

Mission Herald, (Q) National Baptist Convention, U.S.A., Inc., Dr. Bruce N. Alick, 701 S. 19th Street, Philadelphia, PA 19146 Tel. (215)735-9853 Fax (215)735-1721

Missionary Church Today, (Q) Missionary Church, Rev. Thomas Murphy, P.O. Box 9127, Ft. Wayne, IN 46899 Tel. (260)747-2027 Fax (260)747-5331
Email: tommurphy@mcusa.org
Website: www.mcusa.org

The Missionary Messenger, (bi-M) Cumberland Presbyterian Church, George Estes, 8207 Traditional Place, Cordova, TN 38016 Tel. (901)276-9988 Fax (901)751-2104
Email: gestes@cumberland.org
Website: cumberland.org

The Missionary Messenger, (bi-M) Cumberland Presbyterian Church, George R. Estes, 8207 Traditional Place, Cordova, TN 38016-7414 Tel. (901)276-9988 Fax (901)276-4578
Email: messenger@cumberland.org
Website: ww.cumberland.org/bom/Communication_and_Publication_Unit/Missionary Messenger.htm

Missionary Seer, (bi-M) African Methodist Episcopal Zion Church, Rev. Kermit J. DeGraffenreidt, 475 Riverside Dr., Rm. 1935, New York, NY 10115 Tel. (212)870-2952 Fax (212)870-2808
Email: domkd5@aol.com

The Missionary Signal, (bi-M) Churches of God, General Conference, Rachel Foreman, P.O. Box 926, Findlay, OH 45839 Tel. (419)424-1961 Fax (419)424-3433
Email: communications@cggc.org
Website: cggc.org

The Moravian, (10-Y) Moravian Church in North America (Unitas Fratrum), Michael Riess-Dir. Of Communication, Interprovincial Bd. Of Communication, 1021 Center St., P.O. Box 1245, Bethlehem, PA 18016 Tel. (610)867-0593/800-732-0591 Fax (610)866-9223
Email: pubs@mcnp.org
Website: www.moravian.org

The Mother Church, (bi-M) Western Diocese of the Armenian Church of North America, Archpriest Fr. Sipan Mekhsian, 3325 N. Glenoaks Blvd., Burbank, CA 91504 Tel. (818)558-7474 Fax (818)558-6333
Email: mgizlechyan@armenianchurchwd.com
Website: www.armenianchurchwd.com

Multiply, (Q) Presbyterian Church in America, Fred Marsh, Mission to North America, 1700 North Brown Road, Ste. 101, Lawrenceville, GA 30044 Tel. (678)825-1200 Fax (678)825-1201
Email: mna@pcanet.org
Website: www.pca-mna.org

NABtoday for you, (2 -Y) North American Baptist Conference, Julie Ripoli, 1 So 210

Summit Ave., Oakbrook Terrace, IL 60181 Tel. (630)495-2000 Fax (630)495-3301
Email: serve@nabconference.org
Website: www.nabconference.org

NAE Insight, (Q) Interdenominational, Vacant, 701 G St SW, Washington, DC 20024 Tel. (202)789-1011 Fax (202)842-0392
Email: info@nae.net
Website: www.nae.net

NAE Washington Insight, (Q) Interdenominational, Vacant, 701 G Street, SW, Washington, DC 20024 Tel. (202)789-1011 Fax (202)842-0392
Email: info@nae.net
Website: www.nae.net

National Catholic Reporter, (44-Y) The Catholic Church, Tom Roberts, P.O. Box 419281, Kansas City, MO 64141 Tel. (816)531-0538 Fax (816)968-2280
Email: trobert@ncr.org
Website: www.NCRonline.org

The National Spiritualist Summit, (M) National Spiritualist Association of Churches, Rev. Sandra Pfortmiller, 3521 W. Topeka Dr., Glendale, AZ 85308-2325 Tel. (623)581-6686 Fax (623)581-5544
Website: www.nsac.org

Network, (Q) Presbyterian Church in America, Marty Davis, 1600 North Brown Road, Lawrenceville, GA 30043 Tel. (678)823-0004 Fax (678)823-0027
Email: info@mfw.org
Website: www.mtw.org

New Church Life, (M) General Church of the New Jerusalem, Rev. Donald L. Rose, Box 277, Bryn Athyn, PA 19009 Tel. (215)947-6225 ext. 209 Fax (215)938-1871
Email: DonR@BACS-GC.org
Website: www.newchurch.org

New Horizons in the Orthodox Presbyterian Church, (11-Y) The Orthodox Presbyterian Church, Danny E. Olinger, 607 N. Easton Rd., Bldg. E, Willow Grove, PA 19090-2539 Tel. (215)830-0900 Fax (215)830-0350
Email: olinger.1@opc.org
Website: www.opc.org/

New Oxford Review, (10-Y) The Catholic Church, Pieter Vree, 1069 Kains Ave., Berkeley, CA 94706 Tel. (510)526-5374 Fax (510)526-3492
Email: pietervree@newoxfordreview.org
Website: www.newoxfordreview.org

New World Outlook, (bi-M) Mission Magazine of The United Methodist Church, Christie R.

House, 475 Riverside Dr., Rm. 1476, New York, NY 10115 Tel. (212)870-3765 Fax (212) 870-3654
Email: NWO@gbgm-umc.org
Website: gbgm-umc.org/now

Newscope, (W) The United Methodist Church, Mary Catherine Dean, P.O. Box 801, Nashville, TN 37202 Tel. (615)749-6385 Fax (615)749-6061
Email: umnewscope@umpublishing.org
Website: www.umph.org

Newsline, (Bi-W, I) Church of the Brethren, Cheryl Brumbaugh-Cayford, 1451 Dundee Ave., Elgin, IL 60120-1694 Tel. (847)742-5100 (800) 323-8039 Fax (847)742-6103
Email: cobnews@brethren.org
Website: http://www.brethren.org/ genbd/newsline/index.htm

The North American Catholic, (M) North American Old Roman Catholic Church, Theodore J. Remalt, 4154 W. Berteau Ave, Chicago, IL 60641 Tel. (312)685-0461 Fax (312)485-0461
Email: chapelhall@aol.com

The North American Challenge, (M) Home Missions Division of The United Pentecostal Church International, Joseph Fiorino, 8855 Dunn Rd., Hazelwood, MO 63042-2299 Tel. (314)837-7300 Fax (314)837-5632

NRB Today, (9-Y Online) Nondenominational, Laurel MacLeod, National Religious Broadcasters, 9510 Technology Drive, Manassas, VA 20110 Tel. (703)330-7000 Fax (703)330-7100
Email: lmacleod@nrb.org
Website: www.nrb.org

On Course, (bi-M) Assemblies of God, Kristi Arnold and Amber Weigand-Buckley (Interim co-editors), 1445 N. Boonville Ave., Springfield, MO 65802-1894 Tel. (417)862-2781 Fax (417)862-1693
Email: oncourse@ag.org
Website: oncourse.ag.org

On Mission, (Q) Southern Baptist Convention, Carol Pipes, 4200 North Point Pkwy., Alphretta, GA 30202-4174 Tel. (770)410-6394 Fax (770)410-6105
Website: www.onmission.com

ONE Magazine, (bi-M) National Association of Free Will Baptists, Eric Thomsen, P.O. Box 5002, Antioch, TN 37011-5002 Tel. 615-731-6812 Fax 615-731-0771
Email: eric@nafwb.org
Website: http://www.onemag.org/ plymouth_rock.htm

One Voice, (M) Bible Fellowship Church, Rev. Ralph Ritter, 3000 Fellowship Drive, Whitehall, PA 18052-3343 Tel. (877) 795-1212 Fax (215)536-2120
Email: bfc.onevoice@gmail.com
Website: www.bfc.org

OnSite, (Q) United Pentecostal Church International, Bryan Abernathy, 8855 Dunn Rd., Hazelwood, MO 63042 Tel. (314)837-7300 Fax (314)837-2387
Email: fmmail@upci.org
Website: www.foreignmissions.com

Orthodox America, (8-Y) The Russian Orthodox Church Outside of Russia, Mary Mansur, P.O. Box 383, Richfield Springs, NY 13439-0383 Tel. (315)858-1518
Email: info@orthodoxamerica.org
Website: www.orthodoxamerica.org

The Orthodox Church, (M) The Orthodox Church in America, Very Rev. John Matusiak, Managing Editor-Very Rev. Leonid Kishkovsky, Editor, Editorial Office, One Wheaton Center #912, Wheaton, IL 60187 Tel. (630)668-3071 Fax (630)668-5712
Email: tocmed@hotmail.com
Website: www.oca.org

Orthodox Family, (Q) The Russian Orthodox Church Outside of Russia, George Johnson and Deborah Johnson, 10760 Baltimore Avenue, Beltsville, MD 20705 Tel. (301)931-3400 Fax (301)890-3552
Email: apostlebird@aol.com
Website: www.holyapostlesorthodoxchurch.org

Orthodox Life, (bi-M) The Russian Orthodox Church Outside of Russia, Fr. Luke, Holy Trinity Monastery, P.O. Box 36, Jordanville, NY 13361-0036 Tel. (315)858-0940 Fax (315)858-0505
Email: orthlife@telenet.net

The Orthodox Observer, (M) Greek Orthodox Archdiocese of America, Jim Golding (Chryssoulis), 8 E. 79th St., New York, NY 10075 Tel. (212)570-3555 Fax (212)774-0239
Email: observer@goarch.org
Website: www.observer.goarch.org

Orthodox Russia (English translation of Pravoslavnaya Rus), (24-Y) The Russian Orthodox Church Outside of Russia, Archbishop Laurus, Holy Trinity Monastery, P.O. Box 36, Jordanville, NY 13361-0036 Tel. (315)858-0940 Fax (315)858-0505
Email: orthrus@telenet.net

Our Daily Bread, (Bi-M) The Swedenborgian Church, Kevin Baxter and Leah Goodwin, 11 Highland Avenue, Newtonville, MA 02460 Tel. (617)964-4240
Email: ourdailybreadmag@gmail.com
Website: www.swedenborg.org

Our Little Friend, (W) Seventh-day Adventist Church, Aileen Andres Sox, P.O. Box 5353, Nampa, ID 83653-5353 Tel. (208)465-2500 Fax (208)465-2531
Email: ailsox@pacificpress.com
Website: www.pacificpress.com

Our Sunday Visitor, (W) The Catholic Church, Gerald Korson, 200 Noll Plaza, Huntington, IN 46750 Tel. (219)356-8400
Email: oursunvis@osv.com
Website: www.osv.com

Outreach, (6-Y) Armenian Apostolic Church of America, Iris Papazian, 138 E. 39th St., New York, NY 10016 Tel. (212)689-7810 Fax (212)689-7168
Email: email@armenianprelacy.org
Website: www.armenianprelacy.org

The Path of Orthodoxy (Serbian), (M) Serbian Orthodox Church in the U.S.A. and Canada, V. Rev. Nedeljko Lunich, 300 Striker Ave., Joliet, IL 60436 Tel. (815)741-1023 Fax (815)741-1883
Email: nedlunich300@comcast.net

Paul, (Q) Netherlands Reformed Congregations, J. Spans, 47 Main Street E., Norwich, ON N0J 1PO Tel. (519)863-3306 Fax (519)863-2793

Today's Pentecostal Evangel, (W) Assemblies of God, Ken Horn, Gospel Publishing House, 1445 N. Boonville Ave., Springfield, MO 65802-1894 Tel. (417)862-2781 Fax (417)862-0416
Email: pe@ag.org
Website: www.pe.ag.org

The Pentecostal Herald, (M) United Pentecostal Church International, Rev. J. L. Hall, 8855 Dunn Rd., Hazelwood, MO 63042 Tel. (314)837-7300 Fax (314)837-4503

Pentecostal Leader, (bi-M) The International Pentecostal Church of Christ, Clyde M. Hughes, P.O. Box 439, London, OH 43140 Tel. (740)852-4722 Fax (740)852-0348
Email: hqipcc@aol.com
Website: www.IPCC.CC

The Pentecostal Messenger, (M) Pentecostal Church of God (Joplin, MO), John Mallinak, P.O. Box 850, Joplin, MO 64802 Tel. (417)624-7050 Fax (417)624-7102
Email: johnm@pcg.org
Website: www.pcg.org

Perspectives, (10-Y) Reformed Church in America, Christian Reformed Church in North America, Steve Mathonnet-VanderWell, Arika Theule-VanDam (co-editors), 4500 60th St., SE, Grand Rapids, MI 49512 Tel. (616)392-8555 ext. 131 Fax (616)392-7717
Email: perspectives@rca.org
Website: www.perspectivesjournal.org

Perspectives on Science and Christian Faith, (Q) Nondenominational, Dr. Arie Leegwater, Calvin College, De Vries Hall, 1726 Knollcrest Circle, S.E., Grand Rapids, MI 49546-4403
Email: leeg@calvin.edu
Website: www.asa3.org

The Pilot: America's Oldest Catholic Newspaper, (W 49-Y) The Catholic Archdiocese of Boston, Antonio Enrique, 66 Brook Drive, Braintree, MA 02184 Tel. (617)746-5839 Fax (617)779-4563
Email: editorial@pilotcatholicnews.com
Website: www.pilotcatholicnews..org

Pockets, (11-Y) The United Methodist Church, Lynn W. Gilliam, P.O. Box 340004, Nashville, TN 37203-0004 Tel. (615)340-7333 Fax (615)340-7267
Email: pockets@upperroom.org
Website: www.pockets.org

Polka, (Q) Polish National Catholic Church of America, Cecelia Lallo, 1127 Frieda St., Dickson City, PA 18519-1304 Tel. (570)489-4364 Fax (570)346-2188

Pravoslavnaya Rus (Russian), (24-Y) The Russian Orthodox Church Outside of Russia, Father Abbot Luke, Holy Trinity Monastery, P.O. Box 36, Jordanville, NY 13361-0036 Tel. (315)858-0940 Fax (315)858-0505
Email: info@jordanville.org
Website: www.jordanville.org

Pravoslavnaya Zhisn (Monthly Supplement to Pravoslavnaya Rus), (M) The Russian Orthodox Church Outside of Russia, Archbishop Laurus, Holy Trinity Monastery, P.O. Box 36, Jordanville, NY 13361-0036 Tel. (315)858-0940 Fax (315)858-0505
Email: Orthrus@telenet.net

Presbyterian News Service "The News", (On-Line) Presbyterian Church (U.S.A.), Jerry L. VanMarter, 100 Witherspoon St., Rm. 5418, Louisville, KY 40202 Tel. (502)569-5493 Fax (502)569-8073
Email: jerry.vanmarter@pcusa.org
Website: www.pcusa.org/pcnews

Presbyterian Outlook, (43-Y) Presbyterian Church (U.S.A.), Rev. Dr. Jack Haberer, 2112 W. Labaurnum Ave., Suite 109, Richmond, VA 23227 Tel. (800)446-6008 Fax (804)353-6369

Email: jhaberer@pres-outlook.com
Website: www.pres-outlook.com

Presbyterians Today, (10-Y) Presbyterian Church (U.S.A.), Eva Stimson, 100 Witherspoon St., Louisville, KY 40202-1396 Tel. (502)569-5637 Fax (502)569-8632
Email: today@pcusa.org
Website: www.pcusa.org/today

Primary Bible Study Guide (English Braille), (Q) Seventh-day Adventist Church, Falvo Fowler/Richard Clark, Jr., Christian Record Services for the Blind, P.O. Box 6097, Lincoln, NE 68506-0097 Tel. (402)488-0981 Fax (402)488-7582
Email: editorial@christianrecord.org
Website: www.christianrecord.org

Primary Source, (Q) American Baptist Historical Society and American Baptist Churches in the USA, Deborah Van Broekhoven, 3001 Mercer University Dr., Atlanta, GA 30341 Tel. (678)547-6680 Fax (678)547-6682
Website: www.abhsarchives.org

Primary Treasure, (W) Seventh-day Adventist Church, Aileen Andres Sox, P.O. Box 5353, Nampa, ID 83653-5353 Tel. (208)465-2500 Fax (208)465-2531
Email: ailsox@pacificpress.com
Website: www.pacificpress.com

Priority, (M) Missionary Church, Dr. Thomas Murphy, P.O. Box 9127, Ft. Wayne, IN 46899 Tel. (260)747-2027 Fax (260)747-5331
Email: mcdenomusa@aol.com
Website: mcusa.org

The Progressive Voice, (Q.electronic format) The United Methodist Church, Methodist Federation for Social Action, 212 East Capitol St., NE, Washington, DC 20003 Tel. (202)546-8806 Fax (202)546-6811
Email: mfsa@mfsaweb.org
Website: www.mfsaweb.org

Purpose, (Q in montly parts) Mennonite Church Canada and Mennonite Church USA, Carol Duerksen, 616 Walnut Ave., Scottdale, PA 15683 Tel. (724)887-8500 Fax (724)887-3111
Email: purposeeditor@mph.org
Website: www.mph.org

PYM Today, (5-Y) Philadelphia Yearly Meeting of the Religious Society of Friends, Philadelphia Yearly Meeting of the Religious Society of Friends, 1515 Cherry St., Philadelphia, PA 19102-1479 Tel. (215)241-7000 Fax (215)241-7045
Email: news@pym.org
Website: www.pym.org

Quaker Life, (6-Y) Friends United Meeting, Katie Terrell, 101 Quaker Hill Dr., Richmond, IN 47374-1980 Tel. (765)962-7573 Fax (765)966-1293
Email: QuakerLife@fum.org
Website: www.fum.org

Quarterly Review, A.M.E. Zion, (Q) African Methodist Episcopal Zion Church, Rev. James D. Armstrong, P.O. Box 33247, Charlotte, NC 28233 Tel. (704)599-4630 Fax (704)688-2544
Email: jaarmstrong@amezhqtr.org

Reflections, (bi-M) United Pentecostal Church International - Women, Melody Reeber, 8855 Dunn Rd, Hazelwood, MO 63042 Tel. (918)371-2659 Fax (918)371-6320
Email: ladies@upci.org
Website: www.upci.org/ladies

Reformed Worship, (Q) Christian Reformed Chuch in North America, Rev. Joyce Borger, 2850 Kalamazoo Ave. SE, Grand Rapids, MI 49560-0001 Tel. (800)777-7270 Fax (616)224-0834
Email: info@reformedworship.org
Website: www.reformedworship.org

Rejoice!, (Q) Mennonite Church, Byron Remple-Burkholder, 600 Shaftesbury Blvd., Winnipeg, MB R3P 0M4 Tel. (204)488-0610 Fax (204)831-5675
Email: byronrb@mennomediaorg
Website: www.mpn.net/rejoice

Rejoice!, (Q) Mennonite & Mennonite Brethren Church, Byron Remple-Burkholder, 600 Shaftesbury Blvd., Salem, MB R3P 0M4 Tel. (204)488-0610 Fax (204)831-5675
Email: byronrb@mennomedia.org

Report From The Capital, (10-Y) Baptist Joint Committee, Jeff Huett, 200 Maryland Ave. NE, Washington, DC 20002-5797 Tel. (202)544-4226 Fax (202)544-2094
Email: jhuett@bjconline.org
Website: www.bjconline.org

Reporter, (M) The Lutheran Church—Missouri Synod, Joe Isenhower Jr., Managing Editor, 1333 S. Kirkwood Rd., St. Louis, MO 63122-7295 Tel. (314)996-9000 Fax (314)966-1126
Email: reporter@lcms.org
Website: www.lcms.org/reporter

Reporter Interactive, (D.) Independent, Protestant, Cynthia B. Astle, UMR Communications, P.O. Box 660275, Dallas, TX 75266-0275 Tel. (214)630-6495 Fax (214)630-0079
Email: news@umr.org
Website: www.lumicon.org

The Rescue Herald, (3-Y) American Rescue Workers, Deborah La Valla, 25 Ross Street, Williams Port, PA 17701 Tel. (860)741-0727
Email: deborah@arwcanton.com
Website: www.arwus.org

Response, (M) The United Methodist Church, Dana Jones, 475 Riverside Dr., Room 1356, New York, NY 10115 Tel. (212)870-3755 Fax (212)870-3940

The Restitution Herald and Church of God Progress Journal, (bi-M) Church of God General Conference (Oregon, Ill. & Morrow GA) & McDonough, GA 30253, Joe Martin, Box 2950, McDonough, GA 30253 Tel. (678)833-1853 Fax (404)833-1853
Email: info@abc-coggc.org
Website: www.abc-coggc.org

Restoration Herald, (M) Christian Churches and Churches of Christ, H. Lee Mason, 7133 Central Parks Blvd., Mason, OH 45040 Tel. (513)229-8000 Fax (513)229-8003
Email: thecra@aol.com
Website: www.thecra.org

Restoration Quarterly, (Q) Churches of Christ, James W. Thompson, Box 28227, Abilene, TX 79699-8227 Tel. (915)674-3781 Fax (915)674-3776
Email: rq@bible.acu.edu
Website: www.rq.acu.edu

Review for Religious, (Q) The Catholic Church, Michael G. Harter, S. J., 3601 Lindell Blvd., St. Louis, MO 63108 Tel. (314)663-4160 Fax (314)633-4611
Email: reviewrfr@gmail.com
Website: www.reviewforreligious.org

Review of Religious Research, (Q) Non-denominational, Adair Lummis, Faculty Associate in Research, Hartford Seminary, 77 Sherman Street, Hartford, CT 06105-2260 Tel. (860)509-9547 Fax (860)509-9551
Email: alummis@hartsem.edu
Website: rra.hartsem.edu

Road to Emmaus, (Q) Orthodox Christian, Nun Nectaria, 1516 N. Delaware, Indianapolis, IN 46202 Tel. (317)631-1344 Fax (317)637-1897
Email: csb@indy.net
Website: www.roadtoemmaus.net

Rocky Mountain Christian, (M) Churches of Christ, Ron L. Carter, P.O. Box 803, Eastlake, CO 80614-0803. Tel. (719)598-4197 Fax (719)528-1549
Email: rmcnews@q.com

Sabbath Recorder, (M) Seventh Day Baptist General Conference, USA and Canada, Rev.

Kevin J. Butler, 3120 Kennedy Rd., P.O. Box 1678, Janesville, WI 53547 Tel. (608)752-5055 Fax (608)752-7711
Email: editor@seventhdaybaptist.org
Website: www.seventhdaybaptist.org

Sabbath School Toolbox, (Q) Seventh-day Adventist Church, Jim Zackrison, Review and Herald Publishing Assoc., 55 W. Oak Ridge Dr., Hagerstown, MD 21740 Tel. (301)393-4095 Fax (301)393-4055
Email: sabbathschooltoolbox@rhpa.org
Website: www.rhpa.org

Saint Anthony Messenger, (M) The Catholic Church, Fr. Pat McCloskey, O.F.M., St. Anthony Messenger Editorial, Dept., 28 W. Liberty St., Cincinnati, OH 45202 Tel. (513)241-5615 Fax (513)241-0399
Email: StAnthony@AmericanCatholic.org
Website: www.AmericanCatholic.org

Saint Willibrord Journal, (Q) Christ Catholic Church, The Rev. Monsignor Charles E. Harrison, 2710 W. Alabama, Houston, TX 77098 Tel. (713)515-8206 Fax (713)622-5311
Website: www.christcatholic.org

Saints Herald, (M) Community of Christ, Linda Booth, The Herald Publishing House, P.O. Box 390, Independence, MO 64051-0390 Tel. (816)521-3015 Fax (816)521-3066
Email: Herald@CofChrist.org
Website: www.heraldhouse.org

SBC Life, (6-Y) Southern Baptist Convention, John Revell Exec. Ed.: Dr. Roger S. (Sing) Oldham, VP for Convention Communications and Relations, 901 Commerce St., Nashville, TN 37203 Tel. (615)244-2355 Fax (615)782-8684
Email: jrevell@sbc.net
Website: sbc.net

The Schwenkfeldian, (3-Y) The Schwenkfelder Church, Gerald Heebner, 105 Seminary Street, Pennsburg, PA 18073 Tel. (215)679-3103 Fax (215)679-8175
Email: info@schwenfelder.com
Website: www.schwenkfelder.com

Searching Together, (Q) Non-denominational, Jon Zens, Box 548, St. Croix Falls, WI 54024 Tel. (715)338-2796
Email: jzens@searchingtogether.org
Website: www.searchingtogether.org

The Secret Place, (Q) American Baptist Churches USA, Kathleen Hayes, Editor, P.O. Box 851, Valley Forge, PA 19482-0851 Tel. (610)768-2434 Fax (610)768-2441
Email: thesecretplace@abc-usa.org
Website: www.judsonpress.com

Seeds for the Parish, (bi-M) Evangelical Lutheran Church in America, Janice Rizzo, 8765 W. Higgins Rd., Chicago, IL 60631 Tel. (773)380-2949/(800)638-3522 Fax (773)380-2406
Email: Janice.Rizzo@elca.org
Website: www.elca.org/seeds

Shalom!, (Q) Brethren in Christ Church, Harriet Bicksler, P.O. Box A, 431 Grantham Rd., Grantham, PA 17027 Tel. (717)697-2634
Email: bickhouse@aol.com
Website: www.bic-church.org/connect/publications/Shalom/ default.asp

Shiloh's Messenger of Wisdom, (M) Israelite House of David, William Robertson, P.O. Box 1067, Benton Harbor, MI 49023

The Shofar, Apostolic Catholic Church, 7813 N. Nebraska Ave., Tampa, FL 33604 Tel. (813) 238-6060
Email: Bishop-Chuck@apostoliccatholic church.com
Website: www.ApostolicCatholicChurch.com

Signs of the Times, (M) Seventh-day Adventist Church, Marvin Moore, P.O. Box 5353, Nampa, ID 83653-5398 Tel. (208)465-2577 Fax (208)465-2531
Email: mmoore@pacificpress.com
Website: www.signstimes.com

The Silver Lining, (M) Apostolic Christian Churches of America, Bruce Leman, 1389 County Road 1600 N, Box 50, Roanoke, IL 61561-9625 Tel. (309)923-7192 Fax (309)923-7359
Email: cleman@mtco.com

Sojourners, (M) Ecumenical, Jim Wallis, 3333 14th Street NW, Suite 200, Washington, DC 20010 Tel. (202)328-8842 Fax (202)328-8757
Email: sojourners@sojo.net
Website: www.sojo.net

Solia Calendar, (Y) The Romanian Orthodox Episcopate of America, The Department of Publications of the Romanian Orthodox Episcopate of America, P.O. Box 185, Grass Lake, MI 49240-0185 Tel. (517)522-4800 Fax (517)522-5907
Email: solia@roea.org
Website: roea.org

Solia - The Herald, (bi-M) The Romanian Orthodox Episcopate of America, Rev. Archdeacon David Oancea, P.O. Box 185, Grass Lake, MI 49240-0185 Tel. (517)522-3656 Fax (517)522-5907
Email: solia@roea.org
Website: www.roea.org

341

Sound of Grace, (Q) Sovereign Grace Believers, 5317 Wye Creek Dr, Frederick, MD 21703-6938

The Southern Methodist, (bi-M) Southern Methodist Church, Thomas M. Owens, Sr., 425 Broughton Street, Orangeburg, SC 29115 Tel. (803)534-9853 Fax (803)535-3881 Email: foundry@bellsouth.net

Spirit, (Q) Volunteers of America, Arthur Smith and Denis N. Baker, 1809 Carrollton Ave, New Orleans, LA 70118-2829 Tel. (504)897-1731

The Spiritual Sword, (Q) Churches of Christ, Alan E. Highers, 1511 Getwell Rd., Memphis, TN 38111 Tel. (901)743-0464 Fax (901)743-2197 Email: mail@getwellchurchofchrist.org Website: www.getwellchurchofchrist.org

The Standard Bearer, (21-Y) Protestant Reformed Churches in America, Russell Dystra, 4949 Ivanrest Ave. SW, Grandville, MI 49418 Tel. (616)531-1490 Fax (616)531-3033 Email: dystra@prca.org; mail@rfpa.org Website: www.rfpa.org/catalog

The Star of Zion, (bi-W) African Methodist Episcopal Zion Church, Mr. Mike Lisby, P.O. Box 26770, Charlotte, NC 28221-6770 Tel. (704)599-4630 ext.318 Fax (704)688-2546 Email: service@starofzion.org Website: www.starofzion.org

The Student (Braille & Cassette), (M) Seventh-day Adventist Church, Clifford Goldstein/Bert Williams, Christian Record Services for the Blind, P.O. Box 6097, Lincoln, NE 68506-0097 Tel. (402)488-0981 Fax (402) 488-7582 Email: editorial@christianrecord.org Website: www.christianrecord.org

The Student, Spanish edition (Audio), (M) Seventh-day Adventist Church, Clifford Goldstein/Marcos Blanco, Christian Record Services for the Blind, P.O. Box 6097, Lincoln, NE 68506-0097 Tel. (402)488-0981 Fax (402) 488-7582 Email: editorial@christianrecord.org Website: www.christianrecord.org

Sunday, (Q) Interdenominational, Timothy A. Norton, 2930 Flowers Rd., S., Atlanta, GA 30341-5532 Tel. (770)936-5376 Fax (770)936-5385 Email: tnorton@ldausa.org Website: www.sundayonline.org

The Tablet, (W) The Catholic Church, Ed Wilkinson, 310 Prospect Park West, Brooklyn, NY 11215 Tel. (718)965-7333 Fax (718)965-7337 Email: TheTablet@aol.com Website: http://www.thetablet.org/default.aspx

The Anchor Newsletter, (M) The Anglican Orthodox Church, The Most Rev. Jerry L. Ogles, Anglican Orthodox Church, P.O. Box 128, Statesville, NC 28625 Tel. (704)873-8365 Fax (704)873-5359 Email: usa@anglicanorthodoxchurch.org; standrews.church@gmail.com Website: www.anglicanorthodoxchurch.org

Theology Digest, (Q) The Catholic Church, Bernhard Asen, Rosemary Jermann (co-editors), 3800 Lindell Blvd., St. Louis, MO 63108 Tel. (314)977-3410 Fax (314)977-3704 Email: thdigest@slu.edu

Theology Today, (Q) Nondenominational, James F. Kay, Reviews Editor: Gordon S. Mikoski, P.O. Box 821, Princeton, NJ 08542-0803 Tel. (609)497-7714 Fax (609)497-1826 Email: theology.today@ptsem.edu Website: theologytoday.ptsem.edu

These Days, (Q) Interdenominational, Vince Patton, 100 Witherspoon St., Louisville, KY 40202-1396 Tel. (502)569-5080 Fax (502)569-5113 Website: www.ppcpub.com

The Three-Fold Vision, (M) Apostolic Faith Mission Church of God, Alice Walker, 156 Walker Street, Munford, AL 36268 Tel. (256)358-9763 Email: alicemtwalker@aol.com

Timbrel: The Publication for Mennonite Women The, (bi-M) Mennonite Church Canada and USA, Patty Burdette, 718 Main Street, Corvallis Omit, Newton, KS 67114 Tel. (316) 281-4396 Email: office@MennoniteWomenUSA.org; PattyB@MennoniteWomenUSA.org Website: www.mennonitewomenusa.org

Today's Christian, (bi-M) Nondenominational, Ed Gilbreath, 465 Gundersen Dr., Carol Stream, IL 60188 Tel. (630)260-6200 Fax (630)480-2004 Email: tceditor@todays-christian.com Website: www.christianity.com

Today's Christian Woman, (bi-M) Non-denominational, Jane Johnson Struck, 465 Gundersen Dr., Carol Stream, IL 60188 Tel. (630)260-6200 Fax (630)260-0114 Email: TCWedit@christianitytoday.com Website: www.todayschristianwoman.com

Pentecostal Evangel, (W) Assemblies of God, Ken Horn, Gospel Publishing House, 1445 N. Boonville Ave., Springfield, MO 65802 Tel. (417)862-2781 Fax (417)862-0416 Email: pe@ag.org Website: www.pe.ag.org

Together With God, (bi-M) National Association of Free Will Baptists, Sarah Fletcher, Women Nationally Active for Christ, P.O. Box 5002, Antioch, TN 37011-5002 Tel. (877)767-7662/(615)731-6812 Fax (615)731-0771
Email: twg@wnac.org
Website: www.wnac.org

Tomorrow Magazine, (Q) American Baptist Churches in the USA, Sara E. Hopkins, 475 Riverside Dr., Room 1700, New York, NY 10115-0049 Tel. (800)986-6222 Fax (800)986-6782

Truth, (Q) Grace Gospel Fellowship, Phil Cereghino, P.O. Box 9432, Grand Rapids, MI 49509 Tel. (616)245-0100 Fax (616)241-2542
Email: info@ggfusa.org
Website: www.ggfusa.org

Truth Magazine, (bi-W) Churches of Christ, Mike Willis, Box 9670, Bowling Green, KY 42102 Tel. (800)428-0121
Website: truthmagazine.com

Ubique, (Q) The Liberal Catholic Church—Province of the United States, Mrs. Erin S.W. Satterlee, 2033 22nd Ave. #302, Greeley, CO 80631
Email: ubiquetlcc@fastmail.fm
Website: www.TheLCC.org

Ukrainian Orthodox Herald, Ukrainian Orthodox Church of America (Ecumenical Patriarchate), Rev. Dr. Anthony Ugolnik, P.O. Box 774, Allentown, PA 18105

Ukrainian Orthodox Word, (M) Ukrainian Orthodox Church of the USA, Bishop Daniel (Zelinskyy), P.O. Box 495, South Bound Brook, NJ 08880 Tel. (732) 356-0090 Fax (732)356-5556
Email: FatherVZ@aol.com
Website: www.uocofusa.org

UMR Communications, Inc., (W, Bi-W) Independent, United Methodist, Robin Russell, 1221 Profit Drive, Dallas, TX 75266-0275 Tel. (214)630-6495 Fax (214)630-0079
Email: rrussell@umr.org
Website: www.umr.org; www.umportal.org (news site); www.lumicon.org

United Church News, (10-Y) United Church of Christ, W. Evan Golder, 700 Prospect Ave., Cleveland, OH 44115 Tel. (216)736-2218 Fax (216)736-2223
Email: goldere@ucc.org
Website: www.ucc.org

The United Methodist Reporter, (W) Independent, Protestant, Sam Hodges, UMR Communications, 1221 Profit Dr., Dallas, TX 75247 Tel. (214)630-6495 Fax (214)630-0079
Email: news@umr.org
Website: www.umr.org

United Methodists in Service (Korean), (6-Y) United Methodist Church (Korean), Jacob Lee, UMCom, P. O. Box 320, Nashville, TN 37202-0320 Tel. 615-742-5400 Fax 615-742-5469
Email: jlee@umc.org
Website: www.koreanumc.org

UOL Bulletin (Ukrainian Orthodox League Bulletin), (7-Y) Ukrainian Orthodox Church of the USA, Natalie Bilynsky, 703 Pine Ridge Rd., Wallingford, PA 19086 Tel. (610)892-7315
Email: nsufler@aol.com
Website: www.uocofusa.org

The Upper Room, (bi-M) The United Methodist Church, Sarah Wilke, P.O. Box 340004, Nashville, TN 37203-0004 Tel. (877)899-2780 Fax (615)340-7289
Email: sbryant@upperroom.org
Website: www.upperroom.org

U.S. Catholic, (M) The Catholic Church, Rev. John Molyneux, 205 W. Monroe St., Chicago, IL 60606 Tel. (312)236-7782 Fax (312)236-8207
Email: editors@uscatholic.org
Website: www.uscatholic.org

UU World, (Q) Unitarian Universalist Association of Congregations, Christopher L. Walton, Executive Editor, 25 Beacon St., Boston, MA 02108-2803 Tel. (617)948-6518 Fax (617)742-7025
Email: world@uua.org
Website: www.uuworld.org

Vantage Point (Audio), (Q) Seventh-day Adventist Church, Bert Williams, Christian Record Services for the Blind, P. O. Box 6097, Lincoln, NE 68506 Tel. (402)488-0981 Fax (402)488-7582
Email: editorial@christianrecord.org
Website: http://www.christianrecord.org

Vibrant Life, (bi-M) Seventh-day Adventist Church, Heather Quintana, 55 W. Oak Ridge Dr., Hagerstown, MD 21740 Tel. (301)393-4019 Fax (301)393-4055
Email: vibrantlife@rhpa.org
Website: www.vibrantlife.com

Victory (Youth Sunday School/Bible Study Curriculum), (Q) Church of God of Prophecy, David Bryan, P.O. Box 2910, Cleveland, TN 37320-2910 Tel. (423)559-5321 Fax (423)559-5461
Email: david@cogop.org
Website: www.cogop.org

The Vindicator, (M) Old German Baptist Brethren Church, Steven L. Bayer, 6952 N. Montgomery Co. Line Rd., Englewood, OH 45322-9748 Tel. (937)884-7531 Fax (937)884-7531

Vira/Faith, (Q) United Ukrainian Orthodox Sisterhoods of the Ukrainian Orthodox Church of the U.S.A., Bishop Daniel (Zelinskyy), P.O. Box 495, South Bound Brook, NJ 08880 Tel. (732)356-0090 Fax (732)356-5556
Email: virafaith@aol.com
Website: uocofusa.org

Vista, (Q) International Fellowship of Christian Assemblies, Kerrie Evans, 1294 Rutledge Rd., Transfer, PA 16154 Tel. (412)962-3501 Fax (412)962-1766
Email: ifcahq@neohio.twcbc.com
Website: www.ifcaministry.com

Vital Signs, (bi-M) Conservative Baptist Association of America (CBAmerica), Rev. Stanley Rieb, 3686 Stagecoach Rd Unit F, Longmot, CO 80504 Tel. (720)283-3030
Email: info@CBAmerica.org
Website: www.CBAmerica.org

The Voice, (bi-M) IFCA International, Inc., Les Lofquist, P.O. Box 810, Grandville, MI 49468-0810 Tel. (616)531-1840 Fax (616)531-1814
Email: office@ifca.org

The Voice, (Q) The Bible Church of Christ, Inc., Montrose Bushrod, 1358 Morris Ave., Bronx, NY 10456 Tel. (718)588-2284 Fax (718)992-5597
Website: www.thebiblechurchofchrist.org

Voice of Mission, (Q) African Methodist Episcopal Church, Dr. John W.P. Collier, 1587 Savannah Highway, Ste. A, Charleston, SC 29407 Tel. (843)852-2645 Fax (843)852-2648
Email: gwmame@bellsouth.net
Website: amegobalmissions.com

Voices, (Q. - Online) , Mary Andreolli, 3939 Lavista Rd. Ste., E-122, Atlanta, GA 30084 Tel. (866) 7457609
Email: mary@allianceofbaptists.org
Website: www.allianceofbaptists.org

The War Cry, (bi-M) The Salvation Army, Ed Forster, Editor in Chief; Jeff McDonald, Managing Editor, 615 Slaters Lane, Alexandria, VA 22314 Tel. (703)684-5500 Fax (703)684-5539
Email: war_cry@usn.salvationarmy.org

Watchtower, (bi-W) Jehovah's Witnesses, Watch Tower Society, 25 Columbia Heights, Brooklyn, NY 11201-2483 Tel. (718)560-5000 Fax (718)560-8850
Website: www.watchtower.org

Weavings: A Journal of the Christian Spiritual Life, (Q) The United Methodist Church, Pamela C. Hawkins, 1908 Grand Avenue, P.O. Box 30004, Nashville, TN 37203-0004 Tel. (615)340-7254 Fax (615)340-7267
Email: weavings@upperroom.org
Website: www.upperroom.org/weavings

Wesleyan Life, (Q) The Wesleyan Church, Norman G. Wilson, P.O. Box 50434, Indianapolis, IN 46250-0434 Tel. (317)774-7909 Fax (317)774-7913
Email: wilsonn@wesleyan.org
Website: www.wesleyan.org

GP WorldView, (Q) The Wesleyan Church, Elaine Eckhardt, P.O. Box 50434, Indianapolis, IN 46250 Tel. (317)774-7950 Fax (317)774-7958
Email: ghpm@wesleyan.org
Website: www.globalpartnersonline.org; www.praygivego.com

The White Wing Messenger, (bi-W) Church of God of Prophecy, Virginia E. Chatham, P.O. Box 2970, Cleveland, TN 37320-2970 Tel. (423)559-5129/24 Fax (423)559-5128
Website: www.cogop.org

Window on the World, (3-Y) The Evangelical Congregational Church, Rev. Randy Sizemore, 100 W. Park Ave, Myerstown, PA 17067 Tel. (717)866-7584 Fax (717)866-7383
Email: ecglobal@eccenter.com
Website: www.eccenter.com

Wineskins, (bi-M) Churches of Christ, Mike Cope and Rubel Shelly, Box 41028, Nashville, TN 37024-1028 Tel. (615)346-5533 Fax (615)296-4064
Email: ericnoahwilson@gmail.com
Website: www.wineskins.org

Wisconsin Lutheran Quarterly, (Q) Wisconsin Evangelical Lutheran Synod, John F. Brug, 11757 N. Seminary Dr., Mequon, WI 53092 Tel. (262)242-8139 Fax (262)242-8110
Email: brugj@wls.wels.net
Website: www.wls.wels.net

The Witness, (10-Y) Nondenominational, Julie A. Wortman, 7000 Michigan Ave., Detroit, MI 48210 Tel. (313)841-1967 Fax (313)841-1956
Email: office@thewitness.org
Website: www.thewitness.org

Woman to Woman, (M) General Association of General Baptists, Patti Thornton, 100 Stinson Dr., Poplar Bluff, MO 63901 Tel. (573)785-7746 Fax (573)785-0564
Email: wmofc@generalbaptist.com
Website: www.generalbaptist.com

The Woman's Pulpit, (Q) Nondenominational, LaVonne Althouse, 14 St. Mark Avenue, Lititz, PA 17543 Tel. (717)626-0463
Email: revla32@dejazzd.com
Website: www.womenministers.org

Women's Missionary Magazine, (9-Y) African Methodist Episcopal Church, Dr. Bettye J. Allen, 17129 Bennett Dr, South Holland, IL 60473 Tel. (708)339-5997 Fax (708)339-5987
Email: bettye1901@aol.com

The Word, (10-Y) The Antiochian Orthodox Christian Archdiocese of North America, V. Rev. John Abdalah, 635 Miranda Dr., Pittsburgh, PA 15241-2041 Tel. (412)681-2988 Fax (412)831-5554
Email: frjpa@aol.com
Website: www.antiochian.org

Word and Work, (11-Y) Churches of Christ, Alex V. Wilson, 209 South Galt Ave., Louisville, KY 40206 Tel. (502)897-2831
Email: avwilson4@gmail.com
Website: www.wordandwork.org

The Worker, (Q) Progressive National Baptist Convention, Inc., Evelyn Andrews, 601 50th St. NE, Washington, DC 20019 Tel. (202)396-0558 Fax (202)398-4998
Email: jsmith@pnbc.org
Website: www.pnbc.org

World Parish: International Organ of the World Methodist Council, (E-mailed Monthly) Interdenominational Methodist (Christian World Communion of Methodist and WMC-Wesleyan Related Churches), Dr. George Freeman, P.O. Box 518, Lake Junaluska, NC 28745 Tel. (828)456-9432 Fax (828)456-9433

Email: georgefreeman@charter.net
Website: www.worldmethodistcouncil.org

Worship, (bi-M) The Catholic Church, R. Kevin Seasoltz, St. John's Abbey, Collegeville, MN 56321 Tel. (320)363-3883 Fax (320)363-3145
Email: kseasoltz@csbsju.edu
Website: www.sja.org/worship

Worship Arts, (bi-M) United Methodist Church, David A Wiltse, P.O. Box 24787, Nashville, TN 37202 Tel. (800)952-8977
Email: WorshipArts@UMFellowship.org
Website: www.UMFellowship.org

Woman's Touch, (bi-M) Assemblies of God, Arlene Allen, 1445 N. Boonville Ave., Springfield, MO 65802-1894 Tel. (417)862-2781 Fax (417)862-0503
Email: womanstouch@ag.org
Website: www.womanstouch.ag.org

Youth Ministry Accent, (Q) Seventh-day Adventist Church, Jonathán Tejel, 12501 Old Columbia Pike, Silver Spring, MD 20904-6600 Tel. (301)680-6180 Fax (301)680-6155
Email: dunchiem@gc.adventist.org
Website: Gcyouthministries.org

YPD Newsletter, (3-M) African Methodist Episcopal Church, Adrienne A. Morris and Andrea Smith, 327 Washington Avenue, Wyoming, OH 45215 Tel. (513)821-1481 Fax (513)821-3073
Email: amconndri@cs.com
Website: ameypd.org

Zion's Advocate, (M) Church of Christ, Gordon McCann, P.O. Box 472, Independence, MO 64051-0472 Tel. (816)796-6255

11. Religious Periodicals in Canada

Religious periodicals listed below constitute a basic core of important journals and periodicals circulated in Canada. The list does not include all publications prepared by religious bodies, and not all the publications listed here are necessarily the official publication of a particular church. Each entry gives: the title of the periodical, frequency of publication, religious affiliation, editor's name, address, telephone and fax number, and email and website addresses when available. The frequency of publication, which appears in parenthesis after the name of the publication, is represented by a "D" for daily, "W" for weekly, "M" for monthly, "Y" for yearly, "Q" for quarterly, and "I" for Internet.

The Anglican, (10-Y) The Anglican Church of Canada, Stuart Mann, 135 Adelaide St. E., Toronto, ON M5C 1L8, Tel. (416)363-6021 Fax (416)363-7678
Email: smann@toronto.anglican.ca
Website: www.toronto.anglican.ca

Anglican Journal, (10-Y) The Anglican Church of Canada, Kristin Jenkins, 80 Hayden St., Toronto, ON M4Y 3G2, Tel. (416)924-9199 ext. 307 Fax (416)968-7983
Email: kjenkins@national.anglican.ca
Website: www.anglicanjournal.com

Armenian Evangelical Church Newsletter, (Q) Armenian Evangelical Church, Rev. Samuel Albarian, 2600 14th Avenue, Markham, ON L3R 3X1, Tel. (905)305-8144 Fax (905)305-8125
Email: aectoronto@yahoo.com

Aujourd'hui Credo, (10-Y) The United Church of Canada, Lydie Descroix, 1332 Victoria, Longueuil, QC J4V 1L8, Tel. (450)446-7733 Fax (450)466-2664
Email: jlamarre@egliseunie.org
Website: www.united-church.ca/credo

The Baptist Horizon, (4-Y) Canadian Convention of Southern Baptists, Debbie Shelton, 100 Convention Way, Cochrane, AB T4C 2G2, Tel. (403)932-5688 Fax (403)932-4937
Email: office@cnbc.ca
Website: www.cnbc.ca

Blackboard Bulletin, (10-Y) Old Order Amish Church, Old Order Amish Church, Rt. 4, Aylmer, ON N5H 2R3

Die Botschaft, (W) Old Order Amish Church, James Weaver, Brookshire Publishing, Inc., 200 Hazel St., Lancaster, PA 17603, Tel. (717)392-1321 Fax (717)392-2078

The Budget, (W) Old Order Amish Church, Fannie Erb-Miller, P.O. Box 249, Sugarcreek, OH 44681, Tel. (330)852-4634 Fax (330)852-4421
Email: budgetnews@thebudgetnewspaper.com

Cahiers de Spiritualite Ignatienne, (3-Y) The Roman Catholic Church in Canada, Etienne Pouliot, 965 Avenue Loius-Fréchette, Québec, QC G1S 4V1, Tel. (418)653-6353 Fax (418)653-1208
Email: cahiersi@centremanrese.org
Website: www.centremanrese.org

Canada Lutheran, (8-Y) Evangelical Lutheran Church in Canada, Lucia Carruthers, Editor; Trina Gallop, Editorial Director; Catherine Crivici, Graphic Designer, 302-393 Portage Avenue, Winnipeg, MB R3B 3H6, Tel. (204) 984-9150 Toll Free: (888) 786-6707 Fax (204) 984-9185
Email: canaluth@elcic.ca
Website: www.elcic.ca/clweb

Canada Update, (Q) The Church of God of Prophecy - Eastern Canada Administrative Office, Editor, 5145 Tomken Road, Mississaugh, ON L4W 1P1, Tel. (905)625-1278 Fax (905)625-1316
Website: www.coqop.ca

Canadian Adventist Messenger, (12-Y) Seventh-day Adventist Church in Canada, Crystal D. Steeves, 1148 King St. E., Oshawa, ON L1H 1H8, Tel. (905)433-0011 Fax (905) 433-0982
Email: steeves.crystal@adventist.ca
Website: adventistmessenger.ca

The Canadian Baptist, (4-Y) Canadian Baptists of Ontario and Quebec, Jacob Buurma, 100 - 304 The East Mall, Etobicoke, ON M9B 6E2, Tel. (416)622-8600 Fax (416) 622-0780
Email: publications@baptist.ca; cboq@baptist.ca
Website: www.baptist.ca

The Canadian Friend, (5-Y) Canadian Yearly Meeting of the Religious Society of Friends, Sherryll Harris, 91A Fourth Ave., Ottawa, ON K1S 2L1, Tel. (613)235-8553 Fax (613)235-1753
Email: cym-office@quaker.ca
Website: www.quaker.ca/Publications/cfriend/cfriend.html

The Canadian Lutheran, (6-Y) Lutheran Church—Canada, Dr. Ian Adnams, Editor, 3074 Portage Ave., Winnipeg, MB R3K 0Y2, Tel. (204)895-3433 ext.2224 Fax (204)832-3018
Website: www.lutheranchurch.ca

Canadian Mennonite, (bi-W) Mennonite Church Canada, Dick Benner, Suite C5, 490 Dutton Dr., Waterloo, ON N2L 6H7, Tel. (519) 884-3810 Fax (519)884-3331
Email: editor@canadianmennonite.org
Website: www.canadianmennonite.org

Canadian Orthodox Messenger, (Q) Orthodox Church in America (Canada Section), Nun Sophia (Zion), 15, Le Breton Street, North, Ottawa, ON K1R 7H1, Tel. (613)233-7780 Fax (613)233-1931
Email: vladyka@archdiocese.ca

The Catalyst, (6-Y) Nondenominational, Karen Diepeveen, Citizens for Public Justice, 501-309 Cooper St., Ottawa, ON K2P 0G5, Tel. (613)232-0275 Fax (613)232-1275
Email: david@cpj.ca
Website: www.cpj.ca

The Catholic Register, (W) The Roman Catholic Church in Canada, Joseph Sinasac, 1155 Yonge St., Ste. 401, Toronto, ON M4Y 1W2, Tel. (416)934-3410 Fax (416)934-3409
Email: editor@catholicregister.org
Website: www.catholicregister.org

The Catholic Times (Montreal), (Q) The Roman Catholic Church in Canada, Eric Durocher, 2005 St. Marc St., Montreal, QC H3H 2G8, Tel. (514)937-2301 x259 Fax (514) 937-3051
Email: info@catholiccentre.ca

Channels, (3-Y) Presbyterian Church in Canada, Calvin Brown Managing Editor, Dal Schindell, Renewal Fellowship, 3819 Bloor St W, Etobicoke, ON M9B 1K7, Tel. (416)233-6581 Fax (416)233-1743
Email: cbbrown@rogers.com
Website: www.presbycan.ca

Chinese Herald, (bi-M) Canadian Conference of Mennonite Brethren Churches, Joseph Kwan, 8143 Burnlake Drive, Burnaby, BC V5A 3R6, Tel. (604)421-4100 Fax (604)421-4100
Email: chineseherald@mbconf.ca

Church of God Beacon, (Q) Church of God (Cleveland, Tenn.), Dr. Daniel J. Vassell Sr., P.O. Box 2036, Brampton Commercial Service Center, Brampton, ON L6T 3S3, Tel. (905)790-8777 Fax (905)790-8781
Email: bishop@coginontario.org
Website: www.coginontario.org

Clarion- The Canadian Reformed Magazine, (bi-W) Canadian and American Reformed Churches, J. Visscher, One Beghin Ave., Winnipeg, MB R2J 3X5, Tel. (204)663-9000 Fax (204)663-9202
Email: clarionadmin@premierpublishing.ca
Website: premierpublishing.ca

CLBI-Cross Roads, (5-Y) Lutheran, Jonnie Scrivens, 4837-52A St., Camrose, AB T4V 1W5, Tel. (780)672-4454 Fax (780)672-4455
Email: communications@clbi.edu
Website: www.clbi.edu

The Communicator, (3-Y) The Roman Catholic Church in Canada, Editor, 1070 Waterloo Street, London, ON N6A 3Y2, Tel. (519)433-0658 x227 Fax (519)433-0011
Email: info@arccc.ca
Website: www.dioceseoflondon.ca/

Connexions, (4-Y) Interdenominational, Ulli Diemer, 489 College St., Ste. 305, Toronto, ON M6G 1A5, Tel. (416)964-1511
Website: www.connexions.org

The Covenant Messenger, (Q) The Evangelical Covenant Church of Canada, Doug Wildman, Box 93, Norquay, SK S0A 2V0, Tel. (204)269-3437 Fax (204)269-3584
Email: messengr@escape.ca
Website: www.canadacovenantchurch.org

Crux, (Q) Transdenominational, Julie Lane Gay, Regent College, 5800 University Blvd., Vancouver, BC V6T 2E4, Tel. (604)221-3386 Fax (604)224-3097/(800)663-8664
Email: cruxsubs@regent-college.edu
Website: www.regent-college.edu/crux

Cruxifusion, (2-Y) The United Church of Canada, Rev. Diane Walker, Box 237, Barrie, ON L4M 4T2, Tel. (705)737-0114 or (800) 678-2607 Fax (705)737-0114
Email: felmag@csolve.net

Diakonia-A Magazine of Office-Bearers, (4-Y) Canadian and American Reformed Churches, J. Visscher, Brookside Publishing, 3911 Mt. Lehman Rd., Abbotsford, BC V4X 2M9, Tel. (604)856-4127 Fax (604)856-6724

The Diary, (M) Old Order Amish Church, Don Carpenter, P.O. Box 98, Gordonville, PA 17529, Tel. (717)529-3938 Fax (717)529-3292

Ecumenism-Oecumenisme, (Q) Interdenominational, Exec. Dir. Anthony Mansour, 1819 Rene-Levesque West # 003, Montreal, QC H3H 2P5, Tel. (514)937-9176 x33/877-645-6863 Fax (514)937-4986
Email: info@oikoumene.ca
Website: www.oikoumene.ca

The Edge (Christian Youth Magazine), (10-Y) The Salvation Army in Canada, John McAlister, 2 Overlea Blvd., Toronto, ON M4H 1P4, Tel. (416)467-3185 Fax (416)422-6120 Email: edge@can.salvationarmy.org Website: www.salvationarmy.ca

Eesti Kirik, (Q) The Estonian Evangelical Lutheran Church Abroad, Rev. U. Petersoo, 383 Jarvis St., Toronto, ON M5B 2C7, Tel. (416)925-5465 Fax (416)925-5688

EMMC Recorder, (bi-M) Evangelical Mennonite Mission Conference, Lil Goertzen, 757 St. Anne's Road, Winnipeg, MB R2N 4G6, Tel. (204)253-7929 Fax (204)256-7384 Email: recorder@gomission.ca Website: www.gomission.ca

En Avant!, (12-Y) The Salvation Army in Canada, Marie-Michele Roy, 1655 Rue Richardson, Montreal, PQ H3K 3J7, Tel. (514) 288-2848 x 2236 Fax (514)288-4657 Email: enavant@can.salvationarmy.org Website: www.Salvationarmy.org

Evangel- The Good News of Jesus Christ, (4-Y) Canadian and American Reformed Churches, D. Moes, 21804 52nd Ave., Langley, BC V2Y 1L3, Tel. (604)576-2124 Fax (604)576-2101 Email: office@langleycanrc.org

The Evangelical Baptist, (4-Y) The Fellowship of Evangelical Baptist Churches in Canada, Dr. John Kaiser, P O Box 457, Guelph, ON N1H 6K9, Tel. (519)821-4830 Fax (519)821-9829 Email: president@fellowship.ca Website: www.fellowship.ca

Faith & Friends, (M) The Salvation Army in Canada, Geoff Moulton, 2 Overlea Blvd., Toronto, ON M4H 1P4, Tel. (416)422-6110 Fax (416)422-6120 Website: faithandfriends.sallynet.org

Faith Today, (bi-M) The Evangelical Fellowship of Canada (a cooperative organization of more than 40 Protestant denominations), Gail Reid, Bill Fledderus, Karen Stiller, M.I.P. Box 3745, Markham, ON L3R 0Y4, Tel. (905)479-5885 Fax (905)479-4742 Email: info@faithtoday.ca Website: www.faithtoday.ca

Family Life, (11-Y) Old Order Amish Church, Joseph Stoll and David Luthy, Old Order Amish Church, Rt. 4, Aylmer, ON N5H 2R3

Family Life Network Newsline, (3-Y) Canadian Conference of Mennonite Brethren Churches, Leona Krahn, 225 Riverton Ave., Winnipeg, MB R2L 0N1, Tel. (204)667-9576 Fax (204) 669-6079

Email: info@fln.ca Website: www.fln.ca

Foi & Vie, (12-Y) The Salvation Army in Canada, Marie-Michele Roy, 1655 Rue Richardson, Montreal, PQ H3K 3J7, Tel. (416) 422-6112 Fax (514)288-4657 Email: pamela_richardson@can.salvationarmy.org Website: www.SalvationArmy.ca

Glad Tidings, (6-Y) Presbyterian Church in Canada, Colleen Wood, Women's Missionary Society, 50 Wynford Dr., Toronto, ON M3C 1J7, Tel. (800)619-7301/(416)441-1111 Fax (416)441-2825 Email: cwood@presbyterian.ca Website: www.wmspcc.ca/gladtidingsA/gladtidings.html

Good Tidings, (6-Y) The Pentecostal Assemblies of Newfoundland and Labrador, H. Paul Foster, 57 Thorburn Rd., P.O. Box 8895, Sta. A, St. John's, NL A1B 3T2, Tel. (709)753-6314 Fax (709)753-4945 Email: marylynnem@paonl.ca Website: www.paonl.ca

The Gospel Contact, (4-Y) Church of God (Anderson, Ind.), The Church of God in Western Canada, 4717 56th St., Camrose, AB T4V 2C4, Tel. (780)672-0772 Fax (780)672-6888 Email: wcdncog@telus.net Website: www.chog.ca

Gospel Herald, (M) Churches of Christ in Canada, Wayne Turner, Editorial Editor; Paul Birston, Theme Edition Editor; and Max E. Craddock, Managing Editor, 4904 King St., Toronto, ON M4J 4W7, Tel. (905)563-7506 Email: editorial@gospelherald.org Website: www.gospelherald.org

The Gospel Standard, (M) Nondenominational, Perry F. Rockwood, Box 1660, Halifax, NS B3J 3A1, Tel. (902)423-5540 Fax (902)423-0820

Gospel Tidings, (M) Independent Holiness Church, Marilyn E. Votary, 1564 John Quinn Rd., Greely, ON K4P 1J9, Tel. (613)821-2237 Fax (613)821-4663 Email: gtmvotary@live.com Website: www.holiness.ca

The Grape Vine, (12-Y) Reformed Episcopal Church in Canada, Ingrid Andreller, 626 Blanshard Street, Victoria, BC V8W 3G6, Tel. (250)383-8915 Fax (250)383-8916 Email: office@churchofourlord.org Website: www.churchofourlord.org

Hallelujah!, (Q) The Bible Holiness Movement, Wesley H. Wakefield, 311 Falcon Place,

Penticton, BC V2A 8K6, Tel. (250)492-3376
Website: www.bible-holiness-movement.com/
magazine.html

Herold der Wahrheit, (M) Old Order Amish
Church, Cephas Kauffman, 1827 110th St.,
Kalona, IA 52247, Tel. (319)646-8810

Horizons, (bi-M) The Salvation Army in
Canada, 2 Overlea Blvd., Toronto, ON M4H
1P4, Tel. (416)425-6118 Fax (416)422-6120

Insight*Insound*In Touch, (6-Y (Insight); 6-Y
(In Sound); 4-Y (In Touch)) Interdeno-
minational. Insight (large print newspaper); In
Sound (audio magazine); In Touch (braille
newspaper), Rebekah Chevalier, Graham
Down, John Milton Society for the Blind in
Canada, 40 St. Clair Ave. E., Ste. 202, Toronto,
ON M4T 1M9, Tel. (416)960-3953 Fax (416)
960-3570
Email: admin@jmsblind.ca

ISKRA, (20-Y) Union of Spiritual Communities
of Christ (Orthodox Doukhobors in Canada),
Lisa Poznikoff, Box 3024, Castlegar, BC V1N
3H4, Tel. (250) 365-3613 ext. 27 Fax (250)
365-5477
Email: info@iskra.ca
Website: www.iskra.ca

Istocnik, (4-Y) Serbian Orthodox Church in
North and South America, Diocese of Canada,
Very Rev. Ljubomir Rajic, 7470 McNiven Rd.,
RR 3, Campbellville, ON L0P 1B0, Tel.
(905)878-0043 Fax (905)878-1909
Email: vladika@istocnik.com
Website: www.istocnik.com

Leader, (Q) Mennonite Church USA and
Mennonite Church Canada, Sr Editor: Richard
A. Kaufman, Editor: June Mears Driedger,
1918 Clifton Avenue, Lansing, MI 48910, Tel.
(517)346-7610
Email: junemd@mpn.net
Website: www.leaderonline.org

**Leader: Equipping the Missional Congre-
gation**, (Q) Mennonite Church, Managing
Editor: June Mears Driedger, Faith & Life
Resources/Mennonite Publishing Network,
1918 Clifton Ave., Langsing, MI 48910, Tel.
(517)346-7610 Fax (204) 831-5675
Email: junemd@mpn.net

Le Lien, (6-Y) Canadian Conference of
Mennonite Brethren Churches, Jean Bieri,
4824, ch. de la Cote-des-Neiges, Suite 301,
Montreal, QC H3V 1G4, Tel. (514)331-0878
Fax (514)331-0879
Email: lelien@mbconf.ca
Website: www.mbconf.ca/home/products_and
_services/resources/publications/le_lien/

Vivre et Celebrer, (4-Y) The Roman Catholic
Church in Canada, Service des Editions de la
CECC, Office national de liturgie, 3530 rue
Adam, Montreal, QC H1W 1Y8, Tel. (514)
522-4930 Fax (514)522-1557
Email: onl@cecc.ca
Website: www.cccb.ca

Mandate, (4-Y) The United Church of Canada,
Rebekah Chevalier, 3250 Bloor St W., Ste.
300, Toronto, ON M8X 2Y4, Tel. (416)231-
5931 Fax (416)231-3103
Email: rchevali@united-church.ca
Website: www.ucrdstore.ca/magazines/mandate

The Mantle, (M) Independent Assemblies of
God International (Canada), Philip Rassmussen, P.O. Box 2130, Laguna Hills, CA
92654-9901, Tel. (514)522-4930 Fax (514)
522-1557

Mennonite Brethren Herald, (M) Canadian
Conference of Mennonite Brethren Churches,
Laura Kalmar, 1310 Taylor Ave., Winnipeg,
MB R3M 3Z6, Tel. (204)654-5760 Fax (204)
654-1865
Email: mbherald@mbconf.ca
Website: www.mbherald.com

Mennonite Historian, (Q) Canadian Conference
of Mennonite Brethren Churches, Mennonite
Church Canada, Conrad Stoesz, Ctr. for Menn.
Brethren Studies, 1310 Taylor Avenue,
Winnipeg, MB R3M 3Z6, Tel. (204)669-6575
Fax (204)654-1865
Email: cstoesz@mbconf.ca
Website: mbconf.ca/mbstudies

Die Mennonitische Post, (bi-M) Mennonite
Central Committee Canada, Kennert
Giesbrecht, 383 Main St., Steinbach, MB R5G
1Z1, Tel. (204)326-6790 Fax (204)326-6302
Email: office@mennpost.org
Website: www.mennonitischepost.com

The Messenger, (bi-M) Church of God (in
Eastern Canada), Rosemary Krashel, 10
Cloverhill Ave, Dundas, ON L9H 2P2, Tel.
(514)938-9994
Email: info@chogec.ca
Website: www.chogec.ca

The Messenger, (Q) The Reformed Episcopal
Church of Canada, Rt. Rev. Michael Fedechko,
P.O. Box 2532, New Liskeard, ON P0J 1P0,
Tel. (705)630-2071 Fax (705)647-4481
Email: bishopfedechko@yahoo.com
Website: www.rececan.org

The Messenger, (12-Y) The Evangelical
Mennonite Conference, Rev. Terry M. Smith,
Editor; Rebecca Roman, Assistant Editor, 440
Main Street, Steinbach, MB R5G 1Z5, Tel.
(204)326-6401 Fax (204)326-1613

Email: messenger@emconf.ca
Website: www.emconference.ca/messenger

Missions Today, (bi-M) Roman Catholic, Paul Coady, Society for the Propagation of the Faith, 3329 Danforth Ave., Scarborough, ON M1L 4T3, Tel. (416)699-7077 or 800-897-8865 Fax (416)699-9019
Email: missionsocieties.ca
Website: www.eda.net/~missions

Mosaic, (Q) Canadian Baptist Ministries, Jennifer Lau, 7185 Millcreek Dr., Mississauga, ON L5N 5R4, Tel. (905)821-3533 Fax (905) 826-3441
Email: mosaic@cbmin.org
Website: www.cbmin.org

The New Freeman, (W) The Roman Catholic Church in Canada, Margie Traftan, One Bayard Dr., Saint John, NB E2L 3L5, Tel. (506)653-6806 Fax (506)653-6818
Email: tnf@nbnet.nb.ca

News of Québec, (3-Y) Christian Brethren (also known as Plymouth Brethren), Richard E. Strout, P.O. Box 1054, Sherbrooke, QC J1H 5L3, Tel. (819)820-1693 Fax (819)821-9287

News of Quebec, Christian Brethren (also known as Plymouth Brethren), Christian Brethren Churches in Quebec, P.O. Box 1054, Sherbrooke, QC J1H 5L3, Tel. (819)820-1693 Fax (819)821-9287

Orthodox Way, (M) Greek Orthodox Metropolis of Toronto (Canada), Orthodox Way Committee, 86 Overlea Blvd., 4th Floor, Toronto, ON M4H 1C6, Tel. (416)429-5757 Fax (416)429-4588
Email: metropolis@gocanada.org
Website: www.gocanada.org

Passport, (3-Y) Interdenominational, Mike Benallick, Briercrest Family of Schools, 510 College Dr., Caronport, SK S0H 0S0, Tel. (306)756-3200 Fax (306)756-3366
Email: passport@briercrest.ca
Website: www.briercrest.ca

Prairie Messenger, (W) The Roman Catholic Church in Canada, Peter Novecosky, O.S.B., Box 190, 11 College Drive, Muenster, SK S0K 2Y0, Tel. (306)682-1772 Fax (306)682-5285
Email: pm.editor@stpeterspress.ca
Website: www.prairiemessenger.ca

The Presbyterian Message, (10-Y) Presbyterian Church in Canada, Joan Cho, 11 Vista Ridge Crescent, Saint John's, NB E2J 4K4, Tel. (709)754-0773
Email: joan@thechos.ca
Website: www.presbyterian.ca/resources

Presbyterian Record, (11-Y) The Presbyterian Church in Canada, Rev. David Harris, 50

Wynford Dr., Toronto, ON M3C 1J7, Tel. (416) 441-1111 Fax (416)441-2825
Email: pcrecord@presbyterian.ca
Website: www.presbyterian.ca/record

Presence, (8-Y) The Roman Catholic Church in Canada, Jean-Claude Breton, Presence Magazine Inc., 2715 chemin de la Côte Ste-Catherine, Montreal, QC H3T 1B6, Tel. (514)739-9797 Fax (514)739-1664
Email: presence@presencemag.qc.ca

The Pulse, (4-Y) Evangelical Free Church of Canada, Dr. Ron Unruh, Editor-in-Chief; Tracy Morris, Managing Editor, Box 850, LCDI, Langley, BC V3A 8S6, Tel. (604)888-8668 Fax (604)888-3108
Email: efcc@twu.ca
Website: www.efcc.ca

Quaker Concern, (3-Y) Canadian Yearly Meeting of the Religious Society of Friends, Jane Orion Smith, 60 Lowther Ave., Toronto, ON M5R 1C7, Tel. (416)920-5213 Fax (416) 920-5214
Email: info@quakerservice.ca
Website: www.quakerservice.ca

Reformed Perspective - A Magazine for the Christian Family, (M) Canadian and American Reformed Churches and United Reformed Churches in North America, Jon Dykstra, 503A Forest Circle, Lynden, WA 98264, Tel. (360)739-7480
Email: editor@reformedperspective.ca
Website: www.reformedperspective.ca

Relations, (8-Y) The Roman Catholic Church in Canada, Elizabeth Garant, 25 Jarry Ouest, Montreal, QC H2P 1S6, Tel. (514)387-2541 Fax (514)387-0206
Email: relations@cjf.qc.ca
Website: www.cjf.qc.ca

RESCUE, (bi-M) Association of Gospel Rescue Missions, Brad Lewis, 7222 Commerce Center Dr., Suite 120, Colorado Springs, CO 80919, Tel. (719)266-8300 Fax (719)266-8600
Email: editor@agrm.org
Website: www.agrm.org

Revival News, (Q) Interdenominational, John McGregor, Canadian Revival Fellowship, Box 584, Regina, SK S4P 3A3, Tel. (306)522-3685 Fax (306)522-3686
Email: crfellowship@accesscomm.ca
Website: www.revivalfellowship.com

Rupert's Land News, (10-Y) The Anglican Church of Canada, Irvin J. Kroeker, Anglican Centre, 935 Nesbitt Bay, Winnipeg, MB R3T 1W6, Tel. (204)992-4205 Fax (204)992-4219
Email: rlnews@rupertsland.ca

St. Luke Magazine, (M) Christ Catholic Church International, Donald W. Mullan, 4695 St. Lawrence Ave, Niagara Falls, ON L2E 6S8, Tel. (905)354-2329 Fax (905)354-9934 Email: dmullan1@cogeco.ca

Salvationist, (M) The Salvation Army in Canada and Bermuda, Geoff Moulton, Managing Editor, 2 Overlea Blvd., Toronto, ON M4H 1P4, Tel. (416)425-2111 Fax (416)422-6120 Email: salvationist@can.salvationarmy.org Website: www.salvationist/CAN/Sarmy.ca

Scarboro Missions, (7-Y) The Roman Catholic Church in Canada, Kathy Gillis, 2685 Kingston Rd., Scarborough, ON M1M 1M4, Tel. (416)261-7135 or 800-260-4815 (In Canada) Fax (416)261-0820 Email: editor@scarboromissions.ca Website: www.scarboromissions.ca

The Shantyman, (1-Y) Nondenominational, John Noble, Editor in Chief; Mary Noble, Managing Editor, Box 66, McLeese Lake, B.C. V0L 1P0, Tel. Fax (905)427-0334 Email: john.cynthia@scainternational.org Website: scainternational.org/wp-content/uploads/2010/04/Shantyman-Magazine-Jan.-2011.pdf

Sister Triangle, (Q) Churches of Christ, Marilyn Muller, 150 Oak Avenue, Dauphin, MB R7N 2S3, Tel. (204)638-9812 Fax (204)638-6231 Email: dmmuller@mymts.net

SR- Studies in Religion- Sciences religieuses, (Q) Nondenominational, Dr. Aaron Hughes, Dept. of Religious Studies, University of Calgary, 2500 University Avenue NW, Calgary, AB T2N 1N4, Tel. (403)220-7063 Email: rels@ucalgary.ca Website: www.wlupress.wlu.ca

Testimony, (11-Y) The Pentecostal Assemblies of Canada, Steve Kennedy, 2450 Milltower Ct., Mississauga, ON L5N 5Z6, Tel. (905)542-7400 Fax (905)542-7313 Email: testimony@PAOC.org Website: www.testimonymag.com

Topic, (10-Y) The Anglican Church of Canada, Randy Murray, 580-401 W. Georgia St., Vancouver, BC V6B 5A1, Tel. (604)684-6306 ext. 223 Fax (604)684-7017

Email: rmurray@vancouver.anglican.ca Website: www.vancouver.anglican.ca

United Church Observer, (M) The United Church of Canada, David Wilson, 478 Huron St., Toronto, ON M5R 2R3, Tel. (416)960-8500 Fax (416)960-8477 Email: general@ucobserver.org Website: www.ucobserver.org

La Vie Chretienne (French), (M) Presbyterian Church in Canada, Jean Porret, P.O. Box 272, Suzz. Rosemont, Montreal, QC H1X 3B8, Tel. (514)737-4168

La Vie des Communautes religieuses, (5-Y) The Roman Catholic Church in Canada, Religious Communities (Consortium), 251 St-Jean-Baptiste, Nicolet, QC J3T 1X9, Tel. (819)293-8736 Fax (819)293-2419 Email: viecr@sogetel.net

Vie Liturgique, (6-Y) The Roman Catholic Church in Canada, Jean Grou, 4475, rue Frontenac, Montreal, QC H2H 2S2, Tel. (800)668-2547 Fax (514)278-3030 Email: jean.grou@novalis.ca Website: www.novalis.ca

VIP Communique, Foursquare Gospel Church of Canada, Barry Buzza, B307-2099 Lougheed Highway, Port Coquitlam, BC V3S 1A8, Tel. (604)941-8414 Fax (604)941-8415 Email: foursquare@foursquare.ca Website: www.foursquare.ca

Visnyk- The Herald, (M) Ukrainian Orthodox Church of Canada, Rev. Fr. Eugene Maximiuk, 9 St. John's Ave., Winnipeg, MB R2W 1G8, Tel. (204)586-3093 ext 236 Fax (204)582-5241 Email: visnyk@uocc.ca Website: www.uocc.ca

Word Alive, (Q) Nondenominational, Dwayne Janke, Wycliffe Bible Translators of Canada Inc., 4316 10 St. NE, Calgary, AB T2E 6K3, Tel. (403)250-5411 Fax (403)250-2623 Email: editors_wam@wycliffe.ca Website: www.wycliffe.ca

Young Companion, (11-Y) Old Order Amish Church, Joseph Stoll and Christian Stoll, Old Order Amish Church, Rt. 4, Aylmer, ON N5H 2R3

12. Church Archives and Historical Records Collections

American and Canadian history is interwoven with the social and cultural experience of religious life and thought. Most repositories of primary research materials in North America will include some documentation on religion and church communities. This directory is not intended to replace standard bibliographic guides to those resources. The intent is to give a new researcher entry to major archival holdings of religious collections and to programs of national scope. In the interest of space, no attempt has been made to list the specific contents of the archives or to include the numerous specialized research libraries of North America. The repositories listed herein are able to re-direct inquirers to significant regional and local church archives, and specialized collections such as those of religious orders, educational and charitable organizations, and personal papers.

Repositories marked with an asterisk (*) are designated by their denomination as the official archives. The reference departments at these archives will assist researchers in locating primary material of geographic or subject focus.

UNITED STATES

Adventist

Adventist World Headquarters, Office of Archives and Statistics, 12501 Old Columbia Pike, Silver Spring, MD 20904-6600, Director: Bert Haloviak, Tel. (301)680-5020 Fax (301) 680-5038, Email: haloviakb@gc.adventist.org, Website:ast.gc.adventist.org

Repository of the records created at the world administrative center of the Seventh-day Adventist Church and includes the period from the 1800s to the present.

Aurora University, Aurora University, Charles B. Phillips Library, 347 S. Gladstone, Aurora, IL 60506, Curator: Dr. Susan L. Palmer, Tel. (630)844-5445 Fax (630)844-3848, Email: jenks@@aurora.edu

Jenks Memorial Collection of Adventual Materials. Adventual archival materials on the Millerite/Early Adventist movement (1830-1860); also denominational archives relating to Advent Christian Church, Life and Advent Union, and to a lesser extent, Evangelical Adventists and Age-to-Come Adventists.

Center for Adventist Research, James White Library, Andrews University, Berrien Springs, MI 49103-1440, Director: Dr. Merlin D. Burt, Tel. (269)471-3209 Fax (269)471-2646, Email: car@andrews.edu, Website: www.andrews.edu/library/car

Large collection of Seventh-day Adventist material.

Ellen G. White Estate Branch Office, Loma Linda University Library, Department of Archives and Special Collections, 11072 Anderson Street, Loma Linda, CA 92350, Chair of Archives and Special Collection: Lori Curtis, Tel. (909)558-4942 Fax (909)558-0381, Email: whiteestate@ llu.edu, Website: www.llu.edu/llu/ library/heritage

Photographs, sound and video recordings, personal papers, and library pertaining to the Seventh-day Adventist Church.

Ellen G. White Estate, Inc., 12501 Old Columbia Pike, Silver Spring, MD 20904, Archivist: Tim Poirier, Tel. (301)680-6540 Fax (301)680-6559, Email: mail@whitestate.org, Website: www. whiteestate.org

Records include letters and manuscripts (1840s to 1915), pamphlets and publications, and the White papers.

Assemblies of God

*Flower Pentecostal Heritage Center, 1445 Boonville Ave., Springfield, MO 65802, Director: Darrin Rodgers, Tel. (417)862-2781 ext. 4400 Fax (417)862-6203, Email: archives @ag.org, Website: www.ifphc.org

Official repository for materials related to the Assemblies of God, as well as materials related to the broader Pentecostal and charismatic movements.

Baptist

*American Baptist Historical Society, 3001 Mercer University Dr., Atlanta, GA 30341, Exec. Director: Dr. Deborah B. Van Broekhoven, Reader Services: Betsy Dunbar, Tel. (678) 547-6680 Fax (678) 547-6682, Email: abhs@creds.edu, Website: abhsarchives.org

Official archives of the American Baptist Churches, USA and the Baptist World Alliance. Collections also include original manuscripts of Baptist ministers, missionaries and scholars; some original church records; printed reports of national, state and association minutes for over two centuries covering numerous Baptist denominations; serials representing the Baptist worldwide press; books and pamphlets which are by, about, for and against Baptists.

American Baptist-Samuel Colgate Historical Library, *See American Baptist Historical Society*.

*Seventh-day Baptist Historical Society, 3120 Kennedy Rd., P.O. Box 1678, Janesville, WI 53547, Librarian-Historian: Nicholas J. Kersten, Tel. (608)752-5055 Fax (608)752-7711, Email: sdbhist@seventhdaybaptist.org, Website: www.sdbhistory.org

Serves as a depository for records of Seventh-day Baptists, Sabbath and Sabbath-keeping Baptists since the mid-seventeenth century.

*Southern Baptists Historical Library & Archives, 901 Commerce St., Suite 400, Nashville, TN 37203-3630, Director and Archivist: Bill Sumners, Tel. (615)244-0344 Fax (615)782-4821, Email: bill@sbhla.org, Website: www.sbhla.org

Central depository of the Southern Baptist Convention. Materials include official records of denominational agencies; personal papers of denominational leaders; records of related Baptist organizations; and annual proceedings of national and regional bodies.

Primitive Baptist Library of Carthage, Illinois, 416 Main St., Carthage, IL 62321, Director of Library: Elder Robert Webb, Tel. (217)357-3723 Fax (217)357-3723, Email: bwebb9@juno.com, Website: www.carthage.lib.il.us/community/churches/primbap/pbl.html

Collects the records of congregations and associations.

Baptist and United Church of Christ

Andover Newton Theological School, Andover Newton Theological School, Franklin Trask Library, 169 Herrick Rd., Newton Centre, MA 02459, Co-Director for Special Collections: Diana Yount, Tel. (617)831-2415 Fax (617)831-1616, Email: dyount@ants.edu, Website: www.ants.edu/library

The collections document Baptist, Congregational and United Church history, including personal papers relating to national denominational work and foreign missions, with emphasis on New England Church history.

Brethren in Christ

*Brethren in Christ Historical Library and Archives, One College Avenue, P.O. Box 3002, Grantham, PA 17027, Director: Glen A. Pierce, Tel. (717)691-6048 Fax (717)691-6042, Email: archives@messiah.edu, Website: www.messiah.edu/archives/

Records of general church boards and agencies, regional conferences, congregations and organizations; also includes library, manuscripts, and oral history collection.

Catholic Church

American Catholic History Research Center and University Archives, Catholic University of America, 101 Life Cycle Institute, Washington, DC 20064, Archivist: Timothy Meagher, Tel. (202)319-5065 Fax (202)319-6554, Email: meagher@cua.edu, Website: libraries.cua.edu/achrcua

Department of Special Collections and Archives, Marquette University, P.O. Box 3141, , Milwaukee, WI 53233-3141, Department Head and Archivist: Matt Blessing, Tel. (414)288-7256 Fax (414)288-6709, Email: matt.blessing@marquette.edu, Website: www.marquette.edu/library/ collections/archives

Collection strengths are in the areas of Catholic social action, American missions and missionaries, and other work with Native Americans and African Americans.

United States Catholic Historical Society, 201 Seminary Ave., Yonkers, NY 10704, Tel. (914)337-8381 Fax (914)337-6379, Email: Website: www.uschs.com

University of Notre Dame Archives, 607 Hesburgh Library, Notre Dame, IN 46556, Archivist and Curator of Manuscripts: William Kevin Cawley, Tel. (574)631-6448 Fax (574)631-7980, Email: archives@nd.edu, Website: www.archives.nd.edu

Papers of bishops and prominent Catholics and records of Catholic organizations. Includes parish histories, but few parish records.

Salvation Army

*Salvation Army Archives and Research Center, 615 Slaters Lane, Alexandria, VA 22313, Archivist: Susan Mitchem, Tel. (703)684-5500 Fax (703)299-5552, Email: archives@usa.salvationarmy.org, Website: www.salvationarmy.org

Holds the documents of Salvation Army history, personalities, and events in the United States from 1880.

Churches of Christ

Center for Restoration Studies, Abilene Christian University, 760 Library Court, P.O. Box 29208, Abilene, TX 79699-9208, Archivist: Dr. Carisse Berryhill, Tel. (325)674-2000 Fax (325)674-2202, Email: carisse.berryhill@acu.edu, Website: www.bible.acu.edu/crs

Archival materials connected with the Stone-Campbell Movement. The chief focus is on the Church of Christ in the twentieth century.

Emmanuel School of Religion Library, One Walker Drive, Johnson City, TN 37601-9438, Director: Thomas E. Stokes, Tel. (423)926-

1186 Fax (423)926-6198, Email: library@ esr.edu, Website: esr.edu

Materials related to the Stone-Campbell/ Restoration Movement tradition. Collection includes items from the Christian Church and Churches of Christ, the a cappella Churches of Christ, and the Christian Church (Disciples of Christ).

Churches of God General Conference

*Winebrenner Theological Seminary Library, Winebrenner Theological Seminary, 950 N. Main St., Findlay, OH 45840, Director of Library Services: Margaret Hirschy, Tel. (419)434-4260 Fax (419)434-4267, Email: library@winebrenner.edu, Website: www.wine brenner.edu/Library

Archival materials of the Churches of God, General Conference including local conference journals.

Disciples of Christ

Christian Theological Seminary Library, Christian Theological Seminary Library, 1000 W. 42nd St., Indianapolis, IN 46208-3301, Archives Manager: Don Haymes, Tel. (317) 931-2368 Fax (317)931-2363, Email: don.haymes@cts.edu, Website: www.cts.edu

Archival materials dealing with the Disciples of Christ and related movements.

*Disciples of Christ Historical Society, 1101 19th Ave. S, Nashville, TN 37212, Director of Library and Archives: Sara Harwell, Tel. (615) 327-1444 Fax (615)327-1445, Email: harwell @discipleshistory.org, Website: www.dis histsoc.org

Collects documents of the Stone-Campbell Movement.

Episcopal

*Archives of the Episcopal Church, 606 Rathervue Place, P.O. Box 2247, Austin, TX 78768-2247, Canonical Archivist and Director: Mark J. Duffy, Tel. (512)472-6816 Fax (512) 480-0437, Email: research@episcopalarchives.org, Website: www.episcopal archives.org

Repository for the official records of the national Church, its corporate bodies and affiliated agencies, personal papers, and some diocesan archives. Contact the Archives for reference to diocesan and parochial church records.

Evangelical and Reformed

*Evangelical and Reformed Historical Society, Lancaster Theological Seminary, 555 W. James St., Lancaster, PA 17603, Archivist: Richard R. Berg, Tel. (717)290-8704 Fax (717)393-4254, Email: erhs@lancaster seminary.edu, Website: www.erhs.info

Manuscripts and transcriptions of early German Reformed Church (U.S.) 1725-1863; Reformed Church in the United States 1863-1934, and Evangelical and Reformed Church 1934-1957 records of coetus, synods, and classes, pastoral records, and personal papers.

Evangelical Congregational Church

*Archives of the Evangelical Congregational Church, Evangelical Seminary, Rostad Library, 121 S. College St., Myerstown, PA 17067, Archivist: Terry M. Heisey, Tel. (717) 866-5775 Fax (717)866-4667, Email: theisey@ evangelical.edu, Website: www.evangelical. edu

Repository of records of the administrative units of the denomination, affiliated organizations, and closed churches. Also collected are records of local congregations and materials related to the United Evangelical Church and the Evangelical Association.

Friends

*Historical Library of Swarthmore, Swarthmore College, 500 College Ave., Swarthmore, PA 19081-1399, Curator: Christopher Densmore, Tel. (610)328-8496 Fax (610)328-7329, Email: friends@swarthmore.edu, Website: www.swarthmore.edu/library/friends

Official depository for the records of the Philadelphia, Baltimore, and New York Yearly Meetings. Comprehensive collection of originals and copies of other Quaker meeting archives.

Special Collections-Quaker Collection, Haverford College, 370 Lancaster Ave., Haverford, PA 19041-1392, Manuscript Librarian and College Archivist: Diana Franzusoff Peterson, Tel. (610)896-1161 Fax (610)896-1102, Email: elapsans@ haverford.edu, Website: www.haverford. edu/library/special

Repository for material relating to the Society of Friends (Quakers), especially to the segment known from 1827 to the mid-20th century as "Orthodox" in the Delaware Valley.

Interdenominational

American Bible Society Library and Archives, 1865 Broadway, New York, NY 10023-9980, Curator: Liana Lupas, Tel. (212)408-1200 Fax (212)408-1526, Email: llupas@american bible.org, Website: www.americanbible.org/ BiblicalHeritage/library.dsp

Core of collections includes founders' documents, minutes, and correspondence related to the worldwide mission of the ABS.

Billy Graham Center Archives, Wheaton College, 500 College Ave., 3rd Floor, Wheaton, IL 60187-5593, Director of Archives: Paul Ericksen, Tel. (630)752-5910,

Email: archives@gtu.edu, Website: www.gtu. edu/library/special-collections

Graduate Theological Union Archives, 2400 Ridge Road, Berkeley, CA 94709, Archivist: Lucinda Glenn, Tel. (510)649-2507 Fax (510)649-2508, Email: archives@gtu.edu, Website: www.gtu.edu/library/archives

Holy Spirit Research Center, Oral Roberts University, LRC 5E 02, 7777 S. Lewis Ave., Tulsa, OK 74171, Director: Mark E. Roberts, Tel. (918)495-6898 Fax (918)495-6662, Email: mroberts@oru.edu, Website: www.oru. edu/university/library/holyspirit

Pentecostal and Charismatic records, with emphasis on divine healing.

National Council of the Churches of Christ Archives, Presbyterian Historical Society, 425 Lombard St., Philadelphia, PA 19147-1516, Dir. of Programs: Nancy J. Taylor, Tel. (215)627-1852 Fax (215)627-0509, Email: refdesk@history.pcusa.org, Website: www. history.pcusa.org

Schomburg Center for Research in Black Culture, 515 Malcolm X Blvd., New York, NY 10037, Manuscripts, Archives, and Rare Books Division, Curator: Diana Lachatanere, Tel. (212)491-2297 Fax (212)491-2037, Email: scmarbref@nypl.org, Website: www. schomburgcenter.org

The Burke Library at Union Theological Seminary, Union Theological Seminary, Burke Library, 3041 Broadway, New York, NY 10027, Archivist: Ruth Tonkiss Cameron, Tel. (212)280-5607 Fax (212)280-1456, Email: mboddy@uts.columbia.edu, Website: www. columbia.edu/cu/lweb/indiv/burke

The largest theological library in the western hemisphere with extensive rare and antique holdings.

University of Chicago, University of Chicago, Regenstein Library, 1100 E 57th St., Chicago, IL 60637-1502, Acting Bibliographer for Religion: David Larsen, Tel. (773)702-8626, Email: d-larsen@uchicago.edu, Website: guides.lib.uchicago.edu/religion

Yale Divinity School Library, 409 Prospect St., New Haven, CT 06511, Research Services Librarian: Suzanne Estelle-Holmer, Tel. (203) 432-5290 Fax (203)432-3906, Email: divinity. library@yale.edu, Website: www.library.yale. edu/div

Jewish

American Jewish Historical Society (NY Location), Center for Jewish History, 15 W. 16th St., New York, NY 10011, Director of

Research: Michael Feldberg, Tel. (212)294-6160 Fax (212)294-6161, Email: info@ajhs.org, Website: www.ajhs.org

Archival repositories of the Jewish people in America, including significant religious contributions to American life.

American Jewish Historical Society (MA Location), Friedman Memorial Library, 101 Newbury Street, Boston, MA 02116, Managing Archivist: Judi Garner, Tel. (617) 226-1245 Fax (617)226-1248, Website: www.ajhs.org

Archival repositories of the Jewish people in America, including significant religious contributions to American life.

Jacob Rader Marcus Center of the American Jewish Archives, Hebrew Union College, 3101 Clifton Ave., Cincinnati, OH 45220, Senior Archivist: Kevin Proffitt, Tel. (513)221-1875 Fax (513)221-7812, Email: kprofitt@huc.edu, Website: www.huc.edu/aja

Materials documenting the Jewish experience in the Western Hemisphere with emphasis on the Reform movement. Included in the collection are congregational and organizational records, personal papers of rabbis and secular leaders, and genealogical materials.

Latter-day Saints

*Archives, Church of Jesus Christ of Latter-day Saints, 15 E. North Temple, Salt Lake City, UT 84150-3800, Director: Elder Martin K. Jensen, Tel. (801)240-2272 Fax (801)240-2804

Repository of official records of church departments, missions, congregations, and associated organizations. Includes personal papers of church leaders and members.

Family History Library, 35 North West Temple, Salt Lake City, UT 84150-1600, Acquisition and Receiving Center, Tel. (801)240-5696 Fax (801)240-5551, Email: FHL@family search.org, Website: familysearch.org

Primarily microfilmed vital, church, probate, land, census, and military records including local church registers.

Lutheran

*Archives of the Evangelical Lutheran Church in America, 321 Bonnie Lane, Elk Grove Village, IL 60007, Tel. (847)690-9410 Fax (847)690-9502, Email: archives@elca.org, Website: www.elca.org/archives

Official repository for the churchwide offices of the ELCA and its predecessors. For further information on synod and regional archives, contact the Chicago archives or check the ELCA World Wide Web site. For ELCA college and seminary archives, contact those institutions directly, or consult the ELCA Archives.

*Concordia Historical Institute, Concordia Seminary, 804 Seminary Place, St. Louis, MO 63105, Director: Larry E. Lumpe, Tel. (314) 505-7900 Fax (314)505-7901, Email: chi@lutheranhistory.org, Website: www.lutheranhistory.org

Official repository of The Lutheran Church-Missouri Synod. Collects synodical and congregational records, personal papers and records of Lutheran agencies.

Lutheran History Center of the West, , 1712 Greentree Dr., Concord, CA , Editor: Duane A. Peterson, Tel. (925)825-2109, Email: duanep@astound.net

Mennonite

Center for Mennonite Brethren Studies, 1717 S. Chestnut, Fresno, CA 93702, Archivist: Kevin Enns-Rempel, Tel. (559)453-2225 Fax (559) 453-2124, Email: kennsrem@fresno.edu, Website: fresno.edu/dept/library/cmbs

Official repository for the General Conference of Mennonite Brethren Churches.

*Mennonite Church USA Archives-Goshen, 1700 South Main, Goshen, IN 46526, Archivist: Colleen McFarland, Tel. (574)523-3080 Fax (574)535-7756, Email: history@MennoniteUSA.org, Website: www.MennoniteUSA.org

Repository of the official organizational records of the Mennonite Church and personal papers of leaders and members.

*Mennonite Church USA Archives-North Newton, Bethel College, 300 E. 27th St., North Newton, KS 67117-0531, Archivist: John Thiesen, Tel. (316)284-5304 Fax (316)284-5843, Email: mla@bethelks.edu, Website: www.bethelks.edu/services/mla

An official repository for the Mennonite Church USA and several other organizations related to the denomination.

Methodist

B. L. Fisher Library, Asbury Theological Seminary, 204 N. Lexington Ave.,Wilmore, KY 40390, Archivist and Special Collections Librarian: Grace Yoder, Tel. (859)858-3581 Fax (859)858-2350, Email: graceyoder@asburyseminary.edu, Website: www.asburyseminary.edu

Documents the Holiness Movement and evangelical currents in the United Methodist Church. Holdings include records of related associations, camp meetings, personal papers, and periodicals.

Center for Evangelical United Brethren Heritage, United Theological Seminary, 1810 Harvard Blvd., Dayton, OH 45406-4599, Interim

Director: Sarah D. Brooks Blair, Tel. (937) 529-2234 Fax (937)275-5701, Email: sblair@united.edu, Website: www.united.edu/#jans_2

Documents predecessor and cognate church bodies of the United Methodist Church including the Evangelical Association, United Brethren in Christ, United Evangelical, Evangelical, Evangelical United Brethren, Evangelical Congregational, and Evangelical of North America.

*General Commission on Archives and History, The United Methodist Church, P.O. Box 127, Madison, NJ 07940, Archivist/Records Administrator: L. Dale Patterson, Tel. (973) 408-3189 Fax (973)408-3909, Email: dpatterson@gcah.org, Website: www.gcah.org

Collects administrative and episcopal records, and personal papers of missionaries and leaders. Holds limited genealogical information on ordained ministers. Will direct researchers to local and regional collections of congregational records and information on United Methodism and its predecessors.

*Heritage Hall at Livingstone College, 701 W. Monroe St., Salisbury, NC 28144, Director: Phyllis H. Galloway, Tel. (704)216-6094 Fax (704)216-6246, Website: www.livingstone.edu/heritage_hall.htm

Records of the African Methodist Episcopal Zion Church.

*Office of the Historiographer of the African Methodist Episcopal Church, P.O. Box 301, Williamstown, MA 02167, Historiographer: Dennis C. Dickerson, Tel. (413)597-2484 Fax (413)597-3673, Email: dennis.c.dickerson@williams.edu

General and annual conference minutes; reports of various departments such as missions and publications; and congregational histories and other local materials. The materials are housed in the office of the historiographer and other designated locations.

Moravian

Moravian Archives-Northern Province, 41 W. Locust St., Bethlehem, PA 18018-2757, Archivist: Dr. Paul Peucker, Tel. (610)866-3255 Fax (610)866-9210, Email: morarchbeth@enter.net, Website: www.moravianchurcharchives.org

Records of the Northern Province of the Moravian Church in America, including affiliated provinces in the Eastern West Indies, Nicaragua, Honduras, Labrador, and Alaska.

Moravian Archives-Southern Province, 457 S. Church St., Winston-Salem, NC 27101, Archivist: C. Daniel Crews, Tel. (336)722-

1742 Fax (336)725-4514, Email: info@moravian churcharchives.org, Website: www.moravian archives.org

Repository of the records of the Moravian Church, Southern Province, its congregations, and its members.

Nazarene

*Nazarene Archives, Church of the Nazarene, 17001 Praire Star Parkway, Lenexa, KS 66220, Archives Manager: Stan Ingersol, Tel. (913) 577-0641, Email: singersol@nazarene.org, Website: www.nazarene.org/ministries/administration/achives/display.html

Collections are international in scope, including general and district materials, leaders, agencies, study commissions, congregations, church universities and seminaries world-wide, medical work, and social ministries.

Pentecostal

Center for the Study of Oneness Pentecostalism, 8855 Dunn Road, Hazelwood, MO 63042, Chair, Historical Committee: Robin Johnston, Tel. (314) 837-7300 Fax (314)837-4503, Email: rjohnston@upci.org, Website: www.upci.org

Collects a variety of Pentecostal archives, primarily the United Pentecostal (Oneness) Branch.

David du Plessis Archives, Fuller Theological Seminary, 135 North Oakland Ave., Pasadena, CA 81182, Archivist: Roger Robins, Tel. (626)584-5311 Fax (626)584-5644, Email: archive@fuller.edu, Website: www.fuller.edu/archives

Collects material related to the Pentecostal and Charismatic movements; also includes material related to Charles Fuller and the Old Fashioned Revival Hour broadcast, Fuller Theological Seminary, and neo-evangelicalism.

*Hal Bernard Dixon Jr. Pentecostal Research Center, 260 11th St. NE, Cleveland, TN 37311, Director: David G. Roebuck, PhD, Tel. (423) 614-8576 Fax (423)614-8555, Email: dixon_research@leeuniversity.edu, Website: cogheritage.org

Official repository of the Church of God (Cleveland, TN). Also collects other Pentecostal and Charismatic materials.

*International Pentecostal Holiness Church Archives and Research Center, P.O. Box 12609, Oklahoma City, OK 73157, Director: Dr. Harold D. Hunter, Tel. (405)787-7110 ext. 3132 Fax (405)789-3957, Email: archives@iphc.org, Website: www.iphc.org/archives

Official repository for records and publications produced by the international headquarters, conferences, and influential leaders.

Polish National Catholic

*Polish National Catholic Church Commission on History and Archives, 1031 Cedar Ave., Scranton, PA 18505, Chair: Joseph Wieczerzak, Tel. (717)343-0100

Documents pertaining to the Church's national office, parishes, Prime Bishop, leaders, and organizations.

Presbyterian

*Historical Foundation of the Cumberland Presbyterian Church and the Cumberland Presbyterian Church in America, 8207 Traditional Place, Cordova, TN 38016, Director and Archivist: Susan Knight Gore, Tel. (901)276-8602 Fax (901)272-3913, Email: archives@cumberland.org, Website: www.cumberland.org/hfcpc

*Presbyterian Historical Society Headquarters, 425 Lombard St., Philadelphia, PA 19147-1516, Dir. of Programs and Services: Nancy J. Taylor, Tel. (215)627-1852 Fax (215)627-0509, Email: refdesk@history.pcusa.org, Website: www. history.pcusa.org

Collects the official records of the Presbyterian Church (USA)'s national offices and agencies, synods, presbyteries, and some congregations. The Society also houses records of the Church's predecessor denominations, personal papers of prominent Presbyterians, and records of ecumenical organizations. In addition, the Southern Regional Office in Montreat, NC holds local and regional records for the fourteen southern states.

*Presbyterian Church in America Historical Center, 12330 Conway Rd., St. Louis, MO 63141, Director: Wayne Sparkman, Tel. (314) 469-9077 Fax (314)469-9077, Email: wsparkman @pcanet.org, Website: www.pca history.org

Center serves as the official archive of the Presbyterian Church in America. The Center also holds the records of five other Presbytrerian denominations and the manuscript collections of over one hundred individuals connected with these church bodies.

*Presbyterian Historical Society Southern Regional Office, See *Presbyterian Historical Society Headquarters*

Princeton Theological Seminary Libraries, Library Place and Mercer Street, P.O. Box 111, Princeton, NJ 08542, Curator of Spec. Coll.: Clifford Anderson, Tel. (609)497-7953 Fax (609) 497-1826, Email: special.collections@ptsem.edu Website: www. library.ptsem.edu/collections

Reformed

*Heritage Hall, Calvin College, 1855 Knollcrest Circle SE, Grand Rapids, MI 49546, Curator

of Archives: Richard H. Harms, Tel. (616)957-6313 Fax (616)957-6470, Email: crcarchives@calvin.edu, Website: www.calvin.edu/hh

Repository of the official records of the Christian Reformed Church in North America, including classes, congregations, and denominational agencies and committees.

*Reformed Church Archives, 21 Seminary Place, New Brunswick, NJ 08901-1159, Archivist: Russell Gasero, Tel. (732)246-1779 Fax (732)249-5412, Email: rgasero@rca.org, Website: www.rca.org/archives

Official repository for denominational records including congregations, classes, synods, missions, and national offices.

Swedenborgian

*Swedenborg Library, Bryn Athyn College of the New Church, 2925 College Drive, P.O. Box 740, Bryn Athyn, PA 19009-0740, Director: Carroll C. Odhner, Tel. (267)502-2547 Fax (267)502-2637, Email: carroll.odhner@brynathyn.edu, Website: www.brynathyn.edu/academics/swedenborg-library/

Unitarian Universalist

*Andover-Harvard Theological Library, Harvard Divinity School, 45 Francis Ave., Cambridge, MA 02138, Curator: Frances O'Donnell, Tel. (617)496-5153 Fax (617)496-4111, Email: frances_odonnell@harvard.edu, Website: www.hds.harvard.edu/library

Institutional archives of the Unitarian Universalist Association including the Unitarian Universalist Service Committee; also houses records of many congregations; personal papers of ministers and other individuals.

Meadville-Lombard Theological School Library, Meadville/Lombard Theological School Library, 5701 S. Woodlawn Ave., Chicago, IL 60637, Director: Neil W. Gerdes, Tel. (773)256-3000 ext. 225 Fax (773)256-3008, Email: ngerdes@meadville.edu, Website: www.meadville.edu/library.html

Repository for materials relating to Unitarian Universalism in particular and liberal religion in general. Includes personal papers of several noted UU ministers, and church records from many UU churches in the Midwestern USA.

United Church of Christ

Archives of the Evangelical Synod, Eden Theological Seminary, Luhr Library, 475 E. Lockwood Ave., Webster Groves, MO 63119-3192, Sr. Research Consultant: The Rev. Dr. Lowell Zuck, Tel. (314)252-3140, Email: lzuck@eden.edu, Website: www.eden.edu/EducationalResources/Archives.aspx

Archival records include organization records, personal papers and immigration records.

Congregational Library, Congregational Library, 14 Beacon St., Boston, MA 02108, Archivist: Jessica Steytler, Tel. (617)523-0470 Fax (617)523-0491, Email: jsteytler@14beacon.org, Website: www.congregational library.org

Documentation on the Congregational, Congregational Christian, Christian, and United Church of Christ throughout the world, including local church records, associations, charitable organizations, and papers of clergy, missionaries and others.

Elon University Library, Elon University Library, 2550 Campus Box, Elon, NC 27244, Archivist/Technical Services Librarian: Connie L. Keller, Tel. (336)278-6599 Fax (336)278-6639, Email: keller@elon.edu, Website: www.elon.edu/library

Collection of membership records and other archival material on the predecessor churches of the UCC: Christian Church and the Southern Conference of the Christian Church; also maintains records of churches that no longer exist.

*United Church of Christ Archives, 700 Prospect Ave, Cleveland, OH 44115, Archivist: Bridgette Kelly, Tel. (216)736-2106, Email: kellyb@ucc.org, Website: www.ucc.org/about us/archives

Records created in the national setting of the Church since its founding in 1957, including the General Synod, Executive Council, officers, instrumentalities, and bodies created by and/or related to the General Synod.

CANADA

Anglican

*General Synod Archives, 80 Hayden St., Toronto, ON M4Y 3G2, Archivist: Nancy Hurn, Tel. (416)924-9199 ext. 279 Fax (416)968-7983, Email: archives@national.anglican.ca, Website: anglican.ca/resources/gsarchives/

Collects the permanent records of the General Synod, its committees, and its employees. The Archives has a national scope, and provides referral services on local Church records.

Baptist

*Atlantic Baptist Archives, Vaughan Memorial Library, P.O. Box 4, Wolfville, NS B4P 2R6, Tel. (902)585-1011 Fax (902)585-1748, Email: archives@acadiau.ca, Website: library.acadiau.ca/archives

Records of associations and churches of the Convention of Atlantic Baptist Churches; also personal papers of pastors and missionaries.

Canadian Baptist Archives, McMaster Divinity College, 1280 Main St. W, , Hamilton, ON L8S 4K1, Director: Dr. Gordon Heath, Tel. (905)525-9140 ext. 23511 Fax (905)577-4782, Email: gheath@mcmaster.ca, Website: divinity. mcmaster.ca/academics/resources/baptist Archives

Friends
Canadian Yearly Meeting Archives, Pickering College, 16945 Bayview Ave., Newmarket, ON L3Y 4X2, Yearly Meeting Archivist: Jane Zavitz-Bond, Tel. (905)895-1700 ext. 247 Fax (905)895-9076, Email: cym-archivist@ quaker.ca, Website: www.quaker.ca/archives. html

Holds the extant records for Quakers in Canada beginning with Adolphus in 1798 to the present, including the records of the Canadian Friends Service Committee.

Interdenominational
Canadian Council of Churches Archives, National Archives of Canada, 395 Wellington, Ottawa, ON K1A 0N3, Tel. (613)992-3884 Fax (613)995-6274, Email: reference@ archives.ca, Website: www.archives.ca

Genealogical assistance: (613) 996-7458

Library and Archives of Canada, 395 Wellington, Ottawa, ON K1A 0N3, Librarian and Archivist of Canada: Dr. Daniel J. Caron, Tel. (613)992-3884 Fax (613)995-6274, Email: reference@ bac-lac.gc.ca, Website: www.collectionscanada. gc.ca

Records of interdenominational and ecumenical organizations, missionary societies, denominational churches, parish registers, and papers of prominent clergy.

Jewish
Canadian Jewish Congress National Archives, 1590 Avenue Docteur Penfield, Montreal, QC H3G 1C5, Director of Archives: Janice Rosen, Tel. (514)931-7531 ext. 2 Fax (514)931-0548, Email: archives@cjc.ca, Website: www.cjc.ca

Collects documentation on all aspects of social, political, and cultural history of the Jewish presence in Quebec and Canada.

Lutheran
*Archives of the Evangelical Lutheran Church in Canada, Lutheran Theological Seminary, 114 Seminary Crescent, Saskatoon, Saskatchewan, S7N-0X3, National Secretary: Murray Walter, Tel. (306)966-7850, Email: info@elcic.ca, Website: www.elcic.ca

Official repository for the ELCIC and its predecessor bodies, the Evangelical Lutheran Church of Canada and the Evangelical Lutheran Church of America-Canada Section.

Lutheran Historical Institute, 7100 Ada Blvd., Edmonton, AB T5B 4E4, Archivist: Karen Baron, Tel. (780)474-8156 Fax (780)477-9829, Email: abclcc@connect.ab.ca, Website: www.lccarchives.ca

Mennonite
*Centre for Mennonite Brethren Studies, 169 Riverton Ave., Winnipeg, MB R2L 2E5, Archivist: Conrad Stoesz, Tel. (204)669-6575 Fax (204)654-1865, Email: cstoesz@mb conf.ca, Website: www.mbconf.ca/mbstudies

Institutional records of the boards and agencies of the Mennonite Brethren Church in Canada with some holdings pertaining to other parts of North America; also personal papers of leaders.

*Mennonite Heritage Centre, Mennonite Church Canada, 600 Shaftesbury Blvd., , Winnipeg, MB R3P OM4, Director: Alf Redekopp, Tel. (204)888-6781 Fax (204)831-5675, Email: aredekopp@mennonitechurch.ca, Website: www.mennonitechurch.ca/programs/archives

Institutional records and personal papers of leaders within the Mennonite Community. Holdings include the records of the national church, area church, congregations, institutions, and related agencies

Pentecostal
*Pentecostal Assemblies of Canada, 2450 Milltower Court, Mississauga, ON L5N 5Z6, Director of Archives: Marilyn Stroud, Tel. (905)542-7400 Ext. 5282 Fax (905)542-7313, Email: mstroud@paoc.org, Website: www. paoc.org/about/archives

Repository of archival records created by the Pentecostal Assemblies of Canada.

Presbyterian
*Presbyterian Church in Canada Archives and Records, 50 Wynford Dr., , Toronto, ON M3C 1J7, Archivist/Records Administrator: Kim M. Arnold, Tel. (416)441-1111 ext. 310 Fax (416) 441-2825, Email: karnold@presbyterian.ca, Website: presbyterianarchives.ca

Records of the Presbyterian Church in Canada, its officials, ministers, congregations and organizations.

Roman Catholic
Research Centre for the Religious History of Canada, St. Paul University, 223 Main St., Ottawa, ON K1S 1C4, Director: Pierre Hurtubise, Tel. (613)236-1393 ext. 2270 Fax (613)782-3001, Email: crh-rc-rhc@ustpaul. uottowa.ca, Website: www.ustpaul.ca

Holds 900 linear feet of documents, mainly records on deposit from other institutions; and also guides to many Canadian Catholic archives.

Salvation Army

George Scott Railton Heritage Centre, 2130 Bayview Ave., North York, ON M4N 3K6, Director: Ira Barrow, Tel. (416)481-4441 Fax (416)481-6096, Email: Ira.Barrow@sally net.org

Records include publications; also financial, personnel, social welfare, and immigration records.

United Church of Canada

*United Church of Canada Central Archives, Victoria University, 73 Queens Park Crescent E., Toronto, ON M5S 1K7, Chief Archivist: Sharon Larade, Tel. (416)585-4563 Fax (416)585-4584, Email: info@unitedchurch archives.ca, Website: vicu.utoronto.ca/archives/ archives.htm

Records of the United Church and its antece-dent denominations and local and regional records of the Church in Ontario. Call or view the web page for information on other regional archives.

III

STATISTICAL SECTION

Guide to Statistical Tables

Since questions regarding religious affiliation are no longer a part of the United States Census, the *Yearbook of American & Canadian Churches* is as near an "official" record of denominational statistics as is available.

Because these data represent the most complete annual compilation of church statistics, there is a temptation to expect more than is reasonable. These tables provide the answers to very simple and straightforward questions. Officials in church bodies were asked: "How many members does your organization have?" "How many clergy?" and "How much money does your organization spend?" Each respondent interprets the questions according to the policies of the organization.

Caution should, therefore, be exercised when comparing statistics across denominational lines, comparing statistics from one year to another and adding together statistics from different denominations.

Some particular methodological issues and therefore cautions in interpretation include the following considerations:

1. Definitions of membership, clergy, and other important characteristics differ from religious body to religious body. In this section, ***Full or Confirmed Membership*** refers to those with full communicant status. ***Inclusive Membership*** refers to those who are full communicants or confirmed members plus other members baptized, non-confirmed or non-communicant. Each church determines the age at which a young person is considered a member. Churches also vary in their approaches to statistics. For some, very careful counts are made of members. Other groups only make estimates.

2. Each year the data are collected with the same questions. While most denominations have consistent reporting practices from one year to the next, any change in practices is not noted in the tables. Church mergers and splits can also influence the statistics when they are compared over a number of years. Churches have different reporting schedules and some do not report on a regular basis.

3. The two problems listed above make adding figures from different denominations problematic. However, an additional complication is that individuals who attend two different churches may be included more than once. For example, a person who attends the Church of God in Christ Wednesday evening and an AME service on Sunday morning will likely be included in both counts.

4. Churches were asked to report figures for the full year ending December 31, 2010. Churches actually collect statistics according to their own ecclesial calendars. Data collected consistently from year to year accurately reflect trends over time, irrespective of when customarily collected. Caution should, therefore, be exercised when comparing statistics across denominational lines, comparing statistics from one year to another and adding together statistics from different denominations.

Table 1. Membership Statistics in Canada

Religious Body	Year Reporting	Number of Churches Reporting	Full Communicant or Confirmed Members	Inclusive Membership	Number of Pastors Serving Parishes	Total Number of Clergy	Number of Sunday or Sabbath Schools	Total Enrollment
The Anglican Church of Canada	2007	2,884	641,845	641,845	1,930	3,591	1,633	54,345
The Antiochian Orthodox Christian Archdiocese of North America	2007	18	130,000	130,000	35	36	18	1,605
Apostolic Christian Church (Nazarene)	1985	14		830	49	49		
The Apostolic Church in Canada	2002	20	1,450	1,740	22	28	17	687
Apostolic Church of Pentecost of Canada Inc.	2008	147	26,000	26,000	311	403		
Armenian Evangelical Church of Toronto	2010	-	100	250	1	3	1	-
Associated Gospel Churches	2008	154	11,547	11,547	138	273		
Baptist Convention of Ontario and Quebec	2008	363	42,513	56,852	309	621		
Baptist General Conference of Canada	1999	103	7,500	14,000	150	240		
The Bible Holiness Movement	2010	19	482	993	14	16	15	
Brethren in Christ Church, Canadian Conference	2003		3,287	3,287	81	81		
Canadian and American Reformed Churches	2010	54	10,202	17,490	53	77	-	
Canadian Baptist Ministries	1996	1,133	129,055	129,055				
Canadian Baptists of Western Canada	2008	158	18,200	18,200	400	550	142	15,432
Canadian Conference of Mennonite Brethren Churches	2009	246	33,916	33,916				
Canadian Convention of Southern Baptists	2009	279	15,180	15,180	279	250	124	4,907
Canadian District of the Moravian Church in America, Northern Province	2010	9	1,033	1,347	11	15	9	343

Table 1. Membership Statistics in Canada *(continued)*

Religious Body	Year Reporting	Number of Churches Reporting	Full Communicant or Confirmed Members	Inclusive Membership	Number of Pastors Serving Parishes	Total Number of Clergy	Number of Sunday or Sabbath Schools	Total Enrollment
Canadian Yearly Meeting of the Religious Society of Friends	2009	25	1,148	1,742			25	56
Christian Brethren (also known as Plymouth Brethren)	2006	580		47,000		250	500	
Christian Church (Disciples of Christ) in Canada	2010	25	1,599	2,631	24	32	23	390
Christian Churches / Churches of Christ	2004	65	5,500	9,500	75	105	60	3,300
Christian and Missionary Alliance in Canada	2009	430	47,927	125,945	1,244	1,682	304	31,548
Christian Reformed Church in North America	2008	250	51,500	78,460	220	378		
Church of God (Anderson, Ind.)	2002	48	3,711	3,711	41	88	37	1,794
Church of God (Cleveland, Tenn.)	2010	143	15,390	15,390	116	376	95	2,903
Church of God in Christ (Mennonite)	2010	57	5,187	5,187	194	208	57	
The Church of God of Prophecy Canada East	2009	31	4,600	4,600	53	102	22	1,865
The Church of Jesus Christ of Latter-Day Saints in Canada	2007	481	164,617	178,102	1,443	1,623	481	125,930
Church of the Lutheran Brethren	2010	11	466	796	8	10	11	272
Church of the Nazarene in Canada	2008	177	13,293	13,354	141	285	133	15,477
Churches of Christ in Canada	2005	149	6,857	6,857	122	122		
Community of Christ	2007	68	8,483	8,483	976	976		
Congregational Christian Churches in Canada		73		7,200	141	184		
Convention of Atlantic Baptist Churches	2010	510	58,924	58,924	321	677		7,382

Table 1. Membership Statistics in Canada *(continued)*

Religious Body	Year Reporting	Number of Churches Reporting	Full Communicant or Confirmed Members	Inclusive Membership	Number of Pastors Serving Parishes	Total Number of Clergy	Number of Sunday or Sabbath Schools	Total Enrollment
The Coptic Orthodox Church in Canada	2006	37	55,000	55,000	33	33		
The Estonian Evangelical Lutheran Church Abroad	2004	11	4,996	4,996	7	10	4	55
Evangelical Christian Church in Canada	2010	47	669	809	141	141	65	1,285
The Evangelical Covenant Church of Canada	2010	27	1,384	1,384	41	55		
Evangelical Free Church of Canada	2004	140	8,441	8,441	199	199		
Evangelical Lutheran Church in Canada	2006	623	174,555	174,555	485	866	447	17,926
Evangelical Mennonite Conference	2006	60	7,455	7,455			55	
Evangelical Mennonite Mission Conference	2007	27	5,160	5,160	27	57	27	
The Evangelical Missionary Church of Canada	2010	160	11,322	11,322	218	309		
The Fellowship of Evangelical Baptist Churches in Canada	2004	499	71,073		318	348		
Foursquare Gospel Church of Canada	2007	61	3,307	3,307	117	141		860
Free Methodist Church in Canada	2009	147	7,696	7,696	120	210		
Free Will Baptists	1998	10	347	797	3	4	8	
General Church of the New Jerusalem	2007	3	276	797	5	5	2	59
Greek Orthodox Metropolis of Toronto (Canada)	2008	76	350,000	350,000	58	78	58	
Independent Holiness Church	2010	5	80	175	4	5	4	
Jehovah's Witnesses	2010	1,354	113,989	113,989				

Table 1. Membership Statistics in Canada *(continued)*

Religious Body	Year Reporting	Number of Churches Reporting	Full Communicant or Confirmed Members	Inclusive Membership	Number of Pastors Serving Parishes	Total Number of Clergy	Number of Sunday or Sabbath Schools	Total Enrollment
Lutheran Church-Canada	2009	319	51,650	68,735	219	397	259	4,222
Mennonite Church Canada	2009	230	33,000	33,000				
North American Baptist Conference	2008	140	17,222	17,222	130	201	140	
The Old Catholic Church of Canada	2000	4	30	100	4	5		
Open Bible Faith Fellowship of Canada	2003	75	2,500	9,000	164	256	77	3,900
Orthodox Church in America (Archdiocese of Canada)	2004	68	2,000	10,000	59	73	20	450
Patriarchal Parishes of the Russian Orthodox Church in Canada	2007	24	1,200	3,200	5	6	4	108
The Pentecostal Assemblies of Canada	2009	1,124	69,397	234,385	1,561	2,196	95	5,770
The Pentecostal Assemblies of Newfoundland	2004	128	8,864	26,432	212	308		300
Presbyterian Church in America (Canadian Section)	2010	20	1,117	1,534	38	38		
Presbyterian Church in Canada	2010	910	105,886	183,233		1,343	910	17,759
Reformed Church in Canada	2010	39	3,488	5,095	29	72	6	43
The Reformed Episcopal Church of Canada	2007	10	805	1,035	9	12	5	347
Reinland Mennonite Church	2007	6	898	1,922	10	13		
The Roman Catholic Church in Canada	2003	5,391	12,987,637	12,987,637		8,641		
Romanian Orthodox Church in America (Canadian Parishes)	2007	26	3,700	8,200	32	36	20	352
The Romanian Orthodox Episcopate of America (Jackson, MI)	2008	23	1,005	1,611	30	32	12	
The Salvation Army in Canada	2007	321	20,935	72,481	567	2,064		

365

Table 1. Membership Statistics in Canada *(continued)*

Religious Body	Year Reporting	Number of Churches Reporting	Full Communicant or Confirmed Members	Inclusive Membership	Number of Pastors Serving Parishes	Total Number of Clergy	Number of Sunday or Sabbath Schools	Total Enrollment
Serbian Orthodox Church in the U.S.A. and Canada, Diocese of Canada	2008	26	10,000	235,000	26	30	15	2,070
Seventh-day Adventist Church in Canada	2010	358	62,559	62,559	198	301	444	31,846
Syriac Orthodox Church of Antioch	1995	5	2,500	2,500	3	4		
Ukrainian Orthodox Church of Canada	2009	203	9,700	29,700	67	89	30	598
Union d'Eglises Baptistes Françaises au Canada	2004	34	1,868	1,868	29	40	62	629
United Brethren Church in Canada	2008	12	825	825	12	14		
The United Church of Canada	2009	3,255	510,650	1,248,500	1,811	4,035	2,277	33,700
Universal Fellowship of Metropolitan Community Churches	1992	12	50	1,500	8	9	1	36
The Wesleyan Church of Canada	2002	89	5,977	6,481	131	201	80	5,306
TOTALS		**24,863**	**16,192,725**	**17,669,255**	**16,032**	**36,208**	**9,386**	**395,857**

Table 2. Membership Statistics in the United States

Religious Body Year Reporting	Number of Churches Reporting	Full Communicant or Confirmed	Members	Inclusive Membership	Number of Pastors Serving Parishes	Total Number of Clergy	Number of Sunday or Sabbath Schools	Total Enrollment
Advent Christian Church	2007	294	23,629	23,629	220	481	285	12,516
African Methodist Episcopal Church*	2009	4,100		2,500,000	6,000	6,000	6,128	
The African Methodist Episcopal Zion Church*	2010			1,400,000	3,883	4,554	2,835	76,251
Albanian Orthodox Diocese of America	2010	3	3,000	3,000	5	5	2	63
The Allegheny Wesleyan Methodist Connection (Original Allegheny Conference)	2010	99	1,296	1,385	68	153	97	4,101
Alliance of Baptists*	2006	127	65,000	65,000	320	465		
The American Association of Lutheran Churches	2008	70	9,000	16,000	50	120	40	1,635
The American Baptist Association	2009	1,600	100,000	100,000				
American Baptist Churches in the U.S.A.*	2010	5,366	1,308,054	1,308,054	3,055	6,114		94,849
The American Carpatho-Russian Orthodox Greek Catholic Church	2010	79	12,660	12,660	96	127		
American Evangelical Christian Churches	2006	192	16,000	17,400	192	224	192	
American Rescue Workers	2007	5	3,500	3,500	20	29	6	318
Anglo-Lutheran Catholic Church	2010	19	8,900	11,100	20	22	6	
The Antiochian Orthodox Christian Archdiocese of North America	2007	256	430,000	430,000	480	545	250	21,850
Apostolic Catholic Church*	2010	29	7,289	7,414	19	32	14	851
Apostolic Catholic Orthodox Church	2010	8	1,500	8,500	8	24	2	
Apostolic Christian Church (Nazarene)	2008	54	3,527	3,527	202	211	48	1,524

367

Table 2. Membership Statistics in the United States *(continued)*

Religious Body	Year Reporting	Number of Churches Reporting	Full Communicant or Confirmed Members	Inclusive Membership	Number of Pastors Serving Parishes	Total Number of Clergy	Number of Sunday or Sabbath Schools	Total Enrollment
Apostolic Christian Churches of America	2010	93	12,850	12,850	336	461	89	6,375
Apostolic Episcopal Church	2006	200	6,200	12,000	250	255	10	800
Apostolic Faith Mission Church of God	2009	16	5,300	6,880	39	45	16	3,285
Apostolic Faith Mission of Portland, Oregon	1994	54	4,500	4,500	60	85	54	
Apostolic Orthodox Catholic Church of North America	2005	25	15,900	15,900	40	49		
Armenian Apostolic Church of America	2010	38	350,000	350,000	28	41	25	1,670
Armenian Apostolic Church, Dioceses of America*	2010	81	65,000	65,000	75	70	40	2,505
Assemblies of God	2010	12,457	1,753,881	3,030,944	19,514	35,023	11,283	1,090,346
Associate Reformed Presbyterian Church (General Synod)	2010	293	35,721	39,639	255	462		
The Association of Free Lutheran Congregations	2009	280	32,287	44,473	159	277	219	12,167
Association of Independent Evangelical Lutheran Churches	2010	45	7,635	7,760	55	71	27	371
Baptist Bible Fellowship International	2010	4,000	110,000	110,000	4,000	4,190	4,000	
Baptist Missionary Association of America	2010	1,272	137,909	137,909	1,225	3,513	426	28,540
Beachy Amish Mennonite Churches	2009	201	11,611	11,611	284	293	201	
Berean Fellowship of Churches	2005	56	12,000	12,000				
The Bible Church of Christ, Inc.	1993	6	4,150	6,850	11	52	6	
Bible Fellowship Church	2010	65	7,627	7,627	75	150	59	5,167

Table 2. Membership Statistics in the United States *(continued)*

Religious Body	Year Reporting	Number of Churches Reporting	Full Communicant or Confirmed Members	Inclusive Membership	Number of Pastors Serving Parishes	Total Number of Clergy	Number of Sunday or Sabbath Schools	Total Enrollment
Brethren in Christ Church	2001	232	20,739	20,739	151	295		12,404
Brethren Church (Ashland, Ohio)	2009	112	10,227	10,227	135	219		
Calvary Chapel	2008		9,000	10,000				
The Catholic Church	2010	18,199	68,202,492	68,202,492	27,311	40,291		
Christ Catholic Church	2005	6	1,797	2,887	7	7	1	23
Christ Community Church (Evangelical-Protestant)	2005	3	1,149	1,819	3	7	1	265
Christian Brethren (also known as Plymouth Brethren)	2006	1,145		86,000		600	1,000	
Christian Church (Disciples of Christ) in the United States and Canada*	2010	3,624	405,308	639,551	3,835	6,982	2,897	163,067
Christian Churches and Churches of Christ	1988	5,579	1,071,616	1,071,616	5,525			
The Christian Congregation, Inc.	2004	1,496	122,181	122,181	1,574	1,575	1,347	41,891
Christian Methodist Episcopal Church*	2006	3,500	850,000	850,000	3,106	3,548	2,500	69,368
The Christian and Missionary Alliance	2010	2,042	198,118	436,428	2,852	4,587		97,599
Christian Reformed Church in North America	2010	808	131,323	180,502	668	1,452		
Christian Union	2008	107	3,647	4,014	154	225	102	3,143
Church of the Brethren*	2010	1,043	120,041	120,041	789	1,816	690	27,598
Church of Christ	2008		8,000	8,000				
The Church of Christ (Holiness) U.S.A.	2007	148	11,468	11,468	193	221	148	6,276
Church Communities International	2010	13	1,040	1,776	40			40

Table 2. Membership Statistics in the United States (continued)

Religious Body	Year Reporting	Number of Churches Reporting	Full Communicant or Confirmed Members	Inclusive Membership	Number of Pastors Serving Parishes	Total Number of Clergy	Number of Sunday or Sabbath Schools	Total Enrollment
Church of God (Anderson, Indiana)	2010	2,187	249,521	249,521	2,787	3,493	2,187	249,521
The Church of God in Christ	1991	15,300	5,499,875	5,499,875	28,988	33,593		
Church of God in Christ, Mennonite	2010	150	14,804	14,804	537	589	150	
Church of God (Cleveland, Tennessee)	2010	6,481	1,074,047	1,074,047	5,121	17,420	4,412	353,182
Church of God by Faith, Inc.	2004	149	35,000	35,000	152	235		
Church of God General Conference (McDonough, GA)	2010	84	3,121	3,421	61	79		
Church of God, Mountain Assembly, Inc.	2009	3,390	7,000	7,000		4,530	107	10,925
Church of God of Prophecy	2007	1,860	89,674	89,674	4,340	4,340	1,860	64,000
The Church of Illumination	2000	4	1,200	1,200		16	1	216
The Church of Jesus Christ (Bickertonites)	2010		2,700	2,700	250			3,500
The Church of Jesus Christ of Latter-day Saints	2010	13,601	5,523,124	6,157,238	40,803	45,330	13,601	4,707,703
Church of the Living God (Motto, Christian Workers for Fellowship)	2006	170	42,000	42,000	105	214	65	
Church of the Lutheran Brethren of America	2010	105	8,362	13,099			105	6,355
Church of the Lutheran Confession	2006	87	6,365	8,390	64	90	67	943
Church of the Nazarene	2010	5,058	640,966	649,836	5,576	10,900	4,459	772,445
Church of the United Brethren in Christ, USA	2010	193	21,000	21,000	143	213		
Churches of Christ	2006	13,000	1,250,000	1,639,495			10,500	
Churches of Christ in Christian Union	2008	230	11,234	11,234	148	328		8,485

Table 2. Membership Statistics in the United States *(continued)*

Religious Body	Year Reporting	Number of Churches Reporting	Full Communicant or Confirmed Members	Inclusive Membership	Number of Pastors Serving Parishes	Total Number of Clergy	Number of Sunday or Sabbath Schools	Total Enrollment
Churches of God, General Conference	2010	332	32,560	32,560	456	601	332	11,742
Community of Christ*	2007	935	178,328	178,328		20,420		
Congregational Holiness Church	2005	225	25,000	25,000	225	225		
Conservative Baptist Association of America (CBAmerica)	2006	1,200	200,000	200,000	1,800	2,200		
Conservative Congregational Christian Conference	2010	298	42,296	42,296	274	517	262	11,736
Conservative Lutheran Association	2002	3	852	1,267	8	29	3	120
Converge Worldwide (BGC)	2009	1,100		16,000	1,100			
Coptic Orthodox Church*	2000	100	250,000	300,000	140	145	100	5,500
Cumberland Presbyterian Church	2010	657	71,809	72,167				24,640
Cumberland Presbyterian Church in America	1996	152	15,142	15,142	141	156	152	9,465
The Episcopal Church*	2010	6,794	1,576,721	1,951,907			5,673	203,774
The Estonian Evangelical Lutheran Church	2001	21	3,508	3,508	10	12		
The Evangelical Church	2000	133	12,475	12,475	164	255	125	8,000
The Evangelical Church Alliance	2010		300,000	300,000	2,535	2,538		
The Evangelical Congregational Church	2010	141	17,577	17,577	149	255		
The Evangelical Covenant Church	2006	783	114,283	114,283	1,486	1,833	750	106,022
The Evangelical Free Church of America	2008	1,475	159,166	356,000	1,503	2,201		
Evangelical Friends International – North American Region	2008	284	27,844	38,428				

Table 2. Membership Statistics in the United States *(continued)*

Religious Body	Year Reporting	Number of Churches Reporting	Full Communicant or Confirmed Members	Inclusive Membership	Number of Pastors Serving Parishes	Total Number of Clergy	Number of Sunday or Sabbath Schools	Total Enrollment
Evangelical Lutheran Church in America*	2010	9,995	3,258,847	4,274,855	8,176	17,258	6,547	477,823
Evangelical Lutheran Synod	2010	132	15,301	19,394	108	173	108	2,368
Evangelical Methodist Church	2005	108	7,348	7,348	101	202	102	4,920
Evangelical Presbyterian Church	2007	207	77,794	89,190	385	608	171	39,153
Fellowship of Evangelical Bible Churches	2009	19	2,103	2,103	15	43	19	1,460
Fellowship of Evangelical Churches	2010	46	7,754	7,754	106	185	46	4,343
Fellowship of Fundamental Bible Churches	2007	20	980	1,760	32	46	20	1,140
Fellowship of Grace Brethren Churches	1997	260	30,371	30,371		564		
Free Methodist Church—USA	2010	1,051	67,132	75,020		1,947		30,017
Friends General Conference	2010	832	32,000	32,000			400	
Friends United Meeting*	2008	600	36,302	36,302	327	576	273	
Full Gospel Assemblies International	2007	11	2,786	2,786	220		22	
Full Gospel Fellowship of Churches and Ministers International	2007	1,273	430,000	432,632	2,631	3,381		
Fundamental Methodist Church, Inc.	1993	12	682	787	17	22	12	454
General Association of General Baptists	2010	1,154	61,040	61,040		995		
General Association of Regular Baptist Churches	2007	1,321	132,700	132,700			1,321	
General Church of the New Jerusalem	2009	37	3,783	7,052	60	89		
General Conference of The Church of God (Seventh Day), Denver, Colorado	2010	233	10,000	14,000	123	155	233	
General Conference of Mennonite Brethren Churches	1996	368	50,915	82,130	590			34,668

Table 2. Membership Statistics in the United States *(continued)*

Religious Body	Year Reporting	Number of Churches Reporting	Full Communicant or Confirmed Members	Inclusive Membership	Number of Pastors Serving Parishes	Total Number of Clergy	Number of Sunday or Sabbath Schools	Total Enrollment
Grace Gospel Fellowship	1992	128	60,000	60,000	160	196	128	
Greek Orthodox Archdiocese of America*	2006	560	1,500,000	1,500,000	553	840	550	
The Holy Eastern Orthodox Catholic and Apostolic Church in North America, Inc.	2001	17	4,138	4,138	9		17	
Hungarian Reformed Church in America*	2001	27	6,000	6,000	27	30		
Hutterian Brethren	2000	444	36,800	43,000	600	600		
IFCA International, Inc.	1998	659	61,655	61,655			659	57,768
International Church of the Foursquare Gospel	2006	1,875	255,773	353,995	6,738	8,486	1,450	61,000
International Council of Community Churches*	2010	148	68,300	68,300	552	631		
International Fellowship of Bible Churches, Inc	2009		850	850	36	99	30	
International Fellowship of Christian Assemblies	2009	82	357	357	100	168	85	85
The International Pentecostal Church of Christ	2010	62	1,435	3,760	59	125	52	1,867
International Pentecostal Holiness Church	2008	2,024	265,744	330,054	2,946	4,239		
Jehovah's Witnesses	2010	13,021	1,184,249	1,184,249				
The Korean Presbyterian Church Abroad*	2003	302	38,500	55,000	465	583		17,760
The Latvian Evangelical Lutheran Church in America	2007	60	9,700	10,950	41	61	14	
The Liberal Catholic Church— Province of the United States of America	2006	21	5,800	5,800	41	44		
The Lutheran Church— Missouri Synod (LCMS)	2010	6,158	1,764,024	2,278,586	5,369	8,927	4,944	363,389
Malankara Orthodox Syrian Church, Diocese of America*	2006	80	30,000	30,000	100	120	77	3,780

Table 2. Membership Statistics in the United States (continued)

Religious Body	Year Reporting	Number of Churches Reporting	Full Communicant or Confirmed Members	Inclusive Membership	Number of Pastors Serving Parishes	Total Number of Clergy	Number of Sunday or Sabbath Schools	Total Enrollment
Mar Thoma Syrian Church of India*	2010	80	30,000	50,000	60	70	70	6,800
Mennonite Church USA	2009	920	104,684	104,684	1,503	2,831		
The Missionary Church	2008	431	38,206	38,206	362	746		23,656
Moravian Church in America (Northern Province, Southern Province)*	2010	84	16,220	20,220	74	166	80	3,910
National Association of Congregational Christian Churches	2001	432	65,392	65,392	507	650		
National Association of Free Will Baptists	2007	2,369	185,798	185,798	3,915	2,369	106,397
National Baptist Convention of America, Inc.*	2000		3,500,000	3,500,000			9,000	
National Baptist Convention, U.S.A., Inc.*	2010	10,358	5,197,512	5,197,512			10,358	
National Missionary Baptist Convention of America*	1992		2,500,000	2,500,000				
National Organization of the New Apostolic Church of North America	2009	303	39,532	39,532	1,643	1,643	303	2,530
National Primitive Baptist Convention, Inc.	2002	1,565	600,000	600,000				
Netherlands Reformed Congregations	2010	27	5,146	10,493	9	9		
North American Baptist Conference	2006	272	47,150	47,150	296	418	272	
North American Old Roman Catholic Church (Archdiocese of New York)	2008	5	2,750	2,785	4	7	3	15
Old Calender Orthodox Church of Greece (Holy Synod in Resistance), American Exarchate	2010	14	1,095	1,095	18	21		
The Old Catholic Orthodox Church		11	11,000	11,470	29	29		
Old German Baptist Brethren Church	2010	46	3,766	3,766	194	194		

Table 2. Membership Statistics in the United States (continued)

Religious Body	Year Reporting	Number of Churches Reporting	Full Communicant or Confirmed Members	Inclusive Membership	Number of Pastors Serving Parishes	Total Number of Clergy	Number of Sunday or Sabbath Schools	Total Enrollment
Old Order Amish Church	2001	898	80,820	80,820	3,592	3,617	55	
Old Order (Wisler) Mennonite Church	2004	47	7,100	7,100	135	135		
Open Bible Churches	2009	275	45,000	45,000	361	972		
The Orthodox Church in America*	2010	750	105,000	131,000	850	970	650	12,107
The Orthodox Presbyterian Church	2010	269	22,134	29,842		494		
Patriarchal Parishes of the Russian Orthodox Church in the U.S.A.*	2008	31	7,000	17,000	37	63		
Pentecostal Assemblies of the World, Inc.	2010	2,550	1,300,000	1,800,000	2,700	11,000	2,500	
Pentecostal Church of God	2008	1,134	44,850	98,579	1,134	1,572		
The Pentecostal Churches of Christ	2010	45	5,000	5,000	300	300	45	
Pentecostal Fire-Baptized Holiness Church	1996	27	223	223		28	25	400
Philadelphia Yearly Meeting of the Religious Society of Friends*	2009	103	11,319	11,511			80	2,500
Polish National Catholic Church of America*	2008	126	60,000	60,000	103	127		
Presbyterian Church in America	2010	1,737	271,633	341,482	3,760	3,760		103,611
Presbyterian Church (U.S.A.)*	2010	10,560	2,016,091	2,675,873	7,843	21,161	8,070	899,610
Primitive Advent Christian Church	1993	10	345	345	11	11	10	292
Primitive Methodist Church in the U.S.A.	2010	67	3,294	3,601	30	70	60	1,652
Progressive National Baptist Convention, Inc.*	2009	1,500	1,000,000	1,010,000	3,200	3,500	1,700	29,000
Protestant Reformed Churches in America	2010	31	4,552	7,806	26	43	23	
Reformed Catholic Church	2006	100	57,000	57,000	187	227	6	412

375

Table 2. Membership Statistics in the United States *(continued)*

Religious Body	Year Reporting	Number of Churches Reporting	Full Communicant or Confirmed Members	Inclusive Membership	Number of Pastors Serving Parishes	Total Number of Clergy	Number of Sunday or Sabbath Schools	Total Enrollment
Reformed Church in America*	2010	886	152,134	246,024	843	2,133		2,133
Reformed Church in the United States	2002	48	3,258	4,369	42	50	48	951
Reformed Episcopal Church	2009	149	9,342	15,573	168	221		
Reformed Mennonite Church	2009	8	243	268	30	33	-	
Reformed Presbyterian Church of North America	2010		4,881	6,799	78	152		
Religious Society of Friends (Conservative)	2004	1,200	104,000	104,000				
The Romanian Orthodox Church in America	2008	32	3,200	9,700	33	37	28	562
The Romanian Orthodox Episcopate of America	2006	64	7,135	10,635	116	138		
The Russian Orthodox Church Outside of Russia	2008	190	480,000	480,000	221	269	30	2,642
The Salvation Army	2010	1,232	107,846	413,961	2,464	5,237	1,008	96,786
The Schwenkfelder Church	2008	5	2,300	2,300	6	8	5	
Separate Baptists in Christ	1992	100	8,000	8,000	95	140	100	
Serbian Orthodox Church in the U.S.A. and Canada*	2005	68	67,000	67,000	60	82		
Seventh-day Adventist Church	2010	4,916	1,060,386	1,060,386	2,542	5,084		
Seventh Day Baptist General Conference, USA and Canada	2010	97	5,300	6,300	58	83		
Southern Baptist Convention	2010	45,727	16,136,044	16,136,044	105,536	121,989	44,915	7,607,390
Southern Methodist Church	2006	101	6,000	6,000	109	158	105	3,774
Sovereign Grace Believers	2002	350	4,000	4,000	450	450	350	

Table 2. Membership Statistics in the United States (continued)

Religious Body	Year Reporting	Number of Churches Reporting	Full Communicant or Confirmed Members	Inclusive Membership	Number of Pastors Serving Parishes	Total Number of Clergy	Number of Sunday or Sabbath Schools	Total Enrollment
The Swedenborgian Church*	2010	39	1,096	1,534	25	69		
Syriac-Greek Antiochian Orthodox Catholic Church	2010	160	17,000	17,108	135	146	26	780
Syrian (Syriac) Orthodox Church of Antioch*	2009	32	32,500	32,500	24	25	22	1,585
Ukrainian Orthodox Church of the U.S.A.*	2006	118	30,000	50,000	99	114	67	640
Unitarian Universalist Association of Congregations	2009	1,048	221,367	221,367	1,773	1,773	1,048	56,683
The United Catholic Church, Inc.	2010	14	2,227	3,946	18	28		
United Christian Church	2006	9	280	280	9	15	7	577
United Church of Christ*	2010	5,227	1,058,423	1,058,423	3,764	10,174		209,260
The United Methodist Church*	2009	33,583	7,679,850	7,679,850	24,341	45,230	164,742	2,647,201
United Pentecostal Church International	2006	4,358		646,304	9,224	9,224		
United Zion Church	2008	14	774	774	17	27	11	490
Unity of the Brethren	1998	27	2,548	3,218	25	39	24	1,442
Universal Catholic Church	2007	3	25	75	3	3		
Universal Fellowship of Metropolitan Community Churches	2006	115	15,666	15,666	293	425		
Vineyard USA	2010	554	181,474	181,474	604	2,852		
The Wesleyan Church	2010	1,715	121,429	139,330	2,469	3,772	1,488	
Wisconsin Evangelical Lutheran Synod	2010	1,287	305,558	385,321	1,347	1,875	1,127	34,964
TOTALS		330,222	147,983,687	159,848,057	403,129	600,922	348,067	21,307,879

* Indicates National Council of Churches USA member communions. NOTE: Rounding may make totals appear inaccurate.

Table 3. Membership Statistics
for the National Council of Churches USA

Religious Body	Year Reporting	Number of Churches Reporting	Inclusive Membership	Number of Pastors Serving Parishes
African Methodist Episcopal Church	2009	4,100	2,500,000	6,000
The African Methodist Episcopal Zion Church	2010		1,400,000	3,883
Alliance of Baptists	2006	127	65,000	320
American Baptist Churches in the U.S.A.	2010	5,366	1,308,054	3,055
Apostolic Catholic Church	2010	29	7,414	19
Armenian Apostolic Church, Dioceses of America	2010	81	65,000	75
Christian Church (Disciples of Christ) in the United States and Canada	2010	3,624	639,551	3,835
Christian Methodist Episcopal Church	2006	3,500	850,000	3,106
Church of the Brethren	2010	1,043	120,041	789
Community of Christ	2007	935	178,328	
Coptic Orthodox Church	2000	100	300,000	140
The Episcopal Church	2010	6,794	1,951,907	
Evangelical Lutheran Church in America	2010	9,995	4,274,855	8,176
Friends United Meeting	2008	600	36,302	327
Greek Orthodox Archdiocese of America	2006	560	1,500,000	553
Hungarian Reformed Church in America	2001	27	6,000	27
International Council of Community Churches	2010	148	68,300	552
The Korean Presbyterian Church Abroad	2003	302	55,000	465

Table 3. Membership Statistics
for the National Council of Churches USA *(continued)*

Religious Body	Year Reporting	Number of Churches Reporting	Inclusive Membership	Number of Pastors Serving Parishes
Malankara Orthodox Syrian Church, Diocese of America	2006	80	30,000	100
Mar Thoma Syrian Church of India	2010	80	50,000	60
Moravian Church in America (Northern Province, Southern Province)	2010	84	20,220	74
National Baptist Convention of America, Inc.	2000	3,500,000		
National Baptist Convention, U.S.A., Inc.	2010	10,358	5,197,512	
National Missionary Baptist Convention of America	1992	2,500,000		
The Orthodox Church in America	2010	750	131,000	850
Patriarchal Parishes of the Russian Orthodox Church in the U.S.A.	2008	31	17,000	37
Philadelphia Yearly Meeting of the Religious Society of Friends	2009	103	11,511	
Polish National Catholic Church of America	2008	126	60,000	103
Presbyterian Church (U.S.A.)	2010	10,560	2,675,873	7,843
Progressive National Baptist Convention, Inc.	2009	1,500	1,010,000	3,200
Reformed Church in America	2010	886	246,024	843
Serbian Orthodox Church in the U.S.A. and Canada	2005	68	67,000	60
The Swedenborgian Church	2010	39	1,534	25
Syrian (Syriac) Orthodox Church of Antioch	2009	32	32,500	24
Ukrainian Orthodox Church of the U.S.A.	2006	118	50,000	99
United Church of Christ	2010	5,227	1,058,423	3,764
The United Methodist Church	2009	33,583	7,679,850	24,341
Totals		**100,956**	**39,664,199**	**72,745**

Table 4. Selected Statistics of Church

Religious Body	Year	Full or Confirmed Members	Inclusive Members	TOTAL CONTRIBUTIONS		
				Total Contributions	Per Capita Full or Confirmed Members	Per Capita Inclusive Members
The Apostolic Church in Canada	2002	1,450	1,740	$1,705,737	$1,176.37	$980.31
Armenian Holy Apostolic Church - Canadian Diocese	2007	87,000	87,000	$895,000	$10.29	$10.29
Baptist Convention of Ontario and Quebec	2004	42,513	56,852	$42,120,960	$990.78	$740.89
The Bible Holiness Movement	2010	482	993	$60,002	$124.49	$60.42
Canadian Baptists of Western Canada	2008	18,200	18,200	$5,681,170	$312.15	$312.15
Canadian District of the Moravian Church in America, Northern Province	2010	1,033	1,347	$2,102,038	$2,034.89	$1,560.53
Christian Church (Disciples of Christ) in Canada	2002	1,599	2,631	$1,449,009	$906.20	$550.74
Christian and Missionary Alliance in Canada	2009	47,927	125,945	$159,717,856	$3,332.52	$1,268.16
Church of the Nazarene in Canada	2008	13,293	13,354	$14,820,938	$1,114.94	$1,109.85
Evangelical Christian Church in Canada	2010	669	809	$80,005	$119.59	$98.89
Evangelical Lutheran Church in Canada	2002	174,555	174,555	$61,270,705	$351.01	$351.01
Free Methodist Church in Canada	2009	7,696	7,696	$18,502,437	$2,404.16	$2,404.16
The Latvian Evangelical Lutheran Church in America	1995	4,162	4,647	$1,201,332	$288.64	$258.52
Lutheran Church-Canada	2009	51,650	68,735	$29,666,220	$574.37	$431.60
North American Baptist Conference	2006	17,222	17,222	$34,886,910	$2,025.72	$2,025.72
The Pentecostal Assemblies of Canada	2009	69,397	234,385	$330,544,677	$4,763.10	$1,410.26
The Pentecostal Assemblies of Newfoundland	2004	8,864	26,432	$5,624,770	$634.56	$212.80
Presbyterian Church in America (Canadian Section)	2010	1,117	1,534	$2,911,769	$2,606.78	$1,898.15
Reformed Church in Canada	2010	3,488	5,095	$7,575,565	$2,171.89	$1,486.86
The Reformed Episcopal Church of Canada	2007	805	1,035	$437,525	$543.51	$422.73
Seventh-day Adventist Church in Canada	2010	62,559	62,559	$113,932,205	$1,821.20	$1,821.20
Union d'Eglises Baptistes Françaises au Canada	2004	1,868	1,868	$888,230	$475.50	$475.50
The United Church of Canada	2009	510,650	1,248,500	$367,131,000	$718.95	$294.06
TOTALS		**1,128,199**	**2,163,134**	**$1,203,206,060**	**$1,066.48**	**$556.23**

NOTE: Rounding may cause some totals to appear inaccurate.

Finances—Canadian Churches

CONGREGATIONAL FINANCES			BENEVOLENCES			
Total Congregational Contributions	Per Capita Full or Confirmed Members	Per Capita Inclusive Members	Total Benevolences	Per Capita Full or Confirmed Members	Per Capita Inclusive Members	Benevolences as a Percentage of Total Giving
$1,506,104	$1,038.69	$865.58	$199,633	$137.68	$114.73	12%
$475,000	$5.46	$5.46	$440,000	$5.06	$5.06	49%
$35,540,033	$835.98	$625.13	$6,580,927	$154.80	$115.76	16%
$32,984	$68.43	$33.22	$27,018	$56.05	$27.21	45%
$566,299	$31.12	$31.12	$5,114,871	$281.04	$281.04	90%
$1,959,250	$1,896.66	$1,454.53	$142,788	$138.23	$106.00	7%
$1,230,384	$769.47	$467.65	$218,625	$136.73	$83.10	15%
$135,803,273	$2,833.54	$1,078.27	$23,914,583	$498.98	$189.88	15%
$12,112,273	$911.18	$907.01	$2,708,665	$203.77	$202.84	18%
$62,000	$92.68	$76.64	$18,005	$26.91	$22.26	23%
$52,343,354	$299.87	$299.87	$7,518,028	$43.07	$43.07	12%
$15,648,538	$2,033.33	$2,033.33	$2,853,899	$370.83	$370.83	15%
$1,014,766	$243.82	$218.37	$186,566	$44.83	$40.15	16%
$25,774,666	$499.03	$374.99	$3,891,554	$75.34	$56.62	13%
$28,670,810	$1,664.78	$1,664.78	$6,216,100	$360.94	$360.94	18%
$288,953,931	$4,163.78	$1,232.82	$41,590,746	$599.32	$177.45	13%
$3,948,770	$445.48	$149.39	$1,676,000	$189.08	$63.41	30%
$2,446,928	$2,190.62	$1,595.13	$464,841	$416.15	$303.03	16%
$6,127,867	$1,756.84	$1,202.72	$1,447,698	$415.05	$284.14	19%
$432,525	$537.30	$417.90	$5,800	$7.20	$5.60	1%
$44,284,505	$707.88	$707.88	$69,647,700	$1,113.31	$1,113.31	61%
$430,230	$230.32	$230.32	$458,000	$245.18	$245.18	52%
$321,746,000	$630.07	$257.71	$45,385,000	$88.88	$36.35	12%
$981,110,490	**$869.63**	**$453.56**	**$220,707,047**	**$195.63**	**$102.03**	**18%**

Table 5. Selected Statistics of Church

Religious Body	Year	Full or Confirmed Members	Inclusive Members	TOTAL CONTRIBUTIONS		
				Total Contributions	Per Capita Full or Confirmed Members	Per Capita Inclusive Members
Albanian Orthodox Diocese of America	2010	3,000	3,000	$106,000	$35.33	$35.33
The Allegheny Wesleyan Methodist Connection (Original Allegheny Conference)	2010	1,296	1,385	$5,072,039	$3,913.61	$3,662.12
American Baptist Churches in the U.S.A.*	2010	1,308,054	1,308,054	$289,345,336	$221.20	$221.20
The Antiochian Orthodox Christian Archdiocese of North America	2007	430,000	430,000	$6,648,954	$15.46	$15.46
Apostolic Faith Mission Church of God	2009	5,300	6,880	$1,154,686	$217.87	$167.83
Associate Reformed Presbyterian Church (General Synod)	2010	35,721	39,639	$53,379,344	$1,494.34	$1,346.64
Association of Independent Evangelical Lutheran Churches	2010	7,635	7,760	$9,125	$1.20	$1.18
Baptist Missionary Association of America	2010	137,909	137,909	$54,537,217	$395.46	$395.46
Berean Fellowship of Churches	2000	12,000	12,000	$10,309,605	$859.13	$859.13
Bible Fellowship Church	2010	7,627	7,627	$22,502,164	$2,950.33	$2,950.33
Brethren in Christ Church	2001	20,739	20,739	$36,431,223	$1,756.65	$1,756.65
Brethren Church (Ashland, Ohio)	2009	10,227	10,227	$1,509,512	$147.60	$147.60
Christian Church (Disciples of Christ) in the United States and Canada*	2010	405,308	639,551	$489,365,802	$1,207.39	$765.17
The Christian and Missionary Alliance	2010	198,118	436,428	$469,726,502	$2,370.94	$1,076.30
Christian Union	2008	3,647	4,014	$7,816,278	$2,143.21	$1,947.25
Church of the Brethren*	2010	120,041	120,041	$92,270,210	$768.66	$768.66
The Church of the Christ (Holiness) U.S.A.	2007	11,468	11,468	$13,571,278	$1,183.40	$1,183.40
Church of God General Conference (McDonough, GA)	2010	3,121	3,421	$4,158,243	$1,332.34	$1,215.51
Church of the Lutheran Confession	2003	6,365	8,390	$5,855,961	$920.03	$697.97
Church of the Nazarene	2010	640,966	649,836	$774,827,069	$1,208.84	$1,192.34
Churches of God, General Conference	2010	32,560	32,560	$36,429,878	$1,118.85	$1,118.85
Community of Christ*	2007	178,328	178,328	$39,121,403	$219.38	$219.38
Conservative Congregational Christian Conference	2010	42,296	42,296	$70,496,255	$1,666.74	$1,666.74
Cumberland Presbyterian Church	2010	71,809	72,167	$52,531,185	$731.54	$727.91
Cumberland Presbyterian Church in America	1996	15,142	15,142	$40,408,524	$2,668.64	$2,668.64

382

Finances—United States Churches

\multicolumn{3}{CONGREGATIONAL FINANCES}			BENEVOLENCES		
Total Congregational Contributions	Per Capita Full or Confirmed Members	Per Capita Inclusive Members	Total Benevolences	Per Capita Full or Confirmed Members	Per Capita Inclusive Members	Benevolences as a Percentage of Total Giving
$95,000	$31.67	$31.67	$11,000	$3.67	$3.67	10%
$3,967,845	$3,061.61	$2,864.87	$1,104,193.67	$852.00	$797.25	22%
$241,463,947	$184.60	$184.60	$47,881,389	$36.61	$36.61	17%
$3,098,954	$7.21	$7.21	$3,550,000	$8.26	$8.26	53%
$576,200	$108.72	$83.75	$578,486	$109.15	$84.08	50%
$44,654,927	$1,250.10	$1,126.54	$8,724,417	$244.24	$220.10	16%
$2,000	$0.26	$0.26	$7,125	$0.93	$0.92	78%
$43,311,114	$314.06	$314.06	$11,226,103	$81.40	$81.40	21%
$9,277,940	$773.16	$773.16	$1,031,665	$85.97	$85.97	10%
$18,752,540	$2,458.70	$2,458.70	$3,749,624	$491.63	$491.63	17%
$29,566,287	$1,425.64	$1,425.64	$6,864,936	$331.02	$331.02	19%
$569,985	$55.73	$55.73	$939,527	$91.87	$91.87	62%
$443,712,948	$1,094.75	$693.79	$45,652,854	$112.64	$71.38	9%
$399,763,262	$2,017.80	$915.99	$69,963,240	$353.14	$160.31	15%
$2,951,783	$809.37	$735.37	$4,864,495.29	$1,333.83	$1,211.88	62%
$72,339,775	$602.63	$602.63	$19,930,435	$166.03	$166.03	22%
$12,855,697	$1,121.01	$1,121.01	$715,581	$62.40	$62.40	5%
$3,692,900	$1,183.24	$1,079.48	$465,343	$149.10	$136.03	11%
$4,999,122	$785.41	$595.84	$856,839	$134.62	$102.13	15%
$648,769,174	$1,012.17	$998.36	$126,057,895	$196.67	$193.98	16%
$30,369,402	$932.72	$932.72	$6,060,476	$186.13	$186.13	17%
$22,270,216	$124.88	$124.88	$16,851,187	$94.50	$94.50	43%
$60,595,568	$1,432.65	$1,432.65	$9,900,687	$234.08	$234.08	14%
$43,118,256	$600.46	$597.48	$9,412,929	$131.08	$130.43	18%
$34,921,064	$2,306.24	$2,306.24	$5,487,460	$362.40	$362.40	14%

Table 5. Selected Statistics of Church

Religious Body	Year	Full or Confirmed Members	Inclusive Members	TOTAL CONTRIBUTIONS		
				Total Contributions	Per Capita Full or Confirmed Members	Per Capita Inclusive Members
The Episcopal Church*	2010	1,576,721	1,951,907	$2,088,449,676	$1,324.55	$1,069.95
The Evangelical Church	2000	12,475	12,475	$15,632,985	$1,253.15	$1,253.15
The Evangelical Congregational Church	2010	17,577	17,577	$20,221,005	$1,150.42	$1,150.42
The Evangelical Covenant Church	2006	114,283	114,283	$291,847,011	$2,553.72	$2,553.72
Evangelical Lutheran Church in America*	2010	3,258,847	4,274,855	$2,235,550,861	$685.99	$522.95
Evangelical Lutheran Synod	2010	15,301	19,394	$14,960,758	$977.76	$771.41
Fellowship of Evangelical Bible Churches	2009	2,103	2,103	$3,104,496	$1,476.22	$1,476.22
Fellowship of Evangelical Churches	2010	7,754	7,754	$24,607,538	$3,173.53	$3,173.53
Free Methodist Church —USA	2010	67,132	75,029	$170,204,990	$2,535.38	$2,268.52
General Conference of Mennonite Brethren Churches	1996	50,915	82,130	$65,851,481	$1,293.36	$801.80
International Church of the Foursquare Gospel	2003	255,773	353,995	$533,993,579	$2,087.76	$1,508.48
The International Pentecostal Church of Christ	2010	1,435	3,760	$2,983,693	$2,079.23	$793.54
International Pentecostal Holiness Church	2007	265,744	330,054	$14,928,490	$56.18	$45.23
The Latvian Evangelical Lutheran Church in America	2004	9,700	10,950	$3,934,000	$405.57	$359.27
The Lutheran Church— Missouri Synod (LCMS)	2010	1,764,024	2,278,586	$1,375,784,215	$779.91	$603.79
Mar Thoma Syrian Church of India*	2010	30,000	50,000	$2,353,524	$78.45	$47.07
The Missionary Church	2008	38,206	38,206	$88,233,789	$2,309.42	$2,309.42
Moravian Church in America (Northern Province figures)*	2010	16,220	20,220	$18,220,682	$1,123.35	$901.12
National Association of Free Will Baptists	2007	185,798	185,798	$131,462,428	$707.56	$707.56
North American Baptist Conference	2006	47,150	47,150	$72,279,470	$1,532.97	$1,532.97
The Orthodox Presbyterian Church	2010	22,134	29,842	$48,356,529	$2,184.72	$1,620.42
Presbyterian Church in America	2010	271,633	341,482	$703,852,802	$2,591.19	$2,061.17
Presbyterian Church (U.S.A.)*	2010	2,016,091	2,675,873	$2,614,472,933	$1,296.80	$977.05
Primitive Methodist Church in the U.S.A.	2010	3,294	3,601	$5,006,926	$1,520.01	$1,390.43
Progressive National Baptist Convention, Inc.*	2009	1,000,000	1,010,000	$1,020,000	$1.02	$1.01

Finances—United States Churches *(continued)*

CONGREGATIONAL FINANCES			BENEVOLENCES			
Total Congregational Contributions	Per Capita Full or Confirmed Members	Per Capita Inclusive Members	Total Benevolences	Per Capita Full or Confirmed Members	Per Capita Inclusive Members	Benevolences as a Percentage of Total Giving
$1,825,640,740	$1,157.87	$935.31	$262,808,936	$166.68	$134.64	13%
$12,784,502	$1,024.81	$1,024.81	$2,848,483	$228.34	$228.34	18%
$18,183,077	$1,034.48	$1,034.48	$2,037,928	$115.94	$115.94	10%
$266,614,225	$2,332.93	$2,332.93	$25,232,786	$220.79	$220.79	9%
$2,009,373,401	$616.59	$470.04	$226,177,460	$69.40	$52.91	10%
$13,842,672	$904.69	$713.76	$1,118,086	$73.07	$57.65	7%
$2,472,226	$1,175.57	$1,175.57	$632,270	$300.65	$300.65	20%
$22,776,188	$2,937.35	$2,937.35	$1,831,350	$236.18	$236.18	7%
$150,770,675	$2,245.88	$2,009.50	$19,435,315	$289.49	$259.02	11%
$50,832,814	$998.39	$618.93	$15,018,667	$294.98	$182.86	23%
$490,130,528	$1,916.27	$1,384.57	$43,863,051	$171.49	$123.91	8%
$2,172,089	$1,513.65	$577.68	$811,603.88	$565.58	$215.85	27%
$5,310,313	$19.98	$16.09	$9,618,177	$36.19	$29.14	64%
$3,473,000	$358.04	$317.17	$461,000	$47.53	$42.10	12%
$1,254,192,118	$710.98	$550.43	$121,592,097	$68.93	$53.36	9%
$1,846,487	$61.55	$36.93	$507,037.54	$16.90	$10.14	22%
$77,967,320	$2,040.71	$2,040.71	$10,266,469	$268.71	$268.71	12%
$17,312,747	$1,067.37	$856.22	$907,935	$55.98	$44.90	5%
$105,481,483	$567.72	$567.72	$25,980,945	$139.83	$139.83	20%
$62,175,197	$1,318.67	$1,318.67	$10,104,273	$214.30	$214.30	14%
$41,396,760	$1,870.28	$1,387.20	$6,959,769	$314.44	$233.22	14%
$581,396,399	$2,140.37	$1,702.57	$122,456,403	$450.82	$358.60	17%
$2,254,593,261	$1,118.30	$842.56	$359,879,672	$178.50	$134.49	14%
$4,503,734	$1,367.25	$1,250.69	$503,192.00	$152.76	$139.74	10%
$370,000	$0.37	$0.37	$650,000.00	$0.65	$0.64	64%

385

Table 5. Selected Statistics of Church

Religious Body	Year	Full or Confirmed Members	Inclusive Members	Total Contributions	Per Capita Full or Confirmed Members	Per Capita Inclusive Members
				TOTAL CONTRIBUTIONS		
Reformed Church in America*	2010	152,134	246,024	$302,162,041	$1,986.16	$1,228.18
Reformed Church in the United States	2002	3,258	4,369	$6,241,428	$1,915.72	$1,428.57
Reformed Presbyterian Church of North America	2010	4,881	6,799	$11,502,305	$2,356.55	$1,691.76
The Schwenkfelder Church	2005	2,300	2,300	$1,910,513	$830.66	$830.66
Seventh-day Adventist Church	2010	1,060,386	1,060,386	$1,268,582,205	$1,196.34	$1,196.34
Southern Baptist Convention	2010	16,136,044	16,136,044	$11,720,820,320	$726.38	$726.38
Syriac-Greek Antiochian Orthodox Catholic Church	2010	17,000	17,108	$49,000	$2.88	$2.86
United Church of Christ*	2010	1,058,423	1,058,423	$938,000,522	$886.22	$886.22
The United Methodist Church*	2009	7,679,850	7,679,850	$6,218,009,630	$809.65	$809.65
Unity of the Brethren	1998	2,548	3,218	$165,184	$64.83	$51.33
Universal Fellowship of Metropolitan Community Churches	2006	15,666	15,666	$19,509,664	$1,245.35	$1,245.35
The Wesleyan Church	2010	121,429	139,330	$316,205,810	$2,604.04	$2,269.47
Wisconsin Evangelical Lutheran Synod	2010	305,558	385,321	$316,674,402	$1,036.38	$821.85
TOTALS		**41,318,464**	**44,890,724**	**$34,244,730,678**	**$820.80**	**$762.85**

* National Council of Churches USA member communions. NOTE: Rounding may cause some totals to appear inaccurate.

Summary Statistics

Nation	Number Reporting	Full or Confirmed Members	Inclusive Members	Total Contributions	Per Capita Full or Confirmed Members	Per Capita Inclusive Members
CANADA	24	1,128,199	2,163,134	$1,203,206,060	$1,066.48	$556.23
UNITED STATES	63	41,318,464	44,890,724	$34,244,730,678	$820.80	$762.85

Finances—United States Churches *(continued)*

CONGREGATIONAL FINANCES			BENEVOLENCES			
Total Congregational Contributions	Per Capita Full or Confirmed Members	Per Capita Inclusive Members	Total Benevolences	Per Capita Full or Confirmed Members	Per Capita Inclusive Members	Benevolences as a Percentage of Total Giving
$257,415,342	$1,692.03	$1,046.30	$44,746,699	$294.13	$181.88	15%
$5,309,445	$1,629.66	$1,215.25	$931,98	$286.06	$213.32	15%
$10,133,258	$2,076.06	$1,490.40	$1,369,047	$280.48	$201.36	12%
$1,682,568	$731.55	$731.55	$227,946	$99.11	$99.11	12%
$400,622,149	$377.81	$377.81	$867,960,056	$818.53	$818.53	68%
$10,418,340,666	$645.66	$645.66	$1,302,479,654	$80.72	$80.72	11%
$38,000	$2.24	$2.22	$11,000	$0.65	$0.64	22%
$867,668,652	$819.77	$819.77	$70,331,870	$66.45	$66.45	7%
$5,020,514,489	$653.73	$653.73	$1,197,495,141	$155.93	$155.93	19%
$51,465	$20.20	$15.99	$113,719	$44.63	$35.34	69%
$19,290,664	$1,231.37	$1,231.37	$219,224	$13.99	$13.99	1%
$271,863,678	$2,238.87	$1,951.22	$44,342,132	$365.17	$318.25	14%
$257,940,369	$844.16	$669.42	$58,734,033	$192.22	$152.43	19%
$28,982,178,607	**$701.43**	**$645.62**	**$5,262,552,296**	**$127.37**	**$117.23**	**15%**

# of Church Finances

Total Congregational Contributions	Per Capita Full or Confirmed Members	Per Capita Inclusive Members	Total Benevolences	Per Capita Full or Confirmed Members	Per Capita Inclusive Members	Benevolences as a Percentage of Total Contributions
$981,110,490	$869.63	$453.56	$220,707,047	$195.63	$102.03	18%
$28,982,178,607	$701.43	$645.62	$5,262,552,296	$127.37	$117.23	15%

Trends in Seminary Enrollment

Data Provided by The Association of Theological Schools (ATS) in the United States and Canada

Table 1: ATS total student enrollment figures include the number of individuals enrolled in degree programs as well as persons enrolled in non-degree programs of study. From fall 2009 to 2010, the total head count enrollment reported by ATS member schools increased by 398 students. It should be noted, however, that this was the net effect of an influx of eleven new member schools with approximately 1,000 new students. Looking instead at a constant set of 245 schools that have been members of the Association for at least five years, the enrollment figures reflect a decline of 0.8% that follows four straight years of declines in the 2–3% range.

Table 1. Number of Member Schools from 2000 to 2010

Year	Number of Schools	Total Enrollment	Canada		United States		By Membership	
			Head Count	FTE	Head Count	FTE	Accredited	Non-Accredited
2000	243	72,728	5,868	3,251	66,860	44,627	69,850	2,878
2001	243	73,925	6,254	3,342	67,671	45,094	70,942	2,983
2002	244	76,530	6,643	3,512	69,887	44,557	73,615	2,895
2003	243	78,709	6,925	3,653	71,784	46,559	75,660	3,017
2004	251	80,773	7,036	3,597	73,737	48,093	77,513	2,627
2005	251	81,302	6,950	3,523	74,352	48,398	79,083	2,050
2006	253	81,063	6,395	3,205	74,668	47,377	79,618	1,445
2007	253	79,639	5,922	2,991	73,717	46,902	78,050	1,589
2008	252	77,861	5,827	3,081	72,034	44,611	76,333	1,528
2009	251	75,500	5,719	3,019	69,781	44,723	73,609	1,891
2010	257	75,898	5,466	2,931	70,432	44,499	73,747	2,151

Table 2: ATS analyzes enrollment both by the total number of individual students (Head Count) and the equivalent of full-time students (FTE). FTE is a calculation of the number of full-time students that would be represented by the combined time commitment of all students, including those attending part time. Decreasing full-time equivalent enrollment as a percentage of head count enrollment over recent years indicates an increasing number of part-time students. In 2010, head count enrollment increased, while FTE remained flat; as a result, FTE percentage of head count decreased slightly in 2010.

Table 2. Head Count and FTE for all Member Schools 2000 to 2010

Year	Head Count	% Change	FTE	% Change	FTE % of Head Count
2000	72,728	3.26	47,876	6.76	65.8%
2001	73,925	1.65	48,435	1.17	65.5%
2002	76,550	3.50	48,130	-0.76	62.8%
2003	78,709	2.82	50,206	4.3	63.8%
2004	80,773	2.62	51,690	2.9	64.1%
2005	81,302	0.65	51,922	0.4	63.9%
2006	81,063	-0.29	50,582	-2.6	62.4%
2007	79,639	-1.76	49,893	-1.36	62.6%
2008	77,861	-2.23	47,692	-4.41	61.3%
2009	75,500	-3.03	47,742	0.1	63.2%
2010	75,898	.53	47,430	-.65	62.5%

Table 3: ATS member schools offer a variety of degree programs. Table 3 displays enrollment by categories of degree programs. The Master of Divinity (MDiv) degree is the normative degree to prepare persons for ordained ministry and for pastoral and religious leadership responsibilities in congregations. Over the past four years, from fall 2007 to fall 2010, the MDiv experienced a 4.8% decrease in the number of students enrolled.

Table 3. Head Count Enrollment by Degree Categories 2000 to 2010

Year	Basic Ministerial Leadership (M.Div.)	(Non-M.Div.)	General Theological Studies	Advanced Ministerial Leadership	Advanced Theological Research	Other
2000	30,427	9,098	8,436	8,758	5,692	10,317
2001	31,128	8,652	8,503	8,790	5,756	11,096
2002	32,005	9,493	8,626	9,209	5,653	11,544
2003	33,287	10,343	8,708	9,213	5,804	11,354
2004	34,096	10,417	9,257	9,435	5,541	11,394
2005	34,505	11,018	9,831	9,330	5,790	10,828
2006	34,442	11,057	9,811	9,366	5,876	10,511
2007	34,123	11,031	9,608	9,411	5,937	9,529
2008	33,319	11,071	9,221	9,554	5,938	8,758
2009	32,861	11,104	9,060	9,480	5,886	7,109
2010	32,780	11,225	9,264	9,455	5,944	7,230

Table 4: In Fall 2010, women constituted 34.2% of the total enrollment in all ATS schools and 29.8% of the enrollment in the MDiv degree program. When ATS first began gathering enrollment data by gender in 1972, women represented 10% of the total enrollment and 5% of the MDiv enrollment.

Table 4. Women Student Head Count Enrollment 2000 to 2010

Year	Head Count	% Change	FTE % of Head Count
2000	25,391	5.55	34.91%
2001	25,999	2.39	35.17%
2002	27,328	5.06	35.70%
2003	27,920	2.19	35.50%
2004	28,875	3.42	36.03%
2005	29,257	1.32	35.98%
2006	27,921	-4.57	34.44%
2007	27,481	-1.58	34.51%
2008	26,870	-2.22	34.51%
2009	26,326	-2.02	34.87%
2010	25,976	-1.33	N/A

Tables 5, 6, 7: Enrollment of North American racial/ethnic students in ATS schools has grown generally both in overall numbers and as a percent of total enrollment over several decades. Over the past year, head counts and percentages are up for African American and Hispanic students but down for Pacific/Asian American students. These numbers to not take into account the 6.543 Visa students, 263 Native American students, or 7,839 students who did not report ethnicity.

STATISTICAL SECTION

389

Table 5. African American Student Head Count Enrollment 2000 to 2010

Year	Number of Students	% Annual Increase	% of Total Enrollment
2000	7,161	4.48	9.85%
2001	7,462	4.20	10.09%
2002	8,192	9.78	10.71%
2003	8,144	-0.60	10.30%
2004	8,393	3.06	10.47%
2005	8,946	6.59	12.10%
2006	8,344	-6.73	10.29%
2007	8,839	5.93	11.09%
2008	9,049	2.38	11.62%
2009	8,654	-4.37	11.46%
2010	8,933	3.22	11.77%

Table 6. Hispanic Student Head Count Enrollment 2000 to 2010

Year	Number of Students	% Annual Increase	% of Total Enrollment
2000	2,685	19.02	3.69%
2001	2,756	2.64	3.72%
2002	2,449	-11.14	3.20%
2003	2,863	16.9	3.60%
2004	2,842	-0.73	3.54%
2005	2,899	2.00	3.90%
2006	3,104	7.07	3.83%
2007	3,296	6.19	4.12%
2008	3,217	-2.39	4.13%
2009	3,221	0.12	4.27%
2010	3,506	8.85	4.62%

Table 7. Pacific/Asian American Student Head Count Enrollment 2000 to 2010

Year	Number of Students	% Annual Increase	% of Total Enrollment
2000	5,003	1.44	6.88%
2001	5,021	0.36	6.79%
2002	5,005	-0.32	6.54%
2003	5,499	9.90	7.00%
2004	5,226	-4.96	6.52%
2005	5,189	-7.08	7.00%
2006	5,370	3.49	6.62%
2007	5,524	2.87	6.94%
2008	5,208	-5.72	6.69%
2009	5,203	-0.10	6.89%
2010	5,001	-3.88	6.59%

IV

A CALENDAR FOR CHURCH USE
2012–2014

This calendar presents the major days of religious observances for Christians, Jews, Bahá'is, and Muslims; and, within the Christian community, major dates observed by Catholic, Eastern and Oriental Orthodox, Episcopal, and Lutheran churches. Within each of these traditions many other observances, such as saints' days, exist, but only those generally regarded as the most important are listed. Dates of interest to many Protestant communions are also included.

In the Orthodox dates, immovable observances are listed in accordance with the Gregorian calendar. Movable dates (those depending on the date of Easter) often will differ from Western observance, since the date of Easter (Pascha) in the Orthodox communions does not always correlate with the date for Easter of the Western churches. For Orthodox churches that use the old Julian calendar, observances are held thirteen days later than listed here.

Jewish and Muslim holidays begin after sunset the day previous to the date listed in this calendar. For Jews and Muslims, who follow differing lunar calendars, the dates of major observances are translated into Gregorian dates. Since the actual beginning of a new month in the Islamic calendar is determined by the appearance of the new moon, the corresponding dates given here on the Gregorian calendar may vary by geographic location and practice. Following the lunar calendar, Muslim dates fall roughly eleven days earlier each year on the Gregorian calendar. Practice concerning transliteration of the titles of holidays varies widely as well.

(Note: This listing reflects the first full day of holidays extending over two or more days. "C" stands for (Roman) Catholic; "O" stands for Orthodox; "E" stands for Episcopal; "L" stands for Lutheran; "ECU" stands for Ecumenical.)

Religious Event	2012	2013	2014
New Year's Day (C- Solemnity of Mary; O- Circumcision of Jesus Christ; E- Feast of Holy Name; L- Naming of Jesus) (*C, O, E, L*)	1/1/2012	1/1/2013	1/1/2014
Epiphany (O-Theophany) (*C, O, E, L*)	1/6/2012	1/6/2013	1/6/2014
Armenian Christmas (*O*)	1/6/2012	1/6/2013	1/6/2014
Epiphany Sunday (*C*)	1/8/2012	1/6/2013	1/5/2014
Feast Day of St John the Baptist (*Armenian O*)	1/13/2012	1/13/2013	1/13/2014
Ecumenical Sunday (*ECU*)	1/15/2012	1/20/2013	1/19/2014
First Sunday After Epiphany (Feast of the Baptism of Our Lord) (*Christian*)	1/15/2012	1/13/2013	1/12/2014
Week of Prayer for Christian Unity, Canada (*ECU*)	1/16/2012	1/21/2013	1/20/2014
Week of Prayer for Christian Unity (*ECU*)	1/18/2012	1/18/2013	1/18/2014
Theophany (*Oriental O*)	1/19/2012	1/19/2013	1/19/2014
Presentation of Jesus in the Temple (Candlemas; Purification of the Virgin Mary; O- The Meeting of Our Lord and Savior Jesus Christ) (*Christian*)	2/2/2012	2/2/2013	2/2/2014
Mawlid al-Nabi (Anniversary of the Prophet Muhammed's Birthday) (*Muslim*)	2/4/2012	1/24/2013	1/13/2014
Tu B'Shevat (*Jewish*)	2/8/2012	1/26/2013	1/16/2014
Brotherhood Week (*Interfaith*)	2/19/2012	2/17/2013	2/16/2014
Ash Wednesday (*Western Churches*)	2/22/2012	2/13/2013	3/5/2014
Great Lent (First Day of Lent) (*O*)	2/26/2012	2/17/2013	3/3/2014
Baha'i Fasting Season begins (19 days) (*Baha'i*)	3/2/2012	3/2/2013	3/2/2014
World Day of Prayer (*ECU*)	3/2/2012	3/1/2013	3/7/2014
Purim (*Jewish*)	3/8/2012	2/24/2013	3/15/2014
Joseph, Husband of Mary (*C, E, L*)	3/19/2012	3/19/2013	3/19/2014
Feast of Naw-Ruz (Baha'i New Year) (*Baha'i*)	3/21/2012	3/21/2013	3/21/2014

Religious Event	2012	2013	2014
The Annunciation (*Christian*)	3/25/2012	3/25/2013	3/25/2014
Holy Week (Western Churches)	4/1/2012	3/24/2013	4/13/2014
Holy Thursday (*Western Churches*)	4/5/2012	3/28/2013	4/17/2014
Good Friday (Friday of the Passion			
of Our Lord) (*Western Churches*)	4/6/2012	3/29/2013	4/18/2014
Passover (Pesach) (8 days) (*Jewish*)	4/7/2012	3/26/2013	4/14/2014
Holy Week (*O*)	4/8/2012	4/28/2013	4/13/2014
Palm Sunday (*O*)	4/8/2012	4/28/2013	4/13/2014
Easter (*Western Churches*)	4/8/2012	3/31/2013	4/20/2014
Holy Thursday (*O*)	4/12/2012	5/2/2013	4/17/2014
Holy Friday (Good Friday;			
Burial of Jesus Christ) (*O*)	4/13/2012	5/3/2013	4/18/2014
Pascha (Orthodox Easter) (*O*)	4/15/2012	5/5/2013	4/20/2014
Yom Hashoah (*Jewish*)	4/19/2012	4/7/2013	4/27/2014
Feast of Ridvan (Declaration			
of Baha'u'llah) (12 days) (*Baha'i*)	4/21/2012	4/21/2013	4/21/2014
Yom Haatzma'ut (*Jewish*)	4/26/2012	4/15/2013	5/6/2014
National Day of Prayer (*ECU*)	5/3/2012	5/2/2013	5/1/2014
May Friendship Day (*ECU*)	5/4/2012	5/3/2013	5/2/2014
Lag B'Omer (*Jewish*)	5/10/2012	4/28/2013	5/18/2014
Rural Life Sunday (*ECU*)	5/13/2012	5/12/2013	5/11/2014
Ascension Thursday (*Western Churches*)	5/17/2012	5/9/2013	5/29/2014
Declaration of the Bab (*Baha'i*)	5/23/2012	5/23/2013	5/23/2014
Ascension Day (*O*)	5/24/2012	6/13/2013	5/29/2014
Pentecost (Whitsunday) (*Western Churches*)	5/27/2012	5/19/2013	6/8/2014
Shavuot (Pentecost) (2 days) (*Jewish*)	5/27/2012	5/15/2013	6/4/2014
Ascension of Baha'u'llah (*Baha'i*)	5/29/2012	5/29/2013	5/29/2014
Visitation of the Blessed			
Virgin Mary (*C, E, L*)	5/31/2012	5/31/2013	5/31/2014
Holy Trinity (*C, E, L*)	6/3/2012	5/26/2013	6/15/2014
Pentecost/Holy Trinity (*O*)	6/3/2012	6/23/2013	6/8/2014
Martyrdom of the Bab (*Baha'i*)	6/9/2012	6/9/2013	6/9/2014
Corpus Christi (*C*)	6/10/2012	6/2/2013	6/19/2014
Apostles' (Peter & Paul) Fast begins (*O*)	6/11/2012	7/1/2013 *	6/16/2014
Sacred Heart of Jesus (*C*)	6/15/2012	6/7/2013	6/27/2014
Laylat al-Miraj (Ascension			
of the Prophet) (*Muslim*)	6/17/2012	6/6/2013	5/25/2014
Nativity of St. John the Baptist (*C, O, E, L*)	6/24/2012	6/24/2013	6/24/2014
Saint Peter and Saint Paul, Apostles of Christ (*O*)	6/29/2012	6/29/2013	6/29/2014
Feast Day of the Twelve Apostles of Christ (*O*)	6/30/2012	6/30/2013	6/30/2014
Laylat-ul-Bara'h (Night			
of Forgiveness) (*Muslim*)	7/5/2012	6/24/2013	6/12/2014
Ramadan Begins (First day			
of the month of Ramadan) (*Muslim*)	7/20/2012	7/9/2013	6/26/2014
Tish'a B'Av (*Jewish*)	7/29/2012	7/16/2013	8/5/2014
Dormition (Theotokos) Fast begins (*O*)	8/1/2012	8/1/2013	8/1/2014
Transfiguration of the Lord (*C, O, E*)	8/6/2012	8/6/2013	8/6/2014
Laylat al-Qadr (Night of Destiny,			
Revelation of the Holy Qur'an) (*Muslim*)	8/15/2012	8/4/2013	7/23/2014
Assumption of the Blessed Virgin Mary			
(E- Feast of the Blessed Virgin Mary;			
O- Falling Asleep (Dormition)			
of the Blessed Virgin) (*C, O, E*)	8/15/2012	8/15/2013	8/15/2014
'Id al-Fitr (Festival of the End			
of Ramadan; First day of the month			
of Shawwal) (*Muslim*)	8/19/2012	8/8/2013	7/28/2014
The Birth of the Blessed Virgin (*C, O*)	9/8/2012	9/8/2013	9/8/2014
Holy Cross Day (C- Triumph of the Cross;			
O- Adoration of the Holy Cross (*Christian*)	9/14/2012	9/14/2013	9/14/2014
Rosh Hashanah (New Year) (2 days) (*Jewish*)	9/17/2012	9/5/2013	9/25/2014
Yom Kippur (Day of Atonement) (*Jewish*)	9/26/2012	9/14/2013	10/4/2014

Religious Event	2012	2013	2014
Michaelmas (St. Michael and All Angels)			
(*Christian*) 9/29/2012	9/29/2013	9/29/2014	
Sukkot (Tabernacles) (7 days) (*Jewish*) 10/1/2012	9/19/2013	10/9/2014	
World Communion Sunday (*ECU*) .10/7/2012	10/6/2013	10/5/2014	
Shmini Atzeret (Solemn Assembly) (*Jewish*) 10/8/2012	9/26/2013	10/16/2014	
Thanksgiving Day (Canada) (*National*) 10/8/2012	10/14/2013	10/13/2014	
Simchat Torah (Rejoicing of the Law) (*Jewish*) 10/9/2012	9/27/2013	10/17/2014	
Laity Sunday (*ECU*) 10/14/2012	10/13/2013	10/12/2014	
Birth of the Bab (*Baha'i*) 10/20/2012	10/20/2013	10/20/2014	
Waqf al-Arafah (Eve of 'Id al-Adha) (*Muslim*) 10/25/2012	10/14/2013	10/3/2014	
'Id al-Adha (Festival of Sacrifice at time			
of Pilgrimage to Mecca) (*Muslim*) 10/26/2012	10/15/2013	10/4/2014	
Reformation Sunday (*L*) 10/28/2012	10/27/2013	10/26/2014	
Reformation Day (*L*) 10/31/2012	10/31/2013	10/31/2014	
All Saints Day (*C, E, L*) 11/1/2012	11/1/2013	11/1/2014	
World Community Day (*ECU*) 11/1/2012	11/7/2013	11/6/2014	
Birth of Baha'u'llah (*Baha'i*) 11/12/2012	11/12/2013	11/12/2014	
Nativity (St Philip's Fast) begins (*O*) 11/15/2012	11/15/2013	11/15/2014	
Muharram Begins (First Day of the Month			
of Muharram; Muslim New Year) (*Muslim*) 11/15/2012	11/4/2013	10/25/2014	
Thanksgiving Sunday (U.S.A.) (*National*) 11/18/2012	11/24/2013	11/23/2014	
Bible Sunday (*ECU*) 11/18/2012	11/17/2013	11/16/2014	
National Bible Week (*ECU*) 11/18/2012	11/17/2013	11/16/2014	
Presentation of the Blessed Virgin Mary			
in the Temple (Presentation			
of the Theotokos) (*O*) 11/21/2012	11/21/2013	11/21/2014	
Thanksgiving Day (U.S.A.) (*National*) 11/22/2012	11/28/2013	11/27/2014	
Ashura' (Martyrdom of Imam Hussein)			
(*Muslim (Shi'a)*) 11/24/2012	11/13/2013	11/2/2014	
Last Sunday After Pentecost (L- Feast			
of Christ the King) (*C, L*) 11/25/2012	11/24/2013	11/23/2014	
The Day of the Covenant (*Baha'i*) 11/26/2012	11/26/2013	11/26/2014	
Ascension of 'Abdu'l-Baha (*Baha'i*) 11/28/2012	11/28/2013	11/28/2014	
Feast Day of St. Andrew the Apostle			
(*C, O, E, L*) 11/30/2012	11/30/2013	11/30/2014	
First Sunday of Advent (Advent Sunday)			
(*Christian*) 12/2/2012	12/1/2013	11/30/2014	
Hanukkah (Chanukah, Festival of Lights)			
(8 days) (*Jewish*) 12/8/2012	11/27/2013	12/16/2014	
Immaculate Conception of the Blessed			
Virgin Mary (*C*) 12/8/2012	12/8/2013	12/8/2014	
Fourth Sunday of Advent			
(Christmas Sunday) (*Christian*) 12/23/2012	12/22/2013	12/21/2014	
Christmas (*Christian except Armenian*) 12/25/2012	12/25/2013	12/25/2014	

* Orthodox Communions utilizing the New Calendar will not observe this fast

V

INDEXES

Organizations

A

AAR (American Academy of Religion) 217
ABCCM (Asheville-Buncombe
Community Christian Ministry) 260
Action des Chrétiens pour l'Abolition
de la Torture 293
ADRIS-Association for the Development
of Religious Information Services 25
Advent Christian Church 56, 367
Adventist Bodies 181
African Methodist Episcopal
Church 56–57, 367, 378
African Methodist Episcopal
Zion Church, The 57–59, 367, 378
AGAPÉ Deux-Montagnes 293
Akron Area Association of Churches 261
Alaska Christian Conference 238–239
Alban Institute, Inc., The 21
Albanian Orthodox Archdiocese
in America 60, 367, 382
Albanian Orthodox Diocese
of America 60
Alcohol and Drug Concerns, Inc. 48
ALEPH Administrative Office 233
Allegheny Conference, The. See Allegheny
Wesleyan Methodist Connection (Original
Allegheny Conference)
Allegheny Valley Association
of Churches 263
Allegheny Wesleyan Methodist Connection
(Original Allegheny
Conference) 60, 367, 382
Alliance for Christian Media, The 21
Alliance of Baptists, The 60–61, 367, 378
Alliance of Churches 261
AMERC (Appalachian Ministries
Educational Resource Center) 23–24
American Academy of Religion (AAR) 217
American Association
of Lutheran Churches, The 61, 367
American Baptist
Association, The 61–62, 367
American Baptist Churches
in the U.S.A. 62–63, 367, 378, 382
American Bible Society 21–22
American Buddhist Association 227
American Buddhist Congress 227
American Carpatho-Russian Orthodox
Greek Catholic Church, The 63, 367
American Council of Christian Churches 22
American Evangelical Christian
Churches 63–64, 367

American Friends Service Committee 22
American Hindus Against Defamation 230
American Jewish Committee, The 233
American Orthodox Catholic Church. See
Apostolic Orthodox Catholic Church
of North America
American Rescue Workers 64, 367
American Society of Muslims 231–232
American Theological Library
Association, The 22–23
American Tract Society 23
American Waldensian Society, The 23
Amish. See Old Order Amish Church
Anchor Point Counseling Ministry 263
Anglican Bodies 181
Anglican Church of
Canada, The 185–186, 362
Anglo-Lutheran Catholic
Church 64–66, 367
Anti-Defamation League
of B'nai B'rith, The 233–234
Antiochian Orthodox Christian
Archdiocese of North
America, The 66, 186, 362, 367, 382
Apostolic Catholic Assyrian
Church of the East,
North American Dioceses 66–67
Apostolic Catholic Church 66, 367, 382
Apostolic Catholic Orthodox
Church 67–68, 367
Apostolic Christian Church
(Nazarene) 68, 187, 362, 367
Apostolic Christian Churches
of America 68–69, 368
Apostolic Church
in Canada, The 187, 362, 380
Apostolic Church of Pentecost
of Canada, Inc. 187, 362
Apostolic Episcopal Church 69, 368
Apostolic Faith Mission
Church of God 69–70, 368, 382
Apostolic Faith Mission
of Portland, Oregon 70, 368
Apostolic Lutheran Church of America 70
Apostolic Orthodox Catholic
Church of North America 70–71, 368
Appalachian Ministries Educational
Resource Center (AMERC) 23–24
ARDA (Association of Religion
Data Archives) .218
Arizona Ecumenical Council 239
Arkansas Interfaith Conference 239

INDEX

Armenian Apostolic Church,
Dioceses of America 72, 368, 378
Armenian Apostolic Church
of America..................71–72, 368
Armenian Evangelical Church
of Toronto 187, 362
Armenian Holy Apostolic
Church-Canadian Diocese 187–188, 380
Arrowhead Interfaith Council 252
Asheville-Buncombe Community
Christian Ministry (ABCCM) 260
Assemblies of God 72–73, 368
Assemblies of God International
Fellowship (Independent/Not Affiliated) ...73
Associate Reformed Presbyterian Church
(General Synod) 73–74, 368, 382
Associated Church Press, The 24
Associated Churches of Fort Wayne
& Allen County, Inc., The 244–245
Associated Gospel
Churches, The 24, 188, 362
Associated Ministries
of Tacoma-Pierce County 270
Association for the Development
of Religious Information Services
(ADRIS) 25
Association of Catholic Diocesan
Archivists 24
Association of Christian Churches
in Manitoba 292
Association of Christian Churches
of South Dakota 267
Association of Free Lutheran
Congregations, The 74–75, 368
Association of Gospel Rescue Missions 25
Association of Independent Evangelical
Lutheran Churches 75, 368, 382
Association of Regular Baptist
Churches (Canada) 188
Association of Religion Data
Archives (ARDA) 218
Association of Religious Communities 241
Association of Statisticians of American
Religious Bodies 25–26
Association of Theological
Schools (ATS) 26, 218
Association of Vineyard Churches.
See Vineyard USA
Atlantic Ecumenical Council 293
Atlantic Ecumenical Council
of Churches 292
ATS (Association of
Theological Schools) 26, 218
Attleboro Area Council
of Churches, Inc. 250
Auburn Theological Seminary 218–219
Austin Area Interreligious Ministries 268

B

Bahá'í Faith 226–227
Bahá'í National Center
of the U.S.A., The 227

B.A.P.S. (Bochasanwasi Shri Akshar
Purushottam Swaminarayan Sanstha) 230
Baptist Bible Fellowship
International 75–76, 368
Baptist Bodies (Canada) 215
Baptist Bodies (United States) 181
Baptist Convention of Ontario
and Quebec 188, 362, 380
Baptist General Conference.
See Converge Worldwide
Baptist General Conference
of Canada 188–189, 362
Baptist Missionary Association
of America 76–77, 368, 382
BARCA (Border Association for
Refugees from Central America, Inc.) 268
Barna Group, Ltd., The 219
Bay Area Ecumenical Forum 251
Beachy Amish Mennonite Churches ...78, 368
Berean Fellowship of Churches ..78, 368, 382
Bergen County Council of Churches 255
Berrien County Association of Churches ...251
BGC. See Converge Worldwide
Bible Church of Christ, Inc., The ...78–79, 368
Bible Fellowship Church 79, 368, 382
Bible Holiness Church 79
Bible Holiness Movement,
The 189, 362, 380
Bible Way Church of Our Lord
Jesus Christ World Wide, Inc. 79
Blanton-Peale Institute 26
Bochasanwasi Shri Akshar Purushottam
Swaminarayan Sanstha (B.A.P.S.) 230
Border Association for Refugees from
Central America (BARCA), Inc. 268
Bread for the World 26
Brethren, River 80, 181
Brethren (German Baptists) 181
Brethren Church (Ashland,
Ohio) 80, 369, 382
Brethren in Christ Church ..80, 181, 369, 382
Brethren in Christ Church,
Canadian Conference 189–190, 362
Bridgewater Inter-Church Council 292
British Methodist Episcopal
Church of Canada 190
Brooklyn Council of Churches 256
Broome County Council of Churches, Inc. ..256
Bruderhof Communities Inc. See Church
Communities International
Buddhism 227–229
Buddhist Churches of America 227–228
Buddhist Council of the Midwest 228
Buddhist Council of the Northwest 228
Buddhist Peace Fellowship 228
Burlington Inter-Church Council 293

C

CAIR (Council for American-Islamic
Relations) 231
Calgary Council of Churches 292
Calgary Inter-Faith Community
Action Association 292

California Council of Churches-California
  Church Impact 239
Calvary Chapel 80, 369
Campus Crusade for Christ
  International 26–27
Canadian and American Reformed
  Churches 190, 362
Canadian Baptist Ministries 190, 362
Canadian Baptists of Western
  Canada 191, 362, 380
Canadian Bible Society 48
Canadian Centre for Ecumenism . . .48–49, 293
Canadian Conference of Mennonite
  Brethren Churches 191, 362
Canadian Convention of Southern
  Baptists 191, 362
Canadian Council of Churches, The 49
Canadian District of the Moravian
  Church in America,
  Northern Province 191, 362, 380
Canadian Evangelical Theological
  Association 49–50
Canadian Society of Biblical
  Studies-Société Canadienne
  des Etudes Bibliques 50
Canadian Tract Society 50
Canadian Yearly Meeting
  of the Religious Society
  of Friends 191, 363
Cape Cod Council of
  Churches, Inc., The 250
Capital Area Council of Churches, Inc. 256
Capital Region Ecumenical
  Organization (CREO) 256–257
Capitol Region Conference
  of Churches, The 241
CARA (Center for Applied Research
  in the Apostolate) 220
Catholic Church, The 80–81, 369
Catholic Church in Canada, The. See Roman
  Catholic Church in Canada, The
CB America (Conservative Baptist
  Association of America) 371
CBAmerica (Conservative Baptist
  Association of America) 103–104
CCPD (Christian Council on Persons
  with Disabilities) 35
CEAP (Community Emergency
  Assistance Program) 252
Center City Churches 241
Center for Applied Research
  in the Apostolate (CARA) 220
Center for Parish Development 27
Center for the Study of Religion
  and American Culture 220
Center on Conscience & War 27
Central Maryland Ecumenical Council 249
Centre Emmaüs 293–294
Chaplaincy of Full Gospel Churches 27
Chautauqua County Rural Ministry 257
Christ Catholic Church 82, 369
Christ Catholic Church International . . .191–192
Christ Community Church
  (Evangelical-Protestant) 82, 369

Christadelphians 82
Christian and Missionary
  Alliance, The 87–88, 369, 382
Christian and Missionary Alliance
  in Canada 193, 363, 380
Christian Associates of Southwest
  Pennsylvania 263
Christian Brethren
  (also known as
  Plymouth Brethren) . .82–83, 192, 363, 369
Christian Church (Disciples
  of Christ) in Canada 192, 363, 380
Christian Church (Disciples
  of Christ) in the United States
  and Canada 83–85, 369, 378, 382
Christian Churches United
  of the Tri-County Area 263–264
Christian Churches/Churches of
  Christ 85–86, 182, 192–193,
  . . . . .215, 363, 369
Christian Community Action 241
Christian Conference
  of Connecticut 241–242
Christian Congregation, Inc., The 86, 369
Christian Council of Delaware
  and Maryland's Eastern Shore, The 242
Christian Council on Persons
  with Disabilities (CCPD) 35
Christian Endeavor International 27–28
Christian Leadership Council
  of Downtown Toronto 293
Christian Management Association 28
Christian Methodist
  Episcopal Church 86–87, 369, 378
Christian Ministries of Delaware County . . .245
Christian Ministry in the National Parks, A. . .28
Christian Reformed Church in North
  America 88–89, 193–194, 363, 369
Christian Service Center for Central
  Florida, Inc. 243
Christian Union 89, 369, 382
Christian Youth Council 271
Christian-Jewish Dialogue of Montreal 294
Christians United in Beaver County 264
Church Army in Canada, The 50
Church Communities International 91, 369
Church Community Services 245
Church Council of Greater Seattle 270
Church Federation of Greater
  Indianapolis, Inc., The 245
Church Growth Center-Home
  of Church Doctor Ministries 28
Church of the Brethren 369, 378, 382
Church of Christ 90, 369
Church of Christ, Scientist 90–91
Church of Christ (Holiness)
  U.S.A., The 90, 369, 382
Church of God, The 91–92
Church of God, Mountain
  Assembly, Inc. 97, 370
(Original) Church of God, Inc., The 144
Church of God (Anderson,
  Indiana) 92–93, 194, 363, 370

Church of God (Cleveland, Tenn.) 363
Church of God (Cleveland,
    Tennessee) 95–96, 194–195, 370
Church of God (Seventh Day),
    Denver, Colorado, The 370
Church of God by Faith, Inc. 96, 370
Church of God General Conference
    (McDonough, GA) 96–97, 370, 382
Church of God General Conference (Oregon,
    IL and Morrow, GA). See Church of God
    General Conference (McDonough, GA)
Church of God in Christ, The 93–94, 370
Church of God in Christ, International 94
Church of God in Christ,
    Mennonite 95, 194, 363, 370
Church of God of the Firstborn, The 96
Church of God of Prophecy 97–98, 370
Church of God of Prophecy
    Canada East, The 195–196, 363
Church of Illumination, The 98, 370
Church of Jesus Christ, The
    (Bickertonites) .98, 370
Church of Jesus Christ of
    Latter-day Saints, The 98, 370
Church of Jesus Christ of
    Latter-day Saints in Canada, The . . .196, 363
Church of Our Lord Jesus
    Christ of the Apostolic Faith, Inc. 101
Church of the
    Brethren 89–90, 369, 378, 382
Church of the Living God (Motto,
    Christian Workers for Fellowship) . . .99, 370
Church of the Lutheran
    Brethren 100, 196, 363
Church of the Lutheran Brethren
    of America 99–100, 370
Church of the Lutheran Confession . . .370, 382
Church of the Nazarene 100–101, 370, 382
Church of the Nazarene
    in Canada 196–197, 363, 380
Church of the United Brethren
    in Christ . . . . .USA, 101, 370
Church Women United in the U.S.A. 28–29
Churches' Council on Theological
    Education in Canada,
    An Ecumenical Foundation 50–51
Churches of Christ 101–102, 370
Churches of Christ in Canada 197, 363
Churches of Christ in Christian
    Union 102, 367, 370, 371
Churches of Christ/Christian
    Churches 85–86, 182, 192–193, 215
Churches of God 182
Churches of God, General
    Conference 102–103, 367, 371, 382
Churches of the New Jerusalem 182
Churches United, Inc. 246
Churches United of the Quad City Area 246
Churches Uniting in Christ 29–30
Churchpeople for Change and
    Reconciliation 261
Collegeville Institute for Ecumenical
    & Cultural Research 221

Colorado Council of Churches 241
Columbia Partnership, Inc. 30
Comité Québécois du Dialogue
    musulman-chrétien 294
Community Emergency Assistance
    Program (CEAP) 252
Community Ministries of Rockville 250
Community Ministry of Montgomery
    County 250
Community of
    Christ 103, 197, 363, 367, 371, 382
Community Renewal Society 243–244
Concerned Ecumenical Ministry
    to the Upper West Side 257
Congregational Christian Churches
    in Canada .197, 363
Congregational Holiness Church 103, 367, 371
Conservative Baptist Association
    of America
    (CBAmerica) 103–104, 367, 371
Conservative Congregational Christian
    Conference 104, 367, 371, 382
Conservative Lutheran
    Association 104, 367, 371
Consultation on Church Union. See Churches
    Uniting in Christ
Contact Ministries of Springfield 244
Convention of Atlantic Baptist
    Churches 197–198, 363, 380
Converge Worldwide
    (BGC) 104–105, 181, 367, 371
Cooperative Baptist Fellowship 105
Cooperative Metropolitan Ministries 250
Coptic Orthodox Church . .105, 367, 371, 378
Coptic Orthodox Church
    in Canada, The 198, 364
Cornwallis District Inter-Church Council . . .292
Corpus Christi Metro Ministries 268
Cortland County Council
    of Churches, Inc. 257
Council for American-Islamic
    Relations (CAIR) 231
Council of Christian Communions
    of Greater Cincinnati 261
Council of Churches and Synagogues
    of Southwestern Connecticut 242
Council of Churches of Chemung
    County, Inc. 257
Council of Churches of Greater
    Bridgeport, Bridgeport, CT 242
Council of Churches of Greater
    Springfield 250
Council of Churches of Greater
    Washington, The 242–243
Council of Churches of Santa Clara
    County, The 239
Council of Churches of the City
    of New York 257
Council of Churches of the Ozarks 254
Council of Hindu Temples of
    North America 230
CREO (Capital Region Ecumenical
    Organization) 256–257

Cross-Lines Cooperative Council 247
Cumberland Presbyterian
  Church 106, 367, 371, 382
Cumberland Presbyterian Church
  in America 106–107, 367, 371, 382

D

Des Moines Area Religious Council 246
Direction Chrétienne 294
Disciples of Christ. *See* Christian Church
  (Disciples of Christ) in Canada; Christian
  Church (Disciples of Christ) in the United
  States and Canada
Doukhobars. *See* Union of Spiritual
  Communities of Christ (Orthodox
  Doukhobors in Canada)
Dutchess County Interfaith Council, Inc. . . .257

E

East Dallas Cooperative Parish 268
East End Cooperative Ministry 264
Eastern Area Community Ministries 247
Eastern Orthodox Churches 182
Eastern Orthodox Churches (Canada) 215
Ecclesia 255
Ecumenical Committee 293
Ecumenical Conference of
  Greater Altoona 264
Ecumenical Council of Pasadena
  Area Churches, The 239
Ecumenical Council of San Diego
  County 239
Ecumenical Ministries of Iowa (EMI) 246
Ecumenical Ministries of Oregon 263
Elim Fellowship 117
Elim Fellowship Canada 198–199
EMI (Ecumenical Ministries of Iowa) 246
empty tomb, Inc. 221
Episcopal Church,
  The 107–110, 367, 371, 378, 384
Estonian Evangelical Lutheran
  Church, The 367, 371
Estonian Evangelical Lutheran
  Church Abroad, The 199, 364
Evangelical Christian Church
  in Canada 199, 364, 380
Evangelical Church,
  The 110–111, 367, 371, 384
Evangelical Church Alliance,
  The .111, 367, 371
Evangelical Congregational
  Church, The 111–112, 367, 371, 384
Evangelical Council for Financial
  Accountability 30
Evangelical Covenant Church,
  The 112–113, 367, 371
Evangelical Covenant Church
  of Canada, The 199, 364
Evangelical Fellowship of Canada 51
Evangelical Free Church of
  America, The 113, 367, 371
Evangelical Free Church
  of Canada 199–200, 364

Evangelical Friends International-
  North American Region 113, 372
Evangelical Lutheran Church
  in America 113–116, 372, 378, 384
Evangelical Lutheran Church
  in Canada .200, 364
Evangelical Lutheran Synod 116, 372, 384
Evangelical Mennonite Church.
  See Fellowship of Evangelical Churches
Evangelical Mennonite
  Conference 200–201, 364
Evangelical Mennonite Mission
  Conference 201, 364
Evangelical Methodist Church . . .116–117, 372
Evangelical Missionary Church
  of Canada, The 201, 364
Evangelical Presbyterian Church 117, 372
Evangelical Press Association 30

F

Faith & Values Media30–31, 39. *See also*
  National Interfaith Cable Coalition Inc.
Faith Action Network: A Partnership for the
  Common Good .270
Faith Community Assistance Center 256
Faith In Action Network of
  Rochester, NY .257
FaithTrust Institute 270
Family Endeavors .268
Federation of Christian Ministries 31
Federation of Jain Associations in
  North America (JAINA) 232–233
Federation of Zoroastrian Associations
  of North America (FEZANA) 237
Fellowship of Evangelical Baptist
  Churches in Canada, The 201, 364
Fellowship of Evangelical
  Bible Churches 117–118, 372, 384
Fellowship of Evangelical
  Churches 118, 372, 384
Fellowship of Fundamental
  Bible Churches 118–119, 372
Fellowship of Grace Brethren
  Churches .119, 372
Fern Creek-Highview United Ministries 247
FEZANA (Federation of Zorastrian
  Associations of North America) 237
First Miramichi Inter-Church Council 292
Florida Council of Churches 243
FOCUS Churches of Albany, Inc. 257–258
Foursquare Gospel Church
  of Canada 201–202, 364
Free Christian Zion Church of Christ 119
Free Methodist Church
  in Canada 202, 364, 380
Free Methodist Church
  of North America 372, 384
Free Methodist Church-USA 119–120
Free Will Baptists 202, 364
Fresno Metro Ministry 239–240
Friends 182
Friends General Conference 120–121, 372

INDEX

399

Friends International. *See* Evangelical
Friends International-
North American Region
Friends United Meeting 121–122, 372, 378
Friends World Committee for
Consultation (Section of the Americas) 31
Full Gospel Assemblies
International 122–123, 372
Full Gospel Fellowship of Churches
and Ministers International 123, 372
Fund for Theological Education,
Inc., The 31–32
Fundamental Methodist Church, Inc. . . .123, 372

G

GCEPC. *See* Lutheran Evangelical
Protestant Church
GEII (Graymoor Ecumenical &
Interreligious Institute) 32
General Association of General
Baptists 123–124, 372, 384
General Association of Regular
Baptist Churches 124, 372
General Church of the New
Jerusalem 124–125, 202, 364, 372
General Conference of Mennonite
Brethren Churches 125, 372, 384
General Conference of the
Canadian Assemblies of God 202–203
General Conference of
The Church of God (Seventh Day),
Denver, Colorado 125
Genesee County Churches United, Inc 258
Genesee-Orleans Ministry of Concern 258
Georgia Christian Council 243
German Baptists (Brethren) 181
Glengarry-Prescott-Russell
Christian Council 293
Glenmary Research Center 32
GRACE (Grand Rapids Area Center
for Ecumenism) .251
Grace Gospel Fellowship 125–126, 373
Grand Rapids Area Center for
Ecumenism (GRACE) 251
Graymoor Ecumenical & Interreligious
Institute (GEII) 32
Greater Birmingham Ministries 238
Greater Chicago Broadcast Ministries 244
Greater Dallas Community of Churches 268
Greater Dayton Christian Connections 261
Greater Fairmont Council of Churches 271
Greater Flint Council of Churches 251–252
Greater Lawrence Council of Churches 250
Greater Minneapolis Council
of Churches 252–253
Greater New Orleans Federation
of Churches 249
Greater Toronto Council of Christian
Churches, The 293
Greater Victoria Council of Churches 292
Greater Waterbury Interfaith
Ministries, Inc. .242

Greek Orthodox Archdiocese
of America 126–127, 373, 378
Greek Orthodox Metropolis
of Toronto (Canada) 203, 364
Greensboro Urban Ministry 260

H

Hanover Area Council of Churches 264
Hartford Institute for Religion Research
of Hartford Seminary, The 222
Hazard-Perry County Community
Ministries, Inc. .247
Hemmingford Ecumenical Committee 294
Highlands Community Ministries 247–248
Hinduism 230–231
Holy Eastern Orthodox Catholic and
Apostolic Church in North
America, Inc., The 127–128, 373
Holy Ukrainian Autocephalic Orthodox
Church in Exile .128
House of God, Which is the Church
of the Living God, The Pillar and
Ground of the Truth, Inc. 128
Humboldt Clergy Council 294
Hungarian Reformed Church
in America 128–129, 373, 378
Hutterian Brethren 129, 373
Hyde Park & Kenwood Interfaith
Council, The 244

I

ICNA (Islamic Circle of North America) . . .231
IFCA International, Inc. 129, 373
IFCO (Interreligious Foundation
for Community Organization) 34
Ignace Council of Churches 293
Illinois Conference of Churches 244
Independent Assemblies of God
International (Canada) 203
Independent Holiness Church 203, 364
Indiana Partners for Christian
Unity and Mission 245
Industrial Cape Breton Council
of Churches 292
Inland Valley Hope Partners 240
Insight Meditation Society 228
Institute for the Study of American
Evangelicals (ISAE) 222
Institute for the Study of American
Religion 223
Inter Church Council of Burlington 293
Interchurch Communications 52
Inter-Church Council of Greater
New Bedford 251
Inter-Church Ministries of Erie County 264
Interchurch Ministries of Nebraska 255
Interfaith Action of Evanston 244
Interfaith Association of Northwest
Washington, The 270
Interfaith Community Council, Inc. 245
Interfaith Community Services 254
Interfaith Conference of Greater
Milwaukee 271

INDEX

InterFaith Conference of Metropolitan
Washington 243
Interfaith Council .271
Interfaith Council of Boulder 241
Interfaith Council of Contra
Costa County 240
Interfaith Council of Montréal 294
Interfaith Federation of Greater
Baton Rouge 249
Interfaith Impact for Justice and Peace . . .32–33
Interfaith Ministries for Greater Houston . . .268
Inter-Faith Ministries-Wichita 247
Interfaith Mission Service 238
Interfaith Partnership of
Metropolitan St. Louis 254
Interfaith Service Bureau 240
Interfaith Worker Justice 33–34
Interfaith Works 271
InterFaith Works of Central New York 258
International Church of the
Foursquare Gospel 129–130, 373, 384
International Council of
Community Churches 130, 373, 378
International Fellowship of
Bible Churches, Inc. 130–131, 373
International Fellowship of
Christian Assemblies 131, 373
International Pentecostal Church
of Christ, The 131–132, 373, 384
International Pentecostal Holiness
Church 132, 373, 384
International Society for Krishna
Consciousness (ISKCON) 230
Interreligious Foundation for Community
Organization (IFCO) 34
Inter-Varsity Christian Fellowship
of Canada 51–52
InterVarsity Christian Fellowship
of the U.S.A 34
Iowa Religious Media Services 246–247
ISAE (Institute for the Study of
American Evangelicals) 222
ISKCON (International Society for
Krishna Consciousness) 230
Islam 231–232
Islamic Circle of North America
(ICNA) 231
Islamic Society of North America
(ISNA), The 231
ISNA (The Islamic Society of North
America) 231

J

Jackson County Interfaith Council, The 252
JAINA: Federation of Jain Associations
in North America 232–233
Jainism 232–233
Jehovah's Witnesses . .132–133, 203, 364, 373
Jewish Council for Public Affairs 234
Jewish Reconstructionist Federation 234
J.M. Dawson Institute of Church-State
Studies at Baylor University 223

John Howard Society of Ontario 52
Joint Religious Legislative
Coalition, The 253
Judaism 233–235

K

Kairos Institute, Inc., The 35
Kansas Ecumenical Ministries 247
Kentuckiana Interfaith Community 248
Kentucky Council of Churches 248
Kentville Council of Churches 292
Kitchener-Waterloo Council of Churches . . .293
Korean Presbyterian Church
Abroad, The 133, 373, 378

L

Lafayette Urban Ministry 245
Lancaster County Council of Churches 264
Latter-day Saints
(Mormons) . . . . .182.
See also Church of Jesus Christ
of Latter-day Saints
Latter-day Saints (Mormons) (Canada) 215
Latvian Evangelical Lutheran Church
in America, The 133, 373, 380, 384
LCMS (Lutheran Church-Missouri
Synod, The) 134–135, 373, 384
Lebanon County Christian Ministries 264
Lehigh County Conference of
Churches 264–265
Lewisburg Council of Churches 265
Liberal Catholic Church-Province
of the United States of America 134, 373
Lift Disability Network 35
Lincoln Interfaith Council 255
Liturgical Conference, The 35
Lombard Mennonite Peace Center 35
London Inter-City Faith Team 293
Long Island Council of Churches, The 258
Lord's Day Alliance of the United
States, The 35–36
Louisiana Interchurch Conference 249
Louisville Institute, The 223–224
Lunenburg Queens Baptist Association
of Convention Baptist Churches 292
Lutheran Association, Conservative.
See Conservative Lutheran Association
Lutheran Bodies (Canada) 215
Lutheran Bodies (United States) 182
Lutheran Church. See American
Association of Lutheran Churches, The;
Evangelical Lutheran Church in Canada
Lutheran Church of America. See Apostolic
Lutheran Church of America; Evangelical
Lutheran Church in America
Lutheran Church-
Canada 203–204, 365, 380
Lutheran Church-Missouri
Synod (LCMS) 134–135, 373, 384
Lutheran Council in Canada 52
Lutheran Evangelical Protestant
Church (GCEPC) 135

INDEX

Lutheran Synod. *See* Evangelical
  Lutheran Synod
Lutheran World Relief 36

M

Madison-area Urban Ministry 271–272
Mahone Bay Interchurch Council 292
Mahoning Valley Association
  of Churches 261
Maine Council of Churches 249
Malankara Orthodox Syrian Church,
  Diocese of America 136, 373, 378
Mall Area Religious Council (MARC) 253
Manchester Area Conference
  of Churches 242
Mar Thoma Syrian Church
  of India 136–137, 374, 378, 384
MARC (Mall Area Religious Council) 253
Marin Interfaith Council 240
Massachusetts Commission on
  Christian Unity .251
Massachusetts Council of Churches 251
Massey Inter-Church Council 293
MCC (Mennonite Central Committee) 36
MCCC (Mennonite Central Committee
  Canada) 52–53
Melville Association of Churches 294
Mennonite. *See* Canadian Conference of
  Mennonite Brethren Churches;
  Reinland Mennonite Church
Mennonite Bodies (Canada) 215–216
Mennonite Bodies (United States) 182–183
Mennonite Brethren Churches.
  See General Conference of
  Mennonite Brethren Churches
Mennonite Central Committee (MCC) 36
Mennonite Central Committee
  Canada (MCCC) 52–53
Mennonite Church Canada 204, 365
Mennonite Church of God in Christ.
  See Church of God in Christ, Mennonite
Mennonite Church USA 137–138, 374
Methodist Bodies (Canada) 216
Methodist Bodies (United States) 183
Methodist Church. *See* United Methodist
  Church, The
Methodist Church, Evangelical. *See*
  Evangelical Methodist Church
Methodist Church, Fundamental. *See*
  Fundamental Methodist Church, Inc.
Metropolitan Area Church Council 261–262
Metropolitan Area Religious Coalition
  of Cincinnati 262
Metropolitan Christian Council: Detroit-
  Windsor 252
Metropolitan Christian Council of
  Philadelphia 265
Metropolitan Ecumenical Ministry 255
Metropolitan Ecumenical Ministry
  Community Development Corp. 255–256
Metropolitan Inter Faith
  Association (MIFA) 267

Metropolitan Interfaith Council
  on Affordable Housing (MICAH) 253
MICAH (Metropolitan Interfaith Council
  on Affordable Housing) 253
MIFA (Metropolitan Inter Faith
  Association) 267
Ministries United South Central
  Louisville (M.U.S.C.L., Inc.) 248
Minnesota Council of Churches 253
Missionary Church, The 138, 374, 384
Mississippi Religious Leadership
  Conference 254
Moncton Area Council of Churches 292
Montana Association of Churches 254–255
Montreal Association for the Blind
  Foundation 294
Moravian Bodies 183
Moravian Church. *See* Canadian District
  of the Moravian Church in America,
  Northern Province; Moravian Church
  in America
Moravian Church in America
  (Northern Province, Southern
  Province) 138–139, 374, 379, 384
Mormons. *See* Church of Jesus Christ of Latter-
  day Saints; Latter-day Saints
Mosque Cares (Ministry of Imam
  W. Deen Mohammed), The 231–232
MPAC (Muslim Public Affairs Council) 232
Multifaith Action Society of
  British Columbia 292
M.U.S.C.L., Inc. *See* Ministries
  United South Central Louisville
Muskegon County Cooperating Churches . . .252
Muslim American Society 232
Muslim Peace Fellowship 232
Muslim Public Affairs Council (MPAC) 232

N

NARF (Native American Rights Fund) 235
National Association of Congregational
  Christian Churches 139, 374
National Association of Ecumenical and
  Interreligious Staff 36–37
National Association of
  Evangelicals, The 37
National Association of Free
  Will Baptists 139, 384
National Baptist Convention,
  U.S.A., Inc. 140, 374, 379
National Baptist Convention of
  America, Inc. 139–140, 374, 379
National Bible Association 37
National Conference for Community
  and Justice, The .37
National Conference on Ministry
  to the Armed Forces 37–38
National Congress of American
  Indians (NCAI) .235
National Council of the Churches
  of Christ in the U.S.A 38–39
National Institute of Business and
  Industrial Chaplains 39

National Interfaith Cable Coalition,
Inc. (NICC) 39
National Interfaith Coalition on Aging . . .39–40
National Missionary Baptist Convention
of America 140–141, 374, 379
National Organization
of the New Apostolic Church
of North America 141, 374
National Primitive Baptist
Convention, Inc. 141, 374
National Religious Broadcasters 40
National Spiritual Assembly of the
Baha'is of the United States 227
National Spiritualist Association
of Churches 141–142
National Woman's Christian T
emperance Union 40
Native American Rights Fund (NARF) 235
Native American traditional spirituality 235
NCAI (National Congress of American
Indians) 235
Netherlands Reformed
Congregations 142, 374
Network of Religious Communities . . .258–259
New Britain Area Conference of
Churches (NEWBRACC) 242
New Church. See General Church
of the New Jerusalem
New Hampshire Council of Churches 255
New Jersey Council of Churches 256
New Mexico Conference of Churches 256
New York Buddhist Council 228–229
New York State Council of
Churches, Inc. 259
NEWBRACC. See New Britain
Area Conference of Churches
Niagara Council of Churches Inc., The 259
NICA (Northside Inter-Church Agency) 269
NICC (National Interfaith Cable
Coalition, Inc.) 39
North American Baptist
Conference . .142, 204, 365, 374, 380, 384
North American Baptist Fellowship 40–41
North American Old Roman Catholic
Church (Archdiocese
of New York) 142–143, 374
North Carolina Council of Churches . . .260–261
North Dakota Conference of Churches 261
North Dallas Shared Ministries 268
Northern California Interreligious
Conference 240
Northern Kentucky Interfaith
Commission, Inc. 248
Northside Common Ministries 265
Northside Inter-Church Agency (NICA) 269
Northwest Harvest-E. M. M. 271
Northwest Interfaith Movement 265

O

Oak Park-River Forest Community
of Congregations 244
Ohio Council of Churches 262

Oikocredit-Ecumenical Development
Cooperative Society 41
Oklahoma Conference of Churches 262
Old Calendar Orthodox Church
of Greece (Holy Synod in Resistance),
American Exarchate 143
Old Catholic Church, Dutch. See
Universal Catholic Church
Old Catholic Church of
Canada, The 204–205, 365
Old Catholic Churches 183
Old Catholic Orthodox
Church, The 143, 374
Old German Baptist
Brethren Church 143, 374
Old Order Amish
Church 143–144, 205, 375
Old Order (Wisler) Mennonite
Church 144, 375
Open Bible Churches 144, 375
Open Bible Faith Fellowship
of Canada 205, 365
Oriental Orthodox Churches (Canada) 216
Oriental Orthodox Churches
(United States) 183
(Original) Church of God, Inc., The 144
Orthodox Anglican Church, The 144–145
Orthodox Church in
America, The 145–146, 375, 379
Orthodox Church in America
(Archdiocese of Canada) 205, 365
Orthodox Presbyterian
Church, The 146, 375, 384
Ottawa Christian Council
of the Capital Area 293

P

Paducah Cooperative Ministry 248
Parish Resource Center, Inc. 41
Patriarchal Parishes of the Russian
Orthodox Church in Canada 205, 365
Patriarchal Parishes of the Russian
Orthodox Church
in the U.S.A. 146, 375, 379
Pennsylvania Conference on
Interchurch Cooperation 265
Pennsylvania Council of Churches, The 265
Pentecostal Assemblies of
Canada, The 205–206, 365, 380
Pentecostal Assemblies of
Newfoundland, The 206–207, 365, 380
Pentecostal Assemblies of
the World, Inc. 146–147, 375
Pentecostal Bodies (Canada) 216
Pentecostal Bodies (United States) 183
Pentecostal Church of God 147, 375
Pentecostal Churches of Christ 147–148
Pentecostal Fire-Baptized
Holiness Church 148, 375
Pentecostal Free Will Baptist
Church, Inc., The 148
Pentecostal-Charismatic Churches
of North America 41–42

INDEX

403

Peoria Friendship House
of Christian Service 244
Philadelphia Yearly Meeting
of the Religious Society
of Friends 148, 375, 379
Pictou Council of Churches 292
Pike Country Outreach Council 262
Pillar of Fire 148–149
Pluralism Project, The 224–225
Plymouth Brethren. See Christian
Brethren
Polish National Catholic Church
of America 149, 375, 379
Prairie Centre for Ecumenism 294
Presbyterian Church. See Evangelical
Presbyterian Church
Presbyterian Church
(U.S.A.) 150–151, 375, 379, 384
Presbyterian Church in
America 149–150, 375, 384
Presbyterian Church in America
(Canadian Section) 207, 365, 380
Presbyterian Church in Canada 207, 365
Primitive Advent Christian
Church 151–152, 375
Primitive Baptists .152
Primitive Methodist Church
in the U.S.A. 152, 375
Progressive National Baptist
Convention, Inc. 152–153, 375, 379
Project Equality, Inc. 42
Project of Easton, Inc. 265
Project Ploughshares 53
Protestant Reformed Churches
in America 153, 375

Q

Quakers. See Friends General Conference
Quakers, Conservative. See Religious
Society of Friends (Conservative)
Quakers, International. See Evangelical Friends
International-North American Region
Quakers, Philadelphia. See Philadelphia Yearly
Meeting of the Religious Society of Friends
Quakers, Unaffiliated Meetings. See Religious
Society of Friends (Unaffiliated Meetings)
Quebec Ecumenical Network (Réseau
Oecuménique du Québec) 294
Queens County Association of Churches . . .293
Queens Federation of Churches 259

R

Radio Ville-Marie 294
Reading Berks Conference of Churches 266
Reformed Bodies 183–184
Reformed Bodies (Canada) 216
Reformed Catholic Church 153, 375
Reformed Church
in America 154, 376, 379, 386
Reformed Church
in Canada 207–208, 365, 380
Reformed Church
in the United States 154–155, 376, 386

Reformed Episcopal Church 155–157, 376
Reformed Episcopal Church
of Canada, The 208, 365, 380
Reformed Mennonite Church 157, 376
Reformed Methodist Union
Episcopal Church 157
Reformed Presbyterian Church
of North America 157, 376, 386
Reformed Zion Union Apostolic Church . . .158
Regina Council of Churches 294
Regional Council for Christian
Ministry, Inc., The 243
Regional Council of Churches
of Atlanta, The .243
Reinland Mennonite Church 208, 365
Religion Communicators Council,
Inc., The 42–43
Religion in America Life (RIAL) 42
Religion News Service 43
Religion Newswriters Association
and Foundation 43
Religions for Peace-USA, Inc. 43–44
Religious Action Center of Reform
Judaism 234
Religious Conference Management
Association, Inc. 44
Religious Society of Friends
(Conservative) 158, 376
Religious Society of Friends
(Unaffiliated Meetings) 158
Religious Television Associates 53
Reorganized Church of Jesus Christ
of Latter-day Saints. See Community
of Christ
Réseau Oecuménique du Québec (Quebec
Ecumenical Network) 294
Réseau Oecuménique Justice et Paix 294
Rhode Island State Council of
Churches, The 267
RIAL (Religion in America Life) 42
River Brethren. See Brethren in Christ Church
Roman Catholic Church in
Canada, The 208–209, 365
Romanian Orthodox Church
in America, The 158–159, 376
Romanian Orthodox Church in
America (Canadian Parishes) 210, 365
Romanian Orthodox Episcopate
of America, The 159, 376
Romanian Orthodox Episcopate
of America, The (Jackson, MI) 210
Rural Migrant Ministry 259
Russian Orthodox Church. See
Patriarchal Parishes of the
Russian Orthodox Church in Canada
Russian Orthodox Church Outside
of Russia, The 159, 376

S

SAHO (Sikh American Heritage
Organization) 236
Saint Paul Area Council
of Churches 253–254

SALDEF (Sikh American Legal
    Defense and Education Fund) 236
Salvation Army, The 159, 376
Salvation Army in
    Canada, The 210–211, 365
San Antonio Community
    of Congregations 269
San Fernando Valley Interfaith Council 240
Schenectady Inner City Ministry 260
Schwenkfelder
    Church, The 159–160, 376, 386
Scripture Union 53
SCUPE (Seminary Consortium
    for Urban Pastoral Education) 44–45
SEAM (South East Associated
    Ministries) .248–249
SEARCH (Southeast Area Churches) 269
Seminary Consortium for Urban
    Pastoral Education (SCUPE) 44–45
Separate Baptists in Christ 160, 376
Serbian Orthodox Church in the
    U.S.A and Canada 160–161, 376, 379
Serbian Orthodox Church in the
    U.S.A and Canada,
    Diocese of Canada 211, 366
Seventh Day Baptist General
    Conference, USA and Canada 162, 376
Seventh-day Adventist
    Church 161–162, 376, 386
Seventh-day Adventist Church
    in Canada 211, 366, 380
Siddhachalam International
    Mahavira Jain Mission 233
Sikh American Heritage
    Organization (SAHO) 236
Sikh American Legal Defense
    and Education Fund (SALDEF) 236
Sikh Coalition 236
Sikh Foundation 236
Sikh Research Institute 236–237
Sikhism 236–237
Soka Gakkai International-USA 229
Soto Zen Buddhist Association (SZBA) 229
South Carolina Christian Action
    Council, Inc. 267
South Coast Interfaith Council 240
South East Associated Ministries
    (SEAM) .248–249
South Hills Interfaith Ministries 266
South Louisville Community Ministries 249
Southeast Area Churches (SEARCH) 269
Southeast Ecumenical Ministry 260
Southern Baptist
    Convention 162–164, 376, 386
Southern Baptists. See Canadian
    Convention of Southern Baptists
Southern California Ecumenical Council . . .241
Southern Methodist Church 164, 376
Sovereign Grace Believers 164, 376
Spadina-Bloor Interchurch Council 293
St. Bruno Ecumenical Group, The 294
St. Catharines & District Clergy
    Fellowship 293

St. John's Area Council of Churches 292
St. Matthews Area Ministries 248
Staten Island Council of Churches 260
Stratford & District Council of Churches . . .293
Student Christian Movement
    of Canada 53–54
Summerside Christian Council 293
Swedenborgian
    Church, The 164–165, 377, 379
Syriac Orthodox Church
    of Antioch 211, 366
Syriac-Greek Antiochian Orthodox
    Catholic Church 165–166, 377, 386
Syrian (Syriac) Orthodox Church
    of Antioch 166–167, 377, 379
Syro-Russian Orthodox Catholic
    Church. See Syriac-Greek Antiochian
    Orthodox Catholic Church
SZBA (Soto Zen Buddhist Association) 229

T

Tarrant Area Community of Churches 269
Tennessee Association of Churches 267
Texas Buddhist Council 229
Texas Conference of Churches 269
Thomist Churches 184
Thorold Inter-Faith Council 293
Thunder Bay Council of Churches 293
Toledo Area Ministries 262
Transnational Association of
    Christian Colleges and Schools 45
Tri-Council Coordinating Commission 254
Triumph the Church and Kingdom
    of God in Christ Inc. (International) 167
Troy Area United Ministries 260
True Orthodox Church of Greece
    (Synod of Metropolitan Cyprian),
    American Exarchate 377
Tulsa Metropolitan Ministry 262–263
Tuscarawas County Council for Church
    and Community 262

U

Ukrainian Orthodox Church
    of Canada 211–212, 366
Ukrainian Orthodox Church
    of the U.S.A. 167–169, 377, 379
Unified Buddhist Church, Inc. 229
Union d'Eglises Baptistes
    Françaises au Canada 212, 366, 380
Union for Reform Judaism 234–235
Union of Orthodox Jewish
    Congregations of America 234
Union of Spiritual Communities
    of Christ (Orthodox Doukhobors
    in Canada) 212–213
Unitarian Universalist Association
    of Congregations 169, 377
UNITAS 294
United Board of Missions 269
United Brethren Bodies 184
United Brethren Church in Canada . . .213, 366

405

United Catholic
Church, Inc., The 169–170, 377
United Christian Church 170, 377
United Church of
Canada, The 213–214, 366, 380
United Church
of Christ 170–172, 377, 379, 386
United Churches of Lycoming County 266
United Holy Church
of America, Inc. 172–173
United House of Prayer 173
United Methodist
Church, The 173–176, 377, 379, 386
United Ministries 267
United Pentecostal Church in Canada 214
United Pentecostal Church
International 176, 377
United Pentecostal
Churches of Christ, The 377
United Religions Initiative 45
United Religious Community
of St. Joseph County 245–246
United States Conference for the
World Council of Churches 45
United Synagogue of Conservative
Judaism, The 235
United Zion Church 176, 377
Unity of the Brethren 176–177, 377, 386
Universal Catholic Church 177, 377
Universal Fellowship of
Metropolitan Community
Churches 177–178, 214, 366, 377, 386

V

Vedanta Society of New York 230–231
Vellore Christian Medical
College Foundation, Inc. 45–46
Vermont Ecumenical Council
and Bible Society 269
Vineyard USA 178, 377
Virginia Council of Churches, Inc. 269–270
Volunteer Ministry Center 267
Volunteers of America 178

W

Wainwright House 260
Weekday Christian Education 246

Wellspring Interfaith Social
Services, Inc. 246
Wesleyan Church, The 178–179, 377, 386
Wesleyan Church
of Canada, The 214, 366
Wesleyan Holiness Association
of Churches 179
West Central Neighborhood Ministry.
See Wellspring Interfaith
Social Services, Inc.
West Side Ecumenical Ministry 262
West Virginia Council of Churches 271
Westside Interfaith Council 241
Wilkinsburg Community Ministry 266
Wisconsin Council of Churches 272
Wisconsin Evangelical
Lutheran Synod 180, 377, 386
Women's Inter-Church Council
of Canada 54
Won Buddhism of American
Headquarters 229
Worcester County Ecumenical Council 251
World Day of Prayer International
Committee 46
World Methodist Council -
North American Section 46
World Sikh Council - American
Region 236
World Vision 46–47
World Vision Canada 54
Wyoming Association of Churches 272
Wyoming Valley Council of Churches 266

Y

YMCA of the USA 47
York County Council of Churches 266–267
Young Men's Christian Association
in Canada 54
Young Women's Christian Association
of Canada 55
Youth for Christ-Canada 55
Youth for Christ–USA 47
YWCA of the U.S.A 47

Z

Zoroastrianism 237

Individuals

A

Aaenz, Agnes 250
Abbott, Grant 254
Abbott, Julie 248
Abboud, Bonnie C. 155
Abboud, Jon W. 155
Abdalah, John 345
Abernathy, Bryan 338
Abraham,
  Raphael 143, 168
Abramov, Alexander 146
Abrams, David 245
Abromaitis, Jonas 209
Abuls, Tija 133
Acosta, Donaldo 92
Acuña, Adolfo 75
Adams, Don 133
Adams, Dorothy 60
Adams, Gladstone
  Bailey, III 108
Adams, James
  Marshall 108
Adams, Lori L. 84
Adams, Margaret 247
Adams, Michael J. 104
Adams, Nate 163
Adams, Ray 92
Adams, Ray D. 92
Adams, Skip 263
Adams, Todd A. 84
Addington, James 254
Addington, Tim 329
Addington, Timothy 113
Adema, Bruce 49, 88
Adimavunkal, Isaac
  Thomas 92
Adnams, Ian 203, 347
Aftimios (Bishop) 71
Agati, Makoha F. 92
Ague, Paul 312
Aiken, Mike 260
Aitken, Ellen B. 319
Aitken, Thomas M. 115
Aja, Antonio (Tony) 248
Aja, Loyda 151
Ajer, Margaret Schmitt . . .114
Akers, Kenneth 139
Akin, Daniel L. 313
Alarie, Yves 198
Albarian, Samuel . . .187, 346
Albert,
  Leonard C. . . .95, 194, 195
Albrecht, Betty 190
Albrecht, Marcus 330
Aldred, Ray 51
Alejo (Bishop) 145
Aleshire, Daniel O. 218
Alexander, Darlene 268
Alexander, J. Gregory 85
Alexander, J. Neil 108

Alexander, Jane 186
Alexander, Paula 250
Alexander (Bishop) 186
Alexios (Metropolitan) . . .127
Alford,
  Delton L. 95, 194, 195
Alicea-Baez,
  Jhonny 154, 208
Alick, Bruce N. 336
Allbee, Judy G. 62
Allen, Arlene 345
Allen, Bettye J. 345
Allen, Cosie 335
Allen, David, Jr. 152, 153
Allen, David T. 79
Allen, David W. 214
Allen, Elizabeth Peale 26
Allen, Lloyd
  Emmanuel 108
Allen, Richard 56
Allen, Sherman 98, 196
Allen,
  Thaddaeus B. 85, 271
Allen, William 85
Allen-Kent, Venita 268
Alley, Robert E. 89
Allinson, Pat 54
Al-Marayati, Salam 232
Alon, Shlomo 45
Alprecht, Ivan Egas 75
Alston, Roosevelt 172
Althouse, LaVonne 345
Alvarez, David 108
Alvis, Rick 25
Ambrose, Richard 238
Ambrus, Zoltan 128
Amerson, Philip A. 302
Amjad-Ali, Charles 33
Ammons, E. Roger 92
Amor, Adlai 26
Amorim, Nilton D. 211
Amos, Kharma 178
Anderle, Joel
  Matthew 251
Anders, Doug 171
Anders, James C. 92
Andersen, Neil L. 98
Andersen, Phoebe 121
Anderson, Barbara 63
Anderson, Billy 103
Anderson, Bonnie 108
Anderson, Brian 178
Anderson, Daniel L. 295
Anderson, Donald C. 267
Anderson, Doug 178
Anderson, E. Byron 35
Anderson, Gail 253
Anderson, Gordon L. 308
Anderson, James 258
Anderson, Jeff 199

Anderson, Jeffrey 113
Anderson, Jon V. 115
Anderson,
  Keith R. 307, 312
Anderson, Kenneth . . .78, 257
Anderson, L. R. 94
Anderson, Leith 37
Anderson, Mark D. 84
Anderson, Moe 293
Anderson, Nancy L. 253
Anderson, Neil 102
Anderson, Neil W. 332
Anderson, Phyllis 309
Anderson, Scott 36, 272
Anderson, Wallace 150
Anderson, William J. 185
Anderson-Develrow,
  Dorothy 269
Anderson-Larson,
  Virginia 114
Andonios (Bishop) 127
Andreller, Ingrid 348
Andreolli, Mary 328, 344
Andres, Oseas 64
Andrews, Barbara 186
Andrews, Evelyn 345
Andrews, Ruth 51
Andrews, Stephen 185
Andriy
  (Archimandrite) 168
Andrus, Marc Handley . . .108
Angie, Frank 132
Ankeny, Mark 113
Annie, Frederick 271
Annotzelberger, E. 142
Annunziato, Anne 255
Anstey, Andrew R. 206
Antal, Jim 172
Anthony, Lewis 242, 243
Anthony, Stephen D. 262
Antony (Archbishop) 168
Apencha, Henry 123
Apollo, Wopicho 123
Apostola,
  Nicholas 158, 159, 210
Appel, Robert 162
Aquila, Dominic 207
Archer, Jason 120
Ard, Herman D. 92
Ardis, Randy 22
Arends, James A. 115
Argue, Don H. 309
Armiger, Thomas E. 179
Armstrong,
  Bill William 299
Armstrong, Calvin 173
Armstrong,
  James D. 58, 340
Arnold, Don 123
Arnold, Kim M. 359

Arnold, Kristi 337
Arnold, Terry 163
Arrando, Angelo S. 241
Arslanian, Hagop . . .187, 188
Arthur (Bishop) 128
Artysiewicz, Chet 32
Asbury, Francis 56
Ascough, Richard 50
Asen, Bernhard 342
Ashby, John 258
Ashdown, David 185, 186
Asher, Raphael 240
Ashmen, John 25
Astin, Claude S., Jr. 64
Astin, Dawn R. 64
Astin, Sam 64
Astle, Cynthia B. 340
Atagotaalnuk,
    Andrew P. 185
Atherly, Joseph 102
Atkinson, Jason 28
Atmore, A. Brian 320
Atsiaya, Hezekiah 123
Attai, Monday S. 189
Attridge, Harold W. 316
Audrain, Calvert 27
Augsburger, Lynette 118
Augson, Albert 173
Aultman,
    Donald S. 95, 194
Aultman, Jason 76
Austin, George 148
Austin, James W. 163
Austin, John 247
Auxentios
    (Bishop) 143, 168
Avakian, Karl 187
Avera, Alan 74
Avery, Michael 302
Avey, Thomas 119
Ayloush, Hussam 33
Aymer, Albert
    J. D. 303, 304
Aymond, Gregory 81

B

Baak, David P. 251
Baarsma, Carol 270
Babb, Ruby 259
Baber, Diane 333
Bach, Jean 32
Bachus, Amanda M. 333
Baek, Han Young 86
Bagley, Louis 172
Baglyos, Paul 115
Bagnall, Ronald B. 335
Bahi, Mor Athanasius
    Elia 211
Bahruth, Dick 28
Bailey, Arnetta 93
Bailey, C. M. 173
Bailey, Danielle 130

Bailey, Dwight 244
Bailey, Jeff 329
Bailey, Joey 151
Bailey, Leslee 103
Bailey, Mark L. 300
Baillargeon, Gaëtan 209
Baker, Arlene Holt 33
Baker, Danette 248
Baker, David 59
Baker, Denis N. 342
Baker, Kenneth 332
Baker, Marsha 23
Bakken, Peter 272
Balasubramanian, S. 46
Balbick, Jane 258
Baldes, Kenneth E. 87
Baldwin, David N. 163
Baldwin,
    Raymond C. 152, 153
Balentine, Sam 333
Baletka, Jim 177
Balke, Fred 61
Ball, Chris 107
Ballantyne, V. A. 110
Ballard, M. Russell 98
Baltimore, Carroll A. 153
Bambans, Vieturs 326
Bancroft, Timothy 39
Bangham, Bill 328
Bankord, Mark A. 28
Bañuelos, José G. 92
Barber, Ray 124
Barber, Ray G. 298
Barbour, Johnny, Jr. 57
Barcott, Patricia 271
Barfoot, Gillian 54
Barger, Don 248
Baril, Gerald 209
Barker, Larry 77
Barker, Lee 307
Barker, Randy 148
Barlow, Jane 250
Barna, George 219
Barnabas, Mathews
    Mar 136
Barnes, Charles 172
Barnes, James 304
Barnes, James, III 297
Barnes, Jay, III 105
Barnes, Kurt . . .104, 107, 108
Barnes, Ronald B. . . .263, 265
Barnes, Simon 22
Barnhouse, James 262
Baron, Karen 359
Barone, Terry 43
Barrentine, Jimmy 163
Barrett, Michael 260
Barrette, Gilles 294
Barrow, Ira 360
Barrow, Jeffrey S. 115
Barrows, Ken 197
Barsamian, Khajag 42, 72
Barsony, Steve 265

Bartel-Wagner,
    Deena 323, 331
Bartlett, William G. 213
Barton, Jonathan 269
Basiletti, Santi E. 88
Baskerville, Yvonne 59
Bass, Steve 163
Bassham, Keith 324
Batchelor, Don 176
Bates, Brandor 117
Bates, Dale 124
Bathurst, Shirley 259
Batman, Kevin J. 179
Battle,
    George E., Jr. 57, 58
Battle-Hodge,
    Jeraldine 59
Batts, Carl 141
Batuyong, Patrick 154
Bauerschmidt, John C. . . .108
Baugham, Billy 24
Baugham, Eva 24
Baumann, Paul 328
Baumgartner, Will 242
Bawai, Mar 67
Baxter, Kevin 338
Baxter, Nathan D. 108
Baxter, Polly 165
Bay, Eugene C. 299
Bayer,
    Steven L. 143, 144, 344
Bayunus, Owais 253
Beach, Maxine C. 301
Beach, Verda 296
Beacham, A. D., Jr. 132
Beachy, Ivan 78
Beachy, LeRoy 144
Beard, C. Ronald 74
Beardsley, Lisa M. 161
Beasley, Kathy 177
Bechil, Shirley 121
Beck, David L. 98
Beck, Julie 98
Beck, Sarai
    Schnucker 247
Becker, Eillen 264
Becker, Susan 29
Beckett, Malcolm 198
Beckmann, David 26
Beckwith, Mark M. 108
Beckwith, Peter H. 108
Becton, C. M. 214
Bedgood, Douglas 131
Bednar, David A. 98
Behr, John 312
Behrakis, George 126
Behrens, James 266
Behrens, Kathy 266
Beimers, Laurinda 88
Beinikis, Vilmars . . .133, 134
Beisner, Barry L. 108
Bekken, Deab 177
Bekker, Gary 88, 89

Belengu, Simon 123
Bell, Brian 189
Bell, Jeremy 191
Bell, John 153
Bell, Nancy 188
Bell, Paul 74
Bellamy, James C. 173
Bellavin, Tikhon 69
Bellefleur, Beverley 207
Bellinger, Carolyn 202
Bellous, Ken 188
Belrose, Darrell 197, 198
Belsole, Kurt 312
Belt, Kerry 321
Belton, Victor T. 135
Benallick, Mike 350
Benedict, Gary M. 87
Benedict XVI (Pope) 81
Benefiel, Ron 308
Benfield, Larry R. 108
Benjamin (Bishop) 145
Benn, Darlene 263
Benn, Mary 88
Benner, Dick 347
Bennethum,
   Amy Simpson 31
Bennett, David 138
Bennett,
   Donald G. 95, 194, 195
Bennett, Renee 105
Bennett, Robert F. 186
Bennett, Robertson H. 42
Bennett, Vicki 209
Benoway, Edward R. 116
Benson, Dan 213
Benson, Willie, Jr. 119
Berberich, Ellen 246
Beresford, Eric 317
Berg, Peter 142
Berg, Richard R. 354
Berg, Ron 142
Berg, Sharon K. 330
Berghes, DeLandes 67
Berman, Lowen 263
Bernard, A. R., Sr. 257
Bernard, David 315
Bernardin, Joseph
   Cardinal 24
Bernstein, Debra
   Ballinger 45
Bernstein, Jules 33
Bernstine, Gwen
   Nelson 266
Bernthal, Mark 100
Berry, Bradford 101
Berry, Laura 39
Berryhill, Carisse 353
Bertalan, Imre 128
Bertham, Gary 70
Berube, Albert J. 143
Betz, Krista 171
Betzer, Dan 73
Beverley, James 223

Beyer, Teresa A. 144
Bhagan, Ken 293
Bianco, Ernie 270
Bibb, Lillie D. 261
Bickerton, Thomas J. 174
Bickerton, William 98
Bicksler, Harriet 341
Bieniek, Barbara 260
Bieri, Jean 349
Biffle, Steven K. 123
Bigaj, Sylvester 149
Bigg, Carla Starrett 263
Biggs, Vicki 134
Bigland-Pritchard,
   Jan 294
Billman, Kathleen D. 329
Bils, Stephen 62
Bilynsky, Natalie 343
Bingham, Maurice D. 90
Birch, Aaron Louis 189
Bird, Jeffrey L. 130
Bird, Madeline 266
Bird, Michael A. 186
Birk, Peg 32
Birkitt, James N., Jr. 324
Birney, Walter 86
Birse, Douglas 190, 191
Birston, Paul 348
Bisaillon, Michael 206
Bishop, Betty 92
Bishop, Cecil 58
Bishop, James A. 248
Bissenden, William 24
Bithos, George P. 269
Bitner, Terry 243
Bjork, Bruce 252
Bjornberg, Allan C. 114
Black, Bernard 141
Black, Geoffrey A. 171
Black , J. Thomas 91
Blackaby, Richard 318
Blackburn, Martha 179
Blackburn, Richard G. 35
Blackmer, Larry D. 161
Blackwell, Phil 244
Blain, Kate 330
Blair, Michael 213
Blair, Sara D. Brooks 356
Blaire, Stephen 81
Blake, C. E. 93
Blakeman, Jeannine 248
Blanchette, David 238
Blanco, Marcos 342
Bland, James C. 150, 151
Blanding, Ann 157
Blanton, Smiley 26
Bledsoe, Earl W. 175
Bleijerveld, Jeff 101, 102
Blessing, Matt 353
Blevins, Jordan 27, 38, 39
Bliese, Richard H. 306
Blodgett, Barbara 24
Bloom, Peter 50

Bloomquist,
   Nessie S. 259
Blount, Brian K. 314, 315
Blount, Robert 173
Blowers, David 60
Bluff, Poplar 124
Blumhofer, Edith 222
Boatner, Paul 45
Bobo, Kim 34
Bock, Delbert G. 92
Bockelman, Karen 114
Boda, Matthew C. 88
Bodt, Brian R. 242
Boeker, Paul 118
Boerger, Wm. Chris 114
Boers, Barbara 154, 208
Boghosian, Rima 71
Bohan, Daniel 209
Bohren, Ben 84
Boice, Paul 154, 208
Bojey, Fred 213
Bolbach, Cynthia 150
Bolick, Leonard H. 116
Bolinder, Garth T. 113
Bolt, John 85, 88, 194
Bond, Jane Zavitz 191
Bond, Judy 243
Bonk, Jonathan J. 333
Bonner, Harrison 29
Bonnot, Bob 261
Boomershine, Tom 334
Boone, Dan 314
Boone, Martha Moody 29
Boot, Joel R. 88
Booth, Linda 341
Booth, Robert H. 156
Booth, William 159
Borden, M. Daniel 173
Borden, Paul D. 63
Bordeur, Adèle 49
Borek, John 305
Borger, Joyce 340
Boris, Walter John 171
Borowsky, Irvin J. 330
Boschman, Ed 125
Bossio, Patrick, Sr. 131
Boto, Augie 162, 163
Bott, Richard 40
Bottorff, Dan 35
Bouffides-Walsh,
   Catherine 127
Boulva, Michèle 209
Bouman, Stephen P. 114
Bouras, Nicholas 127
Bouton, Becky 267
Bowell, Gary 325
Bowen, Kenny 241
Bowen, Mary Lu 259
Bowie, A. Charles 141
Bowie, E. L. 99
Bowman, Robert 169
Boyajcan, Donna 266
Boyce, H. Gene 132

INDEX

409

Boyce, Janice 132, 325
Boyd, Doug 255
Boyd, Marsha Foster 301
Boyd, T. B., III 141
Boyer, M.
  Christopher 270
Boyer, Terry 169
Boyers, Matt 118
Boyle, Daniel 119
Boyles, Lemuel 38
Boynton, Leonard 258
Brackett, Sterling 130
Bradely, Lasserre 325
Bradford, Bose 173
Bradford, James T. 73
Bradford, Karole 247
Bradley, James G. 242
Bradley,
  Lasserre, Jr. 152, 324
Bradley, Leah Ellison 333
Bradley, Paul W. 26
Bradsell, Kenneth . . .154, 208
Brady, A. Glenn 148
Brame, Nick 130
Brandon, Richard
  (Zenyo) 227
Brandt, Michael 74
Branham, Thomas E. 148
Bransfield, Michael 81
Brantley, Paul S. 161
Brantz, Walter 135
Brashear, Kermit 135
Bratton, G. Stanford 258
Braun, Jan 54
Braun, John A. 331
Braver-Rieke,
  David H. 114
Bravo-Guzman, Pedro 75
Brawner, John 113
Braymer, Howard 76
Brazier, Arthus 148
Breakey, Sam 191
Bregar, Janet A. 241
Breidenthal,
  Thomas E. 108
Brennan, Keith R. 312
Brennan, Peter P. 69, 75
Brenton, B. Dean 206
Brenton, Kelly L. 206
Brereton, David 47
Breton,
  Jean-Claude 322, 350
Brewer, John 179, 329
Brickhouse, Smith N. 90
Briden, Gary 164, 313
Bridges, Kermit S. 313
Bridges, Randy J. 310
Briel, Steven C. 135
Briggs, Carrie 97
Briggs, Robert L. 22
Bright, John 96
Briley, Terry 306
Brill, Al 22

Brill, Debra C. 161
Brinks, Robert 151
Brinser, Gerald 170
Britton, Joseph H. 297
Broadfield, Joan 27
Broadway, Beth A. 258
Brock, David 304
Brock, David R. 103
Brock, Lillie 177
Bronner, William L. 101
Brook, Sarah 325
Brooke, Cynthia 33
Brookhart, C.
  Franklin, Jr. 108
Brooks, Barbara 253
Brooks, Brenda 70
Brooks, George 148
Brooks, James W. 172
Brooks, John 114, 199
Brooks, P. A. 93
Brooks, Terry 267
Brooks, Theodore L. 148
Brooks, Thomas 69, 70
Brosseau, Annie 318
Brothers, William
  Francis 67
Broughton, Dave 88
Browder, David 98
Brower, E. Alex 59
Brown, A. J. 298
Brown, Alister 308, 309
Brown, Carroll E. 242
Brown, Charles 176
Brown, Clint 162
Brown, Cynthia Vasil 60
Brown, David 139
Brown, David J. 103
Brown, David M. 62
Brown, Donice 69
Brown, E. 203, 204
Brown, E. Lynn 87
Brown, Eliza 26
Brown, Elizabeth 80
Brown, Eric 263
Brown, Gary 112
Brown, Gerald L. 311
Brown, Gillian 49
Brown, Harry 245, 246
Brown, J. R. 133
Brown, J. Richard 204
Brown, James R. 64
Brown, Jeannett L. 241
Brown, Jeffrey P. 87
Brown, John W. 192
Brown, Larry 84
Brown, Philip 151
Brown, Richard 203
Brown, T. L. 141
Brown, Thomas 249
Brown, Thomas L., Sr. 87
Brown, Timothy L. 316
Brown, Warner H., Jr. 176
Brown, Warren M. 57, 58

Brown-Williams,
  Charlotte 59
Brubacher, Marvin R. 319
Brubaker, Earl 129
Brubaker, John 80
Bruce, George L. R. 186
Bruckner, Ellen 246
Bruehl, J. Roger 27
Brug, John F. 344
Brumbaugh-Cayford,
  Cheryl 89, 337
Bruno, J. Jon 108
Bruno, Lucia 34
Bryan, David 343
Bryan, Jamie Brooke 177
Bryan, Ron 123
Bryant, Darue 78, 79
Bryant, David 295
Bryant, G. Alexander 161
Bryant, John R. 57
Bryant, Juanita 86
Bryant,
  Roy, Sr. 75, 76, 78, 297
Bryant, S. N. 97
Bryant, Sissieretta 78
Buchanan, John 326
Buchanan, John C. 108
Buck, Charles 171
Buckle, Clarence 206
Buckle, Wilfred S. 206
Bueno, L. John 73
Buffet, Allison 208
Bugbee, Robert 203, 204
Buisch, Stuart 259
Bujnak, Lynn 172
Bula, Omega C. 213
Buliva, Hezekiah
  Ngadi 121
Bullard, George 30, 40
Bulloch, Wendy 213
Bullock, Jeffrey 315
Bullock, LaWanda 120
Bullock, Paul 76
Bullock, Warren 73
Bullock, Wyvetta 114
Bulya, Larissa 169
Bumgardner, Pat 178
Bumgarner, Hampton 166
Bunce, Joseph L. 163
Bunker, Douglas 258
Burden, Keith 139
Burdette, Patty 342
Burditt, Andrew 210
Burge, Shane 22
Burgess, Morgan 119
Burgio, Ron 198
Burgio, Ronald V. 107
Burgonio-Watson,
  Thelma 270
Burgoyne, Howard K. 112
Burk, Michael L. 115
Burkat, Claire S. 116
Burke, C. Don 148

Burke, Michael 213
Burke, William 209
Burkhardt, Patricia 29
Burleigh, Elizabeth F. 68
Burnett, Joe G. 108
Burnett, Joni A. 93
Burney, Artie 78
Burnham, Gary 97
Burns, Donald 293
Burns, Patricia 50
Burns, Robert J. 50
Burnside, Bruce H. 115
Burrell, Calvin 325
Burrell, Willie 148
Burris,
  Glenn C., Jr. 42, 130
Burroughs, Colleen 105
Burroughs, Nannie
  Helen 153
Burt, Lindsey 205
Burt, Merlin D. 352
Burton, Craig 206
Busby, Dan 30
Bushkofsky, Linda
  Post 114
Bushrod, Montrose 344
Buslon, Jim 205
Bustle, Louie 101
Bustram, James 119
Butalia, Tarnujit Singh 44
Butin, Philip W. 312
Butler, Jennifer 33
Butler, Kevin J. 162, 341
Butler, Ramsey 148
Butterworth, Daniel 260
Butts, Elvin R. 303
Butts, J. Wayman 261
Butz, Geneva M. 172
Buurma, Jacob 346
Buxton, Zane 151
Buzza,
  Barry 201, 202, 351
Buzza, Rob 320
Byers, Melvin, Jr. 92
Byler, J. Ron 36, 138
Byma, Ralph 198

C

Cabigting, Ruben 134
Cackler-Veazey,
  Cathleen D. 42
Cady, Donald D. 179
Cahill, Brendan 311
Cahoy, William J. 311
Calderon, Samuel 88
Caldwell, Bruce 108
Calhoun, Heidi 270
Calhoun, James 61
Caliandro, Arthur 26
Calkins, Tim 257
Callaghan, Aloysius R. . . .311
Callahan, Leslie G. 21

Calvert, Lorne 321
Calvin, John 153, 159
Camenga, Andrew 162
Cameron, Ruth
  Tonkiss 355
Camp, Peggy Ann 179
Camp, Richard P., Jr. 28
Campbell, Cynthia M. . . .307
Campbell,
  Gary D. 150, 151
Campbell, Jerry D. 299
Campbell, Joseph 90
Campbell, Scott 51
Campbell, Virginia 247
Caner, Ergun 305
Cangy, Gilbert R. 161
Cannada,
  Robert C., Jr. 310
Cannaday, Antoinette 78
Cannon, Douglas 43
Cannon, Edward 78
Canon, Rose 128
Canoy, Robert W. 306
Carcaño, Minerva 175
Carey-Tucker, Pricilla 252
Carfora, Carmel Henry 67
Carlin, Donald 265
Carlson, Kenneth P. 112
Carmi, Laila 46
Carmichael, Cassandra 38
Carmichael, Colin 207
Caron, Kateri 271
Carouthers, David 293
Carpenter, Chris 153
Carpenter, Don 347
Carpenter, Ron 42
Carpenter,
  Ronald W., Sr. 132
Carr, Donna K. 246
Carrell, Dan 150
Carrico, David L. 63
Carriere, Vianney
  (Sam) 185
Carrion, Adolfo, Sr. 257
Carroll, Jeff 119
Carroo, Winston 39
Carruthers, Lucia 346
Carson, Glen T. 84
Carter, Alison 46
Carter, Ethel Ware 243
Carter, James, Jr. 135
Carter, Jeff 259
Carter, Kenneth Wayne 87
Carter, Lanny W. 92
Carter, Larry 303
Carter, Nick 295
Carter, Ron L. 340
Carter, T. Scot 95, 194
Cartes, Ann 141
Cartwright, Dani
  Loving 85
Casal, Jose Luis 38
Casey, Daniel E. 47

Casey-Lee, Diane 250
Cassian (Bishop) 128
Castile, Sue 247
Castillo, R. Ernest 161
Castrejon, Jaime 304
Castro, Manuel S. 92
Catalano, Mario 203
Cavadini, John C. 315
Cavanaugh, Donald 22
Cavanna, Pedro 91
Cave, Mike 269
Cawley, William
  Kevin 353
Cayce, W. Hartsel 152
Cazabon, Gilles 49
Cebula, John W. 258
Cereghino, Phil 343
Chadden, Shane 53
Chadick, Bonnie 247
Chafe, Joanne 209
Chahine, Michelle 154
Chakravarthy, Vijay 258
Chamberlain, Larry 119
Champagne, Claude 209
Champion, Willie C. 86
Chand, Samuel R. 132
Chandler, Linda 177
Chandler, Maurice G. 296
Chandra, T. 189
Chane, John Bryson 108
Chang, Young Choon 257
Chapell,
  Bryan 150, 151, 300
Chapman, Clare J. 38, 39
Chapman, John H. 186
Chapman, Ryan Tristin 54
Chappell, Paul G. 305
Chapple, Richard 59
Charles, Mark 131
Chase, Randall 301
Chatham, Virginia E. 344
Chatlosh,
  DeAnn 326, 328, 334
Chavez, Silvia 24
Cheatham, Shirlie 119
Chell, John 253
Chemberlin, Peg 38, 253
Cherniak, Hanja 168
Cheshier, Carl 303
Chetti, Samuel S. 62
Chevalier, Rebekah 349
Chidsey, Linda 121
Chiomenti, Lyndelle
  Brower 328
Chipchase, Elwood H. . . .298
Chisholm, Alvah 255
Chloyan, Oshagan 71
Cho, Joan 350
Chow, Rita 40
Christian, Deb 43
Christian, William 99
Christie, James 322
Christie, Marge 256

411

Christie, Paul C. 241
Christofferson, D. Todd . . .98
Christopher (Bishop) 128
Christopher
(Metropolitan) 160
Chrysostomos
(Archbishop) 143, 168
Chubenko, Taras 168
Chung, Moses 89
Church, David A. 135
Chute, Nilda 292, 293
Citronnelli, Eddie 78
Citzler, Annette 114
Clark, A. 203
Clark, Cecil 163
Clark, Charles 63
Clark, James I., Jr. 101
Clark, Katharine 121
Clark, Marvin 164
Clark,
Richard, Jr. 326, 339
Clark, Ruth 62
Clark, Terry 244
Clarke, Barry B. 186
Clarke, Kent 50
Clarke, Levi 196
Clarke, R. D. 167
Clay, Doug 73
Clay, Glenn 130
Claycomb, Charles 247
Clayton, Kendra E. 303
Clayton, Kevin W. 76, 77
Cleave, Dwayne 204
Clemenger, Bruce J. 51
Clemens, Dick 65
Clements, Kerry 151
Clements, Larry 62
Clements, Sam 98, 196
Clifford, Mary
Montgomery 142
Cline, Evadna 266
Clock, Becki 245
Clothier, Walter
"Jerry" 117
Cloud, Randy 62
Coady, Paul 350
Coats, John W. 64
Cobarn, Trevor 130
Cobb, Joseph 267
Cochran, Sylvenia F. 259
Coffey, James 97
Coffin, Chris 292
Coffin, John 121
Coffin, Percy D. 186
Coffman, Betsy 164
Cohen, Albert G. 241
Colas, Ralph 22
Cole, David 301
Cole, Jack 124
Cole, John K. 148
Coleman, Catherine 240
Coleman, Karen 251
Coleman, Robert F. 304

Coles, Robert N. 64
Colkmire, Lance 327
Collado, Lorenzo 88
Collett, Darlene 252
Collier, John W. P. 344
Collins, Arnie 47
Collins, Arnold 47
Collins, Bradley 330
Collins, Dean 296
Collins,
Jacqueline 190, 191
Collins, L. C. Firle 140
Collins, Leland C. 243
Collins, Les D. 142
Collins, Michael R. 163
Collins, Thomas 209
Collymore, Carlisle 173
Colon, John 108
Combes, Frances 293
Comperry, David 248
Compton, Gordon 28
Condrea, Nicolae . . .158, 210
Conhue, Terri 260
Conn, Charles
Paul 95, 194, 195
Conniry, Charles, Jr. 302
Connors, Dan 325
Constantine
(Metropolitan) 168
Conteh, Alpha 108
Cook, Andrea 93
Cook, David 328
Cook, David T. 327
Cook,
Heather 121, 122, 259
Cook, Katie 324
Cook, Quentin L. 98
Coomas, Doug 190, 191
Coombs, Gary F. 313
Coon, Carlton 176
Coons-Torn, Marja 172
Coons-Torn, Marjorie 265
Coop, Linda 113
Cooper, Jerome 76, 77
Cooper, Lamar 300
Cooper, Libby 117
Cooper, Sabrina M. 324
Cooper-White,
Michael L. 306
Cope, Kenneth 148
Cope, Mike 344
Cope, William 60, 323
Copeland, Elaine
Johnson 299
Copeland, Shelley 241
Cope-Robinson,
Lyn 121, 122
Copley, Steve 39, 239
Copp, Raymond W. 65
Coppieters, Joel 48
Copple, Donald J. 210
Corbett, Ardelia M. 172
Corbett, Daniel 196

Corbin, Randall B. 87
Corey, Barry H. 314
Corkery, Sara 23
Cormode, James R. 320
Cornelius, D. Murray 206
Coronel, David 92
Corrigan, John 327
Corson-Finnerty,
Susan 331
Corston, Thomas A. 186
Costa, Williams S., Jr. . . .161
Costello, John E. 321
Cottenden, George R. 146
Cotton, Edmund G. 119
Cotton, T. 94
Coulston, James A. 117
Coultas, Amy Real 248
Coulter, Riley 317
Councell, Gary R. . . .161, 331
Councell, George E. 108
Courter, Gini 169
Courtney, John 55
Cowan, A. J. 185
Cowan, Mattew 160
Cox, Ann 268
Cox, Brian 51
Cox, Craig 311
Cox, Jill 271
Cox, John R. 141
Cox, Lindsay 49
Coy, Ken 262
Coyle, Charlotte 268
Coyner, Michael J. 174
Crabtree, Barbara 178
Crabtree, Bruce 102
Craddock, Margaret 267
Craddock, Max 197
Craddock, Max E. 348
Craft, Roger L. 27
Craig, Al 199
Craig, Shayne 320
Crain, James A. 61
Crane, Charles A. 297
Crawford, Eileen K. 23
Crawford, Florence 70
Crawford, Ronald W. 296
Crawford, S. Rea 148
Crawley, Steve 76, 77
Creech, Barry 150, 151
Creech, Ricky O. 62
Creighton, Philip 53
Crenshaw, Carole 332
Crenshaw, Ray 78
Crew, Jim 122
Crews, Bill 163
Crews, C. Daniel 356
Crinnin, Larry 258
Crist, Larry 85
Crist-Graybill, Jessica 114
Crittenden, David 151
Crivici, Catherine 346
Crocker, Richard 35, 78
Croft, Donna 50

412

Croghan, Laurie 254
Cropsey, Marvin W. 335
Crossin, John W. 315
Crossno, Barry 120
Crouse, C. E. 28
Crout, Valorie 270
Crowshoe, Kirk 253
Crowson, Bryan 123
Crum, John 70
Crumes, W. E. 99
Crump, Gene 255
Crutchfield,
  Carmichael 86
Crutchfield, Charles N. . . .174
Cruver, Rob W. 149
Crystal, Robert 257
Csepregi, Gabor 318
Csomor, Marjorie 89
Cubeta, Phil 33
Cueni, R. Robert 305
Cuevas, Jorge 88
Culp, Kristine A. 300
Culpepper, R. Alan 304
Culpepper,
  Raymond F. 42, 95, 194
Culver, Sheldon 171
Cunningham, A. D. 173
Cunningham, Jack 214
Cunningham, Johnny 70
Cunningham,
  Joseph 89, 327
Cunningham, Ronald 30
Cunningham,
  Ronald M. 87
Cupich, Blasé 81
Cupp, Kris 103
Currie, Martin William . . .209
Currie, Susannah 164
Curry, Michael Bruce 108
Curry, Thomas 81
Curtis, Cheryl 185
Curtis, Larry 268
Curtis, Lori 352
Cusack, Thomas 31
Cushman-Wood, Darren . . .33
Custer, James 119
Cuthbert, Richard 64
Cutler, Lelia 141
Cutts, Debbie 271

D

Dabney, Cary 261
Dadds, David 244
Dae, Choe Chong 189
D'Agostino, Frank 119
Dahulich, Michael G. 311
Dale, Diana C. 39, 68
Dale, Fritz 113
Dale, William 144
Dallenbach, Robert B. . . .149
Dalton, Elaine 98
Daman, Jim 61

Damsgaard-Rodriguez,
  Beth 254
D'Angelo, Mary Rose 50
Daniel, Audrey 166
Daniel, Clifton, III 108
Daniel, Eapen 335
Daniel, Henrietta 59
Daniel, Hieromonk 168
Daniel, Lillian 34
Daniel, Vinoy 137
Daniel (Bishop) 343, 344
Daniels, Anthony 209
Daniels, Antoinette
  (Toni) 108
Daniels, David
  Rwhynica, Jr. 57
Daniels, Mary Martha 107
Danielson, Duane 261
Danks, Sandy 246
Dantzler, Debbie 267
Daoust, Joseph P. 304
Darby, James 101
Darby, John Nelson 83
Darby, Joseph 267
Darden, Samuel 70
Darling, Richard 293
Darr, Steve 269
Dart, Helen 158
Daub, Peggy 121
Daughters, Kenneth
  Alan 301
Davidson, Brian 75
Davies, Fran 260
Davies, James L. 57
Davies, Pat 205
Davies, S. J. P. 292
Davis, Ashley 247
Davis, Charles 148
Davis, Derek 223
Davis, Dollie 148
Davis, James L. 57
Davis, Jim 239
Davis, Kathleen 241
Davis, Lindsey 175
Davis, Mark 106
Davis, Mark J. 329
Davis, Marty 337
Davis, Melvin 249
Davis, Millicent 258
Davis, Nehemiah 141
Davis, Patricia 205
Davis, Phil 91
Davis, R. Paul 103
Davis, Randy 163
Davis, Richard 176
Davis, Robert 248
Davis, Sarah F. 57
Davis, Stephanie 172
Davis, Stephen P. 163
Davis, Tyrone T. 86
Davolt, Philip 79
Davolt, Susan 331
Dawkins, David 148

Dawkins-Smith,
  Monica 264
Dawley, William G. 327
Dawson, Rachel R. 59
Day, Jeff 249
Day, Warren 131
Dayton, Susan 259
De Los Reyes, Mary 31
De Los Reyes, Nick 31
De Marco, Eugene 131
De Vries, Thomas 208
Dean, Amy Jacks 61
Dean, Mary
  Catherine 337
Dearolf, Pieter 22
DeBoer, Wayne 88
DeBree, Su 254, 255
Deckenback, John R. 172
Decker, William A. 335
deFreese, David L. 115
Degges, Ron 84
Deggett, Steve 105
DeGraffenreidt,
  Kermit 58, 336
DelHousaye,
  Darryl 309, 310
Delmonte, Elisabeth 46
Delsaut, Phil 201
Demarse, Mary Grace 258
Demchuk, David 321
Demeter, Andor 129
Demetrios
  (Archbishop) 63, 126
Demetrios
  (Bishop) 126, 127
DeMoor, Robert 324
Demos, Emanuel G. 127
den Hoed, J. 324
Denis, Mary-Frances 213
Dennie, Steve 101, 102
Dennison, Don 103
Densmore, Christopher . . .354
Denton, A. Louis 265
Denton, Michael 171
Derderian, Hovnan . . .72, 187
Dermody, Roger 151
Derr, Wayne 179
Derrenbacker,
  Robert A., Jr. 50
Derry, John 304
Descroix, Lydie 346
Detema, Ralph S. 84
Devadhar, Sudarshana . . .174
DeVeaux, Phillips 57
DeVoe, Jerry M., Jr. 157
Dewberry, A. T. 92
DeWinter, Deborah C. 38
DeWitt, Jesse 34
Dewling, Gregory R. 206
Dewling, Robert H. 206
DeYoung, Terry 24
Diakiw, William 168
Diaz, Javier 92

INDEX

413

Dicaire, Louis 209
DiCicco, Mario 302
Dickerson,
  Dennis 57, 356
Dickerson,
  Dennis C. 57, 353
Dickerson, Tom 135
Diefenbach, Joan 256
Diehl, Paul J., Jr. 85
Diemer, Ulli 347
Diepeveen, Karen 347
Dieppa-Baez, Roberto 62
Dietrich, Lisa 246
Dietz, Harry 266
Diller, Edward 137
Dimitrios (Bishop) 126
Dimitriou, Jerry 127
DiNardo, Daniel 81
Dinatale, Wenda 264
Dinkha, Mar IV 67
Dipboye, Carolyn 333
Dipboye, Larry 333
Diskin, Michael 239
DiStaulo, David 202
DiTommaso, Barbara 256
Dixon, Brad 102
Dixon, Judy 262
Dixon, Melissa 329
Djaballah, Amar 318
Djigo, Jean-Luc 294
Dmitri (Archbishop) 145
Dobbin, Karen 247
Dobbs, H. A. 331
Dobiash, Sandra 166
Dobrowolski,
  Kristoph Franz 292
Dobush, Christine 75
Dockalek, Hendrina 199
Dodge, Gary W. 161
Dodge, Hollis 169
Dodo, Amos A. 122
Doezema, Don 153, 154
Doherty, Margaret 258
Dohner, Stephanie 255
Dolan, Timothy 81
Domanik, Janice 121
Donahue, James A. 303
Donald (Bishop) 128
Donaldson, Blain 118
Donley, Brian C. 305
Dorff, James E. 174, 175
Dorhauer, John 171
Dorland, Arthur G. 191
Dorn, William 135
Dorr,
  Adriane 134, 330, 335
Dorrington,
  Charles W. 157, 208
Dorsey, Derrick 258
Dortch, Mimi 239
Douglas, Chris 89
Douglas, Scott 238
Douglas, William O. 97

Douglass,
  Benjamin T. 148, 176
Douglass, Steve 27
Dow, Thomas E. 318
Dowd, Susan Jackson 333
Dowden, Blair 304
Dowden,
  G. Blair 101, 102
Dowell, W. E. 75
Dowie, John
  Alexander 82
Down, Graham 349
Downey, William S. H. . . .134
Downin, Janet 262
Downs, Michael A. 171
Downs, Timothy C. 172
Doyle, Barrie 193, 194
Doyle, C. Andrew 108
Doyle, Danial 266
Doyle, William 214
Drainville, Dennis 186
Drake, Paul 130
Draper, David E. 316
Dresselhaus, Richard 73
Drew, Nancy K. 135
Drews, Julie 29, 327
Driedger, June Mears 349
Driesen, Robert L. 116
Drilling, Peter J. 299
Driscoll, Virginia 121
Drisner, John 206
Drum, Cindy 244
Drury, Stephen 176
Dua, Barbara E. 256
Duangmala, Prasert 88
Duarte, Eugénio R. 101
Dueholm, Ben 44
Duerksen, Carol 339
Duff, Donald J. 145
Duff, Susan 247
Duffy, Mark 108, 354
Dugan, Laura 122
Dugas, Jacqueline 51
Duhaime, Jean 294
Duke, Ralph 41
Duke, Thomas 254
Dulyea-Parker, Teresa 85
Dumond, Franklin 124
Dunahoo, Charles . . .150, 330
Dunbar, Betsy 352
Dunbar, David G. 297
Duncan, Larry 196
Duncan, Lucy 331
Duncan, Philip M., II 108
Duncan, Ronald V. 93
Duncan, Victoria 108
Dundas, Steven L. 68
Dunham, Guy W. 266
Dunkerson, Roddy 171
Dunkin, Ralph W. . . .116, 271
Dunn, Craig A. 179
Dunn, James A. 179
Dunn, Sharon R. 94

Dunn, Wesley 168
Dupre, Ray D. 92
Duque, Francisco 108
Duracin, Jean Zache 108
Durakis, Thomas 22
Durance, George 317
Durden, John 296
During, Elizabeth 38
Durley, Gerald 243
Durocher, Eric 347
Durocher, Paul-André 209
Dursi, Elsie L. 261
Durso, Pamela R. 324
Duvall, Joe 102
Dwight, David A. 112
Dybdahl, Jon 315
Dybdal, Myrdell 240
Dyck, Dan 204
Dyck, Sally 169, 174, 253
Dyck, Tim 201
Dykstra, Gerard 193, 194
Dykstra, Gerard L. 88
Dykstra, Jon 350
Dystra, Russell 342

E
Eads, Ora W. 86
Earheart-Brown,
  Daniel J. 307
Earheart-Brown, Jay 106
Easley, Michael J. 307
Easter, Deborah 253
Eaton, Elizabeth A. 115
Eberlin, Mary Ellen 211
Echols, James
  Kenneth 306
Eck, Diana 217
Eck, Diana L. 224
Eckhardt, Brian 111
Eckhardt, Elaine 344
Eckhardt, Ellen E. 141
Eckman, James 303
Eckstrom, Kevin 43
Eddy, Mary Baker 90–91
Eddy, Richard 61
Eden, Yvonne 270
Edgar, Tyler 38
Edge, Jim 296
Edgren, John Alexis 104
Edlund, Mark 163
Edmondson, Robert W. 65
Edney, Lowell 173
Edwards, Bill 262
Edwards, Dale 62
Edwards, Dan T. 108
Edwards,
  David 61, 63, 250
Edwards, Gloria 135
Edwards, Gregory 39
Edwards, Harold 99
Edwards, Herbert 101
Edwards, James L. 90, 93, 295

Edwards, Wendy J.
   Deichman 314, 315
Edwards, William H. 85
Egge, Joel 99, 100, 196
Eggleston, James H. 256
Egnew, Bruce E. 81
Ehinger, Lois 246
Ehrenkrantz, Dan 310
Ehresman, David 248
Eichstadt, Wayne 100
Ekemam, Samuel
   Chuka, Sr. 57, 58
Ekeroth, George E. 73
Ekeroth, M. J. 73
Elam, Betty 31, 39
Elfers, Michelle 249
Elford, Keith 202
Elftmann, Tracy 252
Elgin, Bette 123
Elia, Donna 260
Ellefson, Anne 267
Ellenson, David 303
Elliott, Kate Sprutta 335
Ellis, Charles H., III 147
Ellis, Davis L. 147
Ellis, J. Delano, II 176
Ellis, Jerry 266
Ellis, Mandy 254
Ellis, Rebekah A. 260
Ellis, Sabrina 176
Ellis, Sandra 205
Ellis, Wayne 69
Ellison, Leslie 268, 269
Elloian, Dierdre 242
Ellyatt, David 203
Elrod, Rachael 247
Ely, Duncan C. 108
Ely, Thomas Clark 108
Emanuel, Frank 50
Embree, Dot 250
Emerson, Joe 177
Emory, M. L. 255
Endecott, Clayton 98, 196
Endel, Leo 163
Ene, Daniel 210
Ene, Daniel Adrian 158
Engbrecht, Dave 138
Engebretson, Donn 112
Engelsma, David 334
Enger, Cindy 270
Englemayer,
   Shammai 334
Engstrom, Jon R. 123
Enns-Rempel, Kevin 356
Enrique, Antonio 339
Episcopos, Samuel Cor . . .136
Epps, Barbara J. 59
Epting, C. Christopher . . .108
Erb-Miller, Fannie 346
Erdman, Greg 160
Erhardt, Richard 271
Ericksen, Paul 354
Erickson, Charles R. 268

Erickson, Duane 111
Erickson, Gary 176
Eriks, Kenneth 154, 208
Ervine, Sharon 268
Eschenbrenner, Jim 89
Eskridge, Larry 222
Eslinger, Leslie S. 265
Espinoza, Gabriel 147
Essey, Basil 66
Estelle-Homer,
   Suzanne 355
Esterle, Stan 248
Estes, George 336
Estes, George R. 106, 336
Estes, Kristi 121
Estocin, Frank 168
Estwani, Sheikh
   Bassam 243
Etterman, James 96
Eusebio, Marilee 158
Evangelos
   (Metropolitan) 127
Evans, Alton 144
Evans, Carl 267
Evans, G. Thomas 161
Evans, Gene 123
Evans, Irvin 173
Evans, Kerrie 344
Evans, William B. 323
Evenson, Carl R. 115
Everett, Laura 251
Everett, Randel 163
Everts, Ed 135
Evison, Ian 21
Ewing, Rebecca 240
Ewing, Ward B. 302
Eyring, Henry B. 98
Ezell, Kevin 163

F
Faber, Connie 326
Fabric, Elliot 271
Fadelle, Norman 82
Fagerstrom, Doug 105
Fagerstrom,
   Douglas L. 303
Fagin, Earl 240
Fahey, Brian P. 24
Faigao, Howard F. 161
Failing, Mark 323
Fairbanks, LeBron 101
Fairchild, Darryl 261
Falby, Robert 185
Falconer, Gennae 253
Farabee-Lewis, Iris 249
Faris, Robert 51
Farland, Jean Mac 253
Farley, Lawrence 205
Farlow, David 93, 328
Farmer, Jeff 41, 42
Farmer, Jeffrey E. 144
Farrell, Hunter 81, 151

Farren, John 311
Fast, Rick 52
Faurschou, Bruce 213
Faust, David M. 299
Faustin, Mindy 21
Favreau, Claude 198, 199
Feamster-Roll, Gerry 247
Fedechko,
   Michael 157, 208,
   . . . . .321, 349
Fehr, Wes 320
Feldberg, Michael 355
Felger, Vicki 246
Felipa, Luis F. 88
Felter, David J. 332
Felton, David 171
Fendt, John W., Jr. 141
Ferkenstad, Craig 116
Fernhout, Harry 319
Ferre, Faith 246
Ferrell, Ernest 141
Fetherlin, Robert L. 87
Field, Martin, S. 109
Field, Ronald 40
Fieler, Sean 37
Fietje, Bill 188
Fifagrowicz, Joseph 258
Fillmore, Robin 39
Finch, Dody 45
Finck, Murray D. 114
Fincke, George B. 156
Finke, Roger 218
Finkel, Madelan 46
Finley, J. Lance 103
Finn, Peter G. 311
Finney, Kevin 263
Finney, Peter P., Jr. 328
Finzel, Hans 104
Fiorino, Joseph 337
Firle, Sharon L. 328
Fisch, Deborah 331
Fischer, Brian 246
Fischer, Scott 264
Fish, Valarie 77
Fishell, Randy 332
Fisher, Diane 177, 214
Fisher, Fred S. 97
Fisher, Fred S., Sr. 195
Fisher, Travis 246
Fisk, J. Victor 123
Fison, David 238
Fitchue, Leah Gaskin 309
Fitzgerald, Russell G. 45
Fitzmier, John 217
Fitzpatrick,
   Robert L. 108, 109
Flaaten, Jan Olav 239
Flanagan, James 306
Flanders, Thomas J. 88
Fledderus, Bill 348
Fleischer, Daniel 100
Fleischer, Paul 335
Fleming, Reed 321

INDEX

415

Flemmer, Ken 331
Flesher, Chuck 24
Fletcher, Alfred 62
Fletcher, James 22
Fletcher, Judy R. 151
Fletcher, Keith 139
Fletcher, Ruth A. 85
Fletcher, Sarah 343
Fletcher, Wendy 322
Florkey, Marcia L. 46
Flory-Steury, Mary Jo 90
Flowers, Fort D., Jr. 268
Flowers, George F. 57
Flowers, Mary Lynne 151
Fluit, Charlie 54
Focht, Richard 264
Fogas, Jackie 328
Fogle, Lerry W. 44
Follett, Don 265
Fong, Bruce W. 307
Fontenot, Francis 153
Foran, James 266
Forbes, George C. 92
Ford, C. Barney 34
Ford, C. M. 94
Ford, J. Arthur 319
Ford, Lowell 64
Foreman,
    Rachel 103, 332, 336
Foreman, Rachel L. 327
Foreman, Yolanda
    Waggoner 244
Forhand, Darryl 101
Forlines, James 139
Forlines, Leroy 139
Forro, Alexander . . .128, 129
Forsberg, Robert 240
Forsberg, Tonya M. 155
Forsee, Tom 238
Forshaw, Mark 22
Fortin, Dennis 312
Fortin, Marilyn 46
Fortson, Don 117
Fortune, Marie M. 270
Foster, H. Paul 206, 348
Foster, Jim 193, 194
Fournier,
    Pierre-André 209
Fowler, Douglas 248
Fowler, John M. 328
Fox, Jerry 239
Fox, Margaret A. 262
Fox, Ronald K. 260
Foxe, Moira 240
Foxman, Abraham H. 234
Fozard, John 93
Fozard, John D. 307
Frade, Leopold 109
Fradley, N. 203
Frammolino, Carl 98
Francis, Marilyn 210
Francis, Maureen 38
Francis, Oprah 167

Francis,
    William W. 209, 210
Fraser, Hugh 317
Fraser, Ian S. 213
Fraser, Margaret 31
Fraser, Ronald A. 317
Frazee, David 154
Frazier, David 125
Frazier, Mike 76
Free, Keith A. 180
Freed, Kathy 247
Freelander, Daniel 31, 39
Freeman, David 193, 194
Freeman, George 46, 345
Freeman, Hillary 253
Freeman, Richard 239
Freiheit, Warren D. 115
Fretheim, James A. 112
Frey, Mark 261
Frick, Murray 256
Friend, Kendra 103, 197
Friesen, Frank 201
Friesen, Joan 62
Friesllow, Michael 246
Frieson, Desiree 39
Frisch, Deborah 158
Frische-Mouri,
    Dennis 245
Frischkorn, Frank 62
Frndak, Keith 135
Froehlich, S. H. 68, 187
Froese,
    Donnalyn 318, 319
Frontz,
    Maurice C., III 266
Frowe, Caroline 244
Fry, Gary 331
Fryling, Robert A. 34
Fugh, Clement W. 57
Fulenwider, Douglas 73
Fuller, Brian 318
Fuller, John 40
Fuller, Paula 34
Fuller, Robert H. 176
Fullerton, Howard 121
Fullwood, James 64
Fulton, Trish 319
Fulwider, Bryan 243
Funk, Abe 51, 189
Futral, James R. 163

G
Gable, Nancy 116
Gaddie, Ron 248
Gaddis, Louis E. 92
Gaddy, Todd 176
Gadsden, Al 300
Gaewski, David R. 172
Gage, J. Marshall 37
Gagnon, André L. 319
Gagnon, Jean 209
Galegor, Steve 119

Gallop, Trina 346
Galloway, Phyllis H. 356
Galstanian, Bagrat 72
Galvin, Joan 294
Gambino, Mathew 325
Gammill, Nancy 247
Gammon, Stephen A. 104
Gandolfo, Lucian 131
Gantt, John 171
Garant, Elizabeth 350
Garbidakis, Nicholas 22
Garcia, Angel M. 88
Gardner, Harry G. 317
Gardner, Talmadge 132
Gardner, W. Wayne 314
Garis, Mark 80
Garland, David E. 302
Garment, Robert 117
Garner, Darlene 178
Garner, Judi 355
Garrett, Karen 325
Garrett, Phillip 248
Garrison, Brent D. 313
Garrison, J. Michael 109
Garrison, L. Alton 72, 73
Garriss, Stephen 148
Gascoine, James 263
Gasero, Russell 358
Gast, Mary Susan 171
Gatlin, Alton 94
Gaunt, Thomas P. 220
Gauthier, Guy 293
Gautier, Haggeo 243
Gautier, Mary 220
Gaw, Catherine 294
Gaw, Catherine H. 213
Gay, Julie Lane 347
Geiger, C. Edward 265
Geisler, Norman 313
Geldmacher, Joan 257
Genello, William R. 325
Gentle, Stanley 80
Gentles, Jestina 173
George, Francis 81
George, J. Don 73
George, Michele 185
George, Richard 131
George, Timothy 297
George, William 86
Georgije (Bishop) . . .160, 211
Gepert, Robert R. 109
Gerard, Carrie 247
Gerasimos
    (Metropolitan) 127
Gerbrandt, Gerald . . .317, 318
Gerdes, Neil W. 358
Gerlach, Bryan 180
Gethers, Leroy 157
Getz, Greg 138
Getz, Jeff 138
Geulsgugian, Bernard 187
Geyser, Thomas 131
Gholson, Edith 106

Ghougassian, Vazken 71
Gibbens-Rickman,
    Mark 263
Gibbons, Lorrie H. 206
Gibbons, T. 203
Gibbs, Charles P. 45
Gibbs, Kitty 270
Gibbs, Wendell N., Jr. 109
Gibson, Billy 123
Gibson, Diana 239
Gibson, Marie E. 257
Giesbrecht, Kennert 349
Giesler, Christina 138
Giesy, Samuel 306
Gifford, Carolyn 244
Gilbert, Robert 131
Gilbert, Wanda 223
Gilbert-Cougar, John 191
Gilbertson, Leon C. 52
Gilbreath, Ed 342
Gill, Andrew 166
Gilliam, Lynn W. 339
Gillians, Larry 48
Gillies, Susan E. 255
Gillis, Kathy 351
Gillming, Keith 76
Gillum, Perry 196
Gilmore, Marshall 87
Ginn, Jeffrey B. 163
Giordano, Sally 259
Giordano, Stephen T. 255
Giuliano, David W. 213
Gladfelter, Irl A. 64
Gladish, Michael D. 202
Glasgow, Amber 247
Glenn, Lucinda 355
Glenn, Michael 311
Glenn, Robert 246
Glickman, Marlene 259
Glickstein, Richard 37
Glover, Mary Anne 85
Gnat, Thomas J. 149
Goatley, David
    Emmanuel 41
Godfrey, W. Robert 316
Goebel, Samuel 111
Goertemiller, Alan 245
Goertzen, Lil 201, 348
Goff, Jim 160
Goff, Phillip 220
Goforth, C. W. 147
Gofus, Nancy 178
Gohdes,
    Stephen 138, 139, 191
Goldberger, Pierre 213
Golden, Ira Rudolph 59
Golder, Donald L. 147
Golder, Morris 147
Golder, W. Evan 343
Golding, Jim 338
Goldstein,
    Clifford R. 334, 342
Golumb, Paul 257

Gomez, Jose 81
Gomez, Ray 268
Gonzales Dewey, Don 85
Gonzales Dewey,
    Susan 85
Gonzales-Longoria,
    Ramon 121
Gonzalez, Saturnino 73
Gonzalez, Tony 239, 240
Goodhue, Thomas W. 258
Goodlin, Jeanne 269
Goodman, Jim 76
Goodpaster, Larry M. 175
Goodwin, Douglas 213
Goodwin, Leah 338
Goodyear, Paul 211
Gopal, Renee 261
Gordon, A. 203
Gordon, Dorcas 26
Gordon, Drew 157, 329
Gordon, J. Dorcas 319
Gordon, Lynne 157, 329
Gordy, H. Julian 116
Gore, Susan K. 106, 357
Gori, Giorgio 48
Gorton, Dennis L. . . .103, 104
Gorzinski, Barbara 270
Gosnell, David H. 96, 195
Gosnell, Lorna V. 96, 195
Govantes, Pedro 117
Govier, Gordon 34
Goy, Sonly 87
Grady, J. Lee 326
Grady, Joellen W. 261
Graf, Robert 31
Graf, Virginia 31
Graham, Ricardo B. 161
Graham, Richard H. 116
Graham, Robert L. 259
Graham, William A. 303
Grainger, David 244
Granberg-Michaelson,
    Wesley 154
Grannum, Wilson 138
Grant, A. Elizabeth 73
Grant, James M. 313
Grant, Kenneth G. Y. 251
Grant, Michael A. 92
Grant, Sumner 63
Graves, Charles 271
Graves, David W. 101
Graves, James R. 61
Graves, Sylvia 121
Graves,
    William H., Sr. 87
Gray, Arthur J., II 130
Gray, Brian 43
Gray, Duncan, III 254
Gray, Duncan
    Montgomery, III 109
Graybill, John W. 170
Gray-Reeves, Mary 109
Graz, John 161

Green, Daniel 157
Green, Donald B. 263
Green, S. 173
Green, S. L., Jr. 94
Green, Samuel L., Sr. 57
Green, Stanley 138
Greenfield, Larry L. 62
Greenhaw, David M. 301
Greening, John 124
Greenleaf, Helen 168
Greenler, Robin 121
Greenwood, Greg 249
Grefe, Dagmar 241
Gregersen, Bruce 213
Grégoire, Léo 209
Gregory, Carol 242
Gregory, Chester, Sr. 172
Gregory, Wilton 81
Greiman, Clayton 155
Grell, Janet 22
Grier, David 205
Grieves, Brian 108
Griffes, D. Darrell 112
Griffin, Ashley 249
Griffin, Sharon 92
Griffis,
    David M. 95, 194, 195
Griffith, Dick 130
Griffith, Richard 130
Grigsby, Phillip N. 260
Grimard, Roland 212
Grimm, Libby 263
Griswold, Larry H. 73
Gritters, Barrett L. 314
Grogan, Douglas L. 87
Groome, Thomas H. 297
Groover, Clarence 101
Groover, Gentle L. 101
Grorud, Al 250
Gross, Glenn M. 156, 157
Gross, Joseph 149
Gross, Philip J. 129
Grossman, Randall A. 79
Grossman, William 130
Grossmann, Robert 155
Grote, Royal U. 155, 156
Grote,
    Royal U., Jr. 155, 156
Grotegut, Stan 241
Grou, Jean 351
Groves, Anthony Norris . . .83
Grubbs, Bonita 241
Grubbs, Lari R. 84
Guedes, John 311
Guernsey, Lucy 241
Guerrero, Orlando J. 109
Guess, J. Bennett 171
Guffey, Edith A. 171
Guibord, Gwynne 241
Guido, Sam 69
Guidry, Carolyn Tyler 57
Guillebeau, Julie 254
Guinness, Howard 51

Guirguis, Ammonius 198
Guirguis, Lucy Ishak 46
Gulasekharam, Nesa 48
Gulick, Edwin F., Jr. 109
Gulick, Janet A. 265
Gullette, Reginald 79
Gullixson, Theodore 335
Gumbs, Amanda 37
Gumbs, Carolyn 258
Gumbs, E. Ambrose 109
Gunty, Christopher 325
Gurkin, Rose 261
Gurley, G. Morris 257
Guthrie, David 139
Gwinn, Alfred W., Jr. 175

H

Haas, James H. 264
Haas, Steve 46
Haberer, Jack 339
Hackett, Jean 46
Hackett, Rose 272
Hackney, Lois 122
Hadjinicolaou, John 205
Hadley, Alvin 262
Hadsell, Heidi 303
Hagan, G. Michael 313
Hagemann, Dennis 84
Hagerty, Robert E. 316
Hagiya, Grant 176
Hagopian, Stephen 71
Hagy, Arthur, Jr. 260
Hahn, Daniel 259
Halder, Fran 262
Hale, Rebecca 84
Hales, Robert D. 98
Haley, Richard 250
Hall, A. Z., Jr. 94
Hall, Adam 262
Hall, Christopher A. 309
Hall, Dinah 270
Hall, Gary 312
Hall, Gregory V. 93
Hall, Horace 122
Hall, J. L. 331, 338
Hall, Marvin 122
Hall, Simeon 153
Hallberg, Donald M. 114
Hallman, Don 188
Hallward, Stoph 120
Haloviak, Bert 352
Halpert, Nicole 294
Hamb, Elnora P. 86, 87
Hamel, William J. 113
Hamelink, Crystal 260
Hames, Jerrold 330
Hamilton, Karen 49
Hamilton, W. W. 93
Hamlett, James P. 84
Hamlin, Margaret 269
Hamm, Richard 30
Hammel, Marci 101, 102

Hammock, Cheryl 44
Hammons, Roger 152
Hampar, Armen 72
Hampton, John E. 147
Hancock, Carol L. 213
Handysides, Allan R. 161
Haney, Kenneth F. 176
Haney, Margaret 151
Haney, O. L. 94
Hankins, David E. 163
Hanley, Richard 247
Hanse, Brian W. 36
Hansen, Duane 113
Hansen, Ellen 271
Hansen, Frosty 126
Hansen, Traynor
  ("Frosty"), Jr. 126
Hansen, Yelena 263
Hanson, Lloyd 240
Hanson, Mark S. 114
Harbeson, Christine 244
Harbig, Corinna 46
Harder, Christian 327
Harding King, Amy 257
Hardy, Betsy 269
Hardy, Ralph, Jr. 31, 39
Harfoot, William 159
Hargleroad, Bobbi
  Wells 327
Hargrave, Ervin 132
Harke, Gary L. 265
Harmelink,
  Herman, III 130
Harms, Richard H. 358
Harms, Steve 240
Harper, Terry L. 163
Harrell, Robert 113
Harris, Alvin 90
Harris, David 350
Harris, David A. 233
Harris, Elsie 172
Harris, Forrest E. 295
Harris, Jerome V. 57
Harris, Nanci 48
Harris, Ron L. 40
Harris, Sherryll 346
Harrison, Charles E. 341
Harrison, Dan 102
Harrison, David P. 41
Harrison, Kathy 177
Harrison, Matthew C. 135
Harrison, William
  Anthony 143, 144
Harrold, Bob 208
Hart, Donald G. 171
Hart, Ray L. 297
Hart, Terry R. 96, 195
Harter, Michael G. 340
Harter, Richard 251
Hartke, Gary 101
Hartman, Jean 246
Hartman, Richard 245

Hartnett, Barbara 244
Hartwig, Raymond L. 135
Harvey, Jane Hull 33
Harvey, Timothy P. 89
Harwell, Sara 354
Hasan, John 239
Hassane, Taha 33
Hastey, Stan 60, 61
Hatch, Kenneth 93
Hatcher, Warren 157
Hatlie, Susan Allers 252
Hauptfuhrer, George 21
Hauser, Clarence 293
Hawaweeny, Raphael 66
Hawkins, Charles 248
Hawkins, Don 313
Hawkins, Michael W. 186
Hawkins, O. S. 163
Hawkins, Pamela C. 344
Hawkins, Peggy 261
Hawkins, Robert J., Jr. 92
Hawn, Steven 113
Haworth, Sharon 121
Hay, Thomas 151
Hayes, Alan 322
Hayes, Kathleen 341
Hayes, Lindsey 132
Hayes,
  Robert E., Jr. 174, 175
Haymes, Don 354
Hayner, Stephen A. 300
Haynes, N. 93
Hays, Franklin E. 61
Hays, Richard B. 301
Hazuda, Ronald A. 63
Hazzard, David 319
Hazzard, David E. 206
Headman, Wayne A. 310
Heagy, David 170
Hearn, Greg 132
Heaslip, Clifford 214
Heath, Gordon 359
Heath, Preston 148
Heckman, M. 153
Hedberg, William 256
Hedges, Gary 131
Hedgren, Steve 159
Heebner, Gerald 341
Heerspink, Robert C. 88
Heffernan, Gloria 258
Heichler, Kate 242
Heiman, Tom 271
Hein, Marvin 125
Heiniger, Mike 118
Heinz, Sally Jones 267
Heinze, Ted 293
Heinzelmann, Stefan 141
Heinzl, Dieter 254
Heisey, Terry M. 354
Hejl, James 177
Heleine, Berton G. 64
Hellenbrecht,
  Renee 164, 165

Heller, Bill 153
Helton, Mary Beth 248
Heminway,
    L. Marshall 134
Hemphill, Margaret 157
Hendel, Kurt K. 329
Henderson,
    Dorsey F., Jr. 109
Henderson, Katharine R. . .219
Henderson, Kim 202
Henderson, Veryl F. 163
Hendricks, Harry 99
Hendrickson, Mary Lynn . .24
Henke, Kenneth 357
Henkel, Sarah 266
Henn, Jack 32
Henning, Cornal
    Garnett, Sr. 57
Henry, Kevin 112
Henson, Kevin 106
Henze, Charles 256
Her, Steven X. 87
Herbrandson, DeWayne . . .28
Heretz, Michael 168
Herman, Harry 147
Herman, Raymond 258
Herman
    (Metropolitan) 145, 311
Hermiz, Tom 102
Hernando, Mirasal 189
Hernando, Vincente 189
Heron, Claire 54
Herrera, Marco 22
Herron, Brian 253
Herron, Keith 105
Hertzog, Stephen 322
Herz-Lane, Wolfgang D. . .116
Hess, Henry 193
Hester, Yvonne 251
Heuser,
    Frederick J., Jr. . . .151, 333
Hewett, Fred 163
Hewitt, Michael 197, 198
Heyward, Isaiah 94
Hicken, Michael 261
Hickey, Tim S. 328
Hicks, David 156
Hicks, James T. 138
Hicks,
    Maurice M. 190, 191
Hicks, Wayne 103
Hicks, William 125
Hiemstra, John 259
Higgins, Stan 35
High, Danita 139
Higham, Susan 156
Highers, Alan E. 342
Hilarion
    (Metropolitan) 159
Hill, Alec 34
Hill, Amy 265
Hill, Bruce D. 112
Hill, Dale 120

Hill, John 33
Hill, Kenneth H. 95, 333
Hill, Kenneth L. 195
Hill, Michael 94
Hill, R. Eugene 64
Hill, Roy V., II 269
Hill, Ruth Y. 112
Hill,
    Timothy M. . . .95, 194, 195
Hillouse, Darrell 124
Hiltz, Fred J. 185
Hinckle, Carol 264
Hines, D. 94
Hines, Mildred B. 57, 58
Hinkle, John 36
Hinshaw, Greg 122
Hinshaw, Richard 334
Hinshaw, Seth 158
Hinton, Arthur 107
Hinz, Leo 294
Hinz, Mary Ann 251
Hirschy, Margaret 354
Hiscock, David 211
Hiscox, Don 85
Hisey, Destiny 25
Hixon, Larry 241
Hnatko, George 168
Ho, Esther 240
Hoagland, Alberta 242
Hobbs (Reverend) 148
Hockensmith,
    David W., Jr. 254
Hodges, James 68, 187
Hodges, Sam 343
Hodgins, Donald E. 214
Hoey, Eric 151
Hoffman, David 265
Hoffman,
    Warren L. 80, 189
Hofstad, Robert D. 114
Hogan, Peter 257
Hogston, Delphine 252
Hoke, Terry 80
Holbrook, Mark G. 28
Holbrook, Mike 102
Holdefer, Helen 238
Holden, Ron 197, 198
Holder, Steve 123
Holguin, Julio Cesar 109
Holland, Grace 80
Holland, Jeffrey R. 98
Holland,
    Melford E., Jr. 107
Hollerith, Herman, IV . . .109
Holley, Darrell 139
Hollifield,
    Milton A., Jr. 163
Hollingsworth, J .N., III . . .36
Hollingsworth, Mark, Jr. . .109
Holloway, Callon W., Jr. . .115
Holm, Jim 307
Holmes,
    Charley 74, 76, 296

Holmes, Cynthia 254
Holmes, Jenny 263
Holmes, Mary Swalla 247
Holmes, Roy A. 57, 58
Holmgren, A. A. 73
Holmquist, Victor
    Freeman 189
Holmrod, Mark W. 114
Holmstrom, Virginia 63
Holt, Jeanette 61
Holtz, Janet E. 265
Homoki, Lee 126
Homp, Mark 61
Honcharenko, Natalia 168
Hood, George 159
Hoogendoorn, Case 44
Hoover, Amos B. 144
Hoover, B. Penrose 116
Hope, Monica 79
Hopkins, Jim 61
Hopkins, John L. 174
Hopkins, Sara E. 343
Hopper, David 118
Hopwood, Doug 264
Horan, Nancy 257
Horgan, Ron 117
Horn, Ken 338, 342
Horne, James R. 92
Horne, Martha J. 310
Horsely, Gordon 199
Horst, Patricia L. 161
Hortelliti, David 203
Hoshibata, Robert T. 176
Hoskin,
    Derek B. E. 185, 186
Hoskins, Janet A. 321
Hossler, William 138
Hostetter, Steven 309
Hotchkiss,
    Gregory K. 156
Houle, Jaques 95, 194
House, Alvin 63
House, Christie R. 337
Houston, Barbara 266
Houston, Walter 141
Hovis, Carol 240
Howard, John 33
Howard, R. L. 94
Howard, Randall E. 98
Howard, Randy 42, 196
Howard,
    Randy E., Sr. 196, 196
Howard, S. Johnson 109
Howard-Steele,
    Christy 31
Howden, Lisa 202
Howe, Barry R. 109
Howe, John W. 109
Howe, Sue 255
Howell, Bruce 176
Howery, David G. 254
Hoyt, Thomas L., Jr. 87
Hrabak, Frank 152, 153

419

Hrybowych, Anastasia . . .169
Hsieh, Jeannette 314
Hubbard, Bede 209
Hubbard,
  Howard 81, 251, 256
Hucks, John T., Jr. 164
Huculak, Larence 209
Hudascek, Mary Jane 246
Hudgens, Bobby 76, 77
Hudgins, Tina 323
Hudnut-Beumler,
  James 315
Hudson, James L. 151
Hudson, Jill 151
Huebl, Marc 117
Huebner, James R. 180
Huett, Jeff 340
Huffard, Everett W. 303
Hugh, Ivor T. 241
Hughes, Aaron 351
Hughes,
  Charles R., Jr. 88, 88
Hughes, Clyde 42
Hughes,
  Clyde M. 131, 132, 338
Hughes, Dustin 132
Hughes, Jarrett 253
Hughes, Sarah 247
Hughes, Sherly M. 172
Hughes, Teresa A. 242
Huh, Young Chin 133
Huie, Janice Riggle 175
Hukill, Jim 35
Huleatt, Johann 91
Hull, Rey 256
Hultquist, Timothy A. 42
Humphrey, Sandra 327
Hundeby, Art 196
Hundley, Michael 248
Hundt, Peter 209
Hunerdosse, Marion 89
Hunn, Ken 80
Hunt, Raymon E. 59
Hunte, David "Andy" 147
Hunter, Gwen 252
Hunter, Harold D. 357
Hunter, Louis, Sr. 57, 58
Hunter, Martha J. 328
Hunter, Rhashell 151
Hunter, Ron 139
Hunter, Stewart 51
Huntley, Harvey L., Jr. . . .116
Hurn, Nancy 358
Huron, Rod 82, 85, 86
Hurtubise, Pierre 359
Husband, Paul 117
Huszagh, Elini 127
Hutcheon, Cyprian 205
Hutchins, D. 94
Hutchinson, Moira 53
Hutchinson,
  William W. 175
Hux, Ralph 102, 330

Hying, Donald J. 311
Hynes, Marcus 292
Hyvonen, Randall 171

I
Iaguinta, Joe 132
Iakovos (Metropolitan) . . .126
Ihreborg, Christer 205
Illingworth, Beth 260
Ilpeka, Israel 135
Ingersol, Stan 357
Ingham, Michael C. 186
Ingram, Daryl 33, 57
Ingram, Daryl B. 57
Ingram, Gregory
  Gerald McKinley 57
Iorg, Jeff 302
Iov (Rev.) 205
Ireland, Lisa 258
Irenee (Bishop) 145
Irineu (Bishop) 145
Irish, Carolyn T. 109
Irvin, Dale T. 308
Irving, David M. 186
Irvio, Wanda 248
Irwin, John 53
Irwin, Kevin W. 298
Isaiah (Metropolitan) 127
Isenhower, Joe 134
Isenhower, Joe, Jr. 340
Ishkanian, Charlotte 336
Islam-Majeed, Milia 240
Isom, Dotcy I. 87
Israel, Obispo Jose 153
Israel, Wilma 243
Itty, Johncy 302
Izard, Ralph 77

J
Jackson, Bernice Powell . . .45
Jackson, Daniel R. 161
Jackson, Elmira J. 59
Jackson, Kitt 256
Jackson, Mary 78
Jackson, Phil 139
Jackson, Walter L. 101
Jackson-Skelton,
  Christina L. 114
Jackumin,
  Emile M., Jr. 23
Jacob, Winfred 141
Jacobs, Jill 33
Jacobson, Art 68
Jacobson, Shelley 253
Jacobus, Russell E. 109
Jaharis, Michael 127
James, Eugene 85
James, Jean 269, 270
James, Timothy M. 84
James (Archbishop) 128
Jameson, Debra 257
Jameson, Norman 30

Jamieson, Michael R. 161
Janes, Burton K. 207
Jang, Jacob Se 133
Janke, Dwayne 351
Jans, Kathryn J. 270
Jaramillo, M. Linda 171
Jared, Clive 92
Jarret, Peter A. 307, 308
Jarrett, Nathaniel, Jr. 58
Jarrett, R. Bryan 73
Jasper, Jeremiah 271
Jean, Jean 88
Jeans, Yvonne Tufts 176
Jefferts-Schori,
  Katherine 107, 108
Jeffery, Jim 296
Jeffrey, David 159
Jeffrey, Robert 334
Jehle, Bonnie 259
Jelinek, James L. 109
Jellinek, Nancy 268
Jemerson, Robert 38
Jenkins,
  Charles E., III 109
Jenkins, John 105
Jenkins, Keith A. 304
Jenkins, Kristin 346
Jenkins, Laurie 260
Jenkins, Linda 122
Jenkins, Ronny 81
Jenks, Philip E. 38
Jenness, Jeffery A. 93
Jennings, Charles 64
Jensen, Martin K. 355
Jensen, Paul 166
Jensen, Richard 125
Jeremiah, Jeffrey 117
Jerge, Marie C. 116, 259
Jermann, Rosemary 342
Jernigan, Aleida 263
Jernigan, Paul S. 92
Jessup, Bryce L. 316
Jevert, Mark 47
Jewel, Bill 248
Jewell, Thomas R. 85
Jillions, John 49, 205
Jinkins, Michael 306
Johansen, Ruthann K. 297
Johns, Jackie 24
Johnson, A. Wayne 141
Johnson, Alexandra 270
Johnson, Andrea 336
Johnson, Ben 70
Johnson, Carl 242
Johnson, Chris 34
Johnson, Clifford 63
Johnson, Colin R. . . .185, 186
Johnson, Craig 335
Johnson, Craig E. 115
Johnson, David W. 112
Johnson, Deborah 338
Johnson, Delbert L. 161
Johnson, Diane 104

Johnson, Don E. 109
Johnson, Evelyn M. R. . . .112
Johnson, George 338
Johnson, Henry L. 147
Johnson,
    Jack 245, 251, 256
Johnson, Jarvis 34
Johnson, Jeffrey 120
Johnson, Jeron 147
Johnson, Jerry L. 22
Johnson, Joseph 58
Johnson, M. L. 94
Johnson, Mark 211
Johnson, Michelle
    Laque 324, 325
Johnson, Peggy 174
Johnson, Richard O. 331
Johnson, Rita 153
Johnson, Robert E. 324
Johnson,
    Rockford 262, 263
Johnson, Rodney
    McNeil 176
Johnson, Ron 113
Johnson, Rosie 172
Johnson, Sandy 194
Johnson, Susan 52
Johnson, Thomas S. 42
Johnson, Todd 35
Johnson,
    W. Robert, III 57, 58
Johnson,
    Washington, II 335
Johnson-Pata,
    Jacqueline 235
Johnston, Jessica L. 135
Johnston, Robin 357
Johnston, Thomas 263
Jonah (Archbishop) 145
Jones, A. M. 78
Jones, Abraham 78
Jones, Barbara E. 84
Jones, C. Stephen 255
Jones, Cassandra 172
Jones, Clifton 147
Jones, Collin 77
Jones, Dale 25
Jones, Dana 340
Jones, Danny K. 332
Jones, Darlene 160
Jones, Elbert 99
Jones, G. Daniel 265
Jones, Greg 198
Jones,
    Jacqueline 255, 256
Jones, Jerry 176
Jones, Jesse 173
Jones, Jill 88
Jones, Joyce 211
Jones, Juliette 39
Jones, Kenneth E. 86, 326
Jones, LaJuanda 140
Jones, Larry 198

Jones, Lindsay E. 90
Jones, Paul Griffin, II 254
Jones, Paxton 85
Jones, Perry, III 25
Jones, Ralph E. 116
Jones, Scott J. 174, 175
Jones, Serene 314
Jones, Stephen M. 103
Jones, Terrence J. 59
Jones, Verity A. 329
Jones, Verlene 270
Jones, William H. 299
Jordan, Anthony L. 163
Jordan, Deborah 121
Jordan, Joe 316
Jordan, Larry W. 307
Joseph, Emmanuel 67
Joseph, Igumen 146
Joseph, Thomas 66
Joshua (Bishop) 166
Jost, Randy 188
Joudrey, Patricia 292, 293
Joudrey, Philip 322
Jourdain, Cheryl 213
Joyce, Tom 270
Judge, Beverly 31, 39
Julien, Tom 119
Julius, Nambafu 122
Julliot, Brent 330
Jung, Hee-Soo 174
Jupin, J. Michael 249
Justman, James A. 115

K

Kaada, Virginia 260
Kaaua, Judy 138
Kaboth, Kurt 38
Kadden, Daniel 271
Kahaian, Nancy 151
Kahn, Doug 45
Kai, Matthew 267
Kaiser, John 348
Kalamba, Patrice T. 92
Kalcik, Sharon K. 255
Kalikow, Barnett 271
Kalmar, Laura 349
Kalyniuk, Bohdan 168
Kammerer, Charlene
    Payne 175
Kandel, Andrea C. 37
Kanhouse, Kevin S. 115
Kao, Monica 263
Kapanke, John G. 114
Kapeluck, Michael 168
Kapeluck-Nixon,
    Natalie 168
Kaplan, Clemis
    Eugene 167
Kapteyn, John 208
Karaman, Dennis G. 131
Karanja, Benson M. 297
Karim, Aphrem 167

Karrott, Sandra 266
Karsten, Albert 88
Kaseman,
    Mansfield M. 250
Kasimer, Sol 54
Kathryn, Perri 45
Katra, Ilia 60
Katz, Virginia 263
Kauffman, Cephas 349
Kaufman, Richard A. 349
Kaur, Anahat 237
Kaur, Sapreet 236
Kavanaugh, Susan 271
Kawimbe, Paul Jones
    Mulenga 57
Kay, James F. 342
Kays, Joanne 256
Kazanjian, Shant 71
Keaton, Jonathan D. 174
Keefe, Michael 31
Keeler, William
    Cardinal 42
Keener, Theresa 30
Keeney, Nancy 246
Kehler, Allen 201
Keiller, James B. 132
Keith, Raymond J., Jr. . . .101
Keller, Connie L. 358
Kelley, Charles S. 308
Kelley, Jessica 328
Kellum, Kelly 121
Kelly, Bridgette 358
Kelly,
    Francis D. . . .297, 305, 310
Kelly, Ronald D. 179
Kelly, Sue 268, 269
Kelly, Thomas 256
Kelly, William 83
Kemp, Linda 247
Kemp, Roger 40
Kemper, Ken 126
Kemper, Kenneth B. 302
Kendall, David W. 120
Kendall, Stephen 207
Kennaugh, R. S. 205
Kennebrew, Vernon 90
Kennedy, Alric 258
Kennedy, Joanne 326
Kennedy, Steve 351
Kent, Allen 63
Kent, Brian 141
Kent, Edgar 132
Kent, Lynn 141
Kenyon, Howard 263
Kepa, Peter Mar 128
Kern, Alexander
    Levering 250
Kerr-Wilson,
    Gregory K. 186
Kersey, John 69
Kersey, Tay E. 104
Kersten, David 112
Kersten,
    Nicholas J. 162, 353

INDEX

421

Kesohole, Erastus 121
Kessler, Angela 325
Kessler, Ken 30
Kessler, Mathew 334
Ketcham, Donald 177
Ketcham, Linda 272
Keurian, Alice 127
Keya, Peter Kiliswa 122
Keyes, Randy 176
Keys, Michael F. 114
Keyser, Judy E. 89
Khamis, Aprim 67
Khan, Abdool 34
Khan, Nasir 258
Khatchadorian,
    Arshag 241
Khayisie, Andrew
    Mulupi 122
Khayumbi, Moses S. 122
Khouri, Antoun 66
Khouri, Demetri 66
Kibble, Alvin M. 161
Kibisu, Midikira
    Churchil 122
Kidd, Jerry D. 77
Kidd, William B. 293
Kidwell, Gary W. 84
Kidziiri, John
    Musanga 122
Kieft, Gordon 241
Kiesey, Deborah L. 174
Kikis, Peter 127
Kilgallin, Mike 300
Kilgore, James 97
Killam, Gillis 51
Killoren, Eileen 240
Killpack, Jennifer 103
Kilyk, Gerard 104
Kim, Ko-Eun 270
Kim, Nam Soo 73
Kim, P. Gil 87
Kim, Seenam 304
Kimbrow, Terry 298
Kimer, Stan 178
Kimiya, Alex 122
Kincaid, Daisy 169
Kind, Kerry D. 179
King, Amy Harding 257
King, Arthur 107
King, Donald G. 161
King, Eileen 46
King, Eric 93
King, Fred G. 88
King, James R., Jr. 175
King, John 131
King, Johnny 214
King, Michael A. 301
King, Mike 178
King, Rachele 253
King, Stephen 22
King, Terry 153
Kinnaman, David 219
Kinnamon, Michael 38

Kinney, John W. 312, 315
Kintz, Bruce 135
Kireopoulos, Antonios 38
Kirk, Doug 121
Kirkland, Larry 57
Kirkland, T. Larry 57
Kisago, Timothy 122
Kishkovsky, Leonid 338
Kisiangani, Stephen
    Sikulu 121
Kitchen, Klon, Jr. 27
Kitchens, Sidney Lee 158
Klassen, Arli 36
Klaus, Byron D. 296
Klein, Stephen 252
Kleinfelter, Kenneth 176
Kline, Dale 261
Kline, T. 202
Kline, Thomas L. 125
Klinsing, P. David 88
Klusmeyer, William
    Michie 109
Klutz, C. H. 67
Knaggs, James 159
Kneafsey, Padraig 166
Kneece, Brenda Lynn 267
Knezevic, Drago 211
Knoebel, Thomas 310
Knoedler, Lon 271
Knol, Ron 88
Knoth, Rick 330
Knott, Bill 323
Knott, Felix 77
Knowles, Louis L. 46
Knox, Winston 101
Kochis, Michael 168
Kocian, Dorothy 177
Kocses, Richard 255
Koehn, Dale 95, 194
Koehn, Gladwin 336
Koelpin, Daniel 180
Koepke, Donald R. 40
Koh, Linda Mei Lin 161
Kohl, Ronald L. 79
Kohler, Ann 29
Koikoi, Stephen 122
Kokesch, William 52
Kolb, Leonard R. 141
Kolbaba, Ginger 335
Kolodny, Debra 233
Kolsti, Carol 29
Konieczny, Edward J. 109
Konkel, August H. 320
Konnerup, Jon 76
Kooistra, Paul D. 150
Kopka, Anthony D. 149
Koplow, Cordelia 248
Kopp, Herb 125
Koptak, Paul E. 329
Korpela, Paavo A. 206
Korson, Gerald 338
Kosanke, Charles G. 312
Koscak, Robert 304

Kostura, Carol 241
Kotrla, Claren 177
Kovacs, Luciano 39
Kowalski, Kelly 259
Kowley, Kate 325
Koziol, Edward 257
Krahn, Leona 348
Kramer, Melvin F. 92
Krashel, Rosemary 349
Krebill, Dan 254
Krehbiel, Don 118
Krell, Barbara 244
Krestick, Robert C. 204
Krey, Philip D. W. 306
Krieger, Randy 319
Krieger,
    Randy H. 95, 194, 195
Kriese, Paul 121
Kring, S. 188
Kriska, Chloe Ann 261
Kristof, Dennis 168
Kroeker, Irvin J. 350
Kroeze, Nicholas V. 305
Krog, Karin 90
Kropp, Sarah 37
Krouse, Robert W. 89
Kruesel, Thomas 204
Krutz,
    C. Dana 30, 33, 36, 249
Krywolap, George 168
Krywonos, Mykola 168
Ku, Jeoffery 301
Kucharek, Wilma S. 116
Kuchta, Thomas W. 135
Kuhlman, Dexter 117
Kuhn, Robert 135
Kuliczkowski,
    Czeslaw 149
Kumka, Evhen 168
Kumm, Michael 135
Kun, Zolton 129
Kunder, William 213
Kunselman, James 60
Kuntaraf, Jonathan 161
Kurklin, Joanne 263
Kurtz, Calvin 266
Kurtz, Joseph E. 81
Kusserow, Kurt F. 116
Kutash, Ihor 294
Kutter, Joseph 63
Kuykendall, Russell 193
Kvam, Roger A. 36
Kwan, Joseph 347
Kweri, Chaplen
    Luyimba 65
Kwok, Jack P. 163
Kwok, Meggy 48
Kyrill (Archbishop) 159

L

La Valla, Deborah 340
Lacey, Jon 85

Lacey, Paul 22
Lachatanere, Diana 355
Lacy, Homer, Jr. 247
Ladefaged, Jenny 29
Lage, Eerika 199
Lai, David J. H. 109
Lake, Jan 147
Lakey, Othal H. 87
Lakusta, Victor 212
Lallo, Cecelia 339
Lamarre-Vincent,
    David 255
Lamb, Dan 76
Lamb, Jerry A. 109
Lambie, Rosemary 213
Lamm, Norman 310
Lamm, Tim 121
Lamothe, Richard 191
LaMotte, David 261
Lamson, Shirley 250
Lancaster, Delores 59
Lance, Paul 241
Lance, Rick 163
Land, Richard D. 163
Land,
    Steven J. 95, 194,
                        195, 299
Landon, Dennis L. 84
Lane, Dan G. 248
Lane, Gwendolyn 172
Lane, Hardist 244
Lane, Patty 41
Lane, Stephen T. 109
Lanes, T. A. 73
Lang, Christy 125
Lang, Kristy 125
Lang, Kurt 125
Langille, Fran 251
Langley, Ken 82
Langlois,
    Charles 318, 319
Langsfeld, Paul J. 310
Langston, Ken Brooker . . .34
Larade, Sharon 360
Lariviere, Marilyn 250
Larkin, Michael 130
Larom, Margaret S. 108
Larrabee, Arthur 148
Larsen, David 355
Larson, Duane H. 315
Larson, Paul 100
Lassen, John 245
Last, Michael A. 115
Lau, David 100
Lau, Jennifer 350
Laughlin, Robert 260
Laurence, Steven B. 265
Laurus
    (Archbishop) 338, 339
Lav, Iris 243
Lavanhar, Marlin 263
Lavelle, Peggy 24
Lavigne, David P. 199

Lawrence, James F. 314
Lawrence, Mark J. 109
Lawrence, Stephen 166
Lawrence, William B. 309
Lawson, Jim 34
Lawson, Joyce 262
Lawson, Phil 240
Lawton, Fraser W. 185
Lawton, Gordon 162
Lawton, Gordon P. 312
Lay, Bertha 264
Layne, Samuel A. 147
Lazar (retired
    Archbishop) 145
Leath, Jeffrey N. 57
Leavitt, Robert F. 311
Ledesma, Juanita 268
Lee, Chesie 272
Lee, Darrel D. 70, 332
Lee, David H. 163
Lee, Jacob 343
Lee, Jeffrey D. 109
Lee, Linda 174
Lee, Peter 252
Lee, Peter James 109
Lee, Rob 163
Lee, Robert 298
Lee, Terri 255
Leech, David 267
Leegwater, Arie 339
Leeland, Paul L. 175
Leeper, Trubbie R. 59
Leet, Ian 256
Leflore, David 23
LeGatt, Albert 209
Legge, W. James 263
Lehenbauer, Joel D. 135
Lehman, Edwin 204
Lehman, Richard 258
Lehmann,
    Daniel J. 114, 334
Leigh, Charles 67, 243
Leiper, Henry Smith 45
Leman, Bruce 341
Lemming, Patrick 166
Lemon, Robert E. 161
Lemon, Thomas L. 161
Lennick, Robert B. 42
Leonard, Bill 96, 194, 195
Leonard, Claire 121, 158
Leonard, Darnell 264
Leopold, Phyllis J. 241
Lepper, John 248
LeRoy,
    J. Douglas 95, 194, 195
Leslie, David A. 263
Leslie, Susan 34
Leszczuk, Mary Lee 168
Lettini, Gabriella 23
Leumas, Emilie 24
Leung, Donna 188
LeValley, Elizabeth 257
Levandoski, Michele 24

Levering, William 259
Lévesque, Michèle 319
Levy, B. Barry 319
Lew, Khristina 47
Lewis, Beth A. 114
Lewis, Brad 350
Lewis, C. A. 99
Lewis, D. Ray 139
Lewis, Ed 119
Lewis, Harry 214
Lewis, James W. 224
Lewis, Marc 151
Lewis, Parker 246
Lewis, Richard Allen 57
Lewis, Robert L. 39
Lewis, Robert L., Jr. 68
Lewis, Wilbur 153
Lewis, William L. 103
L'Heureux,
    N. J. L., Jr. 259
L'Heureux,
    N. J., "Skip" 257
Liberto, Thomas M. 98
Licht, Reginald 123
Liggett, J. D. 180
Likis, Betty 238
Lillback, Peter A. 316
Lillibridge, Gary R. 109
Lim, Jimmy Seong G. . . .257
Lima, David 251
Lin, Tom 34
Linaman, Larry 303
Lincoln, Laura
    Vaught 269
Lindbeck, Roberta 247
Lindner, Eileen W. 38
Lindquist, Tonia I. 114
Lindsay, Emery 90
Linsey, Nathaniel L. 87
Linsinbigler, Harry 168
Liolin, Arthur E. 60
Lipps, Robert T. 28
Lisby, Mike 58, 342
Lisherness, Sara 151
Little, Edward S., II 109
Little, Jeannine 247
Little, P. 94
Little, Vanuel C. 147
Litwin, Paul A. 258
Liu, Felix 306
Liu-Beers, Chris 260
Livesay, Don 161
Livingston,
    Michael E. 38, 130
Lobenstine, Clark 37, 243
Lockwood, Daniel R. 308
Lofquist, Les 129
Logsdon, Gary B. 263
Lohre, Kathryn 38, 224
Lohrmann, Marcus C. 115
Lombard, Ted 270
Long, Sotello V. 85
Lopez, Lynne Smouse . . .263

INDEX

423

Lopoukhine, Nikita 205
Lopushinsky, Roman 205
Lorah, Ted, Jr. 192
Lorency,
    David B. 96, 194, 195
Lorentzen, Paul 75
Lorimer, Paul D. 193, 194
Lott, William R. 141
Loucks, Mel 304
Loughery, H. David 41
Loughran, James 32, 329
Louttit, Henry I., Jr. 109
Love, Jan 298
Love, Joshua 178
Love,
    Mary A. 59, 325, 327
Love, Ralph E., Sr. 173
Love, William H. 109
Love-Jones, Vivian 29
Lovett, Leonard 34
Lovingood, Vivian 266
Lowe, Asa 132
Lowe, Derwin 123
Lowe, S. L. 94
Lowen, A. Wayne 302
Lowery, Joseph Echols 34
Lowry, Michael J. 175
Lowry, Randolph, III 306
Loy, David 246
Lubek, Egbert 194
Lucco, Richard 112
Lucero, Karina 22
Ludeki, Ephraim
    Mudoga 122
Ludwig, Robert A. 306
Luginbill, Betty 29
Luginbuhl, David 51
Luke (Father) 338, 339
Luke (Murianka) 303
Lull, Patricia J. 254
Lumasia, Gerishom 122
Lummis, Adair 340
Lumpe, Larry 135, 356
Luna, Leonardo 92
Lundgren, Dean A. 112
Lundgren, Jim 34
Lundgren, Renee 253
Lundy, Sarah E. 96
Lunich, Nedeljko 338
Lupas, Liana 354
Lutatabio, Véronique
    Lusieboko 46
Lutes, Christopher 327
Luthy, David 205, 348
Luz, David W. 160
Luzano, Christine 31
Lyght, Ernest S. 174, 271
Lyke, Lonnie 97
Lykins, Terry 132
Lyle, Dennis J. 308, 315
Lyles, J. H., Jr. 93
Lynch, Brenda S. 84
Lynch, Damon, III 261

Lyon, Jo Anne 179
Lyons, Marsha 28
Lysyj, Anatol 168
Lytch, Carol E. 305

M

MacDonald, Timothy 32
Macharia, Fred M. 135
Mack, Lynda 243
Mack, Paget 69
MacKenzie, Daryl 198
MacKenzie, Margaret 55
Mackey, Bill F. 163
Macklin, J. W. 94
Macklin, Jerry 42
Mackoul, Anne Glynn 45
MacLagan, Bill 250
MacLeod, Laurel 337
MacMillan, Clair 197
MacPherson, D. Bruce . . .109
MacPherson, Damian 293
Madden,
    Thomas A. 95, 195
Maddo, Robert 243
Maggs, Robert W., Jr. 151
Magid, Mohamed 231
Magie, Sandra 315
Magness, James B. 108
Magnus, Brian 213
Magnus, Paul 51
Maher, D'Arcy 30
Maher, Philip 54
Mahlay, Ihor 168
Maier, Paul L. 135
Main, Donald 265
Maki, Lynn I. 213
Makokha,
    Joseph Mamai 121
Malcolm, Barbara 241
Malcolm, W. R. Matt 167
Maldonado, Luis
    Fernando Hoyos 192
Malherbe,
    Jean-François 322
Malick, William W. 88
Malimo, Churchill 122
Malina, Helen 258
Mallinak, John 338
Malloy, David 81
Maly, Milton 325
Manahan, Ron 119
Manahan,
    Ronald E. 119, 302
Mangassarian, Silva 188
Mankin, Bill 272
Mann, David 138
Mann, Eric 80
Mann, Gayle 246
Mann, Rick 300
Mann, Stuart 346
Manning, Donald 147
Manning, Leslie 249

Manning, Robert 316
Manon, John C. 117
Manousos, Anthony 331
Manseau, William 31
Mansholt, Gerald L. 115
Mansour,
    Anthony 49, 347
Mansur, Mary 338
Mantha, Ray 54
Mantz, Dough 242
Mapson, Charlrean B. 59
Maracle, John E. 73
Marangos, Frank 127
March-MacCuish,
    Faith 214
Marcis, Albert M. 135
Marcoux, Gerard 143
Mardirossian,
    Moushegh 71
Marek, James 177
Marini, Christine 131
Mark (Bishop) 145
Marks, Kirk 112
Markuly, Mark S. 312
Markus, Carol O. 47
Marold, Antoinette 31
Marquardt, Kami L. 262
Marrin, Patrick 326
Marsh, Fred 336
Marsh, Jack 261
Marsh, Stephen G. 115
Marshall, Dennis 211
Marshall, Jay Wade 301
Marshall, Molly T. 298
Marshall, Paul 51
Marshall, Paul V. 109
Martens, Ed 201
Martin, Clyde 176
Martin, J. Bruce 157
Martin, J. Dwayne 268
Martin, Joe 96, 97, 340
Martin, John A. 308
Martin, John David 326
Martin, Joseph 266
Martin, Joyce Emery 151
Martin, Ken 177
Martin, Paul E. 64
Martin, Paul H. 176
Martin, Paul M. 295
Martinez, Danielline 68
Martinez, Juan
    Verdugo 75
Martini, Jeromey 319
Martino, Joseph 265
Martinson, Bradley 100
Marty, Martin 328
Marvel, Misha 256
Marx, Robert 34
Masliuk, Stephen 168
Maslo, William 266
Mason, Debra 43
Mason, H. Lee 340
Massa, Mark 297

424

Massey, Anthony 264
Massey, Stephen K. 64
Mast, Gregg A. 308
Masters, Mary 258
Matchett, Darla 187
Mathai, Anish 46
Mathes, James R. 109
Mathew, Chacko 137
Mathew, Ciby 136
Mathew, Thomson K. 309
Mathewes, Charles T. 333
Mathews, George 126
Mathews,
Vaughn D. 95, 194
Mathiesen, Tim 100
Mathonnet-VanderWell,
Steve 339
Matiosian, Valtan 71
Matiz, Jose Ruben
Garcia 192
Matoon, Gordon 245
Matossian, Joseph D. 187
Matson, Lois 326
Matson, Louise 252
Matthews, Clayton 108
Matthews, Daniel
Paul 31, 39
Matthews, F. Clayton 108
Matthews, Marcus 174
Matthias
(Bishop-Elect) 145
Mattis, Janet 260
Maturan, Zenaida 46
Matusiak, John 338
Mauney, James F. 116
Maus, Janet 166
Maxim (Bishop) 160
Maximiuk, Eugene 351
Maximiuk, Gene 212
Maximos
(Metropolitan) 126
Maximus (Bishop) 71
Maxwell, Anita 268
Maxwell, Arthur W. 317
Maxwell,
James D., III 301
May, David G. 251
Mayan, Ralph 52, 204
Maye, James A. 101
Mayer, J. Scott 109
Maynard, J. L. 94
Mays, Rod 150, 151
Mazur, Francis X. 258
McAdam, Kerry 120, 121
McAfee, Kenneth 249
McAlister, John 348
McAllister, Julius, Sr. 57
McAllister-Wilson,
David F. 316
McAlpin, Allan 197
McAssee, Oral 202
McCain, Jacquelyn B. . . .173
McCallister, Cline 132

McCandles,
Christopher . .118, 121, 269
McCann, Gordon 345
McCartin, Joseph A. 34
McCarty, Vince S. 144
McClain, Erma 70
McClain, Gene 63
McClain, Richard 97
McClatchie, Stephen 319
McCleland, Rob 204
McCloskey, Pat 341
McCloud, E. Earl, Jr. 57
McColgin, Linda 256
McCollum, Odell 172
McConnell, Alvester 173
McCool, Marilyn 101
McCormack, Alan 209
McCormick, Pat 302
McCown, Sue 268
McCoy, Glenda 269
McCoy, James E. 58
McCoy, Myron F. 311
McCray, Trinette 63
McDaniel, Roxanne 147
McDermott, Pat 248
McDonald, Carol 151
McDonald, Delores 74
McDonald,
Jamey S. 188, 189
McDonald, Janet 213
McDonald, Jeff 344
McDonnell, Carol 246
McDonough, Linda 124
McDowell, Andrew
Reesor 204
McEmrys, Aaron 34
McFadden, Joyce 31
McFadden, Wendy 89
McFarland, Colleen 356
McFarland, James K. 157
McFarlane, Dorothy 59
McGarvey, Ken 104, 331
McGibbon, Carol
Ann 44
McGinnis, Pat 160
McGinnis,
Robert S., Jr. 134
McGrath, J. 292
McGregor, John 350
McGuire, Damaris 259
McGuire,
G. Dennis 95, 194, 195
McJunkin, James E. 62
McKain, George E., II 59
McKay, Ginger 177
McKea, David 269
McKee, David 151
McKee, Joan 245
McKenith, William 59
McKenzie, Megan 318
McKenzie, Vashti
Murphy 57
McKinney, Calvin 140

McKinney, G. D. 94
McKnight, James E. 96
McKnight, John 22
McLarty,
Alan 166, 172, 263
McLaughlin,
Bryon K. 332
McLaughlin, Scott 145
McLaughlin, Scott E. 300
McLaverty, John 48
McMahan, Steven C. 157
McMahon, P. John 135
McMillan, Otis T. 59
McMillan, Sean 44
McMillin-Goodwin,
Christy 105
McMillon, Lynn 326
McMullen, Shawn 334
McNair, David C. 36
McNally, Beverly 256
McNamara, Dexter 240
McNamara, Mary 26
McNamara, Mary E. 315
McNaughton,
Robert D. 241, 242
McNeese, Mark 269
McNish, Mary Ellen 22
McNiven, Don 80
McPhail, Paul 203
McPherson, Jeffrey A. 50
McQueen, Arpie 324
Meade, Kenneth 86
Meador, Clyde 163
Meador,
Prentice A., Jr. 323
Meagher, Timothy 353
Mean, John D. 214
Mecham, Marilyn 255
Medinger, Daniel L. 325
Medley, A. Roy 38, 62
Meeks, Bill 117
Meisner, Lorne 189
Mekhsian, Sipan 336
Melchisedek
(Bishop) 71, 145
Melkonian, Mgedich 187
Mellis, John 320
Melton, David 297
Melton, J. Gordon 223
Memphill, Rick 87
Menden, Harvey Allan . . .135
Mendez, Jose Manuel 138
Mendoza, Salvador 42
Mengel, Gail 29
Meno, John 167
Mercer, Amy 249
Mercer, Larry A. 298
Mercurius (Bishop) 146
Merrill, John 64
Merrill, L. J. 65
Mertz, Douglas 120
Meschisen, Eugene 168
Meschisen, Mark 169

INDEX

425

Mesenbring, David 41
Mesiti, Martha 42
Messer, Tom 314
Messiah, Wilfred J. 57
Messias, Pedro 132
Messick, Sandra 85
Metclaf, Jeffrey K. 305
Methodios
  (Metropolitan) 126
Metzger, Judy 259
Metzger, Laura 248
Metzger, Willard 204
Meyer, Dale A. 300
Meyer, Don 315
Meyer, Donald L. 112
Meyer, Elizabeth 120
Meyer, Kurt 38
Meyer, Ron 117
Meyer, Russell L. 243
Mgonja, Assah E. 46
Miamen, Amos B. 88
Micevych, Paul 168
Mich, Marvin K. 257
Michael (Bishop) 145
Michalak, Keith 125
Michelle, Lisa H. 251
Michener, Wendy 121
Micon, Joseph 245, 246
Middendorf, Edward 259
Middendorf, Jesse C. 101
Middleton, J. Richard 50
Middleton, Jane Allen . . .174
Miericke, Kurt A. 112
Mikoski, Gordon S. 342
Mikovsky,
  Anthony A. 312, 332
Mikulski, Mary Jo 245
Milazzo, Louis 69
Miles, Ray 84
Milks, Bob 201
Millen, George 110
Miller, A. Kathleen 293
Miller, Alan C. 172
Miller, Carole 243
Miller,
  Claude E. W. 185, 186
Miller, Cynthia Fisher 269
Miller, Daniel P. 88
Miller, Elizabeth 138
Miller, G. 94
Miller, Gene E. 267
Miller, George 300
Miller, George L. 111
Miller, Jean 34
Miller, Jeffrey A. 87
Miller, JoyAnn 323
Miller, Larry 138
Miller, Marcus J. 306
Miller, Michael 209
Miller, Paul L. 78, 325
Miller, Peter 258
Miller, Randy 336
Miller, Rick 104

Miller, Steven A. 109
Miller, Ted 244
Miller, Terry 262
Miller, Wayne N. 115
Milliken, Michael P. 109
Milliken, Paul 267
Milliken, Richard D. 308
Mills, Bob 163
Mills, Margaret 85
Mills, Wes 187
Miloro, Frank P. 63
Milsap, Cynthia 45
Miner, Dave 26
Miner, Nancy B. 90
Ming, Wayman C., Jr. 147
Minnix, Janet 119
Minor, Marlene 142
Miranda, Jesse, Jr. 73
Miranda, Randy 252
Mirchuk, Nadia 168
Mirek, Art 64
Mitchell,
  Anne 121, 185, 191
Mitchell, Christine 50
Mitchell, James K. 90
Mitchell, Lisa H. 251
Mitchell, Lois P. 198
Mitchell, Philip 250
Mitchelle, Anne 120
Mitchem, Susan 353
Mitrophan (Bishop) 160
Mittman, F. Russell 171
Mmbwavi, Joseph 121
Mobley, John P. 84
Mock, George 251
Moe, Sharon 270
Moes, D. 348
Moffett, Marilyn 245
Mogenson, Cris 256
Mohler, R. Albert, Jr. 313
Mohr, Ken 265
Mojica, Miguel 196
Molczanski, Mark 202
Moldstad, John A. 116
Molinari, Cynthia
  Woolever 26
Mollard, Tikhon 312
Molsberry, Robert 171
Molyneux, John 343
Moncher,
  Gary 95, 194, 195
Moneymaker,
  Richard 257
Monforton, Jeffrey M. . . .310
Monroe, Kenneth 57, 58
Monson, Thomas S. 98
Montañez, Felipe
  Lozada 116
Monteith, Fred 213
Montgomery, Charles 59
Montgomery,
  Kathleen C. 169
Montgomery, Richard . . .240

Mood, Jacques 141
Moody, C. L. 94
Moon, Angelia 267
Mooney, Paul 176
Moore, Alexis 22
Moore, Clark 269
Moore, Donna J. 262
Moore, Graham 211
Moore, Hugh 245
Moore, Karen 246
Moore,
  Kenneth W. 82, 85, 255
Moore, Larry R. 161
Moore, Marlyn 259
Moore, Marvin 341
Moore, P. J. 104
Moore, R. Douglas 206
Moore,
  Robert A. 95, 194, 195
Moore, Sharon 138
Moore, Thomas E. 64
Moore, Willis 243
Moore-Leamon, Silver . . .249
Moorhead, Gaye 239
Moorhead, James H. 333
Morales, Bernardo 169
Morales, Jorge 171
Morales, Jose, Jr. 84
Morales, Peter 169
Moran,
  Carlos S. 95, 194, 195
Morante, Alfredo 109
Moreno, Rene 111
Morgan, Donn F. 299
Morgan, Robert 170
Morin, Darci 246
Morin, Geof 22
Morissette, Pierre 209
Morris, Adrienne A. 345
Morris, Calvin S. 244
Morris, Derek J. 336
Morrison, Ronald J 87
Morrow, William 319
Morse, Daniel R. 157
Morton, Cristopher 270
Morton, Darrell D. 114
Morton, Karon 34
Morton, Raymond E. 157
Moses, Tom D. 97
Mosher, Lucinda 44
Mosley, Steve 267
Mott, Ben 63
Moulton, Geoff 348, 351
Moulton, Jean 210
Moultrie, Henry A., II . . .101
Moury, Frederick, Jr. 112
Mouw, Richard 26
Mouw, Richard J. 302
Mowatt, Ann 55
Moxham, John 267
Moxley, Susan E. 186
Moyer, Bruce 111, 315
Moyer, David 171

426

Mphahlele, Louis 75
Muchow, Donald 135
Mudoga, Lucas 121
Mueller, George 83
Mueller, Herbert C. 135
Mueller, Herbert C., Jr. . . .135
Mufarrij, Alexander 66
Mugalavai, James 121
Muganda, Patrick L. 122
Muhadi, Ephraim
   Konzolo 121
Mullan, Donald W. 351
Mullan, Donald Wm. 192
Muller, Marilyn 351
Muller, Ralf 135
Mulvaney, Elizabeth 266
Mumford, J. David 264
Munday, Robert S. 308
Mungons, Kevin 324
Munro, Victor 293
Muravski, Adolfo 206
Murdoch, John 38
Murdy, Peter W. 104
Murianka, Luke 303
Murphy, D. J. 292, 293
Murphy, Sue 244
Murphy, Susan 244
Murphy,
   Thomas 336, 339
Murphy, Tom 138
Murray, Billy D. 97
Murray, Billy D., Sr. 195
Murray, Edward J. 31, 39
Murray, Harold 53
Murray, James W. 124
Murray, Lydia 44
Murray, Michele 50
Murray, Randy 351
Murray, Scott R. 135
Murray, Yolanda 258
Murry, George V. 81
Musoke, Alan 62
Mussa, Joan 46
Mussatt, David 244
Musudia, Zebedee 122
Musungu, Philip
   Wasike 121
Mutende, Humphrey 121
Mutoigo, Ida Kaastra 89
Mutti, Albert F. 30
Muyskens, Samuel 36
Muzingo, Cathy 148
Mwavali, Gerishom 121
Myers, Andrew 198
Myers, Deborah 25
Myers, Jerry 64
Myers, Joe 96
Myers, Melvin, Jr. 92
Myers-Wirt, Cathy 85

N

Naff, Stephen 124
Nahoolewa, Connie 269

Nainggolan,
   Kalmen E. 92
Nakonachny, John 168
Narula,
   Raymond 202, 203
Narum, Mark E. 114
Nash, Justin 335
Naten, Loyd L. 147
Nathaniel
   (Archbishop) 145
Neal, Carl J 92
Neal, Joseph C., Jr. 86
Neal, Kenneth 258
Nectaria (Nun) 340
Nederveen, G. 191
Neelands, David 322
Nees, Tom 101
Neevel, Mary Ann 271
Nelson, Beter T. 70
Nelson, Christine L. 264
Nelson, Dean W. 114
Nelson, Elden K. 74
Nelson, Gart 190, 191
Nelson, Gary V. 322
Nelson, Jerome O. 112
Nelson, Jodi 253
Nelson, Kim Beyer 255
Nelson, Russell M. 98
Nelson, Saundra 130
Nelson, Steven L. 271
Nelson-Pallmeyer,
   Sara 252
Nemkovich,
   Robert M. 149, 312
Nenson, Daniel 210
Nesmith, Virginia 39
Netterfield, Cal 189
Neufeld, John 50, 320
New, Rebecca 247
Newhouse, Herbert 152
Newland, Terry 151
Newport, Leroy 79
Newton, Alan 62
Newton, Douglas M. 334
Ney, David 50
Ng, Don 62
Ng, G. T. 161
Ngoya, John W. 122
Ngurukiri, Renison
   Mbogo 92
Nguyen, Tai Anh 88
Nguyen, Tai Binh
   Phan 65
Nicholas, David 313
Nicholas, Zachariah
   Mar 136
Nicholas
   (Metropolitan) 127
Nichols, Terrence L. 88
Nicholson, Betty 123
Nickleson, Isaac 245
Nicoll, Niel 47
Nielsen, Pamela 134

Nielson, E. Kenneth 34
Nielson, Niel 150, 151
Nieto, Amelia 240
Nieuwsma, Virginia 332
Nieves, Ramon 45
Nikkel, Lynn 163
Nikolai (Bishop) 146
Nikon (Bishop) 145
Niles, Dennis D. 314
Nippak, Ivar 199
Niswender, Joy 257
Nix, Lan 267
Njegovan, James D. 185
Noble, John 351
Noble, Kathy 333
Noble, Mary 351
Noel, Michael D. 88
Noffsinger, Stanley J. 89
Nolan, Michael 124
Nolan-Elliason,
   Megan 252
Nolde, Nancy L. 265
Noli, Fan Stylian 60
Nolla, Ormara 46
Nolting, Paul 100
Nordgren, Keith 252
Norgren, Phil 242
Norlin, Dennis A. 23
Norman, Clarence 107
Norman,
   David A. 74, 301
Norman, Ron 204
Norris, Jeffrey A. 88
Norris, John 121
Norris, Richard
   Franklin 57
Norton, Jon 257, 259
Norton, Larry 268
Norton, Michael 135
Norton,
   Timothy A. 36, 342
Norvell, David 77
Norvell, John 147
Norwood, Matthew A. . . .101
Notch, Peter 260
Novak, Mark A. 112
Novecosky, Peter . . .209, 350
Nsofwa, Alfred 92
Nunes, John A. 36
Nunn, Harry, Sr. 73
Nusca, A. Robert 321
Nyenhuis, Ron 252
Nyenzo, Evans 121
Nyquist, Paul 307

O

Oakes, Gwyn 176
Oakes, Ronald L. 298
Oaks, Dallin H. 98
Oancea,
   David 159, 210, 341
Obengerger, Glenn 116

O'Brien, Brendan 209
Ocansey, Edmund 253
Ochoa-Krueger,
  Ninfa 268
O'Day, Gail R. 315
Odegaard, Edward 91
Odhner, Carroll C. 358
Odom, Elzie 268
O'Donnell, Frances 358
Oeswein, Craig 249
O'Farrell, Mark T. 314
O'Flaherty,
  Edward 36, 251
Ogilvie, Kevin A. 319
Ogilvie, Rob 191
Ogles, Jerry L. 342
O'Hara, Robert J. 265
Ohl, C. Wallis, Jr. 109
Ohotin, Nicholas A. 159
Ojeda-Carcamo,
  Sergio 301, 312
Okang'a, Seth
  Shikunzi 121
Oldham,
  Roger S. 162, 163, 341
Olekshy, Ovest 205
Olinger, Danny E. . . .146, 337
Oliver, Julia 22
Oliver, Lon D. 23
Oliver, Willie 161
Oliver, Willie B. 157
Olsen, Donald P. 139
Olsen, Rob 28
Olsen, Ron 213
Olsen, Sandra 242
Olsen, Ted 30
Olson, Mark 304
Olson, Norman A. 324
Olszewski, Brian T. 325
Olubalang, Alan A. 64
O'Malley, Sean 81
O'Malley, Todd 34
Ominde, Epainitus
  Adego 121
Omondi, Samuel
  Kaguli 121
O'Neal, Dennis 34
O'Neill,
  Jerry F. 157, 302, 310
O'Neill, Robert J. 109
Onyewuchi, Rufus 292
Oosting, Ken 316
Orcino, Danilo M. 92
O'Reilly, Pat 239
Orians, Thomas 32
Orlando, Peter 169
Orsini, Vanda 213
Ortiz, Francisco 299
Ortiz, Milton 106
Osborn, Sharon 252
Osborne, Brenda 64
Osborne, Fred C. 319
Osborne, Linda 271

Osguthorpe, Russell T. 98
Oskins, Deborah 262
Osmok, Paula 52
Osodo, Lam Kisanya 122
Ottenhoff, Don B. 221
Otzelberger,
  E. Ann 141, 142
Ouellet, M. Bertrand 209
Ough, Bruce R. 174
Ousley, S. Todd 109
Oussoren, Harry 213
Overland, Jon 196
Overlien, Dennis 135
Overton, Tommy 117
Owen, David L. 309
Owen, Dean 46
Owen, Joe 142
Owen, Timothy P. 88
Owens, C. D. 94
Owens, Darrel 61
Owens,
  Thomas M., Sr. 342

P

Pabst, Michael 91
Pace, Diane 332
Packard, George 108
Packer, Boyd K. 98
Padilla, Rafael
  Malpica 114
Paez, Leticia 47
Pagano, Nicholas 22
Page, Frank S. 162, 163
Page, Jerry N. 161
Paige, Lavette 265
Palla, Prasad 46
Palmer, Gregory V. 174
Palmer, Herb 115
Palmer, Michael 310
Palmer, Susan L. 352
Palmieri, Paul 98
Papazian, Iris 338
Paperini, Richard 308
Pappas, Anthony 62
Paprocki, Thomas 24, 81
Paquette, Mario 209
Parchia, Earl 147
Pardy, Marion 292
Park, C. Michael 161
Park, Jeremiah J. 174
Parke, Jim 270
Parker, B. Aaron 253
Parker, George Lee 85
Parker, Jane 247
Parker, Rebecca 314
Parker, William 157
Parkinson, Ward 201
Parks, J. H. 97
Parkyn, David I. 112
Parrish, Donny 76, 77
Parrish, Terry 61
Parrish, Walter L., II 62

Parrish,
  Walter L., III 152, 153
Parshall, Janet 40
Parsley, Henry Nutt, Jr. 109
Parsons, Earline 135
Parsons, Gradye 151
Parsons, Reginald 151
Parsons, Robert G. 207
Pasbrig, Robert 180
Paslay, Mormon, II 176
Pastukhiv, Serhij K. 128
Patel, Bomi 237
Patterson, Deborah 112
Patterson, J. O., Jr. 94
Patterson, L. Dale 356
Patterson, Paige 313
Patton, Marcia 62
Patton, Vince 342
Paulsen, Vivian 331
Paulsen, Wayne 62
Paulson, Bob 329
Pavichevich, Dennis 160
Payne, Aleta 260
Payne, James T. 156
Payne, Margaret G. 116
Payson, Barbara 250
Peale, Norman Vincent 26
Pearson, John 26, 28, 250
Peck, Roger 87
Peddicord, Richard A. . . .295
Pederson, Duane C. 115
Pediso, Marlene 122
Pediso, Steve 122
Peeler, Owen 261
Peifer, Elvin H. 80
Pelchat, Marc 322
Pellechia,
  James N. 133, 204
Pelles, Ros 33
Pelley, Barry D. 207
Peluso-Verdend, Gary 309
Pena, Carlos E. 114
Pence, Jerry G. 179
Pendergast, Arthur J. 293
Pendleton, J. M. 61
Penfield, Jack 242
Penner, Rick 51
Penner, Ron . . .194, 201, 318
Pennywell,
  Clarence C. 140
Penrose, Christina 59
Pentecost, Patricia 307
Peoples, David 153
Peplowski, Thaddeus S. . .149
Pepper, Gail 265
Perkins, D. Clay 307
Perkins, James C. 153
Perkins, Joseph E. 295
Perkins, Larry 320
Perkins,
  Loveleen "Dee" 59
Perkins, William T. 308
Perkins-Hughes, Vera 172

Perpener, A. 94
Perry, L. Tom 98
Perschbacher, Gerald 335
Persson, Bertil 69
Peterkin, Valzie 242
Peters, Arthur 264
Peters, Donald 36, 53
Peters, Judith 262
Peters, Marshall 62
Peters, Ronald E. 304
Peters, Samuel R., Sr. 101
Petersen, Rodney L. 36
Peterson, Cartis D. 113
Peterson,
  Cathy Norman 329
Peterson, David 38
Peterson, Diana
  Franzusoff 354
Peterson, Dwayne A. 356
Peterson, Kathleen 257
Peterson, Nancy 260
Peterson, Wendy 51
Petersoo, U. 348
Petersoo, Udo 199
Petitt, Charles W. 310
Petlak, Michael 168
Petro, John G. 298
Petrochuk, Sherrie 261
Petroff, Valerie 48
Peucker, Paul 356
Peverini, Miguel
  Valdivia/Milton 329
Pezzulo, Neil 32
Pfortmiller, Sandra 337
Pfrimmer, David 322
Phelan,
  John E., Jr. 112, 308
Phillips, Annie Lee 259
Phillips, Carole 190
Phillips, Donald D. 186
Phillips, Stephen 103
Phinney, Allison 91
Phipps, Ron 138
Pierce, David 22, 318
Pierce, Glen A. 353
Pierce, Patrick 135
Pierre, Louis Marcel 75
Pihach, Dennis 205
Piita, Vaieli Fuiono 46
Pile, Gregory R. 116, 265
Pimentel, Juan 92
Pimentel, Serafin 92
Pinkard, Jacqueline R. 59
Pinkett, Leo 87
Pinson, J. Matthew 302
Pinson, Mathew 139
Piovesan, Luciano 209
Pipes, Carol 337
Pishko, Daria 168
Pitches, Donald M. 255
Pitman, Cyrus C. J. 186
Pitt, Benjamin A. 147
Pittman, Rob 317

Pittman,
  Wallace B., Jr. 148
Pitts, Clifford R. 172
Pitts, Tyrone 45
Pizzi, Rosa E. 268
Plantinga,
  Cornelius, Jr. 298
Platt, Allyson D. 251
Player, Michael 131
Pleva, Rich 171
Poe, James 24
Poesnecker, Gerald E. 98
Poest, Donald 154, 208
Pohl, Curtis 135
Pohl, Faye 40
Poirier, James S. 206
Poirier, Jim 197, 198
Poirier, Tim 352
Poist, William 60
Poitier, S. Annette 46
Poitras, François 209
Pokorny,
  Charlie Korin 229
Polite, William 156
Poliziani, Jay 265
Pollard, Alton B., III 304
Pollema, Vernon 155
Pollesel, Michael F. 185
Polston, Jimmy 160
Pomeroy, Betty 256
Pomykal, Janet 177
Pooler, David 247
Poon, Abraham H. 88
Pope, Deidre 253
Pope, Kenneth 64
Popovich, Edward 123
Popp, Nathaniel 159, 210
Porret, Jean 351
Porter, Jerry D. 101
Porter, John 122
Porter, Stanley E. 320
Porterfield, Amanda 327
Posterski, Don 54
Posthumus, Peter 153
Potter, Jim 197, 198
Potterveld,
  Riess W. 304, 305, 309
Pouliot, Etienne 346
Powell, Christopher 78
Powell, Dennis 124
Powell, F. Neff 109
Powell, George H. 292
Powell, Jerry 148
Powell, Joel 147
Powell, Joseph 157
Powell, Larry 139
Powell, Raymond, Sr. 99
Powell, S. J. 94
Powers, Vertie 172
Poznán, Béla 172
Poznikoff, Lisa 349
Prachar, T. 204
Prange, Paul T. 180

Preheim, Richard 335
Preheim-Bartel, Dean 245
Premawardhana,
  Shanta 44
President, D. S. 153
Presler, Titus L. 301
Preus, Daniel 135
Price, Kenneth L., Jr. 109
Price, R. 173
Price, Shane 154
Priest, Catherine 294
Primavera, Wendy 256
Priniski, Mary 34
Prior, Brian 109
Prior, Joseph G. 310
Pritchett, Wayne N. 321
Privett, John E. 185, 186
Probst, Delores Alt 271
Probus, Lawrence 47
Proctor, Dennis V. 58
Proctor, Matt 309
Proffitt, Kevin 355
Prosser, Robert 106
Provance, Terry 41
Provenzano, Lawrence . . .110
Pruter, Karl 82
Puck, Warren 135
Pue, Carson 51
Puglisi, Amy 266
Pulins, Juris 133
Pullen, Kristy Arneson 61
Puni, Erika F. 161
Punter, Dennis 320
Purdy, Michael 98
Puryear, Richard 264
Pusateri, John 264
Putman, Bob 324, 328
Putnam, Andrew 74
Putnam, Lucy 32
Putz, Richard 27
Pyfer, Carolyn 41
Pyles, Franklin 193, 194

Q

Quackenbush, David 203
Quay, Ronald 246
Quevedo, Jose Moises
  Moncada 192
Quick, Bradley 124
Quick, Norman N. 257
Quiett, Harry V. 178
Quinlan (Metropolitan
  Archbishop) 153
Quinn, Michaelita 31
Quinn, Thomas 31
Quintana, Heather 343
Quispe, Benito Ramos 92

R

Racachinas, Demetrios . . .242
Raccah, William 318
Racek, Theresa 265

Racite, Stephen 119
Radius, Lesley M. 244
Radtke, Robert 108
Rahlan, Glik 88
Rainer, Thom 163
Raines, Frank, III 34
Raines, James Ray 76
Rainovs, John 122
Rajic, Ljubomir 349
Ralph, Karen 292
Ralston, Darwin 261
Ramey, Ibrahim 34
Ramos, Michael 265, 270
Ramphal, Dwarka 148
Ramsay, John 211
Ramsden, Pamela 107
Ramseth, Mark R. 314
Randall, Mike 324
Randall-May, Cay 130
Randels, J. Richard 249
Rans, Susan 44
Ransom, Robert 138
Ranum, Mary S. 114
Rasell, Edith 33
Rassmussen, Philip 349
Rathbun, Peter 22
Ratliff, James 62
Ratzinger, Joseph 81
Ravenell, Joseph P. 255
Ray, Keith H. 305
Ray, Rayford J. 110
Raymond, Jonathan S. . . .321
Read, James 51
Reale, Francesco 135
Rebeck, Victoria A. 24
Redal, R. H. 104, 301
Redd, Eugene 147
Reddick,
    Lawrence L., III 87
Redekopp, Alf 359
Redle, Natalie 269
Reeber, Melody 340
Reece, Roger 245
Reed, Elaine 74
Reed, J. George 260
Reed, Jeremiah 147
Reed, John W. 314
Reed, Michael B. 69
Reed, Monica S. 59
Reed, Rodger
    Hall, Sr. 242, 243
Reel, Judy 254
Reel, Robert A. 263
Reese, Jack R. 295
Reese, John D. 323
Reese, Rosemary 265
Reese, Stewart, Sr. 147
Rees-Rohrbacher,
    Paul 256
Reeves, Steve 61
Regan, Tom 292
Regehr, Nancy 53
Regen, Sue 120

Regnier, Julie 47
Rehling, Tom 171
Reich, Paul 319
Reichter, Arlo R. 63
Reid, Gail 348
Reid, Joyce A. 59
Reid, Peter 198
Reid, Sharmaine R. 207
Reierson,
    Gary 248, 252, 254
Reimer, Gerald 201
Reimer, Rob 321
Reinert, Peter 243
Reinheimer, Larry 205
Reist, L. "Gere"
    Fitzgerald, II 174
Reiter, Steven J. 112
Remalt, Theodore J. 337
Rempel, Ron 138
Rempel, Valerie 125
Remple-Burkholder,
    Byron 340
Reno, Russell R. 331
Retzer, Gordon L. 161
Revell, John 341
Revis, Charles 62
Reyes, Emilio 22
Reyes, José, Sr. 196
Reynolds, Paul V. 214
Rhoades, Kevin 81
Rhoden, H. Robert 73
Rhodes,
    Arthur D. 96, 194, 195
Rice, Mark 89
Rich, Arabella 153
Rich, Jonathan W. 87, 88
Richard, Thomas M. 139
Richards, Carmen K. 114
Richards, James W. 163
Richards, Stephen 189
Richards, William (Bill) . .318
Richardson, Adam
    Jefferson, Jr. 57
Richardson, John M. 85
Richardson, Melvin 262
Richardson, Ralph 51
Riches, Leonard W. 155
Riches,
    Leonard W., Sr. 156
Richter, Don 224
Rickel, Gregory H. 110
Ridings, Dean 30
Rieb, Stanley 344
Rieley-Goddard,
    Catherine 257
Riemenschneider, Dan . .138
Ries, Thomas 135
Riess, Michael 336
Riess, Mike 138, 191
Rigdon, Sidney 98
Riitano, Deb 256
Riley, Adle M. 59
Riley, E. Roy, Jr. 114, 116

Rimbo, Robert A. . . .114, 116
Rindy, William E. 114
Rinehart, Michael W. 115
Rinehart, Neil 138
Ringa, Melanie 146
Ringger, Nick 295
Ripoli, Julie 336
Ritter, Judy 122
Ritter, Ralph 338
Ritts, Kerry 153
Rivera, Bavi E. 110
Rivera, Yamil
    Samalot 301
Rivers, Francis 23
Rivers, W. M. 94
Rizzo, Janice 341
Robb, Turtle 158
Robben, Jerome 192
Roberson,
    James T., Jr. 313
Roberts, Mark E. 355
Roberts, R. Philip 307
Roberts, Randal R. 316
Roberts, Tom 337
Roberts, William A. 159
Robertson, C. C. 141
Robertson, Charles 107
Robertson, Clarence 153
Robertson,
    Creighton L. 110
Robertson, Fran 240
Robertson, Larry 186
Robertson, Richard C. . . .135
Robertson, Terry M. 163
Robertson, William 341
Robey, Connie 270
Robins, Roger 357
Robinson, Anita 78
Robinson, Barbara A. 256
Robinson, Dave 325
Robinson, David 123
Robinson, Denis 311
Robinson, Densimore 141
Robinson, Ellen 292
Robinson, John 96
Robinson, Joyce 249
Robinson, Judith 185
Robinson,
    Julian B. 96, 194, 195
Robinson,
    Kenneth O., Sr. 173
Robinson, Riley 121
Robinson, Shawn 117
Robinson, Tommy 78
Robinson, V. Gene 110
Robinson-Rumble,
    Beverly J. 333
Roblyer, Kathy 331
Rocholl, Rocky 118, 330
Rochon, Igumen
    Irenee 205
Rockwell, David 256
Rockwood, Perry F. 348

Rodenberg, Tamara 241
Rodenbough, Jean 261
Rodgers, Bob 163
Rodgers, Darrin 324, 352
Rodman, Geri 52
Rodquist, David 113
Rodriguez, Carlos 163
Rodriguez, Juan 84
Rodriguez-Villa,
    Jorge 143, 144
Rodriquez, Edwin
    Quiles 151
Roebuck, David G. 357
Roehl, Shirley 330
Rogelstad, David . . .190, 191
Rogers, Huie 79
Rogers, Margaret 91
Rogers, Scott 260
Rogers-Witte, Cally 171
Rogness, Matthew 100
Rogness, Peter 115
Rogriguez, Juan 84
Rohlfs, Steven P. 308
Roland, David 112
Roland, John 266
Rolf, Kathy 245
Rolheiser, Ronald 309
Roller, David T. 120
Rollins, Robert L. 172
Roman, Rebecca 349
Roman, Rosilio 88
Romero, Carlos 138
Ronsvalle, John L. 221
Ronsvalle, Sylvia 221
Rood, Althea 162
Root, Rita 172
Roozen, David A. 222
Rorie, Stephen 271
Rosco, Michael 327
Rose, Donald L. 337
Rose, J. Hugh 176
Rose, Maia 271
Rose, Margaret 108
Rose, Whaid 125
Rosen, Janice 359
Rosengarten,
    Richard A. 315
Roso, Henry A. 111, 330
Ross, Kent 334
Ross, Mary Jane 222
Ross, Patricia 238
Ross-Hunt, Lindsay 263
Rossmoore, Ed 269, 270
Rostad, Dean J. 196
Rostan, June 23
Roth, Adam 262
Roth, John D. 335
Rottino, Kathleen 142
Rourk, David C. 96
Rourke, Marguerite 244
Rousseau, Anne 250
Routledge, Donald 292
Rowan, Cathy 41

Rowe, Sean W. 110
Roy, Marie-Michèle 348
Royster, Carl 25
Rubeck, Dustin
    "Dusty" 300
Rubin, Fred 101
Rucker, Jaqueline P. 263
Rudge, Isabel 261
Ruffin, Jeff 99
Ruge, Mark 203
Ruiz, Luis 110
Rumscheidt, Martin 53
Rundbraaten, Edwin 196
Rundell, Jay 330
Rupe, Jolene 306, 307
Rupert, Allen 152
Rusche, Brian A. 253
Rush, Betty 261
Rush, John 83, 192
Russell, Al 331
Russell, Dave 242
Russell, Dorothy 40
Russell, Gary E. 88
Russell, Howard 131
Russell, Joseph 158
Russell, Kathy 270
Russell, Ken 206
Russell, Robin 343
Russell, Rollin 261
Rust, Harold . . .190, 196, 317
Ruth, Lester 35
Rutherford, F. Thomas . . .192
Rutkowski, Ryan 24
Rutland, Mark 313
Rutzler, John 268
Ruyle, Ronald 131
Ryan, Bridget 252
Ryan, James R. 241
Rydman, Phil 25
Ryskamp, Andrew 89
Rystephanuk, David 205
Ryzy, Emigidiusz H. 69

S
Sabourault, Julie 294
Saenz, Agnes 250
Sage, Russell 260
Saile, Kathy 34
Salge, Carol 246
Saliba, Philip 66, 186
Salt, Steve 262
Samad, Djamillah 39
Sambi, Pietro 81
Sammond, Christopher . . .122
Samson, Pearce 211
Samuels, T. W. 141
Sanchez, Grace 125
Sanders, Bill 248
Sanders, Hiram 308
Sanders, Kay 247
Sanders, Nora M. 213
Sanders, Robert L., Sr. . . .101

Sandler, Abraham 88
Sandoval, Robert 256
Sands, Barb 120
Sands, Susan 252
Sandström, Erik E. 124
Sanft, Jim 135
Sanstha,
    Swaminarayan 230
Santelli, Maria 27
Santiago, Felix 98, 196
Saperstein, David 234
Sapp, W. David 36
Sargent, David 152, 153
Sarmazian, Yessayi 187
Sarwa, Andrzej J. 192
Sasita, Harun Wesley 122
Satterlee, Erin S. W. 343
Sauceda, Sam 271
Sauciur, Vasile 168
Sauls, Stacy F. 108, 110
Saunder,
    Gwendolyn G. 176
Saunders, Willard 147
Savage, Becky 103
Savage, Jeffrey 63
Savas (Bishop) 127
Savell, Medrick 313
Sawyer, Luke 28
Sawyer, Rodney J. 113
Saxby, Jill 249
Scales, Michael G. 295
Scalone, Jonathan 68
Scar, William 240
Scarfe, Alan 110
Scarpato, John 264
Schaafsma, Roberta 23
Schaal, David D. 103
Schaefer, Beth 322
Schaefer, Elizabeth 91
Schaeffer, Jonathan G. 87
Schaffer, Charlene 259
Schapansky,
    Dwight R. 206
Schaper, Michael 79
Schemmel,
    Wade 166, 171, 261
Schermerhorn,
    Eunice 264
Schiemann, D. 204
Schierenbeck, John 100
Schindell, Dal 347
Schipper (Mr.) 333
Schirta, Myroslav 168
Schlabach, Darrel 138
Schlatter,
    William R. 68, 69
Schleicher, John D. 115
Schlemmer, Douglas 63
Schlosser, Rick 239
Schmeling,
    G. R. 297, 330, 335
Schmidgall,
    Paul 95, 194, 195

INDEX

431

Schmidt,
  Harry 44, 123, 299
Schmidt, Karen 151
Schmidt, Krystin 121
Schnase, Robert C. 175
Schneider, Elisa 221
Schneider, Francis J. 312
Schnell, William F. 262
Schner, Joseph G. 321
Schnucker-Rice,
  Sarai 246
Schockley, Nathan D. 179
Schoelles,
  Patricia A. 26, 310
Schoenhals, Floyd M. 115
Schol, John R. 174
Scholes, Nancy 256
Scholfield, Douglas 198
Schoonover, Wayne 126
Schori, Katharine
  Jefferts 108
Schorsch, Ismar 304
Schrader, David 197, 198
Schramm, Richard W. 324
Schrock, Simon 78
Schrock, Wayne 78
Schroeder, Mark G. 180
Schueddig, Louis C. 21
Schuler, Mel 180
Schulte, Gary 172
Schulte, Raymond 27
Schulter, Nancy 255
Schultz, Harvey 118
Schultz, John C. 296
Schultz, Raymond L. 200
Schultz, Ronald 135
Schultz, Stephen R. 105
Schutz, Gary 22
Schwab, Alice Anne 264
Schwab, Chloe 38
Schwarr, Carolyn 269
Schwartz, Beth 40
Scolaro, Peter A. 98
Scott, Alphonso 147
Scott, Charles G. 147
Scott, Don 62
Scott, Hopeton 63
Scott, James C., Jr. 130
Scott, Janice 147
Scott, Martha 34
Scott, Philip L. 147
Scott, Raelyn 154
Scott, Richard G. 98
Scrivens, Jonnie 347
Scruggs, Endia 107
Scruggs, Julius 140
Scruton, Gordon Paul 110
Scully, Eileen 185
Scurry, Frank P. 298
Seabury, Samuel 107
Seacat, Jim 267
Searing, Mark R. 88
Searle, Don L. 330

Seasoltz, R. Kevin 345
Seater, Robert P. 271
Seghers, Devin 191
Segura, Elena 34
Seiler, Paul 159
Selby, Richard 268
Seler, Debby 328
Sellers, Karen Smith 171
Sene, Daniel 243, 244
Senior, Donald 298
Senske, Kurt 135
Seraphim
  (Bishop) 145, 199, 205
Serapion
  (Bishop) 105, 323
Seres, Ted 48
Sessions, Jim 33
Seter, Bernhard M. 135
Sewell, Don 41
Sewell, Wayne 62
Shackelford,
  Barbara 251, 252
Shada, Doug 78
Shafer, Kelly
  Kirkendoll 269
Shaffer, Brian 262
Shand, James J. 110
Shannon, S. E. 99
Sharam, Earle 321
Sharp, John R. 249
Sharp, Randy 254
Sharpe, Michael G. 106
Shaver, Ruth 250
Shaw, Barbara 241
Shaw, Barbara L. 59
Shaw, Cass 256
Shaw, M. Thomas, III 110
Shaw, Milton 134
Shaw, Richard 250
Shawl, Sallie 270
Shay, Ajay 230
Sheard, J. 94
Shearer, Marian 256
Sheffield, Dan 202
Sheie, Myrna J. 114
Shelden, Pam 254
Sheldon, William A. 90
Shelley, Marshall 334
Shelly, Rubel 344
Shelton, Debbie 346
Shenk, Sara Wagner 296
Shepard, Beverley 121
Shepard, Morgan D. 162
Sheptak, Stephen 168
Shequel, Sleiman 67
Sherer, Ann
  Brookshire 175
Sherer, Joseph "Chip" 74
Sherry, Brian 22
Sherry, Paul 34
Sheveland, Gerald 105
Shibly, Othman 258
Shields, Andrew 103

Shields, Richard 61, 330
Shin, Jacob S. 315
Shipley, Joseph 131
Shipman, Joan G. 265
Shishko, William 145
Shively, Jonathan S. 89
Shober, Peter 254
Shockley, Howard 117
Shockley, Nathan D. 179
Shoe, Kirk Crow 254
Shoemaker, Charles T. 45
Shoemaker, Doug 122
Shuman, Maryellen 265
Shumate, David 269
Shy, Willie 101
Siakati, Daniel Ole 121
Sibley,
  Wallace J. 96, 194, 195
Sickbert, Bryan W. 171
Sidden, Andy 267
Siderius, Daniel 97
Siebert, Jared 202
Siebert, John 53
Siebert, Jon 319
Sierralta, Jesus 75
Sigman, Michael W. 112
Siker, Jeffrey S. 306
Sikkila, Wilfred 70
Siladi, Kent 171
Sillings, William
  Harrison 130, 131
Simmons, Blanche 29
Simms, John A. 294
Simon, Paula 271
Simons, John 320
Simpson, Andrew 241
Simpson, David 191
Simpson, John 252
Sinasac, Joseph 347
Singh, Mandit 294
Singh, Prince G. 110
Sippert, Steve 334
Sisk, Mark S. 110
Sitaras,
  Constantine L. 127
Situma, Jotham
  Nyongesa 122
Sivulich, Stephen 168
Siwko, Yurij 168
Sizemore, Randall L. 112
Sizemore, Randy 344
Skeene, Andrea 250
Skiles, Joe, Jr. 147
Skiles, Joseph, Sr. 147
Skiles, Neal 89
Skocypec, Emil 169
Skocypec, Shirly 168
Skrenes, Thomas A. 115
Slade, John 253
Slauter, James E. 103
Slavich, Michael 168
Slayden, Linzy 76
Sloan, John 124

Sloan, Robert A., Jr. 79
Sloat, Karen 104
Sly, Margery 151, 357
Small, Hazel 190, 191
Small, Heather-Dawn 161
Small, Joseph 151
Small, P. Douglas 95, 194
Smalley, Stephen 263
Smedberg, Barry 240
Smiley, Wayne 70
Smisko, Nicholas 299
Smit, Pauline 46
Smith, Alexei 241
Smith, Andrea 345
Smith, Andrew D. 110
Smith, Ann 267
Smith, Arthur 342
Smith, Autholene 78
Smith, Brad 296
Smith, Bruce 196
Smith, Dabney T. 110
Smith, David S. 135
Smith, Dennis 258
Smith, Dewayne 92
Smith,
    Donnie W. 96, 194, 195
Smith,
    Edward P. . . .296, 303, 308
Smith, Emma 130
Smith, Eric 138
Smith, Eric C. 249
Smith, Francis L. 147
Smith, George Wayne 110
Smith, Glenn 51, 294
Smith, Guy H., III 74
Smith, Irving, Jr. 257
Smith, J. Morris 266
Smith, James T. 92
Smith, Jane Orion 350
Smith,
    Jimmy D. 95, 194, 195
Smith, John D. 77
Smith, Joseph 98
Smith, Joseph M. 163
Smith, Kenneth A. 157
Smith, Kirk Stevan 110
Smith, Lawrence 134
Smith, Leroy, Jr. 99
Smith, Liz 324
Smith, Lois L. 264
Smith, Marilyn
    McCann 115
Smith, Mark 299
Smith, Michael Gene 110
Smith, Nancy Orders 267
Smith, R. Bruce 50
Smith, Rebecca 245, 246
Smith, Richard 209
Smith, Robert 192
Smith, Ron 242
Smith, Ronald 103
Smith, Ronald E. 316
Smith, Stephen 92

Smith, Susan 250
Smith, Susan J. 238
Smith, T. Randall 269
Smith, Terry M. 201, 349
Smith, Thomas 34
Smith, Velma 271
Smith, Victor P. 90
Smith, William L. 147
Smith, Zollie L., Jr. 73
Smyth, Peter 166
Snair, Karen 263
Snell, Catherine 141
Snelson, J. E. 326
Snodgrass, Wayne 153
Snow, Catherine J. 206
Snowman,
    Sharon L. 141, 142
Snyder, Don 271
Snyder, Joni 247
Sobel, Ronald B. 42
Sokolyuk, Viktor 269
Solbrekken,
    Kenneth A. 206
Solie, Daryl 204
Somerville, Terrell 124
Sommer, Donald 126
Sommers, Gordon 42
Sommers, Larry F. 328
Song, James 307
Sonnenburg, Brian 293
Soper, John F. 87
Sophia (Zion)
    (Mother) 205, 347
Sorensen, Gordon H. 189
Sotirios (Archbishop) 203
Soto, Jaime 81
Sox, Aileen
    Andres 338, 339
Spangler-Dunning, Bill 85
Spans, J. 338
Sparkman, Alan 148
Sparkman, Wayne 357
Sparks, Dennis D. 271
Sparrow, Patti 250
Spatafora, Andrea 321
Spataro, Francis C. 69, 75
Spears, George 252
Spears, Rusty 241
Speas, Philip 305
Speer, James 76, 77
Spelich, Monica 261
Spencer, Shirley 333
Spencer, Tom 268
Sperzel, Ceil 245
Spittal, David J. 313
Spitzer, Lee 62
Spleth, Richard L. 85
Spriggs, J. Wayne 87
Spyridon (Bishop) 71
St. Laurent,
    Daniel 198, 199
St John, Clarence W. 73
Stafford, Beth 242

Stafford, William S. 313
Stair, Randel 150, 151
Stairs, Dale O. 198
Stairs, M. Jean 320
Staller, Thomas 119
Stallings, James O. 62
Stallings, Willona 261
Standen, Michael 260
Stanley, Heidi 48
Stanley, Richie 25
Stanovsky,
    Elaine J. W. 175
Stansbery, Margaret 262
Stanton, James M. 110
Stapert, Craig W. 325
Staples, Charles E. 265
Star, Barbara 142
Starnes, Darryl B., Sr. 58
Starr, Barbara 142
Starr, Michael L 21
Steadman, William 213
Stearns, Richard 46
Steckel, Clyde J. 328
Steele, Edward 65
Steeves, Crystal D. 346
Stefanis, Anthony 127
Stelck, Brian 191
Stelck, Brian F. 318
Stella, Brigitte 256
Stemmle, Carol 248
Stenson, Jane 40
Stephanopoulos,
    Nikki 126
Stephen (Archbishop) 166
Stephen (Metropolitan) . . .166
Stephens, James 238
Stephens, Mary 247
Stephenson, Carl H. 214
Stephenson, Ed 76
Stern, George M. 265
Sterner, Stephen L. 171
Sterrett, Carey 247
Stetler, P. Daniel 303
Stevens, Bruce G. 151
Stevens, Woodie 101
Stevenson, I. 94
Stevenson, Robert E. 103
Steward, Timothy 153
Stewart, A. G., Sr. 87
Stewart, Dan R. 305
Stewart, Danny 85
Stewart, David R. 23
Stewart, Glen J. 85
Stewart, Jewelle 132
Stewart, Kimberly 177
Stewart, Lois R. 148
Stewart-Rhude, Eileen 51
Steytler, Jessica 358
Stieff, Quentin 113
Stiller, Brian 51
Stiller, Karen 348
Stillwell, Jackie 121
Stimson, Eva 339

INDEX

433

Stinnett, Daniel 189
Stinnett, J. Dwight 62
Stinton, Rick 304
Stith, Rhandi M. 59
Stockman, Robert 25
Stoddard, Horace 257
Stoesz, Conrad 349, 359
Stojanovic, Dragan 211
Stokes, Thomas E. 353
Stoll, Christian 351
Stoll, Joseph 348, 351
Stoltzfus, Timothy 78
Stone, Barbara 263
Stone, H. Lynn 95, 194
Stoops, Robin 62
Stopperich, J. R. 246
Stortz, Dennis 135
Stover, George 123
Stover, Thomas 65
Strand, Jim 24
Strand, Sherri 135
Straub, Gregory 108
Strauser, Carol 123
Strauser,
    Simeon 122, 123, 332
Strauss, Sandra L. 265
Straut, Charles H., Jr. 256
Stricker, Thomas 31
Strickland,
    Marshall H. 58
Strobel, David R. 116
Strohmaier, Sharon E. 247
Strong, Robert F. 92
Stroud, Marilyn 359
Strout, Mark 320
Strout, Richard E. 350
Struchen,
    Shirley W. 38, 43
Struck, Jane Johnson 342
Struik, Félix 301
Strunk, Orlo, Jr. 333
Stuart, Robert F. 243
Stuart, Van I. W. 260
Stubenbort, Patricia 31
Stubenbort, Paul 31
Stuck, James R. 115
Studivant, G. W. 158
Sturtevant, Elwood 247
Stutzman, Ervin R. 137
Styles, Donald H. 326
Subotic, Zivorad 211
Subramanian,
    Siva 230, 243
Suderman, Derek 50
Sudhaker, Paul 92
Suhrheinrich, Heidi 248
Suits, Steven 74
Sullivan, Anita 123, 330
Sullivan, Bernard 59
Sullivan, John 163
Sullivan, Phyillis 238
Sullivan, Veronica 32
Sulyok, Peter 23

Sumner,
    George R., Jr. 322
Sumners, Bill 353
Sumter, Tyrone 78
Sundholm, James V. 113
Sutton, Ed 242
Sutton, Edgar N. 62
Sutton, Eugene T. 110
Sutton, Ray R. 155, 156
Swaiko, Herman 312
Swain, Lawrence 62
Swain, Thomas 121, 148
Swan, Tina 255
Swank, Sandy 247
Swanson, Douglas 253
Swanson, Gary B. 329
Swanson, James E., Sr. . . .175
Swanson, Mark N. 329
Swanson-Nystrom,
    Jane K. 329
Swanstrom, James 246
Swartling, David D. 114
Swartwood, Theresa 247
Swartz, Fred W. 89
Swedenborg, Emanuel . . .164
Sweeney, Michael 301
Sweeney, Michael L. 301
Swenson, Kristin 45
Swenson, Liana Salima
    Rael 252
Swenson, Mary Ann 175
Swidler, Leonard 333
Swift, Jorene 269
Swigart, Agnes 262
Swinburne, R. Douglas . . .87
Swindle, Zephaniah 167
Swing, William 45
Switalski, Joe 239
Sydnor,
    Calvin H., III . .57, 324, 327
Sydow, James 100
Szabo, Stephen 128, 335
Szo, Robert 53

T
Tabbernee, William 262
Tackett, Pamela 244
Taillon, Gerald 191
Talbot, Lydia 244
Talbot, Nathan 91
Talmage,
    Stephen S. 114, 239
Talone, Cheryl 258
Tammen, Mark 151
Tan, Daniel 299
Tandon, Atul 47
Tappen, Jerry 271
Tarallo, Pamela 250
Tarnavsky, Roman 168
Tarr, Candace 131
Tarr, Rita 244
Tate, Mary L. 128

Tatosian, Oscar 72
Taturn, Ed 148
Taylor, Ann 257
Taylor, Betty P. 268
Taylor, Bobbie 244
Taylor, Dolores 267
Taylor, G. Porter 110
Taylor, J. Glen 50
Taylor, Joyce 94
Taylor, L. Roy 150
Taylor, Marian
    McClure 248
Taylor, Mark A. 327
Taylor, Mary Virginia 175
Taylor, Nancy 355
Taylor, Steve 119
Taylor,
    Susan 118, 121, 122
Taylor, Thomas 151
Taylor, Victor 86
Taylor, Wayne 132
Taylor, Wesley M. 101
Teague, Peter W. 305
Tedesco, John 131
Tedrow, Allan 257
Tejel, Jonathán 345
Temple, Guy 265
Temple, Jan 265
Tennent, Timothy C. 296
Tenold, Margo 239
Tenzel, Laura Flippen 43
Terpstra, Bruce K. 87
Terrell, Katie 121, 340
Terry, Bill 132
Terry, Reginald 269
Theodosius,
    Geevarghese Mar 137
Theodosius
    (Metropolitan) 145
Theriault, Donald J. 209
Theule-VanDam,
    Arika 339
Thibodeau, Francois 209
Thiesen, John D. 356
Thiessen, David 201
Thiessen, Gin 201
Thiessen, Jake 201
Thiessen, Ken 191
Thistlethwaite, Susan
    Brooks 299
Thom, Brian James 110
Thomas, D. Karl 187
Thomas, Dick 137
Thomas, Everett J. 335
Thomas, Freeman M. 147
Thomas, James P. 103
Thomas, John 82, 136
Thomas, Ronald P., Jr. 56
Thomason, Jim 117
Thomford,
    Christopher M. 307
Thompson, Brice 98, 196
Thompson, Daniel M. 243

434

Thompson, Dean K. 306
Thompson, Doug 267
Thompson,
    Glendon G. 321, 322
Thompson, Henriette 185
Thompson, James W. 340
Thompson, Karen
    Georgia 38
Thompson, Leonard 62
Thompson, Richard
    Keith 58
Thomsen, Eric 337
Thopil, Markose 147
Thorne, Leo S. 62
Thornton, Patti 124, 344
Thorpe, Debbie 268
Thurston,
    Stephen J. 41, 140
Thurton, Winston 51
Thyberg, Chris 22
Tiemann, Ray 115
Tiemeyer, Ann 38
Tiffany, Tim 239
Tifft, Thomas W. 311
Tikhon
    (Bishop), 145 . . . . .146, 311
Tillet, Charles 242
Tillotson, Frederick J. 316
Timothy (Archbishop) . . .166
Tinsley, Charles 240
Tippett-Eggleston,
    Yashika 153
Tisch, Joseph L. 134
Tisdale, Delores 264
Tisdale, Janet 142
Titus, Beth 266
Titus, Richard C. 238
Tizzard, Brian 54
Tkachuk, Rod 205
Tokunaga, Paul 34
Tolbert, Rosa 70
Tolbert, T. C., Jr. 70
Tolborh, Moses 78
Toler, Stan A. 101
Tollefson, Rebecca J. 262
Tolley, S. T. 152, 326
Tolliver, David 163
Tomalty, Wayne 320
Tombaugh, Richard F. . . .108
Tomlinson, A. J. 97
Tomlinson,
    Susanna M. 264
Tomson, Timothy 168
Toner, Margaret 209
Toompuu, Marie 188
Tooze, George 63
Toppins, Helen Garay 121
Torkelsen, Max C., II 161
Torok, Stefan M. 128
Torrance, Iain R. 310
Torrance, John 188
Torraville, F. David 186
Tosi, Eric G. 145, 146

Toulouse, Mark G. 318
Towne, Becky 331
Towner, Phil 22
Townes, Bill 162
Townsend, Fred 293
Toycen, Dave 54
Tracey, Theresa 245
Tracey, Yvonne A. 59
Trachian, Barkev 314
Traedwell, David 25
Traftan, Margie 350
Trammell,
    Mary M. 91, 327, 332
Tremblay, Donald 293
Trent, Earl 38
Tressel, Rose 169
Trevino, Yoland 45
Triantafilou, Nicholas 127

Triantafilou, Nicholas C. . .303
Trickett, David 304
Trimble, Julius C. 174
Tripp, Linda 54
Trippel, Tim 272
Trotti, Melinda 259, 260
Trout, Keith 267
Trouten, Doug 30
Troutman, Frank, Jr. 21
Trowbridge, Kathleen 250
Troyer, Jonathan 60
Truett, Chris 139
Trulson, Reid 63
Truss, James 70
Trusty, Bill 248
Tse, James N. 29, 30
Tunaru, ioan Casian 210
Tunnicliffe, Geoff 51
Turley, Kenneth O. 164
Turnage, Juleen 72, 73
Turner, B. G. 132
Turner, Brent 74
Turner, Carl A., Sr. 147
Turner, Emil 163
Turner, Jay O. 113
Turner, Michael 314
Turner, Michael C. 295
Turner, Robert S. 256
Turner, Wayne 348
Tutrone, Bob E. 135
Tutrone, Robert E. 135
Tweet, Margaret 29
Tyler, Robert 99
Tyler, Robert D. 332
Tyler, Timothy 131
Tyndall, Margaret 47
Tyson, James E. 147
Tyson, Leah 160

U
Uchtdorf, Dieter F. 98
Uglem, Dwayne 317
Ugoletti, Dennis 264

Ugolnik, Anthony 343
Ulery, Kent J. 296
Ullestad, Steven L. 115
Ulmer, Greg 28
Unruh, Ron 199, 350
Updegrove, John H. 265
Upton, John V., Jr. 163
Usgaard, Harold L. 115
Ussery, Dan 130
Utterback,
    J. Michael 95, 194, 195
Uyeded-Kai, Kim 213

V
Vaillancourt, Stephane . . .294
Valentine, Linda 151
Valentine, Pamela R. 59
Valenzuela, Carmen 254
Valerian (Bishop) 71
Valiame, Hebert 211
Vallance, James E. 324
Van Broekhoven,
    Deborah 63, 339, 352
Van Campen,
    Frank 78
van Dalen, Frank 74
Van Eyl, Christina 327
Van Heukelum,
    Richard 124
Van Kampen, Ken 117
Van Marter, Jerry 24
Van Ostran, Steve 62
Van Vallenburgh,
    Gail 260
VanBeusekom, Hein 134
Vance, Kevin 322
Vance, Phillip 123
Vander Wal, Lisa 208
Vandermeulen,
    Neala 49, 294
VanMarter, Jerry L. 339
Vanyi, Laszlo B. 129
Vargas, David A. 84
Varlaam (Bishop) 146
Varley, Peter 48
Varsberga-Paza, Anita . . .133
Vasilac, Vasile 329
Vasko, Rebecca 220
Vassell, Daniel J. 95, 194
Vassell, Daniel J., Sr. 347
Vassiouchkine,
    Alexei 205
Veatch, Melinda 269
Veazey, Stephen M. 103
Veech, Guthrie 311
Veeraswamy, B. 79
Veillette, Martin 209
Veinotte, Rosemary 292
Veitenhans, Michael 47
Veliko, Lydia 30
Velozo, Ruth M. 271
Venema, Cornelius P. 307

INDEX

435

Vennard, Kathryn
(Penny) 35
Verhoef, A. H. 142
Verigin, John J., Sr. 213
Vesely-Flad, Ethan 330
Vest, R. Lamar 22
Veum, David 100, 306
Victor
(Metropolitan) 128
Victorson, Kay 256
Vieliza, Elijah
Mwavalie 121
Vila, Vesna 263
Villanueva, Alfonso 240
Villanueva, Felix 171
Vinton, Samuel 126
Visscher, G. H. 191, 321
Visscher, J. 347
Visser, Wytske G. 240
Vissers, John 320
Vital, Laurie 244
Vogel-Borne, Jonathan . . .122
Vogles, Bill 117
von Rosenberg,
Charles G. 110
Von Wade, Melvin, Sr. 141
Vonk, Nicole 213
Voss, Joel R. 180
Votary, Marilyn E. 348
Votary, R. E. 203, 204
Vourvoulias, George 127
Vree, Peter 337
Vsevolod
(Archbishop) 168
Vuhasio, Simon 122

W

Wade, James 57
Waggoner, Berten A. 178
Waggoner, James
Edward, Jr. 110
Wagner, Gary 35
Wagner, Mark 309
Wagner, Norman 147
Wagner, Rebecca 250
Wahlberg, Curtis 91
Wakefield,
Andrew H. 298
Wakefield, M. J. 189
Wakefield,
Wesley H. 189, 348
Waldner, Jacob 129
Waldon, J. Jon, IV 332
Waliaula, Alex 121
Walker, Alice 342
Walker, Céleste 334
Walker, Dawn L. 59
Walker, Diane 347
Walker, Frank 154, 155
Walker,
George W. C., Sr. . . .57, 58
Walker, John L. 59

Walker, Melissa
(Missie) 267
Walker, Orris G., Jr. 110
Walker, Riley H. 62
Walker, Ted 325
Walker-Smith,
Angelique 245
Wall, Howie 317
Wall, Jim 148
Wallace, Boyce 106
Wallace, Lance 105
Wallace, Peter 21
Wallace, Vicki 174
Waller, Leonara 246
Walles, Charles A. 112
Walley, Wendell 298
Wallis, Jim 341
Walsh, Gary 51
Walsh, Robert 48
Walter, Gary 112
Walter, John 22
Walter, Martin 129
Walter, Murray 359
Walters, Norman 147
Walton,
Christopher L. 343
Walton, Daniel 198
Waltz, David C. 163
Walukhu, John 121
Wamalia, Francis 122
Wang, Karen 38
Wangila, Isaac 121
Wangila, Jared
Waudo 122
Wanner, Janet 245
Ward, Frank 106
Ward, George 47
Ward, Hope Morgan 175
Ward, Marion J. 270
Ward, Michael, Sr. 63
Ward, Mike 248
Ward, Sarah F. 40
Wardlaw, Theodore J. 296
Warkie, Peter 147
Warr, Sterling E. 207
Warren, Leodis 147
Warren, Patty 238
Warren, Sean 124
Warrick, J. K. 101
Warriner, Bob 198, 199
Washeck, Jim 326
Washington, Don A. 250
Wasielewski,
Charles, Sr. 63
Wasserman, Joseph 241
Wassner, William J. 246
Watkins,
Dennis W. 95, 194
Watkins, Sharon E. 38, 84
Watson,
B. Michael 175, 243
Watson, Suzanne E. 108
Watt, Linda 107

Watt, Neil 210
Watts, Michael 248
Wattson, Paul 32
Waugh, Constance 266
Wauls, Robert 147
Waxler, Mel 268
Waynick,
Catherine M. 110
Weakland,
Rembert G. 271
Weaver, Doug 324
Weaver, James 346
Weaver, Peter D. 174
Weavill, George 267
Webb, Robert 353
Webb, Suzanne 29, 30
Webber, Robert 41
Webster, Gordon V. 257
Webster, Joe L. 172
Wedig, Mark E. 296
Weedman, Gary E. 305
Weeks, Dewayne 148
Weeks, Thomas J. 147
Weeks,
Thomas W., Sr. 147
Weems, L. 94
Weigand-Buckley,
Amber 337
Weigley, David 161
Weikel, Calvin 132
Weil, Steven 234
Weinberg, Richard 325
Weinstein, Judy 265
Weirich, Marvin 78
Weise, Dewyan 177
Weisgerber, James 209
Wekesa, Billy 121
Welch, Mike 205
Welch, Shirley 58
Wells, D. L. S. 94
Wells, David R. 42
Wells, Martin D. 114
Wells, N. W. 94
Welsh,
Robert K. 81, 84, 325
Welty, Marcel A. 38
Wendland, Paul O. 316
Wendorf, Jan 135
Wenger, Lee 170
Wennes, Howard E. 114
Wenthe, Dean O. 300
Wentz, Margy 151
Were, Enock 122
Werkheiser, Kevin D. 92
Wernick, Steven 235
Wert, Rita 40
Wesaw, Marchell 246
West, Barbara J. 156
West, Fritz 35
West, James C., Sr. 156
West, Mona 178
West, Suzy 28
Westbrook, Don 123

436

Westbrook, Jill 138
Westbrook, T. L. 94
Westcott, Barbara
  Spaulding 251
Weyeneth, Benedict 68
Whalen, Dennis K. 87
Whalen, Paul 248
Whaley, Danesta 266
Whalon, Pierre 108
Wheaton, Keith D. 323
Wheeler, Edward L. 299
Whipple, Phil 101, 102
Whitaker, Charles 34
Whitaker,
  Timothy 175, 243
White, Cyrus N. 84
White, David O. 241
White, F. O. 94
White, J. C. 94
White, J. Robert 163
White, James Emery 302
White, Jim 254
White, John F. 38, 57
White, K. Gordon 251
White, LaDonna 253
White, Marcus 271
White, R. 94
White, R. Fowler 305
White, Raymond W. 128
White, Terry Allen 110
Whitehead, Evan 188
Whiten, Bennie, Jr. 33
Whitfield, D. Max 175
Whiting, D. Douglas 41
Whitman, Jeffrey 171
Whitney, Dale 240
Whitsitt, Landon 151
Whitt, Dwight
  Reginald 300
Whittaker, Bill 299
Whittaker, Fermin A. 163
Wickstrom, Shelley 114
Widaman, Dwight 30
Wideman, James 163
Wiebe, Dave 191
Wiebe, Henry 208
Wiebe, Jim 194
Wiebe, Virgil 78
Wieczerzak, Joseph 357
Wiedrick, Ken 194
Wiens, Hart 48
Wiersma, Maynard 88
Wieser, Walter W. 189
Wiggins, Donald A. 88
Wilcox, Donald M. 257
Wildman, Charles L. 172
Wildman, Doug 347
Wiley, Galen 119
Wilgus, John 248
Wilke, Sarah 343
Wilkie, Owen 325
Wilkinson, Ed 342

Wilkinson, William 257
Willemsma, Tena 24
Willey, Steve 51
Williams, Arsenia 141
Williams,
  Bert 329, 334, 342, 343
Williams, Bertha 172
Williams, Carl, Jr. 94
Williams, Carol 262
Williams, Dennis L. 84
Williams, Elijah 42, 173
Williams, Elvonia 94
Williams, F. W. 69
Williams, George 47
Williams, Gloria G. 59
Williams, Gregory 334
Williams, H. Drake, Jr. . . .160
Williams, Horace K. 94
Williams, John P., Jr. 113
Williams, John S. 62
Williams, Kevin 38
Williams, Marilyn F. 84
Williams,
  Mark L. 95, 194, 195
Williams, Matthew 94
Williams, Michael 158
Williams, Michael A. 62
Williams, Newell 298
Williams, Patrick J. 309
Williams, Preston
  Warren, II 57
Williams, Ray W. 141
Williams, Robert 107
Williams, Robert J. 336
Williams, Roger 62
Williams, Ron 130, 331
Williams, Sam 113
Williams, Scott 240
Williams, Todd J. 309
Williams, Troy 264
Williams, W. J. 141
Williams, Zane M. 88
Williamson,
  Edward W. 117
Williamson, Elaine 245
Williamson, Henry M. 87
Williamson, Jack 38
Williamson, Stephen 260
Williford, Donald D. 306
Willimon, William H. 175
Willis, Mike 343
Willis, Tim 309
Wills, Richard J., Jr. 175
Wills, Wanda Bryant 84
Wilson, Alex V. 345
Wilson, Cheryl 253
Wilson, Claudia 121
Wilson, David 196, 351
Wilson, David P. 100, 101
Wilson, Dori 241
Wilson, Glenna 266
Wilson, H. C. 179, 214

Wilson, Harold 317
Wilson, Helen Tibbs 238
Wilson, Howard 318
Wilson, Ian E. 359
Wilson, Johanna 247
Wilson, John 245, 246
Wilson, Maureen 199
Wilson, Nancy 177
Wilson, Norman G. 344
Wilson, Robert W. 179
Wilson, Rod 321
Wilson, Ronald 103
Wilson, Ted N. C. 161
Wilson, William 271
Wiltse, David A. 345
Winbush, R. L. H. 93, 94
Winbush, Robina 151
Wind, James P. 21
Windiate, Jena 251
Wine, LeAnn 90
Wine (Sister) 157
Wines, Roger 152
Winger, Brian 213
Wingner, Thomas 318
Winn, Robert 90
Winston, Mervin 252
Winter, Linda 266
Winter, Roy E. 90
Winters, Robert 177
Winz, Mark 30
Wipf, Jacob 129
Wipf, John 129
Wirt, Douglas 85
Wirth, George 243
Wisbey, Randal R. 305
Wisdo, Nancy 81
Wise, Carson E. 153
Wise, Gary 252
Wisehaupt, Dallas 27
Wissel, Sandy 32
Wisthoff, Grace 261
Witt, Richard 259, 260
Wittin, Robert 255
Wittmeyer, Jay A. 90
Witzig, Doug 118
Wixom, Rosemary M. 98
Wlusak, Steven A. 321
Woelbern, James 26
Wohlrabe, John C. 135
Wohlrabe,
  Lawrence R. 115
Wojcicki, Ted L. 305
Woldt, Alice 37, 270
Wolf, Geralyn 110
Wolfe, Bennet 90
Wolfe, Dean E. 110
Wolfram, Donald J. 148
Wolgemuth, Daniel S. 47
Wollersheim,
  Gary M. 115, 244
Woloschak, Gayle 168
Wong, Suk-Ling 46

Wonsik, Katie Terrell 122
Wood, Colleen 348
Wood, Edward W. 132
Wood, George 42
Wood, George O. 72
Wood, George P. 330
Wood, Larry 104
Wood, Mary Ellen 270
Wood, Maudie E. 92
Wood, Robert Stanley 107
Wood, Virginia 121
Wood, Yvonne 251
Woodall, David 213
Woodard, Effie B. 59
Wooden, Glenn 51
Woodrich, Noya 252
Woodring,
  DeWayne S. 44
Woodruff, James 258
Woods, Gayle 305
Woodson, Jessie R. 148
Woodward, George 205
Woolfolk, Thomas E. 101
Woolridge, Phillip 187
Workowski, Joan 156
Worley, Lloyd 134
Worthington,
  Melvin L. 44
Wortman, Julie A. 344
Woyciesjes, Marilyn 258
Wraight, David 47
Wray, J. T. 73
Wright,
  Abraham 29, 30, 130
Wright, Bryant 162, 163
Wright, David W. 303
Wright, Frank 40
Wright, Hilman 158
Wright, Steve 250

Wright, Wayne P. 110, 242
Wright-Riggins,
  Aidsand F. 63
Wruck, Demetrios E. 166
Wuerl, Donald 81
Wurdeman, Bruce 135
Wvertele, Peggy M. 116
Wyatt, Addie 34
Wylie, Ken 244

Y

Yackel, Roberta 258
Yanes,
  Richard P. 239, 240
Yasenka, David 255
Yates, Bernard 141
Yates, Jonathan 141
Yeats, John 162, 163
Yeglikian, Albert . . .187, 188
Yoder, Grace 356
Yoffie, Eric H. 234
Yoos, Herman R., III 116
York, Alaine F. 125
York, Alwyn 104
York, Tim 139
Yost, Wayne A. 263
Young, George D., III 110
Young, M. Norvel 323
Young, Mark S. 300
Young, Martha 249
Young, McKinley 57
Young, Pamela Dickey . .321
Young, Richard E. 147
Young, Ronald L. 147
Young, Suzanne
  Tibbetts 252
Youngman, Judith 171
Youngren, David 205
Yount, Diana 353

Yurij (Metropolitan) 212
Yusavitz, Carl 31

Z

Zabel, Nancy 40
Zabel, Paul 204
Zacharias, Ken 201
Zackrison, Jim 341
Zahl, Paul F. M. 314
Zain, Thomas 66, 186
Zakian, Christopher 72
Zander, Vera 29
Zandier, Don 266
Zangmeister, Pat 29
Zanicky, Robert 266
Zavala, Gabino 33, 81
Zavitz-Bond, Jane 359
Zawierucha, Bazyl 168
Zehlaoui, Joseph 66
Zelenitz, Myrna 264
Zelinskyy, Daniel . . .343, 344
Zeller, Stephanie 107
Zellmer, David B. 114
Zens, Jon 164, 341
Zerbe, Dean 264
Zetick, Edward 168
Zeuch, Manfred 318
Ziegler, Herb 336
Ziemer, Dale 27
Zilmer, Norman D. 82
Zimmer, Thomas 138
Zimmerman, Phillip 154
Zipfel, Paul 261
Zirille, Francis M. 246
Zittel, Robert J. 256
Zottoli, Carmine 131
Zuck, Lowell 358
Zusevics, Lauma 133
Zylla, Phil 317

NOTES

NOTES

CANNOT BE CHECKED OUT